116637981

Japan

Chris Rowthorn

Ray Bartlett, Andrew Bender, Michael Clark, Matthew D Firestone,

Timothy N Hornyak, Wendy Yanagihara

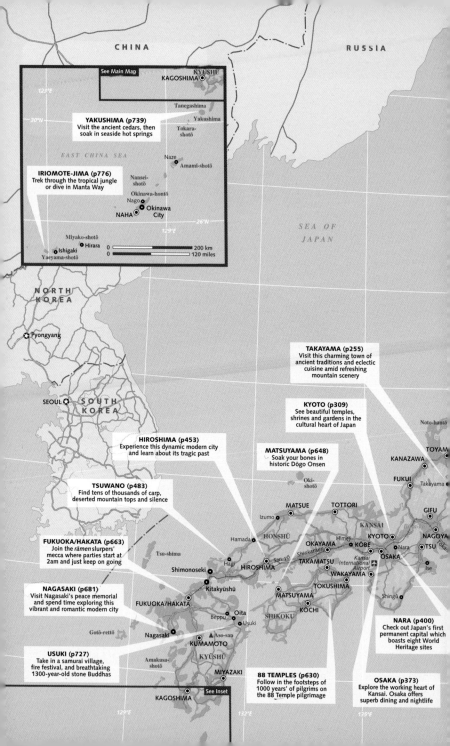

CHINA

RUSSIA

See Main Map

KYŪSHŪ
KAGOSHIMA

123°E

30°N

Tanegashima

Yakushima

YAKUSHIMA (p739)
Visit the ancient cedars, then
soak in seaside hot springs

Tokara-
shotō

EAST CHINA SEA

Naze

Amami-shotō

IRIOMOTE-JIMA (p776)
Trek through the tropical jungle
or dive in Manta Way

Nansei-
shotō

Okinawa-hontō

Nago

Okinawa
City

NAHA

26°N

129°E

Miyako-shotō

Hirara

0   200 km
0   120 miles

Ishigaki

Yaeyama-shotō

SEA OF
JAPAN

NORTH
KOREA

Pyongyang

TAKAYAMA (p255)
Visit this charming town of
ancient traditions and eclectic
cuisine amid refreshing
mountain scenery

Noto-hantō

SEOUL

SOUTH
KOREA

KYOTO (p309)
See beautiful temples,
shrines and gardens in the
cultural heart of Japan

TOYAM

HIROSHIMA (p453)
Experience this dynamic modern city
and learn about its tragic past

MATSUYAMA (p648)
Soak your bones in
historic Dōgo Onsen

KANAZAWA

FUKUI

Takayama

TSUWANO (p483)
Find tens of thousands of carp,
deserted mountain tops and silence

Oki-
shotō

GIFU

MATSUE

TOTTORI

NAGOYA

KANSAI

Izumo

TSU

FUKUOKA/HAKATA (p663)
Join the *rāmen* slurpers'
mecca where parties start at
2am and just keep on going

Hamada

HONSHŪ

OKAYAMA

Himeji

KYOTO

Nara

Tsu-shima

San-yō

Shinkansen

KŌBE

OSAKA

Kansai
International
Airport

Ise

Hagi

Shimonoseki

HIROSHIMA

TAKAMATSU

WAKAYAMA

NAGASAKI (p681)
Visit Nagasaki's peace memorial
and spend time exploring this
vibrant and romantic modern city

Kitakyūshū

TOKUSHIMA

FUKUOKA/HAKATA

MATSUYAMA

Beppu

Ōita

NARA (p400)
Check out Japan's first
permanent capital which
boasts eight World
Heritage sites

Gotō-rettō

Usuki

SHIKOKU

KŌCHI

Shingū

Nagasaki

USUKI (p727)
Take in a samurai village,
fire festival, and breathtaking
1300-year-old stone Buddhas

KUMAMOTO

Aso-san

Amakusa-
shotō

KYŪSHŪ

MIYAZAKI

88 TEMPLES (p630)
Follow in the footsteps of
1000 years' of pilgrims on
the 88 Temple pilgrimage

OSAKA (p373)
Explore the working heart of
Kansai. Osaka offers
superb dining and nightlife

KAGOSHIMA

See Inset

129°E

132°E

135°E

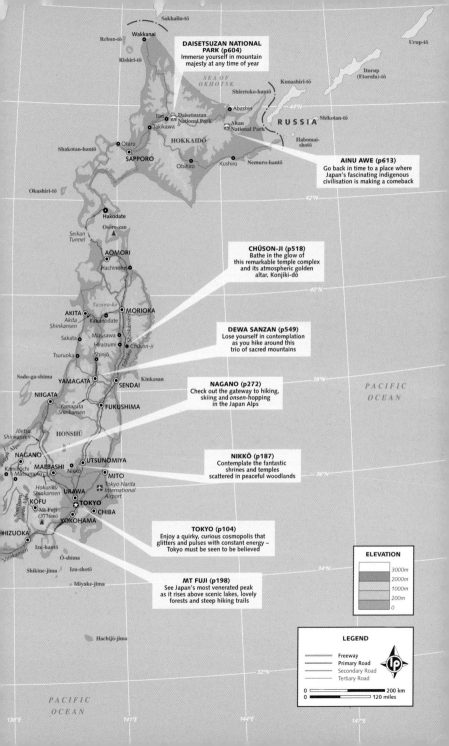

DAISETSUZAN NATIONAL PARK (p604)
Immerse yourself in mountain majesty at any time of year

AINU AWE (p613)
Go back in time to a place where Japan's fascinating indigenous civilisation is making a comeback

CHŪSON-JI (p518)
Bathe in the glow of this remarkable temple complex and its atmospheric golden altar, Konjiki-dō

DEWA SANZAN (p549)
Lose yourself in contemplation as you hike around this trio of sacred mountains

NAGANO (p272)
Check out the gateway to hiking, skiing and onsen-hopping in the Japan Alps

NIKKŌ (p187)
Contemplate the fantastic shrines and temples scattered in peaceful woodlands

TOKYO (p104)
Enjoy a quirky, curious cosmopolis that glitters and pulses with constant energy – Tokyo must be seen to be believed

MT FUJI (p198)
See Japan's most venerated peak as it rises above scenic lakes, lovely forests and steep hiking trails

ELEVATION

3000m
2000m
1000m
200m
0

LEGEND

Freeway
Primary Road
Secondary Road
Tertiary Road

0 ————— 200 km
0 ————— 120 miles

Japan Highlights

Japan packs a mean punch of dazzling cultural attractions and awesome natural wonders. Wander through the ancient Zen gardens of Kyoto and let loose in the neon jungles of Tokyo; ski nose-deep powder snow in Hokkaidō and soak away your cares in steaming natural hot springs; eat mouth-watering sushi in Osaka and wash it down with the best sake you've ever tasted; hike for days and never see another hiker in the Japan Alps, or swim with manta rays off in Okinawa. These are some of our favourites. Why not let the experts speak for themselves? We asked our readers and writers what they liked best. Here is what they had to say:

CHRISTOPHER GROEN

1 KYOTO TEMPLES & GARDENS

Kyoto temples & gardens From the moss garden at Saihō-ji to the shining apparition that is Kinkaku-ji, Kyoto is home to the most beautiful temples in all Japan, and most of them are surrounded by sublime gardens. You've probably got an image of the perfect Japan in your mind – if it exists anywhere, it's probably somewhere in Kyoto waiting for you to discover it.

Chris Rowthorn, Lonely Planet author, Kansai

TSUKIJI FISH MARKET

I'm not awake yet, really, since it's before dawn. But the action at Tokyo's wholesale fish market wakes me up right quick. Motorised carts loaded with produce and enormous frozen tuna zip by. This is where fresh seafood of every variety makes its appearance before being shipped to the city's restaurants and shops. For the full experience, I peruse the trays of octopus and sea urchin, then treat myself to the freshest sushi breakfast ever.

Wendy Yanagihara, Lonely Planet author, Oakland

2

OLIVER STREWE

ONSEN

Making my way through the steam and other naked bodies, I pad self-consciously to the stone pool. Am I doing this right? Is that girl looking at me? Is she staring at my birthmark? My inhibitions, however, soon melt as I touch the water. Snow falls gently on our reddened faces, and a little Japanese boy squeals in delight.

Stephanie Ong, Lonely Planet staff, Australia

3

MASON FLORENCE

TIMOTHY N HORN

4 CLASSIC RYOKAN

Staying at a ryokan is a must while in Japan, but don't settle for the ordinary. Classic ryokan, often in secluded rural areas and made from wood, are the best. One of my favourites is Hōshi Onsen Chōjukan in northern Gunma-ken. Its legendary bathhouse is over a hundred years old, with deep chestnut-wood tubs, arching windows, and rare mixed bathing.

Timothy N Hornyak, Lonely Planet author, Tokyo

ADINA TOVY AI

5 TŌDAI-JI

The largest wooden building in the world, Tōdai-ji also houses the largest enclosed buddha in the world, the Daibutsu. A must-see.

Bluelist, traveller

MIKE BARR

HATTŌJI

The deliciously unspoilt village of Hattōji in rural Okayama features an old-school, thatched-roof farmhouse where you can enjoy the sunken hearth and drum-shaped *goemonburo* bath. Happily, Hattōji isn't entirely devoid of conveniences – down the road there's a Wild West–themed restaurant where a real Japanese cowboy serves up duck hotpot and karaoke.

Timothy N Hornyak, Lonely Planet author, Tokyo

7

TIMOTHY N HORNYAK

6

SKIING

There's nothing like arriving at the top of Happō-One ski area in Nagano and checking out the mind-bending view of the entire Hakuba Range spread out before you. The only thing that tops it is carving perfect telemark turns in new powder on the way down.

Mike Barr, Kyoto resident & recovering ski bum

MASON FLORENCE

8

HIKING IN THE JAPAN ALPS

The long traverse over the northern Japan Alps from Kamikōchi to Tsurugi-dake is world-class by any standard. If you've got a strong back, you can take a backpack and camp it; if not, you can stay in the excellent mountain huts. Either way, I guarantee you that it will be one of the great hikes of your life.

Chris Rowthorn, Lonely Planet author, Kansai

9 KAISEKI

In Japan, the art of presentation enhances the flavour of the food. This art is perfected in *kaiseki* (Japanese haute cuisine), the multi-course meal designed to excite the eye while titillating the palate. Try it.

mrsdoyle, Bluelist, traveller

10 GEISHA-SPOTTING IN KYOTO'S GION DISTRICT

When the cherries are blooming, Kyoto's Shirakawa Minami-dōri in Gion is the most beautiful street in all of Asia (we're not kidding). Spotting a geisha shuffling down the street is the icing on the cake – the quintessential 'only in Japan' moment.

Chris Rowthorn, Lonely Planet author, Kansai

TROPICAL JAPAN

Few travellers are aware of Japan's tropical side. If you're after brilliant coral reefs, mangrove swamps and jungle trekking, head to the southern Islands of Okinawa. Who would have thought that you could swim with manta rays in Japan?

Chris Rowthorn, Lonely Planet author, Kansai

MASON FLORENCE

HIMEJI-JŌ

Japanese castles are pure medieval fantasy, evoking the days of steely samurai and stealthy ninja. Most, though, are postwar ferroconcrete reconstructions. The most spectacular of the authentic fortresses is Himeji-jō, a gem virtually unchanged from four centuries ago. Renowned as the 'White Heron' for its shimmering plaster walls, it towers 92m above sea level and boasts 83 buildings, mazelike paths, and stunning architectural aesthetics. The April cherry blossoms are a delight.

Timothy N Hornyak, Lonely Planet author, Tokyo

TIMOTHY N HORNYAK

SHRINE FESTIVAL

In my old Kyoto neighbourhood of Imakumano, the local men invited me to join the annual shrine festival. They gave me a truly outrageous costume to wear, including a high yellow hat – something King Tut might have worn to parties. We carried the *o-mikoshi* (portable shrine) around the neighbourhood, and my neighbours were delighted to see gaijin-san among the marchers. Later, at the inevitable after-party, the men insisted I make a speech in English. I don't think they understood a word I said, but they were delighted anyway.

Chris Rowthorn, Lonely Planet author, Kyoto

FRANK CA

LOU JONES

13 ## SUMŌ

Even from these cheap seats, the sumō tournaments are riveting. The wrestler's elegant rituals of scattering handfuls of salt before him in the ring, squatting and retreating, staring his opponent down. Each short match culminates in both wrestlers leaping forth in a burst of energy – sometimes slapping madly, scrabbling for one another's thick belts, occasionally tossing one another off the platform altogether. I roam around the stadium listening to the murmur of chattering, punctuated by cheers.

Wendy Yanagihara, Lonely Planet author, Oakland

14

15 ## FUGU: THE LAST SUPPER?

MATT FIRE

Although I'd lived in Japan for years without trying the deadly *fugu* (blowfish), this all changed when I befriended a sushi chef in Izu-honto. After bolstering my courage with a few tumblers of sake, I lifted a thin slice of white flesh to my mouth. My lips and tongue turned numb and, as the fear of death flashed across my face, my friend told me he'd left a bit of poison on the knife for 'dramatic effect.'

Matthew Firestone, Lonely Planet author, Tokyo

SHOPPING IN OMOTE-SANDŌ, TOKYO

A chorus of 'irrashimasssseee' greets me as I enter the store. It begins with a young Japanese boy in tight black jeans, cowboy boots, and a retro shirt. It ends fives voices later. Unable to do anything but smile in response, I let the consumerist fever hit. Before me are boutique adornments and retro one-offs, all immaculately folded and styled. Be warned: Omote-sandō is always chic, and the sales people impossibly well-groomed, so take care of your wallet.

Stephanie Ong, Lonely Planet staff, Australia

GREG ELMS

HIKING FROM MAGOME TO TSUMAGO

To experience the old highway used by ancient travellers between Tokyo and Kyoto, this hiking trail is a must-do. You'll be rewarded with scenery of villages, plantation fields and waterfalls.

Ivy Kwan, Bluelist, traveller

IVY KWAN

FRANK CARTER

OKU-NO-IN GRAVEYARD AT NIGHT

Oku-no-in, in a mountain-top forest, is an enormous graveyard filled with stone monuments. Visit at night, when the path is lit by stone lanterns and the scent of incense creates a sense of otherworldliness.

mrsdoyle, Bluelist, traveller

HANAMI

In springtime, cherry blossoms bloom across Japan, and the Japanese flock to the best parks to eat, drink and be merry, while contemplating the fragile beauty of the snowy pink blossoms. When the wind blows, it's like a soft-pink snow-flurry.

Bluelist, traveller

20

FRANK CA

IVY KWAN

19

MT FUJI FROM YAMANAKA-KO

On a clear day, this is one of the best ways to view the majestic Mt Fuji. We enjoyed the sunset gliding gracefully on the calm water of the lake.

Ivy Kwan, Bluelist, traveller

ROB CHARLTON

21

OGASAWARA-SHOTŌ (OGASAWARA ISLANDS)

The 25-hour ferry ride from Tokyo down to the isolated Ogasawara-shotō is easily the most unusual and rewarding trip you can take in Japan. It's another world, and few non-Japanese ever make the trip (although it was originally settled by New England whalers). The hiking, snorkelling, whale watching and dolphin swimming here is easily worth the cost of the ferry trip.

Chris Rowthorn, Lonely Planet author,

TRAVELLER RANKINGS

We asked travellers like you for their own rankings. Here's what they came up with:

1 Kyoto Temples & Gardens
2 Shrine Festival
3 Himeji-jō
4 *hanami*
5 Tōdai-ji
6 *onsen*
7 Classic Ryokan
8 Mt Fuji from Yamanaka-ko
9 Tsukiji Fish Market
10 Shopping in Omote-sandō, Tokyo
11 sumō
12 Hiking in the Japan Alps
13 Tropical Japan
14 Geisha-spotting in Kyoto's Gion district
15 Ogasawara-shotō (Ogasawara Islands)
16 *kaiseki*
17 Hiking from Magome to Tsumago
18 *Fugu*: The Last Supper
19 Oku-no-in Graveyard at Night
20 Hattōji
21 Skiing

Got a different opinion? Send us your rankings: talk2us@lonelyplanet.com.

Contents

Regional Map Contents

HOKKAIDŌ pp568-9

NORTHERN HONSHŪ p500

CENTRAL HONSHŪ p239

AROUND TOKYO p188

WESTERN HONSHŪ p440

KANSAI p310

TOKYO pp112-13

SHIKOKU p626

KYŪSHŪ pp664-5

OKINAWA & THE SOUTHWEST ISLANDS p737

Destination Japan

When you hear the word 'Japan', what do you think of? Does your mind fill with images of ancient temples or futuristic cities? Do you see visions of mist-shrouded hills or lightning-fast bullet trains? Do you think of suit-clad businessmen or kimono-clad geisha? Whatever image you have of Japan, it's probably accurate, because it's all there.

But you may also have some misconceptions about Japan. For example, many people believe that Japan is one of the world's most expensive countries. In fact, it's cheaper to travel in Japan than in much of North America, Western Europe and parts of Oceania. Others think that Japan is impenetrable or even downright difficult. The fact is, Japan is one of the easiest countries in which to travel. It is, simply put, a place that will remind you why you started travelling in the first place.

If traditional culture is your thing, you can spend weeks in cities such as Kyoto and Nara, gorging yourself on temples, shrines, kabuki, nō (stylised dance-drama), tea ceremonies and museums packed with treasures from Japan's rich artistic heritage. If modern culture and technology is your thing, Japan's cities are an absolute wonderland – an easy peek into the future of the human race, complete with trend-setting cafés and fabulous restaurants.

Outside the cities, you'll find natural wonders the length and breadth of the archipelago. From the coral reefs of Okinawa to the snow-capped peaks of the Japan Alps, Japan has more than enough natural wonders to compete with its cultural treasures.

Then there's the food: whether it's impossibly fresh sushi in Tokyo, perfectly battered tempura in Kyoto, or a hearty bowl of rāmen in Osaka, if you like eating you're going to love Japan.

But for many visitors, the real highlight of their visit to Japan is the gracious hospitality of the Japanese themselves. Whatever your image of Japan, it probably exists somewhere on the archipelago – and it's just waiting for you to discover it!

The Authors

CHRIS ROWTHORN
Coordinating Author, Kansai

Born in England and raised in the USA, Chris has lived in Kyoto since 1992. Soon after his arrival in Kyoto, Chris started studying the Japanese language and culture. In 1995 he became a regional correspondent for the *Japan Times*. He joined Lonely Planet in 1996 and has written or contributed to guidebooks on Japan, Malaysia, the Philippines and Victoria (Australia). When not on the road, Chris spends his time searching out Kyoto's best temples, gardens and restaurants. He also conducts walking tours of Kyoto, Nara and Tokyo. For more on Chris and his tours, check out his website at www.chrisrowthorn.com.

My Favourite Trip

My favourite trip is a route through my 'backyard' in Kansai. It starts in Kyoto (p309), my adopted hometown. From Kyoto, take the Kintetsu Railway down to Nara (p400) to visit the temples and shrines there. After Nara, jump back on the Kintetsu Railway and work your way down to Ise, to check out Ise-jingū (p435), Japan's most impressive Shintō shrine. From Ise, take the JR line around the horn of the Kii-hantō (Kii Peninsula) and stop in Shirahama (p429) for the night, soaking in its fabulous *onsen* (hot springs). From Shirahama head north and east to Wakayama to the mountain-top temple complex of Kōya-san (p417) to spend a night in a temple there. Finally, head back to Kyoto via Osaka (p373).

RAY BARTLETT
Northern Honshū, Hokkaidō

Ray began travel writing at age 18 by jumping a freight train for 500 miles and selling the story to a local newspaper. Almost two decades later he is still wandering the world with pen and camera in hand. He regularly appears on Around the World Radio and has published in *USA Today*, the *Denver Post*, *Miami Herald*, and other newspapers and magazines. His Lonely Planet titles include *Japan, Mexico, Yucatán* and *Korea*. More about him can be found at his website, www.kaisora.com. When not travelling, he surfs, writes and eagerly awaits the end of George W Bush's embarrassing presidency.

LONELY PLANET AUTHORS

Why is our travel information the best in the world? It's simple: our authors are independent, dedicated travellers. They don't research using just the internet or phone, and they don't take freebies in exchange for positive coverage. They travel widely, to all the popular spots and off the beaten track. They personally visit thousands of hotels, restaurants, cafés, bars, galleries, palaces, museums and more – and they take pride in getting all the details right, and telling it how it is. Think you can do it? Find out how at lonelyplanet.com.

ANDREW BENDER Around Tokyo, Central Honshū

France was closed, so after college Andy left his native New England to work in Tokyo, not speaking a word of Japanese. It ended up being a life-changing journey, as visits to Japan so often are. He's since mastered chopsticks, the language and taking his shoes off at the door, and has worked with Japanese companies on both sides of the Pacific. His writing has appeared in *Travel + Leisure*, *Forbes*, the *Los Angeles Times* and many airline magazines, as well as other Lonely Planet titles. In an effort towards ever greater trans-oceanic harmony, Andy also sometimes takes tour groups to Japan and does cross-cultural consulting for businesses. Find out more at www.andrewbender.com.

MICHAEL CLARK Kyūshū

Michael first visited Asia while working aboard a merchant ship in the Pacific bound for Japan. He took his first class in Japanese at the University of Hawaii, and went to Japan to teach at International University of Japan, and then at Keio University. Travelling through Japan sharpened his taste for sumō, sake, bento boxes, trains, kabuki and finally the sound of a baseball striking a metal bat. He has written for the *San Francisco Examiner* and contributed to several Lonely Planet guidebooks. When not on the road, Michael teaches English to Japanese and other international students in Berkeley, California, where he lives with his wife Janet, and kids Melina and Alexander.

MATTHEW D FIRESTONE Shikoku, Okinawa & the Southwest Islands

Matt is a trained anthropologist and epidemiologist who should probably have a real job by now, though somehow he can't pry himself away from Japan. Smitten with love after a 5th grade 'Japan Day' fair, Matt became a self-described Japanophile after being diagnosed with a premature taste for green tea and sushi. After graduating from college, Matt moved to Tokyo where he worked as a bartender while learning a thing or two about the Japanese underworld. As he is fairly certain that he's seen too much to be allowed back in parts of Tokyo, Matt prefers to spend his time in Okinawa where his only worry is whether or not he applied enough sunscreen.

TIMOTHY N HORNYAK Western Honshū

A native of Montreal, Tim Hornyak moved to Japan in 1999 and has written on Japanese culture, technology and history for publications including *Wired*, *Scientific American* and the *Far Eastern Economic Review*. He has lectured on Japanese humanoid robots and traveled to the heart of Hokkaidō to find the remains of a forgotten theme park called Canadian World. His interest in haiku poetry has taken him to Akita-ken to retrace the steps of Basho, as well as to Maui to interview US poet James Hackett. He firmly believes that the greatest Japanese invention of all time is the *onsen*.

WENDY YANAGIHARA — Tokyo

Wendy first toured Tokyo perched on her mother's hip at age two. Between and beyond childhood summers spent in Japan, she has woven travels to other destinations through her stints as psychology and art student, bread peddler, espresso puller, jewellery pusher, graphic designer and more recently as Lonely Planet author for titles including *Mexico*, *Vietnam*, *Indonesia* and *Tokyo*. She is based in Oakland, California.

CONTRIBUTING AUTHORS

Kenneth Henshall English-born Ken Henshall wrote the History chapter and is currently a professor of Japanese Studies at the University of Canterbury, New Zealand. He has published extensively on Japan's writing system, literature, society and history. His recent book *A History of Japan: From Stone Age to Superpower* has been translated into numerous languages.

Dr Trish Batchelor Trish wrote the Health chapter. She is a general practitioner and travel medicine specialist who worked at the Ciwec Clinic in Kathmandu, Nepal. She is a medical advisor to the Travel Doctor New Zealand clinics. Trish teaches travel medicine through the University of Otago and is interested in underwater and high-altitude medicine, and in the impact of tourism on host countries. She has travelled extensively through Southeast and east Asia and particularly loves high-altitude trekking in the Himalayas.

Getting Started

Apart from language difficulties, Japan is a very easy country in which to travel. It's safe and clean and the public transport system is excellent. Best of all, everything you need (with the possible exception of large-sized clothes) is widely available. The only consideration is the cost: Japan can be expensive, although not nearly as expensive as you might fear. While prices have been soaring in other parts of the world, prices in Japan have barely changed in the last 10 years, and the yen is at its weakest level in 21 years according to some calculations.

WHEN TO GO

Without a doubt, the best times to visit Japan are the climatically stable seasons of spring (March to May) and autumn (September to November).

Spring is the time when Japan's famous cherry trees *(sakura)* burst into bloom. Starting from Kyūshū sometime in March, the *sakura zensen* (cherry tree blossom line) advances northward, usually passing the main cities of Honshū in early April. Once the *sakura* bloom, their glory is brief, usually lasting only a week.

Autumn is an equally good time to travel, with pleasant temperatures and soothing colours; the autumn foliage pattern reverses that of the *sakura*, starting in the north sometime in October and peaking across most of Honshū around November.

Travelling during either winter or summer is a mixed bag – midwinter (December to February) weather can be cold, particularly on the Sea of Japan coasts of Honshū and in Hokkaidō, while the summer months (June to August) are generally hot and often humid. June is also the month of Japan's brief rainy season, which in some years brings daily downpours and in other years is hardly a rainy season at all.

See Climate (p790) for more information.

DON'T LEAVE HOME WITHOUT...

The clothing you bring will depend not only on the season, but also on where you are planning to go. Japan extends a long way from north to south: the north of Hokkaidō can be under deep snow at the same time Okinawa and Nansei-shotō (the Southwest Islands) are basking in tropical sunshine. If you're going anywhere near the mountains, or are intent on climbing Mt Fuji, you'll need good cold-weather gear, even at the height of summer.

Unless you're in Japan on business, you won't need formal or even particularly dressy clothes. Men should keep in mind, however, that trousers are preferable to shorts, especially in restaurants.

You'll also need the following:

- Slip-on shoes – you want shoes that are not only comfortable for walking but are also easy to slip on and off for the frequent occasions where they must be removed.

- Unholey socks – your socks will be on display a lot of the time.

- Books – English-language and other foreign-language books are expensive in Japan, and they're not available outside the big cities.

- Medicine – bring any prescription medicine you'll need from home.

- Gifts – a few postcards or some distinctive trinkets from your home country will make good gifts for those you meet along the way.

- Japan Rail Pass – if you intend to do much train travel at all, you'll save money with a Japan Rail Pass, which *must* be purchased outside Japan; see p823 for details.

Also keep in mind that peak holiday seasons, particularly Golden Week (late April to early May) and the mid-August O-Bon (Festival of the Dead), are extremely popular for domestic travel and can be problematic in terms of reservations and crowds. Likewise, everything in Japan basically shuts down during Shōgatsu (New Year period).

All that said, it is worth remembering that you can comfortably travel in Japan at any time of year – just because you can't come in spring or autumn is no reason to give the country a miss.

For information on Japan's festivals and special events, see p794. For public holidays, see p795.

For information on Japan's festivals and special events, see p794. For public holidays, see p795.

COSTS & MONEY

Japan is generally considered an expensive country in which to travel. Certainly, this is the case if you opt to stay in top-end hotels, take a lot of taxis and eat all your meals in fancy restaurants. But Japan does not have to be expensive, indeed it can be *cheaper* than travelling in other parts of the world if you are careful with your spending. And in terms of what you get for your money, Japan is good value indeed.

TRAVEL LITERATURE

Travel books about Japan often end up turning into extended reflections on the eccentricities or uniqueness of the Japanese. One writer who did not fall prey to this temptation was Alan Booth. *The Roads to Sata* (1985) is the best of his writings about Japan, and traces a four-month journey on foot from the northern tip of Hokkaidō to Sata, the southern tip of Kyūshū. Booth's *Looking for the Lost – Journeys Through a Vanishing Japan* (1995) was his final book, and again recounts walks in rural Japan. Booth loved Japan, warts and all, and these books reflect his passion and insight into the country.

SAMPLE DAILY BUDGETS

To help you plan your Japan trip, we've put together these sample daily budgets. Keep in mind that these are rough estimates – it's possible to spend slightly less if you really put your mind to it, and you can spend a heckuva lot more if you want to live large.

Budget

- Youth hostel accommodation (per person): ¥2800
- Two simple restaurant meals: ¥2000
- Train/bus transport: ¥1500
- One average temple/museum admission: ¥500
- Snacks, drinks, sundries: ¥1000
- Total: ¥7800 (about US$65)

Midrange

- Business hotel accommodation (per person): ¥8000
- Two mid-range restaurant meals: ¥4000
- Train/bus transport: ¥1500
- Two average temple/museum admissions: ¥1000
- Snacks, drinks, sundries: ¥2000
- Total: ¥16,500 (about US$135)

JAPAN: IT'S CHEAPER THAN YOU THINK

Everyone has heard the tale of the guy who blundered into a bar in Japan, had two drinks and got stuck with a bill for US$1000 (or US$2000, depending on who's telling the story). Urban legends like this date back to the heady days of the bubble economy of the 1980s. Sure, you can still drop money like that on a few drinks in exclusive establishments in Tokyo if you are lucky enough to get by the guy at the door, but you're more likely to be spending ¥600 (about US$5) per beer in Japan.

The fact is, Japan's image as one of the world's most expensive countries is just that: an image. Anyone who has been to Japan recently knows that it can be cheaper to travel in Japan than in parts of Western Europe, the United States, Australia or even the big coastal cities of China. And the yen has weakened considerably against several of the world's major currencies in recent years, making everything seem remarkably cheap, especially if you visited, say, in the 1980s.

Still, there's no denying that Japan is not Thailand. You can burn through a lot of yen fairly quickly if you're not careful. In order to help you stretch those yen, we've put together a list of money-saving tips.

Accommodation

■ **Capsule Hotels** – A night in a capsule hotel will set you back a mere ¥3000.

■ **Manga Kissa** – These *manga* (comic book) coffee shops have private cubicles and comfy reclining seats where you can spend the night for only ¥2500. For more info, see Missing the Midnight Train on p146.

■ **Guesthouses** – You'll find good, cheap guesthouses in many of Japan's cities, where a night's accommodation runs about ¥3500.

Transport

■ **Japan Rail Pass** – Like the famous Eurail Pass, this is one of the world's great travel bargains. It allows unlimited travel on Japan's brilliant nationwide rail system, including the lightning-fast *shinkansen* bullet trains. See p823.

■ **Seishun Jūhachi Kippu** – For ¥11,500, you get five one-day tickets good for travel on any regular Japan Railways train. You can literally travel from one end of the country to the other for around US$100. See p823.

Eating

■ **Shokudō** – You can get a good filling meal in these all-around Japanese eateries for about ¥700, or US$6, and the tea is free and there's no tipping. Try that in New York. For more, see p88.

■ **Bentō** – The ubiquitous Japanese box lunch, or *bentō*, costs around ¥500 and is both filling and nutritious.

■ **Use Your Noodle** – You can get a steaming bowl of tasty *rāmen* in Japan for as little as ¥500, and ordering is a breeze – you just have to say '*rāmen*' and you're away. *Soba* and *udon* noodles are even cheaper – as low as ¥350 per bowl.

Shopping

■ **Hyaku-en Shops** – *Hyaku-en* means ¥100, and like the name implies, everything in these shops costs only ¥100, or slightly less than one US dollar. You'll be amazed what you can find in these places. Some even sell food.

■ **Flea Markets** – A good new kimono costs an average of ¥200,000 (about US$1700), but you can pick up a fine used kimono at a flea market for ¥1000, or just under US$10. Whether you're shopping for yourself or for presents for the folks back home, you'll find some incredible bargains at Japan's flea markets.

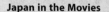

TOP 10

Japan in the Movies

Japan usually fares very poorly in Western movies, which do little but trade in the worst sort of stereotypes about the country and its inhabitants. Thus, if you want to get a clear-eyed view of Japan, it makes sense to check out films mostly by Japanese directors.

- *Marusa-no-Onna* (A Taxing Woman; 1987), directed by Itami Juzo
- *Tampopo* (1987), directed by Itami Juzo
- *Ososhiki* (The Funeral; 1987), directed by Itami Juzo
- *Minbo-no-Onna* (The Anti-Extortion Woman; 1994), directed by Itami Juzo
- *Tokyo Monogatari* (Tokyo Story; 1953), directed by Ōzu Yasujiro
- *Maboroshi no Hikari* (Maborosi; 1995), directed by Koreeda Hirokazu
- *Nijushi-no-Hitomi* (Twenty Four Eyes; 1954), directed by Kinoshita Keisuke
- *Lost in Translation* (2003), directed by Sophia Coppola
- *Rashomon* (1950), directed by Kurosawa Akira
- *Hotaru-no-Haka* (Grave of the Fireflies; 1988), directed by Takahata Isao

Japan Between the Covers

The following is a very subjective list of fiction and nonfiction books about Japan, by Western and Japanese authors. For travel narratives about Japan, see p22.

- *The Roads to Sata* (nonfiction; 1985) by Alan Booth
- *Inventing Japan* (nonfiction; 1989) by Ian Buruma
- *Wages of Guilt* (nonfiction; 2002) by Ian Buruma
- *Memoirs of a Geisha* (fiction; 1999) by Arthur Golden
- *Kitchen* (fiction; 1996) by Banana Yoshimoto
- *A Wild Sheep Chase* (fiction; 1989) by Murakami Haruki
- *Snow Country* (fiction; 1973) by Kawabata Yasunari
- *Nip the Buds Shoot the Kids* (fiction; 1995) by Ōe Kenzaburō
- *Lost Japan* (nonfiction; 1996) by Alex Kerr
- *Dogs and Demons* (nonfiction; 2001) by Alex Kerr

Alex Kerr's *Lost Japan* (1996) is not strictly a travel book, though he does recount some journeys in it; rather, it's a collection of essays on his long experiences in Japan. Like Booth, Kerr has some great insights into Japan and the Japanese, and his love for the country is only matched by his frustration at some of the things he sees going wrong here.

Donald Richie's *The Inland Sea* (1971) is a classic in this genre. It recounts the author's island-hopping journey across the Seto Inland Sea in the late 1960s. Richie's elegiac account of a vanished Japan makes the reader nostalgic for times gone by. It was re-released in 2002 and is widely available online and in better bookshops.

Peter Carey's *Wrong About Japan: A Father's Journey with his Son* (2004) is the novelist's attempt to 'enter the mansion of Japanese culture through its garish, brightly lit back door', in this case, manga (Japanese comics).

MATSURI MAGIC

Witnessing a *matsuri* (traditional festival) can be the highlight of your trip to Japan, and offers a glimpse of the Japanese at their most uninhibited. A lively *matsuri* is a world unto itself – a vision of bright colours, hypnotic chanting, beating drums and swaying crowds. For more information on Japan's festivals and special events, see p794.

Our favourite *matsuri*:

- Yamayaki (Grass Burning Festival), 15 January, Nara, Kansai (p405)
- Yuki Matsuri (Sapporo Snow Festival), early February, Sapporo, Hokkaidō (p577)
- Omizutori (Water-Drawing Ceremony), 1–14 March, Tōdai-ji, Nara, Kansai (p405)
- Takayama Festival, 14–15 April and 9–10 October, Takayama, Gifu-ken, Central Honshū (p259)
- Sanja Matsuri, third Friday, Saturday and Sunday of May, Sensō-ji, Tokyo (p144)
- Hakata Yamagasa Matsuri, 1–15 July, Hakata, Kyūshū (p667)
- Nachi-no-Hi Matsuri (Nachi Fire Festival), 14 July, Kumano Nachi Taisha, Wakayama-ken, Kansai (p432)
- Gion Matsuri, 17 July, Kyoto, Kansai (p351)
- Nagoya Matsuri, mid-October, Nagoya, Central Honshū (p244)
- Kurama-no-himatsuri (Kurama Fire Festival), 22 October, Kyoto (Kurama), Kansai (p351)

Carey and his son Charlie (age 12 at the time the book was written) explore Japan in search of all things manga, and in the process they makes some interesting discoveries.

INTERNET RESOURCES

There's no better place to start your web explorations than at lonelyplanet .com. Here you'll find succinct summaries on travelling to most places on earth, postcards from other travellers and the Thorn Tree bulletin board, where you can ask questions before you go or dispense advice when you get back. You can also find travel news and updates to many of our most popular guidebooks.

Other websites with useful Japan information and links:

Japan Ministry of Foreign Affairs (MOFA; www.infojapan.org) Covers Japan's foreign policy and has useful links to embassies and consulates under 'MOFA info'.

Japan National Tourist Organization (JNTO; www.jnto.go.jp) Great information on all aspects of travel in Japan.

Japan Rail (www.japanrail.com) Information on rail travel in Japan, with details on the Japan Rail Pass.

Kōchi University Weather Home Page (http://weather.is.kochi-u.ac.jp/index-e.html) Weather satellite images of Japan updated several times a day – particularly useful during typhoon season.

Rikai (www.rikai.com/perl/Home.pl) Translate Japanese into English by pasting any bit of Japanese text or webpage into this site.

Tokyo Sights (www.tokyotojp.com) Hours, admission fees, phone numbers and information on most of Tokyo's major sights.

Itineraries
CLASSIC ROUTES

SKYSCRAPERS TO TEMPLES
One to Two weeks / Tokyo to Kyoto

The Tokyo–Kyoto route is the classic Japan route and the best way to get a quick taste of the country. For first-time visitors with only a week or so to look around, a few days in **Tokyo** (p104) sampling the modern Japanese experience and four or five days in the Kansai region exploring the historical sites of **Kyoto** (p309) and **Nara** (p400) is the way to go.

In Tokyo, we recommend that you concentrate on the modern side of things, hitting such attractions as **Shinjuku** (p136), **Akihabara** (p179) and **Shibuya** (p138). Kyoto is the place to see traditional Japan, and we recommend such classic attractions as **Nanzen-ji** (p338) and the **Bamboo Grove** (p344).

This route allows you to take in some of Japan's most famous attractions while not attempting to cover too much ground. The journey between Tokyo and Kyoto is best done by *shinkansen* (bullet train; see p822 for more information) to save valuable time.

This route involves only one major train journey: the three-hour shinkansen trip between Tokyo and Kyoto (the Kyoto–Nara trip takes less than an hour by express train).

Honshū

TOKYO

KYOTO

Nara

CAPITAL SIGHTS & SOUTHERN HOT SPRINGS

Two weeks to One month / Tokyo to the Southwest

Travellers with more time to spend in Japan often hang out in Tokyo and Kyoto and then head west across the island of Honshū and down to the southern island of Kyūshū. The advantage of this route is that it can be done even in mid-winter, whereas Hokkaidō and Northern Honshū are in the grip of winter from November to March.

Assuming you fly into **Tokyo** (p104), spend a few days exploring the city before heading off to the **Kansai area** (p308), notably **Kyoto** (p309) and **Nara** (p400). A good side trip en route is **Takayama** (p255), which can be reached from Nagoya.

From Kansai, take the San-yō *shinkansen* straight down to **Fukuoka/Hakata** (p663) in Kyūshū. Some of Kyūshū's highlights include **Nagasaki** (p681), **Kumamoto** (p695), natural wonders like **Aso-san** (p701) and the hot-spring town of **Beppu** (p727).

The fastest way to return from Kyūshū to Kansai or Tokyo is by the San-yō *shinkansen* along the Inland Sea side of Western Honshū. Possible stopovers include **Hiroshima** (p453) and **Himeji** (p397), a famous castle town. From Okayama, the seldom-visited island of **Shikoku** (p624) is easily accessible. The Sea of Japan side of Western Honshū is visited less frequently by tourists, and is more rural – notable attractions are the shrine at **Izumo** (p487) and the small cities of **Matsue** (p488) and **Tottori** (p494).

This route involves around 25 hours of train travel and allows you to sample the metropolis of Tokyo, the cultural attractions of Kansai (Kyoto and Nara), and the varied attractions of Kyūshū and Western Honshū.

SEA OF JAPAN

Honshū

Takayama

TOKYO

Matsue · Tottori

Izumo · Kansai

Western · KYOTO · Nagoya
Honshū · Himeji · Nara

HIROSHIMA

Okayama

Inland Sea

Shikoku

FUKUOKA

Beppu

Nagasaki

▲ Aso-san
KUMAMOTO

Kyūshū

PACIFIC OCEAN

NORTH BY NORTHEAST THROUGH HONSHŪ

Two weeks to One month / Tokyo / Kansai & Northern Japan

This route allows you to experience Kyoto and/or Tokyo and then sample the wild, natural side of Japan. The route starts in either Kyoto or Tokyo, from where you head to the Japan Alps towns of **Matsumoto** (p282) and **Nagano** (p272), which are excellent bases for hikes in and around places like **Kamikōchi** (p267). From Nagano, you might travel up to **Niigata** (p556) and from there to the island of **Sado-ga-shima** (p560), famous for its *taiko* drummers and Earth Celebration in August. On the other side of Honshū, the city of **Sendai** (p506) provides easy access to **Matsushima** (p513), one of Japan's most celebrated scenic outlooks.

Highlights north of Sendai include peaceful **Kinkasan** (p516) and **Tazawa-ko** (p538), the deepest lake in Japan, **Morioka** (p524), **Towada-Hachimantai National Park** (p538) and **Osore-zan** (p533).

Travelling from Northern Honshū to Hokkaidō by train involves a journey from Aomori through the world's longest underwater tunnel, the **Seikan Tunnel** (p571); rail travellers arriving via the Seikan Tunnel might consider a visit (including seafood meals) to the historic fishing port of **Hakodate** (p580). If you're short on time, **Sapporo** (p572) is a good base, with relatively easy access to **Otaru** (p586), **Shikotsu-Tōya National Park** (p592) and **Biei** (p607). Sapporo is particularly lively during its Yuki Matsuri (Snow Festival; see p577).

The real treasures of Hokkaidō are its national parks, which require either more time or your own transport. If you've only got three or four days in Hokkaidō, you might hit **Shiretoko National Park** (p618) and **Akan National Park** (p613). If you've got at least a week, head to **Daisetsuzan National Park** (p604). More distant but rewarding destinations include the scenic islands of **Rebun-tō** (p603) and **Rishiri-tō** (p601).

This route, which involves around 28 hours of train travel, is for those who want to combine the urban/cultural attractions of Tokyo or Kansai with a few Northern Honshū and Hokkaidō attractions.

ROADS LESS TRAVELLED

ISLAND-HOPPING TO THROUGH THE SOUTHWEST ISLANDS

**Three weeks to One month /
Kyūshū to Iriomote-jima**

For those with the time to explore tropical laid-back Japan, this is a great option. The route starts on the major southern island of Kyūshū, from where you head south from **Kagoshima** (p708) and overnight to **Amami-Ōshima** (p745). **Tokunoshima** (p746) has a 600-year history of bullfighting, while **Okinoerabu-jima** (p746) is an uplifted coral reef with more than 300 caves, which is covered with cultivated flowers in spring. **Yoron-tō** (p747) is surrounded by coral and boasts beautiful Yurigahama, a stunning stretch of white sand inside the reef that disappears at high tide. After a week in the islands of Kagoshima-ken, head to Okinawa, where a day or two in bustling **Naha** (p749) is a must. Take time out for a day trip to nearby **Tokashiki-jima** (p761) to relax on superb Aharen beach, or for a bit of snorkelling, catch a ferry to **Zamami-jima** (p760).

Those who are out of time can fly back to the mainland from Naha, but a great option is to keep island-hopping by ferry, visiting sugar-cane covered **Miyako-jima** (p763) on the way to **Ishigaki-jima** (p769). Ishigaki is a great base for a day trip to the 'living museum' of **Taketomi-jima** (p779). Jungle-covered **Iriomote-jima** (p776) has some brilliant hikes, while divers can swim with the rays in **Manta Way** (p778) between Iriomote-jima and Kohama-jima. Japan's westernmost point, and the country's top marlin fishing spot, is at **Yonaguni-jima** (p781). It's even possible to keep going by ferry from Ishigaki to Taiwan (see p756).

This route takes around 60 hours of travel time, and highlights a laid-back, tropical side of Japan that is relatively unknown outside the country. If you arrive in the dead of winter and need a break from the cold, head to the islands – you won't regret it!

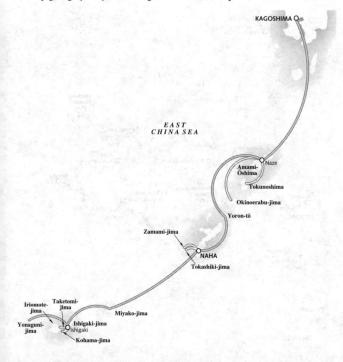

THE WILDS OF HOKKAIDŌ   Two weeks to One month / Hokkaidō

Whether you're on a JR Pass or flying directly, **Sapporo** (p572) makes a good hub for Hokkaidō excursions. A one- or two-night visit to **Hakodate** (p580) should be first on the list. Jump over to the cherry trees of **Matsumae** (p585) if you have time. Be sure to stop between Hakodate and Sapporo at **Tōya-ko** (p592), where you can soak in one of the area's many *onsen* (hot springs) and see Usu-zan's smouldering peak. On the route is **Shiraoi** (p570), Hokkaidō's largest Ainu living-history village. *Onsen* fans may wish to dip in the famed **Noboribetsu Onsen** (p594).

See romantic **Otaru** (p586), an easy day trip out of Sapporo, then head north to **Wakkanai** (p599). Take the ferry to **Rebun-tō** (p603) and check it out for a day, maybe two if you're planning on serious hiking. On the return, see **Cape Sōya** (p599), Japan's northernmost point. Sip Otokoyama sake in **Asahikawa** (p596); from there jump to **Asahidake Onsen** (p608), hike around **Daisetsuzan National Park** (p604) for a day or two, possibly doing a day trip to the lavender fields of **Furano** (p605) or **Biei** (p607).

Head to **Abashiri** (p611). Rent a car there or in **Shari** (p618) if you're planning on going to **Shiretoko National Park** (p618). Do the entire eastern part of the island by car. Not including hiking or other stops this will take one night and two days. Check out **Nemuro** (p620), stop in **Akkeshi** (p621) and return your four-wheeled steed in **Kushiro** (p617).

Watch cranes, deer and other wildlife in **Kushiro Shitsugen National Park** (p617), zip up to **Akan National Park** (p613) to see Mashū-ko, the most beautiful lake in Japan, and then toodle back towards Sapporo.

This route, which involves around 40 hours of travel, is popular as it allows you to do what you have time for. Use Sapporo as a hub and do day trips or overnight to nearby attractions, then loop out eastward, renting a car for the most remote regions.

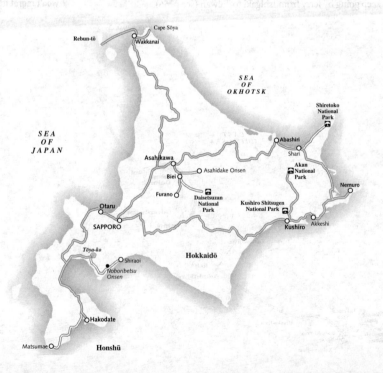

FOLK TALES & CASTLES   One to Two weeks / Northern Honshū

Take the *shinkansen* to Kōriyama, then the local line to **Aizu-Wakamatsu** (p501), a town devoted to keeping alive the tragic tale of the White Tigers (p504), a group of young samurai who committed ritual suicide during the Bōshin Civil War; the cause of their angst was the destruction of Aizu's magnificent Tsuruga-jō (since reconstructed). From Kōriyama, take the *shinkansen* to Ichinoseki, then the local line to **Hiraizumi** (p518). Once ruled by the Fujiwara clan, Hiraizumi was a political and cultural centre informed by Buddhist thought – it rivalled Kyoto until it was ruined by jealousy, betrayal and, ultimately, fratricide. Today, **Chūson-ji** (p518), a mountainside complex of temples, is among Hiraizumi's few reminders of glory, with its sumptuous, glittering Konjiki-dō, one of the country's finest shrines. From Hiraizumi, take the local train to Morioka, then a *shinkansen*/local combination to the **Tōno Valley** (p521), where you might encounter the impish *kappa* (water spirits). The region is famous for its eccentric folk tales and legends, and a number of its attractions will put you in the mood for a spot of old-time ghostbusting. From Morioka, take the *shinkansen* to **Kakunodate** (p541), a charming town that promotes itself as 'Little Kyoto'. With its impeccably maintained samurai district – a network of streets, parks and houses virtually unchanged since the 1600s – it's one of Northern Honshū's most popular attractions.

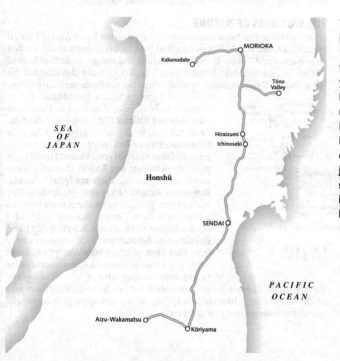

The route, which involves around 19 hours of train travel, takes you through the historically rich regions of northern Honshū. Highlights include the temple complex of Chūson-ji and the restored samurai district in the town of Kakunodate.

TAILORED TRIPS

ON THE TRAIL OF MANGA & ANIME

If names like *Totoro, Howl, Akira, Atom Boy* and *Princess Mononoke* mean something to you, then you'll probably enjoy this trip through the world of Japanese pop culture. It's a journey to the land

of *anime* (Japanese animation) and manga (Japanese comics). Start in **Tokyo** (p104), where you can warm up with a stroll through **Shibuya** (p138), home of all Japanese fads. Then make your way to **Akihabara** (p179), the world's biggest electronics bazaar, where you'll find store after store selling nothing but manga and *anime*. From Tokyo, make the pilgrimage out to the **Ghibli Museum** (p142) in nearby Mitaka, a suburb of Tokyo. This museum is a shrine to director Miyazaki Hayao, sometimes called the Walt Disney of Japan. Return to Tokyo and then hop on a *shinkansen* and get off at **Kyoto** (p309), where you can check out the new **Kyoto International Manga Museum** (p315). From Kyoto, you can make a short side-trip to Takarazuka, outside of Kōbe, where you can visit

the **Tezuka Osamu Memorial Museum** (p394), a shrine to Tezuka Osamu, considered by most Japanese to be the father of *anime* and manga.

THE WONDERS OF NATURE

Japan has some fine natural attractions. Start with the Japan Alps of Central Honshū. **Kamikōchi** (p267) is an excellent base for hikes and is easily reached from Kansai and Tokyo. If you have the time and energy, make the climb to 3180m Yari-ga-take, which starts from Kamikōchi. After checking out the Alps, you must decide: north or south. First, the northern route: from Central Honshū make a beeline for **Hokkaidō** (p566).

If you've only three or four days in Hokkaidō, visit **Shiretoko National Park** (p618) and **Akan National Park** (p613). If you've more time, head to **Daisetsuzan National Park** (p604) and the scenic islands of **Rebun-tō** (p603) and **Rishiri-tō** (p601). On your return to Tokyo or Kansai, stop off at some scenic attractions like **Osore-zan** (p533), **Towada-Hachimantai National Park** (p538), **Tazawa-ko** (p538) and **Kinkasan** (p516). The southern route involves a trip south from Central Honshū to Kyūshū by *shinkansen* to check out **Aso-san** (p701) and **Kirishima-Yaku National Park** (p706). Hop on a ferry from **Kagoshima** (p708) to **Yakushima** (p739). From there, you'll have to return to Kagoshima in order to hop onto another ferry or take an aeroplane

further south. The one really unmissable spot lies at the very southern end of the island chain: **Iriomote-jima** (p776), which has some pristine jungle, mangrove swamps and fine coral reefs.

Snapshot

There won't be an empress, but there may be an army. There is trouble in the west, and the mighty are humbled in the capital. The middle is growing narrow and the edges are growing wider. This is the way it was in Japan in early 2007. Let us explain.

'It's a boy!' The words rang out across the Japanese archipelago on 6 September 2006. The happy mother was Princess Kiko, wife of the current emperor's younger son, Akishino. The birth of Prince Hisahito, the first male child born to the Japanese imperial household in 41 years, shelved talk, for the time being, of an empress in Japan. This had been a real possibility since the Crown Prince and Crown Princess Masako, who were married in 1993, have so far only produced one female child. So, for now, feminist royalists (surely a relatively small minority in Japan) will have to content themselves with fond memories of Japan's last reigning empress, Go-Sakuramachi, who ruled from 1762 until 1771.

While Japan won't be going back to the good old days of matriarchal rule any time soon, the country is making small steps to return to the sort of nation that existed before WWII. In December 2006, the Diet, under the leadership of newly minted Prime Minister Abe Shinzo, passed a law stipulating that the nation's educational system should produce individuals 'who respect their traditions and culture and love their country'. This seemingly innocuous law is a reform of the Fundamental Education Law, which was enacted in 1947, during the occupation, to limit nationalism in education. Liberals in Japan and abroad immediately attacked the law as a return to the kind of curriculum that led the country into WWII. Perhaps significantly, on the very same day, the Diet passed a law that would make overseas missions the 'primary duty' of the country's Jieitai, or Self Defense Forces. This essentially turns the Jietai into a proper army. Of course, those who have been watching the news will note that the Jieitai has already been dispatched abroad, having served in Iraq since.

A driving force behind this revival of nationalism and militarism is Japan's neighbour across the Sea of Japan: North Korea. In October 2006, North Korea conducted a successful test of a nuclear device at a secret location in the northeast of the country. Coming hard on the heels of North Korean ballistic missile tests, the announcement of the successful nuclear test sent shock waves through Japan. Japanese right-wing commentators immediately called for the country to develop its own nuclear weapons. Cooler heads argued for renewed efforts at a diplomatic solution to the problem and the Japanese worked with the United States to force passage of a UN-sponsored sanctions program against North Korea in hopes of forcing the country to give up its nuclear program.

On street level, the test had predictable results: bitter feelings towards the country, already strong due to widely publicised kidnappings of Japanese citizens by North Korea in the 1970s and 1980s, hardened into something approaching outright hatred in some quarters. At the time of writing, six-nation talks were under way in efforts to resolve the problem, but it seems unlikely that North Korea will give up its nuclear ambitions any time soon.

About the only thing that could turn the Japanese public's gaze away from events in North Korea was a juicy home-grown business scandal. It had all the ingredients of a fine kabuki drama: a clash of old and new ways, vain heroes laid low, and plenty of glamour and intrigue thrown in for good measure. Known as the Livedoor Scandal, it was Japan's version of America's Enron

FAST FACTS

Population: 127 million people

Female life expectancy: 84.5 years

Literacy rate: 99%

GDP: US$4.4 trillion (the world's second-biggest economy)

Latitude of Tokyo: at 35.4°N, the same as Tehran, and about the same as Los Angeles (34.05°N) and Crete (35°N)

Islands in the Japanese archipelago: approximately 3900

Number of *onsen* (natural hot-spring baths): more than 3000

World's busiest station: Tokyo's Shinjuku Station, servicing 740,000 passengers a day

Average annual snowfall at Niseko ski area in Hokkaidō: more than 11m

Number of *rāmen* restaurants: more than 200,000

'In 2006, the number of foreign visitors to Japan topped seven million for the first time'

Scandal. At the centre of the storm was Horie Takafumi, a high-flying young Tokyo-based investor who parlayed an internet service provider into one of Japan's most successful companies. In early 2006, Horie was arrested on charges of securities fraud and share price manipulation, delighting Japan's old brick-and-mortar business elite, who had criticised Horie for making money by smoke and mirrors instead of good old-fashioned manufacturing – an echo of Enron if ever there was one.

In some ways, the Livedoor Scandal was a fitting symbol for the changes sweeping Japan, as the country abandons many of its old ways of doing things – cradle-to-grave employment, age-based promotion, a strong social safety net, a preference for manufacturing over service industry – in favour of an economy based more closely on the American model. Now, rather than priding itself on being a country where everyone is a member of the middle class, there is talk of a nation composed of two distinct classes: the *kachi-gumi* (winners) and *make-gumi* (losers). And while this 'brave new economy' may be leading to a roaring stock market and strong corporate earnings, there is the sense that very little of the wealth is trickling down to street level.

However strong the Japanese economy may be, the trade-weighted value of the yen is hovering at a 21-year low. While this means hard times for Japanese travellers abroad, it's a boon for foreign travellers to Japan. In 2006, the number of foreign visitors to Japan topped seven million for the first time, with the greatest growth seen in visitors from other Asian countries: visitors from South Korea, China and Singapore were all up by over 20% compared with 2005. Increasing numbers of Western travellers are also coming to Japan. More than ever, it seems, foreign travellers are waking up to the fact that Japan is an affordable, safe and fascinating destination.

History

ANCIENT JAPAN: FROM HUNTER-GATHERERS TO DIVINE RULE

Once upon a time, two deities, the male Izanagi and the female Izanami, came down from Takamagahara (The Plains of High Heaven) to a watery world in order to create land. Droplets from Izanagi's 'spear' solidified into the land now known as Japan. Izanami and Izanagi then populated the new land with gods. One of these was Japan's supreme deity, the Sun Goddess Amaterasu (Light of Heaven), whose great-great grandson Jimmu was to become the first emperor of Japan, reputedly in 660 BC.

Such is the seminal creation myth of Japan. More certainly, humans were present in Japan at least 200,000 years ago, though the earliest human remains go back only 30,000 years or so. Till around the end of the last Ice Age some 15,000 years ago, Japan was linked to the continent by a number of landbridges – Siberia to the north, Korea to the west and probably China through Taiwan to the south – so access was not difficult.

Amid undoubted diversity, the first recognisable culture to emerge was the Neolithic Jōmon (named after a 'rope mark' pottery style), from around 13,000 BC. The Jōmon were mostly hunter-gatherers, with a preference for coastal regions, though agriculture started to develop from around 4000 BC and this brought about greater stability in settlement and the emergence of larger tribal communities. The present-day indigenous Ainu people of northern Japan are of Jōmon descent.

Jōmon pottery vessels dating back some 15,000 years are the oldest known pottery vessels in the world.

From around 400 BC Japan was effectively invaded by waves of immigrants later known as Yayoi (from the site where their distinctive reddish wheel-thrown pottery was first found). They first arrived in the southwest, probably through the Korean peninsula. Their exact origins are unknown, and may well be diverse, but they brought with them iron and bronze technology, and highly productive wet rice-farming techniques. In general they were taller and less stocky than the Jōmon – though a Chinese document from the 1st century AD nonetheless refers to Japan (by this stage quite heavily peopled by the Yayoi) as 'The Land of the Dwarfs'!

The name of Japan's most famous mountain, Fuji, is an Ainu name for a god of fire.

Opinion is divided as to the nature of Yayoi relations with the Jōmon, but the latter were gradually displaced and forced ever further north. The Yayoi had spread to the middle of Honshū by the 1st century AD, but Northern Honshū could still be considered 'Jōmon' till at least the 8th century. With the exception of the Ainu, present-day Japanese are overwhelmingly of Yayoi descent.

Other consequences of the Yayoi Advent included greater intertribal/regional trade based on greater and more diverse production through new technologies. At the same time there was increased rivalry between tribal/regional groups, often over resources, and greater social stratification.

Agriculture-based fixed settlement led to the consolidation of territory and the establishment of boundaries. According to Chinese sources, by the end of the 1st century AD there were more than a hundred kingdoms in Japan, and by the mid-3rd century these were largely subject to an 'over-queen' named Himiko, whose own territory was known as Yamatai (later Yamato). The location of Yamatai is disputed, with some scholars favouring northwest

TIMELINE	c 13,000 BC	c 400 BC
	First evidence of the Jōmon people and the world's earliest pottery vessels.	The Yayoi people appear in southwest Japan, practising wet rice farming and using metal tools.

Kyūshū, but most preferring the Nara region. The Chinese treated Himiko as sovereign of all Japan – the name Yamato eventually being applied to Japan as a whole – and she acknowledged her allegiance to the Chinese emperor through tribute.

On her death in 248 she is said to have been buried – along with a hundred sacrificed slaves – in a massive barrow-like tomb known as a *kofun*, indicative of the growing importance of status. Other dignitaries chose burial in similar tombs, and so from this point until the establishment of Nara as a capital in 710, this time is referred to as the Kofun or Yamato period.

The period saw the confirmation of the Yamato as the dominant – indeed imperial – clan in Japan. Their consolidation of power often appears to have been by negotiation and alliance with (or incorporation of) powerful potential foes. This was a practice Japan was to continue through the ages where possible, though it was less accommodating in the case of perceived weaker foes.

'Through emulating powerful China, Japan hoped it could also become powerful'

The first verifiable emperor was Suijin (died around 318), very likely of the Yamato clan, though some scholars think he may have been leader of a group of 'horse-riders' who appear to have come into Japan around the start of the 4th century from the Korean peninsula. The period also saw the adoption of writing, based on Chinese but first introduced by scholars from the Korean kingdom of Paekche in the mid-5th century. Scholars from Paekche also introduced Buddhism a century later.

Buddhism was promoted by the Yamato rulers as a means of unification and control of the land. Though Buddhism originated in India it was seen by the Japanese as a Chinese religion, and was one of a number of 'things Chinese' that they adopted to achieve recognition – especially by China – as a civilised country. By emulating China, Japan hoped it could become as powerful. The desire to learn from the strongest/best is another enduring Japanese characteristic.

In 604 the regent Prince Shōtoku (573–620) enacted a constitution of 17 articles, with a very Chinese and indeed Confucianist flavour, esteeming harmony and hard work. Major Chinese-style reforms followed some decades later in 645, such as centralisation of government, nationalisation and allocation of land, and law codes. To strengthen its regime, under Emperor Temmu (r 673–686) the imperial family initiated the compilation of historical works such as the *Kojiki* (Record of Old Things, 712) and *Nihon Shoki* (Record of Japan, 720), with the aim of legitimising their power through claimed divine descent. It had the desired effect, and despite a number of perilous moments, Japan continues to have the longest unbroken monarchic line in the world.

Emulation of things Chinese was not indiscriminate. For example, in China Confucianism condoned the removal of an unvirtuous ruler felt to have lost the 'mandate of heaven', but this idea was not promoted in Japan. Nor was the Chinese practice of allowing achievement of high rank through examination, for the Japanese ruling class preferred birth over merit.

Northern Japan aside, in terms of factors such as effective unification, centralised government, social stratification, systematic administration, external recognition, legitimisation of power, a written constitution and a legal code, Japan, with its estimated five million people, could be said to have formed a nation-state by the early 8th century.

c AD 188–248	c 300
Queen Himiko reigns over Yamatai (Yamato) and is recognised as 'over-queen' of Japan by Chinese visitors.	First verifiable emperor, Suijin, possibly arrived as the leader of 'horse-riders' from Korea.

HISTORICAL PERIODS	
Period	**Date**
Jōmon	c 13,000 BC–c 400 BC
Yayoi	c 400 BC–c AD 250
Kofun/Yamato	c 250–710
Nara	710–94
Heian	794–1185
Kamakura	1185–1333
Muromachi	1333–1568
Azuchi-Momoyama	1568–1600
Edo/Tokugawa	1600–1868
Meiji	1868–1912
Taishō	1912–26
Shōwa	1926–89
Heisei	1989–present

THE AGE OF COURTIERS

In 710 an intended permanent capital was established at Nara (Heijō), built to a Chinese grid pattern. The influence of Buddhism in those days is still seen today in the Tōdai-ji (p403), which houses a huge bronze Buddha and is the world's largest wooden building (and one of the oldest).

In 784 Emperor Kammu (r 781–806) decided to relocate the capital. His reasons are unclear, but may have been related to an inauspicious series of disasters, including a massive smallpox epidemic (735–37) that killed as many as one-third of the population. The capital was transferred to nearby Kyoto (Heian) in 794, newly built on a similar grid pattern. It was to remain Japan's capital for more than a thousand years – though not necessarily as the centre of actual power.

Over the next few centuries, courtly life in Kyoto reached a pinnacle of refined artistic pursuits and etiquette, captured famously in the novel *The Tale of Genji*, written by the court-lady Murasaki Shikibu around 1004. It showed a world where courtiers indulged in amusements, such as guessing flowers by their scent, building extravagant follies and sparing no expense to indulge in the latest luxury. On the positive side, it was a world that encouraged aesthetic sensibilities, such as *mono no aware* (the bitter-sweetness of things) and *okashisa* (pleasantly surprising incongruity), which were to endure right through to the present day. But on the negative side, it was also a world increasingly estranged from the real one. Put bluntly, it lacked muscle. The effeteness of the court was exacerbated by the weakness of the emperors, manipulated over centuries by the intrigues of the notorious and politically dominant Fujiwara family, who effectively ruled the country.

By contrast, while the major nobles immersed themselves in courtly pleasures and/or intrigues, out in the real world of the provinces, powerful military forces were developing. They were typically led by minor nobles, often sent out on behalf of court-based major nobles to carry out 'tedious' local gubernatorial and administrative duties. Some were actually distant imperial family members, barred from succession claims – a practice known as 'dynastic shedding' – and often hostile to the court. Their retainers included skilled warriors known as samurai (literally 'retainer').

The Tale of Genji, written by the court-lady Murasaki Shikibu in around 1004, is widely believed to be the world's first novel.

Mid-5th century	**Mid-6th century**
Writing (Chinese characters) introduced into Japan (from Korea).	Buddhism introduced into Japan (from Korea).

The two main 'shed' families were the Minamoto (also known as Genji) and the Taira (Heike), who were basically enemies. In 1156 they were employed to assist rival claimants to the headship of the Fujiwara family, though these figures soon faded into the background, as the struggle developed into a feud between the Minamoto and the Taira.

The Taira prevailed, under Kiyomori (1118–81), who based himself in the capital and, over the next 20 years or so, fell prey to many of the vices that lurked there. In 1180, following a typical court practice, he enthroned his own two-year-old grandson, Antoku. However, a rival claimant requested the help of the Minamoto, who had regrouped under Yoritomo (1147–99) in Izu. Yoritomo was more than ready to agree.

Both Kiyomori and the claimant died very shortly afterwards, but Yoritomo and his younger half-brother Yoshitsune (1159–89) continued the campaign against the Taira – a campaign interrupted by a pestilence during the early 1180s. By 1185 Kyoto had fallen and the Taira had been pursued to the western tip of Honshū. A naval battle ensued (at Dannoura) and the Minamoto were victorious. In a well-known tragic tale, Kiyomori's widow clasped her grandson Antoku (now aged seven) and leaped with him into the sea, rather than have him surrender. Minamoto Yoritomo was now the most powerful man in Japan, and was to usher in a martial age.

'Minamoto
Yoritomo
was now the
most power-
ful man in
Japan, and
was to usher
in a martial
age'

THE AGE OF WARRIORS

Yoritomo did not seek to become emperor, but rather to have the new emperor confer legitimacy on him through the title of *shōgun* (generalissimo). This was granted in 1192. Similarly, he left many existing offices and institutions in place – though often modified – and set up his base in his home territory of Kamakura, rather than Kyoto. In theory he represented merely the military arm of the emperor's government, but in practice he was in charge of government in the broad sense. His 'shōgunate' was known in Japanese as the *bakufu*, meaning the tent headquarters of a field general, though it was far from temporary. As an institution, it was to last almost 700 years.

The system of government now became feudal, centred on a lord-vassal system in which loyalty was a key value. It tended to be more personal and more 'familial' than medieval European feudalism, particularly in the extended *oya-ko* relationship ('parent-child', in practice 'father-son'). This 'familial hierarchy' was to become another enduring feature of Japan.

But 'families' – even actual blood families – were not always happy, and the more ruthless power seekers would not hesitate to kill family members they saw as threats. Yoritomo himself, seemingly very suspicious by nature, killed off so many of his own family there were serious problems with the shōgunal succession upon his death in 1199 (following a fall from his horse in suspicious circumstances). One of those he had killed was his half-brother Yoshitsune, who earned an enduring place in Japanese literature and legend as the archetypical tragic hero.

Yoritomo's widow Masako (1157–1225) was a formidable figure, arranging shōgunal regents and controlling the shōgunate for much of her remaining life. Having taken religious vows on her husband's death, she became known as the 'nun shōgun', and one of the most powerful women in Japanese history. She was instrumental in ensuring that her own family, the Hōjō, replaced

| Seventeen-Article Constitution (604) drawn up, leading to major reforms (Taika Reforms 645) aimed at emulating China. | Japan's first intended permanent capital established in Nara. Japan arguably a nation-state by this stage. |

the Minamoto as shōguns. The Hōjō shōgunate continued to use Kamakura as the shōgunal base, and was to endure till the 1330s.

It was during their shōgunacy that the Mongols twice tried to invade, in 1274 and 1281. The Mongol empire was close to its peak at this time, under Kublai Khan (r 1260–94). After conquering Korea in 1259 he sent requests to Japan to submit to him, but these were ignored.

His expected first attack came in November 1274, allegedly with some 900 vessels carrying around 40,000 men – many of them reluctant Korean conscripts – though these figures may be exaggerated. They landed near Hakata in northwest Kyūshū and, despite spirited Japanese resistance, made progress inland. However, for unclear reasons, they presently retreated to their ships. Shortly afterwards a violent storm blew up and damaged around a third of the fleet, after which the remainder returned to Korea.

A more determined attempt was made seven years later from China. Allegedly, Kublai ordered the construction of a huge fleet of 4400 warships to carry a massive force of 140,000 men – again, questionable figures. They landed once more in northwest Kyūshū in August 1281. Once again they met spirited resistance and had to retire to their vessels, and once again the weather soon intervened. This time a typhoon destroyed half their vessels – many of which were actually designed for river use, without keels, and unable to withstand rough conditions. The survivors returned to China, and there were no further Mongol invasions of Japan.

It was the typhoon of 1281 in particular that led to the idea of divine intervention to save Japan, with the coining of the term *shinpū* or *kamikaze* (both meaning 'divine wind'). Later this came to refer to the Pacific War suicide pilots who, said to be infused with divine spirit, gave their lives in the cause of protecting Japan from invasion. It also led the Japanese to feel that their land was indeed the Land of the Gods.

Despite the successful defence, the Hōjō shōgunate suffered. It was unable to make a number of promised payments to the warrior families involved, which brought considerable dissatisfaction, while the payments it did make severely depleted its finances.

It was also during the Hōjō shōgunacy that Zen Buddhism was brought from China. Its austerity and self-discipline appealed greatly to the warrior class, and it was also a factor in the appeal of aesthetic values such as *sabi* (elegant simplicity). More popular forms of Buddhism were the Jōdo (Pure Land) and Jōdo Shin (True Pure Land) sects, based on salvation through invocation of Amida Buddha.

Dissatisfaction towards the Hōjō shōgunate came to a head under the unusually assertive emperor Go-Daigo (1288–1339), who, after escaping from exile imposed by the Hōjō, started to muster anti-shōgunal support in Western Honshū. In 1333 the shōgunate despatched troops to counter the rebellion under one of its most promising generals, the young Ashikaga Takauji (1305–58). However, Takauji was aware of the dissatisfaction towards the Hōjō and realised that he and Go-Daigo had considerable military strength between them. He abandoned the shōgunate and threw in his lot with the emperor, attacking the shōgunal offices in Kyoto. Others soon rebelled against the shōgunate in Kamakura itself.

This was the end for the Hōjō shōgunate, but not for the shōgunal institution. Takauji wanted the title of shōgun for himself, but his ally Go-Daigo

Japanese pirates were operating in the islands of present-day Indonesia as early as the 13th century.

The 'divine wind' of 1281 is said to have drowned 70,000 Mongol troops, which, if true, would make it the world's worst maritime disaster.

9th–12th centuries

| Japan's capital moved to Heian (present-day Kyoto), and remains there for over a thousand years. | Court becomes increasingly effete; provincial military clans grow stronger. |

was reluctant to confer it, fearing it would weaken his own imperial power. A rift developed, and Go-Daigo sent forces to attack Takauji. When Takauji emerged victorious, he turned on Kyoto, forcing Go-Daigo to flee into the hills of Yoshino some 100km south of the city, where he set up a court in exile. In Kyoto, Takauji installed a puppet emperor from a rival line who returned the favour by declaring him shōgun in 1338. Thus there were two courts in coexistence, which continued until 1392 when the 'southern court' (at Yoshino) was betrayed by Ashikaga Yoshimitsu (1358–1408), Takauji's grandson and third Ashikaga shogun, who promised reconciliation but very soon 'closed out' the southern court.

Takauji set up his shōgunal base in Kyoto, at Muromachi, which gives its name to the period of the Ashikaga shōgunate. Notable shōguns include Takauji himself and his grandson Yoshimitsu, who among other things had Kyoto's famous Kinkaku-ji (Golden Temple; p343) built, and once declared himself 'King of Japan'. However, the majority of Ashikaga shōguns were relatively weak. In the absence of strong centralised government and control, the country slipped increasingly into civil war. Regional warlords, who came to be known as *daimyō* (big names), vied with each other in seemingly interminable feuds and power struggles. Eventually, starting with the Ōnin War of 1467–77, the country entered a period of virtually constant civil war. This was to last for the next hundred years, a time appropriately known as the Sengoku (Warring States) era.

'In particular, he hated Buddhist priests, whom he saw as troublesome'

Ironically perhaps, it was during the Muromachi period that a new flourishing of the arts took place, such as in the refined *nō* drama, *ikebana* (flower arranging) and *cha-no-yu* (tea ceremony). Key aesthetics were *yūgen* (elegant and tranquil otherworldliness, as seen in *nō*), *wabi* (subdued taste), *kare* (severe and unadorned) and the earlier-mentioned *sabi* (elegant simplicity).

The later stages of the period also saw the first arrival of Europeans, specifically three Portuguese traders blown ashore on the island of Tanegashima, south of Kyūshū, in 1543. Presently other Europeans arrived, bringing with them two important items, Christianity and firearms (mostly arquebuses). They found a land torn apart by warfare, ripe for conversion to Christianity – at least in the eyes of missionaries such as (St) Francis Xavier, who arrived in 1549 – while the Japanese warlords were more interested in the worldly matter of firearms.

REUNIFICATION

One of the most successful warlords to make use of firearms was Oda Nobunaga (1534–82), from what is now Aichi Prefecture. Though starting from a relatively minor power base, his skilled and ruthless generalship resulted in a series of victories over rivals. In 1568 he seized Kyoto in support of the shōgunal claim of one of the Ashikaga clan (Yoshiaki), duly installed him, but then in 1573 drove him out and made his own base at Azuchi. Though he did not take the title of shōgun himself, Nobunaga was the supreme power in the land.

Noted for his brutality, he was not a man to cross. In particular he hated Buddhist priests, whom he saw as troublesome, and tolerated Christianity as a counterbalance to them. His ego was massive, leading him to erect a temple where he could be worshipped, and to declare his birthday a national holiday. His stated aim was *Tenka Fubu* (A Unified Realm under Military

1156–85	1192
Hostilities between Taira and Minamoto clans; Minamoto finally prevails under Yoritomo.	Japan unified under Minamoto Yorimoto, who takes the title *shōgun* (generalissimo) and establishes *bakufu* (shōgunate) in Kamakura.

Rule) and he went some way to achieving this unification by policies such as strategic redistribution of territories among the *daimyō*, land surveys, and standardisation of weights and measures.

In 1582 he was betrayed by one of his generals and forced to commit suicide. However, the work of continuing unification was carried on by another of his generals, Toyotomi Hideyoshi (1536–98), a footsoldier who had risen through the ranks to become Nobunaga's favourite. He, too, was an extraordinary figure. Small and simian in his features, Nobunaga had nicknamed him Saru-chan (Little Monkey), but his huge will for power belied his physical smallness. He disposed of potential rivals among Nobunaga's sons, took the title of regent, continued Nobunaga's policy of territorial redistribution and also insisted that *daimyō* should surrender their families to him as hostages to be kept in Kyoto – his base being at Momoyama. He also banned weapons for all classes except samurai.

Hideyoshi became increasingly paranoid, cruel and megalomaniacal in his later years. Messengers who gave him bad news would be sawn in half, and young members of his own family executed for suspected plotting. He also issued the first expulsion order of Christians (1587), whom he suspected of being an advance guard for an invasion. This order was not necessarily enforced, but in 1597 he crucified 26 Christians – nine of them European. His grand scheme for power included a pan-Asian conquest, and as a first step he attempted an invasion of Korea in 1592, which failed amid much bloodshed. He tried again in 1597, but the campaign was abandoned when he died of illness in 1598.

On his deathbed Hideyoshi entrusted the safeguarding of the country, and the succession of his young son Hideyori (1593–1615), whom he had unexpectedly fathered late in life, to one of his ablest generals, Tokugawa Ieyasu (1542–1616). However, upon Hideyoshi's death, Ieyasu betrayed that trust. In 1600, in the Battle of Sekigahara, he defeated those who were trying to protect Hideyori, and became effectively the overlord of Japan. In 1603 his power was legitimised when the emperor conferred on him the title of shōgun. His Kantō base, the once tiny fishing village of Edo – later to be renamed Tōkyō – now became the real centre of power and government in Japan.

Through these three men, by fair means or more commonly foul, the country had been reunified within three decades.

> 'Hideyoshi became increasingly paranoid, cruel and megalomaniacal in his later years'

STABILITY & SECLUSION

Having secured power for the Tokugawa, Ieyasu and his successors were determined to retain it. Their basic strategy was of a linked two-fold nature: enforce the status quo and minimise potential for challenge. Orthodoxy and strict control (over military families in particular) were key elements.

Policies included requiring authorisation for castle building and marriages, continuing strategic redistribution (or confiscation) of territory, and, importantly, requiring *daimyō* and their retainers to spend every second year at Edo, with their families kept there permanently as hostages. In addition the shōgunate directly controlled ports, mines, major towns and other strategic areas. Movement was severely restricted by deliberate destruction of many bridges, the implementation of checkpoints and requirements for written travel authority, the banning of wheeled transport, the strict monitoring of potentially ocean-going vessels, and the banning of overseas travel for

1274 & 1281	**1333**
The Mongols attempt to invade Japan, and fail in large part due to 'divine wind' of typhoon.	Ashikaga Takauji topples Hōjō shōgunate and establishes Ashikaga shōgunate.

Japanese and even the return of those already overseas. Social movement was also banned, with society divided into four main classes: in descending order, *shi* (samurai), *nō* (farmers), *kō* (artisans) and *shō* (merchants). Detailed codes of conduct applied to each of these classes, even down to clothing and food and housing – right down to the siting of the toilet!

Christianity, though not greatly popular, threatened the authority of the shōgunate. Thus Christian missionaries were expelled in 1614. In 1638 the bloody quelling of the Christian-led Shimabara Uprising (near Nagasaki) saw Christianity banned and Japanese Christians – probably several hundred thousand – forced into hiding. All Westerners except the Protestant Dutch were expelled. The shōgunate found Protestantism less threatening than Catholicism – among other things it knew the Vatican could muster one of the biggest military forces in the world – and would have been prepared to let the British stay on if the Dutch, showing astute commercial one-upmanship, had not convinced it that Britain was a Catholic country. Nevertheless, the Dutch were confined geographically to a tiny trading base on the man-made island of Dejima, near Nagasaki, and numerically to just a few dozen men.

Thus Japan entered an era of *sakoku* (secluded country) that was to last for more than two centuries. Within the isolated and severely prescribed world of Tokugawa Japan, the breach of even a trivial law could mean execution. Even mere 'rude behaviour' was a capital offence, and the definition of this was 'acting in an unexpected manner'. Punishments could be cruel, such as crucifixion, and could be meted out collectively or by proxy (for example, a village headman could be punished for the misdeed of a villager). Secret police were used to report on misdeeds.

As a result, people at large learned the importance of obedience to authority, of collective responsibility and of 'doing the right thing'. These are values still prominent in present-day Japan.

For all the constraints there was nevertheless a considerable dynamism to the period, especially among the merchants, who as the lowest class were often ignored by the authorities and thus had relative freedom. They prospered greatly from the services and goods required for the *daimyō* processions to and from Edo, entailing such expense that *daimyō* had to convert much of their domainal produce into cash. This boosted the economy in general.

A largely pleasure-oriented merchant culture thrived, and produced the popular *kabuki* drama, with its colour and stage effects. Other entertainments included *bunraku* (puppet theatre), *haiku* (17-syllable verses), popular novels and *ukiyoe* (wood-block prints), often of female *geisha*, who came to the fore in this period. (Earlier *geisha* – meaning 'artistic person' – were male.)

Samurai, for their part, had no major military engagements. Well educated, most ended up fighting mere paper wars as administrators and managers. Ironically, it was during this period of relative inactivity that the renowned samurai code of *bushidō* was formalised, largely to justify the existence of the samurai class – some 6% of the population – by portraying them as moral exemplars. Though much of it was idealism, occasionally the code was put into practice, such as the exemplary loyalty shown by the Forty-Seven *rōnin* (masterless samurai) in 1701–03, who waited two years to avenge the unfair enforced suicide by *seppuku* (disembowelment) of their lord. After killing the man responsible, they in turn were all obliged to commit *seppuku*.

'After killing the man responsible, they in turn were all obliged to commit *seppuku*'

In more general terms, Confucianism was officially encouraged with the apparent aim of reinforcing the idea of hierarchy and status quo. Though this was clearly not in the best interests of women, it encouraged learning, and along with this, literacy. By the end of the period as many as 30% of the population of 30 million were literate – far ahead of the Western norm at the time. In some opposition to the 'Chinese learning' represented by Confucianism, there was also a strong trend of nationalism, centred on Shintō and the ancient texts. This was unhelpful to the shōgunate as it tended to focus on the primacy of the emperor. Certainly, by the early-mid-19th century, there was considerable dissatisfaction towards the shōgunate, fanned also by corruption and incompetence among shōgunal officials.

The Japanese religion of Shintō is one of the few religions in the world to have a female sun deity, or a female supreme deity.

It is questionable how much longer the Tokugawa shōgunate and its secluded world could have continued, but as it happened, external forces were to bring about its demise.

MODERNISATION THROUGH WESTERNISATION

Since the start of the 19th century a number of Western vessels had appeared in Japanese waters. Any Westerners who dared to land, even through shipwreck, were almost always met with expulsion or even execution.

The Three Imperial Treasures (*sanshu no jingi*) – a mirror, sword and jewel – are considered the most sacred objects in the Shintō religion.

This was not acceptable to the Western powers, especially the USA, which was keen to expand its interests across the Pacific and had numerous whaling vessels in the northwest that needed regular reprovisioning. In 1853, and again the following year, US Commodore Matthew Perry steamed into Edo Bay with a show of gunships and demanded the opening of Japan for trade and reprovisioning. The shōgunate had little option but to accede to his demands, for it was no match for Perry's firepower. Presently a US consul arrived, and other Western powers followed suit. Japan was obliged to give 'most favoured nation' rights to all the powers, and lost control over its own tariffs.

The humiliation of the shōgunate, the nation's supposed military protector, was capitalised upon by anti-shōgunal samurai in the outer domains of Satsuma (southern Kyūshū) and Chōshū (Western Honshū) in particular. A movement arose to 'revere the emperor and expel the barbarians' (*sonnō jōi*). However, after unsuccessful skirmishing with the Western powers, the reformers realised that expelling the barbarians was not feasible, but restoring the emperor was. Their coup, known as the Meiji (Enlightened Rule) Restoration, was put into effect from late 1867 to early 1868, and the new teenage emperor Mutsuhito (1852–1912), later to be known as Meiji, found himself 'restored', following the convenient death of his stubborn father Kōmei (1831–67). After some initial resistance, the last shōgun, Yoshinobu (1837–1913), retired to Shizuoka to live out his numerous remaining years peacefully. The shōgunal base at Edo became the new imperial base, and was renamed Tōkyō (eastern capital).

The disorienting collapse of the regimented Tokugawa world produced a form of mass hysteria called *Ee Ja Nai Ka* ('Who Cares?'), with traumatised people dancing naked and giving away possessions.

Mutsuhito did as he was told by those who had restored him, though they would claim that everything was done on his behalf and with his sanction. Basically, he was the classic legitimiser. His restorers, driven by both personal ambition and genuine concern for the nation, were largely leading Satsuma/Chōshū samurai in their early 30s. The most prominent of them was Itō Hirobumi (1841–1909), who was to become prime minister on no fewer than four occasions. Fortunately for Japan, they proved a very capable oligarchy.

Late 16th–early 17th centuries	Early 17th–mid-19th centuries
Japan reunified by Oda Nobunaga, Toyotomi Hideyoshi and Tokugawa Ieyasu. The latter becomes shōgun.	Tokugawa shōgunate based at Edo (Tōkyō). Life tightly controlled. Japan closes itself to the outside world.

The rickshaw was not developed till 1869, following the lifting of the Tokugawa ban on wheeled transport.

Japan was also fortunate in that the Western powers were distracted by richer and easier pickings in China and elsewhere, and did not seriously seek to occupy or colonise Japan, though Perry does seem to have entertained such thoughts at one stage. Nevertheless, the fear of colonisation made the oligarchs act with great urgency. Far from being colonised, they themselves wanted to be colonisers, and make Japan a major power.

Under the banner of *fukoku kyōhei* (rich country, strong army), the young men who now controlled Japan decided on Westernisation as the best strategy – again showing the apparent Japanese preference for learning from a powerful potential foe. In fact, as another slogan *oitsuke, oikose* (catch up, overtake) suggests, they even wanted to outdo their models. Missions were sent overseas to observe a whole range of Western institutions and practices, and Western specialists were brought to Japan to advise in areas from banking to transport to mining.

In the coming decades Japan was to Westernise quite substantially, not just in material terms, such as communications and railways and clothing, but also, based on selected models, in the establishment of a modern banking system and economy, legal code, constitution and Diet, elections and political parties, and a conscript army.

The salaries of the foreign specialists invited to Japan in the Meiji period are believed to have amounted to 5% of all government expenditure during the period.

Existing institutions and practices were disestablished where necessary. *Daimyō* were 'persuaded' to give their domainal land to the government in return for governorships or similar compensation, enabling the implementation of a prefectural system. The four-tier class system was scrapped, and people were now free to choose their occupation and place of residence. This included even the samurai class, phased out by 1876 to pave the way for a more efficient conscript army – though there was some armed resistance to this in 1877 under the Satsuma samurai (and oligarch) Saigō Takamori, who ended up committing *seppuku* when the resistance failed.

To help relations with the Western powers, the ban on Christianity was lifted, though few took advantage of it. Nevertheless numerous Western ideologies entered the country, one of the most popular being 'self-help' philosophy. This provided a guiding principle for a population newly liberated from a world in which everything could be prescribed for them. But at the same time, too much freedom could lead to an unhelpful type of individualism. The government quickly realised that nationalism could safely and usefully harness these new energies. People were encouraged to become successful and strong, and in doing so show the world what a successful and strong nation Japan was. Through educational policies, supported by imperial pronouncements, young people were encouraged to become strong and work for the good of the family-nation.

The government was proactive in many other measures, such as taking responsibility for establishing major industries and then selling them off at bargain rates to chosen 'government-friendly' industrial entrepreneurs – a factor in the formation of huge industrial combines known as *zaibatsu*. The government's actions in this were not really democratic, but this was typical of the day. Another example is the 'transcendental cabinet', which was not responsible to the parliament but only to the emperor, who followed his advisers, who were members of the same cabinet! Meiji Japan was outwardly democratic but internally retained many authoritarian features.

The 'state-guided' economy was helped by a workforce that was well educated, obedient and numerous, and traditions of sophisticated com-

1853–54	1868
US Commodore Matthew Perry uses 'gunboat diplomacy' to force Japan to open up.	Meiji Restoration of imperial authority, disestablishment of shōgunate. Japan's formal capital moved to Tōkyō (formerly Edo).

mercial practices such as futures markets. In the early years Japan's main industry was textiles and its main export silk, but later in the Meiji period, with judicious financial support from the government, it moved increasingly into manufacturing and heavy industry, becoming a major world shipbuilder by the end of the period. Improvement in agricultural technology freed up surplus farming labour to move into these manufacturing sectors.

A key element of Japan's aim to become a world power with overseas territory was the military. Following Prussian (army) and British (navy) models, Japan soon built up a formidable military force. Using the same 'gunboat diplomacy' that Perry had used on the Japanese shōgunate, in 1876 Japan was able to force on Korea an unequal treaty of its own, and thereafter interfered increasingly in Korean politics. Using Chinese 'interference' in Korea as a justification, in 1894 Japan manufactured a war with China – a weak nation at this stage despite its massive size – and easily emerged victorious. As a result it gained Taiwan and the Liaotung peninsula. Russia tricked Japan into renouncing the peninsula and then promptly occupied it itself, leading to the Russo-Japanese War of 1904–05, from which Japan again emerged victorious. One important benefit was Western recognition of its interests in Korea, which it proceeded to annex in 1910.

By the time of Mutsuhito's death in 1912, Japan was indeed recognised as a world power. In addition to its military victories and territorial acquisitions, in 1902 it had signed the Anglo-Japanese Alliance, the first ever equal alliance between a Western and non-Western nation. The unequal treaties had also been rectified. Western-style structures were in place. The economy was world ranking. The Meiji period had been a truly extraordinary half-century of modernisation. But where to now?

> 'The Meiji period had been a truly extraordinary half-century of modernisation'

GROWING DISSATISFACTION WITH THE WEST

Mutsuhito was succeeded by his son Yoshihito (Taishō), who suffered mental deterioration that led to his own son Hirohito (1901–89) becoming regent in 1921.

On the one hand, the Taishō period ('Great Righteousness', 1912–26) saw continued democratisation, with a more liberal line, the extension of the right to vote and a stress on diplomacy. Through WWI Japan was able to benefit economically from the reduced presence of the Western powers, and also politically, for it was allied with Britain (though with little actual involvement) and was able to occupy German possessions in East Asia and the Pacific. On the other hand, using that same reduced Western presence, in 1915 Japan aggressively sought to gain effective control of China with its notorious 'Twenty-One Demands', which were eventually modified.

In Japan at this time there was a growing sense of dissatisfaction towards the West and a sense of unfair treatment. The Washington Conference of 1921–22 set naval ratios of three capital ships for Japan to five US and five British, which upset the Japanese despite being well ahead of France's 1.75. Around the same time a racial equality clause that Japan proposed to the newly formed League of Nations was rejected. And in 1924 the US introduced race-based immigration policies that effectively targeted Japanese.

This dissatisfaction was to intensify in the Shōwa period (Illustrious Peace), which started in 1926 with the death of Yoshihito and the formal accession of Hirohito. He was not a strong emperor and was unable to curb the ris-

Late 19th century	1895–1910
Japan modernises through Westernisation, aiming to become a major power, and succeeds.	Japan defeats China in the Sino-Japanese War (1895), gaining Taiwan.

SAMURAI

The prime duty of a samurai, a member of the warrior class from around the 12th century on, was to give faithful service to his lord. In fact, the term 'samurai' is derived from a word meaning 'to serve'. Ideally, 'service' meant being prepared to give up one's life for one's lord, though there were many ranks of samurai and, at least in the early days, it was typically only the hereditary retainers who felt such commitment. At the other end of the ranks, samurai were in effect professional mercenaries who were by no means reliable and often defected if it was to their advantage.

The renowned samurai code, *bushidō* (way of the fighting man), developed over the centuries but was not formally codified till the 17th century, by which stage there were no real battles to fight. Ironically, the intention of the code appears to have been to show samurai as moral exemplars in order to counter criticism that they were parasitic. It was thus greatly idealised.

Core samurai ideals included *gaman* (endurance), *isshin* (whole-hearted commitment) and *makoto* (sincerity). Samurai were supposed to be men of Zen-like austerity who endured hardship without complaint. Though often highly educated and sometimes paralleled with European knights, chivalry was not so dominant as in Europe, and certainly not towards women. Far from romancing women, most samurai shunned them on the grounds that sexual relations with women (who were *yin/in*) weakened their maleness *(yang/yō)*, and as a result most samurai were homosexual or, in many cases, bisexual. There were actually a small number of female samurai, such as Tomoe Gozen (12th century), but they were not given formal recognition.

Warriors, who for one reason or another became lordless, were known as *rōnin* (wanderers), acted more like brigands and were a serious social problem.

Samurai who fell from grace were generally required to commit ritual disembowelment, meant to show the purity of the soul, which was believed to reside in the stomach. Westerners typically refer to this as *harakiri*, but the Japanese prefer the term *seppuku* – though both mean 'stomach cutting'.

The samurai's best-known weapon was the *katana* sword, though in earlier days the bow was also prominent. Arguably the world's finest swordsmen, samurai were formidable opponents in single combat. However, during modernisation in the late 19th century the government – itself comprising samurai – realised that a conscript army was more efficient as a unified fighting force, and disestablished the samurai class. However, samurai ideals such as endurance and fighting to the death were revived through propaganda prior to the Pacific War, and underlay the determination of many Japanese soldiers.

ing power of the military, who pointed to the growing gap between urban and rural living standards and accused politicians and big businessmen of corruption. The situation was not helped by repercussions from the World Depression in the late 1920s. The ultimate cause of these troubles, in Japanese eyes, was the West, with its excessive individualism and liberalism. According to the militarists, Japan needed to look after its own interests, which in extended form meant a resource-rich, Japan-controlled Greater East Asian Co-Prosperity Sphere that even included Australia and New Zealand.

In 1931 Japan invaded Manchuria on a pretext, and presently set up a puppet government. When the League of Nations objected, Japan promptly left the League. It soon turned its attention to China, and in 1937 launched a brutal invasion that saw atrocities such as the notorious Nanjing Massacre of December that year. Casualty figures for Chinese civilians at Nanjing vary between 340,000 (some Chinese sources) and a 'mere' 20,000 (some Japanese sources). Many of the tortures, rapes and murders were filmed

1915–41 (esp 1930s)	1941–45
Japan becomes increasingly disillusioned with much of the West, and its expansionism in Asia becomes more aggressive, especially in China.	Japan attacks Pearl Harbor, entering WWII. It makes initial gains but over-reaches itself and is forced to surrender.

and are undeniable, but persistent (though not universal) Japanese attempts to downplay this and other massacres in Asia remain a stumbling block in Japan's relations with many Asian nations, even today.

Japan did not reject all Western nations, however, for it admired the new regimes in Germany and Italy, and in 1940 entered into a tripartite pact with them. This gave it confidence to expand further in Southeast Asia, principally seeking oil, for which it was heavily dependent on US exports. However, the alliance was not to lead to much cooperation, and since Hitler was openly talking of the Japanese as *untermenschen* (lesser beings) and the 'Yellow Peril', Japan was never sure of Germany's commitment. The US was increasingly concerned about Japan's aggression and applied sanctions. Diplomacy failed, and war seemed inevitable. The US planned to make the first strike, covertly, through the China-based Flying Tigers (Plan JB355), but there was a delay in assembling an appropriate strike force.

So it was that the Japanese struck at Pearl Harbor on 7 December that year, damaging much of the US Pacific Fleet and allegedly catching the US by surprise, though some scholars believe Roosevelt and others deliberately allowed the attack to happen in order to overcome isolationist sentiment and bring the US into the war against Japan's ally Germany. Whatever the reality, the US certainly underestimated Japan and its fierce commitment, which led rapidly to widespread occupation of Pacific islands and parts of continental Asia. Most scholars agree that Japan never expected to beat the US, but hoped to bring it to the negotiating table and emerge better off.

The tide started to turn against Japan from the battle of Midway in June 1942, which saw the destruction of much of Japan's carrier fleet. Basically, Japan had over-extended itself, and over the next three years was subjected to an island-hopping counterattack from forces under General Douglas MacArthur. By mid-1945 the Japanese, ignoring the Potsdam Declaration calling for unconditional surrender, were preparing for a final Allied assault on their homelands. On 6 August the world's first atomic bomb was dropped on Hiroshima (see the boxed text, p457), with 90,000 civilian deaths. On 8 August, Russia, which Japan had hoped might mediate, declared war. On 9 August another atomic bomb was dropped on Nagasaki (see the boxed text, p684), with another 75,000 deaths. The situation prompted the emperor to formally announce surrender on 15 August. Hirohito probably knew what the bombs were, for Japanese scientists were working on their own atomic bomb and seem to have had both sufficient expertise and resources, though their state of progress is unclear.

> 'Whatever the reality, the US certainly underestimated Japan and its fierce commitment'

RECOVERY & BEYOND

Following Japan's defeat a largely US occupation began under MacArthur. It was benign and constructive, with twin aims of demilitarisation and democratisation, and a broader view of making Japan an Americanised bastion against communism in the region. To the puzzlement of many Japanese, Hirohito was not tried as a war criminal but was retained as emperor. This was largely for reasons of expediency, to facilitate and legitimise reconstruction – and with it US policy. It was Americans who drafted Japan's new constitution, with its famous 'no war' clause. US aid was very helpful to the rebuilding of the economy, and so too were procurements from the Korean War of 1950–53. The Occupation ended in 1952, though Okinawa was not returned till 1972 and is still home to US military bases. And Japan still supports US policy in many regards, such as in amending the law to allow (noncombatant) troops to be sent to Iraq.

The Japanese responded extremely positively in rebuilding their nation, urged on by a comment from the postwar prime minister Yoshida Shigeru that Japan had lost the war but would win the peace. Certainly, in economic terms, through close cooperation between a stable government and well organised industry, and a sincere nationwide determination to become 'Number One', by the 1970s Japan had effectively achieved this. It had become an economic superpower, its 'economic miracle' the subject of admiration and study around the world. Even the Oil Shocks of 1973 and 1979 did not cause serious setback.

By the late 1980s Japan was by some criteria the richest nation on the planet, of which it occupied a mere 0.3% in terms of area but 16% in terms of economic might and an incredible 60% in terms of real estate value. Some major Japanese companies had more wealth than many nations' entire GNP.

Hirohito died in January 1989, succeeded by his son Akihito and the new Heisei (Full Peace) period. He must have ended his extraordinarily eventful life happy at his nation's economic supremacy.

The so-called 'Bubble Economy' may have seemed unstoppable, but the laws of economics eventually prevailed and in the early 1990s it burst from within, having grown beyond a sustainable base. Though Japan was to remain an economic superpower, the consequences were nevertheless severe. Economically, Japan entered a recession of some 10 years, which saw almost zero growth in real terms, plummeting land prices, increased unemployment and even dismissal of managers who had believed they were guaranteed 'lifetime' employment. Socially, the impact was even greater. The public, whose lives were often based around corporations and assumed economic growth, were disoriented by the effective collapse of corporatism and the economy. Many felt displaced, confused and even betrayed, their values shaken. In 1993 the Liberal Democratic Party, in power since 1955, found itself out of office, though it soon recovered its position as a sort of resigned apathy seemed to set in among the public.

The situation was not helped by two events in 1995. In January the Kōbe Earthquake struck, killing more than 5000 people and earning the government serious criticism for failure to respond promptly and effectively. A few months later came the notorious sarin gas subway attack by the AUM religious group, which killed 12 and injured thousands. Many people, such as the influential novelist Murakami Haruki, saw the ability of this bizarre cult to attract intelligent members as a manifestation of widespread anxiety in Japan, where people had suddenly experienced the collapse of many of their core values and beliefs were now left on their own – a situation postmodernists term 'the collapse of the Grand Narrative'.

The collapse of corporatism is reflected in increasing numbers of 'freeters' (free arbeiters), who do not commit to any one company but move around in employment, and 'neets' (not in employment or education or training). More people are now seeking their own way in life, which has resulted in greater diversity and more obvious emergence of individuality. On the one hand, this has led to greater extremes of self-expression, such as outland-

---

Until it was occupied by the USA and other Allies following WWII, Japan (as a nation) had never been conquered or occupied by a foreign power.

The Yamato dynasty is the longest unbroken monarchy in the world, and Hirohito's reign from 1926 to 1989 the longest of any monarch in Japan.

1989	Early 1990s
Emperor Hirohito dies after reigning 63 years and his son Akihito succeeds.	Japan's so-called 'Bubble Economy' bursts, heralding a decade of economic recession and a re-orientation of values.

ish clothes and hairstyles (and hair colours) among the young. On the other hand, there's a greater 'Western-style' awareness of the rights of the individual, seen in the recently introduced privacy and official information laws. Direct control by government has also loosened, as seen in the 2004 corporatisation of universities.

The economy started to recover from around 2002, thanks in part to increased demand from China, and is now steady around the 2% to 3% per annum growth mark. The year 2002 was also marked by a successful co-hosting of the football World Cup with rivals Korea. However, relations with Asian nations are still far from fully harmonious. Recent bones of contention include the continued appearance of history textbooks that downplay atrocities such as Nanjing, and controversial visits by Prime Minister Koizumi Junichirō (in office 2001–06) to Yasukuni Shrine to honour Japanese war dead, including war criminals.

There are other worries for Japan. One is that it is the world's most rapidly ageing society, with the birth rate declining to a mere 1.25 per woman, and with its elderly (65 years plus) comprising 21% of the population while its children (up to 15 years) comprise just 13%. This has serious ramifications economically as well as socially, with a growing ratio of supported to supporter, and increased pension and health costs. Along with many ageing Western nations, Japan is doing its best (for example, by introducing nursing insurance schemes), but there is no easy solution in sight, and there are serious calls to redefine 'elderly' (and concomitant retirement expectations) as 75 years of age rather than 65.

Other concerns include juvenile crime and a growing problem of Social Anxiety Disorder in young people, which can lead to serious withdrawal (*hikikomori*) from everyday life. Internationally, the threat from nuclear-capable North Korea, with which Japan has had a particularly troubled relationship, presents a major worry.

Some Japanese were also concerned about there being no male heir to the throne, but in September 2006 Princess Kiko gave birth to Prince Hisahito and allayed those fears. Polls show that most Japanese would have been happy with a reigning empress anyway. That same month Koizumi was followed as prime minister by the 52-year-old Abe Shinzō, the first Japanese prime minister to be born postwar. It remains to be seen how the country will fare under his leadership, for which public support seems somewhat limited as 2007 unfolds.

> 'However, relations with Asian nations are still far from fully harmonious'

2002	2006
Japan's economy starts a sustained recovery, and Japan successfully co-hosts the Soccer World Cup with Korea.	Prince Hisahito born, providing eventual male heir to the throne. Issues such as ageing, relations with Asia and juvenile crime remain.

The Culture

THE NATIONAL PSYCHE

The uniqueness and peculiarity of 'the Japanese' is a favourite topic of both Western observers and the Japanese themselves. It's worth starting any discussion of 'the Japanese' by noting that there is no such thing as 'the Japanese'. Rather, there are 127 million individuals in Japan with their own unique characters, interests and habits. And despite popular stereotypes to the contrary, the Japanese are as varied as any people on earth. Just as importantly, the Japanese people have more in common with the rest of humanity than they have differences.

Why then the pervasive images of the Japanese as inscrutable or even bizarre? These stereotypes are largely rooted in language: few Japanese are able to speak English as well as, say, your average Singaporean, Hong Kong Chinese or well-educated Indian, not to mention most Europeans. This difficulty with English is largely rooted in the country's appalling English education system, and is compounded by a natural shyness, a perfectionist streak and the nature of the Japanese language itself, which contains fewer sounds than any other major world language (making pronunciation of other languages difficult). Thus, what appears to the casual observer to be a maddening inscrutability is more likely just an inability to communicate effectively. Those outsiders who become fluent in Japanese discover a people whose thoughts and feelings are surprisingly – almost boringly – similar to those of folks in other developed nations.

'Japanese people have more in common with the rest of humanity than they have differences'

Of course, myths of Japanese uniqueness are quite useful to certain elements of Japanese society, to whom Japanese uniqueness is evidence of Japanese racial superiority. Among this small minority are writers of a class of books known as Nihonjiron (studies of the Japanese people), which contain absurd claims about the Japanese (including the claim that Japanese brains work differently from other people, and even that Japanese have longer intestines than other races). Some of these beliefs have made headway in general Japanese society, but most well-educated Japanese pay little mind to these essentially racist and unscientific views.

All this said, just like any other race, the Japanese people do have certain characteristics that reflect their unique history and interaction with their environment. The best way to understand how most modern Japanese people think is to look at these influences. First, Japan is an island nation. Second, until WWII, Japan was never conquered by an outside power, nor was it heavily influenced by Christian missionaries. Third, until the beginning of last century, the majority of Japanese lived in close-knit rural farming communities. Fourth, most of Japan is covered in steep mountains, so the few flat areas of the country are quite crowded – people literally live on top of each other. Finally, for almost all of its history, Japan has been a strictly hierarchical place, with something approximating a caste system during the Edo period.

All of this has produced a people who highly value group identity and smooth social harmony – in a tightly packed city or small farming village, there simply isn't room for colourful individualism. One of the ways harmony is preserved is by forming consensus, and concealing personal opinions and true feelings. Thus, the free flowing exchange of ideas, debates and even heated arguments that one expects in the West are far less common in Japan. This reticence about sharing innermost thoughts perhaps contributes to the Western image of the Japanese as mysterious.

The Japanese tendency to put social harmony above individual expression is only strengthened by the country's Confucian and Buddhist heritage. The former, inherited from China, stresses duty to parents, teachers, society and ancestors before individual happiness. The latter, inherited from India by way of China, stresses the illusory nature of the self and preaches austerity in all things.

Of course, there is a lot more to the typical Japanese character than just a tendency to prize social harmony. Any visitor to the country will soon discover a people who are remarkably conscientious, meticulous, industrious, honest and technically skilled. A touching shyness and sometimes almost painful self-consciousness is also an undoubted feature of many Japanese as well. These characteristics result in a society that is a joy for the traveller to experience.

And let us say that any visit to Japan is a good chance to explode the myths about Japan and the Japanese. While you may imagine a nation of suit-clad conformists, or inscrutable automatons, a few rounds in a local *izakaya* (Japanese pub) will quickly put all of these notions to rest. More than likely, the salaryman (white-collar worker) next to you will offer to buy you a round and then treat you to a remarkably frank discussion of Japanese politics. Or, maybe he'll just bring you up to speed on how the Hanshin Tigers are going this year.

LIFESTYLE

The way most Japanese live today differs greatly from the way they lived before WWII. As the birth rate has dropped and labour demands have drawn more workers to cities, the population has become increasingly urban. At the same time, Japan continues to soak up influences from abroad and the traditional lifestyle of the country is quickly disappearing in the face of a dizzying onslaught of Western pop/material culture. These days, the average young Tokyoite has a lot more in common with her peers in Melbourne or London than she does with her grandmother back in her *furusato* (hometown).

In the City

The overwhelming majority of Japanese live in the bustling urban environments of major cities. These urbanites live famously hectic lives dominated by often-gruelling work schedules (the Japanese work week, like the school week, usually runs from Monday to Saturday) and punctuated by lengthy commutes from city centres to more affordable outlying neighbourhoods and suburbs.

Until fairly recently, the nexus of all this activity was the Japanese corporation, which provided lifetime employment to the legions of blue-suited white-collar workers, almost all of them men, who lived, worked, drank, ate and slept in the service of the companies for which they toiled. These days, as the Japanese economy makes the transition from a manufacturing economy to a service economy, the old certainties are vanishing. On the way out are Japan's famous 'cradle-to-grave' employment and age-based promotion system. Now the recent college graduate is just as likely to become a *furitaa* (part-time worker) as he is to become a salaryman. Needless to say, all this has wide-ranging consequences for Japanese society.

The majority of families once comprised of a father who was a salaryman, a mother who was a housewife, kids who studied dutifully in order to earn a place at one of Japan's elite universities and an elderly in-law who had moved in. Though the days of this traditional model may not be completely over, the average family continues to evolve with current social and economic conditions. The father, if he is lucky, still has the job he had 10 years ago, though

Did you know that there are more than six million vending machines in Tokyo alone?

if, like many workers, he has found himself out of a job, it is possible that his wife has found part-time work as he continues to search for emplyoment (the unemployment rate has hovered at around 4% for the last several years – a grim figure by Japanese standards).

The kids in the family probably still study like mad; if they are in junior high, they are working towards gaining admission to a select high school by attending a cram school, known as a *juku;* if they are already in high school, they will be working furiously towards passing university admission exams.

As for the mother- or father-in-law, who in the past would have expected to be taken care of by the eldest son in the family, she or he may have found that beliefs about filial loyalty have changed substantially since the 1980s, particularly in urban centres. Now, more and more Japanese families are sending elderly parents and in-laws to live out their 'golden years' in *rōjin hōmu* (literally, 'old folks homes').

In the Country

Only one in four Japanese live in the small farming and fishing villages that dot the mountains and cling to the rugged coasts. Mass postwar emigration from these rural enclaves has doubtless changed the weave of Japanese social fabric and the texture of its landscape, as the young continue their steady flight to the city leaving untended rice fields to slide down the hills from neglect.

Today only 15% of farming households continue to make ends meet solely through agriculture, with most rural workers holding down two or three jobs. Though this lifestyle manages to make the incomes of some country dwellers higher than those of their urban counterparts, it also speaks clearly of the crisis that many rural communities are facing in their struggle to maintain their traditional way of life.

The salvation of traditional village life may well rely on the success of the 'I-turn' (moving from urban areas to rural villages) and 'U-turn' (moving from country to city, and back again) movements. Though not wildly successful, these movements have managed to attract young people who work at home, company workers who are willing to put in a number of hours on the train commuting to the nearest city, and retirees looking to spend their golden years among the thatched roofs and rice fields that symbolise a not-so-distant past.

Facts, facts and more facts are found at this website (www.stat.go .jp/english/index.htm), managed by the Japanese government.

POPULATION

Japan has a population of approximately 127 million people (the ninth largest in the world) and, with 75% of it concentrated in urban centres, population density is extremely high. Areas such as the Tokyo–Kawasaki–Yokohama conurbation are so densely populated that they have almost ceased to be separate cities, running into each other and forming a vast coalescence that, if considered as a whole, would constitute the world's largest city.

One notable feature of Japan's population is its relative ethnic and cultural homogeneity. This is particularly striking for visitors from the USA, Australia and other multicultural nations. The main reason for this ethnic homogeneity is Japan's strict immigration laws, which have ensured that only a small number of foreigners settle in the country.

The largest non-Japanese group in the country is made up of 650,000 *zai-nichi kankoku-jin* (resident Koreans). For most outsiders, Koreans are an invisible minority. Indeed, even the Japanese themselves have no way of knowing that someone is of Korean descent if he or she adopts a Japanese name. Nevertheless, Japanese-born Koreans, who in some cases speak no language other than Japanese, were only very recently released from the obligation to carry thumb-printed ID cards at all times, and still face discrimination in the workplace and other aspects of their daily lives.

Aside from Koreans, most foreigners in Japan are temporary workers from China, Southeast Asia, South America and Western countries. Indigenous groups such as the Ainu have been reduced to very small numbers and are concentrated mostly in Hokkaidō.

The most notable feature of Japan's population is the fact that it is poised to start shrinking, and shrinking fast. Japan's astonishingly low birth rate of 1.4 births per woman is among the lowest in the developed world and Japan is rapidly becoming a nation of oldsters. Experts predict that the present population will start to decline in 2007, reaching 100 million in 2050 and 67 million in 2100. Needless to say, such demographic change will have a major influence on the economy in coming decades (for more information on the Japanese economy, see p54).

The Ainu

The Ainu, of whom there are roughly 24,000 living in Japan, were the indigenous people of Hokkaidō, and some would argue, the only people who can claim to be natives of Japan. Due to ongoing intermarriage and assimilation, almost all Ainu consider themselves bi-ethnic. Today, less than 200 people in Japan can claim both parents with exclusively Ainu descent.

Burakumin

The Burakumin are a largely invisible (to outsiders, at least) group of Japanese whose ancestors performed work that brought them into contact with the contamination of death – butchering, leatherworking and the disposing of corpses. The Burakumin were the outcasts in the social hierarchy (some would say caste system) that existed during the Edo period. While the Burakumin are racially the same as other Japanese, they have traditionally been treated like an inferior people by much of Japanese society. Estimates put the number of hereditary Burakumin in present-day Japan at anywhere from 890,000 to three million.

While discrimination against Burakumin is now technically against the law, there continues to be significant discrimination against Burakumin in such important aspects of Japanese social life as work and marriage. It is common knowledge, though rarely alluded to, that information about any given individual's possible Burakumin origin is available to anyone (generally employers and prospective fathers-in-law) who is prepared to make certain discreet investigations. Many Japanese dislike discussing this topic with foreigners, and unless you are on very familiar terms or in enlightened company it is probably bad taste to bring it up.

IMMIGRATION

Like many industrialised countries, Japan attracts thousands of workers hoping for high salaries and a better life. At present, there are about 1.9 million foreign residents registered with the government (about 1.5% of the total population of Japan). Of these, 32% are Korean (for more on resident Koreans, see opposite), 24% are Chinese or Taiwanese, 14% are Brazilian and 2.5% are from the USA. In addition, it has been estimated that at least another 250,000 unregistered illegal immigrants live and work in Japan.

Due to its ageing population and low birth rate, Japan may soon have to consider means to increase immigration of skilled workers, something that many Japanese oppose on the grounds that it will disrupt Japan's existing social order (for more on the shrinking population, see opposite).

Almost all Japanese babies are born with a Mongolian spot or *mōkohan* on their bottoms or lower backs. This harmless bluish-grey birthmark is composed of melanin-containing cells. Mongolian spots are common in several Asian races including, as the name suggests, Mongolians, as well as in Native Americans. These birthmarks, which usually fade by the age of five, raise interesting questions about the origins of the Japanese people.

Nakagami Kenji provides a rare insight into the world of the Burakumin, Japan's former untouchable caste, in his book *The Cape and Other Stories from the Japanese Ghetto*. The stories are set in the slums and alleyways of the Kishū, which is now known as the Wakayama-ken.

ECONOMY

The Japanese 'economic miracle' is one of the great success stories of the postwar period. In a few short decades, Japan went from a nation in ruins to the world's second-largest economy. The rise of the Japanese economy is even more startling when one considers Japan's almost total lack of major natural resources beyond agricultural and marine products.

There are many reasons for Japan's incredible economic success: a hard-working populace; strong government support for industry; a strategic Pacific-rim location; infusions of cash during the Korean War (during which Japan acted as a staging point for the American military); and, some would say, protectionist trade policies. What is certain is this: when free-market capitalism was planted in the soil of post-war Japan, it was planted in extremely fertile soil.

Of course, it has not always been smooth sailing for the Japanese economy. During the 1980s, the country experienced what is now known as the 'Bubble Economy'. The Japanese economy went into overdrive, with easy money supply and soaring real-estate prices leading to a stock market bubble that abruptly burst in early 1990. In the years that followed, Japan flirted with recession, and the jobless rate climbed to 5%, an astonishing figure in a country that had always enjoyed near full employment.

Fortunately, the new millennium has brought good economic news to Japan. In the last three months of 2006, the Japanese economy grew by an astonishing 4.8%. This expansion led the Bank of Japan to abandon its long-held zero interest policy, finally raising its prime lending rate to a modest 0.25% in July 2006, followed by another incremental increase in February 2007. At the same time, the stock market enjoyed a near-record year and companies reported robust profits. Despite the rosy figures, many ordinary Japanese contend that corporate profits aren't filtering down to the person on the street. And when Japanese travel abroad, they may indeed wonder if they come from the world's second-richest country: at the time of writing, the yen stood at a 20-year low in terms of real purchasing power (which is, conversely, good news for travellers to Japan).

RELIGION
Shintō & Buddhism

There are three sacred regalia in Shintō: the sacred mirror (stored in Mie-ken's Ise-jingū; p435); the sacred sword (stored in Atsuta-jingū near Nagoya; p243); and the sacred beads (stored in the Imperial Palace in Tokyo; p110). Some speculate that the sacred treasures were brought over by the continental forerunners of the Yamato clan.

The vast majority (about 86%) of Japanese are followers of both Buddhism and Shintō, a fact puzzling to many Westerners, most of whom belong to exclusive monotheistic faiths. The Japanese are fond of saying that Shintō is the religion of this world and this life, while Buddhism is for matters of the soul and the next world. Thus, births, marriages, harvest rituals and business success are considered the province of Shintō, while funerals are exclusively Buddhist affairs. When one looks at the beliefs and metaphysics of each religion, this makes perfect sense, for Shintō is a religion that holds that gods reside in nature itself (this world), while Buddhism stresses the impermanence of the natural world.

Shintō, or 'the way of the gods', is the indigenous religion of Japan. More than a monolithic faith, Shintō is a collection of indigenous folk rituals and practices, many concerned with rice production, and wedded to ancient myths associated with the Yamato clan, the forerunners of the present-day imperial family. It is revealing that Shintō didn't even have a name until one was given to distinguish it from Japan's imported religion, Buddhism.

In Shintō there is a pantheon of gods (kami) who are believed to dwell in the natural world. Consisting of thousands of deities, this pantheon includes both local spirits and global gods and goddesses. Shintō gods are often enshrined in religious structures known as jinja, jingū, or gū (usually

> **TEMPLE OR SHRINE?**
>
> One of the best ways to distinguish a Buddhist temple from a Shintō shrine is to examine the entrance. The main entrance of a shrine is a *torii* (Shintō shrine gate), usually composed of two upright pillars, joined at the top by two horizontal cross-bars, the upper of which is normally slightly curved. *Torii* are often painted a bright vermilion, though some are left as bare wood. In contrast, the main entrance gate *(mon)* of a temple is often a much more substantial affair, constructed of several pillars or casements, joined at the top by a multitiered roof, around which there may even be walkways. Temple gates often contain guardian figures, usually Niō (deva kings). Keep in mind, though, that shrines and temples sometimes share the same precincts, and it is not always easy to tell where one begins and the other ends.

translated into English as shrine; see above). The greatest of these is Ise-jingū in Kansai's Mie-ken (p435), which enshrines the most celebrated Shintō deity, Amaterasu, the goddess of the sun to whom the imperial family of Japan is said to trace its ancestry. At the opposite end of the spectrum, you may come across waterfalls, trees or rocks decorated with a sacred rope (known as a *shimenawa*), which essentially declare that these things contain *kami* (and make them natural shrines in their own right).

In contrast to Shintō, which evolved with the Japanese people, Buddhism arrived from India via China and Korea sometime in the 6th century AD. For most of its history, it has coexisted peacefully with Shintō (the notable exception being the WWII period, during which Buddhism was suppressed as a foreign import). Buddhism, which originated in southern Nepal in the 5th century BC, is sometimes said to be more of a way or method than a religion, since, strictly speaking, there is no god in Buddhism. In practice, the various forms of Buddha and *bodhisattvas* (beings who have put off entering nirvana to help all other sentient beings enter nirvana) are worshipped like gods in most branches of Buddhism, at least by laypeople.

The four noble truths of Buddhism are as follows: 1) life is suffering; 2) the cause of suffering is desire; 3) the cure for suffering is the elimination of desire; and 4) the way to eliminate desire is to follow the Eightfold Path of the Buddha. Thus, Buddhism can be thought of as an operating manual for the human mind when faced with the problem of existence in an impermanent world.

All the main sects of Japanese Buddhism belong to the Mahayana (Greater Vehicle) strain of Buddhism, which is distinguished from Theravada (Lesser Vehicle) Buddhism by its faith in *bodhisattvas*. The major sects of Japanese Buddhism include Zen, Tendai, Esoteric, Pure Land and True Pure Land Buddhism. The religious structure in Buddhism is known as a *tera*, *dera*, *ji* or *in* (temple; see above).

> Until Buddhism arrived in Japan in the 6th century AD, Japanese emperors were buried in giant earth and stone burial mounds known as *kofun* (see p413). The largest of these is said to contain more mass than the Great Pyramid at Cheops.

WOMEN IN JAPAN

Traditional Japanese society restricted the woman's role to the home, where as housekeeper she wielded considerable power, overseeing all financial matters, monitoring the children's education and, in some ways, acting as the head of the household. Even in the early Meiji period, however, the ideal was rarely matched by reality: labour shortfalls often resulted in women taking on factory work, and even before that, women often worked side by side with men in the fields.

As might be expected, the contemporary situation is complex. There are, of course, those who stick to established roles. They tend to opt for shorter college courses, often at women's colleges, and see education as an asset in the marriage market. Once married, they leave the role of breadwinner to their husbands.

VISITING A SHRINE

Entering a Japanese shrine can be a bewildering experience for travellers. In order to make the most of the experience, follow these guidelines and do as the Japanese do.

Just past the *torii* (shrine gate), you'll find a *chōzuya* (trough of water) with long-handled ladles *(hishaku)* perched on a rack above. This is for purifying yourself before entering the sacred precincts of the shrine. Some Japanese forgo this ritual and head directly for the main hall. If you choose to purify yourself, take a ladle, fill it with fresh water from the spigot, pour some over one hand, transfer the spoon and pour water over the other hand, then pour a little water into a cupped hand and rinse your mouth, spitting the water onto the ground beside the trough, *not* into the trough.

Next, head to the *haiden* (hall of worship), which sits in front of the *honden* (main hall) en-shrining the *kami* (god of the shrine). Here you'll find a thick rope hanging from a gong, with an offerings box in front. Toss a coin into the box, ring the gong by pulling on the rope (to summon the deity), pray, then clap your hands twice, bow and then back away from the shrine. Some Japanese believe that a ¥5 coin is the best for an offering at a temple or shrine, and that the luck engendered by the offering of a ¥10 coin will come further in the future (since 10 can be pronounced *tō* in Japanese, which can mean 'far').

If photography is forbidden at a shrine, it will be posted as such; otherwise, it is permitted and you should simply use your discretion when taking photos.

Increasingly, however, Japanese women are choosing to forgo or delay marriage in favour of pursuing their own career ambitions. Of course, changing aspirations do not necessarily translate into changing realities, and Japanese women are still significantly under represented in upper management and political positions, but over represented as office fodder, such as 'OLs' (office ladies). Part of the reason for this is the prevalence of gender discrimination in Japanese companies. Societal expectations, however, also play a role: Japanese women are forced to choose between having a career and having a family. Not only do most companies refuse to hire women for career-track positions, the majority of Japanese men are simply not interested in having a career woman as a spouse. This makes it very intimidating for a Japanese woman to step out of her traditional gender role and follow a career path.

'Those women who do choose full-time work suffer from from one of the worst gender wage gaps in the developed world'

Those women who do choose full-time work suffer from one of the worst gender wage gaps in the developed world: Japanese women earn only 66% of what Japanese men earn, compared to 76% in the USA, 83% in the UK and 85% in Australia (according to figures released by the respective governments). In politics, the situation is even worse: Japanese women hold only 9% of seats in the Diet, the nation's governing body.

MEDIA

Like all democratic countries, Japan constitutionally guarantees freedom of the press. In general, journalists do have quite a bit of freedom, though both Japanese and foreign media analysts have noted that exercise of this liberty is not always easy.

For reasons that are not completely clear, many Japanese journalists practise a form of self-censorship, often taking governmental or police reports at face value rather than conducting independent investigations that might reveal what is hidden beneath the official story. Some have speculated that this practice is symptomatic of journalists working closely, perhaps too closely, with political figures and police chiefs, who tacitly encourage them to omit details that might conflict with official accounts.

Added to the problem of self-censorship is that of exclusive press clubs, also known as *kisha clubs*. These clubs provide a privileged few with access to the halls of government. Journalists who are not members of a *kisha club* are unable to obtain key information and thus are shut out of a story. Some reporters have argued that this constitutes a form of information monopoly and have put pressure on the Japanese government to abolish the clubs.

Despite some problems with the free flow of information, the Japanese press is considered trustworthy by most people in Japan. Newspapers enjoy wide circulation, aided perhaps by the nation's incredible 99% literacy rate, and almost all households have TVs. Internet usage is also high: an estimated 86 million Japanese use the internet regularly.

ARTS
Contemporary Visual Art

In the years that followed WWII, Japanese artists struggled with issues of identity. This was the generation that grappled with duelling philosophies: 'Japanese spirit, Japanese knowledge' versus 'Japanese spirit, Western knowledge'. This group was known for exploring whether Western artistic media and methods could convey the space, light, substance and shadows of the Japanese spirit, or if this essence could only truly be expressed through traditional Japanese artistic genres.

Today's emerging artists and the movements they have generated have no such ambivalence. Gone is the anxiety about coopting, or being coopted by, Western philosophies and aesthetics; in its place is the insouciant celebration of the smooth, cool surface of the future articulated by fantastic colours and shapes. This exuberant, devil-may-care aesthetic is most notably represented by Takashi Murakami, whose work derives much of its energy from *otaku*, the geek culture that worships characters that figure prominently in manga, Japan's ubiquitous comic books (see the boxed text, p65). Murakami's exuberant, prankish images and installations have become emblematic of the Japanese aesthetic known as *poku* (a concept that combines pop art with an *otaku* sensibility), and his *Super Flat Manifesto*, which declares that 'the world of the future might be like Japan is today – super flat,' can be seen as a primer for contemporary Japanese pop aesthetics.

Beyond the pop scene, artists continue to create works whose textures, layers and topics relay a world that is broader than the frames of a comic book. Three notable artists to look for are Yoshie Sakai, whose ethereal oil paintings, replete with pastel skies and deep waters, leave the viewer unsure whether they are floating or sinking; Noriko Ambe, whose sculptural works with paper can resemble sand dunes shifting in the Sahara, or your high-school biology textbook; and the indomitable Hisashi Tenmyouya, whose work chronicles the themes of contemporary Japanese life, echoing the flat surfaces and deep impressions of wood-block prints while singing a song of the street.

Traditional Visual Art
PAINTING

From 794 to 1600, Japanese painting borrowed from Chinese and Western techniques and media, ultimately transforming them into its own aesthetic ends. By the beginning of the Edo period (1600–1868), which was marked by the enthusiastic patronage of a wide range of painting styles, Japanese art had come completely into its own. The Kanō school, initiated more than a century before the beginning of the Edo era, continued to be in demand for its depiction of subjects connected with Confucianism, mythical Chinese creatures or scenes from nature. The Tosa school, which followed the *yamato-e* style of painting (often used on scrolls during the Heian period, 794–1185), was also kept busy with commissions from the nobility who were eager to see scenes re-created from classics of Japanese literature.

Scream Against the Sky (edited by Alexandra Monroe) provides a comprehensive look at some of the finest Japanese postwar art, photography and sculpture. Includes wonderful glossy photos throughout.

Finally, the Rimpa school (from 1600) not only absorbed the styles of painting that had preceded it, but progressed beyond well-worn conventions to produce a strikingly decorative and delicately shaded form of painting. The works of art produced by a trio of outstanding artists from this school – Tawaraya Sōtatsu, Hon'ami Kōetsu and Ogata Kōrin – rank among the finest of this period.

CALLIGRAPHY

Shodō (the way of writing) is one of Japan's most valued arts, cultivated by nobles, priests and samurai alike, and still studied by Japanese schoolchildren today as *shūji*. Like the characters of the Japanese language, the art of *shodō* was imported from China. In the Heian period (794–1185), a fluid, cursive, distinctly Japanese style of *shodō* evolved called *wayō*, though the Chinese style remained popular in Japan among Zen priests and the literati for some time later.

In both Chinese and Japanese *shodō* there are three important types. Most common is *kaisho*, or block-style script. Due to its clarity, this style is favoured in the media and in applications where readability is key. *Gyōsho*, or running hand, is semicursive, and often used in informal correspondence. *Sōsho*, or grass hand, is a truly cursive style. *Sōsho* abbreviates and links the characters together to create a flowing, graceful effect.

UKIYO-E (WOOD-BLOCK PRINTS)

The term *ukiyo-e* means 'pictures of the floating world' and derives from a Buddhist metaphor for the transient world of fleeting pleasures. The subjects chosen by artists for these wood-block prints were characters and scenes from the tawdry, vivacious 'floating world' of the entertainment quarters in Edo (latter-day Tokyo), Kyoto and Osaka.

The floating world, centred in pleasure districts, such as Edo's Yoshiwara, was a topsy-turvy kingdom, an inversion of the usual social hierarchies that were held in place by the power of the Tokugawa shōgunate. Here, money meant more than rank, actors and artists were the arbiters of style, and prostitutes elevated their art to such a level that their accomplishments matched those of the women of noble families.

The vivid colours, novel composition and flowing lines of *ukiyo-e* caused great excitement in the West, sparking a vogue that one French art critic dubbed 'Japonisme'. *Ukiyo-e* became a key influence on impressionists (for example, Toulouse-Lautrec, Manet and Degas) and post-impressionists. Among the Japanese the prints were hardly given more than passing consideration – millions were produced annually in Edo. They were often thrown away or used as wrapping paper for pottery. For many years, the Japanese continued to be perplexed by the keen interest foreigners took in this art form, which they considered of ephemeral value.

CERAMICS

Ceramics are Japan's oldest art form: Jōmon pottery, with its distinctive chord-like decorative patterns, has been dated back as far as 10,000 BC. When the Jōmon people were conquered by the Yayoi people, starting around 400 BC, a more refined style of pottery appeared on the scene. While Jōmon pottery was an indigenous Japanese form, Yayoi pottery had clear continental influences and techniques. Continental techniques and even artisans continued to dominate Japanese ceramic arts for the next millennia or more: around the 5th century AD, Sue Ware pottery was introduced from Korea, and around the 7th century, Tang Chinese pottery became influential.

'Among the Japanese, the prints were hardly given more than passing consideration'

FAMOUS CERAMIC CENTRES

The suffix '~*yaki*' denotes a type of pottery. Thus, the term 'Bizen-yaki' refers to a type of pottery made in the Bizen area of Western Honshū. Some of Japan's main ceramic centres include the following:

- **Arita-yaki** known in the West as Imari, this colourful pottery is produced in the town of Arita, in Kyūshū (p679).
- **Satsuma-yaki** the most common style of this porcelain, from Kagoshima (p708) in Kyūshū, has a cloudy white, crackled glaze enamelled with gold, red, green and blue.
- **Karatsu-yaki** Karatsu (p676), near Fukuoka in northern Kyūshū, produces tea-ceremony utensils that are Korean in style and have a characteristic greyish, crackled glaze.
- **Hagi-yaki** the town of Hagi (p478) in Western Honshū is renowned for Hagi-yaki, a type of porcelain made with a pallid yellow or pinkish crackled glaze.
- **Bizen-yaki** the ancient ceramics centre of Bizen (p446) in Okayama-ken, Honshū, is famed for its solid unglazed bowls, which turn red through oxidation. Bizen also produces roofing tiles.
- **Kiyomizu-yaki** the approach road to the temple Kiyomizu-dera (p335), in Kyoto, is lined with shops selling Kiyomizu-yaki, a style of pottery that can be enamelled, blue painted or red painted in appearance.
- **Kutani-yaki** the porcelain from Ishikawa-ken (p295), in Central Honshū, is usually green or painted.

In the medieval period, Japan's great ceramic centre was Seto, in Central Honshū. Here, starting in the 12th century AD, Japanese potters took Chinese forms and adapted them to Japanese tastes and needs to produce a truly distinctive pottery style known as Seto Ware. One Japanese term for pottery and porcelain, *setomono* (literally, 'things from Seto'), clearly derives from this still-thriving ceramics centre.

Today, there are more than 100 pottery centres in Japan, with scores of artisans producing everything from exclusive tea utensils to souvenir folklore creatures. Department stores regularly organise exhibitions of ceramics and offer the chance to see some of this fine work up close (for more information, see above).

SHIKKI (LACQUERWARE)

The Japanese have been using lacquer to protect and enhance the beauty of wood since the Jōmon period (10,000–300 BC). In the Meiji era (1868–1912), lacquerware became very popular abroad and it remains one of Japan's best-known products. Known in Japan as *shikki* or *nurimono*, lacquerware is made using the sap from the lacquer tree (*urushi*), a close relative of poison oak. Raw lacquer is actually toxic and causes severe skin irritation in those who have not developed immunity. Once hardened, however, it becomes inert and extraordinarily durable.

The most common colour of lacquer is an amber or brown colour, but additives have been used to produce black, violet, blue, yellow and even white lacquer. In the better pieces, multiple layers of lacquer are painstakingly applied and left to dry, and finally polished to a luxurious shine.

'Raw lacquer is actually toxic and causes severe skin irritation'

Contemporary Theatre & Dance

Contemporary theatre and dance are alive and well in Japan, though you'll quickly notice that most major troupes are based in Tokyo. If you're interested in taking in contemporary theatre, your best bet is to enlist the help of a translator and to hit the *shogekijō* (little theatres; see p60) scene. If contemporary dance is what you seek, check the *Japan Times, Metropolis* or the *Tokyo Journal* in Tokyo, or the *Kansai Time Out* in Kansai, to see what's on when you're in town.

UNDERGROUND THEATRE

Theatre the world over spent the 1960s redefining itself, and it was no different in Japan. The *shōgekijō* movement, also called *angura* (underground), has given Japan many of its leading playwrights, directors and actors. It arose as a reaction to the realism and structure of *shingeki* (a 1920s movement that borrowed heavily from Western dramatic forms), and featured surrealistic plays that explored the relationship between human beings and the world. Like their counterparts in the West, these productions took place in any space available – in small theatres, tents, basements, open spaces and on street corners.

The first generation of *shōgekijō* directors and writers often included speedy comedy, wordplay and images from popular culture in their works to highlight the lunacy of modern life. More recent *shōgekijō* productions have dealt with realistic and contemporary themes, such as modern Japanese history, war, environmental degradation and social oppression. Changing cultural perceptions have propelled the movement in new directions, notably towards socially and politically critical dramas.

BUTOH

In many ways, butoh is Japan's most accessible (there are no words except for the occasional grunt) and exciting dance form. It is also its newest dance form, dating only to 1959, when Hijikata Tatsumi (1928–86) gave the first butoh performance. Butoh was born out of a rejection of the excessive formalisation that characterises traditional forms of Japanese dance. It also stems from the desire to return to the ancient roots of the Japanese soul, so is also a rejection of Western influences that flooded Japan in the post-war years.

Displays of butoh are best likened to performance art happenings rather than traditional dance performances. During a butoh performance, one or more dancers use their naked or semi-naked bodies to express the most elemental and intense human emotions. Nothing is sacred in butoh, and performances often deal with taboo topics such as sexuality and death. For this reason, critics often describe butoh as scandalous, and butoh dancers delight in pushing the boundaries of what can be considered tasteful in artistic performance.

Butoh tends to be more underground than the more established forms of Japanese dance and it is, consequently, harder to catch a performance. The best way to see what's on while you're in town is to check the local English-language media (the *Japan Times, Metropolis* or the *Tokyo Journal* in Tokyo, or the *Kansai Time Out* in Kansai), or to ask at a local tourist information office.

'Butoh tends to be more underground than the more established forms of Japanese dance'

Traditional Theatre & Dance

NŌ

Nō is a hypnotic dance-drama that reflects the minimalist aesthetics of Zen. The movement is glorious, the chorus and music sonorous, the expression subtle. A sparsely furnished cedar stage directs full attention to the performers, who include a chorus, drummers and a flautist. There are two principal characters: the *shite,* who is sometimes a living person but more often a demon, or a ghost whose soul cannot rest; and the *waki,* who leads the main character towards the play's climactic moment. Each *nō* school has its own repertoire, and the art form continues to evolve and develop. One of the many new plays performed over the last 30 years is *Takahime,* based on William Butler Yeats' *At the Hawk's Well.*

KABUKI

The first performances of kabuki were staged early in the 17th century by an all-female troupe. The performances were highly erotic and attracted enthusiastic support from the merchant classes. In true bureaucratic fashion, Tokugawa officials feared for the people's morality and banned women from the stage in 1629. Since that time, kabuki has been performed exclusively by men, giving rise to the institution of *onnagata,* or *ōyama,* male actors who specialise in female roles.

Over the course of several centuries, kabuki has developed a repertoire that draws on popular themes, such as famous historical accounts and stories of love-suicide, while also borrowing copiously from *nō, kyōgen* (comic vignettes) and *bunraku* (classical puppet theatre). Most kabuki plays border on melodrama, although they vary in mood.

Formalised beauty and stylisation are the central aesthetic principles of kabuki; the acting is a combination of dancing and speaking in conventionalised intonation patterns, and each actor prepares for a role by studying and emulating the style perfected by his predecessors. Kabuki actors are born to the art form, and training begins in childhood. Today they enjoy great social prestige and their activities on and off the stage attract as much interest as those of popular film and TV stars.

> 'Kabuki actors are born to the art form, and training begins in childhood'

BUNRAKU

Japan's traditional puppet theatre developed at the same time as kabuki, when the *shamisen* (a three-stringed instrument resembling a lute or a banjo), imported from Okinawa, was combined with traditional puppetry techniques and *joruri* (narrative chanting). *Bunraku,* as it came to be known in the 19th century, addresses many of the same themes as kabuki, and in fact many of the most famous plays in the kabuki repertoire were originally written for puppet theatre. *Bunraku* involves large puppets – nearly two-thirds life-sized – manipulated by up to three black-robed puppeteers. The puppeteers do not speak; a seated narrator tells the story and provides the voices of the characters, expressing their feelings with smiles, weeping, and fits of surprise and fear.

RAKUGO

A traditional Japanese style of comic monologue, *rakugo* (literally, 'dropped word') dates back to the Edo period (1600–1868). The performer, usually in kimono, sits on a square cushion on a stage. Props are limited to a fan and hand towel. The monologue begins with a *makura* (prologue), which is followed by the story itself and, finally, the *ochi* (punch line or 'drop', which is another pronunciation of the Chinese character for *raku* in *rakugo*). Many of the monologues in the traditional *rakugo* repertoire date back to the Edo and Meiji periods, and while well known, reflect a social milieu unknown to modern listeners. Accordingly, many practitioners today also write new monologues addressing issues relevant to contemporary life.

MANZAI

Manzai is a comic dialogue, with its origins in the song-and-dance and comedy routines traditionally performed by itinerant entertainers during Shōgatsu (New Year celebrations; p794). It is a highly fluid art that continues to draw large audiences to hear snappy duos exchange clever witticisms on up-to-the-minute themes from everyday life.

Architecture

CONTEMPORARY ARCHITECTURE

Contemporary Japanese architecture is currently among the world's most exciting and influential. The traditional preference for simple, natural and harmonious spaces is still evident in the work of modern architects, but this style is now combined with hi-tech materials and the building techniques of the West.

Japan first opened its doors to Western architecture in 1868 during the Meiji Restoration, and its architects immediately responded to the new influence by combining traditional Japanese methods of wood construction with Western designs. Some 20 years later, a nationalistic push against the influence of the West saw a surge in the popularity of traditional Japanese building styles, and Western technique was temporarily shelved.

This resistance to Western architecture continued until after WWI, when foreign architects such as Frank Lloyd Wright came to build the Imperial Hotel in Tokyo. Wright was careful to pay homage to local sensibilities when designing the Imperial's many elegant bridges and unique guest rooms (though he famously used modern, cubic forms to ornament the interiors of the hotel). The building was demolished in 1967 to make way for the current Imperial Hotel, which shows little of Wright's touch.

By WWII many Japanese architects were using Western techniques and materials and blending old styles with the new, and by the mid-1960s had developed a unique style that began to attract attention on the world stage. Japan's most famous postwar architect Tange Kenzō was strongly influenced by Le Corbusier. Tange's buildings, including the Kagawa Prefectural Offices at Takamatsu (1958) and the National Gymnasium (completed 1964), fuse the sculptural influences and materials of Le Corbusier with traditional Japanese characteristics, such as post-and-beam construction and strong geometry. His Tokyo Metropolitan Government Offices (1991; p137), in Nishi-Shinjuku (west Shinjuku), is the tallest building in Tokyo. It may look a little sinister and has been criticised as totalitarian, but it is a remarkable achievement and pulls in around 6000 visitors daily. Those with an interest in Tange's work should also look for the UN University, close to Omote-sando subway station in Tokyo.

In the 1960s, architects such as Shinohara Kazuo, Kurokawa Kisho, Maki Fumihiko and Kikutake Kiyonori began a movement known as Metabolism, which promoted flexible spaces and functions at the expense of fixed forms in building. Shinohara finally came to design in a style he called Modern Next, incorporating both modern and postmodern design ideas combined with Japanese influences. This style can be seen in his Centennial Hall at Tokyo Institute of Technology, an elegant and uplifting synthesis of clashing forms in a shiny metal cladding. Kurokawa's architecture blends Buddhist building traditions with modern influences, while Maki, the master of minimalism, pursued design in a modernist style while still emphasising the elements of nature – like the roof of his Tokyo Metropolitan Gymnasium (near Sendagaya Station), which takes on the form of a sleek metal insect. Another Maki design, the Spiral Building, built in Aoyama in 1985, is a favourite with Tokyo residents and its interior is also a treat.

Isozaki Arata, an architect who originally worked under Tange Kenzō, also promoted the Metabolist style before later becoming interested in geometry and postmodernism. His work includes the Cultural Centre (1990) in Mito, which contains a striking, geometrical snakelike tower clad in different metals.

A contemporary of Isozaki's, Kikutake, went on to design the Edo-Tokyo Museum (1992; see p142) in Sumida-ku, which charts the history of the Edo period, and is arguably his best-known building. It is a truly enormous structure, encompassing almost 50,000 sq metres of built space and reaching

'Contemporary Japanese architecture is currently among the world's most exciting and influential'

62.2m, which was the height of Edo-jō at its peak. It has been likened in form to a crouching giant and it easily dwarfs its surroundings.

Another influential architect of this generation is Hara Hiroshi. Hara's style defies definition, but the one constant theme is nature. His Umeda Sky Building (1993; see p376), in Kita, Osaka, is a sleek, towering structure designed to resemble a garden in the sky. The Yamamoto International Building (1993) on the outskirts of Tokyo, is the headquarters of a textile factory. Both these buildings, though monumental in scale, dissolve down into many smaller units upon closer inspection – just like nature itself.

In the 1980s, a second generation of Japanese architects began to gain recognition within the international architecture scene, including Andō Tadao, Hasegawa Itsuko and Toyo Ito. This younger group has continued to explore both modernism and postmodernism, while incorporating a renewed interest in Japan's architectural heritage.

Andō's architecture in particular blends classical modern and native Japanese styles. His buildings often combine materials such as concrete, with the strong geometric patterns that have so regularly appeared in Japan's traditional architecture. Some critics contend that Andō's work is inhuman and monolithic, while others are taken by the dramatic spaces his buildings create. Why not judge for yourself? The most accessible of Andō's work is the new Omotesandō Hills shopping complex in Tokyo's Aoyama area (2006; p137).

Fans of modern Tokyo architecture may be surprised to discover that Tokyo's most famous modern building, the new Roppongi Hills complex (2003; p139) wasn't designed by a Japanese architect at all – it was designed by the New York–based firm of Kohn Pedersen Fox Associates.

TRADITIONAL SECULAR ARCHITECTURE
Houses
With the exception of those on the northern island of Hokkaidō, traditional Japanese houses are built with the broiling heat of summer in mind. They are made of flimsy materials designed to take advantage of even the slightest breeze. Another reason behind the gossamer construction of Japanese houses is the relative frequency of earthquakes, which precludes the use of heavier building materials such as stone or brick.

Principally simple and refined, the typical house is constructed of post-and-beam timber, with sliding panels of wood or rice paper (for warmer weather) making up the exterior walls. Movable screens, or *shōji*, divide the interior of the house. There may be a separate area for the tea ceremony – the harmonious atmosphere of this space is of the utmost importance and is usually achieved through the use of natural materials and the careful arrangement of furniture and utensils.

A particularly traditional type of Japanese house is the *machiya* (townhouse), built by merchants in cities such as Kyoto and Tokyo. Until very recently, the older neighbourhoods of Kyoto and some areas of Tokyo were lined with neat, narrow rows of these houses, but most have fallen victim to the current frenzy of construction. These days, the best place to see *machiya* is in Kyoto (p309).

Farmhouses
The most distinctive type of Japanese farmhouse is the thatched-roof *gasshō-zukuri*, so named for the shape of the rafters, which resemble a pair of praying hands. While these farmhouses look cosy and romantic, bear in mind that they were often home for up to 40 people and occasionally farm animals as well. Furthermore, the black floorboards, soot-covered ceilings and lack of windows guaranteed a cavelike atmosphere. The only weapon against this darkness was a fire built in a central fireplace in the floor, known as an *irori*,

Though this site (www .tokyoq.com) focuses exclusively on Tokyo, its art and architecture reviews are up to the minute and some of the best you'll find.

which also provided warmth in the cooler months and hot coals for cooking. Multistorey farmhouses were also built to house silkworms for silk production (particularly prevalent during the Meiji era) in the airy upper gables.

Castles

Japan has an abundance of castles, most of them copies of originals destroyed by fire or war or time.

The first castles were simple mountain forts that relied more on natural terrain than structural innovations for defence, making them as frustratingly inaccessible to their defenders as they were to invading armies. The central feature of these edifices was the donjon, or a keep, which was surrounded by several smaller towers. The buildings, which sat atop stone ramparts, were mostly built of wood that was covered with plaster intended to protect against fire.

The wide-ranging wars of the 16th and 17th centuries left Japan with numerous castles, though many of these were later destroyed by the Edo and then the Meiji governments. Half a century later, the 1960s saw a boom in castle reconstructions, most built of concrete and steel, and like Hollywood movie sets they're authentic-looking when viewed from a distance but distinctly modern in appearance when viewed up close.

Some of the best castles to visit today include the dramatic Himeji-jō (p398), also known as the White Egret Castle, and Edo-jō (p110), around which modern Tokyo has grown. Little of Edo-jō actually remains (the grounds are now the site of the Imperial Palace), though its original gate, Ōte-mon, still marks the main entrance.

Literature

Interestingly, much of Japan's early literature was written by women. One reason for this was that men wrote in kanji (imported Chinese characters), while women wrote in hiragana (Japanese script). Thus, while the men were busy copying Chinese styles and texts, the women of the country were producing the first authentic Japanese literature. Among these early female authors is Murasaki Shikibu, who wrote Japan's first great novel, *Genji Monogatari (The Tale of Genji)*. This detailed, lengthy tome documents the intrigues and romances of early Japanese court life, and although it is perhaps Japan's most important work of literature, its extreme length probably limits its appeal to all but the most ardent Japanophile or literature buff.

In this exquisite haiku travelogue, *Narrow Road to the Deep North,* Matsuo Bashō captures the wonders and contradictions of Honshū's northern region.

Most of Japan's important modern literature has been penned by authors who live in and write of cities. Though these works are sometimes celebratory, many also lament the loss of a traditional rural lifestyle that has given way to the pressures of a modern, industrialised society. *Kokoro,* the modern classic by Sōseki Natsume, outlines these rural/urban tensions, as does *Snow Country,* by Nobel laureate Kawabata Yasunari. Each of these works touches upon the tensions between Japan's nostalgia for the past and its rush towards the future, between its rural heartland and its burgeoning cities.

Although Mishima Yukio is probably the most controversial of Japan's modern writers, and is considered unrepresentative of Japanese culture by many Japanese, his work still makes for very interesting reading. *The Sailor Who Fell from Grace* and *After the Banquet* are both compelling books. If you're looking for unsettling beauty, reach for the former; history buffs will want the latter tome, which was at the centre of a court case that became Japan's first privacy lawsuit.

Ōe Kenzaburo, Japan's second Nobel laureate, produced some of Japan's most disturbing, energetic and enigmatic literature. *A Personal Matter* is the work for which he is most widely known. In this troubling novel, which echoes Ōe's frustrations at having a son with autism, a 27-year-old

MANGA – JAPANESE COMICS

Despite the recent popularity of graphic novels in the West, it's fair to say that comics occupy a fairly humble position in the Western literary world. In Japan, however, manga (Japanese comics) stand shoulder to shoulder with traditional text-based books. Indeed, hop on any morning train in Japan and you could be excused for thinking that the Japanese refuse to read anything that isn't accompanied by eye-popping graphics, long-legged doe-eyed heroines, and the Japanese equivalents of words like 'POW!' and 'BLAM!'

Manga, written with the Japanese characters for 'random' and 'picture', have their roots way back in Japanese history – some would say as early as the 12th century, when ink-brush painters drew humorous pictures of humans and animals (these pictures are known as *chōjū jinbutsu giga*). The direct antecedents of manga, however, are the *ukiyo-e* prints of the 18th century. Following WWII, Japanese artists worked with Western artists to produce the first true manga. These were sometimes called *ponchi-e,* a reference to the British magazine *Punch,* which often ran comics of a political or satirical nature.

The father of modern manga was Tezuka Osamu who, in the late 1940s, began working cinematic effects based on European movies into his cartoons – pioneering multipanel movements, perspectives that brought the reader into the action, close-ups, curious angles and a host of movie-like techniques. His adventurous stories quickly became movie-length comic strips – essentially films drawn on paper. What Tezuka started took off in a big way once weekly magazines realised they could boost sales by including manga in their pages. Tezuka's most famous works include *Tetsuwan Atomu* (Astro Boy), *Black Jack* and *Rion Kōtei* (*Jungle Emperor Leo,* which Disney adapted to make the film *The Lion King*).

These days manga have proliferated and diversified to an almost unimaginable degree, and there is literally no topic that manga do not explore. There are manga for young boys and girls, manga for salarymen, manga for studying, historical manga and even high literary manga. And let's not forget the inevitable *sukebe* manga (pornographic manga), which contain some truly bizarre and often disturbing sexual images.

Unfortunately, almost all manga available in Japan are written in Japanese. These days, however, some of Japan's better English-language bookshops stock English translations of famous Japanese manga. Try the Kyoto branch of Junkudō bookshop (p312) or the giant Kinokuniya bookshop in Tokyo's Shinjuku area (p106).

If you want to get a quick taste of what's out there in the manga world, drop into any Japanese convenience store and check out the magazine rack. If you want to delve deeper, head for a *manga-kissa* (manga coffee shop), where buying one drink will give you access to a huge library of manga (and internet access to boot). Finally, real manga fans will want to check out Kyoto's International Manga Museum (p315).

cram-school teacher's wife gives birth to a brain-damaged child. His life claustrophobic, his marriage failing, he dreams of escaping to Africa while planning the murder of his son.

Of course not all Japanese fiction can be classified as literature in highbrow terms. Murakami Ryū's *Almost Transparent Blue* is strictly sex and drugs, and his ode to the narcissistic early 1990s, *Coin Locker Babies,* recounts the toxic lives of two boys who have been left to die in coin lockers by their mothers. Like Murakami Ryū, Banana Yoshimoto is known for her ability to convey the prevailing zeitgeist in easily, um, digestible form. In her novel *Kitchen,* she relentlessly chronicles Tokyo's fast-food menus and '80s pop culture, though underlying the superficial digressions are hints of a darker and deeper world of death, loss and loneliness.

Japan's most internationally celebrated living novelist is Murakami Haruki, a former jazz club owner gone literary. His most noted work, *Norwegian Wood,* set in the late '60s against the backdrop of student protests, is both the portrait of the artist as a young man (as recounted by a reminiscent nar-

Abe Kobo's beautiful novel *Woman in the Dunes* (1962) is a tale of shifting sands and wandering strangers. One of the strangest and most interesting works of Japanese fiction.

rator) and an ode to first loves. Another interesting read is his *A Wild Sheep Chase* in which a mutant sheep with a star on its back inspires a search that takes a 20-something ad man to the mountainous north. The hero eventually confronts the mythical beast while wrestling with his own shadows.

In April 2004, the Akutagawa Prize, one of the nation's most prestigious, was awarded to the Kanehana Hitomi and Wataya Risa. At the time they received the award, they were 19 and 20, respectively, making them the youngest writers ever to receive the award. Interestingly, prior to these two, the record for youngest writer ever to receive the award was jointly held by Ōe Kenzaburō, and Ishihara Shintarō, a sometimes writer who is now the mayor of Tokyo (both men received the award when they were 23 years old). Kanehana's novella *Snakes and Earrings* is now available in English translation. If you're interested in the work of Wataya, however, you've only got two choices: read it in the original Japanese or read it in Italian (her novel *Install* has been translated into Italian).

'The jazz scene is enormous, as are the followings for rock, house and electronica'

Music

Japan has a huge, shape-shifting music scene supported by a local market of audiophiles who are willing to try almost anything. International artists make a point of swinging through on global tours, and the local scene surfaces every night in one of thousands of live houses. The jazz scene is enormous, as are the followings for rock, house and electronica. More mainstream gleanings are the *aidoru,* idol singers whose popularity is generated largely through media appearances and is centred on a cute, girl-next-door image. Unless you're aged 15, this last option probably won't interest you.

These days, J-pop (Japan Pop) is dominated by female vocalists who borrow heavily from such American pop stars as Mariah Carey. The most famous of these is Utada Hikaru, whose great vocal range and English ability (she peppers her songs with English lyrics) make her a standout from the otherwise drab *aidoru* field.

Cinema

Japan has a vibrant film industry and proud, critically acclaimed cinematic traditions. Renewed international attention since the mid-1990s has reinforced interest in domestic films, which account for an estimated 40% of box-office receipts, nearly double the level in most European countries. Of course, this includes not only artistically important works, but also films in the science-fiction, horror and 'monster-stomps-Tokyo' genres for which Japan is also known.

TRADITIONAL MUSIC & ITS INSTRUMENTS

■ *Gagaku* is a throwback to music of the Japanese imperial court. Today ensembles consist of 16 members and include stringed instruments, such as the *biwa* (lute) and *koto* (zither), and wind instruments such as the *hichiriki* (Japanese oboe).

■ *Shamisen* is a three-stringed instrument resembling a lute or banjo with an extended neck. Popular during the Edo period, particularly in the entertainment districts, it's still used as formal accompaniment in kabuki and *bunraku* (classical puppet theatre) and remains one of the essential skills of a geisha.

■ *Shakuhachi* is a wind instrument imported from China in the 7th century. The *shakuhachi* was popularised by wandering Komusō monks in the 16th and 17th centuries, who played it as a means to enlightenment as they walked alone through the woods.

■ *Taiko* refers to any of a number of large Japanese drums. Drummers who perform this athletic music often play shirtless to show the rippled movements of their backs.

At first, Japanese films were merely cinematic versions of traditional theatrical performances, but in the 1920s, Japanese directors starting producing films in two distinct genres: *jidaigeki* (period films) and new *gendaigeki* films, which dealt with modern themes. The more realistic storylines of the new films soon reflected back on the traditional films with the introduction of *shin jidaigeki* (new period films). During this era, samurai themes became an enduring staple of Japanese cinema.

The golden age of Japanese cinema arrived with the 1950s and began with the release in 1950 of Kurosawa Akira's *Rashōmon*, winner of the Golden Lion at the 1951 Venice International Film Festival and an Oscar for best foreign film. The increasing realism and high artistic standards of the period are evident in such landmark films as *Tokyo Story* (*Tōkyō Monogatari*, 1953), by the legendary Ōzu Yasujirō; Mizoguchi Kenji's classics *Ugetsu Monogatari* (*Tales of Ugetsu*, 1953) and *Saikaku Ichidai Onna* (*The Life of Oharu*, 1952); and Kurosawa's 1954 masterpiece *Shichinin no Samurai* (*Seven Samurai*). Annual attendance at the country's cinemas reached 1.1 billion in 1958, and Kyoto, with its large film studios, such as Shōchiku, Daiei and Tōei, and its more than 60 cinemas, enjoyed a heyday as Japan's own Hollywood.

As it did elsewhere in the world, TV spurred a rapid drop in the number of cinema goers in Japan in the high-growth decades of the 1960s and '70s. But despite falling attendance, Japanese cinema remained a major artistic force. These decades gave the world such landmark works as Ichikawa Kon's *Chushingura* (*47 Samurai*, 1962) and Kurosawa's *Yōjimbo* (1961).

The decline in cinema going continued through the 1980s, reinforced by the popularisation of videos, with annual attendance at cinemas bottoming out at just over 100 million. Yet Japan's cinema was far from dead: Kurosawa garnered acclaim worldwide for *Kagemusha* (1980), which shared the Palme d'Or at Cannes, and *Ran* (1985). Imamura Shōhei's heartrending *Narayama Bushiko* (*The Ballad of Narayama*) won the Grand Prix at Cannes in 1983. Itami Jūzō became perhaps the most widely known Japanese director outside Japan after Kurosawa, with such biting satires as *Osōshiki* (*The Funeral*, 1985), *Tampopo* (*Dandelion*, 1986) and *Marusa no Onna* (*A Taxing Woman*, 1988). Ōshima Nagisa, best known for controversial films such as *Ai no Corrida* (*In the Realm of the Senses*, 1976), scored a critical and popular success with *Senjo no Merry Christmas* (*Merry Christmas, Mr Lawrence*) in 1983.

In the 1990s popular interest in Japan seemed to catch up with international attention as attendance rates began to rise once again. In 1997 Japanese directors received top honours at two of the world's most prestigious film festivals: *Unagi* (*Eel*), Imamura Shohei's black-humoured look at human nature's dark side, won the Palme d'Or in Cannes – making him the only Japanese director to win this award twice; and 'Beat' Takeshi Kitano took the Golden Lion in Venice for *Hana-bi*, a tale of life and death, and the violence and honour that links them. The undisputed king of popular Japanese cinema, Takeshi is a true Renaissance man of media: he stars in and directs his films, and is a newspaper columnist, author and poet. In 2002 he released *Dolls,* a meditation on the sadness of love told in three parts, and in 2003 he followed this up with the release of *Zatoichi,* a tale of a blind swordsman set in the Edo period.

Of course, since 2000, the major story in Japanese film has been *anime*, which has captured Western interest in a way unknown since the days when Godzilla was tearing up Tokyo (see the following Anime section).

ANIME

The term *anime*, a contraction of the word 'animation', is used worldwide to refer to Japan's highly sophisticated animated films. Unlike its counterparts in other countries, *anime* occupies a position very near the forefront of the

Tokyo Story (*Tōkyō Monogatari*, 1953) is Ōzu Yasujirō's tale of an older couple who come to Tokyo to visit their children, only to find themselves treated with disrespect and indifference.

The film *Distance* (2001) is a subtle meditation on togetherness and loneliness. Koreeda's sequel to *After Life* tracks four people into the woods as they seek the truth about lovers and friends who belonged to a mysterious cult.

film industry in Japan. *Anime* films encompass all genres, from science fiction and action adventure to romance and historical drama.

Unlike its counterparts in many other countries, *anime* targets all age and social groups. *Anime* films include deep explorations of philosophical questions and social issues, humorous entertainment and bizarre fantasies. The films offer breathtakingly realistic visuals, exquisite attention to detail, complex and expressive characters, and elaborate plots. Leading directors and voice actors are accorded fame and respect, while characters become popular idols.

Some of the best-known *anime* include *Akira* (1988), Ōtomo Katsuhiro's psychedelic fantasy set in a future Tokyo inhabited by speed-popping biker gangs and psychic children. Ōtomo also worked on the interesting *Memories* (1995), a three-part *anime* that includes the mind-bending 'Magnetic Rose' sequence where deep-space garbage collectors happen upon a spaceship containing the memories of a mysterious woman. Finally, there is *Ghost in a Shell* (1995), an Ōishii Mamoru film with a sci-fi plot worthy of Philip K Dick – it involves cyborgs, hackers and the mother of all computer networks.

MIYAZAKI HAYAO – THE KING OF ANIME

Miyazaki Hayao, Japan's most famous and critically acclaimed *anime* director, has given us some of the most memorable images ever to appear on the silver screen. Consider, for example, the island that floated through the sky in his 1986 classic *Laputa*. Or the magical train that travelled across the surface of an aquamarine sea in *Spirited Away* (2001). Or the psychedelic dreamworlds that waited outside the doors of *Howl's Moving Castle* (2004). Watching scenes like this, one can only conclude that Miyazaki is gifted with the ability to travel to the realm of pure imagination and smuggle images back to this world intact and undiluted.

Miyazaki Hayao was born in 1941 in wartime Tokyo. His father was director of a firm that manufactured parts for the famous Japanese Zero fighter plane. This early exposure to flying machines made a deep impression on the young Miyazaki, and one of the hallmarks of his films are skies filled with the most whimsical flying machines imaginable: winged dirigibles, fantastic flying boats and the flying wings of *Nausicaa of the Valley of the Winds* (to see one is to want one).

In high school, Miyazaki saw one of Japan's first *anime*, *Hakujaden,* and resolved to become an animator himself. After graduating from university in 1963, he joined the powerful Tōei Animation company, where he worked on some of the studio's most famous releases. He left in 1971 to join A Pro studio, where he gained his first directorial experience, working on the now famous (in Japan, at least) *Lupin III* series as co director. In 1979, he directed *The Castle of Cagliostro,* another *Lupin* film and his first solo directorial credit.

In 1984, Miyazaki wrote and directed *Nausicaa of the Valley of the Winds*. This film is considered by many critics to be the first true Miyazaki film, and it provides a brilliant taste of many of the themes that run through his later work. The film enjoyed critical and commercial success and established Miyazaki as a major force in the world of Japanese *anime*. Capitalising on this success, Miyazaki founded his own animation studio, Studio Ghibli, through which he has produced all his later works.

In 1988, Studio Ghibli released what many consider to be Miyazaki's masterwork: *My Neighbor Totoro*. Much simpler and less dense than many Miyazaki films, *Totoro* is the tale of a young girl who moves with her family to the Japanese countryside while her mother recuperates from an illness. While living in the country, she befriends a magical creature who lives in the base of a giant camphor tree and is lucky enough to catch a few rides on a roving cat bus (a vehicle of pure imagination if ever there was one). For anyone wishing to make an acquaintance with the world of Miyazaki, this is the perfect introduction.

Serious Miyazaki fans will want to make a pilgrimage to his Ghibli Museum (p197), located in the town of Mitaka, a short day trip out of Tokyo.

Of course, one name towers above all others in the world of *anime*: Miyazaki Hayao, who almost single-handedly brought *anime* to the attention of the general public in the West (see the boxed text, opposite).

FASHION

It's impossible to visit Japanese cities and not notice their incredible sense of style. From the ultra chic ensembles sported by the beautiful people of Aoyama in Tokyo to the retro chic of the young things in Kyoto, people here think carefully about design and trends and beauty.

In the last 20 years, the fashion scene has been loosely organised around the work of three designers – Issey Miyaki, Rei Kawakubo and Yohji Yamamoto – all of whom show in London, Paris and New York, in addition to maintaining a presence in Tokyo. Together they are revered as some of the most artistic and innovative designers in the business, though it has often been said that their pieces are simply too radical to wear.

SPORT

Sumō

A fascinating, highly ritualised activity steeped in Shintō beliefs, sumō is the only traditional Japanese sport that pulls big crowds and dominates primetime TV. The 2000-year-old sport, which is based on an ancient combat form called *sumai* (to struggle), attracts huge crowds on weekends. Because tournaments take place over the span of 15 days, unless you're aiming for a big match on a weekend, you should be able to secure a ticket. Sumō tournaments (*bashō*) take place in January, May and September at the Ryōgoku Kokugikan Sumō Stadium (p178) in Tokyo; in March at the Furitsu Taiiku-kan Gymnasium in Osaka; in July at the Aichi Prefectural Gymnasium (p244) in Nagoya; and in November at the Fukuoka Kokusai Centre in Fukuoka (p670). Most popular are matches where one of the combatants is a *yokozuna* (grand champion). At the moment, sumō is dominated by foreign-born *rikishi* (sumō wrestlers), including Mongolian Asashōryū and Bulgarian Kotoōshū.

'Japan was already soccer crazy when the World Cup came to Saitama and Yokohama in 2002'

Soccer

Japan was already soccer crazy when the World Cup came to Saitama and Yokohama in 2002. Now, it's a chronic madness, and five minutes of conversation with any 10-year-old about why they like David Beckham should clear up any doubts you might have to the contrary. Japan's national league, also known as J-League (www.j-league.or.jp/eng/), is in season from March to November and can be seen at stadiums around the country.

Baseball

Baseball was introduced to Japan in 1873 and became a fixture in 1934 when the Yomiuri started its own team after Babe Ruth and Lou Gehrig had swung through town. During WWII, the game continued unabated, though players were required to wear unnumbered khaki uniforms and to salute each other on the field.

Today, baseball is still widely publicised and very popular, though many fans have begun to worry about the future of the sport in Japan as some of the most talented national players, such as Matsui Hideki, Suzuki Ichirō and Matsuzaka Daisuke, migrate to major league teams in the USA. If you're visiting Japan between April and October and are interested in catching a game, two exciting places to do so are the historic Kōshien Stadium (Map p375), which is located just outside Osaka and was built in 1924 as Japan's first stadium, and Tokyo Dome (p177), affectionately known as the 'Big Egg' and home to Japan's most popular team, the Yomiuri Giants.

Environment

Stretching from the tropics to the Sea of Okhotsk, the Japanese archipelago is a fantastically varied place. With everything from coral reef islands to snow-capped mountains, few countries in the world enjoy such a richness of different climes and ecosystems. Unfortunately, this wonderful landscape is also one of the world's most crowded, and almost every inch of the Japanese landscape and coastline bears the imprint of human activity (see the boxed text, opposite).

Although Japan's environment has been manipulated and degraded by human activity over the centuries, there are still pockets of real beauty left, some quite close to heavily populated urban areas. Indeed, there is decent hiking in the mountains within two hours of Tokyo, an hour of Osaka and a few minutes from downtown Kyoto.

Nature lovers are likely to be most troubled by the condition of Japan's rivers and coasts: almost all of Japan's rivers are dammed, forced into concrete channels and otherwise bent to the human will, and an astonishing amount of Japan's coast is lined with 'tetrapods' (giant concrete structures in the shape of jacks used to prevent erosion).

Given the incredibly active nature of the Japanese archipelago – the country has always been plagued by volcanoes, earthquakes, typhoons, landslides and other natural disasters – it's perhaps not surprising that the Japanese are eager to tame the wild nature of their islands. Unfortunately, this means that the visitor to Japan is often forced to try to imagine what the land looked like before the industrial revolution. Fortunately, environmental consciousness is on the rise in Japan, and more effort is being put into recycling, conservation and protection of natural areas. We can only hope that some of Japan's remaining areas of beauty will be preserved for future generations.

THE LAND

Japan is an island nation but it has not always been so. As recently as the end of the last ice age, around 10,000 years ago, the level of the sea rose enough to flood a land bridge that connected Japan to the Asian continent. Today, Japan consists of a chain of islands that rides the back of a 3000km-long arc of mountains along the eastern rim of the continent. It stretches from around 25°N at the southern islands of Okinawa to 45°N at the northern end of Hokkaidō. Cities at comparable latitudes are Miami and Cairo in the south and Montreal and Milan in the north. Japan's total land area is 377,435 sq km, and more than 80% of it is mountainous.

Japan consists of some 3900 small islands and four major ones: Honshū (slightly larger than Britain), Hokkaidō, Kyūshū and Shikoku. Okinawa, the largest and most significant of Japan's many smaller islands, is about halfway along an archipelago that stretches from the western tip of Honshū almost all the way to Taiwan. It is far enough from the rest of Japan to have developed a culture that differs from that of the 'mainland' in many respects.

There are several disputed islands in the Japanese archipelago. The most important of these are the Kuril Islands, north of Hokkaidō. Seized by Russia at the close of WWII, they have been a source of tension between Japan and Russia ever since. While the Japanese have made some progress towards their return in recent years, they remain, for the time being, part of Russia.

If Japanese culture has been influenced by isolation, it has equally been shaped by the country's mountainous topography. A number of the moun-

Japan incinerates an estimated 75% of its solid waste.

Dogs and Demons: Tales from the Dark Side of Modern Japan – Alex Kerr's book is essential for anyone who wants to understand why Japan's environment is in such a sorry state. In particular, Kerr explores the power of the construction industry over the government.

tains are volcanic, and more than 40 of these are active, many of them on the southern island of Kyūshū. On the plus side, all this geothermal activity is responsible for Japan's fabulous abundance of *onsen* (hot springs).

In addition to its volcanoes, Japan has the dubious distinction of being one of the most seismically active regions of the world. It has been estimated that Japan is hit by more than 1000 earthquakes a year, most of which are, fortunately, too small to notice without sophisticated seismic equipment. This seismic activity is particularly concentrated in the Kantō region, in which Tokyo is situated. But earthquakes can strike just about any part of the archipelago, as the citizens of Kōbe discovered in the disastrous earthquake of January 1995, which killed more than 6000 people.

Friends of the Earth Japan (FoEJ; www.foejapan.org/en/), the Japan chapter of Friends of the Earth International, runs weekly hikes in the Tokyo area and has a good list of environmental events on its site.

WILDLIFE

The latitudinal spread of the islands of Japan makes for a wide diversity of flora and fauna. The Nansei and Ogasawara archipelagos in the far south are subtropical, and flora and fauna in this region are related to those found on the Malay peninsula. Mainland Japan (Honshū, Kyūshū and Shikoku), on the

WHAT HAPPENED TO THE HILLS?

Visitors to Japan are often shocked at the state of the Japanese landscape. It seems that no matter where you look, the hills, rivers, coastline and fields bear the unmistakable imprint of human activity. Indeed, it is only in the highest, most remote mountains that one finds nature untouched by human hands. Why is this?

Undoubtedly, population density is the crucial factor here. With so many people packed into such a small space, it is only natural that the land should be worked to the hilt. However, it is not just simple population pressure that accounts for Japan's scarred and battered landscape: misguided land management policies and money-influenced politics also play a role.

Almost 70% of Japan's total land area is wooded. Of this area, almost 40% is planted, most of it with uniform rows of conifers, known as *sugi* (cryptomeria). Even national forests are not exempt from tree farming and these forests account for 33% of Japan's total lumber output. The end result of this widespread tree farming is a rather ugly patchwork effect over most of Japan's mountains – monotonous stands of *sugi* interspersed with occasional swathes of bare, clear-cut hillside.

To make matters worse, the planting of monoculture forests and the practice of clear cutting reduces the stability of mountain topsoil, resulting in frequent landslides. To combat this, land engineers erect unsightly concrete retaining walls over huge stretches of hillside, particularly along roadsides or near human habitations. These, combined with high-tension wire towers and the patchwork forests, result in a landscape that is quite unlike anything elsewhere in the world.

As if this weren't enough, it is estimated that only three of Japan's 30,000 rivers and streams are undammed. In addition to dams, concrete channels and embankments are built around even the most inaccessible mountain streams. Although some of this river work serves to prevent flooding downstream, much of it is clearly gratuitous and can only be understood as the unfortunate result of Japanese money-influenced politics.

In Japan, rural areas wield enormous power in national politics, as representation is determined more by area than by population. In order to ensure the support of their constituencies, rural politicians have little choice but to lobby hard for government spending on public works projects, as there is little other work available in these areas. Despite the negative effects this has on the landscape and economy, Japanese politicians seem unable to break this habit.

The upshot of all this is a landscape that looks, in many places, like a giant construction site. Perhaps the writer Alex Kerr put it best in his book *Lost Japan:* 'Japan has become a huge and terrifying machine, a Moloch tearing apart its own land with teeth of steel, and there is absolutely nothing anyone can do to stop it'. For the sake of the beauty that remains in Japan, let's hope he is wrong.

other hand, shows more similarities with Korea and China, while subarctic northern and central Hokkaidō have their own distinct features.

Animals

Japan's land bridge to the Asian continent allowed the migration of animals from Korea and China. The fauna of Japan has much in common with these regions, though there are species that are unique to Japan, such as the Japanese giant salamander and the Japanese macaque. In addition, Nansei-shotō, which has been separated from the mainland for longer than the rest of Japan, has a few examples of fauna (for example the Iriomote cat) that are classified by experts as 'living fossils'.

Japan's largest carnivorous mammals are its bears. Two species are found in Japan – the *higuma* (brown bear) of Hokkaidō, and the *tsukinowaguma* (Asiatic brown bear) of Honshū, Shikoku and Kyūshū. The brown bear can grow to a height of 2m and weigh up to 400kg. The Asiatic brown bear is smaller at an average height of 1.4m and a weight of 200kg.

Japanese macaques are medium-sized monkeys that are found in Honshū, Shikoku and Kyūshū. They average around 60cm in length and have short tails. The last survey of their numbers was taken in 1962, at which time there were some 30,000. They are found in groups of 20 to 150 members.

According to a 2006 report by the International Union for Conservation of Nature and Natural Resources (IUCN), there are 132 endangered species in Japan. Endangered species include the Iriomote cat, the Tsushima cat, Blakiston's fish owl and the Japanese river otter. For more on these, visit the Animal Info page on Japan at www.animalinfo.org/country/japan.htm.

The Lost Wolves of Japan, by Brett Walker, is a sad tale of how the wolf in Japan went from being considered divine to being considered a vermin, and went extinct in the process. You'll learn a lot about Japanese attitudes towards nature as the tale unfolds.

Plants

The flora of Japan today is not what the Japanese saw hundreds of years ago. This is not just because a lot of Japan's natural landscape has succumbed to modern urban culture, but also because much of Japan's flora is imported. It is thought that 200 to 500 plant species have been introduced to Japan since the Meiji period, mainly from Europe but also from North America. Japanese gardens laid out in the Edo period and earlier are good places to see native Japanese flora, even though you won't see it if it had flourished naturally.

A large portion of Japan was once heavily forested. The cool to temperate zones of Central and Northern Honshū and southern Hokkaidō were home to broad-leaf deciduous forests, and still are, to a certain extent. Nevertheless, large-scale deforestation is a feature of contemporary Japan. Pollution and acid rain have also taken their toll. Fortunately, the sheer inaccessibility of much of Japan's mountainous topography has preserved some areas of great natural beauty – in particular the alpine regions of Central Honshū and the lovely national parks of Hokkaidō.

According to the IUCN's 1999 figures, there are more than 1000 endangered species of vascular plants in Japan. For more information, visit the Japan Integrated Biodiversity Information System's site at www.biodic.go.jp/english/J-IBIS.html.

With offices in Tokyo and Kyoto, theJapan Environmental Exchange (JEE; www.jca.apc.org/jee/indexE.html) is one of the best, foreigner-friendly environmental groups in Japan. Visit its site to check on its upcoming environmental projects.

NATIONAL PARKS

Japan has 28 *kokuritsu kōen* (national parks) and 55 *kokutei kōen* (quasi-national parks). Ranging from the far south (Iriomote National Park) to the northern tip of Hokkaidō (Rishiri-Rebun-Sarobetsu National Park), the parks represent an effort to preserve as much as possible of Japan's natural environment. Although national and quasi-national parks account for less than 1% of Japan's total land area, it is estimated that 14% of Japan's land is protected or managed for sustainable use.

SUSTAINABLE TRAVEL IN JAPAN

As a casual visitor to Japan, you may feel that you have few chances to make a positive environmental impact. There are, however, several things you can do to minimize your impact on the Japanese and the world's environment.

Cut down on packaging One shopping trip in Japan will impress upon you just how fond the Japanese are of packaging – some would say overpackaging – purchases and gifts. The solution to this is simply to refuse excess packaging. One line that will come in handy is: *'Fukuro wa irimasen'* (I don't need a bag). Another is the simple *'Kekkō desu'* (That's alright), which can be used to turn down offers for additional packaging.

Carry your own chopsticks Another way to save trees and cut down on waste is to carry your own chopsticks around with you, which you can use instead of the ubiquitous *waribashi* (disposable chopsticks) that are provided in restaurants. One simple way to acquire your own personal set of choppers is to take away the first nice pair of *waribashi* that you are given in a restaurant.

Think globally, eat locally Food that comes from afar carries a lot of 'carbon mileage' with it. If you eat what's grown locally in Japan, you'll almost certainly save some money, you'll get a better understanding of the local diet, and you won't be consuming foods that came across the ocean in oil-burning ships.

A little less tuna, please When you go to a sushi place, try to stay away from species of fish that are endangered, like *maguro* (tuna), including *toro* (fatty tuna belly). We know, this one hurts!

Stay in ecofriendly places When you travel in Japan, try to stay in ecofriendly places, particularly in areas where the environment is easily harmed by human activities. Mountain huts in the Japan Alps, for example, range from very ecofriendly to downright careless. Similarly, when you're in the southern islands, stay in low-impact places and never, ever, walk on or touch coral.

Reduce fuel consumption There are plenty of ways to reduce your fossil fuel consumption as you travel around Japan. Rental bicycles are widely available in most tourist spots (see p815). Japan's public transport system is the best in the world, and you can traverse almost all the archipelago by train and bus (see p814). And keep in mind that Japan's *shinkansen* (bullet trains) are often faster than planes for getting from one big city to the next, especially when you factor in the time spent travelling to and from airports.

When discussing Japan's national and quasi-national parks, it must be noted that these parks are quite different from national parks in most other countries. Few of the parks have facilities that you might expect in national parks (ranger stations, camping grounds, educational facilities etc). More importantly, national park status doesn't necessarily mean that the area in question is free from residential, commercial or even urban development. Indeed, in many of these parks, you'd have no idea that you were in a national or quasi-national park unless you looked on a map.

The highest concentration of national parks and quasi-national parks is in Northern Honshū (Tōhoku) and Hokkaidō, where the population density is relatively low. But there are also national parks and quasi-national parks, such as Chichibu-Tama and Nikkō, within easy striking distance of Tokyo. The largest of Japan's national parks is the Seto-Nai-Kai National Park (Inland Sea National Park; Seto-Nai-Kai Kokuritsu-kōen), which extends some 400km east to west, reaches a maximum width of 70km and encompasses almost 1000 islands of various sizes.

For an update on the greening of Japan, check out www.greenpeace.or.jp/index_en_html, Greenpeace Japan's excellent URL.

ENVIRONMENTAL ISSUES

Japan was the first Asian nation to industrialise. It has also been one of the most successful at cleaning up the resulting mess, though problems remain. In the early postwar years, when Japan was frantically rebuilding its economy, there was widespread public ignorance of the problems of pollution, and the government did little to enlighten the public.

Industrial pollution was at its worst from the mid-1960s to the mid-1970s. But public awareness of the issue had already been awakened by an outbreak in 1953 of what came to be called Minamata disease, after the town of the

Every year, 24 billion pairs of *waribashi* (disposable chopsticks) are used in Japan.

same name, in which up to 6000 people were affected by mercury poisoning. It was not until 1960 that the government officially acknowledged the cause of the 'disease'.

By the late 1960s public consciousness of environmental problems had reached levels that the government could not ignore. Laws were passed to curb air and water pollution. These have been reasonably successful, though critics are quick to point out that while toxic matter has been mostly removed from Japanese waters, organic pollution remains a problem. Similarly, controls on air pollution have had mixed results: photochemical smog emerged as a problem in Tokyo in the early 1970s; it remains a problem and now affects other urban centres around Japan.

'Laws were passed to curb air and water pollution'

In 1972 the government passed the Nature Conservation Law, which aimed to protect the natural environment and provide recreational space for the public. National parks, quasi-national parks and prefectural parks were established, and it appears that these measures have been successful in increasing wildlife numbers.

More recently, Japan has been facing a new set of problems, including dioxin given off by waste incineration plants and a series of accidents at nuclear reactors and nuclear fuel processing facilities. The only up side is that these accidents have forced the government to revise its safety guidelines for the nuclear power industry.

Of course, the news isn't all bleak. The governor of Kumamoto-ken announced in 2002 that the Arase Dam on Kuma-gawa would be removed, starting in 2010. In a country with a surplus of unnecessary dams, this is a major step in the right direction.

The Onsen

Japan is in hot water. Literally. The stuff percolates up out of the ground from one end of the country to the other. The Japanese word for a hot spring is *onsen,* and there are more than 3000 of them in the country, more than anywhere else on earth – it's like Iceland on steroids. So if your idea of relaxation involves spending a few hours soaking your bones in a tub of bubbling hot water, then you've come to the right place.

With so many *onsen,* it's hardly surprising that they come in every size, shape and colour. There are *onsen* in downtown Tokyo, a few minutes' walk from the nightlife district of Roppongi (you could even have a quick soak between drinks if you were so inclined). There are *onsen* high up in the Japan Alps that you can only get to by walking for a full day over high mountain peaks. There are *onsen* bubbling up among the rocks on the coast that only exist when the tide is just right. The fact is, somewhere on the archipelago, there is the perfect bath of your imagination just waiting for you to take the plunge.

Some Japanese will tell you that the only distinctively Japanese aspect of their culture – that is, something that didn't ultimately originate in mainland Asia – is the bath. There are accounts of *onsen* bathing in Japan's earliest historical records, and it's pretty certain that the Japanese have been bathing in *onsen* as long as there have been Japanese. Over the millennia, they have turned the simple act of bathing in an *onsen* into something like a religion. And, for the average modern Japanese, making a pilgrimage to a famous *onsen* is the closest thing he or she will come to a religious pilgrimage.

Today, the ultimate way to experience an *onsen* is to visit an *onsen* ryokan, that is, a traditional Japanese inn with its own private hot-spring bath on the premises. At an *onsen* ryokan you spend all day enjoying the bath, relaxing in your room and eating sumptuous Japanese food. When you think about it, the Japanese were way ahead of the curve here: for what is an *onsen* ryokan but the ultimate spa retreat? Yes, some *onsen* ryokan even offer massages, saunas and beauty treatments.

Perhaps the best thing about *onsen* is where you find them. Whenever possible, *onsen* are located in areas of stunning natural beauty, with tubs placed so that you can enjoy the views while soaking. More often than not, the tubs will be *rotemburo* (outdoor tubs). Imagine relaxing in a natural tub with a river flowing gently by and mountains all around you. Sound idyllic? Perhaps so, but this describes literally hundreds of *onsen* in Japan.

Like many of the best things in life, some of the finest *onsen* in Japan are free. Just show up with a towel and your birthday suit, splash a little water on yourself and plunge in. No communication hassles, no expenses and no worries. And even if you must pay to enter, it's usually just a minor snip – averaging about ¥700 (US$6) per person.

All too often, after taking a holiday somewhere, you return home feeling like you could use another holiday. If this has happened to you, then we strongly recommend a Japanese *onsen* vacation. As you slip into your futon after a day soaking in a beautiful natural bath, you could be forgiven for thinking, 'Now this is a vacation!'.

'When you think about it, the Japanese were way ahead of the curve here'

TOP ONSEN EXPERIENCES

With so many *onsen* to choose from in Japan, it's a thankless task to pick favourites. And no matter how many *onsen* you try, there's always the suspicion that somewhere out there is the holy grail of *onsen* just waiting to be discovered. That said, we're going to go way out on a limb here and recommend a few of our favourites, broken up into categories to help you choose. Here goes:

'It's located in a rocky cleft in the seashore of lovely little Shikine-jima'

Best Inner-City Onsen

Azabu-Jūban Onsen (Tokyo p142) Azabu-Jūban is the urban *onsen* par excellence. As you ease into the tubs here, you'll have to pinch yourself to believe that the seething masses of Tokyo are only just outside the door. The bland exterior of the place belies the reward inside: the steamy, mineral-rich water piped up from 500m below ground and the classic bathhouse atmosphere. Surprisingly, there's a small *rotemburo* for each gender, and weekends feature live traditional music in the tatami tearoom.

Best Island Onsen

Jinata Onsen (Shikine-jima, Izu-shotō p233) The setting of this *onsen* couldn't be more dramatic: it's located in a rocky cleft in the seashore of lovely little Shikine-jima, an island only a few hours' ferry ride from downtown Tokyo.

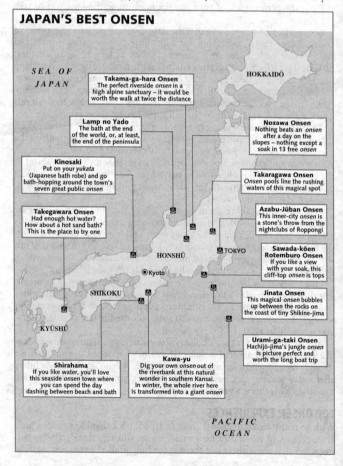

JAPAN'S BEST ONSEN

Takama-ga-hara Onsen
The perfect riverside *onsen* in a high alpine sanctuary – it would be worth the walk at twice the distance

Lamp no Yado
The bath at the end of the world, or, at least, the end of the peninsula

Nozawa Onsen
Nothing beats an *onsen* after a day on the slopes – nothing except a soak in 13 free *onsen*

Kinosaki
Put on your *yukata* (Japanese bath robe) and go bath-hopping around the town's seven great public *onsen*

Takaragawa Onsen
Onsen pools line the rushing waters of this magical spot

Takegawara Onsen
Had enough hot water? How about a hot sand bath? This is the place to try one

Azabu-Jūban Onsen
This inner-city *onsen* is a stone's throw from the nightclubs of Roppongi

Sawada-kōen Rotemburo Onsen
If you like a view with your soak, this cliff-top *onsen* is tops

Jinata Onsen
This magical *onsen* bubbles up between the rocks on the coast of tiny Shikine-jima

Urami-ga-taki Onsen
Hachijō-jima's jungle *onsen* is picture perfect and worth the long boat trip

Shirahama
If you like water, you'll love this seaside *onsen* town where you can spend the day dashing between beach and bath

Kawa-yu
Dig your own *onsen* out of the riverbank at this natural wonder in southern Kansai. In winter, the whole river here is transformed into a giant *onsen*

SEA OF JAPAN

HOKKAIDŌ

HONSHŪ

●Kyoto

SHIKOKU

TOKYO

KYŪSHŪ

PACIFIC OCEAN

The pools are formed by the seaside rocks and it's one of those *onsen* that only works when the tide is right. You can spend a few lovely hours here watching the Pacific rollers crashing on the rocks. And, there are two other excellent *onsen* on the island when you get tired of this one.

Best Riverside Onsen

Takaragawa Onsen (Gunma, Central Honshū p196) Japanese *onsen* maniacs often pronounce Gunma-ken's *onsen* to be the best in the country. Difficult for us to argue. 'Takaragawa' means 'treasure river', and its several slate-floored pools sit along several hundred metres of riverbank. Most of the pools are mixed bathing, with one ladies-only bath. The alkaline waters are said to cure fatigue, nervous disorders and digestive troubles.

Best Onsen Town

Kinosaki (Kinosaki, Kansai p371) Kinosaki, on the Sea of Japan coast in northern Kansai, is the quintessential *onsen* town. With seven public baths and dozens of *onsen* ryokan, this is the place to sample the *onsen* ryokan experience. You can relax in your accommodation taking the waters as it pleases you, and when you get tired of your ryokan's bath, you can hit the streets in a *yukata* (light cotton robe) and *geta* (wooden sandals) and hit the public baths. It doesn't hurt that the town is extremely atmospheric at night, and the local winter speciality, giant crab, goes down pretty nice after a day of *onsen*-hopping.

'The alkaline waters are said to cure fatigue, nervous disorders and digestive troubles'

Best Rotemburo

Sawada-kōen Rotemburo Onsen (Dōgashima, Izu-hantō, Around Tokyo p217) If you like a view with your bath, you won't do any better than this simple *rotemburo* perched high on a cliff overlooking the Pacific Ocean. We liked it early in the day, when you can often have it all to yourself. Of course, if you don't mind a crowd, it's a great place to watch the sunset.

Best Hidden Onsen

Lamp no Yado (Noto-hantō, Central Honshū p304) The Noto-hantō peninsula is about as far as one can go in Central Honshū, and the seaside is about as far as one can go on Noto-hantō. A country road takes you to a narrow 1km path, from where you have to climb down a switchback hill on foot. No wonder this property has been a refuge for centuries of Japanese seeking to cure what ails them. Even if one night here now costs what people would have once spent over weeks here, it's a worthy splurge for a dark-wood and tatami room on a cove, with its own *rotemburo* and Sea of Japan views through craggy rocks.

Best Semitropical Onsen

Urami-ga-taki Onsen (Hachijō-jima, Izu-shotō, Around Tokyo p234) Even in a country of lovely *onsen*, this is a real standout: the perfect little *rotemburo* located next to a waterfall in lush semitropical jungle. It's what they're shooting for at all those resorts on Bali, only this is the real thing. Sitting in the bath as the late-afternoon sunlight pierces the ferns here is a magical experience. Did we mention that's it's free?

Best Onsen/Beach Combination

Shirahama (Shirahama, Wakayama-ken, Kansai p429) There's something peculiarly pleasing about dashing back and forth between the ocean and a natural hot-spring bath – the contrast in temperature and texture is something we never tire of. At Shirahama, a beach town in southern Kansai, there is a free *onsen* right on the beach And, Sakino-yu Onsen here is just spectacular – it's one of our favourite *onsen* in all Japan.

Best Onsen/Sand Bath Combination

Takegawara Onsen (Beppu, Kyūshū p729) Sometimes simplest is best. This traditional Meiji Era *onsen* first opened in 1859, and its smooth wooden floors transport you back to a Japan of neighbourhood pleasures – unpretentious, relaxing and accessible to all. There are separate (and very hot) baths for men and women. Takegawara also offers heated sand baths in which, wearing a cotton *yukata*, you are buried up to your neck with hot sand for 10 to 15 minutes, followed by a rinse and a soak in an adjacent *onsen* bath.

'It's located in a high natural sanctuary with mountains on all sides'

Best Mountain Onsen

Takama-ga-hara Onsen (Northern Japan Alps, Central Honshū below) High, high up in the Japan Alps, if you want to soak in this wonderful free riverside *rotemburo*, you're going to have to hike for at least a full day. It's located in a high natural sanctuary with mountains on all sides. To tell the truth, even if it took three days of walking to get here, it would be worth it. Some Japanese say that this is the highest *rotemburo* in Japan, and it's definitely one of the best. You can spend the night nearby in a creaky old mountain hut.

Best Do-It-Yourself Onsen

Kawa-yu (Kawa-yu, Wakayama-ken, Kansai p433) If you like doing things your own way, you'll love this natural oddity of an *onsen* in southern Kansai. Here, the *onsen* waters bubble up through the rocks of a riverbed. You choose a likely spot and dig out a natural hot pot along the riverside and wait for it to fill with hot water and – *voila* – your own private *rotemburo*. In the winter, it gets even better: they use bulldozers to turn the entire river into a giant 1000-person *onsen*. It doesn't hurt that the river water is a lovely translucent emerald colour.

SO CLOSE TO HEAVEN Chris Rowthorn

Takamama-ga-hara is a natural sanctuary in the heart of the northern Japan Alps. The name means 'high heaven plain' and it's very apt. Most people take at least two days to walk here from the nearest trailhead. But I had only three days to spend in the mountains, and I wanted to check out the sanctuary and then make it all the way down to Yari-ga-take, a fine peak two days' walk south of there, so I rushed things a bit.

I climbed from the Oritate trailhead, over Taro-san and walked down the lovely Yakushi-zawa valley. I made it to Yakushi-koya, a hut located at the bottom of the valley. It was already about 2pm. I asked the hut owner if he thought I could make it to Takama-ga-hara and he looked at me like I was mad. Nonetheless, I set out.

Turns out, the hut owner was right. The light was fading and I was completely exhausted as I finally arrived at Takama-ga-hara-koya hut. I could barely walk, but I knew the *onsen* was only another 20 minutes' walk into the forest.

I dropped my bag and made my way along the trail in the fading light. Finally, I heard the sound of a stream rushing down a mountainside. I crossed the river and there it was – Takama-ga-hara Onsen – the simplest of tubs sitting right beside the river. It was deserted and that suited me just fine.

I stripped down, splashed quick buckets over myself and plunged in. It was pure bliss. It took a few minutes to gather my wits. But, when I did, I realised that I was sitting in one of the most spectacular natural baths anywhere. I was smack dab in the middle of the Japan Alps, with mountains forming a perfect circle around me and a fine alpine river cascading by me. And, I had it all to myself. There was no place in the world I would rather have been.

DO 'YU' SPEAK ONSEN?

yu	ゆ or 湯	hot water
o-yu	お湯	hot water (polite)
dansei-no-yu	男性の湯	male bath
otoko-yu	男湯	male bath
josei-no-yu	女性の湯	female bath
onna-yu	女湯	female bath
konyoku	混浴	mixed bath
kazoku-no-yu	家族の湯	family bath
rotemburo	露天風呂	outdoor bath
kake-yu	かけ湯	rinsing one's body
yubune	湯船	bath tub
soto-yu	外湯	public bath
uchi-yu	内湯	private bath

Best Onsen Ryokan

Nishimuraya Honkan (Kinosaki, Kansai p372) If you want to sample the ultimate in top-end *onsen* ryokan, this is the place. With several fine indoor and outdoor baths and elegant rooms, your stay here will be a highlight of your trip to Japan, and will shed some light on why the Japanese consider an *onsen* vacation to be the ultimate in relaxation.

Best Onsen Ski Town

Nozawa Onsen (Nozawa Onsen, Nagano, Central Honshū p279) What could be better than a day spent on the slopes, followed by a soak in a Jacuzzi? Well, how about a day on the slopes followed by a soak in a real natural hot spring? This is skiing the Japanese way, and we're sure of one thing: try it and you'll like it. This fine little ski town boasts some first-rate skiing, reliable snow, ripping alpine views and no fewer than 13 free *onsen*. Best of all, the *onsen* here are scalding hot, which is a nice contrast to the snow outside and it feels wonderful on tired skier's legs.

ONSEN ETIQUETTE

First: relax. That's what *onsen* are all about. You'll be relieved to hear that there really is nothing tricky about taking an *onsen* bath. If you remember just one basic point, you won't go too far wrong. This is the point: the water in the pools and tubs is for soaking in, not washing in, and it should only be entered after you've washed or rinsed your body.

This is the drill: pay your entry fee, if there is one. Rent a hand towel if you don't have one. Take off your shoes and put them in the lockers or shelves provided. Find the correct changing room/bath for your gender (man: 男; woman: 女). Grab a basket, strip down and put your clothes in the basket. Put the basket in a locker and bring the hand towel in with you.

Once in the bathing area, find a place around the wall (if there is one) to put down your toiletries (if you have them) and wash your body, or, at least, rinse your body. You'll note that some scofflaws dispense with this step and just stride over to the tubs and grab a bucket (there are usually some around) and splash a few scoops over their 'wedding tackle'. Some miscreants can't even be bothered with this step and plunge right into the tubs unwashed and unrinsed. Frankly, we like to think that these people will be reincarnated into a world where there are only cold-water showers for their bathing needs.

'You'll be relieved to hear that there really is nothing tricky about taking an *onsen* bath'

Skiing in Japan

With more than 600 ski resorts and some of the most reliable snow anywhere, Japan may be the skiing world's best-kept secret – the perfect place to combine some world-class skiing with an exotic vacation. Japan offers stunning mountain vistas, kilometres of perfectly groomed runs at all levels of difficulty, along with ripping mogul runs, snowboard parks, friendly locals and good food. There's also great off-piste skiing, cross-country skiing and snowshoeing. And let's not forget Japan's incredible variety of hot spring baths *(onsen)* for that all-important après ski soak.

With so many ski resorts, you're spoiled for choice in Japan. Powder hounds flock to Hokkaidō's Niseko, which offers the world's most reliable lift-served powder snow. Others head to the sprawling Shiga Kōgen resort in Central Honshū, the largest ski resort in the world. Those who want a little European atmosphere gravitate to nearby Nozawa Onsen, which, like its name suggests, offers great hot springs in addition to excellent skiing. There are also plenty of small local areas that are perfect for families and learners.

Of course, you probably think that skiing Japan will cost about as much as a week of heli-skiing and caviar in the Canadian Rockies. If so, you may be surprised to learn that it's actually cheaper to ski in Japan than in North America or Europe – for prices, see below.

Or perhaps you're under the impression that skiing in Japan will involve horrendous communication difficulties – like a sadistic Japanese game show that combines ordering sushi in Japanese and skiing black-diamond runs blindfolded. If so, relax – ski areas in Japan are remarkably foreigner friendly and many even have Aussie, Kiwi and Canadian employees. For useful skiing words and phrases, see p84.

Finally, you may think that getting from the airport to the slopes will be a nightmare. In fact it's easier to get from major airports to ski resorts in Japan than anywhere else in the world – the lift doesn't leave from right outside the arrivals hall, but it sometimes feels that way (for more details, see Getting to the Slopes, below).

According to ski-industry figures, the number of active skiers in Japan is less than half what it was during the peak of the Bubble Economy in the 1980s.

Easily the best source of online information on skiing in Japan can be found at www.snow japan.com. This site has extensive resort info, snow reports, transport and accommodation info, and booking services, as well as information on English ski lessons. And it's all in English.

COSTS

If you're like most skiers, you probably imagine that skiing in Japan is prohibitively expensive. Well, let's check the numbers.

- **Lift tickets** A full-day lift ticket at most areas in Japan costs around ¥4000 (US$35). This is roughly half the cost of big ski areas in the USA, and about two-thirds the cost of most big areas in Europe.
- **Accommodation** You can find plenty of accommodation in the ¥8000 (US65) per person range at most major areas in Japan, and this will often include one or two meals. This is less than half of what you'd expect to pay for similar accommodation in the USA or Europe.
- **Food** On-slope meals average around ¥1000 (around US$9).
- **Transport** Airport-to-resort transport in Japan costs no more than in other countries, and is usually faster and more efficient (and unlike in North America, you most certainly don't need to rent a car). See Getting to the Slopes (below) for more details.

GETTING TO THE SLOPES

Japan's brilliant public transport system makes getting to the slopes a breeze. Take Japan's premier resort, Niseko in Hokkaidō. Say you're coming from abroad and want to go straight to the resort, you'll find the journey painless

SKIING IN JAPAN

ELEVATION

3000m
2000m
1000m
200m
0

Niseko ● Sapporo
Rusutsu

SEA OF
JAPAN

Nozawa Onsen   *Jōetsu Shinkansen*
Happō-One   Shiga-Kōgen
Toyama ●
Northern   ● Nagano
Japan Alps   *Hokuriku Shinkansen*
Nagoya ●   ★ TOKYO
Southern
Kyoto ●   **Japan Alps**
● Osaka

PACIFIC
OCEAN

The first winter Olympics to be held outside Europe or North America were at Sapporo in 1972.

and efficient. First, you fly into Tokyo's Narita International Airport, then change to a domestic flight to Sapporo's Shin-Chitose International Airport. Buses to Niseko depart from right outside the arrivals hall of Chitose and take a mere 2½ hours and cost only ¥2300 (about US$20) to reach the resort. If you arrive in Sapporo in the morning, you can be skiing that afternoon.

The journey from Tokyo to Nagano, the heart of Japan's Central Honshū ski country, takes one hour and 45 minutes and costs ¥7970 (about US$65). And the best part is this: you get to ride on one of the country's ultramodern *shinkansen* bullet trains. You could literally start the day with a look at Tokyo's incredible Tsukiji Fish Market and be skiing in Nagano that afternoon.

The 1998 winter Olympics were held at Nagano, in Central Honshū. The downhill events were held at Happō-One resort, the slalom and giant slalom events were held at Shiga-kōgen resort, and the biathlon was held at Nozawa Onsen resort.

JAPAN'S BEST SKI RESORTS

Japan's best ski resorts are found in the Japan Alps region of Central Honshū (mostly in Nagano and Niigata prefectures) and on the northern island of Hokkaidō. The former lays claim to the highest mountains, while the latter has the deepest and most regular snow. Both regions offer first-class skiing.

If you're interested in doing some sightseeing in cities like Kyoto, Nara and Tokyo in addition to your skiing, you might consider hitting the resorts in the Japan Alps. If skiing is your main goal, then Hokkaidō might be the way to go (although, to be fair, the difference is really only one quick internal flight).

What follows is our very biased list of the five best ski areas in Japan. This is just to whet your appetite – there are more than 600 that we don't mention here.

The world's longest ski lift, the 'Dragondola', a 5.4km gondola, can be found at the Naeba ski resort in Niigata-ken.

■ **Niseko** As far as most Australian skiers are concerned, 'Niseko' is how you say powder in Japanese. This is understandable, since Niseko receives an average of 13m of snow annually. Located on Japan's northern island of Hokkaidō, Niseko is actually three interconnected ski areas: Niseko Annupuri, Niseko Higashiyama and Niseko Grand Hirafu. One lift ticket gives access to all 60 runs and 30 ski lifts. Snowboarding is allowed on all slopes. Needless to say, with so many Aussie skiers making a yearly pilgrimage to Niseko, you'll find that communication is a breeze, and if you like Vegemite on your morning toast, you'll find that, too. If you're heading to Niseko in early February, don't miss Sapporo's famous Yuki Matsuri (see p577). For more information on Niseko, see p589.

Nearly 90% of foreign skiers at Niseko come from Australia.

■ **Happō-One** Nagano-ken's Happō-One (hah poh oh nay) is the quintessential Japan Alps ski resort. With the sprawling Hakuba mountain range as a backdrop, it offers eye-popping views along with excellent and varied skiing. The layout is pretty straightforward here, with plenty of good wide burners heading straight down the fall line from the top of the area. There are both groomed runs and bump runs and you can descend most of the mountain on either. The village at the base of the mountain has several good *onsen* and lots of foreigner-friendly accommodation. For more information on Happō, see p280.

■ **Shiga Kōgen** Also in Nagano-ken, Shiga Kōgen is the world's largest ski area, with an incredible 21 different interlinked areas, all interconnected by trails and lifts and accessible with one lift ticket. Needless to say, with so many different areas, there is something for (almost) everyone here, including one skier-only area. This is a very family-friendly area, and there's lots of accommodation at the base of the slopes, so you can ski right from your lodgings. Like most other major resorts in Japan, there are also some good *onsen* around for soaking out

---

SKI-DŌ: THE JAPANESE WAY OF SKIING

Snow is snow, skis are skis, right? How different can skiing in Japan be? At first glance, you might conclude that ski areas in Japan are exactly like those at home. But, as Vincent Vega observed in the movie *Pulp Fiction*, 'it's the little differences'. Throughout the day, these little differences will keep reminding you that you're not in New Zealand, Colorado or the Swiss Alps.

■ Pop music – often really annoying pop music – is played along ski lifts and in restaurants. Bring an iPod if you prefer real music to the latest girl/boy band.

■ The signposting is inconsistent and irregular, something you may not expect in Japan. It's a good idea to study the map carefully and plan a central meeting point/time at the beginning of the day.

■ Not all resorts use the green/blue/black coding system for difficulty. Some have red, purple, orange, dotted lines or black-numbered runs on the map.

■ The majority of Japanese skiers start skiing at 9am, have lunch at exactly noon and get off the hill by 3pm. If you work on a slightly different schedule, you will avoid a lot of the crowds.

■ You will find young Aussies, Kiwis and Canadians working the lifts and restaurants at many Japanese resorts (a popular way for people from these countries to earn money, do a little skiing and see the country). These folks are always a good source of information.

■ Snowboarders are everywhere in Japan, but unlike areas back home, few of them seem to do much snowboarding. In Japan, the usual position for a snowboarder is sitting on his/her bum surrounded by friends doing the same. Consider them natural hazards and give them a wide berth.

■ Lift-line management is surprisingly poor in Japan. Skiers are often left to jostle and fend for themselves, and even when it's crowded, singles are allowed to ride triple and quad lifts alone.

SKIING LESSONS IN ENGLISH

The following outfits offer skiing lessons in English for both children and adults (usually with foreign instructors). Half-day private ski lessons in Japan average ¥14,000; full-day private ski lessons average ¥21,000.

■ **Canyons** (http://canyons.jp/index_E.htl) With a base at Hakuba (close to Happō-One), Canyons offers skiing, backcountry skiing and snowboarding lessons, as well as snowshoeing tours.

■ **Evergreen** (www.evergreen-hakuba.com) Also in Hakuba, Evergreen offers skiing, snowboarding, powder skiing and telemark lessons.

■ **SAS Snow Sports** (www.sas-net.com/school.html) Based in Niseko, SAS offers skiing and snowboarding lessons.

---

the kinks after a day on the slopes. While you're here, you can make an easy sidetrip to see Japan's famous 'snow monkeys' (see p278). For more information on Shiga Kōgen, see p279.

■ **Nozawa Onsen** This quaint little ski resort/village tucked high up in the Japan Alps of Nagano-ken is the closest thing you'll find to Switzerland in Japan. The main difference is this village has 13 free *onsen* scattered around for your evening entertainment. Of course, skiing is the main reason to visit, and it's excellent here. The area is more compact and easy to get around than Shiga Kōgen, and it has a good variety of runs, including some challenging bump runs. Snowboarders will enjoy the terrain park and half-pipe, and there's a cross-country skiing course up on the mountain as well. For more information on Nozawa Onsen, see p279.

■ **Rusutsu** Hokkaidō's Rusutsu is luring a lot of skiers away from superpopular Niseko. Rusustu gets regular dumps of deep powder snow like Niseko, and allows skiers and boarders to enjoy it both on piste and off piste (there are some great tree runs and the management doesn't try to prevent you from enjoying it). Rusutsu tends to be less crowded than Niseko and as long as the lifts aren't shut down due to high winds, you won't often wait in line here. All in all, if you're going to ski in Hokkaidō, we recommend that you at least give one day to Rusutsu – you may find that you like it as much or even more than Niseko. For more information on Rusutsu, see p591.

'The main difference is this village has 13 free *onsen* scattered around for your evening entertainment'

WHAT TO BRING

With the exception of really large ski boots (see the following list), almost everything you need is available in Japan. However, due to prices or difficulty in finding some items, it's best to bring the following things from abroad:

■ **A small 'around the arm' type case to hold your ski lift chip** You will be scanning this at every lift – having it on your arm is easily the best place to keep it.

■ **Goggles** They're very expensive in Japan, so it's best to bring your own.

■ **A small waterproof bag** For maps and information.

■ **Large size ski boots** Rental places at most resorts have boots up to 30cm (which is equivalent to a men's size 12 in the USA, UK or Australia). If you have larger feet, you'll have trouble finding your size.

■ **Mobile phone(s)** Many of Japan's ski areas are covered by one or more mobile-phone networks, and these are a great way to keep in touch with others in your party. You can easily rent mobile phones in Japan (see p802).

SNOWSHOEING TOURS IN ENGLISH

Snowshoeing is an excellent way to get into the woods and enjoy the winter in Japan. The following operators offer snowshoe tours and instruction.

- **Suisen-Kyō Tours** (www.suisenkyo.com) This friendly outfit offers snowshoe tours of the Kitayama mountains, a short bus trip north of Kyoto. If you can't make it all the way to the Japan Alps, this is a great way to experience the beauty of Japan's mountains.

- **Canyons** (http://canyons.jp/index_E.htl) Located at Hakuba, Canyons offers a variety of backcountry tours, including snowshoe tours and backcountry skiing.

Before you start your skiing day, it's also useful to grab a bunch of ¥1000 notes and ¥500 and ¥100 coins, as many of the rest houses on the mountain have vending machines.

CAN YOU SAY SKI IN JAPANESE?

That's right: it's 'ski' (alright, it's pronounced more like 'sukee'). But the point is, communication won't be much of a problem on your Japan ski trip. First, tackling the language barrier has never been easier: most resorts employ a number of English-speaking foreigners on working holiday visas. They operate the lifts, work in the cafeterias, and are often employed in the hotels or ryokan that are most popular with foreign guests. All major signs and maps are translated into English, and, provided you have some experience at large resorts back home, you'll find the layout and organisation of Japanese resorts to be pretty intuitive. The information counter at the base of the mountain always has someone on staff to answer questions, and, of course, the stereotype regarding politeness holds true.

Snowboarding first debuted as an Olympic sport at the 1998 Nagano Winter Olympics.

Useful Skiing Terms

Some useful words and phrases you may want to try out on the locals:

boots	*bootsu*	ブーツ
cold	*samui*	寒い
difficult	*muzukashii*	難しい
easy	*kantan/yasashii*	簡単・易しい
gondola	*gondora*	ゴンドラ
lesson	*ressun*	レッスン
lift	*rifuto*	リフト
map	*mappu*	マップ
poles	*sutokku*	ストック
run, course, trail	*kōsu*	コース
size	*saizu*	サイズ
ski (noun)	*sukee*	スキー
ski (verb)	*sukee wo suru*	スキーをする
ski area/field/resort	*sukee jō*	スキー場
skis	*sukeezu*	スキーズ
slippery	*suberiyasui*	滑りやすい
snow	*yuki*	雪
(lift) ticket	*chiketto*	チケット
I come from...	*...kara kimashita*	...から来ました
It's cold, isn't it?	*samui desu ne*	寒いですね
Nice weather, isn't it?	*ii otenki desu ne*	いいお天気ですね
You're a good!	*(anata wa) jōzu desu ne*	あなたは上手ですね
I'm not so good.	*(watashi wa) heta desu*	私は下手です

Food & Drink

Those familiar with *nihon ryōri* (Japanese cuisine) know that eating is half the fun of travelling in Japan. Even if you've already tried some of Japan's better-known specialities in Japanese restaurants in your own country, you're likely to be surprised by how delicious the original is when served on its home turf. More importantly, the adventurous eater will be delighted to find that Japanese food is far more than just sushi, tempura or sukiyaki. Indeed, it is possible to spend a month in Japan and sample a different speciality restaurant every night.

Of course, you may baulk at charging into a restaurant where both the language and the menu are likely to be incomprehensible. The best way to get over this fear is to familiarise yourself with the main types of Japanese restaurants so that you have some idea of what's on offer and how to order it. Those timid of heart should take solace in the fact that the Japanese will go to extraordinary lengths to understand what you want and will help you to order. To help you out further, eating reviews in this book recommend specific dishes where no English menu is available; restaurants that do offer English menus are identified with an E.

With the exception of *shokudō* (all-round restaurants) and *izakaya* (pub-style restaurants), most Japanese restaurants concentrate on a speciality cuisine. This naturally makes for delicious eating, but does limit your choice. In the Restaurants & Sample Menus section of this chapter we will introduce the main types of Japanese restaurants, along with a menu sample of some of the most common dishes served (see p88).

For information on how to eat in a Japanese restaurant, see the boxed text, p89. For information on eating etiquette in Japan, see the tips in the boxed text, p87.

Lonely Planet's *World Food Japan* (John Ashburne and Yoshi Abe) provides a detailed introduction to Japanese cuisine. It's an excellent supplement to the information in this chapter.

STAPLES

Despite the mind-boggling variety of dishes throughout the island chain, the staples that make up Japanese cuisine remain the same nationwide: *shōyu* (soy sauce), miso, tofu, *mame* (beans) and above all, the divine crop, *kome* (rice).

Rice (O-kome)

The Japanese don't just consume *kome* (rice) all day, every day. In its uncooked form it is called *o-kome*, the o- denoting respect, *kome* meaning rice. Cooked Japanese style, it is called *go-han* (the go- prefix is the highest indicator of respect), denoting rice or meal. Truck drivers, however, may use the more informal *meshi*, something akin to 'grub'. When it is included in Western-style meals, it is termed *raisu*. On average, Japanese consume an astonishing 70kg of *kome* per person per year. Culturally, most Japanese feel a meal is simply incomplete without the inclusion of *kome*.

Hakumai is the plain white rice that is used in every dish from the humble *eki-ben* (station lunchbox) to the finest *kaiseki* (Japanese formal cuisine). A meal will consist of, for example, a bowl of *hakumai* topped with *tsukudani* (fish and vegetables simmered in *shōyu* – soy sauce – and *mirin* – sweet rice wine), served with a bowl of miso soup, accompanied by a side dish of *tsukemono* (pickles). *Genmai*, unpolished, unrefined brown rice, is rarely spotted outside organic restaurants (with the notable exception of *shōjin-ryōri* – Buddhist vegetarian cuisine) as it lacks that fragrance and glow so desired of simple *hakumai*. Rice is used in *zōsui* (rice soup), *o-chazuke* (where green tea is poured onto white rice), *onigiri* (the ubiquitous rice balls) and vinegared in sushi.

Mame (Beans)

Given the country's Buddhist history, it's no surprise that Japanese cuisine has long been dependent on beans as a source of protein. Top of the Japanese bean pile is the indispensable soy bean, the *daizu* (literally, 'big bean'), which provides the raw material for miso, *shōyu*, tofu, *yuba* (soy milk skin) and the infamous *nattō* (fermented soy beans). It also finds its way into such dishes as *hijiki-mame*, where black spiky seaweed is sauteed in oil, with soy sauce and sugar, and *daizu no nimono*, soy beans cooked with *konbu* (kelp) and dried shiitake mushrooms.

Next is *azuki*, the adzuki bean (written with the characters for 'little bean'), used extensively in preparation of *wagashi* (Japanese sweets), often for the tea ceremony, and in the preparation of *seki-han* (red-bean rice), which is used at times of celebration and to commemorate a teenage girl's first menstruation.

The superb Tokyo Food Page (www.bento.com) offers explanations of Japanese dishes, great places to eat in Tokyo and much, much more.

Miso

A precursor of miso arrived on the Japanese mainland from China sometime around AD 600, not long after Buddhism. Its inhabitants have been gargling it down as *misoshiru* (miso soup) ever since, at breakfast, lunch and dinner. Made by mixing steamed soy beans with *kōji* (a fermenting agent) and salt, miso is integral to any Japanese meal, where it is likely to be present as *misoshiru* or as a flavouring. It is also used in *dengaku* (fish and vegetables roasted on skewers), where it is spread on vegetables such as eggplant and *konnyaku* (devil's tongue).

Misoshiru is a brownish soup made from a mixture of *dashi* (stock), miso and shellfish, such as *shijimi* (freshwater clams) or *asari* (short-necked clams);

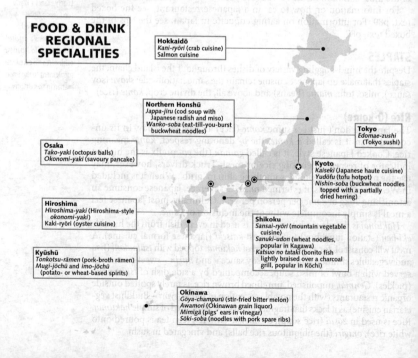

FOOD & DRINK REGIONAL SPECIALITIES

Hokkaidō
Kani-ryōri (crab cuisine)
Salmon cuisine

Northern Honshū
Jappa-jiru (cod soup with Japanese radish and miso)
Wanko-soba (eat-till-you-burst buckwheat noodles)

Tokyo
Edomae-zushi (Tokyo sushi)

Osaka
Tako-yaki (octopus balls)
Okonomi-yaki (savoury pancake)

Kyoto
Kaiseki (Japanese haute cuisine)
Yudōfu (tofu hotpot)
Nishin-soba (buckwheat noodles topped with a partially dried herring)

Hiroshima
Hiroshima-yaki (Hiroshima-style okonomi-yaki)
Kaki-ryōri (oyster cuisine)

Shikoku
Sansai-ryōri (mountain vegetable cuisine)
Sanuki-udon (wheat noodles, popular in Kagawa)
Katsuo no tataki (bonito fish lightly braised over a charcoal grill, popular in Kōchi)

Kyūshū
Tonkotsu-rāmen (pork-broth rāmen)
Mugi-jōchū and *imo-jōchū* (potato- or wheat-based spirits)

Okinawa
Gōya-champurū (stir-fried bitter melon)
Awamori (Okinawan grain liquor)
Mimigā (pigs' ears in vinegar)
Sōki-soba (noodles with pork spare ribs)

EATING ETIQUETTE

When it comes to eating in Japan, there are quite a number of implicit rules, but they're fairly easy to remember. If you're worried about putting your foot in it, relax – the Japanese don't expect you to know what to do, and they are unlikely to be offended as long as you follow the standard rules of politeness from your own country. Here are a few major points to keep in mind:

■ **Chopsticks in rice** Do not stick your chopsticks upright in a bowl of rice. This is how rice is offered to the dead in Buddhist rituals. Similarly, do not pass food from your chopsticks to someone else's. This is another funereal ritual.

■ **Polite expressions** When eating with other people, especially when you're a guest, it is polite to say *'Itadakimasu'* (literally, 'I will receive') before digging in. This is as close as the Japanese come to saying grace. Similarly, at the end of the meal, you should thank your host by saying *'Gochisō-sama deshita'*, which means, 'It was a real feast'.

■ **Kampai** It is bad form to fill your own drink; fill the glass of the person next to you and wait for them to reciprocate. Raise your glass a little off the table while it is being filled. Once everyone's glass has been filled, the usual starting signal is a chorus of '*kampai*', which means 'cheers!'.

■ **Slurp** When you eat noodles in Japan, it's perfectly OK, even expected, to slurp them. In fact, one of the best ways to find a *rāmen* (noodle) restaurant in Japan is to listen for the loud slurping sound that comes out of them!

---

assorted vegetables, such as *daikon* (giant white radish), carrot or burdock (especially good for the digestion); pork; or simply tofu. You may see this up to three times a day in Japan, as it accompanies almost every typical Japanese meal. The simple rule is this: if there's a bowl of rice, then a bowl of *misoshiru* is never far behind.

Tofu

Usually made from soybeans, tofu is one of Japan's most sublime creations. Tofu is sold as the soft 'silk' *kinugoshi* and the firm *momen* (or *momengoshi*). The former is mainly used in soups, especially *misoshiru*. The latter is eaten by itself, deep-fried in *agedashi-dōfu* or used in the Kyoto classic *yudōfu*, a hotpot dish. Both *momen* and *kinugoshi* take their names from the technique used when the hot soy milk is strained – if the material used is cotton, the resulting firm tofu is *momen;* when silk *(kinu)* is used, it's *kinugoshi*.

A classic way to eat tofu is as *hiyayakko*, cold blocks of tofu covered with soy, grated ginger and finely sliced spring onion. This is a favourite on the menus of *izakaya*.

Abura-age is thinly sliced, especially thick tofu traditionally fried in sesame oil (more recently, however, producers use salad oil or soy bean oil). It is a key ingredient in the celebratory *chirashi-zushi* (sushi rice topped with cooked egg and other tidbits like shrimp and ginger) and in *inari-zushi* (where vinegared rice is stuffed into a fried tofu pouch).

Yuba is a staple of *shōjin-ryōri* and a speciality of Kyoto. It is a marvellous accompaniment to sake when it is served fresh with grated wasabi and *shōyu tsuyu* (dipping sauce). Its creation is a time- and labour-intensive process in which soy milk is allowed to curdle over a low heat and then is plucked from the surface.

Shōyu (Soy Sauce)

Surprisingly, *shōyu* is a relatively new addition to Japanese cuisine, although a primitive form of it, *hishio*, was made in the Yayoi period by mixing salt and fish. *Shōyu* in its current form dates back to the more recent Muromachi era.

'Usually made from soybeans, tofu is one of Japan's most sublime creations'

KŌBE BEEF

All meals involving Kōbe beef should come with the following label: warning, consuming this beef will ruin your enjoyment of any other type of beef. We're not kidding, it's that good.

The first thing you should know about Kōbe beef is how to say it: it's pronounced 'ko bay', which rhymes with 'no way'. In Japanese, Kōbe beef is known as Kōbe-gyū. Second, Kōbe beef is actually just one regional variety of Japanese beef, which is known as *wa-gyū* (literally, Japanese beef). *Wa-gyū* can be any of several breeds of cattle bred for the extreme fatty marbling of their meat (the most common breed is Japanese Black). Kōbe beef is simply *wa-gyū* raised in Hyōgō-ken, the prefecture in which the city of Kōbe is located.

There are many urban legends about Kōbe beef, promulgated, we suppose, by the farmers who raise them, or simply imaginative individuals who ascribe to cows the lives they'd like to lead. It is commonly believed that Kōbe beef cattle spend their days drinking beer and receiving regular massages. However, in all our days in Japan, we have never seen a single drunk cow or met a 'cow masseur'. More likely, the marbling pattern of the beef is the result of selective breeding and the cow's diet of alfalfa, corn, barley and wheat straw.

The best way to enjoy Kōbe beef, or any other type of *wa-gyū*, is cooked on a *teppan*, or iron griddle, at a *wa-gyū* specialist, and these restaurants are known as *teppen-yaki-ya*. In the West, a giant steak that hangs off the side of the plate is generally considered a good thing. But due to the intense richness (and price) of a good *wa-gyū* steak, it is usually consumed in relatively small portions, say, smaller than the size of your hand. The meat is usually seared quickly and then cooked to medium rare – cooking a piece of good *wa-gyū* to well done is something akin to making a tuna fish sandwich from the best cut of *toro* sashimi (fatty tuna belly).

Although Kōbe beef and *wa-gyū* are now all the rage in Western cities, like most Japanese food, the real thing consumed on its home turf is a far superior dish. And – surprise, surprise – it can be cheaper to eat it in Japan than overseas. You can get a fine *wa-gyū* steak course at lunch for around ¥5000, and at dinner for around double that. Of course, the best place for Kōbe beef is – you got it – Kōbe. See the Kōbe Eating section (p395) for our favourite Kōbe beef specialist. Just don't blame us if this puts you off the leathery things they call steaks in the West.

Twentieth-century mass production made a household name out of Kikkōman, but *shōyu* is still made using traditional methods at small companies throughout the country. It comes in two forms: the dark brown 'thicker taste' *koikuchi-shōyu*, and the chestnut-coloured 'thinner', much saltier *usukuchi-shōyu* (sweetened and lightened by the addition of *mirin*). *Koikuchi* is used for a variety of applications, especially in the Kantō region around Tokyo, and is perfect for teriyaki, where meat or fish is brushed with *shōyu*, *mirin* and sugar, and grilled. The aromatic *usukuchi-shōyu*, a favourite of the Kansai region, is best suited to clear soups and white fish. It is especially important in enhancing the colour of a dish's ingredients.

RESTAURANTS & SAMPLE MENUS
Shokudō

A *shokudō* is the most common type of restaurant in Japan, and is found near train stations, tourist spots and just about any other place where people congregate. Easily distinguished by the presence of plastic food displays in the window, these inexpensive places usually serve a variety of *washoku* (Japanese dishes) and *yōshoku* (Western dishes).

At lunch, and sometimes dinner, the easiest meal to order at a *shokudō* is a *teishoku* (set-course meal), which is sometimes also called *ranchi setto* (lunch set) or *kōsu*. This usually includes a main dish of meat or fish, a bowl of rice, miso soup, shredded cabbage and some Japanese pickles (*tsukemono*). In addition, most *shokudō* serve a fairly standard selection of *donburi-mono* (rice dishes) and *menrui* (noodle dishes). When you order noodles, you can choose between

We can't recommend *What's What in Japanese Restaurants: A Guide to Ordering Eating and Enjoying* (Robb Satterwhite) highly enough. With thorough explanations of the various types of Japanese dishes and sample English/Japanese menus, this is a must for those who really want to explore and enjoy Japanese restaurants.

soba and *udon*, both of which are served with a variety of toppings. If you're at a loss as to what to order, simply say *kyō-no-ranchi* (today's lunch) and they'll do the rest. Expect to spend from ¥800 to ¥1000 for a meal at a *shokudō*.

RICE DISHES

katsu-don	かつ丼	rice topped with a fried pork cutlet
niku-don	牛丼	rice topped with thin slices of cooked beef
oyako-don	親子丼	rice topped with egg and chicken
ten-don	天丼	rice topped with tempura shrimp and vegetables

NOODLE DISHES

soba	そば	buckwheat noodles
udon	うどん	thick, white wheat noodles
kake soba/udon	かけそば/うどん	*soba/udon* noodles in broth
kitsune soba/udon	きつねそば/うどん	*soba/udon* noodles with fried tofu
tempura soba/udon	天ぷらそば/うどん	*soba/udon* noodles with tempura shrimp
tsukimi soba/udon	月見そば/うどん	*soba/udon* noodles with raw egg on top

Izakaya

An *izakaya* is the Japanese equivalent of a pub. It's a good place to visit when you want a casual meal, a wide selection of food, a hearty atmosphere and, of course, plenty of beer and sake. When you enter an *izakaya*, you are given the choice of sitting around the counter, at a table or on a tatami floor. You usually order a bit at a time, choosing from a selection of typical Japanese foods like *yakitori*, sashimi and grilled fish, as well as Japanese interpretations of Western foods like French fries and beef stew.

Izakaya can be identified by their rustic façades and the red lanterns outside their doors bearing the kanji for *izakaya* (see p96). Since *izakaya* food

> 'An *izakaya* is the Japanese equivalent of a pub'

EATING IN A JAPANESE RESTAURANT

When you enter a restaurant in Japan, you'll be greeted with a hearty *'Irasshaimase!'* (Welcome!). In all but the most casual places the waiter will next ask you *'Nan-mei sama?'* (How many people?). Answer with your fingers, which is what the Japanese do. You will then be led to a table, a place at the counter or a tatami room.

At this point you will be given an *oshibori* (a hot towel), a cup of tea and a menu. The *oshibori* is for wiping your hands and face. When you're done with it, just roll it up and leave it next to your place. Now comes the hard part: ordering. If you don't read Japanese, you can use the romanised translations in this book to help you, or direct the waiter's attention to the Japanese script. If this doesn't work, there are two phrases that may help: *'O-susume wa nan desu ka?'* (What do you recommend?) and *'O-makase shimasu'* (Please decide for me). If you're still having problems, you can try pointing at other diners' food or, if the restaurant has them, dragging the waiter outside to point at the plastic food models in the window.

When you've finished eating, you can signal for the bill by crossing one index finger over the other to form the sign of an 'x'. This is the standard sign for 'bill please'. You can also say *'O-kanjō kudasai'*. Remember there is no tipping in Japan and tea is free of charge. Usually you will be given a bill to take to the cashier at the front of the restaurant. At more upmarket places, the host of the party will discreetly excuse him- or herself to pay before the group leaves. Unlike some places in the West, one doesn't usually leave cash on the table by way of payment. Only the bigger and more international places take credit cards, so cash is always the surer option.

When leaving, it is polite to say to the restaurant staff, *'Gochisō-sama deshita'*, which means 'It was a real feast'. The Useful Words & Phrases section (p102) contains more restaurant words and phrases.

is casual fare to go with drinking, it is usually fairly inexpensive. Depending on how much you drink, you can expect to get away with spending ¥2500 to ¥5000 per person. (See the following Yakitori section for more dishes available at *izakaya*.)

agedashi-dōfu	揚げだし豆腐	deep-fried tofu in a dashi broth
chiizu-age	チーズ揚げ	deep-fried cheese
hiya-yakko	冷奴	a cold block of tofu with soya sauce and spring onions
jaga-batā	ジャガバター	baked potatoes with butter
kata yaki-soba	固焼きそば	hard fried noodles with meat and vegetables
niku-jaga	肉ジャガ	beef and potato stew
poteto furai	ポテトフライ	French fries
sashimi mori-awase	刺身盛り合わせ	a selection of sliced sashimi
shio-yaki-zakana	塩焼魚	a whole fish grilled with salt
tsuna sarada	ツナサラダ	tuna salad over cabbage
yaki-onigiri	焼きおにぎり	a triangle of grilled rice with *yakitori* sauce
yaki-soba	焼きそば	fried noodles with meat and vegetables

Yakitori

Yakitori (skewers of grilled chicken and vegetables) is a popular after-work meal. *Yakitori* is not so much a full meal as an accompaniment for beer and sake. At a *yakitori-ya* (*yakitori* restaurant) you sit around a counter with the other patrons and watch the chef grill your selections over charcoal. The best way to eat here is to order several varieties, then order seconds of the ones you really like. Ordering can be a little confusing since one serving often means two or three skewers (be careful – the price listed on the menu is usually that of a single skewer).

In summer, the beverage of choice at a *yakitori* restaurant is beer or cold sake, while in winter it's hot sake. A few drinks and enough skewers to fill you up should cost ¥3000 to ¥4000 per person. *Yakitori* restaurants are usually small places, often near train stations, and are best identified by a red lantern outside and the smell of grilling chicken.

gyū-niku	牛肉	pieces of beef
hasami/negima	はさみ/ねぎま	pieces of white meat alternating with leek
kawa	皮	chicken skin
piiman	ピーマン	small green peppers
rebā	レバー	chicken livers
sasami	ささみ	skinless chicken-breast pieces
shiitake	しいたけ	Japanese mushrooms
tama-negi	玉ねぎ	round white onions
tebasaki	手羽先	chicken wings
tsukune	つくね	chicken meat balls
yaki-onigiri	焼きおにぎり	a triangle of rice grilled with *yakitori* sauce
yakitori	焼き鳥	plain, grilled white meat

Sushi & Sashimi

Randy Johnson's 'Sushi a là Carte' (www.ease .com/~randyj/rjsushi .htm) is a must for sushi lovers – it explains everything you need to know about ordering and enjoying sushi.

Like *yakitori*, sushi is considered an accompaniment for beer and sake. Nonetheless, both Japanese and foreigners often make a meal of it, and it's one of the healthiest meals around. All proper sushi restaurants serve their fish over rice, in which case it's called sushi; without rice, it's called sashimi or *tsukuri* (or, politely, *o-tsukuri*).

There are two main types of sushi: *nigiri-zushi* (served on a small bed of rice – the most common variety) and *maki-zushi* (served in a seaweed roll). Lesser-known varieties include *chirashi-zushi* (a layer of rice covered in egg and fish toppings), *oshi-zushi* (fish pressed in a mould over rice) and *inari-zushi* (rice in a pocket of sweet, fried tofu). Whatever kind of sushi you try, it will be served with lightly vinegared rice. Note that *nigiri-zushi* and *maki-zushi* will contain a bit of wasabi (hot green horseradish).

Sushi is not difficult to order. If you sit at the counter of a sushi restaurant you can simply point at what you want, as most of the selections are visible in a refrigerated glass case between you and the sushi chef. You can also order à la carte from the menu. When ordering, you usually order *ichi-nin mae* (one portion), which usually means two pieces of sushi. Be careful, since the price on the menu will be that of only one piece. If ordering a la carte is too daunting, you can take care of your whole order with just one or two words by ordering *mori-awase,* an assortment plate of *nigiri-zushi.* These usually come in three grades: *futsū nigiri* (regular *nigiri*), *jō nigiri* (special *nigiri*) and *toku-jō nigiri* (extra-special *nigiri*). The difference is in the type of fish used. Most *mori-awase* contain six or seven pieces of sushi.

Be warned that meals in a good sushi restaurant can cost upwards of ¥10,000, while an average establishment can run from ¥3000 to ¥5000 per person. One way to sample the joy of sushi on the cheap is to try an automatic sushi place, usually called *kaiten-zushi,* where the sushi is served on a conveyor belt that runs along a counter. Here you simply reach up and grab whatever looks good to you (which certainly takes the pain out of ordering). You are charged by the number of plates of sushi that you have eaten. Plates are colour-coded by their price and the cost is written either somewhere on the plate itself or on a sign on the wall. You can usually fill yourself up in one of these places for ¥1000 to ¥2000 per person.

Before popping the sushi into your mouth, dip it in *shōyu,* which you pour from a small decanter into a low dish specially provided for the purpose. If you're not good at using chopsticks, don't worry – sushi is one of the few foods in Japan that is perfectly acceptable to eat with your hands. Slices of *gari* (pickled ginger) will also be served to help refresh the palate. The beverage of choice with sushi is beer or sake (hot in winter and cold in summer), with a cup of green tea at the end of the meal.

Note that most of the items on this sample sushi menu can be ordered as sashimi. Just add the words 'no o-tsukuri' to get the sashimi version ('o-tsukuri' is the more common Japanese expression for sashimi). So, for example, if you want some tuna sashimi, you would order '*maguro no o-tsukuri*'. Note that sashimi often appears in other kinds of restaurants, not just sushi specialists. Shokudō often serve a sashimi set meal (*o-tskuri teishoku*), izakaya usually offer a plate of assorted sashimi (*otsukuri moriawase*) and kaiseki courses usually feature a few pieces of carefully chosen sashimi. When it's eaten at a sushi restaurant, sashimi is often the first course, a warm up for the sushi itself. Note that you'll often be served a different soy sauce to accompany your sashimi; if you like wasabi with your sashimi, you add some directly to the soy sauce and stir. And make no mistake, a bit of good soy sauce and some fresh-grated wasabi is the only way to improve on one of the finest tastes on earth: a piece of top-quality *ō-toro tsukuri* (fatty tuna belly sashimi).

> 'Be warned that meals in a good sushi restaurant can cost upwards of ¥10,000'

ama-ebi	甘海老	sweet shrimp
awabi	あわび	abalone
ebi	海老	prawn or shrimp
hamachi	はまち	yellowtail
ika	いか	squid
ikura	イクラ	salmon roe
kai-bashira	貝柱	scallop
kani	かに	crab
katsuo	かつお	bonito
maguro	まぐろ	tuna
tai	鯛	sea bream

tamago	たまご	sweetened egg
toro	とろ	the choicest cut of fatty tuna belly
unagi	うなぎ	eel with a sweet sauce
uni	うに	sea urchin roe

Sukiyaki & Shabu-shabu

Restaurants usually specialise in both these dishes. Popular in the West, sukiyaki is a favourite of most foreign visitors to Japan. Sukiyaki consists of thin slices of beef cooked in a broth of *shōyu,* sugar and sake, and accompanied by a variety of vegetables and tofu. After cooking, all the ingredients are dipped in raw egg before being eaten. When made with high-quality beef, like Kōbe beef, it is a sublime experience.

Shabu-shabu consists of thin slices of beef and vegetables cooked by swirling the ingredients in a light broth, then dipping them in a variety of special sesame-seed and citrus-based sauces. Both of these dishes are prepared in a pot over a fire at your private table; don't fret about preparation – the waiter will usually help you get started, and keep a close watch as you proceed. The key is to take your time, add the ingredients a little at a time and savour the flavours as you go.

Sukiyaki and *shabu-shabu* restaurants usually have traditional Japanese décor and sometimes a picture of a cow to help you identify them. Ordering is not difficult. Simply say sukiyaki or *shabu-shabu* and indicate how many people are dining. Expect to pay from ¥3000 to ¥10,000 per person.

Tempura

Tempura consists of portions of fish, prawns and vegetables cooked in fluffy, non-greasy batter. When you sit down at a tempura restaurant, you will be given a small bowl of *ten-tsuyu* (a light brown sauce) and a plate of grated *daikon* to mix into the sauce. Dip each piece of tempura into this sauce before eating it. Tempura is best when it's hot, so don't wait too long – use the sauce to cool each piece and dig in.

While it's possible to order à la carte, most diners choose to order *teishoku* (full set), which includes rice, *miso-shiru* and Japanese pickles. Some tempura restaurants offer courses that include different numbers of tempura pieces.

Expect to pay between ¥2000 and ¥10,000 for a full tempura meal. Finding these restaurants is tricky as they have no distinctive façade or décor. If you look through the window, you'll see customers around the counter watching the chefs as they work over large woks filled with oil.

kaki age	かき揚げ	tempura with shredded vegetables or fish
shōjin age	精進揚げ	vegetarian tempura
tempura moriawase	天ぷら盛り合わせ	a selection of tempura

Rāmen

The Japanese imported this dish from China and put their own spin on it to make what is one of the world's most delicious fast foods. *Rāmen* dishes are big bowls of noodles in a meat broth, served with a variety of toppings, such as sliced pork, bean sprouts and leeks. In some restaurants, particularly in Kansai, you may be asked if you'd prefer *kotteri* (thick) or *assari* (thin) soup. Other than this, ordering is simple: just sidle up to the counter and say *rāmen*, or ask for any of the other choices usually on offer (a list follows). Expect to pay between ¥500 and ¥900 for a bowl. Since *rāmen* is derived from Chinese cuisine, some *rāmen* restaurants also serve *chāhan* or *yaki-meshi* (both dishes are fried rice), *gyōza* (dumplings) and *kara-age* (deep-fried chicken pieces).

Rāmen enthusiasts will get hungry just looking at the World Ramen.net (www.worldramen.net/) site. It includes reviews of Tokyo *rāmen* shops and even information about how to open your own *rāmen* shop!

Rāmen restaurants are easily distinguished by their long counters lined with customers hunched over steaming bowls. You can sometimes hear a *rāmen* shop as you wander by – it's considered polite to slurp the noodles and aficionados claim that slurping brings out the full flavour of the broth.

rāmen	ラーメン	soup and noodles with a sprinkling of meat and vegetables
chānpon-men	ちゃんぽん麺	Nagasaki-style *rāmen*
chāshū-men	チャーシュー麺	*rāmen* topped with slices of roasted pork
miso-rāmen	みそラーメン	*rāmen* with miso-flavoured broth
wantan-men	ワンタン麺	*rāmen* with meat dumplings

Soba & Udon

Soba and *udon* are Japan's answer to Chinese-style *rāmen*. *Soba* are thin, brown buckwheat noodles; *udon* are thick, white wheat noodles. Most Japanese noodle shops serve both *soba* and *udon* in a variety of ways. Noodles are usually served in a bowl containing a light, bonito-flavoured broth, but you can also order them served cold and piled on a bamboo screen with a cold broth for dipping.

By far the most popular type of cold noodles is *zaru soba*, which is served with bits of *nori* (seaweed) on top. If you order these noodles, you'll receive a small plate of wasabi and sliced spring onions – put these into the cup of broth and eat the noodles by dipping them in this mixture. At the end of your meal, the waiter will give you some hot broth to mix with the leftover sauce, which you drink like a kind of tea. As with *rāmen*, you should feel free to slurp as loudly as you please.

Soba and *udon* places are usually quite cheap (about ¥900 a dish), but some fancy places can be significantly more expensive (the décor is a good indication of the price). See Noodle Dishes (p89) for more *soba* and *udon* dishes.

zaru soba	ざるそば	cold noodles with seaweed strips served on a bamboo tray

Unagi

Unagi (eel) is an expensive and popular delicacy in Japan. Even if you can't stand the creature when served in your home country, you owe it to yourself to try *unagi* at least once while in Japan. It's cooked over hot coals and brushed with a rich sauce of *shōyu* and sake. Full *unagi* dinners can be expensive, but many *unagi* restaurants offer *unagi bentō* (boxed lunches) and lunch sets for around ¥1500. Most *unagi* restaurants display plastic models of their sets in their front windows, and may have barrels of live eels to entice passers-by.

unagi teishoku	うなぎ定食	full-set *unagi* meal with rice, grilled eel, eel-liver soup and pickles
una-don	うな丼	grilled eel over a bowl of rice
unajū	うな重	grilled eel over a flat tray of rice
kabayaki	蒲焼き	skewers of grilled eel without rice

Fugu

The deadly *fugu* (globefish or pufferfish) is eaten more for the thrill than the taste. It's actually rather bland – most people liken the taste to chicken – but is acclaimed for its fine texture. Nonetheless, if you have the money to lay out for a *fugu* dinner (around ¥10,000), it makes a good 'been there, done that' story back home (see the boxed text, p94).

Although the danger of *fugu* poisoning is negligible, some Japanese joke that you should always let your dining companion try the first piece – if they are still talking after five minutes, you can consider it safe and have some yourself. If you need a shot of liquid courage in order to get you started, try

We consider the film *Tampopo* (Itami Juzo, 1985) just about essential preparation for a visit to Japan – especially if you intend to visit a *rāmen* shop while you're here! It's about two fellows who set out to help a *rāmen* shop owner improve her shop, with several food-related subplots woven in for good measure.

More than five billion servings of instant *rāmen* are consumed each year in Japan.

a glass of *hirezake* (toasted *fugu* tail in hot sake) – the traditional accompaniment to a *fugu* dinner.

Fugu is a seasonal delicacy best eaten in winter. *Fugu* restaurants usually serve only *fugu*, and can be identified by a picture of a *fugu* on the sign out the front.

Fugu is the speciality of Western Honshū, and Shimonoseki (p476) is a good place to give it a try. Of course, you can also find *fugu* in other parts of Japan.

fugu chiri	ふぐちり	a stew made from *fugu* and vegetables
fugu sashimi	ふぐ刺身	thinly sliced raw *fugu*
fugu teishoku	ふぐ定食	a set course of *fugu* served several ways, plus rice and soup
yaki fugu	焼きふぐ	*fugu* grilled on a hibachi at your table

Tonkatsu

Tonkatsu is a deep-fried breaded pork cutlet that is served with a special sauce, usually as part of a set meal (*tonkatsu teishoku*). *Tonkatsu* is served both at speciality restaurants and at *shokudō*. Naturally, the best *tonkatsu* is to be found at the speciality places, where a full set will cost ¥1500 to ¥2500.

ARE YOU A CULINARY DAREDEVIL? *John Ashburne*

There are few cuisines that actively threaten to dispatch you into the next life. Japan's famed, poisonous *fugu*, also known as globefish, blowfish or pufferfish, is one such dish. Its ancient nickname is the *teppō*, 'the pistol', from its tendency to bump off careless eaters. Its active ingredient is tetrodoxin, a clear, tasteless, odourless poison 13 times stronger than arsenic. One species of *fugu* contains enough to kill 33 people. Specially trained chefs remove most of the poison, leaving just enough to numb your lips. Though the danger of *fugu* poisoning is negligible, no one ever pisses off *fugu* chefs.

Yet some consumers actively choose to poison themselves. How's this for bold? A good friend's grandfather, a man of somewhat decadent sensibilities, would eat *fugu* liver (a practice now outlawed) and slip into a state of semiparalysis for three days! Apparently the near-death sensation was rather agreeable, and he was always somewhat disappointed when he regained full control of his limbs. Lonely Planet Publications wishes to remind the reader: DO NOT TRY THIS AT HOME.

Fugu, life threatening as it may be, at least has the saving grace of having shuffled off its own mortal. No such luck with 'dancing-eating' or *odorigui*, the practice of wilfully consuming live animals. It originated in Fukuoka and the chosen Fukuoka victim is usually *shirouo*, a small transparent fish, which wriggles to its suffocating oesophagal doom half-drunk, washed down with sake.

Really bold diners can try the same thing with an octopus. In a Gunma sushi shop I once fatally left the ordering to 'friends', who grinned malevolently and asked for the 'special'. The chef promptly lifted a poor cephalopod from a large tank on the counter, sliced up one tentacle, put it on a plate with some soy sauce, and passed the still twisting and writhing limb to yours truly. The sensation, as the suckers attach to the roof of your mouth, is impossible to convey. Equally difficult to put into words is how it feels to try to murder an octopus leg by chewing it to death.

Same sushi shop. Same evening. It got worse. Dismayed by my refusal to pass out, the said friends brought out the big guns in the shape of *shirako*. Staring at the frothy, white objects shaped like pasta spirals but exuding an unmistakable deep-sea odour, I feebly requested a translation. Poker-faced Mr Suto offered the deadpan 'cod sperm'. I ate. I turned green. I drank large quantities of cold beer.

That was 15 years ago. Since then I have consumed many odd dishes and survived. But it's only now that I can recognise Mr Suto's translation error. *Shirako* is not 'cod sperm' at all. It is the 'sperm-filled reproductive gland of the male cod'.

Enjoy!

When ordering *tonkatsu*, you are able to choose between *rōsu* (a fatter cut of pork) and *hire* (a leaner cut).

hire katsu	ヒレかつ	tonkatsu fillet
kushi katsu	串かつ	deep-fried pork and vegetables on skewers
minchi katsu	ミンチカツ	minced pork cutlet
tonkatsu teishoku	とんかつ定食	a set meal of *tonkatsu*, rice, *miso shiru* and shredded cabbage

Kushiage & Kushikatsu

This is the fried food to beat all fried foods. *Kushiage* and *kushikatsu* are deep-fried skewers of meat, seafood and vegetables eaten as an accompaniment to beer. *Kushi* means 'skewer' and if food can be fit on one, it's probably on the menu. Cabbage is often eaten with the meal.

You order *kushiage* and *kushikatsu* by the skewer (one skewer is *ippon*, but you can always use your fingers to indicate how many you want). Like *yakitori*, this food is popular with after-work salarymen and students and is fairly inexpensive, though there are upmarket places. Expect to pay ¥2000 to ¥5000 for a full meal and a couple of beers. Not particularly distinctive in appearance, the best *kushiage* and *kushikatsu* places are found by asking a Japanese friend.

ebi	海老	shrimp
gyū-niku	牛肉	beef pieces
ginnan	銀杏	ginkgo nuts
ika	いか	squid
imo	いも	potato
renkon	れんこん	lotus root
shiitake	しいたけ	Japanese mushrooms
tama-negi	玉ねぎ	white onion

Okonomiyaki

The name means 'cook what you like', and an *okonomiyaki* restaurant provides you with an inexpensive opportunity to do just that. Sometimes described as Japanese pizza or pancake, the resemblance is in form only. At an *okonomiyaki* restaurant you sit around a *teppan* (iron hotplate), armed with a spatula and chopsticks to cook your choice of meat, seafood and vegetables in a cabbage and vegetable batter.

Some restaurants will do most of the cooking and bring the nearly finished product over to your hotplate for you to season with *katsuo bushi* (bonito flakes), *shōyu*, *ao-nori* (an ingredient similar to parsley), Japanese Worcester-shire-style sauce and mayonnaise. Cheaper places, however, will simply hand you a bowl filled with the ingredients and expect you to cook it for yourself. If this happens, don't panic. First, mix the batter and filling thoroughly, then place it on the hotplate, flattening it into a pancake shape. After five minutes or so, use the spatulas to flip it and cook for another five minutes. Then dig in.

Most *okonomiyaki* places also serve *yaki-soba* (fried noodles) and *yasai-itame* (stir-fried vegetables). All of this is washed down with mugs of draught beer.

One final word: don't worry too much about preparation of the food – as a foreigner you will be expected to be awkward, and the waiter will keep a sharp eye on you to make sure no real disasters occur.

gyū okonomiyaki	牛お好み焼き	beef *okonomiyaki*
ika okonomiyaki	いかお好み焼き	squid *okonomiyaki*
mikkusu	ミックスお好み焼き	mixed fillings of seafood, *okonomiyaki* meat and vegetables
modan-yaki	モダン焼き	okonomiyaki with *yaki soba* and a fried egg
negi okonomiyaki	ネギお好み焼き	thin *okonomiyaki* with spring onions

'All of this is washed down with mugs of draught beer'

Kaiseki

Kaiseki is the pinnacle of Japanese cuisine, where ingredients, preparation, setting and presentation come together to create a dining experience quite unlike any other. Born as an adjunct to the tea ceremony, *kaiseki* is a largely vegetarian affair (though fish is often served, meat never appears on the *kaiseki* menu). One usually eats *kaiseki* in the private room of a *ryōtei* (an especially elegant style of traditional restaurant), often overlooking a private, tranquil garden. The meal is served in several small courses, giving the diner an opportunity to admire the plates and bowls, which are carefully chosen to complement the food and season. Rice is eaten last (usually with an assortment of pickles) and the drink of choice is sake or beer.

All this comes at a steep price – a good *kaiseki* dinner costs upwards of ¥10,000 per person. A cheaper way to sample the delights of *kaiseki* is to visit a *kaiseki* restaurant for lunch. Most places offer a boxed lunch containing a sampling of their dinner fare for around ¥2500.

Unfortunately for foreigners, *kaiseki* restaurants can be intimidating places to enter. If possible, bring a Japanese friend or ask a Japanese friend to call ahead and make arrangements.

bentō	弁当	boxed lunch
kaiseki	懐石	traditional, expensive Kyoto-style cuisine
matsu	松	extra-special course
ryōtei	料亭	a restaurant serving a variety of traditional Japanese dishes
take	竹	special course
ume	梅	regular course

Sweets

'Some Westerners find Japanese sweets a little challenging'

Although most restaurants don't serve dessert (plates of sliced fruit are sometimes served at the end of a meal), there is no lack of sweets in Japan. Most sweets (known generically as *wagashi*) are sold in speciality stores for you to eat at home. Many of the more delicate-looking ones are made to balance the strong, bitter taste of the special *matcha* tea served during the tea ceremony.

Some Westerners find Japanese sweets a little challenging, due to the liberal use of a sweet, red *azuki*-bean paste called *anko*. This unusual filling turns up in even the most innocuous-looking pastries. But don't let anyone make up your mind for you: try a Japanese sweet for yourself.

With such a wide variety of sweets, it's impossible to list all the names. However, you'll probably find many variations on the *anko*-covered-by-*mochi* theme.

Sweet shops are easy to spot; they usually have open fronts with their wares laid out in wooden trays to entice passers-by. Buying sweets is simple – just point at what you want and indicate with your fingers how many you'd like.

anko	あんこ	sweet paste or jam made from adzuki beans
mochi	餅	pounded rice cakes made of glutinous rice
wagashi	和菓子	Japanese-style sweets
yōkan	ようかん	sweet red-bean jelly

DRINKS

Drinking plays a big role in Japanese society, and there are few social occasions where beer or sake is not served. Alcohol (in this case sake) also plays a ceremonial role in various Shintō festivals and rites, including the marriage ceremony. As a visitor to Japan, you'll probably find yourself in lots of situations where you are invited to drink, and tipping back a few beers or glasses of sake is a great way to get to know the locals. However, if you don't drink alcohol, it's no big deal. Simply order *oolong cha* (oolong tea) in place of beer or sake. While some folks might put pressure on you to drink alcohol, you can diffuse this pressure by saying '*sake o nomimasen*' (I don't drink alcohol).

What you pay for your drink depends on where you drink and, in the case of hostess bars, with whom you drink. Hostess bars are the most expensive places to drink (up to ¥10,000 per drink), followed by upmarket traditional Japanese bars, hotel bars, beer halls and casual pubs. If you are not sure about a place, ask about prices and cover charges before sitting down. As a rule, if you are served a small snack with your first round, you'll be paying a cover charge (usually a few hundred yen, but sometimes much more).

Izakaya and *yakitori-ya* are cheap places for beer, sake and food in a casual atmosphere resembling that of a pub. All Japanese cities, whether large or small, will have a few informal bars with reasonable prices. Such places are popular with young Japanese and resident *gaijin* (foreigners), who usually refer to such places as *gaijin* bars. In summer, many department stores open up beer gardens on the roof. Many of these places offer all-you-can-eat/drink specials for around ¥3000 per person.

> There are more than 1500 sake breweries in Japan.

| izakaya | 居酒屋 | pub-style restaurant |
| yakitori-ya | 焼鳥屋 | *yakitori* restaurant |

Beer

Introduced at the end of the 1800s, *biiru* (beer) is now the favourite tipple of the Japanese. The quality is generally excellent and the most popular type is light lager, although recently some breweries have been experimenting with darker brews. The major breweries are Kirin, Asahi, Sapporo and Suntory. Beer is dispensed everywhere, from vending machines to beer halls, and even in some temple lodgings. A standard can of beer from a vending machine is about ¥250, although some of the gigantic cans cost more than ¥1000. At bars, a beer starts at ¥500 and the price climbs upwards, depending on the establishment. *Nama biiru* (draught beer) is widely available, as are imported beers.

| biiru | ビール | beer |
| nama biiru | 生ビール | draught beer |

Sake

Rice wine has been brewed for centuries in Japan. Once restricted to imperial brewers, it was later produced at temples and shrines across the country. In recent years, consumption of beer has overtaken that of sake, but it's still a standard item in homes, restaurants and drinking places. Large casks of sake are often seen piled up as offerings outside temples and shrines, and the drink plays an important part in most celebrations and festivals.

> The Sake World Homepage (www.sake-world.com/) offers an excellent introduction to sake, including some tasting picks.

Most Westerners come to Japan with a bad image of sake, the result of having consumed low-grade brands overseas. Although it won't appeal to all palates, some of the higher grades are actually very good, and a trip to a restaurant specialising in sake is a great way to sample some of the better brews.

There are several major types of sake, including *nigori* (cloudy), *nama* (unrefined) and regular, clear sake. Of these, clear sake is by far the most common. Clear sake is usually divided into three grades: *tokkyū* (premium), *ikkyū* (first grade) and *nikyū* (second grade). *Nikyū* is the routine choice. Sake can be further divided into *karakuchi* (dry) and *amakuchi* (sweet). As well as the national brewing giants, there are thousands of provincial brewers producing local brews called *jizake*.

Sake is served *atsukan* (warm) and *reishu* (cold), with warm sake, unsurprisingly, being more popular in winter. When you order sake, it will usually be served in a small flask called *tokkuri*. These come in two sizes, so you should specify whether you want *ichigō* (small) or *nigō* (large). From these flasks you pour the sake into small ceramic cups called *o-choko* or *sakazuki*. Another way to sample sake is to drink it from a small wooden box called *masu*, with a bit of salt on the rim.

However you drink it, with a 17% alcohol content, sake (particularly the warm stuff) is likely to go right to your head. After a few bouts with sake you'll come to understand why the Japanese drink it in such small cups. Particularly memorable is a real sake hangover born of too much cheap sake. The best advice is not to indulge the day before you have to get on a plane.

amakuchi	甘口	sweet sake
atsukan	あつかん	warm sake
ikkyū	一級	first-grade sake
jizake	地酒	local brew
karakuchi	辛口	dry sake
nama	生	regular clear sake
nigori	にごり	cloudy sake
nikkyū	二級	second-grade sake
o-choko	おちょこ	ceramic sake cup
reishu	冷酒	cold sake
sakazuki	杯	ceramic sake cup
sake	酒	Japanese rice wine
tokkyū	特級	premium-grade sake

Shōchū

The Insider's Guide to Sake (Philip Harper) offers a fine introduction to sake, including information on how to choose a good sake and the history of the drink.

For those looking for a quick and cheap escape route from the sorrows of the world, *shōchū* is the answer. It's a distilled spirit made from a variety of raw materials, including potato (in which case it's called *imo-jōchū*) and barley (in which case it's called *mugi-jōchū*). It's quite strong, with an alcohol content of about 30%. In recent years it has been resurrected from its previous lowly status (it was used as a disinfectant in the Edo period) to become a trendy drink. You can drink it *oyu-wari* (with hot water) or *chūhai* (in a highball with soda and lemon). A 720mL bottle sells for about ¥600, which makes it a relatively cheap option compared to other spirits.

chūhai	チューハイ	*shōchū* with soda and lemon
oyu-wari	お湯割り	*shōchū* with hot water
shōchū	焼酎	distilled grain liquor

Wine, Imported Drinks & Whiskey

Japanese wines are available from areas such as Yamanashi, Nagano, Tōhoku and Hokkaidō. Standard wines are often blended with imports from South America or Eastern Europe. The major producers are Suntory, Mann's and Mercian. Expect to pay at least ¥1000 for a bottle of something drinkable. Imported wines are often stocked by large liquor stores or department stores in the cities. Bargains are sometimes available at ¥600, but most of the quaffable imports cost considerably more.

Prices of imported spirits have been coming down in recent years and bargain liquor stores have been popping up in bigger cities. However, if you really like imported spirits, it is probably a good idea to pick up a duty-free bottle or two on your way through the airport. Whiskey is available at most drinking establishments and is usually drunk *mizu-wari* (with water and ice) or *onzarokku* (on the rocks). Local brands, such as Suntory and Nikka, are sensibly priced, and most measure up to foreign standards. Expensive foreign labels are popular as gifts.

Most other imported spirits are available at drinking establishments in Japan. Bars with a large foreign clientele, including hotel bars, can usually mix anything you request. If not, they will certainly tailor a drink to your specifications.

whiskey	ウィスキー	whiskey
mizu-wari	水割り	whiskey, ice and water
onzarokku	オンザロック	whiskey with ice

Nonalcoholic Drinks

Most of the drinks you're used to at home will be available in Japan, with a few colourfully named additions like Pocari Sweat and Calpis Water. One convenient aspect of Japan is the presence of drink-vending machines on virtually every street corner, and at ¥120, refreshment is rarely more than a few steps away.

COFFEE & TEA

Kōhii (coffee) served in a *kisaten* (coffee shop) tends to be expensive in Japan, costing between ¥350 and ¥500 a cup, with some places charging up to ¥1000. A cheap alternative is one of the newer coffee-restaurant chains like Doutor or Pronto, or doughnut shops like Mr Donut (which offers free refills). An even cheaper alternative is a can of coffee, hot or cold, from a vending machine. Although unpleasantly sweet, at ¥120 the price is hard to beat.

When ordering coffee at a coffee shop in Japan, you'll be asked whether you like it *hotto* (hot) or *aisu* (cold). Black tea also comes hot or cold, with *miruku* (milk) or *remon* (lemon). A good way to start a day of sightseeing in Japan is with a *mōningu setto* (morning set) of tea or coffee, toast and eggs, which costs around ¥400.

'An even cheaper alternative is a can of coffee, hot or cold, from a vending machine'

kafe ōre	カフェオレ	*café au lait,* hot or cold
American *kōhii*	アメリカンコーヒー	weak coffee
burendo kōhii	ブレンドコーヒー	blended coffee, fairly strong
kōhii	コーヒー	regular coffee
kōcha	紅茶	black, British-style tea
orenji jūsu	オレンジジュース	orange juice

JAPANESE TEA

Unlike black tea, which Westerners are familiar with, most Japanese tea is green and contains a lot of vitamin C and caffeine. The powdered form used in the tea ceremony is called *matcha* and is drunk after being whipped into a frothy consistency. The more common form, a leafy green tea, is simply called *o-cha*, and is drunk after being steeped in a pot. In addition to green tea, you'll probably drink a lot of a brownish tea called *bancha,* which restaurants serve for free. In summer, a cold beverage called *mugicha* (roasted barley tea) is served in private homes.

bancha	番茶	ordinary-grade green tea, has a brownish colour
matcha	抹茶	powdered green tea used in the tea ceremony
mugicha	麦茶	roasted barley tea
o-cha	お茶	green tea
sencha	煎茶	medium-grade green tea

CELEBRATIONS

When the Japanese celebrate it must include food and drink, and lots of it, whether it is in a rural festival to appease the rice gods (themselves not averse to the odd glass of sake) or in the party-hard *izakaya* of the big cities. And it's fun. Everyone seems to know about the famous Japanese reserve – everyone, that is, except the Japanese themselves.

The celebratory year begins in homes and restaurants on 1 January, with the multicourse, lavish, colourful *osechi-ryōri.* Served in *jūbako* (four-layered lacquerware boxes), *osechi* originated primarily as a means of giving the overworked Japanese housewife three days' much-needed rest – its ingredients last well.

JAPANESE TEA CULTURE *Morgan Pitelka, Ph.D*

Tea came to Japan from China as part of a cultural package that included kanji and Buddhism, but the beverage did not become popular until the medieval period. Buddhist monks drank tea for its medicinal and stimulatory properties, a practice that gradually spread to warrior society and then to commoners. By the 16th century, elite urban commoners such as the merchant and tea master Sen no Rikyû (1522–91) had elevated the preparation, serving and consumption of powdered green tea *(matcha)* to an elaborate performance art. In the 17th century, tea masters established their own schools of tea, and these institutions codified, spread and protected the practice over subsequent centuries.

Although *chanoyu* (literally, 'hot water for tea') is often referred to in English as the 'tea ceremony', the practice has always been more focused on collaboration, pleasure and artistic appreciation than on dutiful ritual. Tea gatherings can be short and spontaneous or long and extremely formal. They might be held to mark an anniversary, the changing of the seasons, or just as an opportunity to see old friends. Typically, a group of guests arrives at the location of the gathering, perhaps a home or a temple with its own tea house, and waits in the outer garden, a peaceful and meditative space. After entering the tea house, the guests observe while the host arranges the charcoal and serves a special meal known as *kaiseki* cuisine. After the meal, they eat some simple sweets, take a brief intermission and then return for a serving of viscous 'thick tea' *(koicha)* followed, in many cases, by a round of 'thin tea' *(usucha)*. The movements of the host and guests are carefully choreographed and rehearsed, making the sharing of the beverage a satisfying mutual performance. At certain moments during the gathering, the guests have the chance to admire the hanging scroll, the flower arrangement and the host's careful selection of tea utensils *(chadôgu)*.

Tea culture has stimulated and supported the arts and crafts in Japan for centuries, and utensils – including tea bowls, tea caddies, tea scoops and tea whisks – can be purchased in tea shops, galleries or directly from artists. Urban department stores, such as Takashimaya, Daimaru, Seibu and Mitsukoshi, among many others, frequently have whole floors devoted to ceramics, lacquerware and other crafts. There are also galleries in which the finest artists hold solo exhibitions and sales. A trip to a town famous for its crafts, such as Bizen (p446), Hagi (p478) or Karatsu (p676), gives travellers further opportunities to buy tea utensils.

Some tea schools, such as Urasenke, Omotesenke, Mushanokojisenke and Dai Nippon Chado Gakkai, hold tea gatherings that are open to the public, particularly in large cities. Speciality cafés, such as the confectionary Toraya, also offer a serving of sweets and tea. Museums that specialise in art associated with tea, such as Kyoto's Nomura Art Museum (p339), Raku Museum, the Kitamura Museum and Tokyo's Gotoh Museum, display historical tea utensils and on occasion serve tea as well.

Morgan Pitelka is the author of Handmade Culture: Raku Potters, Patrons, and Tea Practitioners in Japan.

The third of February sees beans employed not as a meal ingredient, but as weapons in the fight against evil, at the Setsubun Matsuri. At shrines throughout the country, worshippers and tourists gleefully pepper costumed demons with hard soy beans, to the cry of '*oni wa soto, fuku wa uchi*' (out with the demons, in with good luck).

Common at many celebrations, but especially at the Hina Matsuri (Girls' Day celebration; 3 March) is *seki-han*, red rice, made from glutinous and nonglutinous rice mixed with either *azuki* or black-eyed peas, which give it its sweetness and characteristic pink colour.

Late March or early April sees the much-anticipated coming of the cherry blossoms. The Japanese gather for *hanami* or flower-viewing parties, which during the brief, glorious reign of the pink blossoms transform every inch of open space into a riot of alcohol-drenched, raucous contemplation of the evanescence of life and beauty. As if the cherry blossoms overhead weren't enough, the Japanese eat a variety of pink and white *mochi* on sticks during these parties, which is supposed to resemble the branches from a cherry tree.

The Japanese summer is long, hot and very humid. Its star festival is Kyoto's July Gion Matsuri, nicknamed Hamo Matsuri, the Pike-conger Festival, for the large quantities of the beast consumed during that time. Pike-conger and eel are famed for their invigorating qualities and their ability to restore flagging appetites.

New Year is one of the most food-centred festivals in Japan, the time when distant family members gather for a three-day bout of feasting and drinking, punctuated with the sacred first visit to the local shrine. Inevitably, it's a freezing midwinter night, and the warm *ama-zake* (sweet sake served at winter festivals) served at the shrine helps keep out the winter chill. The first dish of the year will be *toshi-koshi soba,* long buckwheat noodles symbolising long life and wealth, as *soba* dough was once used by gold traders to collect gold dust. To cries of '*yoi o-toshi o'* (Have a Happy New Year) and, postmidnight, '*akemashite omedetō gozaimasu'* (Happy New Year), the cycle of eating and celebration continues anew…

VEGETARIANS & VEGANS

Travellers who eat fish should have almost no trouble dining in Japan: almost all *shokudō, izakaya* and other common restaurants offer a set meal with fish as the main dish. Vegans and vegetarians who don't eat fish will have to get their protein from tofu and other bean products. Note that most *miso-shiru* is made with *dashi* that contains fish, so if you want to avoid fish, you'll also have to avoid *miso-shiru.*

Most big cities in Japan have vegetarian and/or organic restaurants that naturally will serve a variety of choices that appeal to vegetarians and vegans. (See the Eating sections of the destination chapters for specific recommendations.) In the countryside, you'll simply have to do your best to find suitable items on the menu, or try to convey your dietary preferences to the restaurant staff. Note that many temples in Japan serve *shōjin ryōri,* Buddhist vegetarian cuisine, which is made without meat, fish or dairy products. A good place to try this is Kōya-san in Kansai (p429).

For some ways to express your dietary preferences to restaurant staff, see Useful Words & Phrases (p102).

EATING WITH KIDS

Travelling with children in Japan is easy, as long as you come with the right attitudes, equipment and the usual parental patience. There's such a variety of food on offer that even the most particular eaters can find something to their liking, and if noodles and rice begins to pale there are always Japanese fast-food chains in almost every city. At most budget restaurants during the day, you can find '*okosama-ranchi'* (children's special), which is often Western style and actually rather good, though its mini-hamburgers and wiener sausages won't appeal to nonmeat eaters.

The Useful Words & Phrases section (p102) contains a few phrases that will come in handy when dining out with children in tow.

HABITS & CUSTOMS

Japanese people generally eat breakfast at home, where a few slices of bread and a cup of coffee are quickly taking over from the traditional Japanese breakfast of rice, fish and miso soup as the breakfast of choice. If they don't eat at home, a *mōningu setto* (morning set) of toast and coffee at a coffee shop is the norm.

Lunch is often eaten at a *shokudō* or a noodle restaurant, usually in the company of coworkers, but alone if a partner can't be found.

The Tsukiji Fish Market in Tokyo is the world's largest. It handles 2246 tonnes of marine products a day (more than 450 kinds of fish!)

Evening meals are a mixed bag. Many people, of course, eat at home, but the stereotype of the salaryman heading out for drinks and dinner every evening after work with his workmates has some basis in fact.

Weekends are when almost everyone, if they can afford it, heads out for dinner with friends, and at this time, many eateries are packed with groups of people eating, drinking, conversing and generally having a ball.

Mealtimes are pretty much the same as in many parts of the West: breakfast is eaten between 6am and 8am, lunch is eaten between noon and 2pm, and dinner is eaten between 7pm and 9pm.

COOKING COURSES

If you enjoy the food in Japan, why not deepen your appreciation of Japanese cuisine by taking a cooking class? There are good cooking courses available in both Tokyo and Kyoto, and these companies can also arrange market tours:

A Taste of Culture (☎ 03-5716-5751; www.tasteofculture.com; courses from ¥5500) Offers cooking courses, and can create custom courses. For more, see p143.

WAK Japan (☎ 075-212-9993; www.wakjapan.com; 412-506 Iseya-chō, Kamigyō-ku) Offers cooking courses, and can create courses to suit special interests. For more, see p351.

USEFUL WORDS & PHRASES
Eating Out

Table for (one/two/three/...), please.

(hitori/futari/san-nin/...-nin) onegai shimas[u]

(一人/二人/三人/...人),お願いします。

I'd like to reserve a table for eight o'clock (tonight/tomorrow night).

(konban/ashita no ban) hachi-ji ni yoyaku shitai no des[u] ga

(今晩/明日の晩)八時に予約したいのですが。

We have a reservation.

yoyaku shimash[i]ta

予約しました。

We don't have a reservation.

yoyaku sh[i]teimasen

予約していません。

What's that?

are wa nan des[u] ka?

あれは何ですか?

What's the speciality here?

koko no tokubetsu ryōri wa nan des[u] ka?

ここの特別料理は何ですか?

What do you recommend?

o-susume wa nan des[u] ka?

おすすめは何ですか?

Do you have...?

... ga arimas[u] ka?

...がありますか?

Can I see the menu, please?

menyū o misete kudasai!

メニューを見せてください?

Do you have a menu in English?

eigo no menyū wa arimas[u] ka?

英語のメニューはありますか?

I'd like...	... o kudasai	...をください。
Please bring me...	... o onegai shimas[u]	...をお願いします。
some/more bread	pan	パン
some pepper	koshō	コショウ
a plate	sara	皿
some salt	shio	塩
soy sauce	shōyu	醤油
a spoon	supūn	スプーン
a beer	beeru	ビール
some water	mizu	水
some wine	wain	ワイン

Harumi's Japanese Cooking (Kurihara Harumi) is a well-illustrated cookbook and a good introduction to Japanese cuisine. If you want to try making some of the dishes you enjoyed while in Japan, this is an excellent choice.

| **The bill/check, please.** | *(o-kanjō/o-aiso)* | (お勘定/おあいそ) |
| | *o onegai shimas[u]* | をお願いします。 |

You May Hear

May I help you?
irasshaimase   いらっしゃいませ?

Welcome!
irasshai!   いらっしゃい！

By yourself?
o-hitori-sama des[u] ka?   お一人さまですか?

(Two/Three/Four) persons?
(ni/san/yon) -mei-sama des[u] ka?   (二名/三名/四名) さまですか?

This way, please.
kochira e dōzo   こちらへどうぞ。

May I take your order?
(go-chūmon wa) o-kimari des[u] ka?   (ご注文は)お決まりですか?

Vegetarian & Special Needs

I'm a vegetarian.
watashi wa bejitarian des[u]   私はベジタリアンです。

I'm a vegan, I don't eat meat or dairy products.
watashi wa saishoku-shugisha des[u] kara,   私は菜食主義者ですから、
niku ya nyūseihin wa tabemasen   肉や乳製品は食べません。

Do you have any vegetarian dishes?
bejitarian-ryōri ga arimas[u] ka?   ベジタリアン料理がありますか?

Is it cooked with pork lard or chicken stock?
kore wa rādo ka tori no dashi   これはラードか鶏の
o tsukatte imas[u] ka?   だしを使っていますか?

I'm allergic to (peanuts).
watashi wa (pīnattsu) arerugii des[u]   私は(ピーナッツ)アレルギーです。

I don't eat...	*... wa tabemasen*	...は食べません
meat	*niku*	肉
pork	*buta-niku*	豚肉
seafood	*shiifūdo*	シーフード/海産物

Children

Are children allowed?
kodomo-zure demo ii des[u] ka?   子供連れでもいいですか?

Is there a children's menu?
kodomo-yō no menyū wa arimas[u] ka?   子供用のメニューはありますか?

Do you have a highchair for the baby?
bebii-yō no isu wa arimas[u] ka?   ベビー用の椅子はありますか?

Tokyo 東京

You may know Tokyo as glamorous film star, cauldron of technological innovations, self-made capital, funky fashionista, metropolis that runs like clockwork, producer of unique pop culture and city that breeds toddlers on the fast track and salarymen driven to subway suicide. Up close, it's still fascinating, but take a deep breath and step out of Shinjuku station knowing that at street level, all you need to do is tap one shoulder from the swiftly power-walking stream of pedestrians to receive a curious smile and gracious assistance if you need it. For even in this modern megalopolis, there remains a distinct, tangible sense of things inherently Japanese.

Finding a superficial resemblance to old Japan in Tokyo requires scrutiny. If you take an oblique view, you'll find that much of the city's contemporary culture descends from old traditions. The manga that's captivating today's youth in Madrid can trace its origins to Edo-era *ukiyo-e* (wood-block prints of the 'floating world') that inspired the *Japonisme* work of van Gogh in the 1880s. In a city so efficient that you could set your watch by the subway schedules displayed on LED screens, its nameless streets and alleys make the address system medieval by comparison.

And therein lies the contradictory nature of this city that's constantly pushing and pulling on itself towards reinvention. Its massive scale means a stunning abundance of experiences, but the most memorable undoubtedly lie in the meticulous, tiny details that whisper of tradition.

HIGHLIGHTS

- Dodge flying fish on the floor of **Tsukiji Fish Market** (p132) and feast on early-morning sushi

- Attend the seasonal spectacle of *sumō* at **Ryōgoku Kokugikan Sumō Stadium** (p178) for salt-slinging, belly-slapping and solemn ritual

- Stroll around the grounds of **Meiji-jingū** (p137), Tokyo's most impressive Shintō shrine

- Snap shots of goth Lolitas at **Jingū-bashi** (p138), who will pose and preen for your photographic pleasure

- See how the Edo-half lived at the wonderful **Edo-Tokyo Museum** (p142)

- Get down with your funky self, or simply observe the wildlife, in the nocturnal environs of **Roppōngi** (p173)

- Stop at the Hachikō statue, shop pop culture and end your sojourn with a drink in **Shibuya** (p138)

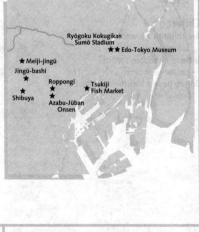

Ryōgoku Kokugikan Sumō Stadium
★★ Edo-Tokyo Museum
★ Meiji-jingū
Jingū-bashi
★
Roppongi
★ Tsukiji
Fish Market
★
Shibuya
Azabu-Jūban
Onsen

TELEPHONE CODE: 03

POPULATION: 12.56 MILLION

HISTORY

Tokyo is something of a miracle, a city that rose from the ashes of WWII to become one of the world's leading economic centres.

Tokyo was formerly known as Edo (literally 'Gate of the River'), so named for its location at the mouth of Sumida-gawa. The city first became significant in 1603, when Tokugawa Ieyasu established his *shōgunate* (military government) there. Edo grew into a city from which the Tokugawa clan governed the whole of Japan. By the late 18th century it had become the most populous city in the world. When the authority of the emperor was restored in 1868, the capital moved from Kyoto to Edo, which was renamed Tokyo (Eastern Capital).

After 250 years of isolation, Tokyo began transforming itself into a modern metropolis. Remarkably, it has succeeded in achieving this despite two major disasters that each practically levelled the city – the Kantō Earthquake and ensuing fires of 1923, and the US air raids of 1944 and 1945.

After the giddy heights of Japan's Bubble Economy of the 80s burst in the 90s, Tokyo has spent much of the interim recovering from resulting recession. But these days, the economy is holding steady. Apart from economics, Tokyo's cultural exports continue to influence the global scene, with its fashion, musical genres, illustration and *anime*, quirky technologies, and uniquely Japanese game shows thriving at home and abroad.

ORIENTATION

Tokyo is a vast conurbation spreading out across the Kantō Plain from Tokyo Bay (Tokyo-wan). The central metropolitan area is made up of 23 *ku* (wards), while outlying areas are divided into 27 separate *shi* (cities), a *gun* (county) and four island-districts. Nearly everything of interest to visitors lies on or near the JR Yamanote line, the rail loop that circles central Tokyo. Areas not on the Yamanote line – like Roppongi, Tsukiji and Asakusa – are nonetheless within easy reach, as the central city is crisscrossed by Tokyo's excellent subway system.

In Edo times, Yamanote referred to 'Uptown': the estates and residences of feudal barons, military aristocracy and other Edo elite, in the hilly regions of the city. Shitamachi or 'Downtown' was home to the working classes, merchants and artisans. Even today the distinction persists. The areas west of the Imperial Palace (Kōkyo) are more modernised, housing the commercial and business centres of modern Tokyo; the areas east of the palace, like Asakusa and Ueno, retain more of the character of old Edo.

A trip around the JR Yamanote line makes a good introduction to the city. You might start at Tokyo station, the first point of arrival for many travellers. Near to the station are the Marunouchi and Ōtemachi office districts and the high-class shopping district of Ginza. Continuing north from Tokyo station brings you to Akihabara, the discount electronics centre of Tokyo. Further along is Ueno, home to many of the city's museums. After rounding the top of the loop you descend into Ikebukuro, a shopping and entertainment district. A few stops further on is Shinjuku, a massive shopping, entertainment and business district considered by many the heart of modern Tokyo. From there, trains continue through to the youth-oriented, fashionable shopping areas of Harajuku, Shibuya and Ebisu. A swing through Shinagawa at the bottom of the loop then brings you back to Tokyo station.

The information in this chapter is presented in an anticlockwise direction around the Yamanote line.

Maps

We strongly recommend you pick up a free copy of the excellent *Tourist Map of Tokyo* from one of the Tourist Information Centres (TICs – see p109). Along with detailed insets of Tokyo's major neighbourhoods, it also includes subway and rail maps. For more in-depth exploration of the city, pick up a copy of *Tokyo City Atlas: A Bilingual Atlas* (Kodansha), which includes *banchi* (street address) numbers essential for finding addresses.

Tokyo's train and subway lines are much easier to navigate with the free, colour-coded *Tokyo Metro Guide* map. It's available at subway stations and TICs around town, and we've included it in the colour section of this guide.

INFORMATION
Bookshops

Tokyo's traditional bookshop area is Jimbōchō. Mostly catering to Japanese readers, it is still a fascinating place to browse for Edo-period gardening manuals or used

TOKYO

TOKYO IN...

One Day

Show up at dawn to **Tsukiji Fish Market** (p132) for a look at the day's catch – the brave can then breakfast on the same. Follow this with coffee and a stroll up Chūō-dōri in **Ginza** (p132), browsing techie toys at the **Sony Building** (p132) or **Leica gallery** (p132). Stop for a weekday lunch in the **Tokyo International Forum plaza** (p111), wander through **Imperial Palace East Garden** (p110) to **Kitanomaru-kōen** (p111) and possibly to **Yasukuni-jinja** (p111). In the evening, head south for a night in **Roppongi** (p174).

One Week

Immerse yourself in crowd culture with a walking tour of **East Shinjuku** (p143). Do the one-day itinerary of Ginza and Central Tokyo, above. Save Saturday night for wild Roppongi, perhaps pulling an all-nighter. Spend a sleepy Sunday afternoon meeting Harajuku's famous **cosplay-zoku** (see the boxed text, p138), visiting **Meiji-jingū** (p137) and a walk in the park at **Yoyogi-kōen** (p138). Shop for records and trinkets in **Shibuya** (p180). Consider taking a classic tour of **Asakusa** (p134) via *jinriksha* (people-powered rickshaw), followed by a soak at a *sentō* (public bath). Devote one afternoon to the **Edo-Tokyo Museum** (p142), **Ghibli Museum** (p142) or five museums in one day in **Ueno-kōen** (p133).

manga. The annual Kanda Furuhon Matsuri (Kanda Secondhand Book Festival) is a bibliophile's paradise, occupying the whole district at the end of October. For places to find manga and *anime*, see p180.

Aoyama Book Center Roppongi-dōri (Map p119; ☎ 3479-0479; 6-1-20 Roppongi, Minato-ku; ☑ 10am-5am Mon-Sat, to 10pm Sun, closed 2nd & 3rd Tue each month; ◉ Hibiya, Toei Ōedo lines to Roppongi, exit 3); Roppongi Hills (Map p119; ☎ 5775-2151; 4th fl, West Walk, Roppongi Hills, 6-10-1 Roppongi, Minato-ku; ☑ 11am-9pm; ◉ Hibiya line to Roppongi, exit C1) The newly remodelled Roppongi-dōri branch is a prime spot for night owls, with a great international selection of reads.

Blue Parrot (Map p114; ☎ 3202-3671; www.blueparrottokyo.com; 3rd fl, Obayashi Bldg, 2-14-10 Takdanobaba, Shinjuku-ku; ☑ 11am-9.30pm; ◉ JR Yamanote line to Takadanobaba, Waseda-dōri exit) One of the best selections of used English-language books in Tokyo.

Good Day Books (Map p121; ☎ 5421-0957; 3rd fl, Asahi Bldg, 1-11-2 Ebisu, Shibuya-ku; ☑ 11am-8pm Mon-Sat, to 6pm Sun; ◉ JR Yamanote line to Ebisu, east exit) Another place to find an excellent selection of used English-language books.

Hacknet (Map p121; ☎ 5728-6611; www.hacknet.tv in Japanese; 1-30-10 Ebisu, Shibuya-ku; ☑ 11am-8pm; ◉ JR Yamanote line to Ebisu, west exit) Carrying a candystore array of art and design books in Ebisu's Q-Flagship Building.

Kinokuniya Shinjuku-dōri (Map p116; ☎ 3354-0131; 3-17-7 Shinjuku, Shinjuku-ku; ☑ 10am-9pm; ◉ JR Yamanote line to Shinjuku, east exit); Takashimaya (Map p116; ☎ 5361-3301; 5-24-2 Sendagaya, Shibuya-ku;

☑ 10am-8pm Sun-Fri, to 8.30pm Sat; ◉ JR Yamanote line to Shinjuku, new south exit) Kinokuniya's newer branch, in the Takashimaya Times Sq annexe, has one of Tokyo's largest selections of English-language books on the 6th floor.

Maruzen (Map pp126-7; ☎ 5288-8881; 1st-4th fl, Oazo Bldg, 1-6-4 Marunouchi, Chiyoda-ku; ☑ 9am-9pm; ◉ JR Yamanote line to Tokyo, Marunouchi north exit) Located across from Tokyo station in central Tokyo, Maruzen houses an impressive selection of books and magazines comparable to Kinokuniya's. The 4th floor houses foreign-language books, a stationery shop and a café. The revamped original branch, near exit B1 of Nihombashi station, was due to reopen by this book's publication.

Tower Books (Map p117; ☎ 3496-3661; 7th fl, Tower Records Bldg, 1-22-14 Jinnan, Shibuya-ku; ☑ 10am-10pm; ◉ JR Yamanote line to Shibuya, Hachikō exit) Tower carries English-language books and a fabulous array of international magazines and newspapers; prices tend to be considerably cheaper than elsewhere around town. It's directly on Jingū-dōri.

Cultural Centres

Cultural centres in Tokyo generally act as focal points of the national groups they represent, and usually have good bulletin boards, events, small libraries and language classes.

British Council (Map pp126-7; ☎ 3235-8031; www.britishcouncil.org/japan.htm; 1-2 Kagurazaka, Shinjuku-ku; ☑ 10am-8.30pm Mon-Fri, 9.30am-5.30pm Sat; ◉ JR Chūō, Sōbu lines to Iidabashi, west exit or Namboku, Tōzai, Yūrakuchō, Toei Ōedo lines to Iidabashi, exit B3) Find it several blocks south along the canal on Sotobori-dōri.

BOOKS ON TOKYO

Several publications might supplement the one you have in your hands, particularly if you're planning to become a resident of Tokyo. For a comprehensive guide to the city, pick up Lonely Planet's *Tokyo*.

Tokyo for Free by Susan Pompian (Kodansha, 1998) lists more than 400 things that you can do for free in this expensive city, while *The Best of Tokyo* by Don Morton and Tsunoi Naoko (Tuttle, 1993) takes a light-hearted look at the city, with recommendations ranging from 'best traditional Japanese dolls' to 'best toilet'.

Tokyo: Exploring the City of the Shogun by Enbutsu Sumiko (Kodansha, 2007) details walking tours of traditional Tokyo with fascinating historical and cultural detail. Rick Kennedy's *Little Adventures in Tokyo* (Kodansha, 1998) introduces some of his secret finds in and around Tokyo.

Tokyo: A Guide to Recent Architecture by Tajima Noriyuki (Elipsis Könemann, 1998) is a great guide to Tokyo's architectural masterpieces and oddities.

Goethe-Institut Tokyo (Map p119; ☎ 3584-3201; www.goethe.de/ins/jp/tok/deindex.htm in Japanese & German; 7-5-56 Akasaka, Minato-ku; ☼ 10am-1pm & 2-5pm Mon-Thu, 10am-1pm & 2-3.30pm Fri; ⊕ Ginza, Hanzōmon, Toei Ōedo lines to Aoyama-itchōme, exit A4) Walk eastward on Aoyama-dōri; turn right at Sōgetsu Kaikan and walk one more block to Goethe Institut.

L'Institut Franco-Japonais de Tokyo (Map pp126-7; ☎ 5206-2500; www.ifjtokyo.or.jp in Japanese & French; 15 Ichigaya Funagawarachō, Shinjuku-ku; ☼ noon-8pm Mon, 9.30am-8pm Tue-Fri, to 7pm Sat, 10am-6pm Sun; ⊕ JR Chūō, Sōbu lines to Iidabashi, west exit or Namboku, Tōzai, Yūrakuchō, Toei Ōedo lines to Iidabashi, exit B3) Head south along Sotobori-dōri and then hang a right at the stoplight before continuing for about 50m uphill.

Emergency

You should be able to get your point across in simple English. See p108 for more information about dealing with a medical emergency.

Emergency numbers:

Fire & ambulance (☎ 119)

Japan Helpline (☎ 0120-461-997; ☼ 24hr) If you have problems communicating, ring this emergency number.

Police (☎ 110)

Immigration Offices

See p793 for information on foreign embassies and consulates in Tokyo.

Tokyo Regional Immigration Bureau (Map pp112-13; ☎ 5796-7112; www.moj.go.jp/ENGLISH/information/iic-01.html; 5-5-30 Kōnan, Minato-ku; ☼ 9am-noon & 1-4pm Mon-Fri; ⊕ Tokyo Monorail to Tennōzu-Isle) A 15-minute walk from Tennōzu-Isle station; board the Tokyo Monorail from Hamamatsuchō JR station. Print a map from the web page for a clear route from Tennōzu-Isle station.

Internet Access

In some neighbourhoods it can be challenging to access the internet. The best bet is finding the local *manga kissa*, 24-hour manga-reading, DVD-viewing internet cafés dotted around the major transport hubs. Though often crowded and smoky, they offer inexpensive internet access, cheap eats and a thousand ways to kill time (see the boxed text, p146).

Café J Net New New (Map p117; ☎ 5458-5935; 7th fl, Saitō Bldg, 34-5 Udagawachō, Shibuya-ku; per hr ¥320; ☼ 24hr; ⊕ JR Yamanote line to Shibuya, Hachikō exit) This *manga kissa* is conveniently located off Bunkamura-dōri in Shibuya.

Marunouchi Café (Map pp124-5; ☎ 3212-5025; 1st fl, Shin-Tokyo Bldg, 3-3-1 Marunouchi, Chiyoda-ku; ☼ 8am-9pm Mon-Fri, 11am-9pm Sat & Sun; ⊕ Marunouchi line to Tokyo, exit 6) Free internet access in aesthetically pleasing surroundings.

TnT Internet Café (Map p114; ☎ 5950-9983; 1st fl, Liberty Ikebukuro Bldg, 2-18-1 Ikebukuro, Toshima-ku; per hr ¥1000; ☼ noon-7pm, closed Sun & some Wed; ⊕ JR Yamanote line to Ikebukuro, west exit) This spot has internet access but no café.

Internet Resources

There are thousands of websites about Tokyo. Here are four of the most useful:

WI-FI

The easiest way to access the internet is at your local *manga kissa* (see the boxed text, p146), but if you're dragging your own laptop around, free wi-fi is easy to find. **Freespot** (www.freespot.com/users/map_e.html) lists a bunch of free hotspots, many in cafés.

TOKYO

Metropolis (www.metropolis.co.jp) The best all-round site for Tokyo. Lots of events, places of interest and hip feature articles.

Tokyo Journal (www.tokyo.to) Has monthly events listings, also interesting articles and interviews from time to time.

Tokyo Food Page (www.bento.com/tf-rest.html) The authority on Tokyo's dining scene, but be aware that a fair number of listings are outdated.

Tokyo Q (www.tokyoq.com) Another great all-round Tokyo site for finding places to shop, drink and explore.

Laundry

Most hotels, midrange and up, have laundry services. If you are in a budget ryokan (traditional Japanese inn), ask the staff for the nearest *koin randorii* (laundrette). Costs start from ¥150 for a load of washing, and drying usually costs ¥100 for 10 minutes.

Kuriningu-yasan (dry-cleaners) are in almost every neighbourhood. The standards are high and some offer rush service. It's about ¥200 for your basic business shirt.

Left Luggage

Travellers wary of hauling unwieldy luggage through Tokyo subways and stations should take advantage of the baggage courier services operating from Narita airport. For about ¥2000 per large bag, a courier will deliver the goods to your hotel the next day (or pick it up the day before your flight out). At Narita, find the courier counters in each terminal hall; signs in English point the way.
ABC (☎ 0120-919-120)
NPS Skyporter (☎ 0120-007-952)

There are coin lockers in all train and bus stations in Tokyo. Smaller lockers start at ¥300 (you can leave luggage for up to three days). Otherwise, the Akaboshi (Red Cap) luggage service on the Yaesu side of Tokyo station will store small/large bags during the day for ¥300/400 (you must pick up your luggage by the end of the day you leave it). For longer periods, there is an overnight luggage-storage service in Tokyo station that will hold luggage for up to two weeks, with rates starting at ¥500 per bag per day. Ask at the main information counter on the Yaesu side for a map to both of these services.

Libraries

Bibliothèque de la Maison franco-japonaise (Map p121; ☎ 5421-7643; biblio@mfj.gr.jp; 3-9-25 Ebisu,

Shibuya-ku; 🕙 10.30am-6pm Mon-Sat; 🚇 JR Yamanote line to Ebisu) From Ebisu station, take the Skywalk to the terminus, turn left at the exit and walk two blocks before turning left at the primary school. The public library, with its formidable collection of French volumes, will be on your right.

British Council (see p106) Comprehensive selection of books and magazines.

Goethe Institut Tokyo Bibliotek (see p107; 🕙 noon-6pm Mon-Thu, to 8pm Fri) With 15,000 volumes.

Japan Foundation Library (Map pp124-5; ☎ 5562-3527; www.jpf.go.jp/e/jfic/lib/index.html; 20th fl, ARK Mori Bldg, 1-12-32 Akasaka, Minato-ku; 🕙 10am-7pm Mon-Fri, to 5pm 3rd Sat each month, closed last Mon each month; 🚇 Namboku line to Roppongi itchôme, exit 3) Has some 30,000 English-language publications and is open only to foreigners.

National Diet Library (Map pp124-5; ☎ 3581-2331; www.ndl.go.jp/en/; 1-10-1 Nagatachô, Chiyoda-ku; 🕙 9.30am-5pm Mon-Sat; 🚇 Hanzômon, Yūrakuchô lines to Nagatachô, exit 2) This small treasure has 1.3 million books in Western languages.

US Embassy Reference Service (Map pp124-5; ☎ 3224-5292; 1-10-5 Akasaka, Minato-ku; 🕙 10am-noon & 1-5pm Mon-Fri; 🚇 Ginza, Namboku lines to Tameike-sannô, exit 13) The US embassy has a reference library relating to US culture, economics and policy; call a day ahead for an appointment.

Media

There's plenty of English-language information on Tokyo, starting with the three English-language newspapers *(Japan Times, Daily Yomiuri, Asahi Shimbun)*. The best listings of Tokyo events can be found in Saturday's *Japan Times*.

The *Tokyo Journal*'s Cityscope listings section makes it worth the purchase price, but the free weekly *Metropolis* is the magazine of choice for most Tokyo residents.

Medical Services

All hospitals listed have English-speaking staff and 24-hour emergency departments. Travel insurance is advisable to cover any medical treatment you may need while in Tokyo. Medical treatment is among the best in the world, but also the most expensive.

Japanese Red Cross Medical Center (Map pp112–13; Nihon Sekijūjisha Iryō Sentā; ☎ 3400-1311; www.med .jrc.or.jp in Japanese; 4-1-22 Hiro-o, Shibuya-ku; 🚇 Hibiya line to Hiro-o, exit 3)

St Luke's International Hospital (Map pp124–5; Seiroka Byōin; ☎ 3541-5151; www.luke.or.jp/eng/index.html; 9-1 Akashichō, Chūō-ku; 🚇 Hibiya line to Tsukiji, exit 3)

Tokyo Medical & Surgical Clinic (Map pp124–5; ☎ 3436-3028; www.tmsc.jp; 2nd fl, 32 Shiba-Kōen Bldg, 3-4-30 Shiba-kōen, Minato-ku; ☺ Toei Mita line to Onarimon, exit A1)

Money

Banks are open from 9am to 3pm Monday to Friday. Look out for the 'Foreign Exchange' sign outside. Some post offices also offer foreign-exchange services, and most have English-language ATMs.

Tokyo has a reasonable number of ATMs that accept foreign-issued cards. The best bet for foreign travellers is Citibank, which has English-language ATMs, open 24 hours a day.

For lost or stolen credit cards, call the following 24-hour, toll-free numbers within Japan.

American Express (☎ 0120-020-120)
MasterCard (☎ 00531-113-886)
Visa (☎ 0120-133-173)

Post

The Tokyo central post office is outside Tokyo station (Map pp126–7; take the Marunouchi exit and then cross the street to the south). Call ☎ 5472-5851 for postal information in English. Poste restante mail will be held at the central post office for 30 days.

Telephone & Fax

Almost all public phones in Tokyo take prepaid phone cards. For domestic directory assistance, call ☎ 104 and ask to be transferred to an English speaker. For details on making international calls from a public phone, see p802.

You can send faxes from the front desk of many hotels (some allow nonguests to use their services for a fee), some convenience stores and from Kinko's copy shops.

Tourist Information

The Japan National Tourist Organization (JNTO) runs two **tourist information centres** (☎ 0476-303-383, 0476-345-877; ☺ 8am-8pm) on the arrival floors of both terminals at Narita airport. Staffed by knowledgeable folks who speak English, this centre is a good place to get oriented or to make a hotel booking if you haven't yet figured out where to stay.

TIC offices will make accommodation reservations, but only for hotels and ryokan that are members of the **Welcome Inn group** (www

.itcj.jp). It can also arrange for tours of the city with volunteer guides. The Metropolitan Government also offers **Teletourist** (☎ 3201-2911), a round-the-clock taped information service on current events in town.

Asakusa Tourist Information Center (Map pp130-1; ☎ 5246-1151; 4-5-6 Higashi-Ueno, Taitō-ku; ☺ 10am-5pm; ☺ Ginza line to Asakusa, exit 2) In Asakusa, stop by the friendly centre where you can arrange free guided tours of the area.

TIC (Map pp124-5; ☎ 3216-1901; www.jnto.go.jp; 10th fl, Kōtsu Kaikan Bldg, 2-10-1 Yūrakuchō, Chiyoda-ku; ☺ 9am-5pm Mon-Fri, to noon Sat; ☺ JR Yamanote line to Yūrakuchō), just outside Yūrakuchō station) Another JNTO-operated TIC. It has by far the most comprehensive information on travel in Tokyo and Japan, and is an essential port of call. The Kōtsu Kaikan Building is just opposite the station as you exit to the right.

Tokyo Tourist Information Center (Map p116; ☎ 5321-3077; 1st fl, Tokyo Metropolitan Government Bldg No 1, 2-8-1 Nishi-Shinjuku, Shinjuku-ku; ☺ 9.30am-6.30pm; ☺ Toei Ōedo line to Tochōmae, exit A4) A good place to pick up a Grutt Pass (¥2000). The pass is a book of tickets entitling the bearer to free or discounted entrance at almost 50 Tokyo museums and zoos. It's valid for two months after the first visit, a terrific deal for multiple museum goers. The pass is also available at participating museums.

Travel Agencies

In Tokyo there are a number of travel agencies where English is spoken and where discounting on flights and domestic travel is the norm. For an idea of current prices check the *Japan Times* or *Metropolis*.

Three well-established agencies where English is spoken:

A'cross Travellers Bureau Ikebukuro (Map p114; ☎ 5391-3227; www.across-travel.com; 3rd fl, Nippon Life Higashi-Ikebukuro Bldg, 1-11-1 Higashi-Ikebukuro, Toshima-ku; ☺ 11am-8pm Mon-Sat; ☺ JR Yamanote line to Ikebukuro, east exit); Shibuya (Map p117; ☎ 5467-0077; 3rd fl, TK Shibuya East Bldg, 1-14-14 Shibuya, Shibuya-ku; ☺ 11am-8pm Mon-Fri, to 7pm Sat; ☺ JR Yamanote line to Shibuya, Hachikō exit); Shinjuku (Map p116; ☎ 3340-6745; 2nd fl, Yamate Shinjuku Bldg, 1-19-6 Nishi-Shinjuku, Shinjuku-ku; ☺ 10am-7pm Mon-Sat; ☺ JR Yamanote line to Shinjuku, west exit)

No 1 Travel Ikebukuro (Map p114; ☎ 3986-4690; www.no1-travel.com; 4th fl, Daini Mikasa Bldg, 1-16-10 Nishi-Ikebukuro, Toshima-ku; ☺ 10am-6.30pm Mon-Fri, 11am-4.30pm Sat; ☺ JR Yamanote line to Ikebukuro, west exit) Just across from the west exit of Ikebukuro JR station, along Azalea-dōri; Shibuya (Map p117; ☎ 3770-1381; 7th fl, Shibuya Ichino Bldg, 1-11-1 Jinnan, Shibuya-ku; ☺ 10am-6.30pm Mon-Fri, 11am-4.30pm Sat; ☺ JR

Yamanote line to Shibuya, Hachikō exit) Walk north up Jingū-dōri and turn right after Tower Records; Shinjuku (Map p116; ☎ 3205-6073; 7th fl, Don Quixote Bldg, 1-16-5 Kabukichō, Shinjuku-ku; ꗳ 10am-6.30pm Mon-Fri, 11am-4.30pm Sat; ◉ JR Yamanote line to Shinjuku, east exit)

STA Travel (Map p114; ☎ 5391-2922; www.statravel .co.jp; 7th fl, Nukariya Bldg, 1-16-20 Minami-Ikebukuro, Toshima-ku; ꗳ 9.30am-5.30pm Mon-Fri, to 12.30pm Sat; ◉ JR Yamanote line to Ikebukuro, south exit)

Useful Organisations & Services

There are innumerable associations for foreign residents and travellers. For the one most suited to your needs and interests, we recommend checking the listings sections of *Metropolis* and *Tokyo Journal*.

Several useful telephone services offer information and support for foreigners in Tokyo.

Foreign Residents' Advisory Center (☎ 5320-7744; ꗳ 9.30am-noon & 1-5pm Mon-Fri) For general information.

JR English Information (☎ 050-2016-1603; ꗳ 10am-6pm) Offers information on train schedules and fares.

Tokyo English Lifeline (TELL; ☎ 5774-0992; www .telljp.com; ꗳ 9am-4pm & 7-11pm) Can help with information and counselling.

DANGERS & ANNOYANCES

Tokyo can be annoying at times but it is rarely dangerous. If possible, avoid the rail network during peak hours – around 8am to 9.30am and 5pm to 7pm – when the surging crowds would try anyone's patience. *Chikan* (gropers) can be a problem, but before you cry *chikan*, be sure it's not just a crowded car.

Some travellers may also be disturbed by the overtly sexual nature of some of the signs and sights in Tokyo's red-light districts, like Shinjuku's Kabukichō and parts of Ikebukuro. Those venturing into hostess clubs should be prepared to spend liberally and to watch their drinks carefully, as both drinks and credit cards of the unwary may be corrupted.

Earthquakes

Check the locations of emergency exits in your hotel and be aware of earthquake safety procedures (see p792). If an earthquake occurs, the Japan Broadcasting Corporation (NHK) will broadcast information and instructions in English on all its TV and radio networks. Tune to channel 1 on your TV, or to NHK

(639kHz AM), FEN (810kHz AM) or InterFM (76.1FM) on your radio.

SIGHTS

Hopping on and off the JR Yamanote loop and crisscrossing town on the metro lines, you can easily catch the major sights from wherever you're based in Tokyo. From Central Tokyo, where Ginza glam is just a short walk from the serene Imperial Palace, the neighbourhoods to the north harbour the big national museums of Ueno Park as well as Shitamachi (Old Town). Moving southeast, Shinjuku's skyscrapers are just a few stops from Harajuku and Shibuya, teeming with trendy young fashionistas. Stylish Ebisu lies further south before the Yamanote line swoops north again. Metro lines whisk you westward towards the diplomatic district of Akasaka and the nightlife of Roppongi. You can even stroll, shop and dine along the waterfront of Tokyo Bay in Odaiba, with a lovely driverless monorail trip over the bay.

Central Tokyo 東京中心部
IMPERIAL PALACE 皇居

The Imperial Palace (Kōkyo; Map pp126–7) occupies the site of the castle Edo-jō, from which the Tokugawa *shōgunate* ruled Japan. In its heyday the castle was the largest in the world, though little remains of it today apart from the massive moat and walls. The present palace, completed in 1968, replaced the palace built in 1888 that was destroyed by Allied bombing in WWII.

As it's the home of Japan's emperor and imperial family, the palace is closed to the public for all but two days of the year, 2 January and 23 December (the emperor's birthday). Though you can't enter the palace itself, you can wander around its outskirts and visit the gardens.

It's an easy walk from Tokyo station, or from Hibiya or Nijū-bashi-mae subway stations, to Nijū-bashi. Crossing Babasaki Moat and the expansive Imperial Palace Plaza (Kōkyo-mae Hiroba), you'll arrive at a vantage point that gives a picture-postcard view of the palace peeking over its fortifications, behind Nijū-bashi.

IMPERIAL PALACE EAST GARDEN
皇居東御苑

The **Imperial Palace East Garden** (Kōkyo Higashi-gyoen; Map pp126-7; ☎ 3213-2050; admission free; ꗳ 9am-4pm Tue-Thu, Sat & Sun, last entry 3pm; ◉ Chiyoda, Marunouchi,

---

TOKYO FOR FREE

Unlike Tokyo's gardens, most city parks are free (Shinjuku-gyoen being the exception), and provide a peaceful backdrop for a picnic – try **Kitanomaru-kōen** (below), **Yoyogi-kōen** (p138) or **Hibiya-kōen** (p133).

Temples and shrines are always free unless you'd like to enter their main halls, and many of Tokyo's skyscrapers, like the **Tokyo Metropolitan Government Offices** (p137) and the **Shinjuku NS Building** (p137), have free observation floors. Galleries, especially around Ginza and Harajuku, welcome visitors. Company showrooms like the **Sony Building** (p132) and **Toyota Mega Web** (p141) in Odaiba are good for gearheads.

And don't forget **Tsukiji Market** (p132), where you could spend hours.

Tōzai lines to Ōtemachi, exit C10) is the only quarter of the palace proper that is open to the public. The main entrance is through **Ōte-mon**, a 10-minute walk north of Nijū-bashi. This was once the principal gate of Edo-jō; the garden lies at what was once the heart of the old castle. You'll be given a numbered token to turn in when you depart. The store inside the garden sells a good map for ¥150.

KITANOMARU-KŌEN 北の丸公園

Kitanomaru-kōen (Map pp126–7) makes an excellent picnicking locale and is good for a leisurely stroll. You can get there from Kudanshita or Takebashi subway stations.

Kitanomaru-kōen contains the **Nihon Budōkan** (Map pp126-7; ☎ 3216-5100; 2-3 Kitanomaru-kōen, Chiyoda-ku; ☒ vary), where you may witness a variety of martial arts. South of the Budōkan is the **Science Museum** (Kagaku Gijutsukan; Map pp126-7; ☎ 3212-2440; www.jsf.or.jp; 2-1 Kitanomaru-kōen, Chiyoda-ku; adult/child ¥600/250; ☒ 9am-4.50pm Tue-Sun), which is a decent rainy-day stop for those with children in tow, especially since most exhibits are interactive. An English booklet is included with entry.

Continuing south from the Science Museum brings you to the **National Museum of Modern Art** (Kokuritsu Kindai Bijutsukan; Map pp126-7; ☎ 5777-8600; www.momat.go.jp/english; 3-1 Kitanomaru-kōen, Chiyoda-ku; adult ¥420, student ¥70-130; ☒ 10am-5pm Tue-Thu, Sat & Sun, to 8pm Fri). The permanent exhibition here features Japanese art from the Meiji period (1868–1912) onwards, but check the website for any special exhibitions. Hold

onto your ticket stub, which gives you free admission to the nearby **Crafts Gallery** (Bijutsukan Kōgeikan; Map pp126-7; ☎ 5777-8600; 1-1 Kitanomaru-kōen, Chiyoda-ku; adult ¥200, student ¥40-70; ☒ 2-5pm Tue-Fri), housing a good display of crafts such as ceramics, lacquerware and dolls.

YASUKUNI-JINJA 靖国神社

If you take the Tayasu-mon exit (just past the Budōkan) of Kitanomaru-kōen, across the road and to your left is the impressive **Yasukuni-jinja** (Map pp126-7; ☎ 3261-8326; 3-1-1 Kudankita, Chiyoda-ku; admission free; ☒ 9am-5.30pm Mar-Oct, to 5pm Nov-Feb; ☒ Hanzōmon, Tōzai, Toei Shinjuku line to Kudanshita, exit 1), the Shrine for Establishing Peace in the Empire. Dedicated to the 2.4 million Japanese war-dead since 1853, it is the most controversial shrine in Japan.

The Japanese constitutional separation of religion and politics and the renunciation of militarism didn't stop a group of class-A war criminals being enshrined here in 1979; it also doesn't stop annual visits by politicians on the anniversary of Japan's defeat in WWII (15 August). The loudest protests are from Japan's Asian neighbours, who suffered most from Japanese aggression.

YASUKUNI-JINJA YUSHŪKAN
靖國神社遊就館

Next to Yasukuni-jinja is the **Yushūkan** (Map pp126-7; ☎ 3261-0998; www.yasukuni.or.jp; adult ¥800, student ¥300-500; ☒ 9am-5.30pm Mar-Oct, to 5pm Nov-Feb, closed 28-31 Aug & 28-31 Dec; ☒ Hanzōmon, Tōzai, Toei Shinjuku line to Kudanshita, exit 1), a war memorial museum that features items commemorating Japanese war-dead. There are limited English explanations, but an English pamphlet is available. Interesting exhibits include the long torpedo in the large exhibition hall that is actually a *kaiten* (human torpedo), a submarine version of the *kamikaze* (WWII suicide pilots). There are also displays of military uniforms, samurai armour and paintings of famous battles. Perhaps most interesting of all are the excerpts from books (some in English) arguing that America forced Japan into bombing Pearl Harbor.

TOKYO INTERNATIONAL FORUM
東京国際フォーラム

A remarkable edifice in central Tokyo, the **forum** (Map pp124-5; ☎ 5221-9000; www.t-i-forum.co.jp /english; 3-5-1 Marunouchi, Chiyoda-ku; ☒ 7am-11.30pm;

(Continued on page 132)

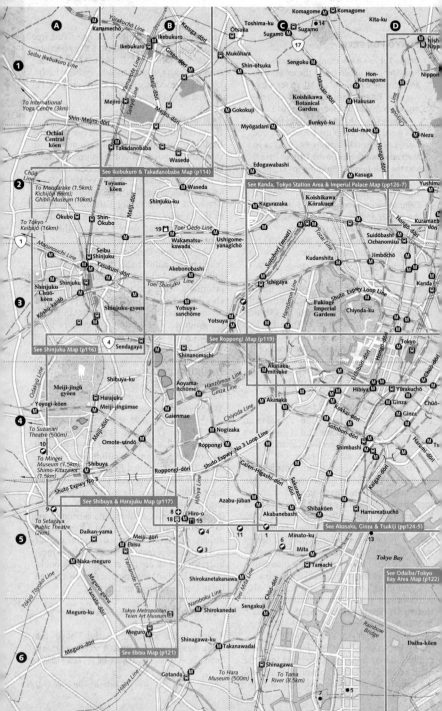

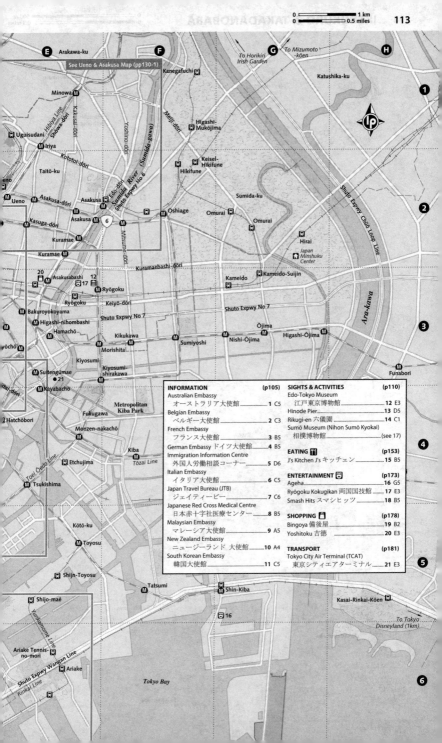

0 — 1 km
0 — 0.5 miles

See Ueno & Asakusa Map (pp130-1)

INFORMATION	(p105)
Australian Embassy オーストラリア大使館	1 C5
Belgian Embassy ベルギー大使館	2 C3
French Embassy フランス大使館	3 B5
German Embassy ドイツ大使館	4 B5
Immigration Information Centre 外国人労働相談コーナー	5 D6
Italian Embassy イタリア大使館	6 C5
Japan Travel Bureau (JTB) ジェイティービー	7 C6
Japanese Red Cross Medical Centre 日本赤十字社医療センター	8 B5
Malaysian Embassy マレーシア大使館	9 A5
New Zealand Embassy ニュージーランド 大使館	10 A4
South Korean Embassy 韓国大使館	11 C5

SIGHTS & ACTIVITIES	(p110)
Edo-Tokyo Museum 江戸東京博物館	12 E3
Hinode Pier	13 D5
Rikugi-en 六儀園	14 C1
Sumō Museum (Nihon Sumō Kyokai) 相撲博物館	(see 17)

EATING	(p153)
J's Kitchen J's キッチン	15 B5

ENTERTAINMENT	(p173)
Ageha	16 G5
Ryōgoku Kokugikan 両国国技館	17 E3
Smash Hits スマシヒッツ	18 B5

SHOPPING	(p178)
Bingoya 備後屋	19 B2
Yoshitoku 吉徳	20 E3

TRANSPORT	(p181)
Tokyo City Air Terminal (TCAT) 東京シティエアターミナル	21 E3

See Shinjuku Map (p116)

IKEBUKURO & TAKADANOBABA (p114)

SHINJUKU (p116)

0   500 m
0   0.3 miles

A   B   C   D

1

2

3

4

5

6

See Ikebukuro & Takadanobaba Map (p114)

Toyama
-köen

Ōkubo-dōri

Shin
Ōkuba

Ōkubo

Ōkubo-dōri

Meiji-dōri

Toei Ōedo Line

Higashi-Shinjuku

To Wakamatsu-kawada
Station (500m)

To Ogikubo
(5km)

Kita-Shinjuku

Shinjuku-ku

Ōme-kaidō

Nishi-Shinjuku

Marunouchi Line

Sakura
House

Kabukichō

Bunka Sentā-dōri

34 2
17
10
6
45

Seibu
Shinjuku

Shinjuku
Ward
Office

Golden
Gai

Hanazono-
jinja
Flea Market

19

Central
Rd

41   7

40
11
43
36
26

Kuyakusho-dōri

Gyoen-dōri

To Ichigaya
(2km)

Shinjuku Nomura
Building

Shinjuku
Island
Tower

Shinjuku
Mitsui Building

Sompo
Japan
Building

1

25

Shinjuku-nishiguchi

28
33

31

Yasukuni-dōri

Hilton
Tokyo

Kita-dōri

Shinjuku
Sumitomo
Building

Shinjuku
Centre
Building

12

47

46

West
Exit

East
Exit

53

5

32

Shinjuku-
sanchōme

Marunouchi Line

Shinjuku
Chūōkōen

Tochōmae

56

54
55
49

My City
Exit

Central
Exit

Mitsukoshi
(South
Building)

37

48

29

39
38
16

30

42

Shinjuku-
nichōme

9   15   20

8

52

Southeast
Exit

Ōedo
Shinjuku

Mitsukoshi
(New
Branch)

Toei Ōedo Line

Season Rd

Ōgido-dōri

Tochō-dōri

Köen-dōri

22

13

KDD
Building

50

1

3

27

New
South
Exit

Shinjuku

35

51

Meiji-dōri

Shinjuku

Shinjuku-
gyoenmae

24

One Day's St

Kōshū-Kaidō

18

Mayods
Tower

4
23

Shinjuku-
gyoen

14

21

Toei Shinjuku Line

Kaiō Line (Underground)

Yoyogi

Yamanote Line

Yoyogi

Meiji-jingū
gyoen

To Harajuku
(1km)

Minami-Shinjuku

Odakyū Line

Saikyō Line

Chūō-Sōbu Line

Sendagaya

To Yotsuya
(2km)

See Shibuya & Harajuku Map (p117)

0 — 500 m
0 — 0.3 miles

A Minami-Shinjuku **B** M Yoyogi **C** Shinjuku-gyoen **D**

To Shinjuku (200m)

Yamanote Line

Saikyō Line

Kita-sandō

See Shinjuku Map (p116)

Sendagaya M

Kokuritsu-Kyōgijō M

Shuto Expwy No 4

Meiji-jingū Treasure Museum

North Gate

27

Sendagaya

61

National Stadium

13

Meiji-kōen

Meiji-jingū gyoen

Jingū Kyūjō (Jingū Stadium)

Gaien-nishi-dōri

Yoyogi-kōen

Shibuya-Ku

Minami-sandō

31

Turkish Embassy

Harajuku

Tōgō-jinja

43

44

18

28

19

South Pond

Chiyoda Line

Takeshita-dōri

10

Gaienmae M

Harajuku

37

14

Killer-dōri

12

Meiji-jingūmae M

68

60

Condomania

Jingūmae

42

Yoyogi National Stadium

33

Omotesandō Hills

Omotesandō

Fire-dōri

Meiji-dōri

51

74

36

77

NHK Hall

Jinnan

NHK Studio Plaza Building

73

72

30

6

Omote-sandō M

70

45

67

Prada Aoyama

Inokashira-dōri

Jingū-dōri-kōen

57

56

16

Kamiyamachō

17

Kōen-dōri

25

41

Miyashita-kōen

5

Mitake-kōen

40

Kita-Aoyama

15

32

48

20

23

69

Parco II

80

76

Parco I

Parco III

Udagawachō

58

3

55

7

53

71

50

29

75

79

49

4

Shibuya

Aoyama Gakuin University

22

Hanzōmon Line

Ginza Line

Keitō-dōri

Shōtō

Love Hotel Hill

47

52

35

39

2

26

1

8

24

64

65

Bunkamura-dōri

Miyamasu-zaka

Aoyama-dōri

Dōgenzaka

46

Maruyamachō

66

62

63

Shibuya Crossing

Shibuya

Keiō Shibuya

11

Shibuya (Tōkyū Department Store)

81

Roppongi-dōri

Sakae-dōri

54

Dōgen-zaka-dōri

Keiō Inokashira Line

59

Shibuya M

To Shimo-Kitazawa

Tamagawa-dōri

Shuto Expwy No 3

21

34

38

Shibuya-gawa

Sakuragaokachō

See Roppongi Map (p119)

See Ebisu Map (p121)

Daikanyama

0   500 m
0   0.3 miles

A   **B**   **C**   **D**

Shinjuku-dōri

Yotsuya

Shuto Expwy

See Kanda, Tokyo Station Area & Imperial Palace Map (pp126–7)

Hirakawachō

1

Akasaka Detached Palace

20

Kioi-Chō

Shinanomachi

Benkei-bori-Moat

Nagatachō

Akasaka-mitsuke

2

Jingū Gaien

Nagatachō

Hitotsugi-dōri

Sotobori-dōri

Prince Chichibu Memorial Rugby Stadium

43

Akasaka-dōri

Gaien-Higashi-dōri

Idō-Namiki

Hanzōmon Line

Ginza Line

3

Akasaka

Tamachi-dōri

3

5

Aoyama-itchōme

Akasaka-dōri

Akasaka

Aoyama-dōri

Toei Ōedo Line

22

Gaienmae

17

Akasaka-dōri

To Ark Hills (500m)

13

15

Kotto-dōri (Antique St)

9

Nogizaka

Gaien-nishi-dōri

Chiyoda Line

21

Defense Agency

Roppongi

Roppongi-dōri

4

Minami-Aoyama

Aoyama Reien (Aoyama Cemetery)

Aoyama-kōen

Roppongi

51

28

31

Roppongi-itchōme

46

8

Roppongi Crossing

49

19

Roppongi

4

38

32

44

52

33

16

37

1

50

24

35

34

6

12

23

2

48

41

25

39

30

26

29

47

40

36

Gaien-Higashi-dōri

27

7

11

Azabudai

Nishi-Azabu Crossing

Shuto Expwy No 3 Loop Line

Roppongi Hills

18

Roppongi Hills Development

5

45

42

Nishi-Azabu

14

TV Asahi

Keyaki-zaka

Tori-zaka

Roppongi-dōri

See Shibuya & Harajuku Map (p117)

Kotto-dōri

Azabu

Azabu-Jūban

Higashi-Azabu

See Akasaka, Ginza & Tsukiji Map (pp124–5)

10

Chinese Embassy

TV Asahi-dōri

Hibiya Line

Austrian Embassy

Azabu-jūban

6

Hiro-o

EBISU (p121)

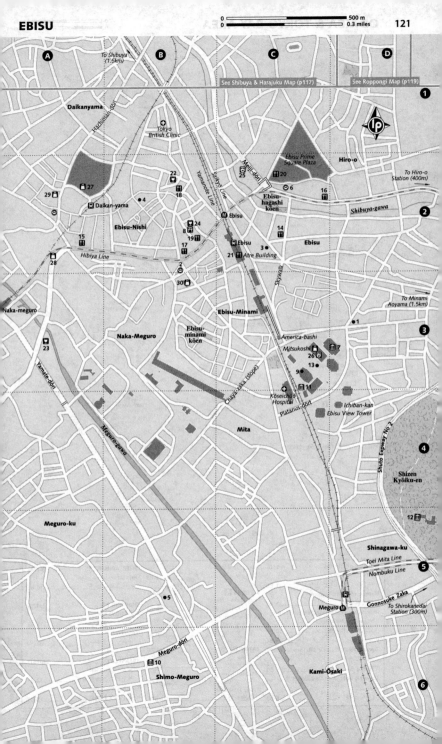

0 — 500 m
0 — 0.3 miles

A **B** **C** **D**

To Shibuya (1.5km)

See Shibuya & Harajuku Map (p117) See Roppongi Map (p119)

1

Daikanyama

Tokyo British Clinic

Ebisu Prime Square Plaza

Hiro-o

27

29

Daikan-yama

4

22
18
25

Meiji-dōri

20

6

Ebisu-hagashi kōen

16

To Hiro-o Station (400m)

Shibuya-gawa

2

Ebisu-Nishi

Ebisu

24
8
19
17

Ebisu

14

21 Atre Building

3

Hibiya Line

15

28

2

30

3

Naka-meguro

Naka-Meguro

Ebisu-minami kōen

Ebisu-Minami

To Minami Aoyama (1.5km)

1

America-bashi

Mitsukoshi

7
26
13
9
11

Kōseichūō Hospital

23

Chaya-zaka (slope)

Platanus-dōri

Mita

Ichiban-kan
Ebisu View Tower

Shuto Expwy No 2

4

Shizen Kyōiku-en

Meguro-ku

Meguro-gawa

Yamate-dōri

12

Shinagawa-ku

Toei Mita Line

Nombuku Line

5

5

Gonnosuke Zaka

To Shirokanedai Station (300m)

Meguro

Meguro-dōri

10

Shimo-Meguro

Kami-Ōsaki

6

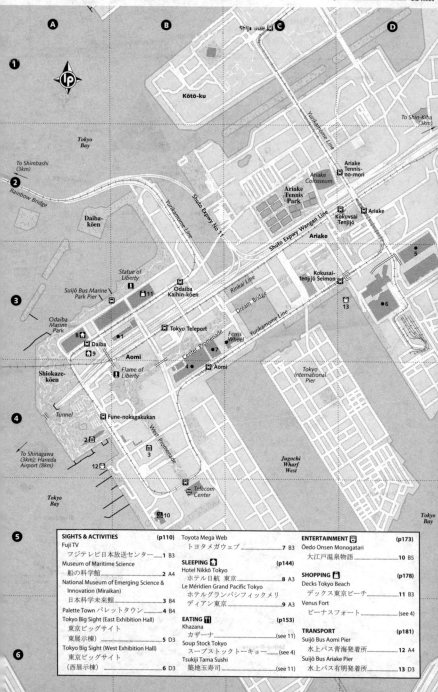

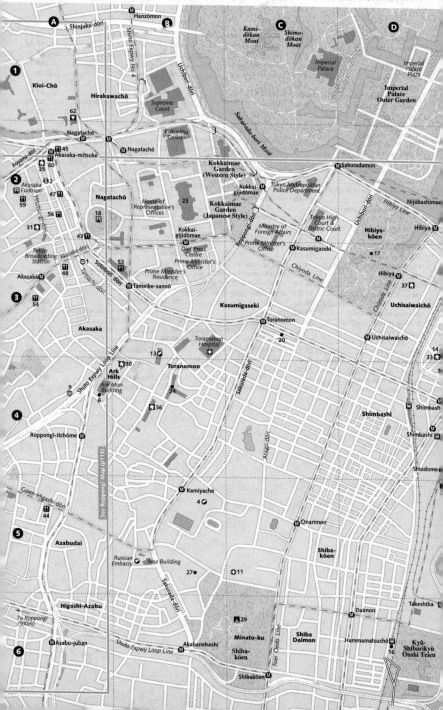

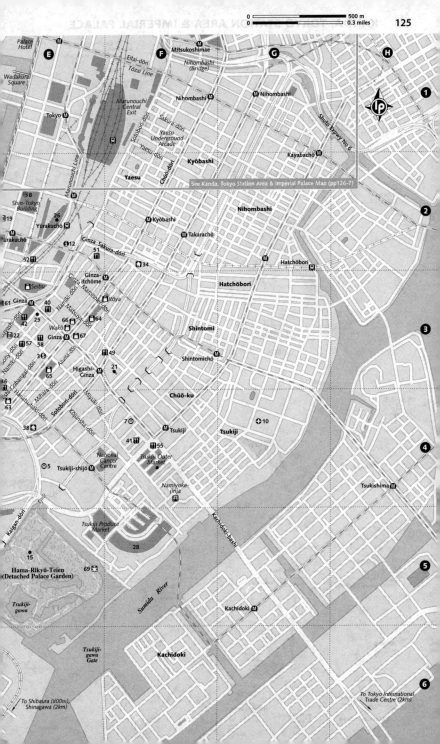

0 — 500 m
0 — 0.3 miles

Palace Hotel

E

F Mitsukoshimae

G

H

Wadakura Square

Eitai-dōri
Tōzai Line

Nihombashi (Bridge)

1

Tokyo Ⓜ

Marunouchi Central Exit

Nihombashi Ⓜ

Ⓜ Nihombashi

Shuto Expwy No 6

Sakura-dōri

Sotobori-dōri

Yaesu Underground Arcade

Yaesu-dōri

Kayabachō Ⓜ

Marunouchi Line

Chūō-dōri

Kyōbashi

Yaesu

See Kanda, Tokyo Station Area & Imperial Palace Map (pp126-7)

Shin-Tokyo Building
⊕8

ℹ19

26
Yūrakuchō

Ⓜ Kyōbashi

Nihombashi

2

Yūrakuchō
ℹ12

52 ⊞

Ⓜ Takarachō

51 ⊞

Ginza Sakura-dōri
⭡34

Ⓜ Hatchōbori

Hatchōbori

Ginza-itchōme
Ⓜ

Hatchōbori

Seibu

Naka-dōri

Ginza-Maronie-dōri

itōya

161 Ginza Ⓜ

40

Namiki-dōri

25 42

66

64

Wakō

3

22

57 58

Ginza Ⓜ

67

Azuma-dōri

Shintomi

Sotobori-dōri

3 S

⊞49

65

21

Shintomichō Ⓜ

Higashi-Ginza Ⓜ

Miyuki-dōri

Hanatsubaki-dōri

Mihara-dōri

Chūō-ku

63

38 ⭡

kojunsha-dōri

7 ⊗

Ⓜ Tsukiji

Tsukiji

⊕10

4

41 55 ⊞

National Cancer Centre

Tsukiji Outer Market

⊗5

Tsukiji-shijō Ⓜ

Namiyoke-jinja

Tsukishima Ⓜ

Kaigan-dōri

Tsukiji Produce Market

28

5

15

69

Hama-Rikyū-Teien
(Detached Palace Garden)

Kachidoki Ⓜ

Kachidoki-bashi

Tsukiji-gawa

Sumida River

Tsukiji-gawa Gate

Kachidoki

6

To Shibaura (800m),
Shinagawa (2km)

To Tokyo International
Trade Centre (2km)

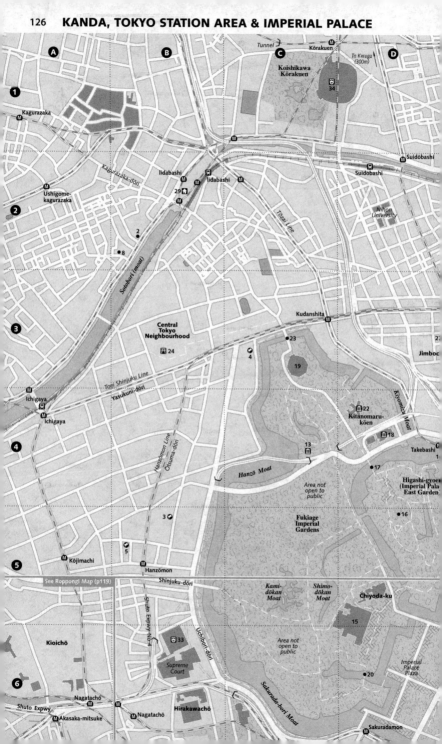

Tunnel

Kōrakuen

Kōrakuen

Koishikawa
Kōrakuen

To Karuga
(300m)

34

Suidōbashi

Kagurazaka

Suidobashi

Nihon
University

Kagurazaka-dōri

Iidabashi

Iidabashi

Ushigome-
kagurazaka

29

Sotobori (moat)

Tōsai Line

2

8

Kudanshita

Central
Tokyo
Neighbourhood

23

Jimboc

24

4

19

Tōei Shinjuku Line

Yasukuni-dōri

Ichigaya

22

Kitanomaru-
kōen

Kiyomichi Moat

Ichigaya

18

Hanzōmon Line

Ōsuma-dōri

13

Takebashi

1

Hanzō Moat

17

Higashi-gyoen
(Imperial Pala
East Garden

Area not
open to
public

3

16

Fukiage
Imperial
Gardens

Kōjimachi

5

Hanzōmon

Shinjuku-dōri

Kami-
dōkan
Moat

Shimo-
dōkan
Moat

Chiyoda-ku

See Roppongi Map (p119)

Shuto Expwy No.4

Uchibori-dōri

Kioichō

33

15

Area not
open to
public

Supreme
Court

Imperial
Palace
Plaza

Nagatachō

Sakurada-hori Moat

20

Shuto Expwy

Nagatachō

Akasaka-mitsuke

Hirakawachō

Sakuradamon

0   500 m
0   0.3 miles

E **F** **G** **H**

To Hongo
San-chôme
(300m)

Naka-
Okachimachi

Ueno-
hirokôji

Kasuga-dôri

Shin-okachimachi

Taitô **1**

See Ueno & Asakusa Map (pp130-1)

Yushima

Suehirochô

Kuramaebashidôri

Sotobori-dôri
Kanda-gawa

Tokyo Medical &
Dental University

Ochanomizu

Suehiro-
Chô

UDX
Building

Sarugakuchô

Ochanomizu

Ochanomizu

Akihabara
Electronic
Town

Akihabara

Asakusabashi **2**

Bookshop
eighbourhood

Nichôdai
Hospital

Nichôlai
Cathedral

Shin-
ochanomizu

Mêiji
University

35 38

7

Akihabara

îbôchô

36

Sporting
Goods
Neighbourhood

26

28

Ogawamachi

Awajichô

Iwamotochô

Bakuroyokoyama **3**

Suzuran-dôri
6

Yasukuni-dôri

Kanda

Kanda-
Nishikichô

Kanda

Iwamotochô

Kodenmachô

Kanda-Keisatsu-dôri

Kanda

Kodemmachô **4**

Shuto Expwy No 5

Uchi-
Kanda

Nihombashi
Muramachi

Ôtemachi

Tunnel

Kôkyo-
Gaien

Museum of
Imperial
Collections

Ôtemachi

12

Bank of
Japan

Ningyôchô

21

Hanzômon Line

25

Mitsukoshimae

40 **5**

Eitai-dôri

See Akasaka, Ginza & Tsukiji Map (pp124-5)

Wadakura
Square

Marunouchi
OAZO Building

Nihombashi
(Bridge)

9

Shin-Marunouchi
Building

Tokyo Stock
Exchange

Nihombashi

**Imperial
Palace
ter Garden**

American
Pharmacy
Marunouchi
Building

Tokyo

Marunouchi
Central Exit

10

30

37

32

31

Yaesu
Central
Exit

39

41

Kayabachô **6**

11

Yaesu
Underground
Arcade

Yaesu

42

43

Yaesu-dôri

Kyôbashi

Sakura-dôri

Nihombashi

Tokyo

UENO & ASAKUSA (pp130-1)

129

UENO & ASAKUSA (pp130–1)

A B C D

1

Nishi
Nippori

To Kita-Senju
(2.5km)

Suwa-jinja

To Keisei
Machiya
(1.8km)

Senkō-ji

Yōfuku-ji

Kejō-ji

Keisei
Nippori

Nippori

Sendagi

Bunkyō-ku

33

2

Ryūsen-ji

Kaizō-in

kannon-ji

3

Chōan-ji

Jōzai-ji

Yanaka
Cemetery

55

Negishi

Yanaka

Kotōtoi-dōri

Kanei-ji

Uguisudani

3

44

26

Iriya

Ueno-
Sakuragi

Hakubutsukan
Dōbutsuen

Tokyo National
University of
Fine Arts & Music

28

40

27

Nezu

Ikenohata

31

11

Rinnō-ji

Ueno-
kōen
32

19

4

45

30

14

20

Daibutsu
Pagoda

16

Gojō-jinja

Tokyo
University
29

Suijōdōbutsu-
ike
Benten-
bashi

Dōbutsuen-dōri

Tokyo Metropolitan
Festival Hall

Ueno

Kita-
Ueno

36

10

Bōto-
ike

Keisei
Ueno

21

Ueno

Tokyo University
Branch Hospital

Shinobazu-ike

23

Inarichō

Ginza Line
Asakusa-dōri

5

Hongō

Tokyo
Regional
Court

51

52

57

Higashi-
Ueno

37

50

60

6

Naka-
Okachimachi

Yushima

Ueno-Okachimachi

Okachimachi

Shin-
okachimachi

Ueno-
hirokōji

See Kanda, Tokyo Station Area & Imperial Palace Map (pp126–7)

Kasuga-dōri

Taitō

6

Yushima

Suehirochō

To Akihabara
(1km)

500 m
0.3 miles

E F G H

1

Arakawa-ku Minamisenju Ⓜ

Joban Line

Minowa Ⓜ

Ⓜ

Meiji-dōri

Yoshino-dōri

Kokusai-dōri

2

Senzoku

Hasiba

4

Imado

3

ototoi-dōri

Taitō-ku 🏯 Banryū-ji Asakusa Sumida-kōen

42 🏯

34 🏯 Hanayashiki Amusement Park 5

7 🏯 🏛 8

22 Kototoi-dōri

Niten-mon

13 Umamichi-dōri

Asakusa- 15

kōen Hanakawado-kōen

9 🏛 Hanakawado

Kapbabashihon-dōri

🏯 12 49

Nishi- 18

Asakusa Asakusa Neighbourhood

Shin-Nakamise-dōri

Nakamise-dōri

Tōbu Asakusa 🏯

47 🏯 58

48 25 🏯 41 Sumida-ku

56 46 🏯 17

54 Kaminarimon

Tokyo Narihirabashi 🏯

Hongan-ji Kaminarimon-dōri 59

1 24 Tobu Isesaki Line

2 Ⓜ Asakusa 5

✉ 35 Azuma-

Asahi bashi

Tawaramachi Ⓜ 4 🏯 Breweries

🏯 39 Complex

6

Honjo-Azumabashi

53 🏯 Ⓜ

Toei-Asakusa Line

Kotobuki

Mitsume-dōri

38 🏯

Ⓜ Kuramac

To Asakusabashi Shuto Expwy No 6

(2km)

6

Kokusai-dōri

Hisago-dōri

Yoshino-dōri

Kototoi-dōri

Kototoi-bashi

Sumida River (Sumida-gawa)

River Cruise Route

Shuto Expwy No 6

Sushiya-dōri

Kappabashi-dōri

Orange-dōri

Metro-dōri

Chinyoko-dōri

Edo-dōri

Komagata-bashi

Shuto Expwy No 6

(Continued from page 111)

JR, Yūrakuchō lines to Yūrakuchō, exit A4b) is mostly used for conventions and events. Its prominent glass wing looks like a transparent ship plying Tokyo's urban waters. In contrast, the west wing is a boxy affair of cantilevered, overhanging spaces and cavernous atria.

GINZA 銀座

Ginza (Map pp124–5) is Tokyo's answer to NYC's Fifth Ave. Back in the 1870s, Ginza was one of the first areas to modernise, featuring a large number of novel (for Tokyoites of that era) Western-style brick buildings. Ginza was also home to Tokyo's first department stores and other harbingers of the modern world, such as gas lamps.

Today other shopping districts rival Ginza in opulence, vitality and popularity, but Ginza retains a distinct snob value – conspicuous consumption continues to be big here. It's therefore a superb place to window-shop and browse the galleries (usually free).

Saturday afternoons and Sundays are the best, when Chūō-dōri and some smaller streets are closed to vehicles, allowing kimono-clad ladies and toddlers to respectively amble and gambol in the middle of the boulevard.

Sony Building ソニービル

Perfect for a rainy day, the **Sony Building** (Map pp124–5; ☎ 3573-2371; www.sonybuilding.jp; 5-3-1 Ginza, Chūō-ku; admission free; 11am-7pm; Ginza, Hibiya, Marunouchi line to Ginza, exit B9) has fascinating hands-on displays of Sony's latest products, and some that are yet to be released. Although there's often a wait, kids (and gamer types) love the free video and virtual-reality games on the 6th floor.

Galleries

Ginza is packed with galleries, many so small that they can be viewed in a few minutes. Wander around a bit and you'll find galleries displaying a mad variety of contemporary art – you're sure to confront something intriguing to your particular sensibilities, especially if you're into graphic design. Though scattered throughout Ginza, they are concentrated in the area south of Harumi-dōri, between Ginza-dōri and Chūō-dōri.

Idemitsu Museum of Arts (Map pp124–5; ☎ 3213-9402; 9th fl, 3-1-1 Marunouchi, Chiyoda-ku; adult/student ¥800/500; 10am-5pm Tue-Thu, Sat & Sun, to 7pm Fri;

Chiyoda, Toei Mita lines to Hibiya, exits A1 & B3) holds Japanese and Chinese art and is famous for its collection of work by the Zen monk Sengai. Find it next door to the Imperial Theatre.

Exhibiting the outstanding work of up-and-coming photographers and long-time professionals, **Leica Ginza Salon** (Map pp124–5; ☎ 6215-7070; www.leica-camera.us/culture/galleries/gal lery_tokyo; 1st & 2nd fl, Tokaido Bldg, 6-4-1 Ginza, Chūō-ku; admission free; 11am-7pm Tue-Fri; Marunouchi line to Ginza, exit C2) remains one of the best photography galleries in the area.

Kabuki-za 歌舞伎座

You may not have the time to take in a long-haul kabuki performance (p177) at **Kabuki-za** (Map pp124–5; ☎ 5565-6000; www.shochiku.co.jp/play/ka bukiza/theater/index.html; 4-12-5 Ginza, Chūō-ku; admission ¥2500-17,000; 11am-9pm; Hibiya, Toei Asakusa lines to Higashi-Ginza, exit 3), but even so, do a walk-by to check out its beautifully dramatic exterior.

HAMARIKYŪ-TEIEN 浜離宮庭園

Walk the garden paths along ponds and tea-houses at **Hama-Rikyū-Teien** (Detached Palace Garden; Map pp124–5; ☎ 3541-0200; admission ¥300; 9am-5pm; Toei Ōedo line to Tsukiji-Shijō, exit A2), perhaps on a journey between Ginza and Asakusa (p134), via the Sumida-gawa Cruise.

TSUKIJI FISH MARKET 築地市場

Tsukiji Fish Market (Map pp124–5; ☎ 3541-2640; www .tsukiji-market.or.jp; 5-2 Tsukiji, Chūō-ku; closed 2nd & 4th Wed most months, Sun & public holidays; Toei Ōedo line to Tsukiji-Shijō, exits A1 & A2) is where all that seafood comes after it's been fished out of the sea and before it turns up on a sashimi platter. The day begins very early, with the arrival of the catch and its wholesale auctioning. The early-morning (that's 5am) auction is not officially open to the general public, but unobtrusive visitors are welcome to attend. Flash photography is not permitted during the auctions – remember that this is a working market and try to keep a respectful profile. To get to the auction, head into the main entrance of the market hall all the way to the end. You can pick up an English guide at the market entrance.

The stalls and shopfront eateries of the outer market are also fun to wander around, and the market is at its best before 8am. Wear shoes you won't mind getting a little set and mucky, and be extremely wary of the motorised carts speeding around the market, especially if you're with small children.

HIBIYA-KŌEN 日比谷公園

If Ginza leaves you yearning for greenery, head west to **Hibiya-kōen** (Map pp124-5; admission free; ⊙ Chiyoda, Hibiya, Toei Mita lines to Hibiya, exits A10 & A14), Tokyo's first Western-style park. It makes for a pleasant break, especially if you claim one of the benches overlooking the pond on the park's eastern side. About midway down on the eastern side is a small café where you can refresh with coffee or ice cream.

Ueno 上野

Ueno is one of the last areas in Tokyo where the old Shitamachi feel still permeates. Ueno's aging but spry shopping arcade, Ameyoko Arcade (Map pp130-1), remains a bustling market that feels worlds away from the monumental marketplace of Roppongi Hills (p139). But Ueno has no need for fancy shopping malls, for its real draw is Ueno-kōen, which boasts the highest concentration of museums and galleries anywhere in Japan.

UENO-KŌEN 上野公園

Ueno Hill was the site of a last-ditch defence of the Tokugawa *shōgunate* by about 2000 Tokugawa loyalists in 1868. They were duly dispatched by the imperial army, and the new Meiji government decreed that Ueno Hill would be transformed into Tokyo's first public park. Today, **Ueno-kōen** (Map pp130-1; ⊙ JR Yamanote line to Ueno, Park exit) may not be the best of Tokyo's parks, but it certainly packs in more attractions than any others. Across the street from the Park exit is a large map showing the layout of the park and museum complex.

The park is famous as Tokyo's most popular site for *hanami* (blossom-viewing) in early to mid-April – which doesn't mean it's the *best* place to see the blossoms (see p137 for an altogether quieter *hanami* spot). In addition to the cherry blossoms, check out the lotuses in the pond, Shinobazu-ike, at the southern end of the park. Ueno-kōen is the centre of Tokyo's sizable but largely invisible homeless population.

Saigō Takamori Statue 西郷隆盛銅像

Near the southern entrance to the park is this unconventional **statue** (Map pp130-1) of a samurai walking his dog. Saigō Takamori started out supporting the Meiji Restoration but ended up ritually disembowelling himself in defeated opposition to it. The turnabout in his loyalties occurred when the Meiji govern-

---

ment withdrew the powers of the military class to which he belonged (see p715).

Tokyo National Museum 東京国立博物館

The **Tokyo National Museum** (Tokyo Kokuritsu Hakubutsu-kan; Map pp130-1; ☎ 3822-1111; www.tnm.jp; 13-9 Ueno-kōen, Taitō-ku; adult/student ¥420/130, 2nd Sat free; ☯ 9.30am-5pm Tue-Thu, Sat & Sun, to 8pm Fri Apr-Sep) is the one museum in Tokyo worth a spot in your itinerary. Not only is it Japan's largest, housing some 87,000 items, it also has the world's largest collection of Japanese art. Only a portion of the museum's works is displayed at any one time.

The museum has four galleries, the most important of which is the **Main Hall** (Honkan). It's straight ahead as you enter, and houses a very impressive array of Japanese art, from sculpture and swords to lacquerware and calligraphy. The **Gallery of Eastern Antiquities** (Tōyō-kan), to the right of the ticket booth, displays a collection of art and archaeological finds from all over Asia. The **Hyōkei-kan**, to the left of the ticket booth, houses Japanese archaeological finds and includes a room devoted to artefacts once used by the Ainu, the indigenous people of Hokkaidō.

Perhaps best of all is the **Gallery of Hōryūji Treasures** (Hōryūji Hōmotsu-kan), which houses some of Japan's most important Buddhist artworks, all from Hōryū-ji in Nara.

Take some air after your museum visit with a stroll around the **Tokugawa Shōgun Cemetery**, behind the museum.

Tokyo Metropolitan Museum of Art
東京都美術館
This **museum of art** (Map pp130-1; ☎ 3823-6921; www.tobikan.jp; 8-36 Ueno-kōen, Taitō-ku; admission varies; ⏱ 9am-5pm Tue-Sun, closed 3rd Mon each month) has several galleries that run temporary displays of contemporary Japanese art. Galleries feature both Western-style art and Japanese-style art, such as *sumi-e* (ink brush) and *ikebana* (flower arrangement). Apart from the main gallery, the rental galleries are not curated by the museum, so exhibitions can be of differing standards.

National Science Museum
国立科学博物館
With limited interpretive signage in English, this **museum** (Kokuritsu Kagaku Hakubutsukan; Map pp130-1; ☎ 3822-0111 Mon-Fri, 3822-0114 Sat & Sun; www.kahaku.go.jp/english; 7-20 Ueno-kōen, Taitō-ku; adult/child ¥500/free; ⏱ 9am-4.30pm Tue-Sun) often installs excellent special exhibitions – usually around ¥500 extra. The interactive exhibits make it a good place to bring kids, especially combined with a trip to the Ueno Zoo.

National Museum of Western Art
国立西洋美術館
The **National Museum of Western Art** (Kokuritsu Seiyō Bijutsukan; Map pp130-1; ☎ 3828-5131; www.nmwa.go.jp; 7-7 Ueno-kōen, Taitō-ku; adult ¥420, student ¥70-130; ⏱ 9.30am-5pm Tue-Thu, Sat & Sun, to 8pm Fri) has a respectable, though rather indifferently displayed, permanent collection. It frequently hosts special exhibits (admission varies) on loan from other museums of international repute.

Shitamachi Museum
下町風俗資料館
This **museum** (Map pp130-1; ☎ 3823-7451; 2-1 Ueno-kōen, Taitō-ku; adult/student ¥300/100; ⏱ 9.30am-4.30pm Tue-Sun) re-creates life in Edo's Shitamachi, the plebeian downtown quarter of old Tokyo. Exhibits include a sweet shop, the home and business of a copper boilermaker and a tenement house. Docents are on hand to teach games or help you try on the clothes, making for a fun, hands-on visit.

Ueno Zoo
上野動物園
Established in 1882, **Ueno Zoo** (Map pp130-1; ☎ 3828-5171; 9-83 Ueno-kōen, Taitō-ku; adult/student ¥600/200; ⏱ 9.30am-5pm Tue-Sun) was the first of its kind in Japan. It's a good outing if you have children; otherwise, it can be safely dropped from a busy itinerary. If you're a panda fan, note that those universally charming creatures are not on view on Fridays.

Tōshō-gū
東照宮
Dating from 1651 this **shrine** (Map pp130-1; ☎ 3822-3455; 9-88 Ueno-kōen, Taitō-ku; admission ¥200; ⏱ 9am-4.30pm Dec-Feb, to 5.30pm Mar-Nov), like its counterpart in Nikkō, is dedicated to Tokugawa Ieyasu, who unified Japan. The shrine is one of the few extant early-Edo structures, having fortunately survived Tokyo's innumerable disasters.

Ameyoko Arcade
アメヤ横丁
Ameyoko Arcade (Ameya-yokochō; Map pp130-1) was famous as a black-market district after WWII, and is still a lively shopping area where many bargains can be found. Shopkeepers are much less restrained than elsewhere in Tokyo, attracting customers with raucous cries that rattle down the crowded alleyways like the trains overhead. Look for its big archway sign opposite Ueno station's south side.

Asakusa
浅草
Long considered the heart of old Shitamachi, Asakusa is an interesting, compact neighbourhood to explore on foot. Asakusa's main attraction is the temple Sensō-ji, also known as Asakusa Kannon-dō. In Edo times, Asakusa was a halfway stop between the city and its most infamous pleasure district, Yoshiwara. Eventually Asakusa developed into a pleasure quarter in its own right, becoming the centre for that most loved of Edo entertainments, kabuki. In the shadow of Sensō-ji a fairground spirit prevailed and a range of very secular establishments thrived, from kabuki theatres to brothels.

When Japan ended its self-imposed isolation with the commencement of the Meiji Restoration, it was in Asakusa that the first cinemas opened, the first music halls appeared and Western opera was first performed before Japanese audiences at Asakusa's Teikoku Gekijo (Imperial Theatre). It was also here that another Western cultural import – the striptease – was introduced.

Unfortunately, Asakusa never quite recovered from the bombing at the end of WWII. Sensō-ji was rebuilt, but other areas of Tokyo assumed Asakusa's pleasure-district role. To its advantage, however, Asakusa may be one of the few areas of Tokyo to have retained something of the spirit of Shitamachi.

SENSŌ-JI 浅草寺

This **temple** (Map pp130-1; ☎ 3842-0181; 2-3-1 Asakusa, Taitō-ku; admission free; 24hr; Ginza line to Asakusa, exit 1 or Toei Asakusa line to Asakusa, exit A5) enshrines a golden image of Kannon (the Buddhist Goddess of Mercy), which, according to legend, was miraculously fished out of the nearby Sumida River by two fishermen in AD 628. The image has remained on the spot ever since, through successive rebuildings of the temple; the present structure dates from 1950.

Approaching Sensō-ji from Asakusa subway station, the entrance is via Kaminarimon (Thunder Gate). The gate's protector gods are Fūjin, the god of wind, on the right; and Raijin, the god of thunder, on the left.

Near Kaminarimon, you'll probably be wooed by *jinriksha* drivers in traditional dress; they can cart you around on tours (10/30/60 minutes for ¥2000/5000/9000 per person), providing commentary in English or Japanese.

Straight ahead is Nakamise-dōri, the temple precinct's shopping street, where everything from tourist trinkets to genuine Edo-style crafts is sold. Need a formal wig to wear with your kimono? Here's where to shop.

Nakamise-dōri leads to the main temple compound. Whether the ancient image of Kannon actually exists is a secret, as it's not on public display. This doesn't stop a steady stream of worshippers from travelling to the top of the stairs to bow and clap. In front of the temple is a large incense cauldron: the smoke is said to bestow health and you'll see visitors rubbing it into their bodies through their clothes.

DEMBŌ-IN 伝法院

To the left of the temple precinct is Dembō-in (Dembō Garden; Map pp130-1). Although it's not open to the public, it is possible to obtain a pass by calling a few days ahead to the **main office** (☎ 3842-0181; 2-3-1 Asakusa, Taitō-ku; admission free; dawn-dusk Mon-Sat, closed for ceremonies; Ginza line to Asakusa, exit 1 or Toei Asakusa line to Asakusa, exit A5) to the left of the Five-Storeyed Pagoda. The garden is one of Tokyo's best, containing a picturesque pond and a replica of a famous Kyoto teahouse.

SUMIDA-GAWA CRUISE 隅田川クルーズ

A Sumida River cruise on the **Suijo Bus** (Map pp130-1; ☎ 0120-977-311; www.suijobus.co.jp; fare to Hamarikyū-teien/Hinode Pier ¥720/760; 9.30am-6pm; Ginza line to Asakusa, exit 4 or Toei Asakusa line to Asakusa, exit A5) may not be the most scenic you've ever experienced, but it's a great way to get to or from Asakusa.

Cruises depart about every half-hour from the pier next to the bridge, Azuma-bashi, and go to Hamarikyū-teien (p132) and Hinode Pier (Map pp112-13). A good way to do the cruise is to buy a ticket to Hamarikyū-teien (where you'll have to pay an additional ¥300 entry fee). After exploring the garden, you can walk into Ginza in about 10 to 15 minutes.

Ikebukuro 池袋

Traditionally Shinjuku's poor cousin, bawdy Ikebukuro shouldn't rate high on a busy schedule, but its attractions include two of the world's largest department stores (Seibu and Tōbu), the second-busiest station in Tokyo and the escalator experience of a lifetime (Tokyo Metropolitan Art Space). Like Shinjuku, Ikebukuro divides into an east side and a west side.

SUNSHINE CITY サンシャインシティ

Billed as a 'city in a building', **Sunshine City** (Map p114; ☎ 3989-3331; 3-1-1 Higashi-Ikebukuro, Toshima-ku; 10am-10pm; JR Yamanote line to Ikebukuro, east exit) is 60 floors of office space and shopping malls, with a few cultural and entertainment options thrown in, all in east Ikebukuro. If you've got ¥620 to burn, you can take a lift (from 10am to 9.30pm) to the lookout on the 60th floor and gaze out on the building blocks below.

On the 7th floor of the Bunka Kaikan Building of Sunshine City is the **Ancient Orient Museum** (☎ 3989-3491; 3-1-4 Higashi-Ikebukuro, Toshima-ku; admission ¥500; 10am-5pm), displaying antiquities and art from across Asia.

Also of interest to some might be the **Sunshine Planetarium** (Sunshine Starlight Dome; ☎ 3989-3475; 10th fl, World Import Mart Bldg, 3-1-3 Higashi-Ikebukuro, Toshima-ku; adult/child ¥800/500; noon-5.30pm Mon-Fri, 11am-6.30pm Sat & Sun), though shows are in Japanese, and the **Sunshine International Aquarium** (☎ 3989-3466; 10th fl, World Import Mart Bldg, 3-1-3 Higashi-Ikebukuro, Toshima-ku; adult/child ¥1800/900; 10am-6pm).

DEPARTMENT STORES

Seibu (Map p114; ☎ 3981-0111; 1-28-1 Minami-Ikebukuro, Toshima-ku; 10am-9pm Mon-Sat, to 8pm Sun, closed some Tue; JR Yamanote line to Ikebukuro, east exit) was for many years the world's biggest department

TOKYO

HELLO, KITTY

If necessity is the mother of invention, Tokyoites have an inventive view of necessity. Where but here would you find a place like **Nekobukuro** (Map p114; ☎ 3980-6111; 8th fl, Tōkyū Hands, 1-28-10 Higashi-Ikebukuro, Toshima-ku; admission ¥600; ☻ 10am-8pm; ◉ JR Yamanote line to Ikebukuro, east exit)? In a city where apartments are tiny and lives busy, adopting a pet is impossible for many…but at Nekobukuro, visitors can play with kitties without the litter. It's basically a petting zoo (for people) slash luxury apartment (for the 20-odd resident cats). Prowl on by if you need a little feline affection.

store. You could easily spend an hour wandering Seibu's *depachika* (basement food hall) sampling the tidbits on offer, while the top floor houses some 50 restaurants, many offering great lunch specials. On the 12th floor of the Seibu department store annexe is **Seibu Art Gallery**, which has changing art exhibits that are usually of fairly high standard.

On the west side, **Tōbu** (Map p114; ☎ 3981-2211; 1-1-25 Nishi-Ikebukuro, Toshima-ku; ☻ 10am-8pm Mon-Sat, closed some Wed; ◉ JR Yamanote line to Ikebukuro, west exit) is the bigger of the two and also has an amazing *depachika*. At the southwestern end of Ikebukuro station lies Tōbu's **Metropolitan Plaza**, packed with classy boutiques, restaurants on the 8th floor and a massive HMV music store on the 6th floor. This is where you'll find the **Japan Traditional Craft Center** (p179), both a showplace and shop featuring traditional crafts, and the **Tōbu Museum of Art** on the 1st through 3rd floors of the plaza.

Tokyo Metropolitan Art Space 東京芸術劇場

Part of the 'Tokyo Renaissance' plan launched by the Department of Education, the **Tokyo Metropolitan Art Space** (Map p114; ☎ 5391-2111; www.geigeki.jp/english/index.html; 1-8-1 Nishi-Ikebukuro; ◉ JR Yamanote line to Ikebukuro, west exit) was plonked down just where Tokyo needed it most – on Ikebukuro's west side. Designed to host performance art, the building has four halls as well as shops and cafés. Those without a ticket for anything should treat themselves to the soaring escalator ride – and the thrills just don't stop.

Shinjuku 新宿

Here in Shinjuku (Map p116), nearly everything that makes Tokyo interesting is crammed into one busy district: upscale department stores, discount shopping arcades, flashing neon, buttoned-up government offices, swarming push-and-shove crowds, streetside video screens, stand-up noodle bars, hostess clubs, shyly tucked-away shrines and seamy strip bars.

Shinjuku is a sprawling business, commercial and entertainment centre that never lets up. Every day approximately three million people pass through the station alone, making it one of the busiest in the world. On the western side of the station is Tokyo's highest concentration of skyscrapers and, presiding over them, Tange Kenzō's Tokyo Metropolitan Government Offices – massive awe-inspiring structures. The eastern side of the station, by contrast, is a labyrinth of department stores, restaurants, boutiques, neon and a glimpse of Tokyo's underbelly.

EAST SIDE 東新宿

Shinjuku's east side is good for roaming rather than a place for seeking out specific sights.

Kabukichō 歌舞伎町

Tokyo's most notorious red-light district lies east of Seibu Shinjuku station, north of Yasukuni-dōri. This is one of the world's more imaginative red-light districts, with 'soaplands' (massage parlours), love hotels, peep shows, pink cabarets ('pink' is the Japanese equivalent of 'blue' in English), porno-video booths and strip shows involving audience participation. The streets here are all crackling neon and drunken salarymen. High-pitched female voices wail out invitations to enter their establishments through distorted speakers, and *freeters* (floating, part-time workers) earn some yen passing out advertisements for karaoke boxes. Most of what goes on is very much off-limits to foreigners, but it's still an interesting area for a stroll.

Kabukichō is not wall-to-wall sex; there are also some straight entertainment options, including cinemas and some good restaurants (p156). For a drink, stroll around the teeny, intriguing alleys of the **Golden Gai** (p163).

Hanazono-jinja 花園神社

Nestled in the shadow of Kabukichō is this quiet, unassuming shrine, **Hanazono-jinja** (Map p116; ☎ 3200-3093; 5-17-3 Shinjuku, Shinjuku-ku; ◉ Maru-nouchi line to Shinjuku-sanchōme, exits B3 & B5). It only takes a few minutes to stroll the grounds, but it's a quiet refuge from the Shinjuku streets. It's particularly pleasant when it's lit up in the evening.

Shinjuku-gyoen 新宿御苑

One of the city's best escapes and top cherry-blossom viewing spots, **Shinjuku-gyoen** (Map p116; ☎ 3350-0151; Naitochō, Shinjuku-ku; adult/child under 15/child under 6 ¥200/50/free; ◉ 9am-4.30pm Tue-Sun; ◉ Marunouchi line to Shinjuku-gyoenmae, exit 1) is also one of Tokyo's largest parks at 57.6 hectares (144 acres). It dates back to 1906 and was designed as a European-style park, though it also has a Japanese garden, a hot-house containing tropical plants and a pond with giant carp.

WEST SIDE 西新宿

Shinjuku's west side is mainly administrative, but photography freaks, take note: the area behind the Keiō department store is home to Tokyo's largest **camera stores**, Yodobashi and Sakuraya (p181). They carry practically every-thing photography-related that you could possibly want, all at very reasonable prices, and even a limited selection of secondhand equipment.

Elsewhere, the attractions of west Shinjuku are mainly centred around the interiors of buildings and the observation floors of the impressive Tokyo Metropolitan Government Offices.

Tokyo Metropolitan Government Offices 東京都庁

These city **offices** (Tokyo Tochō; Map p116; ☎ 5321-1111; 2-8-1 Nishi-Shinjuku, Shinjuku-ku; admission free; ◉ 9.30am-11pm Tue-Sun, North Tower closed 2nd & 4th Mon, South Tower closed 1st & 3rd Tue; ◉ Toei Ōedo line to Tochōmae, exit A4) occupy two adjoining buildings worth visiting for their stunning architecture and for the great views from the **twin observation floors**. On really clear days, you might even spot Mt Fuji to the west. To reach the observation floors, take one of the two 1st-floor lifts.

Most visitors are won over by the build-ings' complex symmetry and computer-chip appearance. Particularly impressive is the spacious Citizen's Plaza in front of the No 1 building, more reminiscent of a Roman am-phitheatre than anything Japanese.

Shinjuku NS Building 新宿 NS ビル

The interior of the **Shinjuku NS Building** (Map p116; 2-4-1 Nishi-Shinjuku, Shinjuku-ku; admission free; ◉ 11am-10pm; ◉ Toei Ōedo line to Tochōmae, exit A2) is hollow, featuring a 1600 sq metre atrium illuminated by sunlight that streams in through the glass roof. The atrium features a 29m-tall pendulum clock. The restaurants on the 29th and 30th floors have excellent views over Tokyo, but if you're not hungry the views are still free.

Pentax Forum ペンタックスフォーラム

Set up as an interactive showroom where photography buffs can play with the latest photography equipment, **Pentax Forum** (Map p116; ☎ 3348-2941; 1st fl, Shinjuku Mitsui Bldg, 2-1-1 Nishi-Shinjuku, Shinjuku-ku; admission free; ◉ 10.30am-6.30pm, closed 1 Jan; ◉ Toei Ōedo line to Tochōmae, exit B2) is a must for shutterbugs.

Harajuku & Aoyama 原宿・青山

Harajuku and Aoyama (Map p117) are where Tokyoites come to be spendy and trendy. They're pleasant areas to stroll and watch lo-cals in contented consumer mode. **Takeshita-dōri** buzzes with bleach-headed teenagers shopping for illiterate T-shirts and fishnet stockings; **Omote-sandō**, with its alfresco cafés and boutiques, is still the closest Tokyo gets to Paris; the bistro alleys of Aoyama harbour some of the best international cuisine in town; and above it all is **Meiji-jingū**, Tokyo's most splendid shrine.

For snaps of the idiosyncratically clad na-tives, check out the Sunday madness at **Jingū-bashi** (see the boxed text, p138).

MEIJI-JINGŪ 明治神宮

Completed in 1920, the **shrine** (Map p117; ☎ 3379-5511; www.meijijingu.or.jp; 1-1 Yoyogi Kamizonochō, Shibuya-ku; admission free; ◉ dawn-dusk; ◉ JR Yamanote line to Harajuku, Omote-sandō exit) was built in memory of Emperor Meiji and Empress Shōken, under whose rule Japan ended its long isolation from the outside world. Unfortunately, like much else in Tokyo, the shrine was destroyed in WWII bombing. Rebuilding was completed in 1958.

Meiji-jingū might be a reconstruction of the original but, unlike so many of Japan's post-war reconstructions, it is altogether authen-tic. The shrine itself was built with Japanese cypress, while the cypress for the huge *torii* (gates) came from Alishan in Taiwan.

The shrine's inner garden, **Meiji-jingū-gyoen** (adult/child ¥500/200; ⏱ 9am-4.30pm), is almost deserted on weekdays. It's particularly beautiful in June, when the irises are in bloom.

YOYOGI-KŌEN 代々木公園

Weekends at **Yoyogi-kōen** (Map p117; admission free; ⏱ dawn-dusk; ⓔ JR Yamanote line to Harajuku, Omote-sandō exit or Chiyoda line to Yoyogi-kōen, exit 4) are prime for stumbling upon the cool and unusual – *shamisen* (three-stringed lute) or punk-rock practice, or fire-eating, for example. At 53.2 hectares (133 acres), its wooded grounds make for a relaxing walk even if there aren't any interesting goings-on. It's at its best on a sunny Sunday in spring or autumn.

ŌTA MEMORIAL ART MUSEUM
太田記念美術館

Pad quietly in slippers through the **Ōta Museum** (Map p117; ☎ 3403-0880; www.ukiyoe-ota-muse .jp/english.html; 1-10-10 Jingūmae, Shibuya-ku; adult/student ¥1000/700; ⏱ 10.30am-5.30pm Tue-Sun, closed from 27th to end of month; ⓔ Chiyoda line to Meiji-jingūmae, exit 5) to view its first-rate collection of *ukiyo-e* (woodblock prints), including works by masters of the art such as Hiroshige. Find it in the alley just northwest of the Laforet Building. Extra charges apply for special exhibits.

GALLERIES

Aoyama is packed with tiny galleries, most of them free. Up Killer-dōri, look for the **Watari-um** (Watari Museum of Contemporary Art; Map p117; ☎ 3402-3001; www.watarium.co.jp; 3-7-6 Jingūmae, Shibuya-ku; adult/student ¥1000/800; ⏱ 11am-7pm Tue & Thu-Sun, 11am-9pm Wed; ⓔ Ginza line to Gaienmae, exit 3). The attached museum shop **On Sundays**

(☎ 3470-1474; ⏱ vary) sells art books, funky gifts and piles of arty postcards. From Gaienmae station, head southwest along Aoyama-dōri and turn right at the Bell Commons building to walk up Killer-dōri.

On the other side of Omote-sandō, the **Spiral Building** (Map p117; ☎ 3498-1171; 5-6-23 Minami-Aoyama, Minato-ku; admission free; ⏱ 11am-8pm; ⓔ Chiyoda, Ginza, Hanzōmon lines to Omote-sandō, exit B1) features changing exhibits, dining and live music. Even more museum-store wares are sold on the 2nd floor.

Just around the corner from the Spiral Building, Kottō-dōri (also billed as 'Antique St') is a good place to seek out both galleries and souvenirs.

Shibuya 渋谷

Shibuya Crossing (Map p117) is probably one of the world's most visually famous four-way intersections, where the green light given to pedestrians releases a timed surge of humanity. Mostly of interest as a stupendous youth-oriented shopping district and people-watching hotspot, the goods for sale and energy of Shibuya offer glimpses into the desires and psyche of a certain generation. Especially on weekends, you might get the feeling that the jammed streets are populated solely by fashionable under 25s.

HACHIKŌ STATUE ハチ公像

In the 1920s, a professor who lived near Shibuya station kept a small Akita dog, who would come to the station every afternoon to await his master's return. The professor died in 1925, but the dog continued to show up and wait at the station until his own death 11

COSPLAY-ZOKU

When Tokyo's forces of law and order donned their riot gear to oust the Takenokozoku – the dancers with 1950s rockabilly hair – from Yoyogi-kōen (above), no-one imagined that the Takenokozoku would be replaced by an even odder, younger crowd.

Enter the Cosplay-zoku, the Costume Play Gang. Mainly teenage girls from the dormitory towns and cities around Tokyo's fringe, the Cosplay-zoku assemble at Harajuku's Jingū-bashi each weekend, bedecked in goth make-up, kimono punk getups, subversive Edwardiana and cartoon-nurse exaggeration.

Cosplay-zoku are united in their fondness for Japanese *visual-kei* (visual type) bands or *anime* and manga characters, and a sense of pride in their alienation. Many of the girls are *ijime-ko*, kids bullied in school, who find release and expression in their temporary weekend identities.

The end result is Tokyo's famous weekend circus of excited photographers, bewildered tourists and cultural voyeurs. The girls revel, primp and pose for the cameras until dusk, when they hop on their trains back to 'normal' life in the faceless housing blocks of Chiba and Kawasaki.

years later. The poor dog's faithfulness was not lost on the locals, who built a statue to honour his memory.

TOBACCO & SALT MUSEUM
たばこと塩の博物館

This unusual little **museum** (Map p117; ☎ 3476-2041; 1-16-8 Jinnan, Shibuya-ku; adult/child ¥100/50; ☼ 10am-6pm Tue-Sun; ◉ JR Yamanote line to Shibuya, Hachikō exit) has some fairly interesting exhibits detailing the history of tobacco and the methods of salt production practised in pre-modern Japan (until recently, Japan harvested all its salt from the sea). While there's little English signage, much of the material is self-explanatory.

TEPCO ELECTRIC ENERGY MUSEUM
電力館

Folks with kids in tow and an interest in electric power might want to stop by the **Tepco Electric Energy Museum** (Denryokukan; Map p117; ☎ 3477-1191; 1-12-10 Jinnan, Shibuya-ku; admission free; ☼ 10am-6pm Thu-Tue; ◉ JR Yamanote line to Shibuya, Hachikō exit). Displays are well presented and cover everything associated with electricity, and each of the seven floors supplies English handouts with explanations. It's just north of the Marui One department store along Fire-dōri.

LOVE HOTEL HILL

Around the top of Dōgenzaka is the highest concentration of **love hotels** (also primly referred to as 'boutique' hotels) in Japan. There's a love hotel for everyone, from miniature Gothic castles to Middle Eastern temples…and these are just the buildings – room themes are even wackier. It's OK to wander in and take a look at the screen with illuminated pictures of available rooms.

The area is also home to alfresco cafés, *izakaya* (pub-style restaurant), performance halls and restaurants. Huge live-music venues and dance clubs line this lively slope.

Ebisu & Daikanyama 恵比寿・代官山

More low-key than crowded Shibuya and Shinjuku, Ebisu and Daikanyama (Map p121) are stylish neighbourhoods that make great spots for a casual afternoon wander. Daikanyama has a very natural Euro-Japanese fusion atmosphere, with abundant alfresco cafés and boutiques featuring imaginative local designers. Neighbouring Ebisu, mean-

while, possesses some of Tokyo's better clubs and bars, and the open-air Yebisu Garden Place complex.

YEBISU GARDEN PLACE
恵比寿ガーデンプレイス

This **complex** (Map p121; ☎ 5423-7111; http://garden place.jp; 4-20 Ebisu, Shibuya-ku; ◉ JR Yamanote line to Ebisu, east exit to Skywalk) of shops, restaurants and a 39-floor **tower** is surrounded by an open mall area – perfect for hanging out on warmer days, when you might catch live music. Located here, the headquarters of Sapporo Breweries contains the **Beer Museum Yebisu** (☎ 5423-7255; 4-20-1 Ebisu, Shibuya-ku; admission free; ☼ 10am-6pm Tue-Sun). There are lots of good exhibits, but the real draw is the Tasting Lounge, where you can sample Sapporo's various brews (¥200 a glass).

You'll find restaurants and outdoor cafés in every building. Check out the views of Tokyo from the Ebisu perspective at restaurants on the 38th and 39th floors of **Yebisu Garden Place Tower**.

Finally, check out the **Tokyo Metropolitan Museum of Photography** (☎ 3280-0099; www.syabi .com/top/top_eng.html; 1-13-3 Mita, Meguro-ku; admission varies; ☼ 10am-6pm Tue-Wed, Sat & Sun, to 8pm Thu & Fri), Japan's first large-scale museum devoted entirely to photography. The emphasis here is on Japanese photography, but international work is also displayed.

Roppongi & Akasaka 六本木・赤坂

Rife with restaurants and bars, Roppongi's nightlife rocks. Though there aren't many compelling reasons to visit the neighbourhood during the daytime, **Roppongi Hills** (Map p119) is worth checking out for shopping, cinema and art exhibitions.

Likewise, Akasaka is of interest less for its sights than for its high concentration of top-end hotels. Still, the area has a few attractions if you find yourself here.

ROPPONGI HILLS 六本木ヒルズ

This massive development was no less than 17 years in the making, conceived by developer Mori Minoru, who envisioned improving people's quality of urban life by centralising home, work and leisure into a microcosm of a city. If a million visitors per weekend is any indication of success, this is overshadowed only by the magnitude of the place itself. The shopping-dining-entertainment-housing complex is embellished with public art and a Japanese garden, and is so big as to warrant **guided tours** (Map p119; ☎ 6406-6677; www.roppongihills.com/jp/tour/detail_019.html; Roppongi 6-chōme, Minato-ku; adult/student/child ¥1500/1000/500; 🕑 9am-6pm; 🚇 Hibiya, Toei Ōedo lines to Roppongi, exits 1c & 3) – book seven days in advance.

Mori Art Museum 森美術館
Making its debut in 2003, this contemporary **art museum** (Map p119; ☎ 5777-8600; www.mori.art.museum; 53rd fl, Roppongi Hills Mori Tower, 6-10-1 Roppongi, Minato-ku; admission incl entry to Tokyo City View about ¥1500; 🕑 10am-10pm Wed-Mon, to 5pm Tue) boasts an enviable location at the top of Mori Tower. Exhibitions tend towards the (mind-bogglingly myriad) multimedia variety and are of a respectably high calibre. As yet lacking a permanent collection, the museum is only open during its temporary exhibitions. Check the website for current shows.

Tokyo City View 東京シティビュー
The eponymous **view** (Map p119; ☎ 6406-6652; 52nd fl, Roppongi Hills Mori Tower, 6-10-1 Roppongi, Minato-ku; adult/student/child ¥1500/1000/500; 🕑 9-1am, last admission midnight) offers 360 degrees' worth of Tokyo. If the floor-to-ceiling windows don't give you enough of an eyeful, there's an open-air deck that's open when weather permits.

HIE-JINJA 日枝神社
This modern shrine is largely cement, but the highlight of **Hie-jinja** (Map pp124-5; ☎ 3581-2471; www.hiejinja.net/jinja/english/index.html; 2-10-5 Nagatachō, Chiyoda-ku; 🚇 Ginza, Marunouchi lines to Akasaka-mitsuke, Belle Vie exit) is the walk up to the shrine through a 'tunnel' of orange *torii* – a spectacular sight during cherry-blossom season. Walking south on Sotobori-dōri, look for the concrete plaza-style entrance leading up to the shrine gates.

TOKYO TOWER 東京タワー
Nine metres taller than the Eiffel Tower, on which it is based, the 333m **Tokyo Tower** (Map pp124-5; ☎ 3433-5111; www.tokyotower.co.jp/333/foreign/eng/index.html; 4-2-8 Shiba-kōen, Minato-ku; main observation deck ¥310-820, special observation deck extra ¥350-600; 🕑 9am-10pm; 🚇 Hibiya line to Kamiyamachō, exits 1 & 2) is a pleasantly retro spire from which to look out across Tokyo. Completed in 1958, it stands as a kind of gaudy orange counterpoint to ultramodern Roppongi Hills.

While the daytime view is unremarkable, the night view is stellar. If you spring for admission to the special observation deck at 250m, the trip up in that wonky elevator is almost as exciting as the view.

Behind Tokyo Tower, **Zōjō-ji** (Map pp124-5; ☎ 3432-1431; 4-7-35 Shiba-kōen, Minato-ku; 🕑 dawn-dusk; 🚇 Toei Ōedo line to Akabanebashi, Akabanebashi exit) was the family temple of the Tokugawas. In the evening, we recommend walking to Tokyo Tower from Hamamatsuchō station on the JR Yamanote line. Cut through Zōjō-ji and admire the bizarre juxtaposition of the illuminated tower leaping skyward above the dark shape of the main hall.

ŌKURA SHŪKOKAN 大倉集古館
The grounds of the venerable Ōkura Hotel contain this small **museum** (Map pp124-5; ☎ 3583-0781; 2-10-3 Toranomon, Minato-ku; adult ¥800, student ¥300-500; 🕑 10am-4.30pm Tue-Sun; 🚇 Ginza line to Tameike-sannō, exit 13), with its collection of sculpture, lacquer writing boxes and no fewer than three National Treasures. The two-storey museum is also surrounded by a small but well-populated sculpture garden.

AOYAMA REIEN 青山霊園
Better known as **Aoyama Botchi** (Map p119; Minami-Aoyama 2-chōme, Minato-ku; 🕑 24hr; 🚇 Ginza line to Gaienmae, exits 1 & 2), this cemetery is a good alternative to Ueno-kōen during *hanami* season, but perfect for a peaceful walk at any time when the masses of the living are too overwhelming. Head south on Gaien-nishi-dōri to get there.

Odaiba & Tokyo Bay お台場・東京湾
A futuristic island in Tokyo Bay, Odaiba (Map p122) was built on reclaimed land and stands as another reminder that Tokyo is a forward-looking, oddball waterfront city.

There's tonnes to do here besides enjoying the views of Tokyo and the bay, most of it in megamall-amusement park complexes. Shopping malls include **Decks Tokyo Beach** (Map p122; ☎ 3599-6500; www.odaiba-decks.com; 1-6-1 Daiba, Minato-ku; 🕑 11am-9pm; 🚇 Yurikamome line to Odaiba Kaihin-kōen), with a Hong Kong–themed mall and Sega amusement centre, or the women-focused shopping experience of **Venus Fort** (Map p122; ☎ 3599-0700; www.venusfort.co.jp/index.html; Palette Town, Aomi 1-chōme, Kōtō-ku; 🕑 shops 11am-9pm Sun-Fri, to 10pm Sat, restaurants to 11pm; 🚇 Yurikamome to Aomi or Rinkai line to Tokyo Teleport) – complete with kitschy 18th-century Italian styling!

The easiest way to get to Ōdaiba is on the driverless Yurikamome line, which connects at Shimbashi station.

OFF THE BEATEN DŌRI

Not far from the city centre are two of Tokyo's coolest, out-of-the-way neighbourhoods that, while as contemporary as they come, seem more low scale and personable than some of central Tokyo's more overwhelming districts.

One favourite is **Kichijōji**, about 10km west of Shinjuku and centred on Inokashira Park, which surrounds a large pond that feeds the Kanda River. If you have a ticket to the **Ghibli Museum** (p142), meander through the park on the way to your appointment with the Cat Bus. On weekends, there's an impromptu arts-and-crafts market and bands playing around the lake. The road leading from station to park is packed with little cafés, shops and bars, making it a wonderful getaway for a few hours, or an entire day and evening. To get there, take the JR Chūō or Sōbu line to Kichijōji and take the park exit. Walk to the Marui department store and hang a left on the road to its right. This road leads down to the park.

Similarly stocked with second-hand shops, bars, cafés and an artsy vibe is **Shimo-Kitazawa**, about 2.5km from Shibuya. Take the Keiō Inokashira line from Shibuya to Shimo-Kitazawa and make a circle through the neighbourhood. From the north exit, turn right and wander the boutique-and-café-filled alleys before heading back towards the train tracks. Cross the tracks to check out more shops, lively restaurants, tiny clubs and bars. Once you've travelled your loop, find the south entrance to the station on that side of the tracks.

MUSEUM OF MARITIME SCIENCE
船の科学館

This ship-shaped **museum** (Fune-no-Kagakukan; Map p122; ☎ 5500-1111; www.funenokagakukan.or.jp; 3-1 Higashi-Yashio, Shinagawa-ku; adult/child ¥1000/600; ⊙ 10am-5pm Mon-Fri, to 6pm Sat & Sun; ◉ Yurikamome line to Fune-no-Kagakukan) has four floors of excellent displays dealing with every aspect of ships and shipping, with loads of highly detailed models. The 4m-long version of the largest battleship ever built, the *Yamato*, is stunning in detail and craftsmanship. There are also lots of hands-on exhibits that kids will love.

NATIONAL MUSEUM OF EMERGING SCIENCE & INNOVATION 日本科学未来館

Also known as the **Miraikan** (Map p122; ☎ 3570-9151; www.miraikan.jst.go.jp; 2-41 Aomi, Kōtō-ku; adult/under 18 ¥500/200, children on Sat free; ⊙ 10am-5pm Wed-Mon; ◉ Yurikamome line to Fune-no-Kagakukan or Telecom Center), this is undoubtedly Japan's best science museum and terrific for kids. Its hands-on exhibits are fun, as well as genuinely educational, whether you're 'driving' a virtual horse around Ōdaiba, building your own robot, or fathoming how Medaka riverfish could copulate in zero gravity aboard the space shuttle.

ŌEDO-ONSEN MONOGATARI
大江戸温泉物語

Modelled on an old Edo town, this **onsen** (Map p122; ☎ 5500-1126; www.ooedoonsen.jp in Japanese; 2-57 Aomi, Kōtō-ku; adult ¥1575-2827, child ¥840-1575; ⊙ 11am-9am, last entry at 2am; ◉ Yurikamome line to Telecom Center) pipes in natural mineral water from 1400m beneath Tokyo Bay. Though it sounds a little hokey, the park is attractively designed, with lovely mixed-gender (clothes required!) outdoor pools as well as traditional baths. Admission fees cover the rental of *yukata* and towels, and there are old-style restaurants and souvenir shops for a postbath bite and browse. Additional charges apply on weekends and holidays if you arrive after 6pm and stay for more than four hours.

TOYOTA MEGA WEB トヨタメガウェブ

Car fiends and kids can get behind the wheel of hybrid and electric cars at **Toyota Mega Web** (Map p122; ☎ 3599-0808; www.megaweb.gr.jp/english; Palette Town, Aomi 1-chōme, Kōtō-ku; admission free; ⊙ 11am-9pm; ◉ Yurikamome line to Aomi), one of Toyota's company showrooms. Some attractions close at 8pm and the whole place closes on varying days each month, so consult the website before cruising by.

Elsewhere in Tokyo
MUSEUMS & GALLERIES

For a more complete listing of museums and galleries in Tokyo, get hold of the TIC's *Museums & Art Galleries* pamphlet. Better still, look for *Tokyo Museums – A Complete Guide* (1993) by Thomas and Ellen Flannigan, which covers everything from the Tombstone Museum to the Button Museum.

You'll have to book several months before your trip if you want to get into the **Ghibli**

Museum (Map pp112-13; ☎ information 0570-000-777; www .ghibli-museum.jp/ticket/overseas.html; 1-1-83 Shimo-Renjaku, Mitaka-shi; adult ¥1000, child ¥100-700; ☯ 10am-6pm Wed-Mon; ☺ JR Chūō line to Mitaka, south exit). This wonderland from *anime* master Miyazaki Hayao's Studio Ghibli is geared towards children, but anyone who fell in love with *Howl's Moving Castle* or *Spirited Away* should try to visit. Each ticket contains an original animation cel from a Studio Ghibli film. Visit the website for ticket-purchase information and directions. You can also access the museum via Inokashira Park in Kichijōji (see the boxed text, p141).

The **Edo-Tokyo Museum** (Map pp112-13; ☎ 3626-9974; www.edo-tokyo-museum.or.jp; 1-4-1 Yokoami, Sumida-ku; adult/child ¥600/free, student ¥300-450; ☯ 9.30am-5.30pm Tue, Wed, Sat & Sun, to 8pm Thu-Fri; ☺ JR Sōbu line Ryōgoku or Toei Ōedo line to Ryōgoku, exit A4) is a gem, with a model of the bridge at Nihombashi dividing this vast display of re-creations of Edo-period and Meiji-period Tokyo. It's just behind Ryōgoku Sumō Stadium & Museum.

Near the main entrance of Ryōgoku Sumō Stadium, the **Sumō Museum** (Map pp112-13; ☎ 3622-0366; www.sumo.or.jp; 1-3-28 Yokoami, Sumida-ku; admission free; ☯ 10am-4.30pm Mon-Fri; ☺ JR Sōbu line Ryōgoku or Toei Ōedo line to Ryōgoku, exit A4) features interesting displays with sumō memorabilia, although there's no interpretive signage in English. During the grand tournaments in January, May and September the museum is open daily, but only to those attending the tournament.

The **Meguro Parasitological Museum** (Map p121; ☎ 3716-1264; 4-1-1 Shimo-Meguro, Meguro-ku; admission free; ☯ 10am-5pm Tue-Sun; ☺ JR Yamanote, Namboku, Toei Mita lines to Meguro, west exit) is not for arachnophobes, but kids will find it irresistible. The crowning glory here is the preserved 8.8m-long tapeworm removed from the gut of a 40-year-old Yokohama man – if this doesn't give you the heebie-jeebies, step right up. Walk west along Meguro-dōri and find it about 400m past the Meguro River.

AMUSEMENT PARKS

Tokyo Disneyland (Map pp112-13; ☎ 045-683-3777; www.tokyodisneyresort.co.jp; 1-1 Maihama, Urayasu-shi, Chiba; one-day ticket adult/youth/child ¥5800/5000/3900; ☯ vary; ☺ JR Keiyō line to Maihama) is a near-perfect replica of the original in Anaheim, California, from Space Mountain to Pirates of the Caribbean. As at the original Disneyland, there are often long queues at popular rides. The resort

is open year-round except for about a dozen days a year (most of them in January), and opening hours vary seasonally, so check the website before heading out. To get there, catch the JR Keiyō line from Tokyo station.

Kōrakuen Amusement Park (Map pp126-7; ☎ 5800-9999; Tokyo Dome City, 1-3-61 Kōraku, Bunkyō-ku; adult/child ¥1200/600, most rides ¥600, unlimited rides adult/child ¥3300/2600; ☯ 10am-10pm; ☺ JR Chūō, Sōbu lines to Suidobashi or Marunouchi line to Kōrakuen, Kōrakuen exit) is of the old shake-rattle-and-roll school, and is popular precisely for that reason. The Ultra Twister roller coaster is a thriller; Geopolis is a hi-tech addition to the amusement park. If you don't want to buy a day pass, you can pay per ride (¥400 to ¥1000).

ACTIVITIES
Sentō & Onsen

A good soak at a *sentō* (public bath) or *onsen* (mineral hot-spring spa) is a great way to relax after a day pounding the pavements of Tokyo. For a primer on bath etiquette, see p75.

Azabu-Jūban Onsen (Map p119; ☎ 3404-2610; 3rd fl, 1-5-22 Azabu-Jūban, Minato-ku; admission ¥1260; ☯ 11am-9pm Wed-Mon; ☺ Namboku, Toei Ōedo lines to Azabu-Jūban, exit 4) is accustomed to foreign visitors (and tattoos) and has some helpful English signage. The dark, tea-coloured water here is scalding hot, and there's a lovely *rotemburo* (outdoor bath). Sunday afternoons mean live traditional music in the tatami tearoom. Downstairs, there's a less expensive, more bare-bones *sentō*. The nondescript building has a small sign in English; it's on the corner of Kurayamizaka and Azabu-Jūban-dōri.

Jakotsu-yu Onsen (Map pp130-1; ☎ 3841-8645; www .jakotsuyu.co.jp in Japanese; 1-11-11 Asakusa, Taitō-ku; admission ¥400; ☯ 1pm-midnight Wed-Mon; ☺ Ginza line to Tawaramachi, exit 3) One of the hottest in town, with mineral-rich dark water at 45°C. This *onsen* has a small *rotemburo* with a garden setting. From Kokusai-dōri, make a right into the second alley north of Kaminarimon-dōri, then slip into the first narrow alley on the right.

In the same neighbourhood, near Sensō-ji, **Asakusa Kannon Onsen** (Map pp130-1; ☎ 3844-4141; 2-7-6 Asakusa, Taitō-ku; admission ¥700; ☯ 6.30am-6pm Thu-Tue; ☺ Ginza line to Asakusa, exits 1, 3 & 6) is a large old bathhouse with lots of room and historic ambience appropriate for a contemplative soak. Look for its ivy-covered exterior.

Kitsch-seekers should head straight for Ōedo-Onsen Monogatari (p141) in Odaiba. Some bigger *sentō* include the following:

Finlando Sauna (Map p116; ☎ 3209-9196; 1-20-1 Kabukichō, Shinjuku-ku; admission noon-5pm ¥1900, 5pm-midnight ¥2100, midnight-noon ¥2600; ⊙ 24hr; ⊕ JR Yamanote line to Shinjuku, east exit) A huge complex of baths and steam rooms in the middle Kabukichō, for men only.

Green Plaza Ladies Sauna (Map p116; ☎ 3207-5411; 9th fl, 1-29-2 Kabukichō, Shinjuku-ku; admission 6am-10pm ¥2700, 10pm-6am ¥3300; ⊙ 24hr; ⊕ JR Yamanote line to Shinjuku, east exit) Another spot in Kabukichō, this one's for the ladies, with the added novel bonus of a rooftop *rotemburo*.

WALKING TOUR

If you've only a day or two in Tokyo, east Shinjuku is a great place to sample a taste of Tokyo's cheery sensory overload. From inside Shinjuku station, follow the east exit or Kabukichō exit signs. Once you've passed through the ticket gates, take the 'My City' exit. As you surface, directly ahead of you is the **Studio Alta Building (1)** and its enormous video screen.

Continue walking east down Shinjuku-dōri past the bargain men's clothing and shoe shops. A little further on is **Kinokuniya bookshop (2**; p106), with its superb collection of English books on the 7th floor. Continue walking and you'll pass **Mitsukoshi department store (3**; p179) on the right and on the left, the Art Deco **Isetan Building (4**; p179), which contains fashionable boutiques and the Isetan Art Gallery on the 5th floor. The gallery hosts a variety of art exhibits by Japanese artists; hours vary and admission is free.

Turn left at Isetan and walk down to Yasukuni-dōri. A lane on the opposite side of the road leads to **Hanazono-jinja (5**; p136), which nestles so close to Tokyo's most infamous red-light district that its clientele can make for some interesting people-watching. The shrine has a reputation for bringing success to business ventures – both legitimate and otherwise.

Exit Hanazono-jinja onto **Golden Gai (6**; p163), a tiny network of alleyways devoted entirely to small, stand-up watering holes. Traditionally the haunt of bohemian Tokyo-ites, it's a safe area to take a walk, even by night (by day it's usually deserted). If you decide to stop for a drink, keep in mind that some bars serve regulars only. It's rumoured that this little maze is gradually being bought up by Seibu department store, but for now the Golden Gai hangs on.

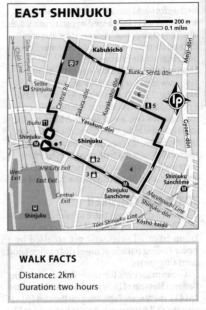

EAST SHINJUKU

WALK FACTS

Distance: 2km
Duration: two hours

Continue in the same direction along the alleyways that run parallel to Yasukuni-dōri and you'll reach **Kabukichō** (p136), Tokyo's notorious red-light district. Despite its reputation, it's a relatively safe area to walk around. Most of what goes on in these environs is pretty much inaccessible to foreigners, though single men are likely to be approached by touts offering to take them to one of the 'pink cabarets'.

Continue along the perimeter of Kabukichō and look for the enormous **Koma Theatre (7)**, which started off as a cinema, but quickly switched to stage shows. It still hosts performances of a more mainstream variety than those elsewhere in Kabukichō. The square facing the Koma is ringed by cinemas and is also a popular busking spot at night, though *yakuza* (mafia) are usually quick about moving anyone too popular along. Take any of the lanes radiating off the square to see Kabukichō at its best.

From this point wander back to Yasukuni-dōri and take one of the lanes that connect it with Shinjuku-dōri.

COURSES

A Taste of Culture (☎ 5716 5751; www.tasteofculture .com; courses from ¥5500) Perhaps your last meal has inspired you to learn how to assemble beautiful, balanced *bentō* (boxed meals) yourself? These folks can teach you how. Courses run by English-speaking culinary pros include informative tastings, cooking classes and market tours. Check out the website for current classes on offer; customised courses can also be arranged.

Sōgetsu School of Ikebana (Map p119; ☎ 3408-1151; www.sogetsu.or.jp/english/index.html; Sōgetsu Kaikan Bldg, 7-2-21 Akasaka, Minato-ku; courses ¥4850; ⏰ 10am-5pm Mon-Thu & Sat, to 8pm Fri; ⊕ Ginza, Hanzōmon, Toei Ōedo lines to Aoyama-itchōme, exit 4) If you're interested in the art of *ikebana*, this offers courses taught in English. The avant-garde Sōgetsu School was founded on the idea that there are no limits to *ikebana*, nor to where or when it can be practised. Call ahead for information about classes; prices include flowers and tax.

TOKYO FOR CHILDREN

Tokyo is a dangerous place to take children, as they'll be doted upon, find sources of stimulation from all sides, and get accosted by a never ending parade of novel distractions and tempting treats.

Great museums for rainy days include the **National Museum of Emerging Science & Innovation** (p141), the **Meguro Parasitological Museum** (p142) and the **Ghibli Museum** (p142). Showrooms like the **Sony Building** (p132) and **Toyota Mega Web** (p141) have terrific interactive activities. Fair-weather jaunts could include **Ueno Zoo** (p134), weekends at **Yoyogi Park** (p138) and Tokyo's **amusement parks** (p142).

Tokyo's toy shops are always a huge hit, notably **Hakuhinkan Toy Park** (p180) and **Kiddyland** (p180).

TOURS

The best way to get under the skin of any city is to have a local show you around, and in Tokyo you can meet up with someone to do just that, gratis.

Mr Oka (www.homestead.com/mroka; half-day from ¥2000) A wonderful, well-informed English-speaking guide who conducts walking tours around the city.

Tokyo Free Guide (www.tokyofreeguide.com) A group of volunteer tour guides who will tailor walking tours according to your interests. You'll have to pay for any admission and transport fees and your own meals. Guides' language skills may vary, but it's a great way to get around and get to know a friendly Tokyoite. Book before you arrive in town.

Several reliable bus companies offer a wide variety of Tokyo tours, from all-day, city-wide affairs to shorter, half-day tours or evenings taking in sukiyaki dinners and performances

at Kabuki-za (p132). All of the following companies provide English-speaking guides and most tours pick up guests at various major hotels around town.

Hato Bus Tours (Map pp124-5; ☎ 3435-6081; www.hato bus.com; World Trade Center Bldg, 2-4-1 Hamamatsuchō, Minato-ku; ⏰ 9am-7pm) Among its variety of tours, the Panoramic Tour (¥9800) takes in most of Tokyo's major sights and includes lunch and a Tokyo Bay cruise. Some tours depart from Hamamatsuchō bus terminal.

Japan Gray Line (Map pp124-5; ☎ 3595-5939; fax 3595-5948; www.jgl.co.jp/inbound/traveler/traveler.htm; 1-4-2 Toranomon, Minato-ku; ⏰ 9am-6pm) Gray Line tours are slightly more limited than JTB's in choice but similar in scope.

JTB's Sunrise Tours (Map pp112-13; ☎ 5796-5454; www.jtbgmt.com/sunrisetour; 2-3-11 Higashi-Shinagawa, Shinagawa-ku; ⏰ 9am-6pm) Sunrise's general sightseeing tours are nearly identical to the Hato Bus offerings. Half-day morning or afternoon tours go for ¥5000.

FESTIVALS & EVENTS

There is a festival of one sort or another every day in Tokyo. Call or visit the JNTO's TIC for up-to-date information. Some of the major celebrations:

Ganjitsu At New Year, Tokyoites head to Meiji-jingū (Map p117), Sensō-ji (Map pp130-1) or Yasukuni-jinja (Map pp126-7).

Hanami (Cherry Blossom Viewing) Chaotic at Ueno-kōen (p133), peaceful at Shinjuku-gyoen (p137); early to mid-April).

Sanja Matsuri A massive festival on the third weekend of May, where 100 *mikoshi* (portable shrines) are paraded through Asakusa.

Samba Matsuri Asakusa's famous wild summer samba extravaganza in late August.

Bōnen-kai Season This last one isn't an official festival at all, but the late-December period leading up to New Year, when the Japanese hold their drink-and-be-merry year-end parties.

SLEEPING

In Tokyo you can choose from the whole range of Japanese accommodation, from capsule hotels to ryokan, but budget accommodation in Tokyo is a bit pricier than elsewhere. Hotels are expensive, and prices quoted here are exclusive of the additional 5% consumption tax as well the accommodation tax of ¥100/200 per person per night on hotel rates over ¥10,000/15,000. Higher-end accommodations add insult to financial injury with service charges of 10% to 18%. Top-end establishments typically accept credit cards, but many midrange hotels do not – best to check beforehand. Booking online usually nets well-discounted rates, especially at higher-end hotels.

Most midrange hotels in Tokyo are business hotels and are reasonably priced. Always check what time your hotel locks its doors before heading out at night – though some hotels stay open all night, many lock up at midnight or 1am.

If you can make a few concessions to Japanese etiquette, ryokan and *minshuku* (Japanese equivalent of a B&B) are quite inexpensive, with rates from around ¥4500 per person. In Tokyo, unlike elsewhere in Japan, ryokan may offer meals for an extra fee and may not supply basic amenities like towels or toiletries.

At youth hostels and so-called 'gaijin houses' (foreigner houses) you can get single rates down to ¥3500 per person (about as low as it gets in Tokyo). But youth hostels impose an early-evening curfew, and *gaijin* houses typically require minimum stays of one month.

The **Welcome Inn Reservation Center** (www.itcj.jp; Narita Airport Terminals 1 & 2; ◷ 8am-8pm), with another location at the TIC (p109) in central Tokyo, is a free service that will make reservations for you at hotels and ryokan in the Japan Welcome Inn hotel group.

If you absolutely must find inexpensive accommodation, book before you arrive. Flying into Narita – particularly at night – without accommodation lined up can be hellish. For hotels near Narita airport, see p230.

For more detailed information on capsule hotels, *gaijin* houses, hostels and love hotels, see p784.

Tokyo International Youth Hostel (Map pp126–7; ☎ 3235-1107, fax 3267-4000; www.tokyo-ih.jp; 1-1 Kagura-kashi, Shinjuku-ku; dm ¥3860; ✕ 🖳 ; ◉ JR Sōbu line to Iidabashi, west exit or Namboku, Tōzai, Yūrakuchō, Toei Ōedo lines to Iidabashi, B2b exit) No membership is required here, credit cards are accepted and you can book ahead online. The hostel is on the 18th floor of the Ramla Building, which towers next to Iidabashi station. Check-in is 3pm to 10pm, and breakfast/dinner costs a paltry ¥450/900. The Narita airport TIC (see p109) has a step-by-step instruction sheet on the cheapest way to get from airport to hostel.

Sakura Hostel (Map pp130–1; ☎ 3847-8111, fax 3847-8112; www.sakura-hostel.co.jp; 2-24-2 Asakusa, Taitō-ku; dm from ¥2940; ✕ 🖳 ; ◉ Ginza line to Tawaramachi, exit 3)

Run by the friendly and eminently helpful Sakura House folks who also run an empire of *gaijin* houses, this cheery hostel requires no membership and includes amenities like laundry facilities, bike rentals and kitchen. Bonus: no curfew. See the website for a map and detailed directions from the airport.

Central Tokyo 東京中心部

Along with Akasaka, Ginza is home to the thickest concentration of elite hotels in Tokyo. Prices here reflect the desirable real estate and proximity to Tokyo station, great shopping, good restaurants, all manner of theatre, and the political and financial districts of the city.

BUDGET

Sakura Hotel (Map pp126–7; ☎ 3261-3939, fax 3264-2777; www.sakura-hotel.co.jp; 2-21-4 Kanda-Jimbōchō, Chiyoda-ku; dm/s/d ¥3780/7140/8200; ✕ 🖳 ; ◉ Hanzōmon, Toei Mita, Toei Shinjuku lines to Jimbōchō, exits A1 & A6) Email ahead for reservations at this reliable, sociable spot in the bookshop district. The helpful staff is bilingual, the bar-café is open 24 hours and there's a coin-operated laundry. From the A6 exit, walk south and turn right at the *kōban* (police box); the hotel is 200m on the right. Check-in is at 1pm.

MIDRANGE

All of the hotels listed in this section accept credit cards, unless indicated otherwise.

Hotel Villa Fontaine Shiodome (Map pp124–5; ☎ 3569-2220, fax 3569-2221; www.villa-fontaine.co.jp /eng/shiodome/index.html; 1-9-2 Higashi-Shimbashi, Minato-ku; s/d/tw from ¥10,000/14,000/18,000, all incl breakfast; ✕ 🖳 ; ◉ Toei Ōedo line to Shiodome, exit 10) This place is a superb midrange deal with an upscale feel. Lighting in lobby areas is dim and subtly spooky, but the rooms are comfortable and modern, with internet-TV and high-speed LAN. No great views here, but it does offer the rarity of a complimentary buffet breakfast. Check-in 3pm.

Yaesu Terminal Hotel (Map pp126–7; ☎ 3281-3771, fax 3281-3089; www.yth.jp; 1-5-14 Yaesu, Chūō-ku; s/d from ¥11,340/16,590; ✕ 🖳 ; ◉ JR Yamanote line to Tokyo, Yaesu north exit or Ginza line to Nihombashi, exit B3) Near Tokyo station, this business hotel sports clean lines. Rooms are quite small, but prices are good for this area and it feels a touch classier than your typical business hotel. The in-house restaurant's wall of plate-glass windows looks onto streetside treetops. Check-in is 1pm.

MISSING THE MIDNIGHT TRAIN

Cinderellas who've stayed out partying past midnight and found that their last train has turned into a *kabocha* (Japanese pumpkin) needn't fret. If dancing the night away doesn't appeal, and an astronomically priced taxi ride doesn't compute, give the capsule hotel a miss and try a *manga kissa* instead.

Kissaten (coffee shops) have long been mainstays for socialising away from home, but the next-generation versions offer a place for watching DVDs, getting some Playstation action, catching up on email or catching some Zs. *Manga kissa* have libraries of DVDs and manga, bottomless cups of coffee and soft drinks, inexpensive food, and have staff making regular rounds to assure safe surfing and sleeping.

Overnight rates – typically around ¥2500 for eight hours – are a bargain. Check in at the reception desk, prepay for your stay and while away the wee hours in a cosy private cubicle. Try one of these if you're stranded:

Aprecio (Map p116; ☎ 3205-7336; www.aprecio.co.jp in Japanese; B1 fl, Hygeia Plaza, 2-44-1 Kabukichō, Shinjuku-ku; 1st 30min ¥300, 10min thereafter ¥100; ⊘ 24hr; ⊘ JR Yamanote line to Shinjuku, east exit) This clean, comfortable spot in Kabukichō offers all the usuals in smoking and nonsmoking wings, plus massage and beauty services, billiards and darts.

Bagus Gran Cyber Cafe (Map p117; ☎ 5428-3676; www.bagus-99.com/netcafe in Japanese; 6th fl, 28-6 Udagawachō, Shibuya-ku; per 8hr ¥1500; ⊘ 24hr; ⊘ JR Yamanote line to Shibuya, Hachikō exit) This popular chain has branches all over Tokyo.

Manga Hiroba (Map p119; ☎ 3497-1751; 2nd fl, Shuwa Roppongi Bldg, 3-14-12 Roppongi, Minato-ku; 1st hr ¥380, 30min thereafter ¥150; ⊘ 24hr; ⊘ Hibiya, Toei Ōedo lines to Roppongi, exit 3) Along Gaien-higashi-dōri, this one's handy for pre- or post-party surfing but is always crowded.

Ginza Nikkō Hotel (Map pp124-5; ☎ 3571-4911; fax 3571-8379; www.ginza-nikko-hotel.com/english/index.html; 8-4-21 Ginza, Chūō-ku; s/d/tw from ¥13,960/29,075/27,920; ✗ ✗ ; ⊘ JR Yamanote line to Shimbashi, Ginza exit or Ginza, Marunouchi line to Shimbashi, exit 5) In a prime location right on Sotobori-dōri between Ginza and Shimbashi, this is a quality business hotel with cosy rooms and decently sized bathtubs. Check-in is at 1pm.

Tokyo Green Hotel Ochanomizu (Map pp126-7; ☎ 3255-4161; fax 3255-4962; www.greenhotel.co.jp/en/hotel_list/ochanomizu.html; 2-6 Kanda-Awajichō, Chiyoda-ku; s/d/tw ¥8400/13,000/14,000; ✗ ✗ ▢ ; ⊘ JR Chūō line to Ochanomizu, Hijiribashi exit or Marunouchi line to Awajichō, exit A5) Though the neighbourhood offers little of interest, this clean, thoughtfully renovated business hotel is the nicest in Kanda. Its visual appeal makes it a lovely oasis within the surrounding monotonous concrete jungle, with comfortable and spotless rooms and a friendly staff. Look for the hotel's bamboo-covered entryway along Sotobori-dōri.

Mitsui Urban Hotel Ginza (Map pp124-5; ☎ 3572-4131; fax 3572-4254; www.mitsuikanko.co.jp/english/map/m_htm/gin.htm; 8-6-15 Ginza, Chūō-ku; s/d ¥14,500/25,000; ✗ ✗ ▢ ; ⊘ JR Yamanote line to Shimbashi, Ginza exit or Ginza, Marunouchi line to Shimbashi, exit 3) Everything about this place is shiny, shiny. Rooms here have an elegant feel and the usual amenities; this is a solid choice for comfortable accommodation at this end of Ginza. The ground-floor café has nice rounded windows for scoping the street over your morning cuppa. Check-in is at 1pm.

Ryokan Ryūmeikan-Honten (Map pp126-7; ☎ 3251-1135; fax 3251-0270; www.ryumeikan.co.jp/honten_e.htm; 3-4 Kanda-Surugadai, Chiyoda-ku; s/d incl breakfast from ¥10,000/17,000; ✗ ▢ ; ⊘ JR Chūō line to Ochanomizu, Hijiribashi exit or Chiyoda line to Shin-Ochanomizu, exit B3) Near Akihabara, this little spot is a good choice for its Japanese-style rooms, offered at rates comparable to most Western-style accommodations, including a continental breakfast. Find it across the boulevard from the Sumitomo Mitsui Insurance building; check-in is at 2pm.

TOP END

Hotel Seiyo Ginza (Map pp124-5; ☎ 3535-1111; fax 3535-1110; www.seiyo-ginza.com; 1-11-2 Ginza, Chūō-ku; r ¥45,000-223,000; ✗ ✗ ▢ ; ⊘ Ginza, Yūrakuchō lines to Ginza-itchōme, exit 7) For an extravagant experience of over-the-top service in impossibly dignified surroundings, book in advance at this exclusive retreat. With only 77 rooms, the Seiyo Ginza is the only hotel in Tokyo providing 24-hour personal butler service for each guest. Check-in is at 2pm; find it on the corner of Chūō-dōri and Sakura-dōri.

Palace Hotel (Map p126-7; ☎ 3211-5211; fax 3211-6987; www.palacehoteltokyo.com; 1-1-1 Marunouchi, Chiyoda-ku; s/d/tw ¥24,000/33,000/38,000; ⊠ ⊠ ⊡ ; ⊖ Chiyoda, Hanzōmon, Marunouchi, Tōzai, Toei Mita lines to Ōtemachi, exit C13b) Directly alongside the Imperial Palace East Garden, this hotel has an classic, old-fashioned atmosphere and arguably the best location in Tokyo. Many rooms here command impressive views over the palace. The service is wonderful, as are the hotel's restaurants. Check-in is at noon.

Imperial Hotel (Map pp124-5; ☎ 3504-1111; fax 3504-9146; www.imperialhotel.co.jp; 1-1-1 Uchisaiwaichō, Chiyoda-ku; s/d from ¥35,700/40,950; ⊠ ⊠ ⊡ ⊠ ; ⊖ Chiyoda, Hibiya, Toei Mita lines to Hibiya, exit A13) One of Tokyo's grand old hotels, the Imperial is within easy walking distance of the Ginza sights and Hibiya-kōen. It has all the amenities of its standard, and rooms are large and tastefully appointed. Check-in is at noon.

Conrad Hotel (Map pp124-5; ☎ 6388-8000; fax 6388-8001; tokyoinfo@conradhotels.com; 1-9-1 Higashi-Shimbashi, Minato-ku; s/d from ¥52,000/57,000; ⊠ ⊠ ⊡ ⊠ ; ⊖ Toei Ōedo line to Shiodome, exit 10) It's Big. Whether you choose city or garden views, you'll find varnished hardwoods and cushy elegance. Enormous bathrooms boast rainshower fixtures, freestanding tubs and floor-to-ceiling glass walls facing the window (automated blinds shut for privacy). Intra-hotel cell phones, a gym overlooking the 25m pool and huge plasma TVs are some of the superlative perks.

our pick **Mitsui Garden Hotel Ginza** (Map pp124-5; ☎ 3543-1131; fax 3543-5531; www.gardenhotels.co.jp/eng /ginza.html; 8-13-1 Ginza, Chūō-ku; s/d from ¥16,800/25,200; ⊠ ⊠ ; ⊖ JR Yamanote line to Shimbashi, Ginza exit or Ginza, Marunouchi lines to Shimbashi, exit 1) Semiorganic urban décor characterises this sleek new hotel. Hardwood details and a minimalist aesthetic meet a glass-walled toilet for, er, two-way views (for very intimate guests). High-tech luxuries include flat-screen TVs and Bose sound systems. Six universal rooms accommodate wheelchair users. Check-in is at 3pm.

Ueno 上野

Ueno may be a bit of a trek from the bright lights, but it's a great sightseeing base – especially for museum buffs – and there are several budget ryokan in the area.

The ryokan here are better value, but if they're all full, the business hotels in the neighbourhood are generally cheaper than those in other areas around Tokyo.

BUDGET

Happily, all of these budget spots accept major credit cards.

Annex Katsutarō Ryokan (Map pp130-1; ☎ 3828-2500; fax 3821-5400; www.katsutaro.com; 3-8-4 Yanaka, Taitō-ku; s/d/tr with bathroom from ¥6300/10,500/14,700; ⊠ ⊠ ⊡ ; ⊖ Chiyoda line to Sendagi, exit 2) All of the bright, Japanese-style rooms at the spotless Annex have Western-style baths attached. Each room has LAN access, but with free internet *and* free coffee in the lobby, why not browse downstairs to chat with the cheery proprietress? Call ahead for directions in English. Credit cards accepted; check-in is at 3pm.

Ryokan Katsutarō (Map pp130-1; ☎ 3821-9808; fax 3821-4789; 4-16-8 Ikenohata, Taitō-ku; s/d/tr without bathroom ¥5200/8400/12,300, d/tr with bathroom ¥9600/13,200; ⊠ ⊠ ⊡ ; ⊖ Chiyoda line to Nezu, exit 2) A pleasant ramble from Ueno Zoo and Ueno Park museums, this tiny, quaint ryokan is run by the friendly brother of the Annex's manager. Western breakfasts cost an extra ¥500. Call for directions from the station or download a map from the website.

Sawanoya Ryokan (Map pp130-1; ☎ 3822-2251; fax 3822-2252; www.tctv.ne.jp/members/sawanoya; 2-3-11 Yanaka, Taitō-ku; s without bathroom ¥4940-5250, d/tr with bathroom ¥9870/14,175; ⊠ ⊡ ⊠ ; ⊖ Chiyoda line to Nezu, exit 1) A cosy, family-run ryokan, Sawanoya is a good choice if you're looking for a home-like atmosphere. Call for walking directions from the station, or download a map from the website. If you're coming from Narita airport, it's inexpensive and easiest to catch a taxi from Ueno station. Check-in is at 2pm.

Sakura Ryokan (Map pp130-1; ☎ 3876-8118; www .sakura-ryokan.com; 2-6-2 Iriya, Taitō-ku; s with/without bathroom ¥6600/5500, d with/without bathroom ¥11,000/10,000; ⊠ ⊡ ; ⊖ Hibiya line to Iriya, exit 1) One stop from Ueno, the modest, family-run Sakura Ryokan is a good base for those interested in staying in contemporary working-class Shitamachi. Definitely opt for a Japanese-style room. Print out a map and directions from the website; check-in is at 3pm. Both Japanese and Western breakfasts cost a reasonable ¥840.

MIDRANGE

Hotel Parkside (Map pp130-1; ☎ 3836-5711; fax 3831-6641; www.parkside.co.jp; 2-11-18 Ueno, Taitō-ku; s/d from ¥9200/15,500, Japanese style d ¥18,000; ⊠ ⊠ ⊡ ; ⊖ JR

Yamanote line to Ueno, Shinobazu exit) Overlooking the gigantic lily pads of Shinobazu Pond, the Parkside is a great choice in this neighbourhood, particularly if you can get a room with a view on the 4th floor or above. It's clean, recently renovated and centrally located, with Japanese-style rooms available. Check-in is at 2pm.

Suigetsu Hotel Ōgaisō (Map pp130-1; ☎ 3822-4611; fax 3823-4340; www.ohgai.co.jp/index-e.html; 3-3-21 Ikenohata, Taitō-ku; Western-style s ¥8000, Japanese-style d ¥25,000; ✗ ✗ ; ◉ Chiyoda line to Nezu, exit 2) On the western side of the park, this hotel combines typical business-hotel comforts with Japanese-style ambience. Though set up like a Western hotel, it offers tatami rooms, several large Japanese-style baths and a lovely garden in the centre of the complex. Check-in is at 3pm.

Hotel Green Capital (Map pp130-1; ☎ 3842-2411; fax 3842-2414; www.thehotel.co.jp/en/green_capital/index .php; 7-8-23 Ueno, Taitō-ku; s/d ¥7875/13,125; ✗ ; ◉ JR Yamanote line to Ueno, Iriya exit) Quite close to Ueno station, this plain-jane business hotel has polite staff and slightly bigger-than-average rooms to recommend it. The rooms are clean and new, and the prices competitive. Check-in is at 3pm.

Asakusa 浅草

If you don't mind sacrificing central location for unpretentious Shitamachi atmosphere, Asakusa (Map pp130–1) is a fine place to stay, with some of Tokyo's best budget accommodations.

BUDGET

Unless otherwise specified, all of the places listed here require payment in full upon check-in, are BYOT (bring your own towel) and none accept credit cards.

Khao San Guesthouse (Map pp130-1; ☎ 3842-8286; www.khaosan-tokyo.com; 2-1-5 Kaminarimon, Taitō-ku; dm/d ¥2200/5000; ✗ ✗ ; ◉ Ginza, Toei Asakusa lines to Asakusa, exits 4 & A2b) Very friendly, remarkably inexpensive and home-like in feel, the Khao San is a warm intro to Tokyo. Located on the bank of the Sumida River, it's central to Asakusa bustle and has a pleasant rooftop terrace. Check-in is at 3pm.

our pick K's House (Map pp130-1; ☎ 5833-0555; fax 5833-0444; http://kshouse.jp/tokyo-e/index.html; 3-20-10 Kuramae, Taitō-ku; per person dm/s/d from ¥2800/3900/3400; ✗ ✗ ; ◉ Toei Asakusa, Toei Ōedo lines to Kuramae, exits A2 & A6) This new guesthouse is spotless, with homey common areas and kitchen.

There's also a coin-operated laundry and even a rooftop terrace overlooking the Sumida River. Check room availability online and book in advance. Credit cards are accepted and it provides towels. Check-in is at 3pm.

Tokyo Ryokan (Map pp130-1; ☎ 090-8879-3599; www .tokyoryokan.com; 2-4-8 Nishi-Asakusa, Taitō-ku; per person with shared bathroom ¥3000; ✗ ✗ ; ◉ Ginza line to Tawaramachi, exit 3) With only three rooms in this immaculate, intimate little ryokan, book well ahead through the website (which contains a detailed map and directions). The English-speaking manager here is helpful and open, and always happy to chat. Check-in is at 11am.

Taitō Ryokan (Map pp130-1; ☎ 3843-2822, 090-5321-3599; www.libertyhouse.gr.jp; 2-1-4 Nishi-Asakusa, Taitō-ku; per person with shared bathroom ¥3000; ✗ ✗ ; ◉ Ginza line to Tawaramachi, exit 3) The tiny, creaky Taitō is good value, run by sociable English speakers. It can be noisy, and palatial it ain't, but who cares at this price. Solo travellers should expect to share a room when demand is high. The website has a map containing detailed directions.

Capsule Hotel Riverside (Map pp130-1; ☎ 3844-5117; fax 3841-6566; www.asakusa-capsule.jp/english; 2-20-4 Kaminarimon, Taitō-ku; capsules ¥3000; ✗ ; ◉ Ginza, Toei Asakusa lines to Asakusa, exits 3 & 4) Within stumbling distance from Asakusa station, this is one capsule hotel that accepts women (the 8th floor is women only). Capsules are a bargain at this cosy place, including *yukata* and use of the bath facilities. Look for the entrance around the back of the building. Check-in is at 3pm.

MIDRANGE

our pick Ryokan Shigetsu (Map pp130-1; ☎ 3843-2345; fax 3843-2348; www.shigetsu.com; 1-31-11 Asakusa, Taitō-ku; Western-style s/d ¥7700/14,700, Japanese-style s/d from ¥9450/16,800; ✗ ✗ ; ◉ Ginza, Toei Asakusa lines to Asakusa, exits 1 & 2) Perfectly situated off Nakamise-dōri, Ryokan Shigetsu comes close to the true ryokan experience. Most rooms have en suite bathrooms, but bathing in the communal baths is a must – both the black granite bath and the Japanese cypress one have unique, stunning views. Lovely Japanese breakfasts cost ¥1300. Check-in is at 3pm.

TOP END

Asakusa View Hotel (Map pp130-1; ☎ 3847-1111; fax 3842-2117; www.viewhotels.co.jp/asakusa/english /index.html; 3-17-1 Nishi-Asakusa, Taitō-ku; s/d/tw from ¥15,000/28,000/28,000; ✗ ✗ ✗ ; ◉ Ginza line to Tawaramachi, exit 3) The ritziest joint in the neighbourhood isn't called the Asakusa View for nothing. While rooms aren't particularly striking, they're spacious and, as the name suggests, have floor-to-ceiling windows with smashing vistas. Try to swing a room on a higher floor for the best views of Sensō-ji or Ueno Park. Check-in is at 1pm.

Ikebukuro 池袋

Ikebukuro, though a convenient stop on the Yamanote line, is not one of Tokyo's sexiest neighbourhoods – but this older district does have its attractions and a certain unflashy appeal.

BUDGET

Kimi Ryokan (Map p114; ☎ 3971-3766; fax 3987-1326; www.kimi-ryokan.jp; 2-36-8 Ikebukuro, Toshima-ku; s/d ¥4500/6500-7500; ✕ 🐾 💻 ; ⊕ JR Yamanote line to Ikebukuro, west exit) Kimi Ryokan is one of Tokyo's best budget accommodations, with clean Japanese-style rooms and a convivial lounge area decorated with the wonderful owner's changing *ikebana*. Shared bathrooms have both showers and a Japanese-style bath. Be sure to book ahead, and print a helpful map from the website. Check-in is at 3pm.

House Ikebukuro (Map p114; ☎ 3984-3399, 3984-3999; www.housejp.com.tw/englishindex.htm; 2-20-1 Ikebukuro, Toshima-ku; d/tr ¥6000/9000, ste from ¥11,000; 🐾 💻 ; ⊕ JR Yamanote line to Ikebukuro, west exit) Also in west Ikebukuro, this house has a variety of smallish tatami rooms, all with shared bathroom and a common kitchen. Better, however, are the apartmentlike suites in the annexe, with kitchenettes and en suite bathrooms. Again, book ahead. Check-in is at 3pm; find directions and maps on the website.

MIDRANGE

There are innumerable business, love and capsule hotels in the Ikebukuro area. Be aware that the local capsule hotels are not as accustomed to foreign guests as their counterparts in Akasaka and Shinjuku.

Hotel Strix Tokyo (Map p114; ☎ 5396-0111, fax 5396-9815; www.strix.jp in Japanese; 2-3-1 Ikebukuro, Toshima-ku; s/d from ¥15,000/20,000; ✕ 🐾 💻 ; ⊕ JR Yamanote line to Ikebukuro, west exit) The most central and stylish option in the neighbourhood, the Strix was recently renovated by a new hotelier. Retro-inspired rooms (and beds) are quite spacious by the usual standard for business hotels. Look for its teal-coloured dome on the corner two blocks from the west exit. Check-in is 2pm.

Hotel Grand City (Map p114; ☎ 3984-5121, fax 3984-5127; www.grand-city.gr.jp in Japanese; 1-30-7 Higashi-Ikebukuro, Toshima-ku; s/d/tw ¥8400/10,500/14,700; ✕ 🐾 💻 ; ⊕ JR Yamanote line to Ikebukuro, east exit) On the east side of Ikebukuro, this is a standard but friendly business hotel with relatively inexpensive rates and even a ladies-only floor. Rooms are on the decidedly small side, and light sleepers should note its location next door to an entertainment complex featuring late-night batting cages. Check-in is at 2pm.

Hotel Sunroute Ikebukuro (Map p114; ☎ 3980-1911, fax 3980-5286; www.sunroute-ikebukuro.com in Japanese; 1-39-4 Higashi-Ikebukuro, Toshima-ku; s/d from ¥10,395/15,750; ✕ 🐾 💻 ; ⊕ JR Yamanote line to Ikebukuro, north exit) Just along the street from the main Bic Camera store, this place has pleasant, clean rooms and a friendly staff, some of whom speak English. Though beds are a bit on the hard side, rooms feel less spartan than the standard. Check-in is at 2pm.

Toyoko Inn (Map p114; ☎ 5960-1045, fax 5960-1046; www.toyoko-inn.com/eng; 2-50-5 Ikebukuro, Toshima-ku; s/d & tw ¥6800/8800, all incl breakfast; ✕ 🐾 wi-fi; ⊕ JR Yamanote line to Ikebukuro, north exit) The Toyoko Inn is one of the most appealing of the cheaper business hotels around here. Rooms are tidy, if tiny, and Japanese-style rooms are available. Room rates even include a Japanese breakfast. Check-in is at 4pm.

More of Ikebukuro's midrange options:

Hotel Theatre (Map p114; ☎ 3988-2251, fax 3988-2260; www.theatres.co.jp/hotel in Japanese; 1-21-4 Higashi-Ikebukuro, Toshima-ku; s/d/tw from ¥9135/12,600/15,750; ✕ 🐾 💻 ; ⊕ JR Yamanote line to Ikebukuro, east exit) Located along Sunshine 60-dōri, this is centrally located and clean. Check-in is at 2pm.

Ark Hotel (Map p114; ☎ 3590-0111, fax 3590-0224; http://tokyo.ark-hotel.co.jp; 3-5-5 Higashi-Ikebukuro, Toshima-ku; s/d/tw from ¥9240/16,800/17,850; 🐾) Another comfortable place with clean rooms and a polite staff; check-in is at 3pm.

Shinjuku 新宿

Shinjuku (Map p116) is full of business hotels accustomed to foreign guests, and the competition keeps prices reasonable. Near massive Shinjuku station, a hub for nearly every rail line snaking in and around Tokyo, this area makes a great base camp and has its own dizzying myriad of attractions.

BUDGET

Green Plaza Shinjuku (Map p116; ☎ 3207-4923; www.hgpshinjuku.jp/hotel in Japanese; 1-29-2 Kabukichō, Shinjuku-ku; capsules ¥4300; ⊠ ; ◉ JR Yamanote line to Shinjuku, east exit) If you have a Y-chromosome, you can spend the night in a curtain-cordoned capsule with 100 snoring salarymen passed out from drinking with colleagues. Capsules are only available to men, but women can crash here at the 9th-floor sauna (p143). Check-in on the 3rd floor after 3pm.

MIDRANGE

Shinjuku Park Hotel (Map p116; ☎ 3356-0241; fax 3352-2733; shinjukuparkhotel.co.jp; 5-27-9 Sendagaya, Shibuya-ku; s/tw from ¥7900/13,800, Japanese-style r ¥24,800; ⊠ 🖳 wifi; ◉ JR Yamanote line to Shinjuku, new south exit) Just south of the Takashimaya Times Sq complex, this pleasant business hotel has larger rooms than most. Solo travellers should spend up for a B-type single for the bigger bed, but everyone should try booking a room with a park view of Shinjuku-gyoen. Check-in is at 3pm.

Hotel Sunlite Shinjuku (Map p116; ☎ 3356-0391; fax 3356-1223; www.sunlite.co.jp; 5-15-8 Shinjuku, Shinjuku-ku; s/d/tw from ¥8715/12,075/14,175; ⊠ ; ◉ Marunouchi, Toei Shinjuku lines to Shinjuku-sanchōme, exit C7) At the lower end of the midrange price scale, the clean and comfortable Sunlite won't break the budget, and it even accepts credit cards. Small rooms are well maintained and cosy, and its central location in east Shinjuku puts you near Shinjuku-gyoen, nocturnal life in Kabukichō and Shinjuku shopping. Check-in is at 3pm.

City Hotel Lornstar (Map p116; ☎ 3356-6511; fax 3350-9505; www.thehotel.co.jp/en/lornstar/index.php; 2-12-12 Shinjuku, Shinjuku-ku; s/d/tw ¥7350/9450/10,500; ⊠ 🖳 🖳 ; ◉ Marunouchi, Toei Shinjuku lines to Shinjuku-sanchōme, exit C8) The modestly proportioned rooms here are a good choice for budget travellers; though it's no frills, it exudes a bit of personality and is probably the most queer-friendly place in Tokyo. Credit cards are accepted and a simple continental breakfast is provided. Check-in is at 2pm.

Shinjuku Washington Hotel (Map p116; ☎ 3343-3111; fax 3342-2575; www.wh-rsv.com/english/shinjuku/index.html; 3-2-9 Nishi-Shinjuku, Shinjuku-ku; s/d/tw from ¥9400/15,000/16,000; ⊠ ; ◉ JR Yamanote line to Shinjuku, south exit) This efficient business hotel has tonnes of room and lots of in-house restaurants. Rooms and windows are small, but views from the upper floors are great. There's also a ladies-only floor. Check-in is at 2pm. From Shinjuku station, take the south exit to Kōshū-kaidō, turn right on Gijido-dōri and take the first left after that.

More midrange options in Shinjuku:

Shinjuku New City Hotel (Map p116; ☎ 3375-6511, 3375-6535; www.newcityhotel.co.jp; 4-31-1 Nishi-Shinjuku, Shinjuku-ku; s/d/tw from ¥9450/15,750/14,700; ⊠ 🖳 🖳 ; ◉ Toei Ōedo line to Tochōmae, exit A4) Some rooms have pretty park views of Chūō-kōen, and staff is friendly. Check-in is at 3pm.

Star Hotel Tokyo (Map p116; ☎ 3361-1111; fax 3369-4216; www.starhotel.co.jp/city/tokyo/guest/e-stand ard.html; 7-10-5 Nishi-Shinjuku, Shinjuku-ku; s/d from ¥9975/14,700; ⊠ 🖳 ; ◉ JR Yamanote line to Shinjuku, west exit) In west Shinjuku, this rather average hotel is very conveniently located. From Shinjuku station, cross Ōme-kaidō and turn left on Yasukuni-dōri. Check-in is at 1pm.

TOP END

Park Hyatt Tokyo (Map p116; ☎ 5322-1234; fax 5322-1288; tokyo.park.hyatt.com; 3-7-1-2 Nishi-Shinjuku, Shinjuku-ku; r/ste from ¥55,650/68,250; ⊠ 🖳 🖳 🖳 ; ◉ JR Yamanote line to Shinjuku, south exit) Views here are legendarily stunning, day and night, and appear to be part of another world from these serene heights. Dignified but relaxed, the stylishly understated rooms are done in naturally finished wood, fabric and marble. Staff is gracefully, discreetly attentive and the restaurants are among Tokyo's best.

Keiō Plaza Hotel (Map p116; ☎ 3344-0111; fax 3345-8269; www.keioplaza.com; 2-2-1 Nishi-Shinjuku, Shinjuku-ku; s/d ¥22,000/26,000, Japanese-style ste ¥80,000; ⊠ 🖳 🖳 🖳) The Keiō Plaza has 47 floors and a simple, refined style. Rooms provide excellent views over west Shinjuku and there's a wealth of restaurants in the hotel. Check-in is at 1pm.

Hotel Century Southern Tower (Map p116; ☎ 5354-0111; fax 5354-0100; www.southerntower.co.jp; 2-2-1 Yoyogi, Shibuya-ku; s/d from ¥16,000/24,000; ⊠ 🖳 🖳 ; ◉ JR Yamanote line to Shinjuku, new south exit) Graced with expansive views, this Shinjuku monolith is very reasonably priced for the intangible sense of space the windows reveal. If it weren't so central and convenient, the views would be this place's winning hand. Find reception on the 20th floor of the Odakyū Southern Tower Building. Check-in is at 2pm.

Shibuya 渋谷
MIDRANGE

Pickings are slim in Shibuya for midrange hotels. Less expensive business hotels in Ueno, Ikebukuro and even Shinjuku represent much better value for money, but then you're not in as fun a spot as in Shib.

Shibuya City Hotel (Map p117; ☎ 5489-1010; fax 5489-1030; www.shibuya-city-hotel.com in Japanese; 1-1

Maruyamachō, Shibuya-ku; s/d from ¥9450/18,900; ✕ ✕ ; ⊙ JR Yamanote line to Shibuya, Hachikō exit) Night owls will love this hotel, strategically located on the lower slope of Love Hotel Hill and a short downhill roll from good live-music venues and clubs. For such a prime location, the prices are a fabulous deal. It has comfortable, spacious rooms, including one tricked-out wheelchair-friendly room (¥14,800).

Shibuya Tōbu Hotel (Map p117; ☎ 3476-0111; fax 3476-0903; sby.shukuhaku@tobuhotel.co.jp; 3-1 Udagawachō, Shibuya-ku; s ¥13,960-16,370, d ¥17,294-25,610; ✕ ✕ ▭ ; ⊙ JR Yamanote line to Shibuya, Hachikō exit) One of Shibuya's nicest business hotels on the upscale end, the rooms here are stylish, clean and relatively spacious. Common areas are pleasant and sparkly, and the friendly, attentive staff speaks English. Check-in is at 2pm.

Shibuya Tōkyū Inn (Map p117; ☎ 3498-0109; fax 3498-0189; www.tokyuhotels.co.jp/en/TI/TI_SHIBU/index .shtml; 1-24-10 Shibuya, Shibuya-ku; s/d/tw from ¥13,650 /21,420/21,840; ✕ ✕ ▭ ; ⊙ JR Yamanote line to Shibuya, east exit) At a similar standard to the Shibuya Tōbu Hotel, the vaguely mod nonsmoking rooms are probably the best of the bunch. They also feature women-only rooms outfitted with nightgowns, special toiletries and humidifiers. Check-in is at 3pm; the hotel is right on Meiji-dōri.

TOP END
Creston Hotel (Map p117; ☎ 3481-5800; fax 3481-5515; www.crestonhotel.co.jp/shibuya/index.html; 10-8 Kamiyamachō, Shibuya-ku; s/d from ¥15,115/22,145; ✕ ✕ ▭ ; ⊙ JR Yamanote line to Shibuya, Hachikō exit) About a 10-minute walk from the station, the unassumingly chic Creston is tucked away in a quiet corner of Shibuya. With a laid-back, classy ambience, it's a sweet deal for this neighbourhood. Find a map to the hotel on its website; check-in is at 3pm.

our pick **Cerulean Tower Tōkyū Hotel** (Map p117; ☎ 3476-3000; fax 3476-3001; www.ceruleantower -hotel.com; 26-1 Sakuragaokachō, Shibuya-ku; s/d from ¥28,875/40,425; ✕ ✕ ▭ ; ⊙ JR Yamanote line to Shibuya, south exit) Sprawl out on huge beds and drink deeply of the big views of the glittery city, because there's room to breathe in these enormous quarters. The sleek lobby opens onto a garden view, an organic complement to the clean modern aesthetic of this place. Arts fiends take note: quality *nō* and jazz performances take place at the impressive in-house theatre and jazz club. Big spenders might consider booking one of the two

gorgeous, enormous Japanese-style rooms (¥77,385).

Roppongi & Akasaka 六本木・赤坂
Akasaka (Map pp124–5, has a high concentration of luxury hotels due to its great location: there are loads of good restaurants nearby, the political and business centres are within walking distance, and Roppongi's nightlife is just down the road. Of course, if nightlife features prominently on your agenda, Roppongi has several convenient digs.

BUDGET
Capsule Hotel Fontaine Akasaka (Map pp124-5; ☎ 3583-6554; www.fontaine-akasaka.co.jp; 4-3-5 Akasaka, Minato-ku; capsules men/women Mon-Fri ¥4800/4500, Sat & Sun ¥4500; ✕ ; ⊙ Ginza, Marunouchi lines to Akasaka-mitsuke, Belle Vie exit) This upmarket capsule hotel is one of the few in Tokyo that accepts women. It also happens to be one of the more luxurious, featuring lovely bath and sauna facilities, and comfortable, bright sitting areas. Check-in is at 5pm.

MIDRANGE
Arca Torre (Map p119; ☎ 3404-5111; fax 3404-5115; www .arktower.co.jp/arcatop01new1.html; 6-1-23 Roppongi, Minato-ku; s/d from ¥11,550/14,700; ✕ ✕ ▭ ; ⊙ Hibiya, Toei Ōedo lines to Roppongi, exit 3) Excellently placed yet reasonably priced, the cosy Arca Torre is made for hard partiers and heavy sleepers. Rooms at the back are considerably quieter than those facing the street. Beds are on the hard side, but even standard singles are furnished with semidoubles. Check-in is at 3pm.

Hotel Sunroute Akasaka (Map pp124-5; ☎ 3589-3610; fax 3589-3619; www.sunroute.jp; 3-21-7 Akasaka, Minato-ku; s/tw ¥14,400/19,500; ✕ ✕ ▭ ; ⊙ Ginza, Marunouchi lines to Akasaka-mitsuke, Belle Vie exit) A bright, friendly spot with well-designed rooms all equipped with high-speed internet access, this is conveniently located near several subway stations and is a 15-minute walk from Roppongi Crossing. Though there's no restaurant, the coffee shop downstairs can serve up your morning caffeine and pastry. Check-in is at 2pm.

Hotel Ibis (Map p119; ☎ 3403-4411; fax 3479-0609; www.ibis-hotel.com; 7-14-4 Roppongi, Minato-ku; s/d/tw from ¥13,382/19,866/22,145; ✕ ✕ ▭ ; ⊙ Hibiya, Toei Ōedo lines to Roppongi, exit 4a) Just this side of noir, the interior of the Ibis suggests some dark drama lurking underneath. Aesthetics notwithstanding, it's a clean, modern hotel just steps from

TOKYO

Roppongi Crossing. Rooms are small, and solo travellers should skip the cramped single rooms in favour of larger semidoubles. Check-in is at 1pm.

Asia Center of Japan (Map p119; ☎ 3402-6111; fax 3402-0738; www.asiacenter.or.jp; 8-10-32 Akasaka, Minato-ku; s/d from ¥8200/10,800; ✗ 🖳 ; ④ Ginza, Hanzōmon, Toei Ōedo lines to Aoyama-itchōme, exit 4) Down a narrow road in a quiet Akasaka neighbourhood, the Asia Center attracts many long-term stayers. As it's often fully booked, call ahead. Old-annexe rooms have wood-panelled walls and an airy, simple charm. Internet access, laundry facilities and ¥795 breakfasts are among the offerings. Find a map on the website. Check-in is at 2pm.

Akasaka Yōkō Hotel (Map p119; ☎ 3586-4050; fax 3586-5944; www.yokohotel.co.jp; 6-14-12 Akasaka, Minato-ku; s/tw from ¥9345/14,700; ✗ ✗ 🖳 ; ④ Chiyoda line to Akasaka, exit 7) All the rooms are nonsmoking and internet access is free at this reasonably priced, basic business hotel. The modest rooms are clean and comfortable and the staff is friendly. From here, you're close enough to walk to Roppongi for a wild night out, but far enough to snooze peacefully afterwards. Check-in is at 3pm.

TOP END

Hotel Ōkura (Map pp124-5; ☎ 3582-0111, 3582-3707; tokyo.okura.com; 2-10-4 Toranomon, Minato-ku; s/d from ¥34,125/42,000; ✗ ✗ 🖳 ; ④ Ginza line to Tameike-sannō, exit 13) A preferred landing place for visiting dignitaries and businesspeople, the unpretentious but graceful Hotel Ōkura exudes old-school elegance. The inviting feel of the hotel's décor and low-lying architecture is complemented by a beautiful Japanese garden. Personable staff, excellent business facilities and top-notch restaurants complete the picture. The hotel grounds also house the Ōkura Shūkokan (p140). Check-in is at 2pm.

ourpick Grand Hyatt Tokyo (Map p119; ☎ 4333-1234; fax 4333-8123; tokyo.grand.hyatt.com; 6-10-3 Roppongi, Minato-ku; s/d from ¥50,400/55,650; ✗ ✗ 🖳 ; ④ Hibiya, Toei Ōedo lines to Roppongi, exits 1c & 3) Set in uber-contemporary Roppongi Hills, the Grand Hyatt gleams with polished refinement. Though the look is decidedly urban, the interior makes liberal use of natural materials, lending an earthy feel to this modern hotel with details like rain-shower fixtures and mahogany walls. Book the west side for views of Mt Fuji; check-in is at 3pm.

These other top-end hotels are also recommended:

ANA Hotel Tokyo (Map pp124-5; ☎ 3505-1111; fax 3505-1155; www.anahoteltokyo.jp/e; 1-12-33 Akasaka, Minato-ku; s/d & tw from ¥31,185/40,425; ✗ ✗ 🖳 ; ④ Namboku line to Roppongi-itchōme, exit 3) Midway between Akasaka and Roppongi, an excellent choice for those seeking straightforward, businesslike glam. Check-in is at 1pm.

Akasaka Prince Hotel (Map pp124-5; ☎ 3234-1111; fax 3262-5163; www.princehotelsjapan.com/akasaka princehotel; 1-2 Kioichō, Chiyoda-ku; Western-style s/d from ¥26,500/32,000, Japanese-style ste ¥92,400; ✗ ✗ 🖳 ; ④ Chiyoda, Hanzōmon, Namboku, Yūrakuchō lines to Nagatachō, exits 5, 7 & 9) Designed by the late Tange Kenzō, this landmark hotel retains a '70s retro appeal with unusually spacious rooms for Tokyo. Check-in is at 2pm.

Hotel New Otani (Map p119; ☎ 3265-1111; fax 3221-2619; www.newotani.co.jp/en/tokyo/index .html; 4-1 Kioichō, Chiyoda-ku; s/d ¥36,005/41,980; ✗ ✗ 🖳 ; ④ Hanzōmon, Namboku, Yūrakuchō lines to Nagatachō, exits 5, 7 & 9) Renowned for the four-century-old Japanese garden around which it is constructed, this hotel is immense. Check-in is at 2pm.

Odaiba お台場

Although it's not the most convenient neighbourhood for exploring Tokyo, you do have breathing room in Odaiba. If it's here you choose to stay, be sure to book a room with a view of Tokyo Bay.

TOP END

Hotel Nikkō Tokyo (Map p122; ☎ 5500-5500; fax 5500-2525; www.hnt.co.jp/index_en.html; 1-9-1 Daiba, Minato-ku; r/ste from ¥38,515/92,800; ✗ ✗ 🖳 ; ④ Yurikamome line to Daiba) What with its spacious real estate on Odaiba, the Hotel Nikkō can afford to splash out on a spa (¥3150), an outdoor hot tub and a sauna. Large rooms are decorated in a low-key palette. Deluxe rooms feature bathrooms with tub views of the Rainbow Bridge. Check-in is at 2pm.

Le Méridien Grand Pacific Tokyo (Map p122; ☎ 5500-6711; fax 5500 4507; grandpacific.lemeridien.com; 2-6-1 Daiba, Minato-ku; s/d from ¥31,000/36,000; ✗ ✗ 🖳 ; ④ Yurikamome line to Daiba) Moderately baroque and polished to a high shine, Le Méridien is plushly outfitted with luxuries like boutiques, an art gallery and a florist, in addition to a pool and gym. It's large and lovely and has all the amenities you would expect from a hotel of this standard.

EATING

No city in Asia can match Tokyo for the sheer variety and quality of its restaurants. As well as refined Japanese cuisine, Tokyo covers the pan-continental spectrum with great international restaurants. One thing to keep in mind is that Japanese food tends to be cheaper than international food. For ¥750 you can get a good bowl of noodles in a *shokudō* (all-round eatery); the same money will buy you a plate of spaghetti in one of Tokyo's many cheap Italian places, though it's a pale imitation of the real stuff. If you fancy international food, be prepared to pay a little extra for a more authentic version.

Whatever you choose to eat, you rarely have to look far for sustenance. Check out the upper floors of the big department stores for *resutoran-gai* (restaurant 'streets'), which invariably have a good selection of Japanese, Chinese and Italian restaurants with inexpensive lunchtime specials. Department stores usually also have *depachika* (food halls) in the basement floors selling *bentō* (boxed meals) amid groceries and gourmet gifts. Train stations are home to *rāmen* shops, *bentō* and *onigiri* (rice ball) stands and *karereisu* (curry rice) restaurants.

During the day the best eating areas are the big shopping districts like Shibuya, Shinjuku, Harajuku and Ginza. By night try Aoyama and Roppongi for some of the city's best restaurants. For something more traditional, try an *izakaya* or Yakitori Alley in central Tokyo, or the down-at-the-heel eating arcade of Omoide-yokochō in Shinjuku.

If you'll be in Tokyo for some time, pick up a copy of John Kennerdell's *Tokyo Restaurant Guide* (Yohan) or Rick Kennedy's *Good Tokyo Restaurants*. Alternatively, check out the **Tokyo Food Page website** (www.bento.com/tokyofood.html) for its gigantic database of restaurant reviews; it's so huge that listings sometimes go stale, so always go forth and dine with a plan B in mind.

For quick, cheap eats, or a cup of coffee in an air-conditioned (albeit smoky) café, chain coffee shops like Doutor, Excelsior and Starbucks dot the city landscape and usually offer sandwiches and snacks at budget prices.

Vegetarian food is less common than you might expect in Tokyo. Luckily, many places that aren't strictly vegetarian – such as Japanese noodle and tofu (bean curd) shops – serve a good variety of no-meat and no-fish dishes. For more information, pick up the TIC's *Vegetarian & Macrobiotic Restaurants in Tokyo* handout. It lists strictly vegetarian restaurants, wholefood shops, *shōjin-ryōri* (Buddhist-temple fare) restaurants and Indian restaurants that offer a good selection of vegetarian dishes.

Central Tokyo 東京中心部

On weekdays, colourful little lunch trucks set up shop in the tree-shaded plaza of the Tokyo International Forum (p111). Cheap eats of an international variety range from falafel to tacos, and most takeaway costs less than ¥1000.

Lunch deals are competitive in and around Ginza; roam the *resutoran-gai* in the Ginza Palmy Building, or in department stores like Matsuzakaya (p179), Matsuya (p179) and Takashimaya (p179). Alternatively, head down to the basement food halls to pick up a *bentō* for later. In the evenings, convivial, atmospheric *yakitori* (charcoal-broiled chicken kebabs, and other meats or vegetables) restaurants can be found under the railway tracks in Yūrakuchō's Yakitori Alley (Map pp124–5).

Sakata (Map pp124-5; ☎ 3563-7400; 2nd fl, 1-5-13 Ginza, Chūō-ku; dishes from ¥850; ⏰ lunch & dinner Mon-Fri, lunch Sat; ✗; ⊕ Yūrakuchō line to Ginza-itchōme, exit 4) You may have to wait for a seat at peak hours at Sakata, widely recognised as Tokyo's best noodle spot. Apart from the sublime *tempura udon* (¥900), Sakata-san is an incredibly gracious host despite the language barrier.

Torigin Honten (Map pp124-5; ☎ 3571-3333; 5-5-7 Ginza, Chūō-ku; meals from ¥840; ⏰ 11.30am-10pm; ✗ E; ⊕ Ginza, Hibiya, Marunouchi lines to Ginza, exit B5) A block south of Harumi-dōri, this place is hidden away down a very narrow back alley, but signposted in English (there's a yellow sign with a chicken on it). This authentic, very popular little place does excellent *yakitori*, and the steamed-rice dish known as *kamameshi*.

Sushi Zanmai (Map pp124-5; ☎ 3541-1117; 4-11-9 Tsukiji, Chūō-ku; dinner from ¥1500; ⏰ 24hr; ✗ Ⓥ E; ⊕ Hibiya line to Tsukiji, exit 1) After the sunrise fish auctions, it serves weary fishermen; then tourists and townsfolk, office workers and retirees. In the evening, it remains open to bar and restaurant trade, and the ladies of the floating world. Zanmai serves up some of the freshest sushi you'll ever sample.

Mikuniya (Map pp126-7; ☎ 3271-3928; 2-5-11 Nihombashi, Chūō-ku; meals ¥1800-3000; ⏰ 11am-4pm Mon-Sat; ✗; ⊕ Ginza, Tōzai, Toei Asakusa lines to Nihombashi, exit B4)

The friendly family running Mikuniya serves tasty *unagi* (eel). Its *unagi bentō* comes in three sizes (¥1800, ¥2300 and ¥3000); plastic food models will help you choose. It's across the street from Takashimaya department store – look for the slab of driftwood above the door, embossed with gold kanji.

Shin-Hi-no-Moto (Map pp124–5; ☎ 3214-8021; 2-4-4 Yūrakuchō, Chiyoda-ku; meals ¥2500; 🕒 5pm–midnight; 🔀; ⊜ Yūrakuchō line to Yūrakuchō, exit A5 or Chiyoda, Hibiya, Toei Mita lines to Hibiya, exit A2) Another great spot under the tracks in Yūrakuchō, this lively *izakaya* is a down-home sort of spot for meeting up with friends. The staff speaks English and can suggest good eats to go with your beer.

Nair's (Map pp124–5; ☎ 3541-8246; 4-10-7 Ginza, Chūo-ku; lunch/dinner ¥1500/3000; 🕒 11am–8.30pm; 🔀 🔽 E; ⊜ Hibiya, Toei Asakusa lines to Higashi-Ginza, exit A2) Japanese showbiz types seem to like dropping by for some incognito Indian here at Nair's. This popular restaurant just up Shōwa-dōri from Kabuki-za always seems to have a queue at lunchtime.

Kyotōfu Fujino (Map pp126–7; ☎ 3240-0012; 6th fl, Marunouchi Bldg, 2-4-1 Marunouchi, Chiyoda-ku; meals from ¥1575; 🕒 lunch & dinner; 🔀 🔀 🔽 🔖; ⊜ Marunouchi line to Tokyo, exit 4) Among the standout dining options in the 'Marubiru' (Marunouchi Building) is this totally vegetarian tofu restaurant. Making the most of seasonal ingredients, the resulting dishes are beautiful as they are delicately tasty. The staff speaks varying degrees of English and can explain your options, but the *teishoku* (lunchtime set; ¥1575) is excellent and includes dessert.

Edogin (Map pp124–5; ☎ 3543-4401; 4-5-1 Tsukiji, Chūo-ku; 🕒 11am–9.30pm Mon-Sat; 🔀 🔀 🔽; ⊜ Hibiya line to Tsukiji, exit 2) Within the alleys northwest of Tsukiji Market, this small place receives steady traffic for good reason. The *teishoku* is a steal at ¥1050. There's no English menu, but a picture menu makes ordering easy.

Robata (Map pp124–5; ☎ 3591-1905; 1-3-8 Yūrakuchō, Chiyoda-ku; meals from ¥3500; 🕒 5.30-11pm Mon-Sat; ⊜ Chiyoda, Hibiya, Toei Mita lines to Hibiya, exit A4) Along the alley parallelling the JR tracks, this is one of Tokyo's most celebrated *izakaya*. A little Japanese ability is helpful here, but the point-and-eat method works just fine. It's hard to spot the sign, even if you can read Japanese; better just to look for the rustic façade and country-style dishes piled on the counter.

Birdland (Map pp124–5; ☎ 5250-1081; B1 fl, Tsukamoto Sogyo Bldg, 4-2-15 Ginza, Chūo-ku; meals from ¥6000; 🕒 5-9pm Tue-Sat; 🔀 E; ⊜ Ginza, Hibiya, Marunouchi lines to Ginza, exit C6) Holy grilled hearts of fowl, Batman! Birdland's obvious draw is *yakitori*. Chefs here know there's more than one way to skewer a chicken, and the resulting array – along with the wine list – honours the humble bird. Only same-day reservations can be made from noon on.

Kyūbei (Map pp124–5; ☎ 3571-6523; 8-7-6 Ginza, Chūo-ku; lunch/dinner from ¥4000/10,000; 🕒 lunch & dinner; 🔀 🔀 🔽; ⊜ Ginza line to Shimbashi, exit 1) Established in 1936, this superb sushi restaurant continues to earn its reputation as one of Tokyo's best. If you treat yourself to one high-end, raw-fish experience, reserve a place at Kyūbei. A picture menu is available and English-speaking staff can translate for you. Its minimalist façade has a discreet flagstone path on the left, one street west of Chūo-dōri.

Ten-Ichi (Map pp124–5; ☎ 3571-1949; 6-6-5 Ginza, Chūo-ku; lunch/dinner from ¥5000/8500; 🕒 11.30am-9.30pm; 🔀 🔀 E; ⊜ Ginza, Hibiya, Marunouchi lines to Ginza, to Ginza, exits A1, B3 & B6) Frying up famously transcendent tempura since 1930, Ten-Ichi is the place to splash out on unbelievably light tempura in elegant surroundings. Reservations are suggested.

Nataraj (Map pp124–5; ☎ 5537-1515; 7th-9th fl, 6-9-4 Ginza, Chūo-ku; meal from ¥2800; 🕒 11.30am-11pm; 🔀 🔀 🔽 E; ⊜ Ginza, Hibiya, Marunouchi lines to Ginza, exit A2) Herbivores have reason to rejoice in Ginza. Nataraj brings warm colours, low-key elegance and vegetarian Indian cuisine to its three-storey branch. Sizable set meals are complemented by beer and wine.

Ueno 上野

The Ueno area is a happy hunting ground for inexpensive food. You'll find a good variety of cheap Japanese places in and around Ameyoko Arcade, where you can also pick up takeaway and fruit from vendors.

Ueno Yabu Soba (Map pp130–1; ☎ 3831-4728; 6-9-16 Ueno, Taitō-ku; meals from ¥650; 🕒 11.30am-9pm Thu-Tue; 🔀 🔖 E; ⊜ JR Yamanote line to Ueno, Hirokōji exit) Near the arcade, this is a famous *soba* (buckwheat noodles) shop. To really fill up, get the *tenseiro* (noodles topped with shrimp and vegetable tempura) set. Look for the black granite sign on the corner shop that says 'Since 1892'. The picture menu makes ordering a snap.

Ganko Sushi (Map pp130–1; ☎ 5688-8845; 6th fl, Nagafuji Bldg, 4-9-6 Ueno, Taitō-ku; meals ¥2500; 🕒 11.30am-3pm & 4.30-11pm; 🔀 🔽; ⊜ JR Yamanote line to Ueno, Hirokōji exit) If you're hankering for decent sushi after a long museum day, Ganko Sushi offers good *teishoku* deals at lunch and dinner. It has a picture menu and is fairly used to foreign customers. Try the sushi *moriawase* (assortment; ¥1000) or the tempura *bentō*.

Futaba (Map pp130-1; ☎ 3835-2672; 2-8-11 Ueno, Taitō-ku; meals ¥1500-3000; 🕙 lunch & dinner; ✗; 🚇 JR Yamanote line to Ueno, Hirokōji exit) Though the nondescript beige exterior doesn't look like much, the proof of Futaba's long-running popularity is in its pudding – or rather, its pork cutlets. Service might be a bit gruff, but you're keeping it real in Ueno if you slide the door open and order up a *tonkatsu teishoku* (deep-fried pork cutlet set; ¥1500).

Izu-ei (Map pp130-1; ☎ 3831-0954; 2-12-22 Ueno, Taitō-ku; meals from ¥2500; 🕙 11am-9.30pm; ✗ ✗ 🍴; 🚇 JR Yamanote line to Ueno, Hirokōji exit) Izu-ei is a smart choice for authentic Japanese food – the speciality here is *unagi*, grilled by pros. The Izu-ei *una toro chō* (¥2625) includes tempura, best eaten near the window for a lovely view of the giant lilypads on Shinobazu-ike. Order from a limited picture menu.

Sasa-no-Yuki (Map pp130-1; ☎ 3873-1145; 2-15-10 Negishi, Taitō-ku; meals from ¥1900; 🕙 11am-9pm Tue-Sun; ✗ ✗ 🍴 E; 🚇 JR Yamanote line to Uguisudani, north exit) Sasa-no-Yuki opened its doors in Edo times, serving beautifully presented *tōfu-ryōri* (multicourse, tofu-based meals). Friendly staff will bend over backwards to help you order. To find it, turn right out the station exit, cross the big intersection at Kototoi-dōri and look for the restaurant on your left about 200m up, past the pedestrian overpass.

Asakusa 浅草

Asakusa's variety of Japanese food makes it difficult to choose where to eat. Poke your head into some of the restaurants in the alleys between Sensō-ji and Kaminarimon-dōri if you can't decide.

Daikokuya (Map pp130-1; ☎ 3844-1111; 1-38-10 Asakusa, Taitō-ku; dishes ¥1500-3000; 🕙 11.30am-8.30pm Mon-Fri, to 9pm Sat; 🍴 E; 🚇 Ginza, Toei Asakusa lines to Asakusa, exit 1) Near Nakamise arcade, this is the place to get authentic tempura, a speciality in Asakusa. The line out the door usually snakes around the corner at lunchtime, but if it looks unbearably long, try your luck at the branch on the next block.

Sometaro (Map pp130-1; ☎ 3844-9502; 2-2-2 Nishi-Asakusa, Taitō-ku; meals ¥1000; 🕙 noon-10pm; ✗ 🍴 E; 🚇 Ginza line to Tawaramachi, exit 3) Sometaro is a fun, funky place to try DIY *okonomiyaki* (meat,

seafood and vegetables in a cabbage-and-vegetable batter). You cook it yourself on a griddle built into your table, and the English menu includes a helpful how-to. Look for the rustic, overgrown façade.

Owariya (Map pp130-1; ☎ 3841-8780; 1-7-1 Asakusa, Taitō-ku; meals ¥1300; 🕙 11.30am-8.30pm; ✗ E; 🚇 Ginza line to Tawaramachi, exit 3) Service is brisk at this busy little corner shop, making it a good choice if you're not willing to wait around at Daikokuya. It does tempura and a variety of noodle dishes – try the *seiro soba* (thin buckwheat noodles with tempura shrimp).

Asakusa Imahan (Map pp130-1; ☎ 3841-1114; 3-1-12 Nishi-Asakusa, Taitō-ku; meals ¥3000-8500; 🕙 11.30am-9.30pm; ✗ E; 🚇 Ginza line to Tawaramachi, exit 3) Here in Shitamachi, the original branch of Imahan feels appropriately dignified for cooking your *shabu-shabu* (hotpot)…but not so staid that you can't get happy on sake while your dinner simmers. The meat is high quality, the vegetables seasonal and the atmosphere enjoyable.

Vin Chou (Map pp130-1; ☎ 3845-4430; 2-2-13 Nishi-Asakusa, Taitō-ku; meals from ¥4000; ✗ E; 🕙 5-11pm Thu-Tue, 4-10pm Sun) In a city enamoured of all things French, this is, *bien sûr*, a French-style *yakitori* joint, offering foie gras with your *tori negi* (chicken and leek). All rather chichi for this neck of the woods. It's around the corner from the Taitō Ryokan.

Komagata Dozeu (Map pp130-1; ☎ 3842-4001; 1-7-12 Komagata, Taitō-ku; dishes ¥1500-3000; 🕙 11am-9pm; ✗ 🍴 E; 🚇 Ginza, Toei Asakusa lines to Asakusa, exits A1 & A5) The sixth-generation chef running this marvellous restaurant continues the tradition of turning the simple *dojō* (a small, eel-like river fish) into rich deliciousness. Floor seating at the shared low, wooden plank tables heightens the traditional flavour, but ladies: don't wear a skirt for this dining expedition.

Ikebukuro 池袋

Though not a dining destination in itself, Ikebukuro has plenty of fine places to chow down. At lunchtime, don't forget the restaurant floors in Seibu, Tōbu and Marui department stores. The eastern side of the station is crammed with *rāmen* shops and *kaiten-zushi*, and is also the place you'll find the Ikebukuro Gyōza Stadium at **Namco Namjatown** (☎ 5950-0765; 2nd fl, World Import Mart Bldg, 3-1-3 Higashi-Ikebukuro, Toshima-ku; adult/child ¥300/200; 🕙 10am-10pm) housing three food 'theme parks', specialising variously in *gyōza* (Chinese dumplings), cream puffs and ice cream. Admission only gets you

TOKYO

in; it doesn't cover the cost of food. We recommend the 'healthy' Kyūshū-based Temujin, which serves its dumplings in a *yuzu* citrus, vinegar-soy sauce dip.

Yamabuki (Map p114; ☎ 3971-1287; 1-27-8 Minami-Ikebukuro; lunch/dinner ¥1280/1600; ☷ 11am-8.45pm; ☷ ; ☷ JR Yamanote line to Ikebukuro, east exit) Call on Yamabuki for that wonderful Japanese delicacy, *unagi*; it serves *unadon* (*unagi* over rice; ¥980), and there's a picture menu. Down a narrow alley off Meiji-dōri across from the east exit, look for all the eel in the window.

Tonerian (Map p114; ☎ 3985-0254; www.tonerian .net/english.htm; 1-38-9 Nishi-Ikebukuro, Toshima-ku; meals ¥3500; ☷ 5-11.15pm) One of Ikebukuro's many *izakaya*, this is a busy place with a friendly staff. Turn up here to learn about good *jizake* (regional sake) – the master, who speaks English, will be glad to make suggestions on food pairings. Just look for the empty sake bottles piled up outside.

Akiyoshi (Map p114; ☎ 3982-0601; 3-30-4 Nishi-Ikebukuro, Toshima-ku; meals ¥3000; ☷ ; ☷ 5-11pm; ☷ JR Yamanote line to Ikebukuro, west exit) If in the mood for *yakitori*, Akiyoshi's open grill at centre stage ignites a festive, sociable atmosphere. Chefs work quickly to move traffic along, but that doesn't mean you can't sit comfortably through several courses and at least one conversation. Ordering is simple with the picture menu.

Sushi Kazu (Map p114; ☎ 3590-4884; 2-10-8 Ikebukuro, Toshima-ku; meals from ¥3500; ☷ 11.30am-5am Mon-Sat; ☷ ; ☷ Marunouchi line to Ikebukuro, exit C6) Off the main boulevards of west Ikebukuro, this good, standard-issue sushi bar is definitely a step up from the *kaiten-zushi* in the neighbourhood. Formal Japanese-style dining rooms are also available for larger groups. It's best to sit at the counter, where you can choose your sushi from the picture menu.

Sasashū (Map p114; ☎ 3971-6796; 2-2-6 Ikebukuro, Toshima-ku; meals from ¥6000; ☷ 5-10pm Mon-Sat; ☷ ; ☷ Marunouchi line to Ikebukuro, exit C5) Sasashū's Japanese-style facade is easy to pick out between the modern concrete strip joints nearby. This dignified *izakaya* is renowned for its high-quality sake selection and traditional hearths. Some Japanese-language ability (or a Japanese friend) would be helpful for ordering here, but consider trying the *kamonabe* (duck stew; ¥3150) or *salmon yaki* (grilled salmon; ¥840).

Malaychan (Map p114; ☎ 5391-7638; www.malay chan.jp/NewFiles/contents_E.html; 3-22-6 Nishi-Ikebukuro, Toshima-ku; meals ¥2000; ☷ dinner Mon, lunch & dinner Tue-Sat, 11am-11pm Sun; ☷ E; ☷ JR Yamanote line to Ikebukuro, west exit) With its sweet location on a corner across from Nishi-Ikebukuro Park, Malaychan is one of Tokyo's few Malaysian restaurants and serves a huge breadth of dishes spanning the country's multiethnic background. The *nasi lemak* (rice with assorted dishes) is a filling introduction to Malaysian food.

Shinjuku 新宿

For a taste of Occupation-era Tokyo, meander through Omoide-yokochō (aka 'Piss Alley'), where tiny restaurants are packed shoulder to shoulder beside the JR tracks just northwest of Shinjuku station. Here, local workers stop off for *yakitori*, *oden* (fishcakes, tofu, vegetables and eggs simmered in a kelp-flavoured broth), noodles and beer before braving the trains back home. Most places serve similar things and few have names, so pick one that appeals to you. What they serve will be piled on the counters; just point to order, and expect to pay about ¥2000 per person. Omoide-yokochō is slated to be razed in late 2008 to make way for new development, but catch it if you can.

Kinkantei (Map p116; ☎ 3356-6556; 2-17-1 Shinjuku, Shinjuku-ku; meals ¥1000; ☷ 7pm-4am Mon-Sat; ☷ ; ☷ Marunouchi, Toei Shinjuku lines to Shinjuku-sanchōme, exit C7) Hemmed in by sex shops and serving the nocturnal life of Shinjuku-sanchōme, Kinkantei has been serving *soba* for longer than some countries have existed. *Tempura soba* (buckwheat noodles served with tempura; ¥1800) is a safe bet, while the unique textures and flavour of *yaki nattō* (fried fermented soybeans; ¥1000) is for the adventurous. From the station, turn right at the first alley, continue to its end, turn right again and look for the green sign.

Court Lodge (Map p116; ☎ 3378-1066; 2-10-9 Yoyogi, Shibuya-ku; lunch from ¥800; ☷ ; ☷ 11am-11pm; ☷ JR Yamanote line to Shinjuku, south exit) In this cramped, clean, bustling restaurant, the super-friendly and efficient staff serves tasty Sri Lankan food. You don't have to go inside if you're claustrophobic or in a hurry; it sells takeaway out the front. While there's no English menu, the staff speak good English and is happy to explain the menu.

Keika Kumamoto Rāmen (Map p116; ☎ 3354-4591; 3-7-2 Shinjuku, Shinjuku-ku; meals ¥800; ☷ 11am-10.45pm; ☷ Marunouchi, Toei Shinjuku lines to Shinjuku-sanchōme, exit C4) This is the place to try authentic *rāmen* in Shinjuku-sanchōme. The noodles are distinctively chewy and the broth is rich. Try the *chashūmen* (*rāmen* with roast pork; ¥830). You order and pay as you enter; navigate towards the kooky, multicoloured mural of a chef and pigs on the exterior.

Ibuki (Map p116; ☎ 3352-4787; 3-23-6 Shinjuku, Shinjuku-ku; sukiyaki course ¥2205, shabu-shabu ¥2970; ⏱ 5-11.30pm; ✗ E; ◉ JR Yamanote line to Shinjuku, east exit) An excellent *sukiyaki* and *shabu-shabu* restaurant in Shinjuku, Ibuki gets a lot of foreign trade. This friendly place offers a traditional atmosphere and sociable dining experience, and even accepts credit cards.

Tsunahachi (Map p116; ☎ 3352-1012; 3-31-8 Shinjuku, Shinjuku-ku; ⏱ 11am-10pm; ✗ ♿ E; ◉ JR Yamanote line to Shinjuku, east exit) Tsunahachi keeps them coming with its reasonably priced, tasty tempura. Sit at the counter for the pleasure of watching the efficient chefs fry each course of your dinner and place it on your dish. From Shinjuku-dōri as you face Mitsukoshi department store, go down the small street to its left; Tsunahachi will be on your left.

Tokyo Dai Hanten (Map p116; ☎ 3202-0121; 4th fl, Oriental Wave Bldg, 5-17-13 Shinjuku, Shinjuku-ku; meals ¥2000; ⏱ 11.30am-10pm; ✗ ; ◉ Marunouchi, Toei Shinjuku lines to Shinjuku-sanchōme, exit B3) Established in 1960, Tokyo Dai Hanten is one of your few possibilities for yum cha (dim sum). For Sunday brunch it serves dim sum á la Hong Kong, rolling it by on trolleys for you to flag down at will.

Canard (Map p116; ☎ 3200-0706; www.jlcjapon.com; B1 fl, 5-17-6 Shinjuku, Shinjuku-ku; lunch/dinner courses from ¥1600/2800; ⏱ lunch & dinner; ✗ E; ◉ JR Yamanote line to Shinjuku, east exit) Tucked into a tiny alley near Hanazono-jinja, an equally tiny Canard serves homemade, seasonal French food in intimate surroundings. With wine the bill adds up, but the meal is worth every yen. Find a map on the website.

Kurumaya (Map p116; ☎ 3352-5566; 3-21-1 Shinjuku, Shinjuku-ku; mains ¥1200; ⏱ 11.30am-11pm Mon-Sat, to 11.30pm Sun; ✗ ✗ E; ◉ JR Yamanote line to Shinjuku, east exit) Kurumaya's seafood and steak sets are good value and it's one of east Shinjuku's classier spots. Highly recommended is the *ise ebi* (Japanese lobster). It's on the corner across from Kirin City beer hall.

Tōfuro (Map p116; ☎ 3204-7772; 7th fl, Oriental Wave Bldg, 5-17-13 Shinjuku, Shinjuku-ku; meals ¥4000; ✗ E; ◉ Marunouchi, Toei Shinjuku lines to Shinjuku-sanchōme, exit B3) Even if you're not a fan of tofu, there's lots to eat in this upscale, Edo-style *izakaya*. Small, private rooms are good for groups, who can order set meals consisting of several courses. The traditional cuisine includes homemade tofu and a full menu of grilled meats, fish, soups and *oden*.

New York Grill (Map p116; ☎ 5323-3458; meals ¥6000; ⏱ lunch & dinner, brunch 11.30am-2.30pm Sun; ✗ ♿ E; ◉ Toei Ōedo line to Tochōmae, exit A4) On the 52nd floor of the Park Hyatt Tower (p150) this is power dining at its best – hearty portions of steak and seafood and drop-dead delicious views. One treat worth indulging in is Sunday brunch (¥5800); the price includes a flute of champagne.

If you can't find anything to your liking on the streets, try the *resutoran-gai* of the big department stores. The Isetan Building has eight floors of restaurants. **Takashimaya Times Square** (☎ 5361-3301; 5-24-2 Sendagaya, Shibuya-ku; ⏱ 10am-9pm) has a *resutoran-gai* on its 12th to 14th floors.

Harajuku & Aoyama 原宿・青山

Harajuku and Aoyama have more bistros, cafés and trattorias than most small European towns. The artery feeding it all is the promenade of Tokyo's young and beautiful: Omote-sandō. A few Japanese eateries are worth seeking out among the French and faddish restaurants.

Tokyo Apartment Café (Map p117; ☎ 3401-4101; 1-11-11 Jingūmae, Shibuya-ku; meals from ¥600; ⏱ 11-4am; ✗ E; ◉ Chiyoda line to Meiji-jingūmae, exit 5 or JR Yamanote line to Harajuku, Omote-sandō exit) A popular, inexpensive option opposite Condomania, the Apartment Café is a good afternoon refuge for snacks like spring rolls, a glass of wine or even Fruits Conscious Frozen. In the evening it transforms into sort of a cocktail lounge.

Bape Cafe!? (Map p117; ☎ 5770-6560; 3-27-22 Jingūmae, Shibuya-ku; lunch specials from ¥800; ⏱ 10.30am-11pm; ✗ ✗ E; ◉ JR Yamanote line to Harajuku, Takeshita exit) One more link in the empire established by Nigo, the underground genius behind A Bathing Ape, Bape Cafe!? serves up well-executed Japanese café comfort food, such as *kareiraisu*. Join the hungry hipsters here, and resist the temptation to pocket the logo-printed glasses.

Pure Café (Map p117; ☎ 5466-2611; 5-5-21 Minami-Aoyama, Minato-ku; lunch ¥1100; ⏱ 8.30am-10.30pm; ✗ ✗ Ⓥ E; ◉ Chiyoda, Ginza, Hanzōmon lines to Omote-sandō, exit B1) This little haven of vegan dining shares a space with nature-friendly Aveda in Aoyama. Using seasonal ingredients, the café creates flavourful, pure food to balance and

TOKYO

energise body and spirit. Actual samples (no plastic models here) of the day's specials are laid out at the counter to help you order.

Hiroba (Map p117; ☎ 3406-6409; B1 fl, Crayon House, 3-8-15 Kita-Aoyama, Minato-ku; lunch buffet ¥1260; 🕙 11am-10pm; 🗶 🗶 Ⓥ ⓖ ; ⓔ Chiyoda, Ginza, Hanzōmon to Omote-sandō, exits B2 & B4) In the Crayon House Building, this bright little spot does an excellent organic lunch buffet that includes both vegetarian and nonvegetarian options; though the descriptions of dishes are only in Japanese, the signs include cute, helpful drawings of fish or pigs to tell you what kinds of animal ingredients are used.

Maisen (Map p117; ☎ 3470-0071; 4-8-5 Jingūmae, Shibuya-ku; lunch sets ¥1500; 🕙 11am-10pm; 🗶 🗶 Ⓥ ⓖ ; ⓔ Chiyoda, Ginza, Hanzōmon lines to Omotesandō, exit A2) Maisen turns out righteous, crisp *tonkatsu* that consistently draws a crowd. Thankfully, the place is housed in a converted bathhouse, so there's plenty of room for the many hungry souls craving Kagoshima *kurobuta* (black pig; ¥1260). If you're on the run, pick up a *bentō* at the takeaway window.

Las Chicas (Map p117; ☎ 3407-6865; www.vision.co.jp /lc/indexe.htm; 5-47-6 Jingūmae, Shibuya-ku; lunch/dinner ¥1300/3000; 🕙 11am-11pm; 🗶 🗶 ⓖ E; ⓔ Chiyoda, Ginza, Hanzōmon lines to Omote-sandō, exit B2) One of the appealing alfresco dining terraces in the city, this hip spot offers casual classics like the Caligula salad (Caesar with a twist). The upmarket grub is tasty and the wine list is solid. Browse adjacent designer boutiques before dinner and repair to the bar afterwards. It should reopen after a renovation in February 2008.

Fujimamas (Map p117; ☎ 5485-2283; www.fujimamas .com; 6-3-2 Jingūmae, Shibuya-ku; lunch/dinner ¥1000/3000; 🕙 11am-11pm; 🗶 🗶 Ⓥ ⓖ E; ⓔ Chiyoda line to Meiji-jingūmae, exit 4 or JR Yamanote line to Harajuku, Omote-sandō exit) Once a tatami-maker's workshop, the airy upstairs dining room and breezy, open ground-floor space now echo the freshness and vitality of Fujimamas' fusion food. Dishes come from multiethnic backgrounds, much like the clientele, and portions are generous. Reservations are recommended.

Natural Harmony Angolo (Map p117; ☎ 3405-8393; 1st fl, Puzzle Bldg, 3-38-12 Jingūmae, Shibuya-ku; lunch/ dinner from ¥1200/3000; 🕙 lunch & dinner Tue-Sun; 🗶 🗶 Ⓥ ⓖ ; ⓔ Ginza line to Gaienmae, exit 2) Downshift to the pace of Natural Harmony, where the wholesome food is as pure as the smoke-free air. The menu is largely vegetarian, augmented with some fish and meat dishes.

Try some cold, cloudy sake with the Angolo set and meditatively decompress.

Mominoki House (Map p117; ☎ 3405-9144; 1st fl, YOU Bldg, 2-18-5 Jingūmae, Shibuya-ku; mains around ¥1500; 🕙 11am-11pm; ⓔ JR Yamanote line to Harajuku, Takeshita exit) You might be all *tonkatsu*-ed out, even if you're not of the vegetarian persuasion. Those seeking some relief from deep-fried delicacies can stop into Mominoki House, where the excellent macrobiotic menu covers the vegan to the vegetarian to…the chicken. Even better, your meals are served in a rambling warren of a space whose corners are filled with jazz and happy plants and whose proprietor will stop and chat about Stevie Wonder, pottery and holistic living.

Good Honest Grub (Map p117; ☎ 3406-6606; www .goodhonestgrub.com; 2nd fl, Belle Pia Bldg, 6-6-2 Jingūmae, Shibuya-ku; meals ¥1500; 🕙 11.30am-11pm Tue-Sun; 🗶 Ⓥ ⓖ E; ⓔ Chiyoda line to Meiji-jingūmae, exit 4) Long the place to go for weekend brunches in Ebisu, this vegetarian-friendly eatery has relocated to Harajuku. Serving smoothies, hearty wraps and sandwiches, and a weekday happy hour from 5.30pm to 7.30pm (all drinks ¥550), it's still a welcoming, airy spot to turn up for a nosh.

Fonda de la Madrugada (Map p117; ☎ 5410-6288; B1 fl, Villa Blanca, 2-33-12 Jingūmae, Shibuya-ku; lunch/dinner from ¥3800/6000; 🕙 5.30pm-2am Sun-Thu, to 5am Fri & Sat; 🗶 🗶 ⓖ E; ⓔ JR Yamanote line to Harajuku, Takeshita exit) Head past the Turkish embassy to this local favourite, where Tokyo's best Mexican food is served. Complete with open courtyards and strolling mariachi musicians, everything from the tiles to the chefs has been imported from Mexico. It's not cheap (¥900 guacamole?! *ay-ay-ay*), but after a few tequila shots you'll be having too much fun to notice.

Shibuya 渋谷

Take the briefest look around Shibuya and it may occur to you that there must be a lot of restaurants lurking in all those department stores – you are correct. Winners: to collect your prize, proceed to the 7th floor of Parco Part 1 or the 8th floor of the 109 Building.

Kushinobō (Map p117; ☎ 3496-8978; 5th fl, J&R Bldg, 33-12 Udagawachō, Shibuya-ku; lunch courses from ¥1000; 🕙 lunch & dinner; 🗶 E; ⓔ JR Yamanote line to Shibuya, Hachikō exit) This is the place to sample that great Japanese treat, *kushi-katsu* – deep-fried goodness. Plan on around ¥3000 for dinner.

Hina Sushi (Map p117; ☎ 3462-1003; B2 fl, 21-1 Udagawachō, Shibuya-ku; meals from ¥2000; 🕙 lunch &

dinner Tue-Fri, 11am-11pm Sat; ⊠ ; Ⓜ JR Yamanote line to Shibuya, Hachikō exit) In the basement of the Seibu A Building, Hina Sushi has a *tabehōdai* (all-you-can-eat) special for ¥4500. It's great value for sushi of this quality, but there's a two-hour time limit, so come ravenous.

Bio Café (Map p117; ☎ 5428-3322; 16-14 Udagawachō, Shibuya-ku; lunch ¥1400; ⏰ 11am-11pm; ⊠ ⊠ Ⓥ ♿ E; Ⓜ JR Yamanote line to Shibuya, Hachikō exit) Nestled amid the accessories shops and all-you-can-eat dessert cafés down this winding alley alongside Cinema Rise lies the peaceful Bio Café, serving healthy, mostly vegetarian meals in this softly lit dining room. Some dishes contain animal products, so strict vegetarians should ask before ordering. Consider sampling the 'alcohol for beautiful skin' cocktail.

Kantipur (Map p117; ☎ 3770-5358; B1 fl, 16-6 Sakuragaokachō, Shibuya-ku; mains around ¥850; ⏰ lunch & dinner Mon-Fri, 11.30am-11pm Sat; ⊠ ⊠ Ⓥ ♿ E; Ⓜ JR Yamanote line to Shibuya, south exit) After crossing the pedestrian overpass above Tamagawa-dōri and spotting its colourful sandwich boards on the street, make your way downstairs into the warmly lit dining room. Kantipur serves generous portions of Nepalese food with a bountiful selection of vegetarian choices.

Loco Moco (Map p117; ☎ 3477-1039; B1 fl, 1-17-5 Jinnan, Shibuya-ku; meals ¥900; ⏰ 11.30am-10.30pm Mon-Fri, 11am-10.30pm Sat & Sun; ⊠ E; Ⓜ JR Yamanote line to Shibuya, Hachikō exit) Lighter versions of the Hawaiian plate-lunch staple *loco moco* – rice topped with a fried egg and hamburger patty smothered in gravy – are this restaurant's bread and butter. Hawaiian embroidery accents the brick and exposed pipes of this basement eatery, and the slack-key guitar soundtrack is immeasurably soothing.

Fujiya Honten (Map p117; ☎ 3461-2128; B1 fl, 1-2-3 Sakuragaokachō, Shibuya-ku; meals ¥1200; ⏰ 5-9pm; ⊠ ; Ⓜ JR Yamanote line to Shibuya, south exit) Bold budget-diners can venture into this marvellous, legendary old *tachi-nomi* (stand-and-drink bar), 99% full of men (who are 94% drunk). Wash down the pub snacks with beer and sake at rock-bottom prices; this is a point-and-eat sort of setup. Cross the pedestrian walkway over Tamagawa-dōri and find it on the small street between Ringer Hut and the spectacles dealer.

Sakana-tei (Map p117; ☎ 3780-1313; 4th fl, Koike Bldg, 2-23-15 Dōgenzaka, Shibuya-ku; meals from ¥3500; ⏰ 5.30-11pm Mon-Sat; ⊠ ; Ⓜ JR Yamanote line to Shibuya, Hachikō exit) This unpretentious but slightly posh *izakaya* is a sake specialist much sought after by connoisseurs, and good value to boot. There's no English menu, but you can point at dishes on the counter to order. Call ahead for reservations, but turn off your mobile phone once you're in.

Gomaya (Map p117; ☎ 3770-8158; B1 fl, Matsubara Bldg, 2-25-13 Dōgenzaka, Shibuya-ku; meals ¥3500; ⏰ dinner; ⊠ E; Ⓜ JR Yamanote line to Shibuya, Hachikō exit) Duck into the alley next to McDonald's along Bunkamura-dōri and find the stairwell for Gomaya on your right. Inside, settle down at the counter and peruse the menu for dishes to go with your *nama biiru* (draught beer). Artistically arranged plates will appear in front of you as you order, but an absolute must-try is the mind-blowing, house-made *gomadōfu* (black sesame tofu).

Sonoma (Map p117; ☎ 3462-7766; www.sonomatokyo.com; 2-25-17 Dōgenzaka, Shibuya-ku; dishes ¥1100-6000; ⏰ 6-11.30pm Sun-Thu, 6pm-4am Fri & Sat; ⊠ ⊠ E; Ⓜ JR Yamanote line to Shibuya, Hachikō exit) As the name might imply, Sonoma's strength is in its well-balanced California cuisine and wines. Signature mains include pork chops with brown sugar, sage and apples. Dinner here gains you entrée to the Ruby Room (p175) upstairs, a fitting place for an all-night nightcap.

Ebisu & Daikanyama 恵比寿・代官山
In Ebisu, have a look around the 6th floor of the Atre building above Ebisu station for all the standard Japanese favourites. Venture forth into the neighbourhood for more variety and worthwhile eating establishments serving international food.

Rivalling Harajuku and Aoyama as the centre of Tokyo café society, Daikanyama is a chic destination to sip a cappuccino and engage in serious people-watching before perusing the local designer wares. You'll also find plenty of trendy foreign restaurants – some good, some merely fashionable.

The Tōkyū Tōyoko line (catch it from Shibuya) stops directly in Daikanyama, but it's also an easy 10-minute walk from Ebisu. From the west exit of Ebisu station, head west along Komazawa-dōri and turn right at the big intersection with Kyu-Yamate-dōri. When you hit the pedestrian overpass, make another right and you'll soon arrive in the heart of Daikanyama (Map p121), with the shopping complex Daikanyama Address on your right.

Fujii (Map p121; ☎ 3473-0088; 1-13-6 Ebisu, Shibuya-ku; ⏰ 11am-10pm Mon-Sat; ⊠ ; Ⓜ JR Yamanote line to Ebisu,

TOKYO

east exit) Fujii is a homey and comfortable place to sample fresh, handmade *udon*. We recommend the *tempura udon* for ¥1500. It's in the corner shop with an electric sign out the front, with a running LED message in Japanese.

Nanaki Soba (Map p121; ☎ 3496-2878; 1-13-2 Ebisu-Nishi, Shibuya-ku; meals ¥650-1600; ⏰ 11.30am-1.50pm & 5-10pm Mon-Sat; ✗ E; ⊚ JR Yamanote line to Ebisu, west exit) One of the best little *soba* shops in the area, this wooden shopfront near Ebisu-jinja may not look like much, but these buckwheat noodles are the pinnacle of tenderness. If you're feeling adventurous, try the gooey *yamakake soba* (grated yam over *soba*).

Ippūdō Rāmen (Map p121; ☎ 5420-2225; 1-3-13 Hiro-o, Shibuya-ku; meals ¥900; ⏰ 11am-4pm; ✗ E; ⊚ JR Yamanote line to Ebisu, east exit) This *rāmen* shop on Meiji-dōri is nationally famous for its Kyūshū-style *rāmen* into which you can grate fresh garlic cloves. You'll have to queue at peak periods – and as at any busy *rāmen* shop, you shouldn't linger longer than 20 minutes to eat – but it's worth every slurp.

Kazuki Rāmen (Map p121; ☎ 3496-6885; 1-10-8 Ebisu-Nishi, Shibuya-ku; dishes ¥800; ⏰ 11am-6pm Mon-Sat, to 5pm Sun; ✗ ; ⊚ JR Yamanote line to Ebisu, west exit) Don't feel the need to dress your *rāmen* with too many sauces and spices at your elbow – these are professionals who've laboured over the broth, after all. Choose from a picture menu or go for the *chashūmen* (¥1000).

Gazebo Café (Map p121; ☎ 3461-4348; 1-33-15 Ebisu-Nishi, Shibuya-ku; meals ¥900; ⏰ 8.30-midnight; ✗ E; ⊚ JR Yamanote line to Ebisu, west exit) Halfway between Ebisu and Daikanyama along Komazawa-dōri, Gazebo Café has outdoor seating and a good selection of teas. The sandwiches and pizzas are pretty good, and the pastry counter contains a few temptations to have with your Earl Grey. Or put your feet up with a beer and people-watch.

Yuuan (Map p121; ☎ 5793-7351; 6th fl, Atre Ebisu, 1-5-5 Ebisu-Minami, Shibuya-ku; set lunch/dinner ¥1050/2500; ⏰ 11am-9.30pm; ✗ ✗ V ♿; ⊚ JR Yamanote line to Ebisu, Atre exit) Names of the tofu-centric specials displayed outside are in English, but descriptions are not. Whatever you choose to eat, go for the tastier brown rice. Strict vegetarians should note that in this, as in most tofu-based restaurants, fish, eggs or meat-derived ingredients may be used.

Mushroom (Map p121; ☎ 5489-1346; 2nd fl, 1-16-3 Ebisu-Nishi, Shibuya-ku; lunch/dinner from ¥2300/5000; ✗ ✗ ; ⊚ JR Yamanote line to Ebisu, west exit) Chef Yamaoka's obsession with the taming of the 'shroom has sprouted this very cosy little French bistro, whose décor is dominated by a fungus motif, of course. Three-course *setto* (set lunches; ¥2500) showcasing mushrooms are amazing value and will transport you – without mind-altering side effects. A little Japanese or French is useful here.

Shunsenbō (Map p121; ☎ 5469-9761; 1st fl, Ebisu Prime Square Tower, 1-1-40 Hiro-o, Shibuya-ku; lunch/dinner ¥1500/3500; ⏰ lunch-dinner; ✗ V ♿ E; ⊚ JR Yamanote line to Ebisu, east exit) Specialising in *tōfu kaiseki* (multicourse dinners) and *shabu-shabu*, Shunsenbo is a bargain considering the quality of the food and the classy surroundings. The excellent, smooth tofu is made in-house.

Roppongi 六本木

It's only logical that there be an abundance of international restaurants in Roppongi, Tokyo's foreign-nightlife playground. From inexpensive burger joints to high-end sushi bars, whatever food you fancy is here. Japanese restaurants tend to be expensive but very accessible to *gaijin*, making it the perfect area for any long-awaited, lavish Japanese meal. But there are also heaps of cheap spots if you just need a quick bite before hitting the bars.

J's Kitchen (Map pp112-13; ☎ 5475-2727; 5-15-22 Minami-Azabu, Minato-ku; meals around ¥1000; ⏰ 11am-11.30pm Mon-Sat, to 4.30pm Sun; ✗ ✗ V ♿ E; ⊚ Hibiya line to Hiro-o, exits 1 & 3) Macrobiotic eating is gaining a foothold in Tokyo, and one little organic gem is the bright, friendly J's Kitchen amid the restaurant row on Gaien-nishi-dōri. Vegan delights include a *tempeh*-and-green-veggie wrap, pumpkin soup and tofu 'cheesecake'. Turn right from exit 1 or left from exit 3.

Bengawan Solo (Map p119; ☎ 3408-5698; 1st fl, Kaneko Bldg, 7-18-13 Roppongi, Minato-ku; meals ¥1100; ⏰ lunch & dinner Mon-Sat; ✗ V E; ⊚ Hibiya, Toei Ōedo lines to Roppongi, exit 2) On Roppongi-dōri, this Indonesian eatery has been around for ages. The indifferent interior isn't much, but the food, importantly, is terrific. The *gado gado* (salad with peanut sauce) lunch is a bargain, and the beef in coconut cream is dreamy. Food models are displayed outside.

Havana Café (Map p119; ☎ 3423-3500; 4-12-2 Roppongi, Minato-ku; meals ¥1000; ⏰ 11.30am-5am Mon-Fri, noon-5am Sat & Sun; ✗ E; ⊚ Hibiya, Toei Ōedo lines to Roppongi, exit 6) One of the best places to start your evening, the casual Havana Café serves respectable grub like burritos and sandwiches for less than ¥1000, and it does a mean burger. It also has good happy-hour drink specials, which you can enjoy in the large-windowed dining room or outside, on the Roppongi backstreet.

Bikkuri Sushi (Map p119; ☎ 3403-1489; 3-14-9 Roppongi, Minato-ku; meals from ¥1000; 🕙 11am-5am; 🍴 E; 🚇 Hibiya, Toei Ōedo lines to Roppongi, exit 3) A long-time favourite for Roppongi revellers, this late-night *kaiten-zushi* place has seen it all. *Bikkuri* means 'surprise' in Japanese, but unless you're picking up dishes blindfolded, there shouldn't be many of those.

Gonpachi (Map p119; ☎ 5771-0170; 1-13-11 Nishi-Azabu, Minato-ku; lunch/dinner ¥2000/4000; 🕙 11.30am-5am; 🍴 🍴 ♿ E; 🚇 Hibiya, Toei Ōedo lines to Roppongi, exit 2) The Edo-village décor and urban buzz in the air makes Gonpachi a great place for celebratory dinners, but do you need a reason to thrill your palate with a dozen new-to-you Japanese morsels? Upstairs you can order everything on the menu, plus sushi. Book ahead.

Erawan (Map p119; ☎ 3404-5741; 13th fl, Roi Bldg, 5-5-1 Roppongi, Minato-ku; meals ¥3000; 🕙 dinner; 🍴 🍴 E; 🚇 Hibiya, Toei Ōedo lines to Roppongi, exit 3) An Asian restaurant that's been on the block for years is Erawan, where spicy curries and green papaya salad are served in a setting reminiscent of an outdoor Thai café on some southern shore…except here, you get a glittering urban view from this top-floor dining venue.

1830 (Map p119; ☎ 3402-1830; 9-6-28 Akasaka, Minato-ku; meals ¥2000; 🕙 lunch & dinner; 🍴 ♿ E; 🚇 Chiyoda line to Nogizaka, exit 3) Pizza catering to Japanese tastes can be found all over Tokyo, but the real beast – with wood-fired crust hand tossed by an Italian *pizzaiolo* – is more elusive. If you must have pizza, then do it right by coming here. Other authentic treats like tender gnocchi, melt-in-your-mouth tiramisu and a strong wine list also await.

Monsoon Café (Map p119; ☎ 5467-5221; 2-10-1 Nishi-Azabu, Minato-ku; meals ¥3500; 🕙 11.30am-3.30am; 🍴 🍴 E; 🚇 Hibiya, Toei Ōedo lines to Roppongi, exit 2) Across from Aoyama Cemetery along Gaien-nishi-dōri, Monsoon serves its takes on Southeast Asian basics like Vietnamese spring rolls, Thai coconut soup and chicken satay. With indoor-outdoor café-style seating, big rattan chairs and an attentive staff, it's a nice place to chill with a fruity drink.

Namban-tei (Map p119; ☎ 3402-0606; 4-5-6 Roppongi, Minato-ku; meals ¥6000; 🕙 5-11pm Mon-Sat; 🍴 E; 🚇 Hibiya, Toei Ōedo lines to Roppongi, exit 6) Namban-tei is something of a local institution, known for its excellent *yakitori* in pleasant, traditional

Japanese surroundings. It won't be cheap but it will be delicious. Look for its unassuming wood shopfront on the alley corner.

Inakaya (Map p119; ☎ 3408-5040; 5-3-4 Roppongi, Minato-ku; meals from ¥10,000; 🕙 5-11pm; 🍴 ; 🚇 Hibiya, Toei Ōedo lines to Roppongi, exit 3) Once you're bombarded with greetings at the door, the action doesn't stop at this old-guard *robatayaki* (rustic bar-restaurant serving charcoal-grilled food that goes beautifully with booze). Point at what you'd like to eat and it will be grilled for you. It's boisterous and joyous – the attitude one must have when the bill arrives.

Kisso (Map pp124-5; ☎ 3582-4191; B1 fl, Axis Bldg, 5-17-1 Roppongi, Minato-ku; meals around ¥10,000; 🕙 lunch & dinner Mon-Sat; 🍴 ; 🚇 Hibiya, Toei Ōedo lines to Roppongi, exit 3) Doubtless the most accessible *kaiseki ryōri* (aesthetically presented multicourse meals) in Tokyo, Kisso is the perfect place to experience this quintessentially Japanese gourmet cuisine. Courses are served on gorgeous lacquerware and ceramics in artistically arranged surroundings. Order *omakase* (chef's choice; ¥10,000) and then let the chef's creativity shine.

Fukuzushi (Map p119; ☎ 3402-4116; 5-7-8 Roppongi, Minato-ku; meals around ¥10,000; 🕙 lunch & dinner Mon-Sat; 🍴 E; 🚇 Hibiya, Toei Ōedo lines to Roppongi, exit 3) Some of the best sushi in town is served here, in an upscale atmosphere that's decidedly more relaxed than some of the more traditional places in Ginza and Tsukiji. The fish here is fresh, the portions are large and there are cocktails. It's in the alley beyond the Hard Rock Café, and has a picture menu.

Seryna (Map p119; ☎ 3402-1051; 3-12-2 Roppongi, Minato-ku; lunch/dinner ¥6000/15,000; 🕙 noon-11pm; 🍴 E; 🚇 Hibiya, Toei Ōedo lines to Roppongi, exit 5) Seryna is the go-to stalwart for those wishing to try Kōbe beef. With several eateries under its roof, you can try *shabu-shabu* and *sukiyaki*, or opt for a slab of steak and *teppanyaki* (table-top grilling). The restaurant surrounds a pretty rock garden.

Akasaka 赤坂

Along with nearby Roppongi, Akasaka is one of Tokyo's more cosmopolitan neighbourhoods. While most of the evening action shuts down on the early side, a stroll through the narrow streets just west of Akasaka-mitsuke subway station will turn up a number of good lunch bargains.

Sunaba (Map pp124-5; ☎ 3583-7670; 6-3-5 Akasaka, Minato-ku; meals ¥1100; 🕙 11am-9pm Mon-Fri, to 4pm Sat;

E; ⊖ Chiyoda line to Akasaka, exit 6) Sunaba has some of the city's finest buckwheat noodles. It invented tempura *soba*, and serves it in an exquisite, dense, smoky *tsuyu* (dipping sauce) – sublime. It's next to the Kokusai Shin-Akasaka building, and it has a sister shop in Nihombashi.

Moti (Map pp124-5; ☎ 3582-3620; 2nd fl, 3-8-8 Akasaka, Minato-ku; lunch/dinner ¥800/2000; ⊙ 11.30am-11pm; V E; ⊖ Ginza, Marunouchi lines to Akasaka-mitsuke, Belle Vie exit) Part of Tokyo's best Indian chain, Moti has two branches in Akasaka, each just a few minutes' walk from Akasaka or Akasaka-mitsuke subway stations. Lunch sets include curry and *lassi* or coffee.

Jangara Rāmen (Map pp124-5; ☎ 3595-2130; 2-12-8 Nagatachō, Minato-ku; meals from ¥580; ⊙ 11am-1am Mon-Thu, to 3am Fri; ⊖ Chiyoda line to Akasaka, exit 2) Near the entrance to Hie-jinja, Jangara is a popular place for a great, inexpensive bowl of *rāmen*. Live a little and order the *zenbu-iri rāmen* (all-in *rāmen*; ¥1000)and it'll come topped with hard-boiled egg, slices of pork and fish cake (among other goodies).

Umaya (Map pp124-5; ☎ 6229-1661; 4-2-24 Akasaka, Minato-ku; lunch/dinner from ¥1100/4000; ⊙ 11am-1.30pm & 5pm-1am Mon-Sat; E; ⊖ Ginza, Marunouchi lines to Akasaka-mitsuke, Belle Vie exit) This lovely, traditionally styled restaurant serves a variety of Japanese dishes, incorporating free-range chicken and house-made tofu. There's no lunch menu in English, but servers can explain the seasonally changing *teishoku*. To find it from Hitotsugi-dōri, head for Akasaka-fudōson-jinja but turn left just inside the shrine gate.

Vietnam Alice (Map pp124-5; ☎ 3588-5020; 2nd fl, Belle Vie, 3-1-6 Akasaka, Minato-ku; lunch/dinner ¥1500/3000; ⊙ 11am-10pm; E; ⊖ Ginza, Marunouchi lines to Akasaka-mitsuke, Belle Vie exit) Dressed up to look like a French-colonial villa, Vietnam Alice delivers a respectable rendition of gourmet Vietnamese food in romantic surroundings. Lunch specials are a good deal, and it does a good *pho*.

Sushi-sei (Map pp124-5; ☎ 3582-9503; 3-11-14 Akasaka, Minato-ku; lunch/dinner ¥1500/4000; ⊙ 11.30am-2pm & 5-11.30pm Mon-Sat; V ; ⊖ Ginza, Marunouchi lines to Akasaka-mitsuke, Belle Vie exit) This branch of the famous Tsukiji sushi chain won't disappoint. Lunch sets (choose from a picture menu) are priced very reasonably for the quality, and with its reputation, you can be sure you're eating some of the freshest fish around. The low-profile shop is set back slightly from the street.

Kushinobō (Map pp124-5; ☎ 3581 6056; 3rd fl, Akasaka Tōkyu Plaza, 2-14-3 Nagatachō, Minato-ku; dinner courses from ¥2500; ⊙ lunch & dinner Mon-Sat; E; ⊖ Ginza, Marunouchi lines to Akasaka-mitsuke, Belle Vie exit) Sometimes it's necessary to give in to those dark cravings for something deep fried, and because these lunches are fairly inexpensive, you can at least console yourself with your budgetary virtue. Come to Kushinobō at times like these for *kushiage* (skewers of deep-fried meat, seafood and vegetables) and *kushi-katsu*, this place's speciality.

Asterix (Map p119; ☎ 5561-0980; B1 fl, 6-3-16 Akasaka, Minato-ku; lunch/dinner from ¥1500/3000; ⊙ lunch & dinner Mon-Sat; ; ⊖ Chiyoda line to Akasaka, exit 7) A French lunch here is a smashing deal, but dinner has its own merits – not as rushed, so you can linger over your wine. Portions are large but the dining room is tiny, so reservations are advised. The menu is in French; servers can translate into English if needed.

Shunju (Map pp124-5; ☎ 3592-5288; 27th fl, Sannō Park Tower, 2-11-1 Nagatachō, Chiyoda-ku; lunch/dinner from ¥1200/6300; ⊙ lunch & dinner Mon-Sat; E; ⊖ Ginza, Namboku lines to Tameike-sannō, exit 7) A great choice for a modern take on traditional Japanese cuisine, Shunju also happens to boast a fabulous view. Lunches are very reasonably priced, as are the dinner sets, which offer a little bit of everything.

Odaiba お台場

Odaiba makes a beautiful stage for enjoying a romantic meal, as most of the restaurants have good views of Tokyo Bay. For fun – and a little dim sum (yum cha) – check out the array of Hong Kong-style eateries at Daiba Little Hong Kong on the 6th and 7th floors of Decks Tokyo Beach.

Soup Stock Tokyo (Map p122; ☎ 3599-2333; 3rd fl, Venus Fort, Aomi-itchōme, Kōtō-ku; meals from ¥580; ⊙ 11am-11pm; V E; ⊖ Yurikamome line to Odaiba Kaihin-kōen, main exit) With its emphasis on wholesome, additive-free soups, Soup Stock Tokyo feeds the health conscious – and those in need of comfort – all across Tokyo. Soup sets come with fresh bread and a drink (¥950), and there are usually around 10 different varieties on offer, from borscht to garlic soup with *onsen tamago* (hot-spring boiled eggs).

Khazana (Map p122; ☎ 3359-6551; 5th fl, Decks Tokyo Beach, 1-6-1 Daiba, Minato-ku; lunch/dinner ¥1000/2000; ⊙ 11am-11pm; V E; ⊖ Yurikamome line to Odaiba Kaihin-kōen, main exit) Khazana's Odaiba outpost is a welcoming perch for taking in the bay views and tucking into some spicy samosa. The staff is warm and the environment pleasantly laid-back.

Tsukiji Tama Sushi (Map p122; ☎ 3599-6556; 5th fl, Decks Tokyo Beach, 1-6-1 Daiba, Minato-ku; meals ¥2000-4000; ☉ 11am-11pm; ⛆ E; ⊕ Yurikamome line to Odaiba Kaihin-kōen, main exit) Settle yourself near the windows and sip from a huge, earthy cup of green tea while you wait for your sushi, which will come immaculately presented and perfectly fresh. The menu also includes set meals and *udon*, if you prefer.

DRINKING

Bar and club life being what it is, the venue of the moment might be passé come tomorrow morning. The following is a rundown on bars and clubs that have proven popular enough to stick around for the past few years and were still going strong at the time of writing. For up-to-the-minute listings, check the websites noted on p107.

For a true Japanese drinking experience, round up a few people and check out an *izakaya*; chains like **Tsubohachi** (Map p117; ☎ 3464-1129; 26-4 Udagawachō, Shibuya-ku; meals ¥3500; ☉ 4pm-midnight Sun-Thu, to 3am Fri & Sat; ⛆ ; ⊕ JR Yamanote line to Shibuya, Hachikō exit) have branches all over Tokyo and huge picture menus to choose what to eat with your *nama-biiru*. During the summer, many of the large department stores like Keiō (p179) in Shinjuku or Matsuya (p179) in Ginza open up their rooftop beer gardens, a treat on hot summer evenings. Join the salarymen after work and hoist a few on these open-air terraces.

Ueno & Asakusa 上野 浅草
Yawn – definitely not the neighbourhoods for a wild night out.

In Asakusa, try the beer halls in the Asahi Breweries complex (look up and follow the Flamme D'Or – aka the 'Golden Turd' – to the east side of the Sumida River).

Kamiya Bar (Map pp130-1; ☎ 3841-5400; 1-1-1 Asakusa, Taitō-ku; ☉ 11.30am-10pm Wed-Mon) Spend an evening at this long-standing bar, which opened in 1880 and is said to be the oldest Western-style bar in Japan. There's a smoky beer hall on the ground floor, where you order and pay for beer and food as you enter. Upstairs, unremarkable Western and Japanese food is served.

Warrior Celt (Map pp130-1; ☎ 3836-8588; www .warriorcelt.com; 3rd fl, Ito Bldg, 6-9-22 Ueno, Taitō-ku; ☉ 5pm-5am; ⊕ JR Yamanote line to Ueno, south central exit) If you do find yourself hanging round old Shitamachi at night, head to this pub in Ueno, where drinks are only ¥500 from 5pm to 7pm. It's a fun, friendly place with a good selection of English and Irish brews, as well as free live music several nights a week.

Ikebukuro 池袋
There are lots of *izakaya* (sans English menus) buried amid the sex shops and strip bars on both sides of Ikebukuro station. Sake fans should seek out the excellent *izakaya* Sasashū, run by a former WWII kamikaze pilot. If you're more in the mood for a pint of Guinness, the following little pubs tend to draw both Japanese and international folks.

Bobby's Bar (Map p114; ☎ 3980-8875; 3rd fl, Milano Bldg, 1-18-10 Nishi-Ikebukuro, Toshima-ku; ☉ 6pm-3am Sun-Thu, to 5am Fri & Sat; ⊕ JR Yamanote line to Ikebukuro, west exit) On the western side of the station is this late-night option, with cocktails from ¥300 and lots of Belgian beers. There's table soccer, darts and good pub grub. Early birds will enjoy the happy hour, 6pm to 8pm Monday to Thursday.

Dubliners (Map p114; ☎ 5951-3614; B1 fl, Sun Glow Bldg, 1-10-8 Nishi-Ikebukuro, Toshima-ku; ☉ 11am-11pm; ⛆ ; ⊕ JR Yamanote line to Ikebukuro, Metropolitan exit) This is a small, standard-issue Irish-style pub offering Kilkenny and Guinness draught; if you're lucky, you'll show up on a night when it has live music.

Shinjuku 新宿
Gaudy Shinjuku is awash with nightspots of every shape and size, many of which fall into the sordid category and don't cater to foreigners. That said, there's still plenty to do here at night if you have the energy to face the madness of an evening on Shinjuku streets.

The Golden Gai is one of the city's most interesting night zones. Even if you don't feel like a drink, take an evening stroll through this maze of tightly packed little establishments, just to soak in the low-slung moodiness – the whole place seems suspended in a time warp. Many of these miniscule bars do not welcome *gaijin* and/or non-Japanese speakers and may charge you a hefty cover for entering, but the first three establishments listed here are friendly to strangers. An easy way to get there is to find Hanazono-jinja and then walk around to the steps at the back of the shrine, which lead right into the Golden Gai.

La Jetée (Map p116; ☎ 3208-9645; 1-1-8 Kabukichō, Shinjuku-ku; admission ¥700; ☷ 7pm till late Mon-Sat; ◉ Marunouchi, Toei Shinjuku lines to Shinjuku-sanchōme, exit B5) A favourite among cineastes (and run by one), this little haven is the namesake for a film much admired by its French-speaking proprietor and a good introduction to these alleys.

Bon's (Map p116; ☎ 3209-6334; 1-1-10 Kabukichō, Shinjuku-ku; admission ¥900; ☷ 7pm-5am; ☒ ; ◉ Marunouchi, Toei Shinjuku lines to Shinjuku-sanchōme, exit B5) Drinks start at ¥700 at this sure-fire spot in the Golden Gai. Look for its corner location with 'Old Fashioned American Style Pub' painted across its exterior wall.

Bar Plastic Model (Map p116; ☎ 5273-8441; 1-1-10 Kabukichō, Shinjuku-ku; admission ¥700; ☷ 8pm-5am Mon-Sat, 6pm-midnight Sun; ☒ ; ◉ Marunouchi, Toei Shinjuku lines to Shinjuku-sanchōme, exit B5) There's a new generation of creative bar owners converting old Golden Gai bars into incarnations of their own visions. This is one such concoction, decorated with tchotchkes c 1980, and sometimes with a DJ spinning beats.

Rolling Stone (Map p116; ☎ 3341-6741; B1 fl, Q-Flat Bldg, 5-4-1 Shinjuku, Shinjuku-ku; admission ¥2000; ☷ 7pm-late; ☒ ; ◉ Marunouchi, Toei Shinjuku lines to Shinjuku-sanchōme, exit C7) This place has been around since the dawn of time, but it's now upgraded to a basement location complete with disco ball and rotating lineup of DJs. There's no admission from 7pm to 9pm, and the admission charge includes two drinks. The stairwell is next door to the Freshness Burger on Yasukuni-dōri.

Garam (Map p116; ☎ 3205-8668; 7th fl, 1-16-6 Kabukichō, Shinjuku-ku; admission from ¥1500; ☷ 8pm-5am; ◉ JR Yamanote line to Shinjuku, east exit) A club that feels like a bar, this is a small, friendly place, where the master DJ spins a range of hip-hop, dub and roots reggae. The admission charge includes one drink.

Harajuku & Shibuya 原宿

These adjoining areas are a good option when the Roppongi crush is too much to bear. Harajuku and Aoyama are all about cafés, and you can spend an evening drinking beer and wine in them rather than mashing yourself into a smoky basement bar. Las Chicas (p158) is a great escape; but check ahead to see if it's reopened yet.

Den Aquaroom (Map p117; ☎ 5778-2090; B1 fl, 5-13-3 Minami-Aoyama, Minato-ku; admission ¥500-1000; ☒ ; ◉ Chiyoda, Ginza, Hanzōmon lines to Omote-sandō, exit B1) Darting fish within the walls of back-lit, blue aquariums make a visual counterpoint to the bop of jazz basslines. Even prettier than the dark décor is the chic clientele floating around here.

Insomnia 2 (Map p117; ☎ 3476-2735; B1 fl, 26-5 Udagawachō, Shibuya-ku; ☷ 6pm-5am; ☒ ; ◉ JR Yamanote line to Shibuya, Hachikō exit) Insomnia is that rare Shibuya find: a bar for grown-ups. Good food, low music and a cosy red interior make it the kind of place to come when you want to hear your conversation. The kitchen's open late, and the oddly eyeballesque mirrored wall behind the bar will induce insomnia if you're not already feeling it.

Hub Pub (Map p117; ☎ 3770-4524; 25-9 Udagawachō, Shibuya-ku; ☒ ; ◉ JR Yamanote line to Shibuya, Hachikō exit) A generally English ambience, pub food and a decent selection of beers attract a mixed crowd of 20-somethings, especially on weekends. The Hub has branches all over the city, though this is probably the most comfortable of the lot.

Ebisu & Daikanyama 恵比寿・代官山

These two neighbourhoods are excellent choices for a night out in Tokyo, striking the perfect balance between hip and casual.

What the Dickens (Map p121; ☎ 3780-2099; www.whatthedickens.jp; 4th fl, Roob 6 Bldg, 1-13-3 Ebisu-Nishi, Shibuya-ku; ☷ 5pm-late Tue-Sat, to midnight Sun; ◉ JR Yamanote line to Ebisu, west exit) Live music, British beers, pub grub and a good time in Ebisu – a combo that works, as the happy crowd will attest. The bands span a variety of styles, and live music happens almost every night.

Enjoy! House (Map p121; ☎ 5489-1591; 2nd fl, Kokuto Bldg, 2-9-9 Ebisu-Nishi, Shibuya-ku; ☷ 1pm-2am Sun & Tue-Thu, to 4am Fri-Sun; ☒ ; ◉ JR Yamanote line to Ebisu, west exit) A multilayered world of sparkly, '70s retro funkiness awaits inside the fairly innocuously named Enjoy! House. The freespirited dude who runs this fun spot will elevate your mood.

Munch-ya (Map p121; ☎ 5722-1333; 1-10-23 Naka-Meguro, Meguro-ku; ☷ noon-3pm & 5pm-late; ☒ E; ◉ Hibiya line to Naka-Meguro) This friendly bar in hip Naka-Meguro serves beer and wine, as well as Japanese small plates, for ¥500 a pop – an easy way to have sort of an *izakaya* experience without leaving you yenless. From the exit, turn right on Yamate-dōri, make a left on Komazawa-dōri and follow the road next to the river.

(Continued on page 173)

GREG ELMS

Sensō-ji (p135) at dusk, Asakusa, Tokyo

GREG ELMS

Frozen tuna, Tsukiji Fish Market
(p132), Tokyo

Roppongi (p139) at night

GREG ELMS

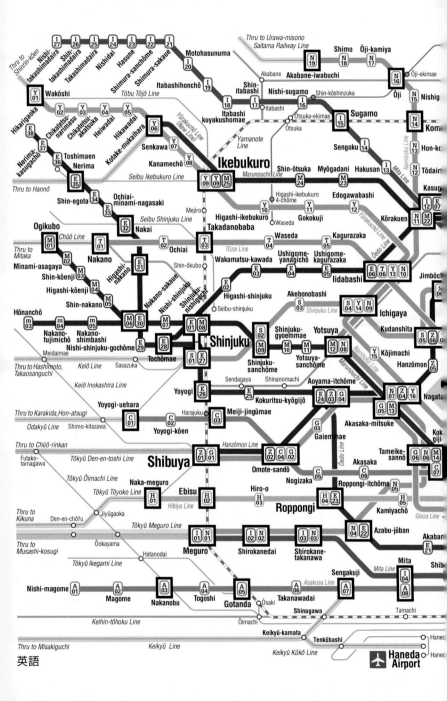

英語

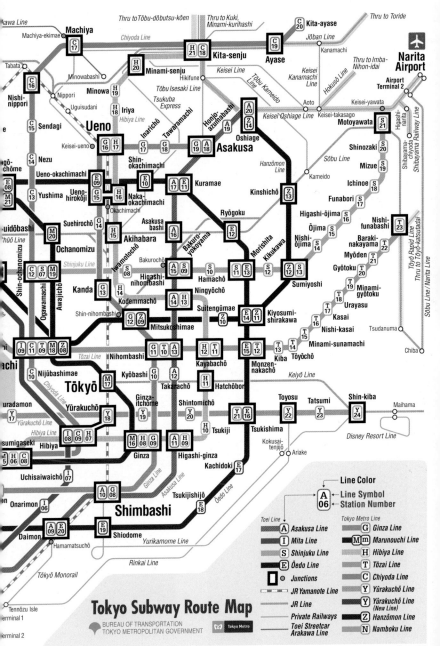

Tokyo Subway Route Map

BUREAU OF TRANSPORTATION
TOKYO METROPOLITAN GOVERNMENT

Line Color

A 06 ← Line Symbol / Station Number

Toei Line

- **A** Asakusa Line
- **I** Mita Line
- **S** Shinjuku Line
- **E** Ōedo Line
- Junctions
- JR Yamanote Line
- JR Line
- Private Railways
- Toei Streetcar Arakawa Line

Tokyo Metro Line

- **G** Ginza Line
- **M** Marunouchi Line
- **H** Hibiya Line
- **T** Tōzai Line
- **C** Chiyoda Line
- **Y** Yūrakuchō Line
- **Y** Yūrakuchō Line (New Line)
- **Z** Hanzōmon Line
- **N** Namboku Line

BUREAU OF TRANSPORTATION TOKYO METROPOLITAN GOVERNMENT   Tokyo Metro Co., Ltd. © 2006.3 P100

ADINA TOVY AMSEL

Boats drift across Ashino-ko (p209) as a cloud drifts across the face of Mt Fuji

A bustling Chinatown (p221) street in Yokohama

JAMES MARSHALL

CHRISTIAN KOBER/ROBERT HARDING PICTURE LIBRARY LTD/PHOTOLIBRARY

Pagoda at Tōshō-gū (p189), Nikkō

FRANK CARTER

A heron wades near a stone lantern in Kenroku-en (p294)

Thatched *gasshō-zukuri* houses at Shirakawa-gō (p264)

MARTIN MOOS

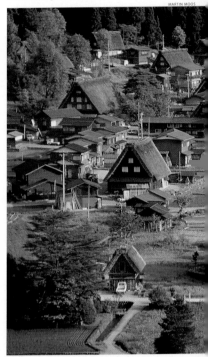

Lazy macaques avoiding the winter chill at Jigokudani Yaen-kōen (p278), Yudanaka

CORBIS/PHOTOLIBRARY

Kyoto's famed Ginkaku-ji (p339) surrounded by spring greenery

FRANK CARTER

PHIL WEYMOUTH

A sacred incense urn sits in front of the main hall of Nanzen-ji (p338), Kyoto

The world's largest wooden building: Tōdai-ji's Daibutsu-den Hall (p403), Nara

STAEVE

FRANK CARTER

Torii tunnels at Fushimi-Inari Taisha (p346), Kyoto

Buildings along the Dōtombori (p378), Osaka

GLOW IMAGES/PHOTOLIBRARY

FRANK CARTER

Cooking *oden* at Nishiki Market (p315), Kyoto

FRANK CARTER

The sun sets on the the banks of the picturesque
Kamo-gawa in Kyoto (p309)

Geisha (p338), Gion, Kyoto

FRANK CARTER

Traditional stone lantern at Kurama-dera (p349), Kitayama Area, Kyoto

OLIVER

(Continued from page 164)

Roppongi & Akasaka 六本木・赤坂

Roppongi is not part of Japan – it's a multinational twilight zone that feels like Mardi Gras blew over on a hurricane from New Orleans, where *gaijin* get together with adventurous locals to boozily schmooze until the first trains at dawn. Because of this, many long-term locals avoid it like the plague, leaving it for punters fresh off the plane, military goons and riff-raff out trolling for local talent. This is the place, above all others in Japan, where you're most likely to get hustled, so just be wary of pushy club promoters and hostess types. Nonetheless, Roppongi still rocks, and you'll want to check it out at least once.

Meet up in front of that pink-painted pastry purveyor, Almond (everyone knows it; you can't miss it), and then jump in.

Heartland (Map p119; ☎ 5772-7600; www.heartland.jp; 1st fl, Roppongi Hills West Walk, 6-10-1 Roppongi, Minato-ku; 🕐 11am-5am; 🏮 ; 🚇 Hibiya, Toei Ōedo lines to Roppongi, exits 1b & 3) At the foot of Roppongi Hills, Heartland is far enough removed from Roppongi Crossing to not be full of sloshed randoms. This crowd has a familiar foreign-male-to-Japanese-female ratio, but these specimens are more nattily dressed than the ones down the road.

Mogambo (Map p119; ☎ 3403-4833; www.mogambo.net; 1st fl, Osawa Bldg, 6-1-7 Roppongi, Minato-ku; 🕐 6pm-6am Mon-Fri, 7pm-6am Sat; 🏮 ; 🚇 Hibiya, Toei Ōedo lines to Roppongi, exit 3) A small shot bar with a long list of cocktails, Mogambo attracts an international crowd with its campy jungle theme. Mogambo is on the southern side of Roppongi-dōri, a block south of Almond.

Agave (Map p119; ☎ 3497-0229; B1 fl, 7-15-10 Roppongi, Minato-ku; 🕐 6.30pm-2am Mon-Fri, to 4am Sat; 🏮 ; 🚇 Hibiya, Toei Ōedo lines to Roppongi, exit 2). This amiable spot is more about savouring the subtleties of its 400-plus types of tequila rather than tossing back body shots of Cuervo. Mariachi musicians will woo you as you sip *añejo* (aged tequila). Walking west from Roppongi Crossing, find it on the small alley on the north side of the street.

Castillo (Map p119; ☎ 3475-1629; 3rd & 4th fl, Win Roppongi Bldg, 3-15-24 Roppongi, Minato-ku; 🕐 7pm-late Mon-Sat; 🏮 ; 🚇 Hibiya, Toei Ōedo lines to Roppongi, exit 3) Still playing its '70s and '80s soul, pop and disco classics in a new venue, Castillo attracts a good mix of locals and foreigners to dance or just kick it for a few drinks between stops on a club crawl.

Propaganda (Map p119; ☎ 3423-0988; 2nd fl, Yua Roppongi Bldg, 3-14-9 Roppongi, Minato-ku; 🕐 6pm-dawn; 🏮 ; 🚇 Hibiya, Toei Ōedo lines to Roppongi, exit 3) Propaganda is the decorating scheme, but the deal is transparent – above Bikkuri Sushi, this is an inexpensive shot bar with half-price happy-hour specials (around ¥400). It's open late and there's no admission, so it's a reliable place to stumble back to if you close another bar.

Motown House 1 (Map p119; ☎ 5474-4605; www.motownhouse.com; 2nd fl, Com Roppongi Bldg, 3-11-5 Roppongi, Minato-ku; 🕐 6pm-5am; 🚇 Hibiya, Toei Ōedo lines to Roppongi, exit 3) Steps from Roppongi Crossing, Motown House plays soul, funk, hip-hop and pop, as well as standard rock and roll. Drinks at the long bar start at ¥800.

Motown House 2 (☎ 5474-2931; B1 fl, Roppongi Plaza Bldg; 🕐 8pm-5am Sun-Thu, to 8am Fri & Sat) On the next block, the second branch has a similar setup to the first.

Gas Panic Bar (Map p119; ☎ 3405-0633; www.gaspanic.co.jp; 2nd & 3rd fl, 3-15-24 Roppongi, Minato-ku; 🕐 6pm-5am; 🏮 ; 🚇 Hibiya, Toei Ōedo lines to Roppongi, exit 3) This concatenation of three ominously named bars forms one of Roppongi's rowdier culs-de-sac. All three are cheap places to drink, so they get crammed with all sorts of sloppy amateurs. You're only welcome as long as you've got a drink in hand.

Akasaka can be an expensive and staid place to drink, especially considering Roppongi is just a 20-minute walk away. But those in search of high-rise views to go with their cocktails can find swish bars at the top of the neighbourhood's luxury hotels. **Top of Akasaka** (Map pp124-5; ☎ 3234-1121; drinks from ¥1500; 🕐 11.30am-2pm & 5pm-2am Mon-Fri, noon-2am Sat, to 11pm Sun) in the Akasaka Prince Hotel and **Bar** (Map p119; ☎ 3265-1111; 🕐 5pm-midnight Mon-Fri, noon-midnight Sat & Sun) in the New Otani tower are both 40th-floor bars.

ENTERTAINMENT

Tokyo is very much the centre of the Japanese arts world, with the best of everything. On the nightlife front, there are those who maintain that Osaka is more cutting edge, but then Osaka offers nowhere near the diversity of entertainment options available in Tokyo – everything from kabuki to avant-garde theatre, cinemas, live houses, pubs and bars. See p59 for more information on Japanese theatre.

Cinemas

Shibuya and Shinjuku are Tokyo's cinema centres, but you'll find cinemas near any

GAY & LESBIAN TOKYO

If you're in Tokyo during the summer, the **Tokyo International Lesbian & Gay Film Festival** (www.tokyo-lgff.org) hits screens in July.

Tokyo's gay and lesbian enclave is Shinjuku-nichōme, the area east of Shinjuku sanchōme station's C8 exit. There are lots of little bars here, and though some can be rather daunting to enter, the following venues have been around awhile and are friendly. For more options, check out www.utopia-asia.com or weekly Cityscope Nightlife listings in *Tokyo Journal* (www.tokyo.to).

Arty Farty (Map p116; ☎ 5362-9720; www.arty-farty.net; 2nd fl, 2-11-7 Shinjuku, Shinjuku-ku; ☽ 7pm-3am Mon-Thu, to 5am Fri & Sat, 5pm-3am Sun; ◉ Marunouchi, Toei Shinjuku lines to Shinjuku-sanchōme, exit C8) Arty Farty is a long-standing place to meet people, with fabulous all-you-can-drink specials and a mixed crowd. It's a good place to start your evening and find out about the area's other possibilities.

Kinswomyn (Map p116; ☎ 3354-8720; 3rd fl, 2-15-10 Shinjuku, Shinjuku-ku; cocktails ¥750; ☽ 7pm-4am Mon-Sat; ◉ Marunouchi, Toei Shinjuku lines to Shinjuku-sanchōme, exit C8) Another well-established and welcoming bar, Kinswomyn is a cosy, women-only spot for Japanese and foreign women alike. The bar mistress Tara is friendly, as are the ladies hanging out here.

Advocates Bar (Map p116; ☎ 3358-8638; B1 fl, 7th Tenka Bldg, 2-18-1 Shinjuku, Shinjuku-ku; ☽ 8pm-4am; ◉ Marunouchi, Toei Shinjuku lines to Shinjuku-sanchōme, exit C8) Advocates Bar is so small that as the crowd gets bigger during the course of an evening, it becomes more like a block party and takes to the streets. Family of all genders are welcome here.

major train station. Check the *Japan Times, Metropolis* or the *Tokyo Journal* to see what's on; imported films are usually subtitled in Japanese, so the sound tends to be in the original language. Discounted tickets are sold in the basement of the Tokyo Kōtsū Kaikan (Map p109) building in Ginza, Shinjuku's Studio Alta building (Map p116; 5th floor), Harajuku's Laforet building (Map p117; 1st floor) and Shibuya's 109 Building (Map p117; 2nd floor). We've listed some of Tokyo's most accessible cinemas here:

Cinema Rise (Map p117; ☎ 3464-0051; www.cinema rise.com in Japanese; 13-17 Udagawachō, Shibuya-ku; adult ¥1500; ◉ JR Yamanote line to Shibuya, Hachikō exit) Screening international and Japanese indie cinema.

Virgin Toho Cinemas Roppongi Hills (Map p119; ☎ 5775-6090; www.tohotheater.jp/theater/roppongi /index.html; 6-10-2 Roppongi, Minato-ku; adult ¥1800-3000, child ¥1000, 1st day of month ¥1000, women on Wed ¥1000; ☽ 10am-midnight Sun-Wed, to 5am Thu-Sat; ◉ Hibiya, Toei Ōedo lines to Roppongi, exit 3) You can book on the internet up to two days in advance for reserved seats at this nine-screen mainstream multiplex with luxurious reclining seats.

Yebisu Garden Cinema (Map p121; ☎ 5420-6161; Yebisu Garden Place, 4-20-2 Ebisu, Shibuya-ku; adult/child ¥1800/1000, 1st day of month ¥1000; ☽ 10am-11pm; ◉ JR Yamanote line to Ebisu, east exit to Skywalk) This small, comfortable movie house screens mainstream and independent films. Tickets are numbered as they're sold and theatregoers are called in by number, preventing competition for seats.

Music

In Tokyo, you might have the luxury of seeing up-and-coming performers playing in intimate venues. Check the latest issue of *Metropolis* or *Tokyo Journal* or pick up some flyers at record shops (p180) in Shibuya to see who's playing around town. Ticket prices generally range from ¥5000 to ¥8000, depending on performer and venue.

DANCE CLUBS

You'll find the greatest concentration and diversity of clubs in Roppongi.

Muse (Map p119; ☎ 5467-1188; 4-1-1 Nishi-Azabu, Minato-ku; admission ¥1000-2000; ☽ 7pm-4am Sun-Thu, to 5am Fri & Sat; ☷ ; ◉ Hibiya, Toei Ōedo lines to Roppongi, exits 1b & 3) With a friendly, international crowd, multilevel Muse has something for everyone – packed dance floor, several bar areas, cosy alcoves big enough for two – but also pool tables, darts and karaoke. Women usually don't pay a cover, which includes a drink or two. Near the Hobson's on the corner of Nishi-Azabu Crossing there's a neon 'Bar' sign marking the entrance.

Club 328 (Map p119; ☎ 3401-4968; www.3-2-8.jp; B1 fl, Kotsu Anzen Center Bldg, 3-24-20 Nishi-Azabu, Minato-ku; admission ¥2000-2500; ☽ 8pm-5am; ◉ Hibiya, Toei Ōedo lines to Roppongi, exits 1b & 3) DJs at San-ni-pa spin a quality mix, from funk to reggae to R&B. With its refreshing un-Roppongi feel and a cool crowd of Japanese and *gaijin*, 328 is a good place to boogie 'til the break of dawn.

Admission includes two drinks. It's on Roppongi-dōri just off Nishi-Azabu Crossing.

Space Lab Yellow (Map p119; ☎ 3479-0690; www .club-yellow.com; B1 & B2 fl, Cesaurus Bldg, 1-10-11 Nishi-Azabu, Minato-ku; admission ¥2000-3500; ◉ Hibiya, Toei Ōedo lines to Roppongi, exit 2) Yellow is one of the best places in Tokyo to head for electronica. It's an inky basement space featuring everything from acid jazz to samba. Look for the glowing yellow sign next to a coin parking lot. Admission includes a drink or two.

Salsa Sudada (Map p119; ☎ 5474-8806; 3rd fl, La Palette Bldg, 7-13-8 Roppongi, Minato-ku; ◷ 6pm-6am; ◉ Hibiya, Toei Ōedo lines to Roppongi, exit 3) Experienced salsa dancers can kick up their heels here for hours, while beginners can take lessons offered on Sunday nights. International dancers flock regularly to this place from Tokyo and beyond for salsa and merengue.

Bul-Let's (Map p119; ☎ 3401-4844; www.bul-lets.com; B1 fl, Kasumi Bldg, 1-7-11 Nishi-Azabu, Minato-ku; admission from ¥1500; ◷ from around 7pm; ◉ Hibiya, Toei Ōedo lines to Roppongi, exit 2) Near Yellow, this mellow basement space plays worldwide trance and ambient sounds for barefoot patrons. Beds and sofas furnish this carpeted club, but don't get the wrong idea – it's not all tranquillity and deadbeats.

Vanilla (Map p119; ☎ 3401-6200; www.clubvanilla .com; TSK Bldg, 7-14-30 Roppongi, Minato-ku; admission from ¥2000; ◷ 9pm-late; ◉ Hibiya, Toei Ōedo lines to Roppongi, exit 4) Aimed more towards a Japanese clientele, Vanilla harbours fewer *gaijin* drunkards than nearby bars. Three floors of dance space are filled with different beats and crowds of peeps. From Roppongi station, head west on Roppongi-dōri, pass Mizuho Bank and turn right down the next alley.

Lexington Queen (Map p119; ☎ 3401-1661; www.lex ingtonqueen.com; B1 fl, Gotō Bldg, 3-13-14 Roppongi, Minato-ku; ◷ 8pm-5am; ◉ Hibiya, Toei Ōedo lines to Roppongi, exit 3) The Lex was one of Roppongi's first discos and is still the place where visiting celebrities end up. Entry starts around ¥2000 unless you've had your visage on the admission of *Vogue* or *Rolling Stone*. But even noncelebs get a free drink with admission.

In Shibuya, you could follow the *kogyaru* ('gals' of Shibuya subcultures) to a 'para-para' club where everyone dances in surreal, mechanical sync, though this will make you feel like a complete alien. If you're over the age of, say, 20, try these clubs for a start.

Ruby Room (Map p117; ☎ 3780-3022; www.rubyroom tokyo.com; 2F, Kasumi Bldg, 2-25-17 Dōgenzaka, Shibuya-ku; admission ¥2000; ◷ 9pm-late; ◉ JR Yamanote line to Shibuya, Hachikō exit) This dark, sparkly cocktail lounge is on a hill behind the 109 Building. The Ruby Room hosts both DJed and live music (admission includes a free drink), and is a fun place for older kids hanging in Shibuya.

Club Asia (Map p117; ☎ 5458-2551; 1-8 Maruyamachō, Shibuya-ku; admission ¥2500; ◷ 11pm-5am; ◉ JR Yamanote line to Shibuya, Hachikō exit) This massive technosoul club is popular with those on the younger end of 20-something. Events here are usually jam-packed no matter what night it is. There's also an OK restaurant serving Southeast Asian food.

Womb (Map p117; ☎ 5459-0039; www.womb.co.jp; 2-16 Maruyamachō, Shibuya-ku; admission ¥1500-4000; ◷ 8pm-late; ◉ JR Yamanote line to Shibuya, Hachikō exit) 'Oomu' (as pronounced in Japanese) plays house, techno and drum 'n' bass, and the four floors get crowded on weekends. If you bring a flyer – make the rounds of Shibuya record shops beforehand, or print one from the website – you'll get ¥500 or ¥1000 off the admission. Picture ID required at the door.

Ageha (Map pp112-13; ☎ 5534-1515; www.ageha.com; 2-2-10 Shin-Kiba, Kōtō-ku; admission ¥2000-3000; ◷ 10pm-5am Tue-Sat; ◉ Yūrakuchō line to Shin-Kiba, main exit) This ginormous club on the water rivals any you'd find in LA or Ibiza. International and Japanese DJs appear here, and counterbalancing the thumping beats are chillout rooms and a small pool area. Free shuttles (ID required) run about every half-hour between the club and Shibuya station's east side bus terminal on Roppongi-dōri.

KARAOKE

Karaoke is ever popular in the land of its birth, and Tokyoites love belting out a few tunes at their local karaoke bars. There's no shortage of places to yowl out your favourites, and most offer at least a limited selection of songs in English and even a few in Spanish, French and Chinese. Oh, by the way, it's not 'carry-okey' in this country, so watch your pronunciation if you're asking the way to kah-rah-oh-kay.

Smash Hits (Map pp112-13; ☎ 3444-0432; www.smash hits.jp; B1 fl, M2 Bldg, 5-2-26 Hiro-o, Shibuya-ku; admission ¥3000; ◷ 7pm-3am Mon-Sat; ◉ Hibiya line to Hiro-o, exit B2) You're spoilt for choice at Smash Hits, where it has thousands of songs to choose from. There's no time limit on karaoke. Entry includes two drinks.

Lovenet (Map p119; ☎ 5771-5511; www.lovenet -jp.com; 3rd-4th fl, Hotel Ibis, 7-14-4 Roppongi, Minato-ku;

rooms per hr from ¥4800; ☒ 6pm-5am; ⊕ Hibiya, Toei Ōedo lines to Roppongi, exit 4a) If you're going for a more unique, upmarket experience, you can rent one of the gajillion themed rooms at Lovenet – one even has a hot tub from which you can warble.

LIVE MUSIC

Tokyo's homegrown live music scene has turned out some good live acts, often found playing around Shibuya and Ebisu.

Crocodile (Map p117; ☎ 3499-5205; B1 fl, New Sekiguchi Bldg, 6-18-8 Jingūmae, Shibuya-ku; admission from ¥2000; ☒ 6pm-2am; ⊕ Chiyoda line to Meiji-jingūmae, exit 4) Crocodile has live music seven nights a week, with enough room for dancing if the music moves you – though you may be the only one. Tunes cover the gamut from night to night, be it jazz, reggae or rock and roll. Admission includes one drink. It's right on Meiji-dōri, in Harajuku.

Milk (Map p121; ☎ 5458-2826; www.milk-tokyo.com; B1 fl, Roob 6 Bldg, 1-13-3 Ebisu-Nishi, Shibuya-ku; admission ¥1000-3000; ☒ 8pm-4am; ⊕ JR Yamanote line to Ebisu, west exit) Beneath What the Dickens, Milk has live music on Thursday and Friday nights. Check out the kitchen – there's no food but it's a great place to chat and sip a cocktail between sets. There's a good mix of musical genres here, from dub and hip-hop to electronica.

La.mama (Map p117; ☎ 3464-0801; info@lamama.net; B1 fl, Primera Dogenzaka Bldg, 1-15-3 Dōgenzaka, Shibuya-ku; admission from ¥2000; ☒ 6pm-late; ⊕ JR Yamanote line to Shibuya, Hachikō exit) For a dose of current local-centric music, this is a good bet for catching live, mainstream-Japanese acts who've arrived or are rocking their way up. The room is fairly spacious, and even when the place gets crowded you'll never be far from the stage.

Eggman (Map p117; ☎ 3496-1561; 1-6-8 Jinnan, Shibuya-ku; admission ¥1000-3000; ☒ 6.30pm-late; ⊕ JR Yamanote line to Shibuya, Hachikō exit) Follow the spiral staircase down to this basement spot to hear blues, rock or light jazz. A smaller venue compared with Shibuya's bigger clubs, Eggman features mostly local, rock-and-roll bands.

Loft (Map p116; ☎ 5272-0382; www.loft-prj.co.jp/LOFT /index.html; B2 fl, Tatehana Bldg, 1-12-9 Kabukichō, Shinjuku-ku; admission from ¥1000; ☒ 5pm-late; ⊕ JR Yamanote line to Shinjuku, east exit) Had they been Japanese, the Rolling Stones would have played here long before they cut their first single. This Shinjuku institution is smoky, loud and lots of fun on a good night. Head into Kabukichō and find Loft a block east of the Koma Theater complex.

Cavern Club (Map p119; ☎ 3405-5207; 1st fl, Saito Bldg, 5-3-2 Roppongi, Minato-ku; admission ¥1500; ☒ from 6pm; ⊕ Hibiya, Toei Ōedo lines to Roppongi, exit 3) Eerily flawless renditions of Beatles covers have to be heard to be believed, sung by four Japanese mop-heads at this club named for the place the originals first appeared in Liverpool. Reserve a table ahead of time.

These bigger Shibuya clubs draw brighter stars, so you'll need to book tickets in advance, rather than turning up in the hope of getting in on the night of a show:

Club Quattro (Map p117; ☎ 3477-8750; 4th & 5th fl, Club Quattro Bldg, 32-13 Udagawachō, Shibuya-ku; admission from ¥3500; ☒ from 6pm; ⊕ JR Yamanote line to Shibuya, Hachikō exit)

O-West (Map p117; ☎ 5784-7088; www.shibuya-o.com /o-west.html in Japanese; 2-3 Maruyamachō, Shibuya-ku; admission from ¥3000; ☒ from 5.30pm; ⊕ JR Yamanote line to Shibuya, Hachikō exit)

O-East (Map p117; ☎ 5458-4681; www.shibuya-o.com /o-east.html in Japanese; 2-14-8 Dōgenzaka, Shibuya-ku; admission from ¥3500; ☒ from 6pm; ⊕ JR Yamanote line to Shibuya, Hachikō exit)

JAZZ

People in this city take their jazz seriously. For listings of performances, check the latest issue of *Tokyo Journal* or *Metropolis*.

Blue Note Tokyo (Map p119; ☎ 5485-0088; www .bluenote.co.jp; Raika Bldg, 6-3-16 Minami-Aoyama, Minato-ku; admission ¥6000-10,000; ☒ from 5.30pm Mon-Sat; ⊕ Chiyoda, Ginza, Hanzōmon lines to Omote-sandō, exit B3) Tokyo's big-name jazz venue in Minami-Aoyama allows aficionados the opportunity to listen up close and personal to the greats of jazz. From Aoyama-dōri walking west, make a left on Kotto-dōri, and make another left when you see Papas Café.

STB 139 (Sweet Basil; Map p119; ☎ 5474-1395; http:// stb139.co.jp; 6-7-11 Roppongi, Minato-ku; admission ¥3000-7000; ☒ 6-11pm Mon-Sat; ⊕ Hibiya, Toei Ōedo lines to Roppongi, exit 3) This is a large, comfortable space that draws big-name domestic and international acts, with performances covering the gamut of jazz genres. Call for reservations between 11am and 8pm.

Shinjuku Pit Inn (Map p116; ☎ 3354-2024; www.pit -inn.com; B1 fl, Accord Shinjuku Bldg, 2-12-4 Shinjuku, Shinjuku-ku; admission ¥1300-3000; ☒ from 2pm; ⊕ Marunouchi, Toei Shinjuku lines to Shinjuku-sanchōme, exit C8) Shinjuku Pit Inn has been going strong for around 40 years now, and is an intimate space hosting performances during the day and evening.

Theatre
BUNRAKU
Kokuritsu Gekijō (National Theatre; Map pp126-7; National Theatre; ☎ 3230-3000; www.ntj.jac.go.jp/english/index .html; 4-1 Hayabusachō, Chiyoda-ku; admission ¥1500-9200; ☒ reservations 10am-6pm; ◉ Namboku, Yūrakuchō lines to Nagatachō, exit 4) Performances are staged several times a year, even though Osaka is the home of *bunraku* (classical puppet theatre). Check the English-language website for a performance schedule.

KABUKI
Kabuki-za (Map pp124-5; ☎ 5565-6000; www.shochiku .co.jp/play/kabukiza/theater/index.html; 4-12-5 Ginza, Chūō-ku; admission ¥2500-17,000; ☒ 11am-9pm; ◉ Hibiya, Toei Asakusa lines to Higashi-Ginza, exit 3) Of the places in Tokyo to see kabuki, historic Kabuki-za is the best theatre overall. Performances and times vary from month to month, so consult the website or contact the theatre directly for programme information. Audio guides providing commentary in English are available for ¥650 plus ¥1000 deposit.

Kabuki performances can be quite a marathon, lasting from four to five hours. If you're not up to it, you can get tickets for the 4th floor from ¥600 to ¥1000 and watch only part of the show (ask for *hitomakumi*). Audio guides are not available for the 4th floor, but tickets can be bought on the day of the performance. There are generally two performances, starting at around 11am and 4pm.

Kokuritsu Gekijō (above), Japan's national theatre, also has kabuki performances, with a range of seat prices. Audio guides are available. Check with the theatre for performance times.

NŌ
Nō (classical Japanese dance-drama) performances are held at various locations around Tokyo. Tickets cost between ¥2100 and ¥15,000, and it's best to get them at the theatre itself. Check with the appropriate theatre for times.

Kanze Nō-gakudō (Map p117; ☎ 3469-6421; 1-16-4 Shōtō, Shibuya-ku; tickets from ¥3000; ◉ JR Yamanote line to Shibuya, Hachikō exit) One of the oldest and most highly respected schools of *nō* in Tokyo, Kanze Nō-gakudō is about a 15-minute walk

west from Shibuya station. Call the theatre or TIC to find out if performances are on while you're in town.

Kokuritsu Nō-gakudō (National Nō Theatre; Map p117; ☎ 3423-1331; 4-18-1 Sendagaya, Shibuya-ku; admission ¥2800-5600; ☒ reservations 10am-6pm; ◉ JR Chūō, Sōbu lines to Sendagaya, main exit) The National Nō Theatre stages its own productions (for which written English synopses are provided), but also hosts privately sponsored *nō* performances. To get there, exit Sendagaya station with Shinjuku to your left and follow the road that hugs the railway tracks. The theatre is on the left.

Tea Ceremonies
A few hotels in Tokyo hold tea ceremonies that you can see and occasionally participate in for a fee of ¥1000 to ¥1500. Call ahead to make reservations.

Hotel New Ōtani (see p152; ☎ 3265-1111; tea ceremony ¥1050; ☒ ceremonies 11am-4pm Thu-Sat)
Hotel Ōkura (see p152; ☎ 3582-0111; tea ceremony ¥1000; ☒ 11am-4pm Mon-Sat)
Imperial Hotel (see p147; ☎ 3504-1111; tea ceremony ¥1500; ☒ 10am-4pm Mon-Sat)

Sports
BASEBALL
Although soccer has made some headway in recent years, baseball remains Japan's most popular team sport. Of the two professional leagues – the Central and the Pacific – several teams are based in the Tokyo area. Within Tokyo, the Yomiuri Giants and Yakult Swallows are crosstown rivals. Taking in a ballgame is a uniquely Japanese spectator-sport experience, what with its teams of cheerleading fans, beer girls with kegs strapped to their backs and the polite crowd bursting into song. Baseball season runs from April through the end of October. Check the *Japan Times* to see who's playing while you're in town. The cheapest unreserved outfield seats start at ¥1500.

Tokyo Dome (The 'Big Egg'; Map pp126-7; ☎ 5800-9999; 1-3-61 Kōraku, Bunkyō-ku; ◉ JR Chūō, Sōbu lines to Suidobashi, west exit or Marunouchi line to Kōrakuen, Kōrakuen exit) Home to Japan's favourite baseball team, the Yomiuri Giants, Tokyo Dome is next to Kōraku-en Amusement Park (p142). Though it's a covered dome, a little dirigible floats around inside.

Jingū Kyūjo (Jingū Stadium; Map p119; ☎ 3404-8999; 13 Kasumigaoka, Shinjuku-ku; ◉ Ginza line to Gaienmae, north exit) Jingū Baseball Stadium was originally built to host the 1964 Olympics, and is where the Yakult Swallows are based.

SUMŌ

Travellers who visit Tokyo in January, May or September should not miss their chance to attend a Grand Tournament at Tokyo's **Ryōgoku Kokugikan Stadium** (Map pp112-13; ☎ 3623-5111; www.sumo.or.jp; 1-3-28 Yokoami, Sumida-ku; ⏰ 10am-4.30pm; JR Sōbu line to Ryōgoku, west exit or Toei Ōedo line to Ryōgoku, exit A4). The best seats are all bought up by those with the right connections, but if you don't mind standing, you can get in for around ¥500. Tickets can be purchased up to a month prior to the tournament, or you can simply turn up on the day (you'll have to arrive very early, say 6am, to be assured of seats during the last days of a tournament).

If you can't attend in person, NHK televises sumō from 3.30pm daily during each tournament. And if you aren't in town during a tournament, you could pick up a handbook at the stadium and take a self-guided walking tour of the neighbourhood, which houses several *heya* (sumō stables).

SHOPPING

Tokyo is a notoriously expensive city, but of course there are bargains to be bagged. The best one-stop shopping options are the department stores, which stock virtually everything, but unless a major sale is on they're pricey places to shop.

Antiques & Vintage Goods

Hanae Mori building (Map p117; 3-6-1 Kita-Aoyama, Minato-ku; ⏰ 11am-7pm; ⊕ Chiyoda, Ginza, Hanzōmon lines to Omote-sandō, exit A1) One great place to look for antiques and eccentric souvenirs is in the basement of this Harajuku building, which has more than 30 antique shops hawking everything from over-the-hill kewpie dolls to antique obi ornaments.

Kurofune (Map p119; ☎ 3479-1552; www.kurofune antiques.com; 7-7-4 Roppongi, Minato-ku; ⏰ 10am-6pm Mon-Sat; ⊕ Toei Ōedo line to Roppongi, exit 7) Kurofune, run for the past quarter-century by a friendly American collector, carries an awesome treasure-trove of Japanese antiques. Correspondingly impressive amounts of cash are necessary for acquiring some of these items, like painstakingly constructed antique *tansu* (Japanese chests of drawers), but it's a nice place to window-shop.

Clothes

Harajuku (Map p117) has reached iconic proportions internationally, becoming synonymous with Tokyo street fashion. While established houses of fashion like Chanel, Comme les Garçons and Gucci line Omotesandō, Ura-Hara (the Harajuku backstreets) is where the small boutiques and studios represent independent designers. Wander the alleys snaking off either side of Omote-sandō – take the alley to the left of Kiddyland for a look at the south side, then backtrack to the pedestrian overpass across Omote-sandō and check out the boutiques and second-hand shops of the north side.

Department stores like **Laforet** (Map p117; ☎ 3475-0411; 1-11-6 Jingūmae, Shibuya-ku; ⏰ 11am-8pm; ⊕ Chiyoda line to Meiji-jingūmae, exit 5) or the **109 Building** (Ichimarukyū; Map p117; ☎ 3477-5111; 2-29-1 Dōgenzaka, Shibuya-ku; ⏰ 10am-9pm Mon-Fri, 11am-10.30pm Sat & Sun; ⊕ JR Yamanote line to Shibuya, Hachikō exit) are good places to dig up the latest hot look you're seeing on the chic young things strutting down Takeshita-dōri. Aoyama (Map p117) and Daikanyama (Map p121) are also good places to find slightly more sophisticated boutiques.

Bapexclusive (Map p117; ☎ 3407-2145; 5-5-8 Minami-Aoyama, Minato-ku; ⏰ 11am-7pm; ⊕ Chiyoda, Ginza, Hanzōmon lines to Omote-sandō, exit A5) A Bathing Ape (BAPE for short), the much-hyped, no-longer-underground label, adorns the backs of young hipsters cruising Harajuku and has perhaps a dozen 'secret' locations squirrelled away around Aoyama. This one has a kaleidoscopic collection of trainers on the 2nd floor.

Evisu Tailor (Map p121; ☎ 3710-1999; www.evisu.com; 1-1-5 Kami-Meguro, Meguro-ku; ⏰ 11am-8pm; ⊕ Hibiya line to Naka-Meguro) In the early '90s, the detail-obsessed founder of Evisu began producing jeans the old-fashioned way using rescued looms and methods, helping to spawn the Japanese selvedge denim craze. Here, you can choose the pair you want and have the Evisu logo custom painted on; discreet denim-heads can opt to go logo-less.

Hysteric Glamour (Map p117; ☎ 3409-7227; www.hystericglamour.jp; B1 & 1st fl, 6-23-2 Jingūmae, Shibuya-ku; ⏰ 11am-8pm; ⊕ JR Yamanote line to Harajuku, Omote-sandō exit) Certainly it isn't the last word on Harajuku fashion, but for many it's the first that comes to mind. Design junkies will favour the sinuous, futuristic interior of the newer Roppongi Hills branch.

Sou-Sou (Map p119; ☎ 3407-7877; www.sousou.co.jp; 2nd fl, From-1st Bldg, 5-3-10 Minami-Aoyama, Minato-ku; ❤ 11am-8pm; ❻ Chiyoda, Ginza, Hanzōmon lines to Omote-sandō, exit A5) In the beautiful way that the old becomes new again, as with denim, the humble *tabi* (split-toed sock) is experiencing a renaissance. Sou-Sou designs whimsical, comfortable and practical *tabi*; it even makes sturdy, rubber-soled models to wear on the street.

Department Stores

Tōkyū Hands (Map p116; ☎ 5361-3111; Takashimaya Times Sq, 5-24-2 Sendagaya, Shibuya-ku; ❤ 10am-8.30pm; ❻ JR Yamanote line to Shinjuku, new south exit) Even if you hate shopping, the one store everyone should hit is ostensibly a DIY home-improvement emporium. If you need lumber or nails, you can get it here; if you need a sheet of stick-on cubic zirconia to add bling to your mobile phone, you can get that here, too. There are two other branches in Ikebukuro and Shibuya.

Tokyo's big *depāto* (department stores) are worth a look for sheer scale and inventory, these opulent shrines to consumerism. Department stores close at least one day each month, usually a Monday or Wednesday. Some of the best things about them are not necessarily the wares, but the eats – with their rooftop beer gardens, *resutoran-gai* and elaborately stocked *depachika*.

Isetan (Map p116; ☎ 3352-1111; 3-14-1 Shinjuku, Shinjuku-ku; ❤ 10am-8pm; ❻ Marunouchi, Toei Shinjuku lines to Shinjuku-sanchōme, exit A1) In addition to having a stunning food basement, Isetan offers a free service called I-club, matching English-speaking staff to visiting shoppers; the membership desk is on the 7th floor of the Isetan annexe building.

Keiō (Map p116; ☎ 3342-2111; 1-1-4 Nishi-Shinjuku, Shinjuku-ku; ❤ 10am-8pm, closed some Thu; ❻ JR Yamanote line to Shinjuku, west exit) Opens its rooftop beer garden in the summer.

Loft (Map p117; ☎ 3462-3807; 21-1 Udagawachō, Shibuya-ku; ❤ 10am-9pm Mon-Sat, to 8pm Sun; ❻ JR Yamanote line to Shibuya, Hachikō exit) The bias here is more towards fun rather than function, and it's a good place to look for cool housewares, gifts and toys for big kids.

Matsuya (Map pp124–5; ☎ 3567-1211; 3-6-1 Ginza, Chūō-ku; ❤ 10.30am-7.30pm; ❻ Ginza, Hibiya, Marunouchi lines to Ginza, exits A12 & A13) Also opens its beer garden during the summer, and has a good *depachika*.

Matsuzakaya (Map pp124–5; ☎ 3572-1111; 6-10-1 Ginza, Chūō-ku; ❤ 10am-8pm Mon-Sat, to 7.30pm Sun; ❻ Ginza, Hibiya, Marunouchi lines to Ginza, exit A4) Another spectacular *depachika*.

Mitsukoshi (Map pp124–5; ☎ 3562-1111; 4-6-16 Ginza, Chūō-ku; ❤ 10am-7.30pm Mon-Sat, to 7pm Sun, closed some Mon; ❻ Ginza, Hibiya, Marunouchi lines to Ginza, exits A7 & A11) Look for the Mitsukoshi lion at the corner entrance.

Takashimaya (Map pp126–7; ☎ 3211-4111; 2-4-1 Nihombashi, Chūō-ku; ❤ 10am-7.30pm; ❻ Ginza, Tōzai, Toei Asakusa lines to Nihombashi, exit B1 & B2) This is one of the more venerable old establishments, where primly dressed, white-gloved attendants operate old-fashioned elevators; have a look at the rooftop patio. There's another branch in Ginza.

Electronics

Akihabara (秋葉原; Map pp126–7), or 'Akiba', is Tokyo's discount electronics neighbourhood – hence the nickname Denki-gai (Electric Town) – though it's also become something of a manga mecca. Nowhere in the world will you find such a range of electrical appliances or *otaku* (geeks). If you have a short attention span, spending half a day flitting from store to noisy store may well be your nirvana. Some larger stores (Laox and Sofmap are reliable options) have tax-free sections with export models of various appliances and gadgets for sale – remember to double-check that they're compatible with your home country's system, and bring along your passport to buy duty-free items.

While prices may be competitive with those in your home country, it's unusual to find prices that match those of dealers in Hong Kong or Singapore. To find the shops, take the Electric Town exit of the JR Akihabara station.

Handicrafts & Souvenirs

While toyshops and department stores sell fun, futuristic and only-in-Japan types of goodies, there's also a wealth of more traditional-style gifts and souvenirs to be found in Tokyo.

Kappabashi-dōri (Map pp130–1; ❻ Ginza line to Tawaramachi, all exits) is where to go if you're setting up a restaurant. You can get custom-made *noren* (doorway curtains) with your restaurant's name, cushions, crockery and, most importantly, your plastic food models. They are carefully crafted and not cheap, but they do make entertaining souvenirs for the fridge or kitchen table back home. Kappabashi-dōri is a five-minute walk northwest of Tawaramachi station.

Takumi Handicrafts (Map pp124-5; ☎ 3571-2017; ginza-takumi.co.jp in Japanese; 8-4-2 Ginza, Chūō-ku; ⊙ 11am-7pm Mon-Sat; ◉ JR Yamanote line to Shimbashi, Ginza exit) Takumi offers an elegant selection of toys, textiles, ceramics and other traditional folk crafts from around Japan. The shop also encloses information detailing the origin and background of pieces you purchase.

Bingoya (Map pp112-13; ☎ 3202-8778; www.quasar .nu/bingoya; 10-6 Wakamatsuchō, Shinjuku-ku; ⊙ 10am-7pm Tue-Sun; ◉ Toei Ōedo line to Wakamatsu-Kawada) Regional ceramics, vibrant batik textiles, richly dyed *washi* (handmade paper), handmade glassware and tatami mats fill out the five floors of this wonderful handicrafts shop.

Japan Traditional Crafts Center (Map p114; ☎ 5954-6066; www.kougei.or.jp/english/center.html; 1st & 2nd fl, Metropolitan Plaza Bldg, 1-11-1 Nishi-Ikebukuro, Toshima-ku; ⊙ 11am-7pm; ◉ JR Yamanote line to Ikebukuro, Metropolitan exit) Demonstrations and temporary exhibitions of handmade crafts, such as weavings, mosaics, bows and arrows, ceramics and *washi* are held on the 3rd floor of this centre. High-quality folk arts and handicrafts are available for purchase on the 1st and 2nd floors.

Kamawanu (Map p121; ☎ 3780-0182; 23-1 Sarugakuchō, Shibuya-ku; ⊙ 11am-7pm; ◉ JR Yamanote line to Ebisu, west exit) In Daikanyama, this little shop specialises in beautifully dyed *tenugui*, those ubiquitous Japanese handtowels that you find in *sentō* and *onsen*. Designs come in a spectrum of colours, incorporating traditional abstract patterns and representations of natural elements.

Haibara (Map p126-7; ☎ 3272-3801; 2-7-6 Nihombashi, Chūō-ku; ⊙ 9.30am-6.30pm Mon-Fri, to 5pm Sat; ◉ Ginza, Tōzai, Toei Asakusa lines to Nihombashi, exits B8 & C3) East of Tokyo station, Haibara stocks a quality range of *washi* and paper handicrafts, such as wallets, handbound notebooks and cards. All the major department stores also have a section devoted to *washi*.

Oriental Bazaar (Map p117; ☎ 3400-3933; 5-9-13 Jingūmae, Shibuya-ku; ⊙ 10am-7pm Fri-Wed; ◉ Chiyoda, Ginza, Hanzōmon lines to Omote-sandō, exit A3) Oriental Bazaar is a good one-stop shop for gifts and souvenirs, with a wide range of items such as fans, folding screens, *yukata* and pottery – many at very affordable prices.

Kids Stuff

Japanese are particularly creative when it comes to finding things to keep their kids occupied, and Tokyo has some great toyshops.

Kiddyland (Map p117; ☎ 3409-3431; www.kiddyland .co.jp; 6-1-9 Jingūmae, Shibuya-ku; ⊙ 10am-8pm, closed 3rd Tue of each month; ◉ Chiyoda line to Meiji-jingūmae, exit 4) Prepare to overdose on the six floors of *kawaii* (cute), here on Omote-sandō in Harajuku. This store is stuffed with toys for kids from age zero onward. You might want to avoid it on the weekends, when teenagers descend in droves.

Hakuhinkan Toy Park (Map pp124-5; ☎ 3571-8008; www.hakuhinkan.co.jp; 8-8-11 Ginza, Chūō-ku; ⊙ 11am-8pm; ◉ JR Yamanote line to Shimbashi, Ginza exit) This multilevel toyshop along Chūō-dōri in Ginza is another great one, full of wacky distractions and objects of desire, with an 8th-floor theatre and two floors of child-friendly restaurants.

Manga & Anime

Along with electronics, Akihabara (see p179) also overflows with shops selling manga and *anime*.

Mandarake Shibuya (Map p117; ☎ 3477-0777; www .mandarake.co.jp; B2 fl, Shibuya Beam Bldg, 31-2 Udagawachō, Shibuya-ku; ⊙ noon-8pm; ◉ JR Yamanote line to Shibuya, Hachikō exit); Nakano (Map p117; ☎ 3228-0007; 2nd-4th fl, Nakano Broadway Bldg, 5-52-15 Nakano, Nakano-ku; ⊙ noon-8pm; ◉ JR Chūō line to Nakano, north exit) Mandarake's Shibuya Beam branch carries a range of new manga and also boasts performances by real, live cosplay kids in full-on *anime* character drag. But the huge flagship store in Nakano, with three floors packed with all manner of new and used manga, *anime*, games and character-related collectibles, is a must-visit for avid fans.

Book Off (Map p117; ☎ 5775-6818; 1-8-8 Jingūmae, Shibuya-ku; ⊙ 10am-9pm; ◉ Chiyoda line to Meiji-jingūmae, exit 5) Find a huge selection of new and gently used, barely bruised manga here. Budget collectors should head for the shelves of ¥105 (!) books – you could feasibly buy up entire series in good condition. This branch is on Meiji-dōri, north of Laforet.

Music

Shibuya (Map p117) is music central, and a great starting point to hunt for music. Udagawachō, the area northwest of Shibuya station, is home to several shops like Recofan and Disk Union, who stock rare and second-hand CDs.

Tower Records (Map p117; ☎ 3496-3661; 1-22-14 Jinnan, Shibuya-ku; ⊙ 10am-11pm; ◉ JR Yamanote line to Shibuya, Hachikō exit) There's a massive branch in Shibuya, with the most extensive range in Tokyo and lots of listening stations. The 7th-floor bookshop is worth a look for its wide selection of foreign magazines. Tower Records, Virgin and HMV all have several branches in Tokyo.

For vinyl, rifle through the record stores in Shibuya. There's a high concentration of little shops around Udagawachō; here's a list of notables in the neighbourhood just to get you started.

Cisco Records (Map p117; ☎ 3462-0366; www.cisco -records.co.jp in Japanese; 2nd fl, 11-1 Udagawachō, Shibuya-ku; ☒ noon-10pm Mon-Sat, 11am-9pm Sun; ◉ JR Yamanote line to Shibuya, Hachikō exit) This is the hip-hop and R&B branch, but Cisco has several other small shops scattered around this area, each specialising in a different genre.

Disk Union (Map p117; ☎ 3476-2627; http://diskunion .net in Japanese; Antenna 21 Bldg, 30-7 Udagawachō, Shibuya-ku; ◉ JR Yamanote line to Shibuya, Hachikō exit) Used and new records along Center-gai, with other branches in Shinjuku (Map p116) and elsewhere. Each floor specialises in a different genre.

Guinness Records (Map p117; ☎ 3464-7752; www .guinness-records.com in Japanese; 4th fl, 10-2 Udagawachō, Shibuya-ku; ☒ 1-8.30pm; ◉ JR Yamanote line to Shibuya, Hachikō exit) Guinness specialises in hip-hop, but also carries soul, R&B and jazz.

Manhattan Records (Map p117; ☎ 3477-7737; 1st fl, 10-1 Udagawachō, Shibuya-ku; ☒ noon-9pm) Bounce into Manhattan for hip-hop and a glimpse of the Japanese B-boys.

Recofan (Map p117; ☎ 5454-0161; www.recofan.co.jp; 4th fl, Beam Bldg, 31-2 Udagawachō, Shibuya-ku; ☒ 11.30am-9pm; ◉ JR Yamanote line to Shibuya, Hachikō exit) Of several branches around town, this place stocks a wide variety of music, including folk, soul, J-pop and reggae.

Ningyō (Japanese Dolls)

Next to JR Asakusabashi station, Edo-dōri (Map pp112–13) is the place for *ningyō*. Both sides of the road have large numbers of shops specialising in both traditional and contemporary Japanese dolls.

Yoshitoku (Map pp112-13; ☎ 3863-4419; 1-9-14 Asa-kusabashi, Taitō-ku; ☒ 9.30am-6pm; ◉ JR Sōbu or Toei Asakusa lines to Asakusabashi, main exit or exit A2) The most famous; has been crafting exquisite *ningyō* since 1711 and is now owned by its 11th-generation descendant.

Photographic Equipment

Ginza's Harumi-dōri is one place to find photographic equipment – there are several good second-hand photographic shops where Japanese gear can often be bought at reasonable prices. For new equipment, the west side of Shinjuku station harbours some of Tokyo's largest camera shops. Be sure to shop around for the best deals.

Bic Camera (Map p116; ☎ 5326-1111; 1-5-1 Nishi-Shinjuku, Shinjuku-ku; ☒ 10am-8.30pm; ◉ JR Yamanote line to Shinjuku, west exit) Bic has infiltrated the entire city, selling not only cameras but also mp3 players, computers, and electronics of all kinds. Just try not to get the endlessly repeated Bic song stuck in your head.

Sakuraya Camera (Map p116; ☎ 3346-3939; 1-16-4 Nishi-Shinjuku, Shinjuku-ku; ☒ 10am-8.30pm; ◉ JR Yamanote line to Shinjuku, west exit) Sakuraya is one of the biggest camera shops in town, selling an incredible selection of lenses, digital cameras and photographic equipment at competitive prices.

Yodobashi Camera (Map p116; ☎ 3346-1010; 1-11-1 Nishi-Shinjuku, Shinjuku-ku; ☒ 9.30am-9.30pm; ◉ JR Yamanote line to Shinjuku, west exit) Yodobashi is one of Tokyo's most highly regarded camera shops, well stocked with photographic equipment. Bring your passport and the consumption tax will be waived.

GETTING THERE & AWAY
Air

With the exception of China Airlines, all international airlines (p809) use Narita airport rather than the more conveniently located Haneda airport.

Immigration and customs procedures are usually straightforward, but they can be time consuming for non-Japanese. Note that Japanese customs officials are probably the most scrupulous in Asia; backpackers arriving from anywhere remotely third-worldish (the Philippines, Thailand etc) can expect some questions and perhaps a thorough search.

You can change money in the customs hall after having cleared customs, and in the arrival hall. The rates are the same as those offered in town.

Narita has two terminals, Nos 1 and 2. This doesn't complicate things much as both have train stations that are connected to JR and Keisei lines. The one you arrive at will depend on the airline you are flying with. Both terminals have clear English signposting for train and limousine bus services.

Be sure to check which terminal your flight leaves from, and give yourself plenty of time to get out to Narita – the train ride itself can take from 50 minutes to 1½ hours.

Boat

A ferry journey can be a great, relatively inexpensive way to get from Tokyo to other parts of the country. Prices given here are for 2nd-class travel. Though we've listed phone numbers, most lines are not staffed by English-speaking operators. It's easiest to book passage through a local travel agency or the JNTO.

From Tokyo is the long-distance **Ocean Tōkyū Ferry** (☎ 5128-0109) going to Tokushima (¥9000, 18 hours) in Shikoku and to Kitakyūshū (¥13,500, 34 hours) in Northern Kyūshū. **Oshima Transport** (☎ 3273-8911) goes to Naha (¥23,500, 44 hours) on Okinawa. Long-distance ferry services to Hokkaidō are no longer available from Tokyo; however, **Higashi Nihon Ferry** (☎ 0120-756-564) has departures from Ibaraki prefecture to Tomakomai in Hokkaidō (¥9500, 19 hours).

Bus

Long-distance buses are generally little or no cheaper than trains, but are sometimes a good alternative for long-distance trips to areas serviced by expressways.

There are a number of express buses running between Tokyo, Kyoto and Osaka. Overnight JR buses leave at 10pm from the Yaesu side of Tokyo station and arrive at Kyoto and Osaka between 6am and 7am the following day. They cost from ¥8000 to ¥8500 (if you're coming back, you'll save money by buying a return ticket). Tickets can be booked at one of the green windows at a JR station.

Buses also run from Tokyo station to Nara (¥8400, 9½ hours), Kōbe (¥8690, 9½ hours), Hiroshima (¥11,600, 12 hours), Fukui (¥8300, eight hours), Nagano (¥4000, four hours), Yamagata (¥6420, 5½ hours), Takamatsu (¥10,000, 9½ hours), Sendai (¥6210, 5½ hours), Morioka (¥7850, 7½ hours) and Aomori (¥10,000, 9½ hours).

From Shinjuku station there are buses running to the Fuji and Hakone regions, including, for Mt Fuji climbers, direct services to the 5th station (see p200). The Shinjuku long-distance bus station is across from the west exit of Shinjuku station.

Train

All major JR lines radiate from Tokyo station; northbound trains stop at Ueno station, which, like Tokyo station, is on the convenient JR Yamanote line. Private lines – often cheaper and

quicker for making day trips out of Tokyo – start from various stations around Tokyo. With the exception of the Tōbu Nikkō line, which starts in Asakusa, all private lines originate somewhere on the Yamanote line.

For fares to major cities from Tokyo, see p822.

SHINKANSEN

There are three *shinkansen* (bullet train) lines that connect Tokyo with the rest of Japan: the Tōkaidō line, which passes through Central Honshū, changing its name along the way to the Sanyō line before terminating at Hakata in Northern Kyūshū; the Tōhoku line, which runs northeast via Utsunomiya and Sendai as far as Morioka, with the Yamagata branch heading from Fukushima to Yamagata and the Akita branch heading from Morioka to Akita; and the Jōetsu line, which runs north to Niigata, with the Nagano branch heading from Takasaki to Nagano-shi. All three *shinkansen* lines start at Tokyo station, though the Tōhoku and Jōetsu lines make a stop at Ueno station, and the Tōkaidō line now stops at Shinagawa station in south-central Tokyo.

Of these lines, the one most likely to be used by visitors to Japan is the Tōkaidō line, as it passes through Kyoto and Osaka. 'Nozomi' trains between Tokyo and Kyoto (¥13,520, 2½ hours) are fastest, as they make only a few stops. Buy tickets at the green JR windows; the way to *shinkansen* platforms in Tokyo station are clearly signposted in English.

PRIVATE LINES

The private lines generally service Tokyo's sprawling suburbia. The most useful are the Tōkyū Tōyoko line, running between Shibuya station and Yokohama; the Odakyū line, running from Shinjuku to Odawara and the Hakone region; the Tōbu Nikkō line, running from Asakusa to Nikkō; and the Seibu Shinjuku line from Ikebukuro to Kawagoe.

OTHER JR LINES

The regular Tōkaidō line serves the stations that the Tōkaidō *shinkansen* line zips through without stopping. Trains start at Tokyo station and pass through Shimbashi and Shinagawa stations on the way out of town. There are *kyūkyō* (express) services to Yokohama and to Izu-hantō via Atami, and from there trains continue – very slowly – to Nagoya, Kyoto and Osaka.

Northbound trains start in Ueno. The Takasaki line goes to Kumagaya and, of course, Takasaki, with onward connections from Takasaki to Niigata. The Tōhoku line follows the Takasaki line as far north as Ōmiya, from where it heads to the far north of Honshū via Sendai and Aomori. Getting to Sendai without paying any express surcharges will involve changes at Utsunomiya and Fukushima. For those intent on saving the expense of a night's accommodation, there are also overnight services.

GETTING AROUND

Tokyo has an excellent public transport system, with everything of note conveniently close to a subway or JR station. Bus services are difficult to use if you don't read kanji, but the average visitor to Tokyo won't need the buses anyway.

To/From Narita Airport

Narita airport is 66km from central Tokyo, and is used by almost all the international airlines but only a small number of domestic operators. Travel to or from Tokyo takes from 50 minutes to over 1½ hours, depending on your mode of transport and destination in town.

Depending on where you're headed, it's generally cheaper and faster to travel into Tokyo by train than by limousine bus. However, rail users will probably need to change trains somewhere, and this can be confusing on a jetlagged first visit. Limousine buses provide a hassle-free direct route to a number of Tokyo's top hotels, and you don't have to be a hotel guest to use the buses.

If you're seriously desperate or have money to burn, taxis from Narita will run you about a cool ¥25,000.

TRAIN

There are three rail services between Tokyo and both terminals at Narita airport: the private **Keisei line** (☎ 3621-2242; www.keisei.co.jp in Japanese); the **JR Narita Express N'EX** (☎ 050-2016-1603; www.jreast.co.jp/e/index.html for information, www.world.eki-net.com for reservations); and the JR 'Airport Narita' service. The Keisei service arrives at Nippori and Ueno, from either of which you can change to the Yamanote line for access to other neighbourhoods. N'EX and the 'Airport Narita' service arrives at Tokyo station (from where you can change to almost any line). N'EX also runs to Shinjuku, Ikebukuro and Yokohama.

The Keisei line has two services: the Keisei Skyliner, which does the trip between Narita and Ueno (¥1920, one hour); and the Keisei *tokkyū* (limited express; ¥1000, one hour and 11 minutes). Times and fares to and from Nippori are marginally less. *Tokkyū* services are much more frequent than the Skyliner, and what's another 11 minutes? If you're heading to Asakusa, it's probably most convenient to take a *tokkyū* train to Aoto station and transfer to the Toei Asakusa line to Asakusa station.

The N'EX services are fast, extremely comfortable, and include amenities like drink-dispensing machines and telephones. They

---

DAY-TRIPPING FROM NARITA

If you face a long layover at Narita airport, consider these alternatives to dazed, interminable hours in the terminals.

Assuming you have several hours to kill – including at least 2½ hours to get out, away and back into the airport – make a quick detour into Narita town. The town's highlight is its impressive temple, **Naritasan Shinsōji** (☎ 0476-222-111; 1 Narita, Narita-shi, Chiba-ken), surrounded by a pretty park laced with walking paths, trees and ponds. Along Omote-sandō, the main road leading from station to temple, explore the little shops and restaurants in town. To get there, take a limited express Keisei or JR train to Narita station (¥250, 10 minutes). Pick up a Narita map from the friendly TIC outside the east exit of the JR station.

If your layover is longer than eight hours, you can spend a couple of those hours in Tokyo. Hit the airport ATM for at least ¥10,000, check your bag through or stow it in a left-luggage locker, and catch the next JR Narita Express (above) or Keisei Skyliner (above) into Tokyo. To save time later, buy a round-trip ticket that departs from Tokyo at least three hours before your flight. Stick around one neighbourhood on the Yamanote line and don't miss your train back to the airport!

go to or from Tokyo station (¥2940, 53 minutes), to Shinjuku station (¥3110, 1½ hours), to or from Ikebukuro station (¥3110, one hour and 40 minutes) and to or from Yokohama station (¥4180, 1½ hours). N'EX services run approximately half-hourly between 7am and 10pm, but Ikebukuro services are infrequent; in most cases you're better off heading to Shinjuku and taking the Yamanote line from there. Seats are reserved only, but can be bought immediately before departure if they are available.

'Airport Narita' trains cost ¥1280 and take 1½ hours to or from Tokyo. Trains only run approximately once an hour.

The Keikyū rail line runs between Narita and Haneda airports (¥1560, two hours), but you'll have to transfer to or from the Keisei line at Aoto station.

LIMOUSINE BUS

Don't be misled by the name; they're just ordinary buses and take 1½ to two hours to travel between Narita airport and a number of major hotels around Tokyo. Check departure times before buying your ticket, as services are not all that frequent. The fare to or from hotels around Asakusa, to or from Ikebukuro, Akasaka, Ginza, Shiba, Shinagawa, Shinjuku or Haneda airport costs around ¥3000. There's also direct service between Narita airport and Yokohama (¥3500, two hours).

To/From Haneda Airport

Most domestic flights and China Airlines to/from Taiwan use the convenient Haneda airport.

Transport to or from Haneda airport is a simple matter, as the **Tokyo Monorail** (www.tokyo -monorail.co.jp) runs from 5.15am to 11.15pm between the airport and Hamamatsuchō station on the JR Yamanote line (¥470, 22 minutes, every 10 minutes).

Taxis from the airport to places around central Tokyo cost around ¥6000. Limousine buses connect Haneda with TCAT (¥900), Tokyo station (¥900), Ikebukuro and Shinjuku (¥1200), and several other destinations in Tokyo.

There is a direct bus service between Haneda and Narita airports (¥3000, two hours).

Bus

Pick up a copy of the free TOEI Bus Route Guide from the TIC. When using a bus, have the name of your destination written in Japanese so you can either show the driver or match up the kanji with the route map yourself (there's very little English signposting on buses or at bus stops). It's a flat ¥200 for city destinations.

Car

For those who enjoy a challenge and who obtain an International Driving Permit before arriving in Japan. Three companies that usually have English speakers on hand are **Mazda Rent-a-Lease** (☎ 5286-0740), **Nippon Rent-a-Car** (☎ 3485-7196) and **Toyota Rent-a-Lease** (☎ 3264-0100). Typical rates for small cars are ¥8000 or ¥9000 for the first day, and ¥5500 to ¥7000 each day thereafter. On top of this there is a ¥1000-per-day insurance fee. Mileage is usually unlimited.

Taxi

Flagfall is ¥660, and if you don't speak Japanese, taxi drivers can plug a venue's telephone number into the GPS system to find its location.

Train

Tokyo has a crowded but otherwise awesome rail network. Between the JR and private above-ground and subway lines, you can get to almost anywhere in town quickly and cheaply. But night owls beware: it closes from around midnight until 5am or 6am.

Avoiding Tokyo's rush hour is not often possible, though things tend to quiet down from 10am to 4pm.

JR LINES

Undoubtedly, the most useful line in Tokyo is the JR Yamanote line, which does a 35km loop around the city, taking in most of the important areas. You can do the whole circuit in an hour for the ¥130 minimum charge – a great introduction to the city. Another useful aboveground JR route is the Chūō line, which cuts across the city centre between Shinjuku and Akihabara. Tickets are transferable on all JR lines.

The major JR stations (Tokyo, Shibuya, Shinjuku, Ikebukuro and Ueno) are massive places with thronging crowds and never enough English signposting. Just working out how to buy a ticket can drive a newcomer to the edge of madness. If it's a JR train you're taking, look for the JR sign (usually green)

TOKYO

and the rows of vending machines. If you don't know the fare, put in the minimum ¥130 and push the top left-hand button (the one with no price on it). When you get to your destination you can pay the balance at a fare adjustment machine, found near the ticket gates. English signposting points the way to the railway platforms.

If you'll be doing a lot of travelling on JR lines (even just the Yamanote line), we strongly suggest buying a JR 'IO' card. These work like debit cards that you can insert directly into automated ticket wickets (the correct fare will be deducted automatically). IO cards come in denominations of ¥1000, ¥3000 and ¥5000, and can be purchased from ticket machines marked with, er, a large watermelon and a penguin, or from JR windows.

Travellers planning to spend an extended period of time in Tokyo might consider getting a Suica smart card – the Suica card can be swiped over the wicket without being removed from a wallet, and they can be recharged. They can even be used to purchase items at convenience stores in the stations. Suica cards require a ¥500 deposit, refundable when you return it to a JR window.

For English-language train information, you can call the **JR English Information line** (☎ 3423-0111; ☺ 10am-6pm Mon-Fri).

SUBWAY LINES

Ticket prices start at ¥160 for short hops, but if your trip involves a change of train, it will probably cost upwards of ¥190. As with the JR system, if you're in doubt at all (there are still subway stations where the only pricing maps are in Japanese), buy a ticket for ¥160 and upgrade if necessary at your destination.

There are 12 subway lines in Tokyo (13 if you include the Yūrakuchō New Line), of which eight are TRTA lines and four are TOEI lines. This is not particularly important to remember, as the subway services are essentially the same and have good connections from one to another; however, you'll need a special transfer ticket to switch between TRTA and TOEI subway lines. If you can't read Japanese, the easiest way to get around this is to buy a Passnet (or SF Metro) card. It comes in denominations of ¥1000, ¥3000 and ¥5000 and is inserted just like a ticket in the automatic ticket gates. It's good for travel on both subway systems and saves you time, money and confusion when switching between the two systems.

DISCOUNT TICKETS & TRAIN PASSES

There are no massively discounted tickets available for travel around Tokyo. The best deal is the Tokyo Combination Ticket (¥1580), which allows travel on any subway, tram, TOEI bus or JR train in the metropolitan area until the last train of the day. It's available from subway and JR stations and post offices.

Taxi

Taxis are so expensive that you should only use them when there's no alternative. Rates start at ¥660, which gives you 2km (1.5km after 11pm), after which the meter starts to clock an additional ¥100 for every 350m; you also click up ¥100 for every two minutes you sit idly gazing at the scenery in a Tokyo traffic jam.

Around Tokyo
東京近郊

Sometimes you need a break from the world's largest city, and on clear days Mt Fuji beckons you from the west. In summer, you can climb through forests towards the jagged summit of Japan's national symbol, as pilgrims have done for centuries, or the towns of Hakone or the Fuji Five Lakes make for ideal hiking and soaking anytime of year.

North of the capital, Nikkō looms equally large in the cultural landscape; its gilded shrines and exquisitely crafted temples are spectacularly set amid verdant woodlands. Further north, Gunma-ken is the nation's hot-spring capital, with riverbank *onsen*, mountain *onsen*, even *onsen* towns where walking the streets in your *yukata* (cotton bathrobe) and clip-clopping *geta* sandals is *de rigueur*.

South of the capital, Kamakura was Japan's capital from AD 1194–1333, boasting a treasury of temples and sylvan hiking trails. Nearby Yokohama has grown from a blip 150 years ago to Japan's second-largest city, with crackling entertainment districts, shopping galore and longstanding foreign influence.

Continuing south, the peninsula Izu-hantō offers quite different temptations: charming seaside towns, lovely windswept beaches and cliff-top *onsen* overlooking the Pacific. And you needn't leave Tokyo Prefecture for an island getaway; Izu-shotō is a chain of volcanic islands with white-sand beaches and a lush subtropical landscape for hiking, surfing and beachcombing; some would swear that the immaculately fresh sashimi alone is worth the journey.

HIGHLIGHTS

- Watch the sunrise from the majestic of **Mt Fuji** (p198), Japan's highest mountain and national symbol

- Find your spiritual centre while exploring the dazzling temples of **Nikkō** (opposite)

- Recover from the madness of the metropolis at idyllic *onsen* on **Izu-hantō** (p217) or in **Gunma-ken** (p195)

- Hike forest trails in search of hidden shrines around **Kamakura** (p224)

- Relax in a natural seaside *onsen* while gazing over the Pacific on one of the easily accessible **Izu-shotō Islands** (p231)

- Spend a day out in **Yokohama** (p218), and the sunset over its harbour may make you want to spend the night

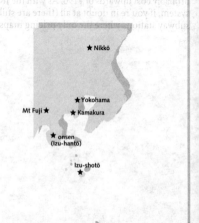

★ Nikkō
★ Yokohama
Mt Fuji ★ ★ Kamakura
★ *onsen* (Izu-hantō)
Izu-shotō ★

NORTH OF TOKYO

The big-ticket item of travel north of Tokyo is Nikkō with its amazing shrines. Further north is Gunma-ken, home to numerous hot-spring resorts.

NIKKŌ 日光

☎ 0288 / pop 95,000

The path from Tōshōgu to Futarasan-Jinja may very well be the Japan you've dreamt of. On your left, years (decades? centuries?) of moss cling to a stone wall, while to the right are dozens of stone lanterns in precise alignment, framed with aching perfection by a vermillion wall and towering cedars.

Scattered among hilly woodlands, Nikkō is one of Japan's major attractions. If there's any drawback, it's that plenty of other people have discovered it too, and at peak season and on weekends any time of year it can be extremely crowded. Although Nikkō is certainly possible as a day trip from Tokyo, try to spend the previous night here so you arrive at its World Heritage shrines and temples before the crowds do. Gorgeous natural scenery west of the city merits another night.

History

Nikkō's history as a sacred site stretches back to the middle of the 8th century, when the Buddhist priest Shōdō Shōnin (735–817) established a hermitage here. It was a training centre for Buddhist monks, before declining into obscurity. That is, until it was chosen as the site for the mausoleum of Tokugawa Ieyasu, the warlord who took control of all Japan and established the shōgunate that ruled for more than 250 years, until the Meiji Restoration ended the feudal era.

Ieyasu was laid to rest among Nikkō's towering cedars in 1617, and in 1634 his grandson, Tokugawa Iemitsu, commenced work on the shrine that can be seen today. The original shrine, Tōshō-gū, was completely rebuilt using an army of some 15,000 artisans from across Japan, taking two years to complete the shrine and mausoleum. Whatever one's opinion of Ieyasu (he is said to have had his wife and eldest son executed because it was politically expedient), the grandeur of Nikkō is intended to awe, a display of wealth and power by a family that for 2½ centuries was Japan's supreme arbiter of power.

Orientation

Both JR Nikkō station and the nearby Tōbu Nikkō station lie within a block of Nikkō's main road (Rte 119, the old Nikkōkaidō), southeast of the town centre. From here, it's a 30-minute walk uphill to the shrine area, past restaurants, hotels and the main tourist information centre. From the stations to the shrines, you can take buses to the Shin-kyō bus stop for ¥190. The area north of the Daiya-gawa from the town centre is greener but less well served by public transport.

Information

INTERNET ACCESS

Kyōdo Center tourist information office (☎ 53-3795; per 30 min ¥100; ⏰ 9am-5pm) Has several computers available.

INTERNET RESOURCES

Nikko Perfect Guide (www.nikko-jp.org/english/index .html)

MEDICAL SERVICES

Kawaii-inn Clinic (☎ 54-0319) On the main road, three blocks southeast of the Kyōdo Centre tourist information office.

POST

Post office (⏰ 8.45am-7pm Mon-Fri, 9am-5pm Sat) On the main road, three blocks northwest of the Kyōdo Center tourist information office. Has international ATM and currency exchange.

TOURIST INFORMATION

The *Tourist Guide of Nikkō* has about everything you need, and the bilingual *Central Nikko* shows the small streets. Hikers should pick up a copy of *Yumoto-Chūzenji Area Hiking Guide* (¥150) with maps and information on local flora and fauna. The small *Guidebook for Walking Trails* (¥150) is useful for short walks.

Kyōdo Center tourist information office (☎ 53-3795; ⏰ 9am-5pm) Has a wealth of pamphlets and maps, with a friendly English speaker always on hand. Here you can also arrange for free guided tours in English through TVIGA (adminTVIGA@hotmail.com).

Tourist information desk (☎ 53-4511; ⏰ 8.30am-5pm) Tōbu Nikkō station has a small desk with hard-working staff.

Sights

The World Heritage sites around Tōshō-gū are Nikkō's centrepiece. A ¥1000 'combination

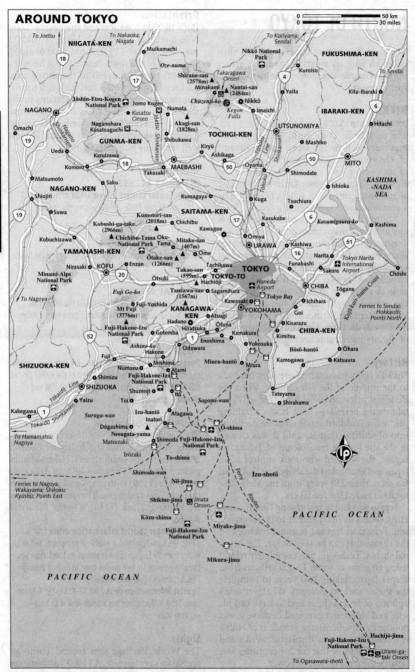

AROUND TOKYO

ROAD-TRIPPING, EDO-STYLE

You know that old chestnut about all roads leading to Rome? Well, in Edo-era Japan all of the important roads literally led to the shogun's capital.

Under a system called *sankin-kotai, daimyō* (feudal lords) were required to maintain residences in Edo as well as in their home provinces and go back and forth to attend to affairs in both places. Their families, meanwhile, remained in Edo in order to suppress temptation towards insurrection. Travel to the provinces was via main 'trunk' roads, including the Tōkaidō ('Eastern Sea road', connecting Edo to Heian-kyō, now Kyoto), the Nikkō Kaidō (Nikkō road) and the Nakasendō ('Central Mountain road' most notably through Nagano-ken).

These roads became celebrated, notably through Hiroshige's series of *ukiyo-e* (woodblock prints), *53 Stations of the Tōkaidō*. At the 'stations', inns thrived and nobles and their retainers could unwind after long days. Strategically located stations housed checkpoints, 50 in all, called *sekisho*. Travelling commoners had to present a *tegata* (a wooden plaque that served as a passport) and subject themselves to inspection for contraband, such as weaponry. Violation of these rules – including trying to circumnavigate the *sekisho* – could bring severe penalties including a particularly ghastly form of crucifixion. The *sekisho* at Hakone and Kiso-Fukushima were among the most important and remain the best preserved. Other atmospheric station towns are Arimatsu (p248) on the Tōkaidō and Tsumago (p288) on the Nakasendō.

---

ticket', valid for two days and available at booths in the area, covers entry to the temple, Rinnō-ji, the shrines, Tōshō-gū and Futarasan-jinja, but not the Nemuri-Neko (Sleeping Cat) in Tōshō-gū and Ieyasu's Tomb.

Most sites are open 8am to 5pm (until 4pm November to March). To avoid hordes, visit early on a weekday.

SHIN-KYŌ 神橋
The lovely red sacred **bridge** (☎ 54-0535; www .shinkyo.net) over the Daiya River is a much-photographed reconstruction of the 17th-century original. Its location is famed as the spot where Shōdō Shōnin was carried across the river on the backs of two giant serpents. Although historically the bridge was only for members of the imperial court and generals, it was temporarily opened to the public in 2005, extended until November 2007. Check when you visit for further openings.

RINNŌ-JI 輪王寺
This Tendai-sect temple was founded 1200 years ago by Shōdō Shōnin, and today some 360m of zelkova trees make up the pillars in the current building. The three gilded images in the Sambutsu-dō (Three Buddha Hall) are the largest wooden Buddhas in Japan (8m). The central image is Amida Nyorai (one of the primal deities in the Mahayana Buddhist cannon) flanked by Senjū (1000-armed Kannon, deity of mercy and compassion) and Batō (a horse-headed Kannon), whose special domain is the animal kingdom. A room to the side contains a healing Buddha, holding his ring finger over a medicine bowl, said to be the origin of the Japanese name for this finger (*kusuri-yubi*, medicine finger).

Rinnō-ji's **Hōmotsu-den** (Treasure Hall; admission ¥300) houses some 6000 treasures associated with the temple; admission is not included in the combination ticket (p187).

Next to Rinnō-ji is the 15m-high, 3m circumference pillar Sōrintō (1643), built by Iemitsu in 1643. Inside are 1000 volumes of sutras.

TŌSHŌ-GŪ 東照宮
A huge stone *torii* is a fittingly grand entrance to this storied Shintō shrine. To the left is a five-storey pagoda (34.3m) dating from 1650 and reconstructed in 1818. The pagoda has no foundations but contains a long suspended pole that swings like a pendulum, maintaining equilibrium in the event of an earthquake.

The entrance to the main shrine is through the *torii* at the gate, **Omote-mon**, protected on either side by Deva kings. Just inside are the **Sanjinko** (Three Sacred Storehouses). On the upper storey of the last storehouse are imaginative relief carvings of elephants by an artist who famously had never seen the real thing. To the left of the entrance is **Shinyōsha** (Sacred Stable), a plain building housing a carved white horse. The stable is adorned with allegorical relief carvings of monkeys, including the famous 'hear no evil, see no evil,

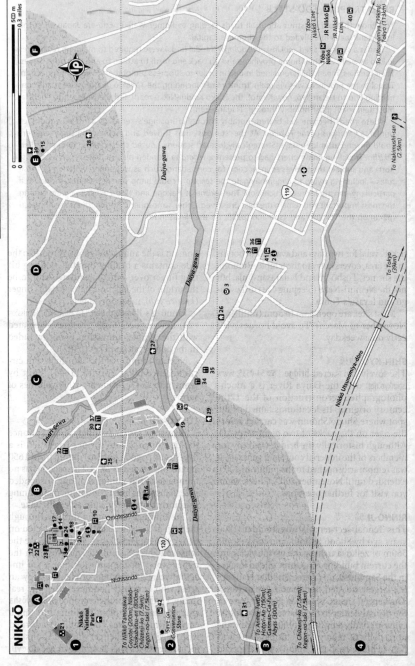

NIKKŌ

Nikkō National Park

Omotesandō

Nishisandō

Daiya-gawa

Daiya-gawa

Daiya-gawa

Inari-gawa

Tōbu Nikkō Line

JR Nikkō Line

Tōbu Nikkō

JR Nikkō

To Utsunomiya (39km);
Tokyo (113km)

To Nakimushi-san
(2.5km)

To Tokyo
(39km)

Nikkō Utsunomiya-dōro

To Nikkō Tamōzawa
Goyōtei (600m); Nikkō
Shōbu-en (800m);
Chūzenji-ko (7.5km);
Kegon-no-taki (7.5km)

Save-on
Convenience
Store

To Annex Turtle
Hotori-An (500m);
Ganman-ga-Fuchi
Abyss (300m)

To Chūzenji-ko (7.5km);
Kegon-no-taki (7.5km)

0   500 m
0   0.3 miles

AROUND TOKYO

speak no evil' monkeys, demonstrating three principles of Tendai Buddhism.

Just beyond the stable is a granite font at which, in accordance with Shintō practice, worshippers cleanse themselves by washing their hands and rinsing their mouths. Next to the gate is a sacred library containing 7000 Buddhist scrolls and books; it's closed to the public.

Pass through another *torii,* climb another flight of stairs, and on the left and right are a drum tower and a belfry. To the left of the drum tower is **Honji-dō** (Yakushido). This hall is best known for the painting on its ceiling of the Nakiryū (crying dragon). Monks demonstrate the acoustical properties of this hall by clapping two sticks together. The dragon 'roars' (a bit of a stretch) when the sticks are clapped beneath the dragon's mouth, but not elsewhere.

Next comes **Yōmei-mon** (Sunset Gate), dazzlingly decorated with glimmering gold leaf and intricate, coloured carvings and paintings of flowers, dancing girls, mythical beasts and Chinese sages. Worrying that its perfection might arouse envy in the gods, those responsible for its construction had the final supporting pillar placed upside down as a deliberate error. Although the style is more Chinese than Japanese and some critics deride it as gaudy, it's a grand spectacle.

To the left of Yōmei-mon is the **Jin-yōsha**, storage for the *mikoshi* (portable shrines), used during festivals.

Tōshō-gu's **Honden** (Main Hall) and **Haiden** (Hall of Worship) are across the enclosure. Inside (open only to *daimyō* during the Edo Period) are paintings of the 36 immortal poets of Kyoto, and a ceiling painting pattern from the Momoyama period; note the 100 dragons, each different. Fusuma (sliding door) paintings depict a *kirin,* a mythical beast that's part giraffe and part dragon. It's said that it will appear only when the world is at peace.

Through Yōmei-mon and to the right is **Nemuri-Neko**, a small wooden sculpture of a sleeping cat famous throughout Japan for its lifelike appearance (though admittedly the attraction is lost on some visitors). From here, **Sakashita-mon** opens onto an uphill path through towering cedars to Ieyasu's tomb, appropriately solemn. There's a separate entry fee (¥520) to see the cat and the tomb.

FUTARASAN-JINJA 二荒山神社

Shōdō Shōnin founded this shrine; the current building dates from 1619, making it Nikkō's oldest. It's the protector shrine of Nikkō itself, dedicated to the nearby mountain, Nantai-san (2484m), the mountain's consort, Nyotai-san, and their mountainous progeny, Tarō. If you are charmed by this shrine, you can visit the other two portions of it, on Nantai-san and by Chūzenji-ko (p194).

TAIYŪIN-BYŌ 大猷院廟

Taiyūin-byō enshrines Ieyasu's grandson Iemitsu (1604–51). Though it houses many of the same elements as Tōshōgu (storehouses, drum tower, Chinese style gates etc), its smaller, more intimate scale and setting in a cryptomeria forest make it very appealing. It's unusual in that it's both a Buddhist temple and a mausoleum.

Among Taiyūin-byō's many structures, look for dozens of lanterns donated by *daimyō*, and the gate Niō-mon, whose guardian deities have a hand up (to welcome those with pure hearts) and a hand down (to suppress impure hearts). Inside the main hall, 140 dragons painted on the ceiling are said to carry prayers to the heavens; those holding pearls are on their way up, and those without are returning to gather more prayers.

GAMMAN-GA-FUCHI ABYSS 含満ヶ淵

If the crowds of Nikkō leave you yearning for a little quiet, take the 20-minute walk to Gamman-Ga-Fuchi Abyss, a collection of *jizō* statues (the small stone statues of the Buddhist protector of travellers and children) set along a wooded path. One of the statues midway along is known as the Bake-jizō, who mocks travellers foolish enough to try to count all the *jizō* (they're said to be uncountable). Take a left after crossing the Shin-kyō bridge and follow the river for about 800m, crossing another bridge en route.

NIKKŌ TAMOZAWA GOYŌTEI
日光田母沢御用邸

The 1899 **Nikkō Tamozawa Goyōtei** (☎ 53-6767; adult/child ¥500/250; ♥ 9am-4.30pm Wed-Mon) was the largest wooden imperial villa (106 rooms) in two generations of Emperors, and it was where the Emperor Shōwa (aka Hirohito) spent WWII. It has been painstakingly restored to its former glory and is well worth a visit. It's about 1km west of the Shin-kyō bridge.

NIKKŌ WOODCARVING CENTER
日光木彫りの里

After marvelling over the craftsmanship of Nikkō's World Heritage sites, this workshop and sales **shop** (☎ 53-0070; 2848 Tokorono; admission free; ♥ 9am-5pm Fri-Wed) has more contemporary (and utilitarian) pieces in the tradition. Exhibits on the 2nd floor include *yatai* (festival floats), *tansu* (wooden chests), and woodworking demonstrations of kitchen and other accessories. You can try your own hand with a week's notice (fax 53-0310; fee based on what you want to produce).

Festivals & Events

Yayoi Matsuri (16 & 17 April) Procession of *mikoshi* (portable shrines), held at Futarasan-jinja.

Tōshō-gū Grand Festival (17 & 18 May) Nikkō's most important annual festival features horseback archery on the first day and a 1000-strong costumed re-enactment of the delivery of Ieyasu's remains to Nikkō on the second.

Tōshō-gū Autumn Festival (16 & 17 October) Autumnal repeat of the May festival, minus the equestrian archery.

Sleeping

Most places in Nikkō are used to foreign guests.

BUDGET

Nikkō Daiyagawa Youth Hostel (☎ /fax 54-1974; www5 .ocn.ne.jp/%7Edaiyayh/; 1075 Nakahatsuishi-machi; dm ¥2730; ☒) This six-room, 24-bed hostel earns commendations for its hospitable hostess. It's a four-minute walk from the Shiyakusho-mae (City Hall) bus stop, behind the post office and near the river. Reserve meals in advance; breakfast/dinner is ¥420/840.

Nikkō Park Lodge (☎ 53-1201; fax 53-4332; www .nikkoparklodge.com; 2825 Tokorono; dm/r per person from ¥2990/3990) Friendly, cute, unpretentious and well kept, on the green side of town (pick-up available on request). It's mostly twin and double rooms, plus a couple of dorms, run by English-speaking Zen Buddhist monks; look for yoga classes. Breakfast/dinner costs ¥395/1500.

Jōhsyū-ya Ryokan (☎ 54-0155; fax 53-2000; www .johsyu-ya.co.jp; 911 Nakahatsuishi; r per person ¥3900) This 100-plus-year-old inn, on the main road beside the post office, is nothing fancy but good honest value. No private facilities or English spoken, but rooms have phone and TV, and there's a hot-spring bath and woodwork on the doors that's funky (in a good way). Breakfast/dinner costs ¥1000/2000.

MIDRANGE

Turtle Inn Nikkō (☎ 53-3168; www.turtle-nikko.com; 2-16 Takumi-cho; s/d without bathroom ¥5100/9000, s/d with bathroom ¥5600/10,600; ☐) One of Nikkō's more popular pensions, with large Japanese and Western-style rooms, some English-speaking staff and hearty meals (breakfast/dinner ¥1050/2100). Downsides: rather institutional feel, décor that's more 'outdated' than 'traditional'. Take a bus to Sōgō-kaikan-mae, backtrack about 50m, turn right along the river and walk for about five minutes; you'll see the turtle sign on the left. Rates vary seasonally.

Annex Turtle Hotori-An (☎ 53-3663; www.turtle
-nikko.com; 8-28 Takumi-cho; s/d with bathroom ¥6500/12,400;
🖳) For a little more money and a few more
minutes' walk, the Turtle Inn's newer Annex
is a more modern, pleasant option. It has a
windowed dining room (breakfast/dinner
¥1050/2100), well-tended *tatami* and Western-style rooms, and greenery surrounding
the *onsen* (plus in-room baths). Internet access is at Turtle Inn, and your dinner may
be, too. From Turtle Inn, bear left and cross
the river; the annex is about 100m ahead on
the right.

Nikkō Tōkan-sō Ryokan (☎ 54-0611; fax 53-3914;
www.tokanso.com; 2335 Sannai; r per person incl 2 meals
¥8400-14,000, min 2 people) Clean and spacious,
Tōkansō provides a welcoming (if not luxurious) ryokan experience. From the Shinkyō
bus stop, continue uphill, cross the street, turn
right and bear left again uphill.

TOP END

Nikkō Kanaya Hotel (☎ 54-0001; www.kanayahotel
.co.jp/nkh/index-e.html; 1300 Kami-Hatsuishi-machi; s/d
from ¥9240/11,500; 🏊 🖳) Nikkō's oldest Western style hotel (1893) wears its history like a
fine suit. Uphill from Rte 119 and with views
of the river and Shin-kyō, the best rooms have
fine views, spacious quarters and private bathrooms. Rates do not include meals and rise
steeply in peak seasons.

Hotel Seikōen (☎ 53-5555; fax 53-5554; www
.hotel-seikoen.com; 2350 Sannai; d per person incl 2 meals
¥12,000-17,000) About as close as you can get to
Tōshōgu, this 24-room hotel was built in the
1980s but somehow looks older. That's forgotten in the neat rooms (mostly Japanese) and
onsen, including indoor and outdoor baths
(the latter of cypress) and sauna, and meals
offering local specialities. It's past Tōkan-sō
Ryokan, about 100m on the left-hand side.

Eating & Drinking

Nikkō's overnight visitors often eat where
they're staying, but there are a number of
places on the main road between the stations
and the shrine area; most close by 8pm or
9pm. A local speciality is *yuba* – the skin that
forms when making tofu – cut into strips; better than it sounds, it's a staple of *shōjin-ryōri*
(Buddhist vegetarian cuisine).

Hippari Dako (☎ 53-2933; 1011 Kami-Hatsuishi-machi;
meals ¥500-850; 🕙 11am-8pm; E) This three-table
shop is an institution among foreign travellers, as years of business cards tacked to the

walls testify. It serves filling sets, including
yakitori (chicken on skewers) and *yaki-udon*
(fried noodles). It's on the left side of Rte 119,
about 100m before the Shin-kyō bridge.

Skylark Gusto (☎ 50-1232; 595-1 Gokōmachi; mains
¥500-1000; 🕙 10am-2am Mon-Fri, 7am-2am Sat; E)
Nikkō's only late-night restaurant is a branch
of Skylark, a national chain of 'family restaurants'. It makes up in value and variety what
it lacks in individuality. Offerings include pizzas, pasta and *tonkatsu* (pork cutlet).

Hi no Kuruma (ひの車; ☎ 54-2062; 597-2 Gokōmachi;
mains ¥500-1500; 🕙 lunch & dinner Thu-Tue; E) A local
favourite for *okonomiyaki* (savoury pancakes),
which you cook by yourself on a *teppan* (hot-
steel table). Most choices are under ¥1000,
or splurge for the works: pork, squid, beef,
shrimp, corn etc (¥1500).

Kikō (☎ 53-3320; 1007 Kami-Hatsuishi-machi; mains
¥700-1300; 🕙 lunch & dinner; E) Welcoming, home-
style spot for Korean dishes, like *ishiyaki
bibimpa* (rice with beef and vegetables in a
hot stone bowl), *chapchae* (fried clear noodles
with vegetables) and *kimchi rāmen* (noodles
with spicy Korean pickles). *Yakiniku* (grilled
meats) is cooked in the kitchen (other places
make you cook it yourself at the table), and
large dishes like *samgyetang* (stewed ginseng
chicken) are enough for two. It's a few doors
downhill from Hippari Dako, with a scrolling
electronic sign.

Yuba Yūzen (☎ 53-0355; 1-22 Yasukawa-cho; sets
¥2625-3150; 🕙 lunch) This *yuba* speciality house
serves its sashimi-style, with tofu and soy milk,
and with a variety of seasonal side dishes.
There's no English menu, but there are only
two choices for sets: ¥2625 if you're hungry
and ¥3150 if you're really hungry. Look for
the two-storey tan building across from the
first left turn after Shinkyō.

Gyoshintei (☎ 53-3751; 2339-1 Sannai; meals around
¥4000; 🕙 lunch & dinner) For *shojin-ryōri* in a setting to die for, Gyoshintei is worth the splurge.
It overlooks an elegant garden, about 250m
north of the Shin-kyō bridge.

Nikkō Beer (☎ 54-3005; 2844-1 Tokorono; beer from
¥525; 🕙 9.30am-5.30pm) Sample the local brew in
the hills above town, a light lager-style Pilsner
that's won beer competitions both internationally (in 2004) and in Japan (2006). Snacks
include sausages and ice cream.

Stalls around the shrine precincts sell
snacks grilled on a stick, including *yakitori*,
yaki-tomorokoshi (grilled corn) and *ayu* (river
trout).

Getting There & Away

Nikkō is best reached from Tokyo via the Tōbu-Nikkō line from Asakusa station. You can usually get last-minute seats on reserved *tokkyū* (limited express) trains (¥2740, one hour 50 minutes) about every 30 minutes from 7.30am to 10am, hourly thereafter. *Kaisoku* (rapid) trains (¥1320, 2½ hours, hourly from 6.20am to 4.30pm) require no reservation. For either train, you may have to change at Shimo-imaichi. Be sure to ride in the first two cars to reach Nikkō (some cars may separate at an intermediate stop).

JR makes four daily runs between Nikko and Tokyo's Shinjuku (¥3900) and Ikebukuro (¥3770) stations, in about two hours. Otherwise, travelling by JR is time-consuming and costly without a JR Pass. Take the *shinkansen* (bullet train) from Tokyo to Utsunomiya (¥4800, 50 minutes) and change there for an ordinary train to Nikkō (¥740, 45 minutes).

TRAIN/BUS PASSES

Tōbu Railway offers two passes covering rail transport from Asakusa to Nikkō (though not the *tokkyū* surcharge, from ¥1040) and unlimited hop-on-hop-off bus services around Nikko. The All Nikko Pass (adult/child ¥4400/2210,) is valid for four days and includes buses to Chūzenji-ko (right), Yumoto-Onsen (p195) and other regional destinations. The World Heritage Pass (Sekai-isan Meguri Pass; adult/senior high/junior high/child ¥3600/3200/3000/1700, two days) includes buses to the World Heritage sights, plus admission to Tōshōgu, Rinnō-ji and Futarasan Jinja. Purchase these passes at the Tōbu **Sightseeing Service Center** (✆ 8am-2.30pm) in Asakusa station. Bus stops are announced in English.

TŌBU NIKKŌ BUS FREE PASS

If you've already got your rail ticket, two-day bus-only passes allow unlimited rides between Nikkō and Yumoto Onsen (¥3000) or Nikkō and Chuzenji Onsen (¥2000), including the World Heritage sites. Alternatively, the Sekai-isan-meguri (World Heritage Bus Pass; ¥500) covers the area between the stations and shrine precincts. Buy these at Tōbu Nikkō station.

AROUND NIKKŌ 日光周辺

✆ 0288

Nikkō is part of the Nikkō National Park, 1402 sq km sprawling over Fukushima, Tochigi,

Gunma and Niigata prefectures. This mountainous region features extinct volcanoes, lakes, waterfalls and marshlands. There are good hiking opportunities and some remote hot-spring resorts.

Yashio-no-yu Onsen やしおの湯温泉

A 5km bus ride from central Nikkō, this modern **onsen** (admission ¥500; ✆ 10am-9pm Fri-Wed) is a good place to relax after a day of exploring shrines and temples. It has several different baths, including a *rotemburo* (outdoor bath). Take a Chūzenji-bound bus from either train station in Nikkō and get off at the Kiyotaki Itchōme stop. The *onsen* is across the river from the bus stop; walk back towards Nikkō, under the Rte 120 bypass and across the bridge.

Chūzenji-ko 中禅寺湖

This area 10km west of Nikkō is (relatively) natural and offers a bit of seclusion, even if the namesake lake has the usual tourist facilities. The big-ticket attraction is the humbling, 97m-high falls, **Kegon-no-taki** (華厳滝; ✆ 55-0030; adult/child return ¥530/320; ✆ 7.30am-6pm May-Sep, 9am-4.30pm Dec-Feb, sliding hr in btwn). Take the elevator down to a platform to observe the full force of the plunging water. **Futarasan-jinja** (二荒山神社; ✆ 55-0017; ✆ 8am-5pm Apr-Oct, 9am-4pm Nov-Mar) complements the shrines at Tōshō-gū and on the mountain, Nantai-san (2484m). The shrine is about 1km west of the falls, along the lake's north shore.

For good views of the lake and Kegon-no-taki, get off the bus at the Akechi-daira bus stop (the stop before Chūzenji Onsen) and take the **Akechi-daira Ropeway** (Akechi Plateau Cable Car; 明智平ロープウェイ; ✆ 55-0331; adult one way/return ¥390/710, child ¥190/360; ✆ 8.30am-4.30pm Apr-Nov, 9am-4pm Dec-Mar) up to a viewing platform. From here, it's a pleasant 1.5km walk across the Chanoki-daira to a vantage point with great views over the lake, the falls and Nantai-san. From here you can walk down to the lake and Chūzenji Onsen.

Chūzenji-ko has the usual flotilla of sightseeing boats at the dock (prices vary). The lake (161m deep) is a fabulous shade of deep blue in good weather, with a mountainous backdrop.

SLEEPING & EATING

Chūzenji Pension (中禅寺ペンション; ✆ 55-0888; fax 55-0721; s/d without meals from ¥6300/9450, per person incl 2 meals from ¥8925) This pink hostelry set back from the lake's eastern shore has nine mostly Western-style rooms that feel a bit like grandma's house. All have private facilities, and there's bike rental available.

our pick **Hotel Fūga** (楓雅; ☎ 55-1122; fax 55-1100; www.nikko-hotelfuga.com; d per person incl 2 meals from ¥23,000) *Ay caramba!* The common baths here are bigger than entire inns elsewhere, the rest of the building is fitted with contemporary art and hallways are lined with carpets you may want to dive into. All 28 palatially proportioned Japanese-style rooms have views of the lake and Mt Nantai. It's about 150m beyond Chūzenji Pension.

Feu de Bois (フゥドボワ; ☎ 55-1223; bread & pastry ¥100-500; ⏰ 8am-6pm while supplies last) A block off the main street by the bus Chūzenji bus stop is this darling *boulangerie* selling walnut bread, Danish with apricot or choco-banana, croissants and more. Stock up before that Senjōgahara hike.

GETTING THERE & AWAY

Buses run from the Nikkō station area to Chūzenji Onsen (¥1100, 50 minutes).

Yumoto Onsen 湯元温泉

From Chūzenji-ko, you might continue on to the quieter hot-springs resort of Yumoto Onsen by bus (¥840, 30 minutes) or reach it by a rewarding three-hour hike on the Senjōgahara Shizen-kenkyu-rō (Senjōgahara Plain Nature Trail; 戦場ヶ原自然研究路).

From Chūzenji Onsen, take a Yumoto-bound bus and get off at Ryūzu-no-taki (竜頭ノ滝; ¥410, 20 minutes), the start of the hike. The hike follows the Yu-gawa across the picturesque marshland of Senjōgahara (partially on wooden plank paths), alongside the 75m-high falls Yu-daki (湯滝) to the lake Yu-no-ko (湯の湖), then around the lake to Yumoto Onsen and the bus back to Nikkō (¥1650, 1½ hours).

Before leaving Yumoto Onsen, you might stop off at the hot-spring temple **Onsen-ji** (温泉寺; admission ¥500; ⏰ 10am-2pm late Apr–Nov), a good spot to rest hiking-weary muscles.

To hike downhill, take the bus to Yumoto and follow this route in reverse.

GUNMA-KEN 群馬県

The Japanese archipelago is filled with *onsen*, but the star in the Kanto area hot-spring firmament is Gunma-ken. Mineral baths seem to bubble out of the ground at every turn in this mountainous landscape, and some small towns feel delightfully traditional. Here's just a small selection.

Kusatsu Onsen 草津温泉

☎ 0279 / pop 7625

Kusatsu has been famous for its waters since the Kamakura Period. Their source is Yubatake (湯畑, 'hot water field') in the town centre, flowing at 5000L per minute and topped with wooden tanks from which Kusatsu's *ryokan* fill their baths. A stroll here in your *yukata* (cotton bathrobe) is a must. Kusatsu's waters are relatively heavy with sulphuric acid, which sounds scary until you realise that it destroys harmful microbes.

Stop in or phone the **city hall tourist section** (☎ 88-0001; ⏰ 8.30am-5.30pm), next to the bus station (English speaker on hand, who can help book accommodation). On the web, visit www.kusatsu-onsen.ne.jp.

There are plenty of *onsen* open to the public, including **Ōtakinoyu** (大瀧乃湯; adult/child ¥800/400; ⏰ 9am-9pm), known for its tubs at a variety of temperatures; try different ones for an experience known as *awase-yu* (mix-and-match waters). At the park Sai-no-kawara-kōen (西の河原公園) west of town is a 500 sq metre **rotemburo** (separated by gender; ☎ 88-6167; adult/child ¥500/300; ⏰ 7am-8pm Apr-Nov, 9am-8pm Dec-Mar).

Kusatsu also offers a unique opportunity to see *yumomi*, in which local women stir the waters to cool them, in folk-dance style while singing a folk song. It's next to Yubatake at the bathhouse **Netsu no Yu** (熱の湯; ☎ 88-3613; adult/child ¥500/200, ⏰ 3 performances Dec-Mar, 4 performances late Mar-Nov, 6 performances May-late Oct).

Inns in the town centre are mostly pretty expensive, but the 12-room Alpine-vibe **Pension Segawa** (ペンションセガワ; ☎ 88-1288; fax 88-1377; r per person incl 2 meals from ¥8025) is a 10-minute walk from the bus terminal (owners will pick you up). Choose a Western- or Japanese-style room and three different bathtubs, and look for fresh-baked bread. Plus, there's a tennis court (in season).

Though you might not know from looking at its tower next to Yubatake, **Hotel Ichii** (ホテル一井; ☎ 88-0011; fax 88-0111; r per person incl two meals from ¥14,000; ⏰) has been a Kusatsu institution in business for 300-plus years. In addition to in-room baths, of course there are indoor and outdoor baths separated by gender. Expect *sansai* (mountain vegetable) cuisine.

Transport to Kusatsu Onsen is by bus from Naganohara Kusatsuguchi station. From Ueno, *tokkyū* Kusatsu trains take about 2½ hours (¥5130) to Naganohara-Kusatsuguchi station, then local bus to Kusatsu Onsen (¥670, 30 minutes). Alternatively, take the *shinkansen* to Takasaki and transfer to the Agatsuma line (¥5650, 2¼ hours). **JR Highway Buses** (www.jrbuskanto.co.jp/mn/aetop.cfm) from Shinjuku station south exit cost ¥3100/5600 (one way/return) and take about 3¾ hours each way; reservations required.

Minakami & Takaragawa Onsen
水上温泉・宝川温泉
☎ 0278

In eastern Gunma-ken, Minakami is a thriving *onsen* town with outdoor activities to match. The town of Minakami also encompasses Takaragawa Onsen (about 30 minutes away by road), a riverside spa oft-voted the nation's best.

The train station is in the village of Minakami Onsen, as are most of Minakami's lodgings. **Minakami Tourist Information Centre** (水上観光協会; ☎ 72-2611; www.minakami-onsen.com; ☻ 9am-5.15pm) is across from the station, has English pamphlets and can make accommodation reservations (in Japanese). Ask which inns in town have *higaeri nyuyoku* (day-use baths) open when you visit.

Tanigawadake Ropeway (谷川岳ロープウェイ; ☎ 72-3575; return ¥2000; ☻ 8am-5pm Mon-Fri, 7am-5pm Sat & Sun) takes you via gondola to the peak Tenjin-daira, from where hiking trips, ranging from a couple of hours to all day, are available from May to November, conditions permitting. There's skiing and snowboarding in winter (December to May). From Minakami station, take a bus to Ropeway-Eki-mae bus stop (¥650, about hourly).

A number of operators lead rafting and kayaking trips in warmer months and winter expeditions, such as snowshoeing, from about ¥6000 for a half-day. Inquire at the tourist information centre. **Max** (☎ 72-4844) is a typical outlet, with English-speaking guides.

Takaragawa Onsen (☎ 75-261; adult/child ¥1500/1000; ☻ 9am-4pm) is idyllic and rangey. Most of its several pools on the riverbanks (with slate, not natural, flooring) are mixed bathing, with one women-only bath. Women are encouraged to take modesty towels into the mixed baths. The covered walkway down to the baths is lined with collections of…well…*stuff* that must have taken decades to assemble: antique teapots to Pooh bears and plastic flowers. A small restaurant serves udon, *soba* and *kamameshi* (rice topped with other ingredients in a metal pot).

our pick The adjacent inn, **Ōsenkaku** (☎ 75-2121; fax 75-2038; r per person incl 2 meals from ¥9600) is spectacular, with gorgeous riverfront rooms over several buildings, a mighty old-style feel and 24-hour use of the outdoor onsen, *and* you get to avoid the covered walkway. Prices rise steeply for nicer rooms with better views.

To reach Minakami station, take the *shinkansen* from Ueno to Takasaki and transfer to the Jōetsu line (¥5650, two hours), or *tokkyū* Minakami trains run direct (¥5130, 2½ hours). You can also catch the *shinkansen* to Jōmō Kōgen (1¼ hours) from Tokyo/Ueno (¥5240/5040), from where buses run to Minakami (¥600) and Takaragawa Onsen (¥1450, April to early December).

MITO 水戸
☎ 029 / pop 264,000

Capital of Ibaraki Prefecture and a one-time castle town, Mito is best known for the garden, **Kairaku-en** (偕楽園; ☎ 244-5454; garden/Kobuntei pavilion free/¥190; ☻ garden 6am-7pm Apr–mid-Sep, 7am-6pm mid-Sep–Mar, pavilion 9am-4pm). It's one of the three most-celebrated landscape gardens in Japan; the other two are Kenroku-en (p294)in Kanazawa and Kōraku-en in Okayama (above).

The 18-acre Kairaku-en dates back to 1842 when it was built by the *daimyō* of the Mito *han* (domain), a member of the clan of the Tokugawa shogun. 'Kairaku-en' means 'the garden to enjoy with people', and it was one of the first gardens in the nation to open to the public, decades before the advent of public parks following the Meiji Restoration.

The gardens remain popular for their 3000 *ume* (plum blossom) trees, some 100 varieties of which bloom in late February or early March. A plum blossom festival takes place here around this time (contact the JNTO or local tourist office ☎ 224-0441 for dates). Other flowering trees (azaleas, camellias, cherry etc) make for impressive viewing in other seasons, and the hillside setting allows broad views. The three-storey pavilion Kobun-tei is a faithful 1950s reproduction of the *daimyo's* villa (the original was destroyed during WWII).

From Tokyo, JR Jōban line trains depart from Ueno station for Mito (*tokkyū*; ¥3820, 80 minutes); connect by local train to Kairaku-en station (¥180, five minutes), take a bus to Kairaku-en bus stop (¥230, 15 minutes) or walk (about 30 minutes) from the station's south exit along the lake Senba-ko.

WEST OF TOKYO

Tokyo-to (Tokyo Prefecture) includes many cities in addition to Tokyo proper; most are along the Chūō line as it heads towards Yamanashi-ken. South and west of these are the scenic Fuji Go-ko region, Mt Fuji itself, the tourist mecca of Hakone, and the *onsen* and beach resorts of the Izu-hantō.

Ghibli Museum 三鷹の森ジブリ美術館

When you saw *Spirited Away* by Miyazaki Hayao (or *Princess Mononoke*, *Howl's Moving Castle*, *My Neighbour Totoro* and so on), you probably fell in love with its mythical themes, fanciful characters and outrageous landscapes. So did every kid in Japan, which means you need to arrange tickets long before you arrive at this **museum** (☎ 0570-055777; www.ghibli-museum .jp/ticket_info.html; 1-1-83 Shimorenjaku, Mitaka-shi, Tokyo; adult ¥1000, child ¥100-700; ☉ 10am-6pm Wed-Mon) in Tokyo's Mitaka City of the work of Ghibli, Miyazaki's animation studio.

Exhibits cover the animation process from concept to screen (English-speaking docents are usually on hand). There's a zoetrope presentation of a half-dozen Ghibli characters in motion, a mini-theatre presenting short films (in Japanese but usually easy enough to follow), 5m worth of robot from *Castle in the Sky* and a gift shop with exclusive merchandise (at exclusive prices).

From Mitaka station on the Chūō line (from Shinjuku: ¥210, 13 minutes), follow the sign-posted walk along the Tamagawa Waterworks for 15 minutes to Inokashira Park and turn right. Alternatively, a community bus (one way/return ¥200/300, approximately every 10 minutes) goes directly to the museum from the station.

Takao-san 高尾山

☎ 042

Easily reached from Shinjuku, Mt Takao is one of Tokyo's most popular day trips, although it's often busy on weekends and holidays and rather built up compared to other regional hikes.

One of the chief attractions on this 599m mountain is the temple **Yaku-ō-in** (薬王院; ☎ 661-1115; ☉ 24hr), best known for the Hiwatari Matsuri (fire-crossing ceremony; second Sunday in March, 1pm near Takaosanguchi station). Priests walk across hot coals in bare feet amid the ceremonial blowing of conch shells. The public is also welcome to participate; expect lots of company.

The rest of the year, Takao-san offers nature hikes with six trails. Keio line offices have free trail maps in English. The most popular trail (No 1) leads you past the temple; allow about 3¼ hours return for the 400m ascent. Alternatively, a cable car and a chair lift can take you partway up (one way adult/child ¥470/230, return ¥900/450).

From Shinjuku station, take the private Keio line (*jun-tokkyū*; ¥370, 47 minutes) to Takaosanguchi. The tourist village (with snack and souvenir shops), trail entrances, cable car and chairlift are a few minutes away to the right. JR Pass holders can travel to Takao station on the Chūō line (45 minutes) and transfer to the Keio line to Takaosanguchi (¥120, three minutes).

Oku-Tama Region 奥多摩周辺

☎ 0428

The upriver region of the Tama-gawa, in Ōme city, has some splendid mountain scenery and good hiking trails, making it a fine day trip or an easygoing overnight. The highlight of the area is the mountaintop shrine complex of Mitake-jinja and the quaint village surrounding it.

MITAKE-SAN 御岳山

Buses run from Mitake station to the Mitake-san cable-car terminus at **Takimoto** (elevation 407m) where a cable car (¥270, 10 minutes) takes you near the summit (elevation 926m, one way/return ¥570/1090, six minutes, 7.30am to 6.30pm). Alternatively, allow one hour to hike from Takimoto to Mitake-san cable-car station (elevation 831m). About 20 minutes on foot from the top of the cable car is the rustic, wooded Mitake-jinja (御岳神社), a Shintō shrine said to date back some 1200 years, making it a historic pilgrimage site. Around the shrine are stunning views of the surrounding mountains.

Mitake Visitors Center (御岳ビジターセンター; ☎ 78-9363; ☉ 9am-4.30pm Tue-Sun) is 250m beyond the top of the cable car, near the start of the village.

ŌTAKE-SAN HIKE 大岳山

If you've got time, the five-hour round-trip hike from Mitake-jinja to the summit of Ōtake-san (大岳山; 1266m) is highly recommended. Although there's some climbing involved, it's a fairly easy hike and the views from the summit are excellent – Mt Fuji is visible on clear days. On the way, detour down to Nanoyono-taki (waterfalls set amid lush forest), Ganseki-en rock garden (a beautiful path that crosses back and forth across a gurgling stream) and Ayahirono-taki (another waterfall).

If you're not spending the night on Mitake-san, be sure to note the hours of the cable car before setting out.

SLEEPING & EATING

The following are all on Mitake-san.

Mitake Youth Hostel (御嶽ユースホステル; ☎ 78-8501; fax 78-8774; www.jyh.or.jp; dm incl 2/no meals ¥4550/2880, add ¥1000 for nonmembers) This comfortable hostel has fine tatami rooms inside a handsome old building that used to be a pilgrims' lodge. It's midway between the top of the cable car and Mitake-jinja, about a minute beyond the visitor centre.

Komadori San-sō (駒鳥山荘; ☎ 78-8472; fax 78-8472; r per person ¥5250-6300; ☐) On a promontory below the shrine, this 10-room *shukubō* (temple lodging) is higgledy-piggledy with bric-a-brac but friendly and at ease with foreigners. There's a balcony with mountain views, and a gigantic bathtub made of *hinoki* cypress. Breakfast/dinner costs from ¥800/2000. To reach the inn, walk around the hill where the shrine is and follow the signs.

Reiunso (嶺雲荘; ☎ 78-8501; fax 78-8774; r per person incl 2 meals from ¥8400) In the same building as the Mitake Youth Hostel, Reiunso has upgraded facilities and more elaborate meals.

Momiji-ya (紅葉屋; ☎ 78-8475; mains ¥735-1155; ☺ noon-5pm, closed irregularly) The little shopping street just before the shrine entrance has a number of small restaurants and shops. This *soba* shop is typical, with views out the back windows and *kamonanban soba* (noodles in hearty duck broth; ¥1155). There's a picture menu.

GETTING THERE & AWAY

To reach Mitake-san, take the JR Chūō line from Shinjuku station to Tachikawa station (¥450, 26 minutes), where you will probably have to change to the JR Ōme line to Mitake (¥440, 45 minutes).

MT FUJI AREA 富士山周辺
☎ 0555

Mt Fuji, emblem of Japan, dominates the region west of Tokyo. Climbing the mountain is a tradition with sacred overtones, while many visitors are content to view the mountain from its foothills. Although Hakone is probably the most famous spot for Fuji viewing, the scenic Fuji Go-ko region offers similar views and fewer crowds.

Mt Fuji 富士山

On clear days, particularly in winter, Mt Fuji (*Fuji-san* in Japanese) is visible from as far as Tokyo, 100km away. When Japan's highest mountain (3776m) is capped with snow, it's a picture-postcard perfect volcanic cone.

For much of the year you need to be closer, and even then the notoriously shy mountain is often covered in haze or cloud. Autumn and spring are your next best bets for Fuji-spotting, yet even during these times the mountain may be visible only in the morning before it retreats behind its cloud curtain.

ORIENTATION

If Fuji-san is the centre of this region, other attractions radiate around it like the numerals on a clock. At 5 o'clock is Izu-Hantō, while 4 o'clock points you towards Hakone. The Fuji-go-ko (Fuji Five Lakes) region begins at about 2 o'clock and heads west, through the towns of Fuji-Yoshida and Fuji-Kawaguchiko, continuing along the mountain's northern flank to the lovely, remote lake Motosu-ko at about 10-thirty. Much of this land is part of the noncontiguous Fuji-Hakone-Izu National Park.

INFORMATION

Brochures available from the **Tokyo Tourist Information Center** (TIC; ☎ 03-3201-3331) provide exhaustive detail on transport to the mountain and how to climb it, complete with climbing schedules worked out to the minute.

The best tourist information centres near the mountain are the **Fuji-Yoshida Information Center** (☎ 22-7000; ☺ 9am-5.30pm), to the left as you exit the Fuji-Yoshida train station, and the **Kawaguchi-ko Tourist Information Center** (☎ 72-6700; ☺ 8.30am-5pm Sun-Fri, 8.30am-6.30pm Sat

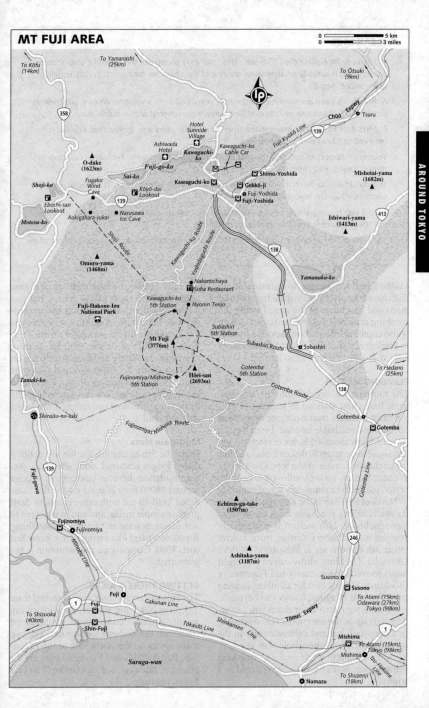

MT FUJI AREA

0 — 5 km
0 — 3 miles

To Kōfu
(14km)

To Yamanashi
(25km)

To Ōtsuki
(9km)

358

Chūo Expwy

Tsuru

Fuji Kyūkō Line

139

Hotel
Sunnide
Village

Ashiwada
Hotel

Kawaguchi-ko
Cable Car

Kawaguchi-ko

O-dake
(1623m)

Fuji-go-ko

Sai-ko

Shimo-Yoshida

Mishotai-yama
(1682m)

Shoji-ko

Fugaku
Wind
Cave

Kōyō-dai
Lookout

Kawaguchi-ko

Gekkō-ji

Fuji-Yoshida

Fuji-Yoshida

Eboshi-san
Lookout

139

Aokigahara-jukai

Narusawa
Ice Cave

Ishiwari-yama
(1413m)

413

Motosu-ko

Kawaguchi-ko Route

Yoshidaguchi Route

138

Omuro-yama
(1468m)

Nakanochaya
Soba Restaurant

Yamanaka-ko

Fuji-Hakone-Izu
National Park

Kawaguchi-ko
5th Station

Nyonin Tenjo

Subashiri
5th Station

Mt Fuji
(3776m)

Subashiri Route

Subashiri

Tanuki-ko

Fujinomiya/Mishima
5th Station

Hōei-san
(2693m)

Gotemba
5th Station

To Hadano
(25km)

Gotemba Route

138

Shiraito-no-taki

Fujinomiya/Mishima Route

Gotemba

Gotemba

Fuji-gawa

139

Gotemba Line

Echizen-ga-take
(1507m)

Fujinomiya

Fujinomiya

Minobu Line

Ashitaka-yama
(1187m)

246

Susono

Susono

To Atami (15km);
Odawara (27km);
Tokyo (98km)

Fuji

Fuji

Gakunan Line

Tōmei Expwy

1

To Shizuoka
(40km)

Shin-Fuji

Shinkansen Line

Tōkaidō Line

Mishima

Mishima

To Atami (15km);
Tokyo (98km)

Izu-Hakone Line

Suruga-wan

To Shuzenji
(18km)

Numazu

FUJI-SAN FAQS

■ In Japanese Mt Fuji is called 'Fuji-san'. This '-san' may sound like the honorific after someone's name, but it is actually an alternative reading of the character for mountain (山), usually pronounced 'yama'.

■ Although it's been dormant for hundreds of years, Fuji-san's a volcano. When it last blew its top, in 1707, the streets of Tokyo, 100km away, were covered with volcanic ash.

■ Experts date Fuji-san's current shape from about 8000 years ago. Before that, Fuji-san is believed to have been two volcanoes.

■ Your best chances of spotting the mountain are from November to February. Lotsa luck in August, unless you climb it.

■ The classic way to climb the mountain is to reach it in time for sunrise. The special name for sunrise on Fuji-san is goraikō.

■ Even if you're just passing on the shinkansen, you may be able to spot the mountain. Look out the northern side of the train around Fuji city.

■ The view of Mt Fuji on the back of the ¥1000 note is from Motosu-ko, the westernmost of the Fuji Go-ko.

& holidays), next to Kawaguchi-ko train station. Both have friendly, English-speaking staff and maps and brochures of the area. During the climbing season (1 July to 31 August), there is also climbing information provided by staff in English at a special office at **Fuji-Yoshida city hall** (☎ 24-1236; ◷ 8.30am-5.15pm Mon-Fri).

CLIMBING MT FUJI

The mountain is divided into 10 'stations' from base (first station) to summit (10th), but most climbers start from one of the four 5th stations, reachable by road. From the 5th stations, allow about 4½ hours to reach the top and about three hours to descend, plus an hour for circling the crater at the top. The Mt Fuji Weather Station, on the southwest edge of the crater, marks the mountain's actual summit.

North of Fuji-san is the Kawaguchi-ko 5th station (2305m), reachable from the town of Kawaguchi-ko. This station is particularly popular with climbers starting from Tokyo. Other 5th stations are at Subashiri (1980m), Gotemba (1440m; allow seven to eight hours to reach the summit) and Fujinomiya (Mishima; 2380m) best for climbers coming from the west (Nagoya, Kyoto and beyond).

To time your arrival for dawn you can either start up in the afternoon, stay overnight in a mountain hut and continue early in the morning, or climb the whole way at night. You do not want to arrive on the top too long before dawn, as it's likely to be very cold and windy.

Trails below the 5th stations are now used mainly as short hiking routes, but you might consider the challenging but rewarding hike from base to summit on either the Yoshidaguchi Route (see p203) from Fuji-Yoshida (p201) or on the Shoji Route from near Shoji-ko. There are alternative trails on the Kawaguchi-ko, Subashiri and Gotemba routes, which, assuming strong knees and expendable clothing, you can descend rapidly by running, schussing and sliding down loose, clay-red sand.

Mountain Huts

From the 5th to the 8th station are about a dozen lodges scattered along the trails. Accommodation here is basic: most charge around ¥5000 for a blanket on the floor sardined head-to-toe with other climbers. Staff prepare simple meals, and you're welcome to rest inside as long as you order something. If you don't feel like eating, a one-hour rest costs ¥500. Camping on the mountain is not permitted.

GETTING THERE & AWAY

The Fuji-san area is most easily reached from Tokyo by bus; from Kansai, the journey can require multiple connections via Mishima station on the Kodama shinkansen. The two main towns on the north side of the mountain, Fuji-Yoshida and Kawaguchi-ko, are the principal gateways. See Fuji Go-ko (Fuji Five Lakes, opposite).

Daily direct buses (¥2600, 2½ hours) run from Shinjuku bus terminal to the Kawaguchi-ko 5th station. For details call ☎ 03-5376-2217. This is by far the fastest and cheapest way of getting from Tokyo to the 5th station. If you take two trains and a bus, the same trip can cost nearly ¥6000. If you're already in Kawaguchi-ko, there are bus services up to Kawaguchi-ko 5th station (¥1700, 55 minutes) from April to mid-November. The schedule varies considerably during that period – call **Fuji Kyūkō bus** (☎ 72-2911) for details. At the height of the climbing season, there are buses until quite late in the evening – ideal for climbers intending to make an overnight ascent. Taxis operate from Kawaguchi-ko train station to the Kawaguchi-ko 5th station for around ¥10,000, plus tolls.

From Subashiri, buses to the Subashiri 5th station cost ¥1220 and take 55 minutes. From Gotemba station they cost ¥1500.

From Gotemba, buses to the Gotemba 5th station (¥1080, 45 minutes) operate four to six times daily during climbing season only.

Coming from western Japan, buses run from the *shinkansen* stations at Shin-Fuji (¥2400) and Mishima (¥2390) to Fujinomiya (Mishima) 5th station in just over two hours. There are reservation centres in **Tokyo** (☎ 03-5376-2217) and **Fuji** (☎ 72-5111).

Fuji go-ko 富士五湖
☎ 555

Yamanashi-ken's Fuji-go-ko (Fuji Five Lakes) region is scattered around the mountain's northern foothills; its lakes provide perfect reflecting pools for the mountain's majesty. Yamanaka-ko is the largest, easternmost lake, followed by Kawaguchi-ko, Sai-ko, Shōji-ko (the smallest) and Motosu-ko. Particularly during the autumn *kōyō* (foliage) season, the lakes make a good overnight trip out of Tokyo, for a stroll or a drive, and the energetic can hike in nearby mountains. Hiking maps are available from the information centres in the two principal towns, Fuji-Yoshida and Kawaguchi-ko.

SIGHTS & ACTIVITIES
Although adjacent, Fuji-Yoshida and Kawaguchi-ko are separate administrative districts, with separate visitor facilities.

Fuji-Yoshida 富士吉田
Fuji-Yoshida's *oshi no ie* (pilgrims' inns) have served visitors to the mountain since the days when climbing Mt Fuji was a pilgrimage rather than a tourist event. A necessary preliminary to the ascent was a visit to the deeply wooded, atmospheric shrine **Sengen-jinja** (1615, thought to have been the site of a shrine as early as 788), still worth a visit for its 1000-year-old cedar, the main gate rebuilt every 60 years (slightly larger each time) and the two one-tonne *mikoshi* used in the annual Yoshida no Himatsuri (Yoshida Fire Festival).

From Fuji-Yoshida station you can walk (15 minutes) or take a bus to Sengen-jinja-mae bus stop (¥150, five minutes).

Central Fuji-Yoshida's **Gekkō-ji district** (月江寺) feels like the little town that time forgot. While developers elsewhere spend fortunes building nostalgic shopping centres through-

---

MT FUJI: KNOW BEFORE YOU GO

Although children and grandparents regularly reach the summit of Fuji-san, this is a serious mountain and not to be trifled with. It's high enough for altitude sickness and, as on any mountain, the weather can be volatile. On the summit it can go from sunny and warm to wet, windy and cold remarkably quickly. Even if conditions are fine, you can count on it being close to freezing in the mornings even in summer.

Mt Fuji's official climbing season is from 1 July to 31 August, and the Japanese pack in during those busy months, meaning occasional nighttime queues reminiscent of the Marunouchi Line. Authorities strongly caution against climbing outside of the regular season, when services are suspended; hiking from October to May is definitely discouraged. The first half of this decade saw a number of high-profile deaths of off-season climbers from overseas.

At a minimum, bring clothing appropriate for cold and wet weather, including a hat and gloves, as well as drinking water (unless you like shelling out ¥500 per half-litre) and snacks. If you're climbing at night, bring a torch (flashlight) or headlamp, and spare batteries. Descending the mountain is much harder on the knees than ascending; bending your knees and using your thigh muscles can help.

out Japan, the original mid-20th century façades here have barely had an update. Inside are some surprisingly hip cafes and shops.

Outside the town centre, the **Mt Fuji Radar Dome Museum** (富士山レーダードーム館; ☎ 20-0223; adult/child ¥600/400; ☉ 9.30am-5pm Wed-Mon, daily Jul & Aug) honours the weather radar that was the world's highest when it was built on the mountaintop in 1963, following a typhoon that killed some 1000 people in coastal lowlands. The radar is credited with saving countless lives. English-language signage was in the works as of this writing. The wind simulator needs no explanation.

Further down Rte 138, Yamanaka-ko is the largest of the lakes, but it doesn't offer much for visitors – unless you count an enormous

swan-shaped hovercraft that does 35-minute circuits of the lake for ¥900.

One stop west of Fuji-Yoshida station is **Fuji-Q Highland** (☎ 23-2111; admission only adult/child ¥1200/600, 1-day pass incl amusements ¥4500/3300; ☉ 9am-5pm Mon-Fri, 9am-8pm Sat & Sun, 8am-9pm 20 Jul–20 Sep), an amusement park with roller coasters, Gundam the Ride, bumper cars and more.

Kawaguchi-ko 河口湖
On the lake of the same name, the town of Fuji-Kawaguchi-ko is closest to four of the five lakes and a popular departure point for climbing the mountain. Around 600m north of Kawaguchi-ko station, on the lower eastern edge of the lake, is the **Kawaguchi-ko cable car** (☎ 72-0363; one way/return ¥400/700) to

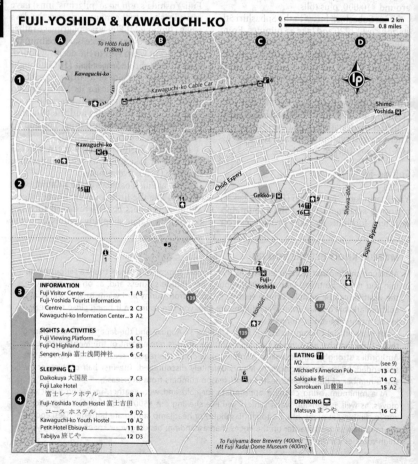

THE YOSHIDAGUCHI TRAIL UP MT FUJI

Before the construction of the road to the 5th station, Fuji pilgrims began at Sengen-jinja near present-day Fuji-Yoshida, walking among towering cryptomeria trees and old stone lanterns, paying their homage to the shrine gods, and beginning their 19km ascent up Japan's most sacred mountain.

Today, this path offers climbers a chance to participate in this centuries-old tradition. Purists feel this is the best way to climb, saying that the lower reaches are the most beautiful, through lush forests along a path that you'll have almost entirely to yourself. Through sunset, the sunrise and a night in a mountain hut, you'll perhaps get a sense of that elusive spirit so deeply sought by pilgrims in the past.

Of all the routes up Mt Fuji, the Yoshidaguchi trail is the oldest. To reach the trail from the shrine, veer to the right before the main building and turn left onto the main road. This is paved, and you'll soon see a walking path alongside the road. When this roadside trail ends, take the first turn to the right to meet up with the woodland path.

After about 1¼ hours of walking you'll reach **Nakanochaya**, an ancient site marked by carved stones left by previous climbers. You'll also find a quaint **tea and soba restaurant** here (the last place to refuel before the 5th station). From here you enter Fuji's lush forests.

Around 90 minutes later is Umagaeshi, which once housed the old stables where horses were left before pilgrims entered the sacred area of the mountain. A big yellow sign to your left marks the path. Follow this through the *torii* with monkeys on either side, as it continues uphill. Another 20 minutes and you'll pass the 1st station.

Between the 2nd and the 3rd stations, just a bit of navigation is required. The Fuji path meets up with the **Nyonin Tenjo** (Women's Holy Ground), which until 1832 was as far up as women were allowed to go. All that remains is an altar, hidden in the forest. Just before entering you'll cross through a set of posts. Take a right, walk for 150m and look for the posts on the left, which mark the continuation of the path. Around an hour later, the path meets up with the 5th station road. You'll find the Fuji path 150m on, cutting up to the right. You can stay at one of the 5th stations in the vicinity or if you still have energy, continue up another two hours to one of the 7th station huts.

It takes about five hours to reach the 5th station from the Sengen-jinja. The next day, you'll have a much harder 4½-hour ascent up the scarred, barren mountain. Many rise at midnight and climb in darkness, but you can let the crowds go, get up at 4.30am and complete the ascent as the sun peeks through the clouds. On the descent, you can catch a bus at the Kawaguchi-ko 5th station, which will take you to Kawaguchi-ko station.

Pick up maps and get the latest climbing information from the **Fuji-Yoshida Information Center** (☎ 22-7000; ◷ 9am-5.30pm). The *Climbing Mt Fuji* brochure is invaluable.

For more information, visit the excellent website www.city.fujiyoshida.yamanashi.jp.

---

the Fuji Viewing Platform (1104m). Ask at Kawaguchi-ko's Tourist Information Center (p198) for a map.

If the mountain isn't visible, **Fuji Visitor Centre** (富士ビジターセンター; ☎ 72-0259; admission free; ◷ 9am-10pm late Jul-late Aug, 9am-4pm Dec-Feb, sliding closing time rest of year) shows what you've missed. An English video gives a great summary of the mountain and its geological history, worth viewing even in good weather.

The western lakes are relatively undeveloped. At Sai-ko, **Sai-ko Iyashi-no-Sato Nenba** (西湖いやしの里根場; ☎ 20-4677; adult/child ¥200/100; ◷ 9am-5pm) opened in 2006 on the site of some historic thatched-roof houses, washed away in

a typhoon 40 years earlier. Inside these dozen reconstructed frames are demonstrations of crafts including silk and paper; restaurants specialise in *soba* and *konyakku* (arrowroot gelatin).

There are good views of Mt Fuji from the western end of the lake and from the Kōyō-dai lookout, near the main road. Close to the road are the Narusawa Ice Cave and the Fugaku Wind Cave, both formed by lava flows from a prehistoric eruption of Mt Fuji.

Further west, tiny Shoji-ko is said to be the prettiest of the Fuji Go-ko, though it has no Fuji view. However, you can continue to Eboshi-san, a one- to 1½-hour climb from the road, for a fine view of it over the Aokiga-hara-jukai (Sea of Trees). The last lake along is Motosu-ko, the deepest and least visited of the lakes.

FESTIVALS & EVENTS

The **Yoshida no Hi Matsuri** (Fire Festival; 26 to 27 August) is an annual festival held to mark the end of the climbing season and to offer thanks for the safety of the year's climbers. The first day involves a *mikoshi* procession and the lighting of bonfires on the town's main street. On the second day, festivals are held at Sengen-jinja (p201).

SLEEPING

If you're not overnighting in a mountain hut, Fuji-Yoshida and Kawaguchi-ko make good bases. **Tourist information offices** (Kawaguchi-ko ☎ 72-6700; Fuji-yoshida ☎ 22-7000) can make reservations for you.

Fuji-Yoshida

Fuji-Yoshida Youth Hostel (☎ 22-0533; www.jyh.or.jp; dm ¥2835; ☒) Popular lodging in a former public bath near Fuji-Yoshida's old town. Both Western and Japanese style are available, some with mountain views, though on our visit the public spaces smelled vaguely of dog. The hostel is around 600m south of Shimo-Yoshida station; walk down the main street, keeping Lawson's on the left. Go through three sets of lights and turn down the small alley on the right.

Tabijiya (☎ 20-0500; fax 24-0200; s/d/tw from ¥5750/10,600/11,600; ☒ ☒ ☒) You're tired after all-day hiking and just want a reliable Western-style bed for not a lot of money. Tabijiya's simple but new and clean business hotel about 10 minutes' walk from the town centre. A large, fresh-cooked breakfast is ¥750.

Daikokuya (☎ 22-3778; Hanchō-dōri; d per person ¥6600) Fuji-Yoshida's main street is lined with old *oshi-no-ie* (pilgrim's inns). Set back from the road, this one has elegant tatami rooms, a traditional setting and a handsome private garden. It's 10-minutes' walk from Fuji-Yoshida station.

Kawaguchi-ko

Most inns far from Kawaguchi-ko station offer free pick-up.

Kawaguchi-ko Youth Hostel (☎ /fax 72-1431; dm ¥3360; ☾ mid-Mar–early Nov) This rather plain hostel is about 500m southwest of Kawaguchi-ko

station, with a mix of Japanese and bunk-bed rooms and a 9pm curfew. From the station, turn left, left again after the 7-Eleven, right at the first set of lights and, finally, left in front of the power station. Bike rental per day costs ¥800.

Hotel Sunnide Village (ホテルサニーデビレッジ; ☎ 76-6004; fax 76-7706; info@sunnide.com; backpacker plan rate per person ¥4200, r per person with bathroom ¥6300; ☒ ☒) A lovely, welcoming hillside lodge commanding a great view over Kawaguchi-ko towards Mt Fuji; enjoy it from the outdoor bath. Same-day travellers qualify for discounted 'backpacker' rates if rooms are available; phone (some English spoken) or ask at the tourist office. Meals are available from breakfast/dinner ¥1050/2100 (¥1575 backpacker dinner).

Ashiwada Hotel (足和田ホテル; ☎ 82-2587; fax 82-2548; s/d ¥6000/12,000; ☒ ☒ ☒) This friendly hotel boasts impressive views of Kawaguchi-ko (though not Fuji-san) and generously proportioned, mostly Japanese rooms with private bath. There are also well-kept common baths and *rotemburo*. It's at the western end of the lake, in a more residential neighbourhood.

Fuji Lake Hotel (☎ 72-2209; fax 73-2700; r per person without/with 2 meals from ¥8000/12,000) Just off the town centre and right on the lakefront, this seven-storey historic (1935) hostelry offers mountain and lake views from its Japanese-Western combo rooms. In addition to private facilities (some rooms have their own *rotemburo*), there are common *onsen*, too.

EATING & DRINKING

Fuji-Yoshida is known for its *teuchi udon* (homemade, white wheat noodles); some 62 shops sell it! Try yours with tempura, *kitsune* (fried tofu) and *niku* (beef). The **Fuji-Yoshida Tourist Information Center** (☎ 22-7000) has a map and list of restaurants (around ¥500).

Kawaguchi-ko's local noodles are *hōtō*, sturdy, hand cut and served in a thick miso stew with pumpkin, sweet potato and other vegetables.

Fuji-Yoshida

Sakigake (☎ 090-3815-6405; most dishes ¥600-800; ☾ dinner Tue-Sun) Down an alley, behind a low door and through some curtains in the middle of Gekkōji, this candlelit basement café is almost an alternative universe. No English menu, but kindly, arty, young staff dish up *tofu salada* (tofu salad), *yakitori*, sashimi and *shochu* in excellent crockery. It's across from Onoue barber shop.

M2 (☎ 23-9309; mains ¥700-1300; ◷ 11am-10pm; 🖳) One block away from the Fuji-Yoshida Youth Hostel, this quaint restaurant serves Western and Japanese dishes at good prices. Curry rice, pork sauté and burger sandwiches are among the offerings. The miniature toys and kitschy artwork adds to the charm.

Michael's American Pub (☎ 24-3917; meals ¥800-1100; ◷ 8pm-2am Fri-Wed, lunch Sun-Fri) For traditional Americana – burgers, pizzas and brew – drop by this expat and local favourite. From Fuji-Yoshida station, walk north to the main road (Akafuji-dōri) and take a right. After crossing the river, take the third left.

Fujiyama Beer Brewery (☎ 24-4800; most dishes ¥714-1300; ◷ 11am-10pm) This beer hall near the Radar Dome is positively Teutonic inside. Wash down sausages, pizzas, salads and cheeses with house-brewed pilsner, weissen or dunkel. Picture menu.

Café Matsuya (☎ 22-5185; ◷ 9am-7pm Tue-Thu, 9am-10pm Fri, 11am-10pm Sat & Sun; 🖳) A fitting emblem for arty Gekkōji, this charming café is also a craft store. Come for coffee, tea or a chat with the equally charming English-speaking owner. It's on the main drag.

Kawaguchi-ko

Hōtō Fudō (ほうとう不動; ☎ 72-5560; hōtō ¥1050; ◷ lunch) A few branches around town serve this massive stew bubbling in its own cast-iron pot. The *honten* (main branch) is a barn of a restaurant north of the lake, near the Kawaguchi-ko Art Museum via retro-bus.

Sanrokuen (山麓園; ☎ 73-1000; meals ¥2100-4200; ◷ 11am-8pm Fri-Wed) This charming *irori* (fireplace) restaurant allows diners to grill their own meals around charcoal pits set in the floor: skewers of fish, chicken, tofu, steak and veggies are available. From Kawaguchi-ko station, turn left, left again after the 7-Eleven and after 600m you'll see the thatched roof on the right.

GETTING THERE & AWAY

Buses (¥1700, 1¾ hours) operate directly to Kawaguchi-ko from outside the western exit of Shinjuku station in Tokyo. There are departures up to 16 times daily at the height of the Fuji climbing season. Some continue on to Yamanaka-ko and Motosu-ko. In Tokyo, call **Keiō Kōsoku Bus** (☎ 03-5376-2217) for reservations and schedule info. In Kawaguchi-ko,

make reservations through **Tōmei Highway Bus** (☎ 72-2922).

Trains take longer and cost more. JR Chūō-line trains go from Shinjuku to Ōtsuki (*tokkyū* ¥2980, one hour; *futsū* ¥1280, 1¾ hours), where you transfer to the Fuji Kyūkō line to Kawaguchi-ko (*futsū* ¥1110, one hour) via Fuji-Yoshida (¥990, 50 minutes). On Sundays and holidays from March to November there is a direct local train from Shinjuku and Tokyo stations (¥2390 from Shinjuku, ¥2560 from Tokyo, both two hours).

GETTING AROUND

The new Fuji-Kawaguchi-ko Sight-seeing bus (retro-bus) has hop-on-hop-off service to all of the sightseeing spots in the western lakes costing ¥1000/500 per adult/child for two days. One route follows Kawaguchi-ko's northern shore, and the other heads south and around Sai-ko and Aokigahara.

Buses run from Fuji-Yoshida station to Fujinomiya (¥2050, 80 minutes) via the four smaller lakes and around the mountain. From Kawaguchi-ko, there are nine to 11 buses daily to the *shinkansen* stop of Mishima (¥2130, two hours).

HAKONE 箱根

☎ 0460 / pop 15,227

Hakone is Tokyo's original tourist mecca and remains popular for views of Mt Fuji, mountainous topography, art museums, *onsen* (and eggs boiled in them) and the opportunity to ride a variety of transport. The tourist track lets you explore the region via switchback train, funicular, ropeway (gondola) and pirate ship.

Unfortunately – particularly during the height of summer and on weekends year-round – Hakone can be quite busy and feel highly packaged. To beat the crowds, plan your trip during the week. For more information, try www.hakone.or.jp/english.

FESTIVALS & EVENTS

Ashino-ko Kosui Matsuri (31 July) At Hakone-jinja near Moto-Hakone, this festival features firework displays over Hakone's landmark lake.

Hakone Daimonji-yaki Matsuri (6 August) During this summer festival, the torches are lit on Myojoga-take so that they form the shape of the Chinese character for 'big' or 'great'.

Hakone Daimyō Gyoretsu Parade (3 November) On the national Culture Day holiday, 400 costumed locals re-enact a feudal lord's procession.

AROUND TOKYO

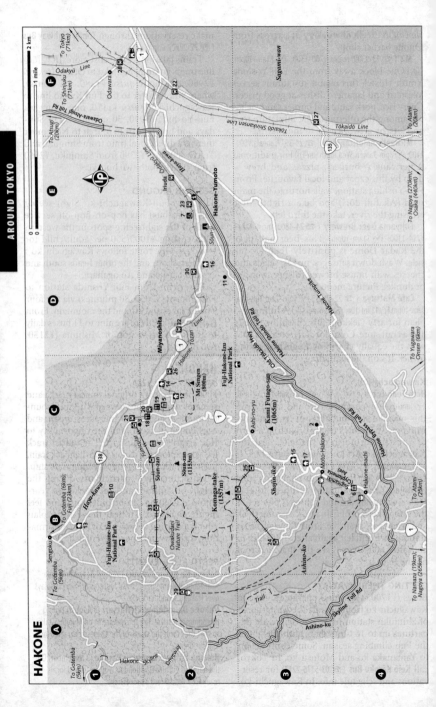

HAKONE

AROUND TOKYO

SLEEPING

In addition to places listed beneath individual destinations are these longtime favourites:

Hakone Sengokuhara Youth Hostel (☎ 84-8966; fax 84-6578; www.jyh.or.jp; dm/r per person ¥3195/5400; ✕ ▢) Run by the same family, this pleasant hostel is directly behind the Fuji Hakone Guest House. It has Japanese-style dorms and private rooms, hot-spring baths, cooking facilities and English-speaking staff.

Fuji Hakone Guest House (☎ 84-6577; fax 84-6578; www.fujihakone.com; r per person ¥5250-6300; ✕ ▢) Run by a welcoming, English-speaking family, the guesthouse has handsome tatami rooms and a cosy *onsen*. It's a popular spot with foreign travellers. Expect rates to increase by ¥1000 per person at busy times. Take bus 4 from Odawara station to Senkyōrō-mae bus stop (50 minutes). There's an English sign close by.

GETTING THERE & AWAY
Bus

Odakyū's express bus service runs directly from the west exit of Shinjuku station to Hakone-machi (¥1950, two hours, 20 daily), but you lose the fun of the combination of rail, cable and water-borne conveyances.

Train

The private **Odakyū line** (www.odakyu.jp) from Shinjuku station takes you directly into Hakone-Yumoto, the region's transit hub. If you are travelling on a Japan Rail Pass, you can save the intercity fare by taking the JR train to Odawara and changing trains for Hakone-Yumoto.

Odakyū's Hakone Freepass (箱根フリーパス; adult/child from Shinjuku ¥5500/2750, from Odawara ¥4130/2070) is an excellent deal for the standard Hakone circuit, covering the return fare to Hakone and unlimited use of most modes of transport within the region for three days, plus a number of other discounts. There's also a Hakone Weekday Pass, valid for two days with similar benefits (¥4700/3410 from Shinjuku/Odawara). Transport prices in this section are without the Freepass, except as noted.

The most convenient service is Odakyū's inscrutably named Romance Car to Hakone Yumoto (with/without Freepass ¥870/2020, 85 minutes). There is also *kyūkō* (regular express) service (¥1150, two hours), although you may have to change trains at Odawara.

JR trains run between Shinjuku and Odawara (¥1450, 80 minutes). From Tokyo station, take the Kodama *shinkansen* (¥3440, 35 minutes) or the Tōkaidō line (*futsū* ¥1450, 1½ hours; *tokkyū* ¥2660, one hour).

At Odawara, change to the narrow gauge, switchback Hakone-Tōzan line, via Hakone Yumoto to Gōra (¥650, 55 minutes). If you've arrived in Hakone Yumoto on the Odakyū line, you can change to the Hakone-Tōzan line (¥390 to Gōra, 40 minutes) in the same station.

GETTING AROUND

Part of Hakone's popularity comes from the chance to ride assorted *norimono* (modes of transport): switchback train (from Hakone-Yumoto to Gōra), funicular, ropeway (gondola), ship and bus. Check out www.odakyu.jp, which describes this circuit. Stops along the way have snack and souvenir shops.

Cable Car & Ropeway

Gōra is the terminus of the Hakone Tōzan Railway and the beginning of the cable car (funicular) to Sōunzan, from where you can catch the Hakone Ropeway (gondola) line to Ōwakudani and Tōgendai.

Boat

From Tōgendai, sightseeing boats crisscross Ashino-ko to Hakone-machi and Moto-Hakone (¥970, 30 minutes). The boats look like pirate ships and Mississippi River paddlewheelers – tourist kitsch but fun all the same.

Bus

The Hakone-Tōzan and Izu Hakone bus companies service the Hakone area, linking up most of the sights. Hakone-Tōzan bus routes are included in the Hakone Freepass. If you finish in Hakone-machi, Hakone-Tōzan buses run between here and Odawara for ¥1150. Hakone-en to Odawara costs ¥1270. Buses run from Moto-Hakone to Hakone-Yumoto for ¥930 every 30 minutes from 10am to 3pm.

Luggage forwarding

At Hakone-Yumoto station, deposit your luggage with **Hakone Baggage Service** (箱根キャリ ーサービス; ☎ 86-4140; baggage per piece from ¥600; ☺ 8.30am-7pm) by noon, and it will be delivered to your inn within Hakone by 3pm. From inns, pick-up is at 10am for 1pm delivery at Hakone-Yumoto. Hakone Freepass holders get ¥100 discount per bag.

Hakone-Yumoto Onsen 箱根湯元温泉

A pleasant town nestled at the foot of the mountains, Yumoto is Hakone's busiest hot-springs resort, in both senses. Still, if the weather looks dodgy, it makes sense to stop off between Odawara and the Tōzan Railway, and spend the day soaking in the baths. You can also approach the town on foot from Moto-Hakone via the Old Tōkaidō Highway (see p210).

Pick up a local and regional maps and info at the excellent **Tourist Information Center** (☎ 85-8911; ☺ 9am-6pm), by the bus stops across the main road from the train station. There's always an English speaker on hand.

Onsen are the main attraction of Hakone-Yumoto. **Kappa Tengoku Rotemburo** (☎ 85-6121; adult/child ¥750/400; ☺ 10am-10pm), behind the station, is a popular outdoor bath, worth a dip if the crowds aren't too bad; it's three minutes on foot from Hakone-Yumoto station. More upmarket are the fantastic *onsen* of **Ten zan Notemburo** (天山野天風呂; ☎ 86-4126; admission ¥1200; ☺ 9am-11pm), which has a larger selection of indoor and outdoor baths. To get there, take the free shuttle bus from the bridge outside the station (except Fridays and second and fourth Thursdays each month).

SLEEPING & EATING

Hotel Okada (☎ 85-6000; fax 85-5774; r per person incl 2 meals from ¥14,000; ☒ ☒) Most travellers prefer staying further up the mountain, but for a bit of pampering, try this large hotel on the edge of the Sukumo-gawa. It has excellent Japanese- and Western-style rooms and a large bath complex. Take bus A from the train station (¥100, 10 minutes).

Yumoto Onsen's dozens of restaurants (from hamburgers to *soba*) are used to foreign visitors.

Miyanoshita 宮ノ下

This village is the first worthwhile stop on the Hakone-Tōzan railway towards Gōra. You'll find a handful of antique shops along the main road (head down the hill from the station and continue in the same direction), some splendid ryokan, and a pleasant hiking trail skirting up the 800m Mt Sengen. The entrance to the trail is 20m from the road from the station, up an incline.

OURPICK Miyanoshita also has one of Japan's finest hotels. Opened in 1878, the **Fujiya Hotel** (☎ 82-2211; fax 82-2210; www.fujiyahotel.co.jp; d from ¥21,090) is one of the first Western-style hotels in the nation. Now sprawled across several wings, it remains impressive for the woodwork in its old-world-lounge areas, dining room, a hillside garden, historic hot-spring baths (though in truth others are nicer) and guest rooms with hot-spring water piped into each one. Even if you don't stay here, it's worth a visit to soak up the atmosphere and maybe have tea in the lounge. Foreign travellers should inquire about the weekday special of US$128 for double rooms (you can pay the equivalent sum in yen). The hotel is around 250m west of the station.

If you don't fancy paying resort prices for dinners at the Fujiya, a short walk away are the friendly sushi shop **Miyafuji** (鮨みやふじ; ☎ 82-2139; most dishes ¥1575-2310; 🕑 lunch & dinner Wed-Mon; E), known for its *aji-don* (brook trout over rice), or **La Bazza** (ラバッツァ; ☎ 87-9223; lunch/dinner courses from ¥1050/1480; 🕑 lunch & dinner Wed-Mon; E) for pizzas, pasta and Italian grills.

Chōkoku-no-Mori 彫刻の森

Two stops beyond Miyanoshita is the excellent **Hakone Open-Air Museum** (☎ 82-1161; www .hakone-oam.or.jp; adult/child/concession ¥1600/800/1100; 🕑 9am-5pm Mar-Nov, to 4pm Dec-Feb). Although tickets are pricey, there's an impressive selection of 19th- and 20th-century Japanese and Western sculptures in a soaring hillside setting: with works by Henry Moore (26 sculptures, one of the world's largest collections), Rodin, Maillol and Miro, while interior galleries contain works by Giacometti and Calder; there's also a Picasso pavilion (with some 300 pieces) and paintings by Takamura Kotaro, Fujikawa Yuzo and other Japanese artists. Several decent restaurants and a teahouse are inside. Hakone Freepass holders receive a discount.

A charming ryokan lies 300m uphill from the museum on the left. **Chōraku-sō** (☎ 82-2192; fax 82-4533; r per person with/without meals ¥8800/5150; 🗶) has simple but nicely maintained tatami rooms with kitchenettes and private toilet. There's an *onsen* on the 1st floor, available for day use ¥550.

For exquisite sushi, don't miss **Kappeizushi** (☎ 82-3278; mixed sushi around ¥1500; 🕑 9am-8pm Wed-Mon), a nondescript spot that delivers fresh, tender slices of sashimi. A picture menu is available. It's a few metres downhill from the museum on the same side of the street.

Gōra 強羅

Gōra is the terminus of the Hakone-Tōzan line and the starting point for the funicular and cable-car trip to Tōgendai on Ashinoko. The town also has a couple of its own attractions that may be of minor interest to travellers.

Just a short walk beside the funicular tracks towards Sōun-zan is the park, **Hakone Gōra-kōen** (☎ 82-2825; adult/child ¥500/free, free for Freepass holders; 🕑 9am-5pm), with a rock garden, alpine and seasonal plants, a fountain and several greenhouses with tropical flowers. Adjacent to the park, **Hakone Museum of Art** (☎ 82-2623; adult/junior high & younger/student ¥900/free/400; 🕑 9.30am-4.30pm Apr-Nov, to 4pm Dec-Mar) has a stately collection

of Japanese ceramics from back as far as the Jōmon period (10,000 years ago).

Pola Museum of Art (☎ 84-2111; www.polamuseum .or.jp; adult/junior high & elementary/university & high school/ senior ¥1800/700/1300/1600; 🕑 9-5pm) is a worthy detour from Gōra. The collection comprises some 9500 works of European and Japanese painting from the impressionists onward, as well as ceramics and glass art, in changing displays. It's almost as renowned for its futuristic building (2002). Admission is free for elementary and junior-high school students on Saturdays. From Gōra station, take the Sightseeing Shuttle bus to Shissei-kaen (¥290, 13 minutes).

Gyōza Center (☎ 82-3457; mains ¥735-945, set meals ¥1155-1365; 🕑 11.30am-3pm & 5-8pm Fri-Wed) is famous for its *gyōza* (dumplings) a dozen different ways, including in soup (*sui-gyōza*), in soup with *kimchi (kimchi sui-gyōza)* and plain pan-fried (*nōmaru…*sound it out). Set menus include rice and miso soup. It's 200m downhill from the Gōra station, or about as far up from Chōkoku-no-mori.

Sōun-zan & Ōwakudani 早雲山・大桶谷

From Gōra, continue to near the 1153m-high summit of Sōun-zan by funicular (¥410, 10 minutes).

From Sōun-zan, there are several hiking trails including one to Mt Kami (1¾ hours); another up to Owakudani (1¼ hours) was closed as of this writing owing to the mountain's toxic gases.

Sōun-zan is the starting point for the Hakone Ropeway, a 30-minute, 4km gondola ride to Tōgendai (one way/return ¥1330/2340), stopping at Ōwakudani en route. In fine weather Mt Fuji looks fabulous from here.

Ōwakudani is a volcanic cauldron of steam, bubbling mud and mysterious smells. The 25-minute **Ōwakudani Nature Trail** (Ōwakudani Shizen Sansakuro, 大桶谷自然散策路) leads uphill through the charred, somewhat apocalyptic landscape to some of the boiling pits. Here you can buy boiled eggs, turned black in the sulphurous waters. Numerous signs warn travellers not to linger too long, as the gases are poisonous.

Ashino-ko 芦ノ湖

Between Tōgendai and Hakone-machi and Moto-Hakone, this leg-shaped lake is touted as the primary attraction of the Hakone region; but it's Mt Fuji, with its snow-clad slopes glimmering in reflection on the water, that lends the lake its poetry. If the venerable mountain is hidden behind clouds (as often happens), you have the consolation of a trip across the lake with recorded commentary in English about the history and natural surroundings. See p815 for details about lake transport.

Komaga-take 駒ヶ岳

The mountain Koma-ga-take (1357m) is a good place from which to get a view of the lake and Mt Fuji. From Tōgendai, boats run to Hakone-en, where a cable car (one way/return ¥620/1050) goes to the top. You can leave the mountain by the same route or by a five-minute funicular descent (¥370/630) to Komaga-take-nobori-guchi. Note that this trip is not covered by the Hakone Free Pass. Buses run from here to Hakone-machi (¥300), Hakone-Yumoto (¥820) and to Odawara (¥1050).

Hakone-machi & Moto-Hakone
箱根町・元箱根

The sightseeing boats across Ashi-no-ko deposit you at either of these two towns, both well touristed but with sights of historical interest. The main attraction in Hakone-machi is the **Hakone Sekisho Shiryōkan** (Hakone Checkpoint Museum; ☎ 83-6635; adult/child ¥300/150; ⏱ 9am-5pm), a recent reconstruction of the checkpoint on the Old Tōkaidō Hwy. Be sure to check out the museum with Darth Vader armour and grisly implements used on lawbreakers. Nearby is the garden of the **Onshi Hakone Kōen** (Hakone Detached Palace) former summer digs of the imperial family, with Fuji views across the lake.

Suginamiki (杉並木; Cryptomeria Ave) is a 2km stone path beside the busy lakeside road connecting Hakone-machi and Moto-Hakone, lined with cryptomeria cedars that were planted more than 360 years ago.

It is impossible to miss **Moto-Hakone's Hakone-jinja** (箱根神社; ☎ 83-7213; treasure hall ¥300; ⏱ 9am-4pm) with its red *torii* rising from the lake. A pleasant stroll around the lake to the *torii* leads along a path lined with huge cedars. A wooded grove surrounds the shrine.

For a bit more exercise, a 3½-hour walk leads you back to Hakone-Yumoto along the Old Tōkaidō Hwy. Start up the hill from the lakeside Moto-Hakone bus stop, and along the way you'll pass the 350-year-old **Amazake-jaya** (☎ 83-6418; ⏱ 7am-5.30pm), where you can enjoy

a cup of *amazake* (warm, sweet sake). You can also stop in the small village of Hatajuku, and end your walk at the historic temple of Sōun-ji near Hakone-Yumoto station.

SLEEPING & EATING

Hakone Lake Villa Youth Hostel (☎ 83-1610; dm ¥3000) Hidden in a wooded spot over the lake, this hostel offers Japanese- and Western-style dorm rooms, a large outdoor deck, *onsen* and tasty meals. From Moto-Hakone, take a bus towards Odawara (小田原) station and get off at the Futako Jaya bus stop (¥210, five minutes). From the stop, head downhill 80m, continue along the dirt road and you'll see it on the right.

Moto-Hakone Guesthouse (☎ 83-7880; fax 84-6578; www.fujihakone.com; r per person ¥5250) A popular spot with foreign tourists, this guesthouse offers simple but pleasant Japanese-style rooms without private facilities, and an informative website. From Hakone-machi/Moto-Hakone, take an Odawara-bound bus to Ashinokōen-mae (¥210/160, 10 minutes), from where the guest house is one minute's walk.

There are a number of more or less reasonably priced *shokudō* and cafés near the Hakone-machi dock.

IZU-HANTŌ 伊豆半島

This peninsula, about 100km southwest of Tokyo in Shizuoka-ken, is a popular destination for its history, including the Black Ships (p212), its lush greenery, rugged coastline, abundant *onsen*, and foods like *himono* (sun-dried fish), *mikan* (oranges) and *wasabi*. Weekends and holidays can be crowded, particularly in summer, but crowds usually thin out once you get past the touristy resort of Atami. Over on the west coast it's always much quieter.

An easy loop takes you by train to Itō on the east coast (reachable by JR from Tokyo), from where you can enjoy drop-dead coastal views on the train or bus to historic Shimoda. Then journey by bus across a landscape of hilly countryside, farms and rural townships to Matsuzaki and Dōgashima on Izu's west coast. Finish at the intimate *onsen* village Shuzenji before catching the Izu-Hakone Tetsudō line to Mishima to connect back to the JR.

Atami 熱海
☎ 0557 / pop 42,000

Atami may be the gateway to Izu, but this overdeveloped hot-springs resort has little to detain foreign travellers, aside from its museum. Overlooking the coastline, the sleek **MOA Museum of Art** (☎ 84-2511; www.moaart.or.jp; admission ¥1600; ⏰ 9.30am-4.30pm Fri-Wed, closed 6-12 Jan & 25-31 Dec) has a collection of Japanese and Chinese paintings, ceramics, calligraphy and sculpture, spanning over 1000 years and including some national treasures. Take the bus

from stop 4 outside Atami station to the last stop, MOA Bijitsukan (¥160, eight minutes).

Discount tickets to the museum (¥1300) and town information are available at the **tourist office** (☎ 81-5297; ⏰ 9.30am-5.30pm), at the station building.

Because of Atami's popularity with domestic tourists, rooms are overpriced; head down

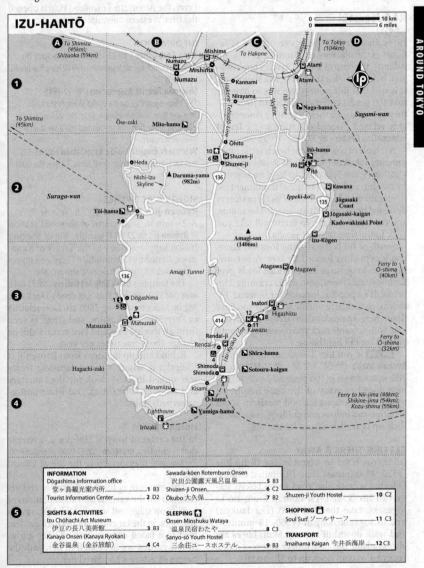

IZU-HANTŌ

to Itō or Shimoda to find more reasonable lodgings.

GETTING THERE & AWAY

JR trains run from Tokyo station to Atami on the Tōkaidō line (Kodama *shinkansen* ¥4080, 55 minutes; Odoriko ¥4070, 1¼ hours; Acty *kaisoku* ¥1890, 1½ hours).

Itō & Jōgasaki 伊東・城ヶ崎
☎ 0557

Itō is another hot-springs resort and is famous as the place where Anjin-san (William Adams), the hero of James Clavell's book *Shogun*, built a ship for the Tokugawa shōgunate. It is said that this resort town was so popular that 100 geisha entertained here in Itō a century ago, although these days it's a commendably relaxed place. Itō station has a **Tourist Information Center** (☎ 37-6105; ◷ 9am-5pm).

A couple of blocks off the beach is the monumental **Tōkaikan** (東海館; ☎ 36-2004; adult/child ¥200/100; ◷ 9am-9pm, closed 1st Tue of the month), a former inn and now a national monument for its elegant woodwork, each of its three storeys designed by a different architect. The rooms, and the canal views from them, will take you back to the time of those geisha.

South of Itō is the striking Jōgasaki coast, windswept cliffs formed by lava. A harrowing 48m-long suspension bridge leads over Kadowakizaki Point, with waves crashing 23m below. It's a popular location for film and TV shoots, particularly suicide scenes. If you have time, there's a moderately strenuous cliffside hike with volcanic rock and pine forests, south of the 17m tall lighthouse.

our pick If you like Tōkaikan, the splendid **Ryokan Inaba** (旅館いな葉; ☎ 37-3178; fax 37-3180; www.inaba-r.co.jp; r per person incl 2 meals ¥13,000) next door has many of the same traditional touches, sumptuous seafood meals, in-room facilities, and indoor and outdoor *onsen* baths. Pick-up is available from Itō station.

GETTING THERE & AWAY

Itō is connected to Atami by the JR Itō line (¥320, 25 minutes). The JR limited express Odoriko service also runs from Tokyo station to Itō (¥3820, 1¾ hours). From Itō to Jōgasaki, take the Izukyūkō (aka Izukyū) line to Jōgasaki-kaigan (¥560, 18 minutes) and walk downhill about 1.5km; buses are also available but take longer and cost more. Izukyū also continues on to Shimoda.

Shimoda 下田
☎ 0558 / pop 26,700

Shimoda has a fabulous mix of history and seashore. It holds a pivotal place in history as the spot where Japan officially opened to the outside world after centuries of isolation. Following the opening of Japan by the *Kurofune* (Black Ships) under Commodore Matthew Perry, the American Townsend Harris opened the first Western consulate here.

INFORMATION

Main Post Office (☎ 22-1531; ◷ 10am-5pm) The main post office has an international ATM; it's a few blocks from Perry Rd.

Shimoda Tourist Association (☎ 22-1531; ◷ 10am-5pm) Pick up the useful *Shimoda Walking Map* and book accommodation. From the station, take a left, walk to the first intersection and you'll see it on the southwest corner.

Volunteer English Guide Association (☎ 23-5151; maimai-h@i-younet.ne.jp; ◷ 8.30am-5.15pm Tue-Sun) Offers free guided tours.

SIGHTS & ACTIVITIES

Ryōsen-ji & Chōraku-ji 了仙寺・長楽寺

A 25-minute walk south of Shimoda station is **Ryōsen-ji** (☎ 22-0657) temple, site of another treaty, supplementary to the Treaty of Kanagawa, signed by Commodore Perry and representatives of the Tokugawa shōgunate.

The temple's **Black Ship Art Gallery** (☎ 22-0657; adult/child ¥500/150; ◷ 8.30am-5pm, closed 1-3 Aug & 24-26 Dec) includes more than 2800 artefacts relating to Perry, the Black Ships, and Japan as seen through foreign eyes and vice versa. Exhibits change about five times per year.

Behind and up the steps from Ryōsen-ji is Chōraku-ji, where a Russo-Japanese treaty was signed in 1854; look for the cemetery and *namako-kabe* (black and white lattice-patterned) walls.

Hōfuku-ji 宝福寺

In the centre of town is Hōfuku-ji, a temple that is chiefly a **museum** (☎ 22-0960; admission ¥300; ◷ 8am-5pm) memorialising the life of Okichi (p214).

The museum is filled with scenes and artefacts from the various movie adaptations of her life on stage and screen. Okichi's grave is also here, in the far corner of the back garden, next to a faded copper statue. Other graves in this garden are dedicated to her, with the names of actors who played her.

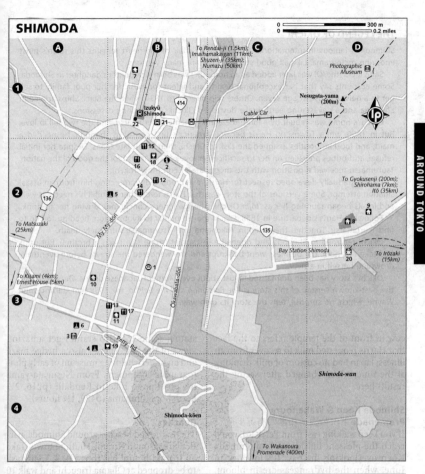

SHIMODA

Gyokusenji 玉泉寺

Founded in 1590, this **temple** (☎ 22-1287; admission free, Harris museum adult/child ¥300/150; ⏰ 8am-5pm) is most famous as the first Western consulate in Japan, in 1856. The museum here is filled with artefacts of the life of Townsend Harris, the first consul general, and life-size models of him and Okichi (p214). The bas-relief of a

THE LEGEND OF OKICHI

Shimoda is famous in international affairs, but an affair of the heart remains this town's most enduring melodrama. Like all good stories, there are many versions.

Saito Kichi (the 'O' was later added as an honorific) was born a carpenter's daughter in Shimoda. Some accounts say that her exceptional beauty and talent for music led her poor family to sell her to a geisha house at age seven. Others skip directly to 1854, when the Black Ships arrived in Shimoda and a devastating earthquake destroyed Okichi's home and possessions.

Okichi's home was rebuilt by a longtime admirer named Tsurumatsu, and the two fell in love. But in 1856, when Townsend Harris became America's first consul in Shimoda, he needed a maid, and local authorities assigned the task to Okichi, then in her late teens. Despite her initial refusal, authorities prevailed on her to sacrifice her love of Tsurumatsu for the good of the nation. Tsurumatsu received a position with the shōgunate in Edo (now Tokyo).

Okichi gradually developed respect for Harris, even reportedly protecting him from an assassination attempt. Some versions of the story say that Harris forced her to fulfill his needs as well, and locals began taunting her as 'tōjin Okichi' (the foreigner's concubine), driving her to drink.

Following Harris's departure in 1858, Okichi moved briefly to Kyoto before heading to Edo to find Tsurumatsu. Together they lived in Yokohama until Tsurumatsu's untimely death.

Okichi returned to Shimoda and opened a restaurant (some say it was a brothel). But drink had taken its hold, the business went bankrupt and she wandered the streets before eventually drowning herself in a river.

Okichi's story has been dramatised in just about every form of Japanese drama. Outside Japan, the best-known version of this story is *The Barbarian and the Geisha,* the 1958 film starring John Wayne, which, no surprise, tells the story its own way.

cow in front of the temple refers to the fact that Harris requested milk to recover from an illness; Japan had no custom of milk drinking at the time, which changed after seeing the results here.

Shimoda Kōen & Wakanoura Promenade 下田公園・和歌の浦遊歩道

If you keep walking east from Perry Rd, you'll reach the pleasant hillside park of Shimoda Kōen overlooking the bay. It's loveliest in June, when the hydrangeas are in bloom. Before entering the park, the coastal road is also a fine place to walk. If you have an hour or so, keep following it around the bay, passing an overpriced aquarium, and eventually you'll meet up with the 2km-long Wakanoura Promenade, a stone path along a peaceful stretch of beach. Turn right when you meet up with the road to return to Perry Rd.

Nesugata-yama 寝姿山

About 200m east of Shimoda station is the cable-car station to Nesugata-yama (Mt Nesugata; 200m). The **Shimoda Ropeway** (☎ 22-1211; adult/child ¥1200/600 return, incl park admission; ⏰ 9am-5pm) runs cable cars every 10 minutes to a mountaintop park, where the temple Aizendō houses a Kamakura period Buddha

statue; some 150 Jizō statues get amazing views of the bay. There's also a hedge maze and an underwhelming museum of early photographic equipment. From Nesugata-yama it's possible to hike to Rendaiji (p216, 2½ hours) or Shirahama (p429, 1¼ hours).

Beaches

There are good beaches around Shimoda, particularly around Kisami, south of town. Take an Irōzaki-bound bus (bus 3 or 4; ¥340); ask to be dropped at Ōhama Iriguchi and walk 10 minutes towards the coast. North of Shimoda is the lovely white-sand beach of Shirahama (bus 9; ¥320), which can get packed in July and August.

Bay Cruises

Several cruises depart from the Shimoda harbour area. Most popular with Japanese tourists is the *Kurofune* (Black Ships) cruise around the bay (adult/child ¥920/460, 20 minutes), which departs every 30 minutes (approximately) from 9.10am to 3.30pm.

Three boats a day (9.40am, 11.20am and 2pm) travel to Irōzaki. You can leave the boat at Irōzaki (adult/child ¥1530/770, 40 minutes) and head northwards up the peninsula by bus, or stay on the boat to return to Shimoda.

FESTIVALS & EVENTS

Kurofune Matsuri (Black Ships Festival; Friday, Saturday and Sunday around the 3rd Saturday in May) Shimoda commemorates the first landing of Commodore Perry with parades by the US Navy Marine band and firework displays. It's fascinating to see virtue has been made out of this potentially bitter historical event.

Shimoda Taiko Matsuri (Drum Festival; 14 & 15 August) A spectacular parade of *dashi* floats and some serious Japanese-style drumming.

SLEEPING

There are lots of *minshuku* around and the **Shimoda Tourist Association** (☎ 22-1531; ☯ 10am-5pm) can help with reservations.

Ōizu Ryokan (☎ 22-0123; r per person ¥3500; ☒) Popular with international travellers for its excellent prices, Ōizu has plain but comfy Japanese-style rooms with TV, and a two-seater *onsen*. It's at the south end of town, two blocks north of Perry Rd. Check-in is from 3pm. It's often closed on weekdays, so phone ahead.

Kokumin-shukusha New Shimoda (☎ 23-0222; fax 23-0025; r per person without/with meals ¥4855/7480) This drab but friendly inn offers spacious tatami rooms with shared facilities and a large *onsen*. Take a right out of the station, another right at the first light, walk 2½ blocks and it's on your right. Expect to pay up to ¥2000 more at peak times.

Shimoda-ya (☎ 22-0446; r per person without meals ¥5380) This *minshuku* offers pleasant Japanese rooms and a 24-hour *onsen*. It's a few blocks past Hofuku-ji on the left-hand side. No English is spoken.

Ernest House (☎ 22-5880; fax 23-3906; www.ernest-house.com; s/d ¥6300/10,500; ☒ ▯) A great escape, two minutes' walk from the beach in Kisami Ōhama. In an attractive, Western-style house, this 13-room pension is friendly and youthful, with hardwood furniture, a restaurant and a café. It gets lots of surfers, and guests can order picnic breakfasts (¥1050), best enjoyed on the beach. Dinners cost ¥2520. Reservations are recommended, and note that rates can more than double at peak times. From Izukyū Shimoda station, take an Irōzaki-bound bus (stop 3 or 4; ¥360); ask to be dropped off at the Kisami stop, from where it's a 15-minute walk towards the coast. A taxi from the station costs about ¥1500.

Shimoda Bay Kuroshio (下田ベイクロシオ; ☎ 27-2111; fax 27-2115; www.baykuro.co.jp; r per person without meals/with 2 meals from ¥12,000/18,000; ☒)

This futuristic 42-room hotel rather gleams above Shimoda-wan. Texas-sized rooms are festooned with textiles, woodworked headboards, designer bedspreads, and relics, shells and fossils inlaid in its poured-in-place concrete. Outside: *rotemburos* (naturally) and summer barbecues.

Kurofune Hotel (☎ 22-1234; kurofune@ever.ocn.ne.jp; r per person incl 2 meals from ¥15,000; ☒) On the hillside across from Shimoda's boat dock and with dead-on bay views, this old-line hotel has both Japanese- and Western-style rooms – some have their own *rotemburo* – plus heaping seafood meals and huge common *onsen* with *rotemburo*. The lobby décor is a little over the top, but squint as you walk through and you'll be fine.

EATING

Seafood is the speciality in Shimoda.

Musashi (☎ 22-0934; mains ¥630-1000; ☯ lunch) This casual spot serves tasty Japanese *shokudō* (cafeteria) favourites, including tempura *soba* and *rāmen* with grilled pork. Take a left out of the station, turn right down the narrow lane and take the first left. Look for the giant badger.

Matsu Sushi (☎ 22-1309; sets from ¥1000; ☯ 11am-8pm Thu-Tue) This home-style, good-value sushi bar is close to the station, across from Akitsu camera. Go for the *jizakana* set of local fish.

Porto Caro (☎ 22-5514; mains ¥1050-1360; ☯ lunch & dinner Thu-Tue; E) A 2nd-floor trattoria serving tasty pastas, pizzas (at night) and other Italian fare. Try seafood pasta with local wasabi, or paella (¥3000). It's two blocks north of Perry Rd, on the same road as the post office.

Isoka-tei (☎ 23-1200; meals ¥1155-2100; ☯ 11.30am-3pm & 5.30-10pm) This friendly spot serves hearty seafood sets that you can choose from a picture menu. From the Tourist Association, head three blocks down My My-dōri, take a left and it'll be on the next corner.

Hiranoya (☎ 22-2525; meals ¥1260-3150; ☯ lunch & dinner Wed-Mon; E) A former private home, filled with antiques, elegant woodwork and funky Western-style seating. It serves steaks, sandwiches, burgers and curry; set meals include soup, salad and coffee. Look for the *namakokabe* (lattice pattern walls).

Gorosaya (☎ 23-5638; lunch/dinner ¥1575/3150; ☯ lunch & dinner Fri-Wed; E) Elegant but understated ambience and fantastic seafood. The *Isōjiru* soup is made from over a dozen varieties of shellfish. From the Tourist Association, head two blocks down My My-dōri, take a left and it'll be on your left. Look for the wooden fish decorating the entrance.

DRINKING

Ja Jah (☎ 27-1611; ☯ 7pm-2am Tue-Sun) This cosy bar is a good place to kick back with fun tunes and friendly people. DJs sometimes spin (R&B, soul, hip-hop) on weekends.

Cheshire Cat Jazz House (☎ 23-3239; ☯ 11am-1am Thu-Sun) For live jazz, visit this low-key spot on My My-dōri. It's easily spotted by its English sign.

GETTING THERE & AWAY

Shimoda is as far as you can go by train on the Izu-hantō. You can take the Odoriko *tokkyū* from Tokyo station (¥6090, 2¾ hours) or Atami (¥3400, 80 minutes). From Itō, Izu Kyūkō runs from Itō station (¥1570, one hour). Trains also run from Atami (¥1890, 1½ hours). Try to catch Izukyū's Resort 21 train cars, with sideways-facing seats for full-on sea views.

South and west, transit is by bus to Dōgashima (¥1360, one hour) or Shuzen-ji (¥2180, two hours).

Car rental is available at **Nippon Rent-a-Car** (☎ 22-5711) just outside the train station on the right.

Around Shimoda

IMAIHAMA 今井浜

This relaxing seaside village is one of Izu's few towns with a sandy beach and a laid-back surfer vibe. Just what the doctor ordered for an overdose of culture and history.

You can rent body boards or fins from ¥1500 a day at **Soul Surf** (☎ 32-1826) on the main street. **Onsen Minshuku Wataya** (☎ 32-1055; fax 32-2058; s/d incl 2 meals ¥9075/1650) is a kindly, family-run, eight-room place facing the beach, with tiny sea-view *rotemburo*. Look for the Kirin beer sign about 100m past the surf shop.

Imaihama-kaigan station is on the Izukyū line between Itō (¥1330, one hour) and Izukyū Shimoda (¥480, 20 minutes).

RENDAI-JI & KANAYA ONSEN
蓮台寺 • 金谷温泉

The town of Rendai-ji is home to one of the best *onsen* on the peninsula, **Kanaya Onsen** (admission ¥1000; ☯ 9am-10pm). Its rangey, rambling building houses the biggest all-wood bath in the nation (on the men's side), called the sen-

nin-furo (1000-person bath, a vast exaggeration). The women's bath is nothing to sneeze at, and both sides have private outdoor baths as well. BYOT (towel), or buy one for ¥200.

The same building also houses the fabulously traditional **Kanaya Ryokan** (金谷旅館; ☎ 22-0325; fax 23-6078; r per person without/with meals from ¥7350/15,750), which was built in 1929 and feels like it. Some of the tatami rooms are simple, while others are vast suites with private toilet. There are no restaurants nearby, so go for the inn's meals or pack you own.

Take the Izukyū line to Rendai-ji station (¥160, five minutes), go straight across the river and main road to the T-junction and turn left; the *onsen* is 50m on the right.

IRŌZAKI 石廊崎

The southernmost point of the peninsula is noted for its cliffs and lighthouse and some fairly good beaches. You can get to the cape from Shimoda by boat (see p214) or by bus (¥930, 45 minutes) from bus 4 platform. **Izukyū Marine** (☎ 22-1151; adult/child ¥1120/5600) runs frequent 25-minute cruises around the harbour.

Matsuzaki 松崎
☎ 0558

The sleepy coastal village of Matsuzaki is known for its streetscapes: some 200 traditional houses with *namako-kabe* walls – diamond-shaped tiles set in plaster. They're concentrated in the south of town, on the far side of the river. There is no tourist information in English.

The **Izu Chōhachi Art Museum** (☎ 42-2540; adult/child ¥500/free; ☯ 9am-5pm) showcases the work of Irie Chōhachi (1815–99). His plaster, fresco and stucco paintings are unimaginably detailed. Each colour, no matter how intricate the design (be it a pine needle or a stitch on a kimono), gets its own layer of plaster. You'll want to use a magnifying glass (supplied by staff) to examine the works in detail.

Amid rice fields 3km east of town is the **Sanyo-sō Youth Hostel** (三余荘ユースホステル; ☎ /fax 42-0408; dm member/nonmember ¥3045/4095), a marvellously antique former landowner's home with fine (shared) tatami rooms. If this building were not a hostel, it would probably be some kind of important cultural property. From Shimoda take a Dōgashima-bound bus and get off at the Yūsu-hosteru-mae bus stop (¥1160, 50 minutes); it's another ¥240 to

Matsuzaki. Breakfast/dinner costs ¥630/1050. Rental bikes are available for exploring the countryside. Check-in is between 4pm and 6.30pm.

To central Matsuzaki, the bus fare from Shimoda is ¥1230; from Dōgashima ¥520.

Dōgashima 堂ヶ島

For help booking accommodation and info on onward transport, stop by the **information office** (☎ 52-1268; ⏰ 8.30am-5pm Mon-Sat) in front of the bus stop and above the tourist jetty. Staff will also rent you a bicycle for free.

The main attraction at Dōgashima is the dramatic rock formations that line the seashore. The park just across the street from the bus stop has some of the best views. It's also possible to take a return boat trip (¥1880/920 50/20 minutes) from the nearby jetty to visit the town's famous shoreline cave. The cave has a natural window in the roof that allows light to pour in. You can look down into the cave from paths in the aforementioned park.

About 700m south of the bus stop, you'll find the stunning **Sawada-kōen Rotemburo onsen** (沢田公園露天風呂温泉; admission ¥500; ⏰ 7am-7pm Wed-Mon Sep-Jul, 6am-8pm Wed-Mon Aug) perched high on a cliff overlooking the Pacific. Go early in the day if possible; around sunset it's standing room only. Males and females bathe separately.

GETTING THERE & AWAY

Buses to Dōgashima (¥1360, one hour) leave from platform 5 in front of Shimoda station. From Dōgashima you can catch a bus onward to Shuzen-ji (¥1970, 1½ hours), complete with fantastic views over Suruga-wan to Mt Fuji. When the air is clear and the mountain is blanketed by snow, you'll swear you're looking at a Hokusai print. The best views are between Ōkubo (大久保) and Toi (土肥).

Shuzen-ji Onsen 修善寺温泉
☎ 0558

Although it's not on any coast, Shuzen-ji Onsen is the peninsula's most charming town, a hot-spring village in a lush valley bisected by the rushing Katsura-gawa. Lucky, too, since Shuzen-ji, along with Atami, is one of the two gateways to Izu (Shuzen-ji Onsen is a 10-minute bus ride from Shuzen-ji station). There are some fine places to stroll, and at dusk the town bells play 'Moon River'.

SIGHTS & ACTIVITIES

In the middle of Shuzen-ji Onsen is the tranquil namesake temple **Shuzen-ji** (☎ 72-0053; admission free; ⏰ 5am-6pm) dating from 807. It's said to have been founded by Kōbō Daishi, the Heian-period priest credited with spreading Buddhism throughout much of Japan. The present structure dates from 1489.

The real reason to visit Shuzen-ji is to take a dip in one of its famous onsen. Right in the on the river is **Tokko-no-yu** (とっこの湯; iron-club waters), said to be Izu's oldest hot spring. Its name comes from a legend that its waters sprung from the rock when it was struck by Kōbō Daishi himself. Unfortunately, it was closed for bathing at the time of writing.

Inns around town offer day-use bathing, or try **Hako-no-yu** (筥湯; admission ¥350; ⏰ noon-9pm), an elegant new facility identified by its wonderful wooden tower.

SLEEPING & EATING

Shuzen-ji Youth Hostel (修善寺ユースホステル; ☎ 72-1222; shuzenji@jyh.gr.jp; dm member/nonmember ¥3045/3645; ⏰ closed 18-22 Jan & 30 May-3 Jun; ✉ 🖥) In the hills west of town, this large (100-bed) hostel feels a little institutional but a good choice nonetheless, featuring tasty meals (breakfast/dinner ¥630/1050), decent rooms and a peaceful setting. It's a 12-minute bus ride from Shuzen-ji station; take a bus from the platform 6 at Shuzen-ji station to the New Town-guchi stop (last bus 6.45pm). It's a five-minute walk from the bus stop.

Onsen Minshuku Fukui (温泉民宿福井; ☎ 72-0558; fax 72-3529; r per person ¥4875) This simple but friendly minshuku is a popular choice for foreign guests. Decent tatami rooms and a small garden-side rotemburo. From the bus stop, head about 350m up hill. Look for the Maruko convenience store on the right and 'tourist home Fukui' in the world's tiniest letters on a white signboard, and follow the path.

Goyōkan (五葉間; ☎ 72-2066; fax 72-8212; www.goyokan.co.jp; r per person without/with breakfast ¥6450/7500) A midrange B&B minshuku in the centre of everything, with river views. No private facilities, but the shared (indoor) baths are made of stone and hinoki cypress. Some English is spoken.

ourpick Yukairo Kikuya (湯回廊菊屋; ☎ 72-2000; fax 72-2002; s/d/tr per person from ¥25,000/23,000/20,000) Spanning the Katsura-gawa, this splendid, romantic ryokan has been an inn since the mid-17th century. Rooms feature wa-beds (futons on platforms), and, unusual for *kaiseki* cuisine, you get to choose your own meals. Naturally, the baths are splendid, too.

Zendera Soba (禅寺そば; ☎ 72-0007; meals ¥630-1890; ☯ lunch Fri-Wed; E) This cosy local institution – it looks like a temple – serves *zaru soba* (cold soba) and the *tempura teishoku* (tempura set meal), but the real speciality is the namesake Zendera *soba* (¥1260), served with your own stalk of wasabi root to grate. It's steps from the bus station on the river side of the street.

GETTING THERE & AWAY

From Tokyo, access to Shuzen-ji is via Mishima on the Tōkaidō line (Kodama *shinkansen* ¥4400, one hour) and then Izu-Hakone Tetsudō trains between Mishima and Shuzen-ji (¥500, 35 minutes). Buses connect Shuzen-ji station and Shuzen-ji Onsen (¥210, 10 minutes). Long-distance buses run between Shuzen-ji and Shimoda (¥2180, two hours) and Shuzen-ji and Dōgashima (¥1970, 1½ hours).

SOUTH OF TOKYO

The coastal towns of Kanagawa-ken are just a short train ride from Tokyo, yet can seem eons away.

The vibrant port of Yokohama is Japan's second-largest city, though it's a much less chaotic metropolis than its big sister to the north. Further south lies the fascinating old capital of Kamakura, often called a Little Kyoto for its wealth of Buddhist temples and Shinto shrines.

YOKOHAMA 横浜

☎ 045 / pop 3,579,000

Around the time of the Black Ships, Yokohama was home to barely 600 people. A century-and-a-half later, it's Japan's second metropolis, with a breezy atmosphere, fine food, parks and historic districts, and loads of shopping. Unlike most Japanese cities, it's also a city of distinct neighbourhoods, including Chinatown, the historic Motomachi and Yamate districts, and the new seaside development of Minato Mirai 21.

Yokohama is barely 20 minutes from central Tokyo, meaning that it's an easy day trip or nighttime excursion. Among Japanese it's a popular date spot.

History

For most of history, Yokohama was an unnoticed fishing village near a rest stop called Kanagawa on the Tōkaidō. Its fate changed abruptly in 1853–54, when the American fleet under Commodore Matthew Perry arrived off the coast to persuade Japan to open to foreign trade; in 1858 this little village was designated an international port.

Westerners were first relegated to an area within a moat in a district called Kannai ('inside the barrier') but later began to own property up the mountainside (Yamate). A Chinese community burgeoned as well, and the city expanded on reclaimed land, eventually encompassing the original Kanagawa rest stop.

Although Yokohama is unquestionably Japanese, foreign influence is in its blood. Among Yokohama's firsts-in-Japan: daily newspaper, gaslamps and train terminus (connected to Shimbashi, in Tokyo).

The Great Kantō Earthquake of 1923 destroyed much of the city, with the rubble used to reclaim more land, including Yamashita Kōen. The city was devastated yet again in WWII air raids; occupation forces were initially based here but later moved down the coast to Yokosuka. The late 20th century saw redevelopment of the harbour area, including some fancy skyscrapers, and in 2002 Yokohama hosted the finals of the FIFA World Cup.

Orientation

Central Yokohama sits on the southern side on the western part of Tokyo-wan (here called Yokohama-wan). Most of the sights are within about 1km of the water, near Sakuragi-chō, Kannai and Ishikawa-chō stations on the JR Negishi line, or Minato Mirai or Motomachi-Chūkagai stations on the Minato Mirai Line.

Information

Information about Yokohama is available on the web at www.welcome.city.yokohama.jp/eng/tourism.

Animi (☎ 222-3316; 4-2-7 Minato Mirai; per hr ¥100; ☯ 10am-8pm) Internet access. Walk 15 minutes northwest of Minato Mirai 21 station.

Chinatown 80 Information Center (☎ 662-1252; Honcho-dōri; ☯ 10am-10pm) For the latest goings-on in Chinatown, the centre is a few blocks from the Motomachi subway station.

Citibank (✆ 24hr) International ATM is outside the western exit of Yokohama station, on the 2nd floor of the First Building, near the Yokohama Bay Sheraton.

Minato Mirai 21 Information Center (☎ 211-0111; 1-1-62 Sakuragi-chō; ✆ 9am-7pm) English speakers here can provide a wealth of information, including the free *Yokohama City Guide*. It's outside the northern exit of Sakuragi-chō station.

Post office A block east of the Sakuragi-chō station, with foreign ATM service.

Sights & Activities

MINATO MIRAI 21 みなとみらい 21

This district of man-made **islands** (🚇 Sakuragi-chō, Minatomirai, Bashamichi) used to be shipping docks, but the last two decades have transformed them into a metropolis-of-the-future ('Minato Mirai' means 'port future'), with a buzzing street scene by day and glowing towers by night (Landmark tower and the three-towered Queens Sq). In addition to the attractions listed here, there's one of the world's largest convention complexes, several hotels, and lots of shopping and dining.

These sights are arranged as a possible walking tour.

Landmark Tower

Japan's tallest building (70 storeys, 296m) has one of the world's fastest lifts (45km/h). The **Landmark Tower Sky Garden** (☎ 222-5030; Minato-Mirai 2-2-1-1; adult/child/senior & student ¥1000/500/800; ✆ 10am-9pm Sep-Jun, to 10pm Sat, to 10pm Jul & Aug) observatory is on the 69th floor; on clear days there are views to Tokyo, Izu-hantō and Mt Fuji.

Yokohama Museum of Art

Behind Landmark Tower, this contemporary **art museum** (☎ 221-0306; 3-4-1 Minato Mirai; adult/elementary & junior high/college & high school ¥500/100/300; ✆ 10am-6pm Fri-Wed) has a decent collection displayed in changing exhibitions. It's noted for its building, designed by Pritzker Prize winner Tange Kenzō (1989).

Mitsubishi Minato Mirai Industrial Museum

This is one of Japan's better science and technology **museums** (☎ 224-9031; 3-3-1 Minato Mirai; adult/child ¥500/200; ✆ 10am-5.30pm Tue-Sun), with a wildly enjoyable helicopter simulator and good hands-on exhibits.

For a less-simulated airborne adventure, take a helicopter tour of Yokohama. **Yokohama Heli Cruising** (横浜ヘリクルージング; ☎ 223-1155; flight per 5/10min ¥4000/12,500; ✆ Fri-Sun) offers short but exhilarating flights from its heliport in Rinko Park, a seven-minute walk northeast of Queen's Sq. Flights depart around sunset.

Yokohama Maritime Museum

On the harbour in front of Landmark Tower, this fan-shaped **museum** (☎ 221-0280; 2-1-1 Minato Mirai; admission to museum & ship ¥600; ✆ 10am-6.30pm Tue-Sun Jul & Aug, 10am-4.30pm Tue-Sun Sep-Jun) is largely dedicated to the *Nippon Maru* sailing ship docked adjacent. The ship (built 1930) retains many original fittings, including captain's and officers' rooms and the engine room.

Cosmo World

Next to the Maritime Museum, this **amusement park** (☎ 641-6591; 2-8-1 Shinkō; rides ¥200-700; ✆ 11am-9pm Mon-Fri, to 10pm Sat & Sun) features one of the world's tallest Ferris wheels, **Cosmo Clock** (112.5m; admission ¥700).

Manyō Club

The fact that there is no *onsen* in Yokohama (that we know of) doesn't matter. This new **hot-spring facility** (☎ 663-4126; 2-7-1 Shinkō; adult/child ¥2620/1470; ✆ 10am-9am) trucks in water daily from Atami and gives you five storeys' worth of ways to enjoy them: pool to pool, sauna to sauna in your custom *yukata*. Spa treatments are available (extra charge), and 'relax rooms' have hundreds of TVs in front of hundreds of comfy chairs. Check-in is on the 7th floor.

Japan Overseas Migration Museum

Yokohama has long welcomed the world, but this fine **museum** (☎ 663-3257; 2-3-1 Shinkō; admission free; ✆ 10am-6pm Tue-Sun) looks at Japanese who went overseas. Agricultural labourers, fishermen and performers later became merchants, doctors and priests in the USA, Brazil and more. It's a must for anyone of Japanese heritage, with signage in English. It's inside the offices of the charitable organisation Japan International Cooperation Agency (JICA).

Akarenga Sōko

It means red brick **warehouses** (☎ 211-1515; admission free; ✆ 11am-8pm, some restaurants later), and these century-old structures have been refurbished into chichi speciality shops, restaurants, cafés, changing art exhibits and special events. Well worth a visit.

AROUND TOKYO

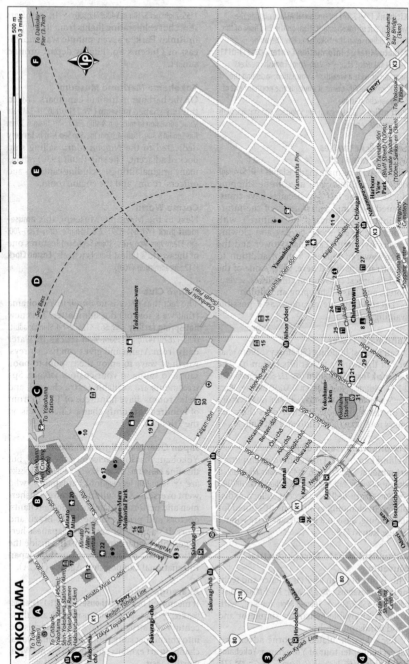

YOKOHAMA

AROUND TOKYO

YAMASHITA-KŌEN AREA 山下公園周辺

Moored alongside this seaside **park** (🚇 Motomachi-Chukagai) you'll find the **Hikawa Maru** (☎ 641-4362; adult/child ¥800/400; ⏱ 9.30am-6pm conditions permitting), a retired luxury 1930 passenger liner (one of the staterooms was used by Charlie Chaplin).

Across the street, the **Silk Museum** (☎ 641-0841; 1 Yamashita-kōen-dōri; adult/child/student/senior ¥500/100/200/300; ⏱ 9am-4.30pm Tue-Sun) pays tribute to Yokohama's history as a silk trading port, with all aspects of silk production and some lovely kimono and *obi* (sashes). The nearby **Yokohama Archives of History** (☎ 201-2100; 3 Nihon Ōdōri; adult/child ¥200/100; ⏱ 9.30am-5pm Tue-Sun) chronicles the city (displays in English) from the opening of Japan to the mid-20th century; it's inside the former British consulate. The **Marine Tower** (☎ 641-7838; 15 Yamashita-kōen-dōri; adult/child/student/senior ¥700/300/350/500; ⏱ 9.30am-9pm conditions permitting), one of the world's tallest inland lighthouses (106m), offers a less-razzle-dazzley view over the harbour than does Landmark Tower.

MOTOMACHI & YAMATE 元町・山手

This area south of **Yamashita-kōen** (🚇 Motomachi-Chukagai, Ishikawa-chō) combines the gentle intimacy of Motomachi's shopping street with early-20th-century Western-style architecture and fantastic views from the brick sidewalks of Yamate-hon-dōri ('Bluff St'). Private homes and churches here are still in use. Attractions include Harbour View Park and the Foreign-

ers' Cemetery, final resting place of 4000 foreign residents and visitors – the headstones carry some fascinating inscriptions. A stroll from near Yamashita-kōen to Ishikawa-chō station should take about one hour.

CHINATOWN 中華街

Always wanted to go to China? Yokohama's **Chinatown** (Chūkagai; 🚇 Motomachi-Chukagai, Ishikawa-chō) has the sights, sounds, aromas of Hong Kong without the airfare, rivalling Minato Mirai in popularity. Within its 10 elaborately painted gates are all manner of Chinese speciality shops and some 500 food shops and (often expensive) restaurants, and enchanting neon displays at night. Chinatown's heart is the Chinese temple **Kantei-byō** (admission free; ⏱ 10am-8pm), dedicated to Kanwu, the god of business. See the box text (p223) for information about Yokohama Daisekai, a Chinese theme park.

SANKEI-EN 三渓園

Opened to the public in 1906, the beautifully landscaped gardens of **Sankei-en** (☎ 621-0634; www.sankeien.or.jp; 58-1 Honmoku-sannotani; adult/child ¥500/200; ⏱ 9am-5pm) feature walking paths among ponds, 17th-century buildings, several fine tea-ceremony houses and a 500-year-old, three-storey pagoda. The inner garden is a fine example of traditional Japanese garden landscaping. From Yokohama or Sakuragi-chō station, take bus 8 to Honmoku Sankei-en-mae bus stop (10 minutes).

Sleeping

Most people day trip to Yokohama from Tokyo, but there are some worthy lodgings even if no bargains. Look for internet specials.

Toyoko Inn Sutajium-mae (☎ 664-1045; fax 664-1046; www.toyoko-inn.com/eng; Osanbashi-dōri; s/d ¥6090/8400; ⓡ Kannai; ❄ ✕ ▯ wi-fi) Simple but nicely outfitted business hotel with small, comfortable rooms in a main building (Honkan) and marginally nicer new building (Shinkan). Rates include breakfast, internet and more. From the station, walk along the main road, turn left after the stadium and take the first left. It's two blocks further.

Navios Yokohama (☎ 633-6000; fax 63-6001; www .navios-yokohama.com; 2-2-1 Shinkō; s/tw from ¥8140/15,750; ⓡ Bashamichi; ❄ ▯ wi-fi) In Minato Mirai, it's Yokohama's best deal in this price range; rooms are spacious, spotless and central. Choose city views (across the harbour to Landmark Tower or sea view towards Akarenga Sōkō).

Hotel New Grand (☎ 681-1841; fax 681-1895; www .hotel-newgrand.co.jp; 10 Yamashita-kōen-dōri; s/tw from ¥13,860/20,000; ⓡ Motomachi-Chūkagai; ❄ ✕ ▯) This old-line (1927) 251-room hotel has a prime waterfront location and was once a favourite of visiting foreign dignitaries (check out the timeless original lobby). Now it's a classy, upmarket option with some old-world charm, despite the addition of a tower in 1992.

Yokohama Royal Park Hotel (☎ 221-1111; 224-5153; www.yrph.com; 2-2-1-3 Minato Mirai; s/tw/d from ¥31,500/35,700/36,750; ❄ ✕ ▯ ▩) You can't get any higher than this, on the upper floors of Landmark Tower, and it hardly gets more luxe either, with fitness centre, pool, oodles of space, marble, burlwood, blackout curtains and an aromatherapy salon.

Pan Pacific Yokohama (☎ 682-2222; fax 682-2223; www.panpacific.com; 2-3-7 Minato Mirai; d from ¥40,000; ⓡ Minatomirai; ❄ ✕ ▯ ▩) Right by the convention centre, this superbly stylish hotel boasts designer furnishings, rooms with balconies and excellent views, and several good but pricey restaurants.

Eating

For generations, people have come to China-town (ⓡ Ishikawachō or Motomachi-Chūkagai) for a bang-up dinner. Plan on spending about ¥5000 per person for a fancy dinner and perhaps half that for lunch – look for set menus – although there are certainly less expensive eateries. For an eclectic mix of cuisines visit the restaurant floors of Landmark Plaza and Queen's Sq.

Baikōtei (☎ 681-4870; 1-1 Aioicho; mains around ¥800-1300; ⏱ 11am-8.30pm Mon-Sat; E; ⓡ Kannai or Nihon Ōdōri) This weathered classic with red-velour seating is famed for its Hayashi rice (with meat, vegetables and demiglace), and a mean *katsu-don* (pork cutlet). Look for the sign that announces Baikō Emmies.

Chano-ma (☎ 650-8228; 3rd fl, Akarenga Sōkō Bldg 2; mains from ¥700; ⏱ 11am-midnight Sun-Thu, to 5am Fri & Sat; E) Dine on sushi, salads and croquettes at high tables with high chairs or on mattresses arranged around an open kitchen, while serious club beats play under tall ceilings.

Yamate Jyuban-kan (山手十番館; ☎ 621-4466; 247 Yamatechō; mains/courses from ¥2000/3500; ⏱ 11am-9pm; E) Overlooking the Foreigners' Cemetery in Yamate, this French restaurant serves consistently good cuisine in a building like a mansion from the American south. A casual café occupies the 1st floor, while upstairs is the classic restaurant, dishing out longstanding favourites like the Kaika steak set. Reservations recommended.

Manchinrō Honten (☎ 681-4004; 153 Yamashita-chō; mains from ¥1100, dinner for 2 ¥8400; ⏱ lunch & dinner Tue-Sun; E) One of Chinatown's oldest and most popular Cantonese restaurants, with a respected Hong Kong chef. Expect specialities like wok-fried seafood with XO sauce and shrimp with mayonnaise, plus *yum cha* (dim sum; ¥480 to ¥700). Look for the stone lions out the front.

Heichinrō Honten (☎ 681-3001; 149 Yamashita-chō; lunch/dinner ¥3000/5000; ⏱ 11am-10.15pm; E) Neck and neck with Manchinrō, the equally elegant Heichinrō is another Cantonese favourite. Separate dining rooms for main dishes and *yum cha* (¥420 to ¥1020), including *ebi no kingyo* (shrimp in the shape of goldfish) and popular noodle soups.

Drinking & Entertainment

Yokohama buzzes at night. Many of the city's bars are near Kannai station, and there's a growing scene around Minato Mirai.

Peace (☎ 650-2200; Osanbashi-dōri; cocktails from ¥650, mains ¥600-950; ⏱ 11am-2am Sun-Thu, to 4am Fri & Sat; ⓡ Kannai) Diagonally across from Yokohama Stadium, this airy, stylish bistro and lounge attracts a young, attractive crowd for its extensive cocktail menu, decent food and groovy beats. Live music some nights.

IT'S A RESTAURANT! IT'S A THEME PARK!

In 1994 Nelson Mandela became president of South Africa, Israel and Jordan signed a peace treaty, Netscape launched Navigator and the first passengers travelled through the Chunnel. But here in Yokohama, something *really* important happened: the **Shin-Yokohama Rāmen Hakubutskan** (☎ 471-0503; 2-14-21 Shinyokohama; adult/child ¥300/100, most meals from ¥900; ☿ 11am-11pm) opened, inaugurating the age of the food theme park throughout Japan. This museum of *rāmen* continues to show the history and culture of these Chinese-style noodles about which it's fair to say Japan is bonkers. Downstairs, nine *rāmen* restaurants from around the country were hand-picked to sell their wares in a replica of a 1958 Shitamachi (downtown district).

The concept has been copied many times since, not least here in Yokohama. In Chinatown, the eight-storey **Yokohama Daisekai** (Daska; ☎ 681-5588; 3 Minami-mon; adult/child ¥500/400, mains from ¥900; ☿ 10am-9pm Oct-Jun, to 10pm Jul-Sep) models itself on Shanghai's gilded age of the 1920s and '30s, with silks, carvings and crafts, performances of jazz and Chinese opera, and three floors of restaurants. To beat the crowds, visit on weekdays.

Japan is also obsessed with curry rice, a large bowl filled with rice on one side and meat or vegetables in curry sauce on the other. The **Yokohama Curry Museum** (☎ 250-0833; 1-2-3 Isezaki-chō; admission free, most meals ¥650-1350; ☿ 11am-10pm) offers nine styles of curry, including Indian, Okinawan and, er, French. The cocktail bar here serves a 'currytini'. We dare you.

Windjammer (☎ 662-3966; 215 Yamashitachō; live music cover ¥400-600, drinks from ¥900; ☿ 6pm-1.30am; ▣ Kannai) The setting feels like the inside of a yacht (especially after the potent Jacktar cocktail, ¥1050). All the better to listen to live jazz nightly.

Bank ART Studio (☎ 663-4697; 3-9 Kaigan-dōri; ☿ 11.30am-11pm; ▣ Nihon-Ōdori) This art gallery opened in 2004, with flexible space for exhibitions, views of Minato Mirai skyscrapers, and a simple bar and snack menu. It will erase any doubts whether Yokohama is cool. Look for the arcade made of wire clothes hangers.

Motion Blue (☎ 226-1919; 3rd fl, Akarenga Sōkō Bldg 2; most tickets free-¥4200; ☿ 5-11.30pm Mon-Sat, 4-10pm Sun; ▣ Bashamichi) Yokohama's hottest music club books jazz, fusion, world music, J-pop and more. It's in the Akarenga-Sōkō.

Nana's Green Tea (☎ 664-2707; Akarenga Sōkō Bldg 2; drinks around ¥500) Contemporary takes on traditional Japanese drinks: latte of frozen *maccha* (powdered green tea) with whipped cream, drinks with azuki beans, and a steaming bowl of *zensai* (azuki bean soup).

Yokohama Stadium (☎ 661-1251; Yokohama Kōen; tickets ¥1800-5500; ☿ games Apr-early Oct; ▣ Kannai) If you're looking to see a Japanese baseball game, Yokohama's stadium is a great place: it's centrally located, and the local team, the Bay Stars, is usually middling, meaning that tickets are generally easy to come by.

Sirius (☎ 221-1111; 2-2-1-3 Minato Mirai; drinks from ¥1000; ☿ 5pm-1am; ▣ Sakuragi-chō) Elegant cocktail lounge on the top (70th floor) of the Yokohama Royal Park Hotel. The place to go for a view over cocktails like the Two Hearts, with apple and cherry syrups, Calpis and fresh apple, topped with Champagne (¥1900).

Shopping

In Minato Mirai, Yokohama World Porters is a huge shopping complex with lots of restaurants on the ground floor, including Vivre, possibly the world's cleanest supermarket. Landmark Tower and Queens Sq are similarly filled with shopping and dining, and Akarenga Sōkō with craft, antique and speciality shops. There are often street performances throughout Minato Mirai. The more intimate shopping strip of Motomachi is lined with lovely boutiques.

Getting There & Away

Frequent JR and private-line trains from Tokyo serve Yokohama station, where you can change for Sakuragichō and Kannai (¥130, three and five minutes) or Ishikawachō (¥150, eight minutes), or the more expensive local subway. Take the Keihin Kyūkō line from Shinagawa station (¥290, 18 minutes), or the Tōkyū Tōyoko line from Shibuya station (¥260, about 25 minutes), which becomes the Minato Mirai subway line to Minatomirai (¥440, 28 minutes) and Motomachi-Chūkagai (¥460, 30 minutes).

From Tokyo station, JR's Keihin Tōhoku and Tōkaidō lines stop at Yokohama station

(¥450, 40 minutes); some continue on to Sakuragichō, Kannai and Ishikawa-chō (all ¥540). The Tōkaidō *shinkansen* stops at Shin-Yokohama station, northwest of town, connected to the city centre by the Yokohama line.

TO/FROM THE AIRPORT
Yokohama station connects frequently with Narita and Haneda airports via Narita Express trains (N'EX; ¥4180, 1½ hours) or JR Airport Narita line (¥1890, two hours, including transfers) and limousine buses to/from the Yokohama City Air Terminal (YCAT, Sky Building east of Yokohama station, next to Sogō department store; Narita airport ¥3500, two hours; Haneda airport ¥560, 35 minutes).

Getting Around
BICYCLE
Bike rental (☎ 641-7838; per 2hr ¥300) is available near the Marine Tower (p221).

BOAT
Sea Bass (☎ 661-0347) ferries connect Yokohama station, Minato Mirai 21 and Yamashita-kōen. Boats run between approximately 10am and 8pm. Full fare from Yokohama station to Yamashita-kōen is ¥600 (20 minutes). **Suijō Bus** (☎ 201-0821; adult/child ¥400/200; ☯ 1-5pm Tue-Fri, noon-6pm Sat & Sun) runs ferries between Minato Mirai, Ōsanbashi and Renga Park.

BUS
Although trains are more convenient, Yokohama has an extensive bus network (¥210 per ride). A special Akai-kutsu (red shoe) bus loops every 30 minutes during daytime through the tourist areas for ¥100/300 per ride/day pass.

KAMAKURA 鎌倉
☎ 0467 / pop 171,000
The capital of Japan from 1185 to 1333, Kamakura rivals Nikkō as the most culturally rewarding day trip from Tokyo. An enormous number of Buddhist temples and the occasional Shinto shrine dot around the countryside. If you start early you can cover a lot of ground in a day, but two days will also allow you to visit the temples of East Kamakura and take some nice walks. Kamakura is small and pleasant, although it gets packed on weekends and in holiday periods.

History
The end of the Heian period was marked by a legendary feud between two great warrior families, the Minamoto (Genji) and the Taira (Heike). After the Taira routed the Minamoto, the third son of the Minamoto clan, called Yoritomo, was sent to live at a temple in Izu-hantō. When the boy grew old enough, he began to gather support for a counterattack on his clan's old rivals. In 1180 Yoritomo set up his base at Kamakura, far away from the debilitating influences of Kyoto court life, close to other clans loyal to the Minamoto and, having the sea on one side and densely wooded hills on the others, easy to defend.

After victories over the Taira, Minamoto Yoritomo was appointed shōgun in 1192 and governed Japan from Kamakura. When he died without an heir, power passed to the Hōjō, the family of Yoritomo's wife.

The Hōjō clan ruled Japan from Kamakura for more than a century until, in 1333, weakened by the cost of maintaining defences against threats of attack from Kublai Khan in China, the Hōjō clan was defeated by Emperor Go-Daigo. Kyoto once again became the capital.

Orientation
Kamakura's main attractions can be covered on foot, with the occasional bus ride. Cycling is also practical (p229). Most sights are signposted in English and Japanese. You can start at Kamakura station and travel around the area in a circle (Komachi-dōri 'shopping town' and broad Wakamiya-ōji are the main streets east of the station), or start one station north at Kita-Kamakura station and visit the temples between there and Kamakura station on foot. The itinerary in this section follows the latter route.

Information
Kamakura Green Net (www.guide.city.ka makura .kanagawa.jp) Has useful information about both living and sightseeing here.
Post office (1-10-3 Komachi; ☯ 9am-7pm Mon-Fri, to 3pm Sat) With ATMs, a short walk from Kamakura station's east exit.
Tourist Information Center (☎ 22-3350; ☯ 9am-5.30pm Apr-Sep, to 5pm Oct-Mar) Just outside Kamakura station's east exit, this helpful office distributes maps and brochures, and can also make bookings for same-day accommodation.

Sights & Activities

ENGAKU-JI 円覚寺

Engaku-ji (☎ 22-0478; admission ¥200; ☯ 8am-5pm Apr-Sep, to 4pm Oct-Mar) is on the left as you exit Kita-Kamakura station. It is one of the five main Rinzai Zen temples in Kamakura. Engaku-ji was founded in 1282, allegedly as a place where Zen monks might pray for soldiers who lost their lives defending Japan against Kublai Khan. Today the only real reminder of the temple's former magnificence and antiquity is the gate San-mon, a 1780 reconstruction. At the top of the long flight of stairs through the gate is the Engaku-ji bell, the largest bell in Kamakura, cast in 1301. The Hondō (Main Hall) inside San-mon is a recent reconstruction, dating from the mid-1960s.

TŌKEI-JI 東慶寺

Tōkei-ji (☎ 22-1663; admission ¥100; ☯ 8.30am-5pm Mar-Oct, to 4pm Nov-Feb), across the railway tracks from Engaku-ji, is notable for its lush grounds as much as for the temple itself. On weekdays, when visitors are few, it can be a pleasantly relaxing place.

Historically, the temple is famed as having served as a women's refuge. A woman could be officially recognised as divorced after three years as a nun in the temple precincts. Today there are no nuns; the grave of the last abbess can be found in the cemetery, shrouded by cypress trees.

JŌCHI-JI 浄智寺

A couple of minutes further on from Tōkei-ji is **Jōchi-ji** (☎ 22-3943; adult/child ¥150/80; ☯ 9am-4.30pm Mar-Oct, to 4.30pm Nov-Feb), another temple with pleasant grounds. Founded in 1283, this is considered one of Kamakura's five great Zen temples, prized for its moss-covered entry, its bell tower and for the flowers that seem to explode here each spring.

DAIBUTSU HIKING COURSE

If time permits, consider taking the Daibutsu Hiking Course, which begins at the steps just up the lane from Jōchi-ji and follows a wooded path for 3km to the Daibutsu (allow about 1½ hours). Along the course you'll pass the small shrine of **Kuzuharagaoka-jinja**, from which you'll see signs to the landscaped park of **Genjiyama-kōen** (where you'll see a statue of Minamoto Yoritomo). From here, head down the stairs, keep going down the hill and take a right to reach **Zeniarai-benten** (Money-washing Shrine; ☎ 25-1081), one of Kamakura's most al-luring Shintō shrines. A cave-like entrance leads to a clearing where visitors come to bathe their money in natural springs with the hope of bringing financial success. You can either return back up the steps to the path or continue down the paved road, turning right at the first intersection, walking along a path lined with cryptomeria and ascending up through the shrine of **Sasuke-inari jinja** (typical of inari shrines, it's recognized by the succession of *torii* gates) before meeting up with the Daibutsu path once again.

KENCHŌ-JI 建長寺

Continuing towards Kamakura along the main road from Jōchi-ji, on the left you'll pass the turn-off to this **temple** (☎ 22-0981; adult/child ¥300/100; ☯ 8.30am-4.30pm), the first-ranked of the five great Zen temples. Founded in 1253, Kenchō-ji once comprised seven buildings and 49 subtemples, most of which were destroyed in the fires of the 14th and 15th centuries. However, the 17th and 18th centuries saw its restoration, and you can still get a sense of its splendour. Today, Kencho-ji functions as a working monastery with 10 subtemples. Among the highlights are the **Butsuden** (Buddha hall), brought piece by piece from Kyoto; the painstakingly landscaped **Zen garden**, shaped like the kanji for 'mind'; and the **juniper grove**, believed to have sprouted from seeds brought from China by Kencho-ji's founder some seven centuries ago.

TEN-EN HIKING COURSE

Another excellent walk through the countryside begins by walking around the Kenchō-ji's Hojo (main hall) and up the steps to the entrance of the Ten-en Hiking Course. From here it's a two-hour walk to Zuisen-ji, along one of the most scenic spots in Kanagawa-ken; those with less time can take a shorter (80-minute) trail to Kamakura-gū.

ENNŌ-JI 円応寺

Across the road from Kenchō-ji is **Ennō-ji** (☎ 25-1905; adult/child ¥200/150; ☯ 9am-4pm Mar-Nov, to 3pm Dec-Feb), which is distinguished primarily by its collection of statues depicting the judges of hell. Presiding over them is a statue of Emma (Sanskrit name: Yama; an important cultural property), an ancient Hindu deity and ruler of the hell's 10 kings. The statue is noted for its fierce gaze meant for the wicked (hopefully you won't have anything to worry about). Hell

AROUND TOKYO

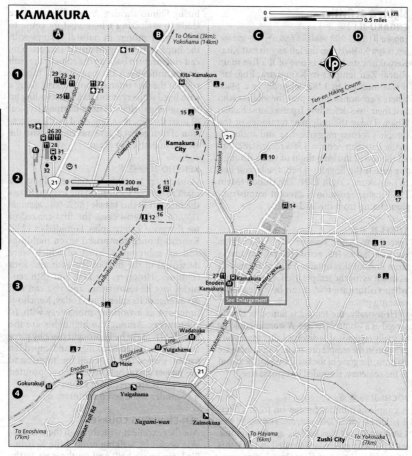

KAMAKURA

and judgement became important concepts with the rise of the Jōdō (Pure Land) school of Buddhism (see p54).

TSURUGAOKA HACHIMAN-GŪ 鶴岡八幡宮
Further down the road, where it turns towards Kamakura station, is **Tsurugaoka Hachiman-gū** (☎ 22-0315; admission free; ☒ 7am-9pm), the main Shintō shrine of Kamakura. It was founded by Minamoto Yoriyoshi, of the same Minamoto clan that ruled Japan from Kamakura. This shrine's sprawl, with elongated paths, broad vistas and lotus ponds, presents the visitor with an atmosphere drastically different to the repose of the Zen temples clustered around Kita-Kamakura station. The Gempei Pond (the name comes from the kanji for the Genji

and Heike clans) is divided by bridges, said to symbolise the rift between the clans.

DAIBUTSU 大仏
The **Kamakura Daibutsu** (Great Buddha; ☎ 22-0703; adult/child ¥200/150; ☒ 7am-6pm Apr-Sep, to 5.30pm Oct-Mar) is at Kōtoku-in temple. Completed in 1252, it is Japan's second-largest Buddha image and Kamakura's most famous sight. It was once housed in a huge hall, today the statue sits in the open, the hall having been washed away by a tsunami in 1495. Cast in bronze and weighing close to 850 tonnes, the statue is 11.4m tall. Its construction is said to have been inspired by Yoritomo's visit to Nara (where Japan's biggest Daibutsu holds court) after the Minamoto clan's victory over

AROUND TOKYO

the rival Taira clan. Even though Kamakura's Daibutsu doesn't quite match Nara's in stature, it is commonly agreed that it is artistically superior.

The Buddha itself is the Amida Buddha (*amitābha* in Sanskrit), worshipped by the followers of the Jōdo school as a figure of salvation.

Buses from stop 1 to 6 in front of Kamakura station run to the Daibutsu-mae stop. Alternatively, take the Enoden Enoshima line to Hase station and walk north for about five minutes. Better yet, take the Daibutsu Hiking Course.

HASE-DERA 長谷寺

About 10 minutes' walk from the Daibutsu, **Hase-dera** (☎ 22-6300; adult/child ¥300/100; ⏰ 8am-5pm Mar-Sep, to 4.30pm Oct-Feb) is one of the most popular temples in the Kantō region, also known as Hase Kannon.

The walls of the staircases leading up to the main hall are lined with thousands of tiny statues of Jizō; ranked like a small army of urchins, many of them clothed to keep them warm. It's quite charming until you realise that Jizō is the patron *boddhisatva* of travellers and departed children, and the statues were placed there by women who lost children through miscarriage or abortion. The effect can be quite haunting.

The focal point of the temple's main hall is the Kannon statue. Kannon (*avalokiteshvara* in Sanskrit), the goddess of mercy, is the Bodhisattva of infinite compassion and, along with Jizō, is one of Japan's most popular Buddhist deities. This 9m-high carved wooden *jūichimen* (11-faced Kannon) is believed to date from the 8th century. The 11 faces are actually one primary face and 10 secondary faces, the latter representing the 10 stages of enlightenment. It is said that the 11 faces allow Kannon, ever vigilant for those in need of her assistance, to cast an eye in every direction. The temple dates back to AD 736, when it is said the statue washed up on the shore near Kamakura.

OTHER SHRINES & TEMPLES

If you're still in the mood for temples, there are plenty more in and around Kamakura, which has some 60 more temples and shrines.

From the Daibutsu it is best to return to Kita-Kamakura station by bus and take another bus out to the temples in the peaceful eastern part of town. While these lack the grandeur compared to Kamakura's more famous temples, they more than make up for with their charm and lack of crowds.

The grounds of this secluded Zen temple, **Zuisen-ji** (☎ 22-1191; admission ¥100; ⏰ 9am-5pm) make for a pleasant stroll and include Zen gardens laid out by Musō Kokushi, the temple's esteemed founder. It is possible to get there from the Egara Ten-jin shrine on foot in about 10 to 15 minutes; turn right where the bus turns left in front of the shrine, take the next left and keep following the road. From Zuisen-ji you can access the Ten-en Hiking Course.

The small **Sugimoto-dera** (☎ 22-3463; admission ¥200; ⏰ 8am-4.30pm), founded in AD 734, is reputed to be the oldest in Kamakura. Its ferocious-looking guardian deities and a statue of Kannon are its main draw. Take a bus from stop 5 at Kamakura dtation to the Sugimoto Kannon bus stop.

Down the road (away from Kamakura dtation) from Sugimoto-dera, on the right-hand side, **Hōkoku-ji** (☎ 22-0762; admission ¥200; ⏰ 9am-4pm) is a Rinzai Zen temple with quiet, landscaped gardens where you can relax under a red parasol with a cup of Japanese tea. This is also one of the more active Zen temples in Kamakura, regularly holding *zazen* (Soto-school meditation) classes for beginners. Take a bus from stop 5 at Kamakura Station (¥190, 10 minutes) to Gyōmyōji.

Festivals & Events

Bonbori Matsuri (7-9 August) Hundreds of lanterns are strung up around Tsurugaoka Hachiman-gū.

Hachiman-gū Matsuri (14-16 September) Festivities include a procession of *mikoshi* (portable shrines) and, on the last day, a display of horseback archery.

Kamakura Matsuri A week of celebrations held from the second Sunday to the third Sunday in April. It includes a wide range of activities, most of which are centred on Tsurugaoka Hachiman-gū.

Sleeping

Kamakura Hase Youth Hostel (☎ /fax 24-3390; dm member/nonmember ¥3000/4000; ✖ ✖) Four rooms, 12 beds, three minutes from both Hasedera and the beach. Simple but contemporary and tidy, this hostel is mostly bunk beds, with one tatami room and laundry facilities. From Kamakura station take an Enoden Enoshima train to Hase station. Breakfast/dinner available for ¥300/700.

Hotel New Kamakura (☎ 22-2230; fax 22-0223; s/d without bathroom from ¥4200/11,000, with bathroom from ¥7500/11,000; ✖) Within sight of the train platform, this handsome 1924 hotel in two buildings has Western- and Japanese-style rooms with large windows, dark wood floors, exposed beams and comfortable furnishings. Exit west from Kamakura station and take a sharp right down the alley. It's at the car park. Reservations recommended.

Komachi-sō (☎ 23-2151; s/tw ¥5000/9000; ✖) Tiny, pleasant and affordable *minshuku* with decent rooms. It's located on a narrow lane parallel to Wakamiya-ōji, just behind the back entrance to the Tsurugaoka Kaikan. Look for the *torii* in the street. Check-in is from 4pm.

Classical Hotel Ajisai (☎ 22-3492; r per person from ¥6830; ✖) Across from Tsurugaoka Hachimangū, the Ajisai is an intimate, affordable option with basic Western-style rooms and a friendly, no-nonsense host. Fourth-floor rooms have shrine views. Breakfast (¥1000) is *kamameshi* (rice in a hot pot; vegetarian version available).

Tsurugaoka Kaikan (☎ 24-1111; fax 24-1115; s/tw or d ¥8400/16,800; ✖) This 14-room hotel, with Japanese-Western combination rooms, is a popular wedding venue – great kimono-spotting on weekends. The blinding-white lobby glows with early '80s glam. Look for the sign on the front reading 'Kamakura Marriage Avenue', facing Wakamiya-ōji.

Eating

The station area bursts with restaurants and snack stands. The streets around Komachi-dōri and Wakamiya-ōji are happy hunting grounds.

Komachi-Ichiba (☎ 24-7921; most dishes ¥500-1000; ✖ lunch & dinner) Two sister restaurants make up the 'Komachi market', upstairs from Kamakura station. Fūrin is a smart *izakaya* (Japanese pub/eatery) specialising in fish and seafood like sashimi and grills, while Tenten offers tempura. Expect the sake and spirits to flow at night.

Caraway (☎ 25-0927; dishes ¥630-940; ✖ 11.30am-8pm Tue-Sun; E) This Japanese-style curry shop has an old-world charm and some unusual preparations. Go for the classic beef curry, or spring for chicken curry with Edam cheese.

Horetaro (☎ 23-8622; most dishes ¥900-1300, all you can eat from ¥1575; ✖ lunch & dinner Tue-Sun; E) *Okonomiyaki* and *monjayaki* (Osaka- and Tokyo-style savoury pancakes respectively) are the thing here, along with fried rice and other dishes you grill yourself on a teppan (steel plate) at the table. All-you-can-eat-and-drink sets including alcoholic drinks are ¥3150 for 2½ hours.

Milk Hall (☎ 22-1179; most dishes ¥700-900; ✖ 11am-10.30pm; E) *Sweet!* This quaint café-bar-antique shop serves light meals (small plates like boiled sausages or baked camembert), coffees and cocktails, and it features live jazz some nights. From Kamakura station's east exit, head two blocks down Komachi-dōri, take a left and then another left down the first alley.

Kawagoe-ya (☎ 24-2580; most meals ¥945-1365; ✖ lunch & dinner Fri-Wed) Cosy and country style, specializing in a range of Japanese foods like *soba* and *donburi* (rice with assorted toppings). The *mini-maguro-don* set (¥1365) comes with *soba* and more. It's outside Kamakura station's east exit, in the basement below McDonald's. Picture menu and plastic models available.

Snackers will love Komachi-dōri. **Kamakura Ichibanya** (☎ 22-6156) specialises in *sembei* (rice crackers); watch staff grilling them in the window or buy some 100 packaged varieties, including curry, garlic, *mentaiko* (spicy cod roe) or *uni* (sea urchin). **Imo no Kichikan** (☎ 25-6038) is famous for soft-serve sweet-potato ice cream (look for the giant plastic cone with lavender-hued ice cream), while **Toshimaya** (☎ 25-0505) sells Kamakura's *omiyage* (souvenir) of record, the *hato sabure,* large butter cookies in the shape of a dove (¥84 each or from ¥451 for five). For picnic foods for hiking or beaching, **Kinokuniya** (☎ 25-1911; ☾ 9.30am-8pm) is a ritzy supermarket out Kamakura station's west exit, with freshly made sushi, deli specialties and baked goods.

Getting There & Away

Yokosuka line trains run to Kamakura from Tokyo (¥890, 56 minutes) and Shinagawa stations, via Yokohama (¥330, 27 minutes). Alternatively, the Shōnan Shinjuku line runs from the west side of Tokyo (Shibuya, Shinjuku and Ikebukuro, all ¥890) in about one hour, though some trains require a transfer at Ōfuna, one stop before Kita-Kamakura.

The JR Kamakura–Enoshima Free Pass (from Tokyo/Yokohama ¥1970/1130) is valid for two days, covering the trip to and from Tokyo/Yokohama and unlimited use of JR trains around Kamakura, the Shōnan monorail between Ōfuna and Enoshima, and the Enoden Enoshima line.

Getting Around

You can walk to most temples and shrines from Kamakura or Kita-Kamakura station. Sites in the west, like the Daibutsu, can be reached via the Enoden Enoshima line from Kamakura station to Hase (¥190) or bus from Kamakura station stops 1 to 6. Bus trips around the area cost either ¥170 or ¥190. Another good option is renting a bicycle; **Rental Cycles** (☎ 24-2319; per hr/day ¥500/1500 Mon-Fri, ¥550/1600 Sat & Sun; ☾ 8.30am-5pm) is outside the east exit of Kamakura station, and right up the incline.

EAST OF TOKYO

Much of Chiba-ken, to the east and southeast of Tokyo, is suburbia with not many compelling reasons to visit. One notable exception is the town of Narita which, fortunately, most visitors to Japan will pass through anyway as it is the hub of the nation's international air traffic.

NARITA 成田

☎ 0476 / pop 120,000

Narita is chiefly known as the home of Japan's main international airport, but the town of Narita is a pleasant stop, with a traditional atmosphere. Its quiet streets lead to a lovely, historic temple with lush gardens – perfect for unwinding before or after a long flight or if you have a layover of a half-day or more.

You can pick up a copy of the Narita map/pamphlet at the **Narita Tourist Information Center** (☎ 24-3198; ☾ 8.30am-5.15pm) just outside the eastern exit of JR Narita station, or at the tourist information counters at Narita International Airport (p808). Maps, including local restaurants, are available at the tourist info center by the station. You might also stop by the **Narita Tourist Pavilion** (☎ 24-3232; Omotesandō; ☾ 9am-5pm Tue-Sun Oct-May, 10am-6pm Jun-Sep) for exhibits on local history. Either of the offices in town can book accommodation.

Orientation

Both the Keisei Narita and JR Narita lines stop in Narita, a couple of hundred metres apart. Both are within a block of Omotesandō, the town's very pleasant main drag lined with restaurants and shops. It winds like an eel (more on that shortly) downhill to Narita's main attractions, Narita-san-kōen and Shinshōji.

Sights & Activities

The town's centrepiece is the impressive temple **Narita-san Shinshō-ji** (成田山新勝寺; ☎ 22-2111; admission free; ☾ 24hr) and the attractive park around it, Narita-san-kōen (成田山公園). While the temple was founded in the 10th century (five of its buildings are Important Cultural Properties), the main hall is a 1968 reconstruction. The temple itself remains an important centre of the Shingon sect of Buddhism and attracts as many as 10 million visitors a year.

Amid the 165,000 sq metres of ponds and greenery of Narita-san-kōen (be sure to stroll the ponds), you'll find two museums good for real aficionados: the **Narita-san Calligraphy Museum** (成田山書道美術館; ☎ 24-0774; adult/child ¥500/300; ☾ 9am-4pm Tue-Sun), which has a good collection of *shodō* (calligraphy), and the **Reikōkan Historical Material Museum** (成田山霊光館; ☎ 22-0234; adult/child ¥300/150; ☾ 9am-4pm Tue-Sun), under the temple's upper pagoda, with artefacts from 18th-century Japanese life and various temple treasures.

Festivals & Events

Hatsumōde (New Year's Day) On a day when a large proportion of the Japanese populace visits shrines and temples to receive blessing for the new year, things get hectic at Narita-san Shinshō-ji. A high level of crowd-tolerance is a must.

Setsubun (3 February) Another notable festival at Narita-san Shinshō-ji, commemorating the last day of winter in the Japanese lunar calendar.

Taiko Matsuri (Drum Festival; first Saturday and Sunday in April) Some 30 to 40 drumming troupes from all over Japan converge on the city for a noisy, energetic weekend.

Gion Festival (Held for three days at the beginning of July) This 300-year-old festival is Narita's most spectacular, featuring colourful floats and costumed processions.

Sleeping

Narita lodging is both in the town centre (accessible by train) and closer to the airport (with airport shuttle service). Japanese-style inns are relatively scarce.

Kirinoya Ryokan (桐の屋旅館; ☎ 22-0724; www .root.or.jp/kirinoya; s/d ¥5250/9450; 🌐 🖳) OK, so it's far from the station, sights, restaurants and nightlife, it's not much to look at from the outside, the ground floor is concrete and rooms don't have private facilities. So what's the attraction? History. Billing itself as a 'ryokan museum', it's filled with armour, swords and other bric-a-brac passed down from the owners' ancestors; some rooms have carvings and paintings. It's on Higashi-sandō; take the first left after passing the entrance to Narita-san-kōen, follow the road for the next 400m and it's on the left. Meals are available.

Comfort Hotel Narita (コンフォートホテル成田; ☎ 24-6311; fax 24-6321; www.choicehotels .com; Hanazaki-chō 968; s/d/tw from ¥5800/8000/10,000; 🌐 🗶 🖳 wi-fi) This excellent-value, new business hotel lives up to its name. Within sight of Keisei Narita station, its rooms are spotless (if business-hotel small), staff have English-language maps to restaurants and such, there's a coin laundry, and breakfast and wi-fi or LAN internet connections are free. From the station, descend the east exit stairs and the hotel is on your left.

Ohgiya Ryokan (扇屋旅館; ☎ 22-1161; fax 24-1663; www.naritakanko.jp/ohgiya; s/d without bathroom ¥6300/10,500, s/d with bathroom ¥7350/13,650; 🌐 🖳) This friendly, 27-room Japanese inn has comfortable rooms; some have traditional art and woodwork and open onto a lovely garden. It's a 10-minute walk from JR Narita or Keisei Narita stations, down Omotesandō towards the temple, but forking to the left just before the tourist pavilion. It's 200m further on the left. Breakfast/dinner is available from ¥800/1575.

Airport hotels are typically big chains. For the following, it's best to go to the airport and then take the shuttle bus to your hotel:

Narita Excel Hotel Tokyū (成田エクセルホテル東急; ☎ 33-0109; fax 33-0148; www.tokyu hotels.co.jp/en/TE/TE_NARIT/index.shtml; s/d from ¥13,860/23,100; 🌐 🗶 🖳 🖳) In addition to in-room facilities, there are common baths and saunas as well as tennis court and a swimming pool (though it's open midsummer only). Women-only rooms available.

ANA Hotel Narita (全日空ホテル成田; ☎ 33-1311; fax 33-0244; www.anahotel-narita.com/english; s/d from ¥18,480/23,100; 🌐 🗶 🖳 🖳) Pick of the bunch, with fitness and sauna facilities. If you're flying ANA, you can check in at the hotel and avoid queues at the airport.

Eating & Drinking

Because of the airport, there's a higher concentration of foreigners here than just about anywhere else in Japan and Omotesandō is happy hunting ground for international cuisine. The local speciality is eel. Many places have English menus and staff who are at least somewhat proficient.

Grill House Hero's (ヒローズ; ☎ 22-9002; 845-8 Hanazaki-chō; most dishes ¥630-890; 🕑 dinner; E) The menu of this *izakaya* careens from sashimi to tempura, *okonomiyaki* to sausages, in a warehouse-like room with rustic dark beams and *ranma* (room dividers) panels dividing the booths. From JR Narita station east exit, turn where you see Mister Donut. After a couple of bends in the road, you'll see the restaurant at the bottom of a hill.

Kikuya (菊屋; ☎ 22-0236; 385 Nakamachi; sets ¥1050-2310; 🕑 lunch & dinner; E) A simple but stylish place on Omotesandō, across from the Tourist Pavilion, serving a variety of lunch and dinner sets, including sashimi, tempura and other Japanese fare. Look for the English sign reading 'Chrysanthemum Housu' (sic).

Kawatoyo Honten (川豊本店; ☎ 22-2711; 386 Nakamachi; meals ¥1260-1890; 🕑 10am-5pm Tue-Sun; E) This landmark eel house is across from the Tourist Pavilion. The most popular preparation is *unajū*, grilled, sauced and served over rice in a lacquer box. Arrive at the right time and you can watch your own eel being fished from the tank and prepared before your eyes.

Barge Inn (バージイン; ☎ 23-2546; Omotesandō; meals around ¥1500; ⓨ 10am-2am; E) A popular gathering spot for expats (especially flight crews), this sprawling, nicely aged British-style pub features billiards, a generous front patio and eclectic eats, including English meat pies and Indian tandoori chicken. There are evenings dedicated to jazz, sports, DJs or quiz nights.

Getting There & Away

From Narita International Airport you can take either the private Keisei line (¥250, five minutes) or JR (¥190/230 from Terminal 2/1, five minutes). From Tokyo, the easiest way to get to Narita is via the Keisei line from Ueno (*kyūkō* ¥810, 65 minutes). JR trains from central Tokyo usually involve a transfer at Chiba and Sakura (¥1110, 1½ hours). Note that most Keisei Skyliner or JR Narita Express trains do not stop at Narita. For more information, see p183.

IZU-SHOTŌ 伊豆諸島

Known in English as the Izu Seven Islands, the Izu-shotō are peaks of a submerged volcanic chain that starts just east of Izu-hantō and extends some 300km south into the Pacific Ocean. Although the islands are easily reached by ferry from Tokyo, they feel worlds away. Five of the seven islands are suitable for tourism, and each has a completely different character – with excellent interisland connections you could spend an enjoyable week island hopping and checking them all out. No matter which island you visit, you're sure to find yourself thinking: 'Can I really be only a few hours from downtown Tokyo?'.

Soaking in an *onsen* while gazing at the Pacific is the classic Izu-shotō activity. There is also excellent hiking up the *mostly* dormant volcanoes (Mitake-jima is still venting volcanic gases). And, in the summer, the surprisingly good beaches fill up with Tokyoites escaping the city.

The islands can be crowded in the summer high season – it's often better to visit just outside this season, but keep in mind that typhoons can wreak havoc with your plans from late summer into early fall; just leave time in your schedule for delays.

Unless you're planning to camp, we recommend getting a Japanese speaker to reserve your accommodations before you arrive.

Otherwise, tourist association offices on the islands can help with accommodation.

Getting There & Away

Tōkai Kisen Ferry Company (東海汽船; ☎ 03-5472-9999 in Japanese; www.tokaikisen.co.jp in Japanese) operates ferries between Tokyo and the Izu-shotō.

The inner group of islands (Ōshima, Toshima, Nii-jima, Shikine-jima and Kōzu-shima) is serviced by high-speed hydrofoils departing mornings from Tokyo (usually around 8am) and returning from the islands to Tokyo that same afternoon. Fares and travel times to/from Tokyo are as follows: Ōshima ¥7220, two hours; Nii-jima ¥9320, 3¼ hours; Shikine-jima ¥9320, 3¼ hours; and Kōzu-shima ¥10,020, four hours.

The inner islands are also serviced by the large passenger ferry *Camellia-maru,* which departs around 11pm and arrives in the islands early the next morning (it stops at all the islands from north to south). It returns to Tokyo the same evening. Fares (2nd class) and travel times are as follows: Ōshima ¥4440, 6¼ hours; Nii-jima ¥5960, 8¾ hours; Shikine-jima ¥5960, 9¼ hours; and Kōzu-shima ¥6330, 10¼ hours. Some of these islands are also serviced by ferries from Izu-hantō.

The outer group of islands (Miyake-jima, Mikura-jima and Hachijō-jima) is serviced by the large passenger ferry *Salvia-maru,* departing daily around 10.30pm and arriving in the islands the following morning, returning to Tokyo late the same evening. The journey between Tokyo and Hachijō-jima takes 10 hours and costs ¥8360 in 2nd class.

Ferries sail to/from from Tokyo's Takeshiba Pier, a 10-minute walk from the north exit of Hamamatsu-chō station.

ANA (全日空グループ　エアーニッポン; ☎ 0120-029-222; www.air-nippon.co.jp in Japanese) has flights between Tokyo's Haneda airport and Ōshima (¥10,500, 35 minutes) and Hachijō-jima (¥16,500, 45 minutes). **Shinchūō Kōkū** (新中央航空; ☎ 0422-31-4191; www.central-air.co.jp in Japanese) has flights between Chōfu airport (on the Keiō Line about 20 minutes from Shinjuku) and Ō-shima (¥6500, 35 minutes), Nii-jima (¥13,700, 45 minutes) and Kōzu-shima (¥14,900, 55 minutes).

Getting Around

Island hopping is easy on the daily ferries that run up and down the island chains. In addition, three ferries daily between Nii-jima and Shikine-jima (¥420, 10 minutes) make day trips possible.

Buses run on the larger islands, infrequently. Hitching, while possible, is not that easy (folks here are less inclined to stop than those elsewhere of Japan). Cars and scooters are ideal on all the islands, though you'll need an international license to rent them. Bicycle rentals are widely available, but the granny bikes on offer are no joy on hills; consider bringing your own bike.

Ō-SHIMA 大島

☎ 04992

The largest of the Izu islands and closest to Tokyo, Ōshima makes an easy overnight trip out of the city. It is dominated by 754m Mihara-san (三原山), a semi-dormant volcano that last erupted in 1986. The south coast has some good beaches, and you can round out your stay with a dip in one of the island's fine *onsen*.

Due to its proximity to the mainland, Ōshima is the most popular island in the group. It can fill up with young Tokyoites on weekends and holidays.

Information

Ō-shima Tourist Association (大島観光協会; Ō-shima Kankōkyōkai; ☎ 2-2177) Near the pier in Motomachi.

Sights & Activities

If you've never peered into the maw of a recently erupted volcano, then we highly recommend a trip to the summit of **Mihara-san**. It's an awesome experience, and the concrete eruption shelters that line the path to the crater add a certain frisson to the approach. To get there, take a bus from Motomachi port to Mihara-sancho-guchi (¥860, 50 minutes, around seven departures daily) and walk to the Kaguchi-tenbōdai observation point (about 45 minutes).

Ōshima's southernmost point, **Toushiki-no-hana** (トウシキの鼻) is rocky and wave beaten with good swimming in sheltered pools below Toushiki Camp-jo. Don't even try to swim when the waves are high. To get there, take a Seminaa-bound bus from Motomachi port to Minami-kōkō-mae (¥620, 35 minutes). About 5km east of this point is the island's best beach, **Suna-no-hama** (砂の浜), a fine stretch of black volcanic sand. Take a Seminaa-bound bus from Motomachi port to Suna-no-hama-iriguchi (¥420, 20 minutes).

Onsen are Ōshima's other main attraction. **Motomachi Hama-no-yu** (元町浜の湯; admission ¥400; 1-7pm, to 11pm Jul & Aug), 10 minutes' walk north of the port, is a fine outdoor *onsen* with great ocean views. It's mixed bathing, so swimsuits are mandatory, and it can be crowded in summer. A quieter place is **Ōshima Onsen Hotel** (大島温泉ホテル; admission ¥800; 1-9pm), an outdoor *onsen* with a good view of Mihara-yama. Take a Mihara-sancho-guchi-bound bus from Motomachi port to Mihara-yama Onsen Hotel (¥630, 20 minutes).

Sleeping & Eating

Tōshiki Camp-jō (トウシキキャンプ場; free) Very close to the Minami-kōkōmae stop, this campground has a nice location right near the sea, as well as showers and a communal cooking area.

Ryokan Kifune (旅館喜船; ☎ 2-1171; fax 2-2853; r per person incl 2 meals ¥6500) They call it a ryokan, but it's actually a collection of small cabins with a communal dining area. All rooms have private bathrooms. It's midway between Motomachi and Okadakō. Call in Japanese and the owners will pick you up at the pier.

Otomodachi (お食事処おともだち; ☎ 2-0026; meals from ¥1000; 11am-3pm & 5-9pm) This simple shokudō 50m north of the pier serves simple Japanese fare, like the *jōsashimi teishoku* (special sashimi set, ¥1200). Look for the large white menu out the front.

NII-JIMA 新島

☎ 04992

Nii-jima competes with neighbouring Shikine-jima as the most appealing island in the Izu-shotō. It's got a ripping white-sand beach, two fine *onsen* and an easy laid-back vibe that'll make you think they hauled a bit of Okinawa right to the doorstep of Tokyo. And there's a great camping ground within walking distance of the beach!

Information

Nii-jima Tourist Association (新島観光協会; Nii-jima Kankōkyōkai; ☎ 5-0048) About 200m south of the pier.

Sights & Activities

The best beach anywhere near Tokyo is Nii-jima's fantastic Habushi-ura, a blazing 6.5km stretch of white sand that runs over half the length of the island. Although it's really just a beach break, it attracts surfers from all over

Kantō. We reckon, however, that it's better for plain old swimming (as long as the waves aren't too big). On the port side of the island, Mae-hama stretches 4km and is a good alternative when Habushi-ura is too rough.

The island's other main attraction is one of Japan's most whimsical *onsen*: **Yunohama Hot Springs** (湯の浜温泉; ⏰ 24hr). This free *onsen* consists of several outdoor tubs built into the rocks overlooking the Pacific with a few Parthenon-inspired columns and structures thrown in for good measure. It's a lot of fun and it's only five minutes, walk south of the Tourist Association. Bathing suits are required. About five minutes, walk away, up the hill and inland a bit, **Mamashita Onsen** (間下温泉; regular bath ¥300, sand bath ¥700; ⏰ 10am-10pm Thu-Tue) has a good indoor bath and a sand bath – you're buried in hot sand and you lie there sweating and feeling like you're being crushed. Sounds awful, but we felt good when it was over!

Niijima's other attractions include the **Niijima Modern Glass Art Museum** (新島現代ガラスアートミュージアム; Niijima Gendai Garasu Aato Mujiamu; ☎ 5-5140; www.niijimaglass.com), 1km south of the port. There's some fine work made from naturally magnetic Koga stone (which is found only in Nii-jima and in Sicily). You can often see glassblowers in action.

Sleeping

Habushi-ura Camp-jo (羽伏浦キャンプ場; free) With a stunning mountain backdrop and spacious grassy sites, this campsite is a winner, and it's only about 10 minutes' walk to the beach. There are showers, a cooking area and fresh water.

Minshuku Hamashō (民宿 浜庄; ☎ 5-0524; fax 5-1318; r per person incl 2 meals from ¥6000) Very close to Mae-hama beach, this rambling *mishuku* has friendly owners, good seafood and a great location.

Nii-jima Grand Hotel (新島グランドホテル; ☎ 5-1661; fax 5-1668; www15.ocn.ne.jp/~nghotel in Japanese; r per person incl 2 meals from ¥8500; 🖥 wi-fi) The island's only proper hotel, only 15 minutes' walk from Habushi-ura, has pleasant, large, clean rooms with private bathrooms and a friendly young staff. The large communal bath is also a winner.

SHIKINE-JIMA 式根島
☎ 04992

About 6km south of Nii-jima is tiny Shikine-jima, only 3.8 sq km. What this island lacks

in size, it more than makes up for in charm. It's got a couple of great seaside *onsen* (all of which are free) and several good little beaches. You can easily make your way around the island on foot, or on *mama-charis* (granny bikes) that can be rented on the island.

Information

Shikine-jima Tourist Association (式根島観光協会; Shikine-jima Kankōkyōkai; ☎ 7-0170) At the pier.

Sights & Activities

Jinata Onsen (地鉈温泉; admission free; ⏰ 24hr) is one of the most dramatically located *onsen* we've seen in Japan: at the end of a narrow cleft in the rocky coastline, it looks like the work of an angry axe-wielding giant (hence the Japanese name, which translates as 'earth axe'). Try to go midway between high tide and low tide, when the temperature is ideal. Pick up a map at the Tourist Association and look for the stone sign with red arrows at the access road.

Near Ashitsuki Port, you'll find another *onsen*: picturesque **Matsugashita Miyabi-yu** (松が下雅湯; admission free; ⏰ 24hr). It's not affected by the tide and the view of the harbour is great; look for the entrance near the boat ramp. A minute or so further down the coast is **Ashizuki Onsen** (足付温泉; admission free; ⏰ 24hr), another fine *onsen* built into the rocks right at the water's edge. Like Jinata Onsen, the water temperature depends on the tide.

Tomarikō-kaigan (泊港海岸) is a picturesque little beach in a sheltered cove with calm waters perfect for children. It's about 500m northwest of the ferry port, up and over the hill. **Naka-no-ura** (中の浦海岸) and **Ō-ura** (大浦海岸) beaches are an easy walk along the same coast.

Sleeping

Kamanoshita Camp-jo (釜の下キャンプ場; free; ⏰ Sep-Jun) Right near a fine little beach and two great free *onsen*, this little camping ground is great, especially in the quieter times of year, when you might have it to yourself. No showers here, but there is one *onsen* nearby.

Ō-ura Camp-jo (大浦キャンプ場; free; ⏰ Jul & Aug) Right on a good beach, this camping ground is rather cramped and not well maintained, but the location is hard to beat. There are showers.

Kutsuroginoyado Fuminoya (くつろぎの宿ふみのや; ☎ 7-0062; fax 7-0814; r per person incl 2 meals from ¥6000) Conveniently located in the centre of the island, this classic *minshuku* has clean rooms, good food and a pleasant owner.

KŌZU-SHIMA 神津島
☎ 04992

Dominated by 572m Tenjō-san (天上山), a table-topped mountain that takes up the entire northern end of the island, Kōzu-shima is somewhat less enticing than its neighbouring islands, but it does have a couple of decent beaches, one good *onsen* and some interesting hiking trails. For thrill seekers, the island's airport, on a plateau on the southern end of the island, is the closest most of us will ever get to flying off an aircraft carrier.

Information
Kōzu-shima Tourist Association (神津島観光協会; Kōzu-shima Kankōkyōkai; ☎ 8-0321) Near the pier.

Sights & Activities
Hiking around the summit area of Tenjō-San is Kōzu-shima's main activity. The information office has excellent Japanese-language hiking maps. The hike up to the 524m **Kuroshima-Tenbō-Dai** (黒島展望台) point is a three-hour roundtrip; on clear days you'll be rewarded with a fine view of Fuji-san. From the point, you can continue along the summit plateau to **Ura-Sabaku** (裏砂漠), a sandy 'desert', and **Babaa-Ike** (ババア池), a small pond.

Back at sea level, about 1km north of the pier, the fine **Kōzu-shima Onsen** (admission ¥800; ○ 10am-9pm Thu-Tue) has three outdoor baths built into the wild rocks of the coast, plus some excellent indoor baths. You'll need a swimsuit to enter the outdoor baths.

About 2km north of the *onsen,* along the coastal road, you'll find **Akazaki Yūhodō Shiokaze-No-Michi** (赤崎遊歩道潮風の道; admission free; ○ 24hr), a fantasy land of wooden walkways, bridges, diving platforms and observation towers built around a great natural swimming inlet in the craggy coast. It's the sort of place you'd see more of if the world was ruled by children.

Sleeping
Nagahama Camp-jo (長浜キャンプ場; free) Right on the beach, with showers and barbeque grills, this camping ground is fairly close to the *onsen,* about 2km north of the pier.

Hotel Kōzukan (ホテル神津館; ☎ 8-1321; fax 8-1323; www.kozukan.yad.jp in Japanese; r per person from ¥10,500) The island's only hotel has both Japa-

nese- and Western-style rooms, with toilets but shared bathrooms. Rooms are fairly spacious and there are sunset views.

MIYAKE-JIMA 三宅島
At the time of writing, Miyake-jima, 180km south of Tokyo, was not suitable for tourism due to the 2002 eruption of its volcano, Osu-yama (雄山). Island residents have been permitted to return and ferries stop here, but tourists are not encouraged to visit. This may change, however. Check with the **Izu Seven Islands Tourist Federation** (東京諸島観光連盟 (旧名称:伊豆七島観光連盟); ☎ 03-3436-6955) for the latest conditions.

HACHIJŌ-JIMA 八丈島
☎ 04996

About 290km south of Tokyo, Hachijō-jima is the second-largest and next-to-last island in the Izu-shotō chain. Basically two dormant volcanoes connected by a flat strip of land, it's a relaxing place to spend a few days away from the Tokyo rat race. While the rocky beaches are no match for those of Nii-jima or Shikine-jima, the island has some great hiking, fine *onsen* and a laid-back vibe.

Information
Hachijōjima Tourism Association (八丈島観光協会; Hachijō-jima Kankōkyōkai; ☎ 2-1377) Next to the town hall, in the centre of the island on the main road.

Sights & Activities
The island is dominated by two dormant volcanoes, 854m Hachijō-Fuji (八丈富士) and 701m Mihara-yama (三原山), covered with lush semitropical vegetation. There is good hiking on both mountains, but if your time is limited take the three-hour trip up Hachijō-Fuji. The one-hour walk around the rim of the crater is awesome, but be careful as the footing is treacherous in places. On the Mihara-yama end of the island, try the hike to **Kara-taki** (唐滝), a lovely waterfall about an hour's hike inland and uphill from the settlement of Kashidate (get a map from the Tourist Association).

Urami-ga-taki Onsen (裏見ケ滝温泉; admission free; ○ 10am-9pm) is not to be missed. It's tucked into a thick forest overlooking a waterfall – in the late afternoon and early evening it's pure magic. You'll need a swimsuit since it's mixed bathing. Take a Sueyoshi-bound bus from the port (you may have to change at Kashitate

Onsen Mae) to Nakata-Shōten-mae and walk 20 minutes towards the ocean. Before you enter the *onsen*, take the trail from the road above and follow it upstream for a few minutes to the lovely waterfall, **Urami-ga-taki** (裏見ケ滝).

A 15-minutes walk below Urami-ga-taki Onsen, towards the sea, is **Nakanogō-Onsen Yasuragi-no-yu** (中之郷温泉 やすらぎの湯; admission ¥300; 🕙 10am-9pm Fri-Wed), a quaint local *onsen* with a fine view over the Pacific from its inside baths.

Project WAVE (🕾 2-5407; wave@isis.ocn.ne.jp) offers a variety of ecotourism options, including hiking, bird-watching, sea kayaking and scuba diving. Its owner, Iwasaki-san, speaks English.

Sleeping

Sokodo Camp-jō (底土キャンプ場; 🕾 2-1121; free) This excellent camping ground is 500m north of Sokodo pier. Toilets, cold showers and cooking facilities are available and there are two good beaches nearby. You must reserve (in Japanese only) a spot at the ward office (number above).

Ashitaba-sō (あしたば荘; 🕾 7-0434; fax 7-0434; www.8jou.com/owners/asitabahp.htm in Japanese; r per person incl 2 meals ¥6500) The owner of this good *minshuku* is a friendly, chatty fellow who serves heaped portions of locally caught seafood. It's in the hamlet of Nakanogō; the owner will pick you up at the pier provided you've made reservations in advance (in Japanese).

Kokuminshukusha San Marina (国民宿舎サンマリーナ; 🕾 2-3010; fax 2-0952; www6.ocn.ne.jp/~marina-6 in Japanese; r per person incl 2 meals ¥6825) This is a clean, fairly new, well-maintained guesthouse with good food and a convenient location, about 500m north of Sokodo pier. Turn left off the coastal road at a sign that reads 'Ocean Boulevard' and look for a big whitish building.

OGASAWARA-SHOTŌ
小笠原諸島

🕾 04998

About 1000km out in the blue expanse of the Pacific Ocean, this far-flung outpost of Tokyo Prefecture is one of Japan's most interesting destinations, a nature-lover's paradise surrounded by clear tropical waters and coral reefs. Snorkelling, whale watching, dolphin

swimming and hiking are all on the bill, as is simply lazing around on the great beaches.

The only way to get here is by a 25-hour ferry ride from Tokyo. The ferry docks at Chichi-jima (父島; Father Island), the main island of the group (population 1938). A smaller ferry connects this island to Haha-jima (母島), the other inhabited island (population 462).

The islands see few Western visitors, despite the fact that the earliest inhabitants were Westerners who set up provisioning stations for whaling ships working the Japan whaling grounds. You still see the occasional Western family name and vaguely Western visage. You'll also see disused gun emplacements at the ends of most of the islands' beaches, built by the Japanese in hopes of repelling an anticipated Allied invasion in WWII (the big battles were fought further south on Iwo-jima).

Given the islands' nature, history and location, a trip here is one of Japan's great little adventures. When your boat sails from Chichi-jima and the entire island turns out to wave you off, you'll know you've done something special.

CHICHI-JIMA 父島

Chichi-jima has plenty of accommodation, restaurants, even a bit of tame nightlife. But the real attractions are the excellent beaches and outdoor activities.

Information

Chichi-jima Tourism Association (父島観光協会; Chichi-jima Kankōkyōkai; 🕾 2-2587) In the B-Ship building, about 250m west of the pier, near the post office.

Sights & Activities

The two best beaches for snorkelling are on the north side of the island, a short walk over the hill from the village. **Miya-no-ura** (宮之浦) has decent coral and is sheltered, making it suitable for beginners. About 500m along the coast (more easily accessed from town) is Tsuri-hama (釣浜), a rocky beach that has better coral but is more exposed.

Good swimming beaches line the west side of the island, getting better the further south you go. **Kominato-kaigan** (小港海岸) is the best, easily accessible beach on this side by bus from town or by hitching. From here, you can walk over the hill and along the coast to the excellent Jinny and John Beaches, but note that it's a two-hour walk in each direction and there is no drinking water – bring at least 3L per person.

On Chichi-jima's east side is another fine beach, **Hatsune-ura** (初寝浦), at the bottom of a 1.2km trail with a 200m vertical drop. Hitching or going by scooter to the trailhead is the best bet.

Many operators, including **Chichijima Taxi** (父島タクシー; ☎ 2-3311 in Japanese) offer dolphin swimming and whale watching, as well as trips to Minami-jima, an uninhabited island with a magical secret beach called **Ōgi-ike** (扇池). Don't expect these operators to speak much English.

Sleeping & Eating

Camping is not permitted on the island.

Ogasawara Youth Hostel (小笠原ユースホステル; ☎ 2-2692; fax 2-2692; www.oyh.jp in Japanese; dm members/nonmembers incl 2 meals ¥4500/5500; ▯) This is a clean, well-run, regimented hostel about 400m southwest of the pier, near the post office.

Chichi-jima View Hotel (父島ビューホテル; ☎ 2-7845; fax 2-7846; www16.ocn.ne.jp/~view1/page006 .html; chichijimaview@alpha.ocn.ne.jp; r per person from ¥10,000) Just a minute's walk west of the pier, this hotel has large, airy rooms with private bathroom and kitchen.

Marujyō-shokudō (丸丈食堂; ☎ 2-3030; set meals from ¥800) This simple *shokudō* is where the locals come for simple but tasty sets like the sashimi set (¥840, ask for *kyō no sashimi teishoku*). It's in a blue-and-white building next to an island gift shop.

Getting There & Away

The *Chichijima Maru* sails about once a week between Tokyo's Takeshiba Pier (10 minutes from Hamamatsu-chō station) and Chichi-jima (2nd class ¥26,100 in July and August, ¥22,570 September to June, 25 hours). Contact **Ogasawara Kaiun** (小笠原海運株式会社; ☎ 03-3451-5171; www.ogasawarakaiun.co.jp/index.html in Japanese).

HAHA-JIMA 母島

Haha-jima is a quieter, less developed version of Chichi-jima, with some fine beaches on its west side and good hiking along its spine. If you really want to get away from it all, this is the place.

Information

Haha-jima Tourist Association (母島観光協会; Haha-jima Kankōkyōkai; ☎ 3-2300) In the passenger waiting room at the pier.

Sights & Activities

A road runs south from the village to the start of the **Minami-zaki Yūhodō** (南崎遊歩道), a hiking course that continues all the way to the **Minami-zaki** (南崎; literally, southern point). Along the way you'll find **Hōraine-kaigan** (蓬莢根海岸), a narrow beach with a decent off-shore coral garden, Wai Beach, the best beach on the island, with a drop-off that sometimes attracts eagle rays, and finally, Minami-zaki itself, which has a rocky, coral-strewn beach with ripping views of smaller islands to the south. Above Minami-zaki you'll find **Kofuji** (小富士), an 86m-high mini Fuji-san with fantastic views in all directions.

Sleeping & Eating

Camping is not permitted on the island.

Minshuku Nanpū (民宿ナンプー; ☎ 3-2462; fax 3-2458; r per person incl 2 meals ¥7350) This clean, new *minshuku* is about 500m northeast of the pier, with friendly owners, good food, clean rooms and a nice bath.

Getting There & Away

The *Hahajima Maru*, sails about four times a week between Chichi-jima and Haha-jima (¥3780, two hours). Contact **Ogasawara Kaiun** (小笠原海運株式会社; ☎ 03-3451-5171; www .ogasawarakaiun.co.jp/index.html in Japanese).

Central Honshū
本州中部

Central Honshū is Japan's heartland in both geography and attitude. Stretching between the two great megalopolises of Kantō (Greater Tokyo) and Kansai (Osaka–Kyoto–Kobe), the Pacific Ocean and the Sea of Japan, this region is filled with commercial centres and traditional towns, the massive Japan Alps and a rugged northern coastline.

In Central Honshū's southern prefectures, called 'Chūbu' in Japanese, trekking takes you through valleys and summits in the Japan Alps National Park, and *onsen* (mineral hot-spring) towns offer welcome recovery for the hikers and skiers, drawn to the Olympic slopes of Nagano-ken. The Sea of Japan side of this region ('Hokuriku' in Japanese) boasts cliff-top vistas, remarkable temples and incredibly fresh seafood.

Busy Nagoya, Japan's fourth-largest city, is the nation's industrial heart, with a can-do spirit and unique foods. Hokuriku's hub is Kanazawa, a historic yet thriving city whose handsome streets once housed samurai and geisha. Lovely Takayama is admired for its traditional riverside houses, delicious cuisine and verdant countryside. Matsumoto is another favourite with visitors for its striking 16th-century black-and-white castle and many galleries.

The mountainous Unesco World Heritage sites of Shirakawa-gō and Gokayama showcase Japan's rich architectural tradition, and Central Honshū is traversed by the Nakasendō, the Edo-period trunk road through the mountains.

HIGHLIGHTS

- Stroll the streets of **Takayama** (p255), with its traditional architecture and skilled woodworkers
- Hike the stunning mountain scenery of the **Kamikōchi** (p267)
- Step back in time at the National Treasure castles **Inuyama-jō** (p250) and **Matsumoto-jō** (p283)
- Discover the rugged beauty of **Noto-hantō** (p299), a windswept peninsula of fishing hamlets and seafood feasts
- Ski, ski, ski at the Olympic resorts **Shiga-Kōgen** (p279), **Nozawa Onsen** (p279) and **Hakuba** (p280)
- Take in arts in **Kanazawa**, from the ancient garden Kenroku-en (p294) to the architecturally daring 21st Century Museum (p294)
- Train with Zen Buddhist monks in the 13th-century **Eihei-ji temple** (p305) or be awed by Nagano's **Zenkō-ji** (p274)
- Sleep in a thatched-roofed house in **Shirakawa-gō** (p263)

★ Noto-hantō

Hakuba
Kanazawa ★ ★Nagano
★Hakuba

Takayama Matsumoto-jō
Eihei-ji ★ ★ ★
Kamikōchi

★Inuyama-jō

Climate

Central Honshū's climate varies with its landscape. In the Japan Alps, winters are cold and long with abundant snowfall from November to February, with the highest peaks covered until June. July and August tend to be most agreeable for hikers; the snows are generally melted and temperatures warmest. In the lowlands the best times to visit are April and May or late September to early November; temperatures are mild and clear sunny skies are the norm. Expect heavy rains in the early summer *tsuyu* (monsoon) season followed by sticky summers in the lowlands; typhoon season usually peaks in September.

National Parks

Japan Alps National Park (p267), accessible via Matsumoto or Takayama, is dotted with spectacular peaks and features *onsen* towns, ski slopes and some excellent hiking trails. A few hours west, Hakusan National Park (p304) is another fine place to enjoy the mountains, attracting skiers in the winter, hikers in the summer and *onsen*-lovers year-round.

Getting There & Away

Nagoya is the gateway to Central Honshū; its new international airport (Centrair) provides easy access. Nagoya is one of Japan's major *shinkansen* stops on the Tōkaidō line; a separate *shinkansen* line links Tokyo with Nagano.

Travellers coming from Russia can arrive by sea. Ferries operated by **FKK Air Service** (☎ 0766-22-2212; http://fkk-air.toyama-net.com in Japanese; one-way adult/child from ¥27,600/18,000) travel between Fushiki in Toyama-ken and Vladivostok, departing Vladivostok on Monday at 6pm and arriving 39 hours later in Fushiki. From Japan ferries leave on Friday at 6pm, arriving in Russia on Sunday morning.

Getting Around

Nagoya is Chūbu's transport hub. The mountainous inland is served by the JR Takayama and Chūō lines, roughly parallel from north to south with hubs in Takayama (Takayama line) and Matsumoto and Nagano (Chūō line). The JR Hokuriku line follows the coast along the Sea of Japan, linking Fukui, Kanazawa and Toyama.

Bus is the main form of transport in Chūbu's mountains, but schedules can be inconvenient or, between November and May, stop entirely (except for ski resorts).

For some destinations – particularly Noto-hantō, Shirakawa-gō and Gokayama – hiring a car makes sense.

NAGOYA 名古屋

☎ 052 / pop 2.2 million

Japan's fourth-largest city, Nagoya is an industrial powerhouse; it's also the birthplace of *pachinko* (Japanese pinball). None of this marks Nagoya as a top-rank tourist destination, but it offers a worthy castle, museum and gardens, fine foods, and plenty of urban amusement, on a far more relaxed scale than Tokyo.

Despite its size, locals and expats alike take pride in the hometown character of this friendly city that's often overlooked on tourist itineraries. Nagoya is also a convenient base for day trips nearby and to Ise-jingū (p435).

HISTORY

Nagoya did not become a unified city until 1889, but it had a strong influence for centuries before. It is the ancestral home of Japan's 'three heroes': Oda Nobunaga, the first unifier of Japan, followed by the *shōgun* Toyotomi Hideyoshi and Tokugawa Ieyasu, whose dictatorial reign from Edo also ushered in an era of peace, prosperity and the arts. Ieyasu ordered the construction of Nagoya Castle, an important outpost for 16 generations of the family.

Nagoya grew into a commercial, financial, industrial, transport and shipping hub; during WWII some 10,000 Zero fighters were produced here. This manufacturing prominence led to massive Allied bombing – citizens were evacuated and roughly one quarter of the city was obliterated. The resulting blank slate allowed officials to plan the city you see today: wide avenues, subways, gleaming skyscrapers and green space.

Today Nagoya and its surrounding prefectures would rank among the top 10 economies worldwide. Leading industries include car manufacturing, machinery, electronics and ceramics, and one look at its many department stores shows the city's thriving commercial sector.

ORIENTATION

On the western edge of the city centre, JR Nagoya station (known locally as Meieki) is

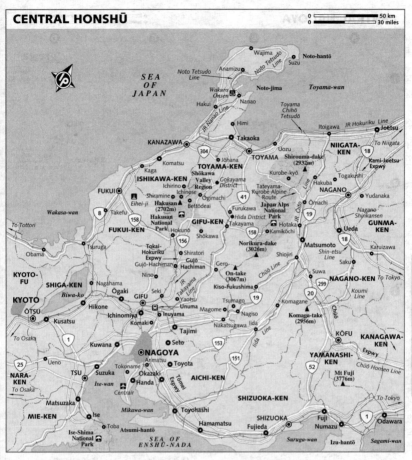

CENTRAL HONSHŪ

a city in itself with department stores, boutiques, restaurants, hotels and observation decks around the two semi-cylindrical 50-plus-storey JR Central Towers. Several train lines converge here. *Shinkansen* platforms are on the station's west side, other JR lines are in the centre, and on the east side are the private regional lines Meitetsu and Kintetsu, as well as subway and bus stations.

From the east exit, Sakura-dōri runs towards the massive TV tower, in the centre of the narrow Central Park (Hisaya-ōdōri-kōen). South and west of the TV tower are the Sakae and Nishiki districts, more atmospheric than Meieki and booming with shopping, dining and nightlife. The castle, Nagoya-jō, is just north of the city centre, while the Ōsu Kan-

non and, much further, Nagoya Port areas are to the south.

English-language signs make navigating Nagoya relatively easy.

INFORMATION
Bookshops

Nagoya has English-language bookshops both in Sakae and Meieki.

Kinokuniya Books (Map p240; ☎ 585-7526; 5th fl, Meieki 1-2-1; ⏱ 10am-8pm) In the Meitetsu Melsa building, two blocks west of Yaba-chō station.

Maruzen (Map p240; ☎ 261-2251; 3-2-7 Sakae; 🚇 Sakae) On busy Hirokoji-dōri.

Sanseidō (Map p240; ☎ 450-6004; 1-1-4 Meieki; 🚇 Nagoya) On the 11th floor of JR Takashimaya department store at Nagoya station.

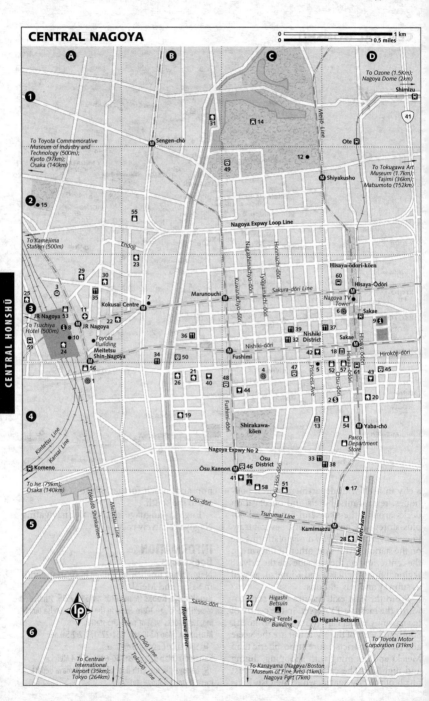

CENTRAL NAGOYA

Emergency

Kyukyuiryō Jōhō Sentā (Emergency Medical Information Centre; ☎ 263-1133) Advice (in Japanese only) on where to receive weekend and holiday emergency treatment.

Nagoya International Centre (Map p240; ☎ 581-0100; 1-47-1 Nagono; ⏰ 9am-8.30pm Tue-Sat, 9am-5pm Sun & holidays; 🚇 Kokusai Centre) Provides emergency advice; the best place to call (English is spoken).

Internet Access

Chikōraku (Map p240; ☎ 587-2528; 1-25-2 Meieki; 1st hr ¥490; ⏰ 24hr; 🚇 Nagoya) In the basement of the Meitetsu Lejac building.
Kinko's (Map p240; ☎ 231-9211; 2-3-31 Sakae; 1st 10min ¥100, 1st hr ¥1100; ⏰ 24hr; 🚇 Fushimi station)
Media Café Popeye (Map p240; ☎ 955-0059; 3-6-15 Nishiki; per hr from ¥300; ⏰ 24hr; 🚇 Sakae). One block south of Hisaya-Ōdōri station, on the 3rd floor of the Tatenomachi building facing the TV tower.
Nagoya International Centre (Map p240; ☎ 581-0100; 1-47-1 Nagono; per 15min ¥100; ⏰ 9am-7pm Tue-Sun; 🚇 Kokusai Centre)

Internet Resources

Nagoya Convention and Visitors Bureau (www .ncvb.or.jp) Good overview, including accommodation and transport.
Nagoya International Centre (www.nic-nagoya .or.jp) Up-to-date listings of local events, plus cultural and practical info.

Medical Services

Nagoya's Prefecture, **Aichi-ken** (☎ 249-9799; www .qq.pref.aichi.jp) has a list of medical institutions with English-speaking staff, including specialities and hours of operation.
Tachino Clinic (Map p240; ☎ 541-9130; Dai-Nagoya Bldg, 3-28-12 Meieki) Opposite the east exit of Nagoya station, with English-speaking staff.

Money

Citibank has some 24-hour Cirrus ATMs that are located in the Sugi building (🚇 Sakae, exit 7), in the arrival lobby at Centrair airport, and also on the 33rd floor of the JR Nagoya Towers.

Post

Eki-mae post office (Map p240) North of the station's east exit.

Nagoya station post office Off the main concourse.

Tourist Information

Useful publications for visitors include *Live Map Nagoya*, a handy brochure with just about all the tourist information you'll need, the advertising-sponsored *Info Guide* and a public transport map. English-language listings publications include *Japanzine*, *Avenues* and *Nagoya Calendar*.

Nagoya International Centre (Map p240; ☎ 581-0100; 3rd fl, Kokusai Centre Bldg, 1-47-1, Nagono; ☻ 9am-8.30pm Tue-Sat, 8am-5pm Sun & holidays; ⊚ Kokusai Centre station, exit 2) Has English-speaking staff and info on both Nagoya and regional destinations. There's a library, overseas TV newscasts and a bulletin board for postings.

Nagoya Tourist Information Nagoya station (Map p240; ☎ 541-4301; ☻ 9am-7pm) In the central concourse; Kanayama station (☎ 323-0161; ☻ 9am-7pm; ⊚ Kanayama); Oasis 21 Building (Map p240; ☎ 963-5252; ☻ 10am-8pm; ⊚ Sakae) In Sakae. All locations have at least one English speaker on hand.

SIGHTS & ACTIVITIES
Nagoya Station Area

NORITAKE GARDEN ノリタケの森
Take a stroll around the tree-planted grounds of the original factory of one of Japan's best-known **porcelain makers** (Map p240; ☎ 561-7290; www.noritake-elec.com/garden; 3-1-36 Noritake-shinmachi; garden admission free; ⊚ Kamejima). The **craft centre** (☎ 561-7114; adult/high school student/child & senior ¥500/300/free; ☻ 10am-5pm) offers a peek at the production process and a museum of old Noritake pieces, plus a chance to glaze your own dish (¥1500). The **Noritake Gallery** (☎ 562-9811; ☻ 10am-6pm Tue-Sun) has changing exhibitions of paintings, sculpture and ceramic works. Signage is in English throughout the grounds.

Naturally, there are shopping opportunities including the Box outlet store, which offers a 40% discount on discontinued items.

TOYOTA COMMEMORATIVE MUSEUM OF INDUSTRY & TECHNOLOGY
トヨタテクノミュージアム産業技術記念館
Japan may be synonymous with cars these days, but Toyota, now the world's largest auto maker, started in another very Japanese industry: weaving. A short walk northwest of Noritake Garden, this **museum** (Map p249; ☎ 551-6115; www.tcmit.org; 4-1-35 Noritake-shinmachi; adult/child ¥500/300; ☻ 9.30am-5pm Tue-Sat; ⊚ Sako, Meitetsu Nagoya line) is on the site of the company's original Nagoya weaving plant (1911). It's filled with displays and demonstrations of metal processing and textile machinery, and hands-on experiences on principles of force, electronics and such, but the rubber meets the road in the 7900-sq-metre automotive pavilion. (See boxed text, p251, for information on factory tours.)

Sakae Area

ROBOT MUSEUM ロボットミュージアム
Otaku (geeks) will be in heaven, and just about anyone will find it fascinating. This appropriately futuristic **building** (Map p240; ☎ 0120-156-610; 3-25-20 Nishiki; adult/student/child ¥1300/1000/700; ☻ 10am-8pm Mon-Fri, 10am-8pm Sat & Sun, closed 3rd Wed of month; ⊚ Sakae, exit 9), near the heart of Sakae, is a legacy of the 2005 World Expo. A ground-floor gallery displays robots, art and robot-art, while the upstairs showcases robots both real and imaginary. English-language versions of the audio guide were in the works as we went to press. A large shop sells robots both practical and fanciful.

RAN NO YAKATA ORCHID GARDENS
ランの館
These **gardens** (Map p240; ☎ 243-0511; 4-4-1 Osu; adult/child ¥700/free; ☻ 10am-8pm Thu-Tue; ⊚ Yaba-chō) contain more than 250 species of orchid presented inside a greenhouse and a walled garden, with a path leading through the flowering plants. There are indoor and outdoor cafés.

INTERNATIONAL DESIGN CENTRE NAGOYA
国際デザインセンター
Just a short walk from Sakae, the futuristic swooping skyscraper Nadya Park houses this **museum** (Map p240; ☎ 265-2106; 4th fl, 3-18-1 Sakae; adult/student/child under 16 ¥300/200/free; ☻ 11am-8pm Wed-Mon; ⊚ Yaba-chō, exit 5 or 6). It's a secular shrine to the deities of conceptualisation, form and function, from Art Deco to the present, from the Electrolux to Isamu Noguchi, from Arne Jacobsen to the Mini Cooper. Signage is in English.

Also in Nadya Park is the Loft department store, which design-shoppers will find equally alluring. Nadya Park is about five minutes walk from Yaba-chō station.

North of the City Centre

NAGOYA-JŌ 名古屋城

Tokugawa Ieyasu ordered **Nagoya Castle** (Map p240; ☎ 231-1700; 1-1 Honmaru; adult/child under 15 yrs ¥500/100; ☒ 9am-4.30pm; ⓡ Shiyakusho, exit 7) to be built for his ninth son on the site of an older castle, from 1610 to 1614. Although it was destroyed in WWII and replaced in 1959 with a ferroconcrete replica, it's worth a visit for the fine museum inside featuring armour, treasures and histories of the Oda, Toyotomi and Tokugawa families. A lift will save you climbing stairs. Note the 3m-long replicas of the famous *shachi-hoko*, gilded dolphinlike sea creatures, at either end of the roof (and in every souvenir shop).

Within the castle grounds, the garden, Ninomaru-en (二の丸園), has a teahouse in an attractive setting. It's lovely during the cherry-blossom season, and on Fridays ceremonial tea is served here from a golden urn (¥525). Nearby is the elegant **Nagoya Noh Theatre** (Map p240; ☎ 231-0088; 1-1-1 San-no-maru; admission free; ☒ 9am-5pm), which has a small museum.

TOKUGAWA ART MUSEUM 徳川美術館

A must for anyone with even a passing interest in Japanese culture and history, this **museum** (Map p240; ☎ 935-6262; www.tokugawa-art-museum.jp; 1017 Tokugawa-chō; adult/senior/student/child/child under 7 ¥1200/1000/700/500/free; ☒ 10am-5pm Tue-Sun) has a 10,000-plus piece collection that includes national treasures and important cultural properties that once belonged to the *shōgunal* family: furnishings, arms and armour, tea-ceremony implements, calligraphy, painted scrolls, masks and costumes from the Nō theatre, and lacquerware. A priceless 12th-century scroll depicting *The Tale of Genji* (see p64) is locked away except for a short stint in late November; the rest of the year, visitors must remain content with a video.

The museum is three minutes' walk from the Tokugawaen-Shindeki bus stop, east of Nagoya-jō. Several buses serve the stop from the Nagoya station and Sakae areas.

South of the City Centre

ŌSU KANNON AREA 大須観音周辺

The much-visited **Ōsu Kannon temple** (admission free; ☒ 5.30am-7pm; ⓡ Ōsu Kannon, exit 2) traces its roots back to 1333. The temple was considered so auspicious that Tokugawa Ieyasu ordered that it be moved here around 1610. Although the current buildings are 20th-century reconstructions, it still retains a traditional atmosphere. It's not uncommon to hear chanting piped in throughout the temple grounds.

Ōsu is equally famous for the vibrant shopping district that draws bargain hunters. See Shopping (p247).

ATSUTA-JINGŪ 熱田神宮

Hidden among 1000-year-old cypress trees, the 1900-year-old **Atsuta-jingū** (Map p249; ☎ 671-4151; www.atsutajingu.or.jp; 1-1-1 Jingū; admission free; ☒ 24hr; ⓡ Jingū-mae, Meitetsu Honsen line or Jingu-nishi, exit 2) is one of the most sacred shrines in all of Shintō. It is said to house the *kusanagi-no-tsurugi* (sacred sword: literally, the 'grass-cutting sword'), one of the *sanshu no jingi* (three regalia) that were, according to legend, handed down to the imperial family by the goddess Amaterasu Ōmikami. (The other two are the curved jewels at the Imperial Palace in Tokyo, p110, and the sacred mirror housed at Ise Jingū, p435.) You won't be able to view the regalia but don't feel left out; no one but the emperor and a few selected Shintō priests ever gets to see them.

There is a small **museum** (Treasure Hall; Hōmotsu-kan; ☎ 671-0852; adult/child ¥300/150; ☒ 9am-4.30pm, closed last Wed of month), housing Tokugawa-era swords, masks and paintings, including some important cultural properties.

The shrine is about three minutes' walk west from Jingū-mae station on the Meitetsu Nagoya Honsen line, or five minutes' walk east from Jingū-nishi station on the Meijō subway line.

NAGOYA/BOSTON MUSEUM OF FINE ARTS 名古屋ボストン美術館

This excellent **museum** (Map p249; ☎ 684-0786; www.nagoya-boston.or.jp; 1-1-1 Kanayama-chō; adult/senior & student/child special & long-term exhibitions ¥1200/900/free, long-term exhibitions only ¥400/300/free; ☒ 10am-7pm Tue-Fri, 10am-5pm Sat & Sun; ⓡ Kanayama station JR, Meitetsu or Meijō subway lines) is a collaborative effort between Japanese backers and the Museum of Fine Arts, Boston. Rotating exhibitions showcase both Japanese and non-Japanese masterpieces, and have good English signage.

The museum is to the right of the south exit of Kanayama Station.

NAGOYA PORT AREA 名古屋港

Redeveloped to attract tourists, the **cargo port** (ⓡ Nagoya-kō station, Meijō subway line) now boasts several attractions. The hi-tech **Port of Nagoya Public Aquarium** (Map p249; ☎ 654-7000; www .nagoyaaqua.jp; 1-3 Minatomachi; adult/child ¥2000/1000; ◷ 9.30am-8pm Tue-Sun 21 Jul-31 Aug, 9.30am-5.30pm Apr-20 Jul & Sep-Nov, 9.30am-5pm rest of year) is one of Japan's largest and it's generally a hit with kids. The **Port Building** (Map p249; ☎ 652-1111; 1-3 Minatomachi; ◷ 9museum .30am-5pm Tue-Sun) offers good views of the harbour and Ise Bay from 53m up and also contains a Maritime Museum on the 3rd floor and the Fuji Antarctic Exploration Ship outside. Admission to any of the Port Building attractions is ¥300/200 (adult/child) individually, ¥700/400 for all three, or ¥2400/1200 including the aquarium. Attractions are signposted in English.

Allow 30 minutes to reach Nagoya Port from Nagoya station by train.

FESTIVALS & EVENTS

Atsuta Matsuri Displays of martial arts, sumō and fireworks in early June at Atsuta-jingū (p243).

Tennō Matsuri On the first Saturday and Sunday of June there's a parade of floats with large *karakuri* (mechanical puppets) around the shrine, Susano-o-jinja, near the Tokugawa Art Museum (p243).

Nagoya Basho sumō tournament One of six annual championship tournaments, held on the first to third Sunday of July at Aichi Prefectural Gymnasium (Map p240; ☎ 962-9300; 1-1 Honmaru; seats from ¥2800). Arrive early in the afternoon to watch the lower-ranked wrestlers up close.

Minato Matsuri Street parade in Nagoya Port, around 20 July, with 1500-plus dancers, a water-logging contest dating back to the Edo period and fireworks.

Nagoya Matsuri At Hisaya-ōdōri-kōen, Nagoya's big annual event (mid-October) includes costume parades, processions of floats with *karakuri* puppets, folk dancing, music and a parade of decorated cars.

Kiku-no-hana Taikai Chrysanthemum Exhibition at Nagoya-jō in late October to late November. A *ningyō* (doll) pavilion incorporates the flowers into scenes from Japanese history and legend.

SLEEPING

Accommodation in Nagoya is clustered around Nagoya station and Sakae. As a rule, Nagoya's ryokan do not have en-suite toilet or bathing facilities except as noted.

Budget

Aichi-ken Seinen-kaikan Youth Hostel (Map p240; ☎ 221-6001; fax 204-3508; www.jyh.or.jp; 1-18-8 Sakae; dm ¥2992; ☒ Fushimi, exit 7) This central, 50-bed hostel is usually the first budget place to fill

up. It has dorms, private single rooms and Japanese-style family rooms. From the station, walk three blocks west and take a left after the Hilton, from where it's two blocks further south. Check-in is 3pm to 8pm, curfew 11pm.

Kimiya Ryokan (Map p240; ☎ 551-0498; fax 565-0465; hott@hotmail.com; 2-20-16 Nagono; r per person ¥4500; ☒ ; ☒ Kokusai Centre, exit 1) This friendly 14-room family-run ryokan is good value for its tatami rooms. The best ones overlook the garden. Not much English is spoken, but the owners dispense a helpful map and prepare Japanese meals (extra charge). From the subway, walk north about five minutes. It's on the left; if you reach Endōji shopping arcade, you've passed it.

Ryokan Meiryū (Map p240; ☎ 331-8686; fax 321-6119; www.japan-net.ne.jp/~meiryu; 2-4-21 Kamimaezu; s/d ¥5250/8400; ☒ ☐ ; ☒ Kamimaezu, exit 3) This 22-room ryokan doesn't look like much from the outside, but inside it's quite professional, with friendly English-speaking staff, coin laundry, women's communal bath and a steam room in the men's. Home-style Japanese meals are available. From the station, walk along the street and take the first left. It's 1½ blocks down, on the left.

Ryokan Marutame (Map p240; ☎ 321-7130; fax 321-3626; www.jin.ne.jp/marutame; 2-6-17 Tachibana; s/tw/tr ¥5040/8820/11,340; ☒ ; ☒ Higashi Betsuin, exit 4) Narrow staircases testify to this ryokan's 50-plus–year history, yet it's modern with clean but basic rooms, English-speaking staff, coin-operated laundry and simple Japanese meals (extra charge). Try for the lovely private *hanare* (apart) room in the back garden. From the station, cross the street, walk past the Nagoya Terebi building and Higashi Betsuin temple and turn right. It's on the left.

The Nagoya station area also offers a couple of capsule hotels, although they're available for male visitors only. For approximately ¥3500, guests get a sarcophagus-sized cubicle with air vent and TV, and use of the common baths. Ask at tourist information offices for referrals.

Midrange

Petit Ryokan Ichifuji (Map p249; ☎ 914-2867; fax 981-6836; www.jin.ne.jp/ichifuji; 1-7 Saikōbashi-dōri, kita-ku; s/d incl breakfast from ¥6100/9600; ☒ ☐ ; ☒ Heiandori, exit 2) Well worth the 20-minute subway ride from Nagoya station. It's dramatically lit, clean and comfortable with designer basins and a communal cypress-wood bath. Japanese-Western fusion dinner is available with advance notice; after dinner the dining room turns into a little bar. From the station, walk south (right) for three minutes. The ryokan is signposted in English, down a gravel alley across from the Pola store.

Tōyoko Inn Nagoya-eki Sakura-dōri-guchi Shinkan (Map p240; ☎ 562-1045; fax 562-1046; www.toyoko-inn .com; 3-9-16 Meieki; s/d or tw ¥6510/8610; ✗ ✗ ☐ wifi; ☒ Nagoya, Sakura-dori exit) Everyone likes free stuff, and this new business hotel gives simple Japanese breakfast, water and coffee, internet access and even short phone calls…all before you leave the lobby. It's almost enough to make up for the microscopic rooms. Note: this is the *shinkan* (new building); there's an older building *(honkan)* diagonally across the street.

Roynet Hotel Nagoya (Map p240; ☎ 212-1055; fax 212-1077; www.roynet.co.jp; 1-2-7 Sakae; s/d/tw from ¥7800/10,800/15,500; ✗ ✗ ☐ ; ☒ Fushimi, exit 7) This new business hotel offers relatively large, spic-n-span rooms in a handsome shell, with darkwood furniture, hi-tech desk lamps and English-language news on flat-panel TVs. Rates quoted here are 'member' rates; become a member on registration. It's four minutes' walk from the station, past the Hilton along Hirokōji-dōri.

B Nagoya (Map p240; ☎ 241-1500; fax 264-1732; www .ishinhotels.com; 4-15-23 Sakae; s/d or tw from ¥8800/12,000; ✗ ✗ ☐ ; ☒ Sakae, exit 13) Finally, a hotel in Sakae that's as stylish as it is functional. Opened in 2006, its rooms make up in panache (think PJs with piping and embroidered logos) for what they lack in space. Buffet breakfast is a bargain at ¥500.

Tsuchiya Hotel (Map p249; ☎ 451-0028, toll-free 0120-144-028; fax 451-9361; www.tsuchiya-hotel.co.jp; 1-1-2 Meieki; per person from ¥8400; ✗ ☐ ; ☒ Nagoya, west exit) This Tsuchiya oozes character despite its nondescript neighbourhood. Craft-style tiles line the hallways to Japanese-style rooms. Some have private facilities, but you'll want to use the common baths: a pottery tub in this region's famous *Mino-yaki* style for the ladies or stone for the gents. Meals and station pick-up available with advance notice.

Hotel Castle Plaza (Map p240; ☎ 581-2121; fax 582-8666; www.castle.co.jp/plaza; 4-3-25 Meieki; s/d or tw from ¥10,972/15,015; ✗ ✗ ☐ ☒ ; ☒ Nagoya, Sakura-dōri exit) A sane, reasonably priced choice a few minutes cast of Nagoya station. Kind, efficient and English-speaking staff; the café-bar has a

retro-mod mid-century charm; and there's a fitness club with swimming pool.

Natural Hotel Elséreine (Map p240; ☎ 459-5344, toll free 0120-793-489; fax 453-7188; www.htl-el.com; 1-23 Tsubaki-cho; s/tw from ¥11,500/18,480; ✗ ✗ ☐ ; ☒ Nagoya, west exit) Walk past those drab business hotels out Meieki's west exit to this new, gracious, all-nonsmoking hotel. Beds of flowering plants grace the lobby. Rooms, while not breaking any size records, are comfy and sparkling clean.

Top End

Hilton Nagoy (Map p240; ☎ 212-1111, toll-free 0120-489-852; fax 212-1225; www.hilton.com; 1-3-3 Sakae; s/d from ¥16,500/23,500; ✗ ✗ ☐ ☒ wi-fi; ☒ Fushimi, exit 7) You are greeted by a soaring lobby with piano player and manicured shrubs. Western-style rooms have Japanese touches like *shoji* and blackout panels on the windows. There's a well-equipped fitness centre and great views from the top-storey bar.

Sofitel the Cypress Nagoya (Map p240; ☎ 571-0111; fax 569-1717; www.sofitelthecypress.com; 2-43-6 Meieki; s/d from ¥20,000/25,000; ✗ ✗ ☐ ; ☒ Nagoya) A quiet atmosphere prevails steps from Meieki in this 115-room European-style hotel. Deluxe doubles offer extra space and interesting layouts. From Nagoya station, exit on the Sakura-dori side, turn left and cross by the post office.

our pick Nagoya Marriott Associa Hotel (Map p240; ☎ 584-1111; fax 584-1112; www.associa.com/english /nma; 1-1-2 Meieki; s/d from ¥20,000/28,000; ✗ ✗ ☐ ; ☒ Nagoya) The Marriott literally begins where other hotels leave off. The palmy lobby (accessed via elevator from Nagoya station) is on the 15th floor, and 774 spacious rooms start from the 20th, fitted with deluxe everything. The 18th-storey gym has views across the city.

Westin Nagoya Castle (Map p240; ☎ 521-2121; fax 531-3313; www.castle.co.jp; 3-19 Hinokuchi-cho; s/d from ¥16,000/33,000; ✗ ✗ ☐ ☒ ; ☒ Sengen-chō) You can't get closer to Nagoya-jō than this, across the moat. The Castle is popular with executives for its 'heavenly beds', spacious bathrooms, fitness facilities and restaurants. Look for web-only specials. Shuttle bus to/from Nagoya station.

EATING

Nagoya is famous for local specialities which, unlike elsewhere in Japan, are also palatable to non-Japanese tastes. *Kishimen* are flat, hand-made noodles; *miso-nikomi udon* is noodles in hearty miso broth, and *miso-katsu* is breaded, fried pork cutlet with miso sauce. *Kōchin* (free-range chicken) and *hitsumabushi* (*unagi* – eel – sets) are also popular, and there's plenty of international fare.

Sakae has the best restaurant browsing.

Yamamotoya-Sōhonke (Map p240; ☎ 222-0253; 2-2-16 Nishiki; dishes ¥924-1606; ☷ 11am-midnight Sun-Thu, 11am-3am Fri & Sat; ☳ Sakae) Since 1925 Yamamotoya has been dishing out *miso-nikomi udon*. The branch near Sakae is open good and late.

Ebisuya (Map p240; ☎ 961-3412; 3-20-7 Sakae; dishes from ¥650; ☷ lunch & dinner Mon-Sat; ☳ Sakae) One of the city's best-known *kishimen* chains, Ebisuya has a laid-back atmosphere and tasty, inexpensive bowls of noodles, which you can often catch chefs making. Picture menu available.

Torigin Honten (Map p240; ☎ 973-3000; 3-14-22 Nishiki; dishes ¥450-1750; ☷ dinner; E; ☳ Sakae) For top *kōchin*, Torigin has been going strong for decades. Chicken is served in many forms, including *kushiyaki* (skewered), *kara-age* (deep-fried chicken pieces), *zōsui* (mild rice hotpot) and sashimi (what you think it is). Individual dishes are a bit dainty for the price, but *teishoku* (set menus; from ¥3000) are more substantial. It's next door to Sabatini.

Yabaton (Map p240; ☎ 252-8810; 3-6-18 Ōsu; dishes ¥735-1365; ☷ lunch & dinner Tue-Sun; E; ☳ Yaba-chō, exit 4) Throw dietary caution to the wind at this spotless, workmanlike local institution for *miso-katsu* since 1947. *Waraji-tonkatsu* is a cutlet flattened to big-as-your-head, or try *kani-korokke* (crab croquettes). *Yabaton-salada* (boiled pork with miso sesame sauce over vegetables) is almost good for you. Look for the pig-in-an-apron logo.

Misen (Map p240; ☎ 238-7357; 3-6-3 Ōsu; dishes ¥580-1680; ☷ 5.30pm-2am; ☳ Yaba-chō, exit 4) Around the corner from Yabaton, Misen has little atmosphere and no English menu, but the *Taiwan rāmen* (¥580) induces rapture, a spicy concoction of ground meat, chilli, garlic and green onion, served over noodles in a hearty clear broth. Other faves include *gomoku mame-itame* (stir-fried green beans with meat; ¥800) and *mabō-dōfu* (tofu in spicy meat sauce; ¥700).

Atsuta Horaiken (Map p249; ☎ 682-5598; 2-10-26 Jingu, Atsuta-ku; mains ¥1680-2520; ☷ lunch & dinner Wed-Mon; ☳ Temma-chō) Near Atsuta Shrine, this revered *hitsumabushi* shop has been in business since 1873. Expect a long queue during the summer peak season for Horaiken's charcoal-grilled eel, basted in a secret *tare* (sauce) and served atop rice in a lacquered box. Set menus (from ¥2520) include sides like green onion and wasabi for making *ochazuke* (tea-based broth).

Tarafuku (Map p240; ☎ 566-5600; 3-17-26 Meieki; dishes ¥400-800, omakase course from ¥3000; ☷ dinner; ☳ Nagoya) Ambitious, young gourmets have turned the *izakaya* (Japanese pub) concept on its head, installing a stainless-steel kitchen in a falling-down house. Fusion dishes include airy potato croquettes in a fried tofu crust; tomato and eggplant au gratin; house-cured ham, or beef in wine sauce. There are 150-plus varieties of wine, plus *shochu*, sake and 50-plus cocktails. It's diagonally across from both Tōyoko Inns.

Nanaya Colonial (Map p240; ☎ 587-5778; 5-24-1 Meieki; dishes ¥480-980; ☷ lunch Mon-Fri, dinner; E; ☳ Fushimi, exit 8) This fashionable restaurant overlooking the Hori-kawa serves beautifully presented Pan-Asian dishes to match its Asian-modern style. Among the eclectic choices: Chinese yam with scallops, rare tuna steak and grilled eel with rice. Open 'til midnight for stylish drinks, too.

Tiger Café (Map p240; ☎ 220-0031; 1-8-26 Nishiki; sandwiches/lunch specials from ¥500/800; E; ☷ 11am-3am Mon-Sat, 11am-midnight Sun; ☳ Fushimi) Fashionistas grace the windows of this re-creation of a Parisian bistro, with tiled floors, sidewalk seating and Deco details. Smoked salmon sandwich and the *croque-monsieur* (toasted ham and cheese sandwich) are favourites, as are the good-value lunch specials.

DRINKING

Heaven's Door (Map p240; ☎ 971-7080; 3-23-10 Nishiki; ☷ 6pm-4am Tue-Sun; ☳ Sakae, exit 8) Probably Nagoya's best bar, Heaven's Door follows a simple recipe: cosy ambience, friendly staff and fantastic music (all vinyl, no less). Rolling Stones fans should visit just to see the loo. From Sakae station, walk one block west down Nishiki-dōri and take a left. It's on the right, down the stairs next to CoCo Curry House.

Eric Life (Map p240; ☎ 222-1555; 2-11-18 Ōsu; ☷ noon-midnight Thu-Tue; ☳ Ōsu Kannon, exit 2) Minimalist and kitsch-free café behind Ōsu Kannon, perfect for chilling over a coffee, cocktail or snack. Being in the Ōsu district it gets a youngish crowd.

Shooters (Map p240; ☎ 202-7077; 2-9-26 Sakae; ☷ 5pm-3am Mon-Fri, 11.30am-3am Sat & Sun; ☳ Fushimi, exit 5) This US-style sports bar attracts a mostly *gaijin* (foreign), mostly raucous crowd. Japanese and foreign staff pour daily drink specials, and the menu includes burgers, pasta and Tex-Mex.

Elephant's Nest (Map p240; ☎ 232-4360; 1-4-3 Sakae; ✆ 5.30pm-1am Sun-Thu, 5.30am-2am Fri & Sat; 🚇 Fushimi, exit 7) Near the Hilton, Elephant's Nest is another favourite expat haunt, with a welcoming vibe, darts and traditional English fare. It's on the 2nd floor.

Red Rock Bar & Grill (Map p240; ☎ 262-7893; 4-14-6 Sakae; ✆ 5.30pm until late Tue-Sun) In Sakae, the Aussie-owned Red Rock has a warm ambience and plenty of tasty pub food.

ENTERTAINMENT

Nagoya's nightlife might not match Tokyo's or Osaka's, but what it lacks in scale it makes up for in ebullience.

For movie listings in English, www.nagoya movies.com has detailed info including maps showing the theatres. Check English-language listings magazines for dates and times of clubs. The website www.mangafrog.com also has updated club gig listings.

Misono-za (☎ 222-1481; www.misonoza.co.jp in Japanese; 1-6-14 Sakae; 🚇 Fushimi, exit 6) The city's venue for kabuki theatre in April and October, although it does not have the translation facilities of theatres in other cities.

Nagoya Noh Theatre (Map p240; ☎ 231-0088; 1-1-1 San-no-maru) In the grounds of Nagoya-jō.

Nagoya Dome (Map p249; ☎ 719-2121; 🚇 Nagoya Dome-mae Yada) Baseball fans will want to visit this 45,000-seat stadium, home of the Chunichi Dragons baseball team. Large concerts also take place here.

Electric Lady Land (☎ 201-5004; www.ell.co.jp in Japanese; 2-10-43 Ōsu; 🚇 Ōsu Kannon, exit 2) An intimate concert venue purveying the underground music scene in a cool post-industrial setting. Nationally known bands perform in the 1st-floor hall, while the 3rd floor sees more up-and-coming acts.

Club JB's (Map p240; ☎ 241-2234; www.shscity.com/jbs; 4-3-15 Sakae) Club kids (20 and over) come for an excellent sound system and famous DJs.

Emporium (Map p240; ☎ 269-1731; www.statexs.co.jp /english/index.html; 3-10-14 Sakae, 9th floor Lion Bldg Sakae) An English owner brings a bit of Brit-club culture to Nagoya. Salarimen are known to frequent the place, but don't let that put you off. The interior and sound system are primo.

Shu (Map p240; ☎ 223-3788; www.geocities.com /mensbar_shu_japan; 10-15 Nishiki 1-chome; ✆ Wed-Mon;

🚇 Fushimi, exit 7) There aren't a whole lot of options for gay visitors to Nagoya (especially those from overseas), but this bar for gay men, opened earlier this decade, welcomes all ages and nationalities.

SHOPPING

Nagoya and the surrounding area are known for arts and crafts, including *Arimatsu-narumi shibori* (elegant tie-dying from Arimatsu, p248), cloisonné, ceramics and *Seki* blades (swords, knives, scissors etc).

The streets around the Ōsu Kannon temple host some of Nagoya's most enthusiastic browsers. Along Ōsu Kannon-dōri and its continuation, Banshō-ji-dōri, a youthful energy fills vintage clothing shops, electronics and music shops, cafés and a hodge-podge of old and new; look for **yen=g** (Map p240; ☎ 218-2122; 2-20-25 Ōsu), which sells used clothing by weight, or **Kurazanmai** (Map p240; ☎ 0120-553-584; 3-25-25 Ōsu) for discount kimono, obi and accessories (though still not *cheap*-cheap). Just east of this district, Ōtsu-dōri is called the Akihabara of Nagoya for its proliferation of manga shops. The temple itself hosts a colourful antique market on the 18th and 28th of each month, while the temple **Higashi-Betsuin** (Map p240; ☎ 321-9201; 🚇 Higashi Betsuin, exit 4) has a flea market on the 12th of each month.

The speciality in the Meidōchō district, north of Nagoya station and west of Nagoya-jō, is *okashi*, Japanese snacks and penny nibbles (*sembei* rice crackers to sweet-potato sticks, dried fish to sponge cake), plus small toys like action figures, beads and balloons. Dozens of wholesalers display their wares in a manner that may dispel any notion of Japanese neatness.

Other major shopping districts are in Sakae and around Nagoya station with malls above ground and below. For crafts, browse in the giant department stores, such as Matsuzakaya (two locations, next to Nagoya station and in Sakae), Maruei and Mitsukoshi in Sakae, or Takashimaya or Meitetsu & Kintetsu near Nagoya station.

For more shopping possibilities, see Noritake Garden (p242).

GETTING THERE & AWAY
Air

Nagoyans rave about **Central Japan International Airport (Centrair)** (NGO; ☎ 0569-38-1195; www.centrair

.jp/en/), the city's newest gateway. It opened in 2005 on a manmade island in Ise-wan (Ise Bay), 35km south of the city, with a shopping mall and *onsen* bath in the building. Coming from Tokyo, the *shinkansen* is generally quicker (two hours) than flying.

Nagoya is well served by about 30 airlines from around the world. Some 430 flights per week connect Centrair with 32 international cities (in Europe, North America, Australia and especially Asia) and 22 Japanese cities. Check with travel agents for the latest schedules and fares. Note that if you're coming from Tokyo, Osaka or Kyoto, the *shinkansen* is quicker than flying once you add in airport transfers and such.

Boat

Taiheiyo ferry (☎ 582-8611) runs between Nagoya and Tomakomai (Hokkaidō, from ¥9400, 38½ hours) via Sendai (from ¥6100, 21 hours) every second evening at 8pm. Take the Meijō subway south to its terminus at Nagoya-kō Station and head for Nagoya port.

Bus

JR and **Meitetsu Highway buses** (☎ 563-0489) operate services between Nagoya and Kyoto (¥2500, 2½ hours, hourly), Osaka (¥2900, three hours, hourly), Kanazawa (¥4060, four hours, 10 daily) and Tokyo (¥5100, six hours, 14 daily). Overnight buses run to Hiroshima (¥8400, nine hours).

Train

Nagoya is a major *shinkansen* hub, including *Nozomi* trains, with fares and times as follows: Tokyo (¥10,580, two hours), Osaka (¥6380, one hour), Kyoto (¥5440, 44 minutes) and Hiroshima (¥13,530, three hours). The Kintetsu line also has indirect services to Nara (*tokkyū*, ¥3750, 2¼ hours), though services are faster via *shinkansen* with a transfer in Kyoto.

To the Japan Alps, you can take the JR Chūō line to Nagano (Shinano *tokkyū*, ¥7330, 2¾ hours) via Matsumoto (¥6070, two hours). A separate line serves Takayama (Hida *tokkyū*, ¥6070, 2¼ hours).

GETTING AROUND
To/From the Airport

Central Japan International Airport is accessible from Nagoya station via the Meitetsu Kūkō (Airport) line. Express trains take 28 minutes (¥870).

Bus

Trains run a few times per hour between central Nagoya and the airport terminal. We can't imagine why you'd want to take the bus, but some 17 buses a day run between the airport and Nagoya Station area (¥1500, 80 minutes). Alternatively, you can expect to pay as much as ¥13,100 from central Nagoya by taxi.

Subway

Nagoya's **Transportation Bureau** (www.kotsu.city .nagoya.jp) operates an excellent subway system with six lines, clearly signposted in English and Japanese. The most useful lines for visitors are the Meijō (purple), Higashiyama (yellow) and Sakura-dōri (red) lines. The last two serve Nagoya station. Fares cost ¥200 to ¥320. If you plan to do a lot of travel by bus and subway, a one-day pass (¥850, ¥740 for subway only), available at subway stations, includes all transport plus discounted admission to many attractions. On Saturday and Sunday the *donichi eco-kippu* (Saturday-Sunday eco-ticket) gives the same benefits for ¥600.

AROUND NAGOYA
名古屋近辺

The main destinations in this area, consisting of outlying Aichi-ken and southern Gifu-ken, are easy day trips from Nagoya. Inuyama has a National Treasure castle and some worthwhile side trips, and both Inuyama and the city of Gifu are famed for *ukai* (cormorant fishing), in which the trained birds, with cords around their necks, dive for river trout and smelts. Gujō-Hachiman is an attractive mountain town crisscrossed by rivers and is the workshop of the nation's plastic food samples.

ARIMATSU 有松
☎ 052

For centuries, this suburb southeast of central Nagoya has been famous for the art of *shibori* (tie-dyeing). No 1960s flower-power here: Arimatsu *shibori* artists tie cotton threads to create precise patterns. The tiny boxes of the *kanoko* (fawn spot) pattern are perhaps the most recognisable style, but there over 100 others. To tie and dye the fabric for a full kimono takes four to six months.

At the **Arimatsu-Narumi Shibori Kaikan** (有松 鳴海絞会館; Tie-Dyeing Museum; ☎ 621-0111; www

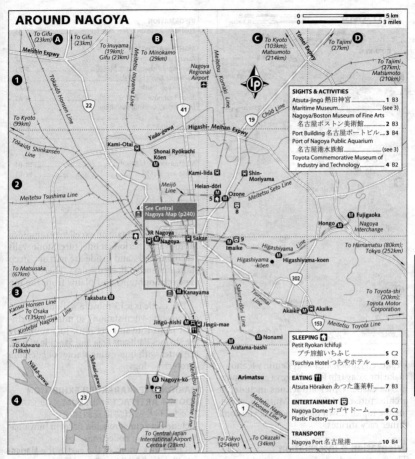

AROUND NAGOYA

0 — 5 km
0 — 3 miles

SIGHTS & ACTIVITIES
Atsuta-jingū 熱田神宮 **1** B3
Maritime Museum ....(see 3)
Nagoya/Boston Museum of Fine Arts
名古屋ボストン美術館 **2** B3
Port Building 名古屋ポートビル ... **3** B4
Port of Nagoya Public Aquarium
名古屋港水族館 ....(see 3)
Toyota Commemorative Museum of
Industry and Technology................ **4** B2

SLEEPING
Petit Ryokan Ichifuji
プチ旅館いちふじ **5** C2
Tsuchiya Hotel つちやホテル **6** B2

EATING
Atsuta Hōraiken あつた蓬莱軒..... **7** B3

ENTERTAINMENT
Nagoya Dome ナゴヤドーム **8** C2
Plastic Factory.................................. **9** C3

TRANSPORT
Nagoya Port 名古屋港.................... **10** B4

CENTRAL HONSHŪ

.shibori-kaikan.com/kaikan-e.html; admission free, film &
exhibitions adult/child ¥300/100; 9.30am-5pm Thu-Tue),
a video in English explains the process and
artisans are on hand to demonstrate. Shops
at the museum and along the main street sell
shibori products.

Floats used in the town's festival feature
kakakuri depicting – wait for it – *shibori*. The
oldest float dates from 1674, and you can see
one on display at the small **Arimatsu Dashi Kaikan**
(有松山車会館; Festival Float Museum; 621-3000;
admission ¥200; 9am-4pm).

Arimatsu was also a stop along the Tōkaidō
(see boxed text, p189); you can see it in Hiroshige's 53 Views of the Tōkaidō. The main
street, with its Edo-period wooden structures
including some historic merchant homes,

has been designated a historic preservation
zone.

Arimatsu is a stop on the Meitetsu Nagoya
line from Meitetsu-Nagoya station (¥340, 20
minutes, frequent departures). From the station, turn left onto the street perpendicular to
the tracks and another left at the first corner
(at Shinseidō bookshop).

INUYAMA 犬山

0568 / pop 71,800

Dubbed the 'Japan Rhine' by a 19th-century
geologist, Inuyama's Kiso River sets a picturesque scene beneath the town's striking castle.
At night the setting becomes all the more cinematic as fishermen come to practise *ukai*. By
day, Inuyama's quaint streets, its manicured

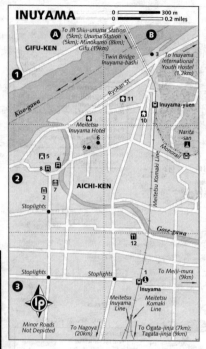

INUYAMA

Uraku-en garden and 17th-century teahouse make for a day trip from Nagoya after exploring its castle. Other attractions include the architecture of Meiji-mura Museum, shooting the rapids down the Kiso-gawa and some rather racy shrines.

Orientation & Information

The castle and *ukai* area are within easy walking distance of Inuyama-yūen station on the Meitetsu Komaki line. However, the **tourist information office** (☎ 61-6000; ◷ 9am-5pm) is in Inuyama station, one stop south, where the Meitetsu Komaki line meets up with the Meitetsu Inuyama line. It has useful English-language pamphlets and maps, and can book accommodation. On the web, visit www.city .inuyama.aichi.jp/english/index.html.

Sights & Activities

INUYAMA-JŌ 犬山城

A national treasure, Japan's oldest **castle** (☎ 61-1711; adult/child ¥500/100; ◷ 9am-5pm) is said to have originated with a fort in 1440; the current donjon (main keep) dates from 1537 and has withstood war, earthquake and restoration to remain an excellent example of Momoyama-period architecture. Stone walls reach 5m high, and inside are narrow, steep staircases and military displays. There's a fine view of mountains and plains from the top storey.

The castle is a 15-minute walk to the west of Inuyama-yūen station (20 minutes northwest from Inuyama station). Just south are the shrines **Haritsuna Jinja** and **Sankō-Inari Jinja**, the latter with interesting statues of *komainu* (protective dogs).

MARIONETTE (KARAKURI) EXHIBITION ROOM & ARTEFACTS MUSEUM からくり展示館 ・ 犬山市文化資料館

Included in your admission ticket to Inuyama-jō are these two collections.

One block south of the castle, the **Marionette (Karakuri) Exhibition Room** (☎ 61-3932; admission purchased separately ¥100; ◷ 9am-5pm) contains a small display of Edo- and Meiji-era puppets. On Saturday and Sunday you can see the wooden characters in action (10.30am and 2pm).

To see the puppets as they were meant to be used, visit during the **Inuyama Matsuri** (Inuyama Festival, first Saturday and Sunday in April), designated an Intangible Cultural Asset by the Japanese government. Dating back to 1650, the festival features a parade of 13 three-tiered floats decked out with lanterns and *karakuri*, which perform to music. At night, it's lit by 365 lanterns.

Nearby, the **Artefacts Museum** (☎ 65-1728; admission purchased separately ¥100; ◷ 9am-5pm) has one of the festival floats on display.

CENTRAL HONSHŪ

URAKU-EN & JO-AN TEAHOUSE
有楽園・茶室如安

The garden **Uraku-en** (☎ 61-4608; admission ¥1000; ⏰ 9am-5pm Mar-Nov, 9am-4pm Dec-Feb) is 300m east of Inuyama-jō, in a corner of the grounds of the Meitetsu Inuyama Hotel. One of the finest teahouses in Japan and a National Treasure, **Jo-an** was built in 1618 in Kyoto by Oda Urakusai, a younger brother of Oda Nobunaga, and it spent time in Tokyo and Kanagawa prefecture before moving here in 1972.

Urakusai was a renowned tea master who founded his own tea-ceremony school. He was also a closet Christian whose adopted name (the Portuguese 'João') was bestowed on the teahouse. Visitors may peek into the teahouse but are not allowed inside, except for four days in March and November.

CORMORANT FISHING 鵜飼い

Ukai takes place close to Inuyama-yūen station, by Twin-Bridge Inuyama-bashi. Book your ticket at the Inuyama tourist office in the morning or at the **dock office** (☎ 61-0057; Jul & Aug from ¥2800, Jun & Sep from ¥2500), near the cormorant-fishing pier.

Boats depart nightly at 5.30pm from June to August, with the show starting around 7.45pm. In September boats depart at 5pm, with things kicking off at 7.15pm.

KISO-GAWA RAPIDS TRIP

Flat-bottomed wooden boats shoot the rapids on a 13km section of the Kiso-gawa. With many daily departures, the ride takes an hour and costs ¥3400/1700 for adults/children; it entails little risk, except of a soaking. Contact **Nihon Rhein Kankō** (☎ 0574-28-2727; ⏰ mid-Mar–late Nov).

Festivals & Events

In addition to the **Inuyama Festival** (first weekend in April; opposite), the city also hosts the summer **Nihon Rhine Festival**, every 10 August on the banks of the river, culminating in fireworks.

Sleeping & Eating

Inuyama International Youth Hostel (犬山国際ユースホステル; ☎ 61-1111; fax 61-2770; tatami r s/d ¥3700/5800, Western-style tw ¥6400) Inuyama's cheapest option (25 minutes' walk northeast of Inuyama-yūen station – access it from along the river) has comfortable rooms, friendly staff and a stone bath. Reservations recommended. Meals available by advance notice – and recommended (no restaurants nearby).

Minshuku Yayoi (☎ /fax 61-0751; r per person incl 2 meals from ¥6300; ✖) Across from Inuyama-yūen station, this friendly inn has simple but comfy tatami rooms and shared bathrooms. Prides itself on its home cooking.

CENTRAL HONSHŪ

FAMOUS FACTORIES FOR FREE

Nagoya is the hub of a major industrial centre and visitors have a unique opportunity to visit some of the world's leading manufacturers. Bookings are required.

As we went to press, Toyota Motor Corporation had its first quarter outselling GM as the world's largest auto-maker. Two-hour tours of its main plant in Toyota city depart from the **Toyota Kaikan Exhibition Hall** (☎ 0565-23-3922; fax 0565-23-5712; www.toyota.co.jp/en/about_toyota /facility/toyota_kaikan; ⏰ 11am Mon-Fri). Tours are by reservation only and must be booked at least two weeks in advance. Check the website for details and directions; allow at least one hour to get to Toyota city from central Nagoya. See also Toyota Commemorative Museum of Industry and Technology (p242).

The Nagoya brewery of **Asahi Beer** (☎ 052-792-8966; fax 052-792-8967; admission free; ⏰ 9.30am-3pm, closed irregularly most days) welcomes visitors for 1¼ hours. Sample the wares for the tour's final 20 minutes; woo-hoo! Request about one week in advance for English guidance. Take the JR Chūō line to Shinmoriyama station; it's a 15-minute walk.

The town of Okazaki, southeast of Nagoya, is the home of *hatchō* miso, a 600-year-old recipe for an especially healthful miso variety. **Hatchō Miso no Sato** (☎ 0564-21-1355; admission free; ⏰ 8.30am-6pm) claims to be the world's most popular miso museum, although we're not sure there's a heck of a lot of competition. Production here is low-tech: 2m-tall cedar vats where miso is fermented as in days of old: three years with lids weighted down by stones. Book for tours in English at least one week in advance. From Nagoya, Meitetsu Honsen line trains serve Okazaki-Koen-Mae (¥650, 40 minutes); you may have to change trains at Chiryu.

If none of that starts your motor, visit www.sangyokanko.jp for more ideas.

Rinkō-kan (☎ 61-0977; fax 61-2505; rinkokan@triton .ocn.ne.jp; r per person incl 2 meals from ¥12,750; ☒) Overlooking the river, this cheery, flower-filled hot-spring hotel has handsome Japanese rooms. It is known for its fabulous stone baths, *rotemburo* (open-air baths), Jacuzzi and local cuisine.

Narita (なり多; ☎ 61-0120; courses from ¥2000; ❤ lunch & dinner) Chichi French restaurant in a cultural heritage building. Weekday lunches are a good deal, including hors d'oeuvres, soup, main and coffee. It's near the Goze-gawa, a block west of the Inuyama Miyako Hotel.

Getting There & Away

Inuyama is connected with Nagoya (¥540, 30 minutes) and Shin-Gifu station in Gifu city (¥440, 35 minutes) via the Meitetsu Inuyama line. JR travellers can connect via Gifu to Unuma (¥320, 20 minutes) and walk across the river from Inuyama.

AROUND INUYAMA 犬山近辺
Museum Meiji-mura 明治村
Few Meiji-period buildings have survived war, earthquake or rabid development, but this open-air **museum** (☎ 67-0314; www.meijimura.com; 1 Uchiyama; adult/senior/student/elementary & junior high school student ¥1600/1200/1000/600; ❤ 9.30am-5pm Mar-Oct, 9.30am-4pm Nov-Feb, closed Mon Dec-Feb) has brought together more than 65 of them from all over Japan. Opened in 1965, this museum houses one-time public offices, private homes and banks, as well as some trains and buses. Among them is the entryway designed by Frank Lloyd Wright for Tokyo's Imperial Hotel (since replaced by a more generic version), the home of Sōseki Natsume (the novelist whose image appears on the ¥1000 bill) and early Kyoto trams. Note the coming-together of Western and Japanese architectural styles. Allow at least half a day to enjoy it at an easy pace.

A bus to Meiji-mura (¥410, 20 minutes) departs every 30 minutes from Inuyama station's east exit.

Ōgata-jinja 大縣神社
This 2000-year-old **shrine** (☎ 67-1017) is dedicated to the female Shintō deity Izanami and draws women devotees seeking marriage or fertility. The precincts of the shrine contain rocks and other items resembling female genitals.

The popular **Hime-no-Miya Grand Festival** takes place here on the Sunday before 15 March (or on 15 March if it's a Sunday). Locals pray for good harvests and prosperity by parading through the streets bearing a *mikoshi* (portable shrine) with replicas of female genitals.

Ōgata-jinja is a 30-minute walk southeast of Gakuden station on the Meitetsu Komaki line.

Tagata-jinja 田県神社
Izanagi, the male counterpart of Izanami, is commemorated at this **shrine** (☎ 76-2906). The main hall has a side building containing a collection of phalluses, left as offerings by grateful worshippers.

The **Tagata Hōnen Sai Festival** takes place on 15 March at the Tagata-jinja when the highly photogenic 2m-long, 60kg 'sacred object' is paraded, amid much mirth, around the neighbourhood. Arrive well before the procession starts at 2pm.

Tagata-jinja is five minutes' walk west of Tagata-jinja-mae station, one stop south of Gakuden station on the Meitetsu Komaki line.

Yaotsu 八百津
☎ 0574 / pop 13,500
This Kiso River town has become a pilgrimage site as the birthplace of Sugihara Chiune (1900–86), Japan's consul in Lithuania during early WWII. Sugihara saved some 6000 Jews from the Nazis by issuing transit visas against Japanese government orders; the 'Sugihara survivors' escaped to Kōbe and Japanese-controlled Shanghai and, later, to other countries. The story is the subject of the 1997 Academy Award–winning film *Visas and Virtue*.

On Yaotsu's Jindō-no-oka (Hill of Humanity; 人道の丘) is a **museum** (adult/child ¥300/100; ❤ 9.30am-5pm Tue-Sun) with photos and thought-provoking exhibits related to this inspiring story. Further information can be found at www.town.yaotsu.gifu.jp, or contact the **city office** (☎ 43-2111, ext 2253), which has an English speaker available.

Yaotsu is easiest reached by car, but from Inuyama you can take the Meitetsu Hiromi train line to Akechi (¥440, 30 minutes, via Shin-Kani), then transfer to the Yao bus (¥400, 25 minutes) to Yaotsu; it's a short bus or taxi ride to the museum. The city office may be able to help with logistics if you phone with enough advance notice.

GIFU 岐阜

☎ 058 / pop 423,730

Historically, Gifu has a strong association with Oda Nobunaga (p40), *daimyō* (regional lords under the *shōgun*) of the castle and bestower of the city's name in 1567. It was later visited by famed haiku poet Matsuō Bashō, who witnessed *ukai* here in 1688; Charlie Chaplin did the same in his day.

Contemporary Gifu shows little evidence of those historic times. In 1891 Gifu was hit by a colossal earthquake, followed by a thorough drubbing in WWII, so the city centre is not much to look at. Still, it remains a popular destination for *ukai* on the Nagara-gawa and handicrafts, as well as a reasonably colourful district of sidestreets near the station and a post-war reconstruction of the castle Gifu-jō atop the nearby mountain, Kinka-zan.

Orientation & Information

JR Gifu station and Meitetsu Shin-Gifu station are separated by several minutes' walk in the southern part of the city centre.

The **tourist information office** (☎ 262-4415; ⏰ 9am-7pm Mar-Dec, to 6pm Jan-Feb) on the 2nd floor of the JR Gifu station provides useful English-language city maps and can make same-day hotel reservations. Some English is spoken.

Sights & Activities

UKAI

During Gifu's **cormorant fishing** season (11 May to 15 October), boats depart nightly (except after heavy rainfall or on the night of a full moon) from the bridge, Nagara-bashi, or you can view the action from a distance by walking along the river east of the bridge.

Bookings are strongly advised. Tickets are sold at hotels or, if any tickets remain after 6pm, at the **booking office** (☎ for advance reservations 262-0104; adult/child ¥3300/2900; ⏰ departures 6.15pm, 6.45pm & 7.15pm) just below Nagara-bashi. Food and drink are not provided on the boats; you can bring food aboard the first departure of the evening but not on later departures. On Monday to Friday, fares for the two later departures are ¥3000/2600 per adult/child.

Nagara-bashi can be reached by bus 11 (¥200) from JR Gifu station.

GIFU-KŌEN 岐阜公園

A few of the attractions of this lush, hillside park are the **Gifu City History Museum** (岐阜市歴史博物館; ☎ 265-0010; 2-18-1 Ōmiya-chō; adult/child ¥300/150; ⏰ 9am-5pm Tue-Sun) and the **Mt Kinka Ropeway** (金華山ロープウエー; ☎ 262-6784; 257 Senjōjiki-shita; return adult/child ¥1050/520; ⏰ 9am-5pm mid-Oct–mid-Mar, to 10.30pm late Jul-Aug, to 6pm mid-Mar–late Jul & Sep–mid-Oct) up to the summit of Kinka-zan (329m). From here you can check out **Gifu-jō** (岐阜城; ☎ 263-4853; 18 Kinka-zan, Tenshukaku; adult/child ¥200/100; ⏰ closes 30min before ropeway), which is a small but picturesque modern reconstruction of the original castle. Those who'd rather huff it can hike to the castle (one hour). To reach the park take bus 11 from Gifu station to Gifu-kōen mae (¥200, 20 minutes).

SHŌHŌ-JI 正法寺

The main attraction of this orange-and-white **temple** (☎ 264-2760; 8 Daibutsu-chō; admission ¥150; ⏰ 9am-5pm) is the papier-mache *daibutsu* (Great Buddha; 1832), which is nearly 14m tall and is said to have been fashioned over 38 years using about a tonne of paper sutras. The temple is a short walk southwest of Gifu-kōen.

Sleeping & Eating

The narrow streets between Gifu's two stations are happy hunting ground for cafés, restaurants and *izakaya*.

Comfort Hotel Gifu (コンフォートホテル岐阜; ☎ 267-1311; fax 267-1312; s/tw incl breakfast ¥6090/11,550; ✉ ⏰ 🖥 wi-fi) Practically across from JR Gifu station, this simple business hotel offers liquid crystal TVs, wireless internet access from rooms and a coin laundry.

Daiwa Roynet Hotel Gifu (ダイワロイネットホテル岐阜; ☎ 212-0055; fax 212-0056; s/d from ¥6800/9000; ✉ ⏰ 🖥) A posher choice, with nice linens and rooms outfitted for business. It's steps from Meitetsu Gifu station (look for the Lawson convenience store on the ground floor).

Shopping

Gifu is famous for *wagasa* (oiled paper parasols/umbrellas) and Gifu *chōchin* (paper lanterns elegantly painted with landscapes etc). You can find mass-produced versions in souvenir shops, or the tourist information office has a map to high-quality speciality stores.

Sakaida Eikichi Honten (坂井田永吉本店; ☎ 271-6958; ⏰ 9am-5pm Mon-Fri) and **Hirano Shōten** (平野商店; ☎ 271-0468; ⏰ irregular) make and sell *wagasa*. The shops are near each other, a 12-minute walk southeast of JR Gifu station. Given these shops' irregular hours, it's wise to phone before setting out. Expect to pay ¥8400 and up for a quality *wagasa*.

For Gifu *chōchin*, try **Ozeki Chōchin** (小関提灯; ☎ 263-0111). Prices start at around ¥10,000. Take bus 11 to Ken-Sōgōchōsha-mae, then walk towards the temple Higashi Betsuin.

Getting There & Away

The JR Tōkaidō line will get you here from Nagoya (*tokkyū*, ¥1180, 20 minutes; *futsū*, ¥450, 30 minutes). Meitetsu line trains from Shin-Nagoya station serve Shin-Gifu (¥540, 35 minutes) and continue to Inuyama (¥440, 35 minutes).

GUJŌ-HACHIMAN 郡上八幡

☎ 0575 / pop 16,000

Nestled in the mountains at the confluence of several rivers, Gujō-Hachiman is a small, pleasant town famed for its **Gujō Odori Matsuri**, Japan's third-largest folk dance festival, and as the place where all those plastic food models you see in restaurant windows come from.

The **tourist office** (観光協会; ☎ 67-0002; ☯ 8.30am-5pm) is by the bridge Shin-bashi in the centre of town, about five minutes' walk from the Jōka-machi Plaza bus terminal.

The festival first: following a tradition dating to the 1590s, townsfolk let down their hair with frenzied dancing on 31 nights between July and early September. Visitor participation is encouraged, especially during the four main days of the festival (13–16 August) and during *tetsuya odori* days, when the dancing goes all night. At other times of year the town's sparkling rivers, narrow lanes and stone bridges make for a relaxing stopover.

Those incredibly realistic **food models** are one of life's great mysteries, and here's your chance to suss them out. In an old *machiya* (merchant

house), **Shokuhin Sample Kōbō Sōsakukan** (食品サンプル工房創作館; ☎ 67-1870; admission free; ☯ 9am-5pm Mar-Nov, 9am-5pm Fri-Wed Dec-Feb) lets you view the almost-good-enough-to-eat treats and try creating them yourself (by reservation). Tempura (¥1000 for three pieces) and lettuce (free) make memorable, only-in-Japan souvenirs. It's three minutes' walk from Jokamachi Plaza.

Gujō-Hachiman's other attractions include the tiny hilltop castle **Gujō Hachiman-jō** (郡上八幡城; ☎ 65-5839; adult/child ¥300/150; ☯ 8am-6pm Jun-Aug, 9am-5pm Sep-May), which had been a humble fortress dating back to about 1600; the current, grander building dates from only 1933. It contains weapons, armour and the like, and offers fine views. From the bus terminal it's about 20 minutes' walk.

Gujō-Hachiman is also known for its waterways. A famous spring, **Sōgi-sui**, near the centre of town, is something of a pilgrimage site, named for a Momoyama-era poet. People who rank such things place Sōgi-sui at the top of the list for clarity.

Gujō Tōsenji Youth Hostel (郡上洞泉寺ユースホステル; ☎ 67-0290; fax 67-0549; dm per person ¥3200; ☯ closed mid-Aug; ✗) is an attractively refurnished hostel pleasantly situated on the grounds of a temple, though there is no bath on the premises (there's a *sentō* – public bath – nearby). Breakfast is ¥500.

Bizenya Ryokan (備前屋旅館; ☎ 65-2068; fax 67-0007; r per person incl 2 meals from ¥11,550; ✗) boasts large rooms with shared facilities around a handsome garden. This 30-bed ryokan provides a relaxing, quietly upscale experience. It's between the bus terminal and tourist office.

The most convenient access to Gujō-Hachiman is via bus from Gifu (¥1560, one hour, four daily). From Nagoya station, the easiest

---

YOU CAN'T KEEP A GOOD ONSEN DOWN

Between Gifu and Takayama is **Gero**, an *onsen* town that's a favourite among Japanese even if its name is an unfortunate homonym for 'vomit'. Gero's concrete sprawl dampens its appeal, but the waters, beneficial for rheumatism, athletic injuries and the complexion, are excellent for a stopover.

Pick up the ¥1200 **Yumeguri Tegata**, a wooden plaque on a rope (and a nice souvenir) that allows one-time access to three among a selection of Gero's *onsen*. It's available at the **tourist information office** (☎ 25-4711; ☯ 8.30am-5.30pm), outside the train station, where staff can tell you which *onsen* are operating that day. You can walk nearly anywhere in Gero within 20 minutes from the train station.

Tokkyū trains serve Gero from Gifu (¥3080, 67 minutes), Takayama (¥1990, 40 minutes) and Nagoya (¥4300, 1½ hours).

way is also by bus (¥3500, three hours). The town centre is easily walkable, or the tourist office hires out bicycles (¥300/1500 per hour/day).

HIDA DISTRICT 飛騨地域

The centrepiece of this ancient, mountainous region is the handsome town of Takayama, where the legacy of a strong craft tradition lives on in its merchant houses, temples and shrines. Hida is known for *gasshō-zukuri* (hands-in-prayer) architecture, which you'll spot in the Unesco World Heritage sites of Shirakawa-gō and nearby Gokayama, though the latter is not part of Hida. Hida's culinary fame rests in its Hida beef and its *soba* (buckwheat noodles).

TAKAYAMA 高山
☎ 0577 / pop 95,904

With its old inns, shops and sake breweries, Takayama is a rarity: a 21st-century city (admittedly a small one) that's also retained its traditional charm. Vibrant morning markets, hillside shrines and a laid-back populace add to the town's allure, and it should be a high priority on any visit to Central Honshū. Give yourself at least two days to enjoy the place; it's easily tackled on foot or bicycle.

Takayama was established in the late 16th century as the castle town of the Kanamori clan, but in 1692 it was placed under direct control of the *bakufu* (shōgunate) in Edo. The present layout dates from the Kanamori period, and its sights include more than a dozen museums, galleries and exhibitions covering lacquer and lion masks, folk craft and architecture.

Takayama remains the region's administrative and transport hub, and it makes a good base for trips around Hida and Japan Alps National Park (p267).

Orientation
All the main sights except Hida-no-Sato (Hida Folk Village) are to be found in the centre of town, within walking distance of the station. Northeast of the station, Kokubun-ji-dōri, the main street, heads east, across the river Miya-gawa (about 10 minutes' walk), where it becomes Yasugawa-dōri. South of Yasugawa-dōri is the historic, picturesque Sanmachi-suji (Sanmachi district) of immaculately preserved old homes.

Hida-no-Sato is a 10-minute bus ride west of the station.

Information
The town's **tourist information office** (☎ 32-5328; ☾ 8.30am-5pm Nov-Mar, 8.30am-6.30pm Apr-Oct), directly in front of JR Takayama station, has English-speaking staff, as well as English-language maps and information on sights (the *Hida Takayama* pamphlet is a good start) and accommodation. It can also provide info on Takayama's festivals, as well as bus schedules between Takayama and Japan Alps National Park and Ogimachi in Shirakawa-go, and has one computer available for internet access. On the web, visit www.hidatakayama.or.jp.

To arrange a home visit, homestay or volunteer interpreter for non-Japanese languages (including sign language), contact the city's **International Affairs Office** (☎ 32-3333, ext 2407; 2-18 Hanaoka), located inside the Takayama Municipal Building, one month in advance.

Internet access is also available at the **City library** (☎ 32-3096; ☾ 9.30am-9.30pm), east of the Sanmachi district, and at **Takayama Municipal Office** (2-18 Hanaoka; ☾ 9am-5pm Mon-Fri), which has two computers.

The main post office is on Hirokōji-dōri, a few blocks east of the station. Ōgaki Kyōritsu Bank has foreign-card ATMs southeast of the station and near the Miya-gawa Morning Market. Jōroku Bank can change cash or travellers cheques.

Sights & Activities
SANMACHI-SUJI 三町筋
The centre of the old town, this district of three main streets (Ichi-no-Machi, Ni-no-Machi and San-no-Machi) is lined with traditional shops, restaurants, museums and private homes. Sake breweries are easily recognised by the spheres of cedar fronds, though most of the year they just sell their wares.

Fujii Folkcraft Art Gallery (☎ 35-3778; 69 San-no-Machi; adult/child ¥700/350; ☾ 9am-5pm) is a private collection in an old merchant's house, with folk craft and ceramics from Japan (particularly from the Muromachi and Edo periods), China and Korea. **Hida Folk Archaeological Museum** (Hida Minzoku Kōkō-kan; ☎ 32-1980; 82 San-no-Machi; adult/high & junior high school student/child ¥500/300/200; ☾ 8.30am-5pm Mar-Nov, 9am-4.30pm Dec-Feb) is a former samurai house boasting interesting secret passageways and an old well in the courtyard.

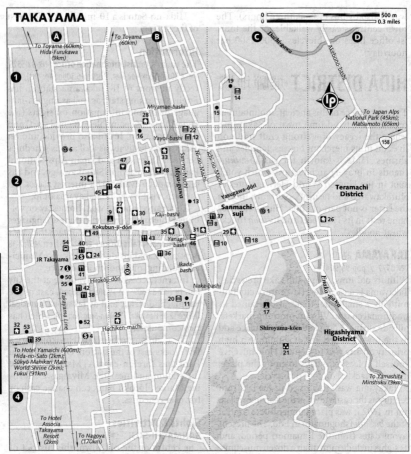

TAKAYAMA

CENTRAL HONSHŪ

Another merchant's house, dating from the turn of the 20th century, **Hirata Folk Art Museum** (Hirata Kinen-kan; ☎ 33-1354; 39 Ni-no-Machi; adult/child ¥300/150; ⏰ 9am-5pm) displays items from everyday rural Japanese life.

Takayama Museum of Local History (☎ 32-1205; 75 Ichi-no-Machi; adult/child ¥300/150; ⏰ 8.30am-5pm Mar-Nov, 9am-4.30pm Tue-Sun Dec-Feb) is devoted to the crafts and traditions of the region, with images carved by Enkū, a woodcarving priest who wandered the region in the 17th century. There are also several small but nicely maintained gardens.

TAKAYAMA-JINYA 高山陣屋
These sprawling grounds south of the Sanmachi district house the only remaining prefectural office building of the Tokugawa shōgunate. **Takayama-jinya** (Historical Government House; ☎ 32-0643; 1-5 Hachiken-machi; adult/child ¥420/free; ⏰ 8.45am-5pm Mar-Oct, 8.45am-4.30pm Nov-Feb) was originally built in 1615 as the administrative centre for the Kanamori clan but was later taken over by the *bakufu*. The main gate was once reserved for high officials. The present main building dates back to 1816 and it was used as a local government office until 1969.

As well as government offices, a rice granary and a garden, there's a torture chamber with explanatory detail. Free guided tours in English are available upon request. Takayama-jinya is a 15-minute walk east of the train station.

CENTRAL HONSHŪ

MERCHANT HOUSES
吉島家, 日下部民芸館

North of Sanmachi are two excellent examples of Edo-period merchants' homes, with the living quarters in one section and the commercial/warehouse areas in another. Design buffs shouldn't miss **Yoshijima-ke** (Yoshijima house; ☎ 32-0038; 1-51 Ōshinmachi; adult/child ¥500/300; ⊙ 9am-5pm Mar-Nov, 9am-4.30pm Wed-Sun Dec-Feb), well covered in architectural publications. Its lack of ornamentation allows you to focus on the spare lines, soaring roof and skylight.

Down the block, **Kusakabe Mingeikan** (Kusakabe Folk Art Museum; ☎ 32-0072; 1-52 Ōshinmachi; adult/child ¥500/300; ⊙ 9am-4.30pm Mar-Nov, 8.30am-4pm Wed-Mon Dec-Feb), built during the 1890s, showcases the striking craftsmanship of traditional Takayama carpenters' skills. Inside is a collection of folk art.

TAKAYAMA YATAI KAIKAN 高山屋台会館

A rotating selection of four of the 23 multitiered *yatai* (floats) used in the Takayama Matsuri can be seen at the **Takayama Yatai Kaikan** (Festival Floats Exhibition Hall; ☎ 32-5100; 178 Sakura-machi; adult/high school student/child ¥820/520/410; ⊙ 8.30am-5pm Mar-Nov, 9am-4.30pm Dec-Feb). These spectacular creations, some dating from the 17th century, are prized for their flamboyant carvings, metalwork and lacquerwork. A famous feature of some floats is the *karakuri* that perform amazing tricks and acrobatics courtesy of eight accomplished puppeteers using 36 strings. A video gives a sense of the festival.

Your ticket also admits you to the **Sakurayama Nikkō-kan** next door, with intricate models of the famous shrines at Nikkō. Lighting takes you from dawn to dusk and back again, allowing you to witness these sites in different kinds of light.

You might pass some unusual slender garages around town with three-storey doors; these house the *yatai* that are not in the museum.

SHISHI KAIKAN 獅子会館

Just south of the Yatai Kaikan is the **Shishi Kaikan** (Lion Mask Exhibition Hall; ☎ 32-0881; 53-1 Sakura-machi; adult/child ¥600/400; ⊙ 8.30am-5.30pm late Apr-late Oct, 9am-5pm late Oct-late Apr). It has a display of over 800 lion masks and musical instruments connected with the lion dances that are commonly performed at festivals in central and northern Japan. Admission includes twice-hourly demonstrations of *karakuri* – a good opportunity to view these marvellous puppets in action.

SHUNKEI KAIKAN 飛驒高山春慶会館

Shunkei lacquerware was introduced from Kyoto several centuries ago but has become Takayama's signature style, used to produce boxes, trays and flower vases. West of the Festival Floats Exhibition Hall and across the river, this **exhibition hall** (☎ 32-3373; 1-88 Kando-chō; adult/child ¥300/200; ☑ 8am-5.30pm Apr-Oct, 9am-5pm Nov-Mar) has more than 1000 pieces, including some dating from the 17th century. Unlike many other Japanese lacquer styles, shunkei is designed to show off the wood grain. A display shows production techniques, and the shop has occasional specials.

HIDA KOKUBUN-JI 飛驒国分寺

Takayama's oldest **temple** (☎ 32-1295; 1-83 Sōwa-chō; treasure hall adult/child ¥300/250; ☑ 9am-4pm) was originally built in the 8th century and subsequently ravaged by fire; the oldest of the present buildings dates from the 16th century. The temple's treasure hall houses some Important Cultural Properties, and the courtyard boasts a three-storey pagoda and an impressively gnarled gingko tree, which is in remarkably good shape considering it's believed to be 1200 years old. The temple is a five-minute walk northeast of the station, on Kokubun-ji-dōri.

MORNING MARKETS 朝市

Asa-ichi (morning markets) take place every morning from 7am to noon, starting an hour earlier from April to October. The **Jinya-mae Market** is in front of Takayama-jinya; the **Miya-gawa Market** is larger, along the east bank of the Miya-gawa, between Kaji-bashi and Yayoi-bashi. The markets provide a pleasant way to start the day, with a stroll past gnarled farmers at their vegetable stands and stalls selling crafts, pickles, souvenirs and that all-important steaming cuppa joe.

TERAMACHI & SHIROYAMA-KŌEN
寺町・城山公園

The hilly districts in the east side of town are linked by a walking trail, particularly enjoyable in the early morning or late after-noon. Teramachi has over a dozen temples (one houses the youth hostel) and shrines that you can wander around before taking in the greenery of the park, Shiroyama-kōen. Various trails lead through the park and up the mountainside to the ruins of the castle, **Takayama-jō**. As you descend, you can take a look at the temple, **Shōren-ji**, which was trans-ferred to this site from the Shōkawa Valley when a dam was built there in 1960.

The walk takes a leisurely two hours and from the temple it's a 10-minute walk back to the centre of town. The tourist information office has descriptions of the temples and a simple map, or the *Hida Takayama* pamphlet has a more detailed map.

HIDA-NO-SATO 飛驒の里

This large open-air **museum** (Hida Folk Village; ☎ 34-4711; 1-590 Okatmoto-chō; adult/child ¥700/200; ☑ 8.30am-5pm) is highly recommended for its dozens of traditional houses, dismantled at their original sites throughout the region and rebuilt here. During clear weather, there are good views across the town to the peaks of the Japan Alps.

Hido-no-Sato is in two sections. The west-ern section features 12 old houses and a com-plex of five traditional buildings with artisans (see opposite). Displays are well presented and offer an excellent chance to see what rural life was like in previous centuries.

The eastern section of the village is centred around the Omoide Taikenkan, where you can try making candles, *sembei* (rice crackers) etc. Other buildings include the Go-kura Store-house (used for storage of rice as payment of taxes) and the Museum of Mountain Life. Allow at least three hours to explore the whole place on foot.

Hida-no-Sato is a 30-minute walk west from Takayama station, but the route is not enjoyable. Either hire a bicycle in town (p262), or take the Hida-no-Sato bus (¥200, 10 minutes) from stop 6 at the bus station. A discount ticket 'Hida-no-Sato setto ken' combines return fare and admission to the park for ¥900. Be sure to check return times for the bus.

SŪKYŌ MAHIKARI MAIN WORLD SHRINE
真光教

Dominating Takayama's western skyline is the golden roof of the **Main World Shrine** (☎ 34-7008; admission free; ☑ 9.30am-4pm, except during religious

---

GASSHŌ-ZUKURI ARCHITECTURE

Winter in the Hida region can be fierce, and inhabitants faced snow and cold long before the advent of propane heaters and 4WD vehicles. One of the most visible symbols of that adaptability is *gasshō-zukuri* architecture, seen in the steeply slanted straw-roofed homes that still dot the landscape around the region.

The sharply angled roofs were designed to prevent heavy snow accumulation, a serious concern in a region where nearly all mountain roads close from December to April. The name *gasshō* comes from the Japanese word for praying, because the shape of the roofs was thought to resemble two hands clasped in prayer. *Gasshō* buildings often featured pillars crafted from stout cedars to lend extra support. The attic areas were ideal for silk cultivation.

Larger *gasshō* buildings were inhabited by wealthy families, up to 30 people under one roof. Peasant families lived in huts of the size that are now used as tool sheds.

The *gasshō-zukuri* building has become an endangered species. Most examples have been gathered and preserved in folk villages, including Hida-no-Sato in Takayama (opposite) and in Shirakawa-gō (p264) and Gokayama (p266). So two homes that are now neighbours were once separated by several days or weeks of travel on foot or sled. But local authorities have worked hard to re-create their natural surroundings, making it possible to imagine what life in the Hida hills might have looked like hundreds of years ago.

---

observances) of Sūkyō Mahikari, a new religion whose teachings are said to include healing via training courses and amulets that transmit divine light rays. Guided tours are available (call in advance for an English-speaking guide).

Festivals & Events

Takayama's famed festival is in two parts. On 14 and 15 April is the **Sannō Matsuri**; a dozen *yatai*, decorated with carvings, dolls, colourful curtains and blinds, are paraded through the town. In the evening the floats are decked out with lanterns and the procession is accompanied by sacred music. **Hachiman Matsuri**, on 9 and 10 October, is a slightly smaller version (p257).

From January to March several of the sake breweries in Sanmachi-suji, many dating back to the Edo period, arrange tours and tastings.

Sleeping

The tourist information office assists with bookings. If visiting Takayama during festival times, book accommodation months in advance and expect to pay a 20% premium. You could also stay elsewhere and commute to Takayama.

BUDGET

Hida Takayama Temple Inn Zenkō-ji (☎ 32-8470; www .geocities.jp/zenkojitakayama; 4-3 Tenman-chō; dm/r per person ¥2500/3000) Although it's in a temple (a branch of Nagano's famous Zenkō-ji), around

a courtyard garden, private-use rooms are generously proportioned and even the dorm-style rooms are handsome. Plus, there's a kitchen for guest use, no curfew and a master who speaks excellent English. If you want, you can practise Jōdō-style meditation in the main hall.

Hida Takayama Tenshō-ji Youth Hostel (☎ 32-6345; fax 32-6392; 83 Tensho-ji-machi; dm ¥2940) This peaceful hostel occupies an attractive temple in Teramachi, though some guests gripe about its lights-out (9.45pm curfew) and wake-up schedule. It's a 25-minute walk from the train station, or board the bus for Shin-Hotaka, get off at Betsuin-mae and walk east for about five minutes.

Hotel Yamaichi (ホテルやまいち; ☎ 34-6200; www.kbnet.jp.org/11pm/kamaya/hyoshi.html; 181-2 Ishiura-chō; Japanese/Western r per person from ¥4000/5000; ✕ 🖳) In an old building 10 minutes by bus south of town (¥230), this inn has simple, decent rooms (Western rooms have private bathrooms). Discounts are available for more than one person per room. The friendly English-speaking owners often pick up guests from the station; if they can't they'll pay half the taxi fare. Check in from 3pm.

MIDRANGE

Rickshaw Inn (☎ 32-2890; fax 32-2469; www.rickshawinn .com; 54 Suehiro-chō; s with/without bathroom ¥6500/4900, tw ¥11,600/9800; ✕ ✕ 🖳) Excellent value and a travellers' favourite, with pleasant Japanese- and Western-style rooms, a small kitchen, laundry facilities and a cosy lounge. The friendly English-speaking owners are founts of information about Takayama. Book well in advance.

Murasaki Ryokan (☎ 32-1724; fax 33-7512; 1-56 Nanoka-machi; r per person from ¥4000, incl 2 meals from ¥7500; 🏠) The splendid wall of flowers outside this ryokan is the product of decades of work, and inside too it's like a trip back to the mid-20th century: Japanese-style loos, pay TVs and kerosene heaters. There's a lot of heart and a great Japanese breakfast including *hoba miso* (sweet miso paste cooked on a magnolia leaf) and *sansai* (mountain vegetables).

Ō-Machi (☎ 32-3251; 38 Ichi-no-Machi; r per person ¥4000; 🏠) In Sanmachi-suji near the Takayama Museum of Local History, Ō-Machi offers small but clean tatami rooms and has many foreign fans. Staff speak some English and guests can use the kitchen. It's set back from the main street.

Minshuku Kuwataniya (☎ 32-5021; fax 36-3835; www.kuwataniya.com; 1-50-30 Sowa-machi; r per person with/without bathroom ¥6450/4350; 🏠) Takayama's longest-running *minshuku* (family-run accommodation; since the 1920s) has both Japanese- and Western-style rooms, hot-spring bath and free bicycle use. Dinner (available for ¥2310) features Hida's famed beef (vegetarian options available with advance notice). It's half a block north of Hida Kokubun-ji temple.

Sōsuke (☎ 32-0818; fax 33-5570; www.irori-sosuke .com; 1-64 Okamoto-machi; r per person ¥5040; 🏠) West of the train station, across from Takayama Green Hotel, Sōsuke has 13 pleasant tatami rooms and the English-speaking staff prepares excellent dinners (¥2100) including meals for vegetarians. The handsomely reconstructed building dates from the 1800s and retains a traditional style, including an *irori* (hearth), though it is on a busy road.

Takayama City Hotel Four Seasons (☎ 36-0088; fax 36-0080; www.f-seasons.co.jp in Japanese; 1-1 Kanda-machi; s/tw from ¥6900/13,100; 🔀 🏠 🖥 wi-fi) Takayama's Four Seasons has nothing to do with the luxury chain, but it's nicer-than-average business-hotel calibre. Some of the large singles and reasonable-sized doubles have hardwood floors, and there's a communal *onsen* (¥150 charge). It's a 15-minute walk from the station, two blocks west of the river.

Ryokan Gōto (☎ /fax 33-0870; San-no-Machi; r per person incl breakfast from ¥8400) Another of this city's lovely traditional inns, Gōto lies in the heart of Sanmachi-suji, positioning you perfectly for this district's dramatic nightscapes. There's a low door at the entry, eclectic touches throughout and *hoba miso* with your breakfast. No English spoken.

Best Western Hotel (☎ 37-2000; fax 37-2005; www.bestwestern.co.jp; 6-6 Hanasato-machi; s/d/tw from ¥9240/12,600/14,700; 🔀 🏠) Very popular among overseas guests, this 78-room hotel offers crisp service and spacious, comfortably furnished rooms. Lounge and restaurant on-site. It's a block from the station.

Sumiyoshi Ryokan (☎ 32-0228; fax 33-8916; sumiyoshi@beach.ocn.ne.jp; 4-21 Hon-machi; r per person incl 2 meals from ¥11,000; 🏠 🖥) This delightfully traditional inn is set in an old merchant's house; some rooms have river views through windows of antique glass. One room has private bath (¥13,000).

TOP END

Asunaro Ryokan (☎ 33-5551; toll-free 0120-052-536; fax 34-6155; www.yado-asunaro.com; 2-96 Hatsuda-machi; r per person incl 2 meals with/without bathroom from ¥15,750/13,650; 🔀 🖥) This excellent ryokan has handsome tatami rooms, a spacious *onsen* bath and decadent dinners and breakfasts. At night, guests can warm themselves by the *irori*. Staff speak some English.

Tanabe Ryokan (☎ 32-0529; fax 35-1955; tanabe rk@jeans.ocn.ne.jp; 58 Aioi-chō; r per person incl 2 meals from ¥15,000; 🔀 🏠) Family-run inn in the centre of everything with sweet, welcoming staff. There's art throughout, stone paths line the carpeted hallways, rooms are spacious, and dinner is *kaiseki*-style (Japanese cuisine which obeys very strict rules of etiquette for every detail of the meal, including the setting) Hida cuisine. Some English spoken.

Hotel Associa Takayama Resort (ホテルアソシア高山リゾート; ☎ 36-0001; fax 36-0188; www .associa.com/tky; 1134 Echigo-chō; s/tw from ¥15,000/17,000; 🔀 🏠) If you find Takayama too historic, the Associa's three towers south of town provide an escape back to the 21st century. There's a pink and lime-green colour palette and rooms are either Western or Japanese style. To include two meals, add approximately ¥6000 per person to room rates. The real showplace is the three-storey, valley-view hot spring. The Associa's about 10 minutes from town, with shuttle bus service.

Eating

Takayama's specialities include *soba*, *hoba miso* and *sansai*. Street foods include *mi-*

tarashi-dango (skewers of grilled riceballs seasoned with soya sauce), *shio-sembei* (salty rice crackers) and skewers of grilled Hida beef (among the finest grades of meat in Japan, even if less known than its Kobe counterpart).

Myogaya (☎ 32-0426; 5-15 Hanasato-chō; mains around ¥1000; ☽ 8-10.30am, 11.30am-3pm & 5-7pm Wed-Mon; ☒ Ⓥ E) A longtime favourite a block east of the train station, this tiny restaurant and food shop prepares tasty vegetarian curry with brown rice, samosas, fruit juices, dandelion tea and organic coffees. Reservations requested on Saturdays.

Suzuya (☎ 32-2484; 24 Hanakawa-chō; sets ¥1100-3100; ☽ 11am-3pm & 5-8pm Wed-Mon; E) In the centre of town, Suzuya is one of Takayama's longstanding favourites, and it's highly recommended (though often packed) for local specialities like Hida beef, *hoba-miso* and various stews.

Ebisu-Honten (☎ 32-0209; 46 Kami-Ni-no-Machi; soba dishes ¥380-1530; ☽ 10am-5pm Wed-Mon; Ⓥ E) A 110-plus-year-old *teuchi* (handmade) *soba* shop and a town classic. The menu explains the *soba*-making process. Go for *zaru* (cold) *soba* for the real flavour of the buckwheat, or try curry or *miso-nikomi* (in miso broth) style.

Yamatake-Shōten (☎ 32-0571; 1-70 Sōwa-chō; meals per person from around ¥3500; ☽ lunch & dinner Thu-Tue, closed 3rd Thu of month) Butcher shop with a restaurant upstairs, an excellent place to sample Hida's savoury beef. No English menu, but here's the drill: choose your own cut (pay by weight, from ¥1380 per 100g), which is plated and brought to the table for you to cook on an inset charcoal grill. Vegetables and simple desserts are included, and sides like *kimchi* (Korean pickled cabbage) and *gyu tataki* (marinated raw beef) are also for sale.

Origin (☎ 36-4655; 4-108 Hanasato-chō; most dishes ¥315-819; ☽ dinner; E) This wonderful local *izakaya* a minute from the station has the usual *kushiyaki* (grilled, skewered dishes) and tofu steak, plus original dishes like sardines rolled in *yuba* (tofu skin), or big-as-a-beer-can grilled daikon in miso sauce. Or go for broke with Hida beef (¥1575). Look for the bamboo poles out the front.

Holy Grail (☎ 35-3393; 4-68 Hanasato-chō; mains ¥730-1250; ☽ lunch Mon & Wed-Sat, dinner Wed-Mon; E) Italian trattoria-style dishes in a hardwood, home-style setting. Crostini, pizzas, pastas, and more, or lunchtime spaghettis from ¥550. Inexpensive house wines are available by the bottle.

Chapala (☎ 34-9800; mains ¥600-980; ☽ dinner Mon-Sat; closed 1st Mon of each month; E) Two blocks west of the river, this cosy restaurant serves tasty chilli con carne, burritos, quesadillas, guacamole and chips, and other Tex-Mex favourites. Margaritas and Coronas accompany the proceedings nicely.

Jingoro Rāmen (☎ 34-5565; mains from ¥600; ☽ lunch & dinner, closed dinner Sun & some Mon; E) Like a roadhouse south of the station, Takayama's most venerable *rāmen* restaurant is a simple affair: broth, noodles and pork (or not) – but the savoury results are extremely satisfying.

La Viennoiserie de Nicolas (☎ 36-0054; 6-28 Hanasato-chō; pastries from ¥320; ☽ 10am-7pm Fri-Wed) A block from the train station, this tiny pastry shop serves some decadent treats – *pain au chocolat*, cheesecake, rhubarb pie – all lovingly prepared by the French owner.

Drinking

Red Hill Pub (☎ 33-8139; ☽ 7pm-midnight, closed irregularly) Locals and expats gather at this welcoming bar with snacks like pita bread or *karai rāmen* (spicy *rāmen*), an excellent selection of domestic and imported brews and an eclectic mix of tunes.

Bagus (☎ 36-4341; ☽ 7pm-1am Mon-Sat) This friendly reggae bar has a youthful energy. A 10-minute walk from the train station, good music and potent drinks await. It's on the 2nd floor.

Tonio (☎ 34-341; ☽ 6pm-midnight Mon-Sat) This English-style pub lies closer to the river, with Guinness on tap and a startling variety of imported whiskies.

Café Doppio (☎ 32-3638; coffee from ¥300; ☽ 9am-6pm) For a pick-me-up, stop by this pleasant café on the edge of the river. Cappuccinos, espressos, macchiatos and waffles.

Shopping

Takayama is renowned for crafts. *Ichii ittobori* (woodcarvings) are fashioned from yew and can be seen as intricate components of the *yatai* or as figurines or accessories for the home. Woodworking also extends to furniture (see boxed text, p262) in shops such as **Mori no Kotoba** (Words from the Forest; ☎ 36-7005; ☽ 9am-6pm Thu-Tue).

Takayama is also known for its shunkei lacquerware. Around the exhibition hall Shunkei Kaikan (p258) are shops with outstanding lacquerware and porcelain and, occasionally, good deals.

CENTRAL HONSHŪ

Local pottery styles include the rustic *Yamada-yaki* and the decorative *Shibukusa-yaki* styles.

Good places to find handicrafts are Sanmachi-suji, the morning markets (p258) and Kokubun-ji-dōri. A ubiquitous souvenir is *saru-bobo* (monkey babies), dolls of red cloth dressed in blue fabric, with pointy limbs and featureless faces, recalling the days when *obaasan* (grandmas) in this once-impoverished town fashioned dolls for kids out of readily available materials.

Getting There & Away

From Tokyo or Kansai, Takayama is most efficiently reached via Nagoya on the JR Takayama line (Hida *tokkyū*, ¥6070, 2¼ hours); the mountainous train ride is *gorge-ous*. The train line connecting Takayama with Toyama, where a trestle bridge was washed out by floods in 2005, should be back up and running by the time you read this; in the meantime, several local train/bus connections per day will get you there (¥1620, 3¼ hours).

Keiō Highway buses (☎ 32-1688) connect Takayama and Tokyo's Shinjuku (¥6500, 5½ hours, several daily, reservations are required). Takayama's bus station is adjacent to the train station. Many roads in this region close during winter, so bus schedules vary seasonally and don't run at all in winter on some of the routes. Check with the tourist offices for details.

For trips to the Japan Alps (Chūbu-Sangaku National Park) see p268.

By car, you'll find **Eki Rent-a-Car System** (☎ 33-3522) at the train station, **Mazda Rent-a-Car** (☎ 36-1515) across the street and about 100m south, and **Nippon Rent-a-Car** (☎ 34-5121)

southwest of the train station, near Sōsuke *minshuku*.

Getting Around

Most sights in Takayama can be covered easily on foot. You can amble from the train station across to Teramachi in 25 minutes.

The only place you may really need to take the bus is to Hida-no-Sato (¥200, 10 minutes, half-hourly).

Takayama is bicycle-friendly. Some lodgings hire out or lend cycles, or you can hire one from the convenience store **Timely** (タイムリー; ☎ 34-1183; per hr/day ¥300/1200; ☼ 10am-5pm) next to the train station; or **Hara Cycle** (☎ 32-1657; per hr/day ¥300/1300) on Kokubun-ji-dōri.

HIDA-FURUKAWA 飛騨古川
☎ 0577 / pop 18,000

Home of the somewhat mystifying Hadaka Matsuri (Naked Festival), Furukawa (also called Hida-Furukawa to distinguish it from other Furukawas in Japan) is a relaxing riverside town with lovely streetscapes, peaceful temples and interesting museums, all framed against mountains. Just 15 minutes by train from Takayama, Furukawa makes a rewarding day trip: if you are in the region on 19 or 20 April, don't miss the festival.

Orientation & Information

Hida-Furukawa train and bus stations adjoin each other east of the town centre. Sights are within 10 minutes' walk. There's an **information office** (観光案内所; ☎ 73-3180; ☼ 8.30am-5.30pm) at the bus station, dispensing an English pamphlet and Japanese maps, but if you don't speak Japanese you'll be better off getting information in Takayama (p255); staff in either location can book accommodation in Furukawa.

HIDA'S TAKUMI WOODWORKERS

Some 1300 years ago there lived in Hida a carpenter named Takumi, said to be so skilled that word of his work spread as far as the capital, Nara.

At that time, the Japanese regions had to pay taxes in rice, which posed a problem for Hida, with little farmland but many forested mountains. So in the year 718, in lieu of taxes, Hida was permitted to send Takumi – and a cadre of carpenters and carvers – to construct the legendary shrines and temples of Kyoto and Nara.

Today, 'Takumi' has become a general term for woodworkers of great skill and precision. Takumi work appears in homes, furniture and statues, and *karakuri* puppets for Hida's famed *yatai*, festival floats that are storeys tall.

Takumi's name has been adopted by woodworking shops nationwide. You can learn more about Takumi-style woodworking at the Takumi-Bunkakan (opposite) in Furukawa.

Sights

From the train station, walk right (north) two blocks and turn left towards the historic canal district **Setokawa to Shirakabe-dōzō** (瀬戸川と白壁土蔵街), handsome streets filled with white- and darkwood-walled shops, storehouses and private homes. Carp-filled waterways (fish food; ¥50) course through the district.

Here, the **Matsuri Kaikan** (まつり会館; Festival Museum; ☎ 73-3511; adult/high school student/child ¥800/700/400; ☟ 9am-5pm Mar-Nov, 9am-4.30pm Dec-Feb) shows Furukawa's festival in all its glory. You can don 3-D glasses to watch a video of the festivities, see some of the *yatai* that are paraded through the streets, try manipulating *karakuri* like those used on the *yatai*, and watch craftsmen demonstrating *kirie* (paper cut-outs) or *ittobori*.

Across the square, **Takumi-Bunkakan** (匠文化館; Takumi Craft Museum; ☎ 73-3321; adult/child ¥200/100; ☟ 9am-4.30pm Apr-Nov, 9am-4.30pm Tue-Sun Dec-Feb) is a must for woodworkers, craftspeople and design fans. In a hands-on room, you can try assembling blocks of wood cut into different joint patterns – not as easy as it sounds.

Follow the canal street westward for three blocks then turn right to reach the riverside **Honkō-ji** (本光寺), an intricately carved temple showcasing Furukawa's fine craftsmanship. From the temple, instead of retracing your steps, walk back along Ichi-no-Machi, a street sprinkled with craft shops, sake breweries (marked by the large balls of cedar fronds above the entrance) and traditional storehouses. Among them is **Mishima-ya** (三島屋; ☎ 73-4109; ☟ 9am-6pm Thu-Tue), a shop that has made candles for over two centuries; traditional shapes are concave or tapered with the wide end at the top.

Festivals & Events

The **Furukawa Matsuri**, as the Hadaka Matsuri is formally known, takes place every 19 and 20 April. The highlight is the Okoshi Daiko, when squads of boisterous young men dressed in loincloths parade through town at midnight, competing to place small drums atop a stage bearing a giant drum. OK, it's not *naked*-naked, but we didn't make up the name.

During the **Kitsune-bi Matsuri** (Fox Fire Festival) on 16 October, locals make up as foxes, parade through the town by lantern-light and enact a wedding at the shrine, Okura Inari-jinja. The ceremony, deemed to bring good fortune, climaxes with a bonfire at the shrine.

Sleeping & Eating

Hida Furukawa Youth Hostel (飛騨古川ユースホステル; ☎ /fax 75-2979; www.jyh.or.jp/english/tou kai/hidafuru/index.html; hidafyh@d2.dion.ne.jp; dm ¥3300, incl 2 meals ¥4900; ☟ closed 30 Mar-10 Apr; ✗ ☒ ☒ ☐) A friendly and attractive hostel amid farmland across from the park, Shinrin-kōen. It's about 6km from the town centre, or 1.2km west of Hida-Hosoe station (two stops north of Hida-Furukawa). In winter the hostel can help guests get set up for telemark skiing. Pick-up from station available after 6pm with advance notice. Japanese- and Western-style rooms available.

Ryokan Tanbo-no-Yu (旅館たんぼの湯; ☎ 73-2014; fax 73-6454; r per person incl 2 meals from ¥7000) In the town centre, this charming ryokan has spacious Japanese rooms with shared bathrooms, plus a bath with red-brown waters said to be good for cuts, bruises and rheumatism. Visitors can bathe for ¥500. No English is spoken.

Kitchen Kyabingu (キッチンきゃびんぐ; ☎ 73-4706; dishes ¥350-2400; ☟ lunch & dinner Tue-Sun) This cosy lunch spot in the historic district serves *Hida-gyu* (Hida beef). Order the beef curry with rice (¥800) or the *teishoku*, starring sizzling steak on a hot iron plate (¥2400).

Getting There & Around

Some 20 daily trains run each way between Takayama and Furukawa. Hida-Furukawa train station is three stops north of Takayama (*futsū*, ¥230, 15 minutes), or you can bus it (¥360, 30 minutes). Central Furukawa is an easy stroll, or hire bikes at the taxi office **Miyagawa** (☎ 73-2321; per hr ¥200), near the station.

SHIRAKAWA-GŌ & GOKAYAMA
白川郷・五箇山

These remote, dramatically mountainous districts between Takayama and Kanazawa are best known for farmhouses in the thatched, A-frame style called *gasshō-zukuri* ('hands-in-prayer'; see boxed text, p259). They're rustic and lovely, particularly in clear weather or in the snow, and they hold a special place in the Japanese heart.

In the 12th century the region's remoteness and inaccessibility are said to have attracted stragglers from the Taira (Heike) clan, virtually wiped out by the Minamoto (Genji) clan in a brutal battle in 1185. During feudal times Shirakawa-gō, like the rest of Hida, was under direct control of the Kanamori clan, connected to the Tokugawa shōgun, while

Gokayama was a centre for the production of gunpowder for the Kaga region, under the ruling Maeda clan.

Fast-forward to the 1960s: when construction of the gigantic Miboro Dam over the Shōkawa was about to submerge some local villages, many *gasshō* houses were moved to their current sites for safekeeping. Although much of what you'll find has been specially preserved for, and supported by, tourism, it still presents a view of rural life found in few other parts of Japan.

Most of Shirakawa-gō's sights are in the heavily visited community of Ogimachi. In Gokayama (technically not in Hida but in Toyama-ken), the community of Ainokura has the greatest concentration; other sights are spread throughout hamlets over many kilometres along Rte 156. Ogimachi and Ainokura are Unesco World Heritage sites (as is the Gokayama settlement of Suganuma).

Tour buses can diminish the magic of these communities. Get around this by avoiding weekends and holidays. Even better, stay overnight in a *gasshō-zukuri* house that's been turned into an inn. Advance reservations are highly recommended; the Shirakawa-gō tourist office by the parking area in Ogimachi can help with bookings (in Japanese), or Takayama's tourist office can help in English. Don't expect rooms with private facilities, but some inns have *irori* for guests to eat around.

Bus services to and around the region are infrequent and vary seasonally; it's important to check schedules. For maximum flexibility (and perhaps even a cost saving), consider hiring a car. Either way, traffic can be severe on weekends and throughout the peak tourist times of May, August and October. Expect snow, and lots of it, between late December and late March.

Shirakawa-gō 白川郷

☎ 05769

The region's central settlement, **Ogimachi**, has some 600 residents and over 110 *gasshō-zukuri* buildings and is the most convenient place to orient yourself for tourist information and transport.

Ogimachi's main **tourist office** (Deai no Yakata; ☎ 6-1013; www.shirakawa-go.org; 🕑 9am-5pm) is in the centre of town near the Shirakawa-gō bus stop. There's a free English map of Shirakawa-gō including Ogimachi (more detailed maps for ¥100/300). Limited English is spoken.

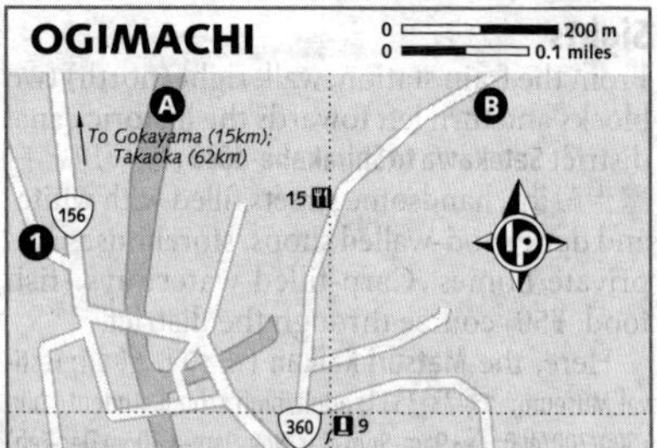

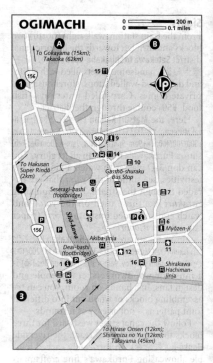

There's a smaller tourist office near the Ogimachi car park in the town centre.

SIGHTS

On the site of the former castle, the observatory **Shiroyama Tenbōdai** provides a lovely overview of the valley. It's a 15-minute walk via the road behind the east side of town. You can climb the path (five minutes) from near the intersection of Rtes 156 and 360, or there's a shuttle bus (¥200 one way) from the Shirakawa-gō bus stop.

Gasshō-zukuri Minka-en (合掌造り民家園; ☎ 6-1231; adult/child ¥500/300; 🕑 8am-5.30pm Aug, 8.40am-5pm Apr-Jul & Sep-Nov, 9am-4pm Fri-Wed Dec-Mar) features over two dozen relocated *gasshō-zukuri* buildings, reconstructed in this open-air museum amid seasonal flowers. Several houses are used for demonstrating regional crafts such as woodwork, straw handicrafts and ceramics; many items are for sale.

You can wander away from the houses for a pleasant stroll through the trees further up the mountain. Feel free to take a picnic, but Shirakawa-gō has a rule that you must carry your rubbish out of town.

Hours listed in this section are subject to change, as some of the old houses have been known to close irregularly. Be sure to call ahead to avoid disappointment.

Shirakawa-gō's largest *gasshō* house, **Wada-ke** (☎ 6-1058; admission ¥300; ⊙ 9am-5pm) is a designated National Treasure. It once belonged to a wealthy silk-trading family and dates back to the mid-Edo period. You'll find silk-harvesting equipment upstairs, as well as a valuable lacquerware collection.

Of the other *gasshō* houses, **Kanda-ke** (☎ 6-1072; adult/child ¥300/150; ⊙ 9am-5pm) is the least cluttered with exhibits, which leaves you to appreciate the architectural details – enjoy a cup of herb tea in the 36-mat living room on the ground floor. **Nagase-ke** (☎ 6-1047; adult/child ¥300/150; ⊙ 9am-5pm) was home of the doctors to the Maeda clan; look for displays of herbal medicine equipment. The *butsudan* (Buddhist altar) dates from the Muromachi period. In the attic, you can get an up-close look at the construction of the roof, which took 530 people to rethatch in 2001.

Next door to Ogimachi's small temple, **Myōzen-ji Folk Museum** (☎ 6-1009; adult/child ¥300/150; ⊙ 8.30am-5pm Apr-Nov, 9am-4pm Dec-Mar) displays the traditional paraphernalia of daily rural life.

Shirakawa-gō's big festival is held on 14 and 15 October at the shrine Shirakawa Hachiman-jinja (other festivals continue until the 19th), and features coordinated dancing groups of locals, including the lion dance and much *niwaka* (improvised buffoonery). The real star is *doboroku*, a very potent unrefined sake. Perhaps the most illustrative part of **Doboroku Matsuri Exhibition Hall** (☎ 6-1655; adult/child ¥300/150; ⊙ 9am-4pm Apr-Nov) is the video of the festival (in Japanese).

There are several *onsen* around Shirakawa-gō. In central Ogimachi, **Shirakawa-gō no Yu** (白川郷の湯; ☎ 6-0026; adult/child ¥700/300; ⊙ 10am-9.30pm) boasts a sauna, small *rotemburo* and large bath. Visitors staying at lodgings in town get a ¥200 discount. About 13km south of Ogimachi, off Rte 156 in Hirase Onsen, **Shiramizu no Yu** (しらみずの湯; ☎ 5-4126; adult/child ¥600/400; ⊙ 10am-9pm Tue-Sun) is a sharp new *onsen* facility with views across the river valley, a treat during the autumn-foliage season; its waters are said to be beneficial for fertility. About another 40km up the Ōshirakawa river (via a mountain road with blind curves and no public transport), **Ōshirakawa Rotemburo** (大白川露天風呂; ☎ 090-2770-2893; admission ¥300; ⊙ 8.30am-5pm Oct-Jun, to 6pm Jul & Aug) is much admired for its views of an emerald-green lake set amid the mountains.

SLEEPING & EATING

Some Japanese is helpful in making reservations at one of Ogimachi's many *gasshō-zukuri* inns. Note that they all close for the festival from 13 to 15 October. All inns include two meals in the rates. The town centre has a few casual restaurants (look for *soba* or *hoba miso*); most open only for lunch.

Kōemon (☎ 6-1446; fax 6-1748; r per person ¥8400) In the town centre, Kōemon has atmospheric rooms with heated floors, darkwood panelling and shared bathrooms. The friendly fifth-generation owner speaks English and his love of Shirakawa-gō is infectious. Try to book the room facing the pond.

Furusato (☎ 6-1033; r per person ¥8500) This much-photographed place near Myōzen-ji is run by a kindly older innkeeper and has quaint touches among the decent-sized tatami rooms.

Magoemon (☎ 6-1167; fax 6-1851; r per person ¥8900) Another friendly place, Magoemon has slightly larger rooms, some with river views. Meals are served around the handsome *irori*. There's a nightly heating surcharge (¥300) during cold weather.

CENTRAL HONSHŪ

Toyota Shirakawa-gō Eco-Institute (トヨタ白川郷自然学校; ☎ 6-1187; fax 6-1287; www.toyota.eco-inst.jp; d per person from ¥12,200) This eco-resort, a five-minute bus ride outside central Ogimachi, offers many opportunities to see and do: bird-watching, climbing Hakusan, and snow activities are just for starters. Organic meals are served. Although it gets school and corporate groups, individual travellers are also welcome. Rates vary widely and include children's discounts.

Irori (☎ 6-1737; mains ¥700-1200; ⏰ 11am-5pm) On the main road near Wada-ke, Irori serves regional specialities like *hoba miso* and *yaki-dofu* (fried tofu), as well as *sansai* or *tempura soba* to patrons who gather around the warm hearths inside.

Masu-en Bunsuke (☎ 6-1268; dishes ¥300-500; teishoku ¥1500-4000; ⏰ 9am-9pm) Uphill from the town centre, this attractive restaurant specialises in fresh trout, which are raised in ponds near the restaurant.

Gokayama District 五箇山
☎ 0763

Along the Shōkawa, Gokayama is so isolated that road links and electricity didn't arrive until 1925.

Villages with varying numbers of *gasshō-zukuri* buildings are scattered over many kilometres along Rte 156. The following briefly describes some of the communities you'll come across as you travel north from Shirakawa-gō or the Gokayama exit from the Tōkai-Hokuriku Expressway; if your time is limited, head straight for Ainokura.

SUGANUMA 菅沼
This riverside World Heritage site (www.gokayama.jp/english/index.html), 15km north of Ogimachi and down a steep hill, features an attractive group of *gasshō-zukuri* houses worth a stroll. The **Minzoku-kan** (民族館; Folklore Museum; ☎ 67-3652; adult/child ¥300/150; ⏰ 9am-4pm May-Nov) consists of two houses, with items from traditional life, and displays illustrating traditional gunpowder production.

About 1km further up Rte 156, **Kuroba Onsen** (くろば温泉; ☎ 67-3741; adult/child ¥600/300; ⏰ 10.30am-10pm Wed-Mon Apr-Oct, 11am-9pm Wed-Mon Nov-Mar) is a complex of indoor-outdoor baths overlooking the river, with fine mountain views from its different storeys. Its low-alkaline waters are good for fatigue and sore muscles, among other ailments.

KAMINASHI 上梨
About 5km beyond Suganuma, the house museum **Murakami-ke** (村上家; ☎ 66-2711; adult/child ¥300/150; ⏰ 8.30am-5pm Apr-Nov, 9am-4pm Dec-Mar, closed 2nd & 4th Wed of each month) is one of the oldest in the region (1578). The proud owner shows visitors around and then sits them beside the *irori* and sings local folk songs. An English-language leaflet is available.

Also close by is the shrine **Hakusan-gū**. The main hall dates from 1502 and has been designated an Important Cultural Property. Its **Kokiriko Festival** (25 and 26 September) features costumed dancers performing with rattles that move like snakes. On the second day everyone joins in.

AINOKURA 相倉
This World Heritage site is the most impressive of Gokayama's villages, with over 20 *gasshō* buildings in an agricultural valley amid splendid mountain views. It's less equipped for visitors than Ogimachi, which can be either a drawback or a selling point. Pick up an English pamphlet at the booth by the central car park.

Stroll through the village to the **Ainokura Museum of Life** (相倉民族館; ☎ 66-2732; admission ¥200; ⏰ 8.30am-5pm) with displays of local crafts and paper.

Continue along Rte 156 for several kilometres until **Gokayama Washi-no-Sato** (五箇山和紙の里; Gokayama Japanese Paper Village; ☎ 66-2223; adult/child ¥200/150; ⏰ 8.30am-5pm), where you will find displays of *washi* (Japanese handmade paper) art and a chance to make your own (¥500, reservations required). It's inside the *michi-no-eki*, a sort of public rest station.

Sleeping
Ainokura is a great place for a *gasshō-zukuri* farmhouse stay. Have a Japanese speaker contact the inns directly for reservations, or approach them yourself; all cost about ¥8000 per person, including two meals. Try the welcoming **Yomoshiro** (与茂四郎; ☎ 66-2377; fax 66-2387); **Goyomon** (五ヨ門; ☎ 66-2154; fax 66-2227), with excellent views from the 2nd storey; or **Chōyomon** (長ヨ門民宿; ☎ 66-2755; fax 66-2765), with its atmospheric dark-wood sliding doors. Ainokura also has a **camping ground** (☎ 66-2123; per person ¥500; ⏰ mid-Apr–late Oct), closed if there's snow.

Getting There & Away
Between April and late November, **Nōhi Bus Company** (☎ 0577-32-1688) operates five buses

daily linking Shirakawa-gō with Takayama (¥2400, 1¾ hours). Two buses a day connect Kanazawa with Shirakawa-gō (¥3300, 3½ hours). Schedules vary from December to March and depend largely on the weather.

Just before Ainokura, buses divert from Rte 156 for Rte 304 towards Kanazawa. From the Ainokura-guchi bus stop it's about 400m uphill to Ainokura.

Between Ogimachi and Gokayama, **Kaetsuno Bus** (☎ 0766-22-4888) operates four buses a day, stopping at all the major sights and continuing to Takaoka on the JR Hokuriku line (one hour). If you want to get off at unofficial stops (eg Kuroba Onsen), tell the driver.

By car it's about two hours from Takayama, with interchanges at Gokayama and Shōkawa. From Hakusan, the scenic toll road Hakusan Super-Rindō ends near Ogimachi (cars ¥3150). During colder months, check road conditions in advance with regional tourist offices.

JAPAN ALPS NATIONAL PARK 中部山岳国立公園

Boasting some of Japan's most dramatic scenery, this mountain-studded park – also called Chūbu-Sangaku National Park – is a favourite of alp-lovers. Highlights include hiking the valleys and peaks of Kamikōchi and Shin Hotaka Onsen, and soaking up the splendour of Shirahone Onsen, a gem of a hot-spring resort. The northern part of the park extends to the Tateyama-Kurobe Alpine Route (p290).

Orientation & Information
The park straddles the border between Gifu-ken and Nagano-ken, with the Gifu-ken (western) side also known as Oku-Hida Onsen, while the Nagano-ken (eastern) side is Azumi-mura. Thanks to recent changes in Japanese zoning laws, the two halves of the park are now administered by Takayama and Matsumoto respectively. Several maps and pamphlets are published by the Japan National Tourist Organization (JNTO) and by local tourist authorities in English, with more detailed hiking maps in Japanese.

Getting There & Around
The main gateway cities are Takayama to the west and Matsumoto to the east. Service from

Takayama is by bus, while most travellers from Matsumoto catch the private Matsumoto Dentetsu train to Shim-Shimashima station (¥680, 30 minutes) to transfer to buses – the ride in, along the Azusa-gawa, is breathtaking. Within the park, the main transit hubs are Hirayu Onsen and Kamikōchi.

Bus schedules are known to change annually, and the schedules short-change visits to some areas and *long*-change others. Check schedules before setting out. See boxed text, p268, for fares and travel times.

Hiring a car may save money, time and nerves. However, some popular routes, particularly the road between Naka-no-yu and Kamikōchi, are open only to buses and taxis.

KAMIKŌCHI 上高地
☎ 0263

Some 50km from Matsumoto and straddling the rushing Azusa-gawa, Kamikōchi is the park's biggest drawcard. It offers some of Japan's most spectacular scenery and a variety of hiking trails from which to see it.

In the late 19th century, foreigners 'discovered' this mountainous region and coined the term 'Japan Alps'. A British missionary, Reverend Walter Weston, toiled from peak to peak and sparked Japanese interest in mountaineering as a sport. He is now honoured with a festival (first Sunday in June, the official opening of the hiking season), and Kamikōchi has become a base for strollers, hikers and climbers. It's a pleasure just to meander Kamikōchi's riverside paths lined with *sasa* grasses.

Kamikōchi is closed from mid-November to late April, and in peak times (late July to late August, and during the foliage season in October) it is busier than Shinjuku station. Arrive early in the day, especially during the foliage season of late September to October. June to mid-July is the rainy season, making outdoor pursuits depressingly soggy. It's perfectly feasible to visit Kamikōchi as a day trip, but you'll miss out on the pleasures of staying in the mountains and taking uncrowded early-morning or late-afternoon walks.

Orientation
Most visitors arrive at Kamikōchi by bus to the bus station, which is surrounded by visitor facilities. A 10-minute walk from the bus station along the Azusa-gawa takes you

SAMPLE BUS ROUTES: JAPAN ALPS NATIONAL PARK

Within the park, bus fares and schedules change seasonally and annually; however, the following are fares and travel times on common bus routes in and around the area. Discounted return fares are listed where available, and if you are doing a lot of back-and-forth travel you may also consider the three-day 'Free Coupon' (¥6400) for unlimited bus transport within the park and to Matsumoto and Takayama. You can find current fare and schedule information at tourist offices in Matsumoto and Takayama, or at www.alpico.co.jp/access/route_k/honsen/info_e.html or www.alpico.co.jp/ac cess/express/kamikochi_takayama/info_e.html.

Bus Fares

From	To	Fare (¥; one way or one way/return)	Duration (mins; one way)
Takayama	Hirayu Onsen	1530	55
	Kamikōchi	2000	80
Matsumoto	Shin-Shimajima	680 (train)	30
		750 (bus – infrequent)	30
	Hirayu Onsen	2300/4100	85
	Kamikōchi	2400/4400	100
	Shin-Hotaka	2800	120
Shin-Shimajima	Naka-no-yu	1550	50
	Kamikōchi	1900/3300	70
	Shirahone Onsen	1400/2300	75
Kamikōchi	Naka-no-yu	600	20
	Hirayu Onsen	1050	30
	Shirahone Onsen	1350	40
Hirayu Onsen	Naka-no-yu	540	45

to the bridge Kappa-bashi, named for a water sprite of Japanese legend, where most of the hiking trails start.

Information

The **Kankō Ryokan Kumiai** (Ryokan Association; ☎ 95-2405; ☻ 9am-5pm late Apr–mid-Nov) at the Kamikōchi bus station is geared to booking accommodation, though non-Japanese speakers may want to book through tourist information offices in Matsumoto (p283) for Kamikōchi and Shirahone Onsen; both have English-speaking staff.

A little bit further along and to the left, the **Kamikōchi Information Centre** (☎ 95-2433; ☻ 8am-5pm late Apr–mid-Nov; E) provides hiking instructions and weather conditions, and also distributes the useful English *Kamikōchi Pocket Guide* with a map of the main walking tracks.

A 10-minute walk from the bus station along the main trail, the spiffy **Kamikōchi Visitor Centre** (☎ 95-2606; ☻ 8am-5pm late Apr–mid-Nov) has displays on Kamikōchi's flora and fauna, and explanations of its geological history.

Serious hikers and climbers might consider **insurance** (*hoken*; ¥1000 per person per day), available from window 3 at the Kamikōchi bus terminal. Weigh the benefits for yourself, but know that the out-of-pocket cost for a rescue 'copter starts at ¥800,000.

Sights & Activities
HIKING & CLIMBING

The river valley offers basically level, short-distance walks. A four-hour round trip starts east of Kappa-bashi along the right-hand side of the river past Myōjin-bashi (one hour) to Tokusawa (another hour) before returning. By Myōjin-bashi is the idyllic pond **Myōjin-ike** (admission ¥300), whose clear waters mark the innermost shrine of the **Hotaka-jinja**. There's also a track on the other side of the river, but it's partly a service road.

West of Kappa-bashi, you can amble along the right-hand side of the river to **Weston Relief** (a monument to Kamikōchi's most famous hiker, Walter Weston; 15 minutes) or keep to the left-hand side of the river and walk to the pond **Taishō-ike** (40 minutes).

The visitor centre offers **ranger-led hikes** (¥300) to Taishō-ike (8.20am) and Myōjin-ike (1pm). **Nature guides** (¥1000-3500) and **climbing guides** (per day ¥30,000) are also on hand. It is always wise to book in advance; some staff members speak English. Other popular hikes include the mountain hut at Dakesawa (2½ hours up) and Yakedake (four hours up, starting about 20 minutes west of the Weston Relief, at Hodaka-bashi). From the peaks, it's possible to see all the way to Mt Fuji in clear weather.

Dozens of long-distance options vary in duration from a couple of days to a week. *Hiking in Japan* by Paul Hunt, Mason Florence et al provides practical advice. Large Japanese-language maps of the area show routes and average hiking times between huts, major peaks and landmarks. Favourite hikes and climbs (which can mean human traffic jams during peak seasons) include Yariga-take (3180m) and Hotaka-dake (3190m) – also known as Oku-Hotaka-dake.

A steep but worthwhile hike connects Kamikōchi and Shin-Hotaka Onsen (p271). The trail from Kappa-bashi crosses the ridge below Nishi Hotaka-dake (2909m) at Nishi Hotaka San-sō (Nishi Hotaka Mountain Cottage; three hours) and continues on to Nishi Hotaka-guchi, which is the top station of the cable car for Shin-Hotaka Onsen. The hike takes nearly four hours (because of a steep ascent). Or you could save an hour of sweat and do the hike in the opposite direction. To reach the cable car, take a bus from Takayama or Hirayu Onsen to Shin-Hotaka Onsen-guchi.

Other more distant hiking destinations include Nakabusa Onsen (allow three days) and Murodō (allow five days), which is on the Tateyama-Kurobe Alpine Route (p78). This allows you to indulge in a soak en route in Takama-ga-hara Onsen, one of the finest in all Japan.

For long-distance hikes there are mountain huts available; enquire at the tourist office for details. Hikers and climbers should be well prepared. Even during summer, temperatures can plummet, or the whole area can be covered in sleeting rain or blinding fog, and in thunderstorms there is no refuge on the peaks.

ONSEN

On cold or drizzly days, the hot baths at the **Kamikōchi Onsen Hotel** (☎ 95-2311; admission ¥600; ⌚ 7-9am & 12.30-3.30pm) are a refreshing respite.

The area's most unusual *onsen* is **Bokuden-no-yu** (☎ 95-2341; admission ¥700; ⌚ 7am-5.30pm), a tiny cave bath dripping with minerals. It's at the intersection at Naka-no-yu, just before the bus-only tunnel towards Kamikōchi proper. Enter the small shop next to the Naka-no-yu bus stop, pay and get the key to the little mountain hut housing the *onsen*. It is yours privately for up to 30 minutes.

CENTRAL HONSHŪ

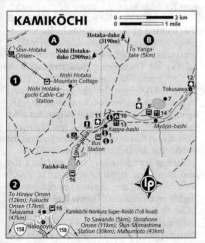

Sleeping & Eating

Accommodation in Kamikōchi is pricey and advance reservations are essential. Lodging rates quoted here include two meals, and some lodgings shut down their electricity generators in the middle of the night (emergency lighting stays on).

Kamikōchi Konashidaira Kyampu-jō (☎ 95-2321; camp sites per person from ¥700, tents/bungalows from ¥2000/6000; ☯ office 7am-7pm) About 200m past the visitors centre, this camping ground can get packed with tents. Rental tents (in July and August) and bungalows are available, and there's a small shop and restaurant open until 6pm.

Kamikōchi Nishiitoya San-sō (☎ 95-2206; fax 95-2208; www.nishiitoya.com; bunk beds ¥7700; d per person ¥10,550; E) Recently refurbished, this friendly lodge with a cosy lounge dates from the early 20th century. Rooms are a mix of Japanese and Western styles, all with toilet and shared bath: a large *onsen* facing the Hotake mountains. It's just west of Kappa-bashi.

Tokusawa-en (徳沢園; ☎ 95-2508; camp sites per person ¥500, Japanese dm per person ¥9000; r per person from ¥13,000) A marvellously secluded place, in a wooded dell about 3km northeast of Kappa-bashi. It's both a camping ground and a lodge and with Japanese-style rooms (shared facilities) and hearty meals served in a busy dining hall.

Kamikōchi Gosenjaku Lodge (上高地五千尺ロッヂ; ☎ 95-2221; fax 95-2511; www.gosenjaku.co.jp; per person 'skier's bed' ¥10,000; d/tr/q ¥17,850/16,800/15,000) This is a polished little place. Its 34 rooms are mostly Japanese-style plus some 'skier's beds', basically curtained-off bunk beds. Rooms all have sink and toilet, but baths are shared. Buffet-style meals are Japanese, Chinese and Western.

Dotted along the trails and around the mountains are dozens of spartan *yama-goya* (mountain huts), which provide two meals and a futon from around ¥8000 per person; some also serve simple lunches. Enquire before setting out to make sure there's one on your intended route.

Kamikōchi's signature dish is actually a signature skewer: *iwana* (river trout) grilled over an *irori*. Some trail huts serve it (along with the usual noodles and curry rice), but **Kamonjigoya** (☎ 95-2418; dishes ¥600-2000, lunch set ¥1500; ☯ 8.30am-4pm; E) is worth seeking out. The *iwana* set is ¥1500, or there's *oden* (fish cake stew), *soba* and *koru*-sake (dried *iwana* in

sake) served in a lovely ceramic bowl. It's near Myōjin-bashi bridge, just outside the entrance to Myōjin-ike pond.

There's a shop at the bus station with cheap trail snacks or, at the other end of the spectrum **Kamikōchi Gosenjaku Hotel** (☎ 95-2111) has pricey restaurants with French food and fancy cakes like Camembert torte with apples (¥630 per slice).

Getting Around

Private vehicles are prohibited between Naka-no-yu and Kamikōchi; access is only by bus or taxi, and then only as far as the Kamikōchi bus station. Those with private cars can use car parks en route to Naka-no-yu in the hamlet of Sawando for ¥500 per day; shuttle buses (¥1800 return) run a few times per hour.

Buses run via Naka-no-yu and Taishō-ike to the bus station. Hiking trails commence at the bridge Kappa-bashi, which is a short walk from the bus station.

SHIRAHONE ONSEN 白骨温泉
☎ 0263

Intimate and dramatic, this hot-spring resort town is easily the most beautiful in the park. Straddling a deep gorge, it's lovely any time of year, but during the autumn foliage season and – especially – in the snow, it is just this side of heaven. All around the gorge are a-dozen-and-a-half traditional inns (some more traditional than others) with open-air baths. Shirahone Onsen could also be a base for trips into Kamikōchi.

Shirahone means 'white bone', and it is said that bathing in the milky-blue hydrogen sulphide waters here for three days ensures three years without a cold; the waters have a wonderful silky feel. The riverside **kōshū rotemburo** (公衆露天風呂; public outdoor bath; admission ¥500; ☯ 8.30am-5pm Apr-Oct) is deep within the gorge, separated by gender; the entrance is by the bus stop. Diagonally opposite, the **tourist information office** (観光案内所; ☎ 93-3251; ☯ 9am-5pm) maintains a list of inns that have opened their baths to the public that day (admission from ¥600).

Budget travellers may wish to take a dip and move on; nightly rates start at ¥9000 with two meals, and advance reservations are highly recommended. **Tsuruya Ryokan** (つるや旅館; ☎ 93-2331; fax 93-2029; www.tsuruya-ryokan.jp in Japanese; r per person incl 2 meals from ¥10,650) has both contemporary and traditional touches and great indoor and outdoor baths, and each of its 28 rooms has fine views of the gorge; rooms with private toilet and sink available for extra charge.

our pick **Awanoyu Ryokan** (泡の湯旅館; ☎ 92-2101; fax 93-2339; www.awanoyu-ryokan.com in Japanese; r incl 2 meals from ¥26,950) may be what you have in mind when you think *onsen ryokan*. Up the hill from most of Shirahone, it's been an inn since 1912 (current building from 1940). It has private facilities in each room as well as single-sex common baths. There's also *kon-yoku* (mixed bathing), but not to worry: the waters are so milky that you can't see below the surface anyway.

Note: many visitors find the bus ride up along the narrow cliff-side roads from the Sawando junction either a thrill ride or a reason to take their happy pills.

HIRAYU ONSEN 平湯温泉
☎ 0578

This hot-spring resort is a busy hub for bus transport on the Takayama side of the park. It has a cluster of *onsen* lodgings and an excellent modern hot-spring complex, and even the bus terminal has a **rotemburo** (admission ¥600; ☺ 8am-5pm). The **information office** (☎ 89-3030; ☺ 9am-5pm), opposite the bus station, has leaflets and maps and can book accommodation. No English is spoken.

The hot-spring complex **Hirayu-no-mori** (ひらゆの森; ☎ 89-3338; admission ¥500; ☺ 10am-9pm), uphill from the bus station, boasts one indoor and six outdoor baths. It's great either for a quick dip between buses, or as part of a day excursion from Takayama.

Although Hirayu is not remote and relaxing in the way other Chūbu-Sangaku villages are, there are some nice inns. **Ryosō Tsuyukusa** (旅荘つゆくさ; ☎ 89-2620; fax 89-3581; r per person incl 2 meals ¥7500) is a friendly spot with decent tatami rooms and a cosy wooden *rotemburo* with mountain views. Turn left out of the bus station and left at the first T-junction. It's on the left before the road curves. The **Eitarō** (栄太郎; ☎ 89-2540; fax 89-3526; r per person incl 2 meals ¥10,650) ryokan offers more nicely outfitted rooms and a pleasant *rotemburo*. Turn left out of the bus station, walk about six minutes and it's on the left.

The elegant **Hirayu-kan** (平湯館; ☎ 89-3111; fax 89-3113; r per person incl 2 meals from ¥13,000) has both Japanese- and Western-style rooms, a splendid garden, and indoor and outdoor baths.

From the bus station, turn left, stay on the main road, go through one T-junction and it will soon be on your right.

To reach the small **Hirayu Camping Ground** (平湯キャンプ場; ☎ 89-2610; fax 89-2130; camp sites per adult/child ¥600/400, parking ¥1500), turn right out of the station, go about 700m and it's on the left-hand side.

For drivers, the 4km-plus Abō tunnel from Hirayu Onsen eastward into the park costs ¥600 each way.

FUKUCHI ONSEN 福地温泉
☎ 0578

This relatively untouristed hot spring, a short ride north of Hirayu Onsen, has rural charm, a morning market and two outstanding baths.

our pick Follow the long, rustic covered walkway to one of Central Honshū's finest *onsen* ryokan, **Yumoto Chōza** (湯元長座; ☎ 89-2146; fax 89-2010; www.cyouza.com in Japanese; r per person incl 2 meals from ¥21,150). Exquisite mountain cuisine is served at *irori* and you're surrounded by elegant traditional architecture and five indoor and two outdoor pools. Half of the 32 rooms have en-suite *irori*. Reservations are essential. By bus, get off at Fukuchi-Onsen-shimo.

A restaurant-cum-hot-spring, **Mukashiba-nashi-no-sato** (昔ばなしの里; ☎ 89-2793; bath ¥500; ☺ 8am-5pm) is set back from the street in a traditional farmhouse with fine indoor and outdoor baths, free on the 26th of each month. Out the front, there's an **asa-ichi** (☺ 6-10.30am daily Apr-Nov, Sat & Sun Dec-Mar). By bus, get off at Fukuchi-Onsen-kami bus stop.

SHIN-HOTAKA ONSEN 新穂高温泉
☎ 0578

North of Fukuchi Onsen, Shin-Hotaka Onsen may have lots of hot springs underground, but above ground the main reason to visit is for the cable car known as the Shin-Hotaka Ropeway. It is reportedly the longest of its kind in Asia, whisking you up close to the peak of Nishi Hotaka-dake (2909m) for a superb mountain panorama. The entrance to the two-stage **Shin-Hotaka Ropeway** (新穂高ロープウェイ; ☎ 9-2252; www.okuhi.jp/Rop/FRTop.html; one way/return ¥1500/2800; ☺ 6am-5.15pm 1 Aug-last Sun in Aug, 8.30am-4.45pm late Aug-Jul) is near the Shin-Hotaka Onsen bus station. Additional hours are offered at peak seasons.

If you are fit, properly equipped and have ample time, there's a variety of hiking options from Nishi Hotaka-guchi (the top cable-car station). One of the most popular is over to **Kamikōchi** (p267), which takes about three hours; it's *much* easier than going the other way.

Adjacent to the bus terminal is a rather spartan **public onsen** (新穂高温泉アルペン浴場; ☎ 9-2361; admission free; ◷ 9am-4pm). During summer it gets crowded with tourists, but in the off-season your only company is likely to be a few weary shift workers from the electric plant across the river.

Information is available at the **Oku-Hida Spa Tourist Information Centre** (奥飛騨温泉郷観光案内所; ☎ 9-2458; ◷ 10am-5pm) across from the bus terminal. Staff can book lodging in Shin-Hotaka Onsen, although lodgings here are not particularly appealing in terms of the price/quality ratio; visitors are better off heading to Kamikōchi, Fukuchi Onsen or Hirayu Onsen instead.

The best access for Shin-Hotaka Onsen is via bus from Takayama or Hirayu Onsen. See boxed text, p268, for details of buses within the park.

NAGANO-KEN 長野県

Known as Shinshū in earlier days, Nagano-ken is one of Japan's most enjoyable visits, not only for the beauty of its mountainous terrain (it claims the title 'the Roof of Japan'), but also for its traditional architecture, rich culture and unique foods.

Nagano-ken's cities, notably Nagano and Matsumoto, are well worth a stay and, apart from the sections of the prefecture in the Japan Alps National Park, there are several quasi-national parks that attract large numbers of skiers, campers, hikers, mountaineers and hot-spring aficionados.

NAGANO 長野
☎ 026 / pop 384,000

Nagano was front-and-centre on the world stage when it hosted the 1998 Winter Olympics, but this mountain-ringed prefectural capital has been around since the Kamakura period. Back then it was a temple town centred around the magnificent Zenkō-ji. The temple is still Nagano's main attraction, drawing more than four million visitors every year.

Since its brief flirtation with international fame, Nagano has reverted to its friendly small-town self, though it's just a bit more worldly. It is also an important transport hub. Not surprisingly, the mountains surrounding the city offer superb recreational opportunities: skiing, hiking, soaking in *onsen* and exploring the region's many mountain shrines.

Orientation

As a temple city, Nagano is laid out on a grid, with Zenkō-ji occupying a prominent position overlooking the city centre from the north. Chūō-dōri leads south from the temple, doing a quick dogleg before hitting JR Nagano station, 1.8km away; it is said that street-planners considered Zenkō-ji so holy that it should not be approached directly. Bus stops and the private Nagano Dentetsu ('Nagaden') train line are just outside JR Nagoya station's Zenkō-ji exit. Buses to various points in the city and surrounds depart from both the Zenkō-ji exit and the opposite east exit.

Information

The website www.nagano-cvb.or.jp has information about sightseeing, transportation, accommodation listings (with websites where available) and annual festivals.

There's a post office and an international ATM in the West Plaza Nagano building opposite the station's Zenkō-ji exit. Another post office is within the Zenkō-ji precincts, just inside the Niō-mon gate.

ANPIE (Association of Nagano Prefecture for Promoting International Exchange; ☎ 235-7186; www.anpie.or.jp; 692-2 Habashita; ◷ 8.30am-5.15pm Mon-Fri) Provides tourist information and assistance to speakers of English and other languages. From Nagano station, take any bus to the Kenchō (prefectural office) and go to the Kenchō-Higashikan (east building).

Boo Foo Woo (☎ 226-0850; 2nd fl, Daita Bldg, Chūō-dōri; per hr ¥390; ◷ 24hr) Internet access; six minutes' walk from the station, just off Chūō-dōri.

Café Planet (☎ 228-5433; B1 fl, 1375 Ishidōchō; per hr ¥400, ◷ 24hr) Internet access; across from the station, beneath the large Chinese restaurant Kinryū Hanten.

Heiandō bookshop (☎ 224-4545; West Plaza Nagano; ◷ 10am-10pm) Facing the station, Nagano's largest bookshop carries English-language books and magazines (4th floor).

Nagano City Hall International Relations Section (長野市役所国際課; ☎ 224-5447; 1613 Midori-chō; ◷ 8.30am-5.15pm Mon-Fri) This office has English speakers available to give tourist info. Take a right out of the station, walk for 10 minutes, and turn right on busy Shōwa-dōri. It's three blocks further, on the right.

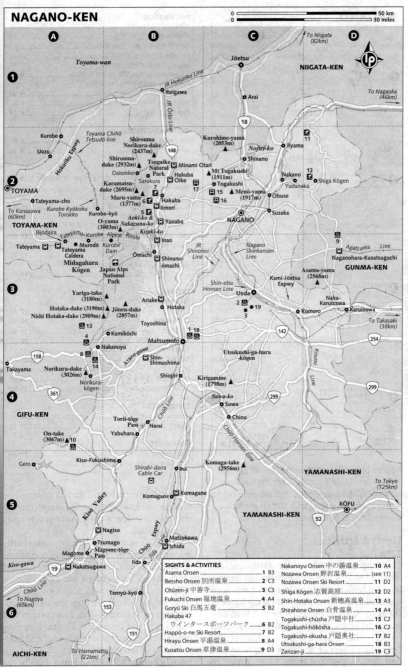

NAGANO-KEN

CENTRAL HONSHŪ

CENTRAL HONSHŪ

Nagano Tourist Information Centre (☎ 226-5626;
🕐 9am-6pm) Inside JR Nagano station, this friendly outfit
has good English-language colour maps and guides to both
Nagano and the surrounding areas. Staff can also book
accommodation in the city centre.

Sights & Activities
ZENKŌ-JI 善光寺

This **temple** (☎ 186-026-234-3591; 491 Motoyoshi-chō;
admission free; 🕐 4.30am-4.30pm summer, 6am-4pm winter, sliding hr rest of year) is believed to have been
founded in the 7th century and is the home of
the Ikkō-Sanzon, allegedly the first Buddhist
image to arrive in Japan (in AD 552, from
Korea). The image has quite a history; it's
been the subject of disputes, lost, recovered
and, finally, installed again. Don't expect to

see it, however; it is said that 37 generations
of emperors have not seen the image, though
visitors may view a copy every seven years
(see opposite).

Zenkō-ji's immense popularity stems partly
from its liberal welcoming of believers from
all Buddhist sects, including women; its chief
officiants are both a priest and a priestess.

The original site was south of the current temple, off what's now the busy shopping street Nakamise-dōri; however, in that
location it was destroyed 11 times by fires
originating in neighbouring homes and businesses – and rebuilt each time with donations
from believers throughout Japan. Finally, the

Tokugawa shōgunate decreed that the temple be moved to its present, safer location. The current building dates from 1707 and is a National Treasure.

Visitors ascend to the temple via Naka-mise-dōri and the impressive gates **Niō-mon** and **Sanmon** (under restoration at time of writing). In the Hondō (main hall), the Ikkō-San-zon image is in an ark left of the central altar, behind a dragon-embroidered curtain. To the right of the altar, visitors may descend a staircase to the Okaidan, a pitch-black tunnel that symbolises death and rebirth and provides the closest access to the hidden image; taller visitors: watch your head! As you navigate the twisting tunnel, dangle your arm along the right-hand wall until you feel something heavy, moveable and metallic – said to be the key to salvation (a bargain for the ¥500 admission).

It's worth getting to the temple shortly after it opens to witness the morning service and the *ojuzu chodai*, in which the priest or priestess touches the Buddhist holy beads to the heads of all who line up and kneel. Check with the tourist information centre or the Zenkō-ji office for the times of the service.

Any bus from bus stop 1 in front of Nagano station's Zenkō-ji exit will get you to the temple (¥100).

M-WAVE SKATING ARENA Mウェーブ

One of the star attractions during the 1998 Olympics, the state-of-the-art **speed-skating arena** (☎ 222-3300; www.nagano-mwave.co.jp; adult/child ¥700/350; museum 10am– 4pm Wed-Mon) today houses an Olympic memorial museum with exhibits relating to the games. Photos, medals, the original torch and uniforms are on display. Visitors can also watch footage from other Olympics and ride a rather amusing bobsled simulator. Skating, while pricey (and hours vary), is perhaps the best way to experience **M-Wave** (admission ¥1500, skate rental ¥600). Take a Yashima-bound bus from stop 1 from Nagano station's east exit and get off at M-Wave (¥260, 20 minutes).

Festivals & Events

Gokaichō Matsuri Five million pilgrims come to Zenkō-ji every seven years from early April to mid-May, to view a copy of Zenkō-ji's sacred Buddha image – the only time it can be seen. Next festival: 2010.

Enka Taikai Fireworks festival with street foods on 23 November.

Sleeping

Perhaps the most Nagano way to stay is in a *shukubō* (temple lodging) at one of Zenkō-ji's subtemples. Contact **Zenkō-ji** (☎ 186-026-234-3591) to book, at least one day in advance. Be sure to dial the '186' to permit caller ID, without which staff might not pick up the phone. Expect to pay ¥7000 to ¥10,000 per person with two meals.

Near Zenkō-ji are several traditional and very old ryokan. The station area is mostly uninspiring business hotels; we've picked out some good station-area options.

Zenkō-ji Kyōju-in Youth Hostel (☎ 232-2768; fax 232-2767; 479 Motoyoshi-chō; dm member/nonmember ¥3360/4360) This atmospheric hostel is housed in a 100-plus-year-old subtemple of Zenkō-ji. Detractors would prefer no curfew and not to have to share a room, but it remains popular nonetheless. Be sure to book. No meals are served.

Oyado Kinenkan (☎ 234-2043; fax 234-6888; 550 Nishimachi; r per person from ¥4200) Old-shoe comfy and exceedingly friendly, this building has been an inn for 100 of its 200 years. Rooms have no private facilities and parts are, shall we say, showing their history; many fans wouldn't have it any other way. Add ¥1300 for breakfast or ¥4600 for two meals. English and French spoken. Take the bus to Daimon Minami, and the inn is one block west – look for the huge inverted bowl on the façade (it's the nose from an early *shinkansen*).

Shimizuya Ryokan (☎ 232-2580; fax 234-5911; 49 Daimon-chō; r per person from ¥4500) On Chūō-dōri, a few blocks south of Zenkō-ji, this friendly, family-run ryokan offers good value, with a smoky dark-wood interior; spotless tatami rooms (no private facilities), laundry machines and lots of ins, outs, ups, downs, nooks and crannies. It's been in the family for 130 years. No meals served.

Comfort Hotel Nagano (☎ 268-1611; fax 268-1621; www.choice-hotels.com; 1-12-4 Minami-Chitose; s/d/tw from ¥4820/7350/9870;) Of the many business hotels near the station, this one has the best combination of value and welcome. Rooms are teeny tiny, but rates include a simple breakfast and internet access in the lobby. From the station, head northeast along Nagano Ōdori, and the hotel is just before Mitsukoshi department store.

Matsuya Ryokan (☎ 232-2811; fax 233-2047; Zenkō-ji Kannai; r per person from ¥4500, incl meals from ¥9000;) Six generations of the Suzuki family have run

CENTRAL HONSHŪ

ZENKŌ-JI LEGENDS

Few Japanese temples have the fascination of Zenkō-ji, thanks in part to the legends related to it. These are just some:

■ **Ikkō-Sanzon** This image, containing three statues of the Amida Buddha, was brought to Japan from Korea in the 6th century and remains the temple's *raison d'être*. It's wrapped like a mummy and kept in an ark behind the main altar, and it's said that nobody has seen it for 1000 years. However, in 1702, to quell rumours that the ark was empty, the shōgunate ordered a priest to confirm its existence and take measurements. That priest remains the last confirmed person to have viewed it.

■ **Following an Ox to Zenkō-ji** Long ago, an impious old woman was washing her kimono when an ox appeared, caught a piece of the cloth on his horn and ran away with it. The woman was as stingy as she was impious, and she gave chase for hours. Finally, the ox led her to Zenkō-ji, and she fell asleep under its eaves. The ox came to her in a dream, revealed himself to be the image of the Amida Buddha and disappeared. The woman saw this as a miracle and became a pious believer. Today, people in Kantō say, 'I followed an ox to Zenkō-ji', to mean that something good happened unexpectedly.

■ **The Doves of Sanmon** Zenkō-ji's pigeon population is renowned, making the rattan *hatto-guruma* (wheeled pigeon) a favourite Nagano souvenir. Locals claim the birds forecast bad weather by roosting on the Sanmon gate. Many visitors claim to also see five white doves in the plaque above the central portal; the five short strokes in the characters for Zenkō-ji do look remarkably dove-like. See if you can spot them too. In the upper character (善, zen) they're the two uppermost strokes; in the middle character (光, kō) they're the strokes on either side of the top; and in the 'ji' (寺) it's the short stroke on the bottom left.

■ **Binzuru** A follower of Buddha, Binzuru trained in healing. He was due to become a Bosatsu (Bodhisattva, enlightened one) and go to the land of the immortals, but the Buddha instructed him to remain on earth and continue to do good works. At most temples with images of Binzuru he's outside the main hall, but at Zenkō-ji you'll find his statue just inside, worn down where visitors have touched it to help heal ailments of the corresponding parts of their own bodies; you can see the lines where the face was once replaced.

---

this traditional inn just inside the Niō-mon of Zenkō-ji. Even if the communal baths are a bit aged, the rest of the ryokan is exceedingly well maintained. Meals are seasonal *kaiseki*. Add ¥1000 per person for rooms with private facilities. It's next to the statue of the Enmei Jizō.

Hotel Sunroute Nagano Higashi-guchi (☎ 264-7700; fax 264-6611; www.sunroute.jp; 995-1 Kurita; s/d/tw from ¥8085/14,385/15,435; ✗ ✗) Business hotel with clean, modern rooms and smart wood touches. Rooms ending in 17 are corner rooms with extra space and good views. Check for internet specials. It's across from the station, outside the east exit.

Hotel Saihokukan (☎ 235-3333; www.saihokukan.com; 528-1 Kenchō; s/d/tw from ¥6825/14,700/15,750) Dating from 1890 (though facilities are recent), this Western hotel has elegant flourishes in its fine rooms, plus stylish restaurants and bars. Less expensive rooms are a bit small; suites are favoured by the imperial family.

From the station's Zenkō-ji exit; head north along Chūō-dōri and turn left after Hachijuni Bank.

Hotel Metropolitan Nagano (☎ 291-7000; fax 291-7007; www.metro-n.co.jp; 1346 Minami-Ishido-chō; s/d/tw from ¥9240/19,635/18,480) An excellent choice next to the station. The modern, elegant Metropolitan features airy, comfortable rooms, with a café, restaurant and top-floor lounge with broad views. Japan Rail Pass holders get a 20% discount. It's just outside the station's Zenkō-ji exit; if you're sensitive to noise, reserve a room facing away from the tracks.

Eating

Tofu Café Gorokutei (☎ 233-0356; 125-1 Higashi-machi; mains ¥600-1200; ☽ lunch & dinner; Ⓥ) From the pancakes to the parfaits, just about everything here is made with Japan's favourite protein (although the 'tofu hamburger' also has a little ground chicken). It's in Patio Daimon, an open-air collection of small buildings built like *kura* (storehouses), by the Daimon and Daimon Minami bus stops. Picture menu available.

Gohonjin Fujiya (Fujiya Gohonjin; ☎ 232-1241; 80 Daimon-chō; mains ¥1000-2400; ☻ lunch Mon-Fri, dinner nightly; E) Until recently, this was Nagano's most venerable hotel (since 1648), but it quit the hotel businesss and is now the city's most venerable Western restaurant. Try potato gnocchi with gorgonzola sauce or *wagyu* sirloin Florentine. The imposing 1923 building mixes Japanese and Art Deco motifs.

Gomeikan (☎ 232-1221; 515 Daimon-chō; mains from ¥1200; ☻ 11am-8pm Thu-Tue; V E) This longtime Nagano favourite serves delicious *tonkatsu* (deep-fried breaded pork cutlet), vegetarian Indian curry, beefsteak, and coffee and cake in an old renovated building next to the post office on Chūō-dōri.

Chō Bali Bali (☎ 243-2891; 1366 Suehiro-chō; mains from ¥600; ☻ noon-2.30pm & 6pm-midnight Tue-Sun; V E) This stylish space gathers a festive crowd most nights and serves eclectic dishes from Indonesia, Thailand and Vietnam with a touch of Italian for good measure; *yam-un-sen* is a spicy Thai salad with vermicelli. Highly recommended.

Marusei (☎ 232-5776; 486 Motoyoshi-chō; dishes ¥600-1300; ☻ 11am-4pm Thu-Tue; E) A stone's throw from the temple on Nakamise-dōri, tiny unassuming Marusei serves *soba* and a well-liked *tonkatsu*; the Marusei *bentō* (boxed lunch; ¥1300) lets you try both.

Munch (☎ 228-7080; 1-16-1 Minami-Chitose; dishes ¥300-580; ☻ 6.30pm-midnight Mon-Sat) Japanese reggae is the soundtrack at this youthful contemporary *izakaya*. Order small plates like *agedashi-dofu* (fried tofu), *basashi* (horsemeat sashimi) or *niku-jaga* (meat and potatoes), washed down with *ichigo* (strawberry) or *mikan* (mandarin orange) sake. Or say how much you want to spend and let the chef surprise you. From the Zenkō-ji exit of the station, turn right through the alley and it's just past the car park.

Sukitei (すき亭; ☎ 234-1123; lunch sets ¥1150-2950; sukiyaki from ¥2500; ☻ lunch & dinner Tue-Sun) Tops in town for splendid sukiyaki. Set menus include *udon*, *gyusashi* (beef sashimi) and more. The price of the top-grade beef is sky-high, but if you try it you may never go back to the cheaper stuff.

Some spots for a quick bite:

Oyaki Kōbō (☎ 223-4537; oyaki each around ¥140; ☻ 8.30am-7.30pm; V) *Oyaki* (filled wheat buns) with tasty flavours like pumpkin, mushroom and eggplant.

Kashin Miwa (☎ 238-3041; ice cream ¥250; ☻ 9am-5pm) Has ice cream made with *soba* (only in Nagano) near Zenkō-ji's Niō-mon

Bakery's Street Café (☎ 232-0269; 1283 Toigosho; mains from ¥480; ☻ 7.30am-7pm; V) Dozens of bakeries from around Shinshu take turns supplying the wares. On Chūō-dōri, en route to Zenkō-ji, 12 minutes' walk from the station.

Drinking

Groovy (☎ 227-0480; http://nagano.cool.ne.jp/jazzgroovy; 1398 Kita-ishidō-machi; cover ¥1000-3500) This music spot is popular with local jazz lovers for its live shows; check the website for schedule info. It's on Chūō-dōri, a six-minute walk from the train station.

Liberty (☎ 235-2870; 1602 Midori-chō; ☻ 11.30am-2pm & 6pm-1am) Nagano's most popular *gaijin* pub has Guinness on tap, decent pub food and a friendly crowd. From the west exit of JR Nagano, take a right on busy Nagano-Odōri and another right (at the second stoplight) on Showa-dōri.

Getting There & Away

Nagano *shinkansen* trains run twice hourly from Tokyo station (Asama, ¥8170, 1½ hours). The JR Shinonoi line connects Nagano with Matsumoto (*tokkyū*, ¥2970, 50 minutes) and Nagoya (*tokkyū*, ¥7330, three hours).

TOGAKUSHI 戸隠

☎ 026 / pop 5200

This mountainous, forested region is northwest of Nagano and makes an excellent day trip. Hikers enjoy the refreshing alpine scenery from late spring to autumn, while winter belongs to the skiers. Togakushi has been famed for *soba* for centuries.

Three **subshrines** (Hōkōsha 宝幸社, Chūsha 中社 and Okusha 奥社), each separated by several kilometres, make up the Togakushi Shrine. The greatest concentration of sights and accommodation is in the community of Chūsha, near the Chūsha-Miyamae bus stop, including the wooded Chūsha; one tree here is said to be 800 years old. It's a good skiing base in the winter. You can hike a meandering 90-minute trail to Okusha, at the foot of Mt Togakushi, passing by **Kagami-ike Pond** (鏡池) and the **Togakushi Botanic Garden** (森林植物園). At the edge of the botanic garden you'll meet up with the long, cedar-lined path (*suginamiki*; 杉並木) to Okusha. Pick up Japanese maps from the Nagano tourist information centre.

CENTRAL HONSHŪ

From Okusha avid alpinists can make the strenuous climb to the top of 1911m-high Mt Togakushi. In winter, Okusha is inaccessible except for hearty snowshoers.

Across from the turn-off to Okusha is **Togakushi Minzoku-kan** (戸隠民俗館; ☎ 254-2395; adult/child ¥500/350; ☷ 9am-5pm), a collection of buildings that attest to the ninja-training school that was once here. A museum displays photos, clothing and weaponry used by the ninja (practitioner of the art of stealth) there. Next door, you can bungle your way through the popular Ninja House, which is full of trick doors, false staircases and curious mazes.

Near Chūsha, **Togakushi Snow World** (戸隠ス ノーワールド; ☎ 254-2106; 1-day pass ¥4000) has a local following for its decent runs (the longest is 3000m) and fewer crowds than other nearby resorts. Opening hours vary.

In Chūsha, **Togakushi Kōgen Yokokura Youth Hostel** (戸隠高原横倉ユースホステル; ☎ 254-2030; dm ¥3050, incl 2 meals ¥4725) is in an early Meiji-era building (Japanese toilets only), near the entrance to the ski area. Ryokan-quality private rooms are available from ¥7000 per person, with two meals. Prices at other ryokan start at around ¥8000 per person. To savour local *soba*, grab lunch at well-known **Uzuraya Soba** (うずら家そば; ☎ 254-2219; dishes ¥800-1700; ☷ lunch), which serves handmade *soba* noodles until they run out. It's also in Chūsha, directly across from the steps to the shrine.

Closer to Okusha (400m before the shrine), **Soba Nomi** (そばの実; ☎ 254-2102; dishes from ¥840; ☷ 10.30am-4.30pm) is another fine choice, with delicious *soba* and large windows overlooking the forest.

Buses via the scenic Togakushi Birdline Highway depart from Nagano approximately hourly (7am to 7pm) and arrive at Chūsha-Miyamae bus stop in about an hour (one-way/return ¥1160) – do not get off at Chūsha bus stop. To Okusha the one way/return fare is ¥1280/2300. If you plan to take many buses, look into the Togakushi Kōgen Free Kippu pass (¥2500 for three days), available from **Kawanakajima Bus Co** (☎ 229-6200), by stop 7 in front of Nagano station.

OBUSE 小布施
☎ 026 / pop 12,000

This little town northeast of Nagano occupies a big place in Japanese art history. The famed *ukiyo-e* (wood-block print) artist Hokusai (1760–1849) worked here during his last years.

The town is also noted for its *kuri* (chestnuts), which you can sample steamed with rice or in ice cream or sweets. Pick up a map of the town from the Nagano tourist information centre before setting out.

The first stop should be the excellent **Hokusai-kan** (北斎館; ☎ 247-5206; adult/high school student/child ¥500/300/free; ☷ 9am-6pm Apr-Sep, 9am-5pm Oct-Mar), displaying some 30 of Hokusai's inspiring prints at any one time as well as several colourful floats decorated with his imaginative ceiling panels. From the train station, cross the street and walk down the road perpendicular to the station; take the second right then look for signs to the museum. It's a 10-minute walk from the station.

A block away, Hokusai's patron, Takai Kōzan, is commemorated in the **Takai Kōzan Kinenkan** (高井鴻山記念館; ☎ 249-4049; admission ¥300; ☷ 9am-5pm). This businessman was also an accomplished artist, albeit of more classical forms than Hokusai's; look for elegant Chinese-style landscapes.

A few blocks east stands the **Taikan Bonsai Museum** (盆栽美術館大観; ☎ 247-3000; adult/child ¥500/300; ☷ 9am-5pm), whose displays of rare species change daily. It's in five sections, to represent different Japanese landscapes including Hokkaidō, the ancient capital and right here in Shinshū.

Nine other **museums** in Obuse showcase everything from Japanese lamps to antique pottery.

To reach Obuse, take the Nagano Dentetsu (Nagaden) line from Nagano (*tokkyū*, ¥750, 22 minutes; *futsū*, ¥650, 35 minutes). You can obtain maps and info and hire bikes (¥400 per half-day) at the **Obuse Guide Centre** (おぶせガイドセンター; ☎ 247-5050; ☷ 9am-5pm), which you'll pass en route to the museums from the station.

YUDANAKA 湯田中
☎ 0269

This hot spring village is famous as the home of Japan's famous 'snow monkeys', a troop of some 200 Japanese macaques who occasionally climb into the hot-spring baths here. The monkeys and their mountain hot tub can be found at **Jigokudani Yaen-kōen** (地獄谷野猿公苑; Wild Monkey Park; ☎ 33-4379; www.jigokudani-yaenkoen.co.jp; adult/child ¥500/250; ☷ 8.30am-5pm Apr-Oct, 9am-4pm Nov-Mar). The park has been operating since 1964, so the monkeys can no longer be described as truly wild, and they're often lured into the tub to gather food that's been placed there. However, it's a unique chance to see Japanese monkeys in a semi-wild setting. It's a popular day trip from Nagano, and in winter it can be combined with a ski excursion to nearby Shiga Kōgen (below).

Across the river from Jigokudani, **Kōraku-kan** (後楽館; ☎ 33-4376; r per person incl 2 meals from ¥10,545; onsen only adult/child ¥500/250; ⏰ 8am-10am & noon-3.30pm) is a simple *onsen* hotel. Accommodation is basic, with small but clean-swept tatami rooms. Aside from the mountain vegetable tempura for overnight visitors, the highlight is indoor and concrete riverside outdoor *onsen*. Bathe outdoors, and uninvited guests – of the decidedly hairy variety – may join you.

Uotoshi Ryokan (魚歲旅館; ☎ 33-1215; fax 33-0074; www.avis.ne.jp/~miyasaka/; s/d/tr/q ¥4300/7980/11, 970/15,960; 💻) In peaceful central Yudanaka, Uotoshi is nothing fancy but commendably hospitable. The English-speaking owner will demonstrate *kyūdō* (Japanese archery), pick you up at Yudanaka station, or drop you off near the start of the Monkey Park trail on request. Dinner (from ¥2520) and breakfast (from ¥530) are available. If you're walking from the station (seven minutes), turn left and follow the road over the river; when the road ends turn right. It's 20m further on.

From Nagano, take the Nagano Dentetsu (Nagaden) line to the Yudanaka terminus (*tokkyū*, ¥1230, 45 minutes; *futsū*, ¥1130, 1¼ hours); note that not all trains go all the way to Yudanaka. For the monkey park, take the bus for Kanbayashi Onsen Guchi and get off at Kanbayashi Onsen (¥220, 15 minutes, eight daily), walk uphill along the road about 400m, and you'll see a sign reading 'Monkey Park' at the start of a tree-lined 1.6km walk.

SHIGA KŌGEN 志賀高原
☎ 0269

Shiga Kōgen (☎ 34-2404; www.shigakogen.gr.jp/english/; 1-day lift ticket ¥4800; ⏰ 9am-9pm Dec-Apr), the site of several events in the 1998 Nagano Olympics, is Japan's largest ski resort and one of the largest in the world: 21 linked areas covering 80 runs. One lift ticket gives access to all areas and the shuttle bus between the various base lodges. There is a huge variety of terrain for all skill levels, as well as ski-only areas. **Shiga Kōgen Tourist Office** (志賀高原観光協会; ☎ 34-2323; ⏰ 9am-5pm) has English speakers who can help you navigate the slopes and

can book accommodation. It's in front of the Shiga Kōgen ropeway station.

Due to its sprawling size, skiers will need to plan carefully or spend their first day at the resort making a full reconnaissance, spending following days at their favourite spots. If you've got limited time, base yourself somewhere central like the Ichinose Family Ski Area, with a central location and wide variety of accommodation and restaurants. You could also start at the Yakebitai area and work your way gradually down the entire resort, taking the bus back up when you're done.

The Nishitateyama area has good wide runs and generally ungroomed terrain. The Terakoya area is a little hard to get to but it is generally uncrowded and has good short runs and a nice atmosphere. Skiers who don't mix well with snowboarders will be happiest at the Kumanoyu area.

During the rest of the year, the mountains' lakes, ponds and overlooks make an excellent destination for hikers.

Hotels are scattered the length of Shiga-kogen, clustered at the bases of the different areas. It makes sense to choose one near the base of your favourite area. **Hotel Shiraka-baso** (ホテル白樺荘; ☎ 34-3311; fax 34-3036; www.shirakaba.co.jp/english/index.html; r per person incl 2 meals from ¥11,000; wi-fi), close to the cable car base station and the Sun Valley ski area, is a pleasant little hotel with a variety of rooms and its own indoor and outdoor *onsen* baths. Near the base of the Kumanoyu ski area, the large **Hotel Heights Shiga Kōgen** (ホテルハイツ志賀高原; ☎ 34-3030; fax 34-2523; www.shigakogen.jp/heights/english/index.htm; r per person incl 2 meals from ¥12,600) boasts clean Japanese- and Western-style rooms and its own *onsen*. Staff are used to foreign guests and make some concessions to foreign palates in the dining room (upon request).

Direct buses run between Nagano station and Shiga-kogen, with frequent departures in ski season (¥1500, 80 minutes). You can also take a train from Nagano to Yudanaka (opposite) and continue to Shiga-kogen by bus – take a Hase-ike–bound bus and get off at the last stop (¥700, 30 minutes).

NOZAWA ONSEN 野沢温泉
☎ 0269 / pop 4264

A compact town that is tucked into a corner of the eastern Japan Alps, Nozawa Onsen is the quintessential Japanese *onsen*/ski resort. It's dominated by the **Nozawa Onsen Ski Resort**

(野沢温泉スキー場; ☎ 85-3155; www.nozawaski
.com/e/; 1-day lift ticket ¥4600; ☑ Dec-Apr), one of
Honshū's best for a day on the slopes followed by an evening in the tubs. Nozawa feels
like a Swiss ski resort, and you may wonder
where you are – until you see a sign written
entirely in kanji.

Although Nozawa is worth visiting any time
of year, skiing is the main attraction for foreign
visitors. The ski area here is more compact
than, say, nearby Shiga-kōgen, and it's relatively easy to navigate and enjoy. The main
base area is right around the Higake gondola
station. There is a good variety of terrain at all
levels, and snowboarders should try the Kara-
sawa terrain park or the halfpipe at Uenotaira.
Advanced skiers will enjoy the steep and often
mogulled Schneider Course, while beginners
and families will enjoy the Higake Course.

For on-slope refreshments, try the rest
house at Uenotaira gondola station, which
has a standard-issue restaurant and snack bar.
There's another restaurant at the top of the
Nagasaka gondola.

There are ski hire places near the base of
both gondolas, and boots of up to 31cm are
available.

After skiing or hiking, check out the 13
free **onsen** (☑ 6am-11pm) dotted about the town.
Our favourite is Ō-yu, with its fine wooden
building, followed by the scalding-hot Shin-
yu, recently renovated, and the atmospheric
old Kuma-no-tearai (Bear's Bathroom). If
you plan on making a full circuit of all the
onsen, leave valuables in your room and wear
easy-on/easy-off clothes like a *yukata* (light
summer cotton kimono) and slip-on shoes
or sandals.

The **Minshuku Information Office** (野沢温泉
民宿組合事務所; ☎ 85-2068; ☑ 8.30am-5.30pm),
in the centre of town, can help with accommodation. **Lodge Nagano** (ロッジながの; ☎ 090-
8670-9597; www.lodgenagano.com/index.html; r per person
from ¥4000) is a popular foreign-run guesthouse
that attracts a lot of Aussie skiers and makes
them feel right at home with Vegemite in the
dining room. It's a friendly, fun place with
both bunk and private rooms.

On the slopes near the Higake gondola base,
the European-style **Pension Schnee** (ペンション
シュネー; ☎ 85-2012; fax 85-3281; pensionschnee@ybb
.ne.jp; r per person incl 2 meals from ¥7000) enjoys the
best location in town. It's a ski-in/ski-out
place with comfortable pension-style rooms
and a woodsy dining room.

Lodge Matsuya (ロッヂ まつや; ☎ 85-2082;
fax 85-3694; r per person incl 2 meals from ¥8000) in the
centre of town is a large, friendly place with
both Western-style and Japanese-style rooms
(though some smell a little of cigarette smoke).
In the centre of the village, **Haus St Anton** (サン
アントンの家; ☎ 85-3597; fax 85-3963; http://nozawa
.com/stanton/; r per person incl 2 meals with/without bathroom from ¥13,125/8925) is a comfortable inn with
an Austrian theme, attractive Western-style
bedrooms and a good kitchen.

There are direct buses between Nagano
station east exit and Nozawa Onsen (¥1300,
85 minutes, six buses per day). Alternatively,
take a JR Iiyama-line train between Nagano
and Togari Nozawa Onsen station (¥740, 1¼
hours). Regular buses connect Togari Nozawa
Onsen station and Nozawa Onsen (¥300, 15
minutes, nine per day).

HAKUBA 白馬
☎ 0261
At the base of one of the highest sections of
the northern Japan Alps, Hakuba is one of
Japan's main ski and hiking centres. In winter,
skiers from all over Japan and increasingly
from overseas flock to Hakuba's seven ski
resorts. In summer, the region is crowded
with hikers drawn by easy access to the high
peaks. There are several *onsen* in and around
Hakuba-mura, the main village, and a long
soak after a day of skiing or hiking is the perfect way to ease your muscles.

For information, maps and lodging assistance, visit the **Hakuba Shukuhaku Jōhō Centre** (白
馬宿泊情報センター; ☎ 72-6900; www.hakuba1
.com in Japanese; ☑ 7am-6pm), to the right of the
Hakuba train/bus station, or **Hakuba-mura
Kankō Kyōkai Annai-jo** (白馬村観光協会案内
所; ☎ 72-2279; ☑ 8.30am-5.15pm), just outside
the station to the right (look for the 'i' symbol). Online, visit www.vill.hakuba.nagano
.jp/e/index.htm.

Sights & Activities
HAPPŌ-ONE SKI RESORT 八方尾根
Host of the men's and women's downhill
races at the 1998 Winter Olympics, **Happō-One**
(☎ 72-3066; www.hakuba-happo.or.jp/ in Japanese; 1-day lift
ticket ¥4600; ☑ Dec-Apr) is one of Japan's best ski
areas. The mountain views here are superb –
the entire Hakuba massif looks close enough
to touch with your ski poles. Beginner, intermediate and advanced runs cater to skiers and
snowboarders.

Most runs go right down the face of the mountain, with several good burners descending from Usagidaira 109, the mountain's centre-point. Above this, two chairlifts run to the top, worth visiting for the views alone. On busy days, you can usually avoid lift-line bottlenecks by heading to areas like the Skyline 2.

The rest house at Usagidaira 109 is the largest eating establishment. There's a *rāmen* restaurant, a McDonald's and the usual curry rice-type selections. The modern Virgin Café Hakuba has upscale ambience, decent food, wait service, cappuccino etc. Café Kurobishi has excellent mountain views to the north and cafeteria-style seating.

There are plenty of hire places in the streets around the base of the mountain, some with boots up to 31cm.

From Hakuba station, a five-minute bus ride (¥260) takes you into the middle of Hakuba-mura; from there it's a 10-minute walk to the base of Happō-One and the main 'Adam' gondola base station. In winter, a shuttle bus makes the rounds of the village, lodges and ski base.

HAKUBA 47/GORYŪ SKI RESORT
HAKUBA47ウインタースポーツパーク/白馬五竜

These two ski-interlinked **ski areas** (☎ 75-4747 Hakuba 47, 75-2636; www.hakubagoryu.com in Japanese, www.hakuba47.co.jp; 1-day lift ticket ¥4500; ☼ Dec-Apr) form the second major ski resort in the Hakuba area. There's a good variety of terrain at both areas, but you'll have to be at least an intermediate skier to ski the runs linking the two. Like Happō-One, this area boasts fantastic mountain views; the restaurant Alps 360 is the place to enjoy them. The Genki Go shuttle bus from Hakuba-mura and Hakuba-eki provides easiest access.

SUMMER ACTIVITIES
In summer, take the gondola and the two upper chairlifts, and then hike along a trail for an hour or so to the pond Happō-ike on a ridge below Karamatsu-dake. From here, follow a trail for an hour up to Maru-yama, continue for 1½ hours to the Karamatsu-dake San-sō (mountain hut) and then climb to the peak of **Karamatsu-dake** (2695m) in about 30 minutes. The return fare is ¥2260 if purchased at the Hakuba tourist office, ¥2600 otherwise.

Other popular hikes include the four-hour ascent of **Shirouma-dake** (白馬岳; 2932m), with spectacular views on clear days. Mountain huts provide meals and basic accommodation, about one hour out from and near the summit (around ¥9000 per person with two meals). **Yari Onsen** (鑓温泉; ☎ 72-2002; onsen ¥300; r per person incl 2 meals ¥8900) is another popular hike for Japan's highest *rotemburo* (2100m) and more breathtaking views.

Buses leave Hakuba station for the trailhead at Sarukura (¥980, 30 minutes, between late May and September). From here you can hike west to Shirouma-dake in about six hours. A track southwest of Sarukura leads uphill for three hours to Yari Onsen.

Ask at tourist offices for information about **Tsugaike National Park** (栂池自然園), renowned for its alpine flora, and **Nishina San-ko** (仁科三湖), three lakes with some short walks.

Evergreen Outdoor Centre (www.evergreen-hakuba .com) offers an array of half-day adventures with English-speaking guides from about ¥5000 year-round, including canyoning and mountain biking, as well as snowshoeing and backcountry treks in the winter.

Sleeping & Eating
The village of Hakuba-mura has a huge selection of accommodation. The Hakuba Shukuhaku Jōhō Centre (opposite) can help arrange accommodation if you arrive without reservations.

Snowbeds (スノーベッズ; ☎ 72-5242; www .snowbedsjapan.com; r per person from ¥3000) One of Hakuba's cheapest, with fairly cramped bunk rooms and a nice communal area with a wood stove. It's foreign-run, so communication is no problem and it's close to some good nightlife options.

Hotel Viola (ホテルヴィオラ; ☎ toll-free 0120-898193; www.hotel-voila.com; d per person incl 2 meals from ¥8000) About 15 minutes' walk from the gondola, this friendly place is a favourite of Aussie skiers and has clean, well-maintained rooms, English-speaking staff and a friendly atmosphere.

Hakuba Highland Hotel (白馬ハイランドホテル; ☎ 72-3450; fax 72-3067; r per person incl 2 meals from ¥8400) Located at the base of the Hakuba Highland ski area, a five-minute drive from Hakuba-mura, this family-friendly hotel boasts a sensational view over the Hakuba range; clean, fairly spacious rooms and a great indoor-outdoor *onsen*.

Getting There & Away

Hakuba is connected with Matsumoto by the JR Ōito line (*tokkyū*, ¥2770, 59 minutes; *futsū*, ¥1110, 99 minutes). Continuing north, change trains at Minami Otari to meet the JR Hokuriku Honsen line at Itoigawa, with connections to Niigata, Toyama and Kanazawa. From Nagano, buses leave from Nagano station (¥1400, one hour). There are also buses between Shinjuku Nishi-guchi, in Tokyo, and Hakuba (¥4700, 4½ hours).

BESSHO ONSEN 別所温泉

☎ 0268 / pop 1800

This intimate, mountain-ringed hot-spring town is known as a 'Little Kamakura' for its dramatic temples and the fact that it served as an administrative centre during the Kamakura period (1185–1333). It was also mentioned in *The Pillow Book* by the Heian-era poetess Sei Shōnagon and was later a retreat for writers including Kawabata Yasunari. Today some of the inns are tall enough to have lifts, but it's still a relaxing place, bisected by a gentle stream.

Bessho's excellent waters, reputed to cure diabetes and constipation while beautifying your complexion, bring in tourists aplenty, but overall it feels undervisited. Web information is available at www.bessho-spa.jp.

Bessho Onsen Ryokan Association (別所温泉旅館組合; ☎ 38-2020; fax 38-8887) is the local tourist office – at the train station – but English speakers will be better off enquiring at the **tourist office** (☎ 26-5001; ☻ 9am-6pm) in Udea station en route to Bessho; staff can book same-day accommodation in Bessho.

The national treasure temple **Anraku-ji** (安楽時; ☎ 38-2062; adult/child ¥300/100; ☻ sunrise-sunset), renowned for its octagonal pagoda, is 10 minutes on foot from Bessho Onsen station. The Tendai temple **Kitamuki Kannon** (北向観音; ☎ 38-2023; admission free; ☻ 24hr) is a few minutes' walk away, with some prodigiously old trees, sweeping views across the valley and a pavilion on stilts like a tiny version of Kyoto's Kiyomizu Temple; its name comes from the fact that this Kannon image faces north, a counterpart to the south-facing image at Zenkō-ji in Nagano. About a 5km hike away are the very enjoyable temples **Chūzen-ji** (☎ 38-4538; admission ¥100; ☻ 9am-4pm) and **Zenzan-ji** (☎ 38-2855; adult/child ¥100/30; ☻ 9am-5pm).

There are three central **public baths** (admission ¥150; ☻ 6am-10pm): Ō-yu (大湯) has a small *ro-temburo*, Ishi-yu (石湯) is famed for its stone bath and Daishi-yu (大師湯), most frequented by the locals, is known for being relatively cool.

The traditional **Ryokan Hanaya** (旅館花屋; ☎ 38-3131; fax 38-7923; r person incl 2 meals ¥20,000) is among lovely, manicured gardens. Spacious tatami rooms open onto the scenery. Some rooms have private hot-springs baths attached; guests without enjoy pleasant indoor and outdoor baths. Book far in advance.

Uematsu-ya (上松屋; ☎ 38-2300; fax 38-8501; www.uematsuya.com in Japanese; r per person incl 2 meals from ¥10,500) is neither historical nor traditional but kindly, well kept and good value. Its 33 rooms (Japanese and Western) are up nine storeys. There's an all-you-can-drink plan (males: ¥3150, females: ¥2100), plus indoor and outdoor baths. Some English is spoken. The 13-bed **Mahoroba Youth Hostel** (上田まほろばユースホステル; ☎ 38-5229; fax 38-1714; dm ¥3040, incl 2 meals ¥4720) is comfortable and secluded, surrounded by lush scenery. It's eight minutes' walk south from the train station (no *onsen*).

Access to Bessho Onsen is via Ueda, on the JR Nagano *shinkansen* (from Tokyo ¥6490, 1½ hours; from Nagano ¥1410, 13 minutes) or the private Shinano Tetsudō line from Nagano (¥660, about 40 minutes). At Ueda, you need to change to the private Ueda Kōtsū line to Bessho Onsen (¥570, 27 minutes, about hourly).

MATSUMOTO 松本

☎ 0263 / pop 289,000

From the moment you step off the train and hear the piped-in voice singing 'Ma-*tsumo-toooh*', you sense you're somewhere different. Matsumoto has a superb castle, some pretty streets and an atmosphere that's both laid-back and surprisingly cosmopolitan.

Nagano-ken's second-largest city has been around since at least the 8th century. Formerly known as Fukashi, it was the castle town of the Ogasawara clan during the 14th and 15th centuries, and it continued to prosper through the Edo period. Today Matsumoto's street aesthetic combines the black-and-white of its castle with *namako-kabe* (lattice-pattern walled) *kura* and 21st-century Japanese architecture; plus, views of the Japan Alps are never much further than around the corner. Parts of the city centre have a more contemporary feel, and the areas by the Metoba-gawa and the Nakamachi district boast smart galleries, comfortable cafés and reasonably priced, high-quality accommodation.

Asama Onsen and Utsukushi-ga-hara are day trips, while Hotaka can be either a day trip or the start of a hiking route. Matsumoto is also a regional transit hub to the Japan Alps National Park, among other destinations.

Orientation & Information

For a castle town, Matsumoto is relatively easy to get around. Although small streets radiate somewhat confusingly from the train station, soon you're on a grid. Any place on the Matsumoto map is within 20 minutes' walk of the train station.

The main post office is located on Hon-machi-dōri. For web information, visit www.city.matsumoto.nagano.jp.

Fureai International Information Centre (☎ 48-7000; 4010-27 Isemachi-dōri; ⏰ 9am-10pm Mon-Fri, 9am-5pm Sat & Sun) Offers free internet use, a lending library and a lounge with news broadcasts in English. It's in the M-Wing building, the entrance marked by sphere in the shape of a *temari* (balls embroidered in gemoetric patterns; see p286).

Tourist information office (☎ 32-2814; 1-1-1 Fukashi; ⏰ 9.30am-6pm Apr-Oct, 9.30am-5.30pm Nov-Mar) Inside Matsumoto Station. English-speaking staff have English-language pamphlets and maps and can book accommodation.

Sights & Activities

MATSUMOTO-JŌ 松本城

Even if you spend only a couple of hours in Matsumoto, be sure to make a visit to this **castle** (☎ 32-2902; 4-1 Marunōchi; adult/child Mar-Nov ¥600/300, Dec-Feb ¥400/200; ⏰ 8.30am-5pm early Sep-early Jul, to 6pm rest of Jul, to 7pm Aug & rest of Sep), Japan's oldest wooden castle and one of four castles

designated National Treasures – the others are Hikone (p369), Himeji (p398) and Inuyama (p250).

The magnificent three-turreted donjon was built c 1595, in contrasting black-and-white, leading to the nickname Karasu-jō (Crow Castle). Steep steps lead up six storeys, with impressive views from each level. Lower floors display guns, bombs and gadgets with which to storm castles, and a delightful

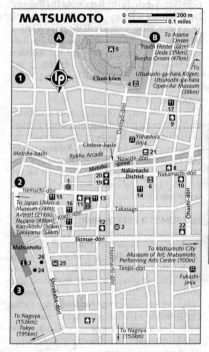

CENTRAL HONSHŪ

CENTRAL HONSHŪ

tsukimi yagura (moon-viewing pavilion). It has a tranquil moat full of carp, with the occasional swan gliding beneath the red bridges. The basics are explained over loudspeakers in English and Japanese. You can also ask at the entrance about a free tour in English; or call the **Goodwill Guide Group** (☎ 32-7140; ☺ 8am-noon), which gives free one-hour tours by advance notice.

The castle grounds (and your admission ticket) also include the **Matsumoto City Museum/ Japan Folklore Museum** (☎ 32-0133; 4-1 Marunōchi; ☺ 8.30am-4.30pm), with small displays relating to the region's history and folklore, including *tanabata* dolls (p286) and the wooden phalluses that play a prominent role in the September Dōsojin festival (opposite).

NAKAMACHI 中町
The narrow streets of this former merchant district make a fine setting for a stroll, as most of its storehouses have been transformed into galleries, craft shops and cafés. **Nakamachi Kura-Chic-Kan** (Classic-kan; ☎ 36-3053; 2-9-15 Chūō; ☺ 9am-10pm) is just one option, showcasing locally produced arts and crafts, with a relaxing coffee house next door.

MATSUMOTO PERFORMING ARTS CENTRE まつもと市民芸術館
Architect Itō Toyō has broken all the rules with this 2004 building, and we love it. Its undulating exterior walls are punctuated with frosted glass cut-outs that look like rocks – very impressive at night. Among other performances, the **Performing Arts Centre** (☎ 33-3800; 3-10-1 Fukashi) is the key venue for the Saitō Kinen festival (opposite). Heading east on Eki-mae-dōri from the city centre, it's just off the map on the right.

MATSUMOTO CITY MUSEUM OF ART 松本市美術館
This sleek **museum** (☎ 39-7400; 4-2-22 Chūō; adult/ high school & college student/child ¥400/200/free; ☺ 9am-5pm Tue-Sun) has a good collection of Japanese artists, many who hail from Matsumoto or depict scenes of the surrounding countryside. Highlights include the striking avant-garde works of Kusama Yayoi (look for the 'Infinity Mirrored Room'), the finely crafted landscapes of Tamura Kazuo, the calligraphy of Kamijo Shinzan and temporary exhibitions. The striking contemporary building (2002) borrows motifs (black façade, stone walls,

impressive greenery and mini-moat) from the castle. It's about 100m past the Performing Arts Centre, across the street.

JAPAN UKIYO-E MUSEUM 日本浮世絵美術館
This **museum** (☎ 47-4440; 2206-1 Koshiba, Shimadachi; adult/child ¥1000/500; ☺ 10am-5pm Tue-Sun) is a must for *ukiyo-e* lovers. Several generations of the Sakai family have collected more than 100,000 prints, paintings, screens and old books – the largest private collection in the world. English signage is minimal, however an explanatory leaflet in English is provided.

The museum is approximately 3km from Matsumoto station or 15 minutes' walk from Ōniwa station on the Matsumoto Dentetsu line (¥170, six minutes), or about ¥2000 by taxi.

ASAMA ONSEN 浅間温泉
This hot-spring resort northeast of town isn't rustic, but its history is said to reach back to the 10th century and include writers and poets. The waters are also said to be good for gastrointestinal and skin troubles, and women's disorders. Among dozens of baths and inns (and the youth hostel), **Hot Plaza Asama** (ホットプラザ浅間; ☎ 46-6278; adult/ child ¥840/420; ☺ 10am-8pm Wed-Mon) has many pools in a traditional building. Buses from Matsumoto station take about 20 minutes (¥350).

UTSUKUSHI-GA-HARA-KŌGEN 美ヶ原高原
This alpine plateau (1990m) is a popular warm-weather excursion from Matsumoto for pleasant walks and the opportunity to see cows in pasture (a constant source of fascination to the Japanese).

Utsukushi-ga-hara-Kōgen Bijutsukan (美ヶ原高原美術館; Utsukushi-ga-hara Open-Air Museum; ☎ 86-2331; adult/student/child ¥1000/800/700; ☺ 9am-4.30pm late Apr-mid Nov), in the same vein (with the same owner) as the Hakone Open-Air Museum (p209), is a large sculpture garden (some 450 pieces) with fine views of the surrounding mountains.

Most Japanese visitors reach the museum by car. Buses (¥1300, 80 minutes) run several times daily in midsummer with spotty-to-nonexistent service the rest of the season; check before you go. Taxis to the museum start at a cool ¥10,700 (yes, one way). See p286 for information on car hire.

Festivals & Events

Matsumoto-jō Sakura Matsuri Cherry-blossom time (late April) coincides with mood lighting at the castle.

Tenjin Matsuri The festival at Fukashi-jinja on 23–24 July features elaborately decorated *dashi* (floats) and a fireworks display. The second day is livelier.

Takigi Nō Matsuri The atmospheric festival during August features nō (classical Japanese dance-drama) by torchlight, performed outdoors on a stage in the park below the castle.

Saitō Kinen Festival About a dozen classical music concerts in memory of revered Japanese conductor and music educator Saitō Hideo (1902–72) held in mid-August to mid-September. Ozawa Seiji, conductor emeritus of the Boston Symphony Orchestra, is festival director.

Dōsojin Matsuri On the fourth Saturday in September phallic merriment is to be had at the festival held in honour of *dōsojin* (roadside guardians) at Utsukushi-ga-hara Onsen.

Yohashira Jinja Matsuri This festival (aka Shintōsai) occurs around the beginning of October, featuring fireworks and large dolls.

Asama Hi-Matsuri Around the start of October Asama Onsen celebrates the spectacular fire festival with torch-lit parades that are accompanied by drumming.

Oshiro Matsuri The Castle Festival, around 3 November, is a cultural jamboree including costume parades, puppet displays and flower shows.

Sleeping

In the station area, you'll mostly find cramped, charmless business hotels; more atmospheric ryokan are in the Nakamachi district.

Asama Onsen Youth Hostel (浅間温泉ユースホステル; ☎ 46-1335; 1-7-15 Asama Onsen; dm ¥3360) Although plain on the outside, this hostel offers quick access to nearby *onsen* and significant discounts to Hot Plaza Asama (opposite). Doors close at 9pm. From Matsumoto bus station, take bus 6 to Shita-Asama (¥300) or bus 7 to Dai-Ichi Kōkō-mae (¥240). Either takes 20 minutes, and the hostel is then five minutes on foot heading south.

Nunoya (☎ /fax 32-0545; 3-5-7 Chūō; r per person ¥5250) Few inns have more heart than this pleasantly traditional charmer in Nakamachi, with shiny wood floors and quality tatami rooms with shared bathrooms. No meals served.

Marumo (☎ 32-0115; fax 35-2251; 3-3-10 Chūō; r per person ¥5250, incl breakfast ¥6300) In the Nakamachi district, this beautiful ryokan dates from 1868 and has lots of traditional charm, including its own bamboo garden and a lovely coffee shop. Although rooms aren't huge and don't have private facilities, it's quite popular, so book

ahead. It's on a side street between Nakamachi-dōri and the rushing Metoba-gawa.

Tōyoko Inn Matsumoto Ekimae Honmachi (☎ 36-1045; www.toyoko-inn.com; 2-1-23 Chūō; s/d or tw ¥5460/8190; ✕ ⊗ ⌨) New business hotel in the centre of everything (across the square from the Parco department store). Rooms are functional, spotless and business-hotel cramped, but there are loads of freebies and a simple Japanese breakfast.

Matsumoto Hotel Kagetsu (☎ 32-0114; www.mcci.or.jp/www/kagetsu; 4-8-9 Ōte; r per person from ¥6825; ⊗ ⌨) Southeast of the castle, this polished, old-line hotel has nice-sized Japanese- or Western-style rooms with full facilities, plus generous communal baths with water from the Japan Alps and a cosy, historic coffee shop. Rooms in the newer building cost a bit more (¥7350 per person) but are smarter. Look for internet specials.

Roynet Hotel (☎ 37-5000; fax 37-5505; www.roynet.jp; 1-10-7 Chūō; s/d from ¥7300/9800; ✕ ⊗ ⌨) Central and crisp, this new-ish business hotel offers decent-sized rooms and a minimum of fuss. Rates are for Roynet *kai-in* (members); to become one, fill out a form and pay a one-time ¥500 charge at check-in. Even cheaper rates are often available online.

Hotel Buena Vista (☎ 37-0111; fax 37-0666; www.buena-vista.co.jp; 1-2-1 Honjo; s/tw from ¥9240/19,645; ✕ ⊗ ⌨) Long Matsumoto's sharpest Western hotel, the Buena Vista has been given a chic Barcelona-style makeover: dark woods, stone, mood lighting and world beats in the lobby. Rooms were being renovated as we went to press. The Salon de Fuego lounge on the top (14th) floor has the city's best views. Frequent internet specials.

Eating & Drinking

Matsumoto is renowned for *Shinshū-soba*, eaten either hot (*kake-soba*; in broth) or cold (*zaru-soba*; with wasabi and soya-based sauce). Other regional specialities include *basashi* (raw horsemeat), *hachinoko* (bee larvae) and *inago* (crickets). Tamer are *oyaki*, little wheat buns filled with various vegetables.

Nomugi (☎ 36-3753; 2-9-11 Chūō; soba ¥1000; ⏰ lunch Thu-Mon) In Nakamachi, this is one of central Japan's finest *soba* shops. Its owner used to run a French restaurant in Tokyo before returning to his home town. There's one dish: *zaru-soba* in a handcrafted wicker basket; in mid-November to mid-April there's also hot *kake-soba* (¥1300).

Ramen Kameya (☎ 32-7515; 1-8-1 Chūō; rāmen ¥550-800; ☽ dinner Tue-Sun) Nothing fancy here, just *ramen* served in traditional Chinese style (*chūka*; ¥550), with Shinshū miso or even *kimchi* (¥800). It's popular with the late-night after-drinking crowd, with all that entails. Look for the chalkboard on the wall across from the hotel car park.

Kura (☎ 33-6444; 2-2-15 Chūō; dishes from ¥300, teishoku ¥900-2000; ☽ lunch & dinner Thu-Tue; E) Located near Nakamachi, Kura serves nicely prepared Japanese dishes for lunch and dinner in a stylish former warehouse. The tempura is exceptional, as is the sashimi and *soba*. For the daring: topnotch *basashi*.

Shizuka (☎ 32-0547; 4-10-8 Ōte; dishes ¥525-1365; ☽ lunch & dinner Mon-Sat; E) Friendly, traditional place east of the castle serving Matsumoto specialities like *basashi* (¥1575) alongside *izakaya* favourites like *oden* and *yakitori* (chicken on skewers). *Inago* (¥735) and *zazamushi* (caddis fly larvae; ¥1575) don't appear on the English menu. We wonder why...

Robata Shōya (☎ 37-1000; 11-1 Chūō; dishes ¥300-980; ☽ dinner; E) On a corner in the town centre, is this classic, lively *yakitori-ya* (restaurant specialising in *yakitori*) with a large selection of grills, seasonal specials and a (sort of) English menu.

Vamonos (☎ 36-4878; 1-4-13 Chūō; mains ¥650-900; ☽ lunch & dinner; E) Two blocks east of the train station, this sweet little Mexican restaurant serves enchiladas, burritos, nachos, large salads and dainty but potent margaritas. Look for the sign in Spanish on the 2nd floor.

Old Rock (☎ 38-0069; 2-30-20 Chūō; mains from ¥750; ☽ lunch & dinner) A block south of the river and across the street from Nakamachi, this popular *gaijin* pub attracts a lively crowd on weekend nights. Good lunch specials and a wide selection of beers.

Coat (☎ 34-7133; 2-3-24 Chūō; ☽ 11am-4pm & 5pm-midnight) This sophisticated little bar is home to Matsumoto's most famous bartender. Hayashi-san's inventive 'otomenadeshiko' cocktail won first prize at the Japan Bartenders Association competition early this decade.

And if you're looking for a quick coffee and cake, cafés line the banks of the Metoba-gawa and Nawate-dōri. **Sweet** (☎ 32-5300; 4-8-9 Ōtemachi; pastries from ¥170; ☽ 7am-7pm) is typical.

Shopping

Matsumoto is synonymous with *temari* and doll-making. You can find both at **Berami** (Belle Amie; ☎ 33-1314; 3-7-23 Chūō; ☽ 10am-5pm Thu-Tue) on Ōhashi-dōri. Doll styles include *tanabata* (flat wood or cardboard cut-outs dressed in paper) and *oshie-bina* (dressed in fine cloth). Takasago street, which is situated one block south from Nakamachi, also has several doll shops.

The Nakamachi district teems with shops selling crafts from textiles to ceramics, and Nawate-dōri north of the river is a colourful place for souvenirs and cafés. The Parco department store has pride of place in the city centre.

Getting There & Away

For information about reaching Japan Alps National Park, see p267.

AIR

Shinshū Matsumoto airport has flights to Fukuoka, Osaka and Sapporo.

BUS

Alpico/Matsumoto Dentetsu (☎ 35-7400) runs buses between Matsumoto and Shinjuku in Tokyo (¥3400, 3¼ hours, 18 daily), Osaka (¥5710, 5¼ hours, two daily), Nagoya (¥3460, 3½ hours, six daily), Centrair Airport (¥4500, 3¾ hours, five daily) and Takayama (¥3100, 2½ hours, four daily). All departures are from Matsumoto bus station, in the basement of the Espa building across from the train station (reservations advised).

CAR

Hiring a car is often the best way to do side trips. **Nippon Rent-A-Car** (☎ 33-1324; 1-1 Fukashi) has the best deals (from about ¥5000 a day), just outside the train station. **Eki Rent-a-Car** (☎ 32-4690; 1-1 Fukashi) is a few doors down.

TRAIN

Matsumoto is connected with Tokyo's Shinjuku station (*Super Azusa, Azusa,* ¥6510, 2½ hours, hourly), Nagoya (Shinano *tokkyū*, ¥5670, two hours) and Nagano (Shinano *tokkyū*, ¥2570, 50 minutes; *futsū*, ¥1110, 70 minutes). On the JR Ōito line, trains serve Hotaka (¥320, 30 minutes) and Hakuba (*Azusa tokkyū*, ¥2570, 55 minutes; *futsū*, ¥1110, 1½ hours).

Getting Around

The castle and the city centre are easily covered on foot, or free bicycles are available for loan. Enquire at the tourist office for locations. Three 'town sneaker' bus routes loop through the centre between 9am and 6pm April to November (to 5.30pm December to March) for ¥100/300 per ride/day; the blue and orange routes cover the castle and Nakamachi.

An airport shuttle bus connects Shinshū Matsumoto airport with the city centre (¥540, 25 minutes). Buses are timed to flights. A taxi costs around ¥4500.

HOTAKA 穂高
☎ 0263

Not to be confused with Shin-Hotaka in Japan Alps National Park, Hotaka is home to Japan's largest wasabi (Japanese horseradish) farm. It is an easy day trip from Matsumoto and a popular starting point for mountain hikes.

The **tourist office** (☎ 82-9363; ⏰ 9am-5pm Apr-Nov, 10am-4pm Dec-Mar) and **bicycle hire** (per hr ¥200), the recommended way to get around, are outside the Hotaka station exit. Both have basic maps, and the tourist office has English-speaking staff.

Sights & Activities

DAI-Ō WASABI-NŌJŌ 大王わさび農場
A visit to the **Dai-ō Wasabi Farm** (☎ 82-2118; admission free; ⏰ 8.30am-5.30pm Jul & Aug, shorter hr rest of year) is *de rigueur* for wasabi lovers, and even wasabi haters may have fun. An English map guides you among wasabi plants (wasabi is grown in flooded fields), restaurants, shops and workspaces, all set amid rolling hills. There are lots of free sampling opportunities; wasabi finds its way into everything from wine to rice crackers, ice cream to chocolate. 'Wasabi juice' (¥400) is a kind of milk shake.

The farm is about 15 minutes' bike ride from Hotaka station. There are also some calmer municipal wasabi fields.

ROKUZAN BIJUTSUKAN 碌山美術館
Ten minutes' walk from the station, the **Rokuzan Art Museum** (☎ 82-2094; adult/student/child ¥700/300/150; ⏰ 9am-5.10pm Mar-Oct, to 4.10pm Nov-Feb, closed Mon Nov-Apr) showcases the work of Meiji-era sculptor Rokuzan Ogiwara (whom the Japanese have labelled the 'Rodin of the Orient') and his Japanese contemporaries. Strolling through the four buildings and garden, you may be struck by how much cross-cultural flow there was between East and West.

NAKABUSA ONSEN 中房温泉
Seasonal buses (late April to mid-November) from Hotaka station (¥1610, 50 minutes) serve these remote **hot springs**. If no bus is available, taxis start at about ¥6500. From Nakabusa Onsen, there are several extended mountain hikes, served by seasonal inns.

JŌNEN-DAKE 常念岳
From Hotaka station, it takes about 30 minutes by taxi to reach Ichi-no-sawa, from where experienced hikers can climb Jōnen-dake (2857m); the ascent takes about 5½ hours. There are many options for mountain hikes extending over several days in the region, but you must be properly prepared. Hiking maps and information are available at regional tourist offices, although the more detailed maps are in Japanese.

Sleeping & Eating
Most people visit Hotaka as a day trip from Matsumoto, but some accommodation is available. Enquire at Hotaka's tourist office for other Nakabusa options.

Azumino Pastoral Youth Hostel (安曇野パストラルユースホステル; ☎ 83-6170; pastoral@po.cnet.ne.jp; dm ¥3360) Amid farmland, 4km west of Hotaka station (a one-hour walk), this pleasant hostel has plenty of rustic charm and rooms sleeping three to five people. Meals are available (breakfast ¥630, dinner ¥1050). Book ahead, as it occasionally closes during the off season (typically in winter).

Nestled up near Nakabusa Onsen, **Ariake-so Kokuminshukusha** (有明荘国民宿舎; ☎ 090-2321-9991; r per person incl 2 meals from ¥9500; ⏰ late Apr-late Nov) is a seasonal 95-person lodge with basic rooms and nourishing *onsen* (day use ¥600).

Getting There & Away
Hotaka is about 30 minutes (¥320) from Matsumoto on the JR Ōito line.

KISO VALLEY REGION 木曽
☎ 0264

Thickly forested and alpine, southwest Nagano-ken is traversed by the twisting, craggy former post road, the Nakasendō (p189). Like the more famous Tōkaidō, the Nakasendō connected Edo (present-day Tokyo) with Kyoto, enriching the towns along the way. Today, several small towns feature carefully preserved architecture of those days, making this a highly recommended visit.

It was not always so. Kiso *hinoki* (cypress) was so prized that it was used in the construction of the Edo and Nagoya castles; it is still used for the reconstruction of Ise Jingū (p435), Shintō's holiest shrine, every 20 years. To protect this asset, the region was placed under control of the Tokugawa shōgunate, and locals could be put to death for cutting down even their own trees; restrictions remained in effect well after the Meiji Restoration. The resulting lack of maintenance left many local buildings beyond repair or unreconstructed after fires. Further economic decline came with the introduction of new roads and commercial centres to the north; the construction of the Chūō train line effectively cut the region off.

However, the 1960s saw a move to preserve the post towns' architecture, and tourism has become a major source of income. Even if most of the remaining buildings are technically Meiji- and Taishō-era reconstructions, the streetscapes are pure Edo and the effect is dramatic.

Tsumago & Magome 妻籠 馬篭

These are two of the most attractive Nakasendō towns. Both close their main streets to vehicular traffic and they're connected by an agreeable hike.

Tsumago feels like an open-air museum, about 15 minutes' walk from end to end. It was designated by the government as a protected area for the preservation of traditional buildings so no modern developments such as telephone poles are allowed to mar the scene. The darkwood glory of its lattice-fronted houses and gently sloping tile roofs is particularly beautiful in early morning mist. Many films and TV shows have been shot on its main street.

Tsumago's **tourist information office** (観光案内館; ☎ 57-3123; fax 57-4036; ☾ 8.30am-5pm) is in the centre of town, by the antique phone booth. Some English is spoken and there's English-language literature.

Down the street and across, **Waki-honjin** (脇本陣; ☎ 57-3322; adult/child ¥600/300; ☾ 9am-5pm) is a former rest stop for retainers of *daimyō* on the Nakasendō. Reconstructed in 1877 under special dispensation from the emperor Meiji, it contains a lovely moss garden and a special toilet built in case Meiji happened to show up (apparently he never did). If some elements remind you of Japanese castles, that's because

the Waki-honjin was built by a former castle builder, out of work due to Meiji's antifeudal policies. The **Shiryōkan** (資料館; local history museum) here houses elegant exhibitions about Kiso and the Nakasendō, with some English signage.

Across from the Shiryōkan, **Tsumago Honjin** (妻籠本陣; ☎ 57-3322; adult/child ¥300/150; ☾ 9am-5pm) is where the *daimyō* themselves spent the night, though this building is more noteworthy for its architecture than its exhibits. A combined ticket (¥700/350) gives you admission to the Waki-honjin and Shiryōkan as well.

Kisoji-kan (木曽路館; ☎ 58-2046; baths ¥700; ☾ 10am-8pm), a few hilly kilometres above Tsumago, is a tourist facility with a raging souvenir shop. The real reason to visit is the *rotemburo* with panoramic mountain vistas. Some Tsumago lodgings offer discount tickets, and there's a free shuttle bus to/from Tsumago's car park No 1 (10 minutes, at least hourly) and Nagiso (opposite).

On 23 November, the **Fuzoku Emaki Parade** is held along the Nakasendō in Tsumago, featuring townsfolk in Edo-period costume.

Magome, the next post town south, is more modern, with houses, restaurants, inns (and souvenir shops) lining a steep, cobblestone pedestrian road. Even if only some structures are Edo-style, Magome is undeniably pretty and has broad views. At the **tourist information office** (観光案内館; ☎ 59-2336; fax 59-2653; ☾ 8.30am-5pm), about halfway up the hill on the right, you can pick up maps and staff will book accommodation.

Magome was the birthplace of the author Shimazaki Tōson (1872–1943). His masterpiece, *Ie* (The Family), records the decline of two provincial Kiso families. A **museum** (藤村記念館; ☎ 59-2047; admission ¥500; ☾ 8.30am-5pm Apr-Oct, 8.30am-4.30pm Nov-Mar, closed 2nd Tue, Wed & Thu Dec) is devoted to his life and times, though it's pretty impenetrable for non-Japanese speakers.

Good gifts from both towns include toys, crafts and household implements made from Kiso *hinoki*.

The 7.8km **hike** connecting Tsumago and Magome peaks at the top of the steep pass, Magome-tōge (elevation 801m). From there, the trail to/from Tsumago passes waterfalls, forest and farmland, while the Magome approach is largely on paved road. It takes around 2½ hours to hike between these towns. It's easier from Magome (elevation 600m) to Tsumago (elevation 420m) than the other way. There are English signs along the way and you'll have the opportunity to stop off at several small waterfalls en route. The Magome–Tsumago bus (¥640, 30 minutes, at least three daily in each direction) also stops at the pass.

If you're hiking between Magome and Tsumago, the towns offer a handy **baggage-forwarding service** (per bag ¥500; ☉ Mon-Sun late Jul-Aug, Sat, Sun & holidays late Mar-late Nov) from either tourist office to the other. Deposit your bags between 8.30am and 11.30am for delivery by 1pm.

SLEEPING & EATING

It's worth a stay in these towns, particularly Tsumago, to have them to yourself once the day-trippers clear out. Both tourist information offices can help book accommodation at numerous ryokan (from around ¥9000 per person) and *minshuku* (from around ¥7000); prices include two meals. Don't expect ensuite bath or toilet, but you will get heaps of atmosphere. For street foods, look for *goheimochi*, skewered rice dumplings coated with sesame-walnut sauce, and in autumn you can't miss *kuri-kinton* (chestnut dumplings).

Minshuku Daikichi (大吉旅館; ☎ 57-2595; fax 57-2203; r per person ¥8400) Popular with foreign visitors, this place feels very traditional – with handsome tatami rooms and fine wood features – despite its 1970s construction. All rooms have a view. At the edge of Tsumago (take the right-hand fork uphill from the centre).

Matsushiro-ya (松代屋旅館; ☎ 57-3022; fax 57-3386; r per person ¥10,500; ☉ Thu-Tue) One of Tsumago's most historic lodgings (parts date from 1804), Matsushiro-ya sits on the village's most picturesque street and offers large tatami rooms.

our pick Fujioto (藤乙; ☎ 57-3009; fax 57-2239; Tsumago; r per person ¥10,500; E) Another much-photographed, excellent ryokan, this place has impressive rooms and a graceful garden. It also serves lovely garden-view lunches, like Kiso valley trout (set menu ¥1500). It's a few doors down from the Waki-Honjin.

Minshuku Kameyama (民宿かめやま; ☎/fax 57-3187; r per person with/without 2 meals ¥7500/6000) For a rustic Nakasendō stay, this 19-bed option is about 20 minutes on foot from Tsumago towards Magome in the hamlet of Ōtsumago; it's known for its meals including *sansai*.

Magome-Chaya (馬籠茶屋; ☎ 59-2038; fax 59-2648; www.magomechaya.com; s/d ¥5250/8190) In Magome, this is a friendly, well-kept place

in the centre of everything, near the water wheel. Meals (breakfast ¥1050, dinner ¥3150) are served across the street in its restaurant; dinners are quite large.

Stalls throughout Tsumago sell street foods, and there are a few little *shokudō* (all-round eateries) near the path to the car park **Yoshimura-ya** (吉村屋; ☎ 57-3265; dishes ¥700-1500; ☉ lunch; E) is typical; its speciality is handmade *soba* – try it with tempura.

GETTING THERE & AWAY

Nakatsugawa and Nagiso stations on the JR Chūō line serve Magome and Tsumago, respectively, though both are still at some distance. Nakatsugawa is connected with Nagoya (Shinano *tokkyū*, ¥2740, 47 minutes) and Matsumoto (Shinano *tokkyū*, ¥3980, 70 minutes). A few *tokkyū* daily stop in Nagiso; otherwise it's about 20 minutes from Nakatsugawa by *futsū* (¥320).

Buses leave hourly from Nakatsugawa station for Magome (¥540, 30 minutes). There's also an infrequent bus service between Magome and Tsumago (¥640, 30 minutes).

From Tsumago, catch the bus to Nagiso station (¥270, 10 minutes, eight per day) or walk there in one hour.

Highway buses operate between Magome and Nagoya's Meitetsu Bus Centre (¥1810, 1½ hours), as well as Tokyo's Shinjuku station (¥4500, 4½ hours). Some of these buses leave from the nearby highway interchange, and not from Magome's own bus terminal.

Kiso-Fukushima 木曽福島

North of Tsumago and Magome and considerably more developed, Kiso-Fukushima's historical significance makes it a worthy side trip en route to these towns or from Matsumoto. It was an important checkpoint on the Nakasendō, and the town centre boasts a picturesque district of old residences.

From the station, cross the street and pick up an English map at the simple **tourist office** (Kisomachi Kankō Kyōkai; 木曽町観光協会; ☎ 22-4000; ☉ 9am-5pm), and head down the hill towards the town centre. Sights are well-signposted. To your right, between the Kiso-gawa and the train tracks, is **Ue-no-dan** (上の段), the old historic district full of atmospheric houses, many of which now serve as shops, cafés and galleries.

Another several minutes' walk leads you to the **Fukushima Sekisho-ato** (福島関所跡; Fukushima

Checkpoint Site; ☎ 23-2595; adult/child ¥300/150; ⊗ 8.30am-5.30pm Apr-Oct, 8.30am-4.30pm Nov-Mar), a reconstruction of one of the most significant checkpoints on the Edo-period trunk roads (p189). From its perch above the river valley, it's easy to see the barrier's strategic importance. Displays inside show the implements used to maintain order, including weaponry and *tegata* (wooden travel passes), as well as the special treatment women travellers received.

Kurumaya Honten (くるまや本店; ☎ 22-2200; mains ¥577-1575; ⊗ 10am-5pm Thu-Tue) is one of Japan's most renowned *soba* shops. The classic presentation is cold *mori* (plain) or *zaru* (with strips of nori seaweed) with a sweetish dipping sauce, or try it hot with *daikon orishi* (grated daikon radish) or *jidori* (free-range chicken). It's just before the first bridge at the bottom of the hill from the station – look for the gears above the doorway.

In Ue-no-dan, **Bistro Matsushima-tei** (ビストロ松島体; ☎ 23-3625; lunch sets from ¥1000; ⊗ lunch & dinner) serves a changing selection of handmade pizzas and pastas in a chichi-atmospheric setting befitting the building's history. Or stop in for coffee and cake.

Kiso-Fukushima is a stop on the JR Chūō line (Shinano *tokkyū*), easily reached from Matsumoto (¥2810, 35 minutes), Nakatsugawa (near Magome; ¥2810, 35 minutes), Nagoya (¥4700, 80 minutes) and Nagano (¥4380, 85 minutes).

Two daily buses travel each way (¥4500, 4¼ hours) travel between Kiso-Fukushima and Tokyo's Shinjuku station (west exit).

TOYAMA-KEN 富山県

TOYAMA 富山

☎ 076 / pop 419,000

This heavily industrialised city has few tourist attractions, but you might pass through en route to the northern Japan Alps or the Sea of Japan coast.

If you have time, **Chōkei-ji** (長慶寺; ☎ 441-5451; admission free; ⊗ 24hr) is famed for 500-plus statues of *rakan* (Buddha's disciples) draped in colourful sashes; and the **Toyama Folkcraft Village** (富山市民俗民芸村; ☎ 433-8270; adult/child ¥630/320; ⊗ 9am-5pm Tue-Sun) exhibits a range of traditional crafts: folk art, ceramics, a tea-ceremony house.

The **information office** (観光案内所; ☎ 432-9751; ⊗ 8.30am-8pm), outside Toyama station's south exit, stocks maps and pamphlets on the Tateyama-Kurobe Alpine Route (below) and Gokayama (p266). Staff speak English. JNTO issues a leaflet entitled *Tateyama, Kurobe & Toyama*, which has details on transport links and accommodation.

There are many lodgings within a few minutes' walk of the train station's south exit. **Toyama Excel Hotel Tōkyū** (富山エクセルホテル東急; ☎ 441-0109; www.tokyuhotels.co.jp; s/d from ¥9817/17,325; ✗ ⊠ wi-fi) has large, comfortable rooms and is conveniently located in a tower above the CIC shopping centre, facing the train station. There are some fine restaurants. **Relax Inn** (リラックスイン; ☎ 444-1010; www.relax-inn.co.jp; s/d from ¥4600/8800; ⊠ wi-fi) is a fairly new business hotel with small but nicely maintained rooms and cheap breakfast (from ¥380). Go straight out of the station and up Ichiban-machi, keeping CIC on your right. It's two blocks up on the left.

One of Toyama's unique offerings, **Yakuto** (薬都; ☎ 425-1873; courses from ¥2100; ⊗ noon-7pm Thu-Tue) serves *yakuzen-ryōri*, cuisine made from medicinal herbs. Book in advance. It's by the Nishi-chō tram stop, 10 minutes' ride from the station (¥200).

For a quick bite inside Toyama station, try *oshi-zushi* (fish pressed down onto rice; from ¥130) from *bentō* merchants, or irresistible cinnamon cream puffs at **Maple House** (☎ 441-1193; cream puffs ¥130).

Daily flights operate between Toyama and major Japanese cities. There are less-frequent flights to Seoul and Vladivostok.

The JR Hokuriku line runs west to Kanazawa (*tokkyū*, ¥2610, 35 minutes; *futsū*, ¥950, 70 minutes), Kyoto (Thunderbird *tokkyū*, ¥7760, three hours) and Osaka (¥8490, 3½ hours). The same line runs northeast to Naoetsu (¥4180, 1¼ hours) and Niigata (¥7130, three hours).

The train line connecting Takayama with Toyama, where a trestle bridge was washed out by floods in 2005, should be back up and running by the time you read this.

TATEYAMA-KUROBE ALPINE ROUTE
立山黒部アルペンルート

This seasonal, 90km route, popular with tourists, connects Toyama with Shinano-ōmachi in Nagano-ken via a sacred mountain, a deep gorge, boiling-hot spring and glory-hallelujah mountain scenery. It is divided into nine sections with different modes of transport: train, ropeway, cable car, bus, trolley bus and your own two feet.

The fare for the entire route is ¥10,560/ 17,730 one way/return; individual tickets are available. The route can be completed in under six hours one way, although you'll probably want to stop en route; some visitors find that a trip as far as Murodō, the route's highest point, is sufficient (¥6530 return). The route is open from mid-April to mid-November. Precise dates vary, so check with a tourist office. During peak season (August to October), transport and accommodation reservations are strongly advised.

Travel is possible in either direction; instructions here are from Toyama. The website www.alpen-route.com/english/index.html has details.

From Toyama station take the chug-a-lug regional Chitetsu line (¥1170, one hour) through rural scenery to **Tateyama** (立山; 475m). There are plenty of ryokan in Tateyama if you make an early start or late finish.

From Tateyama, take the cable car (¥700, seven minutes) to **Bijodaira** (美女平) and then the bus (¥1660, 50 minutes) via the spectacular alpine plateau of Midagahara Kōgen to **Murodō** (室堂; altitude 2450m). You can break the trip at Midagahara and do the 15-minute walk to see **Tateyama caldera** (立山カルデラ), the largest non-active crater in Japan. The upper part of the plateau is often covered with deep snow until late into the summer; the road is kept clear by piling up the snow to form a virtual tunnel (great fun to drive through).

Murodō's beauty has been somewhat spoilt by a monstrous bus station, but short hikes take you back to nature. Just 10 minutes' walk north is the pond **Mikuri-ga-ike** (みくりが池). Twenty minutes further on is **Jigokudani Onsen** (Hell Valley Hot Springs): no bathing here; the waters are boiling! To the east, you can hike for about two hours – including a very steep final section – to the peak of **O-yama** (推山; 3003m) for an astounding panorama. Keen long-distance hikers with several days or a week to spare can continue south to Kamikōchi (p267).

Continuing on the route from Murodō, there's a bus ride (¥2100, 10 minutes) via a tunnel dug through Tateyama to **Daikanbō** (大観峰), where you can pause to admire the view before taking the cable car (¥1260, seven minutes) to Kurobe-daira, where another cable car whisks you down (¥840, five minutes)

to Kurobeko beside the vast **Kurobe Dam** (黒部ダム).

There's a 15-minute walk from Kurobeko to the dam, where you can descend to the water for a cruise, or climb up to a lookout point, before taking the trolley bus to **Ogizawa** (扇沢; ¥1260, 16 minutes). From here, a bus ride (¥1330, 40 minutes) takes you down to Shinano-ōmachi station (altitude 712m). From here there are frequent trains to Matsumoto (one hour), from where you can connect with trains for Tokyo, Nagoya and Nagano.

ISHIKAWA-KEN 石川県

This prefecture, made up of the former Kaga and Noto fiefs, offers a blend of cultural and historical sights and natural beauty. Kanazawa, the Kaga capital and power base of the feudal Maeda clan, boasts traditional architecture and one of Japan's most famous gardens. To the north, the peninsula, Notohantō, has sweeping seascapes, rolling hills and quiet fishing villages. Hakusan National Park, near the southern tip of the prefecture, offers some great hiking, though it can be tough to reach even during peak season.

You can find an overview at www.hot-ishikawa.jp.

KANAZAWA 金沢
☎ 076 / pop 455,000

Blessed with a number of cultural attractions, Kanazawa is a highlight for visitors to Hokuriku. It is most famed for Kenroku-en, the fine former castle garden that dates from the 17th century. The experience is rounded out by handsome streetscapes of the former geisha and samurai districts, attractive temples and a great number of museums for a city of its size.

The city's main sights can be seen in a leisurely two days, and side trips to Notohantō and Eihei-ji in Fukui-ken are highly recommended.

History
'Kanazawa' means 'golden marsh', which is appropriate given its history. During the 15th century, Kanazawa was under the control of an autonomous Buddhist government, which was ousted in 1583 by Maeda Toshiie, head of the powerful Maeda clan of retainers to the shōgun.

Then the fun started.

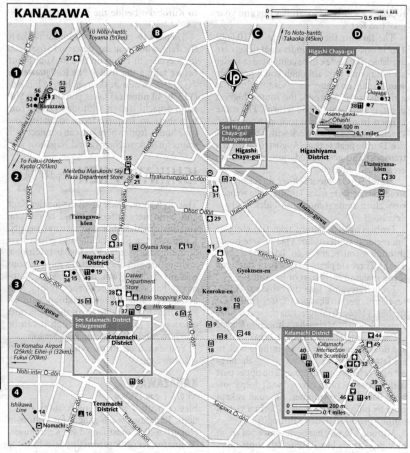

KANAZAWA

Three centuries of bountiful rice production made the Kaga region Japan's wealthiest; it was known as Kaga-Hyaku-Man-Goku for the one million *koku* (about five million bushels) of rice produced annually. Wealth allowed the Maedas to patronise cultural and artistic pursuits (see boxed text, p295), and today Kanazawa is one of Japan's key cultural centres. During WWII, the absence of military targets spared Kanazawa from destruction, preserving its historical and cultural sites, although it is an undeniably modern city with its share of functional (and some fanciful) contemporary architecture.

Orientation

Kanazawa's labyrinthine layout befits its castle-town past, but bus service makes it easy to get from the train station to the main sightseeing districts, which can then be covered on foot.

The site of Kanazawa-jō (Kanazawa Castle) and its gardens including Kenroku-en occupy the centre of town, and the Katamachi district, just to the south, is the commercial and business hub; its busiest intersection is known as the Katamachi Scramble. Another useful orientation point here is the Kōrinbō 109 department store. The Nagamachi samurai district is a short walk west from Kōrinbō 109. Northeast of the castle, across the Asano-gawa, is the picturesque Higashi Chaya-gai (geisha district); the hills of Higashiyama to its east offer walks and city views. Just south of Katamachi, across the Sai-gawa, is the Teramachi temple district.

Information

A good source of information is www.city.kanazawa.ishikawa.jp. The **Ishikawa Foundation for International Exchange** (☎ 262-5931; www.ifie.or.jp; 1-5-3 Honmachi; 9am-6pm Mon-Sat, 9am-5pm Sun) has reams of information, foreign periodicals and satellite TV news, as well as free internet access. It's on the 3rd floor of the Rifare building, a few minutes' walk southeast of the train station.

There are post offices in Katamachi (close to Kōrinbō 109) and in Kanazawa station, and several coin-operated laundries, including in Higashi Chaya-gai and Katamachi. Free internet access is available at Apre (p298).

Kanazawa Goodwill Guide Network (10am-6pm) At the station Tourist Information Office. Two weeks' notice is requested for free guiding in English.

Kanazawa Tourist Information Office (☎ 232-3933; 1 Hiro-oka-machi; 9am-7pm) Friendly office inside Kanazawa station. Pick up the bilingual map *Kanazawa Japan* (with details of sights, crafts and local specialities) and make hotel bookings. Some staff speak English.

Kikuya bookshop (☎ 220-5055; 2-1 Kōrinbō; 10am-10pm) Small selection of English-language titles; beneath Kōrinbō 109.

Libro Books (☎ 232-62502; 1-5-3 Honmachi; 10am-8pm) English-language books and magazines; it's in the Rifare building.

Sights & Activities

This information is arranged in geographical order, to be used as a walking tour. If time is limited, must-sees are Kenroku-en, the 21st Century Museum, the Nagamachi and Higashi Chaya-gai districts and Ōmichō Market.

NAGAMACHI DISTRICT 長町

Once inhabited by samurai, this attractive, well-preserved district (Nagamachi Buke Yashiki) framed by two canals features winding streets lined with tile-roofed mud walls.

Nomura Samurai House (☎ 221-3553; 1-3-32 Nagamachi; adult/student/child ¥500/400/250; 8.30am-5.30pm Apr-Sep, to 4.30pm Oct-Mar), though partly transplanted from outside Kanazawa, is worth a visit for its decorative garden.

Towards the Sai-gawa, **Shinise Kinenkan** (☎ 220-2524; 2-2-45 Naqamachi; adult/child ¥100/free; ☉ 9.30am-5pm) offers a peek at a former pharmacy and, upstairs, a moderate assortment of local traditional products. If the flowering tree made entirely of candy gives you a sweet tooth, slake it at **Murakami** (☎ 264-4223), a handsome *wagashi* (Japanese candy) shop next to the Nomura Samurai House.

In a nontraditional building at the edge of the district, the **Nagamachi Yūzen-kan** (Yūzen Silk Centre; ☎ 264-2811; admission ¥350; ☉ 9am-noon & 1-4.30pm Fri-Wed) allows you to watch the process of *Kaga yūzen* kimono-dyeing (see boxed text, opposite). Enquire about trying the silk-dyeing process yourself (¥4000).

21ST CENTURY MUSEUM OF CONTEMPORARY ART 金沢 21 世紀 美術館
Designed by the critically acclaimed Tokyo architecture firm SANAA, this ultra-modern **museum** (☎ 220-2800; www.kanazawa21.jp; 1-2-1 Hirosaka; permanent collection adult/university student & senior/high school student & child ¥350/280/free; ☉ 10am-6pm Tue-Thu & Sun, 10am-8pm Fri & Sat) opened in late 2004 and instantly became an 'it' building. A low-slung glass cylinder forms the perimeter, inside of which the galleries, auditoria and more are arranged like boxes on a tray.

Oh yes, there's art too, by leading contemporary artists from Japan and abroad, plus music and dance performances. Check the website for upcoming events; the admission price may change during special exhibitions.

KENROKU-EN 兼六園
Kanazawa's star attraction, **Kenroku-en** (☎ 234-3800; 1-1 Marunouchi; adult/child/senior ¥300/100/free; ☉ 7am-6pm Mar-15 Oct, 8am-4.30pm 16 Oct-Feb) is ranked as one of Japan's three top gardens (the other two are Kairaku-en in Mito, p196, and Kōraku-en in Okayama, p443).

The name (*kenroku* means 'combined six') refers to a renowned garden from Sung dynasty China that required six attributes for perfection: seclusion, spaciousness, artificiality, antiquity, abundant water and broad views (on clear days to the Sea of Japan). Originally Kenroku-en formed the outer garden of Kanazawa-jō, but from the 17th century it was enlarged, reaching completion in the early 19th century; the garden opened to the public in 1871. In winter the branches of Kenroku-en's trees are famously suspended with rope via a post at each tree's centre, forming elegant conical shapes that protect the trees from breaking under Kanazawa's heavy snows. In spring, irises turn Kenroku-en's waterways into rivers of purple.

Kenroku-en is certainly attractive, but enormous crowds can diminish its intimacy. Visit at opening time and you'll have the place to yourself.

KANAZAWA CASTLE PARK 金沢城公園
Originally built in 1580, **Kanazawa-jō** (Kanazawa Castle; ☎ 234-3800; 1-1 Marunouchi; grounds admission free, buildings admission ¥300; ☉ grounds 5am-6pm Mar-15 Oct, 6am-4.30pm 16 Oct-Feb, castle 9am-4.30pm) housed the Maeda clan for 14 generations; this massive structure was called the castle of 1000 tatami. That castle was destroyed by fire, but some reconstruction has taken place inside its moated walls, now rechristened Kanazawa Castle Park (Kanazawa-jo Kōen). The elegant gate **Ishikawa-mon**, rebuilt in 1788, provides a dramatic entry from Kenroku-en; holes in its turret were designed for *ishi-otoshi*, hurling rocks at invaders. Two additional buildings, the **Hishi-yagura** (diamond-shaped turret) and **Gojikken-Nagaya** (armoury) were reconstructed in 2001, offering a glimpse of the castle's unique wood-frame construction.

SEISON-KAKU VILLA
Back in Kenroku-en is this stylish retirement **villa** (☎ 221-0580; 2-1 Dewa-machi; adult/student/elementary school student ¥600/300/250; ☉ 8.30am-4.30pm Thu-Tue), built by a Maeda lord for his mother in 1863. It's worth a visit for the elegant chambers and furnishings. A detailed English-language pamphlet is provided.

ISHIKAWA PREFECTURAL MUSEUM FOR TRADITIONAL PRODUCTS & CRAFTS 石川県立伝統産業工芸館
Behind Seison-kaku, this **museum** (☎ 262-2020; 2-1 Dewa-machi; adult/senior/child ¥250/200/100; ☉ 9am-5pm, closed 3rd Thu Apr-Nov, closed Thu Dec-Mar) is not flashy but offers fine displays of over 20 regional crafts. Be sure to pick up the free English-language headphone guide. If you come across a must-buy, the museum has an English-language map to shops on nearby Hirosaka street.

ISHIKAWA PREFECTURAL ART MUSEUM 石川県立美術館
This **museum** (☎ 231-7580; 2-1 Dewa-machi; adult/university student/child ¥350/280/free; ☉ 9.30am-5pm) spe-

GET LACQUERED, GO TO POT, DYE & BE GILDED

Much as the Medici family was the patron of some of the great artists of the Italian Renaissance, during the Edo period Kanazawa's ruling Maeda family fuelled the growth of important crafts. Many of these crafts are still practised today.

Kanazawa & Wajima Lacquerware

This luminous black lacquerware starts with hard, durable wood, such as *keyaki* (zelkova), or Japanese chestnut, finely carved with any defects removed or filled. Many layers of undercoating and middle coating are applied, each rubbed down with *washi* (Japanese paper) before the next application. Before the final topcoat, decoration is applied through *maki-e* (painting) or gilding. With the last coat of lacquer, artists must take great care that dust does not settle on the final product.

Ōhi Pottery

An aesthetic central to tea ceremony is *wabi-sabi:* introspective, humble and understated, yet profound and prepared with great thought. Ōhi pottery seems its ceramic equivalent, with deliberately simple, almost primitive designs, rough surfaces, irregular shapes and monochromatic glazes, typically in black or amber. Little surprise, then, that Ōhi ware has long been favoured by tea practitioners; the same family, with the professional name Chōzaemon, has been keeper of the Ōhi tradition since the early Edo period.

Kutani Porcelain

Known for elegant shapes and bold hues of red, blue, yellow, purple and green, this underglaze ware could hardly be more different from Ōhi pottery. It is said to date back to the early Edo period, and shares design characteristics with Chinese porcelain and Japanese Imari ware. Typical motifs include birds, flowers, trees and landscapes.

Kaga Yūzen Silk Dyeing

This kimono-dyeing technique is characterised by sharp colours (red, ochre, green, indigo and purple) and realistic depictions of nature, such as flower petals that have begun to brown around the edges.

It's highly specialised, labour-intensive work. A pattern is drawn on the fabric with grey-blue ink from spiderwort flowers and the lines are traced over with rice paste using a cone like a fine pastry tube; this keeps the dyes from running as they are painted onto the silk. The colours are filled in and coated with more rice paste, and then the entire sheet of silk is dyed with the kimono's background colour.

Only then is the fabric rinsed clean (traditionally in a river) and steamed to fix the colours. White lines between the elements, where the initial spiderwort ink has washed away, are a characteristic of *Kaga yūzen*. To dye the fabric for one kimono takes about three months.

Gold Leaf

It starts with a lump of pure gold the size of a ¥10 coin, which is rolled to the size of a tatami mat, as little as 0.0001mm thick. The gold leaf is cut into squares of 10.9cm – the size used for mounting on walls, murals or paintings – or then cut again for gilding on lacquerware or pottery. Tiny particles find their way into tea, sweets and hand lotion. Kanazawa makes over 98% of Japan's gold leaf.

CENTRAL HONSHŪ

cialises in antique exhibitions of traditional arts, with special emphasis on colourful Kutani-yaki porcelain, Japanese painting, and *Kaga yūzen* (silk-dyed) fabrics and costumes. Admission prices are more for any special exhibitions.

NAKAMURA MEMORIAL MUSEUM
中村記念美術館

Rotating exhibitions from the 600-piece collection of this **museum** (☎ 221-0751; 3-2-29 Honda-machi; adult/senior/child ¥300/200/free; ☯ 9.30am-5pm) usually include *chanoyu* (tea ceremony) utensils, calligraphy and traditional crafts from the collection of a wealthy sake brewer, Nakamura Eishun. You can enjoy a bowl of powdered tea for ¥100. Reached via a narrow flight of steps below the Ishikawa Prefectural Art Museum.

HONDA MUSEUM 本多蔵品館

The Honda family were chief retainers to the Maeda clan, and this **museum** (☎ 261-0500; 3-1 Dewa-machi; admission ¥500; 9am-5pm daily Mar-Dec, Fri-Wed Nov-Feb) exhibits the family collection of armour, household utensils and works of art. The bulletproof coat and the family vase are particularly interesting, and there's a detailed catalogue in English.

GYOKUSEN-EN 玉泉園

For more intimacy and fewer crowds than Kenroku-en, this Edo-period **garden** (☎ 221-0181; 1-1 Marunouchi; adult/child ¥500/350; 9am-4pm Mar–mid-Nov) rises up a steep slope. Enjoy a cup of tea here for an additional ¥700, while contemplating the tranquil setting.

ŌHI POTTERY MUSEUM 大樋美術館

This **museum** (☎ 221-2397; Hashiba-chō; admission ¥700; 9am-5pm Tue-Sun) was established by the Chōzaemon family, now in its 10th generation. The first Chōzaemon developed this style in nearby Ōhi village, using a special slow-fired amber glaze, specifically for use in *chanoyu*. See boxed text (p295) for further information.

HIGASHI CHAYA-GAI 東茶屋街

North of the Ōhi Pottery Museum and across Asano-gawa, the **Higashi Geisha District** is an enclave of narrow streets that was established early in the 19th century as a centre for geisha to entertain wealthy patrons. The slatted wooden façades of the geisha houses of Higashi Chaya-gai (east teahouse street) are romantically preserved.

One famous, traditional former geisha house is **Shima** (☎ 252-5675; 1-13-21 Higashiyama; adult/child ¥400/300; 9am-6pm); note the case of elaborate combs and *shamisen* (three-stringed traditional instrument) picks; it dates from 1820. Across the street, **Kaikarō** (☎ 253-0591; 1-14-8 Higashiyama; admission ¥700; 9am-5pm) is an early-19th-century geisha house refinished with contemporary fittings and art including a red lacquered staircase.

The **Sakuda Gold Leaf Company** (☎ 251-6777; 1-3-27 Higashiyama; admission free; 9am-6pm) is a good place to observe the *kinpaku* (gold leaf) process and

pick up gilded souvenirs (including pottery, lacquerware and, er, golf balls). The tea served here contains flecks of gold leaf, meant to be good for rheumatism. Even the walls of the loos are lined with gold and platinum.

On most nights you can visit the local *sentō*, **Higashi-yu** (☎ 252-5410; 1-13-2 Higashiyama; admission ¥370; 2pm-12.30am Mon & Wed-Sat, 1pm-12.30am Sun).

TERAMACHI DISTRICT 寺町

Across Sai-gawa, southwest of the centre, this old neighbourhood was established as a first line of defence and still contains dozens of temples. Its narrow backstreets are a good place for a peaceful stroll, even if it's not as picturesque as Kanazawa's other historic districts.

The temple **Myōryū-ji** (Ninja-dera; ☎ 241-0888; 1-2-12 Nomachi; admission ¥800; 9am-4.30pm Mar-Nov, 9am-4pm Dec-Feb, reservations required) is a five-minute walk from the river. Completed in 1643, it was designed as a hideout in case of attack, and contains hidden stairways, escape routes, secret chambers, concealed tunnels and trick doors. The popular name refers to the temple's connection with ninja. Admission is by tour only – it's in Japanese but visual enough. To reach the temple, take Minami Ō-dōri across the river, take a left at the first major intersection, then the first right.

Nearby, **Kutani Kosen Gama Kiln** (☎ 241-0902; 5-3-3 Nomachi; admission free; 9am-4.30pm) is a must for pottery lovers. Short tours give a glimpse of the process and history of this fine craft. You can decorate porcelain yourself (¥1050).

ŌMICHŌ MARKET 近江町市場

A warren of several hundred shops, many of which specialise in seafood, this **market** (35 Ōmichō; 9am-5pm) bustles all day and is a great place for a break from sightseeing and watch everyday people in action. It's between Katamachi district and Kanazawa station; the most convenient bus stop is Musashi-ga-tsuji.

Courses

Japanese-language classes are offered through the **Ishikawa Foundation for International Exchange** (☎ 262-5931; 1-5-3 Honmachi).

Festivals & Events

Kagatobi Dezomeshiki In early January scantily clad firemen brave the cold, imbibe sake and demonstrate ancient fire-fighting skills on ladders.

Asano-gawa Enyūkai Performances of traditional Japanese dance and music are held on the banks of the Asano-gawa during the second weekend of April.

Hyakumangoku Matsuri On the second Saturday in June Kanazawa's main annual festival commemorates the first time the region's rice production hit 1,000,000 *koku* (around 150,000 tonnes). There's a parade of townsfolk in 16th century costumes, *takigi nō* (torch-lit performances of nō drama), *tōrō nagashi* (lanterns floated down the river at dusk) and a special *chanoyu*; at Kenroku-en.

Sleeping

The Kanazawa Tourist Information Office can help with reservations.

BUDGET

Kanazawa Youth Hostel (☎ 252-3414; fax 252-8590; www.jyh.or.jp; 37 Suehiro-machi; dm ¥3150; ☻ closed early–mid-Feb) Commanding a superb position in the hills to the east of the city, this strict, 80-bed hostel has Japanese- and Western-style rooms, with some private rooms available (extra charge). Unfortunately, bus services are infrequent. From the station, take bus 90 for Utatsuyama-kōen and get off after about 25 minutes at the Yūsu-Hosteru-mae bus stop.

Yamadaya (☎ /fax 261-0065; 2-3-28 Nagamachi; r per person ¥4000; ☒ ▣) This friendly place offers decent tatami rooms in a former samurai house in Nagamachi. No English spoken. It's on a side street just west of the Nomura Samurai House.

Murataya Ryokan (☎ 263-0455; fax 263-0456; murataya@spacelan.ne.jp; 1-5-2 Katamachi; s/tw ¥4700/9000; ☒ ☒ ▣) Well-kept rooms with friendly hosts await at this travellers' favourite in Katamachi. It's a convenient base for exploring the area's restaurants and nightlife; there's an English-language map of local establishments.

MIDRANGE

APA Hotel Kanazawa Chūō (☎ 235-2111; fax 235-2112; www.apahotel.com; 1-5-24 Katamachi; s/d/tw from ¥8000/11,000/15,000; ☒ ☒ ▣) Towering above Katamachi, this well-located business hotel offers nicely appointed rooms (though singles are cramped). Guests also have use of indoor and outdoor baths on the 14th floor. Pick up an origami crane.

Hotel Dormy Inn Kanazawa (☎ 263-9888; fax 263-9312; www.hotespa.net in Japanese; 2-25 Horikawa-shinmachi; s/d/tw ¥8500/12,000/15,000; ☒ ☒ ▣) This brand-new hotel steps from the station is filled with futuristic art. Most of its 304 rooms are singles and have an inner door to keep out extraneous noise. There's an *onsen rotemburo* on the top floor, and a coin laundry.

TOP END

New Grand Hotel (☎ 233-1311; fax 233-1591; www.new-grand.co.jp in Japanese; 1-50 Takaoka-machi; s/d or tw from ¥9817/18,480; ☒ ☒) Near both Nagamachi and Katamachi, this business hotel has several restaurants and a 12th-floor bar with views. Nice-sized rooms are spread among its two buildings; the New Grand Annex is newer and more polished; request when booking.

Kanazawa Excel Hotel Tokyū (☎ 231-2411; fax 263-0154; www.tokyuhotels.co.jp; 2-1-1 Kōrinbo; s/d/tw from ¥11,896/19,635/17,902; ☒ ☒ ▣ wi-fi) The city's most upmarket hotel has sleek and stylish rooms with plenty of amenities. It's also a winner for its central location in the heart of Katamachi.

Kanazawa Hakuchōrō Hotel (☎ 222-1212; fax 222-1120; www.hakuchoro.com in Japanese; 6-3 Marunouchi; s/tw from ¥17,000/26,000; ☒ ☒) East meets west with room design (and dimensions) that could be from France or Germany and only-in-Japan touches like sashes across the beds and display cases of local crafts. Its out-of-the-way location means lots of quiet. Common hot-spring baths also available. Enquire about special rates; some include breakfast.

Matsumoto (☎ 221-0302; fax 221-0303; 1-7-2 Owari-chō; r per person incl 2 meals ¥25,000; ☒) This upscale inn bills itself as a *ryōri* (cuisine) ryokan; expect a culinary treat of local specialities. Huge rooms have private bath. It's near the intersection of Hyakumangoku-ō-dōri and Jūhoku-dōri, down a narrow street across from the post office. No English spoken.

Eating

Kanazawa's *Kaga ryōri* (Kaga cuisine) is characterised by seafood; even the most humble train-station *bentō* nearly all feature some type of fish. *Oshi-zushi*, a thin layer of fish pressed atop vinegared rice and cut into pieces, is said by some to be the precursor to modern sushi. Another favourite is *jibuni*, flour-coated duck or chicken that's stewed with shiitake mushrooms and green vegetables. The Katamachi district is the best place to browse, packed with Japanese and international restaurants.

For delicious and relatively cheap sushi, try one of the tiny restaurants in Ōmichō Market (opposite). Not many have English menus, but you should be able to make yourself understood. Another speciality is seafood

CENTRAL HONSHŪ

donburi (seafood served atop a deep bowl of rice). *Teishoku* cost ¥800 to ¥1200. Ōmichō's restaurants close around 7pm or 8pm.

Janome-sushi (☎ 231-0093; 1-1-12 Kōrinbō; sets from ¥2500; ☽ lunch & dinner Mon-Sat) Near Kōrinbō 109, this highly regarded restaurant serves plenty of fresh sashimi and Kaga cuisine. One of our Japanese friends says that when he eats here, he knows he's really in Kanazawa.

Tamazushi (☎ 221-2644; 2-14-9 Katamachi; sets ¥1000-3000) Down near Sai-gawa in Katamachi, this minimalist restaurant is one of Kanazawa's best sushi spots. *Teishoku* are displayed in the front window. It's on your right as you enter from the main street.

Oden Miyuki Honten (☎ 222-6119; 1-10-3 Katamachi; oden ¥100-400, most other dishes ¥400-600; ☽ dinner Mon-Sat) For fish in another form (ground and pressed into cakes and served in broth), *oden* is very satisfying especially on chilly nights. This place has lots of fans, including Ishikawa's most famous son, New York Yankees baseball star Hideki Matsui. Sit at the counter to watch all the action. Some English-speaking staff. It's around the corner to the left of the Washington Hotel.

Jiyūken (☎ 252-1996; 1-6-6 Higashiyama; most mains ¥735-2993; ☽ lunch & dinner) In the Higashi Chaya-gai, this simple but welcoming spot has been serving *yō-shoku* (Japanese takes on Western cuisine: beef stew, grilled chicken, omelettes etc) since 1909. The *teishoku* is a steal at ¥924. Plastic models in the window. Look for the stone front and Art Deco design.

Legian (☎ 262-6510; 2-31-30 Katamachi; most dishes ¥600-1000; Ⓥ E) For popular, authentic Indonesian cuisine head to this tiny spot by the river. Staff make annual trips to Indonesia to bone up on technique, and are happy to make vegetarian versions. Good lunch specials.

Kōtatsu (☎ 261-6310; 32-1 Daiku-machi; mains ¥700-900; ☽ dinner Mon-Sat; E) More sophisticated than your everyday *okonomiyaki* place (see p95), there's a dark atmosphere and an assortment of sakes and shōchūs, *and* they'll cook your *okonomiyaki* (cabbage pancakes) for you. Salads are also available. It's near Mister Donut, two doors down from the Takoya *takoyaki* (octopus dumplings) stand.

Campagne (☎ 261-2156; 2-31-33 Katamachi; mains ¥650-1950, set menu from ¥2500; ☽ dinner Mon-Sat; E) This cosy, quietly fashionable Italian bistro serves lovely set menus including house-made focaccia, salads, pastas, 'plosciutto' (sic) and desserts, plus hors-d'oeuvres you can eat with chopsticks. Friendly, professional staff.

Bistro Yuiga (☎ 261-0978; 4-1 Mizutamemachi; sets from ¥2575; ☽ lunch Mon, Tue, Thu & Fri, dinner Thu-Tue; E) There's a gentle jazz soundtrack to accompany elegantly prepared French delicacies in this one-time private home. Set menus include treats like raw ham and – because this is Kanazawa – seafood. It's a short walk off the main street from Katamachi, down the street opposite Kōtatsu.

Drinking

Most of Kanazawa's bars and clubs are holes-in-the-wall, jam-packed into high-rises in Katamachi. Some are straightforward bars; others are barely disguised girlie clubs. Here are some of the former. Weekdays can be slow, but weekends tend to hop.

Polé Polé (☎ 260-1138; 2-31-30 Katamachi; ☽ 8pm-5am Mon-Sat) In the same building (and sharing the same owners) as Legian restaurant, this dark, grungy and friendly bar has been an institution for decades for *gaijin* and locals – look for the signatures of foreign exchange students. The narrow floor is littered with peanut shells (proceeds from peanut sales go to charity), and the music (reggae) is loud.

Apre (☎ 221-0090; 1-6-12 Kōrinbō; ☽ 6pm-1am) A mix of locals and *gaijin* fill this large two-storey bar near Kōrinbō 109. There's free internet, a pool table, plenty of food and beer selections and a lively crowd (at least on weekends).

Baby Rick (☎ 263-5063; 1-5-20 Katamachi; ☽ 5pm-3am) This classy little shot bar has a billiard table, jazz and whisky (the good kind), and you can get dishes like spaghetti carbonara and homemade pizzas. It's in the basement level beneath Shidax karaoke. If you enter after 10pm there's a ¥500 cover charge.

I no Ichiban (☎ 261-0001; 1-9-20 Katamachi; ☽ 6pm-3am Mon-Sat, 6pm-midnight Sun) This slender *izakaya* serves plenty of cocktails and has ambience in spades – so much so that it's almost unrecognisable from the street; look for the wood-panel screen and tiny stand of bamboo.

Pilsen (☎ 221-0688; 1-9-20 Katamachi; dishes ¥600-1800) Two blocks from the Katamachi Scramble, this German-style place serves lots of beers and a fascinating hybrid menu: where else can you get a sausage plate *and* warm tofu-mushroom salad at the same meal?

Entertainment

Nō theatre is alive and well in Kanazawa, and performances are held once a week during summer at **Ishikawa Prefectural Nō Theatre** (☎ 264-2598; 3-1 Dewa-machi).

Shopping

For a quick view or purchase of Kanazawa crafts, you can visit **Kankō Bussankan** (Ishikawa Local Products Shop; ☎ 222-7788). The Hirosaka district, between Kōrinbō 109 and Kenroku-en, has some upmarket shops on its south side for crafts; and shop for local crafts in department stores. At the Sakuda Gold Leaf Company (p296) you can find business card holders, mirrors, chopstick rests and Buddhist prayer bells, among many dozens of objects covered in gold leaf. At the other end of the spectrum, Tatemachi is to Kanazawa what Takeshita-dōri is to Tokyo: young and trendy. The **100 Yen Shop** (Tatemachi) here has an amazing assortment, from housewares to toys.

Getting There & Away

AIR

Komatsu **airport** (KMQ; www.pref.ishikawa.jp/k_air/index_e.html), serving Kanazawa, has air connections with Tokyo, Narita, Sapporo, Sendai, Fukuoka and Naha (Okinawa), Seoul and Shanghai.

BUS

Hokutetsu Kankō Bus Company (☎ 234-0123; ⏰ reservations 8am-7pm) operates express buses from in front of Kanazawa station's east exit, to Tokyo (¥7840, Ikebukuro seven hours, Shinjuku 7½ hours), Yokohama (¥8250, eight hours), Kyoto (¥4060, 4¼ hours) and Nagoya (¥4060, four hours). See p300 for bus services to Noto-hantō.

TRAIN

The JR Hokuriku line links Kanazawa with Fukui (tokkyū, ¥3140, 50 minutes; futsū, ¥1280, 90 minutes), Kyoto (tokkyū, ¥6910, 2¼ hours), Osaka (tokkyū, ¥7640, 2¾ hours) and Toyama (tokkyū, ¥2810, 35 minutes). From Tokyo take the Jōetsu shinkansen and change at Echigo-Yuzawa in Northern Honshū (¥13,010, four hours).

The JR Nanao line connects Kanazawa with Wakura Onsen on Noto-hantō (tokkyū, ¥2930, one hour).

Getting Around

Airport buses (¥1100, 40 minutes) are timed to aeroplane departures and arrivals, leaving from stop 6 in front of Kanazawa station's east exit. Some buses also stop at Katamachi and Kōrinbō 109 department store but take one hour to reach the airport.

Hire bikes from **JR Kanazawa Station Rent-a-Cycle** (☎ 261-1721; per hr/day ¥200/1200; ⏰ 8am-8.30pm) – take an immediate left from Kanazawa station's west exit – and **Hokutetsu Bicycle Rental** (☎ 263-0919; per 4hr/day ¥630/1050; ⏰ 8am-5.30pm) – by stop 4 on the west exit.

Any bus from station stop 7, 8 or 9 will take you to the city centre (¥200, day pass ¥900). The Kanazawa Loop Bus (day pass ¥500, ⏰ 8.30am to 6pm, every 15 minutes) circles the major tourist attractions in 45 minutes.

Cars can be hired at **Nippon Rent-a-Car** (☎ 263-0919), left of the station's west exit.

NOTO-HANTŌ 能登半島

With its rugged seascapes, traditional rural life, fresh seafood and a light diet of cultural sights, this peninsula atop Ishikawa-ken is highly recommended.

Although day trips from Kanazawa are offered, they don't do the peninsula justice; buzzing through the sights leaves little time to savour the day-to-day pace as the locals do. Unless you're under your own power, a speedy trip may not be an option anyway: public transport is infrequent. With your own car, the Noto Toll Rd offers a quick, not-too-outrageously expensive compromise.

Noto juts out from Honshū like a boomerang, with few sights dotting its flat west coast; the town of Wajima is the hub of the rugged north, known as Oku-Noto.

Kanazawa **tourist information office** (☎ 076-232-6200) stocks the *Unforgettable Ishikawa* map and guide, which includes the peninsula. JNTO's leaflet *Noto Peninsula* also has concise information. On the peninsula, the best tourist office is at Wajima (p302) on the north coast. Telephone information about Noto can be obtained through the **Noto tourist office** (☎ 0767-53-7767) in the city of Nanao (in Japanese).

Particularly in Oku-Noto, you won't have to look far before you see shops groaning with the main regional craft – lacquerware. A large proportion of Wajima's townsfolk is engaged in producing *Wajima-nuri,* renowned for its durability and rich colours. Other good bets are Suzu-style pottery (named for the Oku-Noto town at the end of the peninsula) and locally harvested sea salt and *iwanori* seaweed.

Sleeping

The peninsula has plenty of accommodation, though reservations are advised during the peak months of July and August. A night or two in a Japanese inn will also net you healthy portions of delicious sashimi, grilled fish and shellfish. There are camping grounds tucked away in a few pockets of the peninsula, although most are difficult to reach using public transport. Call ahead to reserve sites, especially in summer.

Getting There & Around

In the Centre of Oku-Noto, the **Noto airport** (NTQ; ☎ 0768-26-2100) connects the peninsula with Tokyo's Haneda airport. **ANA** (☎ 0120-029-222) offers two return flights daily (one way ¥19,800, 65 minutes). The **Furusato Taxi** (☎ 0768-22-7411) is a van service to locations around the peninsula. Fares start at ¥700 to nearby communities including Wajima.

A stay along Noto's west coast should appeal to cyclists as the terrain is mostly flat. However, on the Noto-kongō coast on the west coast, and anywhere east of Wajima, roads can be quite steep and have blind curves. The tourist information offices have a very good map (in Japanese) called *Noto Hantō Kankō Rōdo Mappu* (能登半島観光ロードマップ), which covers the area on a scale of 1:160,000.

Hokutetsu Kankō **bus company** (☎ 076-234-0123) Oku-noto express buses run between Kanazawa and Wajima (¥2200, two hours, 10 daily), with a couple continuing to Sosogi (¥2510). Buses leave from outside Kanazawa station. There are four buses daily between Wakura Onsen and Wajima (¥1200, one hour).

Given the infrequent service, many visitors opt for the daily tour buses from Kanazawa, with one way/return fares from ¥3500 to ¥7200. Depending on the itinerary, the ticket price includes transport, lunch, Japanese-speaking guide and admission fees. Some tours operate all year, others from May to November, and the guide's rapid-fire commentary can be peppered with recorded jungle noises, songs and breaking waves.

Given the lack of bus service, hiring a car has become a popular option. Try **Nippon Rent-a-Car** (☎ 076-263-0919) in Kanazawa. Driving the Noto Toll Rd between Kanazawa and Wajima takes about two hours; the toll road goes only as far as Anamizu: take Rte 1 the rest of the way. If you're planning to visit sights on the west coast, allow a full day to reach Wajima.

Although there are trains – JR Nanao from Kanazawa to Wakura Onsen (¥1280, 1½ hours) and private Noto Tetsudō line to Anamizu (¥660, 30 minutes) – you still have to reach the sights by road. For the west Noto coast, get off the train at Hakui, Noto's western bus hub. Whatever your plan, check departure and arrival times to avoid long waits.

West Noto Coast

☎ 0767

KITA-KE 喜多家

From this sprawling, 300-plus-year-old **house** (☎ 28-2546; admission ¥700; ◷ 8am-5pm), the Kita family once administered over 100 villages at the pivotal crossroads of the Kaga, Echizen and Noto districts. Inside the house and adjacent museum are displays of weapons, ceramics, farming tools, fine and folk art, and documents. The garden was once called the Moss Temple of Noto.

Kita-ke is about 1km from the Komedashi exit on the Noto Toll Rd; by train, take the JR Nanao line to Menden or Hōdatsu stations; it's about 20 minutes' walk.

CHIRIHAMA NAGISA DRIVEWAY 千里浜なぎさドライブウエイ

At times the 8km beach, linking the towns of Chirihama and Hakui, resembles a sandy speedway, with droves of buses, motorcycles and cars roaring past the breakers. **Hakui** (羽咋) is both the western transit hub and Japan's UFO-viewing capital, with flying-saucer-shaped snacks on sale everywhere to prove it.

KETA-TAISHA 気多大社

This **shrine** (☎ 22-0602; admission ¥100; ◷ 8.30am-4.30pm), set in a wooded grove with sea views, was allegedly founded in the 1st century BC, but the architectural style of the present building dates from the 17th century.

Take the Togi-bound bus from Hakui to Ichinomiya bus stop (10 minutes, approximately 10 buses daily).

MYŌJŌ-JI 妙成寺

Founded in 1294 by Nichijō, a disciple of Nichiren, this imposing **temple** (☎ 27-1226; admission ¥500; ◷ 8am-5pm) remains an important temple for the sect. The grounds comprise several buildings, including the strikingly

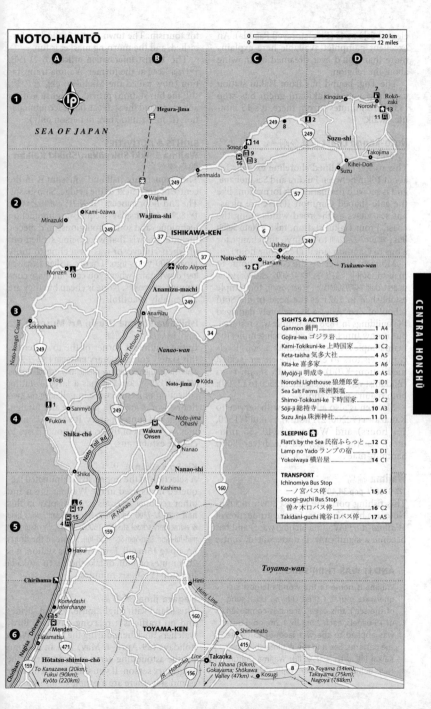

NOTO-HANTŌ

0 ——— 20 km
0 ——— 12 miles

A   B   C   D

SEA OF JAPAN

Hegura-jima

Kinoura

Noroshi   Rokō-zaki   7

249   13
11   Suzu-shi

Gojira-iwa   2   8   249

Sosogi   14   Takojima

16   9   Kihei-Don
3   Suzu

Senmaida   249

57

Wajima

Minazuki   Kami-ōzawa   Wajima-shi

249   6

ISHIKAWA-KEN   Ushitsu   249

37   Noto-chō   Tsukumo-wan

37   Hanami   Noto

Monzen   10   Noto Airport   12

Anamizu-machi

249

Sekinohana   Anamizu

34

Nanao-wan

Noto-jima   Kōda

Togi   Noto-jima   Ōhashi

Sanmyō   249

Wakura   Nanao
Onsen

Fukura   Shika-chō   **Nanao-shi**

Shika   Kashima   160

6
17   JR Nanao Line

4   15

Hakui   159

415   Himi

Chirihama   Himi   **Toyama-wan**

Komedashi   Himi Line
Interchange

160

5   Shinminato   415

Menden   **TOYAMA-KEN**
Takamatsu   471

Hōtatsu-shimizu-chō   Takaoka

159   To Kanazawa (20km);   To Jōhana (30km);   To Toyama (14km);
Fukui (90km);   Gokayama; Shōkawa   Takayama (75km);
Kyōto (220km);   156   Valley (47km);   Kosugi   8   Nagoya (188km)

JR Hokuriku Line

Noto-kongō Coast

Noto Toll Rd

Noto tetsudō Line

Chūbu-en Nagisa Driveway

CENTRAL HONSHŪ

elegant **Gojū-no-tō** (Five-storeyed Pagoda). An excellent pamphlet available here explains more than you'd ever dreamed of knowing about the religion.

The Togi-bound bus from Hakui station can drop you at Takidani-guchi bus stop (¥390, 18 minutes); from there, it's 15 minutes' walk.

Noto-kongō Coast 能登金剛
☎ 0768

This rocky, cliff-lined shoreline extends for about 16km between Fukūra and Sekinohana, and is set with dramatic rock formations like the gate-shaped Ganmon. There are pleasant sea views as the road winds along the coast. From Hakui station, take a **Noto Seibu Bus** (☎ 0767-22-0268) to Sanmyō and change for a bus to Ganmon (total ¥1170, one hour).

Monzen, further up the coast, is home to majestic **Sōji-ji** (総持寺; ☎ 42-0005; adult/high school student/child ¥400/300/150; ☑ 8am-5pm), the temple established in 1321 as the head of the Sōtō school of Zen. After a fire severely damaged the buildings in 1898 the temple was restored, but it now functions as a branch temple; the main temple is now in Yokohama. Sōji-ji welcomes visitors to experience *zazen* (seated meditation; ¥700) and serves *shōjin-ryōri* (Buddhist vegetarian cuisine; ¥2500 to ¥3500); both require reservations.

Monzen is also a bus hub with service to Kanazawa (¥2200, 2½ hours), Hakui (¥1510, 1½ hours) and Wajima (¥740, 35 minutes). For the temple, tell the driver 'Sojiji Sanmon-mae'.

Wajima 輪島
☎ 0768 / pop 34,400

This fishing port, the largest town in Oku-Noto, is a historic centre for the production of *Wajima-nuri* (Wajima lacquerware) and has become a significant, if understated, centre

---

AND IT WAS THIIIIIS BIG...

Wajima is home to the world's largest lacquerware mural. Called *Umi no Uta* ('song of the sea'), this ocean scene is composed of 15 panels, each 2.6m by 1.2m; gold dust was applied to the wet lacquer to create the patterns. See it in the Wajima-shi Bunka Kaikai (輪島市文化会館; Wajima Culture Hall) behind the former Wajima station.

---

for tourism. The town centre is nicely refurbished, and the morning market is fun.

The **tourist information office** (☎ 22-1503; ☑ 7am-10pm) at the former Wajima train station (now called the Michi-no-eki, 道の駅, still the bus station) provides English leaflets and maps, and the staff can book accommodation (from 8am to 7pm, in person only).

SIGHTS & ACTIVITIES
Wajima Shikki Shiryōkan/Shikki Kaikan
輪島漆器会館

The lacquerware hall and museum is in the centre of town next to the bridge, Shin-bashi. The 2nd-floor **museum** (☎ 22-2155; admission ¥200; ☑ 8.30am-5pm) displays lacquerware production techniques and some prodigiously old pieces, including bowls that were being swilled out of when Hideyoshi was struggling to unify Japan 500 years ago. There's a **shop** (admission free) downstairs where you can purchase contemporary works. None is cheap but they are undeniably beautiful.

Ishikawa Wajima Urushi Art Museum
石川輪島漆芸美術館

In the southwest corner of the town centre, this stately contemporary **museum** (☎ 22-9788; adult/student/junior high & elementary school student ¥600/300/150; ☑ 9am-5pm) has a large, rotating collection of lacquerware in galleries on two floors; works are both Japanese and foreign, ancient and contemporary. It's about 15 minutes' walk west of the train station. Closes to change exhibitions.

Kiriko Kaikan キリコ会館

A selection of the impressive illuminated lacquered floats used in the Wajima Taisai and other regional festivals is on display in this **hall** (☎ 22-7100; adult/high school student/junior high & elementary school student ¥600/450/350; ☑ 8am-6pm mid-Jul–Aug, 8am-5pm Sep–mid-Jul). Some of the floats are up to 15m tall. From Wajima station, it is 20 minutes on foot, or take the bus to Tsukada bus stop (¥150, six minutes).

Hegura-jima 舶倉島

This island with a lighthouse, several shrines and no traffic is a relaxing day trip. Birdwatchers flock here during the Golden Week holidays (29 April–6 May) and in autumn for the astounding array of birds during the migratory season. If you want to extend your island stay, there are a couple of *minshuku*.

Weather permitting, Hegura Kōro operates a daily **ferry** (☎ 22-4381; one way ¥2200). It's a 1½-hour trip, departing Wajima at 9am and Hegura-jima at 3pm (March to October) or 2pm (November to February), taking a week off in January for maintenance.

FESTIVALS & EVENTS

Gojinjō Daikō Nabune Matsuri This festival on 31 July and 1 August features wild drumming performed by performers wearing demon masks and seaweed headgear.

Wajima Taisai See Wajima's famous, towering, illuminated *kiriko* festival floats (late August).

SLEEPING & EATING

Wajima has dozens of *minshuku*. This is one town where it's definitely worth going for the meals at the inn, which include copious and delicious seafood. If you're not eating at your inn, there are some lovely restaurants by the harbour, though some close by early evening.

Sodegahama Camping Ground (袖が浜キャンプ場; ☎ 22-2211; fax 22-9920; camp sites ¥600; ☽ late Jul & Aug; ☽ office 4pm-9am) About 10 minutes by bus west of town. Take a Monzen-bound bus to Sodegahama or hike for 20 minutes.

Asunaro (あすなろ; ☎ /fax 22-0652; r per person ¥4800, incl 2 meals ¥7350) Readers have been coming to this *minshuku* for years. Although it's definitely showing its age and is far from the action (15 minutes on foot), the English-speaking owner is kindly and there's an *onsen* and an *irori*. Take route 249 west from the city centre and ask directions once you cross the river.

Wajima (わじま; ☎ 22-4243; fax 22-5969; s/d per person incl 2 meals ¥7875/7350) This 10-room *minshuku* has excellent details in its woodwork, a mineral *onsen* and *Wajima-nuri* bowls and chopsticks for eating your homegrown rice and catch of the day. It's across the bridge Futatsuya-bashi, south of the city centre.

Fukasan (深三; ☎ 22-9933; fax 22-9934; www.wajima-minsyuku.com/fukasan in Japanese; r per person incl 2 meals ¥7500) By the harbour, this is a contemporary *minshuku* with mood-lit rustic elegance, dark beams, high ceilings, an *onsen* and waves crashing outside your window. Known for its meals.

Madara-kan (まだら館; ☎ 22-3453; sets ¥800-3000) This restaurant serves local specialities, including *zosui* (rice hotpot), *yaki-zakana* (grilled fish) and seasonal seafood; there are pictures in the window. From the traffic light at Kawai Shō-gakkō-mae, walk north for about 2½ blocks, almost to the end of the street. The restaurant will be on the right.

Shinpuku (伸幅; ☎ 22-8133; sushi per piece from ¥150, sets ¥1000-2500; ☽ lunch & dinner) This tiny, assiduously local sushi shop serves fabulously fresh fish and seafood, and delicious *iwanori* in the miso soup. Sets are a sure bet, and *asa-ichi-don* is a selection from the morning market. It's on the main street one block east of the Cosmo petrol station. Picture menu. Closed irregularly but mostly Wednesday.

SHOPPING

The **asa-ichi** (morning market; ☽ 8am-noon, closed 10th & 25th of month) is highly entertaining, though undeniably touristy. Fishwives ply their wares with plenty of sass and humour that cuts across the language barrier. To find the market, walk north along the river from the Wajima Shikki Shiryōkan and turn right just before Iroha-bashi. The **yu-ichi** (evening market; ☽ 3.30pm-dusk) is lower key, across the river on the grounds of Sumiyoshi-jinja.

GETTING THERE & AWAY

See p300 for information on reaching Wajima. From Wajima, buses bound for Ushitsu stop in Sosogi (¥740, 40 minutes). Buses to Monzen (¥740, 35 minutes) leave every one to two hours.

Suzu & Noto-chō 珠洲, 能登町
☎ 0768

Heading east from central Wajima towards the end of the peninsula, you'll pass the famous slivered *dandan-batake* (rice terraces) at **Senmaida** (千枚田) before arriving in the coastal village of **Sosogi** (曽々木), technically still part of Wajima city. After the Taira were defeated in 1185 (see p37) one of the few survivors, Taira Tokitada, was exiled to this region. The Tokikuni family, which claims descent from Tokitada, eventually divided into two parts and established separate family residences here. From Wajima station, the bus ride takes about 40 minutes.

The first residence, **Shimo Tokikuni-ke** (下時国家; Lower Tokikuni Residence; ☎ 32-0075; adult/high school student/junior high school student ¥400/400/300; ☽ 8.30am-4.30pm daily Apr-Dec, Sat & Sun Jan-Mar), built in 1590 in the style of the Kamakura period, is a designated National Important Cultural Property and has a *meishō tei-en* (famous garden).

A few minutes' walk away, **Kami Tokikuni-ke** (上時国家; Upper Tokikuni Residence; ☎ 32-0171; admission ¥500; ☉ 8.30am-5.30pm Jul-Sep, 8.30am-5pm Oct-Jun), with its impressive thatched roof and elegant interior, was constructed early in the 19th century. Entry to either home includes an English leaflet.

Close by are the rock formation *mado-iwa* (window rock) and several hiking trails. If you visit this part of the coast in winter, look for *nami-no-hana* (flowers of the waves), masses of foam that form when waves gnash the rocky shore.

The road northeast from Sosogi village leads past the **sea salt farms** and **Gojira-iwa** (ゴジラ岩) – Godzilla Rock: guess why – into the town of Suzu and the remote cape Rokō-zaki, the peninsula's furthest point. At the cape, you can amble up to the lighthouse in the village of **Noroshi** (狼煙); a signpost marks the distances to faraway cities (302km to Tokyo, 1598km to Shanghai). A coastal **hiking trail** runs west along the cape. It's rustic scenery, and during the week when the tourist buses run less frequently, Noroshi reverts to its true role as a sleepy fishing village. As you head south, the road circles around the tip of the peninsula towards less dramatic scenery on the eastern coast, and, reluctantly, back towards Kanazawa.

In Sosogi, **Yokoiwaya** (☎ 32-0603; fax 32-0663; r per person incl 2 meals from ¥8340; ❄) offers comfortable rooms, *onsen* baths and outstanding seafood dinners; in most Japanese cities the dinner alone would easily cost this much. Proprietors will pick you up from Sosogi-guchi bus stop; simple English spoken.

our pick In remotest Suzu, **Lamp no Yado** (☎ 86-8000; www.lampnoyado.co.jp; r per person incl 2 meals from ¥18,000; ❄ ✉) is sublime. A 14-room wooden waterside village, far from the main drag, it's been an inn since the 1970s but the building goes back four centuries when people would escape to its curative waters for weeks at a time. Rooms (some two-storey) have private bath and their own *rotemburo*. The pool is almost superfluous. A very worthy splurge; reservations required.

An Australian-Japanese couple runs the seaside inn-restaurant-bakery **Flatt's by the Sea** (Minshuku Flatto; ☎ 62-1900; www.noto.ne.jp/flatt; r per person incl 2 meals from ¥7500; ☉ Thu-Tue). It has just a few tables, serving Italian-Japanese cuisine, and the three 10-mat rooms all have bang-on water views across the street. For nonguests, lunch and dinner is by reservation only, or just stop in at the shop for bakery basics or adventurous creations like chorizo rolls. It's near the inner elbow of Noto, in the town of Hanami.

HAKUSAN NATIONAL PARK
白山国立公園

☎ 0761

Travellers with a thirst for exercise (and time on their hands) may want to venture into this national park, in the southeast corner of Ishikawa-ken and spilling over into neighbouring Fukui, Toyama and Gifu prefectures. The park has several peaks above 2500m; the tallest is Hakusan (2702m), a sacred mountain that, along with Mt Fuji, has been worshipped since ancient times. In summer, hiking and scrambling uphill to catch mountain sunrises are the main activities, while in winter skiing and *onsen* bathing take over.

For information, you can phone the **Hakusan Visitor Centre** (白山室堂; ☎ 93-1001), which also handles reservations for the Murodō Centre (below), or the **Shiramine Town Hall** (白山市白峰支所; ☎ 98-2011). Japanese language skills are helpful at both places.

The alpine section of the park is crisscrossed with trails, offering hikes of up to 25km. For hikers who are well equipped and in no hurry, there is a 26km trek to Ogimachi (p264) in Shōkawa Valley. However, camping is prohibited in the park except at designated camping grounds, meaning you'll have to hike very fast.

Those looking to hike on and around the peaks are required to stay overnight at either Murodō Centre or Nanryū Mountain Lodge. Getting to either of these requires a hike of 3½ to five hours. That doesn't stop the park from swarming with visitors, however.

The surrounding area of the park is dotted with little villages offering *onsen*, *minshuku* and ryokan accommodation and camping grounds.

Sleeping

Murodō Centre (室堂; ☎ 93-1001; r per person incl 2 meals ¥7700; ☉ 1 May-15 Oct) and **Nanryū Mountain Lodge** (南竜; ☎ 98-2022; camp site per person ¥300; r per person incl 2 meals ¥7300; ☉ Jul-Sep) are your two choices in the alpine area of the park. Both are rather cramped; when the lodges are full, each person gets about one tatami-mat's worth of sleeping space. Murodō can hold up to 750 people in its four lodges. Nanryū is smaller (150 people) but has private cabins for up to five people for ¥12,000 (meals available for extra). There is also a **camping ground** (tent rental ¥2200) at Nanryū, the only place where camping is permitted. During the July to August peak season book at least one week in advance for either place.

The closest access point is Bettōde-ai. From here it's 6km to Murodō (about 4½ hours' walk) and 5km to Nanryū (3½ hours). You can also access the lodges from trailheads at Ichirino and Chūgū Onsen, but these involve hikes of around 20km.

Ichirino, Chūgū Onsen, Shiramine and Ichinose all have *minshuku* and **ryokan**. Rates per person with two meals start at ¥7000.

There are several camping grounds in the area. **Ichinose Yaeijō** (☎ 98-2121; camp sites per person ¥300) has 20 camp sites near Ichinose, which is in turn close to the trailhead at Bettōde-ai. **Midori no Mura Campground** (☎ 98-2716; camp sites per person ¥400, bungalows ¥6000), near Shiramine, has tents and bungalows for rent. There is also a **camping ground** near Chūgū Onsen. Most of the camping grounds open only from June to October, with the exception of the one at Nanryū Sansō Mountain Lodge, which operates year-round.

Getting There & Away

This is not easily done, even during the peak summer period. The main mode of transport is the **Hokutetsu Kankō** (Hokutetsu; ☎ 076-237-5115) bus from Kanazawa station to Bettōde-ai. From late June to mid-October, up to three buses operate daily (¥2000, two hours).

Hokutetsu also has daily round-trip departures for Ichirino and Chūgū Onsen. Check with the Kanazawa tourist information office or the Hokutetsu bus station by Kanazawa station for the latest schedule.

If you're driving from the Shōkawa Valley, you can take the spectacular toll road, Hakusan Super-Rindō (cars ¥3150).

FUKUI-KEN 福井県

FUKUI 福井

☎ 0776 / pop 252,000

Fukui, the prefectural capital, was given quite a drubbing during Allied bombing in 1945, and what was left largely succumbed to a massive earthquake in 1948. It was totally rebuilt and is now a major textile centre. There are no particular attractions in town, but Fukui makes a useful sightseeing base. Between 19

and 21 May, Fukui celebrates the **Mikuni Matsuri** with a parade of giant warrior dolls.

Fukui City Sightseer Information (☎ 20-5348; 1-1-1 Chūō; ☷ 8.30am-5pm) is inside Fukui station, and can provide pamphlets in English. Northwest of the station are the business district and the walls of what was once Fukui castle. On the other side of the grounds of the former castle, **Fukui International Activities Plaza** (福井県国際交流会館; ☎ 28-8800; ☷ 9am-6pm, to 8pm Tue & Thu, closed Mon) has lots of English-language information and free internet access.

Opened in early 2007, **Tōyoko Inn Fukui-Ekimae** (東横イン福井駅前; ☎ 29-1045; fax 29-1046; www.toyoko-inn.com; 2-1-1 Ōte; s/d ¥6090/8190; ✕ ☷ wi-fi) is a minute's walk from Fukui station. Rooms are business-hotel small, but rates include simple Japanese breakfast, internet access with your own computer, and phone calls from the lobby.

Ten minutes' walk from the station, **Hotel Riverge Akebono** (ホテルリバージュアケボノ; ☎ 22-1000, 0120-291-489; fax 22-8023; s/tw from ¥7161/12,705; ✕ ☷ □ wi-fi) is on the bank of the Asuwa-gawa. The smart rooms have private facilities, plus common baths on the top floor 'observation deck' (bathers observe the city, not the other way around). From the main street perpendicular to the station, turn left after Tsuchiya furniture store.

Miyoshiya (見吉屋; ☎ 23-3448; oroshi-soba ¥750; ☷ lunch & dinner, closed irregularly) is a much-loved shop serving Fukui-ken's most famous regional speciality, *oroshi soba* (*soba* noodles topped with grated daikon and shaved bonito flakes). It's about five minutes' walk from Fukui station down Chūō-dōri, near the Shiyakusho-mae bus stop.

The ingenious *izakaya* **Ori-Ori-ya** (織々屋; ☎ 27-4004; skewers ¥100-300, dishes ¥380-980; ☷ dinner) lets you select your own ingredients and grill them yourself at the table. It's near Hotel Riverge Akebono.

The JR Hokuriku line connects Fukui with Kanazawa (*tokkyū*, ¥2940, 50 minutes, *futsū* ¥1280, 1½ hours) and Tsuruga (*tokkyū* ¥2610, 35 minutes; *futsū*, ¥950, 50 minutes); trains also serve Nagoya (¥5550, two hours), Kyoto (¥4810, 1½ hours) and Osaka (¥5870, two hours).

EIHEI-JI 永平寺

☎ 0776

Founded in 1244 by Dōgen, Eihei-ji is now one of the two head temples of the Sōtō sect of Zen Buddhism and is ranked among the most influential Zen centres in the world. It is a palpably spiritual place amid mountains, mosses and ancient cedars. At most times some 150 priests and disciples are in residence, and serious students of Zen should consider a retreat here.

The **temple** (☎ 63-3102; www.sotozen-net.or.jp/kokusai/list/eiheiji.htm; adult/child ¥500/200; 9am-5pm) is geared to huge numbers of visitors who come as sightseers or for rigorous Zen training. Among the approximately 70 buildings, the standard circuit concentrates on seven major ones: San-mon (main gate), *Butsuden* (Buddha Hall), *Hattō* (Dharma Hall), *Sō-dō* (Priests' Hall), plus the *daikuin* (kitchen), *yokushitsu* (bath) and, yes, *tosu* (toilet). You walk among the buildings on wooden walkways in your stockinged feet. The *Shōbōkaku* exhibits many Eihei-ji treasures.

The temple is often closed for periods varying from a week to 10 days. Before you visit, be sure to check ahead with the temple, a nearby tourist office or **Japan Travel-Phone** (☎ 0088-22-4800).

You can attend the temple's four-day, three-night **sanzensha** (religious trainee programme; ☎ 63-3640; fax 63-3631; www.sotozen-net.or.jp/kokusai/list/eiheiji.htm; sanzensha ¥9000), which follows the monks' training schedule, complete with 3.50am prayers, cleaning, *zazen* and ritual meals in which not a grain of rice may be left behind. Japanese ability is not necessary, but it helps to be able to sit in the half-lotus

EASTERN FUKUI-KEN

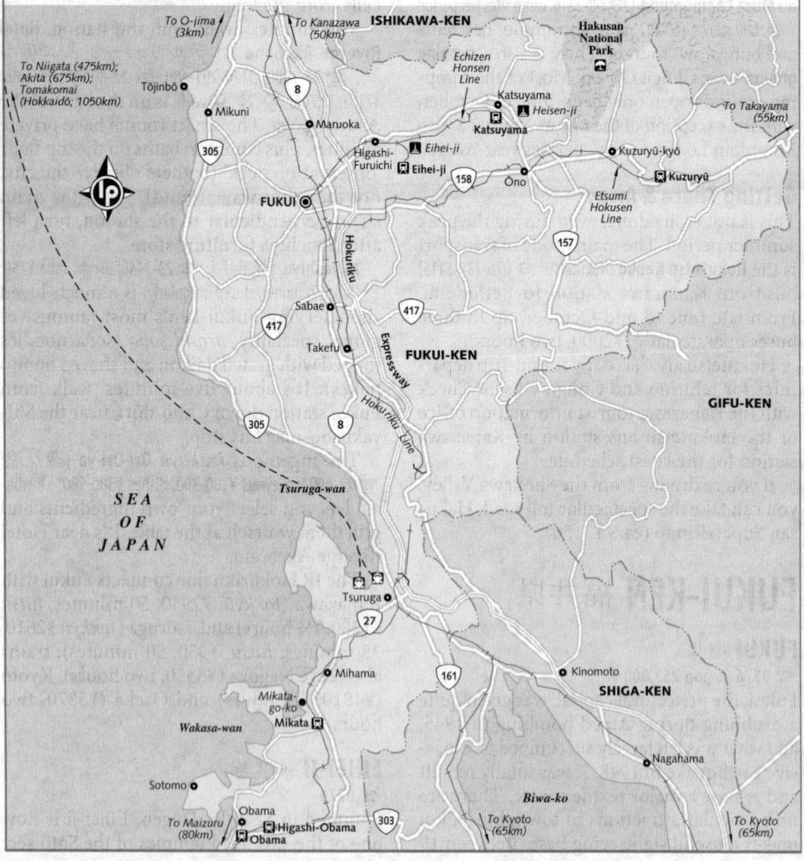

position. Everyone who has completed this course agrees it is a remarkable experience. A single night's stay, *sanrōsha*, is also possible for ¥8000 (with two meals). Book at least one month in advance. If you'd like to eat a special vegan lunch (¥3000) you must confirm this before your arrival.

To get to Eihei-ji from Fukui, take the Kei-fuku bus (¥720, 35 minutes, four daily) from stop 5, a couple of blocks from Fukui station.

TŌJINBŌ 東尋坊

On the coast about 25km northwest of Fukui are these towering **rock columns** and **cliffs**, a too-popular tourist destination that's also a place of legend: one says that Tōjinbō was an evil Buddhist priest who was cast off the cliff by angry villagers in 1182; the sea surged for 49 days thereafter, a demonstration of the priest's fury from beyond his watery grave.

Visitors can take a boat trip (¥1010, 30 minutes) to view the rock formations or travel further up the coast to **O-jima**, a small island with a shrine that is joined to the mainland by a bridge.

At least three buses serve Tōjinbō daily (¥1110, one hour) from bus stop 7 near Fukui station.

TSURUGA 敦賀

Tsuruga, south of Fukui and north of Biwa-ko, is a thriving port and major train junction. The **Shin Nihonkai ferry company** (☎ 0770-23-2222; www.snf.co.jp in Japanese) operates 11 sailings a week to Tomakomai, Hokkaidō (2nd class from ¥9600, 19 hours nonstop, 30½ hours with stops). Several of these stop en route at Niigata (¥5100, 9¼ hours) and Akita (¥6700, 18¾ hours). Buses timed to ferry departures serve Tsuruga-kō port from Tsuruga station (¥340, 20 minutes).

Kansai 関西

For fans of traditional Japanese culture, Kansai is an unmissable destination. Nowhere else in the country can you find so much of historical interest in such a compact area. And, since plenty of international carriers now fly into Kansai International Airport, it is perfectly possible to make Kansai your first port of call in Japan.

Kansai's major drawcards are Kyoto and Nara. Kyoto was the imperial capital between 794 and 1868, and is still considered by most Japanese to be the cultural heart of Japan. Nara pre-dates Kyoto as an imperial capital and also has an impressive array of temples, burial mounds and relics. Both cities should feature prominently in even the busiest travel itinerary.

Osaka is a great place to sample Japanese city life in all its mind-boggling intensity, while Kōbe is one of Japan's most cosmopolitan and attractive cities. Himeji, west of Kōbe, has the best of Japan's many feudal castles. Kyoto is the logical base for an exploration of Kansai, but you could also base yourself in Osaka or Nara. The former allows you to enjoy Japanese modern city life and excellent transport connections; the latter is much quieter and is a good place to relax. You will almost certainly find that Kansai is the perfect place to sample both modern and traditional Japan without having to spend too much time moving from place to place.

The main attractions of the prefecture Mie-ken are Ise-jingū, Japan's most sacred Shintō shrine, and the seascapes around the peninsula, Shima-hantō. Wakayama-ken offers *onsen* (hot-spring spas), a rugged coast and the temple complex of Kōya-san, Japan's most important Buddhist centre. Finally, the northern coast of Kansai has some fabulous scenery, a number of good beaches and the lovely Tango-hantō (Tango Peninsula).

HIGHLIGHTS

- Visit **Kyoto** (opposite), Japan's cultural capital, with more than 2000 temples and shrines
- Uncover the roots of Japanese culture in **Nara** (p400), the country's ancient capital
- Sample the bustling nightlife of **Osaka** (p373), Japan's most down-to-earth city
- Soak in open-air hot springs in mountainous **Kii-hantō** (p415)
- Spend a quiet night in atmospheric temple lodgings atop sacred **Kōya-san** (p417)

★Kyoto
Osaka ★Nara
★
★Kōya-san
★Kii-hantō

Climate

For information on the climate of Kansai, see p311.

Language

The Japanese spoken in Kansai is referred to as Kansai-ben, a rich and hearty dialect that is immediately distinguishable from standard Japanese if you know what to listen for. One thing to listen for is verb endings: in Kansai-ben, verbs often end with '~hen' instead of the standard '~nai' (in simple negative constructions).

Getting There & Away

Travel between Kansai and other parts of Japan is a breeze. Kansai is served by the Tōkaidō and San-yō *shinkansen* lines, several JR main lines, and a few private rail lines. It is also possible to travel to/from Kansai and other parts of Honshū, Shikoku and Kyūshū by long-distance-highway buses. Ferries sail between various Kansai ports (primarily Kōbe/Osaka) and other parts of Honshū, Kyūshū, Shikoku and Okinawa. Ports in northern Kyoto-fu serve ferries that run to/from Hokkaidō. Finally, Kansai has several airports, most notably Osaka's Itami Airport (ITM), which has flights to/from many of Japan's major cities, and Kansai International Airport (KIX), which has flights to dozens of foreign cities. For more information, see the Kyoto Getting There & Away section (p364).

KYOTO 京都

☎ 075 / pop 1.47 million

Kyoto is the storehouse of Japan's traditional culture and the stage on which much of Japanese history was played out. With 17 Unesco World Heritage sites (see boxed text, p313), more than 1600 Buddhist temples and over 400 Shintō shrines, Kyoto is also one of the world's most culturally rich cities. Indeed, it is fair to say that Kyoto ranks with Paris, London and Rome as one of those cities that everyone should see at least once in their lives. And, needless to say, it should rank near the top of any Japan itinerary.

Kyoto is where you will find the Japan of your imagination: raked pebble gardens, poets' huts hidden amid bamboo groves, arcades of vermilion shrine gates, geisha disappearing into the doorways of traditional

restaurants, golden temples floating above tranquil waters. Indeed, most of the sites that make up the popular image of Japan probably originated in Kyoto.

That said, first impressions can be something of an anticlimax. Stepping out of Kyoto station for the first time and gazing around at the neon and concrete that awaits you, you are likely to feel that all you've heard and read about Kyoto is just so much tourist-literature hype. We can only advise you to be patient, for the beauty of Kyoto is largely hidden from casual view: it lies behind walls, doors, curtains and façades. But if you take a little time to explore, you will discover that there are hundreds, perhaps thousands of pockets of incredible beauty scattered across the city. And, the closer you look, the more there is to see.

HISTORY

The Kyoto basin was first settled in the 7th century, and by 794 it had become Heian-kyō, the capital of Japan. Like Nara, a previous capital, the city was laid out in a grid pattern modelled on the Chinese Tang dynasty capital, Chang'an (contemporary Xi'an). Although the city was to serve as home to the Japanese imperial family from 794 to 1868 (when the Meiji Restoration took the imperial family to the new capital, Tokyo), the city was not always the focus of Japanese political power. During the Kamakura period (1185–1333), Kamakura served as the national capital, and during the Edo period (1600–1867), the Tokugawa shōgunate ruled Japan from Edo (now Tokyo).

The problem was that from the 9th century, the imperial family was increasingly isolated from the mechanics of political power and the country was ruled primarily by military families, or shōgunates. While Kyoto still remained capital in name and was the cultural focus of the nation, imperial power was, for the most part, symbolic and the business of running state affairs was often carried out elsewhere.

Just as imperial fortunes have waxed and waned, the fortunes of the city itself have fluctuated dramatically. During the Ōnin War (1466–67), which marked the close of the Muromachi period, the Kyoto Gosho (Imperial Palace) and most of the city were destroyed. Much of what can be seen in Kyoto today dates from the Edo period. Although

KANSAI

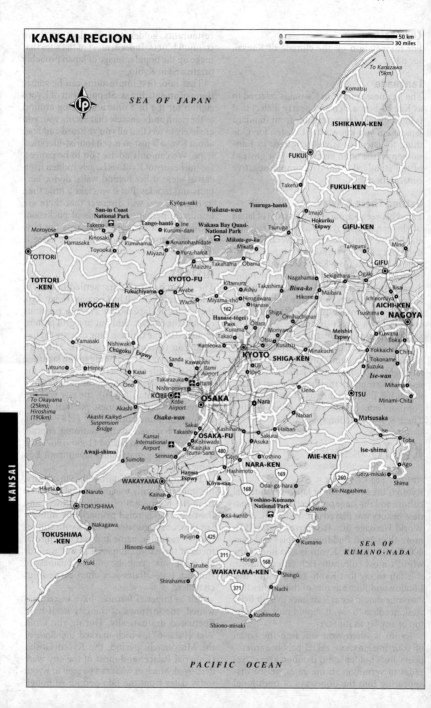

KANSAI REGION

0 — 50 km
0 — 30 miles

SEA OF JAPAN

To Kanazawa
(5km)

Komatsu

ISHIKAWA-KEN

FUKUI

Takefu

FUKUI-KEN

Kyōga-saki

San-in Coast
National Park

Takeno

Kinosaki

Wakasa-wan

Tsuruga-hantō

Imajō

Tango-hantō   Ine

Kurumi-dani   Wakasa Bay Quasi-
National Park

Tsuruga

Hokuriku
Expwy

GIFU-KEN

Moroyose

Hamasaka

Kumihama

Mikata-go-ko

Amanohashidate

Tanigumi

Mino

Toyooka

Miyazu

Yura-hama

Mikata

GIFU

TOTTORI

Maizuru

Takahama   Obama

Nagahama

Sekigahara   Ogaki   Bisai

TOTTORI
-KEN

Fukuchiyama

KYOTO-FU

Ayabe

Kitamura

Takashima

Biwa-ko

Hikone   Maibara

Ichinomiya

AICHI-KEN

Wachi

Miyama-chō   Hirogawara

Shiga

Omihachiman

Tsushima

NAGOYA

HYŌGO-KEN

162

Hanase

Kurama

Ōhara

Moriyama

Hanase-tōgei
Pass

Takao

Ōtsu   Kusatsu

Meishin
Expwy

Kuwana

Tokai   Chita

Yamasaki

Nishiwaki

Chūgoku   Expwy

Kameoka

Minakuchi

Yokkaichi

Suzuka

Tokoname

Sanda

Kawaoshi

KYOTO

SHIGA-KEN

Ise-wan

Tatsuno   Himeji

Kasai

Takarazuka   Itami
Airport

Uji
Jōyō

Ueno

Mihama

Ono

Nishinomiya

Itami

TSU

Minami-Chita

KOBE

Kobe
Airport

OSAKA

Nara

To Okayama
(25km);
Hiroshima
(190km)

Akashi

Takaishi

Nabari

Matsusaka

Akashi Kaikyō
Suspension
Bridge

Osaka-wan

Sakai

OSAKA-FU

Kashihara

Haibari

Ise

Toba

Awaji-shima

Kansai
International
Airport

Kishiwada

Kaizuka

Izumi-Sano

480

Sakurai

Asuka

MIE-KEN

Ise-shima

Ago

Sennan

Cōjō

Yoshino

NARA-KEN

Gōza-misaki

Shima

Sumoto

Hanwa
Expwy

Hashimoto

169

WAKAYAMA

Kōya-san

Odai-ga-hara

260

Kii-Nagashima

Hiketa

Kainan

168

Yoshino-Kumano
National Park

Owase

Naruto

Arita

Kii-hantō

TOKUSHIMA

Nakagawa

Ryūjin

425

Kumano

SEA OF
KUMANO-NADA

TOKUSHIMA
-KEN

Hinomi-saki

311

Hongū

168

Yuki

Tanabe

Shingū

Shirahama

WAKAYAMA-KEN

371

Nachi

Kushimoto

Shiono-misaki

PACIFIC OCEAN

KANSAI

SPECIAL TICKET DEALS

The **Kansai Thru Pass** is an excellent way to get around Kansai on the cheap. This pass – available at the travel counter in the arrivals hall of Kansai International Airport and at the main bus information centre in front of Kyoto station – allows unlimited travel on most bus and train lines in Kansai except the Japan Railways (JR) line. (The pass covers travel on the Nankai line, which serves Kansai International Airport.) It also qualifies you for discounts at several attractions around Kansai. The pass does not cover the Ise-Shima region.

When you buy the pass, be sure to pick up the handy companion English guide-map, which shows all the bus and train lines available.

Two-/three-day passes cost ¥3800/5000. It's possible to purchase multiple passes for longer explorations of Kansai. Like the Japan Rail Pass, however, these passes are only available to travellers on temporary visitor visas (you'll have to show your passport). For more on the pass, visit the **Kansai Thru Pass website** (www.surutto.com/conts/ticket/3dayeng/).

---

political power resided in Edo, Kyoto was rebuilt and flourished as a cultural, religious and economic centre. Fortunately Kyoto was spared the aerial bombing that razed other Japanese urban centres in the closing months of WWII.

Today, even though it has seen rapid industrialisation Kyoto remains an important cultural and educational centre. It has some 20% of Japan's National Treasures and 15% of Japan's Important Cultural Properties. In addition, there are 24 museums and 37 universities and colleges scattered throughout the city. Even though the city centre looks remarkably like the centre of a dozen other large Japanese cities, a little exploration will turn up countless reminders of Kyoto's long history.

CLIMATE

The best and most popular times to visit Kyoto are the climatically stable seasons of spring (March to May) and autumn (late September to November).

The highlight of spring is the cherry-blossom season, which usually arrives in Kyoto in early April. Bear in mind, though, that the blossoms are notoriously fickle, blooming any time from late March to mid-April.

Autumn is an equally good time to travel, with pleasant temperatures and soothing autumn colours, which usually peak between late October and mid-November.

Be warned that Kyoto is crowded with domestic and international tourists during the cherry-blossom and autumn-foliage seasons, and accommodation can be hard to find; if you do come at these times, be sure to book well in advance.

Of course, you can visit Kyoto at any time of year, although the summer, from June to August, can be very hot and humid, and winter can be a little chilly for some people's taste.

ORIENTATION

Like Manhattan, Kyoto is laid out in a grid pattern and is extremely easy to navigate. The main train station, Kyoto station (which serves the JR and Kintetsu lines), is located in the south of the city. The real centre of the city is around Shijō-dōri, which is about 2km immediately north of the station via Karasuma-dōri. The commercial and nightlife centres are between Shijō-dōri to the south and Sanjō-dōri to the north, and between Kawaramachi-dōri to the east and Karasuma-dōri to the west.

Although some of Kyoto's major sights are in the city centre, most of Kyoto's best sightseeing is on the outskirts of the city, along the base of the eastern and western mountains. These areas are most conveniently reached by bus or bicycle. Outside the city itself, the mountain villages of Ōhara, Kurama and Takao make wonderful day trips and are easily accessible by public transport.

Maps

Available at the TIC, the *Tourist Map of Kyoto* is a useful map with decent insets of the main tourist districts on the reverse side. The TIC also stocks the handy *Kyoto City Bus Sightseeing Map*. The TIC also has a leaflet called *Kyoto Walks*, which has detailed walking maps for major sightseeing areas in and around Kyoto (Higashiyama, Arashiyama, Northwestern Kyoto and Ōhara).

KANSAI

INFORMATION

Bookshops

Junkudō (Map p322; ☎ 253-6460; Kyoto BAL Bldg, 2 Yamazaki-chō, Sanjō kudaru, Kawaramachi-dōri, Nakagyō-ku; ⊗ 11am-8pm) In the BAL Building, this shop has a great selection of English-language books on the 5-8 floor.

Random Walk (Map p322; ☎ 256-8231; 273 Enpuku-jimae-chō, Takoyakushi kudaru, Teramachi-dōri, Nakagyō-ku; ⊗ 10am-8.30pm) In the Teramachi shopping arcade, this is the best English-language bookshop in town.

Emergency

Ambulance (☎ 119)

Fire (☎ 119)

Police (☎ 110)

Immigration

Osaka Regional Immigration Bureau Kyoto Branch (Map pp326-7; ☎ 752-5997; 2F Kyoto Second Local Joint Government Bldg, 34-12 Marutamachi Kawabata Higashi iru, Higashi Marutamachi, Sakyō-ku; ⊗ 9am-noon & 1-4pm Mon-Fri)

Internet Access

Kinko's (Map p322; ☎ 213-6802; 651-1 Tearamizu-chō, Takoyakushi kudaru, Karasuma-dōri, Nakagyō-ku; per 10min ¥210; ⊗ 24hr)

Kyoto International Community House (KICH; Map pp326-7; ☎ 752-3010; 2-1 Torii-chō, Awataguchi; per 30min ¥200; ⊗ 9am-9pm Tue-Sun) The machines here have Japanese keyboards and you are limited in the sites you can visit, but it's a fairly cheap place to log on.

Kyoto Prefectural International Centre (Map p321; ☎ 342-5000; 9F Kyoto Eki Bldg, Karasuma-dōri Shiokōji kudaru; per 30min ¥250; ⊗ 10am-6pm, closed 2nd & 4th Tue each month)

Internet Resources

Kyoto Temple Admission Fees (www.templefees.com)

Kyoto Visitor's Guide (www.kyotoguide.com)

Media

The free *Kyoto Visitor's Guide* is the best source of information on upcoming events It has restaurant reviews, day walks, detailed maps, useful information sections and feature articles about various aspects of the city. Pick up a copy as soon as you arrive in Kyoto. It's available at the TIC, Kyoto International Community House and most major hotels.

Another excellent source of information about Kyoto and the rest of the Kansai area is *Kansai Time Out*, a monthly English-language listings magazine. Apart from lively articles, it has a large section of ads for employment, travel agencies, meetings, lonely hearts etc. It's available at the bookshops listed in this section (left) and at the TIC (opposite).

Medical Services

Kyoto University Hospital (Map pp326-7; ☎ 751-3111; 54 Shōgoinkawara-chō, Sakyō-ku; ⊗ 9am-noon) Best hospital in Kyoto. There is an information counter near the entrance that can point you in the right direction.

Money

Most of the major banks are near the Shijō-Karasuma intersection, two stops north of Kyoto station on the Karasuma line subway.

KYOTO IN...

Kyoto is worth considering as a base for travel in Japan, especially as it is within easy reach of Osaka Itami and Kansai International Airports. And Kyoto is by far the best choice as a base for travel in Kansai because it has a wealth of accommodation and is close to Nara, Osaka, Kōbe, Mie-ken and Wakayama-ken.

It is difficult to suggest a minimum itinerary for Kyoto – you should certainly consider it a city you must see while you are in Japan and allocate as much time as possible. The absolute minimum amount of time you should spend in Kyoto is two days, during which you could just about scratch the surface by visiting the **Higashiyama area** (p334) in eastern Kyoto. Five days would give you time to include **Arashiyama** (p344), **northwestern Kyoto** (p342) and **southeastern Kyoto** (p346). A week would allow you to cover these areas, while leaving a day or so for places further afield or for in-depth exploration of museums, shops and culture.

A final word of advice is that it's easy to overdose on temples in Kyoto. If you don't find temples to your liking, there are plenty of other options. Instead, go for a hike in the mountains, browse in the shops around **Shijō-dōri** (p362), do some people-watching on Kiyamachi-dōri in **downtown Kyoto** (p315) or, best of all, find a good restaurant and sample some of the **finest food** (p355) in all of Japan.

International transactions (like wire transfers) can be made at **Tokyo Mitsubishi Bank** (Map p322; ☎ 221-7161; ⏰ 9am-3pm Mon-Fri), which is one block southwest of this intersection. Other international transactions can be made at **Citibank** (Map p322; ☎ 212-5387, ⏰ office 9am-3pm Mon-Fri, ATM 24hr), just west of this intersection. Finally, you can change travellers cheques at most post offices around town, including the Kyoto Central Post Office (below) next to Kyoto station.

INTERNATIONAL ATMS
There's an international ATM (Map p321; open 10am to 9pm) on the B1 floor of the Kyoto Tower Hotel, very close to the TIC and Kyoto station. In the middle of town, you'll find another (Map p322; open 7am to midnight) on the basement floor of the Kyoto Royal Hotel. **Citibank** (Map p322; ☎ 212-5387; ⏰ office 9am-3pm Mon-Fri, ATM 24hr) Has a 24-hour ATM that accepts most foreign-issued cards.

Post
Kyoto Central Post Office (Map p321; ☎ 365-2414; Higashishiokōji-chō; ⏰ 9am-7pm Mon-Fri, to 5pm Sat, to 12.30pm Sun & holidays) Conveniently located next to Kyoto station (take the Karasuma exit, as the post office is on the northwestern side of the station). There's an after-hours service counter on the southern side of the post office, which is open 24 hours a day, 365 days a year.

Tourist Information
Kyoto City Tourist Information Center (Map p321; ☎ 343-6656; ⏰ 8.30am-7pm) Inside the new Kyoto station building, on the 2nd floor just across from Café du Monde. Though it's geared towards Japanese visitors, an English-speaking staff is usually on hand and it's easier to find than the following.
Kyoto Tourist Information Center (TIC; Map p321; ☎ 344-3300; ⏰ 10am-6pm, closed 2nd & 4th Tue of each month & New Year's holidays) The best source of information on Kyoto, this is located on the 9th floor of the Kyoto station building. To get there from the main concourse of the station, take the west escalator to the 2nd floor, enter Isetan department store and take an immediate left and look for the elevator on your left and take it to the 9th floor. It's right outside the elevator, inside the Kyoto Prefectural International Center. There is a Welcome Inn Reservation counter at the TIC that can help with accommodation bookings.

Travel Agency
IACE TRAVEL (Map p322; ☎ 212-8944; 7F Hayakawa Bldg, Sanjō-Kawaramachi; ⏰ office 10am-7pm Mon-

---

KYOTO UNESCO WORLD HERITAGE SITES
In 1994 13 of Kyoto's Buddhist temples, three Shintō shrines and one castle met the criteria to be designated World Heritage sites by the UN. Each of the 17 sites has buildings or gardens of immeasurable historical value and all are open for public viewing.

Castle
- Nijō-jō (p342)

Shrines
- Kamigamo-jinja (p333)
- Shimogamo-jinja (p333)
- Ujigami-jinja in Uji (p347)

Temples
- Byōdō-in (p347)
- Daigo-ji (p346)
- Enryaku-ji (p341)
- Ginkaku-ji (p339)
- Kinkaku-ji (p343)
- Kiyomizu-dera (p335)
- Kōzan-ji (p350)
- Ninna-ji (p343)
- Nishi Hongan-ji (p314)
- Ryōan-ji (p343)
- Saihō-ji (p347)
- Tenryū-ji (p344)
- Tō-ji (p334)

Fri, to 5pm Sat, phone consultation 10am-5pm Sun & holidays)

Useful Organisations
Kyoto International Community House (KICH; Map pp326-7; ☎ 752-3010; 2-1 Torii-chō, Awataguchi; ⏰ 9am-9pm Tue-Sun) An essential stop for those planning a long-term stay in Kyoto, but it can also be quite useful for short-term visitors. Here you can rent typewriters, send and receive faxes, and use the internet. It has a library with maps, books, newspapers and magazines from around the world, and a notice board displaying messages regarding work, accommodation, rummage sales etc. KICH is in

KANSAI

PRIVATE TOURS OF KYOTO

A private tour is a great way to see the sights and learn about the city without having to worry about transport and logistics. There's a variety of private tours on offer in Kyoto.

All Japan Private Tours & Speciality Services (www.kyotoguide.com/yjpt) This company offers exclusive unique tours of Kyoto, Nara and Tokyo as well as business coordination and related services.

Chris Rowthorn's Walks & Tours of Kyoto & Japan (www.chrisrowthorn.com) Lonely Planet *Kyoto* and *Japan* author Chris Rowthorn offers private tours of Kyoto, Nara, Osaka and other parts of Japan.

Johnnie's Kyoto Walking (http://web.kyoto-inet.or.jp/people/h-s-love) Hirooka Hajime, aka Johnnie Hill-walker, offers an interesting guided walking tour of the area around Kyoto station and the Higashiyama area.

Naoki Doi (☎ 090-9596-5546; www3.ocn.ne.jp/~doitaxi/) This English-speaking taxi driver offers private taxi tours of Kyoto and Nara.

eastern Kyoto. You can walk from Keihan Sanjō station in about 30 minutes (1.5km). Alternatively, take the Tōzai line subway from central Kyoto and get off at Keage station, from which it's a 350m (five-minute) walk downhill.

SIGHTS
Kyoto Station Area

Although most of Kyoto's attractions are further north, there are a few attractions within walking distance of the station (Map p321). And don't forget the station building itself – it's an attraction in its own right.

KYOTO TOWER 京都タワー

If you want to orient yourself and get an idea for the layout of Kyoto as soon as you arrive in town, **Kyoto Tower** (Map p321; ☎ 361-3215; Karasuma-dōri-Shiokōji; admission ¥770; ⊙ 9am-9pm) is the place to do so. Located right outside the Karasuma (north) gate of the station, this retro tower looks like a rocket perched atop the Kyoto Tower Hotel. The tower provides excellent views in all directions and you can really get a sense for the Kyoto *bonchi* (how the Japanese describe the Kyoto plain, literally, 'a flat tray'). There are free mounted binoculars to use, and these allow ripping views over to Kiyomizu-dera (p335) and as far south as Osaka.

HIGASHI HONGAN-JI 東本願寺

When Tokugawa Ieyasu engineered the rift in the Jōdo Shin-shū school of Buddhism, he founded this **temple** (Map p321; ☎ 371-9181; Karasuma-dōri-Shichijō; admission free; ⊙ 5.50am-5.30pm, to 4.30pm in winter) as competition for Nishi Hongan-ji (right). Rebuilt in 1895 after a fire, it's certainly monumental in its proportions, but it's less impressive artistically than its counterpart. A curious item on display is a length of rope made from hair donated by female believers, which was used to haul the timber

for the reconstruction. The temple, which is a five-minute walk north of Kyoto station, is now the headquarters of the Ōtani branch of the Jōdo Shin-shū school.

NISHI HONGAN-JI 西本願寺

In 1591 Toyotomi Hideyoshi built this **temple** (Map p321; ☎ 371-5181; Horikawa-dōri-Hanaya-chō; admission free; ⊙ 5.30am-5.30pm, to 6pm in summer), known as Hongan-ji, as the new headquarters for the Jōdo Shin-shū (True Pure Land) school of Buddhism, which had accumulated immense power. Later, Tokugawa Ieyasu saw this power as a threat and sought to weaken it by encouraging a breakaway faction of this school to found Higashi Hongan-ji (*higashi* means 'east') in 1602. The original Hongan-ji then became known as Nishi Hongan-ji (*nishi* means 'west'). It now functions as the headquarters of the Hongan-ji branch of the Jōdo Shin-shū school, with over 10,000 temples and 12 million followers worldwide.

The temple contains five buildings, featuring some of the finest examples of architecture and artistic achievement from the Azuchi-Momoyama period (1568–1600). Unfortunately, the **Goe-dō** (Main Hall) is presently being restored and will be 'under wraps' until 2010. Nonetheless, it's worth a visit to see the **Daisho-in Hall**, which has sumptuous paintings, carvings and metal ornamentation. A small garden and two nō (classical Japanese dance-drama) stages are connected with the hall. The dazzling **Kara-mon** has intricate ornamental carvings. Both the Daisho-in Hall and the Kara-mon were transported here from Fushimi-jō.

If you'd like a guided tour of the temple (in Japanese only), reservations (preferably several days in advance) can be made either at the **temple office** (☎ 371-5181) or through the

KANSAI

TIC. The temple is a 12-minute walk northwest of Kyoto station.

KYOTO STATION 京都駅

Kyoto's **station building** (Map p321; Karasuma-dōri-Shiokōji) is a striking steel-and-glass structure – a futuristic cathedral for the transport age. Unveiled in September 1997, the building met with some decidedly mixed reviews. Some critics assailed it as out of keeping with the traditional architecture of Kyoto; others loved its wide-open spaces and dramatic lines.

Whatever the critics' views, you'll be impressed by the huge atrium that soars over the main concourse. Take some time to explore the many levels of the station, all the way up to the 15th-floor observation level. If you don't suffer from fear of heights, try riding the escalator from the 7th floor on the eastern side of the building up to the 11th-floor aerial skywalk, high over the main concourse.

In the station building you'll find several food courts (see p355), the Kyoto Prefectural International Centre (see p312), a performance space and Isetan department store.

SHŌSEI-EN 渉成園

About five minutes' walk east of Higashi Hongan-ji, the garden **Shōsei-en** (Map p321; ☎ 371-9181; Karasuma-dōri-Kamijuzuyachō; admission free; 9am-3.30pm) is worth a look. The lovely grounds, incorporating the Kikoku-tei villa, were completed in 1657. Bring a picnic (and some bread to feed the carp) or just stroll around the beautiful Ingetsu-ike pond.

Downtown Kyoto

Downtown Kyoto (Map p322) looks much like any other Japanese city, but there are some attractions like Nishiki Market, Kyoto's best food market, the Museum of Kyoto, which has good exhibits on the city, and Ponto-chō, one of the city's most atmospheric lanes. If you'd like a break from temples and shrines, then downtown Kyoto can be a welcome change. It's also good on a rainy day, because of the number of covered arcades and indoor attractions.

NISHIKI MARKET 錦市場

If you are interested in seeing all the really weird and wonderful foods that go into Kyoto cuisine, wander through **Nishiki Market** (Map p322; ☎ 211-3882; Nishikikōji-dōri btwn Teramachi & Takakura; 9am-5pm, varies for individual stalls). It's in the centre of town, one block north of (and parallel to) Shijō-dōri. This market is a great place to visit on a rainy day or if you need a break from temple-hopping. The variety of foods on display is staggering, and the frequent cries of *Irasshaimase!* (Welcome!) are heart-warming.

MUSEUM OF KYOTO 京都文化博物館

Housed in and behind the former Bank of Japan, a classic brick Meiji-period building, this **museum** (Map p322; ☎ 222-0888; Sanjō-dōri-Takakura; admission ¥500, extra for special exhibits; 10am-7.30pm Tue-Sun) is worth visiting if a special exhibit is on or if you need a break from temples. The regular exhibits consist of models of ancient Kyoto, audiovisual presentations and a small gallery dedicated to Kyoto's film industry. On the 1st floor, the Roji Tempō is a reconstructed Edo-period merchant area showing 10 types of exterior latticework (this section can be entered for free; some of the shops sell souvenirs and serve local dishes). The museum has English-speaking volunteer tour guides. The museum is a three-minute walk southeast of the Karasuma-Oike stop on the Karasuma and Tōzai subway lines.

KYOTO INTERNATIONAL MANGA MUSEUM 京都国際マンガミュージアム

This brand-new **museum** (☎ 075-254-7414; www.kyotomm.com/english/; Karasuma-Oike; adult/child ¥500/100; 10am-8pm Thu-Tue) has a collection of some 300,000 manga (Japanese comic books). Set in an atmospheric building that used to house an elementary school, the museum is the perfect introduction to the art of the manga. While most of the manga and displays are, naturally, in Japanese, the collection of translated works is growing.

In addition to the galleries that show both the historical development of manga and original artwork done in manga style, there are beginner's workshops and portrait drawings on weekends. Visitors with children will appreciate the children's library and the humorous traditional Japanese sliding picture shows (in Japanese and unspoken), not to mention the Astroturf lawn where the kids can run free. The museum hosts six month-long special exhibits yearly: check the website for details. While the collection is large, rest assured that it does not hold any of Japan's infamous *sukebe manga* (dirty comics) – trust us: a friend of ours looked.

(Continued on page 332)

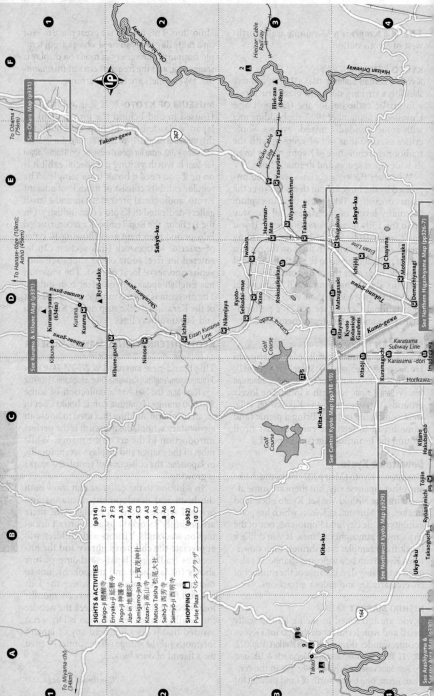

SIGHTS & ACTIVITIES   (p314)
Daigo-ji 醍醐寺 1 E7
Enryaku-ji 延暦寺 2 F3
Jingo-ji 神護寺 3 A3
Jizō-in 地蔵院 4 A6
Kamigamo-jinja 上賀茂神社 5 C3
Kōzan-ji 高山寺 6 A3
Matsuo Taisha 松尾大社 7 A5
Saihō-ji 西芳寺 8 A6
Saimyō-ji 西明寺 9 A3

SHOPPING   (p362)
Pulse Plaza パルスプラザ 10 C7

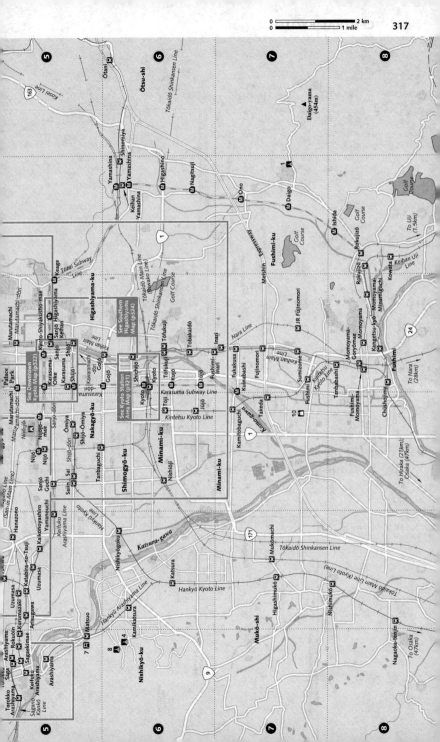

0 — 2 km
0 — 1 mile

Kosei Line

163

Ōtsu-shi

Ōtani

Shinomiya

Yamashina

Yamashina
Keihan
Yamashina

Higashino

Nagitsuji

Ono

Tōkaidō Shinkansen Line

Daigo-yama
(454m)

Daigo

Golf
Course

Ishida

Golf
Course

Golf
Course

Rokujizō

To Uji
(1.5km)

Keihan Uji
Line

Kowata

Rokujizō

Keage

Tōzai Subway
Line

Manutamachi

Marutamachi-dōri

Higashiyama-ku

Biwako Line

Tōkaidō Main Line

Kyoto-Shiyakusho-mae

Higashiyama

Keihan

Sanjō

Shijō

See Southern
Higashiyama
Map (p324)

See Downtown
Kyoto Map (p322)

Keihan Main Line

Tōkaidō Shinkansen Line

Golf Course

Fushimi-ku

Kawarazsaki

Meishin

Nara Line

Tōfukuji

Tōbakaidō

Inari

JR Fujinomori

Palace
Park

Marutamachi

Marutamachi-dōri

Nijō-jō

Karasuma-
oike

Karasuma
Shijō

Shijō

Gojō

See Kyoto Station
Area Map (p321)

Kyoto

Gojō

Kyoto

Tōfukuji

Fushimi-
Inari

Fukakusa

Fujinomori

Keihan Main Line

Momoyama-
Goryōmae

Kangetsu-kyō · Momoyama-
Minamiguchi

Fushimi

24

Karasuma-dōri

Kintetsu Kyoto Line

Sanjō-dōri

Nijō-
mae

Ōmiya

Shijō-Omiya

Nakagyō-ku

Karasuma Subway Line

Tōji

Kujō

Jūjō

Jūjō

Kamitobaguchi

Takeda

Kuinabashi

Sumizome

Fushimi

Tanbabashi

Kintetsu Kyoto Line

Tanbabashi

Fushimi-
Momoyama

Chūshojima

To Nara
(28km)

Sanin Line
(San-in Main Line)

Hanazono

Nijō

Nijō

Shio-dōri

Sanjō
Guchi

Saiin Sai

Tanbaguchi

Nishikyōgoku

Nishōji

Shimogyō-ku

Minami-ku

Minami-ku

10

Kamo-gawa

1

To Hiraka (21km);
Osaka (47km)

Uzumasa

Kalkōnyashiro

Yamanouchi

Keifuku
Arashiyama Line

Katsura-gawa

Hankyū Kyoto Line

Nishikyōgoku

Katsura

Hankyū Kyoto Line

171

Tōkaidō Shinkansen Line

Mukō-shi

Mukōmachi

Higashimukō

Tōkaidō Main Line (Kyoto Line)

Nishimukō

To Osaka
(47km)

Uzumasa

Uzumazaki

Katabira-no-Tsuji

Keifuku
Arashiyama Line

Matsuo

Kamikatsura

Nishikyō-ku

Arashiyama

Saga

Rokuōin

Kurumazaki-mae

Sagaalmae

Arisugawa

7

8

4

9

Nagaoka-tenjin

Torokko
Arashiyama

Keifuku
Arashiyama

Sagano
Kankō Line

Arashiyama

5

6

7

8

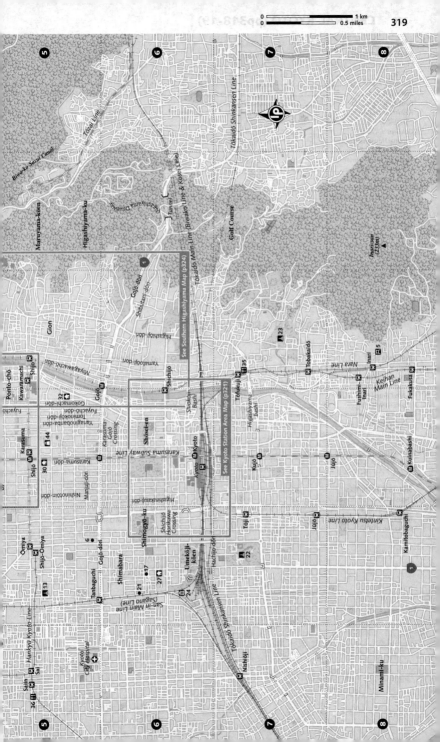

0 ——— 1 km
0 ——— 0.5 miles

See Southern Higashiyama Map (p324)

See Kyoto Station Area Map (p321)

Maruyama-kōen

Higashiyama-ku

Biwa-ko Sosui Canal

Tōkai Line

Tōkaidō Shinkansen Line

Higashiyama Driveway

Tunnel

Tōkaidō Main Line (Biwako Line & Kōsei Line)

Golf Course

Inari-san (233m)

Gion

Gojō-dōri

Shiokoji-dōri

Higashiōji-dōri

Yamatoōji-dōri

Miyagawachō-dōri

Pontochō

Kawaramachi

Shijō

Fuyachō-dōri

Tominokōji-dōri

Fuyachō-dōri

Gokomachi-dōri

Yanaginobanba-dōri

Karasuma

Shijō

Karasuma-dōri

Nishinotōin-dōri

Manjūji-dōri

Shōkoku-ji Bashi

Shichijō

Shichijō

Shōsei-en

Kyoto

Karasuma Subway Line

Higashinakasuji-dōri

Shimogyō-ku

Shichijō Shinkansen Crossing

Kujō

Hachijō-dōri

Umekōji-kōen

Tōji

Tōkaiji

Nara Line

Tobakaidō

Inari

Fushimi-Inari

Fukakusa

Keihan Main Line

Higashiyama-bashi

Kuinabashi

Kintetsu Kyoto Line

Kamitobaguchi

Minami-ku

Nishiōji

Tōkaidō Shinkansen Line

San-in Main Line (Sagano Line)

Shimabara

Tambaguchi

Gojō-dōri

Ōmiya

Shijō-Ōmiya

Hankyū Kyoto Line

Saiin

Sai

Kyoto City Hospital

Sai

36

13

30

44

32

35

23

5

22

24

27

17

21

6

1

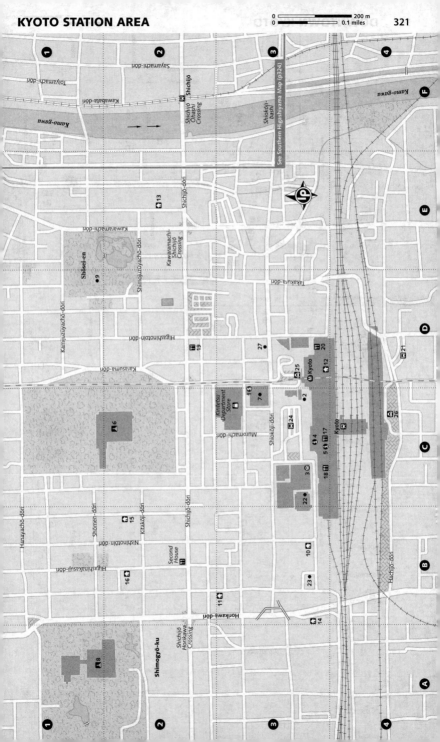

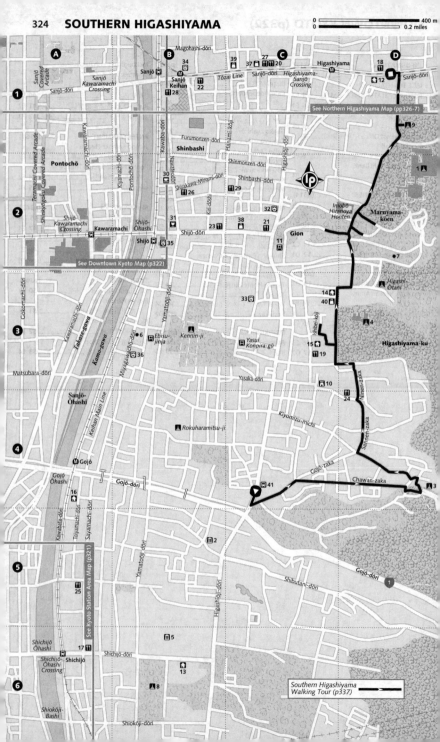

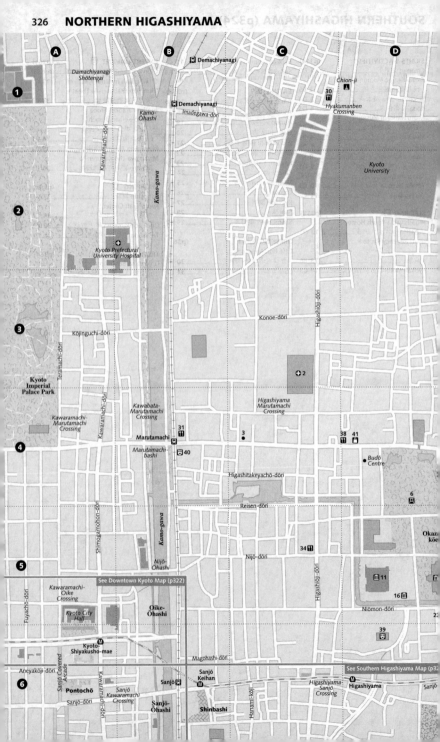

A Demachiyanagi

Damachiyanagi
Shōtengai

B

C

D

Chion-ji

30

Hyakumanben
Crossing

Demachiyanagi

Kamo-
Ōhashi

Imadegawa-dōri

Kyoto
University

Kamo-gawa

Kyoto Prefectural
University Hospital

Higashiōji-dōri

Kawaramachi-dōri

Kōjinguchi-dōri

Konoe-dōri

Teramachi-dōri

Kyoto
Imperial
Palace Park

2

Kawaramachi-
Marutamachi
Crossing

Kawabata-
Marutamachi
Crossing

Higashiyama
Marutamachi
Crossing

Kawaramachi-dōri

Marutamachi

31

3

38 41

Marutamachi-
bashi

40

Budō
Centre

Higashitakeyachō-dōri

6

Shimogamohon-dōri

Reisen-dōri

Okaza
kōe

Kamo-gawa

Nijō-
Ōhashi

34

Nijō-dōri

Higashiōji-dōri

See Downtown Kyoto Map (p322)

Kawaramachi-
Oike
Crossing

Fuyachō-dōri

Oike-
Ōhashi

11

Kyoto City
Hall

16

Niōmon-dōri

Kyoto-
Shiyakusho-mae

39

Magohashi-dōri

22

See Southern Higashiyama Map (p32

Aneyakōji-dōri

Sanjō
Keihan

Higashiyama-
Sanjō
Crossing

Higashiyama

Sanjō

Sanjō Covered Arcade

Pontochō

Sanjō
Kawaramachi
Crossing

Sanjō

Sanjō-
Ōhashi

Hanami-kōji

Shinbashi

Kawaramachi-dōri

Sanjō-dōri

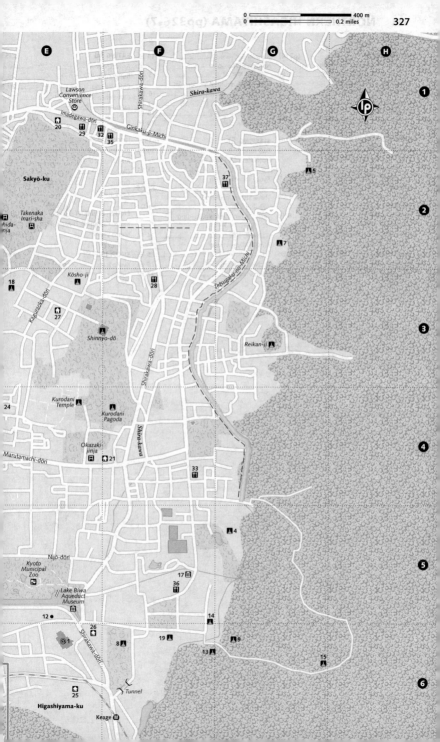

0 — 400 m
0 — 0.2 miles

E   **F**   **G**   **H**

1

Lawson Convenience Store

Imadegawa-dōri
20   29   32   35

Shirakawa-dōri

Shira-kawa

Ginkaku-ji-Michi

5

Sakyō-ku

37

2

7

Takenaka Inari-sha
hidanja

Kōsho-ji   28

18

Kaguraoka-dōri

27

Reikan-ji

3

Shinnyo-dō

Shirakawa-dōri

Tetsugaku-no-Michi

24

Kurodani Temple

Shira-kawa

Kurodani Pagoda

4

Okazaki-jinja

21

Marutamachi-dōri

33

4

Nijō-dōri

5

Kyoto Municipal Zoo

17

Lake Biwa Aqueduct Museum

36

12

14

26

8   19   9

Shirakawa-dōri

1

13   15

6

25

Higashiyama-ku

Tunnel

Keage **M**

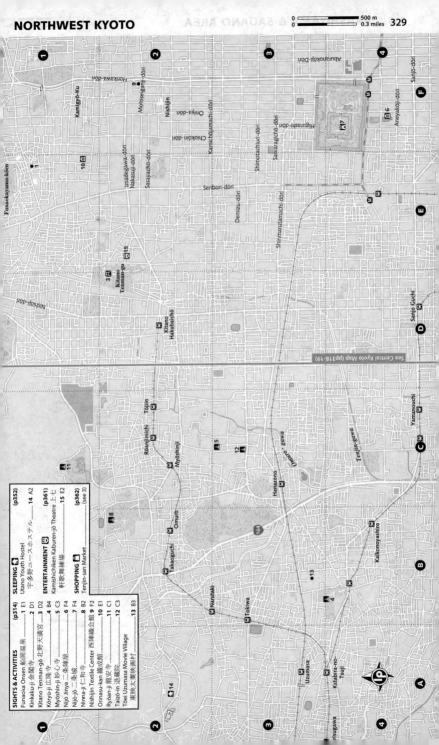

0 — 500 m
0 — 0.3 miles

SIGHTS & ACTIVITIES	(p314)
Funaoka Onsen 船岡温泉	1 E1
Kinkaku-ji 金閣寺	2 D1
Kitano Tenman-gū 北野天満宮	3 D2
Kōryū-ji 広隆寺	4 B4
Myōshin-ji 妙心寺	5 C3
Nijō Jinya 二条陣屋	6 F4
Nijō-jō 二条城	7 F4
Ninna-ji 仁和寺	8 B2
Nishijin Textile Center 西陣織会館	9 F2
Orinasu-kan 織成館	10 E1
Ryōan-ji 龍安寺	11 C1
Taizō-in 退蔵院	12 C3
Tōei Uzumasa Movie Village 東映太秦映画村	13 B3

SLEEPING	(p352)
Utano Youth Hostel 宇多野ユースホステル	14 A2

ENTERTAINMENT	(p361)
Kamishichiken Kaburen-jō Theatre 上七軒歌舞練場	15 E2

SHOPPING	(p362)
Tenjin-san Market	(see 3)

See Central Kyoto Map (pp318-19)

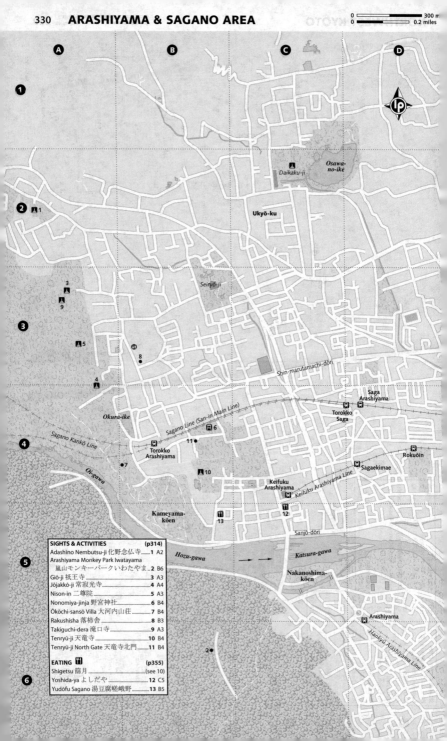

0 ————— 300 m
0 ————— 0.2 miles

KYOTO

A **B** **C** **D**

1

Osawa-no-ike

Daikaku-ji

Ukyō-ku

2 1

Seiryō-ji

3
9

3

5

8

4

Shin-marutamachi-dōri

Saga
Arashiyama

Okura-ike

Torokko
Saga

Sagano Line (San-in Main Line)

6

Sagano Kankō Line

Torokko
Arashiyama

11

4

Ōi-gawa

10

Rokuōin

Sagaekimae

Keifuku
Arashiyama

Keifuku Arashiyama Line

Kameyama-
kōen

13

12

Sanjō-dōri

5

Hozu-gawa

Katsura-gawa

Nakanoshima-
kōen

Arashiyama

Hankyū Arashiyama Line

6

2

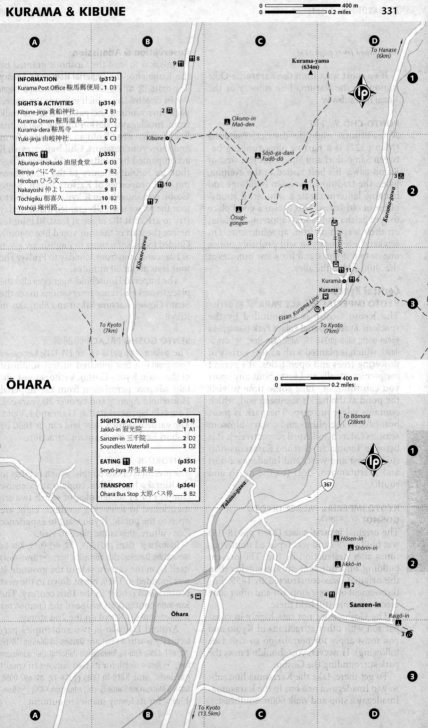

INFORMATION	(p312)
Kurama Post Office 鞍馬郵便局 ...**1** D3	

SIGHTS & ACTIVITIES	(p314)
Kibune-jinja 貴船神社 ...**2** B1	
Kurama Onsen 鞍馬温泉 ...**3** D2	
Kurama-dera 鞍馬寺 ...**4** C2	
Yuki-jinja 由岐神社 ...**5** C3	

EATING	(p355)
Aburaya-shokudō 油屋食堂 ...**6** D3	
Beniya べにや ...**7** B2	
Hirobun ひろ文 ...**8** B1	
Nakayoshi 仲よし ...**9** B1	
Tochigiku 栃喜久 ...**10** B2	
Yōshūji 雍州路 ...**11** D3	

ŌHARA

SIGHTS & ACTIVITIES	(p314)
Jakkō-in 寂光院 ...**1** A1	
Sanzen-in 三千院 ...**2** D2	
Soundless Waterfall ...**3** D2	

EATING	(p355)
Seryō-jaya 芹生茶屋 ...**4** D2	

TRANSPORT	(p364)
Ōhara Bus Stop 大原バス停 ...**5** B2	

(Continued from page 315)

It's a short walk from the Karasuma-Oike station on the Karuma line subway or the Tōzai line subway.

PONTO-CHŌ 先斗町

A traditional nightlife district, **Ponto-chō** (Map p322) is a narrow alley running between Sanjō-dōri and Shijō-dōri just west of Kamo-gawa. It's best visited in the evening, when the traditional wooden buildings and hanging lanterns create a wonderful atmosphere of old Japan. This is also a good place to spot geisha and *maiko* (apprentice geisha) on their way to or from appointments. On weekend evenings you will probably notice one or two if you stand for a few minutes at the Shijō end of the alley.

Central Kyoto

KYOTO IMPERIAL PALACE PARK 京都御所

The Kyoto Gosho is surrounded by the spacious **Kyoto Imperial Palace Park** (Kamigyō-ku Kyoto goen; Map pp318-19; admission free; ☼ dawn-dusk), which is planted with a huge variety of flowering trees and open fields. It's perfect for picnics, strolls and just about any sport you can think of. Take some time to visit the pond at the park's southern end, which contains gorgeous carp. The park is most beautiful in the plum- and cherry-blossom seasons (March and April respectively). It is between Teramachi-dōri and Karasuma-dōri (to the east and west) and Imadegawa-dōri and Marutamachi-dōri (to the north and south).

KYOTO IMPERIAL PALACE (KYOTO GOSHO) 京都御所

The original **imperial palace** (Map pp318–19) was built in 794 and was replaced numerous times after destruction by fire. The present building, on a different site and smaller than the original, was constructed in 1855. Enthronement of a new emperor and other state ceremonies are still held there.

The Gosho does not rate highly in comparison with other attractions in Kyoto and you must apply for permission to visit (see following). However, you shouldn't miss the park surrounding the Gosho.

To get there, take the Karasuma line subway to Imadegawa or a bus to the Karasuma-Imadegawa stop and walk 600m southeast.

Reservation & Admission

Permission to visit the Gosho is granted by the Kunaichō, the **Imperial Household Agency** (Map pp318-19; ☎ 211-1215; ☼ 8.45am-noon & 1-4pm Mon-Fri, closed holidays), which is inside the walled park surrounding the palace, a short walk from Imadegawa station on the Karasuma line. You have to fill out an application form and show your passport. Children can visit if accompanied by adults over 20 years of age (but are forbidden entry to the other three imperial properties of Katsura Rikyū, Sentō Gosho and Shūgaku-in Rikyū). Permission to tour the palace is usually granted the same day (try to arrive at the office at least 30 minutes before the start of the tour you'd like to join). Guided tours, sometimes in English, are given at 10am and 2pm from Monday to Friday. The tour lasts about 50 minutes.

The Imperial Household Agency is also the place to make advance reservations to see the Sentō Gosho, Katsura Rikyū and Shūgaku-in Rikyū.

SENTŌ GOSHO PALACE 仙洞御所

The **palace** (Map pp318-19; ☎ 211-1215; Kamigyō-ku Kyoto goen) is a few hundred metres southeast of the main Kyoto Gosho. Visitors must obtain advance permission from the Imperial Household Agency and be over 20 years old. Tours (in Japanese) start at 11am and 1.30pm. The gardens, which were laid out in 1630 by Kobori Enshū, are the main attraction.

DAITOKU-JI 大徳寺

The precincts of this temple, which belongs to the Rinzai school of Zen, contain an extensive complex of 24 subtemples, of which two are mentioned in following sections; eight are open to the public. If you want to experience Zen culture, this is the place to visit.

Daitoku-ji (Map pp318-19; ☎ 491-0019; Kita-ku Murasakino Daitokuji-chō; admission free; ☼ dawn-dusk) itself is on the eastern side of the grounds. It was founded in 1319, burnt down in the next century and rebuilt in the 16th century. The **San-mon** contains an image of the famous tea master Sen-no-Rikyū on the 2nd storey.

Around Daitoku-ji, two subtemples particularly worth a visit are **Daisen-in** (Map pp318-19; ☎ 491-8346; Kita-ku Murasakino Daitokuji-chō; admission free; ☼ 9am-4.30pm), for its two famous (if small) gardens, and **Kōtō-in** (Map pp318-19; ☎ 492-0068; Kita-ku Murasakino Daitokuji-chō; admission ¥400; ☼ 9am-4.30pm) for its lovely maples in autumn.

Admission charges to the various subtemples vary but are usually around ¥400. Those temples that accept visitors are usually open from 9am to 4.30pm.

The temple bus stop is Daitoku-ji-mae and convenient buses from Kyoto station are buses 205 and 206. Daitoku-ji is also a short walk west of Kitaō-ji subway station on the Karasuma line.

SHIMOGAMO-JINJA 下鴨神社

This **shrine** (Map pp318–19; ☎ 781-0010; Shimogamo, Izumikawa-chō; admission free; ⏰ 6.30am-5.30pm) dates from the 8th century and is a Unesco World Heritage site. It is nestled in the fork of the Kamo-gawa and Takano-gawa rivers, and is approached along a shady path through the lovely Tadasu-no-mori. This wooded area is said to be a place where lies cannot be concealed and is considered a prime location to sort out disputes.

The shrine is dedicated to the god of harvest. Traditionally, pure water was drawn from the nearby rivers for purification and agricultural ceremonies. The Hondō (Main Hall) dates from 1863 and, like the Haiden hall at its sister shrine, Kamigamo-jinja, is an excellent example of *nagare*-style shrine architecture.

The shrine is a only one-minute walk from Shimogamo-jinja-mae bus stop; take bus 205 from Kyoto station.

KYOTO BOTANICAL GARDENS 京都府立植物園

The **Kyoto Botanical Gardens** (Map pp318–19; ☎ 701-0141; Sakyō-ku, Shimogamo; admission ¥200, greenhouse extra ¥200; ⏰ 9am-5pm), opened in 1914, occupy 240,000 sq metres and feature 12,000 plants, flowers and trees. It is pleasant to stroll through the rose, cherry and herb gardens or see the rows of camphor trees and the large tropical greenhouse. The gardens are a two-minute walk from Kitayama subway station (Karasuma line).

KAMIGAMO-JINJA 上賀茂神社

This **shrine** (Map pp318–19; ☎ 781-0011; Kamigamo Motoyama; admission free; ⏰ 8am-4pm) is one of Japan's oldest shrines and predates the founding of Kyoto. Established in 679, it is dedicated to Raijin, the god of thunder, and is one of Kyoto's 17 Unesco World Heritage sites. The present buildings (over 40 in all), including the impressive Haiden hall, are exact reproductions of the originals, dating from the 17th to 19th century. The shrine is entered from a long approach through two torii (shrine gates). The two large conical white-sand mounds in front of Hosodono hall are said to represent mountains sculpted for gods to descend upon.

The shrine is a five-minute walk from Kamigamo-misonobashi bus stop; take bus 9 from Kyoto station.

SUMIYA PLEASURE HOUSE 角屋もてなしの文化美術館

This **house** (Map pp318–19; ☎ 351-0024; Nishishin-yashikiageya-chō; admission ¥1000, Japanese-language tours available; ⏰ 10am-4pm Tue-Sun) is one of the last remaining *ageya* found in Shimabara. This district northwest of Kyoto station was Kyoto's original pleasure quarters. At its peak during the Edo period (1600–1867) the area flourished, with over 20 enormous *ageya* – magnificent banquet halls where artists, writers and statesmen gathered in a 'floating world' ambience of conversation, art and fornication. Geisha were often sent from their quarters (*okiya*) to entertain patrons at these restaurant-cum-brothels. By the start of the Meiji period, however, such activities had drifted north to the Gion district and Shimabara had lost its prominence.

Though the traditional air of the district has dissipated, a few old structures remain. The tremendous **Shimabara-no-ō-mon** gate, which marked the passage into the quarter, still stands, as does the Sumiya Pleasure House, now designated a National Cultural Asset. Built in 1641, this stately two-storey, 20-room structure allows a rare glimpse into Edo-era nirvana. With a delicate latticework exterior, Sumiya has a huge open kitchen and an extensive series of rooms (including one extravagantly decorated with mother-of-pearl inlay).

Sumiya is a seven-minute walk from JR Tanbaguchi station, or a 10-minute walk from Umekōji-kōen-mae bus stop; take bus 205 from Kyoto station.

MIBU-DERA 壬生寺

Founded in 991, **Mibu-dera** (Map pp318–19; ☎ 841-3381; Bōjō-Bukkō-ji; admission free; ⏰ 8.30am-5.30pm) belongs to the Risshū school. In the late Edo period, it became a training centre for samurai. Mibu-dera houses tombs of pro-shōgunate Shinsen-gumi members, who fought bloody street battles resisting the forces that succeeded in restoring the emperor in

1868. Except for an unusual stupa covered in Jizō statues, the temple is of limited interest. It is, however, definitely worth visiting during Mibu kyōgen performances (late April), or the Setsubun celebrations (early February).

The temple is a 10-minute walk from Hankyū Ōmiya station.

TŌ-JI 東寺

This **temple** (Map pp318-19; ☎ 691-3325; Minami-ku Kujō; admission to grounds free, Kondō & Treasure Hall ¥500; ⊗ 9am-4.30pm) was established in 794 by imperial decree to protect the city. In 818, the emperor handed the temple over to Kūkai, the founder of the Shingon school of Buddhism. Many of the buildings were destroyed by fire or fighting during the 15th century; most of those that remain date from the 17th century.

The **Kōdō** (Lecture Hall) contains 21 images representing a Mikkyō (Esoteric Buddhism) mandala. The **Kondō** (Main Hall) contains statues depicting the Yakushi (Healing Buddha) trinity. In the southern part of the garden stands the five-storey pagoda, which burnt down five times, was rebuilt in 1643 and is now the highest pagoda in Japan, standing 57m high.

The **Kōbō-san market-fair** is held here on the 21st of each month. The fairs held in December and January are particularly lively.

Tō-ji is a 15-minute walk southwest of Kyoto station.

UMEKŌJI STEAM LOCOMOTIVE MUSEUM 梅小路蒸気機関車館

A hit with steam-train buffs and kids, this **museum** (Map pp318-19; ☎ 314-2996; Shimogyō-ku Kannon-ji-chō; adult/child ¥400/100, train ride adult/child ¥200/100; ⊗ 9.30am-5pm Tue-Sun) features 18 vintage steam locomotives (dating from 1914 to 1948) and related displays. It's in the former Nijō station building, which was recently relocated here and carefully reconstructed. For an extra ¥200 (¥100 for children), you can take a 10-minute ride on one of the fabulous old trains (departures at 11am, 1.30pm and 3.30pm). From Kyoto station, take bus 33, 205 or 208 to the Umekō-ji Kōen-mae stop (make sure you take a westbound bus).

Southern Higashiyama

The Higashiyama district, which runs along the base of the eastern (Higashiyama) mountains, is the main sightseeing district in Kyoto

and it should be at the top of your Kyoto itinerary. It is, literally, thick with impressive sights: fine temples, shrines, gardens, museums, traditional neighbourhoods and parks. In this guide, we divide the Higashiyama district into two sections: Southern Higashiyama (this section) and Northern Higashiyama (p338).

We start this section with sights in the south, around Shichijō-dōri, and work north, to Sanjō-dōri. You could cover these in the order presented in a fairly long day. Be sure to see the Southern Higashiyama Walking Tour (p337). This is the most interesting route through the area.

SANJŪSANGEN-DŌ 三十三間堂

The original **Sanjūsangen-dō** (Map p324; ☎ 525-0033; Higashiyama-ku Chaya-machi; admission ¥600; ⊗ 8am-5pm Apr–mid-Nov, 9am-4.30pm mid-Nov–Mar) was built in 1164 at the request of the retired emperor Go-shirakawa. The temple burnt to the ground in 1249 but a faithful copy was constructed in 1266.

The temple's name refers to the 33 (*sanjū-san*) bays between the pillars of this long, narrow building that houses 1001 statues of the 1000-armed Kannon (the Buddhist goddess of mercy). The largest Kannon is flanked on either side by 500 smaller Kannon images, neatly lined up in rows.

There are an awful lot of arms, but if you're picky and think the 1000-armed statues don't have the required number of limbs, then you should remember to calculate according to the nifty Buddhist mathematical formula that holds that 40 arms are the equivalent of 1000 arms, because each saves 25 worlds. Visitors also seem keen to spot resemblances between friends or family members and any of the hundreds of images.

At the back of the hall are 28 guardian statues in a great variety of expressive poses. The gallery on the western side of the hall is famous for the annual **Tōshi-ya Matsuri**, held on 15 January, during which archers shoot arrows the length of the hall. The ceremony dates back to the Edo period, when an annual contest was held to see how many arrows could be shot from the southern end to the northern end in 24 hours. The all-time record was set in 1686, when an archer successfully landed over 8000 arrows at the northern end.

The temple is a 1.5km walk east of Kyoto station; alternatively, take bus 206 or 208 and get off at the Sanjūsangen-dō-mae stop. It's also very close to Keihan Shichijō station. From the station, walk north on Karasuma-dōri, then turn right onto Shichijō-dōri and walk east; the temple is on the right.

KYOTO NATIONAL MUSEUM
京都国立博物館
The **Kyoto National Museum** (Map p324; ☎ 531-7509; www.kyohaku.go.jp/eng/index_top.html; Higashiyama-ku Chaya-machi; admission ¥500, extra for special exhibitions; ⏰ 9.30am-5pm Tue-Sun) is housed in two buildings opposite Sanjūsangen-dō. There are excellent displays of fine arts, historical artefacts and handicrafts. The fine arts collection is especially highly regarded, containing some 230 items that have been classified as National Treasures or Important Cultural Properties. Check what special exhibitions are on when you're in town, as these are often superb.

KAWAI KANJIRŌ MEMORIAL HALL
河井寛次郎博物館
This **museum** (Map p324; ☎ 561-3585; Higashiyama-Gojō-zaka; admission ¥900; ⏰ 10am-5pm Tue-Sun, closed around 10-20 Aug & 24 Dec-7 Jan, dates vary each year) was once the home and workshop of one of Japan's most famous potters, Kawai Kanjirō. The house is built in rural style and contains examples of his work, his collection of folk art and ceramics, and his kiln.

The hall is a 10-minute walk north of the Kyoto National Museum. Alternatively, take bus 206 or 207 from Kyoto station and get off at the Umamachi stop.

KIYOMIZU-DERA 清水寺
This ancient **temple** (Map p324; ☎ 551-1234; Higashiyama-ku Kiyomizu; admission ¥300; ⏰ 6am-6pm) was first built in 798, but the present buildings are reconstructions dating from 1633. As an affiliate of the Hossō school of Buddhism, which originated in Nara, it has successfully survived the many intrigues of local Kyoto schools of Buddhism through the centuries and is now one of the most famous landmarks of the city (for which reason it can get very crowded during spring and autumn).

The main hall has a huge veranda that is supported by hundreds of pillars and juts out over the hillside. Just below this hall is the waterfall **Otowa-no-taki** (Map p324), where visitors drink sacred waters believed to have therapeutic properties. Dotted around the precincts are other halls and shrines. At Jishu-jinja, the shrine on the grounds, visitors try to ensure success in love by closing their eyes and walking about 18m between a pair of stones – if you miss the stone, your desire for love won't be fulfilled!

The steep approach to the temple is known as Chawan-zaka (Teapot Lane) and is lined with shops selling Kyoto handicrafts, local snacks and souvenirs.

To get there from Kyoto station take bus 206 and get off at either the Kiyōmizu-michi or Gojō-zaka stop and plod up the hill for 10 minutes.

NINEN-ZAKA & SANNEN-ZAKA
二年坂・三年坂
Just below and slightly to the north of Kiyomizu-dera, you will find one of Kyoto's most lovely restored neighbourhoods, the Ninen-zaka–Sannen-zaka area (Map p324). The name refers to the two main streets of the areas: Ninen-zaka and Sannen-zaka, literally 'Two-Year Hill' and 'Three-Year Hill'. These two charming streets are lined with old wooden houses, traditional shops and restaurants. If you fancy a break, there are many teahouses and cafés along these lanes.

KŌDAI-JI 高台寺
This **temple** (Map p324; ☎ 561-9966; Higashiyama-ku Kōdai-ji; admission ¥600; ⏰ 9am-5pm) was founded in 1605 by Kita-no-Mandokoro in memory of her late husband, Toyotomi Hideyoshi. The extensive grounds include gardens designed by the famed landscape architect Kobori Enshū, and teahouses designed by the renowned master of the tea ceremony, Sen-no-Rikyū.

The temple is a 10-minute walk north of Kiyomizu-dera (left). Check at the TIC for the scheduling of summer and autumn nighttime illuminations of the temple (when the gardens are lit by multicoloured spotlights).

MARUYAMA-KŌEN 円山公園
This **park** (Map p324; Maruyama-chō Higashiyama-ku) is a great place to escape the bustle of the city centre and amble around gardens, ponds, souvenir shops and restaurants. Peaceful paths meander through the trees and carp glide through the waters of a small pond in the centre of the park.

For two weeks in late March/early April, when the park's many cherry trees come into bloom, the calm atmosphere of the park is shattered by hordes of revellers enjoying

KANSAI

hanami (blossom-viewing). The centrepiece is a massive *shidarezakura*, a weeping cherry tree – truly one of the most beautiful sights in Kyoto, particularly when lit from below at night. For those who don't mind crowds, this is a good place to observe the Japanese at their most uninhibited. It is best to arrive early and claim a good spot high on the eastern side of the park, from which point you can safely peer down on the mayhem below.

The park is a five-minute walk east of the Shijō-Higashiōji intersection. To get there from Kyoto station, take bus 206 and get off at the Gion stop.

YASAKA-JINJA 八坂神社

This colourful **shrine** (Map p324; ☎ 561-6155; Higashiyama-ku Gion; admission free; ⏰ 24hr) is just down the hill from Maruyama-kōen. It's considered the guardian shrine of neighbouring Gion and is sometimes endearingly referred to as 'Gion-san'. This shrine is particularly popular as a spot for *hatsu-mōde* (the first shrine visit of the new year). If you don't mind a stampede, come here around midnight on New Year's Eve or over the next few days. Surviving the crush is proof that you're blessed by the gods! Yasaka-jinja also sponsors Kyoto's biggest festival, Gion Matsuri (p351).

GION 祇園周辺

Gion, one minute's walk from Keihan Shijō station, is a famous entertainment and geisha district on the eastern bank of the Kamo-gawa. Modern architecture, congested traffic and contemporary nightlife establishments rob the area of some of its historical beauty, but there are still some lovely places left for a stroll. Gion falls roughly between Sanjō-dōri and Gojō-dōri (north and south, respectively) and Higashiyama-dōri and Kawabata-dōri (east and west, respectively).

Hanami-kōji is a street running north to south that bisects Shijō-dōri. The southern section is lined with 17th-century traditional restaurants and teahouses, many of which are exclusive establishments for geisha entertainment. If you wander around here in the late afternoon or early evening, you can often glimpse geisha or *maiko* on their way to or from appointments.

If you walk north from Shijō-dōri along Hanami-kōji, the fourth intersection you will come to is **Shinmonzen-dōri**. Wander in either direction along this street, which is packed

with old houses, art galleries and shops specialising in antiques. Don't expect flea-market prices.

For more historic buildings in a waterside setting, wander down **Shirakawa Minami-dōri** (sometimes called Shimbashi), which is parallel with, and a block south of, the western section of Shinmonzen-dōri. This is one of Kyoto's most beautiful streets, and, arguably, the most beautiful street in all of Asia, especially in the evening and during cherry-blossom season.

CHION-IN 知恩院

In 1234 **Chion-in** (Map p324; ☎ 531-2111; Shinbashi-dōri-Yamatoōji Higashi iru; admission to grounds/inner buildings & garden free/¥400; ⏰ 9am-4pm Mar-Nov, to 3.40pm Dec-Feb) was built on the site where a famous priest by the name of Hōnen had taught and eventually fasted to death. Today it is still the headquarters of the Jōdo school of Buddhism, which was founded by Hōnen, and a hive of activity. For visitors with a taste for the grand, this temple is sure to satisfy.

The oldest of the present buildings date back to the 17th century. The two-storey **San-mon**, a Buddhist temple gate at the main entrance, is the largest temple gate in Japan and prepares you for the massive scale of the temple. The immense main hall contains an image of Hōnen. It's connected to another hall, the Dai Hōjō, by a 'nightingale' floor (floors that sing and squeak at every move, making it difficult for intruders to move about quietly). The massive scale of the buildings reflects the popularity of the Jōdo school, which holds that earnest faith in the Buddha is all you need to achieve salvation.

The giant **bell**, cast in 1633 and weighing 74 tonnes, is the largest in Japan. The combined muscle-power of 17 monks is needed to make the bell ring for the famous ceremony that heralds the new year.

The temple is close to the northeastern corner of Maruyama-kōen. From Kyoto station take bus 206 and get off at the Chion-in-mae stop or walk up (east) from the Keihan Sanjō or Shijō station.

SHŌREN-IN 青蓮院

This **temple** (Map p324; ☎ 561-2345; Higashiyama-ku Sanjō-Awataguchi; admission ¥500; ⏰ 9am-5pm) is hard to miss, with the giant camphor trees growing just outside its walls. Shōren-in was originally the residence of the chief abbot of

SOUTHERN HIGASHIYAMA WALKING TOUR

- Start: Gojō-zaka bus stop on Higashiōji-dōri, serviced by buses 18, 100, 206 and 207 (see Map p324)
- End: Jingū-michi bus stop on Sanjō-dōri, serviced by buses 5 and 100
- Distance: About 5km
- Time: Half-day

If you had only one day in Kyoto, this walk would be the best way to sample several of Kyoto's most important sights and neighbourhoods. It's pretty much a must-see route, heading right through the heart of Kyoto's premier sightseeing district. Be warned, though, that almost every visitor to Kyoto, both Japanese and foreign, eventually makes their way here, so you'll have to hit it very early in the day to avoid the crush.

The walk begins at Gojō-zaka bus stop (Map p324) on Higashiōji-dōri. From here, walk south for a few metres and turn up Gojō-zaka slope (there is an old noodle shop and pharmacy at the bottom of this street). Head uphill until you reach the first fork in the road; bear right and continue up **Chawan-zaka** (Teapot Lane). At the top of the hill you'll come to **Kiyomizu-dera** (p335), with its unmistakeable pagoda rising against the skyline. Before you enter the main complex of Kiyomizu-dera, we recommend that you pay ¥100 to descend into the **Tainai-meguri**, the entrance to which is just to the left of the main temple entrance.

After touring Kiyomizu-dera, exit down Kiyomizu-michi, the busy approach to the temple. Walk down the hill for about 200m until you reach a four-way intersection; go right here down the stone-paved steps. This is **Sannen-zaka**, a charming street lined with old wooden houses, traditional shops and restaurants. There are many teahouses and cafés along this stretch.

Halfway down Sannen-zaka, the road curves to the left. Follow it a short distance, then go right down a flight of steps into **Ninen-zaka** (p335), another quaint street lined with historic houses, shops and teahouses. At the end of Ninen-zaka zigzag left (at the vending machines), then right (just past the parking lot), and continue north. Very soon, on your left, you'll come to the entrance to **Ishibei-kōji** – perhaps the most beautiful street in Kyoto, though it's actually a cobbled alley lined on both sides with elegant, traditional Japanese inns and restaurants. Take a detour to explore this, then retrace your steps and continue north, passing almost immediately the entrance to **Kōdai-ji** (p335) on the right up a long flight of stairs.

After Kōdai-ji continue north to the T-intersection; turn right at this junction and then take a quick left. You'll cross the wide pedestrian arcade and then descend into **Maruyama-kōen** (p335), a pleasant park in which to take a rest. In the centre of the park, you'll see the giant Gion *shidare-zakura*, Kyoto's most famous cherry tree. Opposite the tree there's a bridge that leads across a carp pond to the lovely upper reaches of the park – this is a good place for a picnic, but you'll have to have brought something with you to eat, since the offerings in the park are limited to junk food.

From the park, you can head west (downhill) into the grounds of **Yasaka-jinja** (opposite) and descend from the shrine to Shijō-dōri and Gion and make your way home (it's about a 400m walk to Keihan Shijō station from here). However, if you've got the energy, it's best to return back through the park and head north to tour the grounds of the impressive **Chion-in** (opposite). From here it's a quick walk to **Shōren-in** (opposite), which is famous for its enormous camphor trees out front. From Shōren-in descend to Sanjō-dōri (you'll see the giant shrine gate of **Heian-jingū** (p340) in the distance). By going left on Sanjō-dōri, you'll soon come to the Jingū-michi bus stop where you can catch bus 5 or bus 100 to Kyoto station, or continue west a little further on Sanjō and you'll soon come to the Higashiyama-Sanjō station on the Tōzai line.

the Tendai school of Buddhism. The present building dates from 1895, but the main hall has sliding screens with paintings from the 16th and 17th centuries. Often overlooked by the crowds that descend on other Higashiyama temples, this is a pleasant place to sit and think while gazing out over the beautiful gardens.

The temple is a five-minute walk north of Chion-in (opposite).

KANSAI

Northern Higashiyama

This is one of the city's richest areas for sightseeing. It includes such first-rate attractions as Ginkaku-ji, Honen-in, Shūgaku-in Rikyū, Shisen-dō and Manshu-in. You can spend a wonderful day in Kyoto walking from Keage station on the subway Tōzai line all the way north to Ginkaku-ji (or vice versa), stopping in the countless temples and shrines en route. The sights in this section are presented from south to north. You could spend a very pleasant day working your way from Nanzen-ji, up the Tetsugaku-no-Michi (Path of Philosophy), to Ginkaku-ji. Sights further north should be tackled separately.

NANZEN-JI 南禅寺

This is one of our favourite **temples** (Map pp326-7; ☎ 771-0365; nanzenji.com/english/index.html; Nanzen-ji Fukuchi-chō; admission to grounds free, inner buildings & garden Hōjō Teien garden/San-mon/Nanzen-in ¥500/500/300; ☉ 8.40am-5pm Mar-Nov, to 4.30pm Dec-Feb) in all Kyoto, with its expansive grounds and numerous subtemples. It began as a retirement villa for Emperor Kameyama but was dedicated as a Zen temple on his death in 1291. Civil war in the 15th century destroyed most of the temple; the present buildings date from the 17th century. It operates now as headquarters for the Rinzai school of Zen.

At its entrance stands the massive **San-mon.** Steps lead up to the 2nd storey, which has a fine view over the city. Beyond the gate is the main hall of the temple, above which you will find the **Hōjō**, where the **Leaping Tiger Garden** is a classic Zen garden well worth a look (try to ignore the annoying taped explanation of the garden). While you're in the Hōjō, you can enjoy a cup of tea while gazing at a small waterfall (¥400, ask at the reception desk of the Hōjō).

Dotted around the grounds of Nanzen-ji are several subtemples (see following sections) that are often skipped by the crowds.

To get to Nanzen-ji from JR Kyoto or Keihan Sanjō station, take bus 5 and get off at the Nanzen-ji Eikan-dō-michi stop. You can also take the subway Tōzai line from the city centre to Keage and walk for five minutes downhill. Turn right (east, towards the mountains) opposite the police box and walk slightly uphill and you will arrive at the main gate of the temple.

Nanzen-ji Oku-no-in 南禅寺奥の院

Perhaps the best part of Nanzen-ji is overlooked by most visitors: **Oku-no-in** (Map pp326-7;

THE LIVING ART OF THE GEISHA

Behind the closed doors of the exclusive teahouses and restaurants that dot the back streets of Kyoto, women of exquisite grace and refinement entertain gentlemen of considerable means. Patrons may pay more than $3000 to spend an evening in the company of two or three geisha – kimono-clad women versed in an array of visual and performing arts, including playing the three-stringed *shamisen,* singing old teahouse ballads and dancing.

An evening in a Gion teahouse begins with an exquisite *kaiseki* (Japanese cuisine that obeys very strict rules of etiquette for every detail of the meal, including the setting) meal. While their customers eat, the geisha or *maiko* (apprentice geisha) enter the room and introduce themselves in Kyoto dialect.

A *shamisen* performance, followed by a traditional fan dance, is often given, and all the while the geisha and *maiko* pour drinks, light cigarettes and engage in charming banter.

It is virtually impossible to enter a Gion teahouse and witness a geisha performance without the introduction of an established patron. With the exception of public performances at annual festivals or dance presentations, they perform only for select customers. While geisha are not prostitutes, those who decide to open their own teahouses once they retire at 50 or so may receive financial backing from well-to-do clients.

Knowledgeable sources estimate that there are perhaps 80 *maiko* and just over 100 geisha in Kyoto. Although their numbers are ever decreasing, geisha (*geiko* in the Kyoto dialect) and *maiko* can still be seen in some parts of Kyoto, especially after dusk in the back streets between the Kamo-gawa and Yasaka-jinja and along the narrow Ponto-chō alley. Geisha and *maiko* can also be found in other parts of the country, most notably Tokyo. However, it is thought that there are less than 1000 geisha and *maiko* remaining in all Japan.

Geisha and *maiko* entertainment can be arranged through top-end hotels, ryokan and some private tour operators in Kyoto.

admission free; ⊙ dawn-dusk), a small shrine-temple hidden in a forested hollow behind the main precinct. To get there, walk up to the redbrick aqueduct in front of the subtemple of Nanzen-in. Follow the road that runs parallel to the aqueduct up into the hills, past several brightly coloured torii until you reach a waterfall in a beautiful mountain glen.

Tenju-an 天授庵

This **temple** (Map pp326–7; ☎ 771-0365; Nanzen-ji Fukuchi-chō; admission ¥400; ⊙ 8.40am-5pm Mar-Nov, to 4.30pm Dec-Feb) stands at the side of the San-mon, a four-minute walk west of Nanzen-in. Constructed in 1337, the temple has a splendid garden and a great collection of carp in its pond.

Konchi-in 金地院

When leaving Tenju-an, turn left and continue for 100m – **Konchi-in** (Map pp326–7; admission ¥400; ⊙ 8.30am-5pm Mar-Nov, 8.40am-4.30pm Dec-Feb) is down a small side street on the left. The stylish gardens fashioned by the master landscape designer Kobori Enshū are the main attraction.

MURIN-AN VILLA 無鄰庵

This elegant **villa** (Map pp326–7; ☎ 771-3909; Nanzen-ji Kusakawa-chō ¥350; ⊙ 9am-4.30pm) was the home of prominent statesman Yamagata Aritomo (1838–1922) and the site of a pivotal 1902 political conference as Japan was heading into the Russo-Japanese War.

Built in 1896, the grounds contain well-preserved wooden buildings including a fine Japanese tearoom. The Western-style annexe is characteristic of Meiji-period architecture and the serene garden features small streams that draw water from the Biwa-ko Sosui canal. For ¥300 you can savour a bowl of frothy *matcha* (green powdered tea) while viewing the 'borrowed scenery' backdrop of the Higashiyama mountains.

Murin-an is a seven-minute walk from subway Tōzai line Keage station.

NOMURA MUSEUM 野村美術館

The **Nomura Museum** (Map pp326–7; ☎ 751-0374; Nanzen-ji Shimokawahara; admission ¥700; ⊙ 10am-4.30pm Tue-Sun) is a 10-minute walk north of Nanzen-ji. Items on display include scrolls, paintings, tea-ceremony implements and ceramics that were bequeathed by the wealthy business magnate Tokushiki Nomura.

EIKAN-DŌ 永観堂

Eikan-dō (Map pp326–7; ☎ 761-0007; www.eikando.or.jp /English/index_eng.htm; Sakyo-ku Eikandō; admission ¥600; ⊙ 9am-5pm) is a large temple famed for its varied architecture, gardens and works of art. It was founded in 855 by the priest Shinshō, but the name was changed to Eikan-dō in the 11th century to honour the philanthropic priest Eikan.

The best way to appreciate this temple is to follow the arrows and wander slowly along the covered walkways connecting the halls and gardens.

In the Amida-dō Hall, at the southern end of the complex, is the statue of Mikaeri Amida (Buddha Glancing Backwards).

From the Amida-dō Hall, head north to the end of the covered walkway. Change into the sandals provided, then climb the steep steps up the mountainside to the **Taho-tō** (Taho Pagoda), where there's a fine view across the city.

The temple is a 10-minute walk north of Nanzen-ji (opposite).

TETSUGAKU-NO-MICHI (PATH OF PHILOSOPHY) 哲学の道

The **Tetsugaku-no-Michi** (Map pp326–7; Sakyō-ku Ginkaku-ji) has long been a favourite with contemplative strollers who follow the traffic-free route beside a canal lined with cherry trees that are spectacular when in bloom. It only takes 30 minutes to complete the walk, which starts just north of Eikan-dō (above) and ends at Ginkaku-ji (below).

HŌNEN-IN 法然院

This fine **temple** (Map pp326–7; ☎ 771-2420; Sakyō-ku Shishigatani; admission free; ⊙ 6am-4pm) was established in 1680 to honour Hōnen, the charismatic founder of the Jōdo school. This is a lovely, secluded temple with carefully raked gardens set back in the woods. Be sure to visit in early April for the cherry blossoms and early November for the maple leaves, when the main hall is opened for a special viewing.

The temple is a 12-minute walk from Ginkaku-ji (below), on a side street that is accessible from the Tetsugaku-no-Michi (above); heading south on the path, look for the English sign on your left, then cross the bridge over the canal and follow the road uphill.

GINKAKU-JI 銀閣寺

Ginkaku-ji (Map pp326–7; ☎ 771-5725; Sakyo-ku Ginkaku-ji; adult ¥500; ⊙ 8.30am-5pm Mar-Nov, 9am-4.30pm Dec-Feb),

KANSAI

is one of Kyoto's premier sights. In 1482 Shōgun Ashikaga Yoshimasa constructed a villa here as a genteel retreat from the turmoil of civil war. The villa's name translates as 'Silver Pavilion', but the shōgun's ambition to cover the building with silver was never realised. After Yoshimasa's death, the villa was converted into a temple.

You approach the main gate between tall hedges, before turning sharply into the extensive grounds. Walkways lead through the gardens, which include meticulously raked cones of white sand (probably symbolic of a mountain and a lake), tall pines and a pond in front of the temple. A path also leads up the mountainside through the trees.

Note that Ginkaku-ji is one of the city's most popular sites, and it is almost always crowded, and it can be ridiculously packed during the spring and autumn. We strongly recommend going right after it opens or just before it closes.

From JR Kyoto or Keihan Sanjō station, take bus 5 and get off at the Ginkaku-ji-michi stop. From Demachiyanagi station or Shijō station, take bus 203 to the same stop.

OKAZAKI-KŌEN AREA 岡崎公園

Right in the heart of the northern Higashiyama area, you'll find Okazaki-kōen (Map pp326–7), which is Kyoto's museum district, and the home of one of Kyoto's most popular and important shrines, Heian-jingū.

Take bus 5 from Kyoto station or Keihan Sanjō station and get off at the Kyoto Kaikan Bijutsu-kan-mae stop and walk north, or walk up from Keihan Sanjō station (15 minutes). All the sights listed here are within five minutes' walk of this stop.

KYOTO MUNICIPAL MUSEUM OF ART 京都市美術館

The **Kyoto Municipal Museum of Art** (Map pp326-7; ☎ 771-4107; Okazaki Enshōji-chō; admission varies by exhibition; ⏰ 9am-5pm Tue-Sun) organises several major exhibitions a year. These exhibitions are drawn from its vast collection of post-Meiji-era artworks. Kyoto-related works form a significant portion of this near-modern and modern collection.

NATIONAL MUSEUM OF MODERN ART 京都国立近代美術館

This **museum** (Map pp326-7; ☎ 761-4111; www.momak.go.jp/English; Okazaki Enshōji-chō; admission ¥420; ⏰ 9.30am-5pm Tue-Sun) is renowned for its collection of contemporary Japanese ceramics and paintings. Check to see what's on while you're in town.

MIYAKO MESSE & FUREAI-KAN KYOTO MUSEUM OF TRADITIONAL CRAFTS みやこめっせ・京都伝統産業ふれあい館

The **museum** (Map pp326-7; ☎ 762-2633; Okazaki Seishōji-chō; admission free; ⏰ 9am-5pm) has exhibits covering things like wood-block prints, lacquerware, bamboo goods and gold-leaf work. It's in the basement of the Miyako Messe (Kyoto International Exhibition Hall).

HEIAN-JINGŪ 平安神宮

This impressive **shrine complex** (Map p326-7; ☎ 761-0221; Okazaki Nishitennō-chō; admission to shrine precincts/garden free/¥600; ⏰ 6am-5.30pm Mar-Aug, to 5pm Sep-Feb) was built in 1895 to commemorate the 1100th anniversary of the founding of Kyoto. The buildings are colourful replicas, reduced to two-thirds of the size of the Kyoto Gosho of the Heian period.

The spacious garden, with its large pond and Chinese-inspired bridge, is also meant to represent the kind of garden that was popular in the Heian period. About 500m in front of the shrine there is a massive steel torii. Although it appears to be entirely separate from the shrine, this is actually considered the main entrance to the shrine itself.

Two major events are held at the shrine: Jidai Matsuri (Festival of the Ages; p351), on 22 October, and Takigi Nō (p406), from 1 to 2 June.

SHISEN-DŌ 詩仙堂

This **temple** (Map pp318-19; ☎ 781-2954; Ichijō-ji Monkuchi-chō; admission ¥500; ⏰ 9am-5pm) was built in 1641 by Jōzan, a scholar of Chinese classics and a landscape architect, who wanted a place to retire to at the end of his life. The garden is a fine place to relax, with only the rhythmic 'thwack' of a bamboo *sōzu* (animal scarer) to interrupt your snooze.

The temple is a five-minute walk from the Ichijōji-sagarimatsu-mae bus stop on the No 5 route.

MANSHU-IN 曼殊院

Founded by Saichō on Hiei-zan, this **temple** (Map pp318-19; ☎ 781-5010; Ichijō-ji Takenouchi-chō; admission ¥500; ⏰ 9am-5pm) was relocated here at the beginning of the Edo period. The architecture, works of art and garden are impressive. The temple is situated around 30 minutes' walk (approximately 3km) to the north of Shisen-dō.

SHŪGAKU-IN RIKYŪ 修学院離宮

This imperial **villa** (Map pp318-19; ☎ 211-1215; Sakyō-ku Shūgakuin; admission free), or detached palace, was begun in the 1650s by the abdicated emperor Go-Mizunoo, and work was continued after his death in 1680 by his daughter Akenomiya.

Designed as an imperial retreat, the villa grounds are divided into three large garden areas on a hillside: lower, middle and upper. The gardens' reputation rests on their ponds, pathways and impressive use of 'borrowed scenery' in the form of the surrounding hills; the view from the Rinun-tei Teahouse in the upper garden is particularly impressive.

Tours, in Japanese, start at 9am, 10am, 11am, 1.30pm and 3pm (50 minutes). Admission is free, but you must make advance reservations through the Imperial Household Agency (see p332 for details).

From Kyoto station, take bus 5 and get off at the Shūgaku-in Rikyū-michi stop. The trip takes about an hour. From the bus stop it's a 15-minute walk (about 1km) to the villa. You can also take the Eiden Eizan line from Demachiyanagi station to the Shūgaku-in stop and walk east about 25 minutes (about 1.5km) towards the mountains.

HIEI-ZAN & ENRYAKU-JI 比叡山・延暦寺

A visit to 848m-high Hiei-zan and the vast **Enryaku-ji complex** (Map pp316-17; ☎ 077-578-0001; Sakamoto Honmachi, Ōtsu city; admission ¥550; ☉ 8.30am-4pm, closes earlier in winter) is a good way to spend half a day hiking, poking around temples and enjoying the atmosphere of a key site in Japanese history.

Enryaku-ji was founded in 788 by Saichō, also known as Dengyō-daishi, the priest who established the Tendai school. From the 8th century the temple grew in power; at its height it possessed some 3000 buildings and an army of thousands of *sōhei*, or warrior monks. In 1571 Oda Nobunaga saw the temple's power as a threat to his aims of unifying the nation and he destroyed most of the buildings, along with the monks inside. This school did not receive imperial recognition until 1823. Today only three pagodas and 120 minor temples remain.

The complex is divided into three sections – Tōtō, Saitō and Yokawa. The **Tōtō** (eastern pagoda section) contains the Kompon Chū-dō (primary central hall), which is the most important building in the complex. The flames on the three Dharma (the law, in Sanskrit) lamps in front of the altar have been kept lit for over 1200 years. The Daikō-dō (great lecture hall) displays life-size wooden statues of the founders of various Buddhist schools. This part of the temple is heavily geared to group access, with large expanses of asphalt for parking.

The **Saitō** (western pagoda section) contains the Shaka-dō, which dates from 1595 and houses a rare Buddha sculpture of the Shaka Nyorai (Historical Buddha). The Saitō, with its stone paths winding through forests of tall trees, temples shrouded in mist and the sound of distant gongs, is the most atmospheric part of the temple. Hold onto your ticket from the Tōtō section, as you may need to show it here.

The **Yokawa** is of minimal interest and a 4km bus ride away from the Saitō area. The Chū-dō here was originally built in 848. It was destroyed by fire several times and has undergone repeated reconstructions (most recently in 1971). If you plan to visit here, as well as Tōtō and Saitō, allow a full day for in-depth exploration.

Getting There & Away

You can reach Hiei-zan and Enryaku-ji by either train or bus. The most interesting way is the train–cable car–ropeway route. If you're in a hurry or would like to save money, the best way is a direct bus from Sanjō Keihan or Kyoto stations.

By train, take the Keihan line north to the last stop, Demachiyanagi, and change to the Yase-yūen/Hiei-bound Eizan Dentetsu Eizan-line train (be careful not to board the Kurama-bound train which sometimes leaves from the same platform). At the last stop, Yase-yūen (¥260), board the cable car (¥530, nine minutes) and then the ropeway (¥310, three minutes) to the peak, from which you can walk down to the temples.

Alternatively, if you want to save money (by avoiding the cable car and ropeway), there are direct Kyoto buses from Kyoto and Keihan Sanjō stations to Enryaku-ji, which take about 70 and 50 minutes respectively (both cost ¥800).

KANSAI

Northwest Kyoto

Northwest Kyoto has many excellent sights spread over a large swath of Kyoto. Highlights include Nijō-jō, a shōgun's castle, Kinkaku-ji, the famed Golden Pavilion, and Ryōan-ji, with its mysterious stone garden. Note that three of the area's main sites – Kinkaku-ji, Ryōan-ji and Ninna-ji – can easily be paired together to form a great half-day tour out of the city centre.

NIJŌ-JŌ 二条城

This **castle** (Map p329; ☎ 841-0096; Nijo-dōri-Horikawa; admission ¥600; ☻ 8.45am-5pm, last entry 4pm, closed Tue in Dec, Jan, Jul & Aug, & 26 Dec-4 Jan) was built in 1603 as the official Kyoto residence of the first Tokugawa shōgun, Ieyasu. The ostentatious style of construction was intended as a demonstration of Ieyasu's prestige and to signal the demise of the emperor's power. As a safeguard against treachery, Ieyasu had the interior fitted with 'nightingale' floors and concealed chambers where bodyguards could keep watch.

After passing through the grand **Kara-mon** gate, you enter **Ninomaru Palace** (admission palace & garden ¥600; ☻ 8.45am-4pm, closed 26 Dec-4 Jan), which is divided into five buildings with numerous chambers. The Ohiroma Yon-no-Ma (Fourth Chamber) has spectacular screen paintings. Don't miss the excellent **Ninomaru Palace Garden**, which was designed by the tea master and landscape architect Kobori Enshū.

The neighbouring **Honmaru Palace** dates from the middle of the 19th century and is only open for special viewing in the autumn.

To reach the castle, take bus 9 from Kyoto station to the Nijō-jō-mae stop. Alternatively, take the Tōzai line subway to the Nijō-jō-mae station.

NIJŌ JINYA 二条陣屋

A few minutes' walk south of Nijō-jō is **Nijō Jinya** (Map p329; ☎ 841-0972; Ōmiya-dōri-Oike; admission ¥1000, reservations necessary in Japanese; ☻ tours in Japanese 10am, 11am, 2pm & 3pm Thu-Tue), sometimes known in English as the 'Ninja House'. Built as a merchant's home in the mid-1600s, it served as an inn for provincial feudal lords visiting the capital. What appears to be an average Edo-period mansion, however, is no ordinary dwelling.

The house contains fire-resistant earthen walls and a warren of 24 rooms that were ingeniously designed to protect the *daimyō* (domain lords) against possible surprise at-tacks. Here you'll find hidden staircases, secret passageways and a whole array of counter-espionage devices. The ceiling skylight of the main room is fitted with a trap door through which samurai could pounce on intruders, and sliding doors feature alternating panels of translucent paper to expose the shadows of eavesdroppers.

One-hour tours are conducted several times a day in Japanese and advance reservations must be made. Those who don't speak Japanese are asked to bring a Japanese-speaking guide.

NISHIJIN 西陣

The Nishijin district (Map p329) is the home of Kyoto's textile industry, the source of the fantastic kimono and obi (ornamental kimono belts) for which the city is famous. It's one of Kyoto's more traditional districts, and there are still lots of good old *machiya* (traditional city houses) scattered about.

NISHIJIN TEXTILE CENTER 西陣織会館

In the heart of the Nishijin textile district, this **centre** (Map p329; ☎ 451-9231; Horikawa-dōri-Imadegawa; admission free; ☻ 9am-5pm) is a good place to observe the weaving of fabrics used in kimono and obi. There are also displays of completed fabrics and kimono. It's on the southwest corner of the Horikawa-dōri and Imadegawa-dōri intersection.

ORINASU-KAN 織成館

This **museum** (Map p329; ☎ 431-0020; Kamigyō-ku Daikoku-chō; admission ¥500; ☻ 10am-4pm Tue-Sun) is housed in a Nishijin weaving factory. It has impressive exhibits of Nishijin textiles. The Susamei-sha building next door is also open to the public and worth a look. With advance reservations, traditional weaving workshops can be attended. It's a short walk from the Nishijin Textile Center (above).

KITANO-TENMAN-GŪ 北野天満宮

This **shrine** (Map p329; ☎ 461-0005; Kamigyō-ku Bakuro-chō; admission free; ☻ 5am-6pm summer, 5.30am-5.30pm winter) is of moderate interest. However, if you're in town on the 25th of any month, be sure to catch the **Tenjin-san market-fair** held here. This is one of Kyoto's two biggest markets and is a great place to pick up some interesting souvenirs. The markets held in December and January are particularly colourful.

From Kyoto station, take bus 50 and get off at the Kitano-Tenmangū-mae stop. From Keihan Sanjō station, take bus 10 to the same stop.

KINKAKU-JI 金閣寺

The famed **Golden Temple** (Kinkaku-ji; Map p329; ☎ 461-0013; Kita-ku Kinkaku-ji-chō; admission ¥400; ◯ 9am-5pm) is one of Japan's best-known sights. The original building was constructed in 1397 as a retirement villa for Shōgun Ashikaga Yoshimitsu. His son converted it into a temple.

In 1950 a young monk consummated his obsession with the temple by burning it to the ground. The monk's story was fictionalised in Mishima Yukio's *The Golden Pavilion*. In 1955 a full reconstruction was completed that exactly followed the original design, but the gold-foil covering was extended to the lower floors.

Note that this temple can be packed almost any day of the year. We recommend going early in the day or just before closing.

To get to the temple from Kyoto station, take bus 205 and get off at the Kinkaku-ji-michi stop. From Keihan Sanjō, take bus 59 and get off at the Kinkaku-ji-mae stop.

RYŌAN-JI 龍安寺

This **temple** (Map p329; ☎ 463-2216; Ukyō-ku Ryōan-ji; admission ¥500; ◯ 8am-5pm Mar-Nov, 8.30am-4.30pm Dec-Feb) belongs to the Rinzai school of Zen and was founded in 1450. The main attraction is the garden arranged in the *kare-sansui* (dry-landscape) style. An austere collection of 15 rocks, apparently adrift in a sea of sand, is enclosed by an earthen wall. The designer, who remains unknown, provided no explanation.

The viewing platform for the garden can be packed solid but the other parts of the temple grounds are also interesting and less of a target for the crowds. Among these, Kyoyo-chi pond is perhaps the most beautiful, particularly in autumn. Probably the best advice for Ryōan-ji is to come as early in the day as possible.

From Keihan Sanjō station, take bus 59 to the Ryōan-ji-mae stop.

NINNA-JI 仁和寺

This **temple** (Map p329; ☎ 461-1155; web.kyoto-inet.or.jp /org/ninnaji/eigo.htm; Ukyō-ku Omuroōuchi; admission ¥500; ◯ 9am-4.30pm) was built in 842 and is the head temple of the Omura branch of the Shingon

school of Buddhism. The present temple buildings, including a five-storey pagoda, are from the 17th century. The extensive grounds are full of cherry trees that bloom in early April.

Admission to most of the grounds is free, but separate admission fees are charged for some of the temple's buildings, many of which are closed most of the year. To get there, take bus 59 from Keihan Sanjō station and get off at the Omuro Ninna-ji stop. From Kyoto station take bus 26.

MYŌSHIN-JI 妙心寺

The vast temple complex **Myōshin-ji** (Map p329; ☎ 461-5226; Ukyō-ku Hanazono Myōshin-ji-chō; admission ¥500; ◯ 9.10am-3.40pm, closed lunch 1hr) dates back to the 14th century, and belongs to the Rinzai school of Zen. There are over 40 temples, but only four are open to the public.

From the northern gate, follow the broad stone avenue flanked by rows of temples to the southern part of the complex.

The real highlight here is the wonderful garden of **Taizō-in** (admission ¥500; ◯ 9am-5pm), a temple in the southwestern corner of the grounds.

The northern gate of Myōshin-ji is an easy 10-minute walk south of Ninna-ji; or take bus 10 from Keihan Sanjō station to the Myōshin-ji Kita-mon-mae stop.

TŌEI UZUMASA MOVIE VILLAGE 東映太秦映画村

In the Uzumasa area, this **attraction** (Tōei Uzumasa Eiga Mura; Map p329; ☎ 864-7716; Ukyo-ku Uzumasa Higashi Hachioka-chō; adult/child under 6/age 6-18 ¥2200/1100/1300; ◯ 9am-5pm Mar-Nov, 9.30am-4pm Dec-Feb) celebrates Kyoto's movie industry and all the films that have been filmed in the city. It has some recreations of Edo-period street scenes that give a decent idea of what Kyoto must have looked like before the advent of concrete. There's no denying that it's a tourist trap, but it's fun for the kids.

The main conceit of the park is that real movies are actually filmed here. While this may occasionally be the case, more often than not this entails a bunch of bored flunkies being ordered around by an ersatz movie 'director' complete with megaphone and a vintage 1930s-era movie camera. This seems to delight some tourists but leaves us a little less than convinced.

Aside from this, there are displays relating to various aspects of Japanese movies and

KANSAI

regular performances involving Japanese TV and movie characters like the Power Rangers. This should entertain the kids – adults will probably be a little bored.

It's a 13-minute walk from JR Sagano line Uzumasa station.

KŌRYŪ-JI 広隆寺

One of the oldest temples in Japan, **Kōryū-ji** (Map p329; ☎ 861-1461; Ukyō-ku Uzumasa Hachioka-chō; admission ¥700; ⊙ 9am-5pm Mar-Nov, to 4.30pm Dec-Feb) was founded in 622 to honour Prince Shōtoku, an enthusiastic promoter of Buddhism.

The Hattō (Lecture Hall), to the right of the main gate, houses a magnificent trio of 9th-century statues: Buddha flanked by manifestations of Kannon.

The Reihōkan (Treasure House) contains numerous fine Buddhist statues, including the Naki Miroku (Crying Miroku) and the world-renowned Miroku Bosatsu, which is extraordinarily expressive. A national upset occurred in 1960 when an enraptured (at least that's what he said) student clasped the statue and snapped off its little finger.

Take bus 11 from Keihan Sanjō station, get off at the Ukyō-ku Sogo-chosha-mae stop and walk north. The temple is also close to Uzumasa station on the Keifuku Arashiyama line.

Arashiyama & Sagano Area

Arashiyama and Sagano, lying at the base of Kyoto's western mountains, is second only to the Higashiyama area as the most important sightseeing district in Kyoto. The attraction here is the temples scattered throughout the area's famous bamboo groves.

The main **bamboo grove**, just outside the north gate of Tenryū-ji (right), is one of Kyoto's most famous sites and is a dead ringer for the bamboo forest in the film *Crouching Tiger, Hidden Dragon*. Note that Arashiyama is wildly popular with Japanese tourists and can be packed, particularly in the cherry-blossom and maple-leaf seasons.

Bus 28 links Kyoto station with Arashiyama. Bus 11 connects Keihan Sanjō station with Arashiyama. The most convenient rail connection is the ride from Shijō-ōmiya station on the Keifuku-Arashiyama line to Arashiyama station. You can also take the JR San-in line from Kyoto station or Nijō station and get off at Saga Arashiyama station (be careful to take only the local train, as the express does not stop in Arashiyama).

The sites in this section are all within walking distance of Arashiyama station. We suggest walking from this station to Tenryū-ji, exiting the north gate, checking out the bamboo grove, visiting Ōkōchi Sansō, then walking north and to Giō-ji. All of these attractions are described in the following sections. If you have time for only one temple in the area, we recommend Tenryū-ji. If you have time for two, we suggest adding Giō-ji.

KAMEYAMA-KŌEN 亀山公園

Behind Tenryū-ji, this **park** (Map p330) is a nice place to escape the crowds of Arashiyama. It's laced with trails, the best of which leads to a lookout over Katsura-gawa and up into the Arashiyama mountains. Keep an eye out for the monkeys; and keep children well away from the occasionally nasty critters.

TENRYŪ-JI 天龍寺

One of the major temples of the Rinzai school of Zen, **Tenryū-ji** (Map p330; ☎ 881-1235; Saga Tenryū-ji; admission ¥600; ⊙ 8.30am-5.30pm Apr-Oct, to 5pm Nov-Mar) was built in 1339 on the former site of Emperor Go-Daigo's villa after a priest had dreamt of a dragon rising from the nearby river. The dream was interpreted as a sign that the emperor's spirit was uneasy and the temple was constructed as appeasement – hence the name *tenryū* (heavenly dragon). The present buildings date from 1900, but the main attraction is the 14th-century Zen garden.

Arashiyama's famous **bamboo grove** lies just outside the north gate of the temple.

ŌKŌCHI SANSŌ 大河内山荘

This **villa** (Map p330; ☎ 872-2233; Saga Ogura-yama; admission ¥1000; ⊙ 9am-5pm) is the home of Ōkōchi Denjiro, an actor in samurai films. The gardens allow fine views over the city and are open to visitors. The admission fee is hefty but includes tea and a cake. The villa is a 10-minute walk through bamboo groves north of Tenryū-ji.

JŌJAKKŌ-JI 常寂光寺

If you continue north of Ōkōchi Sansō, the narrow road soon passes stone steps on your left which lead up to the pleasant grounds of **Jōjakkō-ji** (Map p330; ☎ 861-0435; Saga Ogura-yama; admission ¥300; ⊙ 9am-5pm). The temple is famous for its maple leaves and the Tahōtō pagoda. The upper area of the temple precincts afford

KANSAI

good views east over Kyoto. The temple is a 10-minute walk north of Ōkōchi Sansō.

RAKUSHISHA 落柿舎

This **hut** (Map p330; ☎ 881-1953; Saga Ogura-yama; admission ¥200; ☷ 9am-5pm) belonged to Mukai Kyorai, the best-known disciple of illustrious haiku poet Bashō. Literally meaning 'House of the Fallen Persimmons', legend holds that Kyorai dubbed the house Rakushisha after waking one morning after a storm to find the persimmons he had planned to sell from the garden's trees scattered on the ground. The hut is a short walk downhill and to the north of Jōjakkō-ji.

NISON-IN 二尊院

Near Jōjakkō-ji, **Nison-in** (Map p330; ☎ 861-0687; Saga Nison-in Monzen-chō; admission ¥500; ☷ 9am-4.30pm) is in an attractive setting up the wooded hillside. The long approach to the temple, which is lined with lovely maple trees, is the biggest drawcard. The temple is a short walk north of Jōjakkō-ji.

TAKIGUCHI-DERA 滝口寺

The history of this temple reads like a Romeo and Juliet romance. **Takiguchi-dera** (Map p330; ☎ 871-3929; Saga Kameyama-chō; admission ¥300; ☷ 9am-5pm) was founded by Heian-era nobleman Takiguchi Nyūdō, who entered the priesthood after being forbidden by his father to marry his peasant consort Yokobue. One day Yokobue came to the temple with her flute to serenade Takiguchi, but was again refused by him; she wrote a farewell love sonnet on a stone (in her own blood) before throwing herself into the river to perish. The stone remains at the temple. The temple is about 10 minutes' walk north of Nison-in.

GIŌ-JI 祇王寺

This quiet **temple** (Map p330; ☎ 861-3574; Saga Nisonin Monzen-chō; admission ¥300; ☷ 9am-4.30pm) was named for the Heian-era *shirabyōshi* (traditional dancer) Giō. Aged 21, Giō committed herself here as a nun after her romance with Taira-no-Kiyomori, the mighty commander of the Heike clan. She was usurped by a fellow entertainer Hotoke Gozen (who later deserted Kiyomori to join Giō at the temple). Enshrined in the main hall are five wooden statues: these are Giō, Hotoke Gozen, Kiyomori, and Giō's mother and sister (who were also nuns at the temple). The temple is next to Takiguchi-dera.

ADASHINO NEMBUTSU-JI 化野念仏寺

This rather unusual **temple** (Map p330; ☎ 861-2221; Sagatorii Moto Adashino-chō; admission ¥500; ☷ 9am-4.30pm) is where the abandoned bones of paupers and destitutes without next of kin were gathered. Thousands of stone images are crammed into the temple grounds, and these abandoned souls are remembered each year with candles here in the **Sentō Kuyō ceremony** held on the evenings of 23 and 24 August. The temple is about 15 minutes' walk north of Giō-ji.

ARASHIYAMA MONKEY PARK IWATAYAMA 嵐山モンキーパークいわたやま

Home to some 200 Japanese monkeys of all sizes and ages, this **park** (Map p330; ☎ 861-1616; Arashiyama, Togetsu-kyō; adult/child ¥500/¥150; ☷ 9am-5pm 15 Mar-15 Nov, to 4pm winter) is fun for the kids. Though it is common to spot wild monkeys in the nearby mountains, here you can encounter them at a close distance and enjoy watching the playful creatures frolic about. Refreshingly, it is the animals who are free to roam while the humans who observe them are caged in a box!

You enter the park near the south side of Togetsu-kyō bridge, through the orange torii of Ichitani-jinja. Reaching the monkeys involves a moderate hike uphill. It's a 10-minute walk from Keifuku line Arashiyama station.

HOZU-GAWA TRIP 保津川下り

The **Hozu-gawa river trip** (☎ 0771-22-5846; Hozu-chō Kameoka-shi; admission ¥3900; ☷ 9am-3.30pm, closed 29 Dec-4 Jan) is a great way to enjoy the beauty of Kyoto's western mountains without any strain on the legs. The river winds through steep, forested mountain canyons before it arrives at its destination, Arashiyama. Between 10 March and 30 November, there are seven trips (from 9am to 3.30pm) per day. During the winter, the number of trips is reduced to four per day and the boats are heated.

The ride lasts two hours and covers 16km between Kameoka and Arashiyama through occasional sections of tame white water – a scenic jaunt with minimal danger. The boats depart from a dock that is eight minutes on foot from Kameoka station. Kameoka is accessible by rail from Kyoto station or Nijō station on the JR San-in (Sagano) main line. The train fare from Kyoto to Kameoka is ¥400 one way by *futsū* (local train).

Southeast Kyoto

TŌFUKU-JI 東福寺

Founded in 1236 by the priest Enni, **Tōfuku-ji** (Map pp318-19; ☎ 561-0087; Higashiyama-ku Honmachi; admission to garden/grounds ¥400/free; ⊙ 9am-3.30pm Dec-Oct, 8.30am-4.30pm Nov) now belongs to the Rinzai sect of Zen Buddhism. As this temple was intended to compare with Tōdai-ji and Kōfuku-ji in Nara, it was given a name combining characters from the names of each of these temples.

Despite the destruction of many of the buildings by fire, this is still considered one of the five main Zen temples in Kyoto. The huge **San-mon** is the oldest Zen main gate in Japan. The *tosu* (lavatory) and *yokushitsu* (bathroom) date from the 14th century. The present temple complex includes 24 subtemples; at one time there were 53.

The **Hōjō** was reconstructed in 1890. The gardens, laid out in 1938, are worth a visit. As you approach the northern gardens, you cross a stream over Tsūten-kyō (Bridge to Heaven), which is a pleasant leafy spot – the foliage is renowned for its autumn colour. The northern garden has stones and moss neatly arranged in a chequerboard pattern.

Tōfuku-ji is a 20-minute walk (2km) southeast of Kyoto station. You can also take a local train on the JR Nara line and get off at JR Tōfukuji station, from which it's a 10-minute walk southeast. Alternatively, you can take the Keihan line to Keihan Tōfukuji station, from which it's also a 10-minute walk.

FUSHIMI-INARI TAISHA 伏見稲荷大社

This intriguing **shrine** (Map pp318-19; ☎ 641-7331; Fushimi-ku Fukakusa Yabunouchi-chō; admission free; ⊙ dawn-dusk) was dedicated to the gods of rice and sake by the Hata family in the 8th century. As the role of agriculture diminished, deities were enrolled to ensure prosperity in business. Nowadays the shrine is one of Japan's most popular, and is the head shrine for some 30,000 Inari shrines scattered the length and breadth of Japan.

The entire complex consisting of five shrines sprawls across the wooded slopes of Inari-yama. A pathway wanders 4km up the mountain and is lined with hundreds of red torii. There are also dozens of stone foxes. The fox is considered the messenger of Inari, the god of cereal grains. The Japanese traditionally see the fox as a sacred, somewhat mysterious figure capable of 'possessing' humans –

the favoured point of entry is under the fingernails. The key often seen in the fox's mouth is for the rice granary.

The walk around the upper precincts of the shrine is a pleasant day hike. It also makes for a very eerie stroll in the late afternoon and early evening, when the various graveyards and miniature shrines along the path take on a mysterious air.

To get to the shrine from Kyoto station, take a JR Nara line train to Inari station. From Keihan Sanjō station take the Keihan line to Fushimi-Inari station. There is no admission charge for the shrine. The shrine is just east of both of these stations.

DAIGO-JI 醍醐寺

Daigo-ji (Map pp316-17; ☎ 571-0002; Fushimi-ku Daigo Garan-chō; admission to grounds free, during cherry blossom & autumn foliage seasons ¥600, to Sampō-in ¥600; ⊙ 9am-5pm) was founded in 874 by the priest Shobo, who gave it the name of Daigo. This refers to the five periods of Buddha's teaching, which were often compared to the five forms of milk prepared in India, the highest form of which is called *daigo* (ultimate essence of milk).

The temple was expanded into a vast complex of buildings on two levels – Shimo Daigo (Lower Daigo) and Kami Daigo (Upper Daigo). During the 15th century, the lower-level buildings were destroyed, with the sole exception of the five-storey pagoda. Built in 951, this pagoda still stands and is lovingly noted as the oldest of its kind in Japan and the oldest existing building in Kyoto.

The subtemple **Sampō-in** is a fine example of the amazing opulence of that period. The Kanō paintings and the garden are special features.

Daigo-yama, the mountain that forms the backdrop to the temple, is a steep climb that is enjoyable if you're in good shape and the weather is cool. From Sampō-in, walk up the large avenue of cherry trees, go through the Niō-mon gate and past the pagoda. From there you can continue for a steep climb through the upper part of Daigo-yama, browsing through temples and shrines on the way. Allow at least 50 minutes to reach the top.

To get to Daigo-ji, take the Tōzai line subway from central Kyoto to the last stop, Daigo, and walk east (towards the mountains) for about 10 minutes. Make sure that the train you board is bound for Daigo, as some head to Hama-Ōtsu instead.

UJI 宇治

Uji is a small city to the south of Kyoto. Its main claims to fame are Byōdō-in and tea cultivation. The stone bridge at Uji – the oldest of its kind in Japan – has been the scene of many bitter clashes in previous centuries.

Uji is also home to Ujigami-jinja, a Unesco World Heritage site. Despite this status, it's not one of the Kyoto area's more interesting sights. Those who wish to see it can find it by crossing the river (using the bridge near Byōdō-in) and walking about 10 minutes uphill (there are signs).

Uji can be reached by rail in about 40 minutes from Kyoto on the Keihan Uji line or JR Nara line.

When arriving in Uji by Keihan train, leave the station, cross the river via the first bridge on the right, and then turn left to find Byōdō-in. When coming by JR, the temple is about 10 minutes' walk (towards the river) of Uji station.

Byōdō-in 平等院

This **Buddhist temple** (☎ 0774-21-2861; Uji-shi Uji renge; admission ¥600; ⏰ 8.30am-5.30pm) was converted from a Fujiwara villa in 1052. The Hōō-dō (Phoenix Hall), more properly known as the Amida-dō, was built in 1053 and is the only original remaining building. The phoenix was a popular mythical bird in China and was revered by the Japanese as a protector of Buddha. The architecture of the building resembles the shape of the bird, and there are two bronze phoenixes perched opposite each other on the roof.

The building was originally intended to represent Amida's heavenly palace in the Pure Land. This building is one of the few extant examples of Heian-period architecture, and its graceful lines make one wish that far more of its type had survived Kyoto's past.

Inside the hall is the famous statue of Amida and 52 Bosatsu (Bodhisattvas) dating from the 11th century and attributed to the priest-sculptor Jōchō.

The temple, complete with its reflection in a pond, is one of Japan's top attractions and draws huge crowds. For a preview without the masses, take a look at the ¥10 coin.

Southwest Kyoto

SAIHŌ-JI 西芳寺

The main attraction at this **temple** (Map pp316-17; ☎ 391-3631; Nishikyō-ku Matsuo Jingatani-chō; admission ¥3000, entry as part of tour only, must reserve in advance) is the heart-shaped garden designed in 1339 by Musō Kokushi. The garden is famous for its luxuriant mossy growth, hence the temple's other name, Koke-dera (Moss Temple). Visiting the temple is recommended only if you have the time and patience to follow the reservation rules. If you don't, visit nearby Jizō-in (below) to get a sense of the atmosphere of Saihō-ji without the expense or fuss.

Take bus 28 from Kyoto station to the Matsuo-taisha-mae stop and walk 15 minutes southwest. From Keihan Sanjō station, take Kyoto bus 63 to Koke-dera, the last stop, and walk for two minutes.

Reservations

To visit Saihō-ji, you must make a reservation. Send a postcard at least one week before the date you wish to visit and include details of your name, number of visitors, address in Japan, occupation, age (you must be over 18) and desired date (choice of alternative dates preferred). The address:

Saihō-ji,
56 Kamigaya-chō,
Matsuo, Nishikyō-ku,
Kyoto-shi 615-8286
JAPAN

Enclose a stamped, self-addressed postcard for a reply to your Japanese address. You might find it convenient to buy an Ōfuku-hagaki (send-and-return postcard set) at a Japanese post office.

JIZŌ-IN 地蔵院

This delightful little **temple** (Map pp316-17; ☎ 381-3417; Nishikyō-ku Yamadakitano-chō; admission ¥400; ⏰ 9am-5pm Mar-Nov, to 4.30pm Dec-Feb) could be called the 'poor man's Saihō-ji'. It's only a few minutes' walk south of Saihō-ji, in the same atmospheric bamboo groves. While the temple does not boast any spectacular buildings or treasures, it has a nice moss garden and is almost completely ignored by tourists, making it a great place to sit and think. For directions, see the previous Saihō-ji section.

KATSURA RIKYŪ 桂離宮

This **palace** (Katsura Detached Palace; ☎ 211-1215; Nishikyō-ku Katsura misono; admission free) is considered to be one of the finest examples of Japanese architecture. It was built in 1624 for the emperor's brother, Prince Toshihito. Every

KANSAI

conceivable detail of the villa, the teahouses, the large pond with islets and the surrounding garden has been given meticulous attention.

Tours (around 40 minutes), in Japanese, commence at 10am, 11am, 2pm and 3pm. You should be there 20 minutes beforehand. An explanatory video is shown in the waiting room and a leaflet is provided in English. You must make advance reservations with the Imperial Household Agency (see p332 for details). Visitors must be over 20 years of age.

To get to the villa from Kyoto station, take bus 33 and get off at the Katsura Rikyū-mae stop, which is a five-minute walk from the villa. The easiest access from the city centre is to take a Hankyū line train from Hankyū Kawaramachi station to Hankyū Katsura station, which is a 15-minute walk from the villa. Don't take a *tokkyū* (express) train as they don't stop in Katsura.

Kitayama Area

Starting on the north side of Kyoto city and stretching almost all the way to the Sea of Japan, the Kitayama mountains (literally 'Northern Mountains') are a natural escape prized by Kyoto city dwellers. Attractions here include the village of Ōhara (below), with its pastoral beauty, the fine mountain temple of Kurama (opposite), the rustic beauty of Hanase and Ashiu (opposite) and the trio of mountain temples in Takao (above).

ŌHARA 大原

Since ancient times **Ōhara** (Map p331), a quiet farming town about 10km north of Kyoto, has been regarded as a holy site by followers of the Jōdo (Pure Land) school of Buddhism. The region provides a charming glimpse of rural Japan, along with the picturesque Sanzen-in, Jakkō-in and several other fine temples. It's most popular in autumn, when the maple leaves change colour and the mountain views are spectacular. During the peak foliage season (late October to mid-November) avoid this area on weekends as it will be packed.

Sanzen-in 三千院

Founded in 784 by the priest Saichō, **Sanzen-in** (Map p331; ☎ 744-2531; Ōhara Raikōin-chō; admission ¥700; 8.30am-5pm Mar-Nov, to 4.30pm Dec-Feb) belongs to the Tendai sect of Buddhism. Saichō, considered one of the great patriarchs of Buddhism in Japan, also founded Enryaku-ji (Map p368) on nearby Hiei-zan. The temple's Yusei-en

is one of the most photographed gardens in Japan, and rightly so.

After seeing Yusei-en, head off to the Ojo-gokuraku Hall (Temple of Rebirth in Paradise) to see the impressive Amitabha trinity, a large Amida image flanked by attendants Kannon, goddess of mercy, and Seishi, god of wisdom, respectively. After this, walk up to the hydrangea garden at the back of the temple, where, in late spring and summer you can walk among hectares of blooming hydrangeas.

If you feel like a short hike after leaving the temple, head up the hill around the right side of the temple to the **Soundless Waterfall** (you'll note that it sounds pretty much like any other waterfall). The sound of this waterfall is said to have inspired Shomyo Buddhist chanting.

To get to Sanzen-in, follow the signs from Ōhara's main bus stop up the hill past a long arcade of souvenir stalls. The entrance is on your left as you crest the hill.

Jakkō-in 寂光院

The history of **Jakkō-in** (Map p331; ☎ 744-2545; Ōhara Kusao-chō; admission ¥600; 9am-5pm Mar-Nov, to 4.30pm Dec-Feb) is exceedingly tragic. The actual founding date of the temple is subject to some debate (somewhere between the 6th and 11th centuries), but it acquired fame as the temple that harboured Kenrei Mon-in, a lady of the Taira clan. In 1185 the Taira were soundly defeated in a sea battle with the Minamoto clan at Dan-no-ura. With the entire Taira clan slaughtered or drowned, Kenrei Mon-in threw herself into the waves with her son Antoku, the infant emperor; she was fished out – the only member of the clan to survive.

She was returned to Kyoto, where she became a nun living in a bare hut until it collapsed during an earthquake. Kenrei Mon-in was accepted into Jakkō-in and stayed there, immersed in prayer and sorrowful memories, until her death 27 years later. Her tomb is located high on the hill behind the temple.

Unfortunately the main building of the temple burned down in May 2000 and the newly reconstructed main hall is lacking some of the charm of the original. Nonetheless, it's a nice spot.

Jakkō-in lies to the west of Ōhara. Walk out of the bus station up the road to the traffic lights, then follow the small road to the left. Since it's easy to get lost on the way, we recommend familiarising yourself with the kanji for Jakkō-in (see p331) and following the Japanese signs.

KURAMA & KIBUNE 鞍馬・貴船

Only 30 minutes north of Kyoto on the Eiden Eizan main line, **Kurama** and **Kibune** (Map p331) are a pair of tranquil valleys long favoured by Kyotoites as places to escape the crowds and stresses of the city below. Kurama's main attractions are its mountain temple and its *onsen* (hot-spring bath). Kibune, over the ridge, is a cluster of ryokan overlooking a mountain stream. It is best enjoyed in the summer, when the ryokan serve dinner on platforms built over the rushing waters of the Kibune-gawa, providing welcome relief from the summer heat.

The two valleys lend themselves to being explored together. In the winter one can start from Kibune, walk for an hour or so over the ridge, visit Kurama-dera and then soak in the *onsen* before heading back to Kyoto. In the summer the reverse is best; start from Kurama, walk up to the temple, then down the other side to Kibune to enjoy a meal suspended above the cool river.

If you happen to be in Kyoto on the night of 22 October, be sure not to miss the **Kurama-no-hi Matsuri** (Kurama Fire Festival; p351), one of the most exciting festivals in the Kyoto area.

To get to Kurama and Kibune, take the Eiden Eizan line from Kyoto's Demachiyanagi station. For Kibune, get off at the second-to-last stop, Kibune Guchi, take a right out of the station and walk about 20 minutes up the hill. For Kurama, go to the last stop, Kurama, and walk straight out of the station. Both destinations are ¥410 and take about 30 minutes to reach.

Kurama-dera 鞍馬寺

This **temple** (Map p331; ☎ 741-2003; Sakyō-ku Kurama Honmachi; admission ¥200; ☷ 9am-4.30pm) was established in 770 by the monk Gantei from Nara's Tōshōdai-ji. After seeing a vision of the deity Bishamon-ten, guardian of the northern quarter of the Buddhist heaven, he established Kurama-dera in its present location, just below the peak of Kurama-yama. Originally belonging to the Tendai sect, Kurama has been independent since 1949, describing its own brand of Buddhism as Kurama Kyō.

The entrance to the temple is just up the hill from the Eiden Eizan main line's Kurama station. A tram goes to the top for ¥100; alterna-

tively, hike up by following the main path past the tram station. The trail is worth taking if it's not too hot, as it winds through a forest of towering old-growth *sugi* (cryptomeria) trees. At the top there is a courtyard dominated by the Honden (Main Hall). Behind the Honden, a trail leads off to the mountain's peak.

At the top, those who want to continue to Kibune can take the trail down the other side. It's a 45-minute hike from the Honden of Kurama-dera to the valley floor of Kibune. On the way down there are two pleasant mountain shrines.

Kurama Onsen 鞍馬温泉

One of the few *onsen* within easy reach of Kyoto, **Kurama Onsen** (Map p331; ☎ 741-2131; Sakyō-ku Kurama Honmachi; admission ¥1100; ☷ 10am-9pm) is a great place to relax after a hike. The outdoor bath, with a fine view of Kurama-yama, costs ¥1100. The inside bath costs ¥2300, but even with the use of sauna and locker thrown in, it's difficult to imagine why one would opt for the indoor bath. For both baths, buy a ticket from the machine outside the door of the main building (instructions are in Japanese and English).

To get to Kurama Onsen, walk straight out of Kurama station, turn left up the main road and follow it for about 10 minutes. You'll see the baths down on your right. There's also a free shuttle bus that runs between the station and the *onsen*, leaving approximately every 30 minutes.

Kibune-jinja 貴船神社

This **shrine** (Map p331; ☎ 741-2016; Kibune-chō Kurama; admission free; ☷ 6am-8pm), halfway up the valley-town of Kibune, is worth a quick look, particularly if you can ignore the unfortunate plastic horse statue at its entrance. Admission is free. From Kibune you can hike over the mountain to Kurama-dera, along a trail that starts halfway up the village on the eastern side (or vice versa – see left).

HANASE & ASHIU 花背・芦生

Located directly north of Kurama, over the Hanase-tōge pass, is the quiet rural valley of Hanase (Map p310), which is home to farmers, artists and nature-lovers. Further north, at the end of a Kyoto bus line, is Hirogawara, a small village that even has a small single-lift ski area that is open from January to March. Hirogawara is also the departure point for hikes entering the famous Ashiu virgin forest. The entire Kitayama area is a delight for cyclists, hikers, cross-country skiers and photographers.

Sleeping

There's good camping in the area. Otherwise, a good place to stay is **Hanase Suisen-Kyō** (水仙郷; ☎ 746-0185; fax 712-7023; www.suisenkyo .com; suisenkyo@mac.com; Hanase Harachi-chō; r per person ¥3200, bookings by email/fax only; ✿), which is located 31km north of Kyoto city between the small towns of Ofuse and Hirogawara. It's a secluded riverside getaway near several trailheads that must be reached via footbridge (across the river from the bus stop). Facilities include three guestrooms, full kitchen, traditional living areas and bicycles. Enjoy a relaxing picnic on the deck in the summer or warm your feet by the wood-burning stove and the in-floor hearth in the winter. To get there, take the bus described following and get off at Naka-no-cho (¥930, 1½ hours from Kyoto).

Getting There & Away

Kyoto bus 32 (not Kyoto city bus) runs five times daily (four in winter) from Demachiyanagi (buses depart from the stand outside the Eizan-densha train station). It costs ¥1050 and takes one hour and 40 minutes to the end of the line in Hirogawara. Check the local bus times and incorporate a visit to Kurama to double your sightseeing pleasure.

Takao 高雄

Takao (Map pp316–17) is a secluded district tucked far away in the northwestern part of Kyoto. It is famed for autumn foliage and the temples of Jingo-ji, Saimyō-ji and Kōzan-ji.

Jingo-ji (神護寺; Map pp316-17; ☎ 861-1769; Ukyō-ku Takao-chō; admission ¥400; ✿ 9am-4pm) is the best of the three temples in the Takao district. This mountain temple sits at the top of a long flight of stairs that stretch up from Kiyotaki-gawa to the temple's main gate. The Kondō (Gold Hall) is the most impressive of the temple's structures; it's roughly in the middle of the grounds, at the top of another flight of stairs.

After visiting the Kondō, head in the opposite direction along a wooded path to an open area overlooking the valley. Don't be surprised if you see people tossing small discs over the railing into the chasm below. These are *kawarakenage* – light clay discs that people

throw to rid themselves of their bad karma. Be careful: it's addictive, and at ¥100 for two, it can become expensive. You can buy the discs at a nearby stall. The trick is to flick the discs very gently, convex side up, like a Frisbee. When you get it right, they sail all the way down the valley, taking all that bad karma away with them.

The other two temples are within easy walking distance of Jingo-ji; **Saimyō-ji** (西明寺; Map pp316-17; ☎ 861-1770; Umegahata Toganoo-chō Ukyō-ku; admission free; ✿ 9am-5pm) is the better of the two. It's about five minutes' walk north of the base of the steps that lead up to Jingo-ji (follow the river upstream). To get to **Kōzan-ji** (高山寺; Map pp316-17; ☎ 861-4204; Umegahata Toganoo-chō Ukyō-ku; admission ¥600; ✿ 8.30am-5pm) you must walk back up to the main road and follow it north for about 10 minutes.

There are two options for buses to Takao: an hourly JR bus from Kyoto station which takes about an hour to reach the Takao stop (get off at the Yamashiro-Takao stop); and Kyoto city bus 8 from Shijō-Karasuma (get off at the Takao stop). To get to Jingo-ji from these bus stops, walk down to the river, then look for the steps on the other side.

ACTIVITIES
Baths
FUNAOKA ONSEN 船岡温泉
This old **bath** (Map p329; ☎ 441-3735; 82-1 Minami-Funaoka-chō-Murasakino Kita-ku; admission ¥390; ✿ 3pm-1am Mon-Sat, 8am-1am Sun & holidays) on Kuramaguchi-dōri is the best in all of Kyoto. It boasts an outdoor bath, a sauna, a cypress-wood tub, an electric bath, a herbal bath and a few more for good measure. Be sure to check out the *ranma* (carved wooden panels) in the changing room. Carved during Japan's invasion of Manchuria, the panels offer insight into the prevailing mindset of that era. (Frankly, we're surprised that they haven't been taken down, due to their violent content, which would be sure to upset Chinese visitors to the bath.)

To find the *onsen*, head west about 400m on Kuramaguchi-dōri from the Kuramaguchi-Horiikawa intersection. It's on the left not far past Lawson convenience store. Look for the large rocks out the front.

GOKŌ-YU 五香湯
This popular **bath** (Map pp318-19; ☎ 812-1126; 590-1 Kakinomoto-chō-Gojō agaru Kuromon-dōri; admission ¥390; ✿ 2.30pm-12.30am Mon-Sat, 7am-midnight Sun,

11am-midnight holidays Tue-Sun except for 3rd Tue of each month) is another excellent bath. It has several good tubs and two saunas; one is merely hot, the other is roughly the same temperature as the centre of the sun.

Geisha & Maiko Costume

If you ever wondered how you might look as a geisha or *maiko*, Kyoto has numerous outfits in town offering the chance. **Maika** (Map p324; ☎ 551-1661; www.maica.net/; Higashiyama-ku, Miyagawa suji; maiko/geisha from ¥6720/7350) is in the Gion district. There you can be dressed up to live out your *maiko* fantasy. If you don't mind spending a bit extra, it's possible to head out in costume for a stroll through Gion (and be stared at like never before!). The process takes about an hour. Call to reserve at least one day in advance.

Japanese Culture (Tea Ceremony, Ikebana etc)

Kyoto is a fine place to get a taste of traditional Japanese culture, and there are several organisations that offer introductions to various aspects of Japanese culture, including the following.

WAK Japan (Map pp318-19; ☎ 212-9993; www .wakjapan.com; 412-506 Iseya-chō, Kamigyō-ku) offers a wide variety of excellent introductions to Japanese culture: tea ceremony, ikebana (Japanese flower arrangement), trying on kimonos, home visits, Japanese cooking, calligraphy, origami etc. Presenters-instructors either speak English or interpreters are provided. Pick-up service is available from your lodgings. This is highly recommended.

Club Ōkitsu Kyoto (Map pp318-19; ☎ 411-8585; www .okitsu-kyoto.com; 524-1 Mototsuchimikado-chō, Shinmachi, Kamigyō-ku) offers an upscale introduction to various aspects of Japanese culture including tea ceremony, incense ceremony and traditional Japanese games. The introduction is performed in an exquisite Japanese villa near the Kyoto Gosho and participants get a real sense for the elegance and refinement of traditional Japanese culture. This is also highly recommended.

FESTIVALS & EVENTS

There are hundreds of festivals in Kyoto throughout the year. Listings can be found in *Kyoto Visitor's Guide*, *Kansai Time Out* or weekend editions of the *Japan Times* and the *Yomiuri Daily*. The following are some of the

major or most spectacular festivals. These attract hordes of spectators from out of town, so book accommodation well in advance.

February

Setsubun Matsuri at Yoshida-jinja This festival is held on the day of *setsubun* (2, 3 or 4 February; check with the TIC), which marks the last day of winter in the Japanese lunar calendar. In this festival, people climb up to Yoshida-jinja in the northern Higashiyama area to watch a huge bonfire. It's one of Kyoto's more dramatic festivals. The action starts at dusk.

May

Aoi Matsuri (Hollyhock Festival) This festival dates back to the 6th century and commemorates the successful prayers of the people for the gods to stop calamitous weather. Today the procession involves imperial messengers in ox carts and a retinue of 600 people dressed in traditional costume. The procession leaves at around 10am on 15 May from the Kyosho Gosho and heads for Shimogamo-jinja.

July

Gion Matsuri Perhaps the most renowned of all Japanese festivals, this one reaches a climax on 17 July with a parade of over 30 floats depicting ancient themes and decked out in incredible finery. On the three evenings preceding the main day, people gather on Shijō-dōri, many dressed in beautiful *yutaka* (light summer kimono), to look at the floats and carouse from one street stall to the next.

August

Daimon-ji Gozan Okuribi This festival, commonly known as Daimon-ji Yaki, is performed to bid farewell to the souls of ancestors on 16 August. Enormous fires are lit on five mountains in the form of Chinese characters or other shapes. The fires are lit at 8pm and it is best to watch from the banks of the Kamo-gawa or pay for a rooftop view from a hotel.

October

Kurama-no-hi Matsuri (Kurama Fire Festival) In perhaps Kyoto's most dramatic festival, huge flaming torches are carried through the streets by men in loincloths on 22 October. The festival climaxes around 10pm at Yuki-jinja (Map p331) in the village of Kurama, which is 30 minutes by train from Kyoto station on the Eiden Eizan line.

Jidai Matsuri (Festival of the Ages) This festival is of recent origin, only dating back to 1895. More than 2000 people, dressed in costumes ranging from the 8th century to the 19th century, parade from Kyoto Gosho to Heian-jingū on 22 October.

KANSAI

SLEEPING

The most convenient areas in which to be based, in terms of easy access to shopping, dining and most of the major attractions, are downtown/central Kyoto and the Higashiyama area.

Transport information is from Kyoto station unless otherwise noted.

For details on hotels near Itami airport see p385; near Kansai airport see p385.

Kyoto Station Area

BUDGET

our pick **Tour Club** (Map p321; ☎ 353-6968; fax 353-6968; www.kyotojp.com; Higashinakasuji, Shōmen sagaru; dm ¥2450, d ¥6980-7770, tr ¥8880-9720; ✗ ✗ 🖳 ; ◉ Kyoto station, Karasuma central gate) Run by a charming and informative young couple, this clean, well-maintained guesthouse is a favourite of many foreign visitors. Facilities include internet access, bicycle rentals, laundry, wireless LAN and free tea and coffee. Most private rooms have a private bath and toilet, and there is a spacious quad room for families. This is probably the best choice in this price bracket. It's a 10-minute walk from Kyoto station; turn north off Shichijō-dōri at the Second House coffee shop (looks like a bank) and keep an eye out for the English sign.

Budget Inn (Map p321; ☎ 344-1510; fax 344-1510; www.budgetinnjp.com; Aburanokōji-Shichijō sagaru; dm/tr/q/5-person r ¥2500/10,980/12,980/14,980; ✗ ✗ 🖳 ; ◉ Kyoto station, Karasuma central gate) This well-run guesthouse is an excellent choice. It's got two dorm rooms and six Japanese-style private rooms, all of which are clean and well maintained. All rooms have their own bath and toilet, and there is a spacious quad room which is good for families. The staff here is very helpful and friendly and internet access, laundry and bicycle rental are available. All in all, this is a great choice in this price range. It's a seven-minute walk from Kyoto station; from the station, walk west on Shiokōji-dōri and turn north one street before Horikawa and look for the English-language sign out front.

K's House Kyoto (Map p321; ☎ 342-2444; http://kshouse.jp/kyoto-e/index.html; Shichijō agaru-Dotemachi-dōri; dm ¥2500, s/d/tw per person from ¥3500/2900/2900; ✗ ✗ 🖳 ; ◉ Kyoto station, Karasuma central gate) K's House is a large Western-style guesthouse with both private and dorm rooms. The rooms are simple but adequate and there are spacious common areas. It's about a 10-minute walk from Kyoto station.

Ryokan Shimizu (Map p321; ☎ 371-5538; fax 371-5539; www.kyoto-shimizu.net; Wakamiya Shichijō agaru; r per person from ¥5250; ✗ ✗ 🖳 ; ◉ Kyoto station, Karasuma central gate) A short walk north of Kyoto station, this fine new ryokan is quickly building a loyal following of foreign and Japanese guests, and for good reason: it's clean, well run and friendly. Rooms are standard ryokan style with one difference: all have attached bathrooms and toilets. Bicycle rental is available.

MIDRANGE

APA Hotel (Map p321; ☎ 365-4111; fax 365-8720; www.apahotel.com/hotel_e/ah_kyotoekimae/index.html; Nishinotōin-Shiokōji kudaru; s/tw from ¥10,000/18,000; ✗ ✗ 🖳 ; ◉ Kyoto station, Karasuma central gate) If only all business hotels were like this! Only five minutes on foot from Kyoto station, this excellent and relatively new business hotel is our favourite midpriced hotel near the station. Rooms are on the large size, with firm, clean beds and unit bathrooms. The staff is professional and seems used to dealing with foreign guests.

Hotel Granvia Kyoto (Map p321; ☎ 344-8888; fax 344-4400; www.granvia-kyoto.co.jp/e/index.html; Shiokōji sagaru-Karasuma-dōri; d/tw per r from ¥23,100/25,410; ✗ ✗ 🖳 ; ◉ Kyoto station, Karasuma central gate) Imagine stepping straight out of bed and into the *shinkansen*. This is almost possible when you stay at the Granvia, a fine hotel located directly above Kyoto station. Rooms are clean, spacious and elegant, with deep bathtubs. This is a very professional operation with some good on-site restaurants, some of which have good views over the city.

TOP END

Rihga Royal Hotel Kyoto (Map p321; ☎ 341-1121; fax 341-3073; www.rihga.com/kyoto/; Horikawa-Shiokōji; s/d/tw from ¥15,015/25,410/25,410; ✗ ✗ 🖳 ; ◉ Kyoto station, Karasuma central gate) Though a little dated and too large for some people's taste, this long-running hotel has all the facilities that you'd expect from a first-class hotel, including a revolving rooftop restaurant. The location is convenient to Kyoto station, but a little distant from the Higashiyama sightseeing district.

Downtown Kyoto

MIDRANGE

Sun Hotel Kyoto (Map p322; ☎ 241-3351; fax 241-0616; www.sun-hotel.co.jp/ky_index.htm in Japanese; Kawaramachi-dōri-Sanjō kudaru; s/d/tw from ¥7350/12,810/12,810; ✗ ✗ 🖳 ; ◉ bus 5, Kawaramachi-Sanjō stop) They don't get more central than this downtown business hotel: it's smack dab in the middle of Kyoto's nightlife, shopping and dining district – you can walk to hundreds of restaurants and shops within five minutes. It's a standard-issue business hotel, with small but adequate rooms and unit baths. Nothing special here, but it's clean, well run and used to foreign guests.

TOP END

Hiiragiya Ryokan (Map p322; ☎ 221-1136; fax 221-139; www.hiiragiya.co.jp/en/; Fuyachō-Aneyakōji-agaru; r per person incl 2 meals ¥30,000-90,000; ✕ ✕ 🖳 ; 🚇 Tōzai & Karasuma subway lines, Karasuma-Oike station, exit 3) Impossibly elegant, this classic ryokan is favoured by celebrities from around the world. From the decorations to the service to the food, everything at the Hiiragiya is the best available. It's centrally located downtown within easy walk of two subway stations and lots of good restaurants.

Hiiragiya Ryokan Annex (Map p322; ☎ 231-0151; fax 231-0153; www.hiiragiya.com/index-e.html; Gokōmachi-dōri-Nijō kudaru; r per person incl 2 meals from ¥15,000; ✕ ✕ ; 🚇 Tōzai subway line, Shiyakusho-mae station, exit North-10) Not far from the Hiiragiya main building, the Hiiragiya Ryokan Annex offers the traditional ryokan experience at slightly more affordable rates. The *kaiseki* cuisine (Japanese formal cuisine) served here is delicious, the gardens are lovely and the bathtubs are wonderful. Service is professional, if a little cool.

Kyoto Hotel Ōkura (Map p322; ☎ 211-5111; fax 254-2529; www.kyotohotel.co.jp/khokura/english/index.html; Kawaramachi-Oike; s/d/tw from ¥20,012/37,537/28,875; ✕ ✕ 🖳 ; 🚇 Tōzai subway line, Shiyakusho-mae station, exit 3) This towering hotel in the centre of town commands an impressive view of the Higashiyama mountains. Rooms here are clean and many have great views – we just wish we could open a window to enjoy the breeze. When you exhaust the possibilities here, you can walk downstairs and hop right onto the subway.

Tawaraya Ryokan (Map p322; ☎ 211-5566; fax 221-2204; Fuyachō-Oike kudaru; r per person incl 2 meals ¥42,000-84,000; ✕ ✕ ; 🚇 Tōzai & Karasuma subway lines, Karasuma-Oike station, exit 3) Tawaraya has been operating for over three centuries and is classed as one of the finest places to stay in the world. Guests at this ryokan have included the imperial family, overseas royalty and such celebrities as Alfred Hitchcock, Marlon Brando and Leonard Bernstein. It is a classic in every sense and the downtown location is hard to beat.

Central Kyoto
BUDGET

Ryokan Hinomoto (Map pp318-19; ☎ 351-4563; fax 351-3932; Matsubara agaru-Kawaramachi-dōri; s/d from ¥4000/7500; ✕ ✕ ; 🚌 bus 17 or 205, Kawaramachi-Matsubara stop) This cute little ryokan is very conveniently located for shopping and dining in downtown Kyoto, as well as sightseeing on the east side of town. It's got a nice wooden bathtub and simple rooms. Several readers have reported good things about Hinomoto.

Crossroads Inn (Map pp318-19; ☎ 354-3066; fax 354-3022; www.rose.sannet.ne.jp/c-inn/; Ebisu Banba-chō-Shimogyō-ku; r per person from ¥4000; ✕ ✕ 🖳 ; 🚌 bus 205 Umekō-jikōen-mae stop) Crossroads Inn is a charming little guesthouse with clean, well-maintained rooms and a friendly owner. The entire inn is nonsmoking. It's good value but a little hard to find: turn north off Shichijō-dōri just west of the Umekōji-kōen-mae bus stop across from the Daily Yamazaki convenience store. Reservations are by email only.

Casa de Natsu (Map pp318-19; ☎ 491-2549; natu@sa3.so-net.ne.jp; Koyamamotomachi Kita-ku; r per person ¥4500; ✕ ✕ 🖳 ; 🚇 Karasuma subway line, Kitayama station exit 4) Up in the north of town, this cosy little Japanese-style guesthouse is a good spot for those who want to escape the hubbub of downtown. There are two rooms, each decorated in the traditional style, and a fine little garden. A light breakfast is served.

Ryokan Rakuchō (Map pp318-19; ☎ 721-2174; fax 791-7202; Higashi hangi chō-Shimogamo; s/tw/tr ¥5300/8400/12,600; ✕ ✕ 🖳 ; 🚇 Karasuma subway line, Kitaōji station; bus 205, Furitsudaigaku-mae stop) There is a lot to like about this fine little foreigner-friendly ryokan in the northern part of town: it's entirely nonsmoking, there is a nice little garden and the rooms are clean and simple. Meals aren't served, but it's got a good map of local eateries.

MIDRANGE

Holiday Inn Kyoto (Map pp318-19; ☎ 721-3131; fax 781-6178; Nishibiraki-chō-Takano; s/d/tw ¥9000/12,000/17,000; ✕ ✕ 🖳 ; 🚌 bus 17, Takanobashi-Higashizume stop) Up in the north end of town, near Takano, this hotel has good facilities but is a bit of a hike to the major attractions. The rooms are pretty standard, with nice bathtubs and windows that open to let in the north Kyoto breezes. A short walk away you'll find a large American-style shopping mall with tons of restaurants. There's a shuttle bus to/from Kyoto station.

KANSAI

Karasuma Kyoto Hotel (Map pp318-19; ☎ 371-0111; fax 371-2424; www.kyotohotel.co.jp/karasuma/index_e.html; Karasuma-dōri-Aneyakōji; s/d/tw from ¥10,164/23,100/18,480; ☒ ☒ ▢ ; ☻ Karasuma subway line, Shijō station, exit South-6) This busy downtown hotel occupies the middle ground between a business hotel and a standard hotel, with clean, well-maintained rooms. It's very popular with business people and travellers, many of whom like the convenience of a Starbucks right in the lobby.

Hotel Fujita Kyoto (Map pp318-19; ☎ 222-1511; fax 222-1515; www.fujita-kyoto.com/e/; Kamogawa Nijō-Ōhashi Hotori; s/d/tw from ¥10,395/26,565/16,170; ☒ ☒ ▢ ; ☻ Tōzai subway line, Shiyakusho-mae station, exit 2) Located on the banks of the Kamo-gawa, this hotel has acceptable rooms and a great on-site bar, as well as a few decent rooms. The hotel is usually rather quiet and has a restful feeling. It's a short walk to the downtown entertainment district.

Kyoto ANA Hotel (Map pp318-19; ☎ 231-1155; fax 231-5333; www.anahotels.com/eng/hotels/uky/index.html; Nijō-jō-mae-Horikawa-dōri; s/d/tw from ¥13,000/16,000/16,000; ☒ ☒ ▢ ; ☻ Tōzai subway line, Nijōjō-mae station, exit 2) Directly opposite Nijō-jō on the west side of downtown, this large hotel gets plenty of foreign guests. Rooms are typical for a hotel of this class, and there are all the usual on-site facilities (pool, restaurants and bars) and something you won't find at most other hotels: an on-site fortune teller.

Southern Higashiyama

BUDGET

Higashiyama Youth Hostel (Map p324; ☎ 761-8135; fax 761-8138; www.syukuhaku.jp/english/top.html; Sanjō-dōri-Shirakawabashi; dm from ¥4360; ☒ ☒ ▢ ; ☻ Tōzai subway line, Higashiyama station, exit 1) This YH is very close to the sights of Higashiyama. It's regimented, but if you're the early-to-bed-early-to-rise type, it might suit.

MIDRANGE

Ryokan Uemura (Map p324; ☎ /fax 561-0377; Ishibe-kōji-Shimogawara; r incl breakfast per person ¥9000; ☒ ☒ ; ☻ bus 206, Yasui stop) This beautiful little ryokan is at ease with foreign guests. It's on a quaint cobblestone alley, just down the hill from Kōdai-ji. Rates include breakfast, and there is a 10pm curfew. Book well in advance, as there are only three rooms. Note that the manager prefers bookings by fax and asks that cancellations also be made by fax (with so few rooms, it can be costly when bookings are broken without notice).

TOP END

Ryokan Motonago (Map p324; ☎ 561-2087; fax 561-2655; www.motonago.com; 511 Washio-chō, Kōdaiji-michi, Higashiyama-ku; r per person incl 2 meals from ¥21,000; ☒ ☒ ; ☻ bus 206, Gion stop) This ryokan may have the best location of any ryokan in the city, and it hits all the right notes for a ryokan in this class: classic Japanese décor, friendly service, nice bathtubs and a few small Japanese gardens.

Ryokan Seikōrō (Map p324; ☎ 561-0771; fax 541-5481; www.seikoro.com/top-e.htm; 467 Nishi Tachibana-chō, 3 chō-me, Gojō kudaru, Tonyamachi-dōri, Higashiyama-ku; r per person incl 2 meals from ¥31,500; ☒ ☒ ; ☻ bus 17 or 205, Kawaramachi-Gojō stop) The Seikōrō is a classic ryokan that welcomes foreign guests. It's a fairly spacious place, with excellent, comfortable rooms, attentive service and a fairly convenient midtown location.

Northern Higashiyama

BUDGET

Yonbanchi (Map pp326-7; www.thedivyam.com; 4 Shinnyo-chō; r per person ¥5000; ☒ ☒ wi-fi; ☻ bus 5, Kinrinshako-mae stop) Yonbanchi is a charming B&B ideally located for sightseeing in the Ginkakuji–Yoshida-Yama area. One of the two guest rooms looks out over a small Japanese garden. The house is a late-Edo-period samurai house located just outside of the main gate of Shinnyo-dō, a temple famed for its maples leaves and cherry blossoms. There is a private entrance and no curfew. Reservation by email only.

B&B Juno (Map pp326-7; www.gotokandk.com; Jōdo-ji-Nishida-chō; r per person ¥5000; ☒ wi-fi; ☻ bus 17, Shirakawa-mae stop) Located close to Ginkaku-ji, on the east side of Kyoto University, this large B&B-home, in an old private compound, has two bright Japanese-style rooms on the 2nd floor. It is run by a charming international couple with a wealth of inside information on Kyoto. Reservations by email only.

MIDRANGE

Kyoto Traveller's Inn (Map pp326-7; ☎ 771-0225; fax 771-0226; www.k-travelersinn.com/english/index.php; Heianjingū Torii-mae; s/tw from ¥5775/10,500; ☒ ☒ ▢ ; ☻ bus 5, Kyōto Kaikan Bijyutsukan-mae stop) This small business hotel is very close to Heian-jingū, offering Western- and Japanese-style rooms. The restaurant on the 1st floor is open till 10pm. It's good value for the price and the location is dynamite for exploring the Higashiyama area.

KANSAI

Three Sisters Inn Main Building (Rakutō-sō Honkan; Map pp326-7; ☎ 761-6336; fax 761-6338; Kasugakita-dōri-Okazaki; s/d/tr ¥8900/13,000/19,500; ✗ ☷ ; ☺ bus 5, Dōbutsuen-mae stop) This is a good foreigner-friendly ryokan with a loyal following of foreign guests. It is well situated in Okazaki for exploration of the Higashiyama area.

Three Sisters Inn Annex (Rakutō-so Bekkan; Map pp326-7; ☎ 761-6333; fax 761-6338; Irie-chō-Okazaki; s/d without bathroom ¥5635/11,270, with bathroom ¥10,810/18,170, tr with bathroom ¥23,805; ✗ ☷ ; ☺ bus 5, Dōbutsuen-mae stop) In the same neighbourhood, this is run by another one of the three eponymous sisters, and is a good choice. The features are similar to the main building, but it's somewhat more intimate and the garden walkway adds to the atmosphere.

TOP END

Hotel Heian No Mori Kyoto (Map pp326-7; ☎ 761-3130; fax 761-1333; www.heiannomori.co.jp/in Japanese; Okazaki Higashitenno-chō; d/tw from ¥17,325/18,480; ✗ ☷ ; ☺ bus 5, Tennōchō stop) This large, pleasant hotel is located close to Ginkaku-ji, Nanzen-ji and the Tetsugaku-no-michi (Path of Philosophy). The hotel is getting a little long in the tooth, but the location is excellent. The rooftop beer garden has a great view of the city in summer.

Yachiyo Ryokan (Map pp326-7; ☎ 771-4148; fax 771-4140; www.ryokan-yachiyo.com/top/englishtop.html; Fukuchi-chō; r per person incl 2 meals approx ¥25,000; ✗ ☷ ; ☺ Tōzai subway line, Keage stop, exit 2) Located just down the street from Nanzen-ji temple, this large ryokan is at home with foreign guests. Rooms are spacious and clean, and some look out over private gardens. English-speaking staff is available. For pleasant and convenient evening strolling, this is a good bet.

Westin Miyako Hotel (Map pp326-7; ☎ 771-7111; fax 751-2490; www.westinmiyako-kyoto.com/english/index .html; Sanjō-dōri-Keage; s/d/tw from ¥26,600/28,900/32,400, Japanese-style r from ¥52,000; ✗ ☷ ☐ ; ☺ Tōzai subway line, Keage stop, exit 2) This sprawling complex is perched atop the Higashiyama area, making it one of the best locations for sightseeing in Kyoto. Rooms are clean, well maintained and tastefully decorated, and the staff is at home with foreign guests. On the down side, the main breakfast restaurant is dimly lit and the service here is not up to the prices.

Northwest Kyoto
BUDGET

Utano Youth Hostel (Map p329; ☎ 353-8250; Nakayama-chō; dm ¥2800; ✗ ☷ ☐ ; ☺ bus 10 or 59, Yuusu-hosteru-

mae stop) This is the best youth hostel in Kyoto. Bear in mind, though, that while it is conveniently located for touring sights in northwest Kyoto, it's something of a hike to those in other areas of the city. It is presently under reconstruction and scheduled to reopen in March 2008.

EATING

Kyoto is one of the world's great food cities. First and foremost, it's the place to make a thorough exploration of Japanese cuisine. You could eat here for a month and still not exhaust the specialities on offer. And, if by some miracle you tire of the great Japanese food on offer, you'll find great international restaurants to satisfy every palate and budget.

Because Kyoto gets a lot of foreign travellers, you'll find a surprising number of English menus, and most places are quite comfortable with foreign guests – it's rare to see waitresses running for the exits at the first sign of a foreign face.

Kyoto Station Area

The new Kyoto station building is chock-a-block with restaurants, and if you find yourself anywhere near the station around mealtime, this is probably your best bet in terms of variety and price.

For a quick cuppa while waiting for a train try Café du Monde (Map p321) on the 2nd floor overlooking the central atrium. Or you might want to snag a few pieces of sushi off the conveyor belt at Kaiten-zushi Iwamaru, on the ground floor at the east end of the station building.

For more substantial meals there are several food courts scattered about. The best of these can be found on the 11th floor on the west side of the building: the Cube food court and Isetan department store's Eat Paradise food court.

Outside the station building, there are lots of good places to eat.

Iimura (Map p321; ☎ 351-8023; Shichijō-dōri-Higashinotōin; set lunch ¥650; ☷ 11.30am-2pm; E) About 10 minutes' walk north of the station, this is a classic little restaurant that's popular with locals who come for its ever-changing set Japanese lunch. Just say *kyō no ranchi* (today's lunch) and you should be fine. It's in a traditional Japanese house, set back a bit from the street.

Downtown Kyoto

Downtown Kyoto has the best variety of approachable Japanese and international restaurants. In addition to the choices listed here, don't forget the restaurant floors of the major department stores, which contain many easy-to-enter restaurants of all description.

Park Café (Map p322; ☎ 211-8954; Aneyakō-ji, Nakagyō-ku; drinks from ¥400; ☷ noon-midnight) This hip little café always reminds us of a Melbourne coffee shop. It's on the edge of the downtown shopping district and a convenient place to take a break.

Café Independants (Map p322; ☎ 255 4312; Sanjō-dōri-Gokomachi; salads & sandwiches from ¥400; ☷ 11.45am-midnight) Located beneath a gallery, the cool subterranean café offers a range of light meals and good café drinks in a bohemian atmosphere. A lot of the food offerings are laid out on display for you to choose from – with the emphasis on healthy sandwiches and salads. Take the stairs on your left before the gallery.

Kyō-Hayashi-Ya (Map p322; ☎ 231-3198; Sanjō-dōri, Nakagyō-ku; green tea ¥600; ☷ 11.30am-9.30pm) If you feel like a change from large American coffee chains and want to try some good Japanese green tea and enjoy a nice view over the mountains while you're at it, this is the place.

Merry Island Café (Map p322; ☎ 213-0214; Kiyamachi-dōri-Oike; lunch from ¥800; ☷ 11.30am-midnight, last order 11pm, closed Mon; E) This popular lunch-dinner restaurant strives to create the atmosphere of a tropical resort. The menu is *mukokuseki* (without nationality) and most of what is on offer is pretty tasty. It does a good risotto and occasionally has a nice piece of Japanese steak. In warm weather the front doors are opened and the place takes on the air of a sidewalk café. It's on the 6th floor; take the elevator.

Kōsendō-sumi (Map p322; ☎ 241-7377; Aneyakōji-dōri-Sakaimachi; lunch from ¥870; ☷ 11.30am-4pm, closed Sun; E) A good pick for a pleasant lunch while in the city centre. Kōsendō-sumi, is in an old Japanese house and serves a daily set lunch of simple Japanese fare. It's near the Museum of Kyoto.

Kane-yo (Map p322; ☎ 221-0669; Shinkyōgoku-dōri-Rokkaku; unagi over rice from ¥890; ☷ 11.30am-9pm) This is a good place to try *unagi* (eel). You can sit downstairs with a nice view of the waterfall or upstairs on the tatami. The *kane-yo donburi* set (¥850) is great value; it's served until 3pm. Look for the barrels of live eels outside and the wooden façade.

Musashi Sushi (Map p322; ☎ 222-0634; Kawaramachi-dōri-Sanjō; all plates ¥130; ☷ 11am-10pm, last order 9.50pm; E) This is the place to go to try *kaiten-zushi* (conveyor-belt sushi). Sure, it's not the best sushi in the world, but it's cheap, easy and fun. Look for the mini-sushi conveyor belt in the window. It's just outside the entrance to the Sanjō covered arcade.

Shizenha Restaurant Obanzai (Map p322; ☎ 223-6623; Koromonotana-dōri-Oike; lunch/dinner ¥840/2100; ☷ 11am-2pm & 5-9pm, closed dinner Wed) A little out of the way, but good value, Obanzai serves a good buffet-style lunch-dinner of mostly organic food. It's northwest of the Karasuma-Oike crossing, set back from the street a bit.

Yak & Yeti (Map p322; ☎ 213-7919; Gokōmachi-dōri-Nishikikōji; curry lunch sets from ¥600; ☷ 11.30am-3pm & 5-10pm Tue-Sun; E) This is a little Nepali place that serves reliably good curry sets for lunch and tasty à la carte dinners. One visit and you'll see why many Kyotoites make this a regular pit stop. It's pretty chuffed about being listed in our guides and has posted a picture of an old edition out front – should be no trouble finding it.

Kerala (Map p322; ☎ 251-0141; Kawaramachi-dōri-Sanjō; lunch from ¥850, dinner from ¥3000; ☷ 11.30am-2pm & 5-9pm; E) This is where we go for reliable Indian lunch sets – great *thalis* that include two curries, good naan bread, some rice, a small salad etc. The dinners, however, are a little overpriced. It's on the 2nd floor; look for the display of food in the glass case on street level.

Misoka-an Kawamichi-ya (Map p322; ☎ 221-2525; Fuyachō-dōri-Sanjō; dishes ¥700-3800; ☷ 11am-8pm, closed Thu; E) This is the place to head for a taste of some of Kyoto's best *soba* noodles in traditional surroundings. They've been handmaking noodles here for 300 years. Try a simple bowl of *nishin soba* (*soba* noodles topped with fish), or the more elaborate *nabe* dishes (cooked in a special cast-iron pot). Look for the *noren* (Japanese curtains) and the traditional Japanese exterior.

Katsu Kura (Map p322; ☎ 212-3581; Teramachi-dōri-Sanjō; tonkatsu from ¥820; ☷ 11am-9pm; E) This restaurant in the Sanjō covered arcade is a good place to sample *tonkatsu* (deep-fried breaded pork cutlet). It's not the best in Kyoto, but it's relatively cheap and casual.

Biotei (Map p322; ☎ 255-0086; Sanjō-dōri-Higashinotōin; lunch from ¥840; ☷ 11.30am-2pm & 5-8.30pm Tue-Sat, lunch only Thu, dinner only Sat; E) Located diagonally across from the Nakagyō post office, this is a favourite of Kyoto vegetarians. Best for lunch, it serves a daily set of Japanese vegetarian food (the occasional bit of meat is offered as an option, but you'll be asked your preference). It's up the metal spiral steps.

Tagoto Honten (Map p322; ☎ 221-3030; Sanjō-dōri-Teramachi; noodle dishes from ¥997; ⏰ 11am-9pm; E) One of Kyoto's oldest and most revered *soba* restaurants makes a good break for those who have overdosed on *rāmen* (noodles in a meat broth with toppings). It's in the Sanjō covered arcade and you can see inside to the tables.

A-Bar (Map p322; ☎ 213-2129; Nishikiyamachi-dōri; dishes from ¥500; ⏰ 5-11pm, last order 10.30pm; E) This student *izakaya* (Japanese pub-style venue) with a log-cabin interior is popular with expats and Japanese students for a raucous night out. The food is fairly typical *izakaya* fare, with plenty of fried items and some decent salads. It's a little tough to find – look for the small black-and-white sign at the top of a flight of steps near a place called Reims.

Ganko Zushi (Map p322; ☎ 255-1128; Sanjō-dōri-Kawaramachi; lunch from ¥1000, dinner from ¥3000; ⏰ 11.30am-11pm, last order 10.30pm; E) Near Sanjō-ōhashi bridge, this is a good place for sushi or just about anything else. Look for the large display of plastic food models in the window. There is often a barker outside trying to drum up business.

Tōsai (Map p322; ☎ 213-2900; Takoyakushi-dōri-Sakai-machi East; dinner per person from about ¥3000; ⏰ 5-10pm Tue-Sat; E) A great place to try a range of healthy and well-prepared Japanese dishes, there are plenty of choices here for vegetarians (the name of the place means 'Bean/Vegetable'). It's just east of a corner, next to a tiny parking lot – look for the traditional Japanese exterior.

Mishima-tei (☎ 221-0003; Teramachi-dōri-Sanjō kudaru; sukiyaki sets from ¥4400; ⏰ 11.30am-10pm, last order 9pm, closed Wed; E) In the Sanjō covered arcade, this is an inexpensive place to sample sukiyaki: there is a discount for foreign travellers!

Yoshikawa (☎ 221-5544; Tominokoji-dōri-Oike kudaru; lunch ¥2000-6000, dinner ¥6000-12,000; ⏰ 11am-2pm & 5-8pm) This is the place to go for delectable tempura. It offers table seating, but it's much more interesting to sit and eat around the small counter and observe the chefs at work. It's near Oike-dōri in a recently restored traditional Japanese-style building.

Finally, you'll find a few branches of the coffee chain Doutor in the downtown area, including one set back just off of Kawara-machi-dōri, between Shijō and Sanjō.

Central Kyoto

This section covers a large swath of Kyoto, and includes our picks that fall in the centre of the city, but don't fall on the Kyoto Station Area or Downtown Kyoto maps.

Café Bibliotic HELLO! (Map pp318-19; ☎ 231-8625; Nijo-dōri-Yanaginobanba higashi iru; food from ¥700, coffee ¥400; ⏰ noon-11pm, closed irregularly; E) Like its name suggests, books line the walls of this cool café located in a converted *machiya*. You can get the usual range of coffee and tea drinks here, as well as light café lunches. Overall, this may be our favourite café in Kyoto, and it's worth the walk from the centre of town. Look for the plants out front.

Cocohana (Map pp318-19; ☎ 525-5587; Honmachi-dōri-Kujo; lunch from ¥680; ⏰ 11am-11pm Thu-Mon, to 5.30pm Tue) This place is one of a kind: a Korean café in a converted old Japanese house. Dishes here include *bibimbap* (a Korean rice dish) and *kimchi* (Korean pickles). A full range of coffee and tea drinks is also available. It's a woody rustic place with both table and tatami seating. There is no English menu but the friendly young staff will help with ordering. This makes a great stop while explore south-eastern Kyoto (Tōfuku-ji etc).

Le Bouchon (Map pp318-19; ☎ 211-5220; Nijo-dōri-Tera-machi; lunch/dinner from ¥900/2500; ⏰ 11.30am-2.30pm & 5.30-9.30pm, closed Thu) This reliable French place serves good lunch and dinner sets and has a pleasant, casual atmosphere. The kitchen does very good work with fish, salads and desserts. The owner speaks English and French, as well as Japanese, and will make you feel right at home.

Hiragana-kan (Map pp318-19; ☎ 701-4164; Higash-ioji-dōri-Mikage; lunch/dinner from ¥800; ⏰ 11.30am-4pm & 6-10pm, closed Tue) This place, popular with Kyoto University students, dishes up creative variations on chicken, fish and meat. Most mains come with rice, salad and miso soup for around ¥800. The menu is only in Japanese, but if you're at a loss for what to order try the tasty roll chicken *katsu*, a delectable and filling creation of chicken and vegetables. Look for the words 'Casual Restaurant' on the white awning.

Shuhari (Map pp318-19; ☎ 222-6815; Kawaramachi-dōri-Marutamachi agaru; lunch course from ¥850; ⏰ noon-11pm Mon-Thu, to 2am Fri-Sun) Shuhari is a fine example of Kyoto's newest dining trend – fine

KANSAI

restaurants in renovated *machiya*. In this case, the food is casual French, with an emphasis on light fish dishes and healthy salads. Look for the red stovepipe with the name of the restaurant written on it out front.

Didi (Map pp318-19; ☎ 791-8226; Higashiōji-dōri-Tanaka-Okubo-chō; lunch/dinner from ¥750/900; ⏰ 11am-9.30pm, closed Wed; E) On Higashiōji-dōri, north of Mikage-dōri, you'll find this friendly little smoke-free restaurant serving passable Indian lunch/dinner sets. There are plenty of vegetarian choices on the menu. It's easy to spot from the street.

Den Shichi (Map pp318-19; ☎ 323-0700; 4-1 Tatsumi-chō, Saiin, Ukyō-ku; sushi dinners from ¥3000; ⏰ 11.30am-2pm & 5-11pm, closed Mon) A little out of the way, but well worth the trip, this is our favourite sushi restaurant in Kyoto. While we usually go for a sushi dinner here, the lunch deals are also great, including *tekkadon* (raw tuna over rice) for ¥504. In terms of price and quality, Den Shichi is always a good bet. Look for the black-and-white sign about 100m west of Hankyū Saiin station on Shijō-dōri.

Manzara Honten (Map pp318-19; ☎ 253-1559; Kawaramachi-dōri agaru; dinner courses from ¥4000; ⏰ 5pm-midnight, last order 11.30pm) Manzara is located in a converted *machiya*. The fare here is creative modern Japanese and the surroundings are decidedly stylish. The *omakase* (chef's recommendation) course is good value, with eight dishes for ¥4000.

Southern Higashiyama

Gion Koishi (Map p324; ☎ 531-0331; Higashiyama Gion North; tea from ¥500; ⏰ 10.30am-7.30pm) This is where we go when we want to cool down on a hot summer day in Gion. The speciality here is *uji kintoki* (¥700), a mountain of shaved ice flavoured with green tea, sweetened milk and sweet beans (it tastes a lot better than it sounds, trust us). This is only available in the summer months. Look for the models of the sweets and tea out front.

Kasagi-ya (Map p324; ☎ 561-9562; Higashiyama-ku Kodaiji Masuya chō; sweets from ¥600; ⏰ 11am-6pm, closed Tue) At Kasagi-ya, on the Ninen-zaka slope near Kiyomizu-dera, you can try o-hagi cakes made from *azuki* (sweet red beans). This funky old wooden shop has atmosphere to boot and friendly staff – which makes it worth the wait if there's a line. It's hard to spot; you may have to ask someone in the area to point it out.

Amazon (Map p324; ☎ 561-8875; Shichijō-dōri-Kawabata; coffee from ¥400; ⏰ 7.30am-6pm, closed Wed) A typical Japanese coffee shop that turns out some surprisingly tasty sandwiches. It's good for a bite or a cuppa while heading to/from Sanjūsangen-dō.

Senmonten (Map p324; ☎ 531-2733; Hanamikōji-dōri-Shinbashi; 10 dumplings ¥460; ⏰ 6pm-2am, closed Sun) Senmonten serves only one thing: crisp fried *gyōza* – they're the best in town. Look for the metal-and-glass front door.

Kagizen Yoshifusa (Map p324; ☎ 561-1818; Higashiyama-ku Gion-chō; tea from ¥400; ⏰ 9.30am-6pm, closed Mon; E) One of Kyoto's oldest and best-known *okashi-ya* (sweet shops) sells a variety of traditional sweets and has a cosy tearoom upstairs where you can sample cold *kuzukiri* (transparent arrowroot noodles), served with a *kuro-mitsu* (sweet black sugar) dipping sauce. It's in a traditional *machiya* up a flight of stone steps.

Santōka (Map p324; ☎ 532-1335; Sanjō-dōri-Kawabata; rāmen from ¥750; ⏰ 11am-2am) The young chefs at this sleek new restaurant dish out some seriously good Hokkaidō-style *rāmen*. You'll be given a choice of three kinds of soup when you order: *shio* (salt), *shōyu* (soy sauce) and miso. It's on the east side/ground floor of the new Kyōen restaurant-shopping complex.

Machapuchare (Map p324; ☎ 525-1330; 290 Kamihoritsume-chō, Sayamachi-dōri Shōmen kudaru, Higashiyama-ku; obanzai set from ¥840; ⏰ 11.30am-8pm, closed Tue) This organic vegetarian restaurant serves a sublime vegetarian *obanzai* set (Kyoto home-style cooking). The problem is, the restaurant keeps somewhat irregular hours and the *obanzai* is not always available. Get a Japanese speaker to call and check before trekking here.

Asuka (Map p324; ☎ 751-9809; Sanjō-dōri-Higashiyama Nishi iru; meals from ¥1000; ⏰ 11am-11pm, closed Mon; E) With an English menu, and a staff of old Kyoto *mama-sans* at home with foreign customers, this is a great place for a cheap lunch or dinner while sightseeing in the Higashiyama area. The tempura *moriawase* (assorted tempura set) is a big pile of tempura for only ¥1000. Look for the red lantern and the pictures of the set meals.

Ryūmon (Map p324; ☎ 752-8181; north side, Nishi iru Higashiōji, Sanjō-dōri, Higashiyama-ku; dinner from about ¥1500; ⏰ 5pm-5am) The place looks like a total dive, but the food is reliable and authentic, as the crowds of Kyoto Chinese residents will attest. There's no English menu, but there is a picture menu and some of the waitresses can speak English. Décor is strictly Chinese kitsch, with the exception of the deer head

KANSAI

over the cash register – still trying to figure that one out.

Ichi-ban (Map p324; ☎ 751-1459; Sanjō Ōhashi East; dinner from ¥3000; ☽ 5.30pm-midnight, closed Sun; E) This popular little *yakitori* (skewered meats or vegetables) joint on Sanjō-dōri has an English menu and a friendly young owner to help with ordering. Look for the yellow-and-red sign and the big lantern.

Daikichi (Map p324; ☎ 771-3126; Sanjō Ōhashi East; dinner about ¥3000; ☽ 5pm-1am, closed Wed; E) This is a good *yakitori* joint with a friendly owner. It's a little brightly lit for our taste, but the *yakitori* is tasty and it's easy to enter. It's on Sanjō-dōri; look for the red lanterns outside.

Ōzawa (Map p324; ☎ 561-2052; Gion-Shirakawa Nawate Higashi iru South; lunch ¥2500, dinner from ¥3800; ☽ 5-10pm, last order 9pm, closed Thu, lunch available advance request; E) Located on a beautiful street in Gion, this restaurant offers good tempura in traditional Japanese surroundings. Unless you choose a private tatami room, you'll sit at the counter and watch as the chef prepares each piece of tempura.

Aunbo (Map p324; ☎ 525-2900; Higashiyama-Yasaka Torii mae; lunch ¥2500, dinner ¥6000-10,000; ☽ noon-2pm & 5.30-10pm, closed Wed; E) Aunbo serves elegant, creative Japanese cooking in traditional Gion surroundings – the last time we were here we started with sublime sashimi, went on to fried *yuba* (tofu skimming) pockets and went from there. We recommend asking for the set and leaving the difficult decisions to the master. Aunbo takes reservations in the evening. There is no English sign; look for the traditional Japanese façade.

Northern Higashiyama

Buttercups (Map pp326-7; ☎ 751-7837; 103 Shimobanba-chō-Jōdo-ji Sakyō-ku; coffee/meals from ¥230/580; ☽ noon-10pm, closed Tue; E) This is a favourite of the local expat community and a great place for lunch, dinner or a cup of coffee. There is an international menu and this is one of the only places in town where you can get a proper salad.

Café Carinho/Asian Diner (Map pp326-7; ☎ 752-3636; Imadegawa-dōri-Shirakawa; coffee/lunch from ¥400/750; ☽ 11am-10pm Tue-Thu, to 11pm Fri-Sun; E) Located near Ginkaku-ji, this is a cosy little café. It serves good, strong Brazilian coffee, tasty cakes and some excellent sandwiches. The friendly owner speaks English and the wi-fi internet access is handy.

Hinode Udon (Map pp326-7; ☎ 751-9251; Nanzenji-Kitanobō-chō; noodle dishes from ¥400; ☽ 11am-6pm, closed Sun; E) Filling noodle and rice dishes are served at this pleasant little shop with an English menu. Plain *udon* here is only ¥400, but we recommend you spring for the *nabeyaki udon* (pot-baked *udon* in broth) for ¥800. This is a good spot for lunch when temple-hopping near Ginkaku-ji or Nanzen-ji.

Café Peace (Map pp326-7; ☎ 707-6856; Higashiōji-dōri-Imadegawa; drinks/food from ¥550/600; ☽ 11.30am-11pm Mon-Sat, to 10pm Sun & holidays; E) This is a pleasant spot for a cuppa or a light vegetarian meal. Lunch sets include green curry, sandwiches and Japanese fare. It's on the 3rd floor but there's a small sign on street level.

Karako (Map pp326-7; ☎ 752-8234; Okazaki-Tokusei-chō; rāmen from ¥650; ☽ 11.30am-2pm & 6pm-2am, closed Tue; E) This is our favourite *rāmen* restaurant in Kyoto. While it's not much on atmosphere, Karako has excellent *rāmen* – the soup is thick and rich and the *chāshū* (pork slices) melt in your mouth. We recommend the *kotteri* (thick soup) *rāmen*. Look for the lantern outside.

Earth Kitchen Company (Map pp326-7; ☎ 771-1897; Marutamachi-dōri-Kawabata; lunch ¥700; ☽ 10.30am-6.30pm Mon-Fri, to 3.30pm Sat, closed Sun; E) Located on Marutamachi-dōri near the Kamo-gawa, this is a tiny spot that seats just two people but does a bustling business serving tasty take-away lunch *bentō*. If you fancy a picnic lunch for your temple-hopping, this is the place.

Zac Baran (Map pp326-7; ☎ 751-9748; Higashiōji-dōri-Marutamachi; dishes from ¥500; ☽ noon-3am; E) Near the Kyoto Handicraft Centre, this is a good spot for a light meal or a drink. It serves a variety of spaghetti dishes, as well as a good lunch special. Look for the picture of the Freak Brothers near the downstairs entrance. If you fancy dessert when you're done, step upstairs to the Second House Cake Works.

Omen (Map pp326-7; ☎ 771-8994; Shirakawa-dōri-Imade-gawa; noodles ¥1000; ☽ 11am-10pm, closed Thu; E) This noodle shop is named after the thick, white noodles served in a hot broth with a selection of seven fresh vegetables. Just say *omen* and you'll be given your choice of hot or cold noodles, a bowl of soup to dip them in and a plate of vegetables (you put these into the soup along with some sesame seeds). It's a great bowl of noodles but that's not the end of the story: everything on the frequently changing menu is delicious. Best of all, there's a menu in English. It's about five minutes' walk from Ginkaku-ji in a traditional Japanese house with a lantern outside.

Kushi Hachi (Map pp326-7; ☎ 751-6789; Shirakawa-dōri-Imadegawa; dinner from ¥2000; ☽ 5-11.30pm, closed

Mon; E) Kushi Hachi, part of a popular Kyoto chain, is a fun spot to sample *kushi katsu*, a fried dish that is well suited to Western palates. We like to sit at the counter and watch as the frenetic chefs work the grills and deep-fryers.

Okutan (Map p326-7; ☎ 771-8709; Nanzen-ji; set meals ¥3000; ❋ 10.30am-5pm Fri-Wed) Just outside the grounds of Nanzen-ji, this is a fine restaurant located inside the garden of Chōshō-in. Try a course of *yudōfu* (tofu cooked in a pot) together with vegetable side dishes.

Grotto (Map pp326-7; ☎ 771-0606; Imadegawa-dōri, Sakyō-ku; dinner courses from ¥4000; ❋ 6pm-midnight, closed Mon) This stylish little place along Imadegawa-dōri serves a killer dinner set menu that will take you through the major tastes in the Japanese gastronomy. It's a great way to spend two or three hours with someone special. Reservations are highly recommended.

Arashiyama & Sagano Area

Yoshida-ya (Map p330; ☎ 861-0213; Saga-Tenryū-ji Tsukurimichi-chō; lunch from ¥800; ❋ 10am-6pm, closed Wed) This quaint and friendly little *teishoku-ya* (set-meal restaurant) is the perfect place to grab a simple lunch while in Arashiyama. All the standard *teishoku* favourites are on offer, including things like *oyakodon* (egg and chicken over a bowl of rice) for ¥1000. You can also cool off here with a refreshing *uji kintoki* (sweet *matcha* over shaved ice, sweetened milk and sweet beans; ¥600). It's the first place south of the station and it's got a rustic front.

Shigetsu (Map p330; ☎ 882-9725; Saga-Tenryū-ji; lunch from ¥3000; ❋ 11am-2pm) To sample *shōjin ryōri* (vegetarian meals) try Shigetsu in the precinct of Tenryū-ji. It has beautiful garden views.

Yudōfu Sagano (Map p330; ☎ 871-6946; Sagano-Tenryū-ji; lunch, dinner course from ¥3800; ❋ 11am-7pm; E) This is a good place to try that classic Arashiyama dish: *yudōfu*. Lunch and dinner courses go for ¥3800 (simply ask for the *yudōfu cosu*). Look for the wagon wheels outside.

Ōhara

Seryō-jaya (Map p331; ☎ 744-2301; Ōhara Sanzenin hotori; lunch sets from ¥2756; ❋ 9am-5pm) Just by the entry gate to Sanzen-in, Seryō-jaya serves wholesome *sansai ryōri* (mountain vegetable cooking), fresh river fish and *soba* noodles topped with grated yam. There is outdoor seating in the warmer months. Look for the food models.

Kurama

Aburaya-shokudō (Map p331; ☎ 741-2009; Kurama-honmachi; meals from ¥800; ❋ 9.30am-5pm) Just down the steps from the main gate of Kurama-dera, this classic old-style *shokudō* (all-round restaurant) reminds us of what Japan was like before it got rich. The *sansai teishoku* (¥1700) is a delightful selection of vegetables, rice and *soba* topped with grated yam.

Yōshūji (Map p331; ☎ 741-2848; Kurama-honmachi; meals from ¥1050; ❋ 10am-6pm, closed Tue; E) Yōshūji serves superb *shōjin ryōri* in a delightful old Japanese farmhouse with an *irori* (open hearth). The house special, a sumptuous selection of vegetarian dishes served in red lacquered bowls, is called *kurama-yama shōjin zen* (¥2500). Or if you just feel like a quick bite, try the *uzu-soba* (*soba* topped with mountain vegetables; ¥1050). It's halfway up the steps leading to the main gate of Kurama-dera; look for the orange lanterns out front.

Kibune

Visitors to Kibune from June to September should not miss the chance to cool down by dining at one of the picturesque restaurants beside the Kibune-gawa. Meals are served here on platforms (known as *kawa-doko*) suspended over the river as cool water flows just underneath. Most of the restaurants offer some kind of lunch special for around ¥3000. For a full *kaiseki* spread (¥5000 to ¥10,000) have a Japanese person call to reserve in advance. In the cold months you can dine indoors overlooking the river.

Hirobun (Map p331; ☎ 741-2147; Kurama-Kibune-chō; noodles ¥1200, kaiseki courses from ¥7000; ❋ 11am-9pm) If you don't feel like breaking the bank on a snazzy course lunch, head for this place where you can sample *nagashi-somen* (¥1200), thin white noodles that flow to you in globs down a split bamboo gutter; just pluck them out and slurp away (*nagashi-somen* is served until 5pm). Look for the black-and-white sign and the lantern.

Nakayoshi (Map p331; ☎ 741-2000; Kurama-Kibune-chō; lunch from ¥3500, dinner from ¥8500; ❋ 11am-9pm; E) One of the more reasonably priced restaurants is Nakayoshi, which serves a lunch *bentō* for ¥3500. *Kaiseki* dinners cost ¥8500.

Beniya (Map p331; ☎ 741-2041; Kurama-Kibune-chō; meals from ¥3000; ❋ 11am-7.30pm) This elegant riverside restaurant serves *kaiseki* sets for ¥6000, ¥8000 or ¥10,000, depending on size. There is a wooden sign with white lettering.

KANSAI

Tochigiku (Map p331; ☎ 741-5555; Kurama-Kibune-chō; sukiyaki from ¥8000; 🕑 11am-9pm, closed irregularly) Try this lovely riverside restaurant for sukiyaki and *kaiseki* sets. There is a small English sign.

DRINKING

Kyoto has a great variety of bars, clubs and discos, all of which are good places to meet Japanese folks. And if you happen to be in Kyoto in the summer, many hotels and department stores operate rooftop beer gardens with all-you-can-eat-and-drink deals and good views of the city. Check the *Kyoto Visitor's Guide* for details.

Bars

Kyoto is loaded with great bars and clubs – if you've got the energy left over after sightseeing, Kyoto is a great place to party!

Ing (Map p322; ☎ 255-5087; Nishikiyamachi-dōri-Takoyakushi; meals ¥250-700, drinks from ¥580; 🕑 6pm-2am Mon-Thu, to 5am Fri & Sat; E) Another one of our favourite spots, this little joint is the place for cheap bar snacks and drinks, good music and friendly company. It's on the 2nd floor of the Royal building; you'll know you're getting close when you see all the hostesses out trawling for customers on the streets nearby.

Atlantis (Map p322; ☎ 241-1621; Shijō-Pontochō agaru; drinks from ¥800; 🕑 6pm-2am) This bar is one of the few on Pontochō that foreigners can walk into without a Japanese friend. It's a slick, trendy place that draws a fair smattering of Kyoto's beautiful people and wanna-be beautiful people. In summer you can sit outside on a platform looking over the Kamo-gawa. Drinks average ¥1000.

Café Bon Appétit (Map p324; ☎ 525-0585; Shirakawa Nawate; drinks from ¥500; 🕑 11am-11pm) Not exactly a bar, not exactly a café, this is a fine spot to sip a drink and watch the characters of Gion stroll by. It's near the Shira-kawa canal and right alongside some of Kyoto's best cherry trees.

Zappa (Map p322; ☎ 255-4437; Takoyakushi-dōri-Kawaramachi; dishes from ¥850; 🕑 6pm-midnight Mon-Sat; E) Unbeatable if you're looking for a more intimate venue. It's a cosy little place that once played host to David Bowie (he's said to have discovered it by chance and decided to drop in for a drink). It serves savoury Southeast Asian fare and a few Japanese tidbits for good measure. It's down a narrow alley; turn south at the wooden torii.

McLoughlin's Irish Bar & Restaurant (Map p322; ☎ 212-6339; Empire Bldg, Kiyamachi Sanjō-agaru; 🕑 6pm-late; 💻 wi-fi) This is our favourite expat bar in town. It's got a ripping view over the Higashiyama mountains, great beer on tap, good food and a nice, open feeling. It hosts some great music events as well. There is wi-fi internet access in case you want to do some surfing with your beer.

Rub-a-Dub (Map p322; ☎ 256-3122; Kiyamachi-dōri-Sanjō; meals from ¥500, drinks from ¥600; 🕑 7pm-2am Sun-Thu, to 4am Fri & Sat; E) At the northern end of Kiyamachi-dōri, Rub-a-Dub is a funky little reggae bar with a shabby tropical look. It's a good place for a quiet drink on weekdays, but on Friday and Saturday nights you'll have no choice but to bop along with the crowd. Look for the stairs heading down to the basement beside the popular (and delightfully 'fragrant') Nagahama Rāmen shop.

Tadg's Irish Pub (Map p322; ☎ 525-0680; Yamatōji-dōri-Shijō agaru; drinks from ¥600; 🕑 5pm-1am, later Thu-Sun; E) Tadg's is a good little Irish bar on the doorstep of Gion. It's a great place to meet local expats and see what's going on in town.

Jumbo Karaoke Hiroba (Map p322; ☎ 761-3939; Keihan Sanjō branch, Sanjō-dōri-Kawabata, Sanjō-Ohashi East; per person per hr all-you-can-drink ¥640; 🕑 11am-6am) is one of the cheapest places to indulge in this most Japanese of pastimes, karaoke. Kyoto expats love this place because it's in the same building as a popular *'gaijin bar'*, the Pig & Whistle. There's a decent selection of English songs (ask the attendant to show you the menu) and it's all you can drink. There's a **second branch** (Map p322; ☎ 231-6777; Sanjō Kawaramachi branch, Kawaramachi dōri-Sanjō) in the Sanjō shopping arcade.

ENTERTAINMENT

Most of Kyoto's cultural entertainment is of an occasional nature, and you'll need to check with the TIC or a magazine like *Kansai Time Out* to find out whether anything interesting coincides with your visit. Regular cultural events are generally geared at the tourist market and tend to be expensive and, naturally, somewhat touristy.

Clubs

Metro (Map pp326-7; ☎ 752-4765; Kawabata-dōri-Marutamachi kudaru; admission Wed & Thu free, Fri-Sun ¥2000; 🕑 10pm-3am) This is one of the most popular clubs in town. It's part disco, part live house and even hosts the occasional art exhibition. Every night is a different theme; check the *Kansai Time Out* for forthcoming events. On weekends there's usually an admission charge of between ¥1500 and ¥2000 (with one drink), while Wednesday and Thursday are usually free. It's inside exit 2 of the Keihan Marutamachi station.

World (Map p322; ☎ 213-4119; Nishikiyamachi-dōri-Shijō agaru; admission from ¥1500, drinks from ¥500; ⏰ 10pm-5am) World is Kyoto's biggest club and it naturally hosts some of the biggest events. It has two floors, a dance floor and lockers where you can leave your stuff while you dance the night away. Events include everything from deep soul to reggae to techno to salsa.

Geisha Dances

Annually in autumn and spring, geisha and their *maiko* apprentices from Kyoto's five schools dress elaborately to perform traditional dances in praise of the seasons. The cheapest tickets cost about ¥1650 (unreserved on tatami mats), better seats cost ¥3000 to ¥3800, and spending an extra ¥500 includes participation in a quick tea ceremony. The dances are similar from place to place and are repeated several times a day. Dates and times vary, so check with the TIC.

Gion Odori (祇園をどり; ☎ 561-0224; Higashiyama-ku-Gion; admission/with tea ¥3500/4000; ⏰ shows 1pm & 3.30pm) Held at Gion Kaikan Theatre (Map p324) near Yasaka-jinja; 1 to 10 November.

Kamogawa Odori (鴨川をどり; ☎ 221-2025; Ponto-chō-Sanjō kudaru; normal/special/special with tea ¥2000/3800/4300; ⏰ shows 12.30pm, 2.20pm & 4.10pm) Held at Ponto-chō Kaburen-jō Theatre (Map p322), Ponto-chō; 1 to 24 May.

Kitano Odori (北野をどり; ☎ 461-0148; Imadegawa-dōri-Nishihonmatsu nishi iru; admission/with tea ¥3800/4300; ⏰ shows 1pm & 3pm) At Kamishichiken Kaburen-jō Theatre (Map p329), east of Kitano-Tenman-gū; 15 to 25 April.

Kyō Odori (京をどり; ☎ 561-1151; Kawabata-dōri-Shijō kudaru; admission/with tea ¥3800/4300; ⏰ shows 12.30pm, 2.30pm & 4.30pm) Held at Miyagawa-chō Kaburen-jō Theatre (Map p324), east of the Kamo-gawa between Shijō-dōri and Gojō-dōri; from the first to the third Sunday in April.

Miyako Odori (都をどり; ☎ 561-1115; Higashiyama-ku-Gion-chō South; reserved/nonreserved seat ¥3800/1900, reserved seat with tea ¥4300; ⏰ shows 12.30pm, 2pm, 3.30pm & 4.50pm) At Gion Kōbu Kaburen-jō Theatre (Map p324), near Gion Corner; throughout April.

Kabuki

Minami-za Theatre (Map p322; ☎ 561-0160; Shijō-Ōhashi; ¥4200-12,600; ⏰ irregular) In Gion, this is the oldest kabuki theatre in Japan. The major event of the year is the Kao-mise Festival (1 to 26 December), which features Japan's finest kabuki actors. Other performances take place on an irregular basis. Those interested should check with the TIC. The most likely months for performances are May, June and September.

Musical Performances

Musical performances featuring the koto, *shamisen* and *shakuhachi* are held in Kyoto on an irregular basis. Performances of *bugaku* (court music and dance) are often held at Kyoto shrines during festival periods. Occasionally contemporary *butō* dance is also performed in Kyoto. Check with the TIC to see if any performances are scheduled to be held while you are in town.

Nō

Kanze Kaikan Nō Theatre (Map pp326-7; ☎ 771-6114; Sakyō-ku-Okazaki; admission free-¥8000; ⏰ 9am-5pm Tue-Sun) This is the main theatre for performances of nō. *Takigi-Nō* is a picturesque form of nō performed in the light of blazing fires. In Kyoto this takes place on the evenings of 1 and 2 June at Heian-jingū – tickets cost ¥2000 if you pay in advance (ask at the TIC for the location of ticket agencies) or you can pay ¥3300 at the entrance gate.

Traditional Dance, Theatre & Music

Gion Corner (Map p324; ☎ 561-1119; Gion-Hanamikōji-dōri; admission ¥2800; ⏰ performances nightly at 7.40pm & 8.40pm 1 Mar-29 Nov, closed 16 Aug) The shows presented here are a sort of crash course in Japanese traditional arts. You get a chance to see snippets of the tea ceremony, koto music, ikebana, *gagaku* (court music), *kyōgen* (ancient comic plays), *Kyōmai* (Kyoto-style dance) and *bunraku* (puppet plays). However, these are rather touristy affairs and may not satisfy those in search of more authentic experiences. On top of this, 50 minutes of entertainment for ¥2800 is a little steep by anyone's standards.

SHOPPING

The heart of Kyoto's shopping district is around the intersection of Shijō-dōri and Kawaramachi-dōri. The blocks to the north and west of here are packed with stores selling both traditional and modern goods. Kyoto's largest department stores (Hankyū, Takashimaya, Daimaru and Fujii Daimaru) are grouped together in this area.

Antiques

The place to look for antiques in Kyoto is Shinmonzen-dōri, in Gion (Map p324). The street is lined with great old shops, many of them specialising in one thing or another (furniture, pottery, scrolls, prints etc). You can easily spend an afternoon strolling from shop to shop here, but be warned: if something strikes your fancy you're going to have to break out the credit card – prices here are steep!

Camping & Outdoor Equipment

Kōjitsu (Map p322; ☎ 257-7050; Kawaramachi-dōri-Sanjō agaru; ☯ 10.30am-8pm) If you plan to do some hiking or camping while in Japan, you can stock up on equipment at this excellent little shop on Kawaramachi. You'll find that Japanese outdoor sporting equipment is very high quality (with prices to match).

Food & Kitchen Utensils

Nishiki Market (Map p322), in the centre of town, is Kyoto's most fascinating food market (see p315).

If you do choose to visit, be sure to stop into the knife shop **Aritsugu** (Map p322; ☎ 221-1091; Nishikikōji-dōri-Gokōmachi nishi iru; ☯ 9am-5.30pm) near the eastern end of the market. Here, you can find some of the best kitchen knives available in the world, as well as a variety of other kitchenware.

For an even more impressive display of food, check the basements of any of the big department stores on Shijō-dōri (perhaps Daimaru has the largest selection). It's difficult to believe the variety of food on display, or some of the prices (check out the ¥10,000 melons or the Kōbe beef, for example).

Japanese Arts & Crafts

The paved streets of Ninnen-zaka and Sannen-zaka (close to Kiyomizu-dera), in eastern Kyoto, are renowned for their crafts and antiques. You'll also find lots of pottery shops along Gojō-dōri, between Kawabata-dōri and Higashiōji-dōri.

North of the city hall, Teramachi-dōri, between Oike-dōri and Marutamachi-dōri, there are a number of classic old Kyoto shops and this area is pleasant for strolling around and window-shopping.

Kamiji Kakimoto (Map pp318-19; ☎ 211-3481; Teramachi-dōri-Nijō agaru; ☯ 9am-6pm Mon-Sat, 10am-5pm Sun & holidays) This place sells a good selection of *washi* (Japanese paper). It's not as good as Morita Washi, but it's great for things like *washi* computer paper.

Morita Washi (Map pp318-19; ☎ 341-1419; Higashinotōin-dōri-Bukkōji agaru; ☯ 9.30am-5.30pm, to 4.30pm Sat) Not far from Shijo-Karasuma, it sells a fabulous variety of handmade *washi* for reasonable prices.

Kyūkyo-dō (Map p322; ☎ 231-0510; Teramachi-Aneyakōji agaru; ☯ 10am-6pm Mon-Sat, closed Sun & 1-3 Jan) This old shop in the Teramachi covered arcade sells a selection of incense, *shodō* (calligraphy) goods, tea-ceremony supplies and *washi*. Prices are on the high side but the quality is good.

Ippo-dō (Map pp318-19; ☎ 211-3421; Teramachi-dōri-Nijō; ☯ 9am-7pm Mon-Sat, to 6pm Sun & holidays, café 11am-5pm) This is an old-fashioned tea shop selling

---

MARKETS & MALLS

If you're in town when one of the following markets is on, by all means go! Markets are the best places to find antiques and bric-a-brac at reasonable prices and are the only places in Japan where you can actually bargain for a better price.

On the 21st of each month, **Kōbō-san Market** (Map pp318-19) is held at Tō-ji to commemorate the death of Kōbō Daishi (Kūkai), who in 823 was appointed abbot of the temple.

Another major market, **Tenjin-san Market**, is held on the 25th of each month at Kitano Tenman-gū, marking the day of the birth (and, coincidentally, the death) of the Heian-era statesman Sugawara Michizane (845–903).

If you're not in Kyoto on the 21st, there's also a regular antiques fair at Tō-ji on the first Sunday of each month. In addition, the **Antique Grand Fair** is a major event, with over 100 dealers selling a wide range of Japanese and foreign curios. It is held thrice-yearly at Pulse Plaza (Map pp316–17) in Fushimi (southern Kyoto). Ask at the TIC for more details as times vary each year.

all sorts of Japanese tea. You can ask to sample the tea before buying.

Kyoto Handicraft Center (Map pp326-7; ☎ 761-5080; Marutamachi-dōri-Kumano jinja east; ☺ 10am-6pm, closed 1-3 Jan) Just north of the Heian-jingū, this is a huge cooperative that sells, demonstrates and exhibits crafts (wood-block prints and *yukata* are a good buy here). It's the best spot in town for buying Japanese souvenirs and is highly recommended.

Kyoto Craft Center (Map p324; ☎ 561-9660; Gion-chō-Kitagawa; ☺ 11am-7pm Thu-Tue) Near Maruyama-kōen, this centre also exhibits and sells a wide range of handicrafts and souvenirs.

Kagoshin (Map p324; ☎ 771-0209; Sanjō-dōri-Ōhashi higashi iru; ☺ 9am-6pm) This small shop sells a wide variety of inexpensive bamboo products like flower holders and baskets.

Onouechikuzaiten (Map p324; ☎ 751-2444; Sanjō-dōri-Ōhashi higashi iru; ☺ 10am-7pm) Just a few doors from the previous, it's almost a carbon copy.

Tessai-dō (Map p324; ☎ 531-9566; Shimogawara dōri-Kōdaiji; ☺ 10am-5pm) Just outside Kōdai-ji, this small shop deals in original wood-block prints. Prices average ¥10,000 per piece.

GETTING THERE & AWAY
Air
Kyoto is served by Osaka Itami airport, which handles mostly domestic traffic, and the new Kansai International Airport (KIX), which handles most international flights. There are frequent flights between Tokyo and Itami (¥18,800, 70 minutes) but unless you're very lucky with airport connections you'll probably find it as quick and more convenient to take the *shinkansen*. There are ample connections to/from both airports, though the trip between Kansai International Airport and the city can be both expensive and time consuming.

Bus
The overnight bus (JR Dream Kyoto Go) runs between Tokyo station (Yaesu-guchi long-distance bus stop) and Kyoto station Bus Terminal (Map p321).

The trip takes about eight hours and there are usually two departures nightly in either direction, at 10pm (Friday, Saturday, Sunday and holidays) and 11pm (daily). The fare is ¥8180/14,480 one way/return. You should be able to grab some sleep in the reclining seats. There is a similar service to/from Shinjuku station's Shin-minami-guchi in Tokyo.

Other JR bus transport possibilities include one way/return Kanazawa ¥4060/6600 and Hiroshima ¥5500/10,000.

Hitching
Although we never recommend it, for long-distance hitching head for the Kyoto-Minami Interchange of the Meishin Expressway, about 4km south of Kyoto station. Take bus 19 from Kyoto station and get off when you reach the Meishin Expressway signs. From here you can hitch east towards Tokyo or west to southern Japan.

Train
SHINKANSEN (TOKYO, OSAKA, NAGOYA & HAKATA)
Kyoto is on the Tōkaidō-San-yō Hikari *shinkansen* line to/from Tokyo (¥13,520, two hours 22 minutes); to/from Nagoya (¥5640, 36 minutes); to/from Osaka (¥2930, 14 minutes); and to/from Hakata (¥15,610, three hours 15 minutes). Other stops on this line include Hiroshima, Okayama, Kōbe and Yokohama. The *shinkansen* operates to/from Kyoto station, in the south of town, and it goes to/from Tokyo, Shinagawa and Shin-Yokohama stations at the Tokyo end of the line.

NARA
Unless you have a Japan Rail Pass, the best option is the Kintetsu line (sometimes written in English as the Kinki Nippon railway) linking Kyoto (Kintetsu Kyoto station, on the south side of the main Kyoto station building) and Nara (Kintetsu Nara station). There are direct limited-express trains (¥1110, 33 minutes) and ordinary express trains (¥610, 45 minutes), which may require a change at Saidai-ji.

The JR Nara line connects Kyoto station with JR Nara station (*shinkaisoku*, ¥690, 46 minutes) but departures are often few and far between.

OSAKA
The fastest train other than the *shinkansen* between Kyoto station and Osaka is the JR *shinkaisoku* (special rapid train), which takes 29 minutes (¥540). In Osaka, the train stops at both Shin-Osaka and Osaka stations.

There is also the cheaper private Hankyū line, which runs between Hankyū Kawaramachi, Karasuma and Ōmiya stations in Kyoto and Hankyū Umeda station in Osaka (*tokkyū* or limited express Umeda–Kawara-machi, ¥390, 40 minutes).

Alternatively, you can take the Keihan main line between Demachiyanagi, Sanjō, Shijō or Shichijō stations in Kyoto and Keihan Yo-doyabashi station in Osaka (*tokkyū* to/from Sanjō ¥400, 45 minutes). Yodoyabashi is on the Midō-suji subway line.

TOKYO

The *shinkansen* line has the fastest and most frequent rail links. The journey can also be undertaken by a series of regular JR express trains, but keep in mind that it takes around eight hours and involves at least two (often three or four) changes along the way. The fare is ¥7980. Get the staff at the ticket counter to write down the exact details of each transfer for you when you buy your ticket.

GETTING AROUND
To/From the Airport
OSAKA ITAMI AIRPORT 大阪伊丹空港
There are frequent limousine buses between Osaka Itami airport (Map p310) and Kyoto station (the Kyoto station airport bus stop is opposite the south side of the station, in front of Avanti department store). Buses also run between the airport and various hotels around town, but on a less regular basis (check with your hotel). The journey should take around 55 minutes and the cost is ¥1370. Be sure to allow extra time in case of traffic.

At Itami, the stand for these buses is outside the arrivals hall; buy your tickets from the machines and ask one of the attendants which stand is for Kyoto.

MK Taxi Sky Gate Shuttle limousine van service (☎ 721-2237) also offers limousine van service to/from the airport for ¥2000 (call at least two days in advance to reserve) or ask at the information counter in the arrivals hall on arrival in Osaka.

KANSAI INTERNATIONAL AIRPORT (KIX) 関西国際空港
The fastest, most convenient way to travel between KIX (Map p310) and Kyoto is on the special Haruka airport express, which makes the trip in about 75 minutes. Most seats are reserved (¥3490) but there are usually two cars on each train with unreserved seats (¥2980). Open seats are almost always available, so you don't have to purchase tickets in advance. First and last departures from Kyoto

to KIX are 5.45am and 8.16pm; first and last departures from KIX to Kyoto are 6.29am and 10.18pm.

If you have time to spare, you can save some money by taking the *kanku kaisoku* (Kansai airport express) between the airport and Osaka station and taking a regular *shinkaisoku* to/from Kyoto. The total journey by this method takes about 90 minutes with good connections and costs ¥1800, making it the cheapest option.

It's also possible to travel by limousine bus between Kyoto and KIX (¥2300, about two hours). In Kyoto, the bus departs from the same place as the Itami-bound bus (see left).

A final option is the **MK Taxi Sky Gate Shuttle limousine van service** (☎ 721-2237), which will pick you up anywhere in Kyoto city and deliver you to KIX for ¥3000. Call at least two days in advance to reserve. The advantage of this method is that you are delivered from door to door and you don't have to lug your baggage through the train station. MK has a counter in the arrivals hall of KIX, and if there's room they'll put you on the next van to Kyoto. A similar service is offered by **Yasaka Taxi** (☎ 803-4800).

Bicycle
Kyoto is a great city to explore on a bicycle; with the exception of outlying areas it's mostly flat and there is a new bike path running the length of the Kamo-gawa.

Unfortunately, Kyoto must rank near the top in having the world's worst public facilities for bike parking and the city regularly impounds bikes parked outside of regulation bike-parking areas. If your bike does disappear, check for a poster in the vicinity (in both Japanese and English) indicating the time of seizure and the inconvenient place you'll have to go to pay a ¥2000 fine and retrieve your bike.

There are two bicycle parking lots in town that are convenient for tourists: one in front of Kyoto station and another on Kiyamachi-dōri, halfway between Sanjō-dōri and Shijō-dōri. It costs ¥150 per day to park your bicycle here. Be sure to hang onto the ticket you pick up as you enter.

BICYCLE PURCHASE
If you plan on spending more than a week or so exploring Kyoto by bicycle, it might make

KANSAI

sense to purchase a used bicycle. A simple *mama chari* (shopping bike) can be had for as little as ¥3000. Try the used-cycle shop **Ei Rin** (Map p329; ☎ 752-0292; Imadegawa-dōri) near Kyoto University. Otherwise, you'll find a good selection of used bikes advertised for sale on the message board of the Kyoto International Community House.

BICYCLE RENTAL

Tour Club (see p352) rents large-frame and regular bicycles for ¥800, with a ¥3000 deposit. Bicycles can be picked up between 8am and 9.30pm. It offers a similar deal at its sister inn, Budget Inn (p352).

Another great place to rent a bike is **Kyoto Cycling Tour Project** (KCTP; Map p321; ☎ 354-3636; www .kctp.net/en/index.html). These folks rent mountain bikes (¥1500 per day), which are perfect for getting around the city. KCTP also conducts a variety of bicycle tours of Kyoto, which are an excellent way to see the city (check the website for details).

Most rental outfits require you to leave ID such as a passport or driver's licence.

Bus

Kyoto has an intricate bus network that is an efficient way to get around at moderate cost. Many of the bus routes used by foreign visitors have announcements in English. The core timetable for buses is between 7am and 9pm, though a few run earlier or later.

The bus terminal at Kyoto station is on the northern side of the station and has three main departure bays (departure points are indicated by the letter of the bay and number of the bus stand within that bay).

The TIC's *Kyoto Transportation Guide* is a good map of the city's main bus lines, with a detailed explanation of the routes and a Japanese/English communication guide on the reverse side.

Bus stops throughout the city usually display a map of bus stops in the vicinity on the top section. On the bottom section there's a timetable for the buses serving that stop. Unfortunately, most of this information is written in Japanese, and those who don't read the language will simply have to ask locals waiting at the stop for help.

Entry to the bus is usually through the back door and exit is via the front door. Inner-city buses charge a flat fare (¥220), which you drop into the clear plastic receptacle on top of

the machine next to the driver. The machine gives change for ¥100 and ¥500 coins or ¥1000 notes, or you can ask the driver.

On buses serving the outer areas, you take a *seiri-ken* (numbered ticket) when entering. When you leave, an electronic board above the driver displays the fare corresponding to your ticket number.

To save time and money, you can buy a *kaisū-ken* (book of five tickets) for ¥1000. There's also a one-day card *(shi-basu senyō ichinichi jōshaken kaado)* valid for unlimited travel on city buses and subways that costs ¥500. A similar pass (Kyoto *kankō ichinichi jōsha-ken kaado*) that allows unlimited use of the bus and subway costs ¥1200. A two-day bus/subway pass *(futsuka jōsha-ken)* costs ¥2000. *Kaisū-ken* can be purchased directly from bus drivers. The other passes and cards can be purchased at major bus terminals and at the main bus information centre.

The main bus information centre is located in front of Kyoto station. Here, you can pick up bus maps, purchase bus tickets and passes (on all lines, including highway buses), and get additional information. Nearby, there's an English/Japanese bus information computer terminal; just enter your intended destination and it will tell you the correct bus and bus stop.

When heading for locations outside the city centre, be careful which bus you board. Kyoto city buses are green, Kyoto buses are tan and Keihan buses are red and white.

Scooter

Scooters are a good way to get around the city. Just be sure you have a valid international licence. **Kyoto Rental Scooters** (☎ 864-1635; www .kyoto.zaq.ne.jp/rental-scooter) rents 50cc scooters for ¥4000/14,000 per day/week.

Subway

The quickest way to travel between the north and the south of the city is to take the Karasuma line subway, which operates from 5.30am to 11.30pm. The minimum fare is ¥210.

There's also the new Tōzai line subway, which runs east–west across the city, from Daigo station in the east to Nijō station in the west, stopping at Sanjō-Keihan en route.

Taxi

Kyoto taxi fares start at ¥640 for the first 2km. The exception is **MK Taxis** (☎ 721-2237), whose fares start at ¥580.

MK Taxis also provides tours of the city with English-speaking drivers. For a group of up to four people, prices start at ¥13,280 for a three-hour tour. Another company offering a similar service is **Kyōren Taxi Service** (☎ 672-5111).

Most Kyoto taxis are equipped with satellite navigation systems. If you are going somewhere unusual, it will help the driver if you have the address or phone number of your destination, as both of these can be programmed into the system.

SHIGA-KEN 滋賀県

Just across the Higashiyama mountains from Kyoto is Shiga-ken, a small prefecture dominated by Biwa-ko, Japan's largest lake. The prefecture has a variety of attractions that are easily visited as day trips from Kyoto. The major attractions here are the towns of Nagahama, with its traditional Kurokabe Square neighbourhood of glass artisans, and Hikone, with its fine original castle. Other worthwhile destinations include temples like Mii-dera and Ishiyama-dera, and the Miho Museum, which is worth a trip just to see the building and the compound in which it is located.

ŌTSU 大津
☎ 077 / pop 329,000
Ōtsu has developed from a 7th-century imperial residence (the city was capital of Japan for just five years) into a lake port and major post station on the Tōkaidō highway between eastern and western Japan. It is now the capital of Shiga-ken.

The **information office** (☎ 522-3830; 8.40am-5.25pm) is at JR Ōtsu station.

Mii-dera 三井寺
Formally known as Onjō-ji, **Mii-dera** (☎ 522-2238; 246 Onjōji-chō; admission ¥500; 8am-5pm) is a short walk northwest from Keihan Hama-Ōtsu station. The temple, founded in the late 7th century, is the head branch of the Jimon branch of the Tendai school of Buddhism. It started its days as a branch of Enryaku-ji on Hiei-zan, but later the two fell into conflict, and Mii-dera was repeatedly razed by Enryaku-ji's warrior monks. The Niō-mon gate here is unusual for its roof, which is made of layers of tree bark, rather than tiles. It looks particularly fine when framed by the cherry trees in early April.

Festivals & Events
Ōtsu Dai Hanabi Taikai (Ōtsu Grand Fireworks Festival) If you're in town on 8 August, be sure to catch this. Starting at dusk, the best spots to watch are along the waterfront near Keihan Hama-Ōtsu station. Be warned that trains to and from Kyoto are packed for hours before and after the event.
Ōtsu Matsuri Takes place on 7 and 8 October at Tenson-jinja, close to JR Ōtsu station. Ornate floats are displayed on the first day and paraded around the town on the second day.

Getting There & Away
From Kyoto you can take the JR Tōkaidō line from JR Kyoto station to JR Ōtsu station (¥190, eight minutes), or travel on the Kyoto Tōzai subway line to Hama-Ōtsu station (¥410, 20 minutes from Sanjō Keihan station).

HIRA-SAN 比良山
Hira-san is the high mountain range that rises to the west of Biwa-ko. It is a great hiking destination and there are many excellent hiking courses crisscrossing the peaks. It is best accessed by the JR Kosei line, which leaves from Kyoto station (be careful to board a Kosei-line train, as most Shiga-bound trains head to the other side of the lake).

A good base for hiking in the area is the **Maiko Hut** (☎ 077-596-8190; www.trekstation.co.jp /index5.html; per person from ¥4500). The folks here will happily pick you up at Ōmi-maiko station (about 30 minutes from Kyoto) on the Kosei line if you call ahead to make arrangements. They can also arrange guided walks in the Hira-san range in English.

Several good hikes in the Hira-san range are described in Lonely Planet's *Hiking in Japan*, including the superb Yatsubuchi-no-taki hike, which we reckon is the best one-day hike near Kyoto.

ISHIYAMA-DERA 石山寺
This **temple** (☎ 077-537-0013; 1-1-1 Ishiyama-dera; admission ¥500; 8am-4.30pm), founded in the 8th century, now belongs to the Shingon sect. The room next to the Hondō is famed as the place where Lady Murasaki wrote *The Tale of the Genji*. The temple precincts are in a lovely forest with lots of good trails to explore, including the one that leads up to Tsukimitei hall, from which there are great views over Biwa-ko.

The temple is a 10-minute walk south from Keihan Ishiyama-dera station (continue along

KANSAI

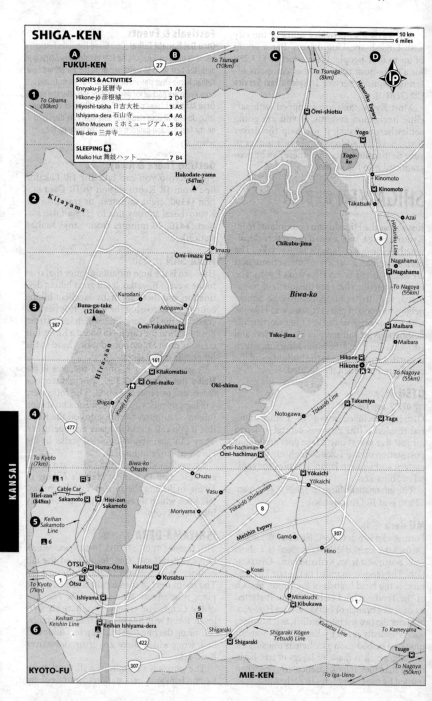

SHIGA-KEN

0 ——————— 10 km
0 ——————— 6 miles

SIGHTS & ACTIVITIES
Enryaku-ji 延暦寺...............................1 A5
Hikone-jō 彦根城...............................2 D4
Hiyoshi-taisha 日吉大社.....................3 A5
Ishiyama-dera 石山寺.........................4 A6
Miho Museum ミホミュージアム.......5 B6
Mii-dera 三井寺.................................6 A5

SLEEPING
Maiko Hut 舞妓ハット.......................7 B4

the road in the direction that the train was travelling). Take the Kyoto Tōzai line subway from Sanjō-Keihan station in Kyoto to Keihan Hama-Ōtsu and change there to a Keihan-line Ishiyama-dera-bound *futsū* (¥540, 36 minutes). Alternatively, take the JR Tōkaidō line from JR Kyoto station to JR Ishiyama-dera station. *Kaisoku* (rapid) and *futsū* trains run this route (¥230, 12 minutes). Switch at JR Ishiyama station to the Keihan line for the short journey to Keihan Ishiyama-dera station (¥160, three minutes).

MIHO MUSEUM

This **museum** (☎ 0748-82-3411; www.miho.or.jp; 300, Momodani, Shigaraki; adult/child ¥1000/300; ☑ 10am-5pm Tue-Sun mid-Mar–mid-Jun, mid-Jul–mid-Aug & Sep–mid-Dec) is visually stunning, located in the countryside of Shiga-ken near the village of Shigaraki. The IM Pei–designed museum houses the Shumei Family art collection, which includes examples of Japanese, Middle Eastern, Chinese and south Asian art.

A visit to the museum is something like a visit to the secret hideout of an archvillain in a James Bond film, and there is no doubt that the facility is at least as impressive as the collection. Since a trip to the museum from Kyoto or Osaka can take the better part of a day, we highly recommend calling the museum to check what's on before making the trip (unless, like a lot of people, you're interested in the building itself).

To get there, take the JR Tōkaidō line from Kyoto or Osaka to Ishiyama station, and change to a **Teisan Bus** (Tanakami Eigyōsho; ☎ 562-3020; www .teisan-bus.co.jp/index.php in Japanese) bound for the museum (¥800, approximately 50 minutes).

HIKONE 彦根

☎ 0749 / pop 111,000

Hikone is the second-largest city in the prefecture and of special interest to visitors for its lovely castle, which dominates the town. The adjoining garden is also a classic and is a must-see after your visit to the castle.

Orientation & Information

There is a good **tourist information office** (☎ 22-2954; ☑ 9am-5pm), which is on your left at the bottom of the steps as you exit the castle (west) exit of Hikone station. It stocks the excellent *Street Map & Guide to Hikone*.

The castle is a 10-minute walk straight up the street from the station.

Hikone-jō 彦根城

This **castle** (☎ 22-2742; 1-1 Konki-chō; admission ¥500; ☑ 8.30am-5pm) was completed in 1622 by the Ii family, who ruled as *daimyō* over Hikone. It is rightly considered one of the finest remaining castles in Japan. Much of it is original, and you can get a great view across the lake from the upper storeys. The castle is surrounded by more than 1000 cherry trees, making it a very popular spot for springtime *hanami* activities.

After visiting the castle, don't miss nearby **Genkyū-en** (admission incl in castle ticket; ☑ 8.30am-5pm), a lovely Chinese-influenced garden that was completed in 1677. Ask someone at the castle to point you in the right direction. There's a teahouse in the garden where ¥500 gets you a cup of *matcha* (powdered green tea) and a sweet to enjoy as you gaze over the scenery.

Yumekyō-bashi Castle Road
夢京橋キャッスルロード

About 400m southwest of the castle (marked on the *Street Map & Guide to Hikone* map and accessible via the Omote-mon gate or the Ōte-mon gate of the castle), this street of traditional shops and restaurants is the ideal spot for lunch after exploring the castle, and a browse in the shops is a nice way to round out the day.

Our favourite spot for a bite here is **Monzen-ya** (もんぜんや; ☎ 24-2297; tori-soba ¥850; ☑ 11am-7pm, closed Tue), a great little *soba* place that serves such things as *tori-soba* (*soba* noodles with chicken; ¥850). Starting from the castle end of the street, it's about 10m on the left – look for the white *noren* curtain with black lettering in the doorway.

Festivals & Events

The **Birdman Contest**, held on the last Friday and Saturday of August at Matsubara Beach in Hikone, is a fantastic celebration of the human desire to fly – ideally without the use of fossil fuels. Here you will find contestants launching themselves over Biwa-ko in all manner of flimsy human-powered flying machines. It's really a whole lot of fun to watch.

Getting There & Away

Hikone is just less than an hour in travelling time (*shinkaisoku*, ¥1110) from Kyoto on the JR Tōkaidō line. If you have a JR Rail Pass or are just in hurry, you can take the *shinkansen* to Maibara (¥2060, 22 minutes

KANSAI

from Kyoto) and then backtrack from there on the JR Tōkaidō line to Hikone (¥180, five minutes).

NAGAHAMA 長浜

☎ 0749 / pop 84,000

Nagahama is a surprisingly appealing little town on the northeast shore of Biwa-ko, which can easily be teamed up with a trip to Hikone. The main attraction here is the **Kurokabe Square** neighbourhood northeast of the station.

If you're in the area from 14 to 16 April, check out the **Nagahama Hikiyama Matsuri**, in which costumed children perform Hikiyama *kyōgen* on top of a dozen festival floats decked out with elaborate ornamentation.

Kurokabe Square 黒壁スクエア

Many of the old *machiya* (traditional city houses) and *kura* (storehouses) in this attractive old neighbourhood have been converted into shops and galleries highlighting the town's traditional (and modern) glass industry. Exit the east side of Nagahama station and take the first major left after the first traffic light and you will find the **Kurokabe Information Centre** (黒壁インフォメーションセンター; ☎ 65-8055; ⏲ 10am-6pm), which has maps of the area.

We like the small collection of glass *objets* at the **Kurokabe Museum of Glass Art** (黒壁美術館; ☎ 62-6364; admission ¥600; ⏲ 10am-4.30pm). While you're there, ask them to demonstrate the *suikinkutsu,* a strange 'musical instrument' formed from an overturned urn into which water is dripped.

Our hands-down favourite attraction in Kurokabe Square is the **Giant Kaleidoscope** (kyodaimangekyō; 巨大万華鏡; admission free; ⏲ dawn-dusk), which is located off the north arcade of the area. It's set back in the open area behind a place with an English sign that reads 'Antique Gallery London'.

Not far from the Giant Kaleidoscope is **Daitsū-ji** (大通じ; ☎ 62-0054; admission to garden/grounds ¥500/free; ⏲ 9am-4.30pm), a True Pure Land sect temple that's worth a quick look (we don't recommend paying to enter the garden, though).

Sleeping & Eating

Kokumin-shukusha Hōkō-sō (国民宿舎豊公荘; ☎ 62-0144; r per person from ¥7000; ⌘) This place is five minutes' walk west of the station in Hōkōen Park (*kokumin-shukusha* are people's lodges – cheap accommodation).

Torikita (鳥善多; ☎ 62-1964; dishes from ¥420; ⏲ 11.30am-2pm & 4.30-7pm, closed Tue) This place specialises in one dish: *oyako-donburi* (chicken and egg over a bowl of rice; ¥580). It has raised this simple dish to a work of art. If you don't like raw egg, ask for *oyako-donburi nama tamago nashi de*. It's located 200m down the main street east of the station, on the left after the second light – look for the traditional front and white *noren* curtain in the doorway.

Getting There & Away

Nagahama is on the JR Tōkaidō line (*shinkaisoku,* ¥1280, 61 minutes from Kyoto) and the Tōkaidō *shinkansen* line. Be aware that not all *shinkaisoku* from Kyoto go all the way to Nagahama; you may have to change in Maibara, which is a 10-minute ride south of Nagahama by *shinkaisoku* (¥190).

NORTHERN KANSAI 関西北部

The spectacular coastline of northern Kansai is known as the San-in Kaigan Kokuritsu Kōen – the San-in Coast National Park. There are sandy beaches, rugged headlands, rocky islets and a laid-back atmosphere.

The JR San-in line runs the length of the area, but it spends a fair bit of time inland and in tunnels. The best way to see the coastline is on wheels, whether it be a rental car, a motorbike, a bicycle or by thumb. If you stick to the trains, make the effort to get off every now and then.

The text in this section moves from west to east, starting at the Tottori-ken–Hyōgo-ken border. It is a continuation of the route along the San-in Coast described in the Western Honshū chapter (see p494). If you're heading east to west, read this section backwards.

MOROYOSE 諸寄

Moroyose, in Hyōgo-ken, near the border with Tottori-ken, is a pleasant little seaside town with a decent sand beach. **Youth Hostel Moroyose-sō** (諸寄荘ユースホステル; ☎ 0796-82-3614; 461 Moroyose; r per person ¥2625-2835) is a good spot to stay for backpackers, with fairly large rooms for a YH and breakfast/dinner for

KANSAI

¥525/945. It's a 10-minute climb uphill from the eastern end of the beach. Moroyose is on the JR San-in line; the station is in the centre of town, very close to the beach.

TAKENO 竹野

Takeno is a pleasant little fishing village–summer resort with two good sandy beaches: **Benten-hama** (弁天浜) to the west and **Takeno-hama** (竹野浜) to the east. To get to Benten-hama, exit Takeno station and turn left at the first light and walk straight for about 15 minutes (you will cross one big street en route). To get to Takeno-hama, go straight out of the station and walk for around 20 minutes. There is an **information office** (☎ 0796-47-1080; ☒ 8.30am-5pm) on the beachfront at Takeno-hama in an orange brick building. This office can help with accommodation in local *minshuku* (B&B-style accommodation) and ryokan.

Bentenhama camping area (弁天浜キャンプ場; ☎ 0796-47-0888; camp sites adult/child ¥800/400) is on the seafront at Benten-hama. It's a decent, if crowded, spot to pitch a tent. **Kitamaekan** (北前館; ☎ 0796-47-2020; adult/child ¥400/250; ☒ 9am-9pm) is an *onsen* complex where the baths are on the 2nd floor with a great view of the beach and sea. It's at Takeno-hama, in a large grey building about 150m west of the information office.

Takeno station is on the JR San-in line, an easy trip from Kinosaki (¥190, 10 minutes). The train trip is a good chance to enjoy some of the coastal scenery.

KINOSAKI 城崎
☎ 0796 / pop 4000

Kinosaki is one of the best places in Japan to sample the classic Japanese *onsen* experience – donning a *yukata* and walking from *onsen* to *onsen*. A willow-lined canal runs through the centre of this town and many of the houses, shops and restaurants retain something of their traditional charm. Add to this the delights of crab fresh from the Japan sea in winter, and you'll understand why this is one of our favourite overnight trips from the cities of Kansai.

Information

Opposite the station is an **accommodation information office** (お宿案内所; ☎ 32-4141; ☒ 9am-6pm) where the staff will gladly help you find a place to stay and make bookings, as well as provide maps to the town. The same office

has rental bicycles available for two hours/a day ¥400/800 (return by 5pm). If you're just passing through, you could leave your bags in a coin locker, pick up a bicycle, go for a ride, have a bath or just soak your feet, and then carry on.

Sights & Activities

Kinosaki's biggest attraction is its seven **onsen** (admission ¥600-800; ☒ 3-11pm, closed irregularly). Guests staying in town stroll the canal from bath to bath wearing *yukata* and *geta* (wooden sandals). Most of the ryokan and hotels in town have their own *uchi-yu* (private baths), but also provide their guests with free tickets to the ones outside (*soto-yu*).

Here is the full list of Kinosaki's *onsen*, in order of preference (get a map from the information office or your lodgings):
Sato-no-yu (さとの湯; admission ¥800; ☒ 7am-11pm) Fantastic variety of baths, including Arab-themed saunas, rooftop *rotemburo* (outdoor bath) and a 'Penguin Sauna' (basically a walk-in freezer – the only one we've seen anywhere – good after a hot bath). Women's and men's baths shift floors daily, so you'll have to go two days in a row to sample all of the offerings.
Gosho-no-yu (御所の湯; admission ¥800; ☒ 7am-11pm) Lovely log construction, a nice two-level *rotemburo* and fine maple colours in autumn. The entry area is decorated like the Kyoto Gosho (Imperial Palace).
Kou-no-yu (鴻の湯; admission ¥600; ☒ 7am-11pm) Nothing fancy, but a good *rotemburo* and pleasant inside baths.
Ichi-no-yu (一の湯; admission ¥600; ☒ 7am-11pm) Wonderful 'cave' bath.
Yanagi-yu (柳湯; admission ¥600; ☒ 3-11pm) Worth a quick soak as you make your way around town.
Mandala-yu (まんだら湯; admission ¥600; ☒ 3-11pm) Small wooden *rotemburo*.
Jizo-yu (地蔵湯; admission ¥600; ☒ 7am-11pm) Small bath with no *rotemburo*. Good if others are crowded.

Sleeping

Suishōen (水翔苑; 32-4571; www.suisyou.com in Japanese; r per person incl 2 meals from ¥19,050; ☒) This excellent modern ryokan is a short drive from the town centre, but they'll whisk you straight to the *onsen* of your choice in their own London taxi and pick you up when you're done. It's a strangely pleasant feeling to ride in the back wearing nothing but a *yukata*! The rooms are clean and well kept and the private *onsen* is great, with indoor and outdoor baths. Taking the price into consideration, it's great value.

KANSAI

Mikuniya (三国屋; ☎ 32-2414; www.kinosaki3928 .com in Japanese; r per person incl 2 meals from ¥13,650; ✖) About 150m on the right on the street heading into town from the station, this fine ryokan is a good choice if you want something more traditional. The rooms are clean, with nice Japanese decorations, and the 'garden view' *onsen* bath is soothing. There is an English sign.

Nishimuraya Honkan (西村屋本館; ☎ 32-2211; honkan@nishimuraya.ne.jp; r per person incl 2 meals from ¥37,950; ✖) This is a classic and the ultimate of inns here. If you would like to try the high-class ryokan experience, this is a good place. The *onsen* baths here are exquisite and the rooms look out over private gardens. The excellent food is the final touch.

Eating

Savoury crab from the Sea of Japan is a speciality in Kinosaki during the winter months. It's called *kani* and the way to enjoy it is in *kani-suki*, cooked in broth with vegetables right at your table.

Heihachirō (☎ 32-0086; ⏰ 11.30am-2pm & 6-11pm, closed Wed) This is a great place to try *kani-suki* (¥4000) in winter. It also serves the usual *izakaya* fare, along with beer and sake. It's just before Mikuniya, on the left near the west end of the main street – look for a stone wall and a small English sign that reads 'Dining Bar Heihachiro'.

For simpler meals, try **Yamayoshi** (山よし), a simple *shokudō* outside the station on the 2nd floor (look for the pictures and food models out front). It serves the usual set meals as well as some local specialities like crab.

Note that most restaurants in Kinosaki shut down very early. This is because most people opt for the two-meal option at their accommodation. You should consider doing the same.

Getting There & Away

Kinosaki is on the JR San-in line, 10 minutes north of Toyooka (¥190, 18 minutes), 2½ hours from Osaka, and three hours from Kyoto. There are occasional *tokkyū* from Kyoto (¥3880, two hours 22 minutes) and (Osaka ¥4620, two hours 36 minutes).

TANGO-HANTŌ 丹後半島

Tango-hantō is a peninsula that juts up into the Sea of Japan on the north coast of Kansai. The inside of the peninsula is covered

with thick forest, idyllic mountain villages and babbling streams, while the serrated coast alternates between good sand beaches and rocky points.

The private Kita-Kinki Tango Tetsudō rail line runs between Toyooka and Nishi-Maizuru, cutting across the southern base of the peninsula and stopping en route at Amanohashidate (below). Thus, if you want to check out the peninsula you'll have to go by road. A bus runs around the peninsula, passing a small number of scenic fishing ports (Tango Ōkoku Romance gō; Tankai Bus ☎ 0772-42-0321; from ¥4300). A large car park and restaurant mark the start of the 40-minute round-trip walk (about 3km) to the **Kyōga-misaki Lighthouse** (経ヶ岬灯台).

The village of **Ine** (伊根), on a perfect little bay on the eastern side of the Tango-hantō, is particularly interesting. There are *funaya* houses that are built right out over the water, under which boats are drawn in, as if in a carport. The best way to check it out is by boat, and **Ine-wan Meguri** (☎ 0772-42-0321) tour boats putter around the bay (¥660, 30 minutes) from March to December. Buses (¥910) reach Ine in half an hour from Amanohashidate.

Sleeping

One of the best ways to see Tango-hantō is with **Two to Tango** (http://thedivyam.com; lodging & 2½-day all-inclusive tour per person ¥100,000), an exclusive tour of the Tango peninsula offered by a French resident of Kyoto-Fu of more than 20 years. You will stay in a secluded farmhouse in Kurumi-dani (a six-house hamlet in the heart of Tango-hantō) and drive over scenic roads to beautiful *onsen*, excellent restaurants and lovely beaches. Everything is taken care of, including driving and guiding. The tour gives you an intimate look at a side of Japan rarely glimpsed by foreign travellers. Perfect for a gentle entry into the country or to unwind after a hectic trip.

There are several fine *minshuku* in the small village of Ine including **Yoza-sō** (与謝荘; ☎ 0772-32-0278; 507 Hirata; per person incl 2 meals from ¥9000; ✖).

AMANOHASHIDATE 天橋立

☎ 0772 / pop 23,000

Amanohashidate (the Bridge to Heaven) is rated as one of Japan's 'three great views', along with Miyajima (p460) and the islands of Matsushima-wan (p513). The 'bridge' is really a long, narrow tree-covered (8000 pine trees!) sand-spit, 3.5km in length. There is good swimming, as well as beach showers, toilet facilities and covered rest areas the length of the spit. It's a good example of a Japanese tourist circus, but it is pleasant enough and there are some decent attractions like Ine (opposite) in the vicinity.

The town of Amanohashidate consists of two separate parts, one at each end of the spit. At the southern end there are a number of hotels, ryokan, restaurants, a popular temple and Amanohashidate station. There's an **information counter** (☎ 22-8030; ☽ 10am-6pm) at the station. To get to the bridge from the staion, take a right out of the station and walk along the main road for 200m to the first light and take a sharp left.

At the southern end of the bridge, **Amanohashidate View Land** (天橋立ビューランド; chairlift/monorail round-trip ¥850; ☽ 9am-5pm) is serviced by chairlift and monorail. From here, you are supposed to view Amanohashidate by turning your back to it, bending over and observing it framed between your legs! (It supposedly makes Amanohashidate look like it is 'floating'.)

At the northern end, **Kasamatsu-kōen** (傘松公園; funicular/chairlift round-trip ¥640; ☽ 8am-5.30pm) offers similar views and another chance to view the world from between your legs.

Sleeping & Eating

Amanohashidate Youth Hostel (天橋立ユースホステル; ☎ 27-0121; per person incl/excl 2 meals ¥4250/2950; ✖) This fine YH has good views down towards Amanohashidate, friendly owners, well-kept rooms and an excellent hillside location. To get there take a bus from JR Amanohashidate station and get off at the Jinja-mae bus stop (¥520; 20 minutes). From the stop, walk to the main hall of the shrine, take a right and leave the shrine precinct and turn left up the hill and walk 50m, take a right and follow the sign for Manai Shrine. Turn at the stone torii, walk 200m uphill and it's on the right.

Amanohashidate Hotel (天橋立ホテル; ☎ 22-4111; per person incl 2 meals from ¥16,800; ✖) This hotel about 100m west of the station commands the best views of Amanohashidate. Rooms are mixed Japanese-Western style and there are several good communal baths that afford views of Amanohashidate and the bay. The hotel serves special crab cuisine in winter.

There are several decent but slightly overpriced *shokudō* at the southern end of Amanohashidate, including **Resutoran Monju** (れすとらん文珠; ☎ 22-2805; meals from ¥1000; ☽ 9.30am-4pm Fri-Wed), which has *asari udon* (*udon* noodles with clams), a local speciality, for ¥1000. Look for the red-and-white sign as you approach Chion-ji (the temple at the southern end of Amanohashidate).

Getting There & Away

The Kita-kinki Tango Tetsudō line runs between JR stations at Toyooka to the west and Nishi-Maizuru to the east. Amanohashidate station is on this line, 1¼ hours from Toyooka (*futsū*, ¥1160) and 40 minutes from Nishi-Maizuru (*futsū*, ¥620). There are several direct trains from Kyoto daily, but JR pass holders will have to fork out for the Kita-kinki Tango Tetsudō part of the route (from Kyoto ¥3770, two hours, from Osaka ¥4630, 2¼ hours).

Getting Around

You can cross Amanohashidate on foot, bicycle or on a motorcycle of less than 125cc capacity. Bicycles can be hired at a number of places for ¥400/1600 for two hours/a day.

MAIZURU 舞鶴

There's nothing overly appealing about the two ports of Nishi-Maizuru and Higashi-Maizuru, but they play an important part in the area's transport networks. If you've come from the west on the Kita-kinki Tango Tetsudō trains, **Nishi-Maizuru** is the end of the line and where the JR Obama line comes out to meet the coast. If you're on your way to Amanohashidate, this is where you'll have to change to the private line.

There are regular ferry services to/from Otaru in Hokkaidō from Higashi-Maizuru. This is a cheap and interesting way of getting to/from Hokkaidō. The cheapest tickets are ¥9600 for the 20-hour journey. Call **Shin-Nihonkai Ferry** (☎ 06-6345-2921; www.snf.co.jp/yoyaku /yoyaku-c.html in Japanese) for details.

OSAKA 大阪

☎ 06 / pop 2.48 million

Osaka is the working heart of Kansai. Famous for its down-to-earth citizens and hearty cuisine, Osaka combines a few historical and cultural attractions with all the delights of a modern Japanese city. Indeed, Osaka is surpassed only by Tokyo as a showcase of the Japanese urban phenomenon.

This isn't to say that Osaka is an attractive city; almost bombed flat in WWII, it appears an endless expanse of concrete boxes punctuated by *pachinko* (pinball) parlours and elevated highways. But the city somehow manages to rise above this and exert a peculiar charm. At night, Osaka really comes into its own; this is when all those drab streets and alleys come alive with flashing neon, beckoning residents and travellers alike with promises of tasty food and good times.

Osaka's highlights include Osaka-jō and its surrounding park, Osaka Aquarium with its enormous whale shark, the *Blade Runner* nightscapes of the Dōtombori area and the wonderful Open Air Museum of Old Japanese Farmhouses. But Osaka has more to offer than its specific sights; like Tokyo, Osaka is a city to be experienced in its totality, and casual strolls are likely to be just as rewarding as structured sightseeing tours.

HISTORY

Osaka has been a major port and mercantile centre from the beginning of Japan's recorded history. It was also briefly the first capital of Japan (before the establishment of a permanent capital at Nara). During its early days, Osaka was Japan's centre for trade with Korea and China, a role which it shares today with Kōbe and Yokohama.

In the late 16th century, Osaka rose to prominence when Toyotomi Hideyoshi, having unified all of Japan, chose Osaka as the site for his castle. Merchants set up around the castle and the city grew into a busy economic centre. This development was further encouraged by the Tokugawa shōgunate, which adopted a hands-off approach to the city, allowing merchants to prosper unhindered by government interference.

In the modern period, Tokyo has usurped Osaka's position as economic centre of Japan, and most of the companies formerly headquartered in Osaka have moved east. However, Osaka is still an economic powerhouse, and the city is ringed by factories churning out the latest in electronics and hi-tech products.

ORIENTATION

Osaka is usually divided into two areas: Kita and Minami. Kita (Japanese for 'north') is the city's main business and administrative centre and contains two of its biggest train stations, JR Osaka and Hankyū Umeda stations.

Minami (Japanese for 'south') is the city's entertainment district and contains the bustling shopping and nightlife zones of Namba and Shinsaibashi. It's also home to two major train stations, JR Namba and Nankai Namba stations.

The dividing line between Kita and Minami is formed by two rivers, the Dōjima-gawa and the Tosabori-gawa, between which you'll find Nakano-shima, a relatively peaceful island that is home to the Museum of Oriental Ceramics. About 1km southeast of Nakano-shima you'll find Osaka-jō and its surrounding park, Osaka-jō-kōen.

To the south of the Minami area you'll find another group of sights clustered around Tennō-ji station. These include Shitennō-ji, Tennō-ji-kōen, Den-Den Town (the electronics neighbourhood) and the retro entertainment district of Shin-Sekai.

The bay area, to the west of the city centre, is home to another set of attractions including the excellent Osaka Aquarium and Universal Studios Japan theme park.

Keep in mind that, while JR Osaka station is centrally located in the Kita area, if you're coming from Tokyo by *shinkansen* you will arrive at Shin-Osaka station, which is three stops (about five minutes) north of Osaka station on the Midō-suji subway line.

Maps

At the visitors information offices (see p376), pick up a free copy of the excellent *Osaka City Map*, which has a subway/tram/train map and insets of the city's most important areas.

INFORMATION
Bookshops

Athens (Map p380; ☎ 6253-0185; ☻ 10am-10pm; ☺ Shinsaibashi station on the Midō-suji subway line)

OSAKA SUBWAY & TRAM MAP

The easiest way to get around Osaka is on the city's excellent subway/tram system. You'll find detailed route maps at every subway station, and the *Osaka City Map*, available at the tourist offices, has a route map. Likewise, this book contains a full Osaka subway/tram map; see p422.

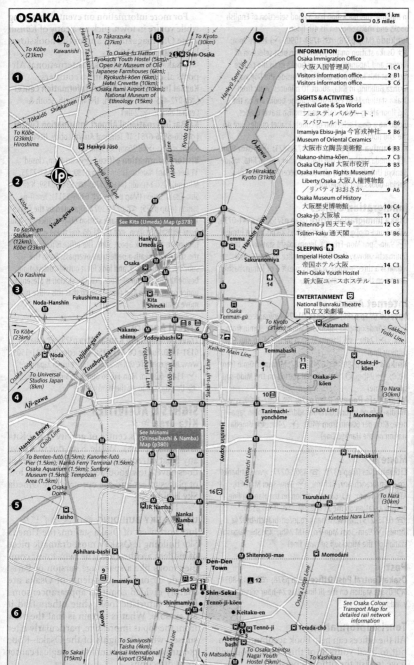

OSAKA

KANSAI

In Minami, this bookshop has a good selection of English books and magazines on its 4th floor.

Junkudō (Map p378; ☎ 4799-1090; ☯ 10am-9pm; ⊕ Osaka station on the JR line) The best selection of foreign and Japanese-language books in Osaka can be found at this huge new bookstore, inside the Dōjima Avanza Building in Kita, about 10 minutes' walk from Osaka station. Most English-language books are on the 3rd floor along with a café, and English travel guides, including a good selection of Lonely Planet guides, are on the 2nd floor.

Kinokuniya (Map p378; ☎ 6372-5821; ☯ 10am-9pm; ⊕ Umeda station on the Hankyū line) Also in Kita, inside Hankyū Umeda station, also has a decent selection of foreign books and magazines.

Immigration Offices

Osaka Immigration Office (Map p375; ☎ 6941-0771; www.immi-moj.go.jp/english/soshiki/kikou/osaka.html; ☯ 9am-5pm Mon-Fri; ⊕ Temmabashi station on the Tanimachi subway line) The main office for the Kansai region is a three-minute walk from exit 3 of Temmabashi station on the Keihan main line.

Internet Access

Aprecio (Map p380; ☎ 6634-0199; www.aprecio.co.jp /namba/index.php in Japanese; Minami; per 30min from ¥200; ☯ 24hr; ⊕ Namba station on the Midō-suji subway line)

Kinko's (Map p380; ☎ 6245-1887; Minami; 10min from ¥200; ☯ 24hr; ⊕ Shinsaibashi station on the Midō-suji subway line)

Media Café Popeye (Map p378; ☎ 6292-3800; www2 .media-cafe.ne.jp/branch/umedadd/index.html in Japanese; Kita; per 60min from ¥400; ☯ 24hr; ⊕ Umeda station on the Hankyū line)

Money

Citibank Kita (Map p378; ☎ 4802-0277; www.citibank .co.jp/en/branch/br025a.html; ☯ 9am-3pm Mon-Fri, ATM 8am-10pm; ⊕ Umeda station on the Hankyū line or Osaka station on the JR line); Minami (Map p380; ☎ 6213-2731; www.citibank.co.jp/en/branch/br024a .html; ☯ 9am-3pm Mon-Fri, ATM 24hr; ⊕ Shinsaibashi station on the Midō-suji subway line)

Post

Osaka Central Post Office (Map p378; ☎ 6347-8034; ⊕ Osaka station on the JR line) Has 24-hour service window.

Tourist Information

All the offices can help book accommodation, but to avail yourself of this service you will have to visit the office in person.

For more information on events happening while you're in town, pick up a copy of *Kansai Time Out* magazine at any of the bookstores listed earlier, p312).

Osaka Itami and Kansai International Airports also have information counters.

Kansai International Airport Information Center (☎ 072-455-2500; 2F/North, 1F&4F/North, South & Central zones; ☯ 24hr)

Kansai International Airport Information Center (☎ 06-6856-6781; 1F Terminal Arrival Lobby, North & South zones; ☯ 8.30am-9.15pm).

Visitors information office (☯ 8am-8pm, closed 31 Dec-3 Jan) Namba station (Map p380; ☎ 6643-2125; Minami); Osaka station (Map p378; ☎ 6345-2189; Kita); Shin-Osaka station (Map p375; ☎ 6305-3311); Tennō-ji station (Map p375; ☎ 6774-3077) Operated by the Osaka Tourist Association, the Osaka station office is tricky to find: from JR Osaka station, exit the Midō-suji ticket gate/exit, turn right, and walk about 50m. The office is just outside the station, beneath a pedestrian overpass. From the subway, go out exit 9, and look for it outside the station, beside the bus terminal. Note that the station is presently under construction and there is word that this office might move again.

Travel Agency

Travel Wonderland Kansai (Map p378; ☎ Asia 06-6131-1500, Europe 06-6131-1504, America 06-6131-1505; www.his-j.com/kix/shiten/kansai-tour.htm in Japanese; ☯ 11am-6.30pm Mon-Fri, to 6pm Sat, Sun & holidays; ⊕ Umeda station on the Hankyū line)

SIGHTS & ACTIVITIES
Kita Area キタ

By day, Osaka's centre of gravity is the Kita area (Map p378). While Kita doesn't have any great attractions to detain the traveller, it does have a few good department stores, lots of places to eat and the eye-catching Umeda Sky building.

UMEDA SKY BUILDING 梅田スカイビル

Just northwest of Osaka station, the Umeda Sky building is Osaka's most dramatic piece of modern architecture. The twin-tower complex looks like a space-age version of Paris' Arc de Triomphe. Residents of Osaka are sharply divided about its appearance: some love its futuristic look while others find it an eyesore. What is certain is that the view from the top is impressive, particularly after sunset, when the lights of the Osaka–Kōbe conurbation spread out like a magical carpet in all directions.

There are two observation galleries: an outdoor one on the roof and an indoor one on the floor below. Getting to the top is only half the fun as you take a glassed-in escalator for the final five storeys (definitely not for vertigo sufferers). Tickets for the **observation decks** (Map p378; ☎ 6440-3855; 1-1-88 Ōyodonaka, Kita-ku; admission ¥700; ⌚ 10am-10.30pm, last entry 10pm; ◉ Osaka station on the JR line) include the white-knuckle escalator ride and can be purchased on the 3rd floor of the east tower.

Below the towers, you'll find **Takimi-kōji Alley** (Map p378), a re-creation of an early Showa-era market street crammed with restaurants and *izakaya*.

The building is reached via an underground passage that starts just north of both Osaka and Umeda stations.

Central Osaka

OSAKA MUSEUM OF HISTORY
大阪歴史博物館

Just southwest of Osaka-jō, the new **Osaka Museum of History** (Osaka Rekishi Hakubutsukan; Map p375; ☎ 6946-5728; 4-1-32 Ōtemae, Chūō-ku; admission ¥600; ⌚ 9.30am-5pm; ◉ Tanimachi-yonchōme station on the Tanimachi subway line) is housed in a fantastic new building adjoining the Osaka NHK Broadcast Center. The display floors of the museum occupy the 7th to the 10th floors of the new, sail-shaped building.

The displays are broken into four sections by floor; you start at the top and work your way down, passing in time from the past to the present. The displays are very well done and there are plenty of English explanations; taped tours are available.

The museum is a two-minute walk northeast of Tanimachi-yonchōme station.

OSAKA-JŌ 大阪城

This **castle** (Osaka Castle; Map p375; ☎ 6941-3044; 1-1 Osaka-jō, Chūō-ku; admission grounds/castle keep free/¥600; ⌚ 9am-5pm, to 8pm Aug, to 6pm Oct; ◉ Osaka-jō-kōen station on the JR Osaka Loop line) was built as a display of power by Toyotomi Hideyoshi after he achieved his goal of unifying Japan. One hundred thousand workers toiled for three years to construct an 'impregnable' granite castle, finishing the job in 1583. However, it was destroyed just 32 years later, in 1615, by the armies of Tokugawa Ieyasu.

Within 10 years the castle had been rebuilt by the Tokugawa forces, but it was to suffer a further calamity when another generation of the Tokugawa clan razed it rather than let it fall to the forces of the Meiji Restoration in 1868.

The present structure is a 1931 concrete reconstruction of the original, which was refurbished at great cost in 1997 (serious fans of Japanese castles should head west to see the castle at Himeji, p398). The interior of the castle houses an excellent collection of displays relating to the castle, Toyotomi Hideyoshi and the city of Osaka. On the 8th floor there is an observation deck offering excellent views of Osaka and surrounding areas.

The castle and park are at their best in the spring cherry-blossom and autumn-foliage seasons.

The Ōte-mon gate, which serves as the main entrance to the park, is a 10-minute walk northeast of Tanimachi-yonchōme station (sometimes written as Tanimachi 4-chome) on the Chūō and Tanimachi subway lines. You can also take the Osaka Loop line, get off at Osaka-jō-kōen station and enter through the back of the castle.

Nakano-shima 中之島

Sandwiched between Dōjima-gawa and Tosa-bori-gawa, this island (Map p375) is a pleasant oasis of trees and riverside walkways in the midst of Osaka's unrelenting grey. It's also home to **Osaka City Hall**, the Museum of Oriental Ceramics and **Nakano-shima-kōen**. The latter park, on the eastern end of the island, is a good place for an afternoon stroll or picnic lunch.

MUSEUM OF ORIENTAL CERAMICS
東洋陶磁美術館

With more than 2700 pieces in its permanent collection, this **museum** (☎ 6223-0055; 1-1-26 Nakanoshima, Kita-ku; admission ¥500; ⌚ 9.30am-5pm, closed Mon; ◉ Yodoyabashi station on the Midō-suji subway line) has one of the finest collections of Chinese and Korean ceramics in the world. At any one time, about 300 of the pieces from the permanent collection are on display, and there are often special exhibits (which cost extra).

To get to the museum, go to Yodoyabashi station on either the Midō-suji line or the Keihan line (different stations). Walk north to the river and cross to Nakano-shima. Turn right, pass the city hall on your left, bear left with the road, and look for the squat brown brick building.

KANSAI

KANSAI

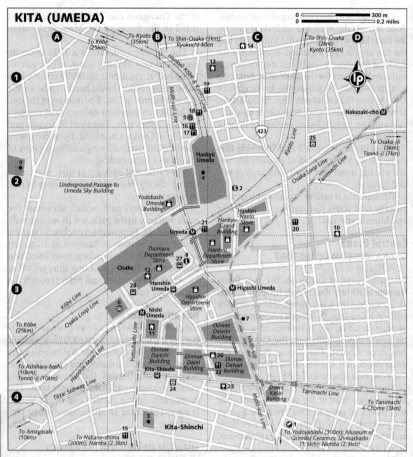

KITA (UMEDA)

Minami Area ミナミ

A few stops south of Osaka station on the Midō-suji subway line (get off at either Shinsaibashi or Namba stations), the Minami area (Map p380) is the place to spend the evening in Osaka. Its highlights include the Dōtombori Arcade, the National Bunraku Theatre, Dōguya-suji Arcade and Amerika-Mura.

Before setting off to explore the sights of Shinsaibashi and Dōtombori, we thoroughly recommend a quick stop at the **Organic Building**, a whimsical building covered with giant flower pots (hence the name). It's situated three blocks north and two blocks west of exit 3 of Shinsaibashi subway station on the Midō-suji line.

DŌTOMBORI 道頓堀

Dōtombori is Osaka's liveliest nightlife area. It's centred around **Dōtombori-gawa** and **Dōtombori Arcade** (Map p380), a strip of restaurants and theatres where a peculiar type of Darwinism is the rule for both people and shops: survival of the flashiest. In the evening, head to **Ebisu-bashi** bridge to sample the glittering nightscape, which brings to mind a scene from the science-fiction movie *Blade Runner*.

Only a short walk south of Dōtombori Arcade you'll find **Hōzen-ji** (Map p380), a tiny temple hidden down a narrow alley. The temple is built around a moss-covered **Fudō-myōō statue**. This statue is a favourite of people employed in *mizu shobai* (water trade) who pause before work to throw some water on the moss-covered statue. Nearby, you'll find **Hōzen-ji Yokochō**, a tiny alley filled with traditional restaurants and bars.

To the south of Dōtombori, in the direction of Nankai Namba station, you'll find a maze of colourful arcades with more restaurants, *pachinko* parlours, strip clubs, cinemas and who knows what else. To the north of Dōtombori, between Midō-suji and Sakai-suji, the narrow streets are crowded with hostess bars, discos and pubs.

DŌGUYA-SUJI ARCADE 道具屋筋

If you desperately need a *tako-yaki* (octopus ball) fryer, a red lantern to hang outside your shop or plastic food models to lure the customers in, this **shopping arcade** (Map p380) is the place to go. You'll also find endless knives, pots, pans and just about anything else that's even remotely related to the preparation and consumption of food.

AMERIKA-MURA アメリカ村

Amerika-Mura (America Village; Map p380) is a compact enclave of trendy shops and restaurants, with a few discreet love hotels thrown in for good measure. The best reason to come is to check out the hordes of colourful Japanese teens living out the myth of America.

In the middle of it all is **Amerika-Mura Triangle Park**, an all-concrete park with benches

where you can sit and watch the parade of fashion victims. Amerika-Mura is one or two blocks west of Midō-suji, bounded on the north by Suomachi-suji and on the south by Dōtombori-gawa.

NATIONAL BUNRAKU THEATRE
国立文楽劇場

Although *bunraku*, or puppet theatre, did not originate in Osaka, the art form was popularised at this **theatre** (☎ 6212-2531; 1-12-10 Nipponbashi, Chūō-ku; ⊕ Nipponbashi station on the Sennichi-mae or Sakai-suji subway line). The most famous *bunraku* playwright, Chikamatsu Monzaemon (1653–1724), wrote plays set in Osaka concerning the classes that traditionally had no place in Japanese art: merchants and the denizens of the pleasure quarters. Not surprisingly, *bunraku* found an appreciative audience among these people, and a theatre was established to put on the plays of Chikamatsu in Dōtombori. Today's theatre is an attempt to revive the fortunes of *bunraku*.

Performances are only held at certain times of the year: check with the tourist information offices. Tickets normally start at around ¥2300; earphones and program guides in English are available.

Tennō-ji & Around 天王寺公園
FESTIVAL GATE フェスティバルゲート

South of Shin-Sekai and west of Tennō-ji-kōen is where you'll find the new entertainment

KANSAI

MINAMI (SHINSAIBASHI & NAMBA)

0 ____ 300 m
0 ____ 0.2 miles

KANSAI

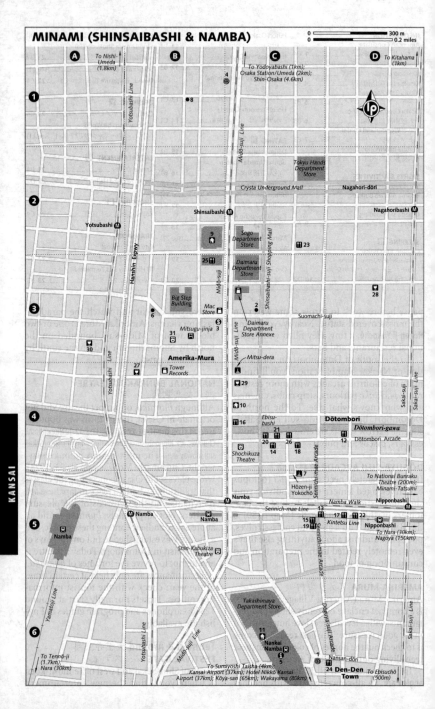

To Nishi-Umeda (1.8km)

To Yodoyabashi (1km);
Osaka Station/Umeda (2km);
Shin-Osaka (4.6km)

To Kitahama (1km)

Yotsubashi Line

Midō-suji Line

Hanshin Expwy

Tokyu Hands Department Store

Crysta Underground Mall   Nagahori-dōri

Shinsaibashi Ⓜ   Nagahoribashi Ⓜ

Yotsubashi Ⓜ

Sogo Department Store

Shinsaibashi-suji Shopping Mall

Daimaru Department Store

Big Step Building

Mac Store

Mitsugu-jinja

Amerika-Mura

Tower Records

Daimaru Department Store Annexe

Mitsu-dera

Suomachi-suji

Ebisu-bashi

Dōtombori

Dōtombori-gawa

Dōtombori Arcade

Shochikuza Theatre

Hōzen-ji Yokochō

To National Bunraku Theatre (200m);
Minami-Tatsumi

Namba Ⓜ

Sennich-mae Line

Namba Walk   Nipponbashi Ⓜ

Namba Ⓜ

Kintetsu Line

Nipponbashi

Sennichi-mae Arcade

To Nara (30km);
Nagoya (150km)

Shin-Kabukiza Theatre

Yamatoji Line

Takashimaya Department Store

Nansan-dōri

To Tennō-ji (1.7km);
Nara (30km)

Midō-suji Line

Nankai Namba Ⓜ

To Sumiyoshi Taisha (4km);
Kansai Airport (37km); Hotel Nikkō Kansai
Airport (37km); Kōya-san (65km); Wakayama (80km)

Dōguya-suji Arcade

Den-Den Town

To Ebisuchō (500m)

Sakai-suji Line

complex of **Festival Gate** (Map p375; ☎ 6635-1000; 3-4-36 Ebisu higashi, Naniwa-ku; admission free, rides average ¥700; ⏱ 10am-7pm, roller coaster operates Sat, Sun & holidays only; ⊕ Shinimamiya station on the JR Osaka Loop line), which is really an amusement park surrounded by a huge shopping-dining complex. The rides are in the open atrium of the complex and the roller coaster snakes its way over and around the walls of the places, offering tantalising glimpses of the city and the nearby Spa World bathing complex. It's a good spot to bring the kids.

SHIN-SEKAI 新世界

For something completely different, take a walk through this retro entertainment district just west of Tennō-ji-kōen. At the heart of it all you'll find crusty old **Tsūten-kaku** tower (Map p375), a 103m-high structure that dates back to 1912 (the present tower was rebuilt in 1969). When the tower first went up it symbolised everything new and exciting about this once-happening neighbourhood (*shin-sekai* is Japanese for 'New World').

Now, Shin-Sekai is a world that time forgot. You'll find ancient *pachinko* parlours, run-down theatres, dirt-cheap restaurants and all manner of raffish and suspicious characters.

SHITENNŌ-JI 四天王寺

Founded in 593, **Shitennō-ji** (Map p375; ☎ 6771-0066; 1-11-18 Shitennō-ji, Tennō-ku; admission free; ⏱ 9am-5pm, closed 28 Dec-1 Jan; ⊕ Shitennōji-mae station on the Tanimachi subway line) has the distinction of being one of the oldest Buddhist temples in Japan, although none of the present buildings are originals; most are the usual concrete reproductions, with the exception of the big stone torii. This dates back to 1294, making it the oldest of its kind in Japan. Apart from the torii, there is little of real historical significance, and the absence of greenery in the raked-gravel grounds makes for a rather desolate atmosphere. The adjoining **museum** (admission ¥200) is of limited interest.

The temple is most easily reached from Shitennōji-mae station on the Tanimachi subway line. Take the southern exit, cross to the left side of the road and take the small road that goes off at an angle away from the subway station. The entrance to the temple is on the left.

SPA WORLD スパワールド

Next door to Festival Gate is the superspa known as **Spa World** (Map p375; ☎ 6631-0001; 3-4-24 Ebisu higashi, Naniwa-ku; per 3hr/full day Mon-Fri ¥2400/2700, Sat, Sun & holidays ¥2700/3000; ⏱ 10am-9pm; ⊕ Dōbutsuen-mae station on the Sakais-uji or Midō-suji subway line). Billed as the world's largest spa, it consists of two floors of baths, one Asian themed and one European themed, and a rooftop waterworld with pools and waterslides, along with restaurants and relaxation areas.

The Asian and European bath floors are segregated by sex; one month the ladies get the Asian bath floor and the men have the European bath floor, and then it switches to the opposite, so you will have to visit twice to sample all the baths (they're fairly similar, so you're not missing much if you don't). We particularly like the *rotemburo* on the roof, where you can show off your tan to folks whizzing by on the Festival Gate roller coaster (and from which you can see Tsūten-kaku tower rising like a retro space ship to the north). Be sure to bring a bathing suit if you want to visit the waterworld (or you can rent one for ¥300).

KANSAI

SUMIYOSHI TAISHA 住吉大社

This **shrine** (☎ 6672-0753; 2-9-89 Sumiyoshi, Sumiyoshi-ku; admission free; ☯ dawn-dusk; ◉ Sumiyoshi-taisha station on the Nankai main line) is dedicated to Shintō deities associated with the sea and sea travel, in commemoration of a safe passage to Korea by a 3rd-century empress.

Having survived the bombing in WWII, Sumiyoshi Taisha actually has a couple of buildings that date back to 1810. The shrine was founded in the early 3rd century and the buildings that can be seen today are faithful replicas of the originals. They offer a rare opportunity to see a Shintō shrine that predates the influence of Chinese Buddhist architectural styles.

The main buildings are roofed with a kind of thatch rather than the tiles used on most later shrines. Other interesting features are a collection of more than 700 stone lanterns donated by seafarers and business people, a stone stage for performances of *bugaku* and court dancing and the attractive Taiko-bashi, an arched bridge set in a park.

It's next to both Sumiyoshi-taisha station on the Nankai main line and Sumiyoshi-torimae station on the Hankai line (the tram line that leaves from Tennō-ji station).

Tempōzan Area 天保山エリア

Trudging through the streets of Kita or Minami, you could easily be forgiven for forgetting that Osaka is actually a port city. A good remedy for this is a trip down to Tempōzan, the best of Osaka's burgeoning seaside developments. On an island amid the busy container ports of Osaka Bay, Tempōzan has several attractions to lure travellers, especially those with children in tow.

Before hitting the main attractions, you might want to get some perspective on it all by taking a whirl on the **Giant Ferris Wheel** (大観覧車; Daikanransha; ☎ 6576-6222; 1-1-10 Kaigan-dōri, Minato-ku; admission ¥700; ☯ 10am-9.30pm; ◉ Osakakō station on the Chūō subway line). Said to be the largest Ferris wheel in the world, the 112m-high wheel offers unbeatable views of Osaka, Osaka Bay and Kōbe. Give it a whirl at night to enjoy the vast carpet of lights formed by the Osaka/Kōbe conurbation.

Next to the Ferris wheel, you'll find **Tempōzan Marketplace** (天保山マーケットプレース; ☎ 6576-5501; 1-1-10 Kaigan-dōri, Minato-ku; admission free; ☯ shops 11am-8pm, restaurants to 9pm; ◉ Osakakō station on the Chūō subway line), a shopping and dining arcade that includes the **Naniwa Kuishinbō Yokochō** (なにわ食いしんぼ横丁; ☎ 6576-5501; 1-1-10 Kaigan-dōri, Minato-ku; admission free; ☯ 10am-8pm; ◉ Osakakō station on the Chūō subway line), a faux-Edo-period food court where you can sample all of Osaka's culinary specialities.

OSAKA AQUARIUM 海遊館

Although it's fairly expensive, **Osaka Aquarium** (☎ 6576-5501; 1-1-10 Kaigan-dōri, Minato-ku; adult/child ¥2000/900; ☯ 10am-8pm; ◉ Osakakō station on the Chūō subway line) is well worth a visit. It's centred around the world's largest aquarium tank, which is home to the aquarium's star attraction, a whale shark, which shares its quarters with an astonishing variety of lesser sharks, rays, tuna and other fish.

A walkway winds its way around the main tank and past displays of life found on eight different ocean levels. The giant spider crabs in the Japan Ocean Deeps section look like alien invaders from another planet. Presentations have both Japanese and English captions and an environmentally friendly slant to them.

Take the Chūō subway line to the Osaka-kō, from where it's about a five-minute walk to the aquarium. Get there for opening time if you want to beat the crowds – on weekends and holidays long queues are the norm.

SUNTORY MUSEUM
サントリーミュージアム

On the southern side of Osaka Aquarium is the **Suntory Museum complex** (☎ 6577-0001; www.suntory.com/culture-sports/smt; 1-5-10 Kaigan-dōri, Minato-ku; admission average ¥1000; ☯ 10.30am-7.30pm, closed Mon; ◉ Osakakō station on the Chūō subway line), which holds an IMAX 3-D theatre and an art gallery with a collection of modern art posters and glass artwork. The building itself, designed by Andō Tadao, is at least as impressive as any of the displays. The **IMAX theatre** (☎ 6577-0001; www.suntory.com/culture-sports/smt; 1-5-10 Kaigan-dōri, Minato-ku; admission ¥1000; ☯ 10.30am-8pm, closed Mon; ◉ Osakakō station on the Chūō subway line) usually has screenings on the hour; check the *Meet Osaka* guide to see what's showing.

Other Areas
OPEN-AIR MUSEUM OF OLD JAPANESE FARMHOUSES 日本民家集落博物館

In Ryokuchi-kōen this fine open-air **museum** (☎ 6862-3137; 1-2 Hattori Ryokuchi, Toyonaka-shi; admission ¥500; ☯ 9.30am-5pm, closed Mon; ◉ Ryokuchi-kōen station on the Midō-suji subway line, west exit) features 11 traditional Japanese country houses and other structures brought here from all over Japan. All have been painstakingly reconstructed and filled with period-era tools and other displays. Most impressive is the giant *gasshō-zukuri* (thatch-roofed) farmhouse from Gifu-ken.

The parklike setting, with plenty of trees and bamboo, gives the whole museum a pleasantly rustic air – and the whole place comes alive with fiery red maple leaves during the November foliage season. For anyone even remotely interested in traditional Japanese architecture, we highly recommend this excellent attraction. An English-language pamphlet is available.

To get there, take the Midō-suji subway line to Ryokuchi-kōen and walk northwest into the park.

UNIVERSAL STUDIOS JAPAN
ユニバーサルスタジオジャパン

Universal Studios Japan (☎ 6465-3000; Universal City; adult/child ¥5800/3900; ⏰ 10am-5pm Mon-Fri, to 6pm Sat, Sun & holidays, with seasonal variations; ⓔ Universal City station on the JR Osaka Loop line) is Osaka's answer to Tokyo Disneyland. Closely based on its two sister parks in the USA, the park features a wide variety of rides, shows, restaurants and other attractions.

To get there, take the JR Loop line to Nishi-kujō station, switch to one of the distinctively painted Universal Studio shuttle trains and get off at Universal City station. From Osaka station the trip costs ¥170 and takes about 20 minutes. There are also some direct trains from Osaka station (ask at the tourist office for times; the price is the same).

OSAKA HUMAN RIGHTS MUSEUM/ LIBERTY OSAKA
大阪人権博物館・リバティおおさか

This **museum** (Map p375; ☎ 6561-5891; 3-6-36 Naniwa nishi, Naniwa-ku; admission ¥250; ⏰ 10am-5pm, closed Mon, closed 4th Fri of every month; ⓔ Ashihara-bashi station on the JR Osaka Loop line), which goes by two names, is dedicated to the suffering of Japan's Burakumin people and other oppressed groups, including Koreans, the handicapped, the Ainu and women. The most fascinating exhibits deal with the Burakumin, outcasts in Japan's four-tiered caste system that was officially outlawed in 1879 under the Emancipation Edict issued by the Meiji government.

An English-language leaflet is available, and you can borrow a tape recorder and English tape for free. Take the JR Osaka Loop line to Ashihara-bashi station, leave via the southern exit, walk south down the main street for five minutes and the museum is on the right of the pedestrian crossing.

NATIONAL MUSEUM OF ETHNOLOGY
国立民族学博物館

Located in Osaka Banpaku-kōen (World Expo Park) this **museum** (☎ 6876-2151; 10-1 Senri Expo Park, Suita; admission ¥420; ⏰ 10am-5pm, closed Wed, closed Thu if the preceding Wed is a national holiday) is arguably Osaka's best, and it's worth the trip from downtown Osaka or Kyoto, especially if there's a good special exhibit on (check the *Kansai Time Out* for upcoming exhibits).

The museum provides a whirlwind tour through the cultural artefacts of many of the world's cultures. Exhibits range from Bollywood movie posters to Thai tuk-tuks, with Ainu textiles, Bhutanese mandalas and Japanese festival floats in between. Exhibits are brilliantly displayed and all seem to merge into a lively kaleidoscope of colours and shapes – the whole is much more than the sum of the parts here. There is almost nothing in the way of English signage or explanations, but most of the materials are self-explanatory. You can also borrow a sheet of English explanations from the reception desk.

To get there from Osaka, take the Midō-suji subway to the last stop, Senri-chūō, and change to the Osaka Monorail and take it two stops east to the Banpaku-kinen-kōen stop. Exit the station, go left, cross the bridge over the highway, buy a ticket from the machines, go through the turnstile and walk towards the huge Tower of the Sun statue. Once past the statue, you will see the museum about 250m in front of you to the northwest (it's got several towers on its roof that resemble cooling towers). From Kyoto, you can take the Hankyū line to Minami Ibaraki station and change there to the Osaka Monorail.

FESTIVALS & EVENTS

Tōka Ebisu Huge crowds of more than a million people flock to the Imamiya Ebisu-jinja (Map p375) to receive bamboo branches hung with auspicious tokens from 9 to 11 January. The shrine is near Imamiya Ebisu station on the Nankai line.

Tenjin Matsuri Held on 24 and 25 July, this is one of Japan's three biggest festivals. Try to make the second day,

KANSAI

when processions of *mikoshi* (portable shrines) and people in traditional attire start at Osaka Temman-gū and end up in O-kawa (in boats). As night falls, the festival is marked with a huge fireworks display.

Kishiwada Danjiri Matsuri Osaka's wildest festival on 14 and 15 September, a kind of running of the bulls except with *danjiri* (festival floats), many weighing over 3000kg. The *danjiri* are hauled through the streets by hundreds of people using ropes, and in all the excitement there have been a couple of deaths – take care and stand back. Most of the action takes place on the second day. The best place to see it is west of Kishiwada station on the Nankai Honsen line (from Nankai station).

SLEEPING

There are plenty of places to stay in and around the two centres of Kita and Minami. Note that it's possible to base yourself in Kyoto when exploring Osaka, and you'll find more budget accommodation in the old capital, which is only about 40 minutes away by train. Keep in mind, however, that the trains stop running a little before midnight, so if you intend to stay out late in Osaka, it makes no sense to stay in Kyoto.

Kita Area
BUDGET
Capsule Inn Osaka/Umeda New Japan Sauna (Map p378; ☎ 6314-2100; 9-5 Dōyama-chō, Kita-ku; men-only capsules ¥2600; 🆇; 🅾 Umeda station on the Hankyū line or Osaka station on the JR line) Located in one of Kita's busiest entertainment districts, this is the place to stay if you miss the last train. It's fairly clean and well maintained, with sauna (from ¥525), Jacuzzi and optional massage services. Note that it's men-only, and if you're over 180cm tall you won't be able to lie flat out.

MIDRANGE
Hotel Sunroute Umeda (Map p378; ☎ 6373-1111; www .sunroute.jp/SunrouteTopHLE.html; 3-9-1 Toyosaki, Kita-ku; s/d/tw from ¥8820/12,600/15,750; 🆇 🖳; 🅾 Nakatsu station on the Midō-suji subway line) A good business hotel, and perhaps the best value in this price range, the Sunroute hits all the right notes: clean rooms, efficient check-in and excellent location. Some of the rooms even have great views over Osaka. It's just north of Hankyū Umeda.

TOP END
Hotel Granvia Osaka (Map p378; ☎ 6344-1235; fax 6344-1130; www.granvia-osaka.jp/english/index.html; 3-1-1 Umeda, Kita-ku; s/d/tw ¥15,592/21,945/23,100; 🆇 🖳;

🅾 Osaka station on the JR line) This hotel can't be beaten for convenience: it's located directly over Osaka station. Rooms and facilities are of a high standard and the views from the restaurants on the upper floors of the building are superb.

Hilton Osaka (Map p378; ☎ 6347-7111; fax 6347-7001; 1-8-8 Umeda, Kita-ku; s ¥18,000-30,800, d ¥22,000-42,000, tw ¥22,000-42,000; 🆇 🖳 🅜; 🅾 Osaka station on the JR line) Just south of JR Osaka station, this is an excellent hotel at home with foreign guests. The rooms are clean and light, with a Japanese touch, and there's a 15m pool in the fitness centre. The views from the 35th-floor Windows on the World bar here are awesome, and there are two floors of great restaurants below the hotel.

ourpick Hotel Hankyū International (Map p378; ☎ 6377-2100; www.hhi.co.jp/new2002/e-index.html; 19-19 Chayamachi, Kita-ku; s/d/tw from ¥34,650/46,200/48,510; 🆇 🖳; 🅾 Nakatsu station on the Midō-suji subway line or Umeda station on the Hankyū line) North of Hankyū Umeda station, this is the most luxurious hotel in town. Rooms are Western size and everything is polished, right down to the marble bathrooms. The *hinoki* (cypress) wooden bathtubs in the Japanese suites are a special touch.

Minami Area
MIDRANGE
Hotel Riva Nankai (Map p380; ☎ 6213-8281; fax 6213-8640; www.hotel-riva.com/in Japanese with English reservation link; 2-5-15 Shinsaibashisuji, Chūō-ku; s/tw/d from ¥11,319/19,404/16,978; 🆇 🖳; 🅾 Namba station on the Midō-suji subway line) Located just a short walk from the Dōtombori area, this is the most reasonably priced hotel (as opposed to business hotel) in Minami. The common areas are nothing special and not particularly intimate, but the rooms are fairly spacious for this price bracket and the staff are friendly.

TOP END
Hotel Nikkō Osaka (Map p380; ☎ 6244-1281; fax 6245-2432; www.hno.co.jp/english/index_e.html; 1-3-3 Nishi-shinsaibashi, Chūō-ku; s/d/tw from ¥21,367/32,917/32,917; 🆇 🖳; 🅾 Shinsaibashi station on the Midō-suji subway line) In Shinsaibashi, this is a good choice, with excellent facilities and a convenient location. All the rooms here are Western style and very clean, including the bathrooms. There is direct access to Shinsaibashi subway station.

Swissotel Nankai Osaka (Map p380; ☎ 6646-1111; fax 6648-0331; http://osaka.swissotel.com; 5-1-60 Namba, Chūō-ku; semidouble/d/tw from ¥31,185/34,650/38,115; 🆇 🖳;

Namba station on the Midō-suji subway line) Minami's most elegant hotel with stunning views and direct connections to KIX via Nankai line trains that depart from Namba station below the hotel. Rooms are clean and well appointed. There is a gym and excellent dining options on-site and nearby.

Other Areas

BUDGET

Osaka Shiritsu Nagai Youth Hostel (大阪市立長居ユースホステル; ☎ 6699-5631; www.nagaiyh.com/english/index.html; 1-1 Nagai-kōen, Higashisumiyoshi-ku; dm HI members/nonmembers from ¥2500/2700, tw ¥3450, r/f per person ¥3000/3500; ✗ ▣; ❶ Tsuruŏaoka station on the JR Hanwa line) This is another good youth hostel, although it's somewhat less conveniently located than the Shin-Osaka Youth Hostel. It's clean, well run, smoke free and many of the staff speak some English. There are private rooms and a family room for up to four people. Take the Midō-suji subway line south from the centre of town to Nagai station, go out exit 1 and walk for 10 minutes towards the stadium. The hostel is at the back of the stadium. Or (for Japan Rail Pass holders), take the JR Hanwa line to Tsurugaoka station and walk southeast for five minutes.

Osaka-fu Hattori Ryokuchi Youth Hostel (大阪府服部緑地ユースホステル; ☎ 6862-0600; www.osakaymca.or.jp/shisetsu/hattori/hattori.html; 1-3 Hattori Ryokuchi, Toyonaka-shi; dm ¥2500; ✗; ❶ Ryokuchi-kōen station on the Midō-suji subway line) Located in Ryokuchi-kōen, this youth hostel is a little long in the tooth and not quite as welcoming as the other two listed here. However, if you fancy a little fresh air in the evening, this is a good choice. No membership is necessary here. It's approximately 15 minutes from Kita or 30 minutes from Minami. Take the Midō-suji line to Ryokuchi-kōen station, take the western exit, enter the park and follow the path past a fountain and around to the right alongside the pond.

Shin-Osaka Youth Hostel (新大阪ユースホステル; Map p375; ☎ 6370-5427; www.osaka-yha.com/shin-osaka/; 1-13-13 Higashinakajima, Higashiyodogawa-ku; dm ¥3300, tw per person ¥4500; ✗ ▣; ❶ Shin-Osaka station on the JR line) Five minutes' walk from Shin-Osaka station, this fine new youth hostel is the closest hostel to the centre of town. On the 10th floor of the impressive Koko Plaza Building, it offers some great views in all directions. The rooms are clean and well taken care of and the staff is friendly. A variety of

private rooms are available, including one barrier-free room. Take the east exit out of Shin-Osaka station (this is only marked from the upper floors of the station); cross the road and go left, passing a small convenience store and a sushi restaurant; turn right just past the sushi restaurant and walk 200m and you will see the large building on your left. Elevators are at the back.

MIDRANGE

Hotel Crevette (ホテル くれべ; ☎ 6843-7201; www.crevette.jp in Japanese; 1-9-6 Kūkō, Ikeda-shi; s/d/tw from ¥7500/13,860/13,860; ✗ ▣; ❶ Hotarugaike station on the Hankyū Takarazuka line) This is the best deal near Itami Airport. Prices are discounted if you make reservations at the main tourist information counter at the airport. The folks at the information counter can also arrange for the hotel's shuttle bus to pick you up. The rooms are fairly small but comfortable enough. They also have a regular shuttle bus to the airport for departures.

TOP END

Hotel Nikkō Kansai Airport (☎ 0724-55-1111; www.nikkokix.com/e/top.html; 1 Senshū Kūkō kita, Izumisano-shi; s/d/tw ¥21,945/32,340/32,340; ✗ ▣ ▣; ❶ Kansai Kūkō station on the JR Kansai Kūkō line) This is the only hotel at KIX and it charges accordingly. But, if you can live with that, it's a good place. The rooms are spacious with some good views, and the staff all speak English. Note that check-in can be slow when a lot of flights are arriving at once.

Imperial Hotel Osaka (Map p375; ☎ 6881-1111; fax 6881-4111; 8-50, Temmabashi 1-chōme, Kita-ku; s/d/tw from ¥31,185/36,960/36,960; ✗ ▣ ▣; ❶ Sakuranomiya station on the JR Osaka Loop line) Within easy walking distance of Osaka-jō, this classic hotel has fairly spacious and well-appointed rooms. There is a fitness club and 25m pool here. The standard of service is very high here and all staff speak English. The location is not particularly convenient, unless you plan to concentrate on Osaka-jō, but there is a shuttle bus to JR Osaka station.

EATING

What Osaka offers is a chance to enjoy what ordinary Japanese enjoy – good food and drink in a rowdy atmosphere. The Osakans call it *kuidaore*, which means 'eat until you drop'. Osaka presents ample opportunities to do just that, with thousands of restaurants lining its cramped streets.

KANSAI

Kita

JAPANESE

Umeda Hagakure (Map p378; ☎ 6341-1409; 1-1-3 Umeda; noodles from ¥600; 🕑 lunch & dinner, closed Sun; ⊙ Osaka station on the JR line) Locals line up outside this place for their fantastic *udon* noodles. It's on the B2 floor of the Ekimae Daisan building. Take the central escalator to the B2 floor, take a right and walk 25m and take another right. It is on the left with a small English sign. There are pictures outside to help with ordering. Our pick here is *tenzaru* (*udon* served on a plate with tempura; ¥1100).

Dōjima Hana (Map p378; ☎ 6345-0141; 2-1-31 Dōjima, Kita-ku; meals from ¥800; 🕑 11am-11pm; ⊙ Osaka station on the JR line) If you crave something a little *kotteri* (rich and fatty), we recommend the tasty *tonkatsu* at this approachable restaurant a stone's throw from the excellent Junkudō bookstore. We recommend the *rosukatsu teishoku* (pork cutlet roast *teishoku*; ¥880/1080 regular/large). There is a limited picture menu and an English sign.

Ganko Umeda Honten (Map p378; ☎ 6376-2001; 1-5-11 Shibata; meals from ¥800; 🕑 11am-late; E; ⊙ Umeda station on the Hankyū line) Big is the operative word at this giant dining hall alongside Hankyū Umeda station that serves a wide variety of Japanese dishes starting with sushi (if you want just sushi, you can sit at the counter and order à la carte). It's very approachable and has an English picture menu. It's just south of the huge DD House entertainment building. Look for the picture of the guy with the headband (the symbol of Ganko).

Isaribi (Map p378; ☎ 6373-2969; 1-5-12 Shibata; dinner from ¥2300; 🕑 11am-2pm & 5-11.15pm Mon-Fri, 4.30-11.15pm Sat, Sun & holidays; ⊙ Umeda station on the Hankyū line) This is a great *robatayaki* place, down a flight of white-tile stairs outside Hankyū Umeda station. Like *yakitori*, this is drinking food, and *nama beeru* (draught beer) really flows at this place. It's a little tricky to spot – look for an English sign near a liquor distributor.

A great place for a cheap lunch or dinner while in Kita is the Shin-Umeda Shokudō-Gai (Map p378), which is located down the escalators and to the right of the main exit of Hankyū Umeda station (just past the McDonald's). There are heaps of good restaurants here that vie for the lunch-dinner custom with cheap set meals, many of which are displayed outside, making ordering easier. Our favourite spot here is a sashimi and grilled fish specialist

called **Maru** (Map p378; ☎ 6361-4552; 9-26 Kakuda-chō; meals from ¥800; 🕑 11.30am-11.30pm; ⊙ Umeda station on the Hankyū line), where the lunchtime sashimi set meal costs about ¥800. It also serves *oden*, the classic Japanese winter dish of meat, vegetables and tofu stewed in broth. To get there, exit Hankyū station via the escalators, walk 10m past the McDonald's, take a left into the corridor and you will see it on the right after about 10m. Pictures of the set meals are on the wall and there's usually a young lady outside beckoning customers.

Another good food court in Kita is the Kappa Yokochō Arcade (marked 'Kappa Plaza' in English) just north of Hankyū Umeda station. Here you'll find **Gataro** (Map p378; ☎ 6373-1484; 1-7-2 Shibata; dinner around ¥3000; 🕑 11am-11pm; E; ⊙ Umeda station on the Hankyū line), a cosy little spot that does creative twists on standard *izakaya* themes. Look for the glass front with credit-card stickers on the left as you head north in the arcade. Unlike most *izakaya*, this one has an English menu.

Another excellent food court is Hilton Plaza, on the B2 floor beneath the Osaka Hilton. Here, you will find the excellent **Shin-kiraku** (Map p378; ☎ 6345-3461; 1-8-16 Umeda, Kita-ku; meals from ¥800; 🕑 11am-2.30pm & 4-11pm; ⊙ Osaka station on the JR line), an excellent tempura specialist that packs 'em in at lunchtime. At lunch try the *ebishio-tendon* (shrimp tempura over rice, ¥880) and at dinner try the *osusume-gozen* (tempura full set; ¥2079). Take the escalator to the B2 floor, go right and look for the small English sign.

INTERNATIONAL

Org...Organic Life (Map p378; ☎ 6312-0529; 7-7 Doyama-chō, Kita-ku; drinks from ¥250, meals ¥900-2500; 🕑 11am-11pm; ⊙ Umeda station on the Hankyū line, Osaka station on the JR line or Higashi Umeda station on the Tanimachi subway line) At this open-plan, casual café you can grab a light meal or a quick pick-me-up while exploring Kita. You can get a pasta or risotto lunch for ¥900 here, and finish it off with cake and coffee. It's easy to spot, with an English sign. There's no English menu, but there is a picture menu and 'pasta lunch' or 'risotto lunch' will get your point across.

Pina Khana (Map p378; ☎ 6375-5828; 1-7-2 Shibata, Kita-ku; lunch/dinner from ¥850/3000; 🕑 11am-3pm & 5-10pm Mon-Thu, 11am-3.30pm & 5-10.30pm Fri-Sun; E, food only; ⊙ Umeda station on the Hankyū line) A crowded spot in the Kappa Yokochō Arcade, this is our favourite Indian restaurant in Kita. The good-value lunch sets usually include a good curry, nan or rice, and tandoori chicken. If you go between noon and 1pm you'll be fighting the salarymen and office ladies for a seat. Look for the Indian flag.

Monsoon Café (Map p378; ☎ 6292-0010; 15-22 Chayamachi, Kita-ku; meals from ¥1000; ☯ 11.30am-4am; E; ◉ Umeda station on the Hankyū line) For a fun night with decent pan-Asian cuisine and a casual international atmosphere, try the Osaka branch of this nationwide chain. It's in the Urban Terrace building, which is across from the Hotel Hankyū International.

Minami
JAPANESE

You will find lots of good Japanese choices in Minami, including a bunch of giant dining halls in Dōtombori Arcade.

Nishiya (Map p380; ☎ 6241-9221; 1-18-18 Higashi Shinsaibashi, Chūō-ku; noodle dishes from ¥630, dinner average ¥4000; ☯ lunch & dinner; E; ◉ Shinsaibashi station on the Midō-suji, Yotsubashi or Nagahori Tsurumiryokuchi subway line) An Osaka landmark that serves *udon* noodles and a variety of hearty *nabe* (iron pot) dishes for reasonable prices, including a *tempura udon* (¥1100). Look for the semirustic façade and the food models about 10m north of the corner.

Tonkatsu Ganko (Map p380; ☎ 6646-4129; 2-2-16 Nambanaka, Naniwa-ku; meals from ¥800; ☯ lunch & dinner; ◉ Namba station on the Nankai Main Line or Midō-suji, Yotsubashi or Sennichi-mae subway line) Sometimes you need something a little heavier than noodles and rice, and *tonkatsu* may be the call. This popular *tonkatsu* specialist near Namba station is easy to spot with food models in the glass case out front (next to an NTT Docomo shop). There's a picture menu.

Gin Sen (Map p380; ☎ 6213-2898; 2-4-2 Shinsaibashi-suji, Chūō-ku; all-you-can-eat kushi-katsu lunch/dinner ¥1980/2980; ☯ 11.30am-11pm; E; ◉ Namba station on the Midō-suji, Yotsubashi or Sennichi-mae subway line) This casual, approachable place serves delicious *kushi katsu* (meat and veggies deep fried on skewers), a greasy but tasty treat. It's on the 2nd floor of the Gurukas building; there's a Lawon convenience store on the ground floor.

Ume no Hana (Map p380; ☎ 6258-3766; OPA Bldg, 11th fl, 1-4-3 Nishi Shinsaibashi, Chūō-ku; dinner from ¥3670; ☯ 11am-4pm & 5-9pm; E; ◉ Shinsaibashi station on the Midō-suji subway line) This is part of an upscale chain that serves a variety of tofu-based dishes. It's on the 11th floor of the OPA building. The

elevator is on the southeast side of the building (entry from the street – look for the sign reading 'OPA Restaurant & Café').

Of course, Minami is all about *shōtengai* (shopping arcades) and the Sennichi-mae Arcade is one of the biggest. In addition to all the *pachinko* parlours here, you'll find lots of cheap, casual restaurants like **Genroku Sushi** (Map p380; 2-11-4 Sennichi-mae; ☯ 10am-10.40pm; ◉ Namba station on the Midō-suji subway line), a bustling automatic sushi place where plates of sushi cost a mere ¥130, and **Izumoya** (Map p380; ☎ 6632-1288; 2-11-10 Sennichi-mae, Chūō-ku; meals from ¥700; 11am-9pm Thu-Tue, closed 2nd & 4th Tue of month; ◉ Namba station on the Midō-suji subway line), an old *unagi* specialist that serves tasty dishes like *mamushi nami* (small *unagi* over rice) for ¥700, or the larger *tokujō* (special *unagi*; ¥1400). It's on the corner with a brownish marble front.

In Osaka half of the action is underground, in the city's vast *chikagai* (underground arcades). Namba Walk, near Nipponbashi station, is particularly packed with restaurants. **Hachisaburō** (Map p380; ☎ 6213-6170; 4-5 Namba Walk, 1 Sennichi-mae, Chūō-ku; sushi meals from ¥2000; ☯ 11am-10pm; E; ◉ Namba station on the Midō-suji, Yotsubashi or Sennichi-mae subway line), a casual sushi restaurant 5m west of the B25 entrance of the arcade, is a decent sushi place where the lunchtime *nigirisushi teishoku* (sushi set) costs only ¥800. Also in Namba Walk, about 5m east of the B29 entrance, is **Minami Taco Ume** (Map p380; ☎ 6213-6218; 5-10 Namba Walk, 1 Sennichi-mae, Chūō-ku; meals from ¥800; ☯ 11am-10pm; ◉ Namba station on the Midō-suji, Yotsubashi or Sennichi-mae subway line), an *oden* specialist that serves an *oden teishoku* for ¥840.

Dōtombori Arcade (Dōtombori, Chūō-ku; Map p380; ◉ Namba station on the Midō-suji, Yotsubashi or Sennichi-mae subway line) is the heart of Minami, and it's crammed with eateries. This is not the place to go for refined dining, but if you want heaping portions of tasty food in a very casual atmosphere, it can be a lot of fun. And because it sees a lot of tourists, most of the big restaurants here have English menus. Here is a quick list of our favourite spots:

Imai Honten (Map p380; ☎ 6211-0319; 1-7-22 Dōtombori, Chūō-ku; noodles from ¥577; ☯ 11am-10pm, closed Wed; E) One of the area's oldest and most revered *udon* specialists and our favourite place on the strip. Try the *tendon* (tempura over rice; ¥1575). It's sandwiched between two *pachinko* parlours. There's no English sign, but the traditional front stands out among the glitter.

Chibō (Map p380; ☎ 6212-2211; 1-5-5 Dōtombori, Chūō-ku; okonomiyaki from ¥800; ☯ 11am-midnight; E)

KANSAI

A great *okonomiyaki* (grilled pancake-like treat) specialist. There's an English sign in addition to the English menu. Try the house special *Dōtombori yaki*, a toothsome treat with pork, beef, squid, shrimp and cheese for ¥1500.

Ganko Zushi (Map p380; ☎ 6212-1705; 1-8-24 Dōtombori, Chūō-ku; set meals from ¥1000; 🕙 11.30am-11pm; E) Giant sushi restaurant (can order à la carte at counter) that serves just about everything else.

Kani Dōraku Honten (Map p380; ☎ 6211-8975; 1-6-18 Dōtombori, Chūō-ku; lunch/dinner from ¥1600/3000; 🕙 11am-11pm; E) Popular crab specialist; look for giant crab on storefront.

Zuboraya (Map p380; ☎ 6211-0181; 1-6-10 Dōtombori, Chūō-ku; fugu sashimi ¥1800, full dinners from ¥3000; 🕙 11am-11pm) A huge *fugu* (Japanese puffer fish) specialist with a good picture menu. Look for the giant *fugu* out front.

INTERNATIONAL

Krungtep (Map p380; ☎ 4708-0088; 1-6-14 Dōtombori, Chūō-ku; lunch buffet/dinner ¥980/2000; 🕙 lunch & dinner, closed Mon; 🚇 Namba station on the Midō-suji, Yotsubashi or Sennichi-mae subway line) Dōtombori's most popular Thai place serves fairly authentic versions of the standard favourites like green curry and fried noodles. Look for the small English sign – it's on the B1 floor.

Finally, if you just feel like a Western-style sandwich or a quick cup of (so-so) coffee, drop into the Doutor (Map p380) at the mouth of the Sennichi-mae Arcade.

DRINKING

Osaka is a hard-working city, but when quitting time rolls around Osakans know how to party. Take a stroll through Minami on a Friday night and you'd be excused for thinking that there is one bar for every resident of the city. Whatever your taste, you're sure to find something to your liking among this vast array of bars and clubs.

Kita キタ

Although Minami is Osaka's real nightlife district, there are plenty of bars, clubs and *izakaya* in the neighbourhoods to the south and east of Osaka station (but be warned that most of the places in Kita-Shinchi cater only to Japanese salarymen on expense accounts).

Canopy (Map p378; ☎ 6341-0339; 1-11-20 Sone-zakishinchi, Kita-ku; 🕙 5pm-6am Mon-Sat, 5pm-midnight Sun; 🚇 Kitashinchi station on the JR Tōzai line) Café-style bar that pulls in a crowd of local expats for after-work snacks and drinks. The happy hour special here is a good and popular deal.

Windows on the World (Map p378; ☎ 6347-7111; 1-8-8 Umeda, Kita-ku; 🕙 11.30am-12.30am; 🚇 Osaka station on the JR line) An unbeatable spot for drinks with a view – it's on the 35th floor of the Hilton Osaka. Be warned that there's a ¥1500-per-person table charge and drinks average ¥1000.

Minami ミナミ

This is the place for a wild night out in Osaka. You simply won't believe the number of bars, clubs and restaurants they've packed into the narrow streets and alleys of Dōtombori, Shinsaibashi, Namba and Amerika-Mura. Go on a weekend night and you'll be part of a colourful human parade of Osaka characters – this is one of Japan's best spots for people-watching.

Pig & Whistle (Map p380; ☎ 6213-6911; meals/drinks from ¥¥500/700; 🕙 5pm-midnight Mon-Thu & Sun, to 1am Fri & Sat; 🚇 Shinsaibashi station on the Midō-suji subway line) Like its sister branch in Kyoto, this is a good place to go for a pint and a plate of fish and chips. It's clearly marked from the street.

Murphy's (Map p380; ☎ 6282-0677; 1-6-31 Higashishinsaibashi, Chūō-ku; average cost per person ¥1000; 🕙 5pm-1am Sun-Thu, to 4am Fri & Sat; 🚇 Nagahoribashi station on the Sakaisuji subway line) This is one of the oldest Irish-style pubs in Japan, and a good place to rub shoulders with local expats and Japanese. It's on the 6th floor of the Reed Plaza Shinsaibashi building, a futuristic building with what looks like a rocket moulded into the front.

SoulFuckTry (Map p380; ☎ 6539-1032; 1-9-14 Minami Horie, Nishi-ku; drinks from ¥700; 🚇 Yotsubashi station on the Yotsubashi subway line) This interestingly named bar-club describes itself as a soul disco, and that pretty much nails it. Like most clubs, it's hit or miss. Turn down the narrow street opposite Eneos gas station.

Cellar (Map p380; ☎ 6212-6437; B1 Shin-sumiya Bldg, 2-17-13 Nishishinsaibashi, Chūō-ku; 🚇 Shinsaibashi station on the Midō-suji subway line) Live music is often the draw at this popular basement bar on the west side of Nishishinsaibashi. Look for the entrance to the stairs a few metres north of the corner.

Tavola 36 (Map p380; ☎ 6646-5125; 5-1-60 Namba, Chūō-ku; 🕙 11.30am-11.30pm Mon-Thu, to midnight Fri, 11am-midnight Sat, to 11.30pm Sun & holidays; 🚇 Namba station on the Nankai Main line) This is where we go when we want something a little swanky. It's an Italian restaurant-bar on the 36th floor of the Swiss Hotel Nankai Osaka. The view is fantastic and the prices are too: there's a

¥1260-per-person table charge after 5.30pm and drinks start at ¥1300.

ENTERTAINMENT

For up-to-date listings of forthcoming club events, check *Kansai Time Out*.

Clubs

Karma (Map p378; ☎ 6344-6181; 1-5-18 Sonezakishinchi, Kita-ku; ⊙ Osaka station on the JR line) A very long-standing club in Kita that is popular with Japanese and foreigners alike. On weekends it usually hosts techno events with cover charges averaging ¥2500.

Grand Café (Map p380; ☎ 6213-8637; 2-10-21 Nishi-shinsaibashi, Chūō-ku; ⊙ Shinsaibashi station on the Mido-suji or Yotsubashi subway line) This hip underground club hosts a variety of electronica-DJ events. There's a comfy seating area and several dance floors. Look for the blue sign at street level.

Traditional Japanese Entertainment

Unfortunately, neither of the following places has regularly scheduled shows. The best thing is to check with the tourist information offices about current shows, check the listings in the *Meet Osaka* guide or look in *Kansai Time Out*.

National Bunraku Theatre (Map p375; ☎ 6212-2531; 1-12-10 Nipponbashi, Chūō-ku; ⊙ Nipponbashi station on the Sennichi-mae or Sakaisuji subway line) This is Osaka's main *bunraku* theatre. It's probably the best place in Japan to see *bunraku*. Just be warned that performances sell out quickly, so plan ahead.

Osaka Nōgaku Hall (Map p378; ☎ 6373-1726; 2-3-17 Nakasakinishi, Kita-ku; ⊙ Osaka station on the JR line) A five-minute walk east of Osaka station, this hall holds nō shows about twice a month, most of which cost ¥4000.

SHOPPING

Osaka has almost as many shops as it has restaurants. Look for department stores in the area around JR Osaka and Umeda stations. Most of the major department stores are represented here.

Osaka's speciality is electronics, and Den Den Town (Map p380) is Osaka's version of Tokyo's Akihabara. Taking its name from the Japanese word for electricity, *denki*, Den Den Town is an area of shops almost exclusively devoted to electronic goods. To avoid sales tax, check if the store has a 'Tax Free' sign outside and bring your passport. Most stores

are closed on Wednesday. Take the Sakaisuji subway line to Ebisu-chō station and take exit 1 or exit 2. Alternatively, it's a 15-minute walk south of Nankai Namba station.

For anything related to cooking and eating, head to the Dōguya-suji Arcade in Minami (p379).

Kōjitsu Sansō (Map p378; ☎ 6442-5267; Osaka Ekimae Daisan Bldg, 1-3 Umeda, Kita-ku; ☉ 10.30am-8pm; ⊙ Osaka station on the JR line) If you need a new backpack or any other kind of outdoor gear, head to this excellent shop on the ground floor at the north-west corner of the Ekimae Daisan building.

GETTING THERE & AWAY

Air

Osaka is served by two airports: the old Osaka Itami airport, which now handles only domestic traffic, and the newer Kansai International Airport (KIX), which handles all international and some domestic flights.

Boat

The **Japan China International Ferry Company** (☎ in Japan 06-6536-6541, in China 021-6325-7642; www.fune.co.jp /chinjif in Japanese) connects Shanghai and Osaka/Kōbe (one way 2nd class ¥20,000/CNY1300, around 48 hours). A 2nd-class ticket costs around US$200.

A similar service is provided by the **Shanghai Ferry Company** (☎ in Japan 06-6243-6345, in China 021-6537-5111; www.shanghai-ferry.co.jp in Japanese). The ferries (one way ¥20,000/CNY1300) leave from the Osaka Nankō international ferry terminal, which can be reached by taking the New Tram service from Suminoe-kōen station to Nan-koguchi station.

Ferries also depart from Nankō ferry terminal and Kanome-futō and Benten-futō piers for various destinations around Honshū, Kyūshū and Shikoku. Destinations and 2nd-class fares include Beppu (from ¥8800, 11½ hours), Miyazaki (from ¥10,400, 12¾ hours), Shibushi (from ¥9900, 14¾ hours) and Shinmoji (from ¥7200, 12 hours) in Kyūshū; Shōdo-shima (from ¥3800, 4½ hours), Mat-suyama (¥6300, 9¼ hours) and Niihama (¥5000, 9¼ hours) in Shikoku.

For detailed information about sailing schedules and bookings contact the tourist information offices.

Bus

There is a long-distance highway bus service between Osaka and cities all across Honshū,

KANSAI

Shikoku and some cities in Kyūshū. Destinations include Tokyo (from ¥4300, eight hours), Nagasaki (¥11,000, 10 hours) and Kagoshima (¥12,000, 11 hours 54 minutes). Most buses depart from JR Osaka station (Map p378); check with the tourist information offices for more details.

Train

KŌBE

The fastest way between Kōbe and Osaka is a JR *shinkaisoku* that runs between JR Osaka station and Kōbe's Sannomiya and Kōbe stations (¥390, 31 minutes).

There is also the private Hankyū line, which takes a little more time but is cheaper. It runs from Osaka's Hankyū Umeda station (Map p378) to Kōbe's Sannomiya station (*tokkyū*, ¥310, 27 minutes).

KYOTO

The fastest way to travel by train between Kyoto and Osaka, other than *shinkansen*, is a JR *shinkaisoku* that runs between JR Kyoto station and JR Osaka station (Map p378; ¥540, 28 minutes).

Another choice is the cheaper private Hankyū line that runs between Hankyū Umeda station in Osaka and Hankyū Kawaramachi, Karasuma and Ōmiya stations in Kyoto (*tokkyū* to Kawaramachi ¥390, 44 minutes).

Alternatively, you can take the Keihan main line between Sanjō, Shijō or Shichijō stations in Kyoto and Keihan Yodoyabashi station in Osaka (*tokkyū* to Sanjō ¥400, 51 minutes). Yodoyabashi is on the Midō-suji subway line.

NARA

The JR Kansai line links Osaka (Namba and Tennō-ji stations) and Nara (JR Nara station) via Hōryū-ji (*kaisoku*, ¥540, 42 minutes).

The private Kintetsu Nara line also connects Osaka (Kintetsu Namba station) with Nara (Kintetsu Nara station). *Kyūkō* (express) and *futsū* services take about 39 minutes and cost ¥540. *Tokkyū* trains do the journey in five minutes less time but at almost double the cost, making them a poor option.

SHINKANSEN

Osaka is on the Tōkaidō–San-yō *shinkansen* line that runs between Tokyo and Hakata (Kyūshū): Hikari *shinkansen* to/from Tokyo (¥13,750, three hours) and Hikari *shinkansen* to/from Hakata (¥14,590, 2¾ hours). Other

cities on this line include Hiroshima, Kyoto, Kōbe and Okayama.

GETTING AROUND
To/From the Airport
OSAKA ITAMI AIRPORT

There are frequent **limousine buses** (Osaka Airport Transport Co; ☎ 06-6844-1124; www.okkbus.co.jp/eng/index.html) running between the airport and various parts of Osaka. Buses run to/from Shin-Osaka station every 20 minutes from about 8am to 9pm (¥490, 25 minutes). Buses run at about the same frequency to/from Osaka and Namba stations (¥620, 30 minutes). At Itami, buy your tickets from the machine outside the arrivals hall.

KANSAI INTERNATIONAL AIRPORT (KIX)

The fastest way by between KIX and Osaka is the private Nankai express Rapit, which runs to/from Nankai Namba station on the Midō-suji subway line (¥1390, 38 minutes). The JR Haruka limited airport express runs between KIX and Tennō-ji station (¥1760, 33 minutes) and Shin-Osaka (¥2470, 51 minutes).

Regular JR express trains called *kankū kaisoku* also run between KIX and Osaka station (¥1160, 70 minutes), Kyōbashi station (¥1160, 66 minutes), Tennō-ji station (¥1030, 53 minutes) and JR Namba station (¥1030, 53 minutes).

The OCAT air terminal, in JR Namba station, allows passengers on Japanese and some other airlines to check in and deposit baggage before boarding trains to the airport. Check with your airline for details.

There are a variety of bus routes between KIX and Osaka. **Limousine buses** (Kansai Airport Transportation Enterprise; ☎ 0724-61-1374; www.kate.co.jp/pc/english/english.html) travel to/from Osaka Umeda, Osaka City Air Terminal (OCAT) Namba, Uehonmachi and Nanko (Cosmo Square) stations. The fare is ¥1300 (¥880 OCAT) for most routes and the journeys take an average of 50 minutes, depending on traffic conditions.

Bus

Osaka does have a bus system, but it is nowhere near as easy to use as the rail network. Japanese-language bus maps are available from the tourist offices.

Train & Subway

Osaka has a good subway network and, like Tokyo, a JR loop line (known in Japanese as the JR Kanjō-sen) that circles the city area. In fact, there should be no need to use any other form of transport while you are in Osaka unless you stay out late and miss the last train.

There are seven subway lines, but the one that most short-term visitors are likely to find most useful is the Midō-suji line, which runs north to south stopping at Shin-Osaka, Umeda (next to Osaka station), Shinsaibashi, Namba and Tennō-ji stations. Most rides cost between ¥200 and ¥300. This book contains a full Osaka subway/tram map; see p422.

If you're going to be using the rail system a lot on any day, it might be worth considering a 'one-day free ticket' (kyōtsū ichinichi jōsha ken). For ¥850 ('no-my car free ticket' ¥600 on Fridays and the 20th of every month only) you get unlimited travel on any subway, the New Tram line and all city buses (but not the JR line). Note, however, that you would really have to be moving around a lot to save any money with this ticket. These tickets can be purchased from some of the ticket machines in most subway stations; push the button for 'one-day free ticket' (kyōtsū ichinichi jōsha ken) then press the illuminated button reading '¥850'.

KŌBE 神戸

☎ 078 / pop 1.5 million

Perched on a hillside overlooking the sea, Kōbe is one of Japan's most attractive cities. It's also one of the country's most cosmopolitan, having served as a maritime gateway to Kansai from the earliest days of trade with China. To this day, there are significant populations of other Asian nationalities in Kōbe, as well as plenty of Westerners, many of whom work in nearby Osaka.

For many, Kōbe will always be associated with the Great Kōbe Earthquake of 17 January 1995, which levelled whole neighbourhoods and killed more than 6000 people. Fortunately, the city has risen, Phoenix-like, from the ashes and is now more vibrant than ever.

One of Kōbe's best features is its relatively small size – most of the sights can be reached on foot from the main train stations. Of course, it must be noted that none of these sights are must-sees: Kōbe is likely to appeal more to residents than to travellers. However, it does have some good restaurants, cafés and

bars and is a good place for a night out in Kansai if you just can't face the mayhem of Osaka.

ORIENTATION

Kōbe's two main entry points are Sannomiya and Shin-Kōbe stations. Shin-Kōbe station, in the northeast of town, is where the shinkansen stops. A subway (¥200, one minute) runs from here to the busier Sannomiya station, which has frequent rail connections with Osaka and Kyoto. It's possible to walk between the two stations in around 20 minutes. Sannomiya station marks the city centre, although a spate of development in Kōbe Harbor Land is starting to swing the city's centre of gravity to the southwest. Before starting your exploration of Kōbe, pick up a copy of the Kōbe City Map at one of the two information offices.

INFORMATION

The city's main **tourist information office** (☎ 322-0220; ☺ 9am-7pm) is on the ground floor on the south side of JR Sannomiya station's west gate (follow the signs for Santica, a shopping mall). There's a smaller information counter on the 2nd floor of Shin-Kōbe station. Both information centres carry the free Kōbe City Map and the Kōbe Guide Map.

Citibank (☎ 392-4122; ☺ 9am-3pm Mon-Fri, ATM 24hr; ◉ Sannomiya station on the Hankyū Kōbe line, Hanshin Main line or JR Kōbe line) Behind Kōbe City Hall; ATM accepts international cards.

H.I.S. (☎ 335-2505; ☺ 10am-6.30pm Mon-Fri, 11am-5pm Sat; ◉ Motomachi station on the Hanshin Main line or JR Kōbe line) Travel agency on the 2nd floor near the corner, diagonally across from Motomachi station.

Random Walk (☎ 332-9200; ☺ 10am-8pm; ◉ Motomachi station on the JR Kōbe line) Small English-language bookshop on 2nd floor in shopping street.

Wantage Books (☎ 232-4517; ☺ 9.30am-5.30pm Mon-Fri; ◉ Shin-Kōbe station on the Seishin-Yamate subway line) Near Shin-Kōbe, used book specialist. Also houses office of Kansai Time Out magazine.

SIGHTS
Kitano 北野

Twenty minutes' walk north of Sannomiya is the pleasant hillside neighbourhood of Kitano, where local tourists come to enjoy the feeling of foreign travel without leaving Japanese soil. A European-American atmosphere is created by the winding streets and ijinkan (literally 'foreigners' houses') that housed some of Kōbe's early Western residents. Admission to

KANSAI

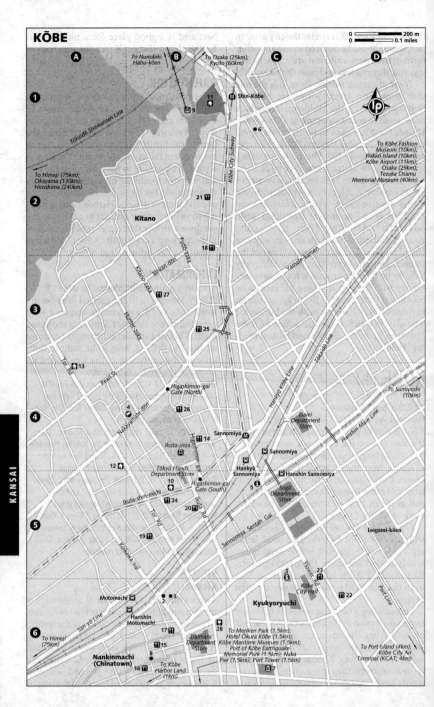

KŌBE

To Nunobiki
Habu-kōen

To Osaka (25km);
Kyoto (60km)

Shin-Kōbe

To Kōbe Fashion
Museum (10km);
Rokkō Island (10km);
Kōbe Airport (11km);
Osaka (25km);
Tezuka Osamu
Memorial Museum (40km)

To Himeji (75km);
Okayama (130km);
Hiroshima (240km)

Tōkaidō Shinkansen Line

Kōbe City Subway

Kitano

Kitano-zaka

Ijinkan-dōri

Fudō-zaka

Yamate-kansen

Tōkaidō Line

Hankyū Kōbe Line

To Sumiyoshi
(10km)

Tor Rd

Hunter-zaka

Nakayamate-dōri

Pearl St

Higashimon-gai
Gate (North)

Ikuta-jinja

Higashimon-gai-dōri

Sannomiya

Daiei
Department
Store

Hanshin Main Line

Tōkyū Hands
Department Store

Higashimon-gai
Gate (South)

Hankyū
Sannomiya

Sannomiya

Hanshin Sannomiya

Ikuta Rd

Ikuta-shin-michi

Sōgō
Department
Store

Isogami-kōen

Tor Rd

Kōnewa-suji

Sannomiya Sentah Gai

Flower Rd

Port Line

Kōbe
City Hall

Kyukyoryuchi

Motomachi

San-yō Line

Hanshin
Motomachi

To Himeji
(75km)

Nankinmachi
(Chinatown)

To Kōbe
Harbor Land
(1km)

Daimaru
Department
Store

To Meriken Park (1.5km);
Hotel Ōkura Kōbe (1.5km);
Kōbe Maritime Museum (1.5km);
Port of Kōbe Earthquake
Memorial Park (1.5km); Naka
Pier (1.5km); Port Tower (1.5km)

To Port Island (4km);
Kōbe City Air
Terminal (KCAT; 4km)

0 — 200 m
0 — 0.1 miles

A   B   C   D

1

2

3

4

5

6

KANSAI

INFORMATION			
Citibank シティバンク	**1** C5	Mon もん	**20** B5
H.I.S エイチアイエス	**2** B6	Nailey's Café ネイリーズ カフェ	**21** B2
Kansai Time Out Office		Okagawa お河川	**22** D6
関西タイムアウト オフィス	(see 6)	Shokutakuya 食卓家	**23** C5
Random Walk ランダムウォーク	**3** B6	Sona Rupa ショナルパ	**24** B5
South Korea Consulate		Tanoshiya 楽舎	**25** B3
大韓民国大使館	**4** B4	Toritetsu とり鉄	**26** B4
Tourist Information Office		Upwards アップワーズ	**27** B3
観光案内所	**5** C5	Wakkoku 和黒	(see 11)
Wantage Books			
ウォンテージ ブックス	**6** C1	**DRINKING** 🍸	
		New Munchen Club	
SIGHTS & ACTIVITIES		ニューミュンヘンクラブ	**28** B6
Kōbe City Museum 神戸市立博物館	**7** C6		
Nankinmachi Square 南京町	**8** B6	**SHOPPING** 🛍	
Shin-Kōbe Cable Car	**9** B1	Avenue shopping centre	
		アベニュー	(see 11)
SLEEPING 🛏			
B Kōbe ザ・ビー神戸	**10** B5		
Crowne Plaza Kōbe			
クラウンプラザ神戸	**11** B1		
Hotel Tor Road ホテルトアロード	**12** A4		
Kōbe Kitano Hotel			
神戸北野ホテル	**13** A4		
EATING 🍴			
Daruma 達磨	**14** B4		
Furuya 古屋	**15** B6		
Ganso Gyōza-en			
がんそぎょうざ苑	**16** B6		
Kintoki 金時	**17** B6		
Mikami 味加味	**18** B2		
Modernark Pharm			
モダナーク ファーム	**19** B5		

some is free, to others ¥300 to ¥700, and most are open from 9am to 5pm daily. Although these brick and weatherboard dwellings may not hold the same fascination for Western travellers that they hold for local tourists, the area itself is pleasant to stroll around and is dotted with good cafés and restaurants.

Shin-kōbe Cable Car & Nunobiki Hābu-kōen
新神戸ロープウェイ・布引ハーブ公園
The **Shin-Kōbe cable car** (Shin-Kōbe Ropeway; one way/return ¥550/1000; ☉ 9.30am-5.30pm, later in summer; ❷ Shin-Kōbe station on the Seishin-Yamate subway line) leaves from behind the Crowne Plaza Kōbe hotel near Shin-Kōbe station and ascends to a mountain ridge 400m above the city. The views from the top over Kōbe and the bay are particularly pretty after sunset. There's a complex of gardens, restaurants and shops below the top station known as the **Nunobiki Hābu-kōen** (Nunobiki Herb Garden; admission ¥200; ☉ 10am-5pm, open later in summer; ❷ Nunobiki Hābu-kōen station on the Shin-Kōbe Ropeway). Note that you can easily walk down to the bottom station from the Herb Garden in about 30 minutes.

Kōbe City Museum 神戸市立博物館
This **museum** (Kōbe Shiritsu Hakubutsukan; ☎ 391-0035; 24 Kyō-machi, Chūō-ku; admission varies by exhibition; ☉ 10am-5pm, closed Mon; ❷ Sannomiya station on the JR Kōbe line) has a collection of so-called Namban (literally 'southern barbarian') art and occasional special exhibits. Namban art is a school of painting that developed under the influence of early Jesuit missionaries in Japan, many of whom taught Western painting techniques to Japanese students. The entrance is on the east side of the building.

Nankinmachi (Chinatown) 南京町
Nankinmachi, Kōbe's Chinatown, is a gaudy, bustling, unabashedly touristy collection of Chinese restaurants and stores that should be familiar to anyone who's visited Chinatowns elsewhere in the world. The restaurants here tend to be overpriced and may disappoint sophisticated palates, but the place is fun for a stroll particularly in the evening, when the lights of the area illuminate the gaudily painted façades of the shops. If you fancy a bite while touring the area, we recommend a plate of *gyōza* and we list two good choices (see p396).

Kōbe Harbor Land & Meriken Park
神戸ハーバーランド
Five minutes' walk southeast of Kōbe station, Kōbe Harbor Land is awash with new megamall shopping and dining developments. This may not appeal to foreign travellers the way it does to the local youth, but it's still a nice place for a stroll in the afternoon. For a good view of the area, take the free glass lift to the 18th floor of the **Ecoll Marine building**.

A five-minute walk to the east of Harbor Land you'll find Meriken Park, on a spit of reclaimed land jutting out into the bay. The main attraction here is the **Kōbe Maritime Museum** (Kōbe Kaiyō Hakubutsukan; ☎ 327-8983; 2-2 Hatoba-chō, Chūō-ku; admission ¥500; ☉ 10am-5pm, closed Mon; ❷ Motomachi station on the JR Kōbe line). The museum has a small collection of ship models and displays, with some English explanations.

Rokkō Island 六甲アイランド
An artificial island, the main attraction here is the **Kōbe Fashion Museum** (Kōbe Fashion Bijutsukan; ☎ 858-0050; 2-9-1 Kōyōchōnaka, Higashinada-ku; admission ¥500; ☉ 10am-6pm, closed Wed; ❷ Island Centre station on

KANSAI

the Rokkō Liner monorail). The museum's collection of mostly foreign fashion is not quite up to the dramatic building in which it's housed but it's worth a look if you're interested in fashion. To reach the museum, take the Rokkō Liner monorail (¥240) from JR Sumiyoshi (four stops east of Sannomiya) and get off at the Island Centre stop.

Hakutsuru Sake Brewery Museum
白鶴記念造酒資料館

The Nada-ku area of Kōbe is one of Japan's major sake-brewing centres and the dominant brewer here is the famous Hakutsuru company. The **Hatsukuru Sake Brewery Museum** (☎ 822-8907; 4-5-5 Sumiyoshi Minami-machi, Higashi-nada-ku; admission free; ☯ 9.30am-4.30pm, closed Mon, New Year & Obon; ☺ Sumiyoshi station on the Hanshin Main line) provides a fascinating look into traditional sake-making methods. There is not much in the way of English explanations, but the free English pamphlet should get you started. Free sake tasting is possible after you tour the facilities (ask at the counter).

Take the Hanshin line eight stops east from Sannomiya (¥180, 15 minutes, express trains do not stop) and get off at Hanshin Sumiyoshi station. Exit the station and walk south to the elevated highway and cross the pedestrian overpass; take a right at the bottom of the steps; take your first left, then a right and look for it on the right (there is no English sign). You have to sign in at the gate. Use the blue-and-white crane logo atop the modern wing of the factory as your guide.

Tezuka Osamu Memorial Museum
手塚治虫記念館

While it's a bit of a hike from downtown Kōbe, this fine **museum** (☎ 0797-81-2970; 7-65 Mukogawa-chō, Takarazuka; adult/child ¥500/100; ☯ 9.30am-5pm, to 8pm in summer, closed Wed) is a must for serious fans of Japanese manga. Located in the town of Takarazuka (a short train ride from Kōbe's Sannomiya station), it celebrates the life and work of Tezuka Osamu, the father of Japanese animation and manga, and a man of such legendary output that his last words were rumoured to be 'I'm begging you, let me work!'.

Tezuka's creations include *Tetsuwan Atomu* (Astro Boy) and *Black Jack* and *Rion Kōtei* (Jungle Emperor Leo, which Disney adapted to make the film *The Lion King*). The museum details Tezuka's life and has several of his childhood drawings and diagrams from his time as a doctor. A small theatre plays an original anime film every 20 minutes (no spoken dialogue) and the 2nd floor has booths where you can watch a variety of old episodes such as the original 1960s *Astro Boy* pilot. First editions of his publications are also on display, and large manga collections are available to peruse.

The museum is a five-minute walk east of Hankyū Takarazuka station. To get to this station, take the Hankyū Takarazuka line from Nishinomiya station, which is on the main Hankyū line between Osaka and Kōbe. From Kōbe's Sannomiya station, the ride costs ¥270 and takes around 45 minutes with good connections (be sure to take the *tokkyū*). After exiting the station, follow the scenic Hana-no-Michi (Flower Ave); when this floral pathway ends, keep going east. Look for the building capped with a glass globe.

FESTIVALS & EVENTS

Luminarie, Kōbe's biggest yearly event, is held every evening from around 12 to 25 December to celebrate the city's miraculous recovery from the 1995 earthquake (check with the Kōbe tourist information office to be sure of the dates as they change slightly every year). The streets southwest of Kōbe City Hall are decorated with countless illuminated metal archways, which when viewed from within look like the interior of some otherworldly cathedral.

SLEEPING

B Kōbe (☎ 333-4880; fax 333-4876; www.ishinhotels.com/theb-kobe/en/index.html; s/d/tw from ¥8400/13,650/15,750; ☒ ▯ ; ☺ Sannomiya station on the Seishin-Yamate subway line) The newly renovated and centrally located B Kōbe is a good utilitarian choice if you've got business in Kōbe or just want a clean place to lay your head in the evening. The windows are tiny and there's not much light, but if you're only there at night this shouldn't matter too much. We recommend springing for the deluxe twin rooms here (¥18,900).

Hotel Tor Road (☎ 391-6691; fax 391-6570; www.hoteltorroad.co.jp in Japanese; s/d/tw from ¥8662/17,325/17,325; ☒ ▯ ; ☺ Sannomiya or Motomachi station on the JR Kōbe line) A step up from the typical business hotel, this Tor Road hotel is a good choice for those who want a little more comfort. Beds are larger than normal for this sort of hotel and quite clean. The friendly staff is another plus.

Crowne Plaza Kōbe (☎ 291-1121; fax 291-1151; www.ichotelsgroup.com/h/d/cp/1/en/hotel/osakb; s/d/tw from ¥15,015/26,565/26,565; 🍴 🖥 ; 🚇 Shin-Kōbe station on the Seishin-Yamate subway line or JR Sanyō Shinkansen) You'll feel on top of the world as you survey the bright lights of Kōbe from this perch atop the city. Conveniently located near JR Shin-Kōbe station, this first-class hotel offers clean and fairly spacious rooms and has an English-speaking staff. Downstairs in the Avenue shopping centre, you'll find several good restaurants to choose from.

our pick **Hotel Ōkura Kōbe** (☎ 333-0111; fax 333-6673; kobe.okura.com; s/d/tw from ¥16,800/22,050/26,250; 🍴 🖥 ; 🚇 Motomachi station on the JR Kōbe line or Hanshin Main line) The Ōkura is the most comfortable and polished hotel in the city, and the harbourside location can't be beat. The rooms are clean, spacious and well maintained. Avoid the lower-floor rooms on the north side as these offer only highway views. There are several good on-site restaurants here.

Kōbe Kitano Hotel (☎ 271-3711; fax 271-3700; www .kobe-kitanohotel.co.jp/en/index.html; 3-3-20 Yamamoto-dōri, Chūō-ku; d/tw from ¥25,200/27,300; 🍴 ; 🚇 Sannnomiya or Motomachi station on the JR Kōbe line) This British-themed hotel is popular with Japanese ladies, who like the European feeling of the Kitano area, with its pleasant strolling and abundant café's. This place does a brisk business in hosting weddings, but it's also a nice place to stay. Unlike many other hotels in Japan, the rooms are fairly large and have bright and spacious bathrooms.

EATING
Japanese
Although Kōbe is more famous for its international cuisine, there are plenty of good Japanese restaurants to be found.

Kintoki (☎ 331-1037; 1-7-2 Motomachi-dōri, Chūō-ku; meals from ¥500; 🕙 10.30am-7pm, closed holidays; 🚇 Motomachi station on the JR Kōbe line or Hanshin Main line) This is a good place to go for a taste of what Japan was like before it got rich. It's an atmospheric old *shokudō* that serves the cheapest food in the city. You can order standard noodle and rice dishes from the menu (plain *soba* or *udon* noodles are ¥250 and a small rice is ¥160) or choose from a variety of dishes laid out on the counter. Look for the blue-and-white awning about 20m north of the shopping street next to Evian Coffee Shop.

Mikami (☎ 242-5200; 2-5-9 Kitano-chō; meals from ¥420; 🕙 11am-3pm & 5-10pm, closed Wed; E; 🚇 Shin-Kōbe station on the subway Seishin-Yamate line) This is a friendly spot for good-value lunch and dinner sets of standard Japanese fare. Noodle dishes are available from ¥420 and *teishoku* from ¥950. Look for the large doghouse outside and a small English sign.

Shokutakuya (☎ 242-4060; 4-2-18 Hachiman-dōri, Chūō-ku; meals from ¥800; 🚇 Sannomiya station on the JR Kōbe line, Hankyū Kōbe line or Hanshin Main line) Near Kōbe City Hall, this simple basement *izakaya/* restaurant serves filling sets of typical Japanese favourites like the *tonkatsu gozen* (fried pork fillet set, ¥890). There's a picture menu and a small English sign on street level (it's at the corner).

Mon (☎ 331-0372; 2-12-2 Ikatsuji, Chūō-ku; meals from ¥1100; 🕙 11am-9pm, closed 3rd Thu of month; E; 🚇 Sannomiya station on the subway Seishin-Yamate line or Hankyū Kōbe line) This Kōbe institution serves a peculiar Japanese speciality known as *yōshoku*: Japanese versions of Western food like steaks and pork cutlets. It's pretty much what the Japanese imagined Westerners ate morning, noon and night when they first started showing up in those black ships. If you're in the mood for something heavier than noodles and rice, this might satisfy. The sign out front has a hilarious picture of two 'barbarians' who look like they could really go for a nice steak.

Okagawa (☎ 222-3511; 4-1-11 Hachiman-dōri, Chūō-ku; tempura from ¥1100; 🕙 lunch & dinner, closed Mon; E; 🚇 Sannomiya station on the JR Kōbe line, Hankyū Kōbe line or Hanshin Main line) Not far from Kōbe City Hall, this fine tempura specialist is an oasis of calm, clean lines and good service. There are plenty of sets to choose from, and you won't go wrong with the *anago tendon* (conger eel tempura over rice; ¥1200). It's hard to spot at the top of a flight of steps over a place called Daiichi (the stairs are on the left – look for the giant black spoon). There is a small English sign on street level.

Daruma (☎ 331-2446; 1-16-3 Nakayamate-dōri, Chūō-ku; yakitori dinner per person from ¥2000; 🕙 5-10.30pm, closed Mon; 🚇 Sannomiya station on the JR Kōbe line, Hankyū Kōbe line or Hanshin Main line) This quaint little mom-and-pop *yakitori* restaurant serves simple skewers of the usual *yakitori* favourites and a very interesting Japan Alps dish known as *hōba miso* (¥550), which is a type of *miso* cooked over a leaf on a hibachi in front of you. There is no English menu, but it's easy to point at what you want. You'll be asked whether you want *shio-yaki* (cooked with salt) or *tare-yaki* (cooked with *yakitori* sauce). There is an English sign (it's 10m in from Higashimon-gai).

Tanoshiya (☎ 242-1132; 1F Matsuda Bldg, 3-14-8 Kanō-chō, Chūō-ku; lunch/dinner from ¥1600/3500; ⏲ 11.30am-2.30pm & 5pm-midnight; E; ◉ Sannomiya station on the JR Kōbe line, Hankyū Kōbe line or Hanshin Main line) This casual spot serves creative and fun food that might be termed 'nouvelle Japonaise'. This might include seared sashimi, skewers of chicken and assorted nibbles on the side. The chef speaks a bit of English. Look for the bamboo sign across from a diving school.

Toritetsu (☎ 327-5529; 1-16-12 Nakayamate-dōri, Chūō-ku; dinner per person from ¥3000; ⏲ 5pm-midnight; ◉ Sannomiya station on the JR Kōbe line, Hankyū Kōbe line or Hanshin Main line) Almost opposite the Daiichi Grand Hotel on Higashimon-gai, this bustling yakitori restaurant is a good place to eat, drink and watch the chefs labour over their grills. The sign says 'yakitori' in English. There is some English on the menu.

Wakkoku (☎ 262-2838; 3F Shin Kōbe Oriental Avenue shopping mall, 1-1 Kitano-chō Chūō-ku; lunch/dinner from ¥2500/8000; ⏲ 11.45am-10.30pm; E; ◉ Shin-Kōbe station on the Seishin-Yamate subway line) If you're a carnivore, you will want to try a bit of Kōbe's famous beef, and you'll find it cheaper and better here than overseas. Our favourite Kōbe beef place is this relatively approachable spot below the Crowne Plaza Kōbe. The steaks here are among the best we've had anywhere. We particularly like the way they 'introduce' your steak to you before they prepare it. It's on the 3rd floor of the Avenue shopping centre at the base of the hotel, just outside the elevator bank on the south side. There is no English sign – look for the black and grey marble exterior.

International

Furuya (☎ 322-1230; 1-6-17 Motomachi-dōri, Chūō-ku; 8 gyōza from ¥320; ⏲ 2-10pm; ◉ Motomachi station on the JR Kōbe line) We can't quite figure this place out: it's a gyōza specialist decorated with skiing, snowboarding and *The Sopranos* memorabilia. Sure, it makes no sense, but the owner is a friendly chap and the dumplings are great. Look above the restaurant for a sign that reads 'Original Gyoza Restaurant' in English.

Ganso Gyōza-en (☎ 331-4096; 2-8-11 Sakaemachi-dōri, Chūō-ku; 6 gyōza ¥380; ⏲ lunch & dinner, closed Mon; ◉ Motomachi station on the JR Kōbe line or Hanshin Main line) This is the best spot in Nankinmachi for

gyōza. Try its wonderful fried dumplings *(yaki gyōza)* at lunch or dinner. At dinner it also makes steamed gyōza *(sui gyōza)*. Use the vinegar, soy sauce and *miso* on the table to make a dipping sauce. It's next to a small parking lot – look for the red-and-white awning.

Nailey's Café (☎ 231-2008; 2-8-12 Kanō-chō, Chūō-ku; coffee from ¥430, lunch/dinner from ¥1050/1200; ⏲ 11.30am-late, closed Tue; E; ◉ Shin-Kōbe station on the Seishin-Yamate subway line) Hip little café that serves espresso, light lunches and dinners. The menu here is European influenced and includes such things as pizza, pasta and salads. This is a good spot for an evening drink.

Modernark Pharm (☎ 391-3060; 3-11-15 Kitanagasa-dōri, Chūō-ku; lunch/dinner from ¥1000/2000; ⏲ 11.30am-10pm, closed irregularly; E; ◉ Motomachi station on the JR Kōbe line) This interesting little restaurant serves tasty sets of Japanese and Western dishes, including burritos and rice dishes. There are some veggie choices here. Look for the plants.

Upwards (☎ 230-8551; 1-7-16 Yamamoto-dōri, Chūō-ku; meals from ¥1000; ⏲ 11.30am-midnight Tue-Sun; ◉ Sannomiya station on the JR Kōbe line, Hankyū Kōbe line or Hanshin Main line) This fashionable eatery in Kitano serves pasta, sandwiches and salads in an airy, open space. It's another good spot for a drink in the evening. There's an English sign.

Sona Rupa (☎ 322-0252; 2-2-9 Yamate-dōri, Chūō-ku; lunch/dinner from ¥1650/3200; ⏲ 11.30am-2pm & 5.30-9.30pm Thu-Tue; E; ◉ Sannomiya station on the JR Kōbe line, Hankyū Kōbe line or Hanshin Main line) We like this small Indian restaurant for its crispy nan bread, tasty curries and tranquil atmosphere. It's on the 3rd floor, with a sign on street level.

DRINKING

Kōbe has a large foreign community and a number of bars that see mixed Japanese and foreign crowds. For Japanese-style drinking establishments, try the *izakaya* in the neighbourhood between the JR tracks and Ikutajinja. Also bear in mind that a lot of Kōbe's nightlife is centred around the city's many cafés, most of which transform into bars come evening (see left).

New Munchen Club (☎ 335-0170; 47 Akashi-chō, Chūō-ku; ⏲ 11am-11pm; ◉ Motomachi station on the JR Kōbe line) A decent German-style pub that draws its share of foreign residents. It's got a picture menu for food. It can be a little smoky, but the beer is good and it's easy to enter. It's close to Daimaru department store, on the basement floor.

GETTING THERE & AWAY
Boat
China Express Line (☎ in Japan 078-321-5791, in China 022-2420-5777; www.celkobe.co.jp in Japanese) operates a ferry (2nd-class ¥23,000, around 48 hours) between Kōbe and Tientsin. It departs Kōbe every Friday at 11.30am.

There are regular ferries between Kōbe and Shikoku (Imabari and Matsuyama) and Kyūshū (Ōita). Most ferries depart from Rokkō Island and are operated by **Diamond Ferry Company** (☎ 857-9525; www.diamond-ferry.co.jp in Japanese). The cheapest fares are as follows: Imabari ¥5400, Matsuyama ¥6300 and Ōita ¥8800.

Train
JR Sannomiya station is on the JR Tōkaidō line as well as the private Hankyū and Hanshin lines (both of which run to/from Osaka).

The fastest way between Kōbe and Osaka station (¥390, 24 minutes) or Kyoto (¥1050, 54 minutes) is the JR *shinkaisoku*.

The Hankyū line is the more convenient of the two private lines, running between Kōbe's Hankyū Sannomiya station and Osaka's Hankyū Umeda station. Osaka has connections to/from Kyoto on the Hankyū line. Fares and times are as follows: Osaka – *tokkyū*, ¥310, 27 minutes; Kyoto – *tokkyū*, ¥600, 63 minutes, change at Jūsō or Umeda.

Shin-Kōbe station is on the Tōkaidō to Sanyō *shinkansen* line. The Hikari *shinkansen* goes to/from Fukuoka (¥14,270, two hours 32 minutes) and to/from Tokyo (¥14,270, three hours 18 minutes).

Note that there are several discount ticket shops near Hankyū Sannomiya station.

GETTING AROUND
To/From the Airport
ITAMI OSAKA AIRPORT
There are direct limousine buses to/from Osaka's Itami airport (¥1020, 45 minutes). In Kōbe, the buses stop on the southwestern side of Sannomiya station.

KŌBE AIRPORT
The easiest way to get to/from Kōbe's spanking-new airport is with the Portliner, which makes the trip between Sannomiya (downtown Kōbe) and the airport in 18 minutes and costs ¥320. A taxi will cost between ¥2500 and ¥3000 and take 15 to 20 minutes.

KANSAI INTERNATIONAL AIRPORT
There are a number of routes between Kōbe and KIX. By train, the fastest way is the JR *shinkaisoku* to/from Osaka station, and the JR *kanku kaisoku* between Osaka station and the airport (total cost ¥1550, total time 87 minutes with good connections). There is also a direct limousine bus to/from the airport (¥1800, 1¼ hours). The Kōbe airport bus stop is on the southwestern side of Sannomiya station.

Public Transport
Kōbe is small enough to travel around on foot. JR, Hankyū and Hanshin railway lines run east to west across Kōbe, providing access to most of Kōbe's more distant sights. A subway line also connects Shin-Kōbe station with Sannomiya station (¥200, two minutes). There is also a city loop bus service that makes a grand circle tour of most of the city's sightseeing spots (per ride/all-day pass ¥200/600). The bus stops at both Sannomiya and Shin-Kōbe stations; look for the retro-style green buses.

HIMEJI 姫路

☎ 079 / pop 536,000

Himeji, a small city halfway between Osaka and Okayama, is home to Japan's most impressive castle: Himeji-jō. In addition to the castle, the city is home to the Hyōgo Prefectural Museum of History and Kōko-en, a small garden alongside the castle. The town may not be much to look at, but it's friendly and there are plenty of good places to eat. Best of all, Himeji can easily be visited as a day trip from Kyoto, Osaka or Kōbe.

ORIENTATION & INFORMATION
In Himeji station, you'll find a **tourist information counter** (☎ 285-3792; ⏱ 9am-5pm) on the ground floor to the left as you exit the central exit on the north side of the station. Between 10am and 3pm, an English-speaking staff is on duty. The castle is a 15-minute walk straight up the main road from the north exit of the station. If you don't feel like walking, free rental cycles are available; enquire at the information counter.

On the way to the castle you'll find **Himeji Tourist Information** (☎ 287-3658; ⏱ 9am-5pm), which has information on movies filmed in Himeji, public toilets, a fantastic model of the castle and free rental bicycles.

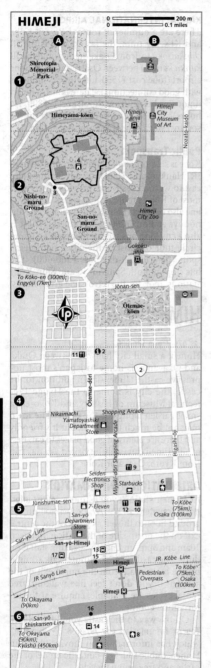

SIGHTS
Himeji-jō 姫路城

This **castle** (☎ 285-1146; 68 Honmachi; admission ¥600; ☯ 9am-5pm, last admission 4pm, 1hr later in summer) is the most magnificent of the handful of Japanese castles that survive in their original (nonconcrete) form. In Japanese the castle is sometimes called *shirasagi*, or 'white heron', a title that derives from the castle's stately white form. Although there have been fortifications in Himeji since 1333, today's castle was built in 1580 by Toyotomi Hideyoshi and enlarged some 30 years later by Ikeda Terumasa. Ikeda was awarded the castle by Tokugawa Ieyasu when the latter's forces defeated the Toyotomi armies. In the following centuries the castle was home to 48 successive lords.

The castle has a five-storey main donjon (heavily fortified central tower) and three smaller donjon, and the entire structure is surrounded by moats and defensive walls punctuated with rectangular, circular and triangular openings for firing guns and shooting arrows. The walls of the donjon also feature *ishiotoshi* – openings that allowed defenders to pour boiling water or oil onto anyone who made it past the defensive slits and was thinking of scaling the walls. All things considered, visitors are recommended to pay the admission charge and enter the castle by legitimate means.

It takes around 1½ hours to follow the arrow-marked route around the castle. English-speaking guides are sometimes available at the castle ticket office. Unfortunately, reservations aren't accepted and there is no regular schedule – ask at the counter and hope for the best. The guide service is free.

Kōko-en 好古園

Just across the moat on the western side of Himeji-jō, you'll find **Kōko-en** (☎ 289-4120; 68 Honmachi; admission ¥300; ♥ 9am-4.30pm, to 5.30pm Jun-Aug), a reconstruction of the former samurai quarters of the castle. There are nine separate Edo-style gardens, two ponds, a stream, a tea arbour (¥500 for *matcha* and a Japanese sweet) and the restaurant **Kassui-ken**, where you can enjoy lunch while gazing over the gardens. While the garden doesn't have the subtle beauty of some of Japan's older gardens, it is well done and especially lovely in the autumn foliage season.

Note that a joint ticket to both the Kōko-en and Himeji-jō costs only ¥720, a saving of ¥180. These can be purchased at both the entrance to Kōko-en and Himeji-jō.

Hyōgo Prefectural Museum of History
兵庫県立博物館

This **museum** (Hyōgo Kenritsu Rekishi Hakubutsukan; ☎ 288-9011; 68 Honmachi; admission ¥200; ♥ 10am-5pm Tue-Sun, closed the day after national holidays) has good displays on Himeji-jō and other castles around Japan. In addition, the museum covers the main periods of Japanese history with some English explanations. At 11am, 2pm and 3.30pm you can even try on a suit of samurai armour or a kimono (ask about this at the front desk).

The museum is a five-minute walk north of the castle.

Engyōji 円教寺

Around 8km northwest of Himeji station, this mountaintop **temple complex** (☎ 266-3327; 2968 Shosha, Himeji-shi; admission ¥300; ♥ 8.30am-5pm) is well worth a visit if you've got time after visiting the castle. The temple and surrounding area are most beautiful in the April cherry-blossom season or November *momiji* (maple-leaf) season. Eight of the temple buildings and seven Buddha images have been designated Important Cultural Properties.

From the top cable-car station, it's about a 25-minute walk (about 2km) to the Maniden,

one of the main structures of the complex, which is dedicated to Kannon (the Goddess of Mercy). Five minutes further on brings you to the Daikō-dō, a lovely wooden auditorium where parts of *The Last Samurai* were filmed. The path to both of these buildings is lined with Senjū-Kannon (Thousand-Armed Kannon) figures.

To get there, take bus 6 or 8 from Himeji station (boarding position 2; ¥260, 25 minutes). Get off at 'Shosha Ropeway', and board the cable car (one way/return ¥500/900). The trip takes about half a day from downtown Himeji.

FESTIVALS & EVENTS

The **Nada-no-Kenka Matsuri**, held on 14 and 15 October, involves a battle between three *mikoshi* that are battered against each other until one smashes. Try to go on the second day, when the festival reaches its peak (around noon). The festival is held five minutes' walk from Shirahamanomiya station (10 minutes from Himeji station on the Sanyō-Dentetsu line); follow the crowds.

SLEEPING

Himeji is best visited as a day trip from other parts of Kansai. If you'd like to stay, however, there are plenty of choices.

Tōyoko Inn (☎ 284-1045; fax 84-1046; 97 Minamieki-mae-chō; s/d/tw ¥5880/7980/7980; 🖳) This new business hotel is a good choice if you want to be close to the station. The rooms are serviceable, well maintained and, as usual in a business hotel, fairly small.

our pick **Himeji Washington Hotel Plaza** (☎ 225-0111; fax 25-0133; 98 Higashiekimae-chō; s/d ¥6754/13,508; 🖳) This is the best midrange choice in town. It's pretty much everything a good business hotel should be: well run and clean with reasonable-size rooms (for a business hotel, that is). It's within easy walking distance of the castle and lots of restaurants.

Hotel Nikkō Himeji (☎ 222-2231; fax 24-3731; 100 Minamiekimae-chō; s/d/tw ¥11,200/20,700/20,700; 🖳) A stone's throw from the south side of the station, this hotel has stylish and fairly spacious rooms and is the best choice for those who want something nicer than a business hotel. Some of the upper rooms on the north side have views of the top of the castle.

EATING

The food court in the underground mall at JR Himeji station has all the usual Western and

KANSAI

Japanese dishes. It's just to the right as you exit the north ticket gate of the station.

Me-n-me (☎ 225 0118; 68 Honmachi; noodles from ¥480; ☻ 11.30am-7pm Thu-Tue; E) They make their own noodles at this homey little noodle joint a few minutes' walk from the castle. It's not fancy, but if you want an honest, tasty bowl of *udon* to power you through the day, this is the spot. They usually put an English sign on the street.

Rāmen-no-Hōryū (☎ 223-0981; 316 Eki-mae-chō; buta miso rāmen ¥990; ☻ 11.30am-midnight Mon-Sat, to 11pm Sun & holidays) For good *gyōza* and hearty bowls of *buta miso rāmen* (pork *miso rāmen*), we recommend this friendly *rāmen* joint near the station. Buy your tickets from the machine. It's roughly opposite Starbucks – look for the faux wooden façade.

Fukutei (☎ 223-0981; 75 Kamei-chō; lunch/dinner ¥1500/3000; ☻ 11am-2.30pm & 4.30-9pm Fri-Wed; E) Japan could use a few more restaurants like this one: It's stylish and serves good food, but at the same time it's very approachable, even for foreigners. The fare here is casual *kaiseki*: a little sashimi, some tempura and the usual nibbles on the side. At lunch try the excellent *omakese-zen* (tasting set; ¥1500). There's a small English sign that reads: 'Omotenashi Dining Fukutei'.

Len (☎ 225-5505; 324 Eki-mae-chō; lunch/dinner ¥1500/3000; ☻ 11.30am-midnight Tue-Sun, closed holidays; E) If you find yourself in Himeji in the evening and feel like a good meal of pan-Asian *izakaya* fare, then try Len, where you can fill up on such tasty dishes as Vietnamese egg soup with crab and asparagus (¥550) or lemongrass grilled pork spareribs (¥800). There's a blue sign in English.

GETTING THERE & AWAY

The best way to reach Himeji from Kyoto, Osaka or Kōbe is by a *shinkaisoku* on the JR Tōkaidō line. Fares and times include: Kyoto (¥2210, 91 minutes); Osaka (¥1450, 61 minutes); and Kōbe (¥950, 37 minutes). From Okayama, to the west, a *tokkyū* JR train on the San-yō line takes 81 minutes and costs ¥1450. You can also reach Himeji from these cities via the Tōkaidō/San-yō *shinkansen* line, and this is a good option for Japan Rail Pass holders.

On the way to Himeji, take a look out the train window at the newly constructed Akashi Kaikyō Suspension Bridge. Its 3910m span links the island of Honshū with Awaji-shima,

making it the longest suspension bridge in the world. It comes into view on the southern side of the train approximately 10km west of Kōbe.

NARA 奈良

☎ 0742 / pop 368,000

Japan's first real capital, Nara is one of the most rewarding destinations in the country. If you've got a day or two to spare after visiting Kyoto, we strongly recommend a trip down to this compact collection of interesting and historically significant sites.

Like Kyoto, Nara is uninspiring at first glance, but careful inspection will reveal the rich history and hidden beauty of the city. Indeed, with eight Unesco World Heritage sites, Nara is second only to Kyoto as a repository of Japan's cultural legacy.

Nara is so small that it's quite possible to pack the most worthwhile sights into one full day. Of course, it's preferable to spend at least two days here if you can. Those with time to spare should allow a day for Nara-kōen and another day for the sights in western and southwestern Nara. If you only have one day available for Nara, spend it walking around Nara-kōen.

HISTORY

Nara is at the northern end of the Yamato Plain, where members of the Yamato clan rose to power as the original emperors of Japan. The remains of these early emperors are contained in *kofun* (burial mounds), some of which date back to the 3rd century AD.

Until the 7th century, however, Japan had no permanent capital, as native Shintō taboos concerning death stipulated that the capital be moved with the passing of each emperor. This practice died out under the influence of Buddhism and with the Taika reforms of 646, when the entire country came under imperial control.

At this time it was decreed that a permanent capital be built. Two locations were tried before a permanent capital was finally established at Nara (which was then known as Heijōkyō) in 710. Permanent status, however, lasted a mere 75 years. When a priest by the name of Dōkyō managed to seduce an empress and nearly usurp the throne, it was decided to move the court to a new location, out of reach of Nara's increasingly powerful clergy. This led to the new capital being established at Kyoto, where it remained until 1868.

Although brief, the Nara period was extraordinarily vigorous in its absorption of influences from China, a process that laid the foundations of Japanese culture and civilisation. The adoption of Buddhism as a national religion made a lasting impact on government, arts, literature and architecture. With the exception of an assault on the area by the Taira clan in the 12th century, Nara was subsequently spared the periodic bouts of destruction wreaked upon Kyoto, and a number of magnificent buildings have survived.

ORIENTATION

Nara retains the grid pattern of streets laid out in Chinese style during the 8th century. The two main train stations, JR Nara station and Kintetsu Nara station, are roughly in the middle of the city, and Nara-kōen, which contains most of the important sights, is on the eastern side, against the bare flank of Wakakusayama. Most of the other sights are southwest of the city and are best reached by buses that leave from both train stations (or by train in the case of Hōryū-ji). It's easy to cover the city centre and the major attractions in nearby Nara-kōen on foot, though some may prefer to rent a bicycle (see p409).

Maps

Nara tourist information offices have two very useful maps: the *Welcome to Nara Sightseeing Map*, which is best for sightseeing within the city limits, and the *Japan: Nara Prefecture* map, which is best for outlying areas. In addition, their handout titled *Nara* has a basic map and useful transport information.

INFORMATION

The **Nara City Tourist Center** (☎ 22-3900; 23-4 Kamisanjō-chō; ◷ 9am-9pm) is the main tourist office and is worth a stop if you start your sightseeing from JR Nara station. If you start from Kintetsu Nara station, try the helpful **Kintetsu Nara station information office** (☎ 24-4858; ◷ 9am-5pm), which is near the top of the stairs above exit 3 from the station.

There are two other information offices in Nara: the **JR Nara station office** (☎ 22-9821; ◷ 9am-5pm) and the **Sarusawa Tourist Information Office** (☎ 26-1991; ◷ 9am-5pm).

The information centres can put you in touch with volunteer guides who speak English and other foreign languages, but you must book at least one day in advance. Two of these services are the **YMCA Goodwill Guides** (☎ 45-5920; www.geocities.com/egg_nara) and **Nara Student Guides** (☎ 26-4753; www.narastudentguide.org).

Outside the NTT telephone company office on Sanjō-dōri there is an IC Card international phone.

Internet Café Suien (☎ 22-2577; 1-58 Aburasaka-chō; per 1hr internet ¥200, 2hr with one drink ¥500; ◷ 7.30am-11pm) Inside Hotel Asyl Nara.

Media-Café Cocoon (☎ 27-2039; 5 Konishi-chō; 1hr internet with drink ¥400; ◷ 11am-10pm).

SIGHTS
Nara-kōen Area 奈良公園

Many of Nara's most important sites are located in Nara-kōen, a fine park that occupies much of the east side of the city. The JNTO's leaflet entitled *Walking Tour Courses in Nara* includes a map for this area. This walking tour is probably the best way to get the most out of a day in Nara and is highly recommended.

The park is home to about 1200 deer, which in pre-Buddhist times were considered messengers of the gods and today enjoy the status of National Treasures. They roam the park and surrounding areas in search of handouts from tourists, often descending on petrified children who have the misfortune to be carrying food. You can buy *shika-sembei* (deer biscuits) from vendors for ¥150 to feed to the deer. Note: don't eat them yourself, as we saw one misguided foreign tourist doing.

NARA NATIONAL MUSEUM
奈良国立博物館

The **Nara National Museum** (Nara Kokuritsu Hakubutsu-kan; ☎ 22-7771; 50 Noborioji-chō; admission ¥500; ◷ 9am-5pm) is devoted to Buddhist art and is divided into two wings. The western gallery has a fine collection of *butsu-zō* (statues of the Buddha), while the new eastern gallery displays sculptures, paintings and calligraphy.

A special exhibition featuring the treasures of the Shōsō-in Hall, which holds the treasures of Tōdai-ji, are displayed here in May, as well as from 21 October to 8 November (call the Nara City Tourist Center to check, as these dates vary slightly each year). The exhibits include priceless items from the cultures along the Silk Road. If you are in Nara during these periods and are a fan of Japanese antiquities,

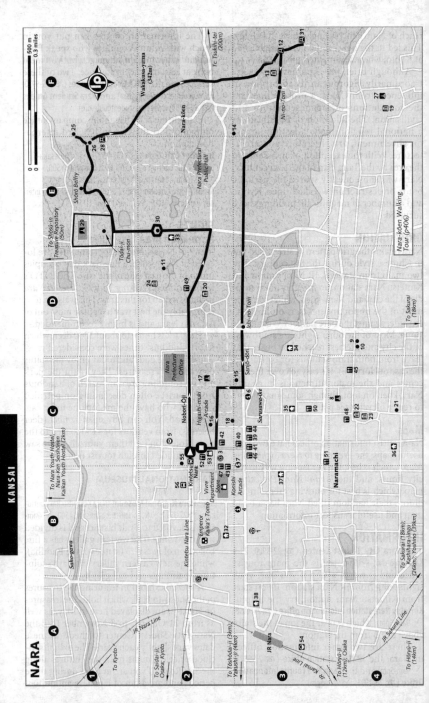

KANSAI

NARA

Nara-kōen Walking
Tour (p406)

you should make a point of visiting the museum, but be prepared for crowds – these exhibits get packed!

KŌFUKU-JI 興福寺

This temple was transferred here from Kyoto in 710 as the main temple for the Fujiwara family. Although the original temple complex had 175 buildings, fires and destruction as a result of power struggles have left only a dozen standing. There are two **pagodas** – three storeys and five storeys – dating from 1143 and 1426 respectively. The taller of the two is the second tallest in Japan, outclassed by the one at Kyoto's Tō-ji by a few centimetres.

The **Kōfuku-ji National Treasure Hall** (☎ 22-7755; 48 Noborioji-chō, Kokuhō-kan; admission ¥500; ☾ 9am-5pm) contains a variety of statues and art objects salvaged from previous structures.

ISUI-EN & NEIRAKU ART MUSEUM
依水園・寧楽美術館

This **garden** (☎ 25-0781; 74 Suimon-chō; admission museum & garden ¥650; ☾ 9.30am-4pm, closed Tue), dating from the Meiji era, is beautifully laid out and features abundant greenery and a pond filled with ornamental carp. It's without a doubt the best garden in the city and well worth a visit. For ¥450 you can enjoy a cup of tea on tatami mats overlooking the garden or you can have lunch in the nearby Sanshū restaurant, which also shares the view.

The adjoining art museum, Neiraku Bijutsukan, displays Chinese and Korean ceramics and bronzes.

TŌDAI-JI 東大寺

This **temple**, with its vast Daibutsu-den Hall and enormous bronze Buddha image, is Nara's star attraction. For this reason, it is often packed with groups of school children being herded around by microphone-wielding tour guides. Nonetheless, it is an awe-inspiring sight and should be high on any sightseeing itinerary.

On your way to the temple you'll pass through **Nandai-mon**, an enormous gate containing two fierce-looking **Niō guardians**. These recently restored wooden images, carved in the 13th century by the sculptor Unkei, are some of the finest wooden statues in all of Japan, if not the world. They are truly dramatic works of art and seem ready to spring to life at any moment.

Most of the temple grounds can be visited free of charge, with the exception of the main hall: the Daibutsu-den Hall.

Daibutsu-den Hall 大仏殿

Tōdai-ji **Daibutsu-den** (Hall of the Great Buddha; ☎ 22-5511; 406-1 Zōshi-chō; admission ¥500; ☾ 8am-5pm) is the

KANSAI

largest wooden building in the world. Unbelievably the present structure, rebuilt in 1709, is a mere two-thirds of the size of the original! The Daibutsu (Great Buddha) contained within is one of the largest bronze figures in the world and was originally cast in 746. The present statue, recast in the Edo period, stands just over 16m high and consists of 437 tonnes of bronze and 130kg of gold.

The Daibutsu is an image of Dainichi Buddha, the cosmic Buddha believed to precede all worlds and their respective historical Buddhas. Historians believe that Emperor Shōmu ordered the building of the Buddha as a charm against smallpox, which ravaged Japan in preceding years. Over the centuries the statue took quite a beating from earthquakes and fires, losing its head a couple of times (note the slight difference in colour between the head and the body).

As you circle the statue towards the back, you'll see a wooden column with a hole through its base. Popular belief maintains that those who can squeeze through the hole, which is exactly the same size as one of the Great Buddha's nostrils, are ensured of enlightenment. It's great fun to watch the kids wiggle through nimbly and the adults get wedged in like champagne corks – you wonder how often they have to call the fire department to extricate trapped visitors. A hint for determined adults: it's a lot easier to go through with both arms held above your head – and station a friend at either end to help with pushing and pulling. And if you do get stuck, we'll be happy to write you up as a more or less permanent part of the temple!

Nigatsu-dō & Sangatsu-dō
二月堂・三月堂

These two halls are an easy walk east of the Daibutsu-den; follow the path that winds uphill starting from the southeast corner of the Daibutsu-den (the normal exit point).

Nigatsu-dō (☎ 22-5511; 406-1 Zōshi-chō; admission free) is famed for its Omizutori Matsuri (see opposite) and a splendid view across Nara, which makes the climb up the hill worthwhile – particularly at dusk. Opening hours here are the same as those of the Daibutsu-den.

A short walk south of Nigatsu-dō is **Sangatsu-dō** (admission ¥500), which is the oldest building in the Tōdai-ji complex. This hall contains a small collection of fine statues from the Nara period. It's open the same hours as the Daibutsu-den.

KASUGA TAISHA 春日大社

This **shrine** (☎ 22-7788; 160 Kasugano-chō; admission free; ☉ dawn-dusk) was founded in the 8th century by the Fujiwara family and was completely rebuilt every 20 years according to Shintō tradition until the end of the 19th century. It lies at the foot of the hill in a pleasant, wooded setting with herds of sacred deer awaiting handouts.

The approaches to the shrine are lined with hundreds of lanterns, and there are many hundreds more in the shrine itself. The **lantern festivals** held twice a year at the shrine are a major attraction (for details see Mantōrō, opposite).

The **Hōmotsu-den** (Treasure Hall; admission ¥420; ☉ 9am-4.30pm) is just north of the entrance torii to the shrine. The hall displays Shintō ceremonial regalia and equipment used in *bugaku*, nō and *gagaku* performances.

While you're in the area, it's worth walking a few minutes south to nearby Wakamiya-jinja.

SHIN-YAKUSHI-JI 新薬師寺

This **temple** (☎ 22-3736; 1352 Takabatake-chō; admission ¥500; ☉ 9am-5pm) was founded by Empress Kōmyō in 747 in thanks for her husband's recovery from an eye disease. Most of the buildings were destroyed or have been reconstructed, but the present main hall dates from the 8th century. The hall contains sculptures of Yakushi Nyorai (Healing Buddha) and a set of 12 divine generals. Unfortunately, last time we were there

---

NARA UNESCO WORLD HERITAGE SITES

In 1998 eight sites in Nara met the criteria to be designated as World Heritage sites by the UN. They are the Buddhist temples of Tōdai-ji, Kōfuku-ji, Gangō-ji, Yakushi-ji and Tōshōdai-ji; the shrine, Kasuga Taisha; Kasuga-yama Primeval Forest; and the remains of Heijō-kyō Palace.

Each of these sites is considered to be of immeasurable historical value. All are open for public viewing. Five are covered in detail in the text; of the remaining three, Kasuga-yama Primeval Forest is directly behind Kasuga Taisha, Gangō-ji is in Naramachi, and the Heijō-kyō Palace ruins are 10 minutes' walk east of Saidai-ji station on the Kintetsu line.

a television was playing a very loud programme about the temple in the main hall.

It's about 15 minutes' walk from Kasuga Taisha/Wakamiya-jinja (see opposite); follow the trail through the woods. When you come to the main street, look for the small signs in English leading up (south) into a suburban neighbourhood.

NARA CITY MUSEUM OF PHOTOGRAPHY 奈良市写真美術館

Around the corner from Shin-Yakushi-ji, this small **museum** (Nara-shi Shashin Bijutsukan; ☎ 22-9811; 600-1 Takabatake-chō; admission ¥500; ☯ 9.30am-5pm Tue-Sun) is worth a visit if you are in the area or interested in a particular exhibit (there is no permanent collection). Ask at any of the tourist offices before making the trek. See Shin-Yakushi-ji for directions.

Naramachi 奈良町

South of Sanjō-dōri and Sarusawa-ike pond you will find Naramachi, with many well-preserved *machiya* and *kura*. It's a nice place for a stroll before or after hitting the big sights of Nara-kōen, and there are several good restaurants in the area to entice the hungry traveller.

Highlights of Naramachi include the **Naramachi Shiryō-kan Museum** (☎ 22-5509; 14 Nishishinya-chō; admission free; ☯ 10am-4pm Tue-Sun), which has a decent collection of bric-a-brac from the area, including a display of old Japanese coins and bills.

Naramachi Koushi-no-Ie (☎ 23-4820; 44 Gangōji-chō; admission free; ☯ 9am-5pm Tue-Sun) is a traditional Japanese house that, unfortunately, has been a little too thoroughly restored.

While you're in the neighbourhood, check out the **Naramachi Monogatari-kan** (☎ 26-3476; 2-1 Nakanoshinya-chō; admission free; ☯ 10am-4.30pm), an interesting little gallery that holds some worthwhile exhibitions.

Imanishike Shoin (☎ 23-2256; 24-3 Fukuchiin-chō; admission ¥350; ☯ 10am-4pm Tue-Sun, last entry 3.30pm) is a lovely old house dating to the Muromachi period and is built in the *shoin*, or library, style. There are a few small gardens here that are well framed by the house itself. Tea is served here. If you are a fan of sake, stop in next door at the **Imanishi Seibei Shōten**, an old sake merchant where for ¥400 you can sample five kinds of sake.

Lastly, Naramachi is also home to **Gangō-ji** (☎ 23-1378; 11 Chūin-chō; admission ¥400; ☯ 9am-5pm,

last entry 4.30pm, closed 29 Dec-4 Jan), a small temple that is listed as one of Nara's Unesco World Heritage sites. Despite its World Heritage listing, it's not particularly interesting and probably only merits a quick glance from outside.

TOURS

Nara Kōtsū (☎ 22-5263) runs daily bus tours on a variety of routes, two of which include Nara city sights only and two of which include more distant sights like Hōryū-ji and the burial mounds around Asuka (see p413). An explanation tape in English is available for all but the Asuka route. Prices for the all-day trips range from ¥800 to ¥10,000 for adults (which includes all temple fees and tape-recorder rental). Lunch at a Japanese restaurant on the route is optional (reserve when buying your ticket). Nara Kōtsū has offices in JR Nara station and across the street from Kintetsu Nara station. For something more intimate, try one of the private tours operated by one of the Kyoto-based private tour operators (see p314) or one of the city's volunteer guide organisations (see p401).

FESTIVALS & EVENTS

Nara has plenty of festivals throughout the year. The following is a brief list of the more interesting ones. Because the dates for some of these festivals vary, it's best to check with the Nara or Kyoto tourist information offices.

January

Yamayaki (Grass Burning Festival) In early January (the day before Seijin-no-hi), this festival commemorates a feud many centuries ago between the monks of Tōdai-ji and Kōfuku-ji: Wakakusa-yama is set alight at 6pm, with an accompanying display of fireworks. Arrive earlier to bag a good viewing position in Nara-kōen.

February

Mantōrō (Lantern Festival) Held in early February at Kasuga Taisha at 6pm, this is a festival renowned for its illumination, with 3000 stone and bronze lanterns; a *bugaku* dance also takes place in the Apple Garden on the last day. Also held around 14 August in O-bon.

March

Omizutori (Water-Drawing Ceremony) The monks of Tōdai-ji enter a special period of initiation during 12 and 13 March. On the evening of 12 March, they parade huge flaming torches around the balcony of Nigatsu-dō (in the temple grounds) and rain down embers on the spectators to purify them. The water-drawing ceremony is performed after midnight.

May

Takigi Nō (Firelight nō performances) Open-air performances of nō held after dark by the light of blazing torches at Kōfuku-ji and Kasuga Taisha, on 11 and 12 May.

October

Shika-no-Tsunokiri (Deer Antler Cutting) Those pesky deer in Nara-kōen are pursued in a type of elegant rodeo into the Roku-en (deer enclosure) close to Kasuga Taisha on Sundays and holidays in October. They are then wrestled to the ground and their antlers sawn off. Tourist brochures hint that this is to avoid personal harm, though it's not clear whether they are referring

to the deer fighting each other or the deer mugging the tourists.

SLEEPING

Although Nara is often visited as a day trip from Kyoto, it is pleasant to spend the night here and this allows for a more relaxing pace.

Budget

Nara Youth Hostel (☎ 22-1334; fax 22-1335; www.jyh .gr.jp/nara/english/neweng.html; narayh@themis.ocn.ne.jp; dm per person from ¥3150; ✖ 🖳) This clean and newish YH is easy to get to and well run. The reception here is efficient but brusque. From bus stand 7 at JR Nara station or bus stand 13

NARA-KŌEN WALKING TOUR

▪ Start: Kintetsu Nara station (see Map p402)

▪ End: Kintetsu Nara station

▪ Distance: about 5km

▪ Time: half a day

This walk meanders through the pleasantly wooded hills of Nara-kōen, taking in some of Nara's most important sights along the way. Start at exit 2 of Kintetsu Nara station. Walk straight up Ōmiya-dōri, passing **Kōfuku-ji (15–18;** p403) on your right (you can visit it now, or leave it until the return leg). After Kōfuku-ji, you have the option of taking a left to visit **Issui-en (11;** p403), one of Nara's finest gardens. Otherwise continue straight on, passing the **Nara National Museum (20;** p401) on your right. At the next traffic light take a left, passing an arcade of souvenir stalls, some of which sell shika-senbei (deer crackers), to the delight of the hordes of deer in the park. At this point, you'll see the massive **Nandai-mon (30)**, the main gate of **Tōdai-ji (29;** p403). Stop in the gate to admire the Niō guardians and then continue to the temple.

After visiting Tōdai-ji, take the path that leads uphill from the southeast corner of the temple (just in front of the torii (main gate) for Tamukeyama-jinja. The path curves around and climbs to the **Shōrō Belfry**, then climbs to an open plaza in front of **Nigatsu-dō (25)** and **Sangatsu-dō (26)** halls (p404). The view from the veranda of Nigatsu-dō is one of the best in Nara, taking in the graceful curves of the Daibutsu-den and most of the Nara plain.

Exit from the plaza heading south, passing between a log cabin–like structure and gaudy **Tamukeyama-hachimangū (28)**. Follow the broad path through the woods, descend two staircases and follow the signs reading 'Kasuga Shrine'. You'll come to a road that leads uphill to the left; follow it along, passing under the bare slopes of Wakakusa-yama. At Musashino Ryokan (look for the small English sign), walk straight down the steps, cross a bridge, jog left, and at the T-intersection take a left up to **Kasuga Taisha (14;** p404; you'll have to work around the side of it to find the main entrance).

After visiting the shrine, leave via the main entrance and bear left up the path to **Wakamiya-jinja (31)**, passing several small shrines on the way. After visiting the shrine, retrace your steps towards Kasuga Taisha, and take a left down the steps which lead back towards the centre of town. You'll pass first through **Ni-no-Torii** and then continue down the broad wooded arcade to **Ichi-no-Torii**. Cross the street and you'll soon see the pagoda of **Kōfuku-ji (15–18;** p403). Walk through the Kōfuku-ji grounds, passing between the **Nanen-dō (17)** and **Hokuen-dō (16)** halls, and take the narrow lane that leads down to **Higashi-muki Arcade**. A quick right here will bring you back to where you started.

at Kintetsu Nara station, take bus 108, 109, 111, 113 or 115 and get off at the Shieikyūjō-mae bus stop – the hostel is almost directly next to the stop.

Nara-ken Seishōnen Kaikan Youth Hostel (☎ / fax 22-5540; www6.ocn.ne.jp/~naseikan in Japanese; naseikan@galaxy.ocn.ne.jp; dm from ¥2650; ✖ ⬛) This YH is older and less pristine than the Nara Youth Hostel, but the warm and friendly staff more than makes up for this. The rooms are large and fairly well maintained; breakfast/dinner is ¥337/900. From bus stand 9 at JR Nara station or bus stand 13 at Kintetsu Nara station, take bus 12, 13, 131 or 140 and get off at the Ikuei-gakuen bus stop, from which it's a five-minute walk. The information offices have maps and directions.

Ryokan Seikansō (☎ /fax 22-2670; seikanso@chive .ocn.ne.jp; per person without bathroom from ¥4200; ✖ ⬛) This traditional ryokan has reasonable rates and a good Naramachi location. The rooms are clean and spacious with shared bathrooms and a large communal bathtub. About two-thirds of the guests are foreigners, so communication should not be an issue. The lovely Japanese garden is the icing on the cake here.

our pick Ryokan Matsumae (☎ 22-3686; fax 26-3927; hanami626@yahoo.co.jp; per person without bathroom from ¥5250; ✖ ⬛) This compact little ryokan gets excellent reviews from our readers, who never fail to mention the warm welcome and convenient location. The rooms are typical of a ryokan: tatami mats, low tables, TVs and futons. Some of the rooms are a little dark, but the feeling here is warm and relaxing. The friendly owner speaks English.

Midrange
HOTELS
Super Hotel (☎ 20-9000; fax 20-9008; www.superhotel .co.jp/s_hotels/jrnara/jrnara.html in Japanese; s/d ¥4980/6980; ✖ ⬛) Directly across from JR Nara station, the Super Hotel is part of a no-frills hotel chain that offers clean, small business hotel rooms at very reasonable prices. As with other business hotels, all rooms have en suite bathrooms. If all you need is a clean place to lay your head, this is a good choice.

Hotel Fujita Nara (☎ 23-8111; fax 22-0255; www .fujita-nara.com; info@fujita-nara.com; s/d/tw from ¥7500/10,500/12,600; ✖ ⬛) Right smack in downtown Nara and close to both main train stations, this efficient midrange hotel hits all the right notes: clean rooms, reasonable prices

and some English-speaking staff. It's a good choice for those who want a conveniently located hotel.

Top End
HOTELS
Nara Hotel (☎ 26-3300; fax 23-5252; www.narahotel .co.jp/english/index.html; s/tw from ¥16,170/31,185; ✖ ⬛) This is the grande dame of Nara hotels, having been in business almost 100 years (97 to be exact). It is a classic, with high ceilings and the smell of polished wood all around. All the rooms are spacious and comfortable with big beds. Unfortunately, some of the bathrooms have cramped unit baths. The rooms in the Shinkan (new wing) are nice, but we recommend the Honkan (main building) for its great retro atmosphere.

RYOKAN
Ryokan Tsubakisō (☎ 22-5330; fax 27-3811; tubaki@pc5 .so-net.ne.jp; per person without bathroom from ¥12,000; ✖ ⬛) Popular with foreign guests, this excellent ryokan is a homey and wonderful place to stay in Nara. The bedrooms and bathrooms are clean and well maintained and the owner can prepare vegetarian meals upon request. Highly recommended.

Kankasō (☎ 26-1128; fax 26-1301; per person from ¥21,500; ✖) A stone's throw from Tōdai-ji, this ryokan offers the classic traditional ryokan experience, with an attentive staff, spacious and tastefully appointed rooms and nice big bathtubs. This is an elegant and pleasing place for those who want something other than a hotel.

Tsukihi-tei (☎ 26-2021; fax 20-3003; homepage3 .nifty.com/tukihitei in Japanese; tukihitei-honten@nifty.com; per person from ¥31,500; ✖ ⬛) Hidden in a valley above Nara-kōen, this traditional high-class ryokan offers fine rooms and excellent service. If you don't mind being a bit of a distance from the centre of town, this hideaway is a tempting choice.

EATING
Nara is full of good restaurants, most of which are in the vicinity of Kintetsu Nara station or in Naramachi. There are not many decent choices up in the Nara-kōen area, so plan accordingly. In a pinch, you can get simple meals of noodles or rice at any of the cheap *shokudō* along the base of Wakakusa-yama, halfway between Tōdai-ji and Kasuga Taisha (the main walking route in the area).

Don (☎ 27-7080; 13-2 Higashimukiminami-machi; donburi from ¥450; ⏰ 11am-8pm; E) In the Higashi-muki arcade, the Don serves the eponymous *donburi* (rice bowl with various toppings) for absurdly low prices. It's healthy Japanese fast food and there's a picture menu to make ordering easier. It's opposite McDonald's, in more ways than one.

Kyōshō-An (☎ 27-7715; 26-3 Hashimoto-chō; green tea & sweets from ¥420; ⏰ 11am-7.30pm, closed Mon; E) This simple shop wins no awards for ambience, but it's a great place to sample Japanese tea and sweets, and unlike most traditional tea-sweet shops in Japan, this one has an English menu. In the hot months, we recommend an *Uji kintoki* (sweetened green tea over shaved ice; ¥570). It's opposite Nanto Bank, up a flight of white steps – look for the pictures of tea and sweets.

Drink Drank (☎ 27-6206; 8 Hashimoto-chō; smoothies from ¥650, lunch sets ¥750-850; ⏰ 11am-8pm, closed Wed; E) This is the sort of place you might just as easily find in New York or Melbourne. It serves a variety of fresh fruit drinks and light lunches including sandwiches and soup. If you want a break from Japanese food and feel like something light and casual, this might be the move.

Nonohana Ohka (☎ 22-1139; 13 Nakashinya-chō; coffee & tea average ¥500; ⏰ 11am-5pm, closed Mon; E) With indoor and outdoor garden seating, this café is one of our favourite places for a drink or a light meal when in Naramachi. The cakes are usually very good here and they go down a treat with the excellent tea. It's easy to spot, with a glass front.

Mellow Café (☎ 27-9099; 1-8 Konishi-chō; lunch from ¥950; ⏰ 11am-11.30pm; E) Located down a narrow alley (look for the palm tree), this open-plan café attempts to create the ambience of a South Seas resort in downtown Nara. Offerings include international and pan-Asian cuisine. Lunch specials are displayed in front to help you choose and order.

Ten Ten Café (☎ 26-6770; 19 Wakido-chō; meals from ¥750; ⏰ 11am-8.30pm; E) Operated by a singer-songwriter, and venue for lots of live-music happenings, this open and airy café is a fine spot for a relaxing drink or light meal in the Naramachi area. It serves a daily lunch special for ¥750. Look for the English sign and plants out front.

Tonkatsu Ganko (☎ 25-4129; 19 Higashimukinaka-machi; meals from ¥780; ⏰ 11am-10pm; E) You'll have to fight the locals to get into this popular new

tonkatsu specialist in the Higashi-muki Arcade, around the corner from Kintetsu Nara. There's a good picture menu with things like *hirekatsu zen* (fillet pork cutlet set; ¥980). Refills of rice, cabbage and pickles are free. It's next to Mr Donuts.

Shizuka (☎ 27-8030; 59-11 Noboriōji-chō; rice dishes from ¥800; ⏰ 11am-8pm, closed Tue; E) The closest decent lunch option to Nara-kōen, Shizuka is a cosy little traditional restaurant that serves a Nara speciality known as *kamameshi* (rice cooked in a small iron pot with various vegetables, meat or fish thrown in). It's in a two-storey building that looks like a private home, with a white-and-black paper lantern-sign.

Ayura Café (☎ 26-5339; 28 Hashimoto-chō; lunch or dinner set from ¥1000; ⏰ 11am-8pm, closed Wed) We highly recommend this tiny café for its wonderful (mostly veggie) set lunch or just a quick cuppa. It's right at the south end of Higashi-muki Arcade, on the 2nd floor. There's a small English sign.

Bikkuri Udon Miyoshino (☎ 22-5239; 27 Hashimoto-chō; meals average ¥1000; ⏰ 11am-8.30pm, closed Wed; E) Miyoshino does good-value sets of typical Japanese fare – noodles and rice dishes predominate. Stop by and check the daily lunch specials on display outside. It's very close to the Ayura Café.

Tempura Asuka (☎ 26-4308; 11 Shōnami-chō; meals ¥1575-3675; ⏰ 11.30am-2.30pm & 5-9.30pm, closed Mon; E) This reliable restaurant serves attractive tempura and sashimi sets in a relatively casual atmosphere. At lunchtime try its nicely presented *yumei-dono bentō* (a lunch box filled with a variety of tasty Japanese foods) for ¥1500. There is an English sign and the staff are used to foreigners here. It is highly recommended.

Beni-e (☎ 22-9493; 1-4 Higashimukiminami-machi; meals from ¥1600/2600; ⏰ 11.30am-2.30pm & 5-9pm, closed Mon; E) If you want tempura without a lot of distractions, this tiny downtown *tempura* specialist is likely to satisfy. It serves good *tempura* sets for ¥1600/2100/2600 (*hana*, *tsuki* and *yuki* lunch sets respectively). It's located a little back from Higashi-muki Arcade, behind Regal Shoes; go down the alley and look for the red writing above the door.

Kana Kana (☎ 22-3214; 13 Kunōdō-chō; ⏰ 11am-8pm, closed Mon) Inside an 80-year-old *machiya* in Naramachi, this simple, relaxing place serves healthy Japanese food, much of it (but not all) vegetarian. We recommend the *kanakana-gohan* set (daily lunch special; ¥1155). It's tricky to spot, since it hardly looks like a restaurant at all; look for the pile of rocks outside next to a house with a tree in its front yard.

Lastly, if you just need a quick cuppa or an eat-in or takeaway sandwich, there is a branch of the coffee shop Doutor in the Konishi Arcade (a five-minute walk from Kintetsu Nara).

SHOPPING

Nara is a great place to stock up on souvenirs, and you'll find plenty of shops selling traditional Japanese crafts and clothing in the streets and shopping arcades between JR Nara station and Kintetsu Nara station.

Daisō (Higashi-muki Arcade) If you've never experienced a *hyaku-en shoppu* (a shop where everything costs ¥100), then be sure to drop in here.

GETTING THERE & AWAY
Bus

There is an overnight bus service between Tokyo's Shinjuku (highway bus terminal) and Nara (one way/return ¥8400/15,120). The bus leaves Nara at 10.27pm and reaches Tokyo the next day at 6.15am. The bus from Tokyo leaves at 11.15pm and arrives in Nara the next day at 6.35am. In Nara, call **Nara Kotsu Bus** (☎ 22-5110; www.narakotsu.co.jp/kousoku/index.html in Japanese) or check with the Nara City Tourist Center for more details. In Tokyo, call **Kanto Bus** (☎ 03-3928-6011; www.kanto-bus.co.jp in Japanese).

Train
KYOTO

Unless you have a Japan Rail Pass, the best option is the Kintetsu line, which runs between Kintetsu Kyoto station (in Kyoto station) and Kintetsu Nara station. There are direct *tokkyū* (¥1110, 33 minutes) and *kyūkō* (¥610, 40 minutes). The *kyūkō* usually require a change at Saidai-ji.

The JR Nara line connects JR Kyoto station with JR Nara station (*kaisoku*, ¥690, 53 minutes) but departures are not frequent.

OSAKA

The Kintetsu Nara line connects Osaka (Kintetsu Namba station) with Nara (Kintetsu Nara station). *Kaisoku* and *futsū* services take about 36 minutes and cost ¥540. *Tokkyū* services do the journey in five minutes less but cost almost double, making them a poor option.

The JR Kansai line links Osaka (Namba and Tennō-ji stations) and Nara (JR Nara station). A *kaisoku* connects Namba and JR Nara station (¥540, 36 minutes) and Tennō-ji and JR Nara station (¥450, 30 minutes).

GETTING AROUND
To/From the Airport

Nara is served by Kansai International Airport. There is a **limousine bus service** (Nara Kotsu; ☎ 22-5110; www.narakotsu.co.jp/kousoku/limousine/nara _kanku.html in Japanese) between Nara and the airport with departures roughly every hour in both directions (¥1800, 85 minutes). At Kansai International Airport ask at the information counter in the arrivals hall, and in Nara visit the ticket office in the building across from Kintetsu Nara station. Reservations are a good idea.

For domestic flights, there are **limousine buses** (Nara Kotsu; ☎ 22-5110; www.narakotsu.co.jp /kousoku/limousine/nara_itami.html in Japanese) to/from Osaka's Itami airport (¥1440, 70 minutes).

Bicycle

Nara is a convenient size for getting around on a bicycle. **Eki Renta Car Kansai** (☎ 26-3929; 1-1 Honmachi, Sanjō; ☑ 8am-8pm) is very close to JR Nara station and rents regular bicycles for ¥300 a day –unbelievable value. If you can't be bothered to pedal along Nara's mostly flat streets, you can opt for electric bicycle (¥1500 a day).

Bus

Most of the area around Nara-kōen is covered by two circular bus routes. Bus 1 runs anticlockwise and bus 2 runs clockwise. There's a ¥170 flat fare. You can easily see the main sights in the park on foot and use the bus as an option if you are pushed for time or get tired of walking (one-day Free Pass ¥500).

AROUND NARA 奈良周辺

Southern Nara-ken was the birthplace of imperial rule and is rich in historical sites that are easily accessible as day trips from Osaka, Kyoto or Nara, provided that you make an early start. Of particular historical interest are the *kofun* that mark the graves of Japan's first emperors; these are concentrated around Asuka. There are also several isolated temples where you can escape the crowds that plague

KANSAI

Nara's city centre. Further afield, the mountaintop town of Yoshino is one of Japan's cherry-blossom meccas.

Easily reached by rail, Yamato-Yagi and Sakurai serve as useful transport hubs for the region. Keep in mind that the Kintetsu line is far more convenient than JR for most of the destinations in this section.

If you're starting from Nara, you may want to pick up a copy of the detailed *Japan: Nara Prefecture* map at any of the tourist information offices in Nara city before starting out.

TEMPLES SOUTHWEST OF NARA

While Nara City has some impressively ancient temples and Buddhist statues, if you want to go right back to the roots of Japanese Buddhism it's necessary to head to three temples southwest of Nara: Hōryū-ji, Yakushi-ji and Tōshōdai-ji.

Hōryū-ji is one of the most important temples in all of Japan, largely for historical reasons. However, its appeal is more academic than aesthetic, and it's quite a slog to get there. Thus, for most people we recommend a half-day trip to Yakushi-ji and Tōshōdai-ji, which are easy to get to from Nara and very pleasant for strolling.

If you do want to visit all three temples, we recommend heading to Hōryū-ji first (it's the most distant from the centre of Nara) and then continuing by bus 52, 97 or 98 (¥560, 39 minutes) up to Yakushi-ji and Tōshōdai-ji, which are a 10-minute walk apart (for more on getting to/from these temples, see the respective entries). Obviously, this can also be done in reverse. Of all the buses that ply the southwest temple route, bus 97 is the most convenient, with English announcements and route maps.

Hōryū-ji 法隆寺

This **temple** (☎ 75-2555; admission ¥1000; ✆ 8am-4pm) was founded in 607 by Prince Shōtoku, considered by many to be the patron saint of Japanese Buddhism. Legend has it that Shōtoku, moments after birth, stood up and started praying. Hōryū-ji is renowned not only as the oldest temple in Japan but also as a repository for some of the country's rarest treasures. Several of the temple's wooden buildings have survived earthquakes and fires to become the oldest of their kind in the world.

The temple is divided into two parts, **Sai-in** (West Temple) and **Tō-in** (East Temple). The

entrance ticket allows admission to Sai-in, Tō-in and the Great Treasure Hall. A detailed map is provided and a guidebook is available in English and several other languages.

The main approach to the temple proceeds from the south along a tree-lined avenue and continues through the Nandai-mon and Chū-mon before entering the Sai-in precinct. As you enter this precinct, you'll see the **Kondō** (Main Hall) on your right and a pagoda on your left.

The Kondō houses several treasures, including the triad of the **Buddha Sakyamuni**, with two attendant Bodhisattvas. Though it is one of Japan's great Buddhist treasures, it's dimly lit and barely visible – you will need a flashlight to see it. Likewise, the pagoda contains clay images depicting scenes from the life of Buddha that are barely visible without a flashlight.

On the eastern side of Sai-in are the two concrete buildings of the **Daihōzō-den** (Great Treasure Hall), containing numerous treasures from Hōryū-ji's long history.

GETTING THERE & AWAY

To get to Hōryū-ji, take the JR Kansai line from JR Nara station to Hōryū-ji station (¥210, 10 minutes). From there, bus 72 shuttles the short distance between the station and the bus stop Hōryū-ji Monzen (¥170, eight minutes). Alternatively, take bus 52, 60 or 97 from either JR Nara station or Kintetsu Nara station and get off at the Hōryū-ji-mae stop (¥760, 37 minutes by bus 60, 60 minutes by others). Leave the bus stop and walk west for about 50m, cross the road and you will see the tree-lined approach to the temple.

Yakushi-ji 薬師寺

This **temple** (☎ 0742-33-6001; admission ¥500; ✆ 8.30am-5pm) houses some of the most beautiful Buddhist images in all Japan. It was established by Emperor Temmu in 680. With the exception of the **East Pagoda**, which dates to 730, the present buildings either date from the 13th century or are very recent reconstructions.

Entering from the south, turn to the right before going through the gate with guardian figures and walk to the **Tōin-dō** (East Hall), which houses a famous Shō-Kannon image, built in the 7th century and showing obvious influences of Indian sculptural styles. Exit the Tōin-dō and walk west to the **Kon-dō** (Main Hall).

AROUND NARA

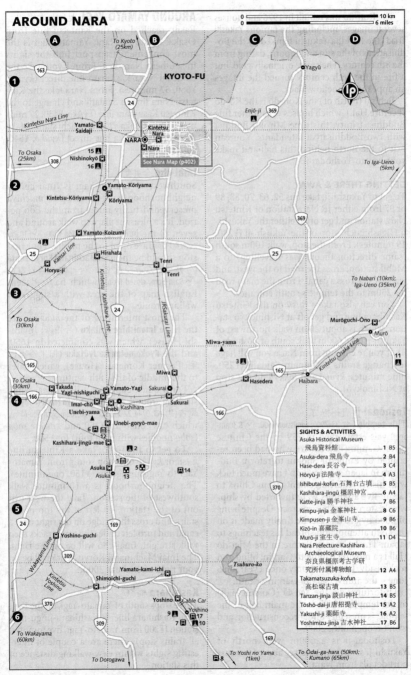

0 ____ 10 km
0 ____ 6 miles

KYOTO-FU

To Kyoto
(25km)

To Yagyū

Enjō-ji

Kintetsu Nara Line

Yamato-Saidaji

Kintetsu Nara

NARA
Nara

See Nara Map (p402)

To Osaka
(25km)

308

15
16
Nishinokyō

To Iga-Ueno
(5km)

Yamato-Kōriyama
Kintetsu-Kōriyama
Kōriyama

Yamato-Koizumi

369

4
25

Kansai Line

Hirahata

Horyu-ji

Tenri
Tenri

25

Kintetsu Kashihara Line

To Nabari (10km);
Iga-Ueno (35km)

24

JR Sakurai Line

To Osaka
(30km)

Murōguchi-Ōno

Murō

11

Miwa-yama

3

165

Kintetsu Osaka Line

Haibara

165
To Osaka
(30km)

Miwa

Hasedera

Takada
Yagi-nishiguchi

Yamato-Yagi
Sakurai

Sakurai

166

166

Imai-chō
Unebi-yama

Unebi Kashihara

6
12

Unebi-goryō-mae

Kashihara-jingū-mae

2

370

1
Asuka
Asuka

5
13

14

24

Yoshino-guchi

309

Kintetsu Yoshino Line

Wakayama Line

169

170

370

Yamato-kami-ichi

Shimoichi-guchi

Tsuburo-ko

Yoshino
Cable Car

Yoshino

9
7
17
10

309

169

6

To Wakayama
(60km)

To Dotogawa

8

To Yoshi no Yama
(1km)

To Ōdai-ga-hara (50km);
Kumano (65km)

K A N S A I

SIGHTS & ACTIVITIES

Asuka Historical Museum 飛鳥資料館	**1** B5
Asuka-dera 飛鳥寺	**2** B4
Hase-dera 長谷寺	**3** C4
Hōryū-ji 法隆寺	**4** A3
Ishibutai-kofun 石舞台古墳	**5** B5
Kashihara-jingū 橿原神宮	**6** A4
Katte-jinja 勝手神社	**7** B6
Kimpu-jinja 金峯神社	**8** C6
Kimpusen-ji 金峯山寺	**9** B6
Kizō-in 喜蔵院	**10** B6
Murō-ji 室生寺	**11** D4
Nara Prefecture Kashihara Archaeological Museum 奈良県立橿原考古学研究所付属博物館	**12** A4
Takamatsuzuka-kofun 高松塚古墳	**13** B5
Tanzan-jinja 談山神社	**14** B5
Tōshō-dai-ji 唐招提寺	**15** A2
Yakushi-ji 薬師寺	**16** A2
Yoshimizu-jinja 吉水神社	**17** B6

The Kon-dō was rebuilt in 1976 and houses several images, including the famous **Yakushi Triad** (the Buddha Yakushi flanked by the Bodhisattvos of the sun and moon), dating from the 8th century. They were originally gold, but a fire in the 16th century turned the images an appealingly mellow black.

Behind (north of) the Kon-dō is the Kō-dō (Lecture Hall), which houses yet another fine Buddhist trinity, this time Miroku Buddha with two Boddhisattva attendants. You can exit to the north behind this hall and make your way to Tōshōdai-ji.

GETTING THERE & AWAY

To get to Yakushi-ji, take bus 52, 63, 70, 88, 89 or 97 from either JR Nara station or Kintetsu Nara station and get off at either the Yakushi-ji Higashiguchi stop or the Yakushi-ji (¥240, 19 minutes). From the stop, walk 100m south (same direction thebus was travelling) to a Mobil station, cross the road to the west, and walk west across a canal. From the main road it's 250m to the temple's south entrance.

You can also take a *futsū* on the Kintetsu Kashihara line and get off at Nishinokyō station, which is about 200m walk northwest of Yakushi-ji (and 600m walk south of Tōshōdai-ji). If you're coming from Nara, you will have to change trains at Yamato-Saidaiji (¥250, nine minutes); *kyūkō* and *tokkyū* do not stop at Nishinokyō.

Tōshōdai-ji 唐招提寺

This **temple** (☎ 33-7900; admission ¥600; 8.30am-5pm) was established in 759 by the Chinese priest Ganjin (Jian Zhen), who had been recruited by Emperor Shōmu to reform Buddhism in Japan. Ganjin didn't have much luck with his travel arrangements from China to Japan: five attempts were thwarted by shipwreck, storms and bureaucracy. Despite being blinded by eye disease, he finally made it on the sixth attempt and spread his teachings to Japan. The lacquer sculpture in the Miei-dō Hall is a moving tribute to Ganjin: blind and rock steady. It is shown only once a year, on 6 June – the anniversary of Ganjin's death.

Unfortunately, the **Kon-dō** (Golden Hall) of the temple, which is the main hall of the temple, is presently under reconstruction and won't reopen until 2009.

Tōshōdai-ji is a 600m walk north of Yakushi-ji's northern gate; see above for transport details from Nara.

AROUND YAMATO-YAGI 大和八木周辺

Easily reached on the Kintetsu line from Osaka, Kyoto or Nara, Yamato-Yagi is the most convenient transport hub for sights in southern Nara-ken. From Kyoto take the Kintetsu Nara/Kashihara line direct (*kyūkō*, ¥860, 57 minutes). From Nara take the Kintetsu Nara line to Saidaiji and change to the Kintetsu Kashihara line (*kyūkō*, ¥430, 27 minutes). From Osaka's Uehonmachi station, take the Kintetsu Osaka line direct (*kyūkō*, ¥540, 34 minutes).

Imai-chō 今井町

Southwest of Yamato-Yagi is Imai-chō, a neighbourhood with around 500 *machiya* preserved virtually intact from the Edo period. It's a pleasant place to walk around and seven of the **buildings** (admission ¥200; 10am-noon & 1-5pm) are open to the public. Your first stop should be the **Imai Machinami Koryū Sentā** (今井まちなみ交流センター; ☎ 0744-24-8719; 9am-5pm, closed Mon), which has a decent English map of the area with a suggested walking route.

The most interesting of the *machiya* are the huge **Imanishike Jyūtaku** (今西家; Imanishi House), which was completed in 1650, and the **Kyukometanike Jyūtaku** (旧米谷家住宅; Former Kometani House), which dates to the middle of the 18th century.

For a quick cuppa or a light meal while strolling around, try **Machiya-jaya Furui** (町家茶屋古伊; ☎ 0744-22-2135; 10.30am-5pm Thu-Mon), which has coffee for ¥350 and *kitsune soba* (*soba* noodles with fried tofu) for ¥500.

To get to Imai-chō, take a Kintetsu line *futsū* or *kyūkō* one stop south from Yamato-Yagi to Yagi-nishiguchi (¥150, one minute). The neighbourhood is a 10-minute walk southwest of the station. Take the west exit out of the station, go left at the top of the stairs, and cross the bridge on the right over a canal and turn left under the train tracks then walk straight. Imai-chō will be on the right. The Imai Machinami Koryū Sentā will be on your right after about 300m.

Kashihara 橿原

Three stops south of Yamato-Yagi, on the Kintetsu Kashihara line, is Kashihara-jingū-mae station (¥200 from Yamato-Yagi, five minutes, all trains stop). There are a couple of interesting sights within easy walking distance of this station.

KASHIHARA-JINGŪ 橿原神宮

This **shrine** (☎ 0744-22-3271; admission free), at the foot of Unebi-yama, dates back to 1889, when many of the buildings were moved here from Kyoto Gosho. The shrine buildings are built in the same style as those of Ise-jingū's Grand Shrine (Japan's most sacred shrine) and are a good example of classical Shintō architecture. The shrine is dedicated to Japan's mythical first emperor, Jimmu, and an annual festival is held here on 11 February, the legendary date of Jimmu's enthronement. The vast, parklike grounds are pleasant to stroll around. The shrine is five minutes' walk from Kashihara-jingū-mae station; take the central exit out of the station and follow the main street in the direction of the mountain.

NARA PREFECTURE KASHIHARA ARCHAEOLOGICAL MUSEUM
奈良県橿原考古学研究所付属博物館

This **museum** (Nara Ken-ritsu Kashihara Kōkogaku Kenkyūjo Fuzoku Hakubutsukan; ☎ 0744-24-1185; admission ¥400; 9am-5pm, closed Mon) is highly recommended for those with an interest in the history of the Japanese people. The objects on display come from various archaeological sites in the area, including several *kofun*. Although most of the explanations are in Japanese, there's enough English to give you an idea of what's going on.

To get there from Kashihara-jingū, walk out the northern gate of the shrine (to your left when you stand with your back to the main hall), follow the wooded avenue for five minutes, cross the main road and continue on in the same direction for 100m before turning left. It's on the left soon after this turn.

ASUKA 明日香
☎ 0744 / pop 6500

The Yamato Plain in central Nara-ken is where the forerunners of Japan's ruling Yamato dynasty cemented their grip on power. In these pre-Buddhist days, huge earthen burial mounds were used to entomb deceased emperors. Some of the best examples of these burial mounds, or *kofun,* can be found around the town of Asuka, an hour or so south of Nara on the Kintetsu line.

The best way to explore the area is by bicycle, which can be rented from one of several rental shops outside the station. There's a **tourist information office** (☎ 54-3624; 8.30am-5pm) outside Asuka station, which stocks an excellent pamphlet with a suggested bicycle route of the area.

Two tombs worth seeing are **Takamatsuzuka-kofun** (高松塚古墳) and **Ishibutai-kofun** (石舞台古墳; admission ¥250; 8.30am-5pm). The former, which was excavated in 1972, is closed to the public but can be observed from outside. The Ishibutai-kofun is open to the public. It is said to have housed the remains of Soga no Umako but is now completely empty.

The best museum in the area is **Asuka Historical Museum** (飛鳥資料館; ☎ 54-3561; admission ¥260; 9am-4pm, closed Mon), which has exhibits from regional digs. It's across the street (take the underpass) from Takamatsuzuka-kofun.

If you have time left after visiting the earlier sights, take a look at **Asuka-dera** (飛鳥寺; ☎ 54-2126; admission ¥300; 9am-4.45pm), which dates from 596 and is considered the first true temple in all of Japan. Housed within is the oldest remaining image of Buddha in Japan – after more than 1300 years of venerable existence, you'll have to excuse its decidedly tatty appearance. You can just glimpse the Buddha image through the open doorway.

Lastly, if you'd like a bite to eat while in Asuka, try **Ashibi-no-sato** (あしびの郷; ☎ 0742-26-6662; simple meals from ¥800; 10am-6pm). To get there, exit the station and follow the canal to the right for about 150m.

Asuka is five stops south of Yamato-Yagi (change at Kashihara-jingū-mae) and two stops south of Kashihara-jingū-mae on the Kintetsu Yoshino line (¥220 from Yamato-Yagi, 20 minutes, *tokkyū* stops at Asuka).

AROUND SAKURAI 桜井周辺

There are a few interesting places to visit close to the town of Sakurai that can be reached directly from Nara on the JR Sakurai line (*futsū,* ¥320, 28 minutes). To reach Sakurai via Yamato-Yagi (when coming from Kyoto or Osaka), take the Kintetsu Osaka line from Yamato-Yagi (*kyūkō,* ¥200, seven minutes).

Tanzan-jinja 談山神社

This **shrine** (☎ 0744-49-0001; admission ¥500; 8.30am-4.30pm) lies south of Sakurai and can be reached by bus 14 from stand 1 outside the southern exit of Sakurai station (¥460, 24 minutes). It's tucked away in the forests of Tōnomine-san, famous for their autumn colours. Enshrined here is Nakatomi no Kamatari, patriarch of the Fujiwara line, which effectively ruled Japan for nearly 500 years. Legend has it that Nakatomi met here secretly with Prince Naka no Ōe over games of kickball to discuss the overthrow of the ruling Soga clan. This event is commemorated on the second Sunday in November by priests playing a game of kickball – call it divine hackey sack.

The central structure of the shrine is an attractive 13-storey pagoda best viewed against a backdrop of maple trees ablaze with autumn colours.

Hase-dera 長谷寺

Two stops east of Sakurai on the Kintetsu Osaka line is Hasedera station. From the station, it's a 20-minute walk to lovely **Hase-dera** (☎ 0744-47-7001; admission ¥500; ⏰ 8.30am-4.30pm). After a long climb up seemingly endless steps, you enter the main hall and are rewarded with a splendid view from the gallery, which juts out on stilts over the mountainside. Inside the top hall, the huge Kannon image is well worth a look. The best times to visit this temple are in the spring, when the way is lined with blooming peonies, and in autumn, when the temple's maple trees turn a vivid red. From the station, walk down through the archway, cross the river and turn right onto the main street that leads to the temple.

Murō-ji 室生寺

This **temple** (☎ 0745-93-2003; admission ¥500; ⏰ 8am-5pm, to 4pm Dec-Feb) was founded in the 9th century and has strong connections with Esoteric Buddhism (the Shingon sect). Women were never excluded from Murō-ji as they were from other Shingon temples, and it is for this reason that it came to be known as 'the Woman's Kōya'. Unfortunately, the temple's lovely five-storey pagoda, which dates from the 8th or 9th century, was severely damaged in a typhoon in the summer of 1999. The newly rebuilt pagoda lacks some of the rustic charm of the old one. Nonetheless, Murō-ji is a secluded place in thick forest and is well worth a visit.

After visiting the main hall, walk up to the pagoda and then continue on behind the pagoda in the direction of **Oku-no-in**, a hall of the temple located at the top of a very steep flight of steps. If you don't feel like making the climb, at least go about 100m past the pagoda to see the mammoth cedar tree growing over a huge rock here – an awesome sight that reminds us of Ta Prohm temple at Angkor Wat.

Murōguchi-Ōno station on the Kintetsu Osaka line is two stops east of Hasedera station. It's a 14-minute bus ride from Murōguchi-Ōno station to Murō-ji on bus 43, 44, 45 or 46 (¥400). In spring, there is a direct bus between Hase-dera and Murō-ji (¥830, end of April to early May, one or two buses per hour between 11am and 3pm).

YOSHINO 吉野

☎ 0746 / pop 10,000

Yoshino is Japan's top cherry-blossom destination, and for a few weeks in early to mid-April the blossoms of thousands of cherry trees form a floral carpet gradually ascending the mountainsides. It's definitely a sight worth seeing, but the narrow streets of the village become jammed tight with thousands of visitors at this time, and you'll have to be content with a day trip unless you've booked accommodation long in advance. Once the cherry-blossom petals fall, the crowds depart and Yoshino reverts to a sleepy village with a handful of shrines and a couple of temples to entertain day-trippers.

Information

Yoshino Visitors Center is about 400m up the main street from the top cable-car station, on your right just after Kimpusen-ji (look for the large tan-and-white building). It can help with *minshuku* bookings if necessary.

Sights

Walk about 500m uphill from the cable-car station and you will come to the stone steps leading to the Ni-ō-mon gate of **Kimpusen-ji** (金峯山寺; ☎ 32-8371; admission ¥400; ⏰ 8.30am-4.30pm). Check out the fearsome **Kongō Rikishi** (guardian figure statues) in the gate and then continue on to the massive **Zaō-dō Hall** of the temple. Said to be the second-largest wooden building in Japan, the hall is most interesting for its unfinished wooden columns. For many centuries Kimpusen-ji has been one of the major centres for Shugendō, and pilgrims have often stopped here to pray for good fortune on the journey to Ōmine-san.

Continuing another 300m up the street brings you to a side road to the left (turn just past the post office) that leads to the small **Yoshimizu-jinja** (吉水神社), a small shrine that has a good view back to Kimpusen-ji. Another 150m up the street is **Katte-jinja** (勝手神社). The road forks just above this shrine.

Take the right (uphill) fork and you will soon pass **Kizō-in** (喜蔵院) on your left and come to **Chikurin-in** (竹林院) on the right, which has a wonderful garden (see below).

A few minutes' walk further on there is another fork, where you'll find some steps leading up to a wooden torii. Take the left fork and the next right up the hill for the 3km hike to **Kimpu-jinja** (金峯神社), a small shrine in a pleasantly wooded mountain setting. If you don't fancy this somewhat strenuous uphill hike, there are plenty of smaller shrines on the streets and alleys off Yoshino's main street.

Sleeping

Yoshino-yama Kizō-in (吉野山喜蔵院; ☎ 32-3014; dm per person incl 2 meals ¥6000; 🅿) This is a temple, Kizō-in, which doubles as the local youth hostel and is the cheapest option in town. It's a pleasant place to stay, and several of the hostel's rooms look out across the valley. See above for directions to the temple.

Chikurin-in Gumpo en (竹林院群芳園; ☎ 32-8081; www.chikurin.co.jp/e/home.htm; r per person incl 2 meals from ¥13,650; 🅿) Not far past Kizō-in, on the opposite side of the street, this is an exquisite temple that now operates primarily as a ryokan. Both present and previous emperors have stayed here, and a look at the view afforded by some of the rooms explains why. Reservations are essential for the cherry-blossom season, and a good idea at all other times. Even if you don't plan to stay at the temple, you should at least visit its splendid garden (admission ¥300), said to have been designed by the famous tea master Sen-no-Rikyū.

Eating

The speciality of Yoshino is *kaki-no-ha* sushi (persimmon-leaf sushi). Almost every store and restaurant in town sells it and you can buy two pieces to take away for ¥250.

Hōkon-an (芳魂庵; ☎ 32-8207; 🕙 9am-5pm, closed irregularly) This is an atmospheric little tea house, where you can sip your tea while enjoying a lovely view over the valley. The *matcha* (¥650) comes with a homemade Japanese sweet. Look for the rustic wooden façade and large ceramic urn on the left, just past the post office.

Nakai Shunpūdō (中井春風堂; ☎ 32-3043; 🕙 9am-5pm, closed irregularly) With a limited picture menu, it serves a *kamameshi teishoku* (rice cooked in an iron pot; ¥1050) and other typical lunch favourites; the view from the

windows is great. It's about 5m past the information office, on the opposite side – look for the ceramic *tanuki* (Japanese raccoon dog) figure out front.

Getting There & Away

The village of Yoshino is on a shoulder of Yoshino-yama, at the bottom of which is Yoshino station. From Yoshino station, you can take the cable car to the village (one way/return ¥350/700) or walk up in 15 minutes on the path that leaves from beside the cable-car station. Note that the cable car stops running at 5pm – plan your day accordingly or you'll have to walk down to the station (30 minutes).

To get to Yoshino station from Kyoto or Nara, take the Kintetsu Nara–Kashihara line to Kashihara-jingū-mae (*kyūkō* from Kyoto, ¥860, 66 minutes; *kyūkō* from Nara, ¥480, 36 minutes) and change to the Kintetsu Yoshino line (*kyūkō*, ¥460, 52 minutes).

You can take a direct train on the Kintetsu Minami–Osaka–Yoshino lines from Osaka (Abenobashi station, close to Tennō-ji station) to Yoshino (*kyūkō*, ¥950, 75 minutes).

The closest JR station to Yoshino is Yoshino-guchi, where you can transfer to trains to/from Nara, Osaka and Wakayama.

KII-HANTŌ 紀伊半島

The remote and mountainous Kii-hantō (Kii Peninsula) is a far cry from central Kansai's bustling urban sprawl. Most of the peninsula's attractions are found in Wakayama-ken, including the mountaintop temple complex of Kōya-san, one of Japan's most important Buddhist centres. Other Wakayama-ken attractions include the *onsen* clustered around the village of Hongū, in the centre of the peninsula, the beachside hot-spring resort of Shirahama, on the west coast of the peninsula, and the rugged coastline of Shiono-misaki and Kii-Ōshima, at the southern tip of the peninsula.

The JR Kii main line (Kinokuni line) runs around the coast of the Kii-hantō, linking Shin-Osaka and Nagoya stations (some trains originate/terminate at Kyoto station). Special Kuroshio and Nankii *tokkyū* trains can get you around the peninsula fairly quickly, but once you step off these express trains you're at the mercy of slow local trains and buses, so

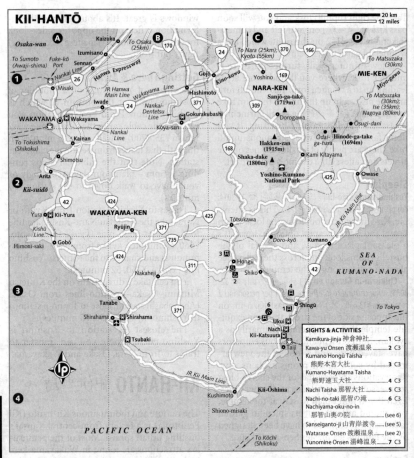

SIGHTS & ACTIVITIES

Kamikura-jinja 神倉神社	1 C3
Kawa-yu Onsen 渡瀬温泉	2 C3
Kumano Hongū Taisha 熊野本宮大社	3 C3
Kumano-Hayatama Taisha 熊野速玉大社	4 C3
Nachi Taisha 那智大社	5 C3
Nachi-no-taki 那智の滝	6 C3
Nachiyama-oku-no-in 那智山奥の院	(see 6)
Sanseiganto-ji 山青岸渡寺	(see 5)
Watarase Onsen 渡瀬温泉	(see 2)
Yunomine Onsen 湯峰温泉	7 C3

plan accordingly. For this reason, renting a car is a good option for exploring this area.

We present the information in this section anticlockwise, working from Wakayama-shi around the horn to Mie-ken, but it's perfectly possible to do this the other way round (perhaps starting in Ise).

WAKAYAMA 和歌山
☎ 073 / pop 374,000

Wakayama, the prefectural capital, is a pleasant little city useful as a transport hub for travellers heading to other parts of the prefecture.

There is a useful **tourist information counter** (☎ 422-5831; ⏰ 8.30am-7pm Mon-Sat, to 5.15pm Sun & holidays) inside JR Wakayama station, which stocks copies of the excellent *Wakayama City Guide* map.

Sights & Activities
WAKAYAMA-JŌ 和歌山城

The city's main attraction is **Wakayama-jō** (☎ 435-1044; 3 Ichiban-chō; admission to grounds/castle keep free/¥350; ⏰ 9am-4.30pm). The original castle was built in 1585 by Toyotomi Hideyoshi and destroyed by bombing in WWII. The present structure is a concrete postwar reconstruction; it's picturesque from afar and unprepossessing up close. However, the gardens surrounding the castle are well worth a stroll if you're in the area.

The castle is a 20-minute walk (about 2km) from JR Wakayama station. Alternatively, it's about a 10-minute (about 1km) walk from Wakayama-shi station.

MUSEUM OF MODERN ART WAKAYAMA
和歌山県立近代美術館

A short walk from the castle, this **museum** (☎ 436-8690; 1-4-14 Fukiage; admission ¥310, extra for special exhibitions; ☯ 9.30am-5pm, closed Mon) is worth a visit for its unique building and small but interesting collection of Japanese and Western 20th-century art. The collection contains, among other things, 4000 block prints, and works by Picasso, Miró and Klee. The museum is across the street south of the castle.

Sleeping & Eating

Kokumin-shukusha Shinwaka Lodge (国民宿舎 新 和歌ロッジ; ☎ 444-9000; 2-3 Shinwakaura; r per person incl/excl 2 meals ¥7000/4800; ☯) Located out in the western Shinwakaura area of the city, this is the most reasonable place in the area. Take bus 24 from stop 2 in front of JR Wakayama station to the last stop, Shinwaka Ura (¥380, 30 minutes). Continue on in the same direction along the main road, go through the tunnel and look for it on your left.

Hotel Granvia Wakayama (ホテルグランヴィ ア和歌山; ☎ 425-3333; hotel@granvia-wakayama.co.jp; 5-18 Tomoda-chō; s/d/tw ¥10,164/17,902/19,635; ☒ ▣) This place is right outside the station and offers new, clean rooms. This hotel has good reports from readers.

Mendori-tei (めんどり亭; ☎ 422-3355; 478 Yoshida; ☯ 8am-11pm) For a bite to eat, head to the restaurant arcade on the basement floor beneath JR Wakayama station. Among the choices here, this serves excellent *tonkatsu* dishes (try the *tonkatsu teishoku* for ¥980). Look for the brown curtains and the all-counter seating.

Otherwise, a short walk from JR Wakayama station you'll find **Ide Shōten** (井出商店; ☎ 436-2941; 4-84 Tanaka-machi; ☯ 11.30am-11.30pm Fri-Wed), where you can sample the local speciality, *shoyū rāmen* (soy sauce *rāmen*) for ¥600. But call it *chuka soba* (Chinese noodles) or you'll get funny looks from the staff! To get there from the station, walk straight out of the station and turn left on the main street – it's six short blocks south on the right, just past a parking lot.

Getting There & Away

Wakayama is serviced by JR *tokkyū* trains from Shin-Osaka and Kyoto, but unless you've got a Japan Rail Pass it's cheaper to take a local train on the JR Hanwa line from Osaka's Tennō-ji station (*kaisoku*, ¥830, 58 minutes). From Osaka's Namba station you can also take the private Nankai line to Wakayama-shi station (*kyūkō*, ¥890, 63 minutes), which is linked to JR Wakayama station by the JR Kisei main line (*futsū*, ¥180, six minutes).

KŌYA-SAN 高野山
☎ 0736 / pop 4000

Kōya-san is a raised tableland in northern Wakayama-ken covered with thick forests and surrounded by eight peaks. The major attraction here is the Kōya-san monastic complex, which is the headquarters of the Shingon school of Esoteric Buddhism. Though not quite the Shangri-la it's occasionally described as, Kōya-san is one of the most rewarding places to visit in Kansai, not just for the natural setting of the area but also as an opportunity to stay in temples and get a glimpse of long-held traditions of Japanese religious life.

Although you could visit Kōya-san as a day trip from Nara, Kyoto or Osaka, it's much better to reduce the travel stress and stay overnight in one of the town's excellent *shukubō* (temple lodgings). Be sure to bring some warm clothes when you go, as up on the mountain it tends to be around 5°C colder than down on the plains.

Whenever you go, you'll find that getting there is half the fun – the train winds through a series of tight valleys with mountains soaring on all sides, and the final vertiginous cable-car leg is not for the faint of heart.

History

The founder of the Shingon school of Esoteric Buddhism, Kūkai (known after his death as Kōbō Daishi), established a religious community here in 816. Kōbō Daishi travelled as a young priest to China and returned after two years to found the school. He is one of Japan's most famous religious figures and is revered as a Bodhisattva, scholar, inventor of the Japanese *kana* syllabary and as a calligrapher.

Followers of Shingon believe that Kōbō Daishi is not dead, but rather that he is meditating in his tomb in Kōya-san's Oku-no-in Cemetery, awaiting the arrival of Miroku (Maitreya, the future Buddha). Food is ritually offered in front of the tomb daily to sustain him during this meditation. When Miroku

KANSAI

returns, it is thought that only Kōbō Daishi will be able to interpret his heavenly message for humanity. Thus, the vast cemetery here is like an amphitheatre crowded with souls gathered in expectation of this heavenly sermon.

Over the centuries the temple complex grew in size and attracted many followers of the Jōdo (Pure Land) school of Buddhism. During the 11th century, it became popular with both nobles and commoners to leave hair or ashes from deceased relatives close to Kōbō Daishi's tomb.

In the 16th century Oda Nobunaga asserted his power by slaughtering large numbers of monks at Kōya-san. The community subsequently suffered confiscation of lands and narrowly escaped invasion by Toyotomi Hideyoshi. At one stage Kōya-san numbered about 1500 monasteries and many thousands of monks. The members of the community were divided into *gakuryō* (clergy), *gyōnin* (lay priests) and *hijiri* (followers of Pure Land Buddhism).

In the 17th century the Tokugawa shōgunate smashed the economic power of the lay priests, who managed considerable estates in the region. Their temples were destroyed, their leaders banished and the followers of Pure Land Buddhism were bluntly pressed into the Shingon school. During the Edo period, the government favoured the practice of Shintō and confiscated the lands that supported Kōya-san's monastic community. Women were barred from entry to Kōya-san until 1872.

Kōya-san is now a thriving centre for Japanese Buddhism, with more than 110 temples remaining and a population of 7000. It is the headquarters of the Shingon school, which numbers 10 million members and presides over nearly 4000 temples all over Japan.

Orientation & Information

The precincts of Kōya-san are divided into two main areas: the Garan (Sacred Precinct) in the west, where you will find interesting temples and pagodas, and the Oku-no-in, with its vast cemetery, in the east. We recommend visiting both sites.

Note that there is a joint ticket (*shodōkyōtsunaihaiken*; ¥1500) that covers entry to Kongōbu-ji, the Kondō, Dai-tō, Treasure

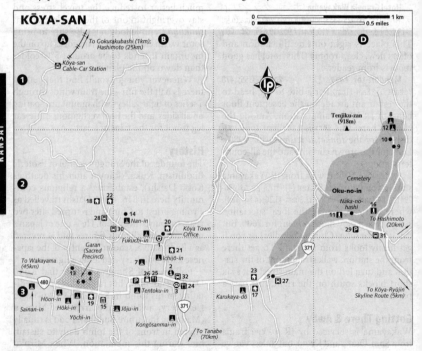

Museum and Tokugawa Mausoleum. It can
be purchased at the information office.

For the best map of the area, pick up a
copy of the Japanese map from the bus office
outside the top cable-car station.

Koyasan Interpreter Guide Club (☎ 080-6148-2588;
www.geocities.jp/koyasan_i_g_c/) This offers four-hour
private tours of Kōya-san for ¥5000 per group for up to
five people. It also offers regularly scheduled tours on
Wednesday from April to September for ¥1000 per person.
The morning tour meets at Ichi-no-hashi at 8.30am and
lasts 2½ hours and covers Oku-no-in. The afternoon tour
meets at Kongōbu-ji at 1pm, takes 1½ hours, and covers
Kongōbu-ji and the Garan.

Kōya-san Tourist Association (☎ 56-2616; fax 56-
2889; ⏰ 8.30am-5.30pm Jul & Aug, to 4.30pm Sep-Jun)
In the centre of town in front of the Senjūin-bashi-mae
bus stop. There are usually English speakers on hand and
brochures and maps are available.

Sights

OKU-NO-IN 奥の院

Any Buddhist worth their salt in Japan has
had their remains, or just a lock or two of
hair, interred in this **cemetery-temple** to ensure
pole position when Miroku Buddha comes
to earth.

The best way to approach Oku-no-in is to
walk or take the bus east to Ichi-no-hashi-mae
bus stop. From here you cross the bridge,
Ichi-no-hashi, and enter the cemetery grounds
along a winding, cobbled path lined by tall
cedar trees and thousands of tombs. As the
trees close in and the mist swirls the atmosphere can be enchanting, especially as night
falls. Among the interesting graves and monuments to look out for are the **North Borneo War
Victim Memorial**, which commemorates Japanese, Malay and Australian soldiers killed in

North Borneo in WWII (look for the flags),
and the **White Ant Memorial**, built by a pesticide
company to expiate its guilt for the murder of
legions of the little critters.

The **Tōrō-dō** (Lantern Hall), the main building of the complex, is at the northern end of
the graveyard. It houses hundreds of lamps,
including two believed to have been burning for more than 900 years. Behind the hall
you can see the closed doors of the Kūkai
mausoleum.

On the way to the Lantern Hall is the bridge
Mimyo-no-hashi. Worshippers ladle water from
the river and pour it over the nearby Jizō statues as an offering for the dead. The inscribed
wooden plaques in the river are in memory
of aborted babies and those who died by
drowning.

Between the bridge and the Tōrō-dō is
a small wooden building the size of a large
phone booth, which contains the **Miroku-ishi**.
Pilgrims reach through the holes in the wall to
try to lift a large, smooth boulder onto a shelf.
The weight of the stone is supposed to change
according to your weight of sin. We can only
report that the thing was damn heavy!

Buses return to the centre of town from the
Oku-no-mae bus stop, or you can walk back
in about 30 minutes.

KONGŌBU-JI 金剛峯寺

This is the headquarters of the Shingon school
and the residence of Kōya-san's abbot. The
present **structure** (☎ 56-2011; admission ¥500;
⏰ 8.30am-4pm) dates from the 19th century
and is definitely worth a visit.

The main hall's Ohiro-ma room has ornate
screens painted by Kanō Tanyu in the 16th
century. The Yanagi-no-ma (Willow Room)

KANSAI

has equally pretty screen paintings of willows but the rather grisly distinction of being the place where Toyotomi Hidetsugu committed *seppuku* (ritual suicide by disembowelment).

The rock garden is interesting for the sheer number of rocks used in its composition, giving the effect of a throng of petrified worshippers eagerly listening to a monk's sermon.

Admission includes tea and rice cakes served beside the stone garden.

GARAN 伽藍

This is a **temple complex** (☎ 56-2011; admission to each bldg ¥200; ☒ 8.30am-4.30pm) of several halls and pagodas. The most important buildings are the **Dai-tō** (Great Pagoda) and **Kondō** (Main Hall). The Dai-tō, rebuilt in 1934 after a fire, is said to be the centre of the lotus-flower mandala formed by the eight mountains around Kōya-san. It's been repainted recently and is an awesome sight. The nearby **Sai-tō** (Western Pagoda) was most recently rebuilt in 1834 and is more subdued. It's well worth entering the Dai-tō to see the Dainichi-nyōrai (Cosmic Buddha) and his four attendant Buddhas.

TREASURE MUSEUM 霊宝館

The **Treasure Museum** (Reihōkan; admission ¥600; ☒ 8.30am-5.30pm May-Oct, to 4.30pm Nov-Apr) has a compact display of Buddhist works of art, all collected in Kōya-san. There are some very fine statues, painted scrolls and mandalas.

TOKUGAWA MAUSOLEUM 徳川家霊台

Built in 1643, the **Tokugawa Mausoleum** (Tokugawa-ke Reidai; admission without joint ticket ¥200; ☒ 8.30am-4.30pm) consists of two adjoining structures that serve as the mausoleums of Tokugawa Ieyasu (on the right) and Tokugawa Hidetada (on the left), the first and second Tokugawa shōguns respectively. They are ornately decorated, as with most structures associated with the Tokugawa shōguns. The mausoleum is not far from the Namikiri-fudō-mae bus stop.

Festivals & Events

Aoba Matsuri Held on 15 June to celebrate the birth of Kōbō Daishi. Various traditional ceremonies are performed at the temples around town.

Rōsoku Matsuri (Candle Festival) This more interesting festival is held on 13 August in remembrance of departed souls. Thousands of mourners light candles along the approaches to Oku-no-in.

Sleeping

There are more than 50 temples in Kōya-san offering *shukubō*. It's worth staying the night at a temple here, especially to try *shōjin-ryōri* (vegetarian food – no meat, fish, onions or garlic). Because *shukubō* is intended for religious pilgrims, in the morning you may be asked to participate in *o-inori* (Buddhist prayer services) or *o-tsutome* (work). While participation is not mandatory, taking part in these practices enables you to appreciate the daily workings of a Japanese temple.

Kōya-san's temples have recently formed a group to fix prices and now most lodgings start at ¥9500 per person including two meals. In practice, there is a lot of variation in prices, not just between temples, but also within temples, depending upon room and season.

You should make advance reservations by fax through the Kōya-san Tourist Association (p419) or directly with the temples. Even if you contact the temples directly, you will be asked to go to the Tourist Association to pick up a reservation slip-voucher.

Kōya-san Youth Hostel (☎ 56-3889; fax 56-3889; dm per person ¥3980; ☒) This YH is a friendly and comfortable budget choice if the prices at the temples are out of your range. It's closed for parts of December and January. Call ahead for reservations.

Haryō-in (☎ 56-2702; fax 56-2936; r per person incl 2 meals from ¥7875; ☒) This temple is an exception to the fixed-price rule and functions as a *kokumin-shukusha*.

Ekō-in (☎ 56-2514; fax 56-2891; ekoin@mbox.co.jp; r per person incl 2 meals from ¥10,000; ☒) One of the nicer temples in town, Ekō-in is run by a friendly bunch of young monks and the rooms look onto beautiful gardens. This is also one of the two temples in town (the other is Kongōbu-ji) where you can study *zazen*. Call ahead to make arrangements.

Henjōson-in (☎ 56-2434; fax 56-3641; r per person incl 2 meals from ¥10,000; ☒) This is another good choice. The rooms here also have good garden views and are quite spacious. High-quality meals are served in the dining hall. The communal bathtubs here are huge and have nice views. And the flowers in the entryway are usually stunning.

Other good choices:

Muryōkō-in (☎ 56-2104; fax 56-4555; r per person incl 2 meals ¥9500; ☒) A fine place with an interesting morning Buddhist ceremony.

(Continued on page 429)

KANSAI

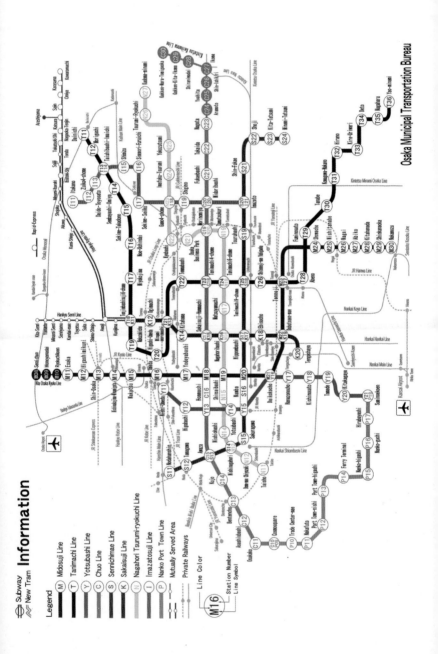

CHRISTIAN KOBER/ROBERT HARDING PICTURE LIBRARY LTD/PHOTOLIBRARY

Dancers celebrating Tokushima's Awa-odori festival (p629)

Page 421:
One of Japan's most photographed sites, the 'floating *torii*' of Itsukushima-jinja (p460)
TIMOTHY N HORNYAK

Acres of greenery at Ritsurin-Kōen (p658), Takamatsu

CORBIS/PHOTO

JOHN ASHBURNE

Thumbs up for the hot spring Tsuru-no-yu (p730), Beppu

The calm face of a 1000-year-old stone Buddha in Usuki (p727)

MARTIN MOOS

MASON FLORENCE

Waterfall and swimming hole in Kirishima-Yaku National Park (p706)

426

Cherry blossoms in Kakunodate (p541)

A young participant in the flamboyant Tōno Matsuri (p523) parade

MARTIN MOOS

Ainu dance at the reconstructed village of Poroto Kotan (p570), Shiraoi

Ice carver preparing for the Sapporo Yuki Matsuri (p577)

OLIVER STREWE

MARTIN MOOS

Mountains to the south of Tokachi-dake (p608) in Daisetsuzan National Park

River kayaking (p776) along the Urauchi-gawa, Iriomote-jima

MASON FLORENCE

Forest in Kirishima-Yaku National Park (p706)

MICHAEL S. YAMASHITA

(Continued from page 420)

Rengejō-in (☎ 56-2233; fax 56-4743; r per person incl 2 meals from ¥11,550; 🔲) An elegant establishment.

Shojōshin-in (☎ 56-2006; fax 56-4770; r per person incl 2 meals from ¥9500; 🔲) Friendly spot.

Eating

The culinary speciality of Kōya-san is *shōjin ryōri*, which you can sample at your temple lodgings. Two tasty tofu specialities are *goma-tōfu* (sesame tofu) and *kōya-tōfu* (local tofu). If you're just in town for the day, you can try *shōjin ryōri* at any of the temples that offer *shukubō*. Ask at the Kōya-san Tourist Association office (p419) and staff will call ahead to make reservations. Prices are fixed at ¥2500, ¥3500 and ¥5000, depending on how many courses you have.

There are various coffee shops and *shokudō* dotted around town where you can have breakfast or lunch (most close before dinnertime). There is also a supermarket in the centre of town.

Maruman (☎ 56-2049; noodle dishes from ¥470; 🕙 9am-5pm, closed irregularly) This simple *shokudō* is a good spot for lunch. All the standard lunch items are represented by plastic food models in the window. *Katsu-don* is ¥810 and noodle dishes start at ¥470. It's just west of the tourist office on the main street – look for the food models in the window and the phone out front (there's no English sign).

Hanabishi Honten (☎ 56-2236; 769 Kōyasan; lunch ¥2100-8400, dinner ¥2100-16,000; 🕙 11am-6pm, reservation required after 6pm, closed irregularly; E) If you fancy something a little nicer than a *shokudō*, you could try this slightly overpriced restaurant. At lunch, the *sankozen* set (a variety of vegetarian dishes; ¥2100) is a good choice. Look for the grey façade and the food models in the window (which will also help with ordering, if necessary).

Getting There & Away

Unless you have a rental car, the best way to Kōya-san is by train. The Nankai-Dentetsu line has trains from Osaka's Namba station to Kōya-san. The trains terminate at Gokuraku-bashi, at the base of the mountain, where you board a funicular railway (five minutes, price included in train tickets) up to Kōya-san itself. From the cable-car station, you must take a bus into the centre of town, as walking is prohibited on the connecting road.

From Osaka (Namba station) you can travel directly on a Nankai–Dentetsu line *kyūkō* to Kōya-san (¥1230, 82 minutes). For the slightly faster *tokkyū* service with reserved seats you pay a supplement (¥760).

From Wakayama you can go by rail on the JR Wakayama line to Hashimoto (¥820, one hour) and then continue on the Nankai–Dentetsu line to Gokurakubashi station (¥430, 38 minutes).

From Kyoto it's best to go via Namba in Osaka. From Nara you can take the JR line to Hashimoto, changing at Sakurai and Takadate en route.

Getting Around

Buses run on three routes from the top cable-car station via the centre of town to Ichi-no-hashi and Oku-no-in. The fare to the tourist office in the centre of town at Senjūin-bashi is ¥280. The fare to the final stop, Oku-no-in, is ¥400. An all-day bus pass (*ichi-nichi furee kippu*; ¥800) is available from the bus office outside the top cable-car station, but once you get into the centre of town you can reach most destinations quite easily on foot (including Oku-no-in, which takes about 30 minutes). Note that buses run infrequently, so you should make a note of the schedule before setting out to see the sights.

If you don't feel like walking, bicycles can be rented (per hour/day ¥400/1200) at the Kōya-san Tourist Association office (p419).

SHIRAHAMA 白浜
☎ 0739 / pop 20,000

Shirahama, on the southwest coast of the Kii-hantō, is Kansai's leading beach-*onsen* resort and has all the trappings of a major Japanese tourist attraction – huge resort hotels, aquariums, amusement parks, the lot. However, because the Japanese like to do things according to the rules – and the rules say the only time you can swim in the ocean is from late July to the end of August – the place is almost deserted outside of the season and you'll have the place to yourself.

Shirahama has several good *onsen* and a great white-sand beach, and the rugged sea coast south of the town is stunning. This is a great place to visit in, say, June or September, and we've swum in the sea here as late as mid-October.

There's a **tourist information office** (☎ 42-2900; 🕙 9.30am-6pm) in the station, where you can pick up a map to the main sights and accommodation. Since the station is a fair distance from the main sights, you'll need to take a bus (one way/all-day pass ¥310/980, 12 minutes to the beach) or rent a bicycle if you arrive by rail. The JR office at the station rents bicycles (¥500 per day).

Sights & Activities

ONSEN

In addition to its great beach, Shirahama has some of Japan's oldest developed *onsen* (they're even mentioned in the Nihon Shoki, one of Japan's earliest literary texts).

The **Sakino-yu Onsen** (崎の湯温泉; ☎ 42-3016; 1688 Shirahama-chō, Nishimuro-gun; admission ¥300; ☷ 7am-7pm Jul & Aug, 8am-5pm Sep-Jun, closed Wed) is sensational. It's built on a rocky point with great views of the Pacific Ocean (and you can climb down the rocks to cool off if the waves aren't too big). Come early in the day to beat the crowds. It's 1km south of the main beach; walk along the seafront road and look for the point below the big Hotel Seymor. The baths are segregated by sex.

Other baths include **Shirara-yu** (白良湯; ☎ 43-2614; 3313-1 Shirahama-chō, Nishimuro-gun; admission ¥300; ☷ 7am-11pm Wed-Mon, noon-10.30pm Tue), a pleasant bath right on the north end of Shirara-hama (the main beach), and **Murono-yu** (牟婁の湯; ☎ 42-0686; 1665 Shirahama-chō, Nishimuro-gun; admission ¥300; ☷ noon-10.30pm Thu, 7am-11pm Fri-Wed), a simple *onsen* not far from Sakino-yu, in front of Shirahama post office, on the way to Sakino-yu.

SENJŌ-JIKI, SANDAN-HEKI & ISOGI-KŌEN
千畳敷・三段壁・いそぎ公園

Just around the point south of the Sakino-yu Onsen are two of Shirahama's natural wonders: Senjō-jiki and Sandan-heki. **Senjō-jiki** (Thousand Tatami Mat Point) is a wildly eroded point with stratified layers that actually resemble the thousand tatami mats it is named for.

More impressive is the 50m cliff face of **Sandan-heki** (Three-Step Cliff), which drops away vertiginously into the sea (there are signs in Japanese warning off suicidal jumpers). While you can pay ¥1200 to take a lift down to a cave at the base of the cliff, it's better simply to clamber along the rocks to the north of the cliff – it's stunning, particularly when the big rollers are pounding in from the Pacific.

If you'd like to enjoy more rugged coastal scenery, walk south along the coast another 1km from Sandan-heki to **Isogi-kōen**, where

the crowds are likely to be thinner and the scenery just as impressive.

These attractions can be reached on foot or bicycle from the main beach in around 30 minutes, or you can take a bus from the station (¥430, 20 minutes to Senjō-jiki), from which you can walk to the others.

SHIRARA-HAMA BEACH 白良浜

Shirara-hama, the town's main beach, is famous for its white sand. If it reminds you of Australia don't be surprised – the town had to import sand from down under after the original stuff washed away. This place is packed during July and August. In the off-peak season, it can actually be quite pleasant. The beach is hard to miss, as it dominates the western side of town.

The only drawback to this excellent beach is the loud music broadcast from loudspeakers during the summer months. The music is uniquely horrible and the only thing you can do to save yourself is to set up shop as far from the speakers as possible.

Shirasuna-yu (しらすな湯; ☎ 43-1126; 864 Shirahama-chō, Nishimuro-gun; ☷ 10am-7pm Tue-Sun) is a free open-air *onsen* off the boardwalk in the middle of the beach. You can soak here and then dash into the ocean to cool off – not a bad way to spend an afternoon.

Sleeping

In Shirahama itself there are several *minshuku, kokumin-shukusha* and hotels of all shapes and sizes.

Ohgigahama Youth Hostel (扇ケ浜ユースホステル; ☎ 22-3433; fax 22-3433; http://ohgigahama.web .infoseek.co.jp; 35-1 Shinyashiki-chō; dm ¥2625; ☒) This is a friendly, comfortable and cheap option if you don't mind staying outside the town of Shirahama. The hostel is 10 minutes on foot from Kii-Tanabe station, which is three stops north of Shirahama station on the JR Kisei line. No meals available.

Minshuku Katsuya (民宿かつ屋; ☎ 42-3814; fax 42-3817; 3118-5 Shirahama-chō, Nishimuro-gun; r per person excl meals ¥4000; ☒) Katsuya is the best-value *minshuku* in town and it's very central, only two minutes' walk from the main beach. It's built around a small Japanese garden and has its own natural *onsen* bath. There is red-and-white Japanese writing on the building and faint English on a small sign.

Kokumin-shukusha Hotel Shirahama (国民宿舎ホテルシラハマ; ☎ 42-3039; fax 42-4643; 813 Shira-

hama-chō, Nishimuro-gun; r per person incl 2 meals ¥6870;
) This is a good bet if Katsuya is full, and offers similar rates. It's a little dark and showing
its age, but the rooms are spacious and there is
an *onsen* bath. It's just off Miyuki-dōri, 100m
past the post office towards the beach (look
for a parking lot and the black-blue-red-and-
white sign). The tourist information office at
the station has maps to both places.

Hotel Marquise (ホテルマーキーズ; 42-4010,
fax 43-2720; www.aikis.or.jp/~marquise/in Japanese; 1905
Yuzaki, Shirahama-chō; r per person incl 2 meals from ¥16,800;
) Very close to Sakino-yu Onsen, this hotel
has excellent sea-view rooms, some with balconies. The Japanese-style rooms are spacious
and clean. This hotel is popular with female
guests and the ladies bath is larger than the
mens (something of a rarity in Japan).

Eating

There are many restaurants in the streets just
in from the beach.

Kiraku (喜楽; 42-3916; 890-48 Shirahama-chō,
Nishimuro-gun; 11am-2pm & 4-9pm Wed-Mon) There
is nothing fancy about this friendly little
shokudō that serves standard *teishoku* for
around ¥800. There is a limited picture menu
to help with ordering. It's about 5m in from
Miyuki-dōri, on the beach side, close to a coin
laundry (look for the plants out front).

Ginchiro (銀ちろ; 42-2514; Ginza-dōri, Shirahama-
chō, Nishimuro-gun; set meals from ¥900; 11am-2pm &
4-9pm Thu-Tue) This is a more upmarket option,
serving tempura and *unagi* set meals (there
is a picture menu). It's on Hama-Ginza-dōri,
directly across from a public foot bath (look
for the traditional front and the black-and-
white sign). The tourist information office at
the station can provide a map to both places.
Alternatively, ask for some directions at your
accommodation.

If you'd like to self-cater, Sakae Supermarket is five minutes' walk from the main
beach.

Getting There & Away

Shirahama is on the JR Kii main line. There is a
tokkyū train from Shin-Osaka station (¥5450,
132 minutes; *futsū*, ¥3260, 207 minutes). The
same line also connects Shirahama to other
cities on Kii-hantō such as Kushimoto, Nachi,
Shingū and Wakayama City. A cheaper alternative is offered by **Meikō Bus** (0739-42-2112;
www13.ocn.ne.jp/~meikobus in Japanese; 9am-6pm),
which runs buses between JR Osaka station

and Shirahama (one way/return ¥2700/5000,
about 3½ hours).

KUSHIMOTO, CAPE SHIONO-MISAKI & KII-ŌSHIMA 串本・潮岬・紀伊大島
 0735

The southern tip of Kii-hantō has some stunning coastal scenery. Shiono-misaki, connected to the mainland by a narrow isthmus,
has some fine rocky vistas, but the real action
is over on Kii-Ōshima, a rocky island accessible by a newly completed bridge.

The main attraction on Kii-Ōshima is the
coastal cliffs at the eastern end of the island,
which can be viewed from the park around
Kashino-zaki Lighthouse (樫野崎灯台). Just before the park, you'll find the **Toruko-Kinenkan
Museum** (トルコ記念館; 65-0628; 1025-25
Kashino, Kushimoto-chō, Higashimuro-gun; admission ¥250;
9am-5pm), which commemorates the sink-
ing of the Turkish ship *Ertugrul* in 1890.

Backtracking about 1km towards the
bridge, there are small English signs to the
Japan-US Memorial Museum (日米修交記念館;
65-0099; 1033 Kashino, Kushimoto-chō, Nishimuro-gun;
admission ¥250; 9am-4pm Tue-Sun), which commemorates the visit of the US ship *Lady
Washington* in 1791, a full 62 years before
Commodore Perry's much more famous
landing in Yokohama in 1853. There is a
lookout just beyond the museum from which
you can see the magnificent **Umi-kongō** (海
金剛) formations along the eastern point of
the island.

If you're without your own transport, the
best way to explore Kii-Ōshima is by renting a
cycle at Kushimoto station (per four hours/full
day ¥600/1000, discount for JR ticket holders),
but be warned that there are a few big hills en
route and these bikes are not performance
vehicles. Otherwise, there are buses from the
station, but take note of schedules as departures are few and far between.

Misaki Lodge Youth Hostel (みさきロッジユー
スホステル; 62-1474; fax 62-0529; 2864-1 Shionomi-
saki, Kushimoto-chō; per person dm excl meals/minshuku incl
2 meals from ¥4410/7350) is the best place to stay in
the area. It's in a good position, on the southern side of the cape overlooking the Pacific.
It's also a *minshuku*, offering large rooms and
two meals. Take a Shiono-misaki-bound bus
from Kushimoto station (20 minutes) and get
off at Koroshio-mae.

Kushimoto is one hour from Shirahama by
JR *tokkyū*, 3½ hours (¥6280) from Shin-Osaka.

KANSAI

Futsū services are significantly cheaper but take almost twice as long.

NACHI & KII-KATSUURA
那智・紀伊勝浦

The Nachi and Kii-Katsuura area has several sights grouped around the sacred **Nachi-no-taki** (那智の滝), Japan's highest waterfall (133m). **Nachi Taisha** (那智大社), near the waterfall, was built in homage to the waterfall's *kami* (Shintō spirit god). It is one of the three great shrines of Kii-hantō, and it's worth the climb up the steep steps to get there. Next to the shrine, **Sanseiganto-ji** (山青岸渡寺) is a fine old temple that is well worth a look.

The most atmospheric approach to the falls and the shrine is the fantastic tree-lined arcade of **Daimon-zaka**. To get to Daimon-zaka, take a bus from Nachi or Kii-Katsuura stations, and get off at the Daimon-zaka stop (ask the bus driver to drop you at Daimon-zaka and he'll point you in the right direction from the stop). The way isn't marked in English, but it's roughly straight uphill just in from the road. From the bus stop to the shrine is roughly 800m, most of it uphill. It's fine in winter, but in summer you'll get soaked, so consider doing it in reverse (check bus schedules carefully before setting out).

Daimon-zaka takes you up to the steps at the base of the shrine. After visiting the shrine, walk down to the falls. At the base of the falls you will find **Nachiyama-oku-no-in** (那智山奥の院), where you can pay ¥200 to hike up to a lookout that affords a better view of the falls.

The **Nachi-no-Hi Matsuri** (Fire Festival) takes place at the falls on 14 July. During this lively event *mikoshi* are brought down from the mountain and met by groups bearing flaming torches.

Buses to the waterfall and shrine leave from Nachi station (¥470, 25 minutes) and from Kii-Katsuura station (¥600, 30 minutes). Buses to the Daimon-zaka stop leave from Nachi station (¥330, 15 minutes) and from Kii-Katsuura station (¥410, 20 minutes).

Sleeping

There are a few places to stay near Nachi station and Kii-Katsuura station.

Hotel Ura-Shima (ホテル浦島; ☎ 0735-52-1011; www.hotelurashima.co.jp in Japanese; per person from ¥11,235 incl 2 meals; 🅿) Laying claim to an entire peninsula in Katsuura-wan, this vast hotel-*onsen* complex is either a lot of fun or an overpriced tourist trap, depending upon your mood. It's got two fantastic baths built into caves looking out over the Pacific, and two others located high atop the peninsula, reached by the longest escalator we've ever seen – we half expected to come out on the South Col of Everest. The fun of the baths is offset by uninspiring food, ageing rooms, and the noisy announcements in the hallways.

Getting There & Away

Nachi and Kii-Katsuura (the stations are only two stops apart) can be reached by JR Kii main line trains from Shin-Osaka station (*tokkyū*, ¥6700, 216 minutes; *futsū*, ¥4310, 332 minutes) and from Nagoya station (*tokkyū*, ¥7510, 213 minutes; *futsū*, ¥3920, 327 minutes). *Futsū* are significantly cheaper but take almost twice as long.

SHINGŪ 新宮
☎ 0735 / pop 34,000

Shingū functions as a useful transport hub for access to the **Kumano Sanzan**, the three major Shintō shrines of the Kii-hantō. The three shrines are Kumano Hayatama Taisha, Kumano Hongū Taisha (opposite) and Nachi Taisha (left).

There's a helpful **information office** (☎ 22-2840; 🕙 9am-5pm) at the station.

Kumano Hayatama Taisha (熊野速玉大社) is actually in Shingū itself. It's a 15-minute walk northwest of Shingū station. The shrine's **Boat Race Festival** takes place on 16 October. Another shrine worth looking at is **Kamikura-jinja** (神倉神社), which is famous for its **Otō Matsuri** (6 February), during which more than 1000 people carrying torches ascend the slope to the shrine. The shrine is a 15-minute walk west of the station.

Station Hotel Shingū (ステーションホテル新宮; ☎ 21-2200; fax 21-1067; station@rifnet.or.jp; s/d/tw from ¥4900/9000/10,000; 🅿), a small business hotel, has decent Western-style rooms. It's 200m southeast of the station. The whitish building is visible from outside Shingū station. Ask for a room in the *shinkan* (new wing).

A two-minute walk north of the station, **Hase Ryokan** (長谷旅館; ☎ 22-2185; fax 21-6677; r per person with 2 meals ¥6300/7350; 🅿) is a comfortable and reasonable choice for those who prefer Japanese-style accommodation. Call from the station and someone will collect you, or ask at the information office for a map.

There are several restaurants near the station. For something nicer, get the folks at the information office to draw you a map to **Ajinosankin** (味のさんきん; ☎ 22-2373; sashimi around ¥1500; ⏱ 11am-1.30pm & 5.30-9.30pm Mon-Sat), which offers excellent sets of locally caught sashimi. It's about a 20-minute walk (approximately 2km) from the station. It has no English menu, however there are some pictures on the menu. Try the *sashimi teishoku* (¥1200). Look for the relatively large white signboard. It is located on the 1st floor of a business hotel.

The JR Kii main line connects Shingū with Nagoya station (*tokkyū*, ¥6990, three hours) and Shin-Osaka station (*tokkyū*, ¥6810, four hours).

There are buses between Shingū and Hongū, about half of which make a loop of the three surrounding *onsen* (Watarase, Yunomine and Kawa-yu). See under Hongū (below) for details.

HONGŪ 本宮

Hongū itself isn't particularly interesting but it makes a good starting point for the *onsen* nearby. Hongū is also home to **Kumano Hongū Taisha** (熊野本宮大社), one of the three famous shrines of the Kumano Sanzan. The shrine is close to the Ōmiya Taisha-mae bus stop (the buses listed in this section stop there).

Buses leave for Hongū from JR Gojō station and Kintetsu Yamato-yagi station in the north (¥4000, 283 minutes), Kii-Tanabe in the west (¥2000, two hours) and Shingū in the southeast (¥1500, 80 minutes). Shingū is the most convenient of these three access points (departures are most frequent from there). Most Hongū buses also stop at Kawa-yu, Watarase and Yunomine *onsen* (in that order), but be sure to ask before boarding. Keep in mind that departures are few in any direction, so jot down the times and plan accordingly.

YUNOMINE, WATARASE & KAWA-YU ONSEN
☎ 0735

These three *onsen* are among the best in all of Kansai. Because each has its own distinct character, it's worth doing a circuit of all three. There are several ryokan and *minshuku* in the area, but if you are on a tight budget it's possible to camp on the riverbanks above and below Kumano Hongū Taisha. See Hongū (above) for transport details.

Note that you can walk between the three *onsen* in this section relatively easily. The tunnel at the west end of the village at Kawa-yu connects to Watarase Onsen (the total journey is a little less than 1km). From Watarase Onsen, it's about 3km west along Rte 311 to reach Yunomine.

Yunomine Onsen 湯峰温泉

The town of Yunomine is nestled around a narrow river in a wooded valley. Most of the town's *onsen* are contained inside ryokan or *minshuku* but charming little **Tsubo-yu Onsen** (つぼ湯温泉; admission ¥250; ⏱ 6am-9.30pm) is open to all. It's right in the middle of town, inside a tiny wooden shack built on an island in the river. Buy a ticket at the *sentō* next to **Tōkō-ji** (東光寺), the temple in the middle of town. The *sentō* itself is open the same hours as the *onsen* and entry is ¥300; of the two baths at the *sentō*, we suggest the *kusuri-yu* (medicine water; ¥380), which is 100% pure hot-spring water.

While you're at Yunomine, try your hand at cooking some *onsen tamago* – eggs boiled in the hot water of an *onsen*. There is a pool of hot-spring water just downstream from Tsubo-yu for cooking. The shop across from the temple sells bags of five eggs for ¥200. Put them in the water before you enter the bath and they should be cooked by the time you get out.

SLEEPING
Yunomine has plenty of *minshuku* and ryokan for you to choose from.

Minshuku Yunotanisō (民宿湯の谷荘; ☎ 42-1620; r per person incl 2 meals ¥7500; 🅿) At the upper end of the village, this simple *minshuku* is exactly what a *minshuku* should be: simple, clean and welcoming. The food is very good and there's an excellent *onsen* bath on the premises.

Ryokan Yoshino-ya (旅館よしのや; ☎ 42-0101; r per person incl 2 meals ¥8550; 🅿) Located very close to Tsubo-yu, this is a slightly more upscale place with a lovely *rotemburo*. It's fairly new and the location can't be beat. Like Yunotanisō, it's a friendly and well-run spot.

Kawa-yu Onsen 川湯温泉

Kawa-yu Onsen is a natural wonder, where geothermally heated water percolates up through the gravel banks of the river that runs through the middle of the town. You can make your own private bath here by digging out some of the stones and letting the hole fill with hot water; you can then spend the rest of the day jumping back and forth between the bath and the cool waters of the river. Admission is free and the best spots along the river are in front of Fujiya ryokan. We suggest bringing a bathing suit unless you fancy putting on a 'naked *gaijin*' show for the whole town.

In the winter, from 1 December to 28 February, bulldozers are used to turn the river into a giant *rotemburo*. Known as the **Sennin Buro** (仙人風呂; admission free; ⏱ 24hr), the name is a play on the word for 'thousand', a reference to the fact that you could just about squeeze 1000 bathers into this open-air tub. It's a lot of fun and you can dazzle locals by jumping into the main flow of the river to cool off.

SLEEPING
Pension Ashita-no-Mori (ペンションあした の森; ☎ 42-1525; fax 42-1333; ashitanomori-kawayu@

za.ztv.ne.jp; r per person incl 2 meals ¥7500; ⊠) This is in a pleasant wooden building with a good riverside location. Rooms are adequate in size and well maintained. It's got its own private *onsen* bath. Inside baths are all *onsen* as well.

Fujiya (富士屋; ☎ 42-0007; fax 42-1115; www .fuziya.co.jp/english/index.html; r per person incl 2 meals from ¥15,900; ⊠) Next door, this is a more upmarket ryokan with tasteful rooms: spacious, clean and tastefully decorated. For a very civilised place to stay after a day in the river baths, this is the spot. Needless to say, it's got its own private *onsen* bath as well.

Watarase Onsen 渡瀬温泉
This *onsen* (admission ¥700; ⏱ 6am-9.30pm) is built around a bend in the river directly between Yunomine Onsen and Kawa-yu Onsen. It's not as interesting as its neighbours, but does boast a nice collection of *rotemburo*. Baths get progressively cooler as you work your way out from the inside bath. Buy tickets from the

---

THE KUMANO KODŌ, KII-HANTŌ'S ANCIENT PILGRIMAGE ROUTE & NEWEST WORLD HERITAGE SITE

From the earliest times, the Japanese believed the wilds of the Kii-hantō to be inhabited by *kami*, Shinto deities. Three of the most powerful deities of the region are enshrined in three famous shrines: Hongū Taisha in Hongū, Hayatama Taisha in Shingū and Nachi Taisha in Nachi Katsuura, all of which are located in present-day Wakayama-ken. Together they are known as the Kumano Sansha – the three shrines of Kumano.

Japan's early emperors made regular pilgrimages to these shrines to petition the deities for power, prosperity and health. The route they followed from Kyoto, via Osaka, Kii Tanabe and over the inner mountains of Wakayama, is known today as the Kumano Kodō – the Old Road of Kumano. The retired emperor Go Shirakawa Jōko performed the pilgrimage no less than 33 times each time with an entourage of about 1000 retainers and 200 horses. Over time, the popularity of this pilgrimage spread from nobles to common folk and yamabushi priests (wandering mountain ascetics). Indeed, it became so popular that the route was sometimes referred to as the Ari Kumano Mōde – the Kumano Ants Pilgrimage. Eventually, the way was paved with stones and graded with well-laid flagstone steps.

In 2004, the 'Sacred Sites and Pilgrimage Routes in the Kii Mountain Range' were granted Unesco World Heritage site status. This new World Heritage site includes the Kumano Kodō and other traditional pilgrimage routes in Wakayama-ken, Mie-ken and Nara-ken. Local governments are now madly scrambling to exploit the tourist potential that this new status confers on their districts, and every footpath and flagstone in sight is being trumpeted as part of the famous Kumano Kodō.

Despite this, plenty of the actual, original route remains passable. While it's possible to walk all the way from Kii Tanabe on the west coast of Wakayama to Nachi Taisha shrine on the east coast, it's better to start from Hongū. From there, it's a two-day hike over mountainous terrain to the shrine at Nachi, overlooking beautiful Nachi falls. There is a private camping ground midway, but many hikers opt to camp along the route at spots of their own choosing. Additional information about the Kumano Kodō is available from the Wakayama Tourist Board.

If you just want a quick taste of the route, combined with a visit to one of the three main shrines, we recommend the incredibly atmospheric Daimon-zaka approach to Nachi Taisha.

machine outside the change room. The *onsen* itself has a restaurant, but you'll find better choices at the adjoining Watarase Onsen Sasa-yuri Hotel (わたらせ温泉ホテルささゆり), which has a restaurant with a picture menu.

ISE-SHIMA 伊勢志摩

The Ise-Shima region, on Mie-ken's Shima-hantō, is most famous for Ise-jingū, Japan's most sacred Shintō shrine. The shrine is located in Ise-shi, the main city of the region. Ise-Shima also encompasses the tourist mecca of Toba and some pleasant coastal scenery around Kashikojima and Goza. Ise-Shima is easily reached from Nagoya, Kyoto or Osaka and makes a good two-day trip from any of these cities.

ISE 伊勢

☎ 0596 / pop 137,000

Although the city of Ise-shi is rather drab, it's worth making the trip here to visit the spectacular Ise-jingū. This is arguably Japan's most impressive shrine; its only rival to this claim is Nikkō's Tōshō-gū, which is as gaudy as Ise-jingū is austere.

Sights & Activities

If you have some time to kill in town after visiting the shrines, take a stroll down atmospheric **Kawasaki Kaiwai** (河崎界隈), a street lined with traditional Japanese houses and shops. It's a little tricky to find; start at the Ise City Hotel (see p437), cross the street, go down the side street next to Eddy's Supermarket (yes, that's the name), and take a left down the street just before the canal; Kawasaki Kaiwai parallels this canal, on its west side.

ISE-JINGŪ 伊勢神宮

Dating back to the 3rd century, Ise-jingū is the most venerated Shintō **shrine** (admission free; ☼ sunrise-sunset) in Japan. Shintō tradition has dictated for centuries that the shrine buildings be replaced every 20 years with exact imitations built on adjacent sites according to ancient techniques – no nails, only wooden dowels and interlocking joints.

Upon completion of the new buildings, the god of the shrine is ritually transferred to its new home in the Sengū No Gi ceremony, first witnessed by Western eyes in 1953. The wood from the old shrine is then used to reconstruct

the torii at the shrine's entrance or is sent to shrines around Japan for use in rebuilding their structures. The present buildings were rebuilt in 1993 (for the 61st time) at a cost exceeding ¥5 billion. They'll next be rebuilt in 2013.

You may be surprised to discover that the main shrine buildings are almost completely hidden from view behind wooden fences. Only members of the imperial family and certain shrine priests are allowed to enter the sacred inner sanctum. This is unfortunate, as the buildings are stunning examples of pre-Buddhist Japanese architecture. Don't despair, though, as determined neck-craning over fences allows a decent view of the upper parts of the buildings. You can also get a good idea of the shrine's architecture by looking at any of the lesser shrines nearby, which are exact replicas built on a smaller scale.

There are two parts to the shrine, **Gekū** (Outer Shrine) and **Naikū** (Inner Shrine). The former is an easy 15-minute walk from Ise-shi station; the latter is accessible by bus from the station or from the stop outside Gekū (below). If you only have time to visit one of the shrines, Naikū is the more impressive of the two.

Smoking is prohibited throughout the grounds of both shrines and photography is forbidden around the main halls of both shrines.

Gekū 外宮

The Outer Shrine dates from the 5th century and enshrines the god of food, clothing and housing, Toyouke-no-Ōkami. Daily offerings of rice are made by shrine priests to the goddess, who is charged with providing food to Amaterasu-Ōmikami, the goddess enshrined in the Naikū. A stall at the entrance to the shrine provides a leaflet in English with a map.

The main shrine building here is the Goshōden, which is about 10 minutes' walk from the entrance to the shrine. Across the river from the Goshōden, you'll find three smaller shrines that are worth a look (and are usually less crowded).

From Ise-shi station or Uji-Yamada station it's a 12-minute walk down the main street to the shrine entrance.

Naikū 内宮

The Inner Shrine is thought to date from the 3rd century and enshrines the sun goddess,

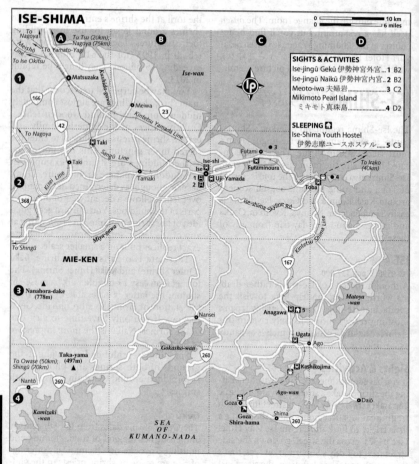

SIGHTS & ACTIVITIES
Ise-jingū Gekū 伊勢神宮外宮...**1** B2
Ise-jingū Naikū 伊勢神宮内宮...**2** B2
Meoto-iwa 夫婦岩...........................**3** C2
Mikimoto Pearl Island
ミキモト真珠島...........................**4** D2

SLEEPING
Ise-Shima Youth Hostel
伊勢志摩ユースホステル...**5** C3

Amaterasu-Ōmikami, who is considered the ancestral goddess of the imperial family and the guardian deity of the Japanese nation. Naikū is held in even higher reverence than Gekū because it houses the sacred mirror of the emperor, one of the three imperial regalia (the other two are the sacred beads and the sacred sword).

A stall just before the entrance to the shrine provides the same English leaflet given out at Gekū. Next to this stall is the Uji-bashi, which leads over the crystal-clear Isuzu-gawa into the shrine. One path leads to the right and passes Mitarashi, a place for pilgrims to purify themselves in the river before entering the shrine.

The path continues along an avenue lined with towering cryptomeria trees to the Goshōden, the main shrine building. As at Gekū, you can only catch a glimpse of the top of the structure here, as four rows of wooden fences obstruct the view. If you're tempted to jump the fence when nobody's around, think again – they're watching you on closed-circuit TV cameras not so cleverly disguised as trees!

A better view of the shrine can be had by walking around the shrine to the left (north) and standing near the Mishinenomikura, the sacred rice storehouse that is No 20 on the shrine map. Here, you can see a large section of the shrine, and on sunny days the cypress wood of the shrine gleams almost as brightly as the gold tips of its roof beams.

To get to Naikū, take bus 51 or 55 from bus stop 11 outside Ise-shi station or the stop on the main road in front of Gekū (¥410, 12 minutes). Note that bus stop 11 is about 100m past the main bus stop outside Ise-shi station (walk south on the main street). Get off at the Naikū-mae stop. From Naikū there are buses back to Ise-shi station via Gekū (¥410, 18 minutes from bus stop 2). Alternatively, a taxi between Ise-shi station/Gekū and Naikū costs ¥2000 to ¥2500.

Festivals & Events

Since Ise-jingu is Japan's most sacred shrine, it's not surprising that it's also a favourite destination for *hatsu-mōde* (first shrine visit of the new year). Most of the action takes place in the first three days of the year, when millions of worshippers pack the area and accommodation is booked out for months in advance.

The **Kagurai-sai Matsuri**, celebrated on 5 and 6 April, is a good chance to see performances of *kagura* (sacred dance), *bugaku*, nō and Shintō music.

Sleeping

Ise City Hotel (伊勢シティホテル; ☎ 28-2111; fax 28-1058; 1-11-31 Fukiage; s/tw ¥6510/13,650; ⚡) This is a good business hotel with small, clean rooms and a convenient location less than 10 minutes' walk from the station. Some staff members speak a bit of English. To get there from Ise-shi station, take a left (east) outside the station, walk past a JTB travel agency, take a left at the first traffic light, and cross the tracks. You'll see it on the left.

Hoshide-kan (星出館; ☎ 28-2377; fax 27-2830; 2-15-2 Kawasaki; r per person incl/excl 2 meals ¥7500/5000; ⚡) Also in Ise-shi, this is a quaint wooden ryokan with some nice traditional touches. Go straight past Ise City Hotel, and it's on the right (there is a small English sign). It's about 400m from the rail tracks.

Ise-Shima Youth Hostel (伊勢志摩ユースホステル; ☎ 0599-55-0226; fax 0599-55-3319; ise@jyh .gr.jp; 1219-82 Anagawa, Isobe-chō; r per person incl breakfast from ¥4620; ⚡) Built on a hill overlooking an attractive bay, this is a great place to stay for budget travellers. It's close to Anagawa station on the Kintetsu line south of Ise-shi (only *futsū* trains stop). Walk east out of the station along the waterfront road; it's uphill on the right.

Eating & Drinking

Daiki (大善; ☎ 28-0281; meals from ¥1500; ⌚ 11am-9pm) Our favourite place to eat in Ise-shi bills itself as 'Japan's most famous restaurant'. Bluff and bluster aside, it's a great place to sample seafood, including *ise-ebi* (Japanese lobsters), served as set meals for ¥5000; ask for the *ise-ebi teishoku* and specify *yaki* (grilled), *niita* (boiled) or *sashimi* (raw). Simpler meals include tempura *teishoku* (tempura set meal; ¥1500). It's outside and to the right of Uji-Yamada station; there's a small English sign reading 'Kappo Daiki'.

Kawasaki-gura (河崎蔵; ☎ 29-1872; 2-13-12 Kawasaki; ⌚ 10am-late Thu-Mon) You'll find more choices along the atmospheric Kawasaki Kaiwai street. This is a good place for a quick pick-me-up. Located inside an old *machiya*, this coffee shop serves good coffee (¥450) and rare tofu cheesecake (¥450). It's 300m from the southern end of the street (the station end). Look for the stones and wooden bench on the right; it's next to a car park.

Tamaya (球家; ☎ 24-0105; 2-17-23 Kawasaki; ⌚ 7pm-midnight, closed Mon; E) Nearby, you'll find an excellent bar-restaurant in an old *kura*. This is a friendly spot for a drink or a light meal. It's just down a narrow street off Kawasaki Kaiwai on the left as you walk north (look for a white-and-red sign on a utility pole that reads 'Tamaya The Lounge').

At Naikū you'll find plenty of good restaurants in the Okage-yokochō Arcade, just outside the shrine (when walking from the bus stop towards the shrine, look to the left and you will see the covered arcade).

In the arcade **Nikōdōshiten** (二光堂支店; ☎ 24-4409; 19 Ujiimazaike-chō; ⌚ 11am-4pm, closed Thu) is a good place to try some of the local specialities in a rough, roadhouse atmosphere. *Ise-udon* (thick noodles in a dark broth; small/large bowl ¥420/570) is the speciality. For a bigger meal, try the *ise-udon teishoku* (*ise-udon* with rice and side dishes; ¥1000). The restaurant is 200m from the shrine end of the arcade, on the right in a three-storey building (look inside for the simple interior). It's 100m north of the arcade entrance. If this doesn't suit, there are many choices along the arcade, and most display food models out front to help you choose.

Getting There & Away

There are rail connections between Ise-shi and Nagoya, Osaka and Kyoto on both the JR and the Kintetsu lines. For those without a Japan Rail Pass, the Kintetsu line is by far the most convenient way to go. Note that there are two stations in Ise: Ise-shi station and Uji-Yamada station. They're only a few hundred metres

KANSAI

apart and most trains stop at both. We recommend using Ise-shi station for the destinations and accommodation described in this section.

Kintetsu fares and travel times to/from Ise-shi include Nagoya (*tokkyū*, ¥2690, 81 minutes), Osaka (Uehonmachi or Namba stations, *tokkyū*, ¥3030, 106 minutes) and Kyoto (*tokkyū*, ¥3520, 123 minutes).

FUTAMI 二見

The attractions here are the **Meoto-iwa** (Wedded Rocks). These two rocks are considered to be male and female and have been joined in matrimony by *shimenawa* (sacred ropes), which are renewed each year in a festival on 5 January. The rocks are 1.5km from the station. The shrine is on the shore opposite the rocks. Futami is reached from Ise by JR (*futsū*, ¥200, 10 minutes). Get off at Futaminoura station.

TOBA 鳥羽

The serrated coast of the Shima-hantō is perfect for the cultivation of pearls and Toba is one of the main centres of Japan's pearl industry. It's also a popular spot for city folk to soak up a bit of coastal ambience. The two main attractions here are Toba Aquarium and Mikimoto Pearl Island. There's no denying that Toba is touristy, but it can be a lot of fun if you're in the mood.

Toba Aquarium (鳥羽水族館; Toba Suizoku-kan; ☎ 0599-25-2555; 3-3-6 Toba; admission ¥2400; ☼ 9am-5pm) has some interesting fish and marine mammal displays and some good shows. It would make a good destination for those with children or if the rain puts a damper on outdoor activities. It's about 10 minutes' walk southeast of the Kintetsu or JR Toba stations; it's on the seafront, across the main road (Rte 42).

Mikimoto Pearl Island (ミキモト真珠島; ☎ 0599-25-2028; 1-7-1 Toba; admission ¥1500; ☼ 9am-4.30pm) is a monument to Kokichi Michimoto, who devoted his life to producing cultured pearls. The demonstration halls show all the oyster tricks from growing and seeding to selecting, drilling and threading the finished product.

There is also a room from which you can watch a boat drop off the *ama* (women pearl divers) in their white outfits. There are several thousand *ama* operating in these areas – but despite efforts by regional tourist organisations to make you think they're after pearls, they are actually after shellfish or seaweed. The island is across a bridge about five minutes' walk southeast of Kintetsu or JR Toba stations.

Ise-wan Ferry Co Ltd (☎ 0599-26-3335; www .isewanferry.co.jp/index1.htm) has ferry connections from Toba-ko port to Irako on Atsumi-hantō in Aichi-ken (¥1500, 55 minutes). Boats leave from Ise-wan ferry terminal. Toba can be reached from Ise in 16 minutes by both the Kintetsu line (*kyūkō*, ¥320) or the JR line (*futsū*, ¥230). Toba is the terminus of the JR line; the Kintetsu line also stops here (and continues all the way south to Kashikojima).

AGO-WAN, KASHIKOJIMA & GOZA 英虞湾・賢島・御座

A short train ride south of Ise-shi, Ago-wan is a scenic bay festooned with islands and inlets. Kashikojima, the main island in the bay, is the terminus of the Kintetsu line. From Ise-shi station, a *futsū* costs ¥670 and takes about 56 minutes. There is no JR service. Kashikojima itself is probably of little interest to foreign travellers as it is dominated by large resort hotels, but it's the jumping-off point for exploration of the bay.

Those in search of peace and quiet might want to take a ferry to Goza on the other side of the bay (¥600, 25 minutes). The ferry terminal is right outside Kashikojima station (buy your tickets from the Kinki Kankōsen office near the terminal). The ride is a good way to see the sights in the bay. There are also sightseeing boats that do a loop around the bay for ¥1500.

Goza is a sleepy fishing community with a fine white-sand beach, Goza Shirahama. There are small signs in English from the ferry pier to the beach; just follow the main road over the hill and across the peninsula. The beach is mobbed in late July and early August but almost deserted at other times.

If you'd like to stay in Goza, there are plenty of *minshuku*, some of which close down outside of summer. **Shiojisō** (潮路荘; ☎ 0599-88-3232; fax 0599-88-3233; Goza Shirahama Kaigan; r per person incl 2 meals from ¥7500), just off the beach (look for the sign reading 'Marine Lodge Shiojisō' in English), is one of the better *minshuku*.

SOUTH OF KASHIKOJIMA 賢島以南

If you want to continue down the Kii-hantō from here, backtrack to Ise-shi and take the JR line to Taki and switch to the JR Kisei main line. This line crosses from Mie-ken into Wakayama-ken and continues down to Shingū on its way round Kii-hantō, finally ending up in Osaka's Tennō-ji station.

Western Honshū
本州西部

A land of exquisite ceramics, tranquil mountain villages and urban vibrance, Western Honshū is most known for the legacy of the atomic bombing of Hiroshima. But this region, known as Chūgoku, offers much more. The Inland Sea (Seto-nai-kai) prefectures of Okayama and Hiroshima boast charming coastal communities, islands dotted with modern art and cities with room to breathe. Superlative museums crowd the canal quarter of Kurashiki, while Bizen abounds in kilns. Yamaguchi prefecture, a trade hub at the end of Honshū, has its 'Kyoto of the west' and limestone caves. Shimonoseki delights in fresh seafood, especially the potentially fatal *fugu* (blowfish). The Inland Sea, meanwhile, is a peaceful microcosm ringed by the twinkling night lights of Honshū and Shikoku.

Shimane and Tottori prefectures, part of an area once pejoratively termed *ura-nihon* (Japan's rear), are especially hospitable. Former gateways for continental culture, they now enjoy a slower pace dedicated to *onsen* (hot springs), rugged nature and quiet mountain towns. With an original castle in Matsue and sand dunes in Tottori, the Sea of Japan coast is like a leisurely historical park stroll. Izumo Taisha, one of the oldest and most important shrines in Japan, is the rendezvous for Shinto's myriad gods.

The Chūgoku mountain range divides Western Honshū. On the southern San-yō coast (literally, 'the sunny side of the mountains'), the mild Inland Sea weather nurtures populous cities; to the north, the San-in coast (literally, 'in the shade of the mountains') is on the cooler Sea of Japan, where nature takes priority.

HIGHLIGHTS

- Ponder the significance of **Hiroshima's** (p453) past and capture its cosmopolitan present
- Clamber up the crumbling volcano of **Daisen** (p494) from the ancient temple Daisen-ji
- Sleep in an old thatched-roof farmhouse **Okayama-ken International Villa** (p464) at Hattōji, on a high plateau
- Gobble up the intriguing marine life from **Karato Ichiba** (p473) in Shimonoseki and watch the sun rise over the Kanmon Strait
- Seek out hidden-away rural health spa **Tawarayama Onsen** (p477) and its curious phallic temple
- Explore the carefully preserved village of **Ōmori** (p486) and the historic Iwami Ginzan silver mines
- Contemplate **Izumo Taisha** (p487), where the Shintō gods go on holiday
- Potter through the well-preserved warehouses and museums along the canal in **Kurashiki** (p447)
- Have a mountaintop to yourself and your own castle ruins in **Tsuwano** (p483)

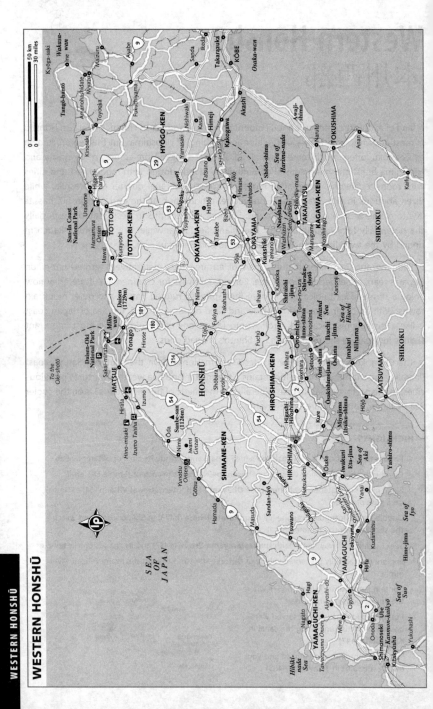

WESTERN HONSHŪ

History

If you tell a Japanese person that you're going to Chūgoku, they might think you're going to China since the region and the country share a name and Chinese characters (kanji). Chūgoku is thus called *chūgoku-chiho* (the Chūgoku region).

Because of its proximity to the Korean peninsula and China, the Chūgoku region was a gateway for Continental influences. There are countless historical reminders of how close Japan, the Koreas and China really are. From the 2nd century AD, China demanded that Japan become a tribute state, and from the 4th century AD it was common for Japanese emperors to take Korean brides. Buddhism and kanji came through from China in the 6th century. During his Korean peninsula campaigns in 1592 and 1598 Toyotomi Hideyoshi abducted whole families of potters as growing interest in the tea ceremony generated desire for *punch'ông* (powder green) ceramics. The campaigns failed to secure the peninsula for Japan and the elusive entrée into China, but the firing techniques and glazes from the period live on in Japanese ceramics today. Up to 10% of Hiroshima bomb victims were Korean (see p456), and the Japanese nationals abducted by North Korea are the focus of constant public outcry and media attention.

Shimonoseki, closer to Seoul than to Tokyo, has always played a vital role in trade and cultural exchange. In 1895 it hosted a Chinese delegation, which, with their Japanese counterparts, took almost a month to sign the Sino-Japanese Peace Treaty. In the 19th century 150 Christians from Nagasaki were sent to and imprisoned in Tsuwano, chosen for its inaccessibility. Hagi was home to 19th-century reformists who were instrumental in bringing about the Meiji Restoration.

Climate

The Chūgoku region is generally mild and comfortable. On the San-yō coast rainfall is light during winter and the air tends to be dry. On the San-in coast the temperatures are a couple of degrees lower, so winters can be cold. The Inland Sea is known as the 'land of fair weather' *(hare no kuni)* due to its moderate temperatures and low rainfall. It's also known for its periodic red tides *(akashio)*, caused by dense concentrations of phytoplankton, which kill large numbers of fish.

Getting There & Away

The *shinkansen* (bullet train) along the San-yō coast is the fastest way to travel in the Chūgoku region from the east or west. Along the San-in coast, express trains will limit train changes and shorten travel times by up to half. Between the San-yō and San-in coasts it's often quicker to go by bus, but most services are not covered by the Japan Rail Pass (see p823). The San-in coast is great to explore by car – Rte 9 is the only major road. An alternative is to take the Chūgoku Expressway, which runs the full length of Western Honshū more or less equidistant from the north and south coasts. Attractions along this route are limited, so it's a quick way to get to Kyūshū or Central Honshū.

OKAYAMA-KEN 岡山県

Okayama-ken is known for its *inaka* (rural) character among the Japanese, and its International Villas (see p445) offer countryside getaways. The cities of Kurashiki and Okayama have compelling cultural charms, while Bizen is perfect for pottery lovers. Okayama-ken is a gateway for Shikoku via the Seto-Ōhashi bridge, the main road and rail link from Honshū. Some of Okayama's islands are included in the Inland Sea section (p463).

OKAYAMA 岡山

☎ 086 / pop 630,000

Prefectural capital Okayama prides itself on its copious sunshine and its connection to Momotarō, a demon-quelling folklore hero. Within easy reach of Kurashiki, this laid-back city offers one of the top three gardens in Japan (Kōraku-en), Okayama Castle and some excellent museums. Most of the sights can be seen in a day.

Orientation

The main street, Momotarō-Ōdōri, leads eastward from the train station to near the castle, Okayama-jō, and the garden, Kōraku-en. Trams (¥100 for the castle area) run down the middle of the street. The *Okayama Culture Zone* map gives a brief overview of the city sights, but the trilingual *Okayama* pamphlet with maps is more useful as it has a larger-scale map of the Kibi Plain bicycle route (see p450).

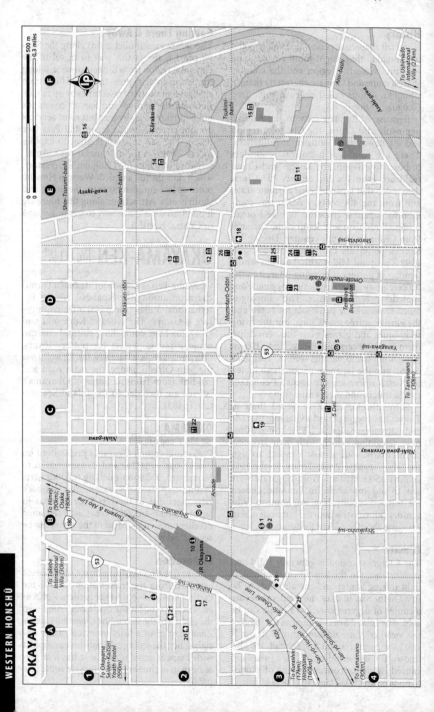

WESTERN HONSHŪ

OKAYAMA

The **Okayama-ken Kanko Bussan Centre** (☎ 234-2270; ☒ 10am-8pm) has products from Okayama-ken, including Bizen-yaki pottery, lacquerware and Kurashiki glass.

Information

BOOKSHOPS
Kinokuniya (☎ 212-2551; 1-8-45 Naka Sange; ☒ 10am-8pm) Has a decent English-language section.

INTERNET ACCESS
Club Mont Blanc (☎ 224-7050; 6-30 Honmachi; 1st 30min ¥290, then per 15min ¥100; ☒ 24hr) Internet café east of the train station.

Okayama International Centre (☎ 256-2000; www .opief.or.jp; 2-2-1 Hōkan-chō; ☒ 9am-5pm Mon-Sat) To the west of the train station. Offers free internet access (until 5pm).

Okayama Prefectural Office (Okayama Kenchō; ☎ 224-2111; 2-4-6 Uchisange; ☒ 8.30am-5pm Mon-Fri) Free internet access.

Megalo (☎ 231-6696; 1-10-25 Omote-chō; per 30min/ 3hr ¥241/1029; ☒ 24hr) In the Omote-chō arcade.

MONEY
There's an exchange service (9am to 5pm) at the Okayama Central Post Office, where travellers cheques (not Thomas Cook) and cash are exchanged.

Bank of Tokyo-Mitsubishi UFJ (☎ 223-9211; 6-36 Honmachi; ☒ 9am-3pm Mon-Fri) Cashes travellers cheques.

POST
Okayama Central Post Office (☎ 227-2755; 2-1-1 Naka Sange; ☒ 8am-8pm Mon-Sat, 8.30am-5pm Sun) On Kenchō-dōri.

Okayama Ekimae Post Office (☎ 224-0809; 1-3-1 Eki-mae-chō; ☒ 9am-5pm Mon-Fri) West of the train station.

TOURIST INFORMATION
Okayama International Centre (☎ 256-2000; www .opief.or.jp; 2-2-1 Hōkan-chō; ☒ 9am-5pm Mon-Sat) Good information source.

Tourist information counter (☎ 222-2912; 1-1 Ekimoto-machi; ☒ 9am-6pm) On the ground floor of the newly renovated JR Okayama station. The *Okayama Culture Zone* brochure covers all the main sights, while *Frontier 21 Okayama* has extensive food coverage.

Sights

KŌRAKU-EN 後楽園
Built by *daimyō* (domain lord) Ikeda Tsune-masa and completed in 1700, **Kōraku-en** (☎ 272-1148; 1-5 Kōraku-en; admission ¥350; ☒ 7.30am-6pm Apr-Sep, 8am-5pm Oct-Mar; ℗) has been called one of the three most beautiful gardens in Japan since the Edo period, along with Kairaku-en in Mito (p196) and Kenroku-en in Kanazawa (p294). Initial impressions may disappoint somewhat since much of it is grass. But several attractive ponds break up the lawns, and structures like the unique Ryuten Pavillion, which has a stream running through it, more than make up for this. Kōrakuen is little changed from feudal times, and you can get a feel for what a *daimyō* did for relaxation here.

Next to the tea plantation you can have a bowl of green tea and try the local dessert, *kibi-dango*, a soft, sweet rice cake, for ¥300. From the station take the Higashi-yama tram to the Shiro-shita stop (¥100) in front of the cylindrical Okayama Symphony Hall building. Then walk east to the riverside (200m, you can't miss it), then north 400m to the bridge, cross it and then turn south and follow the signs to the garden (about 170m from the bridge).

MOMOTARŌ, THE PEACH BOY

Okayama-ken and neighbouring Kagawa-ken, on the island of Shikoku, are linked by the legend of Momotarō, the tiny Peach Boy who emerged from the stone of a peach and, backed up by a monkey, a pheasant and a dog, defeated a three-eyed, three-toed people-eating demon. There are statues of Momotarō at JR Okayama station, and the main road of Okayama is named after him. The island of Megi-jima, off Takamatsu in Shikoku, is said to be the site of the clash with the demon.

Momotarō may actually have been a Yamato prince who was deified as Kibitsuhiko. His shrine, Kibitsu-jinja, lies along the route of the Kibi Plain bicycle ride (p450).

OKAYAMA-JŌ 岡山城

Known to locals as U-jō (Crow Castle), the striking black **Okayama Castle** (☎ 225-2096; 2-3-1 Marunouchi; admission ¥800; 9am-5pm) was built in 1597 by Ukita Hideyoshi and once boasted 35 turrets and 21 gates. It was ruled by 15 successive lords for three centuries. Rebuilt in 1966 after Allied bombing destroyed it in 1945, with only the small *tsukima-yagura* (moon-viewing turret) surviving, its interiors may strike purists as too modern, but the top of the donjon (central tower) has great views of Korakuen. In another room, visitors can dress up in Edo-period costumes and have their photo taken.

MUSEUMS

The Okayama Culture Zone has some fine museums and galleries. Close to the castle's back entrance, near the corner of the moat, the **Hayashibara Museum of Art** (☎ 223-1733; 2-7-15 Marunouchi; admission ¥300; 9am-5pm; P) houses a private collection of Japanese and Chinese artefacts handed down from the local Ikeda clan. Opposite the main entrance to Kōraku-en is the **Okayama Prefectural Museum** (☎ 272-1149; 1-5 Kōrakuen; admission ¥200; 9am-6pm Tue-Sun Apr-Sep, 9.30am-5pm Oct-Mar; P), which has displays on local history including Bizen swords and pottery. North of Kōraku-en is the **Yumeji Art Museum** (☎ 271-1000; 2-1-32 Hama; admission ¥700; 9am-5pm Tue-Sun; P), displaying works by famed local painter Yumeji Takehisa (1884–1934), who has been called Japan's Toulouse-Lautrec.

North of the end of Momotarō-Ōdōri, where the tramline turns south, is the excellent **Okayama Orient Museum** (☎ 232-3636; 9-31 Tenjin-chō; admission ¥300; 9am-5pm Tue-Sun), which houses around 3000 artefacts from the prehistoric to the Islamic Age. Not far behind it is the **Okayama Prefectural Museum of Art** (☎ 225-4800; 8-48 Tenjin-chō; admission ¥300; 9am-5pm Tue-Sun; P).

Festivals & Events

The **Saidai-ji Eyō** (Naked Festival) takes place from midnight on the third Saturday in February at the Kannon-in temple in the Saidai-ji area. A large crowd of near-naked men fight for two sacred *shingi* (wooden sticks), while freezing water is poured over them.

Sleeping

Okayama Seinen-kaikan Youth Hostel (岡山青年会館; ☎ 252-0651; http://homepage3.nifty.com/okayama-yh/; 1-7-6 Tsukura-chō; dm members/nonmembers ¥2940/3570; P) This welcoming old hostel is in a suburban area about 1km west of Okayama station. Catch bus 5 or 15 from the station to Seinen-kaikan Mae bus stop. The manager speaks English and meals are available. Internet access (lobby computer) costs ¥10 per minute and parking is available for ¥500 a night.

Saiwai-sō (☎ 254-0020; http://w150.j.fiw-web.net/in Japanese; 24-8 Ekimoto-chō; s/tw from ¥4200/7600; P) In a quiet area west of the station, this friendly place has Western- and Japanese-style rooms and communal baths.

Matsunoki Ryokan (☎ 253-411; www.matsunoki.com; 19-1 Ekimoto-chō; s/tw ¥5250/8400; P) The Matsunoki has bright, clean rooms with Western- and Japanese- style private bathrooms. There are public laundry facilities, and the friendly staff is very attentive.

Comfort Hotel Okayama (☎ 898-1111; www.choicehotels.com; 1-1-13 Marunouchi; s/tw from ¥5800/7000; P wi-fi) This newly renovated hotel close to the castle has stylish rooms, free breakfast and bicycles that can be borrowed.

Kōraku Hotel (☎ 221-7111; www.hotel.kooraku.co.jp in Japanese; 5-1 Heiwa-chō; s/tw from ¥7500/13,800; P) The Kōraku has spacious rooms and very friendly staff. Laptop computers are available for ¥1050 a night, and the Japanese restaurant on the premises serves Okayama *barazushi* (a kind of chirashi-zushi served in a large bowl topped with fresh seafood, mainly Spanish mackerel and vegetables).

ANA Hotel Okayama (☎ 898-1111; www.anaho tel-okayama.com in Japanese; 15-1 Ekimoto-chō; s/tw from ¥13,860/24,255; P ✕ ☒ ☐) Opened in 2005 right by the station, this luxurious hotel features gorgeous rooms and a chrome-tinted lobby with a wall waterfall behind the front desk. Its 20th-floor bar and restaurant has teppan-yaki and exquisite night views.

Eating & Drinking

Padang Padang (☎ 223-6665; 1-7-10 Omote-chō; dishes ¥550-1900; ☽ dinner Wed-Mon) Despite its Indonesian name, this cosy new restaurant run by chef Daisuke Akagi focuses on French and Italian fare, like herb *peperoncino* pasta (chilli pepper pasta; ¥1500). Located along Shiro-shita-suji near the castle, it's a good spot to have a glass of wine after a day of sightseeing.

Den (☎ 803-3400; 6-36 Honmachi; dishes ¥500-3800; ☽ dinner) Enjoy bone-warming *nabe* (stew) and grilled dishes like *mochibuta sukiyaki* (fatty pork hot pot; ¥1800) in this chic, low-lit hotpot spot in the underground arcade by the station. There's a sign outside saying 'Den'.

Tori-soba (☎ 236-0310; 1-7-24 Omote-chō; dishes ¥600-1000; ☽ 11am-8pm) The name of this jazzy little countertop eatery is also its speciality: *tori-soba* (¥630) means chicken noodles. If one bowl isn't enough, order a small serving of sushi to go with it. Look for the white sign across from Chugoku Bank.

Gonta (☎ 233-4430; 1-2-1 Nodaya-chō; dishes ¥500-10,000; ☽ 11am-11pm Thu-Tue) There are 38 kinds of sushi to choose from at this corner shop. Ask for the Okayama speciality, *barazushi*. There are big green kanji on the outside wall.

Okabe (☎ 222-1404; 1-10-1 Omote-chō; dishes ¥700-750; ☽ lunch Mon-Sat) Order the Okabe *teishoku* (set menu; ¥700) and be surprised by how filling tofu can be. Located on the corner by a bakery, this is a friendly, homey spot.

Saudade Na Yoru (☎ 234-5306; 2nd fl, Shiroshita bldg, 10-16 Tenjin-chō; dishes ¥650-1000; ☽ 12pm-3am) Enjoy views of the symphony hall from this 2nd-floor lounge bar. There are drink and cake set menus until 6pm, after which time the bar takes priority. DJs occasionally play and the desserts are generous.

Quiet Village Curry Shop (☎ 231-4100; 1-6-43 Omote-chō; dishes ¥780-1000; ☽ 11.30am-8.30pm Tue-Sun) This cheerful place is a serious curry house with good service. The chicken curry (¥780) and

dhal are good lunchtime options. There's an English sign outside.

Getting There & Away

Okayama airport (☎ 294-5550; 1277 Nichiyōji) is 20km northwest of the station. There are flights to Japan's major cities as well as Seoul, Shanghai and Guam. A bus (¥680, 30 minutes) runs to the airport from platforms 1 and 3 in front of Okayama station. The first bus leaves at 6.15am, the last at 6.30pm.

Okayama is connected by the San-yō Hikari *shinkansen* to Hakata (Fukuoka; ¥11,550, two hours) to the west; and to Osaka (¥5350, 45 minutes), Kyoto (¥6820, one hour, 16 daily) and Tokyo (¥15,850, 3½ hours, 14 daily). The JR Hakubi line runs between Okayama and Yonago (¥4620, two hours), in Tottori-ken on the San-in coast.

When travelling west to Kurashiki, it's quicker to transfer from the *shinkansen* at Okayama than at Shin-Kurashiki. You also change trains at Okayama if you're heading to Shikoku across the Seto-Ōhashi.

Getting Around

Getting around Okayama is a breeze, since the Higashi-yama tram route will take you to all the main attractions. Trams charge ¥100 to anywhere in the central area.

JR Rent-a-cycle (☎ 223-7081; ☽ 7am-11pm) rents out bikes, costing ¥300 per day. **Eki Rent-a-Car** (☎ 224-1363; 1-1 Ekimoto-chō; ☽ 8am-8pm) is next door.

AROUND OKAYAMA
Okayama International Villas

To attract foreign travellers to the frequently visited areas of the region, Okayama Prefecture established a group of International Villas in 1988. They provide a rare chance for visitors to escape Japan's urban sprawl and get a taste of country living. They are highly recommended, especially Hattōji and Fukiya, but are showing signs of wear and tear.

The villas are in remote locations with few eateries, but they have kitchens and English directions to local attractions, shops and any restaurants. Arrive well before dark, especially for Fukiya and Hattōji, or you'll have trouble finding the way.

Members pay ¥2500 per night and there's a ¥500 joining fee. For reservations and information, contact the **Okayama International Villa Group** (☎ 086-256-2535; fax 086-256-2576; www.harenet

WESTERN HONSHŪ

.ne.jp/villa) at the Okayama International Centre (p443). Staff speak English, and English brochures are available.

FUKIYA 吹屋

This is a remote, picture-postcard town of old wooden buildings lining a road that winds through the mountains; time seems to have stood still here for the past century.

The **Fukiya villa** (吹屋国際交流ヴィラ; ☎ 0866-29-2222; 836 Fukiya Nariwa-chō Takahashi-shi), modelled on a traditional *shoyu-gura* (soya sauce storehouse), has a wood-burning stove and free firewood. The town's history is tied to the making of reddish-brown *bengara* (iron sulphate) seen on the roof tiles, and a nearby former copper mine, the **Sasaune Historic Mine Shaft** (吹屋銅山笹畝坑道; ☎ 0866-29-2145; admission ¥300; ⏲ 10am-4pm Tue-Sun), is open to the public. Buses (¥950, one hour, three daily) connect Takahashi station on the JR Hakubi line with Fukiya.

TAKEBE 建部

Takebe is an *onsen* town along the JR Tsuyama line in central Okayama. The modern **Takebe villa** (建部国際交流ヴィラ; ☎ 0867-22-2500; 586 Takebekami Takebe-chō Mitsu-gun) is beside the Asahi River and right next door is Yahata Onsen, with a variety of hot baths. This is perhaps the most faded of the villas; the surrounding town isn't exactly pastoral, but it is definitely slow-paced. From Okayama, take the JR Tsuyama line to Fukuwatari station. The villa is a 1.5km walk or taxi ride to the south.

HATTŌJI 八塔寺

This is the most picturesque and worthwhile villa destination. Hattōji is a tranquil farming village high up on a plateau in the east of the prefecture.

The **Hattōji villa** (八塔寺国際交流ヴィラ; ☎ 0869-85-0254; 1193 Kagami Yoshinaga-chō Bizen-shi) is a gorgeous, well-preserved thatched-roof farmhouse with an *irori* (hearth) in the floor. The village also has a unique country and western-themed café, **Nozomigaoka** (望ヶ丘; ☎ 0869-85-0252; 1393 Kagami Yoshinaga-chō, Bizen-shi; dishes ¥150-3500; ⏲ 9am-9pm Wed-Mon) run by a one-time Japanese cowboy! Try his hearty *kamo-nabe* (duck hot pot; ¥2500) in colder months. Buses (¥690, 30 minutes) run to Hattōji from Yoshinaga station on the JR Sanyō line, which links with Okayama.

USHIMADO 牛窓

Ushimado is a quiet Inland Sea coastal community with lots of sailboats and olive trees. The **Ushimado villa** (牛窓国際交流ヴィラ; ☎ 0869-34-4218; 496 Ushimado Ushimado-chō Setouchi-shi) is a modern glass-enclosed curved structure perched high above the village. The villa is rather comfortless but the views are stunning; local attractions include an olive garden and Ushimado Beach. From Okayama, take the train to Oku on the JR Akō line, then a bus for Ushimado. Get off at Konnoura (¥370, 25 minutes). The check-in is at Ushimado Town Hall.

SHIRAISHI-JIMA 白石島

our pick On the relaxing island of Shiraishi-jima in the Inland Sea, in the west of the prefecture, the excellent **Shiraishi Island villa** (白石島国際交流ヴィラ; ☎ 0865-68-2095; 317 Shiraishi-jima Kasaoka-shi) has superb views and easy access to the island's main beach and hiking trails (p464). In July and August resident expats Amy Chavez and Paul Hoogland operate **Inland Sea sailboat cruises** (☎ 090-6433-4542; www.moooobar.com; cruises from ¥3000). From Okayama, take the JR Sanyō line to Kasaoka, then the ferry (¥500, 35 minutes) to Shiraishi. The check-in is in the ferry office.

BIZEN 備前

☎ 0869 / pop 42,000

East of Okayama city on the JR Akō line is the 700-year-old pottery region of Bizen, renowned for its unglazed Bizen-yaki pottery and swords. Much prized by tea-ceremony connoisseurs, Bizen ceramics are earthy and dramatic. They're often referred to as 'expensive accidents', as firing can have such mixed results. A morning or afternoon is enough time to enjoy Bizen.

At Imbe station, the drop-off point to explore the area, there's a **tourist information counter** (☎ 64-1100; 1657-7 Imbe; ⏲ 9am-6pm), with useful English pamphlets on the history of Bizen-yaki. Accommodation in the pottery area of Bizen is sparse, so it's best to see it as a day trip.

On the 2nd floor of the station is the **Bizen Ceramic Crafts Museum** (備前焼陶友会; ☎ 64-1001; 1657-7 Imbe; admission free; ⏲ 9.30am-5.30pm Wed-Mon), and on the north side of the station are the **Okayama Prefectural Bizen Ceramics Art Museum** (岡山県備前陶芸美術館; ☎ 64-1400; admission ¥500; ⏲ 9.30am-5pm Tue-Sun) and, further north,

WESTERN HONSHŪ

the **Bizen Ceramics Centre** (備前陶芸センター; ☎ 64-2453; 974-2 Imbe; admission free; ⏰ 10am-4.30pm Tue-Sun), all of which display the pottery of the area. Of the galleries in Bizen's main street, **Tokei-dō** (桃蹊堂; ☎ 64-2147; 1527 Imbe; ⏰ 9am-5pm) is the oldest and most interesting; the staff can show you the kilns out the back. The area's tutelary shrine, Amatsu-jinja, is lovingly decorated with Bizen ceramics.

There are several kilns in the area that offer a chance to try your hand at making Bizen-yaki. The cost is around ¥3000; reservations are necessary. Try **Bishū Gama** (備州窯; ☎ 64-1160; 302-2 Imbe Bizen-shi; ⏰ 9am-3pm), where some English is spoken. In about two hours you can sculpt a masterpiece, but you'll need to arrange to have your creation shipped to you after it's been fired. **Bizen-yaki Traditional Pottery Centre** (備前焼伝統産業会館; ☎ 64-1001; 1657-7 Imbe; ⏰ 9.30am-5.30pm Wed-Mon), on the 3rd floor of Imbe station, holds workshops (¥3150 to ¥3675) on weekends and holidays from April to November.

The station eatery **Shikisai** (四季彩; ☎ 63-0088; dishes ¥500-3000; ⏰ lunch & dinner Wed-Mon) serves everything from simple Japanese dishes to mini-*kaiseki* (Japanese formal cuisine, ¥3150) course meals.

If you have come from Himeji or points east by train, you'll need to change to the JR Akō line at Aioi and get off at Imbe station, possibly after changing trains at Banshū-Akō. You can carry on along the JR Akō line to get to Okayama.

KURASHIKI 倉敷

☎ 086 / pop 476,000

Kurashiki's appeal is a quarter of pretty canal-side buildings. Old black-tiled warehouses have been converted into an eclectic collection of museums, which have become Kurashiki's main draw. Bridges arch over, willows dip into the water, carp cruise the canal and the whole effect is quite delightful.

In the feudal era the warehouses were used to store rice brought by boat from the surrounding rich farmlands. Later, the town's importance as a textile centre increased and the Kurabō Textile Company expanded. Owner Ōhara Keisaburō built up a collection of European art, and opened the Ōhara Museum in the 1920s. It was the first of the museums and is still the finest. Note that many of Kurashiki's main attractions, and most eateries, close on Monday.

Orientation

It's about 1km from the station to the old Bikan area, and Ivy Sq is just beyond. A number of shops along the main street, Kurashiki Chūō-dōri, sell Bizen-yaki.

Information

Just out of the station and to the right, the **tourist information counter** (☎ 424-1220; 2nd fl, Kurashiki City Plaza, 1-7-2 Achi; ⏰ 9am-7pm) has English-speaking staff who can make accommodation bookings. The **Kurashikikan** (☎ 422-0542; 1-4-8 Chuō; ⏰ 9am-6pm Apr-Oct, 9am-5.15pm Nov-Mar), at the bend in the canal, also has a tourist information office and rest area. The **Kurashiki Community Centre** (☎ 423-2135; 2-21 Honmachi; ⏰ 10am-4pm) near Seigan-ji Temple has a computer with free internet access. Travellers can also log on to the net at a computer in the **Terminal Hotel** (倉敷ターミナルホテル; ☎ 426-9001; 1-7-2 Achi) by the front desk (¥200 for the first 30 minutes).

Sights

Ōhara Museum of Art (☎ 422-0005; 1-1-15 Chuō; admission ¥1000; ⏰ 9am-5pm Tue-Sun) is undoubtedly Kurashiki's premier museum and houses the predominantly European art collection of textile magnate Ōhara Keisaburō (1880–1943). Rodin, Matisse, Picasso, Pissarro, Monet, Cézanne, Renoir, El Greco, Toulouse-Lautrec, Gauguin, Degas and Munch are all represented in this superlative collection. The museum's neoclassical façade is Kurashiki's best-known landmark after the canal.

Your ticket is valid all day, allowing multiple entries. It also gives you admission to the museum's folk-art and Chinese-art collections, and to the contemporary-art collection housed in an **annex** behind the main building.

The impressive collection at the **Kurashiki Museum of Folk-craft** (☎ 4221637; 1-4-11 Chuō; admission ¥700; ⏰ 9am-5pm Tue-Sun Mar-Nov, 9am-4.15pm Dec-Feb) is mainly Japanese but also includes furniture and items from other countries. The collection is housed in a rustic complex of linked *kura* (warehouses) dating from the 18th century.

The **Japan Rural Toy Museum** (☎ 422-8058; 1-4-16 Chuō; admission ¥500; ⏰ 9am-5pm) is full of surprises, with folk-craft toys from Japan and around the world in old warehouses. A record-setting giant top that spun for over an hour is housed in a back room.

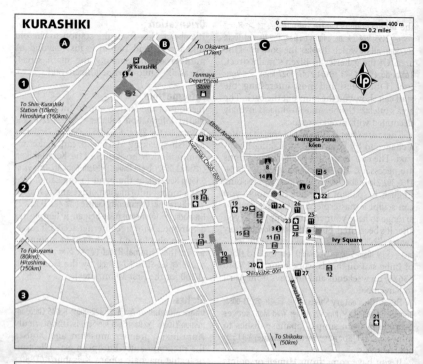

KURASHIKI

The **Kurashiki City Art Museum** (☎ 425-6034; 2-6-1 Chūō; admission ¥200; ☑ 9am-5pm Tue-Sun), featuring works by local artists such as Yoson Ikeda, is worth a look for those with extra time. The restored **Ōhashi-ke** (Ōhashi House; ☎ 422-0007; 3-21-31 Achi; admission ¥500; ☑ 9am-5pm Tue-Sun) is a fine example of a late-18th-century merchant's house and represents this group's rising social status.

IVY SQUARE アイビースクエア
The Kurabō textile factories have moved to more modern premises, and the fine Meiji-era red-brick factory buildings (dating from 1889 and remodelled in 1974) now house a hotel, restaurants, shops and yet more museums. Ivy Sq, with its ivy-covered walls and open-air café, is the centre of the complex. The **Kojima Torajirō Memorial Hall** (☎ 426-1010; 7-1-10 Honmachi;

WESTERN HONSHŪ

admission ¥500, Ōhara Museum ticket holders ¥300; 9am-5pm Tue-Sun) displays work by the impressionist painter who helped Ōhara establish his European collection. Middle Eastern pieces are in the associated **Orient Museum**.

South of the square, the **Kurashiki Piggy Banks Museum** (☎ 425-4577; 1224 Funagura-chō; admission ¥200; 10.30am-5.30pm Fri-Wed) is a remarkable collection of over two thousand coin receptacles. It's on the 2nd floor of the fascinating Sanyo-do antiques shop. Just look for the dozens of porcelain RCA Victor dogs on the roof!

SHRINES & TEMPLES

The shrine **Achi-jinja** (☎ 425-4898; 12-1 Honmachi; 7am-5pm) tops the **Tsurugata-yama-kōen** park, which overlooks the old area of town. The Honei-ji, Kanryū-ji and Seigan-ji temples are also in the park.

Sleeping

Kurashiki is a great town if you're keen to stay in a traditional Japanese inn.

Kurashiki Youth Hostel (☎ 422-7355; fax 422-7364; www.jyh.or.jp/english/chugoku/kurasiki/index.html; 1537-1 Mukoyama; dm members/nonmembers ¥2940/3540; P ☒ ☒) South of the canal area and a 10-minute climb from Ivy Sq through the cemetery, this tidy hostel's hilltop location overlooks the Bikan area. Meals are available.

Minshuku Kamoi (☎ 422-4898; www.kamoi-jp.biz in Japanese; 1-24 Honmachi; s/tw with shared bathroom incl 2 meals ¥6300/12,600; P ☒) Easy to find at the bottom of the steps to Achi-jinja, this place is very quiet and well managed.

Kurashiki Sakura Stay (☎ 435-7001; fax 435-7002; www.sakurastay.jp in Japanese; 1-9-4 Chūō; s/tw ¥6300/10,500; P ☒ ☐) This very white hotel, five minutes west of the canal, is a business hotel masquerading as a wedding centre. The rooms, all Western, are small but clean. There's a scrumptious breakfast for ¥900.

Kurashiki Kokusai Hotel (☎ 422-5141; fax 422-5192; www.kurashiki-kokusai-hotel.co.jp; 1-44-1 Chūō; s/tw from ¥9450/14,700; P ☒ ☒ ☐) Though somewhat faded and with stiff personnel, this excellently located hotel features woodwork, tiles and murals by artists. East-facing rooms have fine views of the Ōhara Museum and its gardens.

Hotel Nikkō Kurashiki (☎ 423-2400; fax 423-2401; www.nikko-kurashiki.com; 3-21-19 Achi; s/tw from ¥19,000/27,000; P ☒ ☒ ☐) A modern highrise behind the Ōhashi House, this hotel's rooms are over 40 sq metres and have fine city views.

Ryokan Kurashiki (☎ 422-0730; fax 422-0990; www.ryokan-kurashiki.jp; 4-1 Honmachi; s/tw incl 2 meals from ¥34,500/56,000; P ☒) With views overlooking the canal, professional service and vast rooms, this is the best ryokan in Kurashiki. The Terrance de Ryokan Kurashiki serves delicious green tea and local sweets in a room overlooking a garden.

Eating

Kamoi Restaurant (☎ 422-0606; 1-3-17 Chūō; dishes ¥500-2000; 10am-6pm Thu-Tue) The canalside Kamoi, facing the Ōhara Museum, serves Japanese noodle dishes, sushi and the

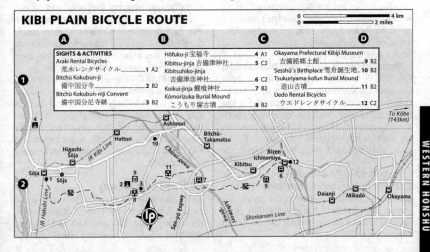

KIBI PLAIN BICYCLE ROUTE

KIBI PLAIN BICYCLE ROUTE

To access this excellent cycling course, take a local JR Kibi line train from Okayama for three stops to Bizen Ichinomiya. You can ride the 15km route to Sōja, drop off your bike and take a JR Hakubi line train back through Kurashiki to Okayama. Most of the course is on a cycling road that cars are not allowed to use.

Rental Bicycles (☎ 0862-84-2311; ◷ 9am-6pm) is just outside JR Bizen Ichinomiya station; if no one is there, call the phone number. Pick up your bike (¥200/1000 per hour/day) and free Japanese-language route map here. You'll want to use this map in conjunction with the one here as it is of a larger scale. Turn right and then right again to cross the railway track and in just 300m you'll reach **Kibitsuhiko-jinja**, a shrine that fronts a large pond. From here you'll soon pick up the bicycle path, which follows a canal through the fields until it rejoins the road just before the temple Fudenkai-ji. Just 200m further on is **Kibitsu-jinja**. This major shrine, built in 1425, is unusual in that it has the oratory and main sanctum topped by a single roof. The legendary Peach Boy, Momotarō (p444), is connected with the shrine.

Pedalling on, you'll pass **Koikui-jinja**, which is connected with the legendary figure of Kibitsuhiko, to reach the huge 5th-century **Tsukuriyama-kofun Burial Mound**, rising like a gentle hill from the surrounding plain. Ideally, you need to be in a hot-air balloon or helicopter to appreciate that it's a 350m-long keyhole-shaped mound, not a natural hill. Just north of here is the birthplace of famous artist **Sesshū** (1420–1506). He was once a novice monk at **Hōfuku-ji**, which is 3km northwest of JR Sōja station.

Finally, you pass the foundation stones of the **Bitchū Kokubun-niji Convent**, the nearby **Okayama Prefectural Kibiji Museum** (◷ 9am-4.30pm Tue-Sun; admission ¥150), the excavated **Kōmorizuka Burial Mound**, and **Bitchū Kokobun-ji** with its picturesque five-storey pagoda. From here it's a few more kilometres into Sōja.

It's worth taking your own water, but occasionally the bicycle path passes close enough to a main road to divert for food. On arrival at Sōja station, return your bicycle to **Araki Rental Bicycles** (☎ 0866-92-0233; ◷ 9am-6pm). If this ride appeals to you, you can easily plot others on the network of tracks that cover the area.

---

mamakari teishoku (sardine set; ¥1365) from a photo menu.

Kana Izumi (☎ 421-7254; 8-33 Honmachi; dishes ¥500-2000; ◷ 10.30am-8pm Tue-Sun) Freshly made udon noodles are served in this modern restaurant with a traditional exterior, just back from the canal. Meals are displayed in the window. Also on offer is *kayaku gohan teishoku* (rice and mixed veggies set; ¥714).

Mamakari-tei (☎ 427-7112; 3-12 Honmachi; dishes ¥600-3500; ◷ lunch & dinner Tue-Sun) Not far from the Ryokan Kurashiki, this is a cosy, traditional spot named after and famed for the local sardine-like fish it serves up daily (both raw and cooked). If you're not a sardine lover, try the *tōfu manjū* (fried tofu patties; ¥525). In an old-fashioned white building with tile trim.

Pasta Marché (☎ 434-4355; 1253-1 Funagura-chō; dishes ¥500-8000; ◷ lunch & dinner Thu-Tue; E) On a corner at the southern part of the city, this sunny little trattoria has great ¥1000 pasta set lunches and dinner items, like beef fillet capriccio (¥1200).

Drinking

El Greco (☎ 422-0297; 1-1-11 Chūō; coffees ¥500; ◷ 10am-5pm Tue-Sun; E) By the canal near the Ōhara Museum (you can't miss its ivy-clad walls), it's a friendly, spacious spot for coffee and cakes.

Coffee-Kan (☎ 424-5516; 4-1 Honmachi; drinks ¥500-1000; ◷ 10am-5pm Tue-Sun) This dark tavern beside the Ryokan Kurashiki is another great coffee spot, and has a garden at the rear. No food served. It has an ornate wooden door.

SWLABR (☎ 434-3099; 2-18-2 Achi; dishes ¥680-1000; ◷ 12pm-3am Fri-Wed) After the Bikan area closes down, relax with the good music and friendly staff at SWLABR. The food stops at 6pm, but the cosy bar-lounge goes until 3am. It's the green weatherboard house on the east side of Kurashiki Chūō-dōri a couple of blocks south of the station.

Getting There & Away

Kurashiki, only 17km from Okayama, is not on the *shinkansen* line. Travelling westwards, it's usually faster to disembark at Okayama and take a San-yō line *futsū* (local train) to

Kurashiki. The trip takes 17 minutes, and *futsū* run frequently. If you're heading east, get off at Shin-Kurashiki station, two stops from Kurashiki on the San-yō line.

Getting Around

It's only a 15-minute walk from the station to the canal area, where almost everything is within a few minutes' stroll. Walking is best for Kurashiki.

HIROSHIMA-KEN 広島県

In addition to Hiroshima city's atomic bomb-related attractions, Hiroshima-ken prefecture boasts Miyajima and its famed shrine, Itsukushima-jinja, the quaint fishing village of Tomo-no-ura and the rather spectacular Sandan-kyō gorge in the north of the prefecture.

SOUTHERN HIROSHIMA-KEN 広島県南部

Fukuyama 福山

☎ 0849 / pop 462,000

Fukuyama is an industrial city, and its convenient location on the Osaka-Hakata *shinkansen* route makes it a good jumping-off point for the pretty fishing port of Tomo-no-Ura or for Onomichi, a gateway to the Inland Sea.

If you have a few hours to spend in Fukuyama, you can visit the art gallery and museum and the reconstructed castle. There's a **tourist information office** (☎ 22-2869; 30-1 Sannomaru-chō; 8.30am-5.15pm) in the station. The unique **Japan Footwear Museum** (日本はきもの博物館; ☎ 34-6644; 4-16-27 Matsunaga-chō; admission ¥1000; 9am-5pm; P) at nearby Matsunaga station chronicles footwear from sandals to moon boots. The excellent **Japan Folk Toy & Doll Museum** is part of it, along with a very elegant coffee house at the entrance.

Tomo-no-ura 鞆の浦

☎ 0849 / 5000

The delightful fishing port of Tomo-no-ura, with its picturesque old streets, is just half an hour south of Fukuyama station by bus. Due to its central location on the Inland Sea, in feudal days the port played an important role as host to fishing boats, which would wait in the harbour to determine the next shift in the tides and winds before heading back out to sea.

Pick up an English-language brochure at JR Fukuyama station information. An enjoyable few hours can be had on foot or by bicycle exploring the village. Bikes can be hired (¥100 for two hours) next to the ferry building.

Sensui-jima island has some accommodation, including a camping area, and some quiet walking trails. Regular ferries to the island run from the harbour area (¥240 return, five minutes).

SIGHTS

Up on the hill behind the ferry terminal, the **Taichōrō** (対潮楼; admission ¥200; 8am-5pm Tue-Sun) temple hall was built at the end of the 17th century to house a Korean delegation that would sometimes pay its respects. The view is quite lovely, and the resident attendant will happily show you the memorabilia on display.

A fascinating snack-food factory, **Uonosato** (うをの里; ☎ 82-3333; 1567-1 Ushiroji Tomo-chō; admission free, food lessons from ¥600; 9am-5pm Tue-Sun) processes most of the locally caught fish. You can watch the workers making prawn *sembei* (rice crackers) and *chikuwa* (ground-fish snacks), and you can even have a go at it yourself. Lessons are worth the price and great for children. Tomo-no-ura is also famed for *houmei-shu*, a sweet Chinese herb liquor. There are breweries offering samples among the houses a few blocks back from the waterfront.

SLEEPING & EATING

Tomo Seaside Hotel (鞆シーサイドホテル; ☎ 83-5111; www.tomonoura.co.jp in Japanese; 555 Tomo Tomo-chō; s/tw incl 2 meals from ¥6800/15,600; P) Close to the sights on the mainland and with great views, this hotel is a little run down and caters to group tours. All rooms are Japanese style with their own bathroom, and the hotel also has a rooftop bath.

Kokuminshukusha Sensui-jima (国民宿舎仙酔島; ☎ 70-5050; fax 70-5035; www.tomonoura.co.jp in Japanese; 3373-2 Ushiroji Tomo-chō; s/tw with shared bathroom incl 2 meals from ¥7800/15,600; P) Right in front of the beach and boasting sea views, this is the most reasonably priced accommodation on nearby Sensui-jima. There are Japanese- and Western-style rooms and wonderful baths. Beware: for dinner you may be served *tai-kabuto* (boiled head of sea bream)!

@Cafe (☎ 82-0131; Jōyatōmae Tomo-chō; meals ¥400-900; 11am-8pm Thu-Tue) This is a hip new café in a 150-year-old *nagaya* building beside the old harbour lighthouse. Panini, parfaits and pastas like *baziru sōsu omakase pasuta* (basil pasta; ¥900) make for a tasty break. **Tabuchiya** (田渕屋; ☎ 83-5085; 838 Tomo Tomo-chō; meals ¥400-1400; ◷ 9am-6.30pm Thu-Tue) A location for the recent film *Yamato*, this lovingly restored, elegant coffee shop on a corner a few blocks back from the harbour has light meals like *hayashi raisu* (hashed beef on rice; ¥1400). Look for the green *noren* (door curtain) with white Chinese characters.

Sensuian (仙酔庵; ☎ 82-2565; 555 Tomo Tomo-chō; dishes ¥580; ◷ 11am-5pm) Right by the Tomo Sea-side Hotel is this tea shop in an old white and black house. Sip some green tea and enjoy a sweet like *tai-yaki* (buns baked in a mold; ¥100) while looking out to sea.

GETTING THERE & AWAY

It's only 14km from Fukuyama to Tomo-no-Ura; buses run every 15 minutes from bus stop 11 outside JR Fukuyama station (¥530, 30 minutes).

Onomichi 尾道

☎ 0848 / pop 150,000

Onomichi may look like an undistinguished industrial town, but give it a chance and you'll warm to its friendly locals and slower pace. Most sights are in the hills. The **tourist information office** (☎ 20-0005; 10-1 Higashigoshō-machi; ◷ 9am-6pm) is to the right of Onomichi station in the Teatro Shell–rune building.

SIGHTS

The Onomichi **Historical Temple Walk** takes in 25 important temples of the original 48. The tourist information office has a very detailed brochure in English about the temple walk and Onomichi. You can catch the **ropeway** (cable car; one way/return ¥280/440) up to **Senkō-ji-kōen**, which is covered with cherry and azalea blossoms in spring. Follow the paths on the way back down and take in the **Path of Literature** on the way, which has memorials to some of the writers who have visited Onomichi. On the waterfront is an old storehouse that's now home to the **Onomichi Motion Picture Museum** (お のみち映画資料館; ☎ 37-8141; 1-14-10 Kubo; admission ¥500; ◷ 9am-6pm Wed-Mon). It has an evocative collection of old movie posters, magazines and memorabilia. *Tokyo Story* (1953) is the most famous movie filmed in Onomichi, and five-minute segments of the film are on show.

SLEEPING & EATING

Onomichi Royal Hotel (尾道ロイヤルホテル; ☎ 23-2111; fax 23-6058; www.kokusai-hotel.com in Japanese; 2-9-27 Tsuchido-chō; s/tw ¥5300/10,500; P ✗ ⏲) On the waterfront, it has simple business-hotel décor and good views. Internet access is dial-up only.

Nishiyama Ryokan (西山旅館; ☎ 37-3145; fax 37-3885; 3-27 Toyohimoto-machi; s/tw incl 2 meals ¥15,750/31,500; ✗) A block before the water-front, the Nishiyama features traditional wooden interiors and gardens.

Uonobu Ryokan (魚信旅館; ☎ 37-4175; fax 37-3849; www.uonobu.jp in Japanese; 2-27-6 Kubo; s/tw from ¥15,000/30,000; ✗) Right on the waterfront, this elegantly old-fashioned furnished place is renowned for its innovative and delicious food.

Onomichi Rāmen Ichibankan (尾道ラーメン壱 番館; ☎ 21-1119; 2-9-26 Tsuchidō-chō; dishes ¥380-1800; ◷ 11am-8pm Thu-Tue) Just past the Royal Hotel on the waterfront, this boisterous noodle shop is the tastiest spot for Onomichi ramen (¥490), characterised by thin noodles and a thick slab of pork.

Yamaneko (やまねこ; ☎ 21-5355; 2-9-33 Tsuchidō-chō; dishes ¥400-900; ◷ 11.30am-10pm Tue-Fri, to mid-night Sat & Sun) By the waterfront next to a lurid junk shop, this very funky corner café serves modern Japanese food, pizza, pasta and a wide range of drinks. The *gyokai no gaarikku supagetti* (garlic seafood spaghetti; ¥780) is a fine choice. It has good music and English-speaking staff.

Casalinga Deux Table (カサリンガ・ドゥタ ーブル; ☎ 722-0035; 1st fl, 1-9-10 Tsuchidō-chō; dishes ¥2000-3000; ◷ lunch & dinner Fri-Wed, closed every 3rd Wed monthly; ✗) For groovy Italian food, look for this place between the shopping arcade and the waterfront about four blocks east of the station; there's a bright red sign outside. Pastas include *bēkon to nasu to tsuna no to-mato sōsu* (bacon, eggplant and tuna pasta with tomato sauce; ¥1300).

GETTING THERE & AWAY

Onomichi is at the Honshū end of the island-hopping Shimanami-kaidō bridge system to Shikoku. As such it's a gateway to Inno-shima (p467), Ikuchi-jima (p467) and Ōmi-shima (p467). The islands can be reached by bus or ferry from Onomichi. The tourist information office has a *Shimanami Kaido Guide Map* in Japanese and a multilingual *I Love Onomichi* brochure.

The Shin-Onomichi *shinkansen* station is 3km north of the JR San-yō line station. Buses connect the two stations, but it's easier to reach Onomichi on the JR San-yō line and change to the *shinkansen* line either at Fukuyama or Mihara.

Mihara 三原

☎ 0848 / pop 105,000

Mihara is on the San-yō *shinkansen* line and on the JR San-yō line. It's a convenient ferry departure and arrival point for Setoda on Ikuchi-jima, for other islands of the Inland Sea and for Shikoku. The harbour is directly south of the station. There's a **tourist information office** (☎ 67-5877; 1-1-1 Shiromachi; ✆ 8am-7pm Mon-Fri, 10am-6pm Sat & Sun) in the modern JR station.

NORTHERN HIROSHIMA-KEN
広島県北部

Sandan-kyō 三段峡

The Sandan-kyō gorge, about 50km northwest of Hiroshima, is an area that you could get lost in for a few days. A mostly paved trail follows the Shiki-gawa through an 11km gorge, providing visitors to Hiroshima with accessible, beautiful Japanese nature. The hike is very popular in autumn when the leaves change colour. Pick up a copy of Lonely Planet's *Hiking in Japan* for details.

Buses run from the Hiroshima bus centre to Sandan-kyō station (¥1400, two hours), at the southern end of the gorge. There is no longer a rail service. The gorge is also accessible by car from Shimane-ken along Rte 191.

HIROSHIMA 広島

☎ 082 / pop 1,154,000

A busy, prosperous, attractive city, Hiroshima will be remembered for that terrible instant on 6 August 1945 when it became the world's first atomic-bomb target. Hiroshima's Peace Memorial Park is a constant reminder of that tragic day and it attracts visitors from all over the world. Yet Hiroshima is a far from depressing place; on the contrary, its citizens have recovered from nuclear holocaust to build a thriving and internationally minded community.

The city dates back to 1589, when feudal lord Mōri Terumoto named the town and established a castle.

Orientation

Hiroshima (literally, 'broad island') is built on a series of sandy islands on the delta of Ōta-gawa. JR Hiroshima station is east of the city centre and, although there are several hotels around the station, the central area, with its very lively entertainment district, is much more interesting.

Peace Memorial Park and most of the atomic-bomb reminders are at the northern end of the island, immediately west of the city centre.

Hiroshima's main east–west avenue is Heiwa-Ōdōri (Peace Blvd), but the busiest road (with the main tramlines from the station) is Aioi-dōri, which runs parallel to Heiwa-Ōdōri. Just south of Aioi-dōri, and again parallel to it, is the busy Hon-dōri shopping arcade.

Information
BOOKSHOPS

Book Nook (☎ 244-8145; 5-17 Kamiya-chō; ✆ 10am-9pm Mon-Fri, to 6pm Sat, 1-6pm Sun; ▣) Has second-hand Western books, mostly trade paperbacks, a notice board and free internet. It's in a language school called Outsider behind Iyo Bank and Yamaha music store. Look for the 2nd-floor sign.

INTERNET ACCESS

The **International Exchange Lounge** (see p455) has free internet access, and there are several Kinko's branches in town.

Futaba@Cafe (per hr from ¥409; ✆ 24hr) JR Hiroshima Station (☎ 568-4792; 2-22 Matsubara-chō, Minami-ku) On the 6th floor of the Futaba Tosho GIGA building with a yellow sign down the side east of JR Hiroshima station; Hondōri Arcade (☎ 542-5455; Basement, Futaba Tosho Kamiya-chō Bldg, 2-2-33 Kamiya-chō, Nakaku-ku) Near the Peace Memorial Park end of Hondōri Arcade. Free drinks are available; there's a ¥105 membership fee.

MONEY

The central post office (see below) changes money during the week, and on weekends the major international hotels have exchange services. The Hiroshima Rest House (see p455) has an extensive list of post offices that change travellers cheques, banks that do cash advances and international ATMs.

Sumitomo Mitsui Bank (☎ 247-2121; 1-3-2 Kamiya-chō, Naka-ku; ✆ 8am-11pm) International cards are accepted by the 1st-floor ATM. Two blocks south of Aioi-Dōri.

POST

Central post office (広島中央郵便局; ☎ 245-5335; 1-4-1 Kokutaiji-chō, Naka-ku; ✆ 9am-7pm Mon-Fri, to 5pm Sat, to 12.30pm Sun) Near the Shiyakusho-mae

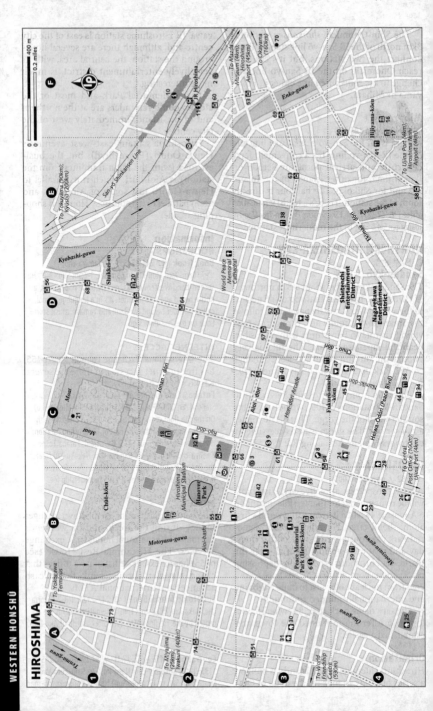

WESTERN HONSHŪ

HIROSHIMA

tram stop. You can change money here between 9am and 4pm Monday to Friday.

Higashi Post Office (☎ 261-6401; 2-62 Matsubara-chō, Minami-ku; ⏰ 9am-7pm Mon-Fri, to 5pm Sat, to 12.30pm Sun) Near the south exit of the station, this branch is more convenient than the 'Central'.

Naka Post Office (☎ 222-1314; 6-36 Motomachi, Naka-ku; ⏰ 9am-7pm Mon-Fri, to 3pm Sat) Next to the Sogō department store.

TOURIST INFORMATION

There are two excellent websites about Hiroshima. The **Hiroshima Convention & Visitors Bureau** (www.hiroshima-navi.or.jp) has extensive information on sightseeing, accommodation and access to/from the city. Check out www.gethiroshima.com for good food and nightlife recommendations, and insights into the local culture not covered by the tourist brochures.

For the benefit of those arriving by sea, Hiroshima's port, Ujina, has an information counter with basic information.

Hiroshima Rest House (☎ 247-6738; 1-1 Nakajima-machi, Naka-ku; ⏰ 9.30am-6pm Apr-Sep, 8.30am-5pm Oct-Mar) In Peace Memorial Park, next to Motoyasu-bashi. Offers the most comprehensive information about the city and the island of Miyajima.

International Exchange Lounge (☎ 247-9715; 1-5 Nakajima-machi, Naka-ku ⏰ 9am-7pm Apr-Sep, to 6pm Oct-Mar; 🖥) Beside the Peace Memorial Museum. Has information in English, newspapers and magazines, a library and a study room. The lounge is geared towards foreigners living in Japan.

Tourist information office JR Hiroshima Station South (☎ 261-1877; 2-31 Matsubara-chō, Minami-ku; ⏰ 9am-5.30pm) At the south exit of the station; JR Hiroshima Station North (☎ 263-6822; 2-37 Matsubara-chō, Minami-ku; ⏰ 9am-7pm) At the north exit. The English-speaking staff can make accommodation bookings.

WESTERN HONSHŪ

Sights

A-BOMB DOME 原爆ドーム

The symbol of the destruction visited upon Hiroshima is the **A-Bomb Dome** (Gembaku Dōmu), across the river from Peace Memorial Park. Declared a Unesco World Heritage site in December 1996, the building was the Industrial Promotion Hall until the bomb exploded almost directly above it. Its propped-up ruins, floodlit at night, have been left as an eternal reminder of the tragedy.

PEACE MEMORIAL PARK 平和記念公園

From the A-Bomb Dome cross over into **Peace Memorial Park** (Heiwa-kōen), which is dotted with memorials, including the **cenotaph** that contains the names of all the known victims of the bomb. The cenotaph frames the **Flame of Peace**, which will only be extinguished once the last nuclear weapon on earth has been destroyed, and the A-Bomb Dome across the river.

Just north of the road crossing through the park is, for many, the most poignant memorial in the park – the **Children's Peace Monument**, inspired by leukaemia victim Sadako Sasaki. When Sadako developed leukaemia at 10 years of age she decided to fold 1000 paper cranes – an ancient Japanese custom through which it is believed that a person's wishes will come true. The crane is the symbol of longevity and happiness in Japan and she was convinced that if she could achieve that target she would recover. She died before reaching her goal, but her classmates folded the rest. The story inspired a nationwide bout of paper-crane folding, which continues to this day.

Nearby is the recently relocated **Korean A-Bomb Memorial**. Great numbers of Koreans were shipped from their homeland to work as slave labourers in Japanese factories during WWII, and more than one in 10 of those killed by the atomic bomb were Korean.

PEACE MEMORIAL MUSEUM 平和記念資料館

The **A-bomb museum** (☎ 241-4004; 1-2 Nakajima-chō, Naka-ku; admission ¥50; ☻ 9am-6pm Apr-Jul & Sep-Nov, 8.30am-7pm Aug,to 5pm Dec-Mar), as the Peace Memorial Museum is commonly known, narrates the events preceding, during and after the atomic bombing of Hiroshima on 6 August 1945. For many it is an overwhelming experience and a potent symbol of the idiocy of war.

HIROSHIMA NATIONAL PEACE MEMORIAL HALL FOR THE ATOMIC BOMB VICTIMS 国立広島原爆死没者追悼平和祈念館

Opened in August 2002, **Peace Memorial Hall** (☎ 543-6271; 1-6 Nakajima-chō, Naka-ku; admission free; ☻ 8.30am-6pm Mar-Jul, to 7pm Aug, to 6pm Sep-Nov, to 5pm Dec-Feb) is a contemplative hall of remembrance and a register where the names and photographs of atomic-bomb victims are kept, along with their testimonies. It was designed by architect Tange Kenzo, who also designed the park's museum, cenotaph and eternal flame. These testimonies, which can be viewed on video, vividly evoke the chaos that Japan was in at this time and the inhumane treatment of civilians by Japanese military personnel. It's worth taking time here to get first-hand accounts of the after-effects of the bomb.

HIROSHIMA-JŌ 広島城

Also known as Carp Castle, **Hiroshima-jō** (☎ 221-7512; 21-1 Moto-machi, Naka-ku; admission ¥320; ☻ 9am-6pm Mar-Nov, to 5pm Dec-Feb) was originally constructed in 1589, but much of it was dismantled following the Meiji Restoration, leaving only the donjon, main gates and turrets. The remainder was totally destroyed by the bomb and rebuilt in modern reinforced concrete in 1958.

SHUKKEI-EN 縮景園

Modelled after Xi Hu (West Lake) in Hangzhou, China, **Shukkei-en** (2-11 Kami-nobori-chō; admission ¥250; ☻ 9am-6pm Apr-Sep, to 5pm Oct-Mar) dates from 1620 but it was severely damaged by the bomb. The garden's name literally means 'contracted view', and it attempts to re-create grand vistas in miniature. It may not be one of Japan's celebrated classic gardens, but it makes for a pleasant stroll.

Next to the garden is the splendid **Hiroshima Prefectural Art Museum** (2-22 Kami-nobori-chō; admission ¥500, combined ticket with garden ¥600; ☻ 9am-5pm Tue-Fri, Sun & to 7pm Sat), featuring Salvador Dali's *Dream of Venus* and the artwork of Hirayama Ikuo, who was in the city during the bombing. Enter the garden through the museum.

OTHER SIGHTS

Hijiyama-kōen, a park noted for its cherry blossoms in spring, lies directly south of JR Hiroshima station and is home to two worthy attractions. The **Hiroshima City Museum of Contemporary Art** (☎ 264-1121; 1-1 Hijiyama-kōen,

HIROSHIMA

'Nothing will grow for 75 years' went the rumours after the *Enola Gay* unleashed the atomic bomb on Hiroshima on 6 August 1945. For many around the world, the bombing is still a potent symbol of people's inhumanity, and even more so for the remaining 125,000 Hiroshima *hibakusha* (atomic-bomb survivors).

The youngest *hibakusha* is 59, in the womb when the bomb was dropped. About 5000 have died every year over the past 10 years. Looking at modern Hiroshima more than 60 years after the bombing, it's easy to forget that it ever happened. Who will tell the *hibakusha* story when the last of their number dies? School children are visiting the Peace Museum in Hiroshima in declining numbers. The Children's Peace Memorial, where thousands of paper cranes are sent annually in memory of leukaemia victim Sadako, has been set alight by vandals. Even though they were protected by a glass enclosure and were under surveillance, the cranes were set alight by a university student from Kōbe a few days before 6 August 2003. The student wished to express frustration over 'grim employment opportunities for university graduates'.

Economic realities and political ambitions are reshaping this most peaceful of nations. Until 2004 the Japanese prime minister would meet with *hibakusha* after the 6 August memorial service. This doesn't happen any longer, as many within the opposition and the dominant Liberal Democratic Party deepen and strengthen their arguments for the development of nuclear weapons in Japan.

As the voices of the *hibakusha* grow fewer, Dr Tanaka Yuki of the Hiroshima Peace Institute, a Hiroshima City Government think-tank, believes that the tragedy of Hiroshima is being discussed less and less, as it is thought of primarily as a nuclear tragedy. He says, 'All warfare is a crime against humanity. Hiroshima, apart from being nuclear, was also an air raid. Sixty-four cities, including Tokyo, were bombed during the Second World War in Japan, and bombing has been used in all modern warfare to some degree – from WWI to Iraq.' Dr Tanaka would like to see Hiroshima reinterpreted for future generations and put into a broader world context, so that it isn't relegated to the historical dustbin once all the *hibakusha* have died.

In a further effort to reinvigorate the antinuclear argument, there are plans for a People's Tribunal on the bombing of Hiroshima and Nagasaki (for details on that atomic explosion see p684), based on crimes-against-humanity trials in places such as Bosnia. As media saturation of modern warfare desensitises people to the realities of war, Dr Tanaka's concern and vision are timely – lest we forget.

Minami-ku; admission ¥360; 10am-5pm Tue-Sun) has excellent displays by modern Japanese and international artists, while the **Hiroshima City Manga Library** (261-0330; 1-4 Hijiyama-kōen, Minami-ku; admission free; 10am-5pm Tue-Sun) is a small comic-book museum.

The **Hiroshima Museum of Art** (223-2530; 3-2 Moto-machi, Naka-ku; admission ¥1000; 9am-5pm) is in an interesting 1970s building built by the Hiroshima Bank and focusing on French masters, and the **Hiroshima Children's Museum** (222-5346; 5-83 Moto-machi, Naka-ku; admission museum/planetarium free/¥500; 9am-5pm Tue-Sun) is good fun for adults and kids. Both are in Hanover Park, just southwest of the castle. The **Mazda Museum** (マツダミュージアム; www .mazda.com/mazdaspirit/museum; 252-5050; 8.30-11am & 12.30-3.30pm Mon-Fri) is quite popular, as you get to see the 7km assembly line – the world's longest. If you feel auto-inclined, check out

the details on the English-language website. Reservations are required; there is one tour in English daily at 1pm. It's two stops from JR Hiroshima station.

Activities

A love of **baseball** is not a prerequisite for having a great time at a Hiroshima Carp game. It's just as much fun watching the rowdy, organised enthusiasm of the crowd, especially when the Tokyo Giants come to town. The stadium is just north of the Peace Memorial Park, and outfield tickets start at ¥1500.

Miyajima (p460), 25km west of the city, can easily be visited as a **day trip** from Hiroshima. The tram company has a special one-day passport that includes a return tram trip to Miyajima-guchi, a return ferry to Miyajima and unlimited daily tram transport for just ¥840. You can buy the ticket at various big

WESTERN

hotels, tram stops and at the Hiroshima Rest House information office (p455).

A variety of lunch and dinner **cruises** run from Hiroshima to Miyajima and back. On weekdays from March to September day cruises operate through the Inland Sea.

Festivals & Events

On 6 August, the anniversary of the atomic bombing, a **memorial service** is held in Peace Memorial Park and thousands of paper lanterns for the souls of the dead are floated down the Ōta-gawa from in front of the A-Bomb Dome.

Sleeping

BUDGET

J-Hoppers Hiroshima (☎ 233-1360; www.hiroshimahostel.jp; 5-16 Dobashi-chō, Naka-ku; dm/s with shared bathroom ¥2500/3000; P ✕ 🖵) This newly opened hostel has small co-ed and female-only dorm rooms but they are clean and staff here are very friendly. Bikes can be rented (¥500 per day) and extended-stay discounts are available.

World Friendship Center (ワールド・フレンドシップ・センター; ☎ 503-3191; fax 503-3179; www.wfchiroshima.net; 8-10 Higashi Kannon-machi Nishi-ku; s/tw with shared bathroom incl breakfast ¥3500/7000; ✕ ✕ wi-fi) Run by an antinuclear nonprofit organisation, the homey World Friendship Center B&B has three bright Japanese-style rooms and hospitable expatriate staff. The city's tourist information offices can supply directions. No credit cards.

Aster Plaza International Youth House (☎ 247-8700; fax 246-5808; www1.ocn.ne.jp/~kokusei1 in Japanese; 4-17 Kako-machi Naka-ku; s/tw ¥3620/6260; P ✕ 🖵) This municipal cultural centre, a block south of the Peace Memorial Park, is the best value in Hiroshima. There's a midnight curfew.

Ikawa Ryokan (☎ 231-5058; fax 231-5995; www.itcj.jp/hdb/634026.html; 5-11 Dobashi-chō, Naka-ku; s/tw from ¥4200/7350; P ✕ 🖵) This is a friendly, family-run complex consisting of several wings with recently renovated rooms. There are Japanese- and Western-style rooms, all very clean, and meals are available in the cafeteria.

Hotel Active! (☎ 212-0001; fax 211-3121; www.hotel-active.com in Japanese; 15-3 Nobori-chō Naka-ku; s/tw ¥5980/8800; P ✕ ✕ 🖵) This newly opened business hotel is one of the most stylish in Japan. The lobby has designer couches, the beds have satiny coverlets, there's a free buffet breakfast and a communal bath (men only). You'll walk out feeling like a star.

Hotel Dormy Inn Hiroshima (☎ 240-1177; fax 240-1755; www.hotespa.net/hotels/hiroshima in Japanese; 3-28 Komachi Naka-ku; s/tw from ¥6000/9000; P ✕ ✕ 🖵) Conveniently located on Heiwa Ōdōri, the Dormy Inn has standard business-hotel singles and a range of amenities, including a large communal bath (men only). There's a good buffet breakfast for ¥950.

MIDRANGE

Comfort Hotel Hiroshima Ōtemachi (☎ 545-7811; fax 545-7812; www.choicehotels.com; 3-7-9 Ōtemachi Naka-ku; s/tw ¥6500/8500; P ✕ ✕ 🖵) Attractively designed, new and friendly, this is a great business hotel, not to be confused with the older Comfort Hotel Hiroshima a block away. It offers free buffet breakfast and internet access via the computers in the bright lobby.

Sera Bekkan (☎ 248-2251; fax 248-2768; www.yado.to in Japanese; 4-20 Mikawa-chō Naka-ku; s/tw ¥7350/14,700, incl 2 meals ¥12,600/25,200; P ✕) A popular and friendly traditional ryokan near Fukurō-machi-kōen. Three of the rooms have a garden view.

ANA Hotel Hiroshima (☎ 241-1111; fax 241-9123; www.anahotels.com; 7-20 Naka-machi Naka-ku; s/tw ¥12,705/23,100; P ✕ 🖵) Rooms are large but plain, and the café downstairs is a mellow place to start the day over a buffet breakfast. Luxury rooms on the 'premier floors' are also available.

Rihga Royal Hotel Hiroshima (☎ 502-1121; fax 228-5415; www.rihga-hiroshima.co.jp; 6-78 Moto-machi; s/tw ¥13,000/17,000; P ✕ ✕ 🖵) With professional English-speaking staff, spacious rooms and great night-time views, this is Hiroshima's tallest hotel, southwest of Hiroshima-jō. Ask for a view of the castle.

Eating

Hiroshima is noted for its seafood (particularly oysters), but especially *hiroshima-yaki*, a local version of *okonomiyaki* (egg-based savoury pancakes) made with *soba* (thin buckwheat noodles) and fried egg.

Peace Pot (☎ 211-0084; 11-7 Hashimoto-chō Naka-ku; dishes ¥650-880; ⏲ 11am-10.30pm) This alfresco soup spot is one of four new eateries along the Kyōbashi river by the Inari-ōhashi bridge. The tasty pork curry soup (¥650) is like a meal; bread or rice sets are available. Oysters and beef are on the menu in the neighbouring restaurants.

Bakudanya (☎ 245-5885; 6-13 Fujimi-chō Naka-ku; dishes ¥650-1000; ⏲ 11.20am-9pm) A rising star of

Hiroshima cuisine is *tsukemen*, a ramen-like soup dish in which noodles and broth are separated. The fun is in the dipping, and this simple counter shop has branched out across Japan. Try the Bakudan set (¥850) and choose the spiciness and volume of noodles. If in doubt, just select *futsū* (regular). Look for the white signboard under the green awning on Jizō-dori.

Hassei (☎ 242-8123; 4-17 Fujimi-chō Naka-ku; dishes ¥450-1200; ☯ lunch & dinner Tue-Sun) For a hole in the wall like this unpretentious little *okonomiyaki* joint run by friendly chef Gaku-san, Hassei gets its share of celeb patrons, like composer Ryūichi Sakamoto. It's a less touristy alternative to Okonomi-mura and even the half-size *soba*- or *udon-yaki* (*hiroshima-yaki* with udon or soba noodles; ¥500) is very filling. If you're famished, try the seafood special (*shīfōdo supeshiaru*; ¥1200). Hassei has a rising sun pattern on the sign over the door.

Okonomi-mura (☎ 241-2210; 5-13 Shintenchi Naka-ku; dishes ¥700-1200; ☯ 11am-2am) This Hiroshima institution is an amazing grouping of 27 eating counters on the 2nd, 3rd and 4th floors of the Shintenchi Plaza building behind the Parco Department Store (look for the red neon sign on the far side of the small square). All specialise in *hiroshima-yaki*, which goes down remarkably well with a tall, cold *nama bīru* (draught beer). Turn to the right as you leave the lift on the 2nd floor to find Sarashina, where Chef Nakamura-san is very welcoming. Sarashina's open Tuesday to Sunday, phone ☎ 241-0564.

Cha Cha Ni Moon (☎ 241-7444; 2-6-26 Otemachi Naka-ku; dishes ¥500-1500; ☯ dinner) Japanese minimalism prevails in this softly lit old house. There's a broad bar downstairs and two other floors of intimate dining rooms that are semiprivate. A house speciality is *yuba* (tofu skin), but most of the beautifully presented dishes here are based on traditional Kyoto cuisine. The ¥3500 *omakase* (chef's discretion) course includes tempura and cow's tongue. Look for the tiny 'Moon' sign across from the small park.

Zucchini (☎ 546-0777; 1-5-18 Otemachi Naka-ku; meals ¥400-2800; ☯ dinner; E) Serves up tapas, paella and other Spanish goodies in very lively style. Waiters shout, the music grooves and everyone seems to have a good time. It's a great alternative if you're tiring of *okonomiyaki*.

Spicy Bar Lal's (☎ 504-6328; 5-12 Tatemachi Naka-ku; dishes ¥500-4200; ☯ lunch & dinner; E) Although Lal himself is no longer here, the Nepalese and Indian fare at this colourful, cosy eatery is still excellent. Filling lunch specials start at ¥880. Truly tasty curries and naan breads make this one of the best South Asian restaurants in town.

Ristorante Mario (☎ 248-4956; 4-11 Nakajima-chō Naka-ku; dishes from ¥1000; ☯ lunch & dinner; E) Good, honest pastas and pizzas (lunch courses start at ¥1800), quick service, a long wine list and an English menu make Ristorante Mario a relaxing option after a visit to the Peace Memorial Museum. This is justifiably a popular spot, so try to reserve on weekends.

Tosho (☎ 506-1028; 6-24 Hijiyama-chō Minami-ku; meals ¥1260-6300; ☯ lunch & dinner) In a quiet wooden building overlooking a carp pond, Tosho has set menus of traditional Japanese food with complimentary coffee. Choose from a photo menu. The walls near the cashier area are covered with signatures from Hiroshima Carp baseball players. Follow the green-and-white signs from Danbara 1 chōme tram stop. It's off an uphill alley right after Hijiyama Shrine.

Drinking

Shintenchi and Nagarekawa are the city's entertainment districts.

Bar Alcoholiday (☎ 090-4659-9072; 3rd fl, Casa Blanca Bldg, 5-19 Nagarekawa-chō Naka-ku; drinks ¥500; ☯ 9pm-5am Tue-Sun) You can hear the karaoke wails as you approach this place, in a building crammed full of bars. Chie will be happy to serve you, particularly between 9pm and 10pm, when drinks are ¥100 off. Look for the bright red Casa Blanca sign outside.

Opium (☎ 504-0255; 3rd fl, Namiki Curl Bldg, 3-12 Mikawa-chō; dishes from ¥500; ☯ noon-4am; E) Sip high-calibre drinks and people-watch in this cool bar. Snacks, pizza and pasta dishes are available. There's a sign on the wall outside. It's above the Kokoroschka shoe shop on the corner.

Lotus (☎ 246-0104; 5th fl, Namiki Curl Bldg, 3-12 Mikawa-chō; drinks from ¥500; ☯ 6pm-3am) Two floors above Opium in the Namiki Curl building is Lotus, a stylish, Zen-like space where you can take off your shoes and relax on the raised floor amid cushions and low tables or sip ¥600 cocktails at the bar. There's a little DJ booth here too playing great tunes.

Koba (☎ 249-6556; 3rd fl, Rego Bldg, 1-4 Naka-machi; dishes ¥700-1200; ☯ 6pm-2am Thu-Tue; E) Koba is a very chill place to enjoy a drink, pizza, pasta or curry and an eclectic range of music; friendly manager Bom is a musician and hosts live acts now and again as well as works by local artists. It's in a concrete building with a pool of water by the entrance, just behind Stussy.

Kuro-sawa (☎ 247-7750; 5th fl, Tenmaya Ebisuclub, 3-20 Horikawa-chō Naka-ku; dishes ¥420-5500; ☯ 6pm-4am Mon-Sat, to 1am Sun; E) This chic *izakaya* (Japanese-style pub) is hewn from bare concrete and attractively low-lit, a fine setting to savour goodies like charcoal-grilled pork with ginger sauce (¥724). Look for the MOS Burger outlet on the ground floor.

J-Café (☎ 242-1234; 4-20 Fujimi-chō Naka-ku; dishes from ¥600; ☯ noon-2am Sun-Thu, to 3am Fri & Sat; E) Homey and comfy are the watchwords at this breezy café-bar on Heiwa-Ōdōri. Big red couches lend a living-room feel, and graffiti art adorns the walls. Scrumptious waffles, crepes and panini are on offer. The sign outside has a stylised 'j' like an ampersand.

Getting There & Away

Hiroshima's main **airport** (☎ 848-86-8151; 64-31 Hiraiwa, Zennyuji, Hongo-chō, Mihara-shi) is 40km east of the city, with bus connections to/from Hiroshima station (¥1300, 48 minutes). There are flights to/from all of Japan's major cities and international flights to Seoul, Dalian, Beijing, Shanghai, Taipei, Bangkok and Guam. **Hiroshima Nishi airport** (☎ 822-95-2650; 4-10-2 Kannon Shin-machi, Nishi-ku) is 4km southwest of the city centre on the coast. It handles more regional services, and there are buses to/from Hiroshima station (¥240).

Hiroshima is an important stop on the Tokyo–Osaka–Hakata *shinkansen* route. The trip from Hiroshima to Hakata (Fukuoka) takes 1¼ hours and costs ¥8700; to Shin-Osaka (Osaka) it's 1½ hours (¥9950), and to Tokyo five hours (¥18,050).

The JR San-yō line passes through Hiroshima onwards to Shimonoseki, hugging the coastline much of the way. The ordinary local services move along fairly quickly and are the best way to visit the nearby attractions of Miyajima and Iwakuni. Long-distance buses connect Hiroshima with all the major cities. Buses depart from the Hiroshima Bus Center, located on the 3rd floor between the Sogo and AQ'A shopping centres by the Kamiya-cho Nishi streetcar stop.

Hiroshima is an important port with ferry connections to other cities. The Hiroshima to Matsuyama ferry (¥2500 to ¥2900, 2¾ hours, 10 daily) and hydrofoil (¥6300, 68 minutes,

15 daily) services are a popular way of getting to/from Shikoku.

Getting Around

Hiroshima has an extensive tram service that will get you almost anywhere you want to go for a flat fare of ¥150 (¥100 on the short route 9). There's even a tram that runs all the way to Miyajima port (¥270). If you have to change trams to get to your destination, you should ask for a *norikae-ken* (transfer) ticket. Pay when you get off.

Two bicycles are available for rent at **Nippon Rent-a-car** (☎ 264-0919; 3-14 Kojin-machi; ☯ 24hr), four blocks southeast of the station. Bike rental costs ¥263/735 per two hours/day.

MIYAJIMA 宮島
☎ 0829 / pop 1970

More correctly known as Itsuku-shima, Miyajima is easily reached from Hiroshima. The famous 'floating' torii (Shintō shrine gate) of Itsukushima-jinja is one of the most photographed tourist attractions in Japan – it's classified as one of Japan's three best views (the other two are the sand spit at Amanohashidate, p372, on the northern coast of Kyoto prefecture, and the islands of Matsushima, p513, near Sendai, in Northern Honshū). Apart from the shrine, the island has other temples, good walks and remarkably tame deer that wander the streets – watch for signs warning of the dangers of fraternising with horned species; some deer will even eat your JR Rail Pass if you're careless!

Information

There's a **tourist information counter** (☎ 44-2011; 1162-18 Miyajima-chō; ☯ 9am-5pm) in the ferry terminal. Turn right as you emerge from the building and follow the waterfront to get to the shrine (a 10-minute walk) and the centre of the island's small town. The shopping street, packed with souvenir outlets and restaurants as well as the world's largest rice scoop (*shakushi*), is a block back from the waterfront.

Sights
ITSUKUSHIMA-JINJA 厳島神社

The **shrine** (☎ 44-2020; 1-1 Miyajima-chō; admission ¥300; ☯ 6.30am-6pm Mar–mid-Oct, to 5.30pm mid-Oct–Nov, Jan & Feb, to 5pm Dec) that gives the island its real name dates from the 6th century (its present form dates from 1168). Its pier-like construction is a result of the island's holy status: commoners were not allowed to set foot on the island and had to approach the shrine by boat, entering through the **floating torii** out in the bay. Much of the time, however, the shrine and torii are surrounded not by water but by mud. The view of the torii that is immortalised in thousands of travel brochures requires a high tide.

On one side of the floating shrine is a **floating nō stage** built by a Mōri lord. The orange torii, dating from 1875 in its present form, is often floodlit at night.

The **Treasure House** (admission ¥300; 8am-5pm) has a collection of painted sutra (Buddhist scriptures regarded as oral teachings of Gautama Buddha) scrolls, dating from the 12th century that is only rarely on display. The

exhibits are perhaps of greatest interest to the scholarly.

TEMPLES & HISTORICAL BUILDINGS

Topping the hill that is immediately north of Itsukushima-jinja is **Senjō-kaku** (Pavilion of 1000 Mats; ☎ 44-2020; 1-1 Miyajima-chō; admission ¥100; 8.30am-4.30pm), built in 1587 by Toyotomi Hideyoshi. This huge and atmospheric hall is constructed with massive pillars and beams, and the ceiling is hung with paintings. It looks out to a colourful five-storey pagoda dating from 1407. Senjō-kaku should have been painted to match but was left unfinished when Toyotomi died (1598).

Miyajima has other temples, including the 1201 **Daigan-ji** (☎ 44-0179; 3 Miyajima-chō;

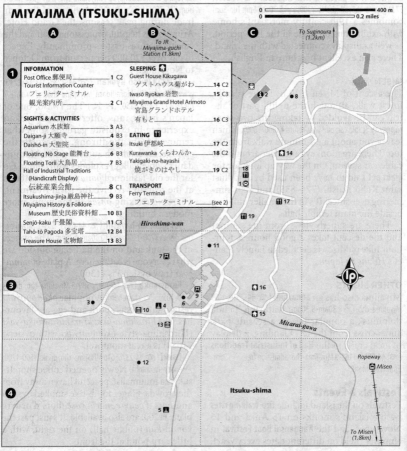

MIYAJIMA (ITSUKU-SHIMA)

0 — 400 m
0 — 0.2 miles

To Suginoura (1.2km)

To JR Miyajima-guchi Station (1.8km)

INFORMATION
Post Office 郵便局 1 C2
Tourist Information Counter
フェリーターミナル
観光案内所 2 C1

SIGHTS & ACTIVITIES
Aquarium 水族館 3 A3
Daigan-ji 大願寺 4 B3
Daishō-in 大聖院 5 B4
Floating Nō Stage 能舞台 6 B3
Floating Torii 大鳥居 7 B3
Hall of Industrial Traditions
(Handicraft Display)
伝統産業会館 8 C2
Itsukushima-jinja 厳島神社 9 B3
Miyajima History & Folklore
Museum 歴史民俗資料館 10 B3
Senjō-kaku 千畳閣 11 C3
Tahō-tō Pagoda 多宝塔 12 B4
Treasure House 宝物館 13 B3

SLEEPING
Guest House Kikugawa
ゲストハウス菊がわ 14 C2
Iwasō Ryokan 岩惣 15 C3
Miyajima Grand Hotel Arimoto
宮島グランドホテル
有もと 16 C3

EATING
Itsuki 伊都岐 17 C2
Kurawanka くらわんか 18 C2
Yakigaki-no-hayashi
焼がきのはやし 19 C2

TRANSPORT
Ferry Terminal
フェリーターミナル .... (see 2)

Hiroshima-wan

Mitarai-gawa

Itsuku-shima

Ropeway
Misen

To Misen (1.8km)

9am-5pm), just south of the shrine, which is dedicated to the god of music. The colourful and glossy Daishō-in (☎ 44-0111; 210 Miyajima-chō; 8am-5pm), just south of town, can be visited on the way down to Misen (below). This is a Shingon sect temple with everything: statues, gates, pools, carp – you name it; there's even a very detailed English pamphlet. You can grope around in the dark beneath the Kannon hall here and view illuminated iconography. The rituals performed at the main Itsukushima-jinja are also administered by Daigan-ji. South of Itsukushima-jinja is the picturesque pagoda Tahō-tō.

MIYAJIMA HISTORY & FOLKLORE MUSEUM 歴史民俗資料館

Set in a fine garden, this museum (☎ 44-2019; 57 Miyajima-chō; admission ¥300; 8.30am-5pm Tue-Sun) combines a 19th-century merchant's home with exhibitions on trade in the Edo period, as well as displays connected with the island. There's an excellent brochure in English.

MISEN 弥山

The ascent of Misen (530m) is the island's finest walk, although the uphill part of the trip can be avoided by taking the two-stage ropeway (cable car; one way/return ¥1000/1800), which leaves you about a 20-minute walk from the top. There are monkeys and deer around the cable-car station. On the way up look for the giant pot said to have been used by Buddhist saint Kōbō Daishi (774–835) and kept simmering ever since! It's in the smaller building beside the main temple hall.

There are superb views from the summit and the descent takes a good hour. A four-hour hike of Misen is detailed in Lonely Planet's *Hiking in Japan*.

OTHER SIGHTS

Miyajima also has an aquarium (☎ 44-2010; 10-3 Miyajima-chō; 8.30am-5.30pm) featuring 'panda dolphins', a popular beach, a seaside park and, across from the ferry landing, a display of local crafts in the Hall of Industrial Traditions (☎ 44-0008; 1165-9 Miyajima-chō; admission free; 9am-5pm Wed-Mon).

Festivals & Events

Festivals on the island include fire-walking rites by the island's monks on 15 April and 15 November, and the Kangensai Boat Festival in summer (held on different dates every year).

Sleeping & Eating

If you can afford to stay on the island, it's well worth it – you'll be able to enjoy the quiet in the evening after the day worshippers have left. Although there are many restaurants and cafés on Miyajima, most cater to day-trippers and close early.

Guest House Kikugawa (☎ 44-0039; fax 44-2773; www.kikugawa.ne.jp; 796 Miyajima-chō; s/tw from ¥6615/11,550; P) This charming inn is comfortable and tastefully decorated, with attractive wooden interiors. There are eight Japanese-style rooms and meals are available. The service is personal and the manager speaks English. Look for the white building with the red *noren*.

Miyajima Grand Hotel Arimoto (☎ 44-2411; www.miyajima-arimoto.co.jp; 364 Miyajima-chō; s/tw incl 2 meals from ¥15,750/31,500; P) A victim of the tour trade during peak seasons, the Grand Hotel Arimoto has helpful, professional staff and the cuisine features oysters prominently. Expect to pay over ¥20,000 per person from October to November.

ourpick Iwasō Ryokan (☎ 44-2233; fax 44-2230; www.iwaso.com; Momijidani Miyajima-chō; s/tw incl 2 meals ¥22,200/42,150; P) The Iwasō, one of Japan's better inns, offers a grand ryokan experience in exquisite gardens somewhat removed from the throng. It's worth the splurge, especially in autumn when Momiji-dani (Maple Valley) explodes with colour. Go for the old-fashioned *hanare* private cottages at the rear and receive the royal treatment. There's a relaxing *onsen* in the main, more modern building.

Yakigaki-no-hayashi (☎ 44-0335; 505-1 Miyajima-chō; dishes ¥700-1400; 10.30am-4.30pm) The oysters in the tank and on the barbecue outside are what everyone is eating here. A plate of *namagaki* (raw oysters) is ¥1300.

Kurawanka (☎ 44-2077; 589-5 Miyajima-chō; dishes ¥730-1050; 11am-6pm) A popular *okonomiyaki* restaurant. Oyster, pork and egg are favourites. The *hiroshima-fū kaki-iri kurawanka-yaki* (Hiroshima-style *okonomiyaki* with oysters; ¥1050) is a real mouthful.

Itsuki (☎ 44-2376; 616 Miyajima-chō; drinks ¥500-1200; noon-midnight) Newly opened coffee shop Itsuki is a minimalist, peaceful haven away from the crowds. Finger foods like smoked oysters and *hors d'oeuvre moriawase* (hors d'oeuvre plate; ¥1200) are also available. It's just past the *kōmin-kan* (public hall) on the right, with a little carp pond at the front.

Getting There & Away

The mainland ferry terminal for Miyajima is near Miyajima-guchi station on the JR San-yō line, between Hiroshima and Iwakuni. Miyajima trams from Hiroshima terminate at the Hiroden-Miyajima-guchi stop by the ferry terminal. The tram (¥270, 70 minutes) takes longer than the *futsū* (¥400, 25 minutes), but it can be boarded in central Hiroshima.

From the terminal, ferries shuttle to Miyajima (¥170, 10 minutes). JR passholders should use the one operated by JR. High-speed ferries (¥1600, 20 to 30 minutes, eight daily) operate direct to Miyajima from Hiroshima's Ujina port. Another ferry (¥1900, 55 minutes, eight daily) links Hiroshima's Peace Memorial Park with Miyajima.

Miyajima can be easily visited as a day trip from Hiroshima. See p457 for details of the Hiroshima tram company's good-value one-day passport.

Getting Around

Bicycles can be hired from the JR office in the ferry building, but walking around is quite easy. A free bus goes from Iwasō Ryokan to the Misen cable-car station.

THE INLAND SEA
瀬戸内海

The Inland Sea (Seto-nai-kai) offers a first-hand experience of a part of Japan that, though rapidly changing, is still much slower-paced than the fast-moving metropolitan centres. It's bound by the major islands of Honshū, Kyūshū and Shikoku. Four narrow channels connect it with the ocean. To the west the Kanmon-kaikyō strait separates Honshū from Kyūshū and leads to the Sea of Japan; to the south, leading to the Pacific, the Hoya-kaikyō separates Kyūshū from Shikoku; at the other end of Shikoku, the Naruto-kaikyō and Kitan-kaikyō straits flow each side of Awaji-shima.

The most interesting area of the Inland Sea is the island-crowded stretch from Takamatsu (Shikoku) and Okayama west to Hiroshima. There are said to be more than 3000 islands and islets.

The Inland Sea can be explored by ferry or sometimes bus from the main islands. There are now three bridge systems linking Honshū with Shikoku; the westernmost, known as Se-tonai Shimanami Kaidō, crosses 10 bridges and nine islands.

Information

Brochures, maps and general tourist information are readily available, but Donald Richie's *The Inland Sea*, originally published in 1971, makes an excellent introduction to the region. Although much of the Inland Sea's slow-moving and easy-going atmosphere has disappeared since this book was published, it still has fascinating insights.

The Inland Sea section of this guidebook starts with its largest island, Awaji-shima, in the east, and then works its way westwards. Islands that are close to and associated with particular places on Honshū or Shikoku are included in those sections. For instance, Miyajima is included in the Hiroshima section and Megi-jima in the Kagawa section of the Shikoku chapter.

Getting Around

Besides the regular ferry services between Honshū, Shikoku and the various islands, **SKK** (Seto Naikai-kisen; ☎ 082-253-1212; ⊙ ticket office 7am-9pm) offers day cruises on the Inland Sea from Hiroshima. The trips are seasonal, and cruises with lunch/dinner cost from ¥5000/7500.

The Japan Travel Bureau (JTB) and other tour operators also run seasonal overnight cruises in the Inland Sea.

It's possible to take a ferry through the Inland Sea from Kansai to Kyūshū. Unless you check the times carefully, though, you may end up going through the Inland Sea at night, and if you just travel through you won't get a chance to taste the lifestyle on any of the islands. **Ferry Sunflower** (☎ 06-6572-5181; www.ferry-sunflower.com in Japanese; ⊙ ticket office 9am-5pm) has two daily Osaka–Beppu ferries, and **Diamond Ferry** (☎ 078-857-9525; www.diamond-ferry.co.jp in Japanese; ⊙ ticket office 9am-5pm) has two ferries a day between Kōbe and Oita on Kyūshū.

AWAJI-SHIMA 淡路島
☎ 0799 / pop 153,000

Awaji-shima, the Inland Sea's largest island, forms the region's eastern boundary and connects with Honshū via **Akashi Kaikyō-Ōhashi** – at 3.91km, the longest suspension bridge in the world. Life on the island has changed considerably since the bridge opened, and

---

TAKING IT EASY IN THE INLAND SEA

If you want to experience the Inland Sea on smaller islands unconnected to the mainland by bridges, consider Shiraishi-jima and Manabe-jima (administratively, the islands are part of Kasaoka city). The starting point is Kasaoka, about 40 minutes west of Okayama on the JR San-yō line. It's only a seven-minute stroll from Kasaoka station down to the rickety ferry terminal.

From there take a ferry to Shiraishi-jima (¥500, 35 minutes or ¥900, 20 minutes, nine daily), where the Okayama International Villa Group has one of its villas (p446). The modern building is in an idyllic location with great views, and it has access to the beach, rocky coastline and hiking trails.

Next up is the ferry to Manabe-jima (¥450, 35 minutes), where the beachside **Santora Youth Hostel** (三虎ユースホステル; ☎ 0865-68-3515; www.jyh.or.jp/english/chugoku/manabe/index.html; 2224 Manabe-jima; dm members/nonmembers ¥3045/4045) is set to take care of your every need. Meals are available at the hostel. Manabe-jima residents call their island *hana-no-shima* (flower island) as a large variety of flowers are cultivated in its mild, frost-free climate.

When you've had enough of island life, head back to Kasaoka or carry on to Tadotsu in Kagawa-ken on Shikoku by ferry, which departs on Thursday and Saturday at 2.30pm (transfer at Sanagi-jima). The ferry company is **San-yō Kisen** (☎ 0865-69-7080).

Awaji-shima is now part of a road link from Kansai to Shikoku. At the southern end of the island, **Naruto-Ōhashi** spans the Naruto-kaikyō (Naruto Channel) across the well-known **Naruto Whirlpools** (see p632) to connect Shikoku with Awaji-shima.

The northern part of the island will be long remembered as the epicentre of the massive 1995 earthquake that claimed over 6000 lives, mostly in and around Kōbe. The island also provided most of the material used to build the island in Osaka Bay on which Kansai's international airport sits.

The island is relatively flat and has some good beaches. It was the original home of *ningyō jōruri* **puppet theatre**, which preceded the development of *bunraku* (classic puppet theatre using huge puppets). Short performances are given several times daily in the small **Awaji Jōruri Puppet Theatre** (淡路人形浄瑠璃館; ☎ 0799-52-0260) in Fukura, at the southern end of the island. Near the Kōshien ferry terminal, at **Onokoro Awaji World Park** (淡路ワールドパークおのころ; ☎ 0799-62-1192; admission ¥1200, rides ¥300-500; ☯ 9.30am-5pm Thu-Tue), there's a bizarre grouping of international sightseeing attractions constructed at 4% their original size. They include the Taj Mahal, the Parthenon, Pisa's leaning tower and other international favourites.

Sandy Ōhama beach, about halfway down the east coast, attracts crowds in summer; Goshiki beach, about halfway down the west coast, is better for swimming and known for its spectacular sunsets.

SHŌDO-SHIMA 小豆島
☎ 0879 / pop 33,000

Famed for its vast olive groves and as the location for the Japanese film classic *Twenty-Four Eyes (Nijūshi-no hitomi)*, Shōdo-shima translates literally as 'island of small beans'. A very mountainous island, it offers a number of interesting places to visit and makes an enjoyable escape from big-city Japan. The second-largest island in the Inland Sea, Shōdo-shima even has a miniature version of neighbouring Shikoku's 88 Temple Circuit. Administratively, Shōdo-shima is part of Shikoku's Kagawa-ken.

Orientation & Information

Tonoshō, at the western end of the island, is the usual arrival point from Takamatsu, Uno or Okayama and makes a good base from which to explore the island, although there are six ports with ferry connections to destinations here and there. At Tonoshō you'll find a **tourist information office** (☎ 62-5300; Tonoshō-chō; ☯ 8.30am-5.15pm) just inside the ferry building, with a very good English brochure on everything the island has to offer.

Sights & Activities
COASTAL AREA

Moving around the island anticlockwise, Shōdo-shima's olive-growing activities are commemorated at **Olive Park** (☎ 82-2200; Nishimura; admission free; ☯ 8.30am-5pm) on the south coast, where there are fake Grecian ruins and olive chocolate for sale. The brand-new **Sun**

Olive Onsen (admission ¥700; ☼ noon-9pm Thu-Tue) is there, featuring stunning views from a variety of baths, a restaurant and a training room. Shōdo-shima is serious about olives – it even has Milos in Greece as a sister island.

Cool off with a soy-sauce–flavoured ice cream at the **Marukin Soya Sauce Historical Museum** (☎ 82-0047; Nouma; admission ¥210; ☼ 9am-4pm), between Kusakabe and Sakate.

Just north of Sakate is the turn-off to the small village of **Tanoura**, the site of the village school in the novel *Twenty-Four Eyes* and the later film of the same name. The real school and its movie-set version are both open for **visits** (☎ 82-2455; Tanoura; combined ticket ¥750; ☼ 9am-5pm). A statue of the film's teacher and her pupils, known as the **Group Statue of Peace**, stands outside the Tonoshō ferry terminal.

CENTRAL MOUNTAINS

The **Kanka-kei cable car** (one way/return ¥700/1250; ☼ 8am-5pm) is the main attraction in the central mountains, making a spectacular trip up through Kanka-kei gorge. An alternative for keen walkers is a 3½-hour return trip climbing up the Omote 12 Views track and down the Ura Eight Views trail. From the cable car's arrival point at the top of the gorge, you can hike to the island's highest peak, Hoshigajō-yama (816m), in an hour.

As you descend on the road from the top towards Tonoshō, you pass **Choshi-kei Valley & Monkey Park** (☎ 62-0768; Nouma; admission ¥370; ☼ 8.10am-4.50pm), where monkeys from around the world are kept in cages. Wild monkeys come for a daily feed – they're used to people and will come right up to you.

Between Tonoshō and Otani is the temple **Hōshō-in** (☎ 62-0682; Kitayama), famed for its huge juniper tree, which is said to have been planted by Emperor Ojin 1500 years ago. The circumference of the trunk is 17m. The temple's opening hours are irregular.

Festivals & Events

The village of Shikoku-mura, in Yashima, just outside Takamatsu on Shikoku, has a village kabuki theatre that comes from Shōdo-shima. **Farmers' kabuki performances** are still held on the island on 3 May at Tonoshō and on Sports Day (around 10 October) in other centres.

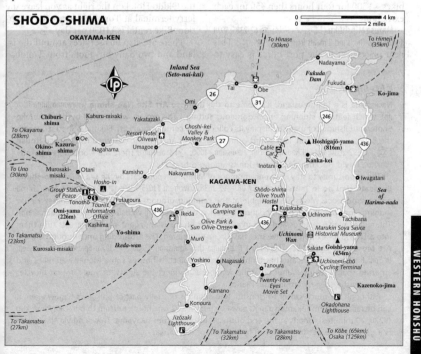

SHŌDO-SHIMA

Sleeping & Eating

The more interesting places to stay are along the southern coast of the island. Tonoshō, though, has a variety of hotels, ryokan and *minshuku* (family-run budget accommodation), particularly along the road running straight back from the waterfront.

Dutch Pancake Camping (ダッチパンケーキ キャンピング; ☎ 82-4616; ww8.tiki.ne.jp/~dpc/Eng-frame.htm; 1869-1 Nishimura Otsu Uchinomi-chō; tents per person ¥1800; P) This friendly place is run by a Dutchman and his Japanese wife who are building a pancake café on site behind the Sun Olive Onsen. Prices are listed on the website. The campsite is on a small signposted road behind the *onsen*.

Shōdo-shima Olive Youth Hostel (小豆島オ リーブユースホステル; ☎ 82-6161; www4.ocn .ne.jp/~olive-yh/index-e.html; Tonoshō-chō; dm members/ nonmembers ¥3100/3700; P X X) On the south coast, this hostel has meals available. It also rents bicycles (per four hours ¥500).

Uchinomi-chō Cycling Terminal (内海町サイク リング・ターミナル; ☎ 82-1099; 1834-15 Ko Sakate Uchinomi-chō; s with/without meals ¥5000/2700) At the Sakate ferry terminal, this place also rents bikes – ¥500 for four hours then ¥50 for each extra hour.

Maruse Minshuku (民宿マルセ; ☎ 62-2385; 5978 Ko Tonoshō-chō; s incl 2 meals from ¥6300; P X) This neat place next to the post office is easy to find, and has a new wing a short distance away with Japanese- and Western-style rooms.

Resort Hotel Olivean (リゾートホテルオ リビアン; ☎ 65-2311; www.artstreet.com/comps /hotel_olivean/Index.htm; Yū-higaoka; s/tw incl 2 meals from ¥21,000/39,000; P X X) If you want something more upmarket, this place has it all and is a good spot to watch the sunrise and sunset. It's a grand complex located towards the northern coast of the island between Tonoshō and Ōbe.

Getting There & Away

There are ferry services from Honshū and Shikoku to various ports on the island. Popular jumping-off points include Uno on Honshū (trains go to Uno from Okayama) and Takamatsu on Shikoku. There are high-speed ferries (¥1140, 30 minutes, 17 daily) and regular ferries (¥570, around an hour, 15 daily) from Takamatsu to Tonoshō.

Getting Around

If you've got plenty of time, cycling is a very enjoyable way to see Shōdo-shima. **Ryobi Rent-a-cycle** (☎ 62-5001; ☉ 7am-10pm) is inside the Ōkido Hotel on the right as you leave the ferry terminal at Tonhsō; ask at the reception. Bike rental is ¥1050 per day.

There are also bus services around the island and two daily bus tours from Tonohsō

NAO-SHIMA 直島

Nao-shima is a unique island. It's home to the **Benesse Art Site Nao-shima** (www.naoshima-is.co .jp), which features stunning art in gorgeous settings. The project was started by the Fukutake Shoten publishing company to display its collection of contemporary art. Fukutake Shoten became the Benesse Corporation, and award-winning architect Andō Tadao designed its **Benesse House** (☎ 087-892-2030; Gotanji Nao-shima-chō; admission ¥1000; ☉ 8am-9pm). There are works here by Andy Warhol, David Hockney and Jasper Johns among others.

The opportunity to stay in an encampment of Mongolian *pao* tents by the sea at the **Nao-shima Furusato Umi no le Tsutsuji-sō** (☎ 087-892-2838; s/tw from ¥3675/7350; P X) makes Nao-shima a rare experience. Meals are available at the camping ground. There's also the Benesse House lodgings for upmarket accommodation – check out rates on the website and preview each room. The museum also restores and preserves old sites on the island; contemporary artists turn them into artworks for exhibition. Five sites have been completed. The astounding underground **Chichū Art Museum** (☎ 087-892-3755; 3449-1 Nao-shima-chō; admission ¥2000; ☉ 10am-6pm Tue-Sun Mar-Sep, to 5pm Tue-Sun Oct-Feb) is another highlight of the project. It houses some Monet waterlilies and amazing sculptures by Walter de Maria. Minibuses connect the sights, or you can rent bicycles and enjoy the scenery around the island.

Although it's much closer to Honshū, Nao-shima is officially part of Shikoku's Kagawa-ken. It can be reached from Takamatsu in Kagawa by ferry (¥510, one hour), or from Uno in Okayama-ken (¥220, 20 minutes). Uno is at the end of the JR Uno line from Okayama. Travelling via Nao-shima is a good way to get from Honshū to Shikoku, or vice versa.

(¥3280/3980, departing 12.40pm/9.40am) and one from Sakate (departing 1.20pm, ¥2500). If having your own car appeals, **Nippon Car Rental** (☎ 62-0680; ⏰ 8.30am-6pm) is on the left as you leave the ferry terminal Tonohsō. Rates are ¥5250 for six hours.

INNO-SHIMA 因島
☎ 084 / pop 27,000

Inno-shima and the islands Ikuchi-jima and Ōmi-shima are now linked with Honshū and Shikoku; they're three of the nine islands linked by the Setonai Shimanami Kaidō system. Famed for its flowers and abundance of fruit, Inno-shima is connected by bridge to Mukai-shima and on to Onomichi. The island has a mildly interesting **pirate castle** (因島水軍城; 3228-2 Nakanosho; admission ¥310; ⏰ 9.30am-5pm Fri-Wed) and atop Shirataki-yama there are 500 statues of *rakan*, the disciples of Buddha, as well as excellent views of the Kaidō. On the first Saturday and Sunday in September the lively **Suigun Furusato Matsuri** has boat races and *jindaiko* drumming.

IKUCHI-JIMA 生口島
☎ 08452 / pop 10,900

Ikuchi-jima is known for its citrus groves and beaches, including the artificial Sunset Beach on its west coast. It may not rival Hawaii's Sunset Beach for waves, but it definitely tops it in terms of summer swimmers.

Sights

Sleepy Setoda, the main town on the island, attracts package tours with the temple **Kōsan-ji** (耕三寺; ☎ 7-0800; 553-2 Setoda; combined ticket ¥1200; ⏰ 9am-5pm), a wonderful if bizarre exercise in kitsch. Starting in 1935, local steel-tube magnate Kanemoto Kōzō devoted a large slab of his considerable fortune to re-creating numerous important temples and shrines, all in this one spot and all in grateful homage to his mother and Buddha. The complex has some 2000 exhibits.

Admission to Kōsan-ji includes the **Art Museum**, **1000 Buddhas Cave**, **Treasure House** and the exquisite **Choseikaku Villa**, where Kōzō's mother lived. The extraordinary 1000 Buddhas Cave includes an introductory 'hell', as well as winding tunnels and spiral stairs lined with statues. The effect is a bit like a Buddhist Disneyland.

To get to the temple, turn right as you leave the boat landing then left up the shop-lined 600m-long street. The **Onomichi City History & Folklore Museum** (尾道市歴史民俗資料館; admission free; ⏰ 10am-4.30pm Sat, Sun & national holidays) is at the start of this street. Halfway up the same street you can turn left towards a temple on the hillside; around the back of this temple and much further up the hill is Kōjō-ji, dating from 1403, with a three-storey pagoda and fine views over the island. You can also get there by turning left from the pier and heading straight up the hill.

Sleeping

Setoda Shimanami Youth Hostel (瀬戸田しまなみユースホステル; ☎ 7-3137; homepage2/nifty .com/shimanami/nab.html in Japanese; 58-1 Tarumi Setoda-chō; dm ¥2700; P X) Right on Sunset Beach, this friendly hostel is popular with cyclists. It's also unique for having an archery dojo and genuine *onsen* baths. Most rooms are Japanese, and meals are available.

Ryokan Tsutsui (旅館つつ井; ☎ 7-2221; www .tsutsui.yad.jp in Japanese; 216 Setoda Setoda-chō; s incl 2 meals from ¥12,000; P X) The rooms at this ryokan are spacious and the gorgeous new wooden baths offer great views. Located in front of the ferry terminal, it's one of the few options left in town since the closure of other businesses.

Getting There & Away

On Honshū, ferries from Onomichi leave every 1½ hours (¥760, 35 minutes) and from Mihara every hour (¥750, 25 minutes). Other services are available. It seems a bit of a shame to do so, but yes, you can get to Setoda by bus from Onomichi.

ŌMI-SHIMA 大三島
☎ 0897 / pop 3900

This hilly island boasts the mountain god's treasure house, **Ōyamatsumi-jinja** (大山祇神社; ☎ 82-0032; 3327 Miyaura; admission incl Kaiji Museum ¥1000; ⏰ 8.30am-4.30pm), which commanded much respect from the Inland Sea's pirates between the 12th and 16th centuries. In fact, the pirates were more like a local navy than real pirates but, until Toyotomi Hideyoshi brought them to heel, they wielded real power in these parts. Along the way, what is reputedly Japan's largest collection of armour was built up in the shrine's treasure house. Around 80% of the armour and helmets designated as National Treasures are held there.

In an adjacent building known as the **Kaiji Museum** (海事博物館; admission ¥1000; 8.30am-4.30pm) there's a boat that was used by Emperor Hirohito in his marine-science investigations, together with a natural-history exhibit. The shrine is one of the most ancient in Japan.

Miyaura port is a 15-minute walk from the shrine. There's a **tourist information counter** in the roadside **Shimanami no eki mishima** (しまなみの駅御島; 82-0002; 3260 Miyaura; 8.30am-5pm), which can help with local *minshuku* reservations. It's just past the shrine on the right. Showers and bicycle rental are available.

Getting There & Away

You can get to Ōmi-shima by high-speed ferry service from Mihara (¥1250, 40 minutes) or from Tadanoumi in Hiroshima-ken (¥290, 20 minutes). A highway bus links Ōmi-shima with JR Shin-Onomichi station (¥1800, 50 minutes). The bus station is on the eastern side of the island below Tatara Ōhashi, the bridge that links Ōmi-shima with Ikuchi-jima.

YAMAGUCHI-KEN 山口県

Yamaguchi, at the western end of Honshū, straddles both the southern San-yō coast and the northern San-in coast. The great Kintai-kyō bridge at Iwakuni is a southern highlight, while Shimonoseki acts as the gateway to Kyūshū and Korea. The northern stretch includes the historically important town of Hagi and, in the central mountains, the vast cave at Akiyoshi-dai. The section of the coast from Tottori eastwards to Wakasa-wan is included in the Kansai chapter (see p370).

IWAKUNI 岩国

☎ 0827 / pop 148,000

The five-arched Kintai-kyō bridge is Iwakuni's major attraction, but this relaxed city has a number of points of interest in the nearby Kikko-kōen area. The main sights can be seen in a couple of hours.

Orientation & Information

Iwakuni has three widely separated areas. To the far west of the town centre is the Shin-Iwakuni *shinkansen* station, which is totally separate from the rest of town. Its **tourist information office** (46-0655; 1055-1 Mishō; 10.30am-3.30pm Thu-Tue) is very helpful. In the central area is the old part of town with the bridge,

the samurai quarter and the castle. There's a **tourist information office** (41-2300; 1-1-42 Iwakuni; 9.35am-5pm) near the bridge. To the east, in the modern part of town, the JR Iwakuni station has a helpful **tourist information office** (21-6050; 1-1-1 Marifu-machi; 10am-4pm Tue-Sun), as well as hotels, restaurants, bars and other conveniences.

At the bridge, the cable car can be seen climbing the mountains on the far side. The castle overlooks the town from the right of the cable car.

Sights

KINTAI-KYŌ 錦帯橋

Kintai-kyō, or the **Brocade Sash Bridge**, was built in 1673 and washed away by a flood in 1950. It was authentically rebuilt in 1953, with some cunningly concealed steel reinforcements, and rebuilt again in 2003–04. The bridge is immediately recognisable by its five steep arches. In the feudal era only samurai could use the bridge, which connected their side of the river with the rest of the town; commoners had to cross by boat. Today visitors pay ¥300 to walk across and back. The ticket office at the entrance to the bridge also sells an all-inclusive *setto-ken* (set ticket; ¥930) covering the bridge (normally ¥300 on its own), the return cable-car trip (normally ¥540) and entry to Iwakuni-jō (normally ¥260) – a saving of ¥170 for all three. The bridge and castle are floodlit nightly. After 4pm or 5pm, there are no attendants at the bridge ticket booth.

SAMURAI QUARTER

Some traces remain of the old samurai quarter on the far side of the bridge. Beside the cable-car station is the **Iwakuni Art Museum** (岩国美術館; 41-0506; 2-10-27 Yokoyama; admission ¥800; 9am-5pm Fri-Wed Mar-Nov, to 4pm Fri-Wed Dec-Feb), a delight for military buffs with its extensive collection of samurai armour and equipment. It's said to be one of the best collections in Japan.

The old samurai quarter is now part of **Kikko-kōen** and includes picturesque moats and remnants of feudal buildings.

IWAKUNI-JŌ 岩国城

The original **castle** (41-0633; admission ¥260; 9am-4.45pm, closed 29 Jan-5 Mar) was built on the mountain between 1603 and 1608, but seven years later the *daimyō* was forced to dismantle it and move down to the riverside. The castle was rebuilt in 1960 as part of Japan's great castle-reconstruction movement, but modern Japanese castles were built for tourism, not warfare, so it now stands photogenically high on the hill.

You can get to the castle by **cable car** (one way/return ¥320/540; ☉ 9am-5pm) or on foot along the road (for walking only) beside the youth hostel. See opposite for details of all-inclusive tickets.

OTHER SIGHTS

Iwakuni is famed for its albino snakes, said to embody the spirit of Benzaiten, the goddess of good fortune. They are unique to the area. On the far side of the bridge, the **Yokoyama White Snake Viewing Facility** (白蛇横山観覧所; ☎ 43-4888; 2-6 Yokoyama; admission ¥100; ☉ 9am-5pm) has four of these strange-looking creatures; other white snake facilities are around Iwakuni station.

Ukai (fishing using trained cormorants) usually takes place at Kintai-kyō every night from June to August, except when rain makes the water muddy or on nights with a full-moon. For ¥3500 you can watch this colourful and exciting method of fishing.

On the mountain side of the bridge, to the right, is a small shop selling *ishiningyō*, curious little rock agglutinations formed by river insects.

Sleeping & Eating

Iwakuni has places to stay on both sides of the river. There's only one restaurant on the west side of the river (by the cable-car station), though you can have tea and snacks. On the east side there are a few places selling takeaway and Japanese food close to the bridge.

Iwakuni Youth Hostel (岩国ユースホステル; ☎ 43-1092; fax 43-0123; www.jyh.or.jp/english/chugoku /iwakuni/index.html; 1-10-46 Yokoyama; dm members/nonmembers ¥2835/3835) This is a large, basic hostel, somewhat institutional but run by a very cheerful young couple. It's close to most of the attractions on the west side of the Kintai-kyō bridge and in a beautiful wooded area. Meals are available. There's a path outside that makes for a nice walk up to the castle area.

Hangetsu-an (半月庵; ☎ 41-0021; fax 43-0121; 1-17-27 Iwakuni; s/tw incl 2 meals from ¥8900/17,800; Ⓟ ✶) This clean, friendly place stresses its traditional service, but the building is modern and there are more-expensive rooms with private bathrooms (single/twin ¥11,000/22,000). It's on the east bank down the street continuing

from the bridge; you'll see the old-fashioned entrance a few blocks along on the left.

Shiratame Ryokan (白為旅館; ☎ 41-0074; fax 41-1174; www.gambo-ad.com/iwakuni/hotel/shiratame /info.htm in Japanese; 1-5-16 Iwakuni; s/tw incl 2 meals from ¥18,110/36,220; Ⓟ ✶) Just in front of the east side of the bridge, this fair-sized, traditional ryokan has well-presented local seafood. All the rooms here have views of the river.

Midori-no-sato (緑の里; ☎ 41-1370; 1-4-10 Iwakuni; meals ¥730-980; ☉ 10am-6pm Wed-Mon) Away from the crowds, a couple of blocks down the street continuing on from the bridge on the right-hand side, Midori-no-sato has set menus including cake-like *iwakuni-zushi* (Iwakuni-style sushi; ¥980), which includes *renkon* (lotus root) salad and *sōmen* noodles.

Cafe de Campagne (カフェ・ド・カンパーニュ; ☎ 43-4477; 2-7-25 Kawanishi; meals ¥1000-3800; ☉ 11am-11pm Mon-Fri, 9am-11pm Sat & Sun) One of the few eatery options open late, this standard trattoria is about 1km from the Kintai-kyō bridge. It has basic pasta dishes, like *peperoncino* pasta (¥880), garlic bread and salads. From the bridge, go south and cross the Garyō-bashi bridge, turn left and continue to the intersection before Kawanishi station; it's by a car dealership.

Getting There & Away

Iwakuni is only 40km from Hiroshima. Shin-Iwakuni station is on the *shinkansen* line, while JR Iwakuni station is on the JR San-yō line. Kintai-kyō is about 5km from either. Buses shuttle back and forth between JR Iwakuni station and the bridge (¥240), and between Shin-Iwakuni station and the bridge (¥280).

YAMAGUCHI 山口

☎ 083 / pop 192,000

During the Sengoku-jidai (Warring States) period (1467–1573), Yamaguchi prospered as an alternative capital to chaotic Kyoto. In 1550 the Jesuit missionary Francis Xavier paused for two months in Yamaguchi on his way to the imperial capital, but quickly returned to the safety of this provincial centre when he was unable even to find the emperor in Kyoto! In the following centuries Yamaguchi took turns with Hagi as the provincial capital and, like Hagi, Yamaguchi played an important part in the Meiji Restoration. Today this 'Kyoto of the West' is a peaceful town with interesting attractions.

WESTERN HONSHŪ

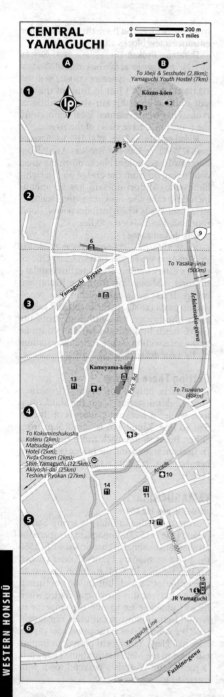

Orientation & Information

Ekimae-dōri is the main shopping street, running straight up from the station and crossing the main shopping arcade before reaching Rte 9. A very helpful **tourist information office** (☎ 933-0090; 2-1 Sodayu-chō; ☽ 9am-6pm Apr-Nov, 8.30am-5.30pm Dec-Mar) is on the 2nd floor of the train station, with English-language brochures and free internet access.

North of Rte 204, the **Ichinosaka-gawa** river has a particularly pretty stretch lined with cherry trees. Naturally, they're at their best during the spring blossoming time, but they're also lovely on summer evenings, when large fireflies flit through the branches.

Sights

ST FRANCIS XAVIER MEMORIAL CHURCH
ザビエル記念聖堂

The **church** (☎ 923-0532; 4-1 Kameyama-chō; suggested donation/ ¥100; ☽ 9am-5.30pm) overlooks the town centre from a hilltop in Kameyama-kōen. Built in 1952 to commemorate the 400th anniversary of Francis Xavier's visit to the city, it burned down under mysterious circumstances in 1991 and was rebuilt in 1998. It now has a very modern design and colourful interior.

ART GALLERY & MUSEUMS

At the foot of the hill stands the **Yamaguchi Prefectural Art Museum** (☎ 925-7788; 3-1 Kameya-chō; admission ¥190; ☻ 9am-5pm Tue-Sun), where frequent special exhibitions are held. Just north of it is the **Yamaguchi Prefectural Museum** (☎ 922-0294; 8-2 Kasuga-chō; admission ¥130; ☻ 9am-4.30pm Tue-Sun), which has exhibitions on wildlife and technology. The **Yamaguchi History Museum** (☎ 924-7001; 5-1 Kasuga-chō; admission ¥100; ☻ 9am-5pm Tue-Sun) is just off Rte 9.

KŌZAN-KŌEN & RURIKŌ-JI 香山公園 瑠璃光寺

Further north again from the town centre is **Kōzan-kōen**, where the **five-storey pagoda** of Rurikō-ji, dating from 1404, is picturesquely sited beside a small lake. A small museum, **Rurikō-ji Shiryōkan** (☎ 924-9139; 7-1 Kōzan-chō; admission ¥300; ☻ 9am-5pm), has photos and details of all 40 Japanese five-storey pagodas, and a map indicating where they're located. It's illuminated at night. The temple **Rurikō-ji**, with which the pagoda is associated, is also in the park and was moved here from a small village.

The park's teahouse was also moved here; the Yamaguchi *daimyō* held secret talks in the house under the pretext of a tea ceremony. The park is also the site of the **Tōshun-ji** temple and the graves of the Mōri lords.

JŌEI-JI 常栄寺

About 3km northeast of the JR station, **Jōei-ji** was originally built as a house and is notable for its Zen garden, **Sesshutei** (☎ 922-2272; 2001 Miyano-shimo; admission ¥300; ☻ 8am-5pm), designed by the painter Sesshū. Visitors bring *bentō* (boxed lunches) and sit on the veranda to eat, admiring the garden.

YUDA ONSEN

Just west of the city is the 800-year-old **Yuda Onsen** hot springs, said to have been discovered when a white fox healed its injured legs in the waters here. It's an eclectic mix of the traditional and the modern, geared to the older tour-group set. There's a **tourist information office** (☎ 901-0150; 2-1-23 Yuda Onsen; ☻ 9am-7pm) about 600m northwest of Yuda Onsen station on Rte 204; internet access is available here. In front of the office is one of the neighbourhood's five *ashi no yu* (foot baths), where you can bathe your feet for free and get friendly with locals. You can also use the baths at the large **Hotel Kamefuku** (ホテルかめ福; ☎ 922-

7000; 4-5 Yuda Onsen; admission ¥800; ☻ 11.30am-10pm), the less-crowded **Kokuminshukusha Koteru** (国民宿舎小てる; ☎ 922-3240; 4-3-15 Yuda Onsen; admission ¥350; ☻ 7am-midnight, 3-10pm) and, for a taste of luxury, the traditional ryokan **Umenoya** (梅乃屋; ☎ 922-0051; 4-3-19 Yuda Onsen; admission ¥800; ☻ 1pm-midnight). Buses run regularly to Yuda Onsen bus stop, near the tourist information office, from Yamaguchi station (¥190, 10 minutes).

Festivals & Events

During **Gion Matsuri**, which takes place on 20, 24 and 27 July, the Sagi no mai (Egret Dance) is held at Yasaka-jinja. From 6 to 7 August, during **Tanabata Chōchin Matsuri**, 10,000 decorated lanterns illuminate the city.

Sleeping

There are more accommodation options in nearby Yuda Onsen than in the Yamaguchi station area, but the youth hostel offers a relaxing getaway in a rural neighbourhood.

Yamaguchi Youth Hostel (山口ユースホステル; ☎ 928-0057; www.jyh.or.jp/english/chugoku/yamaguti/index.html; 801 Miyanoue; dm members/nonmembers ¥2730/3730; ℗ ⊠) This charming home is about 4km from Miyano station (two stops east of Yamaguchi) in a lovely farming area, and features a small crafts gallery. Meals are available, and manager Sugita-san can sometimes pick up guests at Miyano station; otherwise there is a bus.

Kokuminshukusha Koteru (国民宿舎小てる; ☎ 922-3240; fax 928-6177; 4-3-15 Yuda Onsen; s/tw ¥5400/10,800; ℗ ⊠) Two blocks north of the main street in Yuda Onsen, this is a good-value family-run place with Japanese-style rooms and cheery staff. The entrance to the baths is on the side of the building.

Taiyō-dō Ryokan (☎ 922-0897; fax 922-1152; 2-3 Komeya-chō; s/tw incl 2 meals ¥5500/11,000) On the shopping arcade just off Ekimae-dōri and beside a bakery with a green peaked roof, the Taiyō-dō has comfortably large rooms, and original '60s and '70s woodwork and furniture. The place is quite old, but has some character; the elderly manager is welcoming and helpful. It's seven minutes' walk from Yamaguchi station.

Sunroute Kokusai Hotel Yamaguchi (☎ 923-3610; fax 923-2379; www.sunroute.jp; 1-1 Nakagawara-chō; s/tw ¥6825/12,180; ℗ ⊠ ⊠ ⬜) This is the best value in town. Central to the sights in the middle of town and a 10-minute walk from the station, this recently renovated hotel has cheerful staff and stylish rooms. Free bicycles are also available. Indian restaurant Shiva on the 1st floor has great curry and naan lunch sets, as well as English menus.

our pick Teshima Ryokan (てしま旅館; ☎ 665-2248; www.teshimaryokan.com in Japanese; 7418-8 Ajisu-chō; s/tw incl 2 meals from ¥19,950/33,600; P ✗) A 20-minute drive southwest of Shin-yamaguchi station, this inn is a miracle of contemporary design by Kyoto architect Tsujimura Hisa-nobu. It ain't much from the outside, but the interior is a delicious symphony of blonde woods, cosy couches and diaphanous screens. There are baths here and superb cuisine; every detail is seen to by the *bantō-san* (concierge), who can pick up guests at the station.

Matsudaya Hotel (ホテル松田屋; ☎ 922-0125; fax 925-6111; www.matsudayahotel.co.jp in Japanese; 3-6-7 Yuda Onsen; s/tw incl 2 meals from ¥22,000/44,000; P ✗) Ichirō, the famed baseball player, stayed at this very traditional inn when he was in town. The rooms, baths and gardens are gorgeous, with service to match – expect about five staff standing at attention when you enter the lobby – and there's a great selection of dolls and ceramics for sale. The Matsudaya is about 800m north of Yuda Onsen station along the main drag in Yuda Onsen.

Eating

Sabō Kō (☎ 928-5522; 1-2-39 Dōjōmonzen; dishes ¥300-900; ✆ 11.30am-7pm Wed-Mon) 'Kō' means happi-ness, a very apt name for this delightful local coffee shop. It's a very laid-back atmosphere with humble décor and staff who are at turns boisterous or Zen-clam. The speciality here is *wafū omuraisu* (Japanese-style rice ome-lette; ¥800), a delish blend of mushrooms, *daikon* (raddish), garlic and onions. Look for the wooden door with a diamond-shaped window.

Café Galle (☎ 928-2880; 2-4-12 Dōjōmonzen; meals ¥350-800; ✆ 11am-6pm Thu-Tue) This is a stylish little basement café, very attractively designed and popular with local ladies. The *higawari ranchi* (daily lunch set; ¥800) typically consists of a fish and veggies plate. The entrance is easy to miss; it's right by some tall plants along the pavement.

Frank (☎ 932-4836; Dōjōmonzen; meals ¥700-900; ✆ noon-7pm Wed-Mon) Come to Frank if you want a funky place to chill out after sightsee-ing and try the *tai-fū yaki bīfun* (Thai food stall–style rice noodles; ¥700). This spacious

café, two blocks southwest of the arcade, has sofas, drinks and good daily lunch sets, also ¥700. Look for the red F by the door, which is around the corner from the main street.

La Francesca (☎ 934-1888; 7-1 Kameyama; meals ¥1500-4200; ✆ lunch & dinner; ✗) An Italian villa with a terrace that's a great spot for a beer in summer, La Francesca has good food and professional service. The lunch set (¥1575) offers a main course choice of *honjitsu no sakana* (fish of the day), *buta-bara niku* (pork back ribs) and *hoho niku* (beef cheek).

Getting There & Away

The Yamaguchi *futsū* service connects the city with Shin-Yamaguchi (¥230, 25 min-utes). Shin-Yamaguchi is 10km southwest of Yamaguchi in Ogōri, at the junction of the San-yō Osaka-Hakata *shinkansen* line and the JR Yamaguchi line, which passes through Yamaguchi and continues on to Tsuwano and Masuda on the San-in coast.

JR and Bōchō Kōtsū buses run to/from Yamaguchi to Hagi (¥1680, 70 minutes) and Akiyoshi-dai (¥1130, 55 minutes).

The fun *SL Yamaguchi-gō* steam locomotive stops at Yamaguchi and Yuda Onsen stations from March to November (see p486).

Getting Around

Bicycles can be hired from the train station at **Nishi Nihon Bus Net Service** (☎ 922-0774) – a good idea, since the town's attractions are some-what scattered (it's 8km just to Jōei-ji and back) and the pavements are wide. The first two hours cost ¥310, or it's ¥820 daily.

AKIYOSHI-DAI 秋吉台
☎ 0837

The rolling Akiyoshi-dai tablelands are about halfway between Yamaguchi and Hagi on the northern San-in coast. In this unusual land-scape, the green fields are dotted with curi-ous rock spires. Every February locals carry out the centuries-old tradition of *yama-yaki* (grass burning) on the plain to revitalise the vegetation. Beneath this picturesque plateau are hundreds of limestone caverns, the largest of which, **Akiyoshi-dō** (秋芳洞; ☎ 62-0304; admission ¥1200; ✆ 8.30am-5.30pm Mar-Nov, to 4.30pm Dec-Feb), is open to the public.

Akiyoshi-dō is of interest principally for its size; it is the largest limestone cave in Japan. The stalagmites and stalactites are not par-ticularly noteworthy, but the *hyakumai-zara* layered limestone pools are remarkable. In all, the cave extends about 10km, at some points 100m wide, with a river flowing through it and a pathway that runs for about 1km. At the midpoint of the cave trail you can take a lift up to the surface, where there is a lookout over the surrounding country. There are entrances to the cave at both ends of the pathway as well as at the lift. Buses run between the two ends if you don't want to retrace your steps. If you're feeling claustrophobic in the cave, go for a wander along the plentiful hiking trails on Japan's largest karst plateau.

Sleeping

There is scant accommodation around the cave area, and you'd be better off staying in Hagi or Yamaguchi and visiting Akiyoshi-dai as a day trip.

Akiyoshi-dai Youth Hostel (秋吉台ユースホ ステル; ☎ 62-0341; fax 62-1546; www.jyh.or.jp/english /chugoku/akiyoshi/index.html; 4236-1 Akiyoshi Shūho-chō; dm members/nonmembers ¥2730/3730; Ⓟ 🏿) This is a large and somewhat institutional hostel, but foreign guests are usually given rooms in the more modern part of the building. Meals are available, and the elderly managers are quite friendly. It's close to one of the entrances to the cave.

Akiyoshi Royal Hotel (秋芳ロイヤルホテ ル; ☎ 62-0311; fax 62-0231; www.shuhokan.co.jp; Akiy- oshidai; s/tw incl 2 meals ¥12,600/25,200; Ⓟ 🏿) This large hotel that caters to Japanese group tours visiting the plateau. Japanese- and Western- style rooms are available, rather spartan but large, and there are *onsen* baths on the premises with views of the plain, also open to nonguests (¥500, open 5pm to 9pm). It's located about 1.5km north of the main en- trance to the cave along the road.

Getting There & Away

It takes just under an hour by bus to reach the cave from Yamaguchi (¥1130, 55 min- utes) or Higashi-Hagi (¥1710, two daily). If you've got a JR pass, take the JR bus from Yamaguchi. Buses also run to the cave from Shin-Yamaguchi (¥1140, 45 minutes) and Shi- monoseki (¥1730, two hours).

SHIMONOSEKI 下関

☎ 0832 / pop 288,000

Shimonoseki is an important crossroads for travellers and Japanese history. At the extreme western tip of Honshū, it's separated from the island of Kyūshū by only a narrow strait, famous in Japanese history for a decisive 12th- century clash between rival samurai clans. The expressway crosses the Kanmon-kaikyō strait on the Kanmon-bashi bridge; while another road, the *shinkansen* railway line and the JR railway line all tunnel underneath. You can even walk to Kyūshū through a tunnel under the strait! Shimonoseki is also an important connecting point to South Korea, with a daily ferry service to/from Busan. The town has a number of points of interest and some excel- lent, if potentially deadly, cuisine.

Orientation

Beside JR Shimonoseki station is the large Sea Mall Shimonoseki shopping centre, and just east is the 153m Kaikyō Yume Tower, which looks like a midget skyscraper topped by a futuristic billiard ball. A ¥600 ticket to the tower gets you to the **observatory** (☎ 31-5600; 30th fl, 3-3-1 Buzenda-chō; 🕑 9.30am-9.30pm) for a very impressive 360-degree view of the surround- ing scenery.

Information

There's a **tourist information office** (☎ 32-8383; 4-3- 1 Takezaki-chō; 🕑 9am-7pm) in JR Shimonoseki sta- tion and another **tourist office** (☎ 56-3422; 1-11-1 Akine Minami-machi; 🕑 9am-7pm) in the Shin-Shi- monoseki *shinkansen* station, two stops north of the JR station on the JR San-yō line.

Internet access and a small library are available at the **International Exchange Room 'Global Salon'** (☎ 31-5770; 3-3-1 Buzenda-chō; per 30min ¥100; 🕑 10am-8pm Tue-Sun), on the 4th floor of the International Trade Building, which is by the Kaikyō Yume Tower. There's an **internet café** (☎ 28-1638; 1-15-33 Takezaki-chō; per 30min ¥400, wi-fi ¥200; 🕑 10am-10pm) on the 1st floor of Hotel 38 Shimonoseki, which is about a two-minute walk from the station.

If you're arriving from Korea, note that there are no currency-exchange counters in the ferry terminal. The information office in the station can give you a list of interna- tional ATMs and places where you can change money; one is the **Shimonoseki Post Office** (☎ 22- 0957; 2-12-12 Takezaki-chō; 🕑 9am-4pm), which takes cash and travellers cheques.

Sights & Activities

KARATO ICHIBA 唐戸市場

A highlight of any trip to Shimonoseki is an early rise and a visit to the **Karato Ichiba fish**

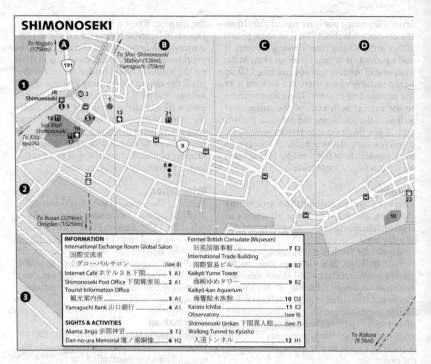

SHIMONOSEKI

markets (☎ 31-0001; 5-50 Karato; ⏰ 4am-3pm Mon-Sat, 7am-3pm Sun; Ⓟ). The interesting stuff is on show from 4am to 8am, so if you like to sleep in, forget it. The markets kick off at 2am for those in the industry, but the public is welcome from 4am – the earlier you get there the better. It's a great opportunity to try sashimi for breakfast or lunch, and the fish doesn't get any fresher – a fair bit will still be moving. People-watching is almost as much fun as goggling at the many different sea creatures.

The market is in Karato, halfway between central Shimonoseki and Hino-yama. The first bus leaves from outside the station at 5.55am (6.14am on weekends) – it costs ¥190 and takes seven minutes. Organise a taxi if you want to go earlier. The markets are closed two Wednesdays a month.

Also in Karato, the **Kaikyō-kan aquarium** (☎ 28-1100; 6-1 Arukapōto; admission ¥1800; ⏰ 9.30am-5.30pm; Ⓟ) has stacks of impressive fish, shows, displays, a huge blue-whale skeleton and a special tank of *fugu* (see p476).

The Meiji-era former **British Consulate building** (☎ 31-1238; 4-11 Karato; admission free; ⏰ 9am-5pm)

of 1906 is close at hand. It has an interesting façade, and there's a small museum inside with the consul's desk still in place. There's a unique coffee house at the rear (see p476).

AKAMA-JINGŪ 赤間神宮
Bright vermilion, this postwar **shrine** (☎ 31-4138; 4-1 Amidaiji-chō; ⏰ 24hr) is dedicated to the eight-year-old emperor Antoku, who died in 1185 in the naval battle of Dan-no-ura. In the Hōichi Hall stands a statue of the splendidly monikered Earless Hōichi, the hero of a traditional ghost story retold by Japanophile Lafcadio Hearn (see p489). The shrine is between Karato and Hino-yama. Get off the bus (¥230, 10 minutes) at the Akama-jingū-mae bus stop.

The **Sentei Festival** (2 to 4 May) is held here to remember the Heike women who worked as prostitutes to pay for rites for their fallen kin. On 3 May women dressed as Heian-era courtesans form a colourful procession at the shrine.

HINO-YAMA 火の山
About 5km northeast of JR Shimonoseki station there are superb views over the Kanmon-

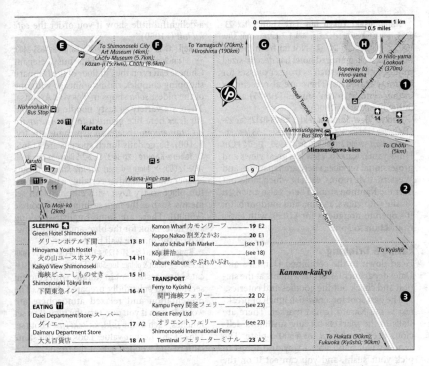

kaikyō from the top of 268m-high **Hino-yama**. Walk or drive to the top, as the ropeway is closed. Take a Ropeway-mae bus (¥360) to the Mimosusōgawa bus stop and walk up to the ropeway station, or take a Kokuminshukusha-mae bus straight to the bottom of the ropeway. By the Mimosusōgawa-kōen bus stop are lifts that take you down to a free **cross-strait walker's tunnel**, popular with local joggers, for a 780m submarine walk to Kyūshū. It's a nice stroll around the seaside promenade on the Kyūshū side, but there are no restaurants.

Across the road from the same bus stop is the **Dan-no-ura Memorial**, marking the spot where the decisive clash between the Minamoto and Taira clans took place in 1185. This is where one of the ladies of the House of Taira plunged into the sea with the infant emperor Antoku in her arms instead of surrendering to the enemy.

CHŌFU 長府

Chōfu is the old castle town area and, while little remains of the coastal castle itself, there are earth walls and samurai gates, along with a museum and some important temples and shrines.

National treasure **Kōzan-ji** (功山時; ☎ 45-0258; 1 Kawabuchi; ⏰ 9am-5pm) has a Zen-style hall dating from 1327, and the **Chōfu Museum** (長府博物館; ☎ 45-0555; 1-2-5 Kawabuchi; admission ¥200; ⏰ 9.30am-5pm Tue-Sun) is also in the temple grounds.

Shimonoseki City Art Museum (下関市立美術館; ☎ 45-4131; 1-1 Kuromon Higashi-machi admission ¥200; ⏰ 9.30am-5pm Tue-Sun) features contemporary Japanese artists.

Sleeping

Hinoyama Youth Hostel (☎ 22-3753; www.e-yh.net /shimonoseki; 3-47 Mimosusogawa-chō; dm ¥2900; P ⌧ ⌧ ▭) Amazing views of the straits and relaxed service make this one of the best youth hostels in Chūgoku. You can take a Hino-yama bus from the station (¥230, 26 minutes). Breakfast is available, but there are few restaurants in the area.

Green Hotel Shimonoseki (☎ 31-1007; fax 31-3603; www.greenhotelshimonoseki.jp in Japanese; 1-16-13 Takezaki-chō; s/tw ¥4800/8800; P ⌧ ▭ wi-fi) Singles in this bright, friendly little chain hotel are small, but it's well kept and only three minutes from the station. A free lobby computer and ¥500 buffet breakfast are available.

Shimonoseki Tōkyū Inn (☎ 33-0109; fax 23-0285; www.tokyu hotels.co.jp; 4-4-1 Takezaki-chō; s/tw ¥6825/12,600; P ✕ ✕ ⬜) Not far from the station, this well-managed hotel has decent-sized rooms with extras such as trouser presses for business travellers. There are also recliners in the 'comfort room' singles (¥9975) and a buffet breakfast (¥1000).

Kaikyō View Shimonoseki (☎ 23-0117; fax 29-0114; www.kv-shimonoseki.com in Japanese; 3-58 Mimosu-sogawa-chō; s/tw incl 2 meals ¥10,500/19,950; P ✕) On Hino-yama, Kaikyō View has great views and professional service. There are Japanese- and Western-style rooms, each of which looks out over the Kanmon strait. There's also an *onsen* on site with views, a sauna and outdoor bath. It's open to nonguests for ¥1050, with entry from 11am to 3pm.

Eating & Drinking

Head down to the combined Daimaru and Daiei department-store basements at the station and check out the goodies and eateries.

The best spot for a raw-fish lunch or breakfast is the Karato Ichiba market. There are stalls in the markets serving sushi and delicious deep-fried *fugu* for ¥500 a plate. The vendors will hand you a tray and tongs to pick your sushi, and you can eat it on the boardwalk while watching the ships sail by. Next door is the Kamon Wharf complex, which has more than 40 shops, the majority of them eateries.

Shimonoseki Ijinkan (☎ 22-2262; 4-11 Karato; drinks ¥500-1500; ⌚ 9.30am-8pm Tue-Sun) Tucked away in the old British consulate courtyard, the Ijinkan coffee house has bygone European elegance and the theatrical ministrations of bow-tied 'coffee meister' Kunio Kanegae, who puts on

a delightful little show if you order the *café au lait* (¥1050).

Kōji (☎ 29-5000; 4-4-10 Takezaki-chō; meals ¥683-8400; ⌚ 11am-9pm; ✕ 11am-3pm) This busy, elegant Chinese eatery on the 7th floor of the Daimaru shopping complex claims a lineage with one of the oldest *soba* shops in Tokyo's Asakusa. There's a variety of tasty noodle dishes and stir-fries here like *gyūniku to gurīn asupara no atamemono* (beef and asparagus stir-fry; ¥2100). Large daily lunch specials are ¥1365.

Yabure-Kabure (☎ 34-3711; 2-2-5 Buzenda-chō; meals ¥800-12,000; ⌚ lunch & dinner) *Yabure kabure* means 'desperation' and this is certainly a boisterous, fun place to try *fugu* with emphasis on set menus, such as the *fugu* sashimi Ebisu course (¥5000). There are some English-speaking staff here. Look for the blue-and-white blowfish on the outside wall by the door.

Kappo Nakao (☎ 31-4129; 4-6 Akama-chō; meals ¥3800-26,250; ⌚ lunch & dinner Tue-Sun) This is a sophisticated *fugu* restaurant in Karato, with graceful service and splendidly prepared dishes. The presentation and relaxed atmosphere are worth it even if you don't try the *fugu*. The set lunches, such as the *fuku kaiseki* (*fugu* course; ¥2625), are decent value. Look for the stone lantern and wooden gate at the front.

Getting There & Away

Shinkansen trains stop at Shin-Shimonoseki station, two stops from JR Shimonoseki station. From Shimonoseki the bridge and tunnels connect roads and rail lines in Honshū with Kyūshū. Eastbound road users can take Rte 191 along the northern San-in coast, Rte 2 along the southern San-yō coast or the Chūgoku Expressway through central Honshū.

DARE TO FUGU?

Fugu are known in English as globefish or blowfish, and you won't have to go to Karato Ichiba (p473) to see your first in Shimonoseki. The city revels in its reputation as the *fugu* capital of Japan, and paintings and sculptures of the fish are everywhere.

Eating raw *fugu* is considered somewhat adventurous, since the fish's liver and other organs contain tetrodotoxin, a poison that makes cyanide look like chicken feed. During the Tokugawa shōgunate and the Meiji Restoration eating *fugu* was banned in certain districts, and since 1958 only specialist chefs have been allowed to prepare and sell the potentially deadly fare. Only 30% of apprentice chefs who train for three years pass the test to get a licence. Despite the precautions, every now and then people die – Kabuki actor Bandō Mitsugoro VIII, considered a national treasure, keeled over after a *fugu* party in 1975, but he had eaten four servings of *fugu* liver.

Fugu used to be a winter dish, eaten mainly between October and March, but it's now available year-round, thanks to *fugu* farms off Kyūshū.

Kanmon Kisen ferries run two or three times hourly from the Karato area of Shimonoseki to Moji-ko in Kyūshū (¥390, five minutes). Kanmon Kaikyō ferries ply the route between Karato and Kokura in Kyūshū (¥200, 13 minutes). From Shin-moji in Kita-Kyūshū there are ferries to Kōbe, Osaka and Tokyo in Honshū and to Matsuyama in Shikoku.

FERRIES TO KOREA & CHINA

Kampu Ferry (☎ in Shimonoseki 24-3000, operating under Pukwan Ferry in Busan 051-464-2700) operates the Shimonoseki–Busan ferry from the Shimonoseki International Ferry Terminal (Shimonoseki-kō Kokusai Taminaru), a short walk from the station. Head up to the **2nd floor** (✆ 10am-noon & 1-6.30pm) for bookings. There are daily departures at 7pm from Shimonoseki, arriving in Busan at 8.30am the following morning. Boarding time is between 6pm and 6.20pm, and one-way fares start at ¥7200 for students (¥9000 for an open tatami area), continuing upwards for cabins; there's a 10% discount on return fares. Shimonoseki City imposes a ¥600 levy on departing passengers.

Ferries from Busan depart from the Busan Port International Passenger Terminal, five-to 10-minutes' walk from Jungang-dong subway station on subway line 1. They follow the same time schedule, leaving Busan at 8pm and arriving in Shimonoseki at 8am. One-way/ return fares start at 85,000/161,500 won.

If you need a visa for South Korea, arrange it before coming to Shimonoseki. There's a Korean consulate in Hiroshima. This route is used by many long-term Western residents in Japan, so expect to have your passport rigorously inspected when you return to Japan.

Orient Ferry Ltd (www.orientferry.co.jp in Japanese; ☎ in Shimonoseki 32-9677, in Qingdao 0532-8387-1160) runs between Shimonoseki and Qingdao, China (27 hours). The cheapest one-way/ return tickets are ¥15,000/27,200 from Shimonoseki (departures 1pm Wednesday, Friday and Saturday) and 1100/1980 yuan from Qingdao, departing from the port ferry terminal north of Qingdao station at 8pm on Monday, Thursday and Saturday.

SHIMONOSEKI TO HAGI

There are three routes between Shimonoseki and Hagi. One goes around the western extremity of Honshū, served by the JR San-in line, and features some great coastal scenery, small fishing villages and interesting country-side. **Ōmi-shima**, with its scenic, rocky coast, is immediately north of **Nagato** and connected to the mainland by a bridge. The island is part of the Kita Nagato Coastal Park, which extends eastwards beyond Hagi. **Ōmi-shima Kanko-kisen** (☎ 0837-26-0834) runs 1½-hour cruises (¥2200) around the island, taking passengers through natural rock archways.

An alternative is to travel via the Akiyoshi cave and tablelands area (see p472).

The third option is to take the JR Mine line from Asa, east of Shimonoseki, to Nagato, and then take the JR San-in line to Hagi.

Tawarayama Onsen 俵山温泉
☎ 0837

Nestled in the mountains, Tawarayama Onsen has escaped developers and maintained its reputation as a favoured hidden spa for *tōji* (curative bathing). It's quite deep in the mountains and serious about its purpose: there are no karaoke bars, no neon and almost no restaurants. Bathers come here for their health, usually staying from four days to a week at a time in the 40-odd ryokan. This *onsen* is so old-style that none of the ryokan has its own bath; water is not all that plentiful. Guests go out to bathe in the three public baths: **Machi-no-yu** (町の湯; ☎ 29-0001; admission ¥360; ✆ 6am-10.30pm); **Kawa-no-yu** (川の湯; ☎ 29-0001; admission ¥360; ✆ 2-10pm), which overlooks the river; and the newer **Hakuen-no-yu** (白猿の湯; ☎ 29-0036; admission ¥700; ✆ 7am-9pm). The latter has one of the only eateries in town, **Ryōfūtei** (風亭; dishes ¥900-5000; ✆ lunch & dinner), serving pastas and meals like *karē raisu* (curry and rice, ¥850). There's a photo menu. An endless stream of lifelong *onsen* devotees wander down the narrow main street in their *yukata* (summer kimonos). If you're looking for a place to stay while in town, the popular **Izumiya** (泉屋; ☎ 29-0231; s/tw incl 2 meals ¥10,500/17,850; P ☒) has Edo-and Meiji-era buildings and a huge garden. The friendly managers can pick up guests at Nagato-Yumoto station.

About 2km west of the *onsen* village is the **Mara Kannon** temple. Kannon is the Buddhist deity of compassion, while *mara* is the most graphic word imaginable for the male procreative organ, somewhere off the vulgar scale beyond 'knob end'. Put the two together, and you've this astonishing little temple asking for compassion for knob ends that aren't working properly. It looks more like a garden shed than a place of worship, and it's festooned with phallic statuary. On 1 May it's the scene of a highly photographic fertility rite, the **Mara Kannon Matsuri**. Call the ryokan and check the date – sometimes it's on the 3rd.

Take the JR Mine line from Asa to the south, or Nagato to the north, to Nagato-Yumoto. Buses run from there up to Tawarayama Onsen (¥510, 25 minutes). There's also a direct bus from Shimonoseki (¥1610, 1½ hours).

HAGI 萩

☎ 0838 / pop 56,000

Hagi is a sleepy but attractive city closely linked with ceramics and the Meiji Restoration. It has an interesting combination of temples and shrines, a fascinating old samurai quarter, some picturesque castle ruins and fine coastal views. It's ironic that Hagi's claim to fame is its role in propelling Japan directly from the feudal to the modern era, while its attractions are principally its feudal past.

Orientation & Information

Western and central Hagi are effectively an island created by the two rivers Hashimoto-gawa and Matsumoto-gawa; eastern Hagi (with the major JR station Higashi-Hagi) lies on the eastern bank of the Matsumoto-gawa. Get off at JR Higashi-Hagi for the main sights of the city.

The main road through central Hagi starts from JR Hagi station in the south and runs north, past the bus centre (*basu senta* in Japanese) in the centre of town. West of this central area is the old samurai quarter of Jōkamachi, with its picturesque streets and old buildings. More such buildings can be found in Horiuchi to the northwest and Teramachi to the northeast of Jōkamachi.

Hagi's **tourist information office** (☎ 25-3145; 2997-3 Chintō; ⏰ 9am-noon & 1-5pm) is just beside the Higashi-Hagi station. There's another south of town near Hagi station.

Free internet access is available at the **Hagi City Library** (☎ 25-6355; 552-26 Emukai; ⏰ 9.30am-5.30pm Tue-Sun) on the 2nd floor; you'll have to fill out a form in Japanese first. There's also **Dagashi-ten** (☎ 080-3622-6961; 90-3 Higashi-tamachi; per 30min ¥100; ⏰ 11am-6pm), a sweet shop in the arcade with a single terminal down the back.

Sights

HAGI POTTERY & KILNS

Connoisseurs of Japanese pottery rank *hagi-yaki*, the pottery of Hagi, second only to Kyo-to's *raku-yaki*. As in other Japanese pottery centres, the craft came from Korea when Korean potters were abducted during Toyotomi Hideyoshi's unsuccessful invasion in the late 1500s. At a number of shops and kilns you can see the pottery being made and browse through the finished products. *Hagi-yaki* is noted for its fine glazes and delicate pastel colours.

The **Hagi-jō Kiln** (☎ 22-5226; Horiuchi; ⏰ 8am-5pm) in Horiuchi has particularly fine pieces. It's closed irregular hours for firing. The western end of Hagi has several interesting pottery kilns near the park, Shizuki-kōen. You can also try your hand at making *hagi-yaki* at the crafts centre **Jōzan** (☎ 25-1666; Horiuchi; lessons ¥1680-5250; ⏰ 8am-4pm). Call for a reservation.

Swede **Bertil Persson** (☎ 25-2693), who has lived in Hagi for over 30 years, has his own kiln and is happy to meet anyone seriously interested in ceramics.

During the first week of May the **Hagi-yaki Matsuri** takes place at the city gymnasium, with works from 51 local kilns on sale.

HAGI-JŌ RUINS & SHIZUKI-KŌEN
萩城跡指月公園

There's not much of the old Hagi-jō to see, apart from the typically imposing outer walls and the surrounding moat. The **castle** (☎ 25-1826; Horiuchi Shizuki-kōen-nai; admission with Mōri House ¥210; ⏰ 8am-6.30pm Mar-Oct, to 4.30pm Nov-Feb) was built in 1604. It was dismantled in 1874 during the Meiji Restoration – since Hagi played a leading part in the end of the feudal era and the downfall of the shōgunate, it was appropriate that the town also led the way in the removal of feudal symbols.

Now the grounds are a pleasant park, with the **Shizukiyama-jinja**, the **Hanano-e Tea House** (Hanano-e Satei; tea ¥500) and other buildings. From the castle ruins you can climb the hillside to the 143m peak of Shizuki-yama.

MŌRI HOUSE 旧毛利家萩屋敷長屋

South of the park is **Mōri House** (☎ 25-2304; Horiuchi Shizuki-kōen; admission with Hagi-jō ¥210; ⏰ 8am-6.30pm Apr-Aug, 8.30am-4.30pm Nov-Feb, to 6pm Mar), a terrace house where samurai soldiers were once barracked. There's an interesting **Christian cemetery** to the south of the samurai house.

JŌKAMACHI, HORIUCHI & TERAMACHI AREAS 城下町・堀内・寺町

Between the modern town centre and the moat that separates western Hagi from central

Hagi is the old samurai residential area, with many streets lined by whitewashed walls. This area is fascinating to wander around and has a number of interesting houses, particularly in the area known as Jōkamachi. Teramachi is noted particularly for its many fine old temples.

The Kikuya family were merchants rather than samurai, but their wealth and special connections allowed them to build a house well above their station. **Kikuya House** (☎ 25-8282; 1-1 Gofuku-machi; admission ¥500; ⏰ 9am-5pm) dates from 1604 and has a fine gate, attractive gardens, and numerous examples of construction details and materials that would normally have been forbidden to the merchant class. Across the street is **Kubota House** (☎ 25-3139; 1-3 Gofuku-machi; admission free; ⏰ 9am-5pm), another renovated residence. At the southern perimeter of the Jōkamachi district, before you reach the little canal, is the green tea–coloured **Ishii Chawan Museum** (☎ 22-1211; 33-3 Minamifuruhagi-machi; admission ¥500; ⏰ 9am-4.45pm Tue-Sun, closed Jan, Jun & Dec), which has an extensive collection of tea-ceremony bowls and utensils. From the museum, go east, cross the canal and turn south to reach the **Hagi Uragami Museum** (☎ 24-2400; 586-1 Hiyako; admission from ¥800; ⏰ 9am-5pm Tue-Sun). This superb private collection, housed in a building designed by Tange Kenzo, consists of oriental ceramics and about 5000 woodblock prints. There are fine works by Katsushika Hokusai and Utamaro Kitagawa. At the main entrance to the Horiuchi district is the **Hagi Museum** (☎ 25-6447; 355 Horiuchi; admission ¥500; ⏰ 9am-5pm), which has exhibitions about Hagi history, as well as astronomy and biology.

Kumaya Art Museum (☎ 22-7547; 47 Imauono Tamachi; admission ¥700; ⏰ 9am-5pm Tue-Sun), in Jōkamachi, has a limited collection including tea bowls, screens and other items, displayed in a series of small warehouses dating from 1768. The Kumaya family handled the trading and commercial operations of Hagi's ruling Mōri family.

The Horiuchi and Teramachi areas are dotted with temples and shrines. **Fukuhara-ke Yashiki-mon** is one of the finest of the samurai gates in Horiuchi. Nearby is the **Tomb of Tenjuin**, dedicated to Mōri Terumoto, the founder of the Mōri dynasty. There are numerous old temples in the Teramachi area, including the two-storey **Kaichō-ji** (☎ 22-0053; 50 Kitafuruhagi-machi Ikku; ⏰ 5am-6pm).

TŌKŌ-JI 東光寺

East of the river stands this pretty **temple** (☎ 26-1052; admission ¥300; 1647 Chintō; ⏰ 8.30am-

THE REVOLUTIONARY WHO WASN'T

Hagi in Honshū and Kagoshima in Kyūshū played major parts in the events leading up to the Meiji Restoration. Japan's long period of isolation from the outside world under the Tokugawa rule had, by about the mid-19th century, created tensions approaching breaking point. The arrival of US Commodore Perry brought matters to a humiliating head, as the 'barbarians' simply dictated their terms to the helpless Japanese and forced the country open.

Japan's modernisation couldn't happen under the calcified feudal shōgunate. Restoring the emperor to power, even if only as a figurehead, was the route the progressive samurai chose, and Yoshida Shōin of Hagi was one of their leaders. On the surface he was also a complete failure. In 1854, in order to study first-hand the ways of the West, he attempted to leave Japan on Perry's ship, only to be handed over to the authorities and imprisoned in Edo (Tokyo).

When he returned to Hagi he hatched a plot to kill a shōgunate official, but he talked about it so much that word leaked out to his enemies. He was arrested again and, in 1859 at the age of 29, he was executed.

Fortunately, where Yoshida failed in acting he succeeded in inspiring. In the years before his death he taught followers at a school he founded called Shoka Sonjuku. In 1865 they led a militia of peasants and samurai that overturned Hagi's Chōshū government. The Western powers supported the new blood in Hagi and Kagoshima and, when the shōgunate army moved against Hagi's young Turks, it was defeated. That the downfall of the shōgunate came at the hands of an army of not just samurai but also peasants was further proof of the changes taking place. In 1867 the emperor was restored to nominal power and Japan was on the road to becoming a modern nation-state thanks to the Sonjuku group; pupil Itō Hirobumi became the first prime minister. Today, the spirit of Yoshida Shōin lives on at Hagi's Shōin-jinja.

WESTERN HONSHŪ

HAGI

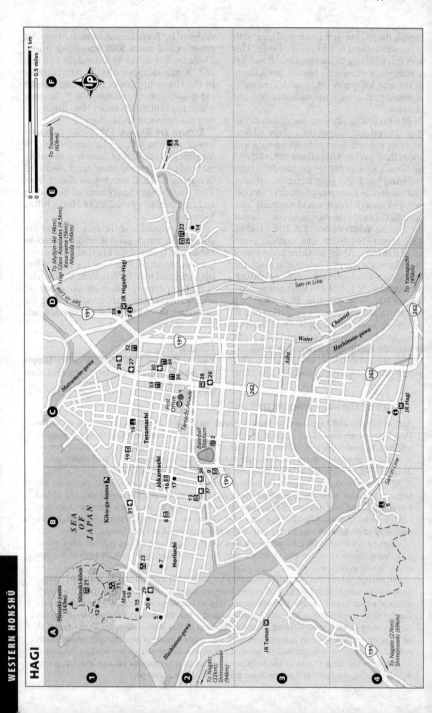

San-in Line

Water Channel

Baseball Stadium

Post Office

Tamachi Arcade

Teramachi

Jōkamachi

Horiuchi

Kiku-ga-hama

SEA OF JAPAN

Matsumoto-gawa

Hashimoto-gawa

Aiba

Shizuki-yama (143m)

Shizuki-kōen

Moat

JR Higashi-Hagi

JR Hagi

JR Tamae

To Nagato (22km); Shimonoseki (94km)

To Nagato (27km); Shimonoseki (69km)

To Yamaguchi (45km)

To Tsuwano (60km)

To Myōjin-ike (4km); Hagi Glass (4.5km); Ojizo-sama (4.5km); Kasa-yama (5km); Masuda (54km)

0   1 km
0   0.5 miles

5pm), home to the tombs of five Mōri lords. The odd-numbered lords (apart from No 1) were buried here; the even-numbered ones were buried at the **Daishō-in** temple. The stone walkways on the hillside behind the temple are flanked by almost 500 stone lanterns, erected by the lords' servants.

SHŌIN-JINJA 松陰神社
This Meiji-era shrine is dedicated to Meiji Restoration movement leader Yoshida Shōin. His life is illustrated in the nearby **Yoshida Shōin Rekishikan** (Yoshida Shōin Historical Museum; ☎ 26-9116; Chintō Matsumoto; admission ¥650; ☯ 9am-5pm). South of the shrine, **Itō Hirobumi House** (伊藤博文旧宅; admission to grounds free; ☯ 9am-5pm) is the early home of the four-term prime minister who was a follower of Yoshida Shōin, and who later drafted the Meiji Constitution. Yoshida Shōin's tomb is near Tōkō-ji.

DAISHŌ-IN 大照院
South of the centre, near JR Hagi station, this **funerary temple** (☎ 22-2124; 4132 Omi; admission ¥200; ☯ 8am-5pm Apr-Nov, to 4.30pm Dec-Mar) was the resting place for the first two Mōri generations and then, after that, all even-numbered generations of the Mōri lords.

MYŌJIN-IKE & KASA-YAMA 明神池・笠山
About 5km east of the town is the 112m dormant volcano **Kasa-yama**. It's hardly a whopper, but there are some great things to do here. The pond at the mountain's base, **Myōjin-ike**, is connected to the sea and shelters a variety of saltwater fish.

Further up the mountain is **Hagi Glass Associates** (萩ガラス工房; ☎ 26-2555; Myōjin-ike Koshigahama; admission free; ☯ 9am-6pm, demonstrations 4.30pm), where quartz basalt from the volcano is used to make extremely tough Hagi glassware. There is a showroom and a shop, and visitors can make their own piece of glassware (courses ¥1050 to ¥3150). Next door is Hagi's own beer factory **Yuzuya Honten** (柚子屋本店; ☎ 25-7511; Myojin-ike Koshigahama; ☯ 9am-5pm), where you can check out how the beer is made and taste the brew; it also bottles citrus juice.

The road continues to the top of Kasa-yama, from where there are fine views along the coast and an intriguingly tiny 30m-deep crater. Kasa-yama is close enough to make a good bicycle ride from Hagi.

Sleeping
Hagi Youth Hostel (☎ 22-0733; fax 22-3558; www.jyh .or.jp/yhguide/chugoku/hagi/index.html in Japanese; 109-22 Horiuchi; dm members/nonmembers ¥2940/3940; ☯ closed mid-Jan–mid-Feb; P ✗) Close to the castle at the western end of the town, the hostel is a 15-minute walk from JR Tamae station. Most of the kilns and hagi-yaki shops are in this quiet area. The hostel is cold and bare, but the manager is very attentive. Bicycles can be rented for ¥500 a day and meals are available.

Nakamura Ryokan (☎ 22-0303; fax 26-0303; naka mura-r.ftw.jp in Japanese; 56 Furuhagi-machi; s/tw ¥5250/8400; P ✗) The Nakamura (no connection to restaurant Nakamura next door) is a friendly place divided into modern and older buildings. It has large tatami rooms and there's a large pine by the tile-roof genkan (entrance).

WESTERN HONSHŪ

Business Hotel Hasegawa (☎ 22-0450; fax 22-4884; www.haqi.ne.jp/004 hasegawa in Japanese, 17 Karahi-machi; s/tw ¥5775/10,500; P 🛇 🖳) Between the station and the sights near Hagi castle, the cheerful Hasegawa has sunny Western- and Japanese-style rooms with bathrooms, but they're quite small. It's right by the bus centre.

Well Heart Pia Hagi (☎ 22-7580; fax 25-7931; www .kjp.or.jp/hp_109 in Japanese; 485-2 Horiuchi; s/tw Western ¥8500/12,000, Japanese ¥11,400/15,400; P 🛇 🛇) Five minutes' walk east of Hagi castle, this modern public lodging facility has huge rooms with great views facing Kiku-ga-hama beach. The Japanese- and Western-style rooms have their own bathroom, and meals are available. The baths are also open to nonguests (11am to 9pm Thur-Tues, 11am-3pm Wed, ¥400).

Hagi Grand Hotel Tenkū (☎ 25-1211; fax 25-4422; www.hagi-gh.com in Japanese; 25 Furuhagi-machi; s/tw ¥8550/13,950; P 🛇 🛇) Here there are large rooms and a huge *onsen* complex at the back. The foyer is a good place to sample local sweets.

Hagi no Yado Tomoe (☎ 22-0150; fax 25-0152; www .tomoehagi.jp in Japanese; 608-53 Kōbō-ji Hijiwara; per person incl 2 meals from ¥26,250; P 🛇) The finest inn in Hagi, the historic Tomoe has gorgeous, refurbished Japanese rooms with garden views, exquisite, artfully prepared cuisine and luxurious baths. There's also a small gallery off the lobby showcasing Hagi ceramics, open to nonguests.

Eating & Drinking

Kurumayado Tenjuppei (☎ 26-6474; 33-5 Minami-furuhagi-machi; dishes ¥350-600; 🕙 9am-6pm) This charming gallery and tea room is in a late-Edo period house with a large garden. Enjoy the *sukon setto* (tea with scone; ¥600) in the European-style drawing room.

Don Don Udonya (☎ 22-7537; 377 San-ku Hijiwara; dishes ¥390-700; 🕙 9am-9pm) Popular with locals, this place has excellent udon noodles and set meals, with plastic food models in the window. Try the *nikuten udon* (beef and tempura over noodles; ¥490). This chain outlet is in a large white building with a check pattern on the lower part.

Cafeteria Ijinkan (☎ 25-6334; 2-61 Gofuku-machi; dishes ¥350-880; 🕙 9.30am-10pm) The Ijinkan is an old-fashioned, brick-walled café with many varieties of coffee available, as well as pizzas, cakes and *sansai pirafu* (pilaf with edible wild plants; ¥850). Close to the museum, it's popular with elderly tourists.

Maru (☎ 26-5050; 78 Yoshida chō, dishes ¥430-1000; 🕙 dinner Tue-Sun) Maru is a fashionable *izakaya* with an inventive menu, mostly side dishes. Sushi, tofu and other Japanese food with a modern twist are on offer. If you really love meat, the *kenrangyū nigirizushi* (raw beef sushi; ¥1000) is something to write home about. Look for the tall white building across the street; Maru has a large wooden door.

San Marco (☎ 25-4677; 18 Higashi-machi; meals ¥730-1950; 🕙 11am-9pm) Hagi pizza and very simple Italian lunch and dinner set menus are on offer at this family restaurant. There's a photo menu and plastic meal displays. It's located above the sports shop on the corner.

Nakamura (☎ 22-6619; 394 Hijiwara; meals ¥1500-5000; 🕙 lunch & dinner) *Unidon* (sea urchin on rice; ¥3150) is the house speciality in the traditional surroundings here. Fronted by bushes, this old fashioned–looking restaurant is behind a carpark by a small canal.

Getting There & Away

The JR San-in line runs along the north coast through Tottori, Matsue, Masuda and Hagi to Shimonoseki. Local services between Shimonoseki and Higashi-Hagi (¥1890) take about three hours, including transfers. They travel around the end of Honshū, giving some great coastal views.

JR buses connect Hagi with Shin-Yamaguchi (¥1970, 1½ hours), which is south of Hagi on the Tokyo–Osaka–Hakata *shinkansen* line. There's a service to Tsuwano (¥2080, two hours) to the east in Shimane-ken, and also to Tokyo (¥14,250, 12 hours), Osaka (¥9480, 12 hours) and Hiroshima (¥3300, four hours). Buses run from Yamaguchi to Hagi (¥1760, one hour).

Hagi is served by Iwami airport, an hour to the northeast near Masuda in Shimane-ken. There are daily flights to/from Tokyo and Osaka. A bus (¥1560, 70 minutes) from in front of Higashi-Hagi station or the Hagi bus centre connects Hagi with all flights.

Getting Around

Hagi is a good place to explore by bicycle and there are plenty of hire places, including one at the youth hostel and several around the castle and JR Higashi-Hagi station. The best is **Smile** (☎ 22-2914; 3000 Shinkawa Minami; bike rental 1hr/day ¥100/800; 🕙 8am-sunset), to the right as you leave the station.

A handy bus system takes in Hagi's main attractions. There are east- and west-bound loops, with two services per hour at each stop. One trip costs ¥100, and one-/two-day passes cost ¥500/700. Pick up a schedule at the tourist information office.

From Hagi, the JR San-in line and Rte 191, the main road, pretty much hug each other and the coastline up to the prefectural border with Shimane-ken. If you're going to Tsuwano, there's a direct bus from Hagi, but if you've got a JR pass you'll want to go by train up the coast to Masuda, then change to the JR Yamaguchi line for Tsuwano.

SHIMANE-KEN 島根県

Along the northern San-in coastline on the Sea of Japan, Shimane-ken is off the beaten track but well worth the effort of visiting. Cities are few and far between, the pace of life is decidedly slower than on the San-yō coast and locals seem particularly friendly towards visitors. Highlights include Tsuwano, a quiet, unspoilt mountain town; the great shrine at Izumo; and Matsue, where the writer and Japanophile Lafcadio Hearn lived.

TSUWANO 津和野
☎ 0856 / pop 9,500

Tsuwano is a relaxing, 700-year-old mountain town with a bit of something for everyone – a fine shrine and castle ruins, buildings reminiscent of the Edo era and literary sites. It's in the far western reaches of Shimane-ken, about 42km east of Hagi, and has a wonderful collection of carp swimming in the roadside water channels – in fact, there are far more carp here than people!

Orientation & Information
Tsuwano is a long, narrow town wedged into a deep north–south valley. Tsuwano-kawa, the JR Yamaguchi line and main road all run down the middle of the valley. A bilingual booklet, *Yū ni shin sai Tsuwano*, is available at the **tourist information office** (☎ 72-1771; Ekimae; ☼ 9am-5pm), just south of the train station. The title means 'make yourself at home in Tsuwano' in the local dialect.

Sights & Activities
TSUWANO-JŌ 津和野城
The ruins of Tsuwano-jō seem to brood over the valley, with the broken stone walls draping along the ridge. The **castle** was originally

constructed in 1295 and remained in use until the Meiji Restoration. An old single-seater chairlift takes you up (and down) the hillside for ¥450, and there's a further 15-minute walk to the castle ruins.

TAIKODANI-INARI-JINJA 太鼓谷稲成神社
Just above the castle chairlift station, this splendid, thriving **shrine** (☎ 72-0219; Tsuwano; ☼ 8am-4.30pm) is one of the largest Inari shrines in Japan. You can walk up to it from the main road through a tunnel created by about 1000 red torii; their lantern light is beautiful at night. Festivals are held here on 15 May and 15 November. The **Sagi Mai Matsuri** (Heron Dance Festival), which includes a procession of dancers dressed as herons, is performed on 20 and 27 July at Yasaka-jinja, near the start of the torii steps.

TONOMACHI DISTRICT 殿町
Only the walls and some fine old gates from the former **samurai quarter** of Tonomachi remain. The water channels that run alongside the picturesque Tonomachi road are home to numerous large, colourful carp, though disease has diminished their numbers. It's said that these fish were bred to provide a potential source of food should the town ever be besieged. (The feared attack never came.)

The Tsuwano **Catholic Church** (☎ 72-0251; Tonomachi; ☼ 8am-5.30pm April-Nov, to 5pm Dec-Mar) is a reminder that Nagasaki Christians were once exiled here. Instead of pews, the church has tatami mats! Just north of the river is the **Yōrō-kan**, a school for young samurai in the late Edo period. The building houses the **Minzoku Museum** (☎ 72-1000; Tonomachi; admission ¥250; ☼ 8.30am-5pm March-November), an interesting little folk-art museum with all sorts of farming and cooking equipment.

Near the post office, the **Katsushika Hokusai Museum** (☎ 72-1850; Ushiroda; admission ¥500; ☼ 9.30am-5pm) features a small collection by the master Edo-period painter Hokusai and his disciples, and interestingly shows the woodblock process plate by plate.

CHAPEL OF ST MARIA マリア聖堂
The tiny **Chapel of St Maria** dates from 1951, when a German priest built it as a memorial to the exiled Catholics who died in the final period of Christian persecution before the anti-Christian laws were repealed in 1872. Today it's a well-kept, peaceful sanctuary.

TSUWANO

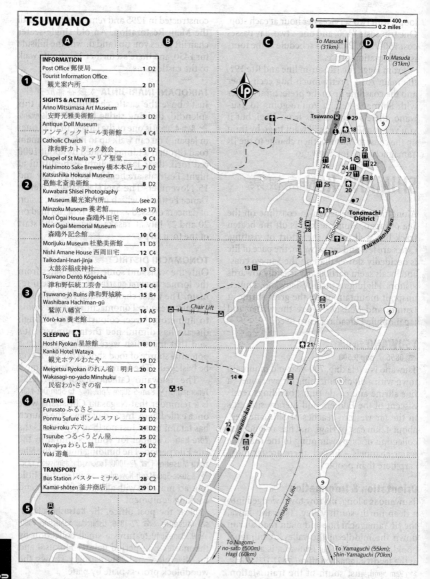

OTHER SIGHTS

The beautiful **former residences** of Nishi Amane, who played an important part in the Meiji Restoration government, and Mori Ōgai, a highly regarded novelist who served as a physician in the Imperial Japanese Army, are in the south of the town. At the rear of the latter is the **Mori Ōgai Memorial Museum** (☎ 72-3210; Machida; museum ¥500, residence grounds ¥100; ⏰ 9am-5pm Tue-Sun), a modern building housing many of the writer's personal effects. The residence grounds are even more interesting than the museum.

The **Antique Doll Museum** (☎ 72-3110; Mori; admission ¥800; ⏰ 9.30am-5.30pm Fri-Wed) houses an astounding collection of fine European antique dolls. Perhaps more interesting (and still with a bit of European flavour) is the **Morijuku Museum** (☎ 72-3200; Mori; admission ¥500; ☺ 9am-5pm), an old farmhouse with a room of etchings by Goya and paintings by local artists. Make sure you see the pinhole camera feature on the 2nd floor (the proprietor will gladly show you). Crafts shop **Tsuwano Dentō Kōgeisha** (☎ 72-1518; Shiroyama-shita; admission free; ☺ 9am-5pm Wed-Mon) has a neat paper-making demonstration and a good range of traditional paper products for sale.

Kuwabara Shisei Photography Museum (☎ 72-3171; Ekimae; admission ¥300; ☺ 9am-4.45pm) has a small but excellent collection dedicated to contemporary photojournalism. It's in the same building as the information office, next to the station. Across the street is the **Anno Mitsumasa Art Museum** (☎ 72-4155; Ekimae; admission ¥800; ☺ 9am-5pm), showing works by local artist Anno Mitsumasa. It has a good gift shop.

There are a number of sake breweries in town, some of which have tastings. Try **Hashimoto**, where Toba-san, one of the resident staff, can answer your questions in English while you sample the local brew.

South of the town is the shrine **Washibara Hachiman-gū**, about 4km from the station, where **archery contests** on horseback are held on 2 April.

If you feel like a long soak in a bath, head down to **Nagomi-no-sato** (なごみの里; ☎ 72-4122; Washibara; admission ¥500; ☺ 10am-10pm, closed 2nd & 4th Tue of month), the Tsuwano *onsen* complex south of town. It has a restaurant, local produce for sale, and mask painting and bamboo weaving on weekends.

Sleeping

Hoshi Ryokan (☎ 72-0136; fax 72-0241; Ekimae; s/tw incl 2 meals ¥6500/13,000; P ☒) This is an older, faded ryokan opposite the bicycle shop and steps away from the station. The Japanese rooms, though, are quite large and some have mountain views. Toilets are shared.

Wakasagi-no-yado Minshuku (☎ /fax 72-1146; Mori; s/tw incl 2 meals ¥7500/15,000; P ☒) This family-run operation is pleasant, friendly and frequently recommended; staff can even pick you up at the station in summer. If you're walking from the station, look for the white building on the left with a checked tile design.

Meigetsu Ryokan (☎ 72-0685; fax 72-0637; Uocho; s/tw incl 2 meals from ¥10,500/21,000; P ☒) A traditional ryokan with old-style, very warm service and a pretty little garden. The wooden interiors and baths are older but well kept. There's an old-fashioned gate with a tiled roof outside the white building.

Kankō Hotel Wataya (☎ 72-0333; fax 72-1543; www.tsuwano.jp in Japanese; Takaokadōri; s/tw incl 2 meals ¥12,600/25,200; P ☒) The Wataya is a modern, sophisticated *onsen* complex with Western- and Japanese-style rooms and some very stylish bathing facilities. You can have your own outdoor bath with mountain views if you want to splash out. Meals here are exquisitely prepared, with emphasis on tofu and *sansai* (edible wild plants).

Eating

Most visitors to Tsuwano usually dine in their *minshuku* or ryokan, so many restaurants are open only during the day.

Roku-roku (☎ 72-0443; Shin-chō; dishes ¥300-780; ☺ 6pm-12.30am Tue-Sun) A short walk southwest of the post office, this small but lively *izakaya* is the best bet in the evening, as it's inexpensive, friendly and a good place for meeting locals. The *kabuto-ebi shio-yaki* (grilled and salted minilobster; ¥500) is highly recommended. The lower half of the building is covered with logs.

Tsurube (☎ 72-2098; Takaokadōri; dishes ¥520-840; ☺ 11am-6.30pm) Here the house speciality is udon noodles handmade on the premises, like the *sansai udon* (udon wild edible plants; ¥785). It's the brown-and-white building by the graveyard.

Waraji-ya (☎ 72-3221; Takaokadōri; dishes ¥400-1600; ☺ 11am-5pm) Rustic and traditional, Waraji-ya serves noodles and is well known for *tendon* (tempura-and-rice dishes; ¥1100). It has an *irori* (open fireplace). There are plastic food models in the window. Closes irregularly for holidays.

Furusato (☎ 72-0403; Gion-chō; meals ¥1200-1300; ☺ lunch) Across from the post office, Furusato serves the local speciality, *uzume-meshi* (rice served in a soup with tofu, mushrooms and mountain vegetables; ¥1200). It's a mostly brown building with a white *noren* over the door.

Yūki (☎ 72-0162; 271-4 Ushiroda; meals ¥1300-3000; ☺ 10.30am-7pm) Yūki's *Tsuwano teishoku* (a sampler of local dishes; ¥2300) is recommended. There are carp swimming in a pool in the floor here, and you can also try the *koi teishoku* (carp course; ¥2300). Look for the old-fashioned building with a small pine tree outside.

Ponmu Sufure (☎ 72-2778; 284 Ushiroda; meals ¥1500-3000; ⏰ 10am-9pm Fri-Wed, to midnight Fri & Sat) There's good pizza and bread at the only Western restaurant in town. It's hard to go wrong with the ¥1500 lunch specials; choose from the *honjitsu* (daily) pasta, pizza or risotto. Look for the white building with a green awning.

Getting There & Away

The JR Yamaguchi line runs from Shin-Yamaguchi on the south coast through Yamaguchi to Tsuwano and on to Masuda on the north coast. There are connections from Tsuwano to Shin-Yamaguchi (¥1110, 1¾ hours) and Masuda (¥570, 40 minutes). Seven buses a day (¥2080, two hours) and two expresses buses (¥2080, 1¼ hours) run between Tsuwano and Hagi.

From mid-March to late November there's a popular steam-locomotive service from Shin-Yamaguchi to Tsuwano. It mainly runs on weekends, the Golden Week holiday (late April to early May) and from late July to late August. The SL *Yamaguchi-gō* service is operated with two restored 1930s locomotives pulling antique carriages that travel between Shin-Yamaguchi and Tsuwano. The trip costs ¥1620 and takes two hours. Ask for up-to-date details and book well ahead at JR and tourist information offices. Details in Japanese at www.c571.jp.

Getting Around

Tsuwano has several bicycle-rental places; rates are ¥500/800 per two hours/day. **Kamai-shōten** (⏰ 8am-7pm) is in front of the station.

ŌDA 大田

☎ 0854 / pop 41,000

Ōda itself is an unremarkable coastal city but its outskirts contain worthwhile attractions seldom visited by foreigners. The old silver mine here is slated to become a Unesco World Heritage site in 2007.

If you're coming from the west, try the old-style baths at **Yunotsu Onsen** (温泉津温泉), a charming little seaside hamlet on the San'in train line from which silver was once shipped. Don't be shy if the local oldsters are crowding the two *sentō* here, which have mineral deposits lining the tubs. **Motoyu Onsen** (元湯温泉; ☎ 0855-65-2052; admission ¥300; ⏰ 5.30am-9pm) is the older of the two and faces a statue of local

Buddhist poet Asahara Saichi, who insisted he be depicted with horns on his head to reflect his sins. A few doors down is **Yakushinoyu Onsen** (薬師湯温泉; ☎ 0855-65-4894; admission ¥300; ⏰ 5am-9pm), which has a pleasant lounge and bay windows on the 2nd floor.

Three stops up the train line is the curious, underground **Nima Sand Museum** (摩サンドミュージアム; ☎ 0854-88-3776; 975Amagōchi Nima-chō; admission ¥700, youth hostel members ¥560; ⏰ 9am-5pm, closed 1st Wed of each month), which houses the world's biggest hourglass – this monster is turned over at midnight on 31 December each year, and has exactly the right number of grains of sand to last through to the same time the next year. The 5m-long timer is suspended high in one of the museum's glass pyramids. There are also displays on the local 'singing sand'. The museum is about 10 minutes' walk from Nima station.

ourpick If you haven't had the chance to stay at a Buddhist temple, **Jōfuku-ji Youth Hostel** (ースホステル城福寺; ☎ 0854-88-2233; www.shimane-yh.jp/jofukuji/jofukuji_e.html; 1114 Nima-machi Nima-chō; members/nonmembers ¥2730/3780) is a lovely spot to try it out. The busy priest and his wife are very friendly, and there's a splendid view out over the coast. Sometimes they can pick visitors up at Nima station. This homey wooden temple is a bit isolated but meals are available.

Iwami Ginzan 石見銀山

About 6km inland from Nima station is the old **Iwami Ginzan Silver Mine**, which in the early 17th century produced an impressive 38 tonnes of silver annually, about one-third of global output. The Tokugawa shōgunate had direct control over the 500 or so mines in the area. Today visitors can explore the small **Ryūgenji Mabu Mine** (龍源寺間歩; ☎ 0854-89-0347; Ōmori-chō Ōda-shi; admission ¥400; ⏰ 9am-5pm 21 March-23 Nov, to 4pm 24 Nov-20 March) but, as Iwami will become a Unesco World Heritage site, the much larger Ōkubo mine shaft is to open to the public in 2007. Shuttle buses are expected to run there from Ōmori.

Ōmori is a charming little town near the mines with carefully restored wooden houses lining the main street. There's an interesting temple, **Rakan-ji** (羅漢時; ☎ 0854-89-0005; Ōmori-chō Ōda-shi; admission ¥500; ⏰ 8am-5pm), which boasts 500 stone arhat statues in two chambers beside graceful stone bridges. Their facial expressions are particularly striking.

A good place for a coffee break is **Gungendō** (群言堂; ☎ 0854-89-0077; 183 Ōmori-chō Ōda-shi; cake sets ¥1000; 10am-6pm Thu-Tue), a large, stylish clothing-shop-cum-café. It's just down the road and over a little bridge from Rakan-ji temple, past the Wilds Gallery. It's a large building on the corner; look for the orange post box outside.

Buses run from Nima station to the Ryūgenji Mabu Mine (23 minutes, ¥510) via the Ōmori Daikansho Ato (Former Intendant's Office) at the centre of town and the nearby **tourist information office** (0854-89-0333; 9am-5pm May-Sep, to 4pm Oct-Apr), also a stop for buses to and from Ōda bus centre (28 minutes, ¥560).

Sanbe-san 三瓶山

About 20km inland from Ōda is Sanbe-san, an old volcano with grassy slopes that reaches 1126m. It has four separate peaks known as the Father, the Mother, the Child and the Grandchild. It takes about an hour to climb from **Sanbe Onsen** and five hours to climb around the caldera. There's a dip in the *onsen* awaiting you on your return. Day-trippers can try **Kokuminshukusha Sanbesō** (民宿舎さんべ荘; 0854-83-2011; Shigaku Sanbe-chō Ōda-shi; admission ¥500; 10.30am-9pm; P), a large lodging facility that has outdoor circular tubs. The area is also a popular ski centre in winter. Buses run between Ōda and Sanbe Onsen (¥830, 40 minutes).

IZUMO 出雲

☎ 0853 / pop 148,000

Only 34km west of Matsue, Izumo has one major attraction – the great **Izumo Taisha shrine** (出雲大社; ☎ 53-3100; 195 Kizuki Higashi Taisha-chō; 6am-8pm), one of Japan's two top Shintō sites along with Ise-jingū. It's hard to see behind its fence but definitely worth a visit if you're in the area.

Orientation & Information

Izumo Taisha is 8km northwest of central Izumo, where accommodation is more plentiful. The shrine area, basically one main, sleepy street, runs straight up to the shrine. It has the Ichibata Line Taisha Ekimae train station and a few accommodation places and restaurants. The friendly **tourist information office** (☎ 53-2298; 1346-9 Kizuki Minami Shinmondōri Taisha-chō; 9am-5.30pm) in the heritage train station building has information in English. There's also a new **tourist information office** (☎ 53-2100; 3286-1 Kizuki Higashi Seidamari Taisha-chō; 10am-3pm) right by the

front gate to the shrine. Izumo Taisha can easily be visited as a day trip from Matsue.

Sights

IZUMO TAISHA 出雲大社

This is the oldest Shintō shrine in Japan and is second in importance only to the shrines of Ise. Although it's only a shadow of its former self – the buildings purportedly once towered to a colossal 48m with a 109m-long staircase, but today they're a modest 24m – this is still an enormously significant structure, both architecturally and spiritually. It's also known as Izumo Ōyashiro.

A shrine has existed on the site for the last 1500 years. The current main shrine was last rebuilt in 1744, its 25th incarnation, whereas the surrounding buildings date back to 1874. All are constructed in the Taisha-zukuri style, considered Japan's oldest form of shrine architecture. The wooded grounds are pleasant to wander through, and the shrine itself enjoys the borrowed scenery of Yakumo Hill as a backdrop.

The shrine is dedicated to Okuninushi, the *kami* (Shintō deity) of marriage, among other things. Hence visitors to the shrine summon the deity by clapping four times rather than the normal two – twice for themselves and twice for their partner or partners to be.

The **Haiden** (拝殿; Hall of Worship) is the first building inside the entrance torii; huge *shimenawa* (twisted straw ropes) hang over the entry. Those who can toss and lodge a coin in them are said to be blessed by good luck. The main building is the largest shrine in Japan, but the **Honden** (本殿; Main Hall) cannot be entered. The shrine compound is flanked by *jūku-sha*, long shelters where Japan's eight million Shintō deities stay when they turn up for their annual shindig.

On the southeastern side of the compound is the **Shinko-den** (神祜殿; Treasure House; admission ¥150; 8.30am-4.30pm), with a collection of shrine paraphernalia. Behind the main shrine building, in the northwestern corner, is the former **Shōkokan** (彰古館; Treasure Hall; admission ¥50; 8.30am-4.30pm), which boasts a large collection of images of Okuninushi in the form of Daikoku, a cheerful chubby character standing on two or three rice bales with a sack over his shoulder and a mallet in his hand. Usually you will see his equally happy son Ebisu standing beside him with a fish tucked under his arm.

Just to the right of the front gate of the shrine is the **Shimane Museum of Ancient Izumo** (島根県立古代出雲歴史博物館; ☎ 53-8600; 99-4 Kizuki Higashi Taisha-chō; admission ¥600; ◷ 9am-6pm, closed 3rd Tue of month; **P**), opened in March 2007 with a collection featuring numerous national treasures and important cultural properties ranging from arms and armour to masks and fans.

If you want to get an idea of the original size of Izumo Taisha, check out the **Kodai Izumo Ōyashiro Mokei Tenjikan** (古代出雲大社模型展示館; Ancient Izumo Shrine Model Hall; ☎ 53-3100; admission free; ◷ 8.30am-4.30pm), which has a one-tenth-scale model of the shrine as it was about 800 years ago. There are also photos of wooden pillars unearthed in 2000 with a diameter of 1.2m, evidence supporting the high-rise shrine theory.

HINOMISAKI 日御碕
It's less than 10km from Izumo Taisha to **Hinomisaki** cape, where you'll find a beautiful lighthouse, some fine views and another ancient shrine. On the way you'll pass the pleasant **Inasa-no-hama**, a good swimming beach just 2km from Taisha Ekimae station. Buses run regularly from the station to the cape via the beach (¥840, 35 minutes). **Hinomisaki-jinja** is near the cape's bus terminus. Coastal paths head north and south from the car park, offering fine views, particularly from the top of the **lighthouse** (日御碕灯台; admission ¥150; ◷ 9am-4.30pm).

Festivals & Events
The lunar calendar month corresponding to October is known throughout Japan as Kannazuki (Month without Gods). In Izumo, however, it is known as Kan-arizuki (Month with Gods), for this is the month when all the Shintō gods congregate for an annual get-together at Izumo Taisha.

In accordance with the ancient calendar, the **Kamiari-sai Matsuri** (*kamiari-sai* means 'the gods are here!') takes place from 11 to 17 October.

Sleeping & Eating
It's easy to take a day trip to Izumo from Matsue or simply pause there while travelling along the coast. If you do want to stop, you'll find a few places along the main street of Izumo Taisha, which runs down from the shrine to the train station.

Ebisuya Youth Hostel (☎ 53-2157; fax 53-5805; www .shimane-yh.jp/ebisuya/ebisuya_e.html; Shinmondōri Taisha-chō; dm members/nonmembers ¥3050/4100; **P** ✗) Just off the main street, near the station, this hostel is a large, older concrete structure with clean Western- and Japanese-style rooms. Look for the tall hedge around a white building.

Fujiwara Ryokan (☎ 53-2009; fax 53-2524; Seimonmae Taisha-chō; s/tw incl 2 meals ¥10,500/21,000; **P** ✗) Full-sized baths and a small internal garden lend charm to this family-run business. It's a little faded but the staff here are very friendly. The cuisine features seasonal dishes. Look for the large pine tree outside.

Yashiroya (☎ 53-2596; 72-5 Kizuki-higashi Taisha-chō; meals ¥700-800; ◷ 10am-7pm Wed-Mon) A local favourite, Yashiroya is down the hill and off to the right from the shrine entrance and has tasty *warigo* (buckwheat) *soba* (¥700), as well as *yamakake soba* (soba topped with grated yam; ¥800). It's the white building with a tiled roof.

Getting There & Away
The private Ichibata line starts from Matsue Shinjiko-onsen station in Matsue and runs on the northern side of Shinji-ko lake to Taisha Ekimae station (¥790, one hour, with a transfer at Kawato). The JR line runs from JR Matsue station to JR Izumo-shi station (¥570, 42 minutes), where you can transfer to an Ichibata-line train to Izumo Taisha. The first option is more frequent, with more than 20 services a day. If you're coming from the west, change at JR Izumo-shi station.

The one-day L&R Free Kippu ticket (¥1000) allows unlimited travel on Ichibata trains going from Izumo Taisha towards Matsue, and on Shinji-ko Lakeline buses, which stop at the Ichibata bus terminal. The one-day Ichin-ichi Free Jōshaken (¥1500) allows unlimited travel on Ichibata trains.

Izumo has an airport with flights to/from most of Japan's major cities.

MATSUE 松江
☎ 0852 / pop 194,000
Home to spectacular sunsets over neighbouring Lake Shinji, Matsue is a pleasant, laid-back city with great food and some fine historical attractions. It straddles the Ōhashi-gawa, the river that connects Shinji-ko with Nakanoumi, a saline lake. There's a compact area in the north with almost all of Matsue's interesting sites: an original castle,

a fine samurai residence, the former home of writer Lafcadio Hearn and garden. It's worth spending a night or two here to enjoy the leisurely pace.

Information

The **tourist information office** (☎ 21-4034; 665 Asahi-machi; ☯ 9am-6pm) in front of JR Matsue station can arrange a free English-language tour – the Matsue Goodwill Guide – if you call a few days in advance. There are guides at the castle on weekends.

You'll also find information, a small library and free internet access at the **Shimane International Centre** (☎ 31-5056; 2nd fl, Kunibiki Messe Bldg, 1-2-1 Gakuen Minami; ☯ 9am-7pm Mon-Fri, to 5pm Sat), about a 12-minute walk from the station.

Sights

MATSUE-JŌ 松江城

Matsue's **castle** (☎ 21-4030; 1-5 Tono-machi; admission ¥550, foreigners with ID ¥280; ☯ 8.30am-6.30pm Apr-Sep, to 5pm Oct-Mar) is hardly imposing but it is picturesque and original, dating from 1611, with a rich wooden interior showcasing treasures from the Matsudaira clan. Known as Plover Castle for the graceful shape of its gable ornaments, Matsue-jō is the only surviving fortress in the San'in region. You can save 20% with a Universal Pass (¥920), which includes entry to the castle, Buke Yashiki Samurai Residence and the Koizumi Yakumo (Lafcadio Hearn) Memorial Museum.

Fun **Horikawa Pleasure Boat tours** (☎ 27-0417; admission ¥1200, foreigners with ID ¥800; ☯ 9am-5pm Mar-Jun & Sep-20 Oct, to 6pm Jul-Aug, to 4pm 21 Oct-Nov, 10am-3pm Dec-Feb) circumnavigate the castle moat and then zip you around some of the city's canals.

KOIZUMI YAKUMO (LAFCADIO HEARN) RESIDENCE 小泉八雲旧宅

Hearn was a Greco-Irish writer born on the Greek island of Lefkada in 1850 and educated in France and the UK. He lived in the USA from 1869, went to Japan in 1890 and remained there for the rest of his life. His adopted Japanese name was Koizumi Yakumo, and his first book on Japan, *Glimpses of Unfamiliar Japan*, is a classic, providing an insight into the country at that time. The Japanese have a great interest in the outsider's view of their country, so Hearn's pretty little house is an important attraction, despite the fact that he only lived in Matsue for just over

a year. Hearn's former **residence** (☎ admission ¥300; ☯ 9am-4.30pm) is at the northern end of Shiomi Nawate.

KOIZUMI YAKUMO (LAFCADIO HEARN) MEMORIAL MUSEUM 小泉八雲記念館

Next door to Hearn's home is this **memorial museum** (☎ 21-2147; 322 Okudani-chō; admission ¥300, foreigners with ID ¥150; ☯ 8.30am-6.30pm Apr-Sep, to 5pm Oct-Mar) with displays about Hearn's life, writing and Matsue residence. There's a stack of Japanese newspapers on which Hearn wrote simple words and phrases to teach English to his son. A brochure and map in English are available, showing points of interest around Matsue that are mentioned in Hearn's writings.

TANABE ART MUSEUM 田部美術館

Family items from generations of the region's Tanabe clan are displayed at the **Tanabe Art Museum** (☎ 26-2211; 310-5 Kitahori-chō; admission ¥600; ☯ 9am-4.30pm Tue-Sun), including tea bowls and other tea-ceremony utensils.

BUKE YASHIKI SAMURAI RESIDENCE 武家屋敷

The well-preserved **Buke Yashiki** (☎ 22-2243; 305 Kitahori-chō; admission ¥300, foreigners with ID ¥150; ☯ 8.30am-6.30pm Apr-Sep, to 5pm Oct-Mar) is a middle Edo–period samurai residence from 1730. A useful leaflet in English describes the various rooms and their uses. The large, spartan residence was clearly not the home of a wealthy samurai.

SHIMANE PREFECTURAL ART MUSEUM 島根県立博物館

This impressive, futuristic-looking **museum** (☎ 55-4700; 1-5 Sodeshi-chō; admission ¥300; ☯ 10am-6.30pm Wed-Mon; Ⓟ) displays work by Monet, Rodin and current Japanese artists. It's in a fabulous location overlooking the lake, and on a sunny day it's fun to wander round the outdoor sculptures. You can also watch the sunset from the 2nd-floor viewing platform or outside by the water. The museum is a 15-minute walk west of the station.

OTHER SIGHTS

The **Matsue onsen** area is just north of the lake near Matsue-onsen station on the Ichihata line. Here there are several hotels and ryokan, as well as O-yu-kake Jizō, a *jigoku* (hell) – very hot springs that are definitely not for bathing.

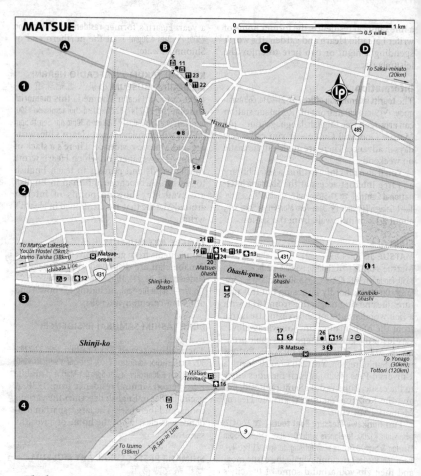

MATSUE

To Sakai-minato
(20km)

To Matsue Lakeside
Youth Hostel (5km);
Izumo Taisha (38km)

Matsue-
onsen

Ichibata Line

Shinji-ko-
ōhashi

Matsue-
ōhashi

Ōhashi-gawa

Shin-
ōhashi

Kunibiki-
ōhashi

Shinji-ko

JR Matsue

To Yonago
(30km);
Tottori (120km)

Matsue
Tenmarig

To Izumo
(38km)

JR San-in Line

The fine sunset views over the lake **Shinji-ko** are best appreciated from the museum area and the Matsue-Ōhashi bridge.

Sleeping
BUDGET

Matsue Lakeside Youth Hostel (松江レークサイドユースホステル; ☎ 36-8620; www.shimane-yh.jp/matsue/matsue_e.html; 1546 Kososhi-chō; dm members/nonmembers ¥2940/3990; ℗ ✖ ▯) This friendly, older hostel is 30 minutes by bus from the city but has a fantastic view of Lake Shinji and sensational sunsets. It's a good spot if you want to get away from it all. Meals are available in the dining room, along with a piano.

Terazuya (☎ 21-3480; fax 21-3422; www.mable .ne.jp/~terazuya/english/index.html; 60-3 Tenjin-machi;

s ¥4000, incl 2 meals ¥7000; ℗ ✖ ▯) This clean, very friendly, family-run ryokan next to the Matsue Tenmangū shrine is by far the best budget option. Some English is spoken here, and there's free internet access. If you ask nicely, the father might sing Noh songs for you and the mother might perform the tea ceremony. Email reservations are preferred. They can pick up guests at the south exit of the station.

Matsue City Hotel (☎ 25-4100; fax 25-4102; www2 .crosstalk.or.jp/sobido/dalian/ctyhote.html in Japanese; 31 Suetsugu Honmachi; s/tw ¥4400/10,000; ℗ ✖ ▯) Right by Matsue-Ōhashi bridge, this is a charming little hotel in an old-fashioned building, with small displays of antique European and Japanese clocks on every floor.

The rooms are small but have good views through the tiny windows. Complimentary *bentō* breakfasts are available. Look for the clocktower; the front desk is at the end of a garage-like tunnel.

Tōyoko Inn Matsue Ekimae (☎ 60-1045; fax 60-1046; www.toyoko-inn.com in Japanese; 498-10 Asahi-machi; s/tw ¥4800/7400; P ✗ ☒ ⬜ wi-fi) The rooms in this national chain are small and what you'd expect for a cheaper business hotel. However, the beds are fairly wide, the hotel itself is new and it's very close to the station. There's a free Japanese breakfast, too.

Hotel Route Inn Matsue (☎ 20-6211; fax 20-6215; www.route-inn.co.jp in Japanese; 2-22 Higashi Honmachi; s/tw ¥4900/10,500; P ✗ ☒ ⬜) Across the river from JR Matsue station and located in Matsue's nightlife district, this hotel has views of the downtown area, very friendly staff and a ¥500 buffet breakfast. It's a little more spacious than the Tōyoko Inn but older.

MIDRANGE

Matsue Tōkyū Inn (☎ 27-0109; fax 25-1327; www.tokyu .co.jp/inn/in Japanese; 590 Asahi-machi; s/tw ¥8610/16,380; P ✗ ☒ ⬜) This is an upscale business hotel with large, quiet rooms, helpful staff and a lobby restaurant with a decent ¥1000 buffet breakfast. It's right across from the station, so for convenience it can't be beaten.

Hotel Ichibata (☎ 22-0188; fax 22-0230; www.ichibata .co.jp/hotel in Japanese; 30 Chidōri-chō; s/tw ¥10,000/17,800; P ✗ ☒ ⬜) On the lake, the luxurious Ichibata has great views and grovelling, impeccable service. Japanese-style rooms face the lake; the cheaper Western-style ones face the city and are a bit faded, but spacious. There's an *onsen* with outdoor baths and fine views at the top of the annex.

Eating

Yakumo-an Bekkan (☎ 22-2400; dishes ¥350-600; ◷ 10am-4pm Thu-Tue) A pleasant teahouse affiliated to Yakumo-an, with a large garden by the Buke Yashiki. *Matcha jelly* (green-tea jelly; ¥600) is the trademark sweet here.

Pasta Factory (☎ 28-0101; 82 Suetsugu Honmachi; dishes ¥580-1400; ◷ 11.30am-10pm; E) Create your own pasta, sandwich or salad at this bright, funky spot, perfect for those tiring of Japanese set courses. Choose the DIY 'signature' dishes or from the menu; large pasta servings are only an extra ¥150.

Yakumo-an (☎ 25-0587; Bukeyashiki-nai 308 Kita Horiuchi; dishes ¥750-1300; ◷ 9am-4pm) This is a good spot to pause for lunch if you're wandering along Shiomi Nawate. The local speciality is *warigo*-style noodles (¥690), but the most popular dish is *kamo nanban* (noodles with slices of duck in broth). Look for the large old gate topped by a lantern; there are plastic food displays inside.

Kawa-kyō (☎ 22-1312; 65 Suetsugu Honmachi; meals ¥1500-4000; ◷ 6-10.30pm Mon-Sat; E) A very friendly, small, family-run eatery near the Hotel Route Inn with a warm, welcoming atmosphere. It offers the seven local 'exotic dishes from the lake' (see p492). It has a rare 1980s guidebook entitled *Along the San'in* that's worth a look.

Minamikan (☎ 27-0373; 14 Suetsugu Honmachi; meals ¥1500-10,000; ◷ lunch & dinner) Enjoy haute cuisine in an exquisite ryokan by the river while overlooking a traditional garden. The menu features elaborate seasonal dishes, sometimes served as a *bentō* presentation. The lunchtime *tai meshi gozen* (sea bream course; ¥3150) is a beautifully arranged treat. Look for a driveway leading to the entrance.

EXOTIC DISHES FROM THE LAKE

Matsue's *kyodo ryōri* (regional cuisine) includes 'seven exotic dishes from Shinji-ko'.

■ *suzuki* or *hōsho yaki* – steam-baked and paper-wrapped bass

■ *shirauo* – whitebait tempura or sashimi

■ *amasagi* – sweet tempura or teriyaki

■ *shijimi* – tiny shellfish in miso soup

■ *moroge ebi* – steamed shrimp

■ *koi* – baked carp

■ *unagi* – grilled freshwater eel

The seven exotic dishes are seasonal, but you can sample up to six of the wonders at any time of year. For a little indulgence, make a lunchtime reservation at Minamikan (p491), an old ryokan. Have a tatami room to yourself overlooking a garden and Shinji-ko. If you order the *omakase* (chef's suggestion), the dishes just keep on coming. The *suzuki-yaki* is particularly good here. For a more laid-back experience, get yourself a counter seat at Kawa-kyō (p491) in the evening. At this very popular local drinking spot the company is as agreeable as the food, and someone will be on hand to translate, suggest sake and make the whole experience a night to remember. Try the trademark dish, tenderised eel with garlic and *tomburi* (plant caviar).

Naniwa Hotori (☎ 21-2835; 21 Suetsugu Honmachi; meals ¥1890-10,000; lunch & dinner) Right on the river and next to Matsue-Ōhashi bridge, this is a very bright and airy modern Japanese restaurant. You can try the lunchtime *unameshi* (eel and rice; ¥1890) and, with a reservation, 'exotic dishes from the lake' (*kyōdofu*; from ¥4200) at the attached Naniwa Honten traditional eatery.

Drinking

Filaments (☎ 24-8984; 5 Hakkenya-chō; drinks ¥500-700; 7.30pm-late) This is a hip bar in a quiet area near the river. Owner Sam has thousands of CDs and likes to chat into the early hours.

Cafe Bar E.A.D. (☎ 28-3130; 36 Suetsugu Honmachi; meals ¥315-1050, drinks ¥525-840; 5pm-midnight Thu-Mon) This stylish little delight has comfy couches, a terrace and some of the best river views in the city. The menu is mostly snacks, but *jikasei* (homemade) pizza (¥735) is on offer, along with cigars. Take the stairs beside EAD used-clothing shop by the bridge and climb to the 3rd floor.

Getting There & Away

Matsue is on the JR San-in line, which runs along the San-in coast. You can head down to Okayama (on the south coast) via Yonago on the JR Hakubi line. It's ¥480 to Yonago (35 minutes), then ¥5360 to Okayama (2½ hours).

Matsue is serviced by both Izumo and Yonago airports, and between them they have flights to all the major cities. Highway buses also operate to/from all of Japan's major cities.

Getting Around

Matsue has an efficient Lake Line bus, which runs a set route around the city's attractions every 20 minutes from 8.40am to 5.40pm. One ride costs ¥200, but a day pass is only ¥500 and includes discounts on many attractions. The Walker loop bus follows smaller loops around the downtown area, taking in the sights, and leaving Matsue station about every 30 minutes. One trip is ¥150 and day passes are ¥400. Lake Line buses are red and look like streetcars. Walker buses are smaller, like minibuses.

If you're planning to visit Izumo Taisha, make sure you invest in the one-day L&R Free Kippu ticket (¥1500), which allows unlimited travel on Ichibata trains and Shinji-ko lakeside buses.

Matsue is a good place to explore by bicycle; these can be rented opposite Matsue station at **Nippon Rent-a-car** (☎ 21-7518; 589-1 Asahimachi; 8am-8pm). Rates are ¥525 for two hours or ¥1155 per day.

AROUND MATSUE & IZUMO

Shinji-ko 宍道湖

Sunset over the Yomega-shima islet in Shinji-ko is a photographer's favourite. The lake also provides the region's seven local delicacies. At the western end of the lake, the garden at Gakuen-ji temple in Hirata is noted for its autumn colours.

At the southwestern corner of the lake, the town of Shinji had one of the finest ryokan in Japan, **Yakumo Honjin** (八雲本陣; ☎ 0852-66-0136; 1335 Shinji-chō, Shinji Yatsuka-gun, Matsue-shi; ☼ 9am-4.30pm Fri-Wed), until its closure in 2006. Parts of the inn are 250 years old, and visitors can still have a look around for ¥300. It's a short walk from Shinji station on the JR San'in Line.

Shimane-hantō 島根半島

North of Matsue, the coastline of the Shimane-hantō peninsula has some spectacular scenery, particularly around Kaga. From April to October you can enter the **Kaga-no-Kukedo cave** boat with 50-minute tours leaving from **Marine Plaza Shimane** (☎ 0852-85-9111; tour ¥1000, min 3 people).

Adachi Art Museum 足立美術館

East of Matsue in Yasugi is this excellent **museum** (☎ 0854-28-7111; 320 Furukawa-chō, Yasugi-shi; admission ¥2200, foreigners with ID ¥1200; ☼ 9am-5.30pm Apr-Sep, to 5pm Oct-Mar; Ⓟ). Founded by businessman and aesthete Adachi Zenko, this renowned collection is set in large, meticulous gardens ranked as the best in Japan, and features wonderful modern works by the likes of painter Yokoyama Taikan, *mingei* (folk craft) potter Kawai Kanjiro and ceramicist and epicure Kitaoji Rosanjin. A beautifully illustrated English pamphlet is available. Take the JR line to Yasugi, where there's a free connecting shuttle bus to the museum (about once an hour).

OKI-SHOTŌ 隠岐諸島

☎ 08512 / pop 24,000

Directly north of Matsue are the islands of the Oki-shotō, with spectacular scenery and steep cliffs. They are strictly for those who want to get away from it all and were once used to exile political prisoners and *daimyō* (as well as two emperors) who came out on the losing side of political squabbles. The group consists of several islands, including the three Dōzen islands and the larger Dōgo. The 7km-long cliffs of the Oki Kuniga coast of **Nishi-no-shima**, at times falling 250 sheer metres into the sea, are particularly noteworthy. **Kokobun-ji** on Dōgo dates from the 8th century. **Bullfights** are an attraction on Dōgo during the summer months – not man versus bull, but bull versus bull.

If you're keen to go, allow at least a couple of days and pop into the information office at Matsue station to sort out a few things before you head off. Pick up the simple English-language brochure and map of the islands called *Oki National Park*. There's also the Japanese-only website www.e-oki.net.

The islands have some *minshuku* and other forms of accommodation, as well as places to camp.

Ferry services to the Oki islands from Shichirui and Sakai-minato, which are northeast of Matsue, are operated by **Oki Kisen** (☎ 08512-2-1122). For Dōgo-shima, from Matsue bus terminal take the 7.55am bus to Shichirui (¥1000, 40 minutes), then the 9am ferry (¥2840, 2½ hours). Flights operate to Dōgo from Izumo and Osaka.

TOTTORI-KEN 鳥取県

Although Tottori is the least populous of Japan's 47 prefectures, it has a wealth of spectacular coastal scenery, sand dunes, *onsen* and volcanoes. It's best to visit in summer.

YONAGO 米子

☎ 0859 / pop 150,000

Yonago is a sizable city and an important railway junction – here the JR San-in line, which runs along the Sea of Japan coast, is met by the JR Hakubi line coming up from Okayama on the San-yō side of the mountains.

There's a **tourist information office** (☎ 22-6317; 2 Yayoi-chō; ☼ 9am-6pm) in JR Yonago station. Attractions include a visit to the **Yonago Waterbirds Sanctuary** (子水鳥公園; ☎ 24-6139; 665 Hikona Shinden; admission ¥300; ☼ 9am-5.30pm Wed-Mon; Ⓟ), which boasts over 50 kinds of birds, including migratory whistling swans from northern Russia. To get there, board a Sakaiminato-bound bus on the Uchihama Line at the station and get off 20 minutes later at Norikoshi.

Kaike Onsen is on the coast, north of the station, and is the largest *onsen* area in the San-in region. It's given over to large group-oriented ryokan and hotels, and the beach is marred by concrete tetrapods. Near the bus station is the reasonably priced *sentō*, hotel and restaurant complex **OU Land** (おーゆランド; ☎ 31-2666; 1-18-1 Kaike Onsen; bathing ¥350; ☼ 10am-11pm; Ⓟ); local accommodation places also allow bathers, generally for ¥500 or ¥1000.

WESTERN HONSHŪ

Yonago **airport** (☎ 45-6121; 1634 Sainokami-chō Sakaiminato-shi) has daily flights to/from Tokyo, Nagoya and Seoul.

If travelling by bus in Tottori-ken, a three-day, ¥1500 pass (in the form of an old-time *tegata* wooden plaque) is available at tourist information offices and allows discounts at some attractions.

DAISEN 大山
☎ 0859

Although it's not one of Japan's highest mountains, at 1729m Daisen looks very impressive because it rises straight from sea level – its summit is only about 10km from the coast.

The popular climb up the volcano is a five- to six-hour return trip from the ancient **Daisen-ji** (大山寺) temple. Up a stone path is **Ogamiyama-jinja** (大神山神社) shrine, the oldest building in western Tottori-ken. From the summit, there are fine views over the coast and, in perfect conditions, all the way to the Oki-shotō. Pick up a copy of Lonely Planet's *Hiking in Japan* for detailed information on hiking Daisen.

Buses run to the temple from Yonago (¥800, 50 minutes), where you will also find the **Daisen-ji Tourist Information Centre** (☎ 52-2502; ◷ 8.30am-5pm Mon-Fri, to 6.30pm Sat & Sun). It has brochures, maps and hiking information in English, as well as updated warnings and conditions on the mountain, and can arrange bookings at the many local ryokan.

The mountain catches the northwest monsoon winds in the winter, bringing deep snow and tonnes of enjoyment for skiers at what is western Japan's top ski area. **Daisen Kokusai Ski Resort** (大山国際スキー場; ☎ 52-2321; www.daisen.net) is one of four linked ski hills on the lower slopes.

ALONG THE COAST TO TOTTORI

Just north of Kurayoshi is **Lake Tōgo**, which has **Hawai Onsen** on its western side and **Tōgo Onsen** on its eastern side. There's lots of accommodation around, including **Kōhō-ji Youth Hostel** (香宝寺ユースホステル; ☎ 0858-35-2054; fax 0858-35-2052; www.jyh.or.jp/english/chugoku/kohoji/index.html; Yurihama-chō Shimoasozu; dm ¥2900, onsen ¥100; ℗), which is attached to a Buddhist temple and serves meals. Nearby is a friendly local *sentō* with a glass ceiling called **Hawai Yūtown** (ハワイゆ～たうん; ☎ 0858-35-4919; admission ¥350; ◷ 9am-9pm Wed-Mon). The likeness

of the town's name to the popular Pacific islands is not lost on the people of Hawaii, but although there's a nice beach, it's not Waimea Bay. It does have a sister city in Hawaii, though.

Travelling eastwards there's a succession of impressive **swimming beaches** split by rocky headlands all the way to Tottori city, notably Ishiwaki, Ide-ga-hama, Aoya and the extremely popular Hakuto. These are packed with surfers on weekends in summer. If you're on the train you'll miss a lot of the coast, as the line runs a fair way inland, so it's worth considering using a car to explore this area. You can also take a dip at **Hamamura Onsen Kan** (浜村温泉館; ☎ 0857-82-4567; admission ¥420; ◷ 10am-10pm, closed 1st Wed of month). It's a seven-minute walk from Hamamura station, and has delightful indoor and panoramic outdoor baths – but you'll have to climb more than 70 steps to reach them!

TOTTORI 鳥取
☎ 0857 / pop 201,000

Tottori is a large, busy city a few kilometres inland but it's a good jumping-off point to explore the area's seaside wonders like Tottori's sand dunes, the main draw here. The principal coast road passes through the city's northern fringe in a blizzard of car dealers, *pachinko* parlours and fast-food outlets. There is a helpful **tourist information booth** (☎ 22-3318; 117 Higashi Honji-chō; ◷ 9.30am-6.30pm) inside the station, with English-language pamphlets and maps. For internet access, try **Comic Buster Dorothy** (☎ 27-7775; 2-27 Tomiyasu; per 30min/3hr ¥280/980; ◷ 24hr) southeast of the station.

Sights

Most of Tottori's attractions are concentrated in a compact little group about 1.5km northeast of the station at the foot of Mt Kyūshō.

Tottori-jō once overlooked the town from the hillside but now only the castle's foundations remain. Below is the elegant, European-style **Jinpū-kaku Villa** (☎ 26-3595; 2-121 Higashi-machi; admission ¥150; ◷ 9am-5pm Tue-Sun), dating from 1907 and now used as a museum. Across from this building is the modern **Tottori Prefectural Museum** (☎ 26-8042; 2-124 Higashi-machi; admission ¥180; ◷ 9am-5pm Tue-Sun).

Tottori also has an interesting little **Folkcraft Museum** (☎ 26-2367; 651 Sakae-machi; admission ¥500; ◷ 10am-5pm Thu-Tue) near the JR station, with

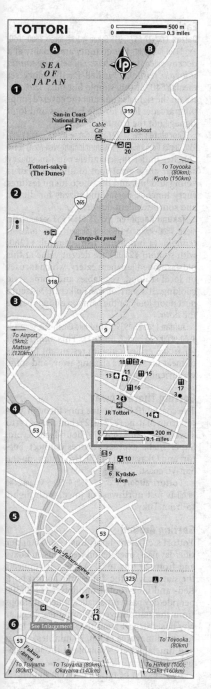

gorgeous items from Japan, Korea, China and Europe. East of the station is the 17th-century temple and garden **Kannon-in** (☎ 24-5641; 162 Ue-machi; admission incl matcha tea ¥600; 🕑 9am-5pm; 🅿).

Ekimae Ichiba (☎ 24-0645; 272 Eiraku Onsen-chō; 🕑 4am-7pm Thu-Tue) is a fun little fish market near the station with a resident cat who loves to be stroked.

The station area also has a number of *onsen* in hotels and ryokan available for public bathing. If you can brave the 47°C waters, try soaking with the local oldsters at the *sentō* **Hinomaru Onsen** (☎ 22-2648; 401 Suehiro Onsen-chō; admission ¥350; 🕑 6am-midnight, closed 2nd Mon of month).

TOTTORI-SAKYŪ (THE DUNES)
鳥取砂丘

Used as the location for Teshigahara Hiroshi's classic 1964 film *Woman in the Dunes* about an entomologist who gets trapped in the sand, the Tottori sand dunes are on the coast about 5km from the city. There's a viewing point on a hillside overlooking the dunes, along with a huge car park and the usual assortment of tourist amenities. The dunes stretch for over

10km along the coast and, at some points, can be about 2km wide. The section where the dunes are highest is popular with paragliders, who fly off on the incoming sea breezes. You can even get a Lawrence of Arabia photo of yourself wearing Arabian headgear and accompanied by a camel. It's quite easy to get away from it all out on the sand, which has footprints going to and fro.

You can stay at the **Tottori Cycling Terminal** (☎ 29-0800; 1157-115 Hamasaka; r per person incl 2 meals ¥4920), but it's a bit isolated; there's a camping area next door. The Cycling Terminal also rents bicycles; rates are ¥310 for four hours.

Use the Loop Bus (right) to get out to Tottori-sakyū. The bus stop for the dunes is Sakyū-Sentā (Dunes Centre); get off at the Kodomo-no-kuni iriguchi (Children's World entrance) for the Cycling Terminal.

Sleeping

Matsuya-sō (☎ 22-4891; 3-814 Yoshikata Onsen; s/tw ¥3500/6000; P ✗) About a 10-minute walk from the station and behind a high-rise apartment building, this *minshuku*-style lodging is very friendly and comfortable. It has simple Japanese rooms and shared toilets. It's also very close to several of the city's scalding public baths.

Tottori Green Hotel Morris (☎ 22-2331; fax 26-5574; www.hotel-morris.co.jp/tottori in Japanese; 2-107 Ima-machi; s/tw ¥5250/9240; P ✗ ✗ ▢) You can choose from nine different kinds of healing pillows to sleep on at this business hotel. A buffet breakfast and large bath (men only) are available. The sign in English outside says 'Hotel Morris'.

Hotel Taihei (☎ 29-1111; fax 29-1125; www.hotel taihei.jp in Japanese; 752 Sakae-machi; s/tw ¥5565/9450; P ✗ ✗ ▢) This is a dark, older business hotel that still has rotary-dial phones in the rooms, some of which have retro couches. The red-brick façade makes it easy to find. Restaurant Taiheiraku in the basement serves reasonably priced Matsuba crab dishes in winter.

Tottori Washington Hotel Plaza (☎ 27-8111; fax 27-8125; wh-at.com in Japanese; 102 Higashi Honji-chō; s/tw ¥7900/16,000; P ✗ ✗ ▢) Standard business hotel-type rooms are on offer from this national chain, conveniently located by the station. In an effort to reduce waste, it no longer provides disposable razors or toothbrushes.

Eating

Daizen (☎ 27-6574; 715 Sakae-machi; meals ¥500-1050; ☺ 11am-midnight) For quantity and quality at a decent price, try the *teishoku* sets like *sanma shioyaki teishoku* (grilled Pacific saury set meal; ¥840) at this simple but busy *izakaya*. It's on the right as you enter the covered shopping arcade; look for the lanterns and loud signage out the front.

Chocolate (☎ 37-2227; 611 Sakae-machi; meals ¥600-950, drinks from ¥550; ☺ 10am-midnight Wed-Mon) The couches under the chandelier in this snazzy café-bar are a great spot to unwind. Staff is young and hip, and the photo menu features curry lunches, pastas and pizzas for dinner and some excellent desserts.

Takumi Kappōten (☎ 26-6355; 653 Sakae-machi; meals ¥800-9000; ☺ lunch & dinner) The *takumi teishoku* (a lunchtime fish set meal; ¥1260; with *sashimi* ¥2100) are decent value at this old-fashioned Japanese eatery, which focuses on local seafood, vegetables and home-style cooking. It's part of the Folkcraft Museum next door; look for the bamboo railings beside the door.

Jujuan (☎ 21-1919; 751 Suehiro Onsen-chō; set meals ¥800-9800; ☺ lunch & dinner; E). This *sumibiyaki* (charcoal grilled cuisine) restaurant has lots of meat on skewers sizzling away, and some very friendly staff.

Getting There & Away

The coastal JR San-in line runs through Tottori from Matsue (¥2210, 2¼ hours) and on to Toyooka (*futsū* ¥1450, 2½ hours) and Kyoto. Super Inaba express services connect Tottori and Okayama (¥4270, two hours) on the San-yō coast.

Tottori **airport** (☎ 28-1150; 4-110-5 Koyama-chō Nishi) is just northwest of town, with flights to/from Tokyo.

Getting Around

Tottori's efficient Loop Bus (¥300/600 per ride/day pass) operates on weekends, holidays and from 20 July to 31 August. It connects the station with the dunes and Tottori port. Red- and blue-roofed minibuses (¥100/300 per ride/day pass) ply smaller, inner-city loops from the station every 20 minutes. Regular city buses depart from the station and leave for the dunes area (¥360, 20 minutes). Maps and timetables are available at the information office.

Bicycles can be rented near the station.

SAN-IN COAST NATIONAL PARK

山陰海岸国立公園

The spectacular coastline east from the Tottori dunes all the way to the Tango-hantō peninsula in Kyoto-fu is known as the San-in Kaigan Kokuritsu Kōen – the San-in Coast National Park. There are sandy beaches, rugged headlands and pines jutting into the blue sky.

Train lines run the length of the area, but they spend a fair bit of time inland and in tunnels. The best way to see the coastline is on wheels, whether it be by rental car, motorbike or bicycle.

Uradome Kaigan 浦富海岸

The first place of interest is Uradome Kaigan, amid the park's bluffs and craggy outcrops. Forty-minute **cruises** (☎ 0857-73-1212; cruise ¥1200; ⊙ Mar-Nov) leave from Ōtani-sanbashi, which is about 35 minutes east of Tottori by bus from JR Tottori station. The bus goes via the dunes, so it's possible to visit the dunes and do the cruise as a day trip from Tottori. Boat is the only way to see the islets and craggy cliffs, with pines clinging precariously to their sides.

Uradome and **Makidani**, two very popular beaches, are a few kilometres east. The closest station is Iwami on the JR San-in line, 2km from the coast, where there's a **tourist information office** (☎ 0857-72-3481; ⊙ 9am-6pm Tue-Sun). You can rent bicycles at the office and arrange accommodation. **Seaside Uradome** (シーサイド浦富; ☎ 0857-73-1555; fax 0857-73-1557; www .seasideuradome.com in Japanese; 2475-18 Uradome Iwamichō Iwami-gun; s/tw ¥4200/84000; ℗ ⊠) is a small hotel with Japanese-style rooms on a 3.5km-long esplanade in Iwami. Camping is possible on Makidani beach.

Said to be the oldest *onsen* in the San'in region and known for having curative waters, **Iwai Onsen** is a small, quiet collection of ryokan about eight minutes by bus from Iwami station along Rte 9. Casual bathers can relax at the modern *sentō* **Iwai Yukamuri Onsen** (岩井ゆかむり温泉; ☎ 0857-73-1670; admission ¥300; ⊙ 6am-10pm). It's right by the bus stop and has an old-fashioned, white and blue exterior.

Higashi-hama 東浜

The next train station heading eastwards is Higashi-hama; if you're coming by train, this is the one to hop off at. It's all of 100m from the station to a long sandy beach where you can take a stroll or a dip and contemplate the fact that Japan is not all urban sprawl after all. A minibus makes runs here from Iwami.

The Tottori-ken–Hyōgo-ken border is on the next headland.

Northern Honshū
本州の北部

> May's gentle showers, collected, become the rushing Mogami River...
>
> *Matsuo Bashō, 1644–94*

Northern Honshū remains less travelled than much of the rest of Honshū – a shame, since its rugged mountains, deep valleys, rushing rivers and friendly people make it rich and rewarding for travellers. Numerous dormant volcanoes make for numerous hot springs, and its clean water and high-quality rice have made the area synonymous with sake.

Some of Japan's most curious customs and oddest traditions are alive and well here, as is pride in the area's fascinating feudal past. Travellers who take the time to step off the *shinkansen* trail into the less travelled areas will find jaw-dropping beauty, incredibly kind people and well-preserved examples of the life of olden days. Anyone familiar with the ordered neon chaos of Tokyo will find Northern Honshū a refreshing and revitalising change. Paradoxically, thanks to the *shinkansen* and excellent local trains, this remote region is remarkably accessible, with many of the prime skiing, rafting, boating, *onsen* or hiking opportunities only a few hours away from Tokyo.

The area is comprised of Fukushima-ken, Miyagi-ken, Iwate-ken, Aomori-ken, Akita-ken and Yamagata-ken (collectively known as Tōhoku), as well as Niigata-ken and the island Sado-ga-shima. Tōhoku was called Michinoku, meaning 'back roads', and that isolation has helped to keep ancient traditions alive in the era of the internet and HDTV (high-definition television).

While English isn't widely spoken in Tōhoku (and its northern dialect is impenetrable even to many native Japanese), you will meet helpful, kind locals who often happily go out of their way to assist a traveller in need.

HIGHLIGHTS

- Learn about bloody feudal history and the tragic White Tiger samurais at **Aizu-Wakamatsu** (p501)

- Soak your worries away in the **Sukayu** (p533) lemony-tasting, 1000-person *onsen* bath

- Go *kappa*-hunting at **Tōno** (p521), where these little goblins dwell

- Sample a small but remarkable taste of Hiraizumi's former glory at the **Chūson-ji** (p518) complex

- Ride the famed Dragondola and tear down the slopes on perfect powder at **Naeba** (p564)

- Get away from the mainland crush on **Sado-ga-shima** (p560), a former island of exile with a rich, quirky history – and lots of persimmons

★ Sukayu

★ Tōno

★ Chūson-ji

Sado-ga-shima
★

★ Aizu-Wakamatsu

★ Naeba

History

Originally inhabited by the Ezo people, who are believed to have been related to the Ainu of Hokkaidō, Tōhoku was settled during the 7th to 9th centuries, when Japanese from the south spread northward, searching for arable new land.

In the 11th century the Northern Fujiwara clan ruled from Hiraizumi, a settlement reputed to rival Kyoto for its majesty and opulence. Aizu-Wakamatsu and Morioka were also important feudal towns.

Date Masamune represents the cornerstone of Tōhoku's feudal history. In 1601 construction commenced on Date's castle at the former fishing village of Sendai; the clan would go on to rule for close to 300 years, a reign that ushered in Tōhoku's Golden Age.

Unfortunately, Tōhoku regained 'backwater' status when the Meiji Restoration wiped out clan rule. It subsequently suffered years of neglect, a trend that was reversed only after WWII and the subsequent drive for development heavily based on industrial growth. Iron, transport, steel, chemical, pulp and petroleum were among the major industries that sprouted during this time. These days tourism is a major player in the region's economic health.

Climate

Depending on when you come, Northern Honshū will either be very comfortable or bone-chillingly cold. Summers are mild and considerably more comfortable than in the south, producing magnificent displays of greenery. In winter, Siberian cold grips the region and temperatures plummet. Snow is at least half of the fun here – making for great skiing, atmospheric *yukimiburos* (snow viewing from an *onsen*'s warmth) and adding winter's white serenity to the mountain ranges.

The Sea of Japan coast – bounded by Aomori, Akita, Yamagata and Niigata prefectures – endures particularly heavy snowfall. This clearly demarcated climate influences the texture of the local culture, most notably in the diversity of Tōhoku's festival programme, and ensures varied culinary harvests, like oysters in winter and mushrooms in autumn (fine seafood is a year-round feature).

Getting There & Away

The best way to get to the region is via the JR Tōhoku *shinkansen* (bullet train) line, which links Tokyo with Morioka in about 2½ hours, and travels as far as Hachinohe. From there, limited express and local trains run to Aomori and further north to Hokkaidō.

Getting Around

Maybe it's the influence of the ninja-poet (see the boxed text, p502), but locals seem to chronically underestimate walking times. If they say it'll take 10 minutes, it's more like 15. If they say it's an hour, it's three hours or more. Be especially cautious when planning hikes, especially if they say it'll take most of an afternoon (that could mean you should plan for a week or more). Unless you really do walk as quickly as Bashō himself, you'll find darkness gathering before you're halfway to your destination.

Local transport revolves around three major JR railway lines. Two of these run down the east and west coasts and the third snakes down between them in the centre, closely following the Tōhoku *shinkansen* line. Transport connections in the region have been accelerated with the opening of the Akita *shinkansen* line from Morioka to Akita and the extension of the Yamagata *shinkansen* line north to Shinjō.

Exploration of the more remote parts of Tōhoku is generally possible with local train and bus connections, but car rental is preferable as there is little traffic and most rentals include GPS positioning, making navigation a breeze. Roads and connections can be severely affected by winter weather, which can change on a dime.

Those without JR Passes should consider investing in the JR East Pass (p823), which provides unlimited travel by JR rail in the Tōhoku region for four flexible days, or five or 10 consecutive days, and – unlike the JR Pass – this one can be purchased after you arrive.

FUKUSHIMA-KEN 福島県

Fukushima-ken, Japan's third-largest prefecture, is closest to Tokyo, though it boasts fewer sites of tourist value than its northern neighbours. At the same time, it shouldn't be overlooked. *Onsen* lovers will be happy to know that the prefecture boasts over 200 hot springs, and sake sippers can delight in numerous local varieties. The Hamadori area, on the coast, was once an important mining

NORTHERN HONSHŪ

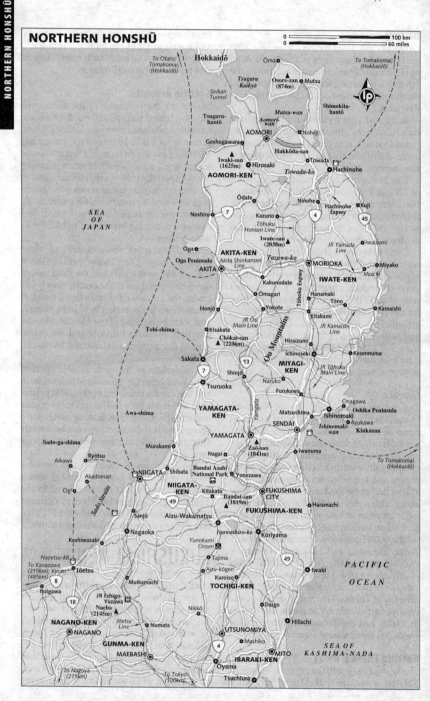

NORTHERN TŌHOKU WELCOME CARD

The Northern Tōhoku Welcome Card was recently introduced as a special incentive for foreign tourists and students residing in Japan. It provides discounts – usually around 10% – on transport, accommodation and sightseeing throughout Akita, Iwate and Aomori prefectures. Some of the listings in this chapter fall under the scheme, although the list of participants is not as comprehensive as it should be; many major sights are not yet included. Still, it's free and worth keeping at hand.

To obtain the card, print it out from the website (www.northern-tohoku.gr.jp/welcome) or pick up a form from tourist offices throughout the region. Fill in your details and present the card with your passport (or foreign student ID) to obtain the discount; the card is valid for one year. Look out for the red-and-white Welcome Card sticker at participating facilities or download a full list from the website.

area and is now known for its seaside resorts (the tourist board also promotes the output of Hamadori's nuclear power plants – perhaps not the best move, given Japan's dubious safety record). Nakadori, the inland region, is the administrative hub, containing the capital, Fukushima City, and most of the population. Aizu, to the prefecture's west, was at the centre of the feudal war.

AIZU-WAKAMATSU 会津若松
☎ 0242 / pop 130,000

In the middle of Fukushima prefecture, this quiet, friendly town makes a relaxed base for exploring the Bandai Asahi National Park (p505), but it is most famous for its Edo-period past. It was the capital of the Aizu clan, a reign that came to an end in the Bōshin Civil War in 1868, when Tsuruga castle fell after the clan sided with the Tokugawa Shōgunate against the imperial faction. A reconstructed castle and re-enactments of samurai battles make Aizu an interesting stop as you meander northward, and it is close enough that a day trip from 'the City' is possible as well.

Information
There's free internet (one hour) at the Tsuruga-jō information desk.

Aizu Wakamatsu Post Office (1-2-17 Chūō) On the main street, and has an international ATM.

Books Fuji (☎ 22-3592; Ekimae-machi 5-25; ⏱ 10.30am-8pm) In the Fuji Grand Hotel; has a microscopic selection of English material.

ePalette (☎ 22-4100; 1-20 Heian chō; membership/per hr ¥300/480) For internet access.

Police box (☎ 22-1877, main office 22-5454) Right next to the train station.

Sightseeing information desk Aizu-Wakamatsu station (☎ 32-0688; ⏱ 9am-5.30pm); Tsuruga-jō (鶴ケ城;

☎ 29-1151; ⏱ 8:30am-5pm). The willing staff at both locations can supply you with English-language maps, brochures and thorough directions. The Japanese map is excellent and exactly to scale – it is worth asking for them to circle the places you want to go on that map instead of using the English one.

Sights
The following, arranged in a ring around the fringes of the city centre, are clearly signposted in English. It's possible to do the lot on foot in a day, but a tourist bus does the loop if you need it (p505).

Iimori-yama (飯盛山) is the mountain where a group of 'White Tiger' samurai killed themselves during the Bōshin Civil War (p504). At the foot of the mountain, the **Byakkotai Memorial Hall** (白虎隊記念館; ☎ 24-9170; Iimori-yama, Ikki-machi; admission ¥400; ⏱ 8am-5pm Apr-Nov, 8.30am-4.30pm Dec-Mar) explains the story, while **Sazae-dō** (さざえ堂; ☎ 22-3163; Iimori-yama, Ikki-machi; admission ¥400; ⏱ 8.15am-sunset Apr-Oct, 9am-sunset Nov-Mar), an 18th-century hexagonal hall, contains 33 statues of Kannon (the Buddhist goddess of mercy). It also has a fabulous spiral staircase that, Escher-esque, allows you to walk up and down without retracing your steps.

Saigō Tanomo was the Aizu clan's chief retainer and **Aizu Bukeyashiki** (会津武家屋敷; ☎ 28-2525; Innai Higashiyama-machi; admission ¥850; ⏱ 8.30am-5pm Apr-Oct, 9am-4.30pm Nov-Mar) is a superbly realised reconstruction of his *yashiki* (villa). Wander through the 38 rooms that include a guestroom for the Aizu lord, a tea-ceremony house, quarters for the clan's judge and a rice-cleaning mill presented here in full, noisy working order. Don't miss the samurai lavatory: underneath is a sandbox on wheels, an 'early-warning system' that could be removed so staff could monitor the health of the warriors. You'll also find the room where Tanomo's wife and children committed suicide, fearing he wouldn't return from combat in the Bōshin War – although the utter impassivity of the wax models re-enacting the scene comically undercuts the drama. There's also a target range where you can try your hand at archery for ¥200.

Oyaku-en (御薬園; ☎ 27-2472; Hanaharu-machi; admission ¥310; ☉ 8.30am-5pm, last entry 4.30pm) is a meditative garden complex with a large, central carp pond. Originally a holiday retreat for the Aizu clan, it features a section devoted to the cultivation of medicinal herbs (available for purchase) – a practice encouraged by the lords.

The Aizu clan made **Tsuruga-jō** (鶴ヶ城; Crane Castle; ☎ 27-4005; Oute-machi; admission ¥400; ☉ 8.30am-5pm, last entry 4.30pm) their headquarters. The present building is a 1965 reconstruction, but parts of the daunting walls remain, as does the castle's moat. Inside, there's a museum with historical artefacts from battle and daily life. Displays are a bit sketchy, although the frequent martial-arts demonstrations, carried out by adepts in full warrior regalia, are engaging. The 5th storey affords a terrific view of the surrounding town and valley, including Iimori-yama.

On the castle grounds, **Rinkaku** (茶室麟閣; ☎ 27-4005; admission ¥200, combined castle ticket ¥500; ☉ 8.30am-5pm, last entry 4.30pm) is an evocative, 400-year-old teahouse that was rescued from the castle's destruction by a local family and returned here in 1990.

For nonfeudal glimpses into Aizu-Wakamatsu's history, try the **Fukushima Prefectural Museum** (福島県立博物館; ☎ 28-6000; 1-25 Jōto-machi; admission ¥260; ☉ 9.30am-4.30pm, closed Mon & day after public holidays except Sat & Sun), with 400 displays ranging from prehistoric times to recent history.

The **Aizu Sake Brewing Museum** (会津酒造歴史館; ☎ 26-0031; 8-7 Higashisakae-machi; admission ¥300; ☉ 8.30am-5pm Apr-Nov, 9.30am-4.30pm Dec-Mar) details

---

MATSUO BASHŌ: POET OR NINJA?

Regarded as Japan's master of haiku, Matsuo Bashō (1644–94) is credited with elevating its status from comic relief to Zen-infused enlightenment. Bashō was born into a samurai family and in his late teenage years served the feudal lord Yoshitada. Moving to Kyoto and then to Edo, Bashō found success as a published poet, but ultimately found the acclaim to be spiritually unsettling. He turned to Zen and the philosophy had a deep impact on his work: many comparisons have been made between his haiku and Zen *kōan* (short riddles), intended to bring about a sudden flash of insight in the listener. Bashō was also influenced by the natural philosophy of the Chinese Taoist sage Chuangzi, and began to examine nature uncritically. Later he developed his own poetic principle by drawing on the concept of *sabi*, a kind of spare, lonely beauty.

When he reached his 40s, Bashō decided to give his career away in favour of travelling throughout Japan, seeking to build friendships and commune with nature as he went. He published evocative accounts of his travels, including *The Records of a Weather-Beaten Skeleton* and *The Records of a Travel-Worn Satchel*, but his collection *The Narrow Road to the Deep North*, detailing his journey throughout Tōhoku in 1689, is perhaps the most famous. Like many Japanese, Bashō had initial misgivings ('I may as well be travelling to the ends of the earth', he lamented), but the north's special charms eventually rendered him lost for words, most famously on his encounter with Matsushima Bay – 'Matsushima, ah! Matsushima! Matsushima!' Bashō famously wrote (although recent evidence suggests that anecdote to be apocryphal).

Some people have tried to read even more into Bashō's life and work. In recent times, a bizarre theory has spread. It claims that Bashō was actually a ninja spy for the shōgunate, sent to Tohokū to report on any unrest that might be fermenting in the provinces; accordingly, his haikus are supposed to be coded missives. There's no real evidence for this, but some of the arguments are intriguing. The conspiracy theorists point out that Bashō covered 2500km on foot in 150 days (sometimes 50km a day) at the ripe old age of 46; only certain ninja, they say, were able to accomplish this, using methods of running and walking that used minute amounts of energy. He was also able to gain access to high-level feudal territory, a feat apparently impossible for ordinary people. Adding fuel to the rumours is the undeniable fact of the poet's early employment history (many ninja were also samurai), as well as the nature of his birthplace, in the Iga province – home of the famous Iga Ninja school.

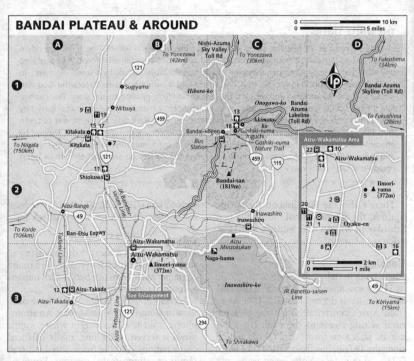

BANDAI PLATEAU & AROUND

the history of rice-wine brewing in the area. A fair number of English signs and an English pamphlet make it easy to get a basic sense of the brewing process. Life-size dioramas and old sake advertisements add to the charm. Naturally you can sample the famous tipple for the price of admission.

Festivals & Events

Aizu-Wakamatsu holds four main festivals, coordinated according to season. The most prominent is the three-day **Aizu Autumn Festival** (会津秋祭り) on 22 to 24 September, an extravagant procession that threads through the city to Tsuruga-jō, accompanied by a drum-and-fife band, a children's parade and an evening lantern parade. The sacrifice of the 20 White Tigers (p504) is dramatised by local high-school boys. The owner of the Aizu-no-sato Youth Hostel is a local expert and can advise, in English, on how to best attend.

THE WHITE TIGERS

In 1868 a group of 20 teenage samurai, known as the Byakkotai (White Tigers), looked down upon Tsuruga-jō, saw it shrouded in smoke, and concluded that imperial forces had captured the castle. Rather than surrender, they committed *seppuku* (ritual suicide by disembowelment). In reality it was the surrounding area that was ablaze and it would be weeks before the Aizu clan would fall; one lad survived and devoted the rest of his life to passing on the story. This strange tale greatly tickles Japanese sensibilities, with its tragi-comic blend of blind loyalty tempered by utter futility and a ruthless universe. To the outsider, there's a dark side: Mussolini was so taken with the Byakkotai he donated a grandiose monument to commemorate the event. Topped by an eagle, it surveys the horizon from the top of Iimori-yama, surrounded by Byakkotai graves and the steady stream of Japanese tourists scanning the horizon to see what the White Tigers couldn't: a fully intact castle.

There's also the **Higanjishi** on the spring equinox, the **Summer Festival** during the first Saturday in August and winter's **Sainokami**, held on 14 January.

Sleeping

Aizuno Youth Hostel (会津野ユースホステル; ☎ 55-1020; www.aizuno.com/e_index.html; 88 Kakiyashiki, Terasaki Aizu-Takada-chō; dm/r from ¥3100/4200) Away from Aizu's centre, although the pleasing rural setting sweetens the deal. It's a 20-minute walk west from Aizu-Takada station along the Tadami line from Aizu-Wakamatsu (¥230, 20 minutes). Note: seven trains run daily, but only one in the afternoon. Find out your train's arrival time in advance and give the hostel notice – the manager will pick you up from the station (he also escorts guests to a hot spring at 6pm daily). Free bike rental and breakfast.

Minshuku Takaku (民宿多賀来; ☎ 26-6299; fax 26-6116; www.naf.co.jp/takaku, in Japanese only; 104 Innai Higashiyama-machi; r incl/excl 2 meals from ¥6300/4200) This cosy place, with well-kept Japanese-style rooms, is east of the Aizu Bukeyashiki bus stop. From there, continue along the road, turn left at the post office and it's just behind, on the left.

There's a slew of business hotels clustered around or near the train station, all at about the same level of cleanliness and comfort, with TVs and phones in the rooms. Of the many options, try these:

Fuji Grand Hotel (駅前フジグランドホテル; ☎ 24-1111; 5-25 Ekimae-machi; s/d from ¥4900/9900; 🖳) Rates depend on views – you pay more to ensure your room doesn't face the sheer concrete wall next door. It's next to the station, to the right as you exit.

Aizu Wakamatsu Washington Hotel (会津若松 ワシントンホテル; ☎ 22-6111; 201 Byakko-machi; s/d from ¥7350/13,650; 🖳) About five minutes' walk southeast of the train station. Roomy and very clean.

Eating

Wappa meshi is a local dish consisting of steamed fish over rice. It's prepared in a round container made from tree bark, which imparts a woody fragrance to the contents.

Takino (田季野; ☎ 25-0808; 5-31 Sakae-machi; wappa meshi from ¥1420; ⏰ lunch & dinner) An atmospheric, split-level restaurant where *wappa meshi* is served in sublime, subtly balanced combinations. Try the finely shredded crab (*kani*) or salmon (*sake*) versions. From the main post office, facing south, turn left onto Nanokomachi-dōri, at the first light turn right (south); go left at the second alleyway, and it's on the right. Ask the obliging staff at the information desk to mark up a map with the exact location. You'll know you've arrived when you see the large penis (plastered with various bills) in the entranceway. No English menu.

Mitsutaya (満田屋; ☎ 27-1345; 1-1-25 Ōmachi; skewers from ¥200; ⏰ 10am-5pm, closed 1st & 3rd Wed of each month & every Wed Jan-Mar) At this atmospheric former bean-paste mill, dating from 1869, the speciality is eight varieties of *dengaku*; these are bamboo skewers with deep-fried tofu and vegetables such as taro basted in sweet *miso* paste and baked over charcoal. Herring (*nishin*) is also superb. Facing west from the main post office, walk down Nanokomachi-dōri, then take the second left; it's just near the intersection with Nanokomachi-dōri. No English, but a picture menu makes ordering easy.

Kagota (籠太; ☎ 32-5380; 8-49 Sakae-machi; food menu ¥500-1000; ⏰ 5-11pm Mon-Sat) Serving mainly local specialities of Aizu Wakamatsu.

Getting There & Around

From Tokyo, take the JR Tōhoku *shinkansen* to Kōriyama (¥7970, 1½ hours), then change to an hourly *kaisoku* (rapid) train on the JR Banetsu-saisen line for Aizu-Wakamatsu (¥1110, 1¼ hours). There are two daily *kaisoku* trains between Aizu-Wakamatsu and Niigata (¥2210, 2¾ hours). Express buses to Niigata run four times daily (¥2000, 1¾ hours).

The **Aizu Town Bus** (まちなか周遊バスハイカラさん; single/day pass ¥200/500) does a loop of the sights. Enquire about bike rental (per day ¥1500) at the tourist info desks.

KITAKATA 喜多方

☎ 0241 / pop 77,000

An old Kitakata saying reflects this town's view towards commerce: 'A man is not a man unless he has built at least one *kura* [a mud-walled storehouse]'. These days, the town's 2600 coloured *kura* – now functioning as living quarters, sake breweries and workshops – are a perennial tourist attraction, as are its 120 *rāmen* (soup noodles) shops.

Staff at the small **tourist information kiosk** (☎ 24-2633; ⏰ 8.30am-5.15pm), left of the station exit, has copies of a small English-language map.

Sample the excellent local sake at **Yamato-gawa Sake Brewing Museum** (大和川酒造北方風土館; ☎ 22-2233; 4761 Teramachi; admission free; ⏰ 9am-4.30pm, closed irregularly), five minutes' walk north of the station.

At **Ohara Brewing Factory** (小原酒造; ☎ 22-0074; www.oharashuzo.co.jp; ⏰ 9am-5pm) staff play Mozart to the yeasts to enhance fermentation. A visit also includes a Mozart-infused tipple. Last entry is at 4.40pm.

Aizu-no-sato Youth Hostel (会津の里ユースホステル; ☎ 27-2054; 36 Hatakeda Kofune-aza, Shiokawa-machi, Kitakata-shi; dm from ¥3200), set among lovely old grounds with well-worn but comfortable Japanese-style rooms, is worth leaving the city centre for. The host is a Byakkotai buff, and a good source of area knowledge as well. The hostel is 15 minutes' walk from Shiokawa station on the JR Banetsu-saisen line. From the station head straight until you hit the first light, then turn left and veer left again when the road merges into Rte 121. Cross the bridge and it's on the left, tucked behind the owner's sake shop.

The **Kitakata Hotel** (キタカタホテル; ☎ 22-0139; 8269-2 Machida; s ¥5250), just across from the station, is a standard business hotel, clean but

characterless, while **Sasaya Ryokan** (笹屋旅館; ☎ 22-0008; Chūō-dōri; r per person incl/excl 2 meals from ¥8800/5500; 🖃) offers traditional accommodation 1km north of the station.

Genraiken (源来軒; ☎ 22-0091; 7745 Ippongiue Kitakata City; sets from ¥800; ⏰ 10am-8pm Wed-Mon, last orders 7.30pm) is Kitakata's best-known *rāmen* shop, with a 70-year history and a devoted lunchtime crowd. Head south on Chūō-dōri and look for the red façade.

Getting There & Around

Kitakata is a relatively easy trip from Aizu-Wakamatsu, accessible by train along the JR Banetsu-saisen line (¥320, 15 minutes). Bicycle rental (per two hours/day ¥500/1500) is available outside Kitakata station, while a **horse-drawn carriage** (☎ 24-4111; tours on demand ¥1300) shaped like a *kura* departs from the train station for an 80-minute tour of the more interesting storehouses. New velo-taxis (three-wheeled bicycles with a covered passenger area) are also a fun way to get around.

BANDAI PLATEAU 磐梯高原

☎ 0241 / pop 4000

On 15 July 1888 **Bandai-san** (磐梯山; 1819m), a once-dormant volcano, suddenly erupted, spewing forth a tremendous amount of debris that's said to have lowered the mountain's height by 600m, while destroying dozens of villages. Over 400 people died. The aftershock completely rearranged the landscape, creating the plateau Bandai-kōgen and damming local rivers that then formed numerous water bodies. Now Japan's second-largest national park, it's hemmed in by the Fukushima, Niigata and Yamagata prefectural boundaries, and offers stirring scenery and stellar opportunities for hiking and skiing.

Information

There's a **visitors centre** (☎ 32-2850; ⏰ 9am-4pm Wed-Mon Dec-Mar, to 5pm Wed-Mon Apr-Nov) not far from the Goshiki-numa Iriguchi trailhead and a **tourist information office** (☎ 0242-62-2048; ⏰ 8.30am-5pm) to the left outside JR Inawashiro station.

Activities

The most popular walk follows a 3.7km nature trail around **Goshiki-numa** (五色沼), an area of around 11 lakes and ponds known as Five Colours Lakes, after mineral deposits from the eruption imparted various hues to the waters – emerald green, cobalt blue and so on – that change with the weather. There are trailheads at the Goshiki-numa Iriguchi and Bandai-kōgen bus stops, the main transport hubs on the edge of Hibara-ko. Bandai-san itself can be climbed in a day with an early start; the most popular route starts from the Bandai-kōgen bus stop and climbs up through the skiing ground to the summit.

Sleeping & Eating

Several *minshuku* (Japanese B&B) cater to hikers and skiers, and cost from ¥6500 per person with two meals. For more details and other information call the **Goshiki-numa Minshuku Information Centre** (☎ 32-2902).

Ura Bandai Youth Hostel (☎ 32-2811; http:// homepage3.nifty.com/urabandai/indexe.html; urabandai-YH@nifty.com; dm from ¥2900; ☽ late Apr-Nov; ▣) This friendly old hostel has a super location, next to one of the Goshiki-numa trailheads. There's an 11pm curfew and bicycles for rent (¥1000 per day). It's a seven-minute walk from the Goshiki-numa Iriguchi bus stop, signposted right from the car park. The adjoining camping ground has ¥1000 tents and ¥5000 cabins.

Fraser Hotel (☎ 32-3470; www012.upp.so-net.ne.jp /fraser in Japanese; fraser@spajoy.com; r per person incl 2 meals from ¥12,600) This upmarket, Canadian-style option has spick-and-span rooms and a great cypress bath. It's in front of the Goshikinuma-Iriguchi bus station; look in the direction of the Italian restaurant.

Getting There & Away

The JR Banetsu-saisen line (*kaisoku* ¥480, 29 minutes) connects Aizu-Wakamatsu with the town of Inawashiro (猪苗代). From outside Inawashiro station, frequent buses depart from stop 3 and pass by the Goshiki-numa Iriguchi stop (¥750, 25 minutes), heading onto the Bandai-kōgen Kyūkamura stop (¥870, 30 minutes).

MIYAGI-KEN 宮城県

Miyagi-ken is a paradoxical gateway between the very rural areas to the north and the rest of Honshū. Its capital, Sendai, is Tohoku's most cosmopolitan city, a fun destination with excellent tourist support and a lively nightlife. Date Masamune developed Sendai into a major culture and trade centre in the 1600s. Miyagi-

ken has several attractions, including Naruko Onsen, a great spot for *onsen* enthusiasts, and Matsushima, a bay studded with atmospheric pine-covered islands, immortalised by Bashō and popular with Japanese sightseers.

SENDAI 仙台
☎ 022 / pop 1,028,000
Sendai, while nowhere near as big as Tokyo, offers travellers the best of both worlds – you get small-town hospitality in, well, a big town – without the cold-shoulder reception one finds southward in that 'even bigger city'. Sendai is famous for souvenirs of *zunda*, a mildly sweet, bright green paste made from soybeans, and *gyutan*, cow's tongue. People are refreshingly friendly here – a bit of a paradox, as Sendai was demolished by Allied bombing during WWII. Lucky for tourists, residents have long forgotten about keeping any grudges, and the city's wide, tree-lined streets make for relaxing strolls. Buildings such as the Mediateque, with its see-through glass and giant columns, defy description. *Wow*.

Sendai's Jōzenji Jazz Festival (p511) is a two-day, open-air extravaganza in early September; the Sendai Tanabata Matsuri (p510) tops that, though, with two million visitors each year.

The city also has a compelling history as the stomping ground of the remarkable feudal lord Date Masamune (1567–1636), known as the One-Eyed Dragon (see the boxed text, p509). A number of intriguing sites around town pay tribute to his overarching presence, as does the name 'Sendai' – it means '1000 generations', apparently an indication of how long Masamune felt his clan would rule.

Sendai marks the last place south of Sapporo that you can find a good English bookshop, and is an ideal base to arrange tickets, exchange your rail pass, check email and see some bright lights before heading to nearby rural *onsen* or along the coast.

Orientation

From Sendai station, located east of most of the action, the broad sweep of Aoba-dōri, lined with many of the major department stores, banks and hotels, leads west to a park, Aoba-yama. The main shopping areas are the series of arcades along Chūō-dōri (also known as CLIS Rd) and Ichibanchō-dōri, which intersect just east of Kokubunchō-dōri, the main drag of Tōhoku's largest entertainment

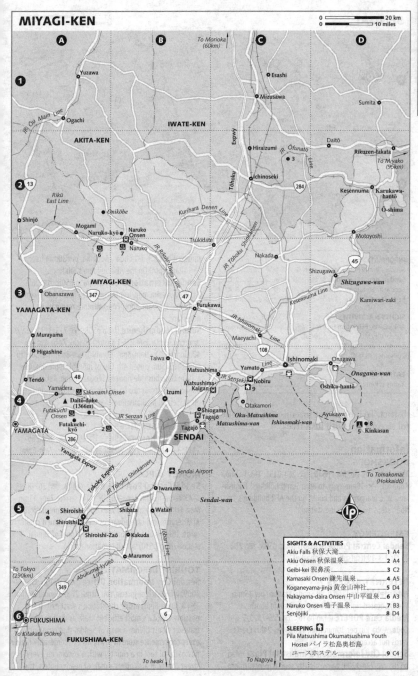

MIYAGI-KEN

0 ——————— 20 km
0 ——————— 10 miles

To Morioka
(60km)

A   **B**   **C**   **D**

1

Yuzawa

Esashi

Mizusawa

Sumita

Ogachi

JR Ou Main Line

IWATE-KEN

Daitō

Rikuzen-takata

AKITA-KEN

Hiraizumi

JR Ōfunato Line

● 3

To Miyako
(95km)

Ichinoseki

284

Kesennuma

Karukawa-hantō

2

13

Rikū East Line

Onikōbe

Kurihara Denen Line

Tsukidate

Ō-shima

Shinjō

Mogami

Naruko-kyō

Naruko Onsen

Motoyoshi

6   7   Naruko

JR Rikuu-Tosego Line

Nakada

45

JR Tōhoku Shinkansen

Shizugawa

Shizugawa-wan

3

Obanazawa

MIYAGI-KEN

347

47

Furukawa

Kesennuma Line

Kamiwari-zaki

YAMAGATA-KEN

Murayama

JR Ishinomaki Line

Maeyachi

Higashine

Taiwa

108

JR Ishinomaki Line

Ishinomaki

Onagawa

Onagawa-wan

Tendō

48

Yamadera

Sakunami Onsen

Matsushima

Yamato

Nobiru

9

Oshika-hantō

4

Futakuchi Onsen

▲ Daitō-dake
(1366m)

● 1

Izumi

Matsushima-Kaigan

JR Senseki Line

Otakamori

Oku-Matsushima

Ayukawa

8

YAMAGATA

Futakuchi-kyō

2

JR Senzan Line

Shiogama

Tagajō

Matsushima-wan

Ishinomaki-wan

5 Kinkasan

286

Tagajō

SENDAI

4

To Tomakomai
(Hokkaidō)

5

4

Shiroishi

Shibata

Watari

Shiroishi

Sendai Airport

JR Tōhoku Shinkansen

Tōhoku Expwy

Yamagata Expwy

Iwanuma

Sendai-wan

Shiroishi-Zaō

Kakuda

Marumori

Abukuma-kyōko Line

Jōban Line

To Tokyo
(290km)

349

6

FUKUSHIMA

6

To Kitakata (50km)

FUKUSHIMA-KEN

To Iwaki

To Nagoya

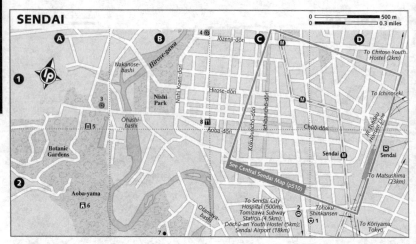

SENDAI

district. To the north is Jōzenji-dōri, a delightful street lined with lush trees.

Information
BOOKSHOPS
Maruzen (丸善; Map p510; ☎ 264-0151; 1-3-1 Chūō, Aoba-ku; ☻ 10am-9pm, to 8pm Sun & holidays) English-language magazines and books on the AER building's 1st floor, steps away from the station.

EMERGENCY
Sendai Central Police Station (Map p508; ☎ 222-7171; 1-3-19 Itsutsubashi, Aoba-ku)

INTERNET ACCESS
Internet kiosks (2nd fl, JR Sendai station; per 15min ¥100) Located right outside the tourist info booth.
Media Café POPEYE (Map p510; ☎ 726-7890; 2-6-4 Chūō, Aoba-ku; per 30min from ¥262, ☻ 24hr) Credit cards not accepted.
Sendai City Information & Industrial Plaza (Map p510; ☎ 724-1200; www.siip.city.sendai.jp/netu/room /indexen.html; 1-3-1 Chūō-, Aoba-ku; per 30min free; ☻ 10am-8pm) On the AER building's 5th floor.
Sendai International Centre (Map p508; ☎ 265-2450; www.sira.or.jp/icenter/en/index.html; Aoba-yama, Aoba-ku; ☻ 9am-8pm) Free; advance reservation necessary.
Sendai Mediatheque (Map p508; ☎ 713-3171; www.smt.city.sendai.jp/en; 2-1 Kasuga-machi, Aoba-ku; per 40min free; ☻ 9am-8pm, library 10am-8pm Tue-Sun, to 6pm Sat & Sun, closed 4th Thu of month) Approximately a 10-minute bus ride from JR Sendai station. Take a bus bound for 'Kōtsūkyoku Daigakubyōin via Jōzenji-dōri'. Get off at 'Sendai Mediatheque-Mae' stop.

MEDICAL SERVICES
Sendai City Hospital (仙台市立病院; ☎ 266-7111; 3-1 Shimizu-kōji, Wakabayashi-ku; ☻ 7am-6pm)

MONEY & POST
Sendai Central Post Office (Map p508; ☎ 267-8035; 1-7 Kitame-machi, Aoba-ku; ☻ ATM service 7am-11pm Mon-Fri, 9am-9pm Sat, to 7pm Sun) Offers international ATM service; and cash advances on foreign-issued credit cards. There is also a branch on the 1st floor of Sendai station (Map p510) with international ATM.

TOURIST INFORMATION
Sendai City Information Office (Map p510; ☎ 222-4069; www.stcb.or.jp/eng/tbic.html; 2F JR Sendai station; ☻ 8.30am-8pm) Inside the station's west exit, it has possibly Tōhoku's most efficient staff, as well as the traveller's best friend: a map of Sendai that pinpoints every convenience store in town, an extraordinarily handy navigational tool in a country with a *konbini* on every street corner. It also offers a map of nearby hotels, the

closest of which (within a 10-minute walk) are marked by an asterisk.

Sendai International Centre (Map p508; ☎ 265-2471; www.sira.or.jp/icenter/en/index.html; Aoba-yama, Aoba-ku; 9am-8pm) Features an information desk with English-speaking staff, international newspaper library, bulletin board, CNN broadcasts, free internet access and a Visa ATM.

Sights & Activities

Sendai is compact and pretty enough to make a full day on-foot tour a possibility, but if time is money, use the Loople tourist bus (see p513). It includes the following sights during its one-hour circuit.

Masamune Date's mausoleum, **Zuihō-den** (Map p508; ☎ 262-6250; 23-2 Otamayashita, Aoba-ku; admission ¥550; 9am-4.30pm Feb-Nov, to 4pm Dec & Jan; Loople stop 4), is at the summit of a tree-covered hill by the Hirose-gawa. It was originally built in 1637, destroyed by Allied bombing during WWII and reconstructed in 1979. The present building is an exact replica of the original, faithful to the ornate and sumptuous Momoyama style: a complex, interlocking architecture, characterised by multicoloured woodcarvings.

Also atop the hill are the mausoleums of Masamune's second and third successors, Date Tadamune and Date Tsunamune. When the reconstruction commenced, the remains of the three lords, as well as personal possessions and items of armour, were excavated. These are now displayed in a museum at the site, as are likenesses of the three. Don't miss the rather curious comparison of the lengths of their noses and the shapes of their foreheads.

Sendai-jō Ato (Map p508; admission free; 24hr; Loople stop 6, regular bus stop 'Sendai Jō Ato Minami') is the second of Sendai's star attractions. Though destroyed during Allied bombing in WWII, the giant, moss-covered walls are as imposing as they are impressive – and the spot makes a great meander. Built on Aoba-yama in 1602 by Date Masamune, it was commonly known as Aoba-jō (Green Leaves Castle), after a nearby spring that flowed even during times of drought. It affords sweeping views over the city, but keep in mind that there's not a lot here other than a stirring statue of Masamune on horseback, views, and little shops and restaurants. For the Japanese it's the spirit that counts, and armed with a little knowledge of the Masamune legend, it's rather easy for the outsider to get caught up in it.

THE ONE-EYED DRAGON

Date Masamune is the most famous figure in Miyagi's feudal history. Nicknamed Dokuganryū (One-Eyed Dragon) after he caught smallpox as a child and went blind in his right eye, he combined military nous with commercial instinct, ranking among the most important lords in feudal Japan. He was also an aesthete with finely developed tastes in *nō* theatre (stylised Japanese dance-drama performed on a bare stage) and calligraphy, and transformed Sendai into a major cultural centre.

Masamune became head of the Date clan at the age of 17 and quickly increased his territory through ferocious skill on the battleground. When Japan was wracked by civil war in 1598, Masamune sided with Tokugawa Ieyasu's victorious faction. For his efforts Masamune was granted control over the Sendai domain, and soon after moved his base of operations to the village of Sendai in order to gain access to the port.

He constructed Aoba Castle in 1601 and then proceeded to build Sendai as a major focus of trade, constructing a salt works and ensuring the region supplied a considerable quantity of the country's grain. He also oversaw the construction of a series of temples, shrines and other sites of spiritual significance. But Date's rule was also remarkable for his developing interest in Christianity. This culminated in his dispatch of Japan's first diplomatic envoy, seeking trade with Mexico and Europe as well as an audience with Pope Paul V.

Many predicted Masamune would soon rise to the shōgunate and control the whole of Japan, but he was never fully trusted by his superiors, due to his unorthodox manner and singular leadership; it was suspected, for example, that Masamune's European envoy was designed to drum up European support for an overthrow of the incumbent shōgun.

But the people of Sendai always remained loyal to Masamune's vision, even today, as illustrated by the recently built Miyagi Stadium: the roof of its west stand is modelled after the unique crescent symbol the warlord wore on his helmet.

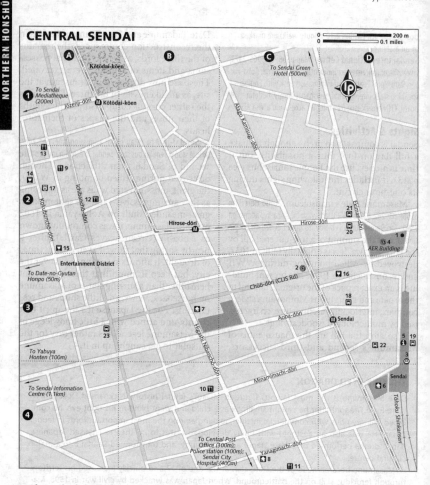

CENTRAL SENDAI

If you don't have that kind of knowledge when you climb the hill, you can get it at the **Aoba Castle Exhibition Hall** (Map p508; ☎ 227-7077; Aobajō Ato, Tenshudai, Aoba-ku, admission ¥700; ⊗ 9am-5pm Apr-Oct, to 4pm Nov-Mar). A computer-generated film depicts the castle's former glory; its graphics are so similar to modern video games that Sony PS3 or XBox aficionados will start expecting samurai warriors to jump out from behind the castle if they don't toss a grenade. You can get English-language headsets.

At **Sendai City Museum** (Map p508; ☎ 225-3074; Sendai Jō Sannomaru Ato, 26 Kawauchi, Aoba-ku; admission ¥400; ⊗ 9am-4.45pm Tue-Sun; Loople stop 5) there's a scale model of Sendai castle, along with an exhaustive account of the Masamune era.

Among some 13,000 artefacts loaned from the Date family is his distinctive armour.

Festivals & Events

Donto-sai (どんと祭) On 14 January men brave subzero weather conditions to hop around almost naked, a ritual supposed to bring good fortune for the new year.

Sendai Tanabata Matsuri (仙台七夕まつり; Star Festival) Sendai's major event, held from 6 to 8 August, celebrates a Chinese legend about the stars Vega and Altair. Vega was the king's daughter who fell in love with and married Altair, a common herder. The king disapproved, so he formed the Milky Way between them. Once a year magpies are supposed to spread their wings across the universe so that the lovers can meet – traditionally on 7 July. Sendai seems to have stretched the dates a bit, but celebrates in grand style by decorating the main streets with bamboo poles festooned with multicoloured streamers and holding afternoon parades on Jōzenji-dōri. A couple of million visitors ensure that accommodation is booked solid at this time of year.

Jōzenji Street Jazz Festival (定禅寺ストリート ジャズフェスティバル) Another highly infectious major festival is held on the second weekend of September when 600 buskers from across Japan perform in Sendai's streets and arcades. Book rooms way, way, *way* in advance.

Sendai Pageant of Starlight (SENDAI光のペー ジェント) Illuminates Aoba-dōri and Jōzenji-dōri with festive lights on 12 to 31 December.

Sleeping

BUDGET

our pick **Dōchū-an Youth Hostel** (道中庵ユースホ ステル; ☎ 247-0511; 31 Kita-yashiki, Ōnoda, Taihaku-ku; dm from ¥3150; 💻) This evocative former farmhouse features genial management, bike rental, free internet, home cooking and a fantastic old cedar bath to soak in. Its only drawbacks are that it's quite a way from the city centre, south of Sendai at the end of the subway line in Tomizawa (¥290, 12 minutes), then a further 15-minute walk. Station attendants have a map of the area and small signs guide the way. Head straight out from the station rather than veering right or left, and follow the road until you cross a major (four-lane) intersection. Cross, then take the first right, a smallish street. The hostel is on the left; if you hit the *rāmen* shop you've gone too far.

Sendai Chitose Youth Hostel (仙台千登勢ユー スホステル; ☎ 222-6329; 6-3-8 Odawara, Aoba-ku; dm from ¥3150; 💻) Closer to the city, this snug hostel, with Japanese-style rooms, is a 20-minute walk from Sendai station's west exit. Take any bus going via Miyamachi from stop 17 at the west bus pool and get off at 'Miyamachi 2

Chōme' bus stop; the hostel is tucked down a small side street three blocks east of the bus stop.

MIDRANGE

Sendai's business hotels have what you would expect: TVs in the rooms and slightly cramped quarters. Except at the top end, of course.

Sendai Green Hotel (仙台グリーンホテル; ☎ 221-7070; 2-5-6 Nishiki-chō, Aoba-ku; s/tw/d from ¥4100/8200/11,000; 💻) Basic, sparse rooms, although the views over the city are good. There's a spacious lounge area and accommodating staff. North of Jōzenji-dōri, straight ahead from Ekimae-dōri.

Hotel Richfield Aoba Dōri (Map p510; ☎ 262-1355; 2-3-18 Chūō, Aoba-ku; s/tw from ¥5700/12,600; 💻) A central hotel with a spiffy 2nd-floor lobby, friendly staff, its own restaurant and surprisingly small rooms. Head straight out on Chūō-dōri and then turn left.

TOP END

Hotel Metropolitan Sendai (Map p510; ☎ 268-2525; www.s-metro.stbl.co.jp/english/index.html; 1-1-1 Chūō, Aoba-ku; s/tw/d ¥11,550/20,790/20,790; 💻) No surprises here at the Metropolitan. Rooms are sweet, well appointed and comfortably plush. It features Japanese and Chinese restaurants, a Sky Lounge, a gym, an indoor pool and even a wedding chapel, presumably for those who strike it lucky during their stay.

Sendai Kokusai Hotel (Map p510; ☎ 268-1112; www .tobu-skh.co.jp/english/english.htm; 4-6-1 Chūō, Aoba-ku; s/d from ¥13,282/20,790; 💻) The Kokusai is a classy option, with a sumptuous baroque dining area, and large rooms done up in brown and cream tones.

NORTHERN HONSHŪ

Eating

JAPANESE

Gyūtan (cow tongue) is much loved by Sendai locals. Apparently the tradition derived from hard times (as so many Tōhoku traditions do) – in the immediate postwar years meat was scarce, so cow tongue was served instead of being thrown out. Expect deep queues and no English at the following first two places.

Umami Tasuke (Map p510; ☎ 262-2539; 1st fl, Sen chimatsushima Bldg, 2-11-11 Kokubunchō, Aoba-ku; gyūtan from ¥1260; 🕑 11.30am-10pm Tue-Sun; E) Serves excellent *gyūtan* in salted (*shioyaki*; ¥1260) and fatty variants.

Aji Tasuke (Map p510; ☎ 225-4641; 4-4-13 Ichiban-chō, Aoba-ku; gyūtan from ¥900; lunch sets from ¥1350; 🕑 lunch & dinner Wed-Mon) Try *gyūtan* cooked over charcoal (¥900), or the set menu (*teishoku*; ¥1400) featuring the famous dish accompanied by oxtail soup and rice with boiled barley. It's right next to the small *torii* shrine gate.

Yabuya Honten (Map p508; ☎ 222-5002; 2-2-24 Ōmachi, Aoba-ku; mains from ¥900; 🕑 11.30-6pm Mon-Sat) A much-loved *soba* (buckwheat noodles) specialist, Yabuya Honten has been around since 1847 – more than enough time to perfect its craft. The *kamo-zaru soba* variation, served with duck, is terrific.

Umai Sushikan (Map p510; ☎ 268-1822; 4-5-6 Ichiban-chō; sets from ¥840; 🕑 11.30am-11pm) This popular restaurant, spotlessly clean and featuring lots of natural wood and friendly smiles, is known for the freshness of its dishes.

INTERNATIONAL

Namaskar (Map p510; ☎ 222-7701; Basement, TK Bldg, 2-2-11 Ichiban-chō, Aoba-ku; lunch set from ¥1200; 🕑 lunch & dinner; E) The menu, with its spice-level warnings, has the usual suspects: tandoori chicken, chicken tikka, tandoori king prawns, prawn masala. It's all good stuff, though, and the portions are generous. Beware: the large video screen showing continuous, loud music videos is highly distracting.

There's a clutch of restaurants, covering the gamut of price ranges, at the top of SS30, Sendai's second-tallest building (with 30 storeys, as opposed to AER's 31).

Drinking

The Kokubunchō area is Northern Tōhoku's largest entertainment district, as noisy and as bright as you might expect, with endless rabbit warrens jammed with hole-in-the-wall bars and clubs.

Simon's Bar (Map p510; ☎ 223-8840; 1st fl, Daishin Bldg, 2-9-1 Kokubunchō) This cosy little stand-up bar, with its talismanic name, glass bar and memorabilia, has a lively crowd of Japanese, the occasional foreigner, and a good selection of beers and cocktails. Take the first left after Club Shaft, heading towards Jōzenji-dōri.

Vilevan (Map p510; ☎ 225-2222; 3rd fl, Sunsquare-Shōji Bldg, 1-8-22 Chūō, Aoba-ku; 🕑 5pm-1am Mon-Thu, to 2am Fri & Sat, 9am-midnight Sun) A mellow jazz bar, well versed in the history of the genre: it was originally called the Village Vanguard, until the famous New York bar of that name 'suggested' it reconsider. There's live music on Saturday nights and decent vegetarian food.

Trad Bar Esprit (Map p510; ☎ 214-3880; 1BF 2-1-3 Kokubun-chō, Aoba-ku; 🕑 6pm-midnight Sun-Thu, to 1am Fri & Sat; E) A popular trend in Japan is the 'olde tyme bar', with loads of wood panelling, photos of leathery jazz men on the walls and bar staff done up like characters from *The Sting*. Esprit is one such place, and its *faux* nostalgia is an easy respite from Kokubunchō madness.

Entertainment

Kokubunchō is Sendai's maze of seedy clubs, strip shows and hostess bars, and as such it doesn't offer much for foreigners. Try asking at the tourist info centre for new Sendai venues, as they frequently change.

Club Shaft (Map p510; ☎ 722-5651; www.clubshaft .com; 4th fl, Yoshiokaya Dai 3 Bldg, Kokubunchō, Aoba-ku) This one's a sports bar during the week, with a high-fibre diet of European soccer and American baseball. On the weekends it's a dance club with house, breaks and hip-hop, as well as 'waving-your-arms-in-the-air-like-you-just-don't-care' retro Manchester nights.

Getting There & Away

AIR

From Sendai airport, 18km south of the city centre, there are international flights to various destinations in Asia, such as Seoul, Beijing, Dailan, Guam and Shanghai. Domestic destinations include Sapporo, Nagoya and Hiroshima. From Tokyo, the *shinkansen* is so fast that it's not worth flying. Taipei and Changchun routes are also available, as are domestic routes: Hakodate, Komatsu, Tokyo, Osaka, Kobe, Fukuoka and Okinawa.

BOAT

Sendai-kō is a major port with ferries once daily to Tomakomai on Hokkaidō (¥7300,

14¾ hours); ferries depart at noon every second day for Nagoya (¥6100, 21 hours). To get to Sendai-kō, take a *futsū* (local) train on the JR Senseki line to Tagajō station (¥230); it's then a 10-minute taxi ride. There are also five direct buses from stop 34 at Sendai station, but only until 6pm (¥490, 40 minutes).

BUS

From stop 42 outside the station's east exit, there are five buses daily to Shinjuku (¥6210, 5½ hours) and Niigata (¥4500, four hours).

From stop 41, north of the station, buses run daily via stop 22 to Tokyo (¥6210, 5¾ hours) at 8am, 11am, 11.40pm and 11.55pm. From stop 40 across the street, night buses to Kyoto/Osaka depart at 7.30pm (¥11,930/12,230, 11 hours), as well as day buses to Morioka (¥2850, 2¾ hours), Akita (¥4000, 3¾ hours) and Aomori (¥5700, five hours).

TRAIN

From Sendai, the JR Tōhoku *shinkansen* line runs south to Tokyo (¥10,390, 1¾ hours) and north to Morioka (¥6090, 45 minutes) for transfers to the Akita *shinkansen* line. Sendai is connected by the JR Senzan line to Yamagata (*kaisoku* ¥1110, 1½ hours) and by the JR Senseki line to Matsushima-kaigan (*kaisoku* ¥400, 34 minutes).

Getting Around

Airport limousines (single/return ¥910/1640, 40 minutes) from stop 15-2 at the station's west bus pool depart frequently for the airport between 6.25am and 6.40pm.

The Loople tourist trolley leaves from the west bus pool's stop 15-3 every 30 minutes from 9am to 4pm, making a useful sightseeing loop around the city (¥250 per ride) in a clockwise direction. A one-day pass costs ¥600 and comes with an English-language booklet detailing the bus route and sightseeing discounts for pass holders. Passes can be purchased from the bus ticket office by stop 15.3.

Sendai's single subway line runs from Izumi-Chūō in the north to Tomizawa in the south but doesn't cover any tourist attractions; single tickets cost ¥200 to ¥350.

AKIU ONSEN 秋保温泉

☎ 022 / pop 5000

Considered one of the three most famous hot springs in Japan, Akiu Onsen was the Date clan's favourite, with a saltwater spring that's said to be a curative for back pain and arthritis. It's also a good base for side trips into the mountains to see **Akiu Ōtaki** (秋保大滝), a 6m-wide, 55m-high waterfall, which is itself designated as one of Japan's three most famous waterfalls (Japanese do love those famous sets of three!). Akiu Onsen is also handy for access to the gorge, **Futakuchi-kyō** (二口渓), with its *banji-iwa* (rock columns). There are hiking trails along the river valley and a trail from Futakuchi Onsen to the summit of **Daitō-dake** (1366m) that takes about three hours.

Hiking maps are available at Akiu Onsen's **tourist information office** (☎ 398-2323; ⏰ 9.30am-6pm). The staff can also advise on the hotels, *minshuku* and camping grounds that are scattered throughout the area, though the *onsen* itself is an easy day trip out of Sendai.

Getting There & Away

Buses leave frequently from stop 8 at Sendai station's west bus pool for Akiu Onsen (¥780, 50 minutes), but only a few continue to Akiu Ōtaki (¥1070, 1½ hours).

MATSUSHIMA & OKU-MATSUSHIMA

松島・奥松島

☎ 022 / pop 19,400

It's easy to see why Bashō was so taken by Matsushima Bay, for it features around 250 islands covered in pines that have been shaped by wind, as well as rock formations that have been misshapen by the ceaseless slapping of waves, resulting in spectacular monuments to natural forces. This conglomeration is one of Japan's Nihon Sankei (Three Great Sights) – the other two are the floating torii (shrine gates) of Miyajima island and the sand-spit at Amanohashidate. As a result of that distinguished reputation, it's heavily touristed, but undeniably picturesque with peculiar charm. Masamune Date was so smitten with one of the rock formations that he offered a reward to anyone who could deliver it to castle headquarters. No one could.

Weekends can be trying in Matsushima, when packed crowds undercut the reflective serenity that so entranced Bashō. On the eastern curve of the bay, Oku-Matsushima is less touristed and offers several trails for exploration by bicycle or on foot. Even the train ride is pretty, affording nice glimpses of the ocean, the isles, boats and birds.

Orientation & Information

There's a Matsushima station, but Matsushima-kaigan is the one you want – it's closer to the main sights.

Outside, the **tourist information office** (☎ 354-2618; ⏰ 8.30am-5pm Apr-Nov, to 4.30pm Dec-Mar) provides maps. Luggage storage is available next door for ¥300 per day. Inside Oku-Matsushima's Nobiru station, the **tourist information office** (☎ 0225-88-2611; ⏰ 9am-6pm) has a few bicycles for rent. From Nobiru you can cycle the 5km to Otakamori, where a 20-minute climb up the hill is rewarded with a fine panorama of the bay.

Sights

MATSUSHIMA

Zuigan-ji (admission ¥700; ⏰ 8am-3.30pm Jan & Dec, to 4pm Feb & Nov, to 4.30pm Mar & Oct, to 5pm Apr-Sep), one of Tōhoku's finest Zen temples, was founded in 828. The present buildings were constructed in 1606 by Date Masamune to serve as a family temple. Look out for the painted screens and interior carvings of the main hall, in the Momoyama style, and the **Seiryū-den** (青龍殿; Treasure Hall) displaying works of art associated with the Date family. The temple is accessed via an avenue lined with tall cedars, with weathered Buddhas and altars to the sides – a frequently spooky, deeply contemplative approach.

The interior of **Godai-dō**, a small wooden temple, opens to the public just once every 33 years. You missed the viewing in 2006, so make do with the sea view and the 12 animals of the Chinese zodiac carved in to the eaves, then come back in 2039.

The **Kanran-tei** (admission ¥200; ⏰ 8.30am-5pm Apr-Oct, to 4.30pm Nov-Mar) pavilion was presented to the Date family by Toyotomi Hideyoshi in the late 16th century. It served as a genteel venue for tea ceremonies and moon viewing – the name means 'a place to view ripples on the water'. Today *matcha* (powdered green tea) is served here, and the garden includes the **Matsushima Hakubutsukan**, a small museum housing a collection of relics from the Date family.

Fukuura-jima (福浦島; admission ¥200; ⏰ 8am-5pm Mar-Oct, to 4.30pm Nov-Feb), an island connected to the mainland by a 252m-long, red wooden bridge, makes for a leisurely half-hour walk around its botanic gardens.

Ojima (雄島) is also connected by bridge to the mainland. It was once a monks retreat and

is renowned for its Buddhist rock carvings, statues, meditation caves and relics.

OKU-MATSUSHIMA

Natural beauty is the order of the day here. **Sagakei** (嵯峨渓) is a 40m-high scenic canyon overhanging the Pacific Ocean, notable for its crashing waves; **Ōtakamori** (大高森) is a small hill in the middle of Miyato Island offering a terrific panorama, including Mt Zaō and Kinkasan; and **Nobiru Beach** (野蒜海岸) is a swimming beach popular with day-trippers from Sendai. Look twice before diving in, however – there's a lot of trash strewn about.

Festivals & Events

Matsushima Kaki Matsuri (松島牡蠣祭り; Matsushima Oyster Festival) Bivalve aficionados will appreciate this festival held the first weekend in February, where you can purchase oysters and cook them on a 100m-long grill.

Zuigan-ji Tōdō The approach to Zuigan-ji is enhanced from 6 to 8 August, when candlesticks are lit along the path for the event.

Matsushima Tōrō Nagashi Hanabi Taikai On 17 August; honours the souls of the departed with the O-Bon (Festival of the Dead) ritual, when lighted lanterns are floated out to sea accompanied by an extensive fireworks display.

Sleeping

MATSUSHIMA

Hotel Daimatsusō (☎ 354-3601; fax 354-6154; www.daimatsuso.co.jp in Japanese; 25 Matsushima; per person incl 2 meals from ¥8400) Just steps away from the station (to the left as you exit, at the end of the parking lot), with welcoming potted plants to greet you. Not as posh as some places, but clean and convenient, and the upper floors have nice views.

Matsushima Century Hotel (☎ 354-4111; www.centuryhotel.co.jp in Japanese; 8 Aza-Senzui; tw from ¥12,700; 🖥) Near the sights, with nice interiors, a pool and sauna. It has Western- and Japanese-style rooms, and rates depend on whether you take a room with a view of the car park or the sea.

OKU-MATSUSHIMA

Pila Matsushima Okumatsushima Youth Hostel (Map p507; ☎ 0225-88-2220; 89-48 Minami-Akazaki, Nobiru, Matsushima; dm from ¥4305) In a lovely pine-clad location just near the beach at Oku-Matsushima. There's bike rental (¥800 per day) and the staff can advise on the best way to tackle hiking trails. To get to the hostel from Nobiru station, walk across the bridge and towards the ocean

MATSUSHIMA

0	200 m
0	0.1 miles

INFORMATION
Tourist Information Office
松島海岸駅前観光案内所...**1** A4

SIGHTS & ACTIVITIES
Godai-dō 五大堂...**2** A3
Kanran-tei 観瀾亭...**3** A3
Zuigan-ji 瑞巌寺...**4** A3

SLEEPING
Hotel Daimatsusō
ホテル大松荘...**5** A4
Matsushima Century Hotel
松島センチュリーホテル...**6** B3
Ryokan Sakuragawa 旅館 桜川...**7** B2

EATING
Santori Chaya さんとり茶屋...**8** A3

To Oku-Matsushima;
Sagakei; Nobiru
Beach (11km);
Ōtakamori; Pila
Matsushima
Okumatsushima
Youth Hostel
(11km);
Ishinomaki
(16km)

Takagimachi

Tōhoku Main Line

JR Senseki Line

To Bistro
Abalon
(400m)

Fukuura-
bashi

Matsushima-
Kaigan

Matsushima-wan

Fukuura-jima

Ōjima

To Sendai
(23km)

for about 15 minutes until you reach an intersection with a blue youth-hostel sign pointing down the road to the right. From there it's about 800m. Staff at the tourist information office can give you a map with directions. A bird-watching blind on the bike trail makes a perfect peek (or photo) that much easier.

Eating

Matsushima has an unimpeachable reputation among oyster lovers. Neither listed option has an English menu.

Santori Chaya (☎ 353-2622; dinner mains ¥1500-2500; ☺ lunch & dinner Thu-Tue, closed 2nd & 4th Wed of month) A small, intimate, Japanese-style eatery favoured by locals. It's great for fried oysters (*kaki yaki*) or *sanma sashimi* (raw saury) in season. If you're feeling adventurous, ask for the *osusume* (chef's suggestion). From Matsushima-Kaigan station, go left out of the parking lot and follow the main road to the third set of lights. You'll find Santori Chaya on the left side of the big parking lot.

Bistro Abalon (びすとろアバロン; ☎ 354-5777; 26-21 Sanjūgari Matsushima; lunch/dinner from ¥1200/2630; ☺ lunch & dinner Thu-Tue) Concentrates on French-style dishes like oyster *gratin*.

Getting There & Around

The most convenient route to Matsushima-kaigan is from Sendai via the JR Senseki line (*kaisoku* ¥400, 34 minutes). Alternatively, boat trips (¥1420, 50 minutes) to Matsushima, along the celebrated coastline, depart from Shiogama Pier every 30 minutes between 9.30am and 3pm from 21 April to November, and hourly the rest of the year. Get off the train two stops before Matsushima Kaigan at Hon-Shiogama (¥320, 28 minutes). The harbour is 10 minutes on foot from Hon-Shiogama station – turn right as you exit.

Otherwise there are loop cruises from Matsushima through the pine-covered islets (¥1420, 50 minutes) between 9.30am and 3pm, but these can be overrun with sightseers.

To reach Oku-Matsushima from Matsushima-kaigan station, take the JR Senseki line six stations east (two stops by *kaisoku*) to Nobiru (¥230).

The sights are eminently walkable. Bike rental is available at the tourist information office inside Oku-Matsushima's Nobiru station, but the crowds and narrow sidewalks make cycling laborious.

ISHINOMAKI 石巻
☎ 0225 / pop 165,800

Manga-maniacs should be sure to put Ishinomaki on their Go To list. Ishinomaki is littered with tributes to cartoonist Shōtarō Ishinomori, a local hero who created some of Japan's best-loved manga characters, but aside from that and its use as a launching pad for Kinkasan, there isn't much else for the traveller. An unpretentious port city ringed by scenic mountains, it sits at the mouth of the Kitakami, Northern Honshū's largest river. This location has ensured its status as a major northeastern channel of commerce since the Edo era. The **tourist information office** (☎ 93-6448; ☺ 9am-5.30pm) is just outside the station, and has combo bus-and-ferry timetables for the

Kinkasan bound, as well as info about Ishinomaki (some in English) and a manga-themed map. With Sendai only an hour away there's no compelling reason to stay here.

Sights

The spaceship-style **Ishinomaki Mangattan Museum** (石ノ森萬画館; ☎ 96-5055; 2-7 Nakase; admission 2nd floor ¥800, 1st & 3rd fl free; ☽ 9am-6pm Mar-Nov, to 5pm, Wed-Mon Dec-Feb, closed 3rd Tue Mar-Nov) is mostly devoted to Shōtarō Ishinomori's work and will appeal most to folks already familiar with the comics Cyborg 009, one of Ishinomori's many cartoon creations.

Old Ishinomaki Orthodox Church (旧石巻ハリストス正教会教会堂; ☎ 95-1111; 3-18 Nakase; admission free; ☽ 9am-5pm Apr-Oct, to 4pm Mon-Fri Nov-Mar) is Japan's oldest wooden church (dating from 1880, but no longer in use). Advance reservation (by phone) is mandatory.

An impressive replica of the galleon **San Juan Bautista** (宮城県慶長使節船ミュージアム; ☎ 24-2210; ww51.et.tiki.ne.jp/~santjuan in Japanese; 30-2 Ōmori Watanoha; adult ¥700; ☽ 9.30am-4.30pm Wed-Mon) is near the wharf. The San Juan is a monument to Date Masamune's forward-thinking rule; with an envoy of 20, it sailed to Rome as Japan's first diplomatic mission (see the boxed text, p509).

Getting There & Around

From Sendai, the JR Senseki line runs to Ishinomaki (*kaisoku* ¥820, one hour and 24 minutes) via Matsushima-kaigan and Nobiru.

From bus stop 2 outside Ishinomaki station, seven buses run daily to Ayukawa between 7am and 6pm (¥1460, 1½ hours). It's a wonderfully scenic trip.

Rental bikes (per two hours ¥500), available right outside the station, make a great way to see the town, even though most of the sights are within walking distance.

KINKASAN 金華山

☎ 0225 / pop 32

Also known as Golden Mountain, Kinkasan is considered one of the three holiest places in Tōhoku, along with Dewa Sanzan (p549) and Osore-san (p533). Its spiritual significance and the fact that it used to be a site for gold prospecting ensure a steady stream of visitors eager for some good fortune to rub off. It's said that if you pay a visit three years running to Kinkasan's impressive shrine, you can kiss your money worries goodbye for the rest of your life. Women were banned on Kinkasan until the late 19th century, but today, for both sexes, an overnight stay is ideal for those seeking tranquillity.

Along with its shrine, the island features the pyramid-shaped Mt Kinka (445m), a handful of houses around the dock, cheeky deer and monkeys, mostly untended trails, a few leeches and the odd snake. Most visitors to Kinkasan seem to be day-trippers, which means the island is delightfully deserted in the early morning and late afternoon.

Information

There's no tourist information, no internet and no convenience store on Kinkasan. Before you leave, check in at the Ishinomaki tourist information office, which has Kinkasan information plus timetables for getting to Ayukawa and from there to Kinkasan. Ayukawa is no longer its own town (it merged with Ishinomaki), but there's a small **Oshika tourist information office** (☎ 0225-45-3456; ☽ 8.30am-5pm).

Sights

Before setting out on foot, take heed: locals advise that it's no longer possible to hike around Kinkasan's northern side because of a landslip; only the southern side is considered safe. If you get lost, head south and downhill towards the sea. The dirt trail that once circled the entire island (24km) along the shore is no longer safe at the northern edge.

Turning left from the boat dock, it's a steep 20-minute walk uphill to **Koganeyama-jinja** (黄金山神社), built in 794 by Emperor Shōmu as thanks for finding the gold used to finish the Great Buddha at Nara's Tōdai-ji.

From Koganeyama-jinja it's a 50-minute hike downhill to **Senjōjiki** (千畳敷; 1000 Tatami Mats Rock), a large formation of white rock on the eastern shore of the island, and a further hour to the lighthouse propping up the southeast corner. It takes roughly 1½ hours to follow the dirt trail along the shore and cross back over the summit to the dock area.

Festivals & Events

Ryūjin Matsuri (龍神祭り; Dragon Festival) On the last weekend in July; features giant dragon floats supported by up to 50 dancers.

Antler-cutting ceremony On the first and second Sunday in October, this tradition is meant to stop the deer from injuring each other during mating season.

Sleeping & Eating

Koganeyama-jinja (黄金山神社; ☎ 45-2264; kinkasan@cocoa.ocn.ne.jp; r per person ¥9000) On the shrine grounds, this offers basic temple lodgings with two meals. If you're awake before 6am, you can attend morning prayers. Advance reservations by phone or email are mandatory.

Minshuku Shiokaze (民宿 潮風; ☎ day/evening 45-2666/2244; r per person ¥6300) This friendly *minshuku* is 500m south along the headland from the pier. Expect simple but airy rooms, great food and panoramic views out to sea. The owners can also advise on the safest hiking routes. You must book well in advance, though, as the owners actually live in Ayukawa and only come out to Kinkasan if there are customers.

Another option is to stay overnight in Ishinomaki or Ayukawa. **Minami-sō** (みなみ荘; ☎ 45-2501; r per person incl/excl 2 meals from ¥6300/4200; 🖳), behind the Ayukawa bus station, is a friendly *minshuku*.

Getting There & Away

From Ishinomaki, seven buses run daily to Ayukawa.

During summer ferries leave from Ayukawa pier – opposite the bus station – for Kinkasan almost hourly between 8.30am and 3.45pm (one way ¥900, 25 minutes); the last return ferry is at 4pm. Service is greatly reduced the rest of the year. Reservations (☎ 53-3121) are required at peak times.

There are three high-speed catamarans daily between Kinkasan and Onagawa, the eastern gateway to the peninsula, from April to early November (one way ¥1600, 25 minutes). The last departure from Onagawa is at 12.10pm. Some of the boats have open-air fantail decks, which make for a pleasant ride. Onagawa is also the terminus for the JR Ishinomaki line, 30 minutes from JR Ishinomaki station (¥320). From Onagawa station walk straight to the waterfront, turn right and walk about 200m to the pier. The ferry ticket office is down a side street opposite the pier, little more than a hole in the wall on the right-hand side.

NARUKO ONSEN 鳴子温泉

☎ 0229 / pop 8570

Come to Naruko Onsen to hear the clip-clop of *geta* (Japanese clogs) as *yukata*-clad (Japanese robe) bathers trot from bath to bath. Stop in a shop window and see an artisan make a *kokeshi* doll (spindle-shaped dolls, often brightly coloured, with round heads) or purchase pottery or lacquerware. Breathe in and smell the sulphurous steam as it rises from street culverts, or stop and soak tired feet in the (free!) *ashiyu* (foot baths). Naruko's charms are quiet, simple and rejuvenating. Like all *onsen*, these waters are said to possess distinct healing qualities. Naruko has a high sulphur count, as well as sodium chloride and sodium bicarbonate, thought to be a relief for the symptoms of high blood pressure and hardened arteries.

The helpful **tourist information office** (☎ 83-3441; www.naruko.gr.jp; 🕙 8.30am-6pm), inside JR Naruko Onsen station, has useful English-language maps and brochures and can also help book your accommodation. It's a dense town; you can easily walk from one end to the other in 25 minutes.

Naruko-kyō (鳴子峡), a scenic, 100m-deep gorge, can be reached in 20 minutes (Bashō time, that is) on foot from Naruko Onsen station. Alternatively, buses (¥200, seven minutes) run from 8.50am to 4pm. From the gorge entrance, a pleasant 4km trail leads along the river valley to Nakayama-daira. If you turn right just after the bridge, but before reaching the gorge, you'll find the historical Shitomae checkpoint, the start of a quiet 5km country path along the route Bashō once walked. The last bus back to the station leaves at 4.29pm.

Taki-no-yu (滝の湯; admission ¥150; 🕙 7.30am-10pm) is a sheer delight – a fabulously atmospheric wooden bathhouse that's hardly changed in 150 years. Water gushes in from *hinoki* (Japanese cypress) channels. Bring your own towel.

The **Japan Kokeshi Museum** (日本こけし館; ☎ 83-3600; admission ¥320; 🕙 8.30am-5pm Apr-Nov, 9am-4pm Dec) features around 5000 *kokeshi* dolls from around the country. During the Meiji era the Tōhoku region was almost totally neglected, with the result that a flood of men and women moved south to find work. Some say that *kokeshi* dolls were symbolic representations of those lost girls, who were often snatched away at a young age.

Ryokan Suimei-sō (旅館水明荘; ☎ 83-2114; r for up to 2 people incl 2 meals ¥8000, each additional person ¥1000; 🖳) has clean rooms. Walking northwest from the station, it's five minutes down the main street on the left before the railway tracks. Functional but far from fancy, the **Ko-kumin Shukusha Ryokan Takishima** (国民宿舎ホ テル瀧嶋; ☎ 83-3054; 2801 Shinyashiki; r per person incl/excl 2 meals from ¥6650/4150) is across the train tracks, about 10 minutes from the station. If you don't feel like walking elsewhere, go for a skin-scaldingly hot dip in its own basement *onsen*.

Getting There & Away

From JR Sendai station, take the JR Tōhoku *shinkansen* to Furukawa (¥2840, 15 minutes) then transfer to the JR Rikuu-tōsen line for Naruko Onsen (¥650, 45 minutes). Naruko Onsen has infrequent connections to Shinjō (¥950, one hour) for transfers to the Yamagata *shinkansen* line or local trains west to Sakata (¥950, one hour) and Tsuruoka (¥1110, one hour).

IWATE-KEN 岩手県

Iwate-ken is a quiet place with rich farmland, sleepy valleys and some pretty serious mountain ranges, too. You'll find it feels more provincial – in the best of ways, and stopping in places like Tōno can seem almost like turning back time. Once rife with feudalism, the region was separated into north, controlled by the Nambu clan, and south, under the rule of the Date clan. Later, breakaway clans – Hachinohe (from Nambu) and Ichinohe (from Date) – divided Iwate further. During WWII, the prefecture was devastated and immediately embarked on a rehabilitation process marked by heavy industrial growth. Iwate-ken is the country's second-largest prefecture.

HIRAIZUMI 平泉

☎ 0191 / pop 8750

Stop here to see some pretty amazing temples and wish that more remained – Hiraizumi's grandeur once rivalled Kyoto's, and the tale of its ruin is one of the most bittersweet sagas in Tōhoku's history. Yet you'd hardly know it from the present looks of this quiet, rural town. From 1089 to 1189, three generations of the Fujiwara family, headed by Fujiwara Kiyohira, created a political and cultural centre in Hiraizumi. Kiyohira had made his fortune from local gold mines and, at the behest of Kyoto priests, he used his wealth and power to commence work on the creation of a 'paradise on earth', devoted to the principles of Buddhist thought

as a reaction against the feudal wars that were plaguing the land. His son and grandson continued along this path. However, Kiyohira's great-grandson, Yoshihira, yielding to both internal and external pressures, brought this short century of fame and prosperity to an end (see the boxed text, p521). Today only a few sights bear testament to Hiraizumi's glory, but they represent a singular experience and are well worth your time.

Information

Turning right outside Hiraizumi station, the **tourist information office** (☎ 46-2110; h-kankou@khaki .plala.or.jp; ☽ 8.30am-5pm) has English-language pamphlets. The post office, with an international ATM, is 400m northwest of the station heading towards Mōtsū-ji. Free internet access is available at the public library (open 9am to 5pm Tuesday to Sunday), 1500m southwest of the station.

Sights & Activities

CHŪSON-JI 中尊寺

This **temple complex** (☎ 46-2211; admission incl Kon-jiki-dō, Sankōzō & Kyōzō ¥800; ☽ 8am-5pm Apr-Oct, 8.30am-4.30pm Nov-Mar) was established in 850 by the priest Ennin, who was responsible for many of Tōhoku's most famous temples. However, it was Fujiwara Kiyohira who decided in the early 12th century to expand the complex into a site with around 300 buildings, including 40 temples. Ironically, in the face of the grand scheme to build a Buddhist utopia, Hiraizumi was never far from tragedy: a massive fire here in 1337 destroyed most of the buildings, although two of the original constructions remain alongside the newer temples. The site is accessed via a steep approach along a tree-lined avenue. Take your time: the views over the valley, intermingled with Jizō monuments scattered among the greenery, make this an absorbing route.

The approach snakes past the **Hon-dō** (Main Hall) to an enclosed area featuring the splendid **Konjiki-dō** (金色堂; Golden Hall; ☽ 8am-4.30pm Apr-Oct, 8.30am-4pm Nov-Mar). Built in 1124, Konjiki-dō is quite a sight, packed with gold detailing, black lacquerwork and inlaid mother-of-pearl (the region was known for its gold and lacquer resources). The centrepiece of the hall is the fabulously ornate statue of the Amida Buddha, along with attendants. Beneath the three side altars are the mummified remains of three generations of the Fujiwara family.

Beside the Konjiki-dō, the temple treasury, **Sankōzō**, contains the coffins and funeral finery of the Fujiwara clan – scrolls, swords and images transferred from long-vanished halls and temples. The sutra treasury **Kyōzō**, built in 1108, is the oldest structure in the complex. The original collection of more than 5000 sutras was damaged by fire and the remains have been transferred to the Sankōzō.

MŌTSŪ-JI 毛越寺
Dating from 850, **Mōtsū-ji** (☎ 46-2331; admission ¥500; ⏰ 8.30am-5pm Apr-Oct, to 4.30pm Nov-Mar) once surpassed Chūson-ji as Tōhoku's largest temple complex; it, too, was established by Ennin. Now the temples are long gone and only the beautiful gardens remain, a so-called Pure Land

garden from the Heian era, designed with the Buddhist notion of preserving 'paradise' in mind – it's as peaceful as that implies. The perimeter of the large pond is a popular walk, and along with the rambling greenery may very well make you pause for reflection in the face of Hiraizumi's history. Keep an eye out for emerald green kingfishers (*kawasemi*), which often perch on the rocks or overhanging tree branches. In season (spring and summer), the lotus and iris both have spectacular blooms.

TAKKOKU-NO-IWAYA BISHAMON-DŌ 達谷窟毘沙門堂
Five kilometres southwest of Mōtsū-ji, **Takkoku-no-Iwaya Bishamon-dō** (☎ 46-4931; admission ¥300; ⏰ 8am-5pm, varies per season) is a cave temple,

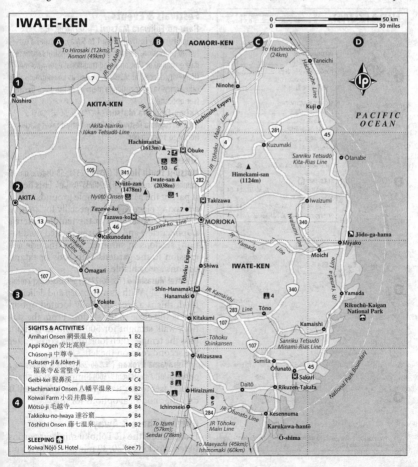

IWATE-KEN

small but very picturesque, dedicated to the deity Bishamon (the Buddhist guardian of warriors) by the famous general Sakanoue no Tamuramaro. It was built in 801 after Sakanoue's victory against the Ezo, the original inhabitants of Northern Honshū; the present structure is a 1961 replica. You can cycle to the cave along a paved path from Mōtsū-ji in about 30 minutes, longer if you stop to snap a picture or two of the stunning rice fields you'll pass along the way.

TAKADACHI GIKEI-DŌ 高館義経堂
A small memorial honouring Minamoto Yoshitsune, **Takadachi Gikei-dō** (☎ 46-3300; admission ¥200; ⏰ 8.30am-5pm Apr-Oct, to 4.30pm Nov-Mar) includes a monument inscribed with Bashō's

'summer grass' lament (see the boxed text, p502). The hall is at the top of a small hill with fine views of the Kitakami-gawa. It's 700m from the entrance to Chūson-ji.

GEIBI-KEI 猊鼻渓
A huge natural gorge, **Geibi-kei** features sheer 100m-high cliffs. Singing boatmen on flat-bottomed **boats** (☎ 47-2341; per 90min ¥1500; ⏰ 8.30am-4.30pm Apr-Oct, 9am-3pm Nov-Mar, varies per season) regale passengers with local folk songs that echo along the cliffs. Take the bus from stop 7 outside Ichinoseki station (¥620, 40 minutes, hourly) or the train from Ichinoseki to Geibi-kei station on the JR Ōfunato line (*kaisoku* ¥480, 25 minutes). Ask at the tourist info booth if a discount is available.

Festivals & Events
Haru-no-Fujiwara Matsuri (春の藤原まつり; Spring Fujiwara Festival) From 1 to 5 May; features a costumed procession, performances of *nō* (classical Japanese dance-drama) at Chūson-ji and traditional *ennen-no-mai* (longevity dances) at Mōtsū-ji, as well as an enormous rice cake–carrying competition in memory of the giant Benkei (see opposite).
Aki-no-Fujiwara Matsuri (秋の藤原まつり; Autumn Fujiwara Festival) A similar festival takes place from 1 to 3 November.

Sleeping
Mōtsū-ji Youth Hostel (☎ 46-2331; 58 Ōsawa; dm HI members/nonmembers from ¥2940/3570; 💻) This hostel is part of the Mōtsū-ji temple grounds and is a relaxing place to stay, especially for anyone wanting a closer look at the temple. There's a 9pm curfew and free *zazen* (seated meditation) sessions in summer. Rates include admission to the garden. Both beds or tatami options are available.

Hotel Musashibō (☎ 46-2241; r per person incl 2 meals from ¥8000; 💻) With its own *onsen* and delicious food, this is a nice, centrally located option that is still close to the station. From the station, walk straight for 500m and turn right, pass the temple, then look on the corner after the second road on the left.

Shirayama Ryokan (☎ 46-2883; 139-8 Shirayama; r per person incl 2 meals from ¥7500) Simple option that's even closer to the station. Ask in advance if it can offer nonmeal options for less.

Getting There & Away
From Sendai the JR Tōhoku *shinkansen* runs to Ichinoseki (¥3720, 32 minutes), where you

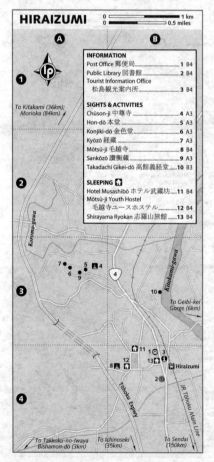

HIRAIZUMI

0 ——— 1 km
0 ——— 0.5 miles

To Kitakami (36km);
Morioka (84km)

To Geibi-kei
Gorge (6km)

To Takkoku-no-Iwaya
Bishamon-dō (3km)

To Ichinoseki
(35km)

To Sendai
(150km)

HIRAIZUMI: A 'BRIEF REMEMBERED DREAM' (BASHŌ)

The dashing warrior Minamoto Yoshitsune grew up with, and trained under, the Fujiwara clan, but left Hiraizumi to fight with his half-brother Minamoto Yoritomo, the great warlord who founded the *shōgunate*, Japan's system of feudal government. Yoritomo was troubled by the Fujiwaras' growing power, eventually ordering his brother's death. Yoshitsune and his loyal retainer, the giant Benkei, disguised themselves as *yamabushi* (mountain priests) and returned to Hiraizumi, where they were taken in by the Fujiwaras...only to be betrayed by Fujiwara Hidehira's son, Yoshihira. Seeing no escape, Yoshitsune killed his family and then committed *seppuku* (ritual suicide by disembowelment). Benkei, so the story goes, defended his master to the very end, remaining standing and blocking the doorway even as his body was 'porcupined' with many arrows, an iconic image that will be familiar to anyone who's seen Akira Kurosawa's films. Yoritomo then ordered the Fujiwara clan to be wiped out and the temples of Hiraizumi to be destroyed – a tragic end to one of the most remarkable periods of the feudal era. There's a twist in the finale: according to local legend, the bodies of Benkei and Yoshitsune were actually those of their doubles. The real duo are said to have fled to Mongolia, where Yoshitsune became...Ghengis Khan.

can either take a bus via Hiraizumi station to Chūson-ji (¥350, 22 minutes) or a local train on the JR Tōhoku Main line (*futsū*, ¥190, eight minutes) to Hiraizumi.

Ichinoseki is connected to Morioka by the JR Tōhoku *shinkansen* (¥3720, 38 minutes) and the JR Tōhoku Main line (*futsū*, ¥1620, 94 minutes).

Getting Around

Frequent buses from Ichinoseki run to Hiraizumi station and on to Chūson-ji (¥310, 18 minutes). **Bicycle rental** (per day ¥1000; 9am-4pm Apr-Nov) is available next to Hiraizumi station.

TŌNO VALLEY 遠野
☎ 0198 / pop 30,980

Tōno is a sleepy little town set amid a dramatic valley region, surrounded by rice fields and mountains that harbour a fair population of wild bears. It's an area that will appeal to those with vivid imaginations and those keen on country air, and it is the birthplace of superstitions and tales that run the gamut from odd to the wildly wacky. The town was also the site of some devastating famines due to poor harvests; much of the lore has a food-prosperity theme.

The present city was formed by the merging of eight villages and much of that rural flavour is preserved today: there are still some examples of the local architectural style of L-shaped farmhouses, known as *magariya*, where farmfolk and their prized horses lived under one roof, albeit in different sections (unlike the fertility goddess, Oshira-sama; see the boxed text, p523). Tōno is the heartland of

some of Japan's most cherished folk legends, including the mischievous *kappa* water spirits, whose likenesses are found everywhere. Even if you don't see spirits, you'll see *kappa*-sized pumpkins, loofah squashes the length of baseball bats and horses that could contend with the Budweiser Clydesdales.

Information

Cho BORA (☎ 63-3535; 5-31 Chūō-dōri; 9:30am-6pm Mon-Sat) There's free internet here.

Tōno City Library (☎ 62-2340; 9am-5pm Tue-Sun) There's also free internet access here, downstairs from the Tōno Municipal Museum.

Tōno post office (遠野郵便局; ☎ 62-2830; 6-10 Chūō-dōri) Ten minutes' walk southeast of the Tōno train station.

Tourist information office (☎ 62-1333; 8am-6pm Apr-Oct, 8.30am-5.30pm Nov-Mar) To the right as you exit Tōno station; staff speak some English and can supply a useful English-language brochure and a map of the three main cycling routes.

Sights

You'll need some form of transport to make the most of your stay; allow at least two days, but don't plan on much in the way of nightlife. A beautiful way to see the countryside is by bicycle, made easier by a fantastic bike trail that runs alongside the river. Renting a car is another option. Bus tours are sporadically available – ask at the tourist info booth before making plans.

On the upper floors of the city library, the **Tōno Municipal Museum** (☎ 62-2340; 3-9 Higashidate-chō; admission ¥310; 9am-5pm, closed last day of each month) has exhibits of folklore and traditional

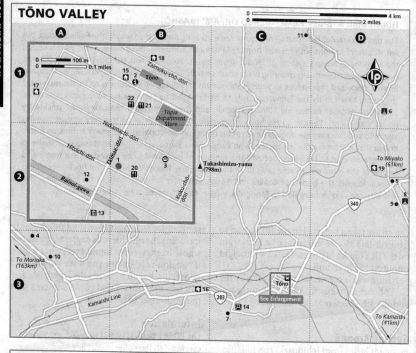

TŌNO VALLEY

life, and some engaging audiovisual presentations of the various legends of Tōno.

Tōno Mukashibanashi-mura (☎ 62-7887; 2-11 Chūō-dōri; admission ¥310; ⊙ 9am-5pm) is a folk village with a restored ryokan, where Kunio Yanagita (see the boxed text, opposite) once stayed. There's also an exhibition hall for folk art. A combined ticket with the Tōno Municipal Museum costs ¥500.

Fukusen-ji (☎ 62-3822; 7-57 Komagi, Matsuzaki; admission ¥300; ⊙ 8am-4.30pm Apr-Dec) is 8.5km northeast of Tōno station. Founded in 1912, the temple's major claim to fame is the wooden Fukusen-ji Kannon statue (17m high and weighing 25

tonnes), which took 12 years to complete and is supposedly the tallest of its type in Japan. Take a bus bound for Sakanoshita and get off at Fukusen-ji (¥370, eight daily).

About 3.5km beyond Fukusen-ji, **Tōno Furusato-mura** (☎ 64-2300; 5-89-1 Kami-tsukimoushi, Tsukimoushi-chō; admission ¥520; ⊙ 9am-5pm) is Tōno's largest folk village, with several different farmhouses, a water wheel and a folkcraft gallery. Buses run hourly from Tōno station (¥490, 25 minutes).

Tsuzuki Ishi is a curious rock formation up a short, steep hike about 8km outside the city. The lush aromatic cedar forest is as impressive as the rock itself. Originally thought to be a natural formation, recent studies indicate it may actually be a dolmen (primitive tomb).

Jōken-ji is a peaceful temple 2.5km south of Fukusen-ji, famous for the deity image **Obinzuru-sama** – some believe it will cure their illness if they rub the parts of its body corresponding to the location of their ailment.

Behind the temple is the **Kappa-buchi** pool. Legend has it that *kappa*, belying their impish nature, once put out a fire in the temple; the lion statue was erected as a gesture of thanks to honour this good deed. It is said that if pregnant women worship at the shrine on the riverbank they'll produce plenty of milk, but only if they first produce a breast-shaped offering. The tiny temple is filled with small cloth bags, either red or white, most replete with nipple.

Also in this vicinity is **Denshōen** (☎ 62-8655; admission ¥310; ☼ 9am-5pm, last entry 4.30pm), a small folk village featuring a hall with 1000 Oshirasama dolls. From Tōno station, take a direct bus to Denshōen-mae (¥300, 15 minutes), or more frequent buses bound for Sakanoshita to the Nitagai stop (¥290, 12 minutes), which is 10 minutes on foot from Denshōen.

Unedori-sama shrine is about 2.5km southwest of Tōno station. Women tie a red strip of cloth to the surrounding pines (using only their left hand) to ensure a healthy birth. In the hills above it are **Gohyaku Rakan**, ethereal rock carvings of 500 disciples of Buddha. They were fashioned by a priest to console the spirits of those who died in a 1754 famine.

Nine kilometres west of Tōno station is the **Chiba Family Magariya** (☎ 62-9529; admission ¥350; ☼ 8.30am-5pm Apr-Oct, 9am-4pm Nov-Mar). This traditional L-shaped farmhouse, with the mountains as its backdrop, has been restored to evoke the traditional lifestyle of a wealthy farming family of the 18th century.

Festivals & Events

The **Tōno Matsuri** takes place on 14 September with *yabusame* (horseback archery, in this case a 700-year-old event), traditional dances and costume parades through the city to Tonogo-hachimangu shrine. It's a flamboyant spectacle, designed to pray for a bountiful harvest, and is deeply connected with the legends of Tōno.

Sleeping

our pick **Tōno Youth Hostel** (☎ 62-8736; 13-39-5 Tsuchibuchi, Tsuchibuchi-chō; dm from ¥3200) Spick-and-span, two-storey hostel that's a super base for exploring the valley. The manager speaks some

---

THE CURIOUS CUSTOMS OF TŌHOKU

At the beginning of the 20th century, a collection of regional folk tales was published under the title *Tōno Monogatari* (Legends of Tōno). They were compiled by Kunio Yanagita (1875–1962), a prominent writer and scholar regarded as the father of Japanese folklore. The collection was based on interviews with Tōno resident Kyōseki Sasaki, who was born into a peasant family and who had committed to memory over 100 *densetsu* (local legends). What Yanagita and Sasaki unearthed immediately captured the nation's imagination, bringing into rich focus the oral storytelling traditions of a region hitherto almost completely ignored.

The cast of characters and situations is truly weird and wonderful and draws heavily on the concept of animism, a system of belief that attributes a personal spirit to everything that exists, including animals and inanimate objects. One of the more striking tales concerns a simple village girl who married her horse. Amazingly, this was against her father's wishes, so the father hung the horse from a mulberry tree and beheaded it. The girl, clutching the horse's head, then flew off to heaven where she became Oshira-sama, the fertility goddess (today, Oshira-sama dolls are still important ceremonial objects for *itako* mediums; see p533).

Elsewhere, we have shape-shifting foxes; elderly folk who are cast off into the wilderness to die; impish water spirits called *kappa*, who sumō-wrestle passers-by to the ground and who like to pull their victim's intestines out through their anus (ew!); *zashiki warashi* spirits, who live in the corners of houses and play tricks on the residents; and wild men who live in the hills and eat children. Throughout all of them is a common theme: the battle with nature and the struggle to tame the elements – everyday features of rural life, of which Tōno is an exemplar.

Legends of Tōno is available, in English, for ¥2000 from the souvenir shop next to the Tōno tourist information office.

English, is quite sociable and is well versed in the local legends (there's a detailed report nightly). Bicycle rental is available (¥800 per day), there's no curfew and there's an extensive manga library. From Tōno station, take a bus bound for Sakanoshita to the Nitagai stop (¥290, 12 minutes). From there, it's a 10-minute walk; the hostel is clearly signposted – minute by minute – along the way.

Folkloro Tōno (☎ 62-0700; 5-7 Shinkoku-chō; r per person incl breakfast ¥6300) Standard business hotel that is curiously located right above the station, with Western-style rooms. The train is infrequent, but when it comes you'll know.

Minshuku Tōno (☎ 62-4395; 2-17 Zaimoku-chō; r per person incl 2 meals ¥6300) Just behind the station, this is a welcoming place where the host speaks English.

Minshuku Rindō (☎ 62-5726; 2-34 Daiku-chō; r per person incl 2 meals ¥6500; 🖵) About a six-minute walk from the station, this is a clean, hospitable place with good food and is a decent value.

Minshuku Magariya (☎ 62-4564; 30-58-3 Niisato, Ayaori-chō; r per person incl 2 meals from ¥9790) About 3km southwest of the station, this is atmospheric accommodation in a traditional farmhouse. No English is spoken. From the station, take a bus to the *basu-sentā* (bus centre), then walk for 30 minutes. Actually, you might want to catch a taxi just this once (for around ¥1000).

Eating

Taigetsu (☎ 62-2436; meals from ¥600; 🕙 10am-9.30pm Thu-Tue) On Ekimae-dōri, 350m south of the train station, this one's good for coffee, *rāmen* and basic snacks.

Shokudō Umenoya (☎ 62-2622; meals from ¥650; 🕙 11.30am-8pm) Across the road from Taigetsu, Ume-no-ya serves good-value set meals, as well as *rāmen* and omelettes.

Ichiriki (☎ 62-2008; meals from ¥800; 🕙 11am-8pm, closed irregularly) With its cosy, traditional interior, this restaurant serves terrific seafood – the delectable tempura tofu is recommended for its extraordinary lightness. There are advisory posters on the walls for those wishing to go *kappa* hunting.

Getting There & Away

The JR Tōhoku line runs from Hiraizumi (¥820, 45 minutes) and Morioka (¥650, 40 minutes) to Hanamaki; the *shinkansen* runs from Morioka (¥2750, 11 minutes) and Sendai (¥5350, 59 minutes) to Shin-Hanamaki. On the JR Kamaishi line, local trains connect

Tōno with Shin-Hanamaki on the Tōhoku *shinkansen* line (¥740, 45 minutes) and Hanamaki on the Tōhoku Main line (¥820, 65 minutes). The approach into town is divine as the train winds through the valley and its mountains. You can also take the (very worthwhile!) scenic route that goes from Tōno to Kamaishi, then along the coast northward, returning inland to Morioka on the JR Yamada line.

There are two afternoon buses from Morioka at 2.15pm and 3.30pm to Kamaishi that stop at Tōno's Topia department store (¥1890, two hours). In the reverse direction, buses to Morioka pass by at 7am and 10am.

Getting Around

Tōno is one place where car rental is a good idea – try **Kankō Rent-a-Car** (遠野観光レンタカー; ☎ 62-1375), inside the train station. Bicycle rental is available from the tourist office at ¥1000 per day, or from the youth hostel.

MORIOKA 盛岡
☎ 019 / pop 300,400

A river runs through it, er, rivers that is: the Kitakami, Nakatsu, and Shizukuishi, making Morioka one of the prettiest cities in Tōhoku. The capital of Iwate-ken, in the early Edo period it was the seat of the Nambu clan. With the grand Mt Iwate volcano as its northwest backdrop and some beautiful old buildings, Morioka is a picturesque place, and its people are very keen to share their city's delights with outsiders. The city's *wanko-soba* culinary ritual is a curious custom that's fun to try, and exchange with Canada means that residents are refreshingly nonchalant about foreigners, far more so than in other Tōhoku towns.

Orientation

The city centre is east of the station, which lies on the southwest corner of the action, on the other side of the Kitakami-gawa. Ōdōri, which heads over the Kaiun-bashi up to Iwate-kōen, is the main shopping street.

Information
INTERNET ACCESS
The tourist information centre has free access.

Cafe α (☎ 653-1288; 1-6-13 Ōdōri; per hr ¥480; 🕙 11am-8am Mon-Fri, 24hr Sat-Sun)

MEDICAL SERVICES
Iwate Medical University Hospital (☎ 651-5111; 19-1 Uchi-maru)

MONEY & POST

Iwate Bank (Ōdōri) Exchanges cash.
Morioka Central Post Office (盛岡中央郵便局;
☎ 624-5353; 1-13-45 Chūō-dōri; ☿ 9am-7pm Mon-Fri,
to 5pm Sat, to 12.30pm Sun, ATM 7am-11pm Mon-Fri,
9am-9pm Sat, to 7pm Sun) Downtown, with international
ATM. There's also a useful branch with ATM facilities five
minutes' walk east of the station.

TOURIST INFORMATION

Iwate International Plaza (国際交流セン
ター; ☎ 606-1750; 5F aiina 1-7-1 Moriokaekinishi-dōri;
☿ 9am-9.30pm) An excellent resource for visitors and
residents, with helpful staff, a foreign-newspaper library,
local 'what's on' information and free internet.
Morioka Tourist Information Centre (☎ 604-3305;
1-1-10 Nakanohashi-dōri; ☿ 9am-8pm, closed 2nd Tue
of each month) On the 2nd floor of Odette Plaza. Free
internet access (30 minutes), tourist brochures, phonecards
and stamps.
Northern Tōhoku Tourist Information Centre
(☎ 625-2090; ☿ 9am-5.30pm) On the 2nd floor of
Morioka station at the north exit, next to the *shinkansen*
ticket gate. Highly efficient, English-speaking staff and a
good supply of regional brochures.

Sights

Morioka is easily navigated on foot, but there
is also a tourist bus. Ask at the info desk for
current schedules as they may change.

Iwate-kōen, 20 minutes' walk east of the station, is the park where Morioka-jō once stood.
Only the castle's moss-covered stone foundation walls remain as a testament to Edo-period
life. The park has pleasing views over the city,
and the grounds, with varicoloured tree foliage, are pretty. The park also contains the
shrine **Sakurayama**, and a totem pole presented
by Morioka's sister city in British Columbia;
it's a collaboration between a Native North
American chief and a local woodcarver.

The Japanese love displays of fortitude, as
the many samurai legends forever enshrined
in the nation's hearts and minds illustrate.

KENJI MIYAZAWA: A 'MAGIC LANTERN OF FONDLY REMEMBERED GREEN WIND'

Kenji Miyazawa (1896–1933) is one of Japan's best-known writers of the 20th century. Born in
Morioka he lived there until his early 20s, although the town and the surrounding environment
continued to influence him. Throughout Miyazawa's life, Tōhoku was very much the backwater
of Japan. Iwate-ken, in particular, was a land barely struggling to survive, as crops failed and new
farming technology proved to be slow making its way north. On top of that, Miyazawa was the
son of a pawnbroker and it caused him great anguish and deep shame to observe how his well-
to-do family preyed on the poor by taking their property in exchange for lending them money.
This experience, combined with an intense Buddhist faith, shaped his life's work.

Miyazawa developed a wondrous cosmology whereby profound empathy is felt between the
animal world, the human world and the world of nature. A man is forced to hunt bears to make
a living, even though he loves bears and deeply understands their ways and customs; the bears,
in turn, understand and respect the bind he is in. Another man chances upon a group of deer;
captivated by them, he hides in the grass to observe and before long realises he can understand
the deer's 'language'. Foxes boast about their knowledge of poetry and astronomy. Stars in
the sky take human form and play the flute. A cellist, rejected from an orchestra because his
playing is atrocious, finds peace with the animals who visit him at night to hear him play. This
communication between species has been understood as a plea for tolerance of other cultures,
particularly as Miyazawa was writing during a time when Japanese society was becoming ever
more closed off as the nation moved towards war.

Connections have also been made between Miyazawa's work and the legends of Tōno (see
the boxed text, p523); certainly the battle against the elements by poor people is a common
thread, as is the belief in animism. But the Tōno stories are filled with casual violence and an
often antagonistic relationship towards the natural world. Tōno's legends depict foxes, for example, as a constant torment to humans, whereas Miyazawa overturns the common notion of
foxes as cunning and devious, and demonstrates that even the most entrenched stereotypes can
be debunked – as in the scholarly fox mentioned earlier.

Ultimately, both realms are deeply infused with the rhythms and paradoxes of everyday Tōhoku
life, and both are worthy additions to the library of anyone seeking to go beyond the platitudes
of tourist brochures to understand what makes the region tick.

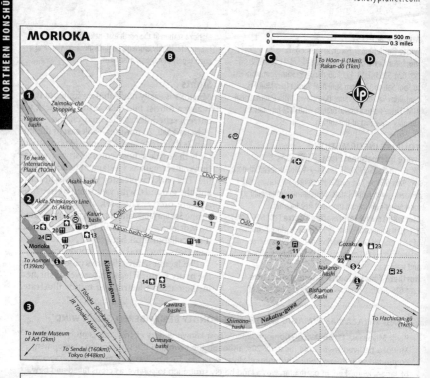

MORIOKA

This applies even if the display is exhibited by an inanimate object, like the **Rock-Splitting Cherry Tree** in front of the Morioka District Court. This 300-year-old tree, sprouting from the crack in a huge granite boulder, has the locals claiming that it's pushed its way through over time. That's clearly an impossible feat, but it makes for a very charming story.

The **Iwate Museum of Art** (岩手県立美術館; ☎ 658-1711; 12-3 Matsuhaba, Motomiya; admission ¥500; ☯ 10am-7pm Tue-Sun) has works by local artists such as Yorozu Tetsugoro, Matsumoto Shunsuke and Funakoshi Yasutake. It's 2km west of the station. Buses from Morioka station stop 10 (¥290, 12 minutes, five daily between 9.10am and 2.10pm) stop outside the museum; the last bus back leaves the museum at 4.38pm.

Hōon-ji (報恩寺) is a quiet Zen temple in Morioka's *teramachi* (temple district), where Kenji Miyazawa lived after being expelled from boarding school. The temple's impressive San-mon (Main Gate) has a Kannon image, but the real attraction here is the musty **Rakan-dō** (羅漢堂; admission by donation ¥300; ☺ 9am-4pm), a small hall containing 18th-century statues of the 500 disciples of Buddha, each posed in a different attitude. Take the Dendenmushi loop bus from stop 15 in front of Morioka station and get off at the Honchō-dōri 1-chōme stop (¥100, 15 minutes).

Appi Kōgen (安比高原; www.appi.co.jp/foreign _country/english/index.html; day lift ticket ¥3300), located about one hour northwest of Morioka, offers skiing, snowboarding and kid-friendly activities. For more information visit the website or enquire at Morioka's friendly tourist information counters (p525). Most of the lodgings are quite a distance from the slopes, so plan on using shuttles once you get there.

Festivals & Events

Chagu-Chagu Umakko Matsuri On the second Saturday of June, features a parade of brightly decorated horses and children in traditional dress. Starting outside town, the procession passes near Iwate-kō in the afternoon (the best views are from Nakano-hashi). Iwate was historically famous for breeding horses and the festival allegedly originated when farmers took their horses to shrines to rest them after harvest and pray for their health. The name 'chagu-chagu' is said to describe the sound of the horses' bells.

Hachiman-gū Matsuri During the festival from 14 to 16 September, portable shrines and colourful floats are paraded to the rhythm of *taiko* (Japanese drums). There are also displays of horseback archery on the 15th. The parades are thoroughly engaging, and feature traditional Japanese floats pushed and wheeled through crowded streets by huffing, puffing men scantily dressed in sumō-type outfits, headed by a flying V of elegant, dancing women.

Sleeping

Minshuku Taishōkan (☎ 622-4436; 2-5-30 Ōsawakawara; r per person from ¥3700) Faded but friendly, about 10 minutes southeast of the station, with clean, Japanese-style rooms. You'll feel more like you're in Grandma's house than at a hotel; that's a good thing, part of the charm.

Kumagai Ryokan (☎ 651-3020; 3-2-5 Ōsawakawara; s/d from ¥4500/8400; ▣) The Ryokan Kumagai is an easy-going place, opposite Taishōkan. The rooms are clean and tidy, and there's a nice Japanese garden and folk-craft displays.

A number of standard business hotels are close to the station:

Hotel Metropolitan Morioka (☎ 625-1211; 1-44 Ekimae-dōri; s/d incl breakfast from ¥8662/16,747) Upmarket, snazzier hotel next to the station.

Hotel Ruiz (☎ 625-2611; www.hyperhotel.co.jp; 7-15 Ekimae-dōri; s/tw from ¥5480/8800; ▣) Reliable business hotel close to the station.

Morioka New City Hotel (盛岡ニューシティ ホテル; ☎ 654-5161; 13-10 Ekimae-dōri; s/d from ¥4980/735; ▣) Across the road from the station. More casual than other business hotels. Has only two of the least expensive rooms.

Eating

Morioka has a great culinary tradition with some Korean influence. *Jājāmen* (soba-type noodles with spicy sauce) is a local speciality. Famished? Let's see you eat 550 bowls of the local noodle dish, *wanko-soba*. More of a competition between you and the waitress (who tries to refill your bowl faster than you can say you're full), it's a fun culinary tradition that is well worth doing once. We managed to stop at 162, but 552 is the current record for this unique experience, which is best appreciated at **Azumaya** (☎ 622-2252; 2nd fl, Miurabiru Bldg, 1-8-3 Naka-no-hashi-dōri; wanko-soba from ¥2600; ☺ 11am-8pm). The Mariah Carey tunes are oddly incongruous with the otherwise traditional flair. Some staff speaks English.

Cappuccino Shiki (☎ 625-3608; 10-6 Ekimae-dōri; snacks ¥420-630; ☺ 9am-10pm Tue-Fri, to 8pm Sat & Sun) An atmospheric old coffee shop that feels like a tavern because of its rustic, dark-wood interior. Serves tasty toasted sandwiches, good breakfast sets and heart-starting espresso.

Banya Nagasawa (☎ 622-2646; 2-6-1 Saien; set meals from ¥2000; ☺ dinner Mon-Sat) Here you can select your seafood for grilling as you relax with a beverage of your choice.

Morioka's other speciality is *reimen*, *soba* noodles served with *kimchi* (spicy Korean pickles). **Pyon Pyon Sha** (☎ 606-1067; 1st fl, Jaren Bldg, 9-3 Ekimae-dōri; reimen from ¥735; ☺ 11am-11pm) has delicious cold *reimen* and hot *reimen* sets. **Seirōkaku** (☎ 654-8752; 2nd fl, Gen Plaza, 15-5 Ekimae-dōri; reimen from ¥900; ☺ lunch & dinner; E) also does a mean *reimen*, as well as dishes made from the (gulp!) first, second and fourth stomachs of cows.

Drinking

No surprises that with all that water, rice, and time on their hands, Morioka-ites made some excellent local sakes.

Fukakusa (☎ 622-2353; 1-2 Konya-chō; drinks ¥400-700; ☺ lunch & dinner Mon-Sat, lunch Sun) This tiny 40-year-old bar-café, just behind the old Iwate Bank, has an unbeatable location on the banks of the Nakatsu-gawa. With its cosy wood-panelled interior, piano, warm lighting and handmade prints, it's a romantic little hideout, and the charming hostess-owner speaks perfect English and can offer suggestions about the local sakes.

Shopping

The Morioka region is famous for its *nanbu tetsubin* (cast ironware). **Kamasada Honten** (☎ 622-3911; 2-5 Konya-chō; ☺ 9am-5.30pm Mon-Sat) is a fine exponent of the craft, selling affordable gift items alongside tea kettles that cost as much as a small car. It's across the Nakatsu-gawa near Gozaku, a traditional merchant's area of *kura* (mud-walled) warehouses, coffee shops and craft studios. Try the Zaimoku-chō district, five minutes from the station, home to craft shops for lacquerware and fabrics.

Getting There & Away

On the JR Tōhoku *shinkansen* line, the fastest trains from Tokyo (Ueno) reach Morioka in 2½ hours (¥13,640). From Morioka, the Akita *shinkansen* line runs west to Akita (¥4300, 1½ hours) via Tazawa-ko and Kakunodate, which can also be reached by infrequent local trains on the JR Tazawa-ko line. From Morioka you can continue north to Aomori on the JR Tōhoku Main line (*tokkyū*, ¥5960, 1¾ hours).

The bus station at Morioka station is well organised. It has abundant English signs and a directory matching buses to their relevant stops, as well as journey times and fares. Popular destinations include Iwate-san, Towada-ko and Tazawa-ko.

The easiest access to the Hachimantai area, northwest of Morioka, is also by bus, from stop 3 at Morioka station to Hachimantai Chōjō (¥1320, two hours, three daily).

Long-distance buses leave the station for Aomori (¥3160, three hours), Hirosaki (¥2930, 2½ hours) and Sendai (¥2850, 2½ hours). There are two night buses to Tokyo leaving at 10.15pm and 10.55pm (¥7850, 7½ hours) and one to Yokohama (¥8950, eight hours) leaving at 10.10pm.

Getting Around

Most local buses depart from the station, although there are also some departures from the Morioka bus centre close to Iwate-kōen. The rather charmingly named tourist bus, Dendenmushi (snail; single ride/day pass ¥100/300), makes a convenient loop around the town, departing in a clockwise direction from stop 15 in front of Morioka station (anticlockwise from stop 16) between 9am and 7pm.

IWATE-SAN 岩手山

The jagged molar of Iwate-san (2038m) is a dominating landmark northwest of Morioka, and a popular destination for hikers. Seven walking trails are open between July and October, but periodically close due to volcanic activity. Check with tourist information in Morioka (p525) for the latest conditions. If you want to stay near Iwate-san, **Amihari Onsen**, at the start of one of the main trails to the summit, has numerous *minshuku*. Railway enthusiasts prefer the **Koiwai Nōjō SL Hotel** (小岩井農場 ホテル; ☎ 692-4316; 21 Apr-6 Nov; r per person from ¥4200) at Koiwai (Japan's largest privately owned farm), where you sleep in old train compartments. From early May to early November, buses from Morioka bound for Amihari Onsen (¥1140, one hour) pass by Koiwai farm (¥720, 35 minutes). Before Amihari, there's a bus stop at Omisaka for the trailhead.

AOMORI-KEN 青森県

Aomori-ken, at the curious northern tip of Honshū, is split in the middle by Mutsu, Noheji and Aomori bays, all cradled in the arm of the axe-shaped Shimokita peninsula. Volcano strewn, it has some fantastic *onsens* and boasts Japan's biggest apple harvest, its oldest cherry tree and (don't go kissing anyone!) the most garlic produced. Rather than ward off the dead, Aomori's people commune with them: Osore-zan, splendidly sulphurous, is famed for its connections to the spirit world. Lake Towada, at the opposite end of the prefecture, puts on airs as Tōhoku's most popular sight. The world's longest submarine tunnel (54km) connects Aomori with Hokkaidō. Yet despite all these amazing superlatives, the city and surrounding countryside are quaintly provincial. It's a fun place, though the more remote areas may require some advance planning...or a car rental.

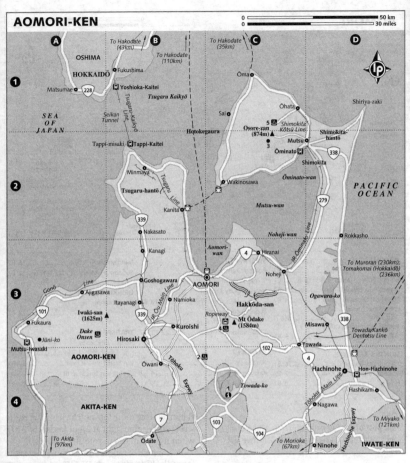

AOMORI-KEN

0   50 km
0   30 miles

AOMORI 青森

☎ 017 / pop 313,200

You won't find much in the way of ancient architecture in Aomori, as the city was 90% destroyed by bombing during WWII; however, Aomori's people seem to have taken that in their stride. The ASPAM building and the Aomori Bay Bridge seem almost too modern, yet ancient festivals such as the Nebuta – raucously wild, with amazing floats – remind you that traditional ways are alive and kicking here. Aomori is a popular place to break up the journey between Tokyo and Hokkaidō, and serves as a convenient transport hub for Shimokita-hantō, Towada-ko and the scenic region around Hakkōda-san.

Information

EMERGENCY

Aomori Police Station (☎ 723-4211; 2-3-1 Shinmachi)

INTERNET ACCESS

Ai Plaza (☎ 735-3232; www.city.aomori.aomori .jp/aiplaza in Japanese; 1-3-7 Shin-machi; per 1hr free; ⏰ 10am-9pm, closed irregularly) On the 4th floor of the AUGA building.

Freaks (フリークス; ☎ 732-5015; 3-10-11 Midori; per hr ¥473; ⏰ 24hr) A 50-minute walk or 10 minutes by taxi.

MEDICAL SERVICES

Aomori City Hospital (青森市民病院; ☎ 734-2171; 1-14-20 Katsuda)

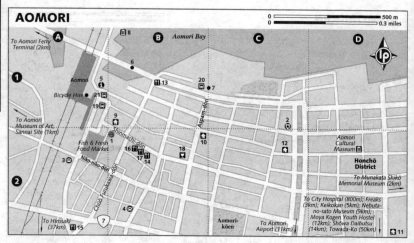

POST

Main post office East of the city centre, with a smaller branch within easy reach of the station. Both have ATM services.

TOURIST INFORMATION

Prefectural tourist information counter (☎ 734-2500; 2F, ASPAM Bldg, 1-1-40 Yasukata; ☺ 9am-6pm, closed irregularly)

Tourist information office (☎ 723-4670; ☺ 8.30am-5.30pm) On the left of the station's central exit. Good English-language pamphlets and an excellent map of the city.

Sights

The futuristic, pyramid-shaped **ASPAM building** (1-1-40 Yasukata) has a top-floor viewing plaza (admission ¥400). The view out across the bay is great but the perspective is equally as good on the lower (free!) floors.

Nearby, **Aomori Bay Bridge** is also remarkably modern. Climb the stairs at the Bay Bridge's station end for more top-notch views; the entire structure is a fine sight at night (as is ASPAM), when it illuminates in rotating colours.

Permanently moored in Aomori Bay is the ferry **Hakkōda-maru** (☎ 735-8150; admission ¥500; ☺ 9am-5pm Nov-Mar, to 6pm Apr-Oct). For 25 years, it was the flagship of the famous Seikan line that linked Honshū with Hokkaidō, before the underground tunnel rendered it obsolete. It's now a maritime museum with some interesting displays. In summer it becomes a 'beer garden', surely the most pleasant surroundings in which to have a drink.

The **Nebuta-no-sato Museum** (ねぶたの里; ☎ 738-1230; 1 Yaegiku, Yokouchi; admission ¥630; ☺ 9am-5.30pm) tells the story of Aomori's legendary Nebuta Matsuri, with an exhibition of the mighty illuminated floats used in the festival. Buses to the museum, 9km south of town, leave frequently from stop 9 outside the train station for the Nebuta-no-sato Iriguchi stop (¥450, 30 minutes).

Shōwa Daibutsu (昭和大仏; ☎ 726-2312; 458 Yamazaki, Kuwabara; admission ¥400; ☯ 8am-5.30pm Apr-Oct, 9am-4.30pm Nov-Mar), Japan's largest outdoor Buddha at a height of 21m and weighing 220 tonnes, is an impressive sight. The breezy temple grounds are full of spinning pinwheels left by parents for their dead children. Buses from Aomori station are timed so that you have about an hour to look around before catching the next bus back (¥540, 45 minutes).

The **Munakata Shikō Memorial Museum** (棟方志功記念館; ☎ 777-4567; 2-1-2 Matsubara; admission ¥500; ☯ 9.30am-5pm Tue-Sun) houses a collection of woodblock prints, paintings and calligraphy by Munakata Shikō, an Aomori native who won international fame. The building itself is *azekura* style, with walls of geometric wooden planks fitted together without upright supports. Buses bound for Nakatsutui leave from stop 2 outside the train station for the Munakata Shikō Kinenkan-dōri stop (¥190, 15 minutes).

The **Aomori Museum of Art** (青森県立美術館; ☎ 783-3000; 185 Yasuta-Aza Chikano; admission ¥500; ☯ 9am-6pm Jun-Sep, 9.30am-5pm Oct-May, closed 2nd & 4th Mon of month) has a variety of works on display, including rotating exhibits. A large outdoor exhibition of Jōmon-era replicas bring the lifestyles of ancient people to life.

Festivals & Events

Even Japanese people muddle up Aomori's Nebuta and Hirosaki's Neputa (p534) festivals – not only do they sound alike but both take place at the start of August. The **Nebuta Matsuri** (www.nebuta.or.jp/english/index_e.htm), held from 2 to 7 August, is renowned for its parades of colossal illuminated floats accompanied by thousands of rowdy, chanting dancers. The parades start at sunset and last for hours; on the final day the action starts around noon.

Sleeping

It's sometimes tricky to find accommodation in Aomori, due to its status as a stop-off for Hokkaidō-bound travellers. Book ahead, especially for the Nebuta Matsuri.

Moya Kogen Youth Hostel (雲谷高原ユースホステル; ☎ 764-2888; 9-5 Yamabuki, Moya; dm from ¥3360; ▣) This modern hostel is 12km from the station. The English-speaking owner loves Ireland and usually has a case of Guinness in the fridge. Buses from stop 9, outside the train station, can drop you off outside the hostel (¥590, 40 minutes). The last bus leaves at 8.20pm.

Super Hotel Aomori (☎ 723-9000; http://www.super hotel.co.jp/s_hotels/aomori/aomori.html; 1-3-14 Hashimoto; s/d incl breakfast ¥4980/6980; ▣) This chain is an attractive option for anyone needing a business hotel. Take bus 4 (¥180) and get off at the NTT building, about 5 minutes away.

our pick **Tako Ryokan** (☎ 722-4825; Yasukata 2-chōme; r per person incl/excl 2 meals from ¥7140/4725) In the town centre, this is a smart option with more charm than a bland business hotel. Japanese-style rooms and (yum!) Japanese meals, mostly local seafood.

Aomori Grand Hotel (☎ 723-1011; 1-1-23 Shin-machi; s/d from ¥6500/10,000; ▣) Just east of the station, this hotel has rooms with sea views and is conveniently located. Staff will exchange money after the banks close.

Hotel JAL City Aomori (☎ 732-2580; 2-4-12 Yasukata; s/tw ¥9400/16,100; ▣) Six minutes east of the station, near ASPAM, it has international-standard facilities, including a decent restaurant.

Eating & Drinking

The *tsugaru jamisen* is a version of the traditional three-stringed *shamisen* (guitar) instrument, but with a thicker neck than what's found in other regions. Practitioners are characterised by their rapid, forceful plectrum style. None of the first four places have an English menu, but pictures, plastic food and friendly service make ordering relatively simple.

Kotobukiya (☎ 773-7134; 1st fl, 2-1-5 Furukawa; meals from ¥6000; ☯ dinner) Offers nightly dinner shows featuring *tsugaru jamisen* music. Reservations are required and it's a 15-minute walk south of Aomori station.

Jintako (☎ 722-7727; 1-6-16 Yasukata; meals from ¥5000; ☯ dinner, closed 1st & 3rd Sun) Another restaurant serving up *tsugaru jamisen* and local seafood.

Kakigen (☎ 727-2933; 1-8-9 Shinmachi; dishes from ¥1300; ☯ 10.30am-9pm) Tiny hole in the wall that's notable for its speciality, Aomori scallops. Ask for mouthwatering *hotate batā yaki teishoku* (scallops grilled with butter).

Nandaimon (☎ 777-2377; 1-8-3 Shinmachi; dishes/set menu from ¥600/1260; ☯ 11am-midnight) A Korean-Japanese place with some authentic treats such as *makkoli* (Korean rice wine). Good range of seafood dishes, including *hotate* as well as grill-your-own meat ensembles.

Supage-tei Aomori (☎ 773-6537; 1-8-8 Shinmachi; dishes from ¥850; ☯ 11am-9pm Tue-Sun) In the basement next door to Kakigen, this has pasta dishes infused with Japanese-style seafood and an English menu.

Bar Centamil (☎ //5-7054; 1-11-16 Shinmachi; ☼ until late) With its industrial aesthetic of concrete and brushed steel, this bar is a minimalist's delight. The soundtrack is organic, though: '60s soul. It's down a small alleyway, which is next to the Doutor coffee shop on Shinmachi.

Getting There & Away

AIR

There are frequent flights from Aomori airport to major Japanese cities (Tokyo, Kyoto, Osaka, Nagoya) and an international connection to Seoul. Airport buses are timed for flights and depart from the front of the ASPAM building and Aomori station (¥560, 40 minutes).

BOAT

Passenger ferries to Hakodate leave year-round (¥1850, 3¾ hours), while one ferry departs for Muroran (Hokkaidō) daily at 1.30pm (¥3460). Coming back, an overnighter leaves Muroran at 11.25pm (¥3460, 6¾ hours each way).

The ferry terminal, on the western side of the city, is a 10-minute taxi ride from Aomori station.

BUS

Between April and mid-November, JR runs five to eight buses daily from stop 8 outside the train station to Towada-ko (¥3000, 4¾ hours); the last bus leaves at 2.30pm. The bus stops at the Hakkōda ropeway (cable car; ¥1070, 50 minutes), then runs via the glorious Sukayu Onsen (p533; ¥1300, one hour) onto the Oirase Valley and the lake.

JR also operates six buses daily to both Morioka (¥3160, three hours) and Sendai (¥5700, five hours), and one night bus to Tokyo (¥10,000, 9½ hours); buses depart from the Highway Bus stop 10 outside the station-side tourist information office.

To visit Osore-zan (Shimokita-hantō), direct buses leave the ASPAM building at 11.55am, 1.55pm and 5pm for Mutsu via Noheji (¥2520, 2¾ hours).

TRAIN

The JR Tsugaru Kaikyō line runs from Aomori via the Seikan Tunnel to Hakodate on Hokkaidō (tokkyū, ¥5140, two hours).

Kaisoku trains do the trip in 2¼ hours, and on some of these services (¥3150) you take the Seikan Tunnel tour (see the boxed text, p571).

The JR Tōhoku Main line runs south from Aomori to Morioka (tokkyū, ¥5960, two hours), from where you can zip back to Tokyo in 2½ hours on the shinkansen. The Ōu Main line runs via Hirosaki to Akita (¥3260 4½ hours) where you can pick up the Akita shinkansen.

SHIMOKITA-HANTŌ 下北半島
☎ 0175 / pop 119,600

Also called Masakari-hantō (Axe peninsula) because of its shape, this isolated peninsula has long stretches of sparsely inhabited coastline and remote mountain valleys. At its western edge, **Hotokegaura** (仏ヶ浦) is a spectacular stretch of coastline dotted with 100m-tall wind-carved cliffs, which are said to resemble Buddhas. Stock up with supplies before heading to the peninsula – facilities are limited.

Mutsu むつ

This is Shimokita's main hub, from where bus services operate across the peninsula. Train connections are centred on Shimokita station, with buses connecting to Mutsu bus terminal. North of Mutsu is Ōhata, where you can get buses to the Yagen Onsen resort. To the east is the cape, Shiriya-zaki, and to the west, Ōma, Honshū's northernmost point. At the bottom tip of the peninsula is Wakinosawa, which is popular with nature lovers, not least for its 'snow monkeys' (Japanese macaques; see www.wakinosawa.com).

The tiny **tourist information office** (☎ 22-0909; ☼ 9am-6pm May-Oct, to 6pm Wed-Mon Nov-Apr) inside Masakari Plaza has few resources; comprehensive information is available in Aomori (p530).

There are numerous accommodation options clustered around the bus terminal. Next to Masakari Plaza, **Murai Ryokan** (むらい旅館; ☎ 22-4755; 9-30 Tanabu-chō, Mutsu; r incl/excl 2 meals from ¥7000/4300) is a safe bet. The rustic **Wakinosawa Youth Hostel** (脇野沢ユースホステル; ☎ 44-2341; 41 Wakinosawasenokawame, Mutsu; dm from ¥2990) is perched on a hillside at Wakinosawa village, 15 minutes west of the ferry pier. The helpful owners drive guests to a local onsen (¥200) before dinner, and conduct excursions to observe 'snow monkeys'. Yagen

Onsen offers upmarket accommodation, like **Hotel New Yagen** (ホテルニュー薬研; ☎ 34-3311; r from ¥13,000), with Western- or Japanese-style rooms.

Osore-zan 恐山

This barren volcanic mountain, with its **Osore-zan-Bodaiji** (恐山菩提寺; admission ¥500; ☼ 6am-6pm May-Oct), is among Japan's most sacred regions. It's a sulphurously atmospheric place that's popular with pilgrims seeking to commune with the dead, especially parents who've lost their children. Several stone statues of the child-guardian deity, Jizō, overlook hills of craggy, sulphur-strewn rocks and hissing vapour; visitors help lost souls with their underworld penance by adding stones to the cairns. With the yellow sulphur tributaries running into **Usori-ko** (宇曽利湖) and ravens swarming about, it's an appropriate setting for Buddhist purgatory – even the name, Osore, means fear or dread.

You can bathe on hell's doorstep at free *onsen* to the side as you approach the main hall (sex-segregated options are on the left). The two annual **Osore-zan Taisai festivals** (20 to 24 July and 9 to 11 October) attract huge crowds of visitors who come to consult blind crones. These *itako* (mediums) contact dead family members for a ¥3000 fee – it's an elaborate show, as the women recite Buddhist sutras and rattle rosary beads to invoke the spirits.

Getting There & Away

Renting a car in Aomori will save you a lot of time; however, the JR Ōminato line has two to four direct *kaisoku* trains daily from Aomori via Noheji to the terminus at Ōminato – get off one stop before at Shimokita station (¥1890, two hours) for buses to Mutsu. Buses run from the Mutsu bus terminal to Ōhata (¥440, 40 minutes).

From Shimokita station, frequent buses run to the Mutsu bus terminal (¥230, 10 minutes). Three direct buses run daily between Mutsu bus terminal and Aomori (¥2520, 2½ hours); others run via Noheji (¥1260, 1½ hours) onto Aomori (¥1260, one hour).

From Ōma, there are two daily ferries (four in summer) to Hakodate on Hokkaidō (¥1170, 1¾ hours). The JR Tsugaru line travels from Aomori to Kanita (¥480, 48 minutes), from where two ferries run daily (three in summer) to Wakinosawa (¥1120, one hour).

Getting Around

Buses to destinations across the peninsula run from the Mutsu bus terminal. Between May and October, regular buses run from Wakinosawa to Mutsu (¥1790, 1½ hours), from where four buses leave for Osore-zan between 9am and 4.45pm (¥750, 40 minutes); the last bus back leaves Osore-zan at 7.30pm.

Nine daily buses ply the northern shore of the peninsula, passing Ōhata, Shimofuro Onsen and Ōma before terminating at Sai (¥2260, two hours). Buses for Yagen Onsen start from Ōhata (¥540, 30 minutes). Six JR buses run daily between Ominato station (not the Mutsu bus terminal) and Wakinosawa (¥1790, 1¼ hours).

Between April and October, round-trip sightseeing boats for Hotokegaura depart from Wakinosawa at 10.45am and 2.45pm (¥3800, two hours), returning from Sai (¥2170, two hours); services are often suspended in poor weather.

HAKKŌDA-SAN 八甲田山

☎ 017

Just south of Aomori, Hakkōda-san is a scenic region of peaks popular as a day trip with hikers, *onsen* enthusiasts and skiers. The Hakkōda **ropeway** (cable car; one way/return ¥1150/1800; ☼ 9am-4.20pm) whisks you up Tamoyachi-dake to the 1324m summit. From there you can follow a network of hiking trails. One particularly pleasant route scales the three peaks of Akakura-dake (1548m), Ido-dake (1550m) and Ōdake (1584m), and then winds its way down to Sukayu Onsen, which is about 10 minutes by bus beyond the ropeway station, in the direction of Towada-ko. This 8km hike can be done in a leisurely four hours.

Sukayu Onsen Ryokan (酸ヶ湯温泉; ☎ 738-6400; r per person incl/excl 2 meals from ¥11700/4350; ☼ 7am-5.30pm) is a place plucked right out of an old *ukiyoe* woodblock painting – a delight for all five senses. Look at the dark wood, milky water and steam; listen to the gurgle of the water; feel its penetrating heat or massage tired shoulders with its *utase-yu* (massaging stream of water); smell the sulphur; if you dare, taste the water itself – it's lemony, almost like *ponzu* (citrusy sauce). On a cold autumn day relaxing here is hard to beat, and one of the baths is rumoured to hold up to 1000 people (though you'll rarely see more than 25 at any one time). Be aware that this is a mixed-sex bath, and that it's off in the mountains, away from everything but a few hiking trails. Those who take the time will be happy they stepped off the beaten 'bath'.

Two JR buses leave from stop 8 outside Aomori station and pass by the Hakkōda Ropeway-eki stop (¥1070, 50 minutes). In winter, buses terminate at the next stop, Sukayu Onsen (¥1300, one hour). Guests of the ryokan can take the twice-daily shuttle.

HIROSAKI 弘前
☎ 0172 / pop 187,600

Tucked about an hour southwest of Aomori, and founded in the 17th century by Lord Tsugaru Tamenobu, this pretty castle town was once one of Tōhoku's leading cultural centres. However, the Meiji Restoration combined Tsugaru's territories with those of the Nambu clan, resulting in the creation of Aomori prefecture, with the city of Aomori as its capital. Unlike Aomori, Hirosaki was spared from damage during WWII (although the castle itself had been previously destroyed by a lightning strike), and the castle grounds are well preserved, with extant keeps and towers, plus numerous beautiful maple and cherry trees. Hirosaki is also the site of the Neputa Matsuri – not to be confused with Aomori's Nebuta but almost as rowdy and just as popular.

Information

Thirty minutes of internet is free at the Hirosaki station's tourist info booth.

Freaks (フリークス; ☎ 29-5255; ⏰ 24hr) Internet access. Too far to walk to, but the city bus (¥100; several each hour) goes there in about 15 minutes.

Hirosaki Sightseeing Information Centre (☎ 37-5501; ⏰ 9am-6pm, later during festivals) Inside the Kankōkan (Tourism building) on the south side of Hirosaki-kōen; has basic information.

Main post office (18-1 Kita Kawarake-chō; ☎ 232-4104) Has postal and ATM service available until 9pm weekdays (7pm weekends); 20 minutes' walk northwest of the station.

Tourist information office (☎ 26-3600; ⏰ 8.45am-6pm) To the right as you exit Hirosaki station; offers a basic brochure/map in English, with some of the friendliest staff you'll find in Tōhoku.

Sights

The **Tsugaruhan Neputa-mura** (☎ 39-1511; 61 Kamenoko-machi; admission ¥500; ⏰ 9am-5pm Apr-Nov, to 4pm Dec-Mar) has a fine, extensive display, over two levels, of the unique fan-shaped floats that are paraded during the Neputa Matsuri.

Visitors get the chance to bang the massive drums used during the parade, while wearing a Neputa smock, all to the accompaniment of a traditional flautist. Addictive fun.

Just south, the **Genbei craft shop** (☎ 38-3377; 4-3 Ourachō; ⏰ 10am-5pm Fri-Wed) has fine examples of Tsugaru lacquerware, nicknamed *baka-nurii* (fool's lacquerware), due to the tedious work involved in applying more than 40 layers of multicoloured designs to its surface.

Hirosaki-kōen (弘前公園), the castle park, is so pretty that it's amazing that much of it is free. Three moats (with lotus plants and overhanging cherry trees) surround the remains of the original castle, **Hirosaki-jō**, which has gates and three corner keeps. It's a satisfying place for a stroll and attracts big crowds for *hanami* (cherry blossom viewing) during late April and early May. A giant murder of crows descends to roost on the trees each evening. Construction of Hirosaki-jō was completed in 1611, but the castle was burnt down in 1627 after being struck by lightning. One of the corner towers was rebuilt in 1810 and now houses a small **museum** (admission ¥300; ⏰ 9am-5pm Apr-Nov) of samurai artefacts, and a **botanical garden** (admission ¥300; ⏰ 9am-5pm Apr-Nov).

Fujita Kinen Tei-en (☎ 37-5525; admission ¥300; ⏰ 9am-5pm Tue-Sun Apr-Nov) is a well-manicured garden outside the southwest corner of the park.

The **Zenrin-gai** (禅林街) temple district is another atmospheric spot, redolent of Old Japan. It follows the central avenue – flanked by temples – to **Chōshō-ji** (長勝寺; ☎ 32-0813; admission ¥300; ⏰ 8am-5pm Apr-Oct, 9am-4pm Nov–mid-Dec), the Tsugaru clan's family temple. After passing through the impressive gate, continue past a large 14th-century bell to the main hall, which dates from the 17th century. Turning left, a path through the trees leads to a row of mausoleums built for the early rulers of the Tsugaru clan, who dominated the region around Hirosaki during the Edo period. Also on display is a collection of 500 statues depicting Buddha's disciples. To get here take a bus from stop 6 outside Hirosaki station to the Daigaku-byōin stop (¥170, 15 minutes); from there it's a further 10-minute walk southwest. Otherwise you could do the 30-minute walk or take a taxi (¥1000).

Festivals & Events

From 1 to 7 August Hirosaki celebrates its **Neputa Matsuri**, a festival famous for its illuminated

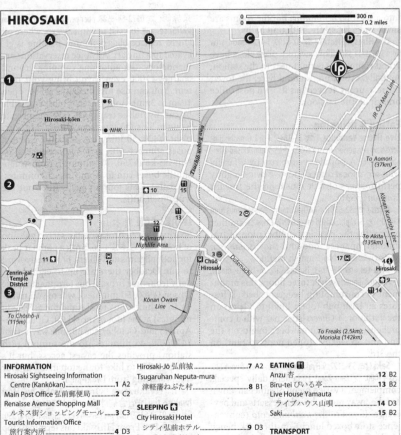

HIROSAKI

floats parading every evening to the accompaniment of flutes and drums. The festival is generally said to signify ceremonial preparation for battle – the fan-shaped floats are rotated during festival parades so that the heroic *kagami-e* painting on the front and the tear-jerker *miokuri-e* (seeing-off picture) on the back can both be viewed. Like its more rowdy counterpart held in Aomori (p531), this festival attracts thousands of visitors – book accommodation well in advance if you plan to attend.

Sleeping

Hirosaki has very few budget and midrange options.

Hirosaki Youth Hostel (☎ 33-7066; 11 Mori-machi; dm from ¥3045) It's quite hard to see the sign for this hostel that's tucked away on a side street near the castle, but at least there's no curfew. Take a bus from stop 6 outside Hirosaki station to the Daigaku-byōin stop (¥100, 15 minutes); the hostel is 250m west down an alleyway. Look up for the small sign that's almost indistinguishable from the other street signs, before you come to Lawson at the corner.

Hirosaki Grand Hotel (☎ 32-1515; 1 Ichiban-chō; s/tw/semi-d from ¥5800/11,000/9000) The lobby and restaurant are snazzy, and the red carpeting will make you feel a bit like you've stepped into a set for *The Shining*, but the rooms are small and a bit stuffy, with unit baths.

City Hirosaki Hotel (☎ 37-0109; 1-1-2 Ōmachi; s/tw from ¥6825/11,550) This swanky place does have grand rooms and is right next to the station. Actually, everything's grand here: the foyer, the restaurant. It even has its own post office branch on the 1st floor.

Eating & Drinking

Live House Yamauta (☎ 36-1835; 1-2-7 Ōmachi; dinner/show per person from ¥3000; 🕙 5-11pm, closed alternate Mon; E) A popular venue run by a family who serve local dishes and give twice-nightly performances of folk music on the *tsugaru jamisen* (p531).

Anzu (☎ 32-6684; 1-44 Oyakata-machi; set menus from ¥3500; 🕙 5-11pm, closed irregularly) This is another option for the pleasing combination of traditional Japanese food and *tsugaru-jamisen* performances. No English menu.

Bīru-tei (☎ 37-7741; Hokusaikan, 26-1 Dote-machi; 🕙 lunch & dinner; E) Over three floors, this monument to consumption hedges its bets. It features an Irish pub (open 11am to 11pm) on the 1st floor, a *Cheers*-style bar with a comprehensive international-beer menu on the 2nd and an *izakaya* (open noon to 1am) on the 3rd.

Saki (☎ 33-2122; 9 Hyakkokumachi; sweets from ¥320, sets ¥1000; 🕙 8am-7pm) Excellent daily specials complement a varied menu of either sit-down or take-away meals, breads, desserts and beverages. If you're the *konbini-bentō* (convenience store boxed lunch)-on-the-park-bench kind of eater, the boxed lunches here are a refreshing change. The high tea set is huge, easily large enough for two, and the scones come with real whipped cream.

Getting There & Away

Hirosaki station is on the JR Ōu Main line north of Aomori (*futsū*, ¥650, 44 minutes) and south of Akita (*tokkyū*, ¥4130, two hours).

Most local buses stop at the train station as well as the Hirosaki bus terminal adjacent to Itō Yōkadō department store. The bus terminal only services connections to Sendai (¥5090, 4½ hours, nine daily) and Iwaki-san (¥1780, 80 minutes, seven daily), with a change at Dake Onsen.

AONI ONSEN 青荷温泉

This seriously atmospheric but seriously isolated rustic group of **Aoni Onsen Ryokan** (青荷温泉旅館; ☎ 0172-54-8588; r per person incl 2 meals from ¥9075) seems to exist in a time warp, where oil lamps replace electricity and bathing is elevated to a fine art. Advance reservations are mandatory; the adjoining camping ground charges ¥1000 even if you bring your own tent. You can use just the baths (¥500, open 10am to 3pm). Aoni Onsen is most accessible by car. By public transport, take the private Kounan Tetsudō line from Hirosaki to Kuroishi (¥420, 30 minutes, six daily); Kounan buses connect with arriving passengers for Niji-no-ko (¥750, 10 minutes), from where shuttle buses run to Aoni (free, 30 minutes, six daily). This journey helps filter out the true *onsen* buffs.

IWAKI-SAN 岩木山

Soaring above Hirosaki is the sacred volcano of **Iwaki-san** (岩木山; 1625m), a popular peak for both pilgrims and hikers. From early April to late October there are up to eight buses daily from the Hirosaki bus terminal to Dake Onsen (¥900, 50 minutes), where you transfer to a shuttle bus to Hachigōme (¥880, 30 minutes) at the foot of the ski lift. Open mid-April to mid-October, the lift (one way/return ¥410/750, 45 minutes) to the summit (8th station) provides the easiest access, but it's also possible to hike to the top in about four hours starting from **Iwaki-jinja**.

In Hyakuzawa Onsen, **Asobe no Mori Iwakisō** (国民宿舎岩木荘 アソベの森いわき荘; ☎ 0172-83-2215; r per person incl 2 meals from ¥7350) is a safe bet. From Hirosaki bus terminal stop 3, take a bus bound for Iwaki-sō and get off at the last stop (¥660, one hour).

TOWADA-KO 十和田湖
☎ 0176 / pop 6000

There's no denying that this 327m-deep **crater lake** (52km in circumference) has some impressive scenery (it's at the top of a 440m mountain), famously transparent water and superb opportunities for hiking and skiing, but people here are oddly unwelcoming – perhaps the only area in Tōhoku where you may be told, 'we're booked solid this evening', in the off season, when there are only two cars in the parking lot. It's best enjoyed as a day trip, unless you've made reservations in advance.

Nenokuchi, a small tourist outpost on the eastern shore of the lake, marks the entrance to the 14km **Oirase Valley Nature Trail**, a three-

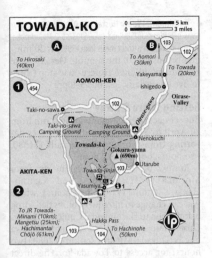

TOWADA-KO

0 —— 5 km
0 —— 3 miles

To Hirosaki
(40km)

To Aomori
(30km)

To Towada
(20km)

Yakeyama

AOMORI-KEN

Ishigedo

Oirase-
Valley

Taki-no-sawa

Taki-no-sawa
Camping Ground

Nenokuchi
Camping Ground

Nenokuchi

Towada-ko

AKITA-KEN

Gokura-yama
(690m)

Towada-jinja

Utarube

Yasumiya

Hakka Pass

To JR Towada-
Minami (10km);
Mangetsu (25km);
Hachimantai
Chōjō (61km)

To Hachinohe
(50km)

trimmings, including fruit sushi. Don't leave here without picking up a stuffed weasel as a souvenir.

Hakubutsukan Youth Hostel (☎ 75-2002; dm from ¥3360) Rooms here are squeezed into the old wing of the Towada-ko Grand Hotel, but are not available when the hotel is 'booked solid'.

Minshuku line the track leading out of Yasumiya away from the lake, but almost all of them close from November through March.

Kokuminshukuha Towada-ko Onsen (国民宿舎十和田湖温泉; ☎ 75-2041; www.laketowada.co.jp/e/; 16 Towada, Okuse-Aza; r per person incl 2 meals from ¥6650; 26 Apr-4 Nov) A few minutes northwest of the bus station, with decent rooms and a refreshingly welcoming owner.

Mangetsu (満月; ☎ 0186-37-3340; 20-1 Towada Ōyu Kaminoyu, Kazunoshi; meals from ¥650; lunch & dinner Tue-Sun) A great place for handmade *soba* noodles, tempura and other Japanese meals, run by a young chef. There's no English menu, but a very helpful, warm staff make dining here a pleasure. It's 25km towards Akita-ken on Route 103.

hour hike along the lakeshore; you might want to hike it in the early morning or late afternoon to avoid the coach parties. The path ends at Yakeyama, from where frequent buses return to Nenokuchi (¥660, 30 minutes) and Yasumiya (¥1100, one hour).

The tourist hub, Yasumiya, offers numerous boat tours of the lake, the best of which is the one-hour cruise between Yasumiya and Nenokuchi (one way ¥1320). Boats leave roughly every hour from April to early November between 8am and 4pm. You can rent mountain bikes at the dock for ¥1500 per day from April to November.

The hole-in-the-wall **tourist information centre** (☎ 75-2425; 8am-5pm), just north of the JR bus station, stocks only Japanese-language hiking maps but can help arrange accommodation.

Sleeping & Eating

There are several camping grounds around the edge of the lake. **Towada-ko Oide Camping Ground** (☎ 75-2368; www.citydo.com/outdoor/akita/0370 .html in Japanese; camp sites ¥300; 25 Apr-5 Nov) is about 4km west of Yasumiya. JR buses from Yasumiya to Towada-Minami pass by the Oide Kyampu-jō-mae stop (¥220, four minutes, two buses a day, depart at 8.45am and 1.10pm).

Towada-ko Grand Hotel (☎ 75-1111; Yasumiya-sanbashi-mae, Towada-kohan, Towada-chō, Kamikita-gun; r per person incl 2 meals from ¥8400) Offers a choice of Western- or Japanese-style rooms, and a dinner buffet that's ¥3500, but has all the

Getting There & Away

There are two bus centres in Yasumiya, one for JR buses and one for other services. Both are a couple of minutes on foot from the pier.

From April to November, JR buses run to Aomori (¥3000, three hours). There are three buses daily between April and early November to Morioka (¥2420, 2¼ hours). From late April to September there is one bus at 8.45am to Hachimantai Chōjō, the main point of access for the Hachimantai region (¥2300, 2¼ hours).

The nearest train station is at Towada-Minami on the JR Hanawa line, with connections to Morioka (*kaisoku* ¥2080, two hours). Up to four connecting buses run daily 8am to 4.40pm (¥330, one hour).

AKITA-KEN 秋田県

In a country created by volcanoes and peppered with *onsen*, many prefectures claim to be the 'Land of the *Onsen*' and Akita-ken is no exception. Japan's sixth-largest prefecture, it consists of 13 cities, six counties, nine towns and three villages, most of which are close to – or in – an *onsen*. People are as warm as the hot-spring water, making Akita a great place to relax before heading northward to Hokkaidō or going back on down south. The Oū Mountain Range and Dewa Mountain Ranges ensure there's plenty of hiking opportunities.

HACHIMANTAI 八幡平

Like a row of giant molars, often snowcapped, the peaks of this volcanic plateau south of Towada-ko are popular with hikers, skiers and *onsen* enthusiasts. Cutting across the Iwate-ken–Akita-ken border, the area features four types of volcano and has spectacular views, including Iwate-san (p528).

Hachimantai Chōjō, the main access point for the summit, offers gentle walks, but longer hikes are possible over a couple of days from nearby **Tōshichi Onsen**, a 2km walk downhill from the Hachimantai Chōjō car park. West of the summit, the Aspite Line Hwy, open late April to November, winds past several hot-spring resorts before joining Rte 341, which leads either south to Tazawa-ko or north towards Towada-ko. In winter some roads may be closed due to snow.

There's a small **visitors centre** (☎ 0186-31-2714; ⊗ 9am-5pm, closed Nov-Apr) next to the car park at Hachimantai Chōjō, where you can purchase regional contour maps (Japanese only) and consult bilingual hiking sketch maps. However, the best place for English-language information on Hachimantai is Morioka's tourist office (p524) or the office at Akita JR station.

The mountain lodge **Yuki-no-Koya** (ゆきの 小舎; ☎ 0186-31-2118; dm from ¥5250; ⊗ closed mid-Nov–Christmas & Feb-late Apr) is in a quiet riverside location at Shibari Onsen, on Rte 341, north of the turn-off for the Aspite Line Hwy to Hachimantai. Buses from Hachimantai Chōjō to Shibari Onsen (and connections to the JR Hanawa line towards Morioka) are, at best, erratic. Do a thorough check at the visitors centre or Morioka's tourist information office before setting out.

Hachimantai Youth Hostel (☎ 0195-78-2031; http:// www.geocities.co.jp/SilkRoad-Lake/5303/; 5-2 Midorigaoka, Matsuo-mura; dm without meals from ¥3990) is 20 minutes by bus east of the summit. Get off at the Hachimantai Kankō Hoteru-mae stop (three to five buses daily, last bus 3.40pm).

Getting There & Away

Bus services to Hachimantai Chōjō run from 20 April to 31 October, with four buses departing from Morioka station daily (¥1380, two hours, hourly until noon).

Kaisoku on the JR Hanawa line run from Morioka to Hachimantai and Kazuno-Hanawa stations (¥1910, two hours), where you can change to infrequent buses departing before noon to Hachimantai Chōjō via Shibari Onsen. Two stops further west on the Hanawa line is Towada-Minami station (¥2080, two hours) for access to Towada-ko. The direct bus to Towada-ko from Hachimantai Chōjō at noon is more convenient.

There are three buses daily from Hachimantai Chōjō to Tazawa Kohan (¥1880, two hours) and Tazawa-ko station (¥1990, 2¼ hours); the last bus departs at 3pm.

TAZAWA-KO 田沢湖
☎ 0187 / pop 13,000

With the atmospheric Nyūtō Onsen, some spectacular views, nice hiking and its own *shinkansen* station, Tazawa-ko has it all. At 423m, it is the deepest lake in Japan. Surrounded by wooded shores, with sandy beaches and boat rentals, Tazawa-ko is fun for kids, adults, couples…just about anyone wanting to slip away for a weekend. In September 2005, it merged with nearby Kakunodate and Nishikimura to create a larger *shi* (city), now known as Nishikishi. Thankfully for travellers, names have otherwise stayed the same.

The main access to the area is via JR Tazawa-ko station, outside of which buses from stop 3 run to Tazawa Kohan (¥350, 10 minutes), the area's hub on the east side of the lake.

Inside Tazawa-ko station, the modern and highly efficient **Folake tourist information office** (☎ 43-2111; ⊗ 8.30am-6.30pm) has excellent bilingual maps and free internet. If you're planning on doing any hiking in the Tazawa-ko or Hachimantai regions, ask for detailed contour maps in Japanese, as well as sketch maps in English.

Activities

Nyūtō Onsen is one of Japan's nicest hot springs, a must visit for any *onsen* buffs. Tucked up at the top of a winding mountain road, this collection of **spas** (each with a different character, and different baths) is famous for its healing waters and its *rotenburo* (outdoor baths). Several offer overnight lodging (see Sleeping, following), and many are *konyoku* (mixed sex). In Tsuru-no-Yu or the streamside Kuroyu, you'll easily feel like you've stepped back into a Japanese woodblock print…or gone to heaven. The former has classic milk-white water, while the latter is particularly beautiful when the maple trees are in full bloom.

Thanks to inconvenient bus schedules, it's wise to check with the tourist information office before heading somewhere. Semi-hourly buses run from Tazawa Kohan to Nyūtō Onsen (¥650, 40 minutes); the last bus back leaves at 6.40pm.

The lake offers boat excursions (¥1170, 40 minutes, from April to mid-November only), swimming beaches and a 20km perimeter road for which you can rent bicycles (¥400 per hour) or scooters (¥1200 per hour) in Tazawa Kohan.

In winter, there's **skiing** at Tazawa-kōgen, about halfway between the lake and Nyūtō Onsen, while a stroll by the lake at sunset is a treat at any time of year. In spring and early summer, skunk cabbage flowers in a nearby swamp, its white blooms carpeting the mud.

Hikers should take a bus from Tazawa-ko station to Komaga-take Hachigōme (8th station) for **Akita Komaga-take** (秋田駒ヶ岳; 1637m). From there, it's a challenging climb to the summit. A popular trail leads across to the peak of Nyūtō-zan (1478m) in about four (Bashō) hours, from where you can hike down to Nyūtō Onsen (another 5km). The whole thing is an all-day trek – make sure you're properly prepared. After soaking in a few of Nyūtō Onsen's renowned *rotenburo*, you can catch a bus back to Tazawa Kohan (¥650, 50 minutes); the last bus leaves at 6.20pm, but the schedule changes each April.

Direct buses travel to Komaga-take Hachigōme from the bus terminal near JR Tazawa-ko station, via Tazawa Kohan, six times daily during July and August, less frequently on weekends and holidays from June to late October (¥1000, one hour). At other times, you can take a bus from Tazawa-ko to Kōgen Onsen (¥580, 30 minutes), from where frequent buses run to Komaga-take Hachigōme (¥600, 30 minutes). If you're stuck, buses travelling to Nyūtō Onsen stop at Komaga-take Tozan-guchi (¥560, 40 minutes), which is 7km from Komaga-take Hachigōme.

Sleeping

Tazawa-ko Youth Hostel (田沢湖ユースホステル; ☎ 43-1281; 33-8 Kami-Ishigami, Obonai; r from ¥3140) Come here for Japanese meals that are equal to many *minshuku*, served with a friendly smile. It's not in great shape, but the rooms are clean and include TVs, and there's a nice *onsen* downstairs. It's 10 minutes from Tazawa Kohan bus station; coming from Tazawa-ko station, get off at the Kōen-iriguchi stop. The hostel's diagonally across the street.

Minshuku Beach House (民宿ビーチハウス; ☎ 43-0396; www.kosui-net.com; 145 Azaharuyama; r incl 2 meals ¥6500) Small, casual *minshuku* with shared baths, a steaming hot *onsen* and worn *tatami* that feels like home. Steps away from the lakeshore, with great sunset views. From the Kōen Iriguchi bus stop continue straight towards the lake – Beach House is the last house on the left.

HOT STUFF

There's an enduring myth attached to Lake Tazawa concerning a beautiful woman, Takko Hime, and her husband, Hachirōtarō. It's a very long and complex legend, and more than a little odd, but the gist of it is this: Takko Hime drank too much of the local water, believing it would make her even more beautiful. Her greed turned her into a water dragon, a metamorphosis that caused violent storms to whip up the elements, creating Lake Tazawa in the process. Meanwhile, Hachirōtarō had eaten a fish that made him very thirsty. He also drank too much water, bloated out and became a water dragon; the fury of his transformation from man to beast created Lake Towada. Later, he fell in love with the beautiful water dragon, Takko Hime, and began to visit her regularly at Tazawa-ko. The passion of their lovemaking on the lake floor supposedly keeps Lake Tazawa from freezing over in winter.

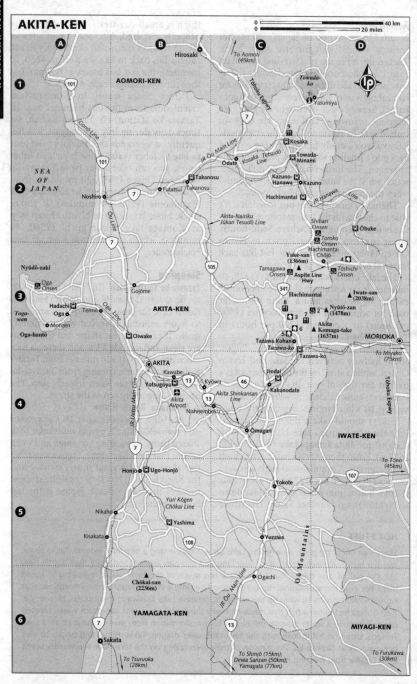

AKITA-KEN

0   40 km
0   20 miles

AOMORI-KEN

Hirosaki

To Aomori
(45km)

Towada-
ko
Yasumiya

Gonō Line

Kosaka

Takanosu
Futatsui
Takanosu

Odate
Kosaka Tetsudō
Line

Towada-
Minami

Kazuno-
Hanawa
Kazuno

SEA
OF
JAPAN

Noshiro

JR Ōu Main Line

Hachimantai

JR Hanawa Line

Ōbuke

Akita-Nairiku
Jūkan Tesudō Line

Shibari
Onsen
Toroko
Onsen

Hachimantai
Chōjō

Nyūdō-zaki

Oga
Onsen

Gojōme

Yake-san
(1366m)

Tamagawa
Onsen
Aspite Line Hwy

Tōshichi
Onsen

Iwate-san
(2038m)

Hadachi
Oga
Monzen

Tennō

Ōu Line

AKITA-KEN

Hachimantai

Nyūtō-zan
(1478m)

Toga-
wan

Oga-hantō

Oiwake

Tazawa Kohan
Tazawa-ko

Akita
Komaga-take
(1637m)

MORIOKA

Tazawa-ko

To Miyako
(75km)

AKITA

Kawabe

Yotsugoya

Kyowa

Jindai

Akita
Airport

Nishisemboku

Akita Shinkansen
Line

Kakunodate

Tōhoku Expwy

Ōmagari

IWATE-KEN

To Tōno
(45km)

JR Ōu Main Line

Honjō
Ugo-Honjō

Yuri Kōgen
Chōkai Line

Nikaho

Yashima

Yokote

Kisakata

Yuzawa

Ōu Mountains

Chōkai-san
(2236m)

Ogachi

JR Ōu Main Line

YAMAGATA-KEN

MIYAGI-KEN

Sakata

To Tsuruoka
(28km)

To Shinjō (15km);
Dewa Sanzan (50km);
Yamagata (77km)

To Furukawa
(30km)

Cafe+Inn That Sounds Good! (サウンズグッド; ☎ 43-0127; www.hana.or.jp/~takko; sanzoku@hana.or.jp; 160-58 Tazawakohan; r per person incl 2 meals from ¥8800; 🖳) A charming place with an excellent atmosphere. The owners are jazz fans and often host impromptu jazz nights; they also help organise outdoor activities. It's a pleasant 30-minute stroll north of Tazawa Kohan bus station, otherwise call ahead for a pick-up; advance reservations are mandatory during peak seasons.

The Nyūtō Onsen area is home to seven rustic ryokan, great for soaking away from it all. At **Tsuru-no-yu Onsen Ryokan** (鶴の湯温泉旅館; ☎ 46-2139; Kokuyurin 50 Senboku-gun, Akita, Towada-Hachimantai National Park; r per person ¥8550, bath ¥500; 🕗 8am-5pm Tue-Sun, day use 10am-3pm) and **Tae-no-yu Onsen Ryokan** (☎ 46-2740; r per person ¥12,855, bath ¥1000; 🕗 10am-3pm), rates include two meals.

If you just fancy a dip in a *rotenburo*, stay at the **Nyūtō camping ground** (sites ¥1000, plus per person ¥500) and then head for **Magoroku Onsen Ryokan** (☎ 46-2224; bath ¥400; 🕗 7am-5pm) or **Ganiba Onsen Ryokan** (☎ 46-2021; bath ¥500; 🕗 8am-5pm), which has a popular outdoor *konyoku* bath.

Eating & Drinking
Both of the following establishments are a 15-minute walk north of the Tazawa Kohan bus station, where you will also find a cluster of snack bars, ice-cream stands and souvenir shops.

Heart Herb (ハートハーブ; ☎ 43-2424; lunch sets ¥880; 🕗 9am-5pm Apr-Nov, 10am-4pm Dec-Mar) Has a good café and local food–inspired menus (no English), plus a weekend all-you-can-eat special for only ¥1500.

Kohan-no-Mori Restaurant ORAE (オラエ 湖畔の杜レストランオラエ; ☎ 58-0608; 37-5 Haruyama; set menus/beers from ¥820/480; 🕗 11am-9pm) A groovy place for snacks and local microbrews with its relaxed outdoor deck. There's no English, but picture menus (no beef, just chicken and veggies) make for easy ordering. Try the *korokke* (croquette) set (¥1200) or one of the daily specials.

Getting There & Away
On the Akita *shinkansen* line, Tazawa-ko is within easy reach of Morioka (¥1980, 33 minutes), Kakunodate (¥1560, 13 minutes) and Akita (¥3280, one hour), and it is only a three-hour trip from Tokyo (¥15,240, 186 minutes). Local trains run infrequently along the JR Tazawa-ko line to Morioka (¥740, 60 minutes) and Kakunodate (¥320, 20 minutes).

If you're heading west, it's easiest to take the bus from Tazawa Kohan via Tazawa-ko station to Kakunodate (¥840, 52 minutes, nine daily); departures before 4.10pm continue to Akita (¥1680, 2¼ hours). From December to March, services to and from Tazawa Kohan, but not Tazawa-ko station, are suspended.

Between 20 April and 31 October, three buses daily leave Tazawa-ko station for Hachimantai Chōjō (¥1990, 2¼ hours); the last bus leaves at 12.40pm.

KAKUNODATE 角館
☎ 0187 / pop 14,390
This quiet castle town was founded in 1620 by the feudal lord Ashina Yoshikatsu, a member of the Satake clan. The location was considered ideal as it was relatively secure, being surrounded on three sides by mountain ranges. Kakunodate is known as 'Little Kyoto', a thoughtful, immersive experience for anyone interested in old Japan. The castle has gone but the feudal layout is very much intact. Wandering through Uchimachi – the samurai district, with its original homesteads surrounded by cherry trees and lush garden expanses – is a splendid way to pass a day, though you may have quite a bit of company during peak holiday times. In September 2005 it merged with nearby Tazawa-ko (p538), but names have remained the same.

Information
Cash service is available at the **Kakunodate Post Office** (☎ 54-1400) and Akita bank.

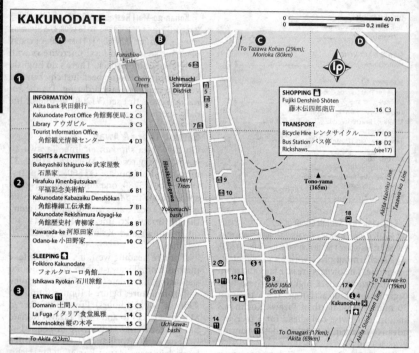

KAKUNODATE

INFORMATION
Akita Bank 秋田銀行	1 C3
Kakunodate Post Office 角館郵便局	2 C3
Library アウガビル	3 C3
Tourist Information Office 角館観光情報センター	4 D3

SIGHTS & ACTIVITIES
Bukeyashiki Ishiguro-ke 武家屋敷 石黒家	5 B1
Hirafuku Kinenbijutsukan 平福記念美術館	6 B1
Kakunodate Kabazaiku Denshōkan 角館樺細工伝承館	7 B1
Kakunodate Rekishimura Aoyagi-ke 角館歴史村 青柳家	8 B1
Kawarada-ke 河原田家	9 C2
Odano-ke 小田野家	10 C2

SLEEPING
Folkloro Kakunodate フォルクローロ角館	11 D3
Ishikawa Ryokan 石川旅館	12 C3

EATING
Domanin 土間人	13 C3
La Fuga イタリア食堂風雅	14 C3
Mominokitei 樅の木亭	15 C3

SHOPPING
Fujiki Denshirō Shōten 藤木伝四郎商店	16 C3

TRANSPORT
Bicycle Hire レンタサイクル	17 D3
Bus Station バス停	18 D2
Rickshaws	(see17)

Outside the station, you can hire a **bicycle** (☎ 53-3002; per hr ¥300) or a Japanese-speaking **rickshaw driver** (per rickshaw 15/30min ¥2000/5000; ☼ 10am-5.30pm Apr-Nov) to explain the local sights.

Library (Sōgō Jōhō Centre; ☼ 9am-5pm Tue-Sun) Free internet access.

Tourist information office (☎ 54-2700; ☼ 9am-6pm mid-Apr–Sep, to 5.30pm Oct–mid-Apr) In a small building that looks like a *kura,* it's outside Kakunodate station. The staff will oblige with reservations and English-language maps.

Sights

The Uchimachi samurai district is a 15-minute walk northwest from Kakunodate station. It's possible to stroll at any time, but most of the action is from April to November.

Bukeyashiki Ishiguro-ke (☎ 55-1496; Omotemachi; admission ¥300; ☼ 9am-5pm) was the residence of the Isihiguro family, advisers to the Satake clan; a descendant of the family still lives there, and has opened some of the rooms to the public. The house dates from 1809 and features an ornate gate, thatched roof and two entrances.

The interiors of the **Kawarada-ke** (☼ mid-Apr–Nov) and **Odano-ke** residences can be viewed for free, while further north **Kakunodate Rekishimura Aoyagi-ke** (☎ 54-3257; www.samuraiworld.com/english/index.html; 3 Omotemachi, Shimochō; admission ¥500; ☼ 9am-5pm Apr-Oct, to 4pm Nov-Mar) is the centrepiece of the district, an agglomeration of mini-museums with folk art and Aoyagi family heirlooms. Not all of the pieces are related to feudal history – in a turn-up for the books, there are also exhibits featuring old-time cameras, gramophones and classic jazz record covers.

Kakunodate Kabazaiku Denshōkan (☎ 54-1700; 10-1 Omotemachi Shimochō; single/combined ¥300/510; ☼ 9am-5pm Apr-Oct, to 4.30pm Nov-Mar) is a museum that houses various exhibits and has demonstrations of *kabazaiku* (cherry-bark craft). The combined ticket also allows entry to the nearby **Hirafuku Kinenbijutsukan** (☎ 54-3888; 4-4 Kamichō Omotemachi; ☼ 9am-5pm Apr-Oct, to 4.30pm Nov-Mar), which displays Japanese and Western modern art.

Festivals & Events

Some of the *shidarezakura* (drooping cherry) trees in the Bukeyashiki (samurai) area are up to 300 years old. On the river embankment, a 2km 'cherry blossom tunnel' comes alive around April/May – many of the trees were originally brought from Kyōtō.

From 7 to 9 September Kakunodate celebrates the **Hikiyama Matsuri**, in which participants haul around enormous seven-tonne *yama* (wooden carts) to pray for peaceful times, accompanied by folk music and dancing.

Sleeping & Eating

It might be more desirable to stay in Morioka or Akita; not only are Kakunodate's sights easily covered in a day trip from either, but those two cities have more accommodation options for travellers.

Sakura is big here, and you'll find pink 'sakura' udon, sakura sweets and other cherry-related products for sale.

Ishikawa Ryokan (☎ 54-2030; Iwasemachi 32; r incl 2 meals from ¥10,500) Close to town, this ryokan, which has been around since Edo times, offers Japanese-style rooms (no surprise there) with private bathroom.

Folkloro Kakunodate (☎ 53-2070; Nakasuga-zawa 14; s/tw/q ¥7350/12,600/21,000) This Western-style hotel is next to Kakunodate station; English is not spoken here; prices decrease for multiple-day stays.

Mominokitei (☎ 52-1705; mains from ¥1000; ☾ lunch & dinner) Mominokitei has a lovely old traditional Japanese interior and friendly staff, but it's an Italian restaurant, sort of. Take the very Italian entrée of bruschetta, antipasto and garden salad: it's served up Japanese style, arranged into minimal configurations, like sushi would be. Crisscrossed and arranged according to complementary colours, a sliver of capsicum might nestle on a bridge of finely chopped carrot, itself resting on a bed of lettuce. No English menu.

La Fuga (☎ 54-2784; 34-8 Kotate; set lunches/pizzas from ¥800/1200; ☾ 11am-2pm Tue-Sun; E) Kakunodate seems to have an Italy fetish. Like Mominokitei, this is one place worth seeking out, with its excellent pizzas and friendly owners.

Domanin (☎ 52-1703; 30 Shimonakamachi; single items ¥600, meals from ¥1575; ☾ lunch & dinner until midnight) This funky *izakaya*-style eatery features no Italian dishes, no English either, just an assortment of the usual suspects: try *yakitori* (chicken meat on skewers) or *agedashidōfu* (fried tofu) if you need suggestions.

Shopping

Kakunodate is renowned for *kabazaiku* (household or decorative items covered in cherry bark), a craft first taken up by poor samurai. It's worth spending more on the genuine article that is made entirely from wood, rather than the cheaper version with a tin inner core.

Fujiki Denshirō Shōten (☎ 54-1151; 45 Shimoshin-machi; ☾ 9am-5.30pm, closed Sun in winter) High-quality *kabazaiku* can be found here; it has its own workshop nearby.

Getting There & Away

The Akita *shinkansen* line connects Kakunodate with Tazawa-ko (¥1560, 14 minutes), Morioka (¥2770, 54 minutes) and Akita (¥2940, 43 minutes). Infrequent local trains run on the JR Tazawa-ko line from Kakunodate east to Tazawa-ko (¥320, 20 minutes) and Morioka (¥1110, 1½ hours). Infrequent connections west to Akita require a change of trains at Ōmagari.

Buses run from Kakunodate to Tazawa Kohan (¥840, 52 minutes) and Tazawa-ko station (¥490, 35 minutes), as well as to Akita (¥1330, 1½ hours). From December to March, these buses do not stop at Tazawa Kohan.

Kakunodate bus station is 10 minutes north of the train station.

AKITA 秋田
☎ 018 / pop 331,800

Akita, the prefectural capital, is a large commercial city that makes a great base for exploration. People-watchers may want to note that Akita's women are famous for their (supposedly) fair skin, and the term 'Akita *bijin*' (an Akita beauty) is well known. Truth or fiction, it's an interesting anecdote about a city that's not particularly beautiful in itself. Still, Akita has some delicious local cuisine and stages the spectacular Kantō Matsuri, ranked among Tōhoku's top three festivals.

Information
EMERGENCY
Akita Central Police Station (☎ 835-1111; 1-9 Meitoku-chō, Senshū)

INTERNET ACCESS
Comic Buster (☎ 884-7472; 2F, ALVE Bldg, 4-1 Higashidōri Nakamachi; per 30min ¥350; ☾ 24hr) Connected to the east exit of the JR station. The building is pronounced 'Aroo-vay'.

Plaza 1 (☎ 889-3588; 2nd fl, Topico station Bldg, 7-1-2 Naka-dōri; per hr ¥350; ☾ 7.30am-8pm)

MEDICAL SERVICES

Akita Red Cross Hospital (秋田赤十字病院; ☎ 829-5000; 222-1 Naeshirosawa Aza Kamikitatesaruta)

POST

Akita Central post office (秋田中央郵便局; ☎ 823-2900; 5-1 Hodono Teppōmachi) Five minutes west of the train station's west exit, in the backstreets near the market.

TOURIST INFORMATION

Tourist information office (☎ 832-7941; www.akita fan.com; 9am-7pm) Opposite the *shinkansen* tracks on the 2nd floor of Akita station.

Sights

The ruins of Akita's castle, Kubota-jō, are 10 minutes west of the station in **Senshū-kōen** (千秋公園). The castle dates from 1604 but, like many other feudal relics, it was destroyed by Meiji 'enlightenment'. At the park's northern end is **Osumi-yagura**, a reconstruction of one of the castle's eight turrets, with an observation platform that delivers appealing views of the city. Near **Hachiman Akita-jinja**, the **Omonogashira-obansho** guardhouse is the only remaining original castle building, while the tiny **Satake Historical Material Museum** (☎ 832-7892; admission ¥100; 9am-4.30pm) borders the southeast corner.

The **Masakichi Hirano Art Museum** (☎ 833-5809; 3-7 Senshū Meitoku-chō; admission ¥610; 10am-5.30pm Tue-Sun May-Sep, to 5pm Tue-Sun Oct-Apr) is noted for its enormous painting, *Events of Akita*. Reputed to be the world's largest canvas painting, it measures 3.65m by 20.5m and depicts traditional Akita life throughout the seasons.

The **Kantō Festival Centre** (☎ 866-7091; Neburi Nagashi-kan; admission ¥100; 9.30am-4.30pm, 9am-9pm during festivals), 10 minutes west of the park across the river, has exhibitions and videos of Akita's famous Kantō Matsuri and a chance for you to heft the famous *kantō* poles. It won't be easy: these babies are 10m long and weigh around 60kg.

Five minutes south, past Daiei department store, the **Akarengakan Museum** (☎ 864-6851; 3-3-21 Ōmachi; admission ¥200; 9.30am-4.30pm), in a Meiji-era, Renaissance-style, red-brick building, has woodblock prints of traditional Akita life by self-taught folk artist Katsuhira Tokushi. A combined ticket with the Kantō Festival Centre is available at either place for ¥250.

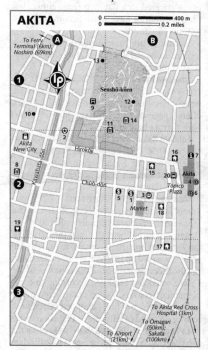

Festivals & Events

From 3 to 6 August, Akita celebrates the visually stunning **Akita Kantō Matsuri** (秋田竿燈まつり; Pole Lantern Festival; www.kantou.gr.jp). Starting in the evening along Kantō Ōdori, more than 160 men skilfully balance giant poles, weighing 60kg and hung with illuminated lanterns, on their heads, chins, hips and shoulders to the beat of *taiko* drumming groups. As the aim of the festival is to pray for a good harvest, the arrangement of the lanterns is designed to resemble an ear of rice. During the day, exhibitions of music and pole balancing are held in Senshū-kōen.

Sleeping

A lot is happening on the east side of Akita JR station– check there for new business hotels, many of which often offer inexpensive 'campaigns' to attract new clientele. Tōyoko Inn, Alpha-1 and other chains are all steps away from the station. Comic Buster's (see Internet, p543) overnight package costs about ¥2000 depending on a whole bunch of options, half the cost of a business hotel. If you're looking for something with more personality, check out the following.

Naniwa Hotel (☎ 832-4570; naniwa@beige.plala.or.jp; 6-18-27 Nakadōri; d per person incl/excl 2 meals ¥6680/3980) Meals here are made with the hotel's own homegrown rice, along with other local ingredients. This friendly place also has free internet, free massage chairs and a beautiful 24-hour *hinoki* (Japanese cyprus) bath.

Ryokan Chikuba-sō (☎ 832-6446; 4-14-9 Naka-dōri; r per person incl 2 meals ¥6800) A Japanese-style spick-and-span choice with decent-sized rooms. It's convenient to the station's west exit; the post office is one street further up on the opposite side.

Akita View Hotel (☎ 832-1111; 2-6-1 Naka-dōri; s/tw from ¥9500/17,000; 🖳) Opposite the Hotel Hawaii, this lush hotel is perhaps the swankiest in town, with its gym, pool, sauna and upmarket restaurants.

Hotel Metropolitan Akita (☎ 831-2225/-2222; 7-2-1 Naka-dōri; s/tw from ¥9200/17,500; 🖳) An upscale business hotel, with clean rooms and all the usual features: TVs, phones, full bathrooms. Compared to the discount business hotels, however, this isn't much of a bargain, considering the latter are less than half the price.

Eating & Drinking

Local specialities include two types of hotpot. One is *shottsuru* – *hatahata* (local fish) with green onions and tofu. The other is the fabulous *kiritanpo*, based on rice that's kneaded and wrapped around bamboo spits then barbecued over a charcoal fire. The rice is then cooked in a soy-flavoured chicken broth with noodles, onions, Japanese parsley and field mushrooms. Yum!

Kawabata-dōri is Akita's main nightlife area, a 15-minute walk west of the station. If you're coming south from Sapporo or north from Sendai, Akita's version of the neon jungle will seem quiet and quaint, but there's still plenty to do.

Ryōtei Hamanoya (☎ 836-0755; www.hamanoya.co.jp; 3rd fl, Hotel Metropolitan; kiritanpo from ¥2887; 🕙 lunch & dinner) This is the real deal: Hamanoya's *kiritanpo* is masterful, both in the preparation and the taste. The hotpot is a perfect blend, the mushrooms, onions and noodles soak the *mochi* (rice cakes) with a subtle mesh of flavours to produce a sticky rice stew. Hamanoya's kimono-clad waitresses prepare this right at your table, with a casual elegance and skill that's as seductive as the dish itself.

Suginoya (☎ 835-8903; 7-1-2 Naka-dōri; set menus from ¥1050; 🕙 10am-9pm) On the 3rd-floor restaurant arcade of Akita station's Topico Plaza, Suginoya does reasonable versions of the two hotpots, as well as other regional dishes.

Green Pocket (☎ 863-6917; 5-1-7 Ōmachi; 🕙 7pm-midnight Mon-Sat) This little gem is decked out in authentic period panelling, with an old-time piano in the corner, the aforementioned soundtrack, Vivien Leigh prints, and a fabulously decadent selection of scotch whiskies and fine wines – classy. The owner-bartender is gregarious and impeccably dressed in a tuxedo. Weeknights attract a lively older crowd; weekends are quieter.

Getting There & Away

There are flights from Akita's airport south of town to Nagoya (¥25,500, 70 minutes), Osaka (¥29,500, 1¾ hours), Sapporo (¥22,300, 55 minutes) and Tokyo (¥22,100, 70 minutes). Buses run from outside JR Akita station (¥890, 40 minutes).

The JR Akita *shinkansen* line runs via Tazawa-ko and Kakunodate to Morioka (¥4500, 1½ hours), cutting the total travel time between Akita and Tokyo to four hours (¥16,810). Painfully infrequent local trains chug along the Ōu line to Ōmagari, where you change to the JR Tazawa-ko line for Kakunodate (¥1280, 1½ hours) and Tazawa-ko

(¥1620, 2½ hours). The JR Uetsu line connects Akita with Niigata via Sakata and Tsuruoka (*tokkyū*, ¥7020, 3¾ hours).

Ten buses run daily from **Akita station** (羽後交通; Ugo Kōtsū; ☎ 863-6570) to Kakunodate (¥1330, 1½ hours) and eight daily to Tazawako (¥1680, 2¼ hours). Direct night buses to Tokyo (Shinjuku) run from the Nagasakiya bus terminal via Akita station at 10pm (one way ¥9450, 8½ hours).

Shin Nihonkai (☎ 880-2600) ferries connect Akita with Niigata (¥4000, 6½ hours, Sunday, Tuesday, Wednesday, Thursday, Saturday) and Tsuruga (¥6700, 21 hours, Sunday, Wednesday, Thursday). Ferries run to Tomakomai on Hokkaidō (¥4400, 12 hours, Monday to Wednesday, Friday and Saturday) as well.

One bus daily at 6.05am runs to Akita's port, 8km northwest of the station (¥390, 30 minutes).

KISAKATA 象潟

☎ 0184 / pop 13,100

This was the most northerly point Bashō reached in his travels through Tōhoku. Kisakata is a small coastal town near **Chōkai-san** (鳥海山; 2236m), Tōhoku's second-highest peak. Known as 'Dewa Fuji', Chōkai-san is an object of veneration by the same *yamabushi* (mountain priests) who worship at Dewa Sanzan (p549) in Yamagata-ken.

The **tourist information office** (☎ 43-2174; 9am-4.30pm), inside the station waiting room, has photocopied contour maps for hiking Chōkai-san and information on local sights, such as **Kanman-ji** (蚶満寺; visited by Bashō) just north of the town centre.

Next door to the youth hostel is a **camping ground** (camp sites ¥500, plus per person ¥400; Jul-Sep), while nearby **Minshuku Rofūsō Nihonkai** (民宿ろうふう草・日本海; ☎ 43-2228; 63-3 Kanmuri Ishishita; r per person incl 1/2 meals ¥5800/6300) is a simple but effective option.

Masaen (マサ苑; ☎ 44-2358; 8-1 Hamadō Aza Kotaki Kisakata-machi; set menus ¥800; 11am-8pm Tue-Sun) is a fantastic little eatery offering up generous serves of *rāmen* and free coffee. It's 300m west of the station.

Getting There & Away

Local trains on the scenic JR Uetsu Main line connect Kisakata with Sakata (¥650, 40 minutes) for connections to Tsuruoka (¥1110, one hour 36 minutes). Local trains head north on the same line to Akita (¥1110, 1¼ hours).

YAMAGATA-KEN 山形県

Yamagata-ken is often overlooked, yet has some beautiful gems that – time permitting – should not be overlooked. At the top of the list is tiny Zaō Onsen, famed for its atmospheric *rotenburo* and, more recently, its ski slopes. Yamadera offers temple buffs some spectacular photo opportunities, while Dewa Sanzan's peaks are revered by *yamabushi* (mountain monks) and hikers. Quieter places like Tobi-shima, Mogami-kyō and Tendō have charm all of their own. Like its neighbour Akita, Yamagata also claims to be an *onsen* capital. Sample all 100 and perhaps you'll be able to make the call for yourself.

TOBI-SHIMA 飛島

☎ 0234

Tiny Tobi-shima's main attractions are rugged cliffs, sea caves, bird-watching, scuba diving and excellent fishing. You can also organise boat trips out to smaller islands.

The coastal town of Sakata is your best bet for **tourist information** (☎ 24-2233; 9am-6pm).

Rates at the island's ryokan vary seasonally from ¥7000 to ¥10,000 per person with two meals; *minshuku* cost around ¥7000 with two meals. **Sawaguchi Ryokan** (沢口旅館; ☎ 95-2246; r per person incl 2 meals from ¥8000), the island's youth hostel, is seven minutes on foot from the ferry pier; bicycle rental is available.

Ferries run at least once (often twice) daily from Sakata-kō to the island (¥2040, 1½ hours); advance reservations (☎ 22-3911) are recommended in summer. To get to Sakatakō, take the Run Run bus from Sakata to the ferry-terminal stop (¥100). The JR Uetsu Main line runs to Sakata via Kisakata (*futsū*, ¥650, 40 minutes), Akita (¥1890, two hours nine minutes), Tsuruoka (¥480, 30 minutes) and Niigata (*tokkyū*, ¥5130, 2¼ hours).

There are up to seven buses daily from Sakata to Sendai (¥3100, three hours, last bus 6.30pm) via the Tsuruoka bus terminal (¥700, 90 minutes). There is one night bus to Tokyo (Shibuya, Ikebukuro) departing from Sakata at 9.30pm (¥7870, nine hours).

MOGAMI-KYŌ 最上峡

Boat tours (最上川舟下り; ☎ 72-2001) are operated through this gorge on a section of the Mogami-gawa between Sakata and Shinjō, complete with a boatman singing a selection of local folk tunes.

YAMAGATA-KEN

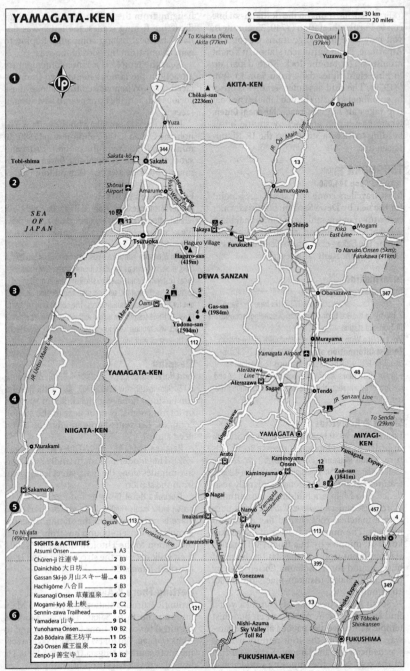

0 ————— 30 km
0 ————— 20 miles

To Kisakata (9km);
Akita (77km)

To Ōmagari
(37km)

Yuzawa

AKITA-KEN

Chōkai-san
(2236m)

Ogachi

Yuza

Tobi-shima

Sakata-kō

Sakata

344

JR Ōu Main Line

13

Mamurogawa

SEA
OF
JAPAN

Shōnai
Airport

Amarume

Mogami-gawa

Riku West Line

10 ☒ 13

Tsuruoka

7

Takaya

☒ 6

7

Furukuchi

Shinjō

Riku
East Line

Mogami

47

To Naruko Onsen (5km);
Furukawa (41km)

Haguro Village

Haguro-san
(419m)

DEWA SANZAN

Akagawa

Ōami

2 3

5

4

Gas-san
(1984m)

Obanazawa

347

Yudono-san
(1504m)

112

YAMAGATA-KEN

Yamagata Airport

Higashine

JR Uetsu Main Line

Aterazawa
Line

Aterazawa

Sagae

Tendō

48

7

NIIGATA-KEN

Mogami-gawa

JR Senzan Line

9 ☒

To Sendai
(29km)

Murakami

YAMAGATA

**MIYAGI-
KEN**

Arato

Sakamachi

Kaminoyama
Onsen

Kaminoyama

12

Zaō-san
(1841m)

Yamagata Expwy

11 8 ☒

Nagai

Oguni

113

Yonesaka Line

Imaizumi

Namyo

Akayu

Yamagata Shinkansen

To Niigata
(49km)

Kawanishi

Takahata

113

457

4

Shiroishi

349

121

Yonezawa

399

13

Tōhoku Expwy

Nishi-Azuma
Sky Valley
Toll Rd

JR Tōhoku
Shinkansen

FUKUSHIMA-KEN

FUKUSHIMA

SIGHTS & ACTIVITIES

Atsumi Onsen	1 A3
Chūren-ji 注連寺	2 B3
Dainichibō 大日坊	3 B3
Gassan Ski-jō 月山スキー場	4 B3
Hachigōme 八合目	5 B3
Kusanagi Onsen 草薙温泉	6 C2
Mogami-kyō 最上峡	7 C2
Sennin-zawa Trailhead	8 D5
Yamadera 山寺	9 D4
Yunohama Onsen	10 B2
Zaō Bōdaira 蔵王坊平	11 D5
Zaō Onsen 蔵王温泉	12 D5
Zenpō-ji 善宝寺	13 B2

From Sakata, trains on the JR Rikuu-sai line run to Furukuchi station (¥740, 35 minutes); you may have to change trains en route at Amarume. From Furukuchi station, it's eight minutes on foot to the dock. Boats depart up to nine eight times daily from 9am to 4pm (¥1970). The chill of winter weather is offset by an onboat *kotatsu* (heated table). The boat trip takes an hour to reach **Kusanagi Onsen**, where passengers are met by shuttle buses heading to Takaya station on the JR Rikuu-saisen line.

TSURUOKA 鶴岡

☎ 0235 / pop 144,000

Most travellers come here as an access point for the nearby Dewa Sanzan, but this former castle town in the middle of the Shōnai plain was once an important city in its own right, run by the Sakai-clan, one of feudal Yamagata's most important families.

Information

Internet access (鶴岡市ネットワークコミュ ニティセンター; ☎ 29-7775; 1hr free; ◷ 9am-7.30pm) On the 3rd floor of the Marica building, opposite JR Tsuruoka station.

Post office With ATM service, 300m south of the station.

Tourist information office (☎ 25-7678; ◷ 10am-5pm Nov-Feb, 9.30am-5.30pm Mar-Oct) To the right as you exit JR Tsuruoka station; can book accommodation and has lots of information about Dewa Sanzan, although little is in English.

Sights & Activities

Founded in 1950 by the former Lord Shōnai in order to develop and preserve local culture, **Chidō Museum** (致道博物館; ☎ 22-1199; 10-18 Kachū-shinmachi; admission ¥700; ◷ 9am-4.30pm) features Sakai family artefacts, a family residence, two Meiji-era buildings, a traditional storehouse and a *kabuto-zukuri* (a farmhouse with a thatched roof shaped like a samurai helmet). The museum is west of Tsuruoka-kōen, 10 minutes by bus from JR Tsuruoka station. From stop 1 at the station, frequent buses bound for Yunohama Onsen pass by the Chidō Hakubutsukan-mae stop (¥200, 10 minutes).

Seven kilometres west of Tsuruoka you'll find **Zenpō-ji** (善寶寺; ◷ 24hr), a Zen Buddhist temple with a five-tier pagoda and large gateway; it dates from the 10th century when it was dedicated to the Dragon King, guardian of the seas. Note the imposing wooden fish

hanging from the ceilings and the paintings depicting fishing scenes; the latter was donated by local fishing companies hoping to gain favour from the gods of the seas.

Near the temple is a more contemporary attraction, the famous *jinmen-gyo* (human-faced carp). When viewed from above, these curious fish actually do appear to have human faces.

From the station, take a bus bound for Yunohama Onsen to the Zenpō-ji stop (¥580, 30 minutes). If you're in the mood for surf and sand, the beach at **Yunohama Onsen** is a 10-minute bus ride away or 4km on foot.

Festivals & Events

Nō performances (黒川能 王祇祭) On 1 and 2 February, these are held at night in Kurokawa village near Tsuruoka; reserve tickets well in advance via the tourist information office.

Tenjin Matsuri Tsuruoka's best-known festival, on 25 May, is also known as the Bakemono Matsuri (Masked Faces Festival). People used to stroll around in masks and costume for three days, serving sake and keeping an eye out for friends and acquaintances. The object is to make it through three festivals in a row without anyone recognising you, whereupon local lore states you'll have good luck for the rest of your life.

Sleeping

Petit Hotel Tsuruoka (プチホテル鶴岡; ☎ 25-1011; 2-1 Suehiro-machi; s/tw ¥5000/9800; 🖵) This family-run business hotel, with its choice of Western or tatami rooms, is right next to the station complex. Let staffs know in advance if you need a meal.

Narakan (奈良館; ☎ 22-1202; r per person from ¥6500) This modern, clean, friendly ryokan is five minutes along the main street leading out from the station.

Tsuruoka Hotel (鶴岡ホテル; ☎ 22-1135; r per person incl 2 meals ¥8400) This atmospheric old place is rather far from the station. Take the Yunohama Onsen–bound bus from stop 1 at the station to the Hitoichi-dōri stop (¥100), then walk back up the street – the hotel is on the right-hand side.

Getting There & Away

From JR Tsuruoka station, the JR Uetsu Main line runs north to Sakata (*tokkyū*, ¥480, 38 minutes) for connections to Kisakata, and to Akita (*tokkyū*, ¥4020, 1½ hours); it takes a scenic route south to Niigata (*tokkyū*, ¥4330, 1¾ hours) across a backdrop of crashing waves.

Taking the train to Yamagata usually requires three changes, one at the very least. Despite the extension of the Yamagata *shinkansen* line to Shinjō, it's still more convenient to take the bus.

A series of scenic local trains along the JR Rikuu-sai and Rikuu-tō lines connects Tsuruoka to Naruko Onsen (Miyagi-ken; ¥1890, two hours 20 minutes) via a change at Shinjō.

Night buses to Tokyo (Ikebukuro, Shibuya) depart from in front of the Tokyo Dai-ichi Hotel in Tsuruoka (¥7540, eight hours). Regular buses between Tsuruoka and Yamagata (¥2400, 1¾ hours) run via the Yudono-san Hotel (¥1370, 50 minutes), which provides access to Yudono-san. Services are often cut back during the winter months due to snowdrifts. Between July and early November, there are also up to four direct buses between Tsuruoka and Yudono-san that stop by the hotel on the way up to the Sennin-zawa trailhead (¥1480, 80 minutes).

DEWA SANZAN 出羽三山
☎ 0235

Dewa Sanzan is the collective title for three sacred peaks: Haguro-san, Gas-san and Yudono-san. The mountains have been worshipped for centuries by *yamabushi* and followers of the Shugendō sect. During the pilgrimage seasons, you can see white-clad pilgrims (equipped with wooden staff, sandals and straw hat) and the occasional *yamabushi* (equipped with conch shell, checked jacket and voluminous white pantaloons) stomping along mountain trails or sitting under icy waterfalls as part of severe ascetic exercises intended to train both body and spirit.

Theoretically, if you hiked at a military pace and timed the buses perfectly you might be able to cover all three peaks in one day. However, this would leave you no time to enjoy the scenery, and the chances of missing a key bus connection are good. If you want to tackle all three mountains, it's best to devote at least two days; book accommodation and stock up on maps at the Tsuruoka tourist office before setting off.

Haguro-san 羽黒山
Because it has the easiest access, Haguro-san (414m) attracts a steady flow of tourists. At the base of the mountain is Haguro village, consisting of *shukubō* (pilgrims lodgings) and

the **Ideha Bunka Kinenkan** (いでは文化記念館; ☎ 62-4727; admission ¥400; ⏰ 9am-4.30pm Wed-Mon Apr-Nov, 9.30am-4pm Wed-Mon Dec-Mar), a small history museum featuring films of *yamabushi* rites and festivals.

The orthodox approach to the shrine on the summit requires pilgrims to climb 2446 steps but buses also run to the top. The climb can be done in a leisurely 50 minutes and you might even be lapped by gaggles of sprightly senior citizens; don't lose heart – just take your time and enjoy the views.

From Haguro centre bus station, walk straight ahead through the *torii* and continue across a bridge into beautiful cryptomeria trees that form a canopy overhead. En route you'll pass **Gojū-no-tō**, a weatherbeaten fivestorey pagoda dating from the 14th century. It's a stirring sight, with its aged, intricate wooden structure blending in with the trees. Then comes a very long slog up the hundreds of stone steps arranged in steep sections. Pause halfway at the **teahouse** (二の坂茶屋; ☎ 62-4287; ⏰ 8.30am-5pm Apr-Nov) for refreshment and breathtaking views. If you detour to the right just past the teahouse, you'll come upon the temple ruins of **Betsu-in**, visited by Bashō during his pilgrimage here.

The scene at the top is an anticlimax. There are several shrines, often crowded with visitors except during early mornings or late afternoons, an uninspiring history museum, and a row of shops and eateries. From the top you can either walk or catch a bus back down to the bottom. In summer there are two buses in the morning that go on to Gas-san.

Gas-san 月山
Accessible from June to September, Gas-san (1984m) is the highest of the three sacred peaks and attracts pilgrims to **Gassan-jinja** (admission with ritual purification ¥500; ⏰ 6am-5pm), a shrine on the peak itself. To enter the shrine you need to be purified: bow your head to receive a priest's benediction before rubbing your head and shoulders with sacred paper, which is then placed in the fountain.

The peak is usually accessed from the trailhead at **Hachigōme** (8th station); the trail passes through an alpine plateau to the Kyūgōme (9th station) in 1¾ hours and then grinds uphill for 70 minutes.

The steep descent to Yudono-san-jinja takes another 2½ hours (keep choosing the right fork). After about 45 minutes of this descent, you also have the choice of taking the trail to Ubazawa, the main ski resort on Gas-san, which has its own cable car. If you continue to Yudono-san, you'll eventually have to descend rusty ladders chained to the cliffside and carefully pick your way down through a slippery streambed at the end of the trail.

For those who can't last the summer without some powder, **Gassan Ski-jō** (☎ 0237-75-2025; ◔ 8am-4.30pm Apr-Jul; per day ¥4600) offers skiers a chance to slide around on snow, but come for the novelty of skiing in July, not because you're expecting great conditions. If you're not up for a whole (pricey) day, you can get per-time tickets for ¥560.

Assuming roads are open, drivers may want to (carefully!) toodle along the snowy roads – sometimes walls of snow tower four to five times the height of the passing cars, a surreal winterscape that's well worth taking time for.

Yudono-san 湯殿山

Accessible from June to October, the Sennin-zawa trailhead for Yudono-san (1504m) is approached via a 3km toll road from the Yudono-san Hotel. From there it's a 10-minute hike further up the mountain to **Yudonosan-jinja** (湯殿山神社; admission ¥500; ◔ 6am-5pm, closed Nov-Apr). This sacred shrine is not a building but a large orange rock continuously lapped by water from a hot spring. It has the strictest rituals of the three, with pilgrims required to perform a barefoot circuit of the rock, paddling through the cascading water.

Dainichibō & Chūren-ji 大日坊・注連寺

Off Rte 112 between Yudono-san and Tsuruoka, these two ordinary country temples house the exotic mummies of former priests who have become 'Buddhas in their own bodies'. The ascetic practice of self-mummification, outlawed since the 19th century, involved coming as close to death as possible through starvation, before being buried alive while meditating. The mummy at **Dainichibō** (admission ¥500; ◔ 8am-5pm) is dressed in bright orange robes and is rather ghoulish. The **Chūren-ji** (admission ¥500; ◔ 8.30am-5pm) mummy, also freakish, is allegedly a reformed murderer who became a powerful Buddhist priest.

Both temples are five minutes on foot from the Ōami bus stop, which is approximately halfway between Tsuruoka (¥950) and Yu-

dono-san (¥910). Buses are spaced about two hours apart, enough time to look around.

Festivals & Events

Dewa Sanzan-jinja, on the peak of Haguro-san, is the site of several major festivals. During the **Hassaku Matsuri** (八朔祭り), yamabushi perform ancient fire rites to pray for a bountiful harvest (31 August to 1 September). During the **Shōrei-sai** (松例祭) festival on New Year's Eve, they perform similar rituals in competition with each other after completing 100-day-long austerities.

Courses

If you haven't yet found your calling, consider becoming a yamabushi in a training camp:
Dewa Sanzan-jinja (☎ 62-2355) 'Real' yamabushi courses that are even more intensive, as well as three-day training programmes for women (¥35,000) in early September. These Buddhist boot camps are not for the faint-hearted.
Ideha Bunka Kinenkan On selected weekends in July and September, three- /eight-day courses for ¥34,600/40,000 that include fasting, mountain sprints and 4.30am wake-up calls.

Sleeping & Eating

There are more than 30 shukubō in the Tōge district of Haguro village, charging around ¥7000 to ¥8000 per person including two meals.
Haguro-san Saikan (斎館 羽黒山斎館; ☎ 62-2357; r per person incl 2 meals ¥7350) This temple lodging is at the top of Haguro-san, with airy rooms and spectacular views. Rates include two gourmet vegetarian meals; advance reservations are mandatory.
Yudono-san Sanrōjo (参籠所 湯殿山参籠所; ☎ 54-6131; r per person incl 2 meals from ¥7350; ◔ closed Nov-Apr) This friendly place can be found beside the Sennin-zawa bus terminal. There's a very good chance that you may be expected to join in prayers.

Saikan and Sanrōjo also serve vegetarian lunches to nonguests from ¥1500; reservations are required.
Yudono-san Hotel (湯殿山ホテル; ☎ 54-6231; r per person from ¥8500) This one's a convenient base to start or finish the Yudono-san to Gas-san hike. The rooms are basic but comfortable and the rate includes a vegetarian dinner.

Getting There & Away

Buses to Haguro centre bus station depart from Tsuruoka roughly every hour (¥680,

35 minutes), continuing to Haguro-sanchō (Haguro summit) less frequently between 7.52pm and 6.47pm (¥990, 55 minutes).

From early July to late August, and then on weekends and holidays until late September, there are four buses from Haguro-sanchō at 7.05am, 8.05am, 11.40am and 2pm, allowing pilgrims to travel towards the peak of Gas-san as far as Hachigōme (¥1240, one hour). Two buses at 6am and 7am also run from Tsuruoka direct to Gas-san Hachigōme (¥1650, two hours) during these times.

Buses from Tsuruoka pass by the Yudono-san Hotel en route to Yamagata (¥1370, 1¼ hours, last bus 3pm), as they do to Tsuruoka via Ōami (¥950, 50 minutes, last bus 6.42pm).

Between June and early November, there are up to four more buses from the Senninzawa trailhead at Yudono-san to Tsuruoka (¥1480, one hour 20 minutes), which also pass by the hotel and Ōami.

YAMAGATA 山形

☎ 023 / pop 255,600

Surrounded by beautiful, often snowcapped mountains, Yamagata is a thriving industrial city with a sizable student population, making for a livelier nightlife and more youthful vibe than in comparable *inaka* (rural) cities. Most travellers use it as a base for day trips to Yamadera, Tendō and Takahata, as well as the skiing, bathing and hiking region around Zaō Onsen.

Information

Free internet access on the 3rd floor of Kajō Central, at a tiny stand adjoining the digital copy centre, is for information on living in Yamagata only.

Prefectural tourism information office (やまがた観光情報センター; ☎ 647-2333; www.yamagatakanko.com/english/index.html; ☺ 10am-6pm) On the 1st floor of the Kajō Central building (joined to the station complex by walkways). Come here for excellent, helpful, English-speaking staff.

Tourist information office (山形市観光案内センター; ☎ 647-2266; ☺ 8.30am-8pm) On the 2nd floor of Yamagata station, in a small glass booth. Very helpful staff.

WIP (☎ 615-0788; www.wip-fe.com/yamagata; per 1hr ¥410; ☺ 24hr) Just outside the east exit of the Akita JR station, diagonally to the left. Overnight packages here are perfect for a backpacker budget.

Yamagata Central Post Office (山形中央郵便局; ☎ 622-2180; 1-7-24 Tōkamachi) Has ATM; a branch

post office is on the 1st floor of the Kajō Central building (☎ 645-9600).

Sights & Activities

HIRASHIMIZU POTTERY DISTRICT 平清水陶器地域

These recently revived kilns along the Hazukashi-kawa (Embarrassed River) turn out beautiful bluish-grey spotted-glaze pieces, nicknamed *nashi-seiji* (pear skin), which are displayed for sale in attached workshops. The renowned **Shichiemon-gama** (七右エ門窯; ☎ 642-7777; 153 Hirachimizu; ☺ 8.30am-5.30pm, pottery making 9am-3pm) offers instruction in pottery making at ¥1800 per 1kg of clay. To get there, buses bound for Nishi-Zaō or Geikō-dai run hourly or half-hourly from stop 5 outside Yamagata station to the Hirashimizu stop (¥200, 15 minutes).

The river's name comes from a folktale about a young girl who lost her beau – grief-struck, she looked down at her reflection while crossing a bridge and thought (as would anyone, no doubt) that she looked so awful she was embarrassed to be seen.

Festivals & Events

Hanagasa Matsuri In early August; features large crowds of dancers wearing *hanagasa* (flower-laden straw hats) and singing folk songs. The lyrics are said to derive from the impromptu, often salacious tunes once improvised by construction workers to keep time to the rhythm of their labour.

Yamagata International Documentary Film Festival This biennial is unique: it was established in 1989 to mark the 100th anniversary of the municipalisation of Yamagata, and was the first of its kind in Asia. During the festival week in October, films from over 70 countries screen, along with retrospectives, symposiums and a Japanese panorama. All screenings have English and Japanese subtitles and most festival publications are bilingual. See www.yidiff.jp for more information.

Sleeping & Eating

Yamashiroya Ryokan (山城屋旅館; ☎ 622-3007; r per person incl/excl 2 meals ¥6000/4000) A simple ryokan elevated to luxury levels by the friendliness of the hosts. It's 150m north of the station's east exit, next to a fruit shop.

Tōyoko Inn Yamagata Eki Nishiguchi (東横イン山形駅西口; ☎ 644-1045; 1-18-13 Jōnan-machi; s/d ¥5880/7980; ▢) If you've seen one, you've seen them all, but if you've got heavy suitcases, a close hotel sure beats lugging them across town. This is a minute's walk from the station's west exit. If it's full, try one of the new business hotels going up nearby.

There are plenty of places hawking marbled Yamagata beef along Nanokamachi-dōri.

Sagorō (五五郎; ☎ 631-3560; 1-6-10 Kasumi-chō; ⏰ lunch & dinner Mon-Sat) An excellent beef joint serving delicious *sukiyaki* (thin slices of beef) and good old steaks. Look for it on the 3rd floor above a butcher's shop, straight out from the east exit. No English menus.

Sakaeya Honten (栄屋本店; ☎ 623-0766; 2-3-21 Honchō; hiyashi rāmen ¥700; ⏰ 11.30am-7.30pm Thu-Tue) Try this place for *hiyashi* (chilled) *rāmen*, another Yamagata speciality. Facing east from the AZ store, take the first side street to your right. No English menus.

Getting There & Away

The JR Senzan line connects Yamagata with Yamadera and Sendai (*kaisoku* ¥1110, one hour 21 minutes). The JR Ōu Main line runs south to Yonezawa (*futsū*, ¥820, 45 minutes) and north to Ōma-gari for connections to Tazawa-ko and Akita (*kaisoku* ¥2520, three hours 18 minutes).

The JR Yamagata and Tōhoku *shinkansen* lines connect Yamagata with Yonezawa (¥2060, 36 minutes), Fukushima (¥3110, 1¼ hours) and Tokyo (¥11,030, two hours 51 minutes).

Travellers to Tsuruoka are advised to take the bus via the Yudono-san Hotel (¥2150, 1¾ hours). Buses start from the Yamakō bus terminal (stop 4) on Ekimae-dōri; most buses stop at Yamagata station before leaving town. There are frequent buses from Yamagata to Zaō Onsen (¥800, 40 minutes). Do not confuse Zaō Onsen with nearby Zaō, as the latter has no connection to the fabled baths.

Frequent highway buses run to Sendai (¥800, one hour) and two buses run daily to Niigata (¥3500, 3¾ hours). A night bus to Tokyo (Asakusa, Ueno) departs at 11.40pm (¥6420, six hours). Reserve in advance for a cheaper Tokyo-bound bus with **Orion Tours** (オリオンツアー; ☎ 022-224-8541; www.orion-tour .co.jp; ¥4500), which goes to Shinjuku and other locations.

TENDŌ 天童
☎ 023 / pop 63,100

Tendō makes an interesting half-day excursion from Yamagata. It produces around 90% of Japan's chess pieces annually, an exquisite art begun by poor samurai during the Edo period (their salaries were cut by the Tendō lord, who had fallen upon hard times).

The **tourist information centre** (天童市観光 物産協会; ☎ 653-1680; ⏰ 9am-6pm, closed every 3rd Mon), on the 2nd floor of JR Tendō station, has details of local attractions, including the eccentric **Tendō Mingeikan** (天童民芸館; ☎ 653-5749; admission ¥500; ⏰ 9am-5pm), a folkcraft museum housed in a *gasshō-zukuri* (thatched 'praying' roof) farmhouse. The **Tendō Shōgi Museum** (天童市将棋資料館; ☎ 653-1690; 1-1-1 Hon-chō; admission ¥300; ⏰ 9am-6pm Thu-Tue) is part of JR Tendō station and displays chess sets from Japan and abroad.

You can see chess pieces being made at **Eishundō** (栄春堂; ☎ 653-2843; 1-3-28 Kamatahonchō; admission free; ⏰ 8am-6pm Wed-Mon), a 15-minute walk straight out from the station, just past the Tendō Park Hotel. Across the street, the **Hiroshige Art Museum** (広重美術館; ☎ 654-6555; 1-2-1 Kamatahonchō; admission ¥600; ⏰ 8.30am-5.30pm Wed-Mon Apr-Oct, 9am-4.30pm Wed-Mon Nov-Mar) displays woodblock prints by famous Edo-period master Hiroshige.

On the last weekend in April, Tendō-kōen hosts the theatrical **Ningen Shōgi**, when outdoor chess matches are played using real people as pieces. The tradition is credited to Toyotomi Hideyoshi, who once played a similar match with his son in Kyoto. If you want to become a human chess piece, visit www.ikechang .com/chess/piece-e.htm.

Tendō is six stops north of Yamagata by local train (¥230, 20 minutes) or 50 minutes by bus from Yamagata station (¥480).

ZAŌ-SAN 蔵王山
☎ 023 / pop 13,600

The Zaō Quasi National Park region (not to be confused with Zaō, a town just outside Yamagata) is one of this prefecture's must visits. It's small, but packed with people, hot springs and great powder. Skiing starts in December and runs through April, but even if there's no snow there are plenty of reasons to come here. Good hikes and great baths are the biggies, but it's also fun to just kick back and bask in the friendly atmosphere and relaxed pace. Zaō's simply stunning vistas are gorgeous year-round. That said, if you come in the off season you should expect to have the town pretty much to yourself, with shops and restaurants closing early. The main ski resorts are around **Zaō Onsen** (☎ 694-9328) and **Zaō Bōdaira** (☎ 679-2042). In winter, free shuttles connect the extensive networks of ropeways and lifts; one-day passes start at ¥4500. Advanced skiers will probably want to pass unless they're with less-skilled friends, and the mountain is small, smaller if any of the upper lifts are closed due to winds or poor snow. But skiing through the 'Ice Monsters' is a wacky thrill, something worth doing once just for the view.

Near Zaō bus terminal, the **tourist information office** (☎ 694-9328; ☉ 9am-5.30pm) has maps and can advise on transport and accommodation options, though the town is small enough that you easily do-it-yourself.

In summer you can make your way up to **Okama** (御釜), a cobalt blue, volcanic crater lake atop Zaō-san, considered by many to be the area's premier sight. Given the right weather, it is indeed beautiful and hiking around it is a joy, with Buddhist statues and monuments hidden among the greenery. The most convenient access is via Katta Chūshajōcar park, where the **Katta Sky Cable** (蔵王スカイケーブル; one way/return ¥700/1200; ☉ 8.30am-5pm) takes you to within spitting distance of the Okama overlook.

There are numerous trails around the area, open except when there's snow. A nice one-hour walk over to Jizōsanchō-eki leads to the **Zaō Ropeway** (蔵王ロープウェイ; ☎ 694-9518; single/return ¥700/1400; ☉ 8.30am-5pm Apr-Nov) down through Juhyō-kōgen (Ice Monster Plateau) to Zaō Onsen. The 'monsters', best viewed from late February to early March, are really frozen conifers covered in snow by Siberian winds; a unique, fascinating winter display.

After a long day of hiking or skiing, you can soak among sulphur-stained rocks at the atmospheric **Zaō Onsen Dai-rotenburo** (蔵王温泉大露天風呂; admission ¥450; ☉ 6am-7pm May-Oct), where each outdoor hot-spring pool can hold up to 200 people. Smaller and much older are two community baths called 'Upper' and 'Lower' (¥200), both on the main cobbled street leading uphill from the bus station. These baths are old school – no soap or towels: just splash yourself clean and hop into water so hot Hell's brimstone will seem chilly in comparison.

Sleeping & Eating

Accommodation abounds, but advance reservations are essential if visiting during high seasons or on weekends. In nonpeak times some places close, as do many shops and res-

taurants. Either way, it pays to call ahead. Very little English is spoken.

Ginrei Honten (銀嶺本店; ☎ 694-9120; www.community-i.com/zao/ginrey.html; 940-5 Zaō Onsen; r per person with shared bathroom ¥3500) is a casual, friendly *minshuku* (love the astroturf carpets!) and souvenir shop. The toilet is shared, and the owners offer a discount coupon for the community *onsen* across the street. Find it by going right from the bus station, cross the bridge and it's on the right corner, just before a large hotel parking lot.

Pension Boku-no-Uchi (ペンション ぼくのうち; ☎ 694-9542; www.bokunouchi.com; 904 Zaō-onsen; r per person incl 2 meals from ¥7185), next to the Lawson convenience store, is a friendly, family-run place with its own restaurant and 24-hour sulphur bath.

The comfortable **Lodge Chitoseya** (ロッジちとせや; ☎ 694-9145; 954 Zaō Onsen; r per person incl/excl 2 meals from ¥6825/4515; 💻) is closer to the bus station. Original meals are served with pride, a mix of Japanese-inspired and fusion favourites.

Shinzaemon-no-Yu (新左衛門の湯; ☎ 693-1212; www.zaospa.co.jp/top.html; 905 Kawa-mae Zaō Onsen; bath ¥600, meals from ¥1500; ☉ bath 10am-9.30pm, lunch & dinner, closed irregularly) Luxurious bath cum banquet – come here to soak those ski pains away or to revel in the simple, natural-wood elegance. Food is pricey; the baths are divine.

Robata Honten (炉ばた本店; ☎ 694-9565; www.t023.com/zao/index.html; 42-7 Zaō Onsen; dinners from ¥1200; ☉ 11am-11.30pm) An *izakaya*-style eatery with a community bath just outside its door. Come here for *jingis-kān*, a mix of lamb and veggies grilled on a skillet, or excellent broiled *sanma* (Japanese saury).

Buses from stop 1 outside Yamagata station depart frequently for Zaō Onsen (¥800, 40 minutes). To cope with the demand during winter – when there are more than a million visitors to the region – there is a regular bus service direct from Tokyo. Between late April and early November, there are two buses daily at 9.30am and 10.30am connecting Yamagata station, via Zaō Onsen, with Katta Chūsha-jō (¥1800, 1½ hours); buses in the reverse direction leave from Katta at 1pm and 2pm.

YAMADERA 山寺
☎ 023 / pop 1600

Yamadera, also known as **Risshaku-ji** (立石寺; ☉ 8am-5pm), is a stunning temple complex, a wondrously atmospheric cluster of buildings and shrines perched on lush, wooded slopes; each turn holds a new place with a character all its own. It's believed that Yamadera's rock faces are the boundary between this world and the afterlife. Founded in 860 with a sacred flame that was brought from Enryaku-ji near Kyoto (supposedly the same flame is still alight today), the complex is often besieged with tourists, so visit early morning or late afternoon for meditative bliss.

From **Hihōkan**, the temple treasury, you pay a ¥300 entry fee to start the steep climb up hundreds of steps through the trees to the Oku-no-in (Inner Sanctuary), where trails lead off on either side to small shrines and lookout points.

There is a small **tourist information office** (☎ 695-2816; ☼ 9am-5pm) near the bridge before Risshaku-ji. Staff provides English-language pamphlets but no English is spoken.

Five minutes from the station, **Bashō Kinenkan** (山寺芭蕉記念館; ☎ 695-2221; admission ¥400; ☼ 9am-4.30pm, closed Mon Dec-Feb) is a very quiet museum exhibiting scrolls and calligraphy related to Bashō's famous northern journey, as well as documentary videos of the places he visited.

For clean accommodation, **Pension Yamadera** (山寺ペンション; ☎ 695-2134; r per person incl 2 meals from ¥8767) is right by the station.

The JR Senzan line links Yamadera with Yamagata station (*kaisoku* ¥230, 19 minutes) and Sendai (¥820, 58 minutes). There are also infrequent buses from Yamagata station to Yamadera (¥580, 40 minutes).

YONEZAWA 米沢
☎ 0238 / pop 92,400

Carnivores should come here to chow down on Yonezawa beef, famous for its tenderness and flavour, similar to Kobe's own. During the 17th century the Uesugi clan built their castle in this town, which later developed into a major centre for silk weaving. You can pick up maps and information at the **tourist information office** (☎ 24-2965; ☼ 8am-6pm) inside the station. Rental bicycles (¥1000 per day) are available outside.

At the south entrance of **Matsugasaki-kōen** (松ヶ崎公園), the small **Uesugi Museum** (米沢市上杉博物館; ☎ 26-8001; admission ¥400; ☼ 9am-4.30pm, closed 4th Wed, closed Mon Dec-Mar) displays Uesugi clan artefacts. **Uesugi-jinja** (上杉神社), built on the castle ruins in 1923, is inside the park grounds with a nearby treasury, **Keishō-den**, (稽照殿; ☎ 22-3189; ☼ 9am-4pm), which displays armour and works of art belonging to several generations of the Uesugi family. Advance reservation

is necessary from December to March. Just south of the shrine is **Uesugi Kinenkan** (上杉記念館; ☎ 21-5121; ☼ 11am-2pm & 5-8pm), a Meiji-era residence with more Uesugi relics. Advance reservation is necessary for dinner.

To get to the park, take a bus from stop 2 from outside the station bound for Shirabu Onsen to the Uesugi-jinja-mae stop (¥190, 10 minutes).

The clan mausoleum **Uesugi-ke Byōsho** (上杉家廟所; ☎ 23-3115; admission ¥200; ☼ 9am-5pm), 1km west of the park, has several generations of the Uesugi clan entombed in gloomy individual mausoleums.

Festivals & Events

The **Uesugi Matsuri** starts off with folk singing on 29 April and mock ceremonial preparation for battle in Matsugasaki-kōen on the evening of 2 May. The real action takes place on 3 May with a re-enactment of the titanic Battle of Kawanakajima (one of the Uesugi clan's more bloody and infamous skirmishes), featuring more than 2000 participants.

Sleeping & Eating

Hotel Otowa (ホテルおとわ; ☎ 22-0124; www.hotel-otowa.com; s/tw ¥4500/8400; ☐) This atmospheric, castle-like building is 100 years old; it's three minutes from the station. It was the only inn in town not destroyed by the Japanese military or US occupying authorities at the end of WWII, and former prime ministers, famous kabuki actors and pop stars have stayed here.

Gourmet Kozō Mankichi (グルメ小僧万吉; ☎ 24-5455; beef ¥2300-5000; ☼ lunch & dinner Tue-Sun) A good bet for, you guessed it, the famous marbled Yonezawa beef.

Getting There & Away

The JR Ōu Main line runs north from Yonezawa to Yamagata (¥820, 51 minutes) and east to Fukushima (¥740, 46 minutes). The JR Yonesaka and Uetsu Main lines link Yonezawa with Niigata (*kaisoku* ¥2520, four hours) via a change at Sakamachi.

NIIGATA-KEN 新潟県

Niigata-ken, while not technically part of Tōhoku proper, makes a wonderful stepping-stone to these beautiful northern lands. Its mountains offer fantastic skiing, it has unique customs and festivals, sublime selections of sake, and remains steeped in history and culture even in the era of HDTV. From persimmon-peppered Sadogashima, where exiles were once banished, to Echigo-Yuzawa, the site of Kawabata's *Snow Country*, to the mellow bars of Niigata City – this is a prefecture not to overlook.

In 2004 the prefecture suffered a devastating earthquake in the Chuetsu region: 35 people died and 80,000 people were left homeless. The scale of the quake caught the entire nation off guard (it caused the *shinkansen's* first-ever train derailment), particularly the prefectural government, who, being in a rural area, found that resources were inadequate to cope with the number of evacuees.

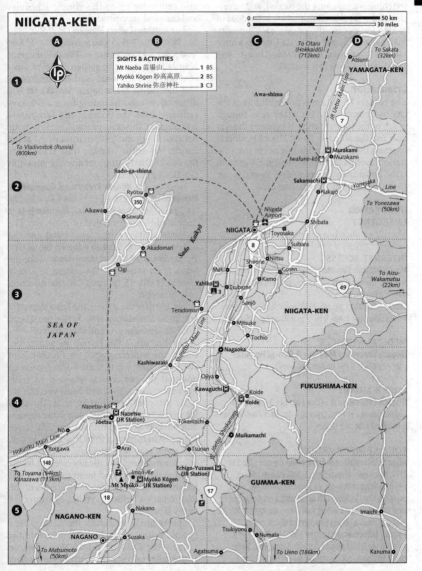

NIIGATA-KEN

0 — 50 km
0 — 30 miles

SIGHTS & ACTIVITIES		
Mt Naeba 苗場山	1	B5
Myōkō Kōgen 妙高高原	2	B5
Yahiko Shrine 弥彦神社	3	C3

To Otaru (Hokkaidō) (712km)
To Sakata (32km)

YAMAGATA-KEN
Atsumi

JR Uetsu Main Line

Awa-shima

To Vladivostok (Russia) (800km)

Murakami
Murakami
Iwafune-ko

Sado-ga-shima

Sakamachi
Yonesaka Line
Nakajō
To Yonezawa (50km)

Ryōtsu
350
Aikawa
Sawata

Niigata Airport
NIIGATA
Toyosaka
Shibata

Akadomari

Suibara
Shirone Niitsu
Maki
Suibara
8

Ogi

Sado Kaikyō

Yahiko
3
Tsubame
Kamo
Gosen

To Aizu-Wakamatsu (22km)
49

Teradomari

Sanjō

NIIGATA-KEN

SEA OF JAPAN

Mitsuke
Tochio

Shinetsu Main Line

Nagaoka

Kashiwazaki

Ojiya

FUKUSHIMA-KEN

Kawaguchi
Koide
Koide

Naoetsu-kō
Naoetsu (JR Station)
Jōetsu

Tōkamachi

Muikamachi

Nō
Itoigawa

Arai

Tsunan

JR Jōetsu Shinkansen

Hokuriku Main Line

148
To Toyama (54km); Kanazawa (113km)

Imori-ike
Mt Myōkō
Myōkō Kōgen (JR Station)

Echigo-Yuzawa (JR Station)

GUMMA-KEN

18
Nakano

1
17

5

NAGANO-KEN

Imaichi

NAGANO
Suzaka

Tsukiyono
Numata

To Matsumoto (50km)

Agatsuma

To Ueno (186km)

Kanuma

NIIGATA 新潟

☎ 025 / pop 812,900

Niigata, the lively capital, has a calm and spacious feel, despite its reputation as a transport hub and springboard to nearby Sadogashima. It's bisected by the Shinano River, which generates a great swathe of blue sky where, in other cities, there'd be skyscrapers (people-watching is a joy along the banks), and street-side ginko trees send miniature tornadoes of golden leaves cascading down each autumn. Sake reigns supreme – Niigata City has a huge sake-tasting festival each year and boasts over 100 different *kura* (breweries).

Orientation

The Niigata JR station is in the middle of the city, with stuff to do on either side, though much of the tourist action is between the station and the Shinano River. Higashi Ōdori is the main thoroughfare leading north from the station. Across the Bandai-bashi, Furumachi is the downtown shopping district and home to the vibrant Honchō market area.

Information

EMERGENCY

There's a police box inside the station.

INTERNET ACCESS

Media Station Banana (30min free; ☽ 11am-7pm Mon-Fri, 10am-7.50pm Sat, 11am-7pm Sun) Inside the station's Bandai exit.

Stock + Niigata (☎ 246-1370; www.stockplus-n.com; 1-2-23 Ōdori; per 15min ¥157; ☽ 9.30am-6pm Mon-Fri)

MEDICAL SERVICES

Niigata University Medican & Dental Hospital (☎ 223-6161; 1-757 Asahimachi-dōri)

POST & MONEY

Niigata Central post office (☎ 244-3429; 2-6-26 Higashi Ōdori) ☽ 7am-11pm Mon-Fri, 9am-7pm Sat, Sun & holidays) ATM cash service.

TOURIST INFORMATION

Niigata International Friendship Centre (☎ 225-2777; Kurosuparu Niigata Bldg, 3-2086 Ishizuechōdori; ☽ 9am-9.30pm Mon-Sat, to 5pm Sun & holidays, closed every 4th Mon) Includes CNN broadcasts, a small library, local information and willing staff. Also publishes the *Niigata English Journal*, a helpful pamphlet of topical events.

Tourist information centre (☎ 241-7914; ☽ 9am-6pm) To the left of Niigata station's Bandai exit. Sweet, kindly English-speaking staff, excellent maps and brochures for both Niigata and Sado-ga-shima. Same-day accommodation bookings, often with a discount.

Sights

The city centre is easily covered on foot, otherwise a flat rate fare of ¥180 operates on city buses. Further destinations, such as the final two, require buses or trains. Ask at the tourist info centre for up-to-the-minute schedules and seasonal suggestions.

The **Northern Culture Museum** (北方文化博物館; ☎ 385-2001; 2-15-25 Sōmi; admission ¥800; ☽ 9am-5pm Apr-Nov, to 4.30pm Dec-Mar) is 10km southeast of Niigata in an attractive garden complex. Situated among traditional earthen warehouses and individual tea arbours, **Sanraku-tei** is a diminutive teahouse dating from 1890; everything – even the flooring and furniture – is triangular. Buses leave roughly every hour between 10am and 4.40pm from stop 7 at the Bandai bus centre (not the train station) for the Nishi Ohata stop outside the museum (¥500, 45 minutes).

Next to the **Niigata Prefectural Government Memorial Hall** (☎ 228-3607; ☽ 9am-4.30pm Tue-Sun, to 6.30pm Jul-Aug, closed 28 Dec-4 Jan), **Hakusan-jinja** is dedicated to the local god of marriage. The grounds contain a fine lotus pond and the historic teahouse **Enkikan** (admission free, tea ¥300; ☽ 9am-5pm, closed 1st & 3rd Mon of month). Take the buses from stop 13 at the station to Showa Ōhashi (¥180, 15 minutes), in the direction of Irihonechō.

Just north of the station, the **Tsurui Museum of Art** (☎ 247-3311; admission ¥500; ☽ 10am-5pm Mon-Sat) exhibits Japanese arts and local crafts.

Further off, Lake Hyoko in winter becomes the wintering spot for thousands of swans. Brilliant white, these flocks have been designated a prefectural treasure. At feeding times (noon, 1pm and 3pm) you can see these graceful, beautiful animals, threshed into a food frenzy – think 13kg white pigeons and buckets of popcorn. It's possible to see them just hanging out in nearby fields as well, and some may want to avoid an area where wild animals are specifically overfed to the point that they depend on human handouts for winter survival. Still, they are beautiful, and remain a beloved symbol of winter for many Japanese.

Spectacularly beautiful is the 'Momiji Tani' (Maple Valley) of nearby Yahiko. In autumn, roughly late October to mid-November, an entire valley (albeit a smallish one) turns fiery

NIIGATA

INFORMATION

Media Station Banana	
メディアステーションbanana........1 E4	
Niigata Chūō Post Office	
新潟中央郵便局............................2 E4	
Niigata International Friendship	
Centre 新潟国際友好会館..............3 C3	
Niigata Naka Post Office	
新潟中郵便局...............................4 C2	
Niigata University Medican Dental	
Hospital	
新潟大学医歯学総合病院..............5 A3	
Police Box 新潟駅前交番..............6 E4	
Stock + Niigata	
ストックプラス新潟.......................7 E4	
Tourist Information Centre	
観光案内センター.........................8 E4	

SIGHTS & ACTIVITIES

Enkikan 燕喜館.......................(see 9)	
Hakusan-jinja 白山神社................9 B4	
Niigata Prefectural Government	
Memorial Hall 新潟県政記念館...10 B4	
Tsuru| Museum of Art 敦井美術館...11 E4	

SLEEPING

Dormy Inn Niigata	
ドーミーイン新潟.......................12 E4	
Hotel Sunroute	
ホテルサンルート新潟...............13 F4	
Ueda Ryokan 植田旅所館.............14 D2	

EATING

Immigrant's Café	
イミグランツ カフェ..................15 E4	
Kurumiya 胡桃屋......................16 E4	
Toritsune 鳥つね......................17 D2	

ENTERTAINMENT

Ryotopia りゅーとぴあ...............18 B4	

TRANSPORT

Bandai Bus Centre	
万代バスセンター.....................19 D4	
Bus Terminal バスターミナル......20 E4	
Sado Kisen Ferry Terminal 佐渡汽船	
フェリーターミナル....................21 E1	

To Niigata Airport (12km)

To Sado-ga-shima

To Sakata (67km)

To Sakata (67km); Akita (220km)

To Northern Culture Museum (10km)

Niigata

Ryōtsu Ōhashi-bashi

Bandai-bashi

Shinano-gawa

Higashi Ōdori

Yachiyo-bashi

To Nagaoka (52km)

Shōwa Ōhashi-bashi

Shōwa-ōhashi

Honchō Market

Furumachi Arcade

Masaya-kōji

Masaya-kōji

Higashi Naka-dōri

Hakusan-kōen

Nishi Ōhata-kōen

To Toyama (254km)

scarlet and orange, as these gorgeous trees blush before dropping their leaves for winter's chill. Photographers and tour groups come by the busload, yet it's still well worth ducking onto the beaten path to see. If you time it right, you can catch the Chrysanthemum Festival, held there from 1 to 24 November, where the walkways of Iyahiko Shrine are festooned with flowers.

Festivals & Events

Niigata Sake no Jin Festival Sake aficionados won't want to miss this, held on the third weekend each March. It's a mammoth bacchanal with a blissfully reasonable all-you-can-drink ¥1000 fee, sake vending tables and a blindfolded tasting contest. Over 170 varieties of sake from all over Japan are available. *Kanpai!*

Niigata Matsuri From the first or second weekend (varies yearly) in August, the streets are filled with afternoon parades of colourful floats and shrines. At night thousands of folk dancers parade across the Bandai Bridge. A bumper fireworks display on the final night lights up the Shinano-gawa, as a passage of decorated boats carries the shrine of the local god of the sea.

Sleeping

If you're stuck and are on a backpacker budget, Niigata has several 24-hour internet cafés, but they're located inconveniently far from the station, a 10- or 15-minute bus ride away.

our pick **Dormy Inn Niigata** (☎ 247-7755; 1-7-14 Akashi; s/d from ¥5775/7350; ☐) Further down the road, this is a modern and clean business hotel with boxy, featureless rooms and its own laundry. There are a couple of cleanliness options: pay extra for a private bathroom, or pay less and use the public bath and sauna.

Ueda Ryokan (☎ 225-1111; 2120 Yonnochō Ishizuchodōri; r per person from ¥3990; ☐) Tucked in the side streets near the Bandai Bridge Lawson, this intimate Japanese-style ryokan isn't fancy, but has clean accommodation and a welcoming host. From the Lawson, cross Ōdōri and follow the small side street past three intersections. When the road narrows, turn right at the next street and Ueda will be on your left, about halfway down.

Hotel Sunroute (☎ 246-6161; 1-11-25 Higashi Ōdōri; s/tw/d from ¥8000/13,800/12,800; ☐) The Sunroute is neat, white and bright, with spacious rooms and excellent amenities.

Eating & Drinking

Niigata is known for the quality of its rice, seafood and, of course, sake. Be aware that at many restaurants, if you order any alcohol at all you get slapped with a table charge *(otōshi)*, and that specials are often listed as costing 'from ¥1000', which may mean your bill ends up more than you expected. This is par for the course here so don't expect complaining to make it go away, but try to ask first if you're pinching your pennies…er, yen.

Kurumiya (☎ 290-6556; 1st fl, Tōkyū Inn, 1-2-4 Benten; dishes from ¥800; ☺ lunch & dinner) Right next to the train station, this place has a comprehensive selection of local sake, terribly tempting seafood set menus (including fresh sushi and zesty seafood salads) and an eclectic assortment of meat dishes, including horse and (gulp!) whale. The specials (see previous note) are mouthwatering; though no English and no pictures makes ordering a challenge. You're best off asking for *osusume* (chef's suggestion) and letting them decide. Yep, tipplers, they hit you with a table charge if you order a drink, even with the meal.

Immigrant's Cafe (☎ 242-2722; www.immigrantscafe .com; Basement Niigata Central Bldg, 1-7-10 Higashi Ōdōri; dishes from ¥600; E) Expats and locals come for good times and an international atmosphere. Asian and Mexican mains are served and there's a happy hour from 5.30pm to 7.30pm Sunday to Thursday. Light electronic beats and a comprehensive drinks list keep everyone juiced up.

Toritsune (☎ 229-3074; 2149-2 Ishizuechō-dōri; chicken skewers from ¥100; ☺ dinner) A nice little hole in the wall, with a friendly, non-intrusive owner who cooks up great yakitori to order over a small fire.

Entertainment

Ryūtopia (☎ 224-5622; www.ryutopia.or.jp; 3-2 Ichiban-bori-dōri; dance performances from ¥4000; ☺ 9am-10pm, closed 2nd & 4th Mon of each month) The city's snazziest attraction is a major performing arts centre with a 1900-seat concert hall, a 900-seat theatre and a 400-seat *nō* theatre.

Getting There & Away

Northeast of the city, **Niigata airport** (☎ 275-2633) has international flights to various Asian destinations. **Kyokushin Air** (☎ 273-0312) links Niigata with Ryōtsu on Sado-ga-shima (¥7350, 25 minutes). Buses run from stop 11 outside Niigata station to the airport every half-hour from 6.40am to 6.40pm (¥370, 25 minutes). A taxi costs about ¥2000.

The JR Jōetsu *shinkansen* line runs from Niigata to Echigo-Yuzawa (¥5240, 53 minutes) and on to Tokyo (Ueno; ¥10,270, two hours); change at Takisaki for the Nagano *shinkansen*. On the JR Uetsu line, there are *tokkyū* trains north from Niigata to Tsuruoka (¥4530, 1¾ hours) and Akita (¥7020, 3¾ hours).

Long-distance buses use the covered Bandai bus centre, which is across the river from the station. Buses link Niigata with Sendai (¥4500, four hours), Yamagata (¥3800, 3¾ hours), Aizu-Wakamatsu (¥2000, 1¾ hours), Kanazawa (¥4580, five hours) and Nagano (¥3060, 3½ hours). There are also night buses to Tokyo (Ikebukuro; ¥5250, five hours) and Kyoto/Osaka (¥9450, 9½ hours). Most buses pass by Niigata station on their way out of town.

Shin-Nihonkai (☎ 273-2171) ferries from Niigata to Otaru (Hokkaidō) are excellent value (¥6200, 18 hours, daily except Monday). Buses leave from stop 3 at Niigata station for Rinkonichōme. For Niigata-kō port, get off at Suehiro-bashi (¥180, 20 minutes).

From the **Sado Kisen** terminal, there are frequent ferries and hydrofoils to Ryōtsu on Sado-ga-shima (p563). Buses to the terminal (¥180, 15 minutes) leave from stop 6 at the station 45 minutes before sailing.

TO/FROM RUSSIA
Every Monday and Friday **Dalavia Far East Airways** (Tokyo office ☎ 03-3431-0687) flies from Niigata to Khabarovsk, Russia, for connections with the Trans-Siberian Railway. **Vladivostok Airlines** (☎ 279-5105) operates flights every Thursday and Sunday to Vladivostok. For information about obtaining a Russian visa, see p804.

MYŌKŌ KŌGEN 妙高高原
☎ 0255
A sprawling collection of over 60 ski resorts along the Myōkō-shi mountain range, with massive Mt Myōkō presiding over it all, this area should not be overlooked, particularly since it's so accessible from Tokyo. Many of the resorts are run by the ubiquitous Prince chain, with ski and snowboard facilities comparable to what one finds in places further north, such as Niseko (p589). No surprise, the season starts later than the Hokkaidō counterparts (early to late December), but it is more than made up for by proximity to Tokyo and Nagano, and for its lack of crowds. Snowboarding is allowed at most of the area slopes.

For information, check www.snowjapan.com for up-to-the minute stats, maps and reviews. Local tourist information, maps and ski reports are at **Myōkō Kōgen Tourist Information** (☎ 86-3911; 291-1 Ōaza Taguchi; ☻ 8.30am-6pm), which is just 100m to the right as you exit Myōkō Kōgen station. There's also info at **Suginohara Tourist Info Centre** (☎ 86-6000; ☻ 8.30am-5pm Mon-Fri, daily during the ski season) at the Suginohara Kankōkyōkai bus stop.

Sights & Activities
MYŌKŌ-YAMA 妙高山
This beautiful mountain, listed as one of Japan's top 100, overlooks it all, and makes for great scenery while you're on the slopes. Hiking is possible when there isn't snow – check at the tourist info booths for trail details and current conditions.

IMORI-IKE
This pretty pond (er, puddle, really) is famous for its beautiful reflections of nearby Mt Myōkō, which make for great pictures, and for *mizubashou* (Asian skunk cabbage), which blooms in spring and early summer. The white blossoms resemble the more familiar Calla lily, and the green leaves have a distinct pungent odour if stepped on (please don't!). There's a **visitors centre** (☎ 86-4599; director@myokovc.jp; ☻ 9am-4.30pm) and a 500m hiking trail that makes for good birding.

MYŌKŌ SUGINOHARA SKI RESORT
妙高杉の原スキー場
One of the numerous resorts in the Myōkō Kōgen area, this Prince-run resort, **Myōkō Suginohara** (妙高杉の原スキー場; ☎ 86-6211; http://ski.princehotels.co.jp/myoko in Japanese; lift ticket ¥4000; ☻ 8am-5pm, night skiing Fri & holidays 6-9pm) has nice views of Mt Myōkō and 17 runs, the majority of them at the intermediate level, with beginner slopes close behind, and a handful of 'black' to round things off. Wide and well groomed, the runs have good powder snow and often seem empty compared to other Japanese ski resorts. Piped muzak makes things less serene, but it's easy to overlook when you're tearing down through moguls or cruising beside the snow-covered trees with only a handful of people to share the slopes with. The area caters to both skiers and snowboarders.

Grab a snack at one of the many restaurants and coffee shops at the base of the mountain or head to the **Rāmen Corner** (ラーメンコーナー; parking lot 1; ☻ 8am-5pm) for a noodle fix. The snazzy **Suginosawa Onsen Centre** (杉野沢温泉セ

ンター 杉野沢温泉苗名の湯; ☎ 86-6565; ☒ daily Dec-Mar, closed Wed Apr-Nov; bath ¥450) offers a relaxing soak after a hard day on the slopes.

For off-piste excitement, check out the local telemark experts, **Myōkō Backcountry Ski School** (妙高バックカントリースキースクール; ☎ 87-2392; fax 87-3278; www.myokokogen.org /mbss/english.php) for guided tours through the backwoods terrain.

Myōkō Suginohara is about 23 minutes from Myōkō Kōgen JR station.

Sleeping & Eating

The massive Myōkō Kōgen area has numerous hotels, *minshuku* and ryokan; many of the packages include an overnight stay.

Canadian House (カナディアンハウス; ☎ 87-2186; www6.ocn.ne.jp/~canadian/zhome.html; 1394 Taguchi; s/d ¥6000/9000, 5 people in 1 room per person ¥3200; ☐) An inexpensive place with Japanese- and Western-style options, kitchenettes (in some rooms), with pick-up at the station if you call in advance. It also rents bicycles for those wanting to roll around instead of hit the white stuff. Meals are optional, and at extra cost.

Sun Village Machida (サン・ヴィレッジまちだ; ☎ 86-6117; 2003 Suginosawa; r per person from ¥8000) Come here for a right-at-the-slopes villa with locally grown seasonal veggies as part of the meals. Rooms are your choice of either Japanese- or Western-style. Find it by (from Myōkō Kōgen station) taking a Suginohara-bound bus and getting off at the Onsen Centre stop. Deals for students or seniors are sometimes possible: ask.

Kumasugi-no-Sato Soba-no-Hana (くま杉の里 そばの花; ☎ 86-6967; noodles ¥700-800; ☒ lunch-dinner Thu-Tue) This small noodle shop uses local produce in its various dishes. Try the *san-sai-soba* (mountain vegetable buckwheat noodles; ¥800). No English menu. Take a bus to Suginosawa Ue and get off at the last stop. It's right there, on the 1st floor of the Kuma-no-Sato building.

Getting There & Away

Package tours out of Tokyo start at about ¥5200 per person, with another ¥500/1000 for ski/snowboard rental gear. Many night departures are available, giving you a whole day on the slopes prior to a return in the evening. Or choose overnight options, which include one night as well (single/double per person ¥11,700/8800). Call **Travel Road** (☎ 042-599-2052; www.roadplan.net; ☒ 10am-7pm Mon-Fri, 11am-7pm Sat

& Sun) or the tourist info booths for package details.

Frequent buses (about nine per day) run from the slopes to Myōkō Kōgen JR station or to Nagano. From there, take the *shinkansen* back to Tokyo (¥7970, 1¾ hours). Bus service runs frequently during the ski season (December to April) and less frequently at other times of year.

SADO-GA-SHIMA 佐渡島
☎ 0259 / pop 69,500

Sado-ga-shima, where out-of-favour intellectuals were banished, is Japan's sixth-largest island. Persimmons are everywhere, and *hoshigaki* (dried winter persimmon) is a common food, even appearing in the traditional *yōkan* (bean jelly) sweets – some flecked with real gold. The island is a very popular destination because of its natural beauty and atmospheric hiking (the southern and northern mountain ranges are connected by a vast, fertile plain), as well as for the eccentric reminders of its rich, evocative history.

Among those banished here were Emperor Juntoku, *nō* master Ze-Ami, and Nichiren, the founder of one of Japan's most influential Buddhist sects. When gold was discovered near Aikawa in 1601, there was a sudden influx of gold-diggers, who were often vagrants press-ganged from the mainland and made to work like slaves.

Sado is famous for the Earth Celebration, with *okesa* (folk dances), *onidaiko* (demon drum dances) and *tsuburosashi* (a phallic dance with two goddesses).

The best time to visit is between late April and mid-October; during winter, not only will the weather be foul, but much of the accommodation will be closed and transport will be slashed to a bare minimum.

The island is well furnished with guesthouses, youth hostels and camping, but you must book accommodation well in advance in the hectic summer months. Ask the tourist information offices for help if necessary, as only a few of the many options are listed here.

Festivals & Events

One of Sado's biggest draws is the **Earth Celebration**, a three-day music, dance and arts festival usually held during the third week in August. The focal point is performances by the world-famous Kodo Drummers, who

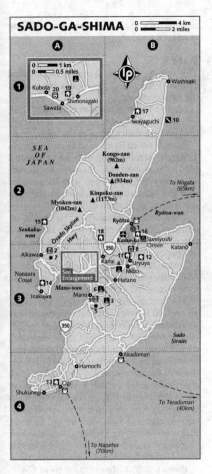

SADO-GA-SHIMA

0 — 4 km
0 — 2 miles

Ogi Minato Matsuri (小木港祭り) Lion dances, folk songs, tub-boat races and fireworks from 28 to 30 August.

Ryōtsu 両津

With its grand mountain backdrop, Sado's main hub is quite pretty, as far as ports go. The central area is a 10-minute walk north of the ferry terminal, which is surrounded by *nō* artefacts; statues pepper the terminal and a giant mask rises above the trees.

The island's main **tourist information centre** (☎ 23-3300; 8.30am-5pm, to 6.50pm Jun-Aug) is in Ryōtsu, in the street behind the coffee and souvenir shops across from the ferry terminal. Staff speaks some English and provides comprehensive maps, timetables and pamphlets for the entire island.

Check internet at tiny **Clever Cat** (☎ 23-3158; 138-1 Minato; per 30min incl 1 drink ¥700; 10am-9pm Wed-Mon), near the ferry terminal.

From bus stop 2 outside the terminal, buses (one way, including entry fee ¥960) run to **Sado Nōgaku-no-sato** (☎ 23-5000; 8.30am-5pm), a hi-tech museum of *nō* drama, with displays of masks and costumes and performances of *nō* enacted by a cast of animatronic actors.

Kunimisō (☎ 22-2316; Niibo-Shomyōji; per person incl 2 meals from ¥7000) is one of Sado's most popular *minshuku*, due to its collection of *bunya*

live in a small village north of Ogi, but who tour eight months a year; all members are required to adhere to strict physical, mental and spiritual training regimens. International guest performers and Japanese artists offer workshops throughout the festival. For more information contact www.kodo.or.jp. You will need to buy tickets and arrange accommodation well in advance.

Other major festivals:

Kōzan Matsuri (鉱山祭) Fireworks, *okesa* and float parades on the fourth weekend of July.

Ryōtsu Tanabata Kawabiraki (両津七夕・川開き) Onidaiko and Sado's biggest firework display, held on 7 and 8 August.

Shishi-ga-jō Matsuri (獅子ケ城まつり) Beach volleyball and fireworks on 11 August.

puppets, which the owner likes to demonstrate to guests. It's 15 minutes by bus from Ryōtsu to the Uryūya bus stop, then a long walk. Phone ahead for a pick-up.

Sado Seaside Hotel (佐渡シーサイドホテル; ☎ 27-7211; kkmasah@mui.bi globe.ne.jp; 80 Sumiyoshi; r per person incl/excl meals from ¥7500/4875; 🖳) is at Sumiyoshi Onsen, about 2km from Ryōtsu. It's cheery enough with free internet, an *onsen*, and an obliging free shuttle service to and from the port. Try for a room with an ocean view.

Sawata 佐和田

The town of Sawata, 15km southwest of Ryōtsu, is on the main road between Ryōtsu and Aikawa. If you get off the bus 1km east of town at Kaminagaki (¥150, from Ryōtsu ¥510), you can walk for about 30 minutes into the hills to **Myōshō-ji**, a temple belonging to the Nichiren sect, with its sizable, five-storey pagoda.

Near the bus terminal in Sawata, the Silver Village resort stages **bunya puppet performances** (佐渡文弥人形芝居; ☎ 52-3961; Kubotahama; admission ¥350; 🕑 4 shows daily Apr-Nov), a traditional form of puppetry that's been a feature of Sado life for over 250 years. From stop 1 outside the Ryōtsu ferry terminal, frequent buses run to Sawata (¥570, 40 minutes) and onto Aikawa (¥390, 20 minutes) on the Hon-sen line.

Green Village Youth Hostel (☎ 22-2719; gvyh@ e-sadonet.tv; 750-4 Niibo Uryuya; dm from ¥3670), south of Ryōtsu, is among the island's top accommodation options because of great food (¥1500), internet access, friendly hosts and spectacular scenery. From Ryōtsu take a bus bound for Sawata on the Minami-sen bus line and get off at the Uryūya stop (¥350, 10 minutes); continue for 10 minutes and turn left at the first bend. If you tell the driver you're going to Green Village, he'll drop you off a bit closer.

Urashima (☎ 57-3751; www.r-urashima.com in Japanese; 978-3 Kubota; r per person incl 2 meals from ¥8000), with its modern space-capsule design, overlooks the beach.

Tōkaen (☎ 63-2221; www.on.rim.or.jp/~toukaen/in Japanese; tokaen@on.rim.or.jp; 1636-1 Otsu; s incl/excl 2 meals from ¥¥8400/4200) is a pleasant *minshuku*. The owners can help you plan all sorts of outdoor activities – hiking, fishing and so on – and they also cook up good vegetarian food. Plus, there's a *shiogama-buro* (rock-salt sauna) that's certainly worth a soak. Tōkaen is a bit out of the way, though. Take the Hon line to the Shinbo Undōkōen-mae stop (¥400, 20

minutes); it's about 3km to the north. Calling ahead is a good idea.

Mano 真野

This was the provincial capital and cultural centre of the island from early times until the 14th century.

Mano's **tourist information office** (☎ 55-3589; 🕑 9am-5.30pm Apr-Oct) rents bicycles (¥1100 per day) and has sketch maps of the hiking trail.

Buses between Ryōtsu and Mano on the No 2 Minami-sen line stop in front of **Konpon-ji** (☎ 22-3751; admission ¥300; 🕑 8am-4pm Nov-Apr, 8am-4.45pm May-Oct). This temple, with its thatched roof and pleasant gardens, is where Nichiren was first brought when exiled.

There are several other temples in the vicinity of Mano, many of which lie along a peaceful 7km nature trail that begins just west of Konpon-ji, near the Danpū-jōbus stop. It's a short walk from there to the **Myōsen-ji** (☎ 55-2061; admission free; 🕑 9am-4pm) temple, also with a distinctive five-storey pagoda.

The trail then passes through rice fields and up old wooden steps set into the hillside to **Kokubun-ji**, Sado-ga-shima's oldest temple (dating from 741); although sadly neglected, it's still beautiful. Another 3km takes you past marvellous lookout points to **Mano Go-ryō**, the tomb of Emperor Juntoku. From there, it's a short walk down to **Sado Rekishi Densetsukan** (☎ 55-2525; admission ¥700; 🕑 8am-5.30pm Apr-Nov, to 5pm Dec-Mar), where more tireless robots illustrate dioramas of Sado's history and festivals, as do various holograms. Next door is **Mano-gū**, a small shrine dedicated to Emperor Juntoku. It's a 15-minute walk back to the main road.

Buses connect Mano with Ryōtsu (¥630, 45 minutes) and Sawata (¥260, 13 minutes) on the Minami-sen line, and Ogi (¥810, 50 minutes) on the Ogi line.

Ogi 小木

This drowsy port on the island's southern tip is kept in business by a ferry connection to Naoetsu. The **tourist office** (☎ 86-3200) is a few minutes' walk west of the post office (which is behind the bus terminal).

The big attraction here is a ride in a **taraibune** (たらい舟; tub boat; 🕑 approx 8.30am-4.30pm), a boat usually made from a barrel and rowed by women in traditional fisherfolk costumes. It looks difficult and it is – those awkward poles at the front are used to steer. You can try your hand at it in Ogi harbour (10 minutes ¥450).

Minshuku Sakaya (民宿さかや; ☎ 86-2535; r per person incl/excl 2 meals ¥7000/4500) has pared-down yet cosy rooms, and is conveniently located a few minutes' walk east of the Ogi ferry terminal.

Buses run hourly between Ogi and Sawata via Mano (¥910, 1¼ hours); direct buses between Ogi and Ryōtsu (¥1070, one hour 25 minutes) run only during certain festivals.

Aikawa 相川

From a tiny hamlet, Aikawa developed almost overnight into a 100,000-person boomtown when gold was discovered nearby in 1601; private mining continued until the end of the Edo period. Today the population has dwindled to a few thousand and tourism is the main business. There's a small **tourist information centre** (☎ 74-2220) beside the bus terminal.

From Aikawa bus terminal, it's a 40-minute walk up a steep mountain (buses run occasionally in the high season) to the bountiful **Sado Kinzan Gold Mine** (☎ 74-2389; 1305 Shimoaikawa; admission ¥700; ⏰ 8am-5pm Apr-Oct, 8.30am-4.30pm Nov-Mar), which produced large quantities of gold and silver until its demise in 1989. Descend into the chilly depths where you'll encounter robots that dramatise the tough existence of former miners. A further 300m up the mountain is Dōyū-no-Wareto, the original opencast mine where you can still see the remains of the workings.

It takes around 30 minutes to return on foot down the mountain road to Aikawa. On the way you'll pass several temples and **Aikawa Kyōdo Hakubutsukan** (☎ 74-4312; Sakashita Machi; admission ¥300; ⏰ 8.30am-5pm), a folk museum with more exhibits from the old mine.

At **Nanaura-sō** (民宿 七浦荘; ☎ 76-2735; nanaura@jasmine.ocn.ne.jp; 1586-3 Tachibana; per person incl 2 meals from ¥7000), there are several rooms with balconies overlooking the ocean and the owners speak some English. From Aikawa, take the Nanaura-kaigan line to the Nagatemi-saki-iriguchi stop (¥330), or better still, call ahead for a pick-up. It can also be reached from Sawata, which is the southern terminus for the Nanaura-kaigan-sen line. Note that the Hon-sen line, which also links Sawata with Aikawa, follows a different road. Avoid it.

Aikawa bus terminal, a major transport hub for bus services on the island, has regular buses to Ryōtsu (¥780, one hour), and connections to Ogi (¥910, 50 minutes, via Sawata) and Sawata (¥390, 20 minutes).

Iwayaguchi 岩谷口

The scenery along the coast road further north is interesting, with its time-worn fishing villages. At Iwayaguchi, you'll find the **Sotokaifu Youth Hostel** (☎ 78-2911; www.sotokaifu-yh.com/en/; info@sotokaifu.net; 131 Iwayaguchi; dm from ¥3360) in a tiny fishing hamlet – just the ticket for solitude seekers. Across, on the opposite side of the island's tip, you'll find the **Underwater Christmas Tree** (☎ 23-3687; tu9t-hnm@asahi-net.or.jp; ¥1500 plus diving fee, usually 2 dives and lunch for ¥15,000; ⏰ 3rd week of Nov), where divers can, yes, go down and see presents, lights, decorations. A similar event happens on Tanabata, with a decorated bamboo.

There are seven buses daily to Iwayaguchi from Aikawa on the Kaifu line (¥1010, 70 minutes).

Senkaku-wan 尖閣湾

A 20-minute bus ride (¥280) north of Aikawa on the Kaifu line, this bay features striking rock formations that can be viewed on **excursions** (30min ¥850; ⏰ 4 daily Apr-Oct) in a glass-bottom vessel.

The **Sado Belle Mer Youth Hostel** (☎ 75-2011; http://sado.bellemer.jp in Japanese; 369-4 Himezu; dm from ¥3360) is in the tourist area of Senkaku-wan. From Aikawa, take the Kaifu line to the Minami-Himezu stop (¥310, 20 minutes); from there it's a five-minute walk in the direction of the shore.

Getting There & Away

Kyokushin Air (旭伸航空; ☎ 23-5005) flights link Ryōtsu with Niigata (one way ¥7350, return ¥11,020, 25 minutes, three flights daily, four in summer). Buses between the airport and Ryōtsu bus terminal are currently suspended indefinitely.

Sado Kisen passenger ferries and hydrofoils run between Niigata and Ryōtsu. There are up to six regular ferries daily (one way from ¥2320, two hours 30 minutes). As many as 10 jetfoils zip across daily in merely an hour, but service is greatly reduced between December and February (one way/return ¥6220/11,250). Before embarking, you need to buy a ticket from the vending machines and to fill in a white passenger ID form.

From Naoetsu-kō, southwest of Niigata, there are ferry and hydrofoil services to Ogi, in the southwest part of Sado-ga-shima. Between April and late November, there are four or more regular ferry departures daily (2½ hours) and two hydrofoils (one hour). During the rest of the year the hydrofoil service is suspended and regular ferries run only twice daily. Fares are the same as for the Niigata-Ryōtsu service. From JR Naoetsu station, it's a 10-minute bus ride (¥160) and then a 15-minute walk to the port.

Getting Around

Local buses are fine on the main routes – between Ryōtsu and Aikawa, for example. However, services to other parts of the island are often restricted to two or three a day and in winter services are sharply restricted.

To explore less-touristed areas, car rental is desirable. There are numerous car-rental firms close to the Ryōtsu terminal; rates start from ¥7000/9000 per day/24 hours. Tell the proprietor your plan, as construction, unpassable bridges or snow may mean the map's routes are unavailable.

If you plan to make extended use of local buses, there's an English-language timetable available from the ferry terminals and tourist information offices. The ¥2000 unlimited ride bus pass, also in English, is a good-value option valid for two consecutive days on weekends only (sightseeing buses excluded). The *teiki kankō* (sightseeing buses) have packaged itineraries with prices from ¥4000 to ¥8000.

Cycling is an enjoyable way to get off the beaten track. Bicycle rental is available in Ryōtsu, Aikawa and Ogi (per day ¥400 to Ÿ1500).

NAEBA 苗場
☎ 025

As home to the Fuji rock festival and with some of Japan's best skiing, Naeba might just be a partygoer's perfect little 'town'. Four ski resorts – Tashiro, Kagura, Mitsumata and Naeba – are all linked by the world's longest gondola (5481m!), meaning that you get four ski resorts in one if you come here. The longest run is 4000m long. The Dragondola (return ¥1800), as it's called, can speed up to eight people to dry, light powder that makes for great trips down the slopes. Snowboarders will want to check out the biggest half-pipe within a day's trip from Tokyo, and because there are so many options, beginners can enjoy a day just as easily as advanced skiers. Naeba itself has 33 ski lifts, so there is plenty to do – the only problem is that with such proximity to Tokyo, you may find long waits in lift

lines and at the restaurant. As of winter 2006, a new ski centre has opened up that caters to night-bus arrivals. It's open from midnight until 10pm and has heated waiting rooms and 'nap rooms' for the truly sleepy.

If you come in late July, the **Fuji Rock Festival** (www.smash-uk.com/frf07; admission ¥39,800) is a three-day-long musical madness – like Woodstock, only with toilets and less mud – and up to 100,000 people show up to hang out, listen to great bands and enjoy the party atmosphere. While pricey, it's like a trip to mecca for many music lovers.

More sedate pleasures can be found on the 18-hole **golf course** or the **swimming pool** (open year-round).

Get here by taking the *shinkansen* to either Echigo-Yuzawa Onsen or Joetsu, then take a bus or free shuttle. Packages often include round-trip transport and can start at around ¥9300 for day trips. One-way shuttles from Tokyo's Prince Hotel in Shinagawa cost ¥4000; purchase through **Seibu Travel** (☎ 03-5296-9165; ☷ 10am-6pm).

ECHIGO-YUZAWA ONSEN 越後湯沢温泉
☎ 025 / pop 8660

Echigo-Yuzawa was the setting for Nobel Prize–winning writer Kawabata Yasunari's *Snow Country*, a novel about decadent *onsen* geisha. Today it's the ski slopes that draw people here, but a few items in his memory are on display at the **Yukiguni-kan** (雪国館; History & Folk Museum; ☎ 784-3965; admission ¥500; ☷ 9am-4.30pm Thu-Tue), 500m north of the station. **Gala Yuzawa** (ガーラ湯沢スキー場; ☎ 785-6543; www .gala.co.jp/2007/GALA_English/index.html; ☷ Dec-May; day lift ticket ¥4300) is one of the area's ski resorts. Check www.snowjapan.com for the latest conditions.

Hike in summer around **Yuzawa Kōgen**, an alpine plateau accessed via ropeway (cable car; return ¥1300) from the town. Discount coupons may be available.

Echigo-Yuzawa's JR station is so complete you hardly need to step outside. What with its own **onsen** (¥800; ☷ 9am-6pm Apr-22 Dec, 9am-8pm 23 Dec-Mar), a **sake tasting bar** (ぽんしゅ館; ☎ 784-3758; www.pon shukan.com in Japanese; per 5 samples ¥500), with over 150 varieties of Niigata's and other speciality brews, a salt-tasting table (ever had rose salt before?) and a mammoth *omiyage* (souvenir) shop – with plenty of samples and some odd gifts, such as a dried whole fish wrapped in rope – all that's missing is a station ski slope.

ROCK FESTIVALS IN JAPAN Simon Bartz

Music lovers head to Japan, late July, for the **Fuji Rock Festival** (www.fujirockfestival.com). There's no better location than the ski resort in Naeba, Niigata Prefecture: mountains rising both sides of a forested valley, and it's littered with several stages. Here you'll find rock, hip-hop, experimental jazz, techno, punk and reggae, all just a two-hour train ride from Tokyo.

As well as foreign acts like the Red Hot Chilli Peppers, Neil Young, Franz Ferdinand, Oasis and New Order, there's plenty of home-grown talent. And the organisers are known for their eccentricities and a sense of humour: when Morrissey pulled out of his headlining slot in 2004, the organisers simply hired a Smiths tribute band to take his place.

More than 100,000 people attend Fuji Rock, and it's about ¥38,000 for the three-day pass. Most camp up on a mountain, as accommodation tends to be booked out. What to bring? You won't need your skis so much as some sunscreen and, yes, Wellington boots. Most years see two days of blue skies and sun followed by rain. You may find yourself swimming in mud.

Held in late September, the two-day **Asagiri Jam** festival is perhaps more deserving of the name 'Fuji Rock Festival' – it's located in the beautiful foothills that surround Mt Fuji. Asagiri Jam is low-key, and the line-up isn't announced beforehand. The emphasis is more on creating a good vibe than pulling in big names. Dub, techno, jazz and, of course, rock are featured; Television, The Pogues and the late Joe Strummer have all performed. There are no hotels around here, so bring a tent or stay up all night.

The two-day **Summer Sonic** (www.summersonic.com) draws major international acts and is held during early August in Chiba, next to Tokyo, and Osaka. Chiba's line-up plays the next day in Osaka, and vice-versa. Then there's the three-day **Rock in Japan** festival, set in acres of green fields in Ibaraki Prefecture, a two-hour train ride from Tokyo. In many ways, this festival epitomises the Japanese music scene today – all performers are Japanese – and it spans J-Pop stars to aging crooners.

Simon Bartz runs a website about Japanese music: www.badbee.net

---

If you must leave, there are two exits from the station. The east exit is the main one, with the **tourist information office** (☎ 785-5505; ۞ 9am-5.30pm) to its left outside the station. To the right of the west exit, an **accommodation office** books rooms at the numerous *minshuku*, hotels and ski lodges in town. You pay a ¥2000 deposit and staff issues you with a receipt to take to your guesthouse.

our pick Right outside the west exit's little rotary is the luxurious **Hatago Isen** (旅籠井仙; ☎ 784-3361; www.isen.co.jp, in Japanese; r per 1 or 2 people incl breakfast from ¥11,500; 🖳), a beautiful ryokan with extremely tasteful décor designed to re-create the feel of an old traveller's lodge. Though modern niceties such as TVs peep through, they've done a great job. The details make all the difference, whether it be artful screens placed to conceal a plasma TV, or a simple flower in a ceramic vase. You *won't* feel at home here – it's just too beautiful.

Overlooking the town and its own skiing grounds, **NASPA New Ōtani** (NASPAニューオータニ; ☎ 780-6111, 0120-227-021; www.naspa.co.jp/english; s/tw from ¥7300/12,000; 🖳) has luxurious Western-style rooms for up to three people – good value if sharing, and most have excellent views. A small *rotenburo* is a great way to soak the soreness away. Free shuttles run between the station and the resort and, in winter, to many major ski areas, making it a superb choice for skiers.

Asahikan (あさひ館; ☎ 787-3205; www.asahikan -yuzawa.com/english.html; 1760 Tsuchitaru, Yuzawa-machi, Minamiuonuma-gun; r per person incl 2 meals from ¥8000) is a friendly *minshuku* in an old-style Japanese house. Homecooked meals, tea and coffee, and close proximity to the Yuzawa Park Ski Jō, are all reasons to stay here. Pick-up is possible if you call ahead. Another Asahikan is nearby the station's west exit, so don't get them confused.

Minshuku Tatsumoto (民宿たつもと; ☎ 784-2371; www.dpl-jp.com/yado/tatumoto in Japanese; 317-2 Yuzawa; r per person incl/excl meals from ¥6000/4000) is very close to the train track. It's cosy, only six rooms. The natural *onsen* is open in the morning as well as at night. Turn right out of the west exit, pass the 7-Eleven and look on the right, about 250m away.

Echigo-Yuzawa station is on the JR Jōetsu *shinkansen* line between Niigata (¥5240, 51 minutes) and Tokyo (Ueno; ¥6490, 91 minutes), within walking distance of all the in-town sights, with shuttles to zip you to the ski slopes.

Hokkaidō 北海道

Few Japanese, and even fewer tourists, make it as far north as Hokkaidō, Japan's final frontier. A shame, since the sweeping vistas, amazing wildlife, wide open roads and spaciousness offer a refreshing contrast to the often claustrophobic density of Honshū. The northernmost of the country's four main islands, Hokkaidō offers skiing, hiking, camping, motorcycling, biking, rafting, canoeing, fishing…even bird-watching. Exciting nightlife in the larger cities lets you get into as much trouble as you want, while luxurious hot springs let you ease those troubles away. Hokkaidō comprises one-fifth of the country's land mass, yet only 5% of the population lives here, in part because of the Siberian cold that descends from November to March. Paradoxically, winter is still a major tourist time. People come to enjoy the skiing and snowboarding, look at the frozen northern waters of Wakkanai and Rebun, or enjoy the ice sculptures of the Yuki Matsuri.

The Ainu, Hokkaidō's indigenous people, have shaped this island's history. Many of the names in the area, such as Sapporo and Noshappu, come from Ainu language. Though marginalised for much of the past century, the Ainu have recently won recognition as an important part of Japanese cultural heritage and are re-establishing themselves. Excellent museums can be found in Sapporo, Hakodate and Shiraoi.

Shaped a bit like the squashed head of a squid, Hokkaidō is often divided into four major regions: Dō-nan (southern), Dō-ō (central), Dō-hoku (northern) and Dō-tō (eastern).

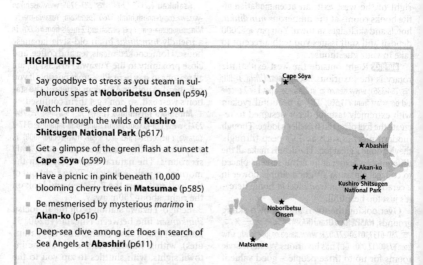

HIGHLIGHTS

- Say goodbye to stress as you steam in sulphurous spas at **Noboribetsu Onsen** (p594)
- Watch cranes, deer and herons as you canoe through the wilds of **Kushiro Shitsugen National Park** (p617)
- Get a glimpse of the green flash at sunset at **Cape Sōya** (p599)
- Have a picnic in pink beneath 10,000 blooming cherry trees in **Matsumae** (p585)
- Be mesmerised by mysterious *marimo* in **Akan-ko** (p616)
- Deep-sea dive among ice floes in search of Sea Angels at **Abashiri** (p611)

★ Cape Sōya

★ Abashiri

★ Akan-ko
Kushiro Shitsugen National Park

★ Noboribetsu Onsen

★ Matsumae

History

After the glaciers receded, the Ainu were the first to settle here. They called it Ainu Moshiri, Ainu meaning 'human', and Moshiri meaning 'world'. Until the Edo period (1600–1868), the Ainu and Japanese had relatively little contact with each other. The Matsumae clan were the first to establish a major foothold in southwestern Hokkaidō, and they successfully bargained with the Ainu, creating a trade monopoly. While lucrative for the Matsumae clan, it would prove disastrous to the Ainu people.

By the end of the Edo period, trade and colonisation had begun in earnest and by the time the Meiji Restoration began in 1868 the Ainu culture was under attack. Many Ainu customs were banned, women were forbidden to get tattoos, men were prohibited from wearing earrings and the Kaitakushi (Colonial Office) was created to encourage mainland Japanese people to migrate northward. By the time the Meiji period ended the Ainu were de facto 2nd-class citizens. By 1900 the mainland Japanese population topped one million.

One look at the rolling farmlands and fields will convince anyone familiar with New England or Europe that Western farming styles were adopted. Indeed, in some areas Hokkaidō resembles the pastoral West more than it does Japan.

With world attention focused on the island when Sapporo hosted the 1972 Winter Olympics, Japan felt the need to ease restrictions on the Ainu; however, it would take another 26 years before significant protections were written into law. Today, the Ainu are proudly continuing their traditions while still fighting for further recognition of their unique culture.

Hokkaidō's main industries are tourism, forestry and agriculture. It remains a top supplier of some of Japan's most revered delicacies, such as snow crab, salmon roe and sea urchin, and scenic kelp production is a major part of many small towns' economies. It remains a tourist destination year-round.

Climate

Hokkaidō's temperature ranges from warm and pleasant in summer to subzero in winter. Spring and early summer can be wet and miserable. The hiking season runs from May through to October, with a peak in the July and August months when the leaves begin

---

EVERYTHING BUT THE KITCHEN SINK

Check web-based email in a *manga-kissa* (comic-book salon), many of which also offer internet access. Rates are hourly and usually include free coffee, tea and other beverages. Some of the larger, 24-hour internet cafés and *manga-kissa* offer showers, private rooms and discount all-night packages that rival the cheapest hotels. Those bringing a notebook computer can find wi-fi or LAN access in most business hotels.

---

to change colour. Prices tend to be 20% to 30% higher during this time, and many of the popular areas will be booked solid. Typhoons, though rare in Hokkaidō, start to hit Japan in mid-August and can continue through to the end of October, causing train delays, power outages and even landslides. September and October are chilly, particularly in the mountains, and by November winter has come, bringing heavy snows and very cold temperatures. Bring plenty of layers and plan on bundling up.

National Parks

Hokkaidō boasts some of Japan's oldest and most beautiful national parks. Daisetsuzan National Park, centrally located near Asahikawa City, is a must see. This stunning expanse of mountain ranges, volcanoes, *onsen* (mineral hot-spring spa), lakes and hiking tracks is Japan's largest, covering 2309 sq km. Skiing and hiking are the main attractions; if you want to escape off the beaten track you should allow a few extra days.

Akan National Park, near Kushiro, has *onsen*, volcanoes and hiking. In spring thousands of cranes flock to Kushiro Shitsugen National Park, one of Japan's largest marshlands; deer, foxes, *shima-risu* (none other than the humble chipmunk!) and a host of birds are abundant. The northern islands of Rebun and Rishiri offer superb hiking and views of seaside cliffs, volcanic mountains and (in season) hillsides of flowers.

Shiretoko National Park, in the northeast, is as remote as it gets: two-thirds of it doesn't even have roads. Ponds as glassy as reflecting pools, rivers with brown bears munching salmon, waterfalls more delicate than ricepaper paintings – the scenery is stunning, but tourists are told quite plainly that if they

HOKKAIDŌ

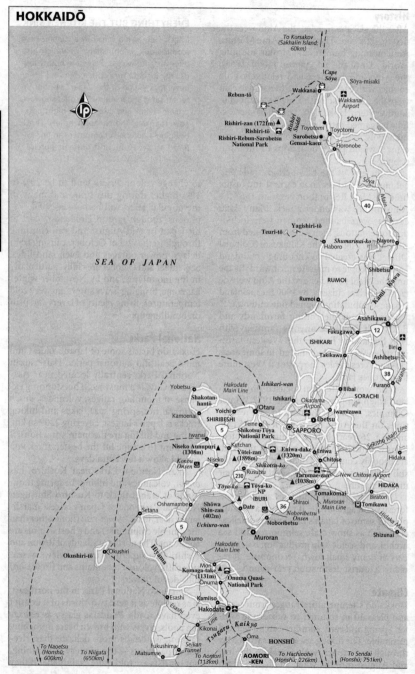

To Korsakov
(Sakhalin Island;
60km)

*Cape
Sōya*

Sōya-misaki

Rebun-tō

Wakkanai

*Wakkanai
Airport*

SŌYA

Rishiri-zan (1721m)

Rishiri-tō

**Rishiri-Rebun-Sarobetsu
National Park**

*Rishiri
Suidō*

Toyotomi

Toyotomi

Sarobetsu
Gensai-kaen

Horonobe

*Sōya
Main Line*

(40)

Teuri-tō

Yagishiri-tō

Shumarinai-ko

Nayoro

Haboro

SEA OF JAPAN

RUMOI

Shibetsu

*Kami
Kawa*

Rumoi

Asahikawa

Fukugawa

(12)

Biei

ISHIKARI

Takikawa

Ashibetsu

*Furano
Line*

(38)

Bibai

Furano

Ishikari-wan

*Hakodate
Main Line*

Yobetsu

SORACHI

**Shakotan-
hantō**

Iwamizawa

Yoichi

Ishikari

*Okadama
Airport*

Kamoenai

SHIRIBESHI

Otaru

Ebetsu

Sekishō Main Line

Teine

SAPPORO

Iwanai

(5)

Niseko Annupuri
(1308m)

Kutchan

Shikotsu-Tōya
National Park

Yōtei-zan
(1898m)

Eniwa-dake
(1320m)

Eniwa

Hidaka

Niseko

Shikotsu-ko

Chitose

*Konbu
Onsen*

Rusutsu

New Chitose Airport

(230)

Tarumae-zan
(1038m)

HIDAKA

Tōya-ko

Tōya-ko
NP

IBURI

Tomakomai

Biratori

Setana

Oshamambe

Shōwa
Shin-zan
(402m)

Date

Shiraoi

*Muroran
Main Line*

Tomikawa

Uchiura-wan

*Noboribetsu
Onsen*

Shizunai

*Hidaka Main
Line*

(36)

(5)

Yakumo

Noboribetsu

Hiyama

*Hakodate
Main Line*

Muroran

Okushiri

Okushiri-tō

*Hakodate
Main Line*

Mori

Konaga-take
(1131m)

Onuma Quasi-
National Park

Onuma

Esashi

Kamiiso

*Esashi
Line*

Hakodate

Kikonai

*Tsugaru
Kaikyō*

Oma

*Seikan
Tunnel*

Fukushima

HONSHŪ

Matsumae

AOMORI
-KEN

To Naoetsu
(Honshū;
600km)

To Niigata
(650km)

To Aomori
(113km)

To Hachinohe
(Honshū; 226km)

To Sendai
(Honshū; 751km)

HOKKAIDŌ

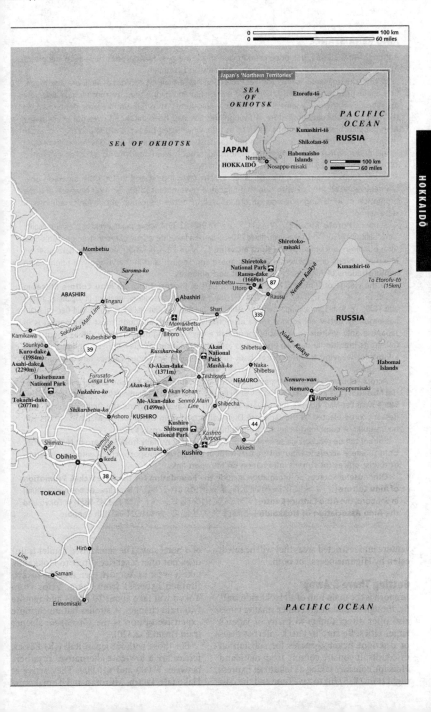

AINU RENAISSANCE

Although Ainu culture was once pronounced dead, the past few decades have seen people of Ainu descent assert their ethnicity both politically and culturally.

In 1899 the Hokkaidō Former Natives Protection Act formalised decades of Meiji-era discrimination against the Ainu, denying them land ownership and giving the governor of Hokkaidō sole discretion over the management of communal Ainu funds. Thus the Ainu became dependent on the welfare of the Japanese state. Although this law had been amended over the years, many Ainu people objected to it, right down to its title, which used the word *kyūdo-jin* ('dirt' or 'earth' people) to describe them. It was once the standard among people of Ainu descent to hide their ethnicity out of fear of discrimination in housing, schools and employment; out of an estimated 100,000 Ainu only 25,000 acknowledged it publicly.

In the 1980s various Ainu groups called for the law's repeal, and in 1998 the Japanese government replaced the law with one that allocated government funds for Ainu research and the promotion of Ainu language and culture, as well as better education about Ainu traditions in state schools.

Shiraoi's **Poroto Kotan** (ポロトコタン; ☎ 0144-82-3914; www.ainu-museum.or.jp/english/english.html; admission ¥750; ⏰ 8.45am-5pm, closed 29 Dec-5 Jan) is a lakeside village of reconstructed traditional Ainu buildings, anchored by the **Ainu Museum** (アイヌ民族博物館; Ainu Minzoku Hakubutsukan). Museum exhibits are labelled in both Japanese and English, and in the village you might catch demonstrations of Ainu crafts and cultural performances.

In the village of Nibutani, in the northern part of Biratori, **Nibutani Ainu Culture Museum** (二風谷アイヌ文化博物館; ☎ 01457-2-2892; www.ainu-museum-nibutani.org in Japanese; admission ¥400; ⏰ 9am-5pm mid-Apr–mid-Nov, 9am-5pm Tue-Sun mid-Nov–mid-Apr, closed mid-Dec–mid-Jan) has arguably better collections more attractively displayed, although most information is in Japanese only. Visitors could easily spend half a day watching documentary videos about Ainu folk crafts, traditional dances, epic songs and traditional ceremonies. Other highlights include a loom for weaving traditional tree-bark cloth and some enormous canoes hewn from entire tree trunks.

Across Nibutani's main street, amid some traditional huts, the **Kayano Shigeru Ainu Memorial Museum** (萱野茂二風谷アイヌ資料館; ☎ 01457-2-3215; admission ¥400; ⏰ 9am-5pm Apr-Nov, 9am-4.30pm Dec-Mar) houses the private collection of Kayano Shigeru, the first person of Ainu descent to be elected to the Japanese Diet. Call ahead from December to March, as hours can be irregular. A combined ticket for both Nibutani museums costs ¥700.

Shiraoi can be reached via several bus or train connections daily from Sapporo or Noboribetsu. Unfortunately, access to Nibutani is a trial without one's own transport – check with the museums or tourist offices for current information on transport links.

Other useful sources of information include the **Foundation for the Research & Promotion of Ainu Culture** (アイヌ文化振興研究推進機構; ☎ 011-271-4171; www.frpac.or.jp/eng/index.html) in Sapporo, the **Ainu Culture Centre** (アイヌ文化交流センター; ☎ 03-3245-9831) in Tokyo and the **Ainu Association of Hokkaidō** (北海道ウタリ協会; ☎ 011-221-0462) in Sapporo.

venture into restricted areas they will be fined, eaten by Higuma bears...or both.

Getting There & Away

Sapporo is the main hub of all Hokkaidō traffic, though Hakodate and other smaller cities also offer direct flights to many of Japan's larger cities. Be sure to check internet deals or discount ticket agencies for substantial discounts. If you are coming from mainland Honshū, consider taking a Hokutosei Express night train (¥25270) to save time and the cost of a hotel stay. The *shinkansen* (bullet train) does not offer a service direct to Hokkaidō; take it as far as Aomori, then take the *tokkyū* (limited express) from there. Trips from Tokyo will take about 10 hours and require two train changes. A similar but much more expensive option is the *Cassiopeia* sleeper train (from ¥32,320).

For those without Japan Rail (JR) Passes, ferries are a low-cost alternative, anywhere between ¥5000 and ¥10,000. They arrive at Hakodate, Otaru, Muroran and Tomakomai

– all relatively close to Sapporo. Ferries are often fancy; some include saunas and gyms. The cheap 2nd-class tickets offer sleeping on open-area mats. Berths in a shared 2nd-class cabin cost about ¥2000 more and may be more relaxing. Though theft is unlikely, you should watch your valuables.

FERRY TO/FROM RUSSIA

For those heading to Japan's most northern city, Wakkanai, a ferry trip to Korsakov, Russia, is an interesting option. Regular services run from early May to mid-September; there are less frequent runs the rest of the year. Most Japanese tourists go with a tour group, but if you plan ahead you can make the trip on your own. Visit www.embassy-avenue.jp for specific details; a Russian visa requires an invitation letter from a Sakhalin tourist agency or hotel, and you must apply at least two weeks in advance (it may be faster, but give yourself two) at the **Consulate General of the Russian Federation** (在札幌ロシア連邦総領事館; ☎ 064-0914, Japan 011-561-3171; Nishi 12-chōme Minami 14-jo, Chūō-ku, Sapporo; ☼ Mon-Fri) in Sapporo. The **Japan Eurasia Association** (日本ユーラシア協会北海道連合会; ☎ 011-707-0933; http://homepage2.nifty.com/eurasia-doren/ in Japanese) can assist with arrangements for Japan residents. **Falcon Japan Co Ltd** (株式会社ロシア旅行社; ☎ 011-207-3370; www.falconjapan.co.jp in Japanese) is a good start for those interested in going with a group.

The **East Japan Sea Ferry Company** (東日本海フェリー; ☎ Wakkanai 0162-23-3780, Sapporo 011-518-2780; www.kaiferry.co.jp/english/index.html) runs ships and has several office locations around Hokkaidō, including one in Sapporo. Ferries take around 5½ hours and cost ¥22,500 to ¥32,500. Return fares begin at ¥35,000, and if you're short on yen you can also pay in US dollars.

Getting Around

In Hokkaidō distances can be deceiving. The website www.hyperdia.com has a schedule calculator that lists up-to-date options and prices for getting around.

Sapporo has flights to all major Hokkaidō locations, but rail, car or motorcycle are preferred. Trains run frequently on the trunk lines, but reaching remote locations (like Nemuro) involves infrequent trains and pricey buses. The foreigner-only Hokkaidō Rail Pass is also available: a four-day pass costs ¥14,500.

Within cities, buses are convenient and usually cheap. Ask about a *norihō dai* (all day) pass if you're going to use them a lot; it's often a substantial discount.

If you have brought an International Driving Permit (you must get it from your home country prior to arrival in Japan), renting a car or motorcycle may save time. Local roads are often just as pretty as expressways and may yield unforeseen surprises. Car-rental rates vary, but if you walk in off the street expect to pay about ¥7000 per day, plus your first-born child for fuel.

For fans of greener ways to get around, Hokkaidō is a good place to tour by bike. *Charida* (bicycle riders) are a common sight on major roads. Rider houses (see p787) are common and cheap.

SEIKAN TUNNEL TOUR 青函トンネルツアー

You can tour Japan's longest tunnel at either the Yoshioka-kaitei (Hokkaidō) or Tappi-kaitei (Honshū) stations. More than 100m below sea level, you'll wind through a maze of service corridors and passageways – staff use bicycles and even cars to make their rounds. Longer tours include some of the tunnel's unique features, such as a 600m-long cable-car link to the shore of Honshū and a narrow passageway between the railway tracks that gives visitors a worm's eye view of the passing trains.

You must reserve your tunnel tour at least one day in advance from travel agencies or Japan Railways (JR) reservation centres in either Aomori (Honshū) or Hakodate (Hokkaidō). Only a few trains a day in either direction allow actual through-train/tour combinations. If you already have paid your train fare or have a rail pass, the standard Yoshioka-kaitei or Tappi-kaitei station tour (in Japanese only) costs ¥840 extra; tours last from one to 2½ hours, depending on train schedules. For ¥2040 you can take the tour that continues from Tappi-kaitei station, via the cable car formerly used by construction workers, up to the Seikan Tunnel Museum on dry land. Return-trip tours from Aomori (¥4320) and Hakodate (¥4040) include the museum.

SAPPORO 札幌

☎ 011 / pop 1.88 million

Japan's fifth-largest city, and also one of its newest, Sapporo is clean, friendly and relaxed, with numerous parks and wide, tree-lined streets. Families play on stone sculptures, people feed pigeons and there are festivals all year round. Museums and a wonderful botanical garden make for fun-filled sightseeing. The variety of shopping arcades, restaurants and nightlife in Susukino gives visitors and residents plenty to do.

History

This bustling metropolis was once nothing but a quiet hunting and fishing town in the Ishikari Plain of Hokkaidō, settled by the Ainu. They were left alone until 1821, when the Tokugawa Shōgunate created an official trading post in what would eventually become Sapporo. The city was declared the capital of Hokkaidō in 1868, and – unlike much of mainland Japan – its growth was carefully planned. In 1880 Japan's third major railway was constructed, which linked Sapporo and the port city of Otaru.

In the 20th century Sapporo emerged as a major producer of agricultural products. Sapporo Beer (see p576), the country's first, was founded in 1876 and quickly became synonymous with the city itself. In 1972 Sapporo hosted the Winter Olympics, and it continues to attract visitors from around the world.

In addition to beer, Sapporo is also famous for its particular style of *rāmen* noodles, which rank among the best.

Orientation

Sapporo, laid out in a Western-style grid pattern, is relatively easy to navigate. Blocks are labelled East, West, North and South in relation to a central point near the TV Tower in the city centre. For example, the famous landmark Tokei-dai (Clock Tower) is in the block of North 1, West 2 (Kita Ichi-jo, Nishi Ni-chōme) – N1W1. Ōdōri-kōen, a narrow grass-covered section ending at the TV Tower, is a major city feature, dividing the city east–west, into north–south halves. South of Ōdōri is the downtown shopping district with shops and arcades. Susukino, the club and entertainment district, is located mainly between the South 2 and South 6 blocks.

Information

BOOKSHOPS

Kinokuniya (☎ 231-2131; 5-7 Kita-Gojō-nishi, Chūō-ku) A stone's throw from the south exit of JR Sapporo station. Look to the right as you leave; it's across the street. Foreign books are on the 2nd floor.

Sapporo Municipal Central Library (札幌中央図書館; ☎ 512-7320; www.city.sapporo.jp/tos yokan/ht/english.html; S22W13 Chūō-ku; ☼ 9.15am-8pm Mon-Fri, 9.15am-5pm Sat & Sun, closed every 2nd & 4th Wed) Has several thousand English-language titles as well as newspapers and magazines. Take the Chūō-Toshokan-mae tram stop.

Tower Records (☎ 241-3851; 7-8F Pibō Bldg, S2W4 Chūō-ku; ☼ 10am-8pm) In the Pivo building. A good resource for English CDs, DVDs and other digital entertainment. Closed irregularly.

INTERNET ACCESS

Comic Land (☎ 200-3003; 2F Hinode Bldg, S1W4 Chūō-ku; per 9hr ¥2000; ☼ 24hr) Has showers and offers fixed fees as well as hourly rates.

i-café (☎ 221-3440; http://sapporocrh.i-cafe.ne.jp; N5W5 Gochōme 2-12, Chūō-ku; ☼ 24hr) Next to the station, with free food (rice porridge, miso soup, ice cream) in addition to the usual coffee/drinks. Heading south, look to the right side, near Kinokuniya bookshop.

MEDICAL SERVICES

Dial ☎ 119 for a medical emergency. JR Sapporo and Sapporo City hospitals require that non-emergency patients arrive before noon.

JR Sapporo Railway Hospital (JR札幌鉄道病院; ☎ 241-4971; N3E1 Chūō-ku) Closest to JR Sapporo station, but no emergency room.

Medical Plaza Sapporo (☎ 209-5410; N5W2 Chūō-ku) Conveniently located on the 7th and 8th floors of the JR Tower in JR Sapporo station. Open until 7pm.

Sapporo City General Hospital (市立札幌病院; ☎ 726-2211; N11W13 1-1 Chūō-ku) Offers 24-hour emergency care as well as the usual gamut of health services.

MONEY

ATMs on the street do not accept non-Japanese issued cards, so the best place to get money is at the Postal ATMs; even the smaller post office branches have these now, and there is even an English 'Visitor Withdrawal' option to make getting yen even easier.

POST

Sapporo Chūō Post Office (☎ 748-2313; N6E1-2-1 Higashi-ku) This branch is located just east of Sapporo JR station. Take the north exit, turn right, walk towards the giant white bowling pin and the building is right across the first major intersection. Like many larger post offices, it is open evenings and weekends and offers a variety of services. The ATMs stay open longer than the window.

Sapporo Ōdōri Post Office (☎ 221-4280; 2-9 Ōdōri-nishi, Chūō-ku)

TOURIST INFORMATION

Several tourist offices offer excellent English brochures and the friendly staff can be relied on for more detailed help. Information can be found at www.welcome.city.sapporo.jp/english/index.html or email convention@plaza-sapporo.or.jp.

Sapporo International Communication Plaza Foundation (☎ 211-3678, 211-3670; www.plaza-sapporo.or.jp/english/index_e.html; 1F MN Bldg, N1W3 Chūō-ku; ☾ 9am-5.30pm) Has an extensive list of English resources, just opposite the Clock Tower (Tokei-dai).

Sapporo Tourist Information Centre (☎ 213-5088; N6W4 Chūō-ku, JR Sapporo station Nishi-dōri Kita-guchi; ☾ 8.30am-8pm) Located on the 1st floor of Sapporo Stellar Place, inside JR Sapporo station. Offers assistance with housing as well as other tourist-related info, along with a host of brochures. The English desk closes at 5.30pm, but other staff can help and many speak excellent English.

Sights

HOKUDAI SHOKUBUTSUEN 北大植物園

Though damaged by a typhoon in 2004, the **Hokudai Shokubutsuen** (☎ 221-0066; N3W8 Chūō-ku; adult ¥400; ☾ 9am-4.30pm 29 Apr-30 Sep, 9am-3.30pm 1 Oct-3 Nov) is one of Sapporo's must sees. This beautiful botanical garden and museum boasts over 4000 varieties of plants, all attractively set on a meandering 14-hectare plot. In addition to the outdoor sights, the Hokudai has two smaller museums: one of local animals (it claims to be the country's oldest, created in 1882) and another of Ainu culture and artefacts, such as tools and clothing. In winter the gardens aren't impressive; head to the greenhouse's hothouse flowers instead.

Across the street, the **Ainu Association of Hokkaidō** (団法人北海道ウタリ協会; ☎ 221-0462; 7F Kaderu 2.7 Community Centre, N2W7 Chūō-ku; www.ainu-assn.or.jp; ☾ 9am-5pm Mon-Sat) has an office and a display room of robes, tools and historical information.

CLOCK TOWER 市時計台

A famous Sapporo landmark, the **Clock Tower** (Tokei-dai; ☎ 231-0838; www15.ocn.ne.jp/~tokeidai/english.html; N1W2 Chūō-ku; admission ¥200; ☾ 8.45am-5.10pm Tue-Sun Nov-May, closed 4th Sat Jun-Oct) is about a 10-minute walk from the JR Sapporo station or a three-minute walk from Ōdōri station. Enter by 5pm. Visitors can look at some clocks and get a brief history of the building, which was built in 1878 and (supposedly) has never missed tolling the hour for 120 years. It's also known as one of Japan's top three *gakkari* (disappointing) spots, mainly because the brochure photos often remove the urban metropolis that dwarfs the small building. You might walk right by before realising it's right in front of you.

SAPPORO TV TOWER さっぽろテレビ塔

There's no way you'd overlook the Eiffel Tower-shaped affair at the east of Ōdōri-kōen: the **TV Tower** (☎ 241-1131; www.tv-tower.co.jp/index_e.html; Ōdōri-nishi 1-chōme, Chūō-ku; admission ¥700; ☾ 9.30am-10pm Apr, 9am-10pm May-Oct, 9.30am-9.30pm Nov-Mar) is 90m high. It has a 360-degree view of the city and souvenir shops below. The city hall's **viewing deck** (Kita 1-jo Nishi 2-chōme, Chūō-ku; ☾ 9.30am-4.30pm Mon-Fri May-Nov) is free. It's just northwest of the TV Tower, on the 19th floor.

HOKKAIDŌ UNIVERSITY 北海道大学

Established in 1876, **Hokkaidō University** (海道大学総合博物館; ☎ 706-2658; www.museum.hokudai.ac.jp/index-e.html; N10W8 Chūō-ku; ☾ 9.30am-4.30pm Tue-Sun Jun-Oct, 10am-4pm Tue-Sun Nov-May) is a scenic place to meander and has a number of unique buildings within its grounds. The bust of William S Clark is a landmark, as are the Poplar and Gingko Aves. (Caution: the odoriferous gingko nuts sometimes cause an itchy rash; it's best not to handle them.) Elms and oaks are also common. Many of the tallest and oldest trees on campus were damaged in 2004 by a severe typhoon. The Furukawa Memorial Hall and the Seikatei are architecturally noteworthy. Several campus museums are open to the public.

NIJŌ FISH MARKET 二条市場

Buy a bowl of rice and select your own sashimi toppings, gawk at the fresh delicacies (some more delicate than others!) or sit down at a shop in **Nijō Fish Market** (S3E1&2 Chūō-ku; ☾ 7am-6pm, individual shops may close at various times), one of Hokkaidō's best. Get there early for the freshest selections and the most variety; things close up by 6pm and individual restaurants have their own hours. Sea urchin and salmon roe are favourites; as is Hokkaidō's version of 'Mother and Child' (Oyakodon), a bowl of rice topped with salmon and roe.

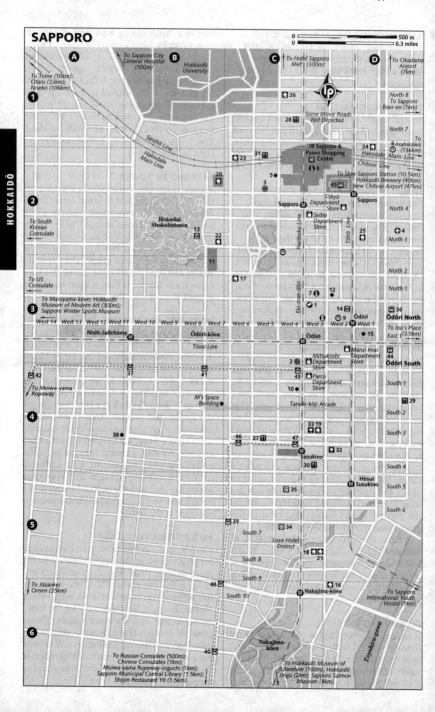

SAPPORO WINTER SPORTS MUSEUM
札幌ウィンタースポーツミュージアム

As well as a variety of other activities, this **museum** (☎ 631-2000; 1274 Miyano-mori Chūō-ku; 8.30am-6pm Apr-Oct, 9am-5pm Nov-Mar) includes the actual ski jump used in the 1972 Olympic Games. Those wishing to ascend the jump can either walk or use the chairlift. Inside, a computerised ski-jump simulator allows you to try your skills without risking a broken leg.

MOIWA-YAMA ROPEWAY
藻岩ロープウェイ

Panoramic views of Sapporo can be had from the **ropeway** (cable car ☎ 561-8177; www.sapporo-dc.co.jp/eng/; 10.30am-9.30pm 9 Apr-May & 1 Oct-19 Nov, 10.30am-10pm Jun-Sep, 11am-8pm 10 Dec-Mar, closed 1-8 Apr), especially at night. The ropeway may be closed due to high winds and has shorter hours on 31 December (11am to 3pm) and 1 January (5am to noon). Be sure to ask for the coupon when you take the tram: there's a ¥200 discount if the conductor stamps your ticket.

OTHER MUSEUMS & TEMPLES
Hokkaidō Jingu (北海道神宮; ☎ 611-0261; www.hokkaidojingu.or.jp) is near Maruyama-kōen, nes-tled in a forest so dense it's easy to forget that the city is just beyond the temple's grounds. Attention has been paid to labelling the natural surroundings: a large plaque lists a number of local birds and the largest trees have identification signs. To the right of the temple, near the toilets, you'll find a small souvenir shop that serves free *ocha* (green tea) and sweets. Purchasing postcards or a confection is not required.

The **Hokkaidō Museum of Literature** (北海道立文学館; ☎ 511-7655; Nakashima-kōen 1-4 Chūō-ku; admission ¥250; Tue-Sun, closed 29 Dec-3 Jan) offers viewers the opportunity to see the private side of many of Japan's famous novelists, primarily those with a Hokkaidō connection. Letters, memorabilia, books and short films all help viewers understand why these writers have earned a place in the canon of Japanese literature. English signage is limited.

Half aquarium, half museum, the interesting **Salmon Museum** (豊平さけ科学館; ☎ 582-7555; 2-1 Makomanai-kōen; www.sapporo-park.or.jp/sake/english/e_index.html; admission free; 9.15am-4.45pm Tue-Sun, closed 29 Dec-3 Jan) is a tribute to one of the world's most delicious fish. It's located across the street from the Sapporo Winter

Sports Museum. Check out over 20 different species of salmon in varying stages of development. Salamanders, turtles and frogs are on display as well. Great place to go with kids.

The **Hokkaidō Museum of Modern Art** (北海道立近代美術館; ☎ 644-6881; N1W17 Chūō-ku; adult/student ¥450/220; ☒ 9.30am-5pm Tue-Sun) has a comprehensive collection of modern works by primarily Japanese artists. Special exhibitions feature a variety of foreign and native artists. Enter by 4.30pm.

Activities

JŌZANKEI ONSEN 定山渓温泉

The Jōzankei area southwest of Sapporo proper has a number of famous *onsen* and hotels, though it's famous mainly because it's conveniently close to Sapporo. The **Jōzankei Grand Hotel** (定山渓グランドホテル; ☎ 598-2214) and **Jōzankei Hot Spring** (定山渓温泉; ☎ 598-2012) are very popular. The area also has several 'foot *onsen*' (*ashiyu*) where you can soak your tired feet. To get there, take the Jozankei-bound Donan or Jōtetsu Bus and get off at the Jozankei stop. It's approximately an hour from JR Sapporo station.

Lesser known but more atmospheric is **Koganeyu Onsen** (小金湯温泉). It's also on the Jozankei bus route; come here to soak in hot, sulphurous waters and *onsen*-steamed vegetables. Some places still have facilities where you can cook your own. Get off at the Koganeyu Onsen stop, about 55 minutes from JR Sapporo station.

WINTER SPORTS

Skiing, snowboarding and snowshoeing can all be done near Sapporo. The closest place is Teine, 10 minutes' train ride away. Try **Teine Highland** (サッポロテイネ; ☎ 681-3191; www.sapporo-teine.com; day pass ¥4550; ☒ 9am-4pm) or **Sapporo KOKUSAI Skiing Resort** (札幌国際スキー場; ☎ 598-4511; www.sapporo-kokusai.co.jp/ski2006/e/index_e.html; day pass ¥4600; ☒ 8.30am-4.30pm). Mainly popular for their proximity to Sapporo, the runs at these places are packed with people, but they're a great getaway.

Sapporo KOKUSAI has five lifts, powder snow and is mainly suitable for beginner and

---

SAPPORO BEER

Let's face it: 'Sapporo' means beer. After visiting Germany (and being favourably impressed) Kihachirō Ōkura returned and selected Sapporo as the lucky place to start what would become Japan's first beer brewery, founded in 1876.

A museum and beer garden, **Sapporo Beer-En** (サッポロビール園; ☎ museum 731-4368, beer garden 0120-15-0550; N7E9 Higashi-ku; ☒ beer garden 11.30am-10pm, tours 9am-3.40pm) is located in the original Sapporo Beer brewery, almost due east of JR Sapporo station. Two tour options are possible: visitors on the short tour (30 minutes) get a carry-home goody bag with a can of beer per person and other miscellaneous items; those wanting to belly up to the trough should take the 50-minute option, which includes a tasting (per beer ¥200). The adjoining beer garden has a variety of beverages and food, serving the local grilled lamb speciality, *jingus kān*, which has become a popular Sapporo dish.

To get here by subway take the Tōhō subway to the Higashi-Kuyakusho-mae stop and take Exit 4. Head south along Higashi-Nana-Chōme-dōri to N8E8 (about 10 minutes) and look to the left. The large brick chimney with the distinct Sapporo trademark star is unmistakable. The building itself is at N7E9. By bus, take the Chūō Bus Higashi 63 and get off at the Kitahachi Higashinana (N8E7) stop. The building will be right in front of you.

Diehard fans will want to take the 40-minute train ride out to the current brewing and bottling facility, **Hokkaidō Brewery** (サッポロビール北海道工場; ☎ 0123-32-5811; hokkaido@sapporobeer.jp; Toiso 542-1 Eniwa-shi). This mammoth production plant seems more like something out of a James Bond movie than a place where beer is made: technicians in white lab coats peer into test tubes; immaculate stainless-steel tanks are covered with computerised gauges and dials; and video cameras monitor the bottles as they whizz by. The tour is self-guided and English is minimal, but you'll be rewarded with a refreshing 20 minutes to tipple at the end.

Take the JR Chitose line towards the airport and get off at the Sapporo Beer Teien station. Head away from the tracks towards the giant white silos with the Sapporo logo; the entrance is a 10-minute walk away.

intermediate snowboarders and skiers. It's very, very crowded, especially on the weekends, but has more of a family vibe than Niseko or Furano.

Teine has 14 lifts and is even more geared towards beginners than KOKUSAI. It's the place to ski if you're wanting to play around for a while; it's probably a disappointment for hard-core skiers, but is good for families with children. As with other skiing resorts, all equipment can be rented when you arrive.

Intermediate to advanced skiers will want to check out Niseko (p589) or Rusutsu (p591) instead.

Festivals & Events

Sapporo Yuki Matsuri (さっぽろ雪まつり; Snow Festival) Come here in early February for fantastic ice sculptures that take weeks to make. They depict historical figures, buildings, celebs and even international pop icons like Hello Kitty or Harry Potter. View them in Ōdōri-kōen and other locations around the city and enjoy food, concerts, karaoke and dancing. Finding reasonably priced accommodation can be extremely difficult, so book as far in advance as possible.

Ōdōri Nōryō Garden (大通納涼ガーデン) The summer beer festival (mid-July to mid-August) is held in Ōdōri Kōen. Sapporo, Asahi and microbrewers set up outdoor beer gardens, offering a variety of beers and other beverages, as well as food and snacks.

Hokkai Bonodori (北海盆踊り) Families welcome back the spirits of the dead in mid-August. The festival provides viewers with glimpses of traditional songs, dances and summer yukata (light, cotton kimonos). Although there are other, more splendid summer festivals in other parts of Japan, this is the largest Hokkaidō has to offer and is well worth a look if you're in town.

Sleeping

If you're just looking for a place to crash in an emergency, the cyber-cafés (see p572) are open 24 hours and are often cheaper than even the cheapest of hotels. Try Comic Land (p572). Love hotels in Susukino are another colourful (often zany!) option, and are as clean as (or cleaner than!) many non-love hotels. Check in after 11pm for the cheapest deals.

BUDGET

OUR PICK Sapporo International Youth Hostel (札幌国際ユースホステル; ☎ 825-3120; www.youthhostel .or.jp/kokusai/ in Japanese; 6-5-35 Toyohira-ku; dm ¥3200, r per person ¥3800; 🖳) A 10-minute subway ride, but nicer and newer than many business hotels. Located in a brand-new facility just behind the

Gakuen-mae station, it is immaculately clean, has inexpensive dial-up internet access, a relaxing Japanese-style bath as well as Western showers, and even those fancy wash-rinse-dry computerised toilet seats. Note: unmarried male/female couples are not allowed to share a private room. The Japanese-language website has a reservation form in English.

Sapporo House Youth Hostel (☎ 726-4235; yh -sappo@crocus.ocn.ne.jp; N6W6-3-1 Kita-ku; dm ¥2940; 🖳) More conveniently located than the International hostel, this is only a 10-minute walk from JR Sapporo station, but definitely not such a good deal. Older and very close to the noisy train tracks, it offers a choice of Western- and Japanese-style rooms.

Kapuseru (Capsule) Inn Sapporo (☎ 251-5571; http://capsule.cside.com in Japanese; S3W3-7 Chūo-ku; per person ¥3200) For men only. Includes a berth with all the usual amenities, plus a sauna, large bathroom, coin laundry and even a 'book corner' with reclining chairs. A stone's throw from the Susukino station on the Nanboku line. Take Exit 1 and go to KFC (on the corner to the right). Turn right on the side street and Kapuseru Sapporo is on the left, about halfway down. A 6am to 6pm 'rest' is also an option (¥1200).

Ino's Place (イノーズプレイス; ☎ 832-1828; http://inos-place.com/e/; dm from ¥3400; 🖳) Come here for no curfew, private rooms and friendly, English-speaking staff. Western-style facilities and internet access (¥10 per minute) make it easy to feel at home. Take the Tōzai line to the Shiroishi stop (four past Ōdōri) and from there it's about a seven-minute walk. Free coffee and tea; breakfast is available for an additional charge. Dorm prices are increased by ¥200 in winter for heating.

MIDRANGE

Tōyoko Inn Sapporo Eki Kita Guchi (☎ 728-1045; www .toyoko-inn.com/eng; N6W1-4-3 Kita-ku; s/d/tw Nov-May ¥4800/6800/6800, Jun-Oct ¥6800/8800/8800; ✖ 🔅 🖳) A chain, yeah, but a simple Japanese-style breakfast is served along with coffee and tea, and the lobbies have free telephones and wi-fi. Five Tōyokos grace the JR station environs.

Hotel Sapporo Met's (ホテル サッポロメッツ; ☎ 726-5511; www.hotelmets.co.jp/index.html in Japanese; N17W5-20 Kita-ku; s/tw ¥7140/10,500; 🖳) One of the few places to offer reasonably priced rooms with kitchenettes and washing machines in each room. Although the website's English is hard to understand in places, reserving over the internet saves an additional ¥1000. Take the Nanboku line north to Kita 18-Jo station; the hotel is a minute's walk westward, across from the Hotel Sapporo-Kaikan. Offers free breakfast.

OUR PICK **Nakamuraya Ryokan** (☎ 241-2111; www .nakamura-ya.com/english.html; N3W7-1 Chūō-ku; r per person high season from ¥7875, low season ¥7350) Attractive tatami rooms and delicious meals. Located directly across from the botanical garden, this is a pleasant place to enjoy the flavours of Hokkaidō, and large baths offer a relaxing way to soothe away the day's travel stress.

Marks Inn Sapporo (☎ 512-5001; www.marks-inn.com /sapporo/english.html; S8W3 Chūō-ku; s/d from ¥5000/7000; 🖳) Another business hotel that offers a simple breakfast and the usual 'cosy' rooms. A Marks Inn discount card allows the holder to get an additional 15% off; it costs ¥1000 and can be bought when you check in.

Hotel Sunlight Sapporo (☎ 562-3111; www.sun light-sapporo.com in Japanese; S8W3-1-4 Chūō-ku; s/tw from ¥6000/11,000; 🅿 🖳) Offers a late-night (after 11pm) check-in of ¥3000 for a single; rooms have to be booked after 11am that day. Parking is from ¥1000 for small cars, from ¥1600 for large vehicles.

Alternative Tōyoko options if the one near the station is full:

Tōyoko Inn Sapporo-eki Nishi Guchi Hokudai-Mae (☎ 717-1045; N8W4 Chūō-ku; 🅿 🗙 📺 🖳)

Tōyoko Inn Sapporo-eki Minami Guchi (☎ 222-1045; N3W1 Chūō-ku; 🅿 🗙 📺 🖳)

TOP END

Hotel Sapporo Garden Palace (☎ 261-5311; www .hotelgp-sapporo.com in Japanese; N1W6 Chūō-ku; s/d/ste low season ¥7738/17,094/28,182, high season ¥9817/20,790/34,650; 🅿 🗙 📺 🖳) A beautiful hotel, convenient for anyone wanting to sightsee downtown or visit the Yuki Matsuri in February, and relatively affordable. The magnificent lobby and attentive staff make checking in a pleasure. Rooms are well appointed; both Japanese and Western styles are available.

Art Hotels Sapporo (☎ 511-0101; www.arthotels .co.jp/sapporo.htm in Japanese; S9W2-2-10 Chūō-ku; s/tw/ ste low season ¥10,972/17,325/27,050, high season ¥15,015/ 23,100/27,050; 📺 🖳) If you can get someone to navigate through the Japanese website, try to do your reservation online: you'll get a buffet-style breakfast with both Japanese and Western options. The *onsen* here seems more like something out of a Roman gala, and a number of in-house restaurant options make

it easy to find something you like. The less expensive rooms seem a bit small for the price; if spaciousness is important, go for the larger suites where you'll have some leg room.

Keiō Plaza Hotel Sapporo (☎ 271-0111; www.keio plaza-sapporo.co.jp/english/index2.html; N5W7 Chūō-ku; s/d from ¥8500/14,000; 🅿 🗙 🖳 🖳) Deluxe, stylish option with a full-sized swimming pool, sauna and athletic training room. Some of the rooms have a 'bath with a view' of the city. Note, when you ask for a nonsmoking room: while it does have a limited number reserved for real nonsmokers, it also feels that an air-cleaner is almost the same thing.

Eating

Rāmen Yokochō (🕑 11-3am) This famous alleyway is crammed with 16 *rāmen* noodle shops in Susukino centre (hours vary from shop to shop). Anyone with a yen for *rāmen* shouldn't miss it, but it can be difficult to find. Take the Nanboku line to Susukino and walk south to the first crossroad. Turn left (east); Rāmen Yokochō is halfway down on the right. Note: there is now a Shin (New) Rāmen Yokochō in the same general vicinity. Either will be fine for a tasty meal, and if you can't find it just ask – it's one place people *will* know. Hours and holidays vary for different shops.

Esta (🕑 7am-9pm) A giant food court under JR Sapporo station; one major path to the subway leads right through it. The variety, from *yakitori* (chargrilled skewered meat, usually chicken) and fish cakes to sandwiches and salads, is awe-inspiring, mouthwatering, even overwhelming. Listen for the singsong 'Ikagadeshou~~ka?' (Take a look?) and you'll know you've arrived.

Kushidori (☎ 758-2989; www.sapnet.ne.jp/kusidori in Japanese; N7W4-8-3, Kita-ku; skewers ¥130-250, beers ¥500; 🕑 4.30pm-12.30am) A Sapporo-only chain serving a variety of *yakitori* and grilled vegetables. The place is usually packed with boisterous college kids and 20-somethings. Try the *tsu-kune* (chicken sausage) or the *okura* (okra).

Shōjin Restaurant Yō (精進　葉; ☎ 562-7020; http://shoujin.com/index.html in Japanese; S17W7-2-12 Chūō-ku; dishes ¥1000-3000; 🕑 11.30am-4.30pm Mon & Tue, 11.30am-8pm Thu-Sun; E) Macrobiotic, organic and vegan fare that's attractively presented and very tasty. The shop is beautifully done with brown paper lanterns, a sushi-style bar and Zen-style flower arrangements. To get there, take the Nanboku line and get off at Horohirabashi. Go left out of the station and veer right at the first traffic signal. The road curves, passing a park (on the right). Go straight through the next signal and turn left when you hit the next one (at the tram line). The restaurant is a few doors down on the right. The small sign is easy to miss.

Nijō Fish Market (S2E1 Chūō-ku; ☼ 7am-6pm) One of the best places for inexpensive sushi and sashimi, some so fresh it's still twitching. Hours vary from shop to shop. For more information, see p573.

Sapporo Beer-En (サッポロビール園; ☎ 742-0505; N7E9 Higashi-ku; mains from ¥1500; E) See the boxed text on p576 for more information. Many come to try the Hokkaidō speciality *jingus kān* (grilled lamb in sauce).

Ebi-kani Gassen (☎ 210-0411; 12F F45 Bldg, S4W5 Chūō-ku; all-you-can-eat ¥3500-5000; ☼ 4pm-midnight) Most people come here for crab, one of Hokkaidō's best-known specialities, but the restaurant serves other items as well. Try to sit by a window if you get the chance, to enjoy the view.

Ambrosia (☎ 271-3279; www.keioplaza-sapporo.co.jp /english/restandb/ambrosia.html; N5W7 Chūō-ku; lunch/dinner from ¥2500/7000; E) Fancy and delicious, this pricey option in the Keio Plaza Hotel offers a 22nd-floor view of the city and is a stylish way to celebrate something special. Not quite the fare you'd find in France, but it's attractively served and flavourful. Ask about the nightly specials and suggested wines.

Soup Curry Kōbō Hirihiri-dō (☎ 643-1710; 2-27 5 chōme Kotoni Nijō Nishi-ku; soups from ¥880; ☼ lunch & dinner Tue-Sun) On the opposite end of the scale, this casual but clean place has fiery curry soup, in a variety of spices and options.

Drinking

If you're just looking for a beer or two, an *izakaya* (Japanese pub) in the M's Space (M'sスペース) building near Tanuki-kōji might fit the bill. It has a variety of small cafés and bars and is a good place to begin a night on the town. The places below are all within easy stumbling distance of the Susukino subway station, but there are literally hundreds of bars and clubs throughout the city.

500 Bar (☎ 562-2556; 1F Hoshi Bldg, S4W2 Chūō-ku; ☼ 6pm-5am Mon-Sat, 6pm-2am Sun & holidays) Usually packed even on weekdays with a mix of foreign and local clientele. Every drink on the menu is ¥500, hence the name (pronounced 'gohyakubaa'), and you can order food as well. This is one of the franchise's several locations

in Sapporo, right across the street from the Susukino subway station's Nanboku line.

Blues Alley (☎ 231-6166; B1F Miyako Bldg, S3W3 Chūō-ku; ☼ 7pm-6am) A night here can be hit or miss depending on what's happening elsewhere, but it's a good place to relax and perhaps play a game or two on the full-sized pool table. Whiskey shots start at ¥700, beers at ¥600.

Entertainment

Susukino is the place to go for clubs and dancing. Cover charges vary substantially from spot to spot and night to night, depending on who's playing where and when. On a Friday or Saturday, be prepared to spend at least ¥1000 to as much as ¥5000, which often includes a drink.

King Xmhu (☎ 531-1388; www.king-xmhu.com in Japanese; S7W4-424-10 Chūō-ku) This mammoth institution is a Susukino landmark, known for its elaborate concrete face (King Xmhu, one presumes) sculpted outside the entrance. Inside, revellers dance and drink on three floors of neon and strobe. Para-para (day-glo makeup and crazy outfits) is just the beginning.

Night Stage SHU (www.nightstage-shu.com; B1F S6W4 Chūō-ku; cover 'charm charge' male/female ¥4000/3500; ☼ from 8pm Mon-Sat) An Okama Bar (all-male dance review) that's about as extravagant as they come. Not just for the gay and lesbian crowd, SHU is 100% chorus line–style Japanese showbiz. A dinner and show set and an all-you-can-drink (three people or more only) discount are attractive options.

Getting There & Away
AIR

Sapporo is connected by direct flights to all major cities in Japan, and many carriers also offer add-ons that allow 'direct' access (you have to change at Narita to Haneda). Look for Asia-related travel agents in your home country for round-trip packages, some of which include hotel package deals.

Sapporo's main airport is **New Chitose Airport** (新千歳空港; Shin-Chitose Kūkō), about 40km south of the city. There's a smaller airport at Okadama, about 10km north of the city.

BUS

Bus services also connect Sapporo with the rest of Hokkaidō. Cheaper than trains and, on some routes, time-competitive as well, buses are an attractive option. Sapporo Eki-mae is the main bus station, just southeast of JR

Sapporo station beneath Bic Camera and Esta. The Chūō bus station (southeast of JR Sapporo station) and Ōdōri bus centre are also departure spots.

Buses depart from Sapporo Eki-mae bus terminal several times a day for destinations all over Hokkaidō, including Wakkanai (¥5500, six hours), Asahikawa (¥2000, two hours), Muroran (¥2000, 2¼ hours), Noboribetsu Onsen (¥1900, one hour and 54 minutes), Tōya-ko Onsen (¥2700, 2¾ hours), Niseko (¥2100, three hours) and Furano (¥2100, two hours and 51 minutes).

From the Chūō bus station there are a few departures a day to Obihiro (¥3670, four hours and 10 minutes) and Abashiri (¥6210, six hours and 10 minutes). Buses to Hakodate depart from both the Chūō bus station and Ōdōri bus centre (¥4680, five hours and five minutes). Discounted round-trip tickets are available for most routes.

TRAIN

Trains are an easy and inexpensive way to get to or from JR Sapporo station, located just north of the city centre – most of the action is less than 10 minutes' walk away. Check www.hyperdia.com for English schedules and up-to-the-minute pricing.

The *Hokutosei Express*, a sleeper train (¥25,270, or ¥9450 with a JR Pass), is the most convenient. It takes 16 hours and runs direct between Tokyo and JR Sapporo station twice a day. The other option is to take a *shinkansen* to Hachinohe, then an express via Aomori (¥22,780, 10 hours).

Sapporo, a central hub, has frequent trains to almost anywhere else in Hokkaidō. If you're Hakodate-bound, a *tokkyū* (limited express) will get you there in 3½ hours (¥8590). Otaru, a popular port nearby, and Asahikawa (to the north) have frequent services.

Getting Around

TO/FROM THE AIRPORTS

New Chitose Airport is accessible from Sapporo by *kaisoku* (rapid) train (¥1040, 36 minutes) or bus (¥1000, 70 minutes). The airport has its own train station, car-rental counters and convenient bus services to various Hokkaidō destinations, including Shikotsu-ko, Tōya-ko Onsen, Noboribetsu Onsen and Niseko.

For Okadama airport, buses leave every 20 minutes or so from in front of the ANA ticket offices, opposite JR Sapporo station (¥400, 30 minutes).

BUS & TRAM

JR Sapporo station is the main terminus for local buses. From late April to early November, tourist buses loop through major sights and attractions between 9am and 5.30pm; a one-day pass costs ¥750, single trips are ¥200 (basic fee).

There is a single tram line that heads west from Ōdōri, turns south, then loops back to Susukino. It's convenient for a trip to Moiwayama, and the fare is a flat ¥170.

SUBWAY

Sapporo's three subways are efficient. Fares start at ¥200, and one-day passes cost ¥800 (weekend only ¥500). There are also ¥1000 day passes that include the tram and buses as well. Or get a pay-in-advance 'With You' card (¥1100), which can be used on subways, buses, trams, Jōtetsu and Chūō buses; unlike the one-day passes, the 'With You' card does not expire at midnight.

DŌ-NAN (SOUTHERN HOKKAIDŌ) 道南

HAKODATE 函館
☎ 0138 / pop 293,000

Hour-glass shaped Hakodate, built on a strip of land between two harbours (Hakodate Harbour to the west and Tsugaru Channel to the east) is, for many, the gateway to Hokkaidō. Pinched in the middle and wider at each end, Hakodate was one of the first ports opened under the Kanagawa Treaty of 1854, and as such had a small foreign community. Much of that influence can still be seen in the Motomachi district, a hillside sprinkled with historic buildings and excellent views of the bay.

Spread out along the water's edge, the city is best accessed by its trams: most of the sights can be walked to from stops along the way. Buses, trams and trains leave the station regularly. Head west, towards Mt Hakodate (hakodateyama; 344m) and the Motomachi district, to find most historical sites; Goryō-kaku, Japan's first Western-style fort, is to the east.

Information

The English maps and information at the **Hakodate Tourist Information Centre** (Map p582; ☎ 23-5440;

9am-7pm Apr-Oct, 9am-5pm Nov-Mar, closed 31 Dec & 1 Jan) inside Hakodate Station are a good starting place. The *Hakodate Guide Map* combined with street signs (many in English and Russian) should make it fairly simple to find what you're looking for. There is also an **information desk** (Map p582; ☎ 27-3333; 12-18 Motomachi; 9am-7pm Apr-Oct, 9am-5pm Nov-Mar) in Motomachi-kōen. Though not fancy, www.city.hakodate.hokkaido.jp has useful information as well.

The PABOTs building has an **i-cafe** (Map p581; ☎ 55-7771; 24hr) advertising 'comfortable time and space' and has great doughnuts and all-you-can-drink coffee and tea. From the station, take the 27Loop 107 (27ループ107) to Tēō PABOTs Mae and it's on the 2nd floor.

Clean but expensive internet can be found straight out from the station (keep going past WAKO, but before Lotteria) at **Hot Web cafe** (Map p582; ☎ 26-3591; www.hotweb.ne.jp/cafe/shop.html; 10am-8pm, Wed-Mon; per 1hr incl 1 drink ¥400).

Sights

If museums are your thing, be sure to ask about a multi-access pass (*kyōtsūken*) for discount entry to two, three or four museums.

MOTOMACHI DISTRICT 元町

On Mt Hakodate's lower slopes, this area has many 19th-century sites and commanding views of the bay – if it's not foggy.

There's a beautiful old **Russian Greek Orthodox Church** (Greek Orthodox Church; Map p582; ☎ 23-7387; 3-13 Motomachi; admission ¥200; 10am-5pm Mon-Fri, 10am-4pm Sat, 1-4pm Sun,), restored in 1916. Remove your shoes before you enter. It's closed in winter from about 26 December through to February (dates vary).

Hakodate City Museum of Northern Peoples (Map p582; ☎ 22-4128; 21-7 Suehiro-chō; admission ¥300; 9am-7pm Apr-Oct, 9am-5pm Nov-Mar) is a good place to learn about the Ainu and their culture. English signs have been added to some exhibits.

Old Public Hall of Hakodate Ward (Map p582; ☎ 22-1001; 11-13 Motomachi; admission ¥300; 9am-7pm Apr-Oct, 9am-5pm Nov-Mar) has a great view of the bay and the outgoing squid boats.

English-style tea-time at the **Old British Consulate** (Map p582; ☎ 27-8159; 33-14 Motomachi; admission ¥300, afternoon tea set ¥1050; 9am-7pm Apr-Oct, 9am-5pm Nov-Mar; E) makes a relaxing afternoon that much more enjoyable. British souvenirs

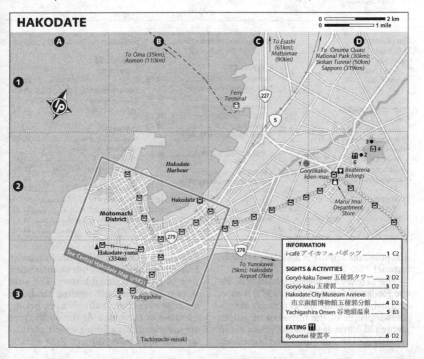

HAKODATE

To Ōma (35km);
Aomori (110km)

To Esashi
(61km);
Matsumae
(90km)

To Ōnuma Quasi
National Park (30km);
Seikan Tunnel (50km);
Sapporo (319km)

Ferry Terminal

Hakodate Harbour

Hakodate

Motomachi District

Goryōkaku-kōen-mae

Beatereria Belongs

Marui Imai Department Store

See Central Hakodate Map (p582)

Hakodate-yama
(334m)

To Yunokawa
(5km); Hakodate
Airport (7km)

Yachigashira

Tachimachi-misaki

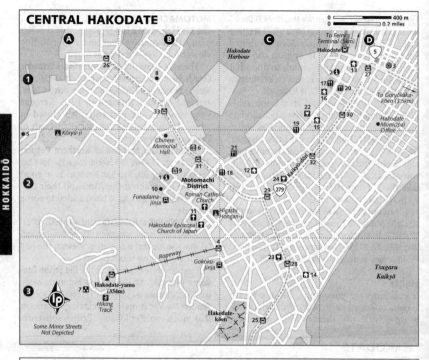

CENTRAL HAKODATE

and postcards add to the nostalgia. Marmite, anyone?

There are several **Buddhist temples** here, but the **Foreigners' Cemetery** (Map p582) is more unusual, as it has the graves not only of well-known people of the time, but of sailors, clergy and others as well, all of whom unfortunately died far away from their homelands.

Many of the graves have English, Russian or French inscriptions, and it is an interesting slice of Japan's colonial history. The walk there is a sight in itself: running parallel to the edge of the bay, it affords some beautiful views of the water. At the docks there are some interesting fishing vessels, particularly the **squid boats**. Lantern-light attracts the squid to the surface; there are few boats as picturesque.

To get to Motomachi, take tram 5 from the station and get off at the Suehirō-chō stop, then walk uphill for 10 minutes. Alternatively, get off at the end of the line and walk along the waterfront first, visit the cemeteries, then stop at the buildings as you walk uphill to Suehirō-chō.

HAKODATE-YAMA 函館山

This small mountain (334m) offers a great view of the city, especially at night. A **cable car** (ropeway; Map p582; ☎ 23-6288; www.334.co.jp/en/index .html; one way/return ¥640/1160; ☼ 10am-10pm May-Oct, to 9pm Nov-Apr) whisks you to the top in a few minutes. Take tram 2 or 5 to the Jūjigai stop (¥200) and walk uphill to the ropeway platform (seven minutes). A summit-bound bus (¥360, 30 minutes) leaves directly from the station, is cheaper and stops at several viewing places as it winds to the top. Those wanting to rough it old-style can take the hiking track (from May to late October).

A 10-minute walk from the summit is Tsutsuji-yama carpark, a hot date spot at night, but relatively crowd free by day. At its far end there is an overgrown path that leads to moss-covered walls and buttresses, the ruins of an old fort, **Hakodateyama Yōsai** (Map p582). Unlike so many of Japan's historic sites, this one is refreshingly deserted and you can clamber around, Indiana Jones–style, among ferns with fronds the size of palm leaves.

GORYŌ-KAKU 五稜郭

Japan's first Western-style **fort** (Map p581) was built in 1864 in the shape of a five-pointed star (*goryō-kaku* means 'five-sided fort') and was designed to trap attackers in deadly crossfire. Nothing remains of the actual fort structure, but the landscaped grounds and moat are picturesque, and one can actually climb around on them. The nearby **Hakodate City Museum Annexe** (Map p581; ☎ 51-2548; 44-2 Goryōkakumachi; admission ¥100; ☼ 9am-4.30pm Apr-Oct Tue-Sun, 9am-4pm Nov-Mar Tue-Sun) offers a taste of the fort's history, including weaponry and bloodstained uniforms (ugh!). **Goryō-kaku Tower** (Map p581; ☎ 51-4785; 43-9 Goryōkakumachi; admission ¥840; ☼ 8am-7pm Apr-Oct, 9am-6pm Nov & Mar, 9am-7pm Dec-Feb), recently rebuilt but to mixed reaction ('looks like Big Brother', said a resident), provides an attractive view of the fort below and the surrounding city. To reach the fort, take tram 2 or 5 to the Goryōkaku-

kōen-mae stop (¥220, 15 minutes). From there it's a 10-minute walk.

Other Attractions

The **Asa-ichi** (morning market; Map p582; ☼ 5am-noon), located just to the right of Hakodate station, is a great place for hungry seafood lovers. Like tightly packed ammo, freshly caught squid glisten in ice-stuffed Styrofoam. Most of the commerce is over by 8am, after which the tourists come for shopping, snacks and souvenirs.

If you want to catch your own squid, the cruiser **Octopus** (Map p582; ☎ 26-4705; 24-1 Bentenmachi; trip ¥6000) offers two-hour expeditions. It costs extra to have them cook the unfortunate cephalopod for you.

Yachigashira Onsen (Map p581; ☎ 22-8371; 20-7 Yachigashira; admission ¥390; ☼ 6am-9.30pm, closed every 2nd & 4th Tue) is an enormous hot spring south of Hakodate proper, one of Hokkaidō's oldest, with dark iron-laden water. To get there, take tram 2 from Hakodate station to Yachigashira, the final stop (¥220), continue to the first intersection and then turn right – you'll see the public bathhouse complex on the left shortly after you turn.

East of the town centre, the Yunokawa district has many high-end hot-spring resorts; some allow day use.

Though quite a distance from Hakodate proper (40 minutes by car, one hour by JR train), **Ōnuma Quasi-National Park** (大沼国定公園; ☎ 67-2170), an unusually large lake and swamp that offers beautiful canoeing, fishing and many scenic hiking tracks, is worth the trip (the JR line between Hakodate and Sapporo does stop here). Bring insect repellent, as tourists are particularly tasty. You're much better off renting a car, as the train connection is inconvenient. Many of the hills have hidden hot springs, but finding them can be difficult – your best bet is to ask a local for directions to their favourite gem.

Festivals & Events

Hakodate Goryōkaku Matsuri (函館五稜郭祭り 函館五稜郭祭) Held on the third weekend in May, this festival features a parade of townsfolk dressed in the uniforms of the soldiers who took part in the Meiji Restoration battle of 1868.

Hakodate Minato Matsuri (函館港祭り 函館港まつり; Hakodate Port Festival) During this festival in early August, groups of seafood-fortified locals (reportedly 10,000 of them!) move like waves doing an energetic squid dance.

HOKKAIDŌ

HOKKAIDŌ

Sleeping

In summer, Hakodate can be swamped with tourists en route to other parts of Hokkaidō, and accommodation can be scarce. If you have trouble booking, call the tourist information centre. Staff will know which lodgings, if any, have vacancies.

Hakodate Youth Guesthouse (Map p582; ☎ 26-7892; www12.ocn.ne.jp/~hakodate/; 17-6 Hōraimachi; dm Oct-Jun ¥3800, Jul & Sep ¥4200, Aug ¥4500) A quick walk from Hōrai-chō tram stop, but accessible from Hakodate station as well (after getting off the tram, turn left at the first light, then go past two more lights and turn right. The guesthouse is across the street from a supermarket and carpark.). Winter hours can be irregular, so call ahead. No meals are served and it's lights out at 11pm, but ice-cream addicts will appreciate the free homemade ice cream.

Niceday Inn (Map p582; ☎ 22-5919; 9-11 Ōtemachi; dm ¥3000) Near the Asa-ichi morning market, this tiny hotel offers bunk-style rooms and has a friendly matron. It might not be for everyone – but it's a great place to pinch pennies. It's directly opposite the Kokusai Hotel, in a small alley. The sign is small, easily visible once you're in the alley but not so much when you're out on the main street.

Auberge Kokian (Map p582; ☎ 26-5753; www .hakodate.or.jp/hotel/kokian/default.htm in Japanese; 13-2 Suehirochō; r per person ¥4725) Built in 1897, this is a typical example of that period's architecture. It has a Japanese-style façade downstairs and Western rooms upstairs. Rooms are 'cosy', but have charm. Add ¥5000 per person for a Japanese-style dinner and breakfast. This place is just a two-minute walk from Jūjigai tram station. Walk three blocks towards the water (dock area) after getting off the tram; the inn is behind one of the old warehouses.

Tōyoko Inn Hakodate Eki-mae Asaichi (Map p582; ☎ 23-1045; www.toyoko-inn.com/e_hotel/00063/index .html; 22-7 Ōtemachi; s/d high season ¥5800/7800, low season ¥4800/6800; ⓟ ✖ ✖ ⌨) Another Tōyoko clone, this modern business hotel is steps away from the Asa-ichi market and only three minutes' walk from Hakodate station. A great, moderately priced option, especially for those who need computer or LAN access. Japanese-style *onigiri* (rice-ball snack) breakfast is complimentary, as are coffee and tea.

our pick **Hakodate Harborview Hotel** (Map p582; ☎ 22-0111; www.hvh.jp in Japanese; 14-10 Wakamatsuchō; s/d/tw from ¥10,350/15,000/20,700; ⓟ ✖ ✖ ⌨) This top-end hotel offers a number of cheap website deals (in Japanese only; prices vary), and the 10th floor is reserved entirely for nonsmokers. Several of the restaurants are western-style, as are the bars.

Eating

A new, fairly trendy place to dine is **Nishi Hatoba** (Map p582), a waterfront district with a variety of eateries in converted warehouses and English-style buildings.

Asa-ichi (朝市; morning market; Map p582; ⓨ 5am-noon) The morning market is the place for fresh fish. Seafood *donburi* (a bowl of rice with toppings) is a local favourite.

If you prefer to eat your seafood in a restaurant, see if one will whip up a Hakodate version of *oyakodon*; meaning 'mother and child *donburi*', it's usually made with chicken and egg in the rest of Japan; in Hokkaidō it's made with salmon and roe.

Hakodate Rāmen Kamome (Map p582; ☎ 22-1727; 8-2 Wakamatsuchō; rāmen ¥580-1150; ⓨ 6am-3pm Apr-Oct, 6.30am-3pm Nov-Mar) Lets you top your noodles how you like it. Choose from roast pork *(buta)*, crab *(kani)*, shrimp *(ebi)*, squid *(ika)* or even sea urchin *(uni)*.

California Baby (Map p582; ☎ 22-0643; 23-15 Suehiro-chō; meals ¥1000; ⓨ lunch-dinner; E) Just around the corner from Nishi-Hatoba, this place has 'the best American coffee' and a variety of inexpensive dishes, such as California sandwiches and 'Sysco Rice', a popular favourite – rice, sausages and Italian meat sauce. Get off at Suehiro-chō and backtrack to the first stoplight. Turn left (towards the water) and look for the teddy-bear museum, then turn right and look for the bright yellow sign.

Ryōuntei (Map p581; ☎ 54-3221; 8-20 Honchō; set menus ¥980-2000; ⓨ lunch & dinner Mon-Sat) Not far from the new Goryōkaku tower, this place has fresh seafood and a choice of counter or tatami seating. No English, but a picture menu makes ordering a straightforward affair.

Hakodate Beer (Map p582; ☎ 23-8000; 5-22 Ōtemachi; dishes ¥500-2500; ⓨ 11am-10pm; E) Next to the Hakodate Kokusai Hotel, this expansive place has live music and sometimes boisterous crowds. A variety of microbrews complement a Western-style menu of pizza and items from the grill. A sample of four (small) glasses of different microbrews is available for ¥1260.

Drinking

Hakodate isn't known for nightlife so the tourist information booth may have suggestions.

Sabou Hishii (Map p582; ☎ 27-3300; www4.ocn
.ne.jp/~hishii/; 9-4 Hōraichō; coffee or tea ¥890) Antique
store, coffee shop and dessert café by day,
quiet bar by night. In an old ivy-covered *kura*
(storage room) with lots of atmosphere. No
English menu.

Yasai Bar Miruya (Map p582; ☎ 26-2688; 7-26
Toyokawachō; drinks from ¥450) Tiny and cheerful,
with veggie-inspired specials often paired with
local sakes or *shōchūs* (distilled spirits). The
sweet, energetic hostess proudly produces a
well-thumbed Japanese-English dictionary
and will pass it around for anyone to share –
but plan on practising your Japanese. Get off
the tram at Uoichiba-dōri and continue for
two blocks, looking on the right for the pastel-
yellow sign. If you reach the next tram stop,
you've gone too far.

Gagyū Lounge (スカイラウンジ「ル・モン
・ガギュー」; Map p582; Sky Lounge Le Mont Gagyū;
☎ 23-8757; 5-10 Ōtemachi; cocktails ¥800-1000; E) In the
Hakodate Kokusai Hotel. If you're dying for a
view (and it's definitely a view to die for), this
is the place to sip a late-night something, but
plan on paying premium yen for that cocktail.
Dress to impress to avoid a frosty reception.

Getting There & Away
Nippon Airways (ANA) and Japan Air-
lines (JAL) connect Hakodate Airport with
Nagoya, Kansai, Sendai, Niigata, Hiroshima,
Fukuoka and (of course) Tokyo. All Nippon
Kōkū has flights from Hakodate to Sapporo's
Okadama airport (low season from ¥9000,
45 minutes).

Trains link Hakodate and Aomori via the
Seikan Tunnel (*tokkyū* ¥5340, two hours).
Some of these trains also give you the option
of taking the Seikan Tunnel Tour (p571).

Hokutosei Express sleeper trains serve Tokyo's Ueno station (¥27,990, nine hours). It
costs ¥9450 with a JR Pass. A combination of
tokkyū and *shinkansen* (from Morioka) takes
about seven hours to Tokyo (¥18,750).

JR's Hakodate main line runs north to
Sapporo (*tokkyū* ¥8790, 3½ hours) via New
Chitose airport.

Hokuto buses (☎ 22-3265) depart from in front
of Hakodate station for Sapporo's Chūō bus
station and Ōdōri bus centres (¥4680, five
hours and 10 minutes, six daily). One night
bus leaves at 11.55pm for the same locations,
same price. Buses for Esashi leave six times
a day (¥1830, 2¼ hours). A tour bus does a
loop of Matsumae and Esashi – check out

www.hotweb.or.jp/hakobus or the tourist info
centre for the current schedule. The tour is in
Japanese only, but English handouts help.

Seikan Ferries (☎ 42-5561; ☾ 24hr) depart year-
round for Aomori (¥1420, 3¾ hours) and
Ōma on the Shimokita-hantō peninsula (from
¥1170, 1¾ hours, two to four daily).

Getting Around
Buses to Hakodate Airport depart frequently
from just outside Hakodate station (¥300, 20
minutes).

A taxi from Hakodate Station to the ferry
terminal costs around ¥1500. City bus 16 runs
much more frequently between the ferry terminal and the Goryō-kaku-kōen-mae tram
stop, from where you can catch a tram to
Hakodate station.

Single-trip fares on trams are ¥200; buses
are ¥250. One-day (¥1000) and two-day
(¥1700) passes offer unlimited rides on both
trams and buses (¥600 for tram alone) and are
available at the tourist information centres or
from the drivers. A pass is also good for the
bus to the peak of Hakodate-yama.

MATSUMAE 松前
☎ 01394 / pop 10,300
Matsumae was once the stronghold of the
Matsumae clan and the centre of Japanese
political power in Hokkaidō until the 19th
century. Among other things, Matsumae is
famous for its 10,000 *sakura* (cherry trees),
which bloom towards the end of April or early
May. Over 250 species can be seen, most of
them in and around Matsumae-jō.

Hokkaidō's only castle, **Matsumae-jō** (前
城; ☎ 2-2275; admission ¥270; ☾ 9am-5pm mid-Apr–
Dec), and the last one to be built in Japan, was
completed in 1854. The restored castle houses
typical feudal relics and a small collection of
Ainu items. There is a small **tourist information
office** (☎ 2-3868; ☾ Apr-Oct) near the castle. Uphill is a 17th-century temple district and the
burial ground of the Matsumae clan. Further
along is **Matsumaehan Yashiki** (松村藩屋敷 松前
藩屋敷; admission ¥350; ☾ closed Nov–mid-Apr), an interesting replica of an Edo-period village built
using authentic materials and construction
techniques. Mannequins are both instructive
and comical.

To reach Matsumae from Hakodate, take
the JR Esashi line to Kikonai (*futsū* ¥810,
1¼ hours), which is also on the JR Tsugaru
Kaikyō line for connections with Honshū.

HOKKAIDŌ

From Kikonai station there are direct buses to Matsumae; get off at the Matsumae-jō stop (¥1220, 1½ hours). Buses then continue to the Matsumae station across town, from where there are buses to Esashi between April and November (¥2720, two hours, four daily).

ESASHI 江差

☎ 0139 / pop 9930

If Matsumae was Hokkaidō's Edo-period political centre, Esashi was the economic centre. It's still an important fishing town (herring – until the stocks were depleted in the early 20th century – and other seafood now). A number of *nishingoten* (herring barons' homes) once dominated the shoreline, and several are still quite well preserved.

Yokoyama House (横山家; ☎ 52-0018; admission ¥300) and **Nakamura House** (旧中村家住宅; ☎ 52-1617; admission ¥300) are good places to start, although there are numerous other houses to view and a trip to Esashi could easily fill the better part of an afternoon. Both are open all year round, but close on Monday during the winter. Call ahead for an appointment at Yokoyama House from November to April.

Listen to performances of Esashi Oiwake, a nationally known music style, at **Esashi Oiwake Museum** (江差追分会館; ☎ 52-0920; admission ¥500; closed Mon in winter). Shows are held at 11am, 1pm and 2.30pm. It's high-pitched, nasal singing that will either fascinate or make you want to cover your ears.

Esashi holds an annual festival, the **Ubagami Matsuri** (姥神祭り 江差姥神大神宮渡御祭; 9-11 August), when streets fill with more than a dozen floats in honour of Ubagami Daijingu, the oldest shrine in Hokkaidō, which was built to invoke a successful herring catch over 350 years ago. Some of the floats are antiques.

Esashi is also the most convenient gateway to Okushiri-tō, a sleepy island with small fishing villages, few foreign visitors, gorgeous coastal scenery and some tourist attractions.

Getting There & Away

There are infrequent local trains between Hakodate and Esashi (¥1790, 2½ hours). From Esashi station, it's a 20-minute walk downhill to the tourist sites. Direct buses from Hakodate (¥1830, 2¼ hours) stop across the street from the terminal. From April to November buses run between Esashi and Matsumae directly (¥2410, two hours, four daily). From Esashi ferry terminal, near the tourist sites,

ferries depart twice daily for Okushiri-tō (¥2200, 2¼ hours), or once daily between January and March. From late April to October ferries also run between Okushiri-tō and Setana (¥1660 one way, 95 minutes), further north along the western coast.

DŌ-Ō (CENTRAL HOKKAIDŌ) 道央

OTARU 小樽

☎ 0134 / pop 141,000

Escape from Sapporo to Otaru for a weekend, a day or even an afternoon. Famous now as a tourist spot and for its music boxes, it has a rich, interesting history. Building buffs will love the old warehouses and the beautiful canal district. It played an important part in the herring industry, was a terminal station for Hokkaidō's first railroad and was also a literary hotspot.

Information

The **tourist information office** (☎ 29-1333; 2-22-15 Inaho; ☼ 9am-6pm Apr-Sep, 9am-5pm Oct-Mar) is inside JR Otaru station. The *Otaru Tourist Guide*, which details most of Otaru's sights, transport and hotels, is particularly useful. There is an additional information booth at **Unga Plaza** (☎ 33-1661; 2-1-20 Ironai; ☼ 9am-6pm, 8am-8pm Apr-Nov) near the Otaru Museum and at Dec-Mar **Asakusa-bashi** (☎ 23-7740; ☼ 9am-6pm) in the canal area. internet access is at **Cafe La Fille** (フェ・ラ・フィーユ; ☎ 32-1234; per 30min ¥400; ☼ 9am-6pm Wed-Mon). Find it by turning right out of the station, pass four lights, then look for it on the right just after the pedestrian bridge.

Sights & Activities

Take a romantic stroll along Otaru Canal beneath the old gas lamps or have a picnic on a sunny afternoon. Numerous old warehouses are still standing, many of them labelled in Japanese, English and Russian. Built in the Meiji-era and Taisho-era, these structures lend themselves to picture taking. More can be seen along Nichigin-dori, once known as the 'Wall Street of the North', including the street's namesake Bank of Japan, the **Former Nippon Yüsen Company building** (旧日本郵船ビル; 旧日本郵船株式会社小樽支店; ☎ 22-3316; admission ¥300; ☼ 9.30am-5pm Tue-Sun) and the old **Mitsui Banking Corporation building**,

---

HOKKAIDŌ'S TOP 10 VIEWS

- Mashū-ko (p614) on a clear day
- Winter drift ice in the Sea of Okhotsk (p611)
- Whales, dolphins and porpoises during summer boat cruises from Muroran (p594)
- Kuril seals basking below the cliffs at the cape Erimo Misaki (p622)
- The white peaks of Tokachidake mountains rising behind the lavender fields of Furano (p605) and Biei (p607)
- Tōya-ko's frisky young volcanoes and terrifying Usu-zan (p593)
- Autumn's red, gold and yellow hillsides from the slopes of the mountain of Daisetsuzan (p604)
- Sapporo skyline from Moiwa-yama Ropeway (p575)
- Sunset over Momo-iwa on Rebun-tō (p603)
- The stunning pools of Kamuiwakka-no-taki and the surrounding mountains from Shiretoko-go-ko (p619)

---

which finally closed in 2002 after 123 years of operation.

Self-styled as the 'Venice of Japan', Otaru is also trying to build a name for itself as a glass-blowing town. **K's Blowing** (☎ 31-5454; www.ks-blowing.net; lessons ¥1800-2200; ☽ 9am-5.30pm) offers short lessons (in English; 25 minutes) in making a cup or bowl, which you may keep. The glass can be a spittoon-shaped thimble or a pretty usable vase. It's in a lively area of craft shops. **Yuzu Kōbō** (☎ 34-1314; www.geocities.jp/yuzu_koubou/ in Japanese; ☽ 9am-6pm summer, 10am-5pm winter), closer to the waterfront, lets you make a ring (¥1500) or bead (¥300). It uses flamework (done with a small torch) to produce small, highly detailed works of art.

The **Otaru Museum** (☎ 33-2439; 2-1-20 Ironai; admission ¥300; ☽ 9.30am-5pm) is in a restored old warehouse that was built in 1893. It's small, but has displays on Hokkaidō's natural history, some Ainu relics, and various special exhibitions on herring, ceramics and literature. English pamphlets are available, although they only scratch the surface of the explanations.

Built in 1897, **Nishin Goten** (鰊御殿; Herring Mansion; ☎ 22-1038; admission ¥300; ☽ 9am-5pm mid-Apr–Nov) was relocated to the coast at Shukustu in 1956. The original owners were herring industry barons during the Meiji and Taishō eras, living in this enormous complex along with their seasonal labourers. To get there, take bus 11 from Otaru station to the last stop at the Otaru Suizokukan (Otaru Aquarium, ¥200, 25 minutes).

Otaru Kihinkan (小樽貴賓館; Former Aoyama villa; ☎ 24-0024; www.otaru-kihinkan.jp in Japanese; admission ¥1000; ☽ 9am-6pm Apr-Oct, 9am-5pm Nov-Mar) is a herring-money mansion, built by the Aoyama family in 1918. This amazing Japanese-style building has all the trimmings: an *uguisu-bari* (squeaking corridor designed to reveal intruders), a 100-tatami room, ornate woodwork and even opulent Arita porcelain pit toilets. Well worth the bus ride. To get there, take bus 11 (¥200) and get off at the Iwaizu-san-chōme stop (20 minutes).

From late April to mid-October you can take a sightseeing boat from Otaru's Pier 3 (¥1550, 85 minutes), which cruises around the shoreline and returns to the pier. It can also drop you off at the herring villa area, where you can catch a bus back to town.

Sleeping

There are several rider houses in and around Otaru, which offer cheap accommodation in the ¥1000 to ¥1500 range. Ask at the tourist information centres for directions; a few are accessible by public transport.

Villa Mountengu Youth Hostel (ヴィラマウンテング; ☎ 33-6944; www.tengu.co.jp/english/index.html; 2-13-1 Mogami; dm per person incl breakfast ¥3930; ☒ 🖳) This is actually two different guest houses connected to the same umbrella organisation Otaru Tengu-yama. Close to Tengu-yama cable-car and ski area. Take bus 3 to the final stop (¥200), about a 20-minute ride. Backtrack from the station just a little and it will be on the right, before you come to a park.

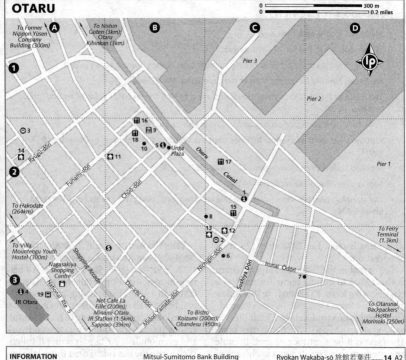

OTARU

Otarunai Backpackers' Hostel MorinoKi (旅
の家　小樽　もりのき; ☎ 23-2175; 4-15 Aioi-chō;
http://back packers-hostel.infotaru.net; dm ¥3400) Quiet,
quaint and cosy, this place gets filled quickly
so book ahead in the summer if you want to
ensure a room. Just 15 minutes on foot from
either Otaru or Minami Otaru JR stations.
Turn right on the main road immediately in
front of the JR station. Follow it and at the
third traffic signal after passing under the
railroad turn left. The road eventually comes
to a dead end at a shrine (Suitengu).The hostel
is on the right of the shrine.

Ryokan Wakaba-sō (☎ 27-3111; Inaho 4-3-17; r per
person incl breakfast ¥3500) On a side street west of
the centre, this place is small but sweet, quiet
yet conveniently located. There's a 2am curfew – but if you're late, ring the inconspicuous
doorbell and a sleepy-eyed owner will let you
in. From the Otaru post office, head towards
Chūō-dōri and look for a small alley on the
right. The Wakaba-sō is halfway up on the
left, across from a parking area.

ourpick Hotel Vibrant Otaru (☎ 31-3939; www
.vibrant-otaru.jp; 1-3-1 Ironai; from s/d/tr incl breakfast
¥5140/6190/10,500; 🖳) Very stylish recent renova-

tion of an old bank building. The lobby is very attractive, with wrought-iron tables and a small souvenir stand. Western-style rooms are bland, and the triples often consist of one double bed and one bunk, though various bed configurations are available. The hotel is on the left side of the road across from the main post office.

Ebiya Ryokan (☎ 22-2317; 2-10-16 Ironai; r per person incl breakfast ¥5800, per person incl 2 meals ¥7800) In a quiet area close to the canal (take the main road from the station; turn left at the third traffic light – the inn is on the second block). The lobby needs some renovation, but the Japanese-style rooms are perfectly up to par and are handsomely decorated.

Otaru Grand Hotel Classic (☎ 22-6500; 1-8-25 Ironai; s/d high season ¥12,600/18,900, low season ¥6300/10,500; **P** **✂**) In another former bank, this nicely done hotel is its own slice of history. It has tastefully styled Western rooms and lovely leaded glass. Take the main road away from the station, turn right at the third traffic light. Go one block and the hotel is before the main post office.

Eating

The Otaru station has the usual fare, but you're better off wandering down to the far more picturesque canal area and finding something more exciting. The street of Sushi-ya Dōri has numerous sushi stands, with everything from the standard to the rather bizarre.

Mangiare Takinami (☎ 33-3394; 2-1-16 Ironai; set lunches ¥920; ☽ lunch & dinner Thu-Tue; E) One block off the canal. A relaxing place with wooden rafters, brick walls and delicious pasta and fish sets. Paella is the speciality.

Bistro Koizumi (ビストロ小泉; ☎ 32-4965; 1-7-10 Inaho; meals ¥850; ☽ lunch & dinner Thu-Tue) A hit with the younger crowd, this place specialises in Hayashi-rice, a tomato-based beef dish served on white rice. Get there early if you want some; it's often sold out. Salmon pasta (sake pasuta) is another favourite. No English menu.

Uminekoya (☎ 32-2914; Ironai 2-2-14; dishes ¥630-1890; ☽ lunch & dinner; E) A combo restaurant and pub, this atmospheric warehouse was built in 1906 and was the setting for several novels of Japanese literary fame. The façade, crumbling brick laced with ivy, has been described by several famous writers.

Otaru Sōko No 1 (☎ 21-2323; 5-4 Minato-machi; dishes ¥800-2000; ☽ 11am-10pm; E) A nice microbrewery with a selection of fresh brews on tap, plus both German and Japanese fare to comple-

ment its Bavarian décor. Potatoes and sausages are big here. Sometimes has live music to accompany your meal.

Kita no Ice Cream Yasan (☎ 23-8983; 1-2-18 Ironai; ☽ 9.30am-7pm; E) Serves up stomach-turning flavours such as nattō (fermented soy beans), tofu, crab, beer…even sea urchin. Squid ink – jet black – is about as bizarre as ice cream gets. Menu in English, Japanese and Korean.

Obandesu (おばんです; ☎ 25-5432; 1-10-8 Hanazono; ☽ dinner-midnight Tue-Sun) A tiny izakaya that's little more than three booths and a bar – but the food is excellent, the owners are gracious, and the beers are fresh. Getting there is tricky: follow Daiichi Ōdōri past Sushiyadōri and continue straight. It's about halfway up the long hill on the left side of the street, on the 2nd floor, with a small white sign.

Getting There & Away

Otaru is just 30 minutes from Sapporo by kaisoku train or 50 minutes away by futsū; fares for both cost ¥620. Special airport kaisoku trains run via Sapporo to New Chitose Airport (¥1740, 75 minutes). Occasional local trains run south to Niseko (¥1410, two hours).

Buses run frequently to Sapporo (¥590, one hour), and less often to Niseko (¥1600, 1¾ hours, three daily).

Ferries run daily between Otaru and Maizuru (from ¥9600, 20 hours), just north of Kyoto, and almost daily to Niigata (¥6200, 18 hours). To get to the Shin-Nihonkai **ferry terminal** (☎ 22-6191), take bus 10 from in front of the station (¥200, 30 minutes). Tourist-loop buses also stop at the port a couple of times a day.

Getting Around

The main part of town is small enough to tackle on foot. Tourist buses loop through the city taking in most of the sights (¥200 per trip or ¥750 for a day pass). Buses leave about every 20 minutes from Otaru station, starting at 9am and finishing at 6.30pm.

You can rent bikes at **Charinko Otaru** (☎ 32-6861; per hr shopping bike/mountain bike ¥500/700; ☽ 8am-10pm); go straight out from the station, turn right at the third corner and it's right near the KFC.

NISEKO ニセコ
☎ 0136 / pop 4700
One of Hokkaidō's prime ski resorts during the winter months and a hiking base during

HOKKAIDŌ

summer and autumn, Niseko sprawls between the mountain Yōtei-zan to the east and Niseko Annupuri to the west. Views at any time of year are splendid, and there is something almost holy about the snow-covered peaks on a chilly winter day.

When snow is falling (and it does a lot), sounds are dampened, making even a walk out to the car seem like a magic sleigh ride. Locals are as laid back and friendly as the tourists (many of whom are Aussies) are boisterous. Skiing at Niseko, with its jaw-dropping views of mountains and its plethora of *onsen*, is unequalled. Like its northern cousin Furano, Niseko enjoys perfect powder snow; if you're one of the first on the slopes, you'll feel like you've left Earth as you float downhill.

Information

Niseko station has a **tourist information office** (☎ 44-2468), which can help plan skiing weekends. Info is also available online at www .niseko.gr.jp.

Sights & Activities

Come here for canoeing, kayaking and river rafting in summer, and ice climbing, snowshoeing or even dogsledding in the winter. Hot springs are open all year round and during the ski season this town has a lively night life (which disappears as soon as the snow is gone). Be sure to check the *Local Rules Guide* as accidents do happen and avalanches are a possibility after heavy snows. The slopes are an equal mix of beginner, medium and advanced levels. A 2m to 3m snow base, the 17 lifts and varied terrain make for a challenging, exciting ski experience for just about anyone. Downsides include long queues and the usual piped music over loudspeakers, but that's standard for skiing in Japan.

The first and most popular of the major Niseko resorts, **Niseko Annupuri Kokusai** (☎ 58-2080; www.niseko.ne.jp/annupuri in Japanese; lift tickets ¥4400, night only ¥1900; 🕐 day 8.30am-4.30pm, night 4.30-9pm) is also often the most crowded. The trails are slightly more advanced, with more than two-thirds at the intermediate or advanced level, with a 60:40 mix of skiers and snowboarders. The season runs from late November to late April or early May. Ask if there's artificial snow and watch people burst out laughing.

You can buy an eight-hour lift ticket for all three resorts – Annupuri, Grand Hiraifu and Higashiyama – for ¥4800.

The **Niseko Outdoor Centre** (ニセコアウトドアセンター; ☎ 44-1133; www.noc-hokkaido.jp/nocindex_eng.html), near the Annupuri ski slope, and the **Niseko Adventure Centre** (ニセコアドベンチャーセンター; ☎ 23-2093; www.nac-web.com), in the village of Hirafu, can organise activities.

At the station is **Kiranoyu** (綺羅乃湯; ☎ 44-1100; bath ¥500; 🕐 10am-9.30pm Thu-Tue), where you can step off the train and into your choice of *hinoki* (cypress), rock, hot steam or bubble baths.

Sleeping

Niseko is spread out, with nothing close to the station. Most places will provide pick up and drop off, or you can take buses or shuttles. The closer you get to the slopes themselves, the more options you'll have. Near the lifts, if you basically walk in a straight line, you'll run into a pension or two.

For really cheap accommodation, check out rider houses.

Niseko Tourist Home (ニセコツーリストホーム; ☎ 44-2517; http://niseko-th.com in Japanese; dm Nov-Apr/Mar-Oct ¥3500/2500, incl 2 meals ¥5500/4500) A perennial favourite – clean and inexpensive – though speaking/reading Japanese will help. It's 4km from JR Niseko station.

Niseko Annupuri Youth Hostel (ニセコアンヌプリユースホステル; ☎ 58-2084; www .annupuri-yh.com in Japanese; 470-4 Niseko; YHA members r per person ¥3250, incl 2 meals ¥4930) A mountain lodge near the Annupuri ski ground. The owner can provide local hiking and cycling maps and plenty of recommendations. Meals are delicious. If you phone ahead, someone can pick you up at Niseko station.

our pick **Niseko Kōgen Youth Hostel** (ニセコ高原ユースホステル; Pooh's House; ☎/fax 44-1171; kogenyh@rose.ocn.ne.jp; dm per person incl 2 meals ¥5935; 🖳) This *Winnie the Pooh* themed hostel may sound cutesy, but it has wonderful Japanese-style meals and the owner performs incredible accordion solos if there are enough guests to warrant a show. Call to arrange to be picked up at the station: you can be dropped off at *onsens*, hiking trailheads or the ski slopes as well.

Jam Garden (ジャムガーデン; ☎ 22-6676; www .jamgarden.com; 37-89 Kabayama, Kucchan-chō; r per person incl 2 meals from ¥6000, group discounts available) Right near the ski lift at Hirafu, this deluxe farmhouse (it has its own Jacuzzi and sauna) has Western-style rooms and meals. If you need to be picked up from either Hirafu or Kucchan stations, just phone ahead. It's a 15-minute taxi ride from JR Niseko station.

Pension Forest Green (ペンション　フォレストグリーン; ☎ 44-2868; www3.ocn.ne.jp/~forest-g in Japanese; per person incl 2 meals ¥7000) This cute five-room place is unique, offering home-cooked Chinese meals as part of the lodging package. In summer it offers fly fishing trips. There's even a pool table.

Niseko Hotel Nikko Annupuri (ニセコホテル日航アンヌプリ; ☎ 58-3311; www.nikko-annupuri.co.jp; 480-1 Niseko, Niseko-chō; r per person incl 2 meals ¥13,000; 🔲) A top-of-the-line establishment near the top of the mountain, this place boasts splendid views of the valley and easy bus access. Take the bus from JR Niseko station to Konbu Onsen, and get off at Annupri Ski Jyo (12 minutes).

Eating

Many of the lodges and ryokan offer great meals cooked to order, and the slopes have plenty of snacks, pizza, *rāmen* and other goodies to stave off the munchies while you're in your gear. After hours, things are tricky because lodging is spread out and buses are surprisingly inconvenient.

Bistare Kana (ビスターレ・カナ; ☎ 58-3330; www10.plala.or.jp/bistare in Japanese; Niseko 431-1; 🕑 11.30am-3pm Mon-Fri, 11.30am-7.30pm Sat-Sun & holidays, lunch & dinner 20 Dec-8 Jan; mains from ¥1500) Offers fantastic Nepalese dishes, curry, dumplings and vegetarian options. It's also a pension with cosy rooms. Irregular hours in December and January.

Sabō Nupuri (茶房ヌプリ; ☎ 44-2619; in Niseko JR station; cakes & curries from ¥500; 🕑 11am-8pm Thu-Tue) Just a snack shop, with cakes, curries and coffee, but it's right in the station and a convenient stop as you go to or from the slopes.

Pizzeria Niseko Paraiso (パライゾ; ☎ 22-2436; http://niseko.cafe-paraiso.com; pizzas from ¥1000; 🕑 11am-10pm; E) Sick of sushi? Swing by here for nice pizzas made with Hokkaidō-grown ingredients, thick wood-slab tables and wide windows, giving it a log cabin–like ambiance. It's very near the Hirafu Skī Jō, across from Seikomart and Hirafu Onsen.

Getting There & Away

Unfortunately, in summer (the low season) there aren't a lot of easy ways to get here unless you want to rent a vehicle.

The tiny JR Niseko station is a shock if you've just come from Sapporo, and don't

expect to walk with your gear to any nearby hotels. Depending on where you're heading, it may make more sense to travel via one of two other stations serving the area, Hirafu and Kucchan.

Direct *kaisoku* trains run from Sapporo (¥2100, 2¼ hours); however, if you don't time it right you may have to wait when changing trains at Otaru (¥1410, two hours). Alternatively, you could hop on a direct bus to Niseko outside Otaru station (¥1530, two hours). From June to September there is a daily bus from New Chitose Airport to the Niseko Hotel Nikko Annupuri (¥2300, 2½ hours).

Winter is an entirely different story: there are frequent direct buses to the area's various ski resorts from Sapporo (¥2190, three hours) as well as New Chitose Airport (¥2300, three hours). A discount round-trip fare is also available from both places for ¥3850. Check out **CB Tours** (シィービーツアーズ; ☎ 011-211-0912; www.cbt.chuo-bus.co.jp in Japanese; 🕑 9am-6pm Mon-Fri) for packages out of Sapporo. One day with a round-trip bus fare and an eight-hour lift ticket at Niseko Annupuri costs ¥3900. One-night, two-day packages start at ¥18,000 per person. If you're stuck in Tokyo, **JAL Tours** (JALツアーズ; ☎ 03-5460-8221; www.jal.co.jp/tours in Japanese) can whisk you to Niseko Annupuri for around ¥40,000 per person, which includes airfare, two nights' stay (double occupancy), lift tickets and breakfasts.

Trains are more frequent during the ski season as well, and all the major ski resorts have shuttles that run to and from the stations.

Onsen fans may want to check out the Niseko Yumeguri Pass, valid for six months, which allows entrance to up to three of the 15 local *onsen* for ¥1400.

RUSUTSU

Niseko's neighbour **Rusutsu** (☎ 46-3331; www.rusutsu.co.jp; lift tickets 1/2 days ¥4950/8900; 🕑 day 9am-5pm, night 4-9pm) is another ski destination that is rapidly gaining fame. Some say skiing in Japan doesn't get any better. It's much less developed here than in Niseko, so the slopes are not as crowded here and you can actually 'get away from it all'. New shuttles make day trips from Niseko a snap, which can be a good plan as there's not much to do in the evenings and meals are pricey (¥3000 to ¥5000).

But wow, what skiing! The well-groomed trails and fantastic tree runs (often you're the first person passing through the powder!) are awesome. The resort has trails of all difficulty levels and a 50:50 mix of skiers and snowboarders. Eighteen lifts, a 100m half pipe, and numerous through-the-trees trail options means there's something for everyone. The season runs from late November to April.

If you're going to stay overnight, try the friendly **Rusutsu Powder Lodge** (www.snowjapan.com), which has firm beds and crisp linens, shared bathrooms and is seconds from the slopes. It's also right next to a convenience store: useful if you don't feel like eating out. It takes online bookings only. **Pension Lilla Huset** (ペンション リッラヒューセット; ☎ 46-3676; http://web.travel .rakuten.co.jp/portal/my/info_page_e.Eng?f_no=14935; 144

Aza Izumikawa; per person incl 2 meals from ¥7000; 🖳) is also right at the bottom of the lifts.

The nearest train station is an hour's drive away at Kucchan.

SHIKOTSU-TŌYA NATIONAL PARK
支笏洞爺国立公園
☎ 0142

Part of Shikotsu-Tōya National Park (983 sq km), Tōya-ko is a large and beautiful lake, though its beauty is somewhat marred by huge hotels on the southern perimeter. Its volcanoes are still making headlines: Usuzan erupted quite violently in 2000, sending boulders thousands of feet into the air.

In 1943, after a series of earthquakes, **Shōwa-Shin-zan** (昭和新山) emerged as an upstart

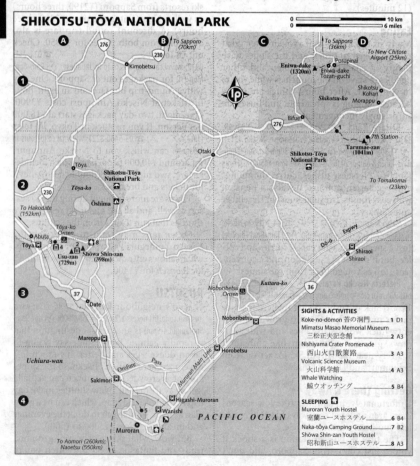

bump in some vegetable fields southeast of Tōya-ko Onsen. It then surged upwards for two more years to reach its present height of 398m. At the time, Japanese officials were keen to hush it up as they thought it was a bad omen and might portend an inauspicious end to WWII. Local officials were urged to douse the volcanic flames (they didn't) so that Allied aircraft couldn't use them for orientation. Shōwa-Shin-zan is still belching sulphurous fumes, creating an awesome spectacle for visitors and keeping local officials nervous about its next move.

Nearby, **Usu-zan** (有珠山; 729m), a taller and more formidable volcano, has also been just as active, erupting violently in March 2000. The ash cloud that rained down on Tōya-ko was 2700m high, and volcanic bombs threatened to down news helicopters. There's a **ropeway** (有珠山ロープウェ イ; cable car; ☎ 75-2401; return ¥1450; ☼ Jan-Nov) to the peak of Usu-zan. It's closed for a week in both January and February.

Behind the tourist shops, the small **Mimatsu Masao Memorial Museum** (☎ 75-2365; admission ¥300; ☼ 8am-5pm Apr-Oct, 9am-4pm Nov-Mar) is devoted to the local postmaster, who purchased the volcano in 1946 (for the princely sum of ¥28,000). He spent years diagramming its growth using an ingenious method that has become a standard among volcanologists today. English signage in the museum is limited.

The **Nishiyama Crater Promenade** (☼ closed 10 Nov-20 Apr) is a bit like walking through an area after a bomb blast. Steam hisses out of fissures, azure ponds bubble from boiling underground springs, and houses and roads are crushed and mangled. The entrance is about 10 minutes by bus (¥160) from Tōya-ko Onsen; it costs ¥300 to park your own vehicle in the expansive carpark. It is sometimes closed due to dangerous levels of toxic gas.

For something sedentary, check out the movie at the **Volcanic Science Museum** (火山科学館; ☎ 75-4400; admission ¥600; ☼ 9am-5pm) above the Tōya-ko Onsen bus terminal.

TŌYA-KO ONSEN 洞爺湖温泉

Despite the volcanic interruptions, Tōya-ko Onsen remains a popular spot for soaking, perhaps because of its proximity to New Chitose Airport and Sapporo. From mid-April to the end of October, this tiny town displays 400 fireworks every evening. Head to the shoreline for the best view. The 37km perimeter of Tōyako is both beautiful and daunting. Cruises out to Ōshima, the island in the middle of the lake, depart every 30 minutes from 8am to 4.30pm (¥1320). An evening firework-viewing cruise (¥1500) is a little more exciting. Get your tickets at the pier.

The Tōya-ko Onsen **tourist office** (☎ 75-2446; info@laketoya.com; 144 Tōyako Onsen; ☼ 9am-5pm Mon-Fri) is downhill from the bus station: head towards the lake, then look for it across from the Hotel Grand Tōya.

Sleeping

Resort hotels line the waterfront; rates begin around ¥12,000 per person per night. Many of them have day-use access to their baths; rates vary from ¥500 to ¥2000. Bring your own towel to save the ¥300 hire fee.

Naka-tōya Camping Ground (☎ 66-7022; camp sites per person ¥330; ☼ May-Sep) On the eastern edge of the lake, several kilometres from Tōya-ko Onsen. Tents can be hired if necessary. Buses from Toya JR station are infrequent (¥630), stopping here only two or three times each day.

Shōwa-Shin-zan Youth Hostel (☎ 75-2283; 103 Soubetsu-onsen, Soubetsu-chō, Usu-gun; dm ¥3150) With comfortable shared-room accommodation, this hostel is on the road leading up to Usu-zan. Bicycles are ¥1000 per day, a good way to cover ground around town. By bus it's eight minutes from Tōya-ko Onsen; get off at the Tozan-guchi stop.

Tōya Green Hotel (洞爺グリーンホテル; ☎ 75-3030; 144-3 Tōyako Onsen, Tōyako-chō, Abuta-gun; r per person incl 2 meals from ¥5250) Calls itself a 'business *minshuku*' (B&B) and has expansive Japanese-style rooms, full facilities (TV, mini-fridge, buffet breakfast and dinner, large and small public baths) and enormous meals. Quieter rooms are at the back, away from the main drag.

Hotel Grand Tōya (ホテルグランドトーヤ; ☎ 75-2288; 144 Tōyako Onsen, Tōyako-chō, Abuta-gun; r per person incl 2 meals ¥7875; ☐) Has nice lake views from every room. Both Japanese and Western styles are available, with bathroom in each room.

Getting There & Away

There are more 'Tōya's here than you can shake a stick at, but don't let that confuse you. There's Tōya JR station, Tōya Onsen (on the south of the lake) and Tōya town, on the north side. And of course, Tōya-ko itself.

HOKKAIDŌ

Tokkyū, kaisoku and local trains to Hakodate (¥5340, 1½ hours) or Sapporo (¥5760, 1¾ hours) all make a brief stop at Tōya JR station. Buses are a less expensive option, running frequently between Tōya Sapporo (¥2700, 2¾ hours) or Muroran (¥1170, 1¾ hours).

Local buses run every 30 minutes between Tōya JR station and Tōya-ko Onsen (¥320, 25 minutes).

From April to November, buses also run via the scenic Orofure pass to Noboribetsu Onsen (¥1530, 1¼ hours); some continue onwards to New Chitose Airport (¥2140, 2½ hours).

MURORAN 室蘭
☎ 0143 / pop 98,400

This dwindling industrial city is in the process of reinventing itself. It's conveniently connected by ferry with the rest of Honshū; the trip from the pier to the **tourist office** (☎ 23-0102), which is in the oldest wooden train station in Hokkaido (built in 1912), is a 15-minute ride. Among other activities, a whale-watching boat run by **KK Elm** (KKエルム; ☎ 27-1822; www.kk-elm.jp/index.htm in Japanese; per 3hr ¥6000) leaves from the pier three times daily in summer. Whales, dolphins, porpoises and seals are best viewed from May to July, and tours are often booked solid weeks ahead.

While the industrialised section of the valley is definitely less than scenic, the shoreline between Wanishi (where the Muroran Youth Hostel is) and **Cape Chikyū** (地球岬) is quite stunning. A well-marked road parallels the shore and offers several spots to stop and admire the view. The observation areas at the cape are also pretty. Cape Chikyū is known for its returning pair of *hayabusa* (peregrine falcons) and for its almost 360-degree panoramic views of the sea.

The black-sand beach behind the youth hostel is gorgeous, a perfect place for an early morning walk as you watch the sunrise. Beautiful white cliffs, giant mystic boulders and ethereal sunlight will make you feel like you've stepped inside a Wyeth painting. Surfing (you'll need your own board and wetsuit) is a popular pastime, and hiking, skiing and snowshoeing are also available nearby.

Gourmands will appreciate Muroran's *yakitori*, but be warned: the preferred meat here is pork. In fact, many of the popular places don't serve chicken at all, only the skin, which is very popular. **Yakitori Fujitori** (焼き鳥ふじ鳥; ☎ 44-4986/4970; 1-36-3 Wanishi-chō; dishes ¥200-1000),

an inconspicuous greasy spoon in the centre of town, is a favourite with locals and serves excellent *yakitori*, tofu in broth and *rāmen* that's hard to beat. No English is spoken, unless by clientele interested in practising their skills with a traveller.

Institutional and old, but clean and practical (it even has a web cam!), **Muroran Youth Hostel** (Map p592; ☎ 44-3357; www.jyh.gr.jp/muroran in Japanese; dm ¥3990; [P] [🖥] [♨]) affords fantastic views of the bay and easy access to hiking tracks along the cliff top. From Wanishi Station, turn left and follow Rte 36 until you see Lawson on the right. Turn right and follow this road all the way until it ends after a steep climb uphill. Look diagonally across the street to the left and you will see a small sign for the hostel. From there it's a three-minute walk to the hostel driveway.

Camping is possible on some of the scenic laybys along the cliffside road between Wanishi and Cape Chikyū. Several secluded areas would be easy to use, but are not officially sanctioned. Use your own judgment and caution.

Long-distance trains depart from Higashi-Muroran station, three stops east of Muroran itself; transfer to central Muroran is included in long-distance fares. Direct *tokkyū* trains run south to Hakodate (¥6180, two hours) and north to Sapporo (¥4680, 1¼ hours).

From the bus station there are frequent departures for Sapporo (¥2000, 2¼ hours), Noboribetsu Onsen (¥710, 80 minutes) and Tōya-ko Onsen (¥1170, 1¾ hours).

Ferries depart from Muroran for Aomori (¥3460, seven hours) year-round, and Naoetsu (¥8230, 17 hours, three per week) between April and December. To get to Hachinohe, head to nearby Tomakomai. The ferry terminal is about a 10-minute walk from Muroran station. The **Higashi Nihon Ferry** (東日本フェリー; ☎ 22-1668) office will have the latest details.

NOBORIBETSU ONSEN 登別温泉
☎ 0143

Nobiribetsu Onsen is the most popular *onsen* resort in Hokkaidō, boasting over 30 hotels and bath houses clustered tightly together along a narrow, winding street, but it's not as atmospheric as you might expect – with convenience stores, hotels and souvenir shops packed with fun sculptures of animals and demons. The water originates from a volcanic sulphurous 'hell' not far above. Some of the higher-end spas are as nice as Japan has to offer. There are various interesting hikes around the surrounding hills and sulphur vents. The **tourist association office** (☎ 84-3311; 60 Noboribetsu onsen machi; ⏰ 9am-6pm Mon-Fri, 10am-4pm Sat & Sun) has English maps, hotel locations and good English info on the bathing hours.

Sights & Activities

Dai-ichi Takimoto-kan (第一滝本館; ☎ 84-3322; www.takimotokan.co.jp/english/; onsen bath ¥2000; ⏰ 9am-5pm) is the cream of the crop of the *onsen* resorts; this luxurious spa has more than 15 different kinds of baths, ranging from take-your-skin-off scalding to icy cool. Several outdoor *rotemburo* (open-air baths) offer beautiful views of the valley, and there's even a swimming pool (where you will require a swimsuit). Its English website offers online booking and reservations.

For half the price, you'll get much of the same luxury (minus the view) at the **Grand Hotel** (登別グランドホテル; ☎ 717-8899; www .nobogura.co.jp/english; onsen bath ¥1000; ⏰ 12.30-5pm & 6.30-8pm), a few steps away from the bus station. The star attraction is the beautiful *hinoki* (Japanese cypress) bath, and a domed ceiling to give the spacious impression of a Roman-era bath. Men's and women's areas alternate to give each gender the chance to see both bathing areas.

Jigokudani (地獄谷; Hell Valley) is a short walk uphill, offering viewers a peek at what may await us in the afterlife: sulphurous gases, hissing vents and vividly coloured rocks. Pools of scalding water can be seen from **Ōyu-numa** (大湯沼; Boiling Water Swamp). For those of us who are far from Heaven-bound, it's good to know that Hell (if the Japanese have anything to say about it!) will surely include a lot of *onsen*.

The simple **public bath** (夢元さぎり湯; ☎ 84-2050; 60 Noboribetsu onsen machi; onsen bath ¥390; ⏰ 7am-10pm), on the 1st floor of an office building next to the tourist association office (above), has three baths, each packed with mainly wizened bathers – you'll feel spry as a spring chicken if you're under 65.

Sleeping

Minshuku Kikusui (民宿菊水; ☎ 84-2437; fax 84-3302; 220-5 Noboribetsu; per person incl 2 meals from ¥6500) A decent place: looks plain on the outside but serves great crab dinners all winter long. Get off the bus at Momijidani-danchi Iriguchi, turn right at the light and then walk about 200m. It's an unassuming white single-storey building.

Kashōtei Hanaya (花鐘亭はなや; ☎ 84-2521; www.kashoutei-hanaya.co.jp/english/index.htm; r per person incl 2 meals ¥12,750-26,400) A great midrange option with Japanese-style rooms, many overlooking the river. The very friendly staff speak some English. It also has its own hot-spring baths, private toilets and basins.

Dai-ichi Takimoto-kan (第一滝本館; ☎ 84-3322; www.takimotokan.co.jp/english/; r from ¥11,175; Ⓟ Ⓧ 🗎) The *onsen* (left) also doubles as a hotel. In addition to immaculate Western- or Japanese-style rooms, meals (prices vary seasonally) are offered either buffet style in the main dining rooms or in your room, and children's menus are available. Barrier-free rooms are also an option for the elderly or those with disabilities.

Getting There & Away

Noboribetsu Onsen and **Noboribetsu JR station** (☎ 84-3111) are about 13 minutes from each other by bus (¥330). Noboribetsu JR Station has local train connections to Higashi-Muroran (¥350, 20 minutes), Shiraoi (¥350, 30 minutes) and Tomakomai (¥810, 45 minutes), all of which have connections to Sapporo.

From Noboribetsu Onsen there are direct buses to Sapporo (Eki-mae terminal ¥1900, 1½ to 2¾ hours). There are also buses to New Chitose Airport (¥1330, 73 minutes, one to three daily) and Muroran (¥710, 80 minutes). In summer (April to November) scenic buses run the length of Orofure Pass and end at Tōya-ko Onsen (¥1530, 1¼ hours).

SHIKOTSU-KO 支笏湖

☎ 0123

Part of the Shikotsu-Tōya National Park, Shikotsu-ko is a caldera lake surrounded by picturesque volcanoes. It's Japan's second-deepest lake after Tazawa-ko in Akita-ken (p538). The area is served by Shikotsu Kohan (支笏湖畔), a tiny town consisting mainly of a bus station, **visitors centre** (支笏湖ビジターセンター; ☎ 25-2404; www15.ocn.ne.jp/~sikotuvc/in Japanese; ⏰ 9.30am-5.30pm Wed-Mon Apr-Oct, 9.30am-4.30pm Wed-Mon Nov-Mar), boat pier, a few souvenir shops and restaurants. **Morappu** (モラップ), nearby, has a few more options. Both can be enjoyed as a day trip from Muroran.

Activities

Leaving from Shikotsu Kohan's pier there are 30-minute **sightseeing cruises** (☎ 25-2031; per person ¥1100; ☺ Apr-Nov). You can take a one-hour walk on the nature trail between the pier and Morappu, which goes through a wild bird forest with two bird-watching blinds. There are birding ID boards with pictures along the way, as well as lakeside views. Not so tame **speedboat cruises** (☎ 0123-20-4131; per person ¥1300) are a faster way to take in the lake and its environs (minimum of three people per cruise).

Cycling is a nice option if the weather is good. A full circuit of the lake is 50km and the youth hostel hires out bikes for ¥400 per hour or ¥2000 per day, with a discount for its own guests.

Freshwater scuba diving in the lake can be arranged through **Blue Note** (ブルーノート; ☎ 0120-43-3340; 107 Shikotsuko Onsen; www2.ocn.ne.jp/~bluenote/ in Japanese; dive ¥13,800). Waterflowers, 100m cliffs and numerous freshwater fish are a few of the attractions.

Mountain **hikes** are one of the area's most popular activities, but check at the visitors centre, as tracks are frequently closed due to bad conditions or erosion. **Eniwa-dake** (恵庭岳; 1320m) lies on the northwestern side of the lake. A 3½-hour hike will bring you to a panoramic view. It's another three hours back down.

On the southern side of the lake is **Tarumae-zan** (樽前山; 1041m), an active volcano. Due to poisonous gas the crater itself is closed, but you can reach the rim from the seventh station in about 40 minutes. Japanese walkers all wear bear bells in this area, and you should stay on the main tracks to avoid an unexpected encounter.

A spectacular mossy gorge, **Koke-no-dōmon** (Map p592; ☺ 9am-5pm Jun-Oct) has recently been damaged by erosion. Visitors are not allowed to enter after 4pm, and may only view it in a specific roped-off area. Brown bears frequent the gorge and should not be trifled with (see p620).

Sleeping

These places are clustered in or around Shikotsu Kohan.

Morappu Camping Ground (モラップキャンプ場; ☎ 25-2439; tent sites from ¥500; ☺ late Apr-late Oct) In Morappu, conveniently situated by the lake.

Shikotsu-ko Youth Hostel (支笏湖ユースホステル; ☎ 25-2311; www.youthhostel.or.jp/English/menu2.htm; dm ¥3645) Has private family rooms as well as dorms; bike hire and a hot-spring bath (¥150) are also available. To reach the hostel head away from the visitors centre; after about a three-minute walk, it's on the other side of a carpark.

Lapland (ラップランド; ☎ 25-2239; dm incl 2 meals ¥4900) In Morappu, this is a great little log cabin with views of the lake. Has carpeted Japanese-style rooms and private rooms are sometimes available (per person ¥5900). The owners will pick you up and take you back to the bus station or mountain trailheads. Buses bound for Koke-no-dōmon from Shikotsu Kohan pass Morappu (¥240, 10 minutes).

Log Bear (ログベアー; ☎ 25-2738; http://web.mac.com/logbear; r per person incl breakfast ¥5000; ☐) An intimate, friendly log cabin right in the town centre. The owner speaks English quite fluently and makes a good cup of coffee as well. Walk straight (east) from the visitors centre to the small alley directly across the street. Log Bear is on the left, just after Tonton (a restaurant). If you reach Tōya-ko Kankō Hotel, you've gone too far.

Shikotsu-sō (支笏荘; ☎ 25-2718; www.shikotsuko.com/s-shikotsusou.htm in Japanese; r per person incl 2 meals ¥5800) A cheerful *minshuku* right behind the bus station, primarily known for its miso, *rāmen* and trout. The owner's hobby is pressing wildflowers, from which she makes postcards, plates and other souvenirs.

Getting There & Away

Between mid-June and mid-October there are three to four buses a day from Shikotsu Kōhan to JR Sapporo station (¥1330, 97 minutes). Other buses run all year round to New Chitose Airport (¥920, 55 minutes).

DŌ-HOKU (NORTHERN HOKKAIDŌ) 道北

ASAHIKAWA 旭川
☎ 0166 / pop 358,500

Asahikawa is one of the largest cities in Hokkaidō, second to Sapporo. It was built on a flat plain along the Ishikari River and was once one of the biggest Ainu settlements. It carries the dual honour of having the most days with snowfall, as well as the record for the coldest temperature (-40°C). Though less picturesque than other Hokkaidō cities, Asahikawa is interesting both historically and as a jumping-off point to other parts: Wakkanai to the north; Daisetsuzan National Park to the southeast; and Biei and Furano due south.

In addition to its Ainu heritage, Asahikawa was also an important part of Meiji-era settlements and has a long history of sake brewing. It was the location of the first ski area in Japan. It has since become one of the major industrial cities of the island, with associated urban development.

Orientation

Asahikawa JR station is on the southwest side of the city. A large pedestrian avenue extends out for a few blocks, and most of the hotels and restaurants listed here are within easy walking distance. Museums and some of the other sights (such as the Asahikawa Zoo) will require a bus ride, and boarding the bus can be a bit confusing, as there are more than 20 bus stops on three different streets, numerous routes and several different bus companies.

Information

Friendly, helpful assistance can be found at the **information counter** (☎ 22-6704; ☼ 9am-7pm Jul-Sep, 9am-5.30pm Oct-Jun) inside Asahikawa station with a number of English pamphlets and sightseeing brochures. Be sure to ask for the very useful bus-stop map. The staff have a wealth of information at their fingertips, quite literally, and can share tips about the city, its sights and activities, and they may also be able to recommend places to stay. The station also has a **hotel booking desk** (☎ 22-5139), which can be relied on to find reasonable deals. If you are getting off the train, turn right once you go through the ticket gate before going out of the station building. The station's post office has a Postal ATM.

Asahikawa has several internet cafés, these are near the station.

Compa37 (コンパ３７; ☎ 21-3249; 7-5 Sanjō; per 30min ¥250; ☼ 24hr) Go straight out from the station on the pedestrian street to the 3rd intersection, turn left, then look on the left. Has a night package if you need to crash on the cheap.

PC Terakoya (PC-Tera屋; ☎ 23-9789; 4F Marutoku Bldg, 9-7 Ichijō-dōri; per hr ¥525; ☼ 10am-7pm Mon-Fri) Closest to the station, a few blocks' walk. When exiting the station, take the pedestrian street for two blocks. Turn

right and go another block or so. It is on your right (if you get to Lawson at the corner, you've gone too far).

Sights & Activities

MUSEUMS

The **Hokkaido Folk Arts & Crafts Village** (北海道伝統美術工芸村; 3-1-1 Minamigaoka) is a collection of three museums. A free shuttle leaves every one or two hours from Kureyon Parking, a three-minute walk from Asahikawa station, next to the Asahikawa Washington Hotel (note: not the Fujitakankō Washington Hotel, which is directly across from the station). Follow the pedestrian street to the first major intersection, then turn left at the light. The carpark will be on your right just after the next light. A combined ticket (¥1400) gives entry to the following three museums. The **International Dyeing & Weaving Art Museum** (国際染織美術館; ☎ 61-6161; admission ¥550; ☼ Apr-Dec) is the most spectacular, displaying textiles from around the world as well as Japanese specialities, such as embroidered Ainu woodbark cloth and a number of spectacular silk kimonos. The **Yukara Ori Folk Craft Museum** (優佳良織工芸館; ☎ 62-8811; admission ¥450; ☼ 9am-5.30pm Apr-Nov, 9am-5pm Dec-Mar) has a number of examples of Ainu cloth in the interesting local weaving style. Paradoxically, the **Snow Crystal Museum** (雪の美術館; ☎ 63-2211; admission ¥650; ☼ 9am-5pm Feb & Mar, 9am-5.30pm Apr-Nov) is closed in the winter months of December and January. This museum has some dainty displays, a concert hall and walk-in freezers with metre-long icicles. Brrr.

Kawamura Kaneto Ainu Memorial Museum (川村カ子トアイヌ記念館; ☎ 51-2461; 11 Kitamonchō; admission ¥500; ☼ 8am-6pm Jul & Aug, 9am-5pm Sep-Jun) has a ticket office that sells an English-language booklet, *Living in the Ainu Moshir*, by Kawamura Shinrit Eoripak Ainu, the present curator and the son of the museum's founder. For more info on the founder, Kawamura Kaneto Ainu, see p598. Take bus 24 from bus stop 14 on Ichijō-dōri to the Ainu Kinenkan-mae stop (¥170, 15 minutes).

BREWERIES

Several breweries located in and around Asahikawa are well worth checking out.

Otokoyama was frequently featured in *ukiyo-e* (wood-block prints) and old literature. Admission is free at **Otokoyama Sake Brewery & Museum** (男山酒造; ☎ 48-1931; www.otokoyama .com/english/index.html; 2-7 Nagayama; ☼ 9am-5pm) and includes tasting. Take bus 67, 68, 70, 71, 667 or 669 from bus stop 18 and get off at Nagayama 2-jō 6-chōme. From there it's a two-minute walk.

A 10-minute bus ride from Asahikawa station, **Takasago Sake Brewery** (高砂酒造; ☎ 23-2251; http://takasagoshuzo.com/ in Japanese; 17 Miyashitadōri; admission free; ⏰ 9am-4.30pm Mon-Fri, 9am-11.30pm Sat & Sun mid-Apr–mid-Oct, 9am-4.30pm daily mid-Oct–mid-Apr) has interesting pictures of the old buildings and brewing process, plus a large display room. From January to March it also has an *aisudōmu* (ice dome), a sake-filled igloo that you can tour. Take bus 1, 3 or 17 from bus stop 17 and get off at 1-jō 18-chōme. It's also possible to walk there from the Asahikwawa JR station: turn right on Miyashita-dōri and walk for about 15 minutes. It's a large white-washed building with a cedar ball hanging outside the door. An English pamphlet and friendly staff help make it worthwhile even if you don't speak Japanese.

OTHER SIGHTS
Asahiyama Zoo (旭山動物園; ☎ 36-1104; Kuranuma; admission ¥580; ⏰ 9.30am-5.30pm 28 Apr-Jul, 9.30am-9pm Aug, 9.30am-5.30pm 1 Sep-21 Oct, 10.30am-3.30pm 3 Nov-7 Apr) Has a round-up of the usual zoo suspects, but a big crowd pleaser is the winter penguin march: because the birds get porky, they have to go for a twice-daily run at 11am and 2.30pm from mid-December through to March. Take bus 41, 42 or 47.

Festivals & Events
Check with local tourist offices for specific dates for Asahikawa's various annual festivals, as many vary slightly from year to year.

KANETO KAWAMURA – AINU GENIUS

While it's indisputable that Ainu culture suffered as mainland Japanese settled in Hokkaidō, a few Ainu managed to prove themselves purely on Japanese terms. Kaneto Kawamura, an Ainu chief, became a master surveyor and helped to lay the tracks for several of Hokkaidō's railways. After eye problems forced him to retire, he used his accumulated wealth to create the first Ainu museum, Kawamura Kaneto Ainu Memorial Museum (p597). Visitors can tour the collection of Ainu and railway-related items, as well as wear Ainu clothing and take a picture for free.

Kotan Matsuri (コタン祭り) Takes place in late September on the banks of the Ishikari-gawa, south of the city. During the festival you can see traditional dances, music and *kamui-nomi* and *inau-shiki*, prayer ceremonies offered to the deities of fire, the river, *kotan* (the village) and the mountains.

Yuki Matsuri (雪祭り) Held in Asahikawa every February. While second to the one in Sapporo (p577), it is still impressive, with ice sculptures, food and fun seasonal events.

Sleeping & Eating
Ryokan Tokiya (時屋旅館; ☎ 23-2237; www.tokiya .net/tokiyaryokan2.html; Nijō-dōri 9-6; r per person with shared/private bathroom ¥4725/5250, incl 2 meals ¥6300/7350; 🖥) North of the station, this place is inviting, well decorated and reasonably priced.

Tōyoko Inn Asahikawa Ekimae (東横イン旭川駅前; ☎ 27-1045; www.toyoko-inn.com/eng/; Ichijō-dōri 9-164-1; s/d high season ¥6400/8800, low season ¥4800/6800; 🖥) This chain's clean, convenient Asahikawa clone.

Asahikawa Terminal Hotel (旭川ターミナルホテル; ☎ 24-0111; www.asahikawa-th.com/contents/intl /Index_english.htm; s/d ¥5800/7600; 🖥 🖥) As you exit JR Asahikawa station, it's just to the left.

Ganso Asahikawa Rāmen Ichikura (山頭火 元祖 旭川らーめん 一蔵; ☎ 24-8887; 7-3 Sanjō, Yamada Bldg 1F; dishes ¥700-1200; ⏰ 11-4am Thu-Tue) One of many popular Asahikawa *rāmen* shops, and there are dozens. Bowls here come with plenty of scallions, and it's open late – really late – if you need a bite before stumbling home. Follow the pedestrian street to the jazz statue and go to one more light, then turn left. It's on the next corner, opposite a 7-11.

Saroma-ko (サロマ湖; ☎ 22-6426; 6-1 Sanjō; meals ¥3500; ⏰ dinner) A little pricey, but if the owner is driving a four-hour round trip daily to get the freshest scallops from Saroma Lake, it's worth it. Come here for the freshest seafood prepared with care by a chef who's not afraid to close the restaurant if the shellfish doesn't meet his finicky standards. Try the scallop sashimi (*ho-tate no sashimi*) or the oysters steamed in sake (*kaki no sakemushi*). Find it by going straight out on the pedestrian street, then turn left at Sanjō street (shortly after the jazz player and cat statue, with Okuno on your left), then pass Compa 37 on your left. Go through the light, then look for Saroma-ko at the left corner of the next intersection. No English menu.

Getting There & Around
Asahikawa is a central location with frequent plane, train and bus access. Flights head di-

rectly to and from Osaka, Nagoya and Tokyo. Buses between the airport and JR Asahikawa station (JR 旭川駅; ¥570, 35 minutes) are timed to connect with arrivals and departures.

Trains link Asahikawa with Sapporo (*tokkyū* ¥4680, 1½ hours) to the south, Wakkanai (¥8070, four hours) to the north, Abashiri (¥7750, 3¾ hours) to the east, and to the smaller sightseeing towns of Biei (¥530, 30 minutes) and Furano (*futsū* ¥1040, 1¼ hours).

Buses leave from 20 different stops spread out over three streets in front of the train station. If you are using Asahikawa as a springboard for a day trip to Daisetsuzan, set your alarm early and catch the 9.10am bus: the next one leaves at 10.45am and arrives an hour later, which does not leave much time for hiking – and don't miss the last bus back to Asahikawa at 5.05pm.

Unless you feel confident reading the frequently changing route schedules, you're best off asking for assistance either at the tourist information counter in the station or at the bus info booth across the street from the train station parking lot. Plan on allowing extra time for navigating if you're on a tight schedule, and be sure to check departure times – it's easy to miss a bus and end up with very little time at your destination.

WAKKANAI 稚内
☎ 0162 / pop 41,400

Wakkanai, Japan's most northern mainland city, is closest to the island's two most northern capes, Noshappu and Sōya, and that's the biggest tourist draw. Depart here for Rishiri-tō and Rebun-tō, islands off the coast, and, further off, Russia's Sakhalin Island. It's a quiet town whose economy depends on kelp fishing and tourism. The views of the water and its fishing boats are very picturesque all year round, and many brave the bitter cold to see the frozen bay in the dead of winter, a majestic (but chilly!) scene.

In late February Wakkanai hosts the **Japan Cup National Dogsled Races** (全国犬ぞり稚内大会). As the name implies, it's the biggest dogsled race in Japan. People come from Tokyo or Osaka to watch or compete – though where someone from Osaka practises their mushing is a bit of a mystery. For those with a plucky pooch of their own, their is the *wan-wan-dash*, where audience dogs can show their speed.

Information

Wakkanai station is right next to the bus terminal and only a 10-minute walk from the ferry port. Internet access is hard to come by. **Tourist information counters** (☎ 22-2384; ☼ 10am-6pm) are at Wakkanai station and the **ferry port** (☼ 7am-3.30pm Jun-Sep). At the time of research there was no internet café – nor any plans for one.

Sights & Activities

Wakkanai-kōen (Map p602), atop a grassy hill a few blocks from the train station, offers a number of walking tracks and the **Centennial Memorial Tower** (稚内開基百年記念塔; ☎ 24-4019; admission ¥400; ☼ closed Nov-Apr) has 360-degree views of Northern Hokkaidō. On clear days Sakhalin Island is visible. One monument is dedicated to the 22 dogs who accompanied Japan's first South Pole expedition. A modest **temple** is right next to the now defunct ropeway's lower terminal. The 19 Tanka (31-syllable poem) Trail leads up to the plateau – in spring, it's full of wildflowers. It's named for the 19 *tanka* poems that are inscribed on boards along the way.

Between Wakkanai and Cape Noshappu are interesting **kelp drying yards** (they look like gravel-covered carparks if they're not covered with kelp) along the shoreline.

Cape Noshappu (ノシャップ岬), the second-most northern point in Japan, is a nice place for a picture or a picnic, or just to watch the water for a while. If it's clear, look for the green flash as the sun slips below the horizon; if you see it, make a wish. It's a pleasant walk (35 minutes) or bike ride (15 minutes) away from town.

Cape Sōya (宗谷岬), 30km from Wakkanai, is the real thing: mainland Japan's most northern point. A bus leaves four times a day (¥1350, 50 minutes). Among Cape Sōya's various monuments is one dedicated to the victims of Korean Flight 007, shot down in 1983 by a Soviet fighter jet. Bird-watchers will love seeing hawks sitting side by side with seagulls and terns on the wave-washed black sand.

Busy and bustling, **Wakkanai Onsen Dōmu** (Map p602; ☎ 28-1160; onsen ¥600; ☼ 10am-10pm, closed 1st Mon of month) is an 18-minute bus ride from the station and offers nice views of the water, though the bath itself is more functional than luxurious.

Harp seal viewing (Map p602) is possible in Bakkai, where 200 harp seals arrive each year

HOKKAIDŌ

and stay from November to the end of March. Rishiri-tō makes a very scenic backdrop on a clear day. A basic viewing hut (free) provides shelter, a toilet and some information about the seals. Dress warmly as the hut is a 30-minute walk from JR Bakkai station and temperatures can be well below freezing.

Sleeping & Eating

Any of the following will be good if you're going to bed down for the night. The tourist counters may have additional suggestions.

Rider House Midori-yu (Map p602; ☎ 22-4275; 1-10-23 Midori; dm with shared bathroom ¥1000) A good place to meet other travellers, but you should have your own bedding. Near Minami-Wakkanai station and close to the *sentō* (public bath). Find it by crossing the tracks (just south) and following that road to the school on the right. Midori-yu is on the left-hand side, on the other side of the small gully, about halfway along the school grounds (if you reach the convenience store you've gone too far). Look for the red and white sign that says 'コインロッカー' (coin locker).

Wakkanai Youth Hostel (Map p602; ☎ 23-7162; www7.plala.or.jp/komadori-house/; 3-9-1 Komadori; dm ¥3900; ☾ check-in 3-8pm). Due to its spot on top of the hill it has a beautiful, commanding view of the surrounding town and ocean. While still a youth hostel, it feels more homey – like a *minshuku* rather than an institution. The on-site coin laundry is a convenience that makes it popular with motorcyclists and bike riders. Bikes can be rented for ¥1000 per day. It's

---

MINSHUKU MEALS

When you book at a remote ryokan or *minshuku* that includes one or two meals, remember that these are set courses, not pick-and-choose (especially at the small, family-run places). Be aware that this will surely include lots of seafood, shellfish, and possibly horsemeat or even whale.

If you have a particular food allergy or you simply can't stomach something for personal or religious reasons, let your host know *as soon as possible* – preferably before you book your stay, and remind them again when you arrive. Most places will try hard to accommodate you. If you're really worried, ask if a no-meal price option is possible and find a restaurant nearby.

---

a 15-minute walk from Minami-Wakkanai station. Credit cards not accepted.

Saihate Ryokan (Map p602; ☎ 23-3556; per person ¥4000) Simple and well maintained, but a bit noisy as it's right next to the bus and ferry terminals. Offers a choice of Japanese- and Western-style rooms.

Wakkanai Moshiripa Youth Hostel (Map p602; ☎ 24-0180; www.moshiripa.net in Japanese; 2-9-5 Chūō-ku; dm ¥4360) An eight-minute walk from Wakkanai station and close to the ferry port. Convenient and hospitable, it is sometimes closed in the winter, so phone ahead.

Hotel Okabe Shiosai-tei (ホテルおかべ汐彩亭; ☎ 22-3411; www.hotel-okabe.co.jp in Japanese; per person high/low season ¥8400/6825; ℗ ☒ 🖳) New and pleasant, this hotel has Western-style rooms, views of the harbour, private facilities and a luxurious Japanese bath (open 24 hours for guests). Turn right as you exit the station and follow the road to a T-junction. The Okabe is on the left-hand corner.

ANA Hotel Wakkanai (Map p602; ☎ 23-8111; www.ana-hotel-wakkanai.co.jp; r per person low/high season from ¥6500/19,500; ℗ ☒ ☒ 🖳) Tall, sleek and stylish, this place seems a bit out of place in empty Wakkanai. Wi-fi is available in the lobby. Depending on the season, discounted rooms may be available. The high-season price includes two meals. Walk to the waterfront and you can't miss it.

If you're feeling adventurous, try *unidon* (sea urchin bowl) or *ikuradon* (salmon roe bowl), fresher here than anywhere else in Hokkaidō. Many places are closed by 9pm, but a few *izakaya* stay open later. Find them behind the shopping arcade.

Getting There & Around

Wakkanai is small enough for most of the sights to be reached on foot or bicycle. Bikes are available for ¥500 per day (June to September) through **TMO** (☎ 29-0277; ☾ Mon-Fri), a Wakkanai city tourism association. Pick one up around the corner from the TMO office in the shopping arcade or, on Saturdays, at the eyeglass shop **Megane no Nagano** (長野めがね; ☎ 22-7070), also in the arcade. Hours vary.

Considering how remote it is, Wakkanai is easy to get to. Between Wakkanai and Sapporo there is one flight daily to New Chitose Airport (50 minutes) and two to Odama (one hour); both cost ¥20,300 during peak times. Wakkanai also has direct flights to Tokyo (¥40,500, 1¾ hours). Buses to Wakkanai airport (35 minutes, for airline passengers only) cost ¥590.

There are a few *tokkyū* trains that travel between Wakkanai and Asahikawa (¥8070, four hours); most continue on to Sapporo (¥10,170, five hours). An overnight train runs in summer, leaving at about 11pm and arriving in Wakkanai at 6am.

There are several daily buses to Sapporo (¥5500, six hours) and a daily bus to Asahikawa (¥4350, 4¾ hours). Discounted return tickets are available for both. Advance **reservations** (☎ 23-5510; ⏱ 5.30am-6pm & 9.30-11pm) are required.

The **Higashi Nihonkai Ferry** (☎ 23-3780) leaves from Wakkanai to Rishiri-tō (¥1980, 1¾ hours) and Rebun-tō (¥2200, two hours), as well as to Russia's Sakhalin Island (¥22,500). Parking at Wakkanai's ferry terminal is ¥1000 per night. For details about a trip to Russia, see p571. You will have to wait for up to two weeks for a visa, so be sure to plan well in advance.

RISHIRI-REBUN-SAROBETSU NATIONAL PARK

利尻礼文サロベツ国立公園

Comprised mainly of two islands, Rishiri-tō and Rebun-tō, just west of Wakkanai, this park offers visitors superb hikes and wild-flower viewing. The park also includes Sarobetsu, a swampy area near Wakkanai on the mainland, which has beautiful flowers, mainly rhododendrons, irises and lilies, in season. The peak flower-viewing time is June and July, but various wildflowers are in bloom in all three areas from May through to early September.

Rishiri-tō 利尻島

☎ 0163 / pop 5920

A near-perfect cinder cone rising like a miniature Mt Fuji from the surrounding sea, Rishiri-zan (1721m) provides numerous hiking opportunities and stunning scenery. If you're feeling energetic and have good footwear you can hike to the summit in a day. A road encircles the island and a bus service links the small fishing villages on the way.

Oshidomari and Kutsugata are Rishiri-tō's main ports; both have ferry services and **information booths** (Oshidomari ☎ 82-2201; ⏱ 8am-5.30pm 15 Apr-15 Oct; Kutsugata ☎ 4-3622; ⏱ 10am-4.30pm May-Sep) that provide maps and details about transport, sights and hiking. Staff can also help you book accommodation.

ACTIVITIES

The two most reliable **hiking tracks** to the summit of Rishiri-zan start about 3km from town at Oshidomari and Kutsugata. A limited bus service runs to the start of each track; otherwise you must either walk (about an hour), hitch, take a taxi or ask your lodgings if they can drop you off.

Prepare properly for a mountain hike and pay particular attention to the season. Hiking in July will be very different from October! Late June through mid-September are best. Aim for an early start and allow about five hours each for the ascent and descent. Excellent maps and hiking details (mainly in Japanese) are available at the information booths and youth hostels.

Just past the eighth station is **Rishiri-dake Yamagoya**, an unstaffed mountain hut that perches on the edge of a precipice and provides the bare minimum for a roof over your head (no water). It is possible to spend the night here, but it is bloody cold, colder still with the wind-chill factor. It's also very beautiful, especially on a crystal-clear night when even Sakhalin Island is visible.

If you don't feel like heading all the way to the summit, there are several other hikes that are pretty but less strenuous. One of these follows the track from Oshidomari for an hour past the Hokuroku Camping Ground towards the summit, veering left into thick forest about 10 minutes after passing a group of A-frame chalets at the end of a paved road. In 1¾ hours, this track leads to Hime-numa, with the option of a 30-minute side trip to Pon-yama. From Hime-numa it's 6km to Oshidomari along Rte 108.

Rishiri-Fuji Onsen (利尻富士温泉; ☎ 82-2388; ¥500) makes the most of its plain building with Jacuzzis, mountain-view *rotemburo*, saunas and indoor baths. The *onsen* is a 30-minute walk from Oshidomari en route to the camping ground and start of the Rishiri-zan track. A couple of buses a day (¥150, 10 minutes) pass the *onsen* from Oshidomari.

SLEEPING

Most lodgings are in Oshidomari and Kutsugata. In July and August, the high season, it's wise to book well in advance.

Rishiri-tō has six camping grounds: all are open from May to October, and some are even free.

Kutsugata-Misaki Camping Ground (☎ 84-2345) Right by the ferry terminal, this camping

HOKKAIDŌ

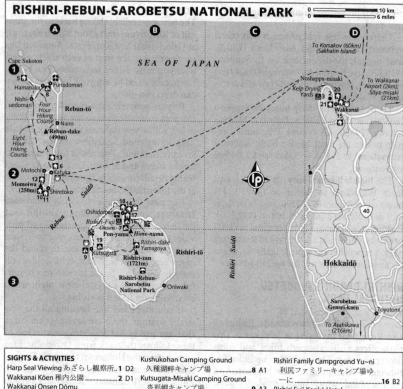

RISHIRI-REBUN-SAROBETSU NATIONAL PARK

ground is free, but often too windy to be particularly comfortable.

Rishiri-tō Family Camp Ground Yu~ni (☎ 82-2166 May-Oct, 82-1114 Nov-Apr; camp site per person ¥500, 4-person cabins ¥4000) This is a new camping ground, catering mainly to families. Get off at the Onsen Hoyōshisetsu bus stop.

Rishiri-shinrin-kōen Camping Ground (☎ 84-3551; 1-/2-person cabins ¥2500/3000) About 25 minutes' walk from the ferry terminal.

Hokuroku Camping Ground (☎ 82-2394; 4-person cabins ¥3000) Quite popular with hikers, perhaps because it's right near the start of the

Rishiri-zan track. Only ¥300 per person if you have a tent.

Rishiri Green Hill Youth Hostel (☎ 82-2507; dm ¥3990; ☷ Mar-Sep) About 25 minutes' walk from Oshidomari-kō port or a short bus ride (¥260) to the Gurīn-Hiru-Yūsu-Hosuteru-mae stop. Staff will be able to provide info on hiking Rishiri-zan, and you can also rent bicycles.

Minshuku Kutsugata-sō (民宿くつがた荘; ☎ 84-2038; r per person incl 2 meals ¥7350) Right in Kutsugata, about 10 minutes' walk from the ferry pier near the town's (only!) traffic light. It's casual and favoured by workers as well as tourists.

Pension Misaki (☎ 82-1659; www.misaki.burari.biz/ in Japanese; r per person incl 2 meals ¥7875, Jun–Aug ¥8925) An informal place with harbour-view Japanese-style rooms and a Japanese bath. It's six minutes' walk from the ferry.

Rishiri Fuji Kankō Hotel (☎ 82-1531; per person incl 2 meals high season ¥23,000; ☼ closed Dec–Feb) A popular spot for those on bus tours, this new hotel has Japanese-style rooms with private facilities as well as a public, onsen-fed bath.

EATING

Rishiri-tō is a great place for fresh seafood of all kinds, but uni (sea urchin) is mouthwatering. People have been known to travel all the way from Tokyo simply to eat it here. The stall **Aji-no-Ichiba** (味の市場; ☎ 82-1105; ☼ 9am–3pm late Jul–Aug) serves seafood straight from the local fishing boats to your mouth, sometimes with no cooking in between. Live uni cost ¥500. Look for a small, nondescript building next to a warehouse with an uni tank and Coca-Cola vending machine; exit to the right from the Oshidomari ferry terminal.

GETTING THERE & AROUND

From Rishiri-tō there are flights to Sapporo (¥23,200, 50 minutes). The island bus runs by the airport only once a day from Oshidomari (¥310, 20 minutes) or Kutsugata-kō port (¥520, 25 minutes). A taxi costs ¥1200. For details of ferry services, see Wakkanai (p601).

Buses (☎ 84-2550) run in both directions around the island's perimeter, completing a circuit in about two hours (¥2200). The trip from Oshidomari to Kutsugata (¥730) takes 30 to 50 minutes, depending on whether the bus stops at the airport and/or onsen.

Bicycling is another great way to see the island. Rent them from the youth hostels or shops near the Oshidomari ferry terminal. A leisurely circuit of the island (56km) takes anywhere from five to seven hours. A 29km cycling path runs through woods and coastal plains from Oshidomari past Kutsugata.

Rebun-tō 礼文島

☎ 0163 / pop 3330

Shaped like an arrowhead (or a dock-dried squid), Rebun Island is a naturalist's dream: fields of over 300 species of wildflower explode from May through to August; the terrain is varied and each walking track is unique; and the beaches harbour all sorts of cool finds, from interesting (and edible!) marine animals to semiprecious stones. Some people may wish to hire a scooter or motorcycle, as its one road leads past some gorgeous coastline.

The only main town is the small port of Kafuka, where the ferry arrives several times a day. From there several of the hiking tracks are within walking distance, and someone at the **tourist information counter** (☎ 86-2655; ☼ 8am–5pm mid-Apr–Oct) in the ferry terminal will point out the best routes or discuss your options in detail, as well as giving you maps and schedules.

ACTIVITIES

Most people come to Rebun-tō to **hike**, whether it is the eight-hour version or some of the tamer three-hour counterparts. It's a good idea to take a bus to the northern tip of the island, Cape Sukoton, and hike your way back past breathtaking cliffside vistas, fields of flowers and dwarf bamboo, thick forests and tiny fishing villages tucked tightly into the island's many coves. Anyone injured has to be rescued by boat, so group hiking is encouraged.

A four-hour hike runs from Cape Sukoton to Nishi-uedomari, then northeast to the bus stop at Hamanaka. The common route is from north to south. Momoiwa-sō Youth Hostel and other lodgings have info about the nearby hiking options and how to get to trailheads.

Another popular hike is from Nairo, halfway down the east coast, to the top of Rebundake. The peak is modest by any standards (490m) but the hike is a pleasant 3½ hours return. Near the port in Kafuka there is a wildflower loop leading across a backbone of spectacular highlands to Momoiwa (enigmatically named 'Peach Rock', as it bears far more resemblance to a breast than to its namesake fruit) and then down through flower fields and dwarf bamboo to the lighthouse at Cape Shiretoko. It's a great two-hour taste of the island's beauty for those without a lot of time.

Watch the weather carefully and plan ahead. Warm layers and rain gear are recommended. Do not, under any circumstances, drink unpurified water, as fox faeces now contaminate the streams (foxes were introduced from Russia in the 1930s).

SLEEPING & EATING

A few of the more attractive minshuku here no longer accept foreigners, a casualty of the fact that many foreigners did not understand they had no choice in what food was served (p600), and many close on 1 September when the relatively short tourist season ends.

Kushukohan camping ground (☎ 87-3110; entrance fee per person ¥600, tent ¥500, 4-person cabins ¥2000; ☷ May-Oct) This lakeside camping ground also has cabins and bungalows.

Momoiwa-sō Youth Hostel (☎ 86-1421; dm ¥5725; ☷ Jun-Sep) Famous for hard hikes by day and camp songs and craziness until lights out at 10pm, this eclectic youth hostel (located in an old herring house) has quite a devoted following. It has an absolutely stunning location on Rebun's west side, is just a few minutes' walk from several hiking tracks and has easy access to the rock-strewn sea. Beds are a combination of Japanese-style dorms (on tatami mats) and bunks. Staff can pick you up when the ferry docks: look for the flags and the enthusiastic guys yelling *okaerinasai!* (Welcome home!). If you're coming by yourself, you can take a Motochi-bound bus and get off at the Yūsu-mae station (15 minutes). From there it's a 17-minute walk to the hostel.

Field Inn Seikan-sō (☎ 87-2818; http://homepage1 .nifty.com/seikanso/main/p030000.htm; dm incl 2 meals ¥6000; ☷ May-Oct) More peaceful than Momoiwa-sō and also convenient for hiking. take a bus to Cape Sukoton (ask the driver to let you off at Seikan-sō). After getting off the bus, take the unpaved road to the west. Staff can pick you up at the ferry if you phone ahead.

Nature Inn Hanashin (☎ 86-1648; www16.plala .or.jp/hanasin in Japanese; r per person with shared bathroom incl 2 meals low/high season from ¥6800/8190) Popular and well kept. However, despite the price, most rooms do not have their own bathroom. It does have a new wing with a toilet and sink in each room (those rooms cost an additional ¥2000). It is a 25-minute walk from Kafuka-kō: walk toward Shimadomari and you'll find it on the left. By bus, head in the Shimadomari direction and get off at 'Youth Iriguchi'.

Kāchan Yado (☎ 86-1406; fax 86-2188; http://web-kutsurogi.net/kaachan/index.html in Japanese; r per person incl 2 meals ¥7500, Jun-Aug ¥8000) Translates to 'Mum's Place'. Warm and (according to travellers!) has nice toilets (these are in the new 'washlet' style, which allow for wash, rinse and blow dry after the morning's business is finished). Get off the bus at the Shiretoko stop, walk five minutes along the road and the inn is on your right. You can arrange to be collected from the port if you call ahead.

Minshuku Shiretoko (☎ 86-1335; per person incl 2 meals ¥8400) Has great views of the water and the presiding Rishiri-zan beyond. The owner is a fisherman and prides himself on hand-catching the evening's meal. To get here just get off the bus at the Shiretoko stop.

Hana Rebun (☎ 86-1177; www.hanarebun.com in Japanese; r incl 2 meals ¥30,000) For honeymooners who really want to remember something special, this super-luxury hotel offers balcony *rotemburo* in each room (a choice of porcelain or slightly pricier *hinoki* – an aromatic Japanese cypress wood often used in high-end *onsen* baths) that look out at Rishiri-tō, sunken *kotatsu* (a heated table with a cover over it to keep the legs and lower body warm) surrounded by beautiful tatami and exquisite meals. Head right as you leave the port and Hana Rebun is about 10 minutes' walk on the left.

GETTING THERE & AROUND

From Wakkanai there are infrequent flights each day to Rebun-tō (¥9930, 20 minutes). The closest bus stop to the airport is Kūkō-shita ('Below the Airport') and you'll need to walk 15 minutes to the terminal. The ferry (two hours) leaves five times a day between May and mid-September, four times a day between mid-September and December and in March and April, and twice a day in January and February.

Many lodgings will help out with transport to walking tracks or the ferry port, but packing light can help make the trip more pleasant; you can leave luggage in coin lockers in Wakkanai JR station if need be. Five buses per day run along the island's main road from Kafuka in the south to Cape Sukoton in the north (¥1180, 70 minutes). There are bus routes to Shiretoko (¥280, 13 minutes) and Motochi (¥440, 16 minutes) as well. Service is greatly reduced from November to April, so check the timetable at the Kafuka ferry terminal on arrival.

Bikes, scooters, motorcycles and cars can all be rented; as a last resort, hitchhiking will often get you where you need to go.

DAISETSUZAN NATIONAL PARK & ENVIRONS 大雪山国立公園

Daisetsuzan, Japan's largest national park (2309 sq km) and one of its first, consists of several stunning mountain groups, volcanoes, *onsen*, picturesque lakes and thick forests. It also includes Asahi-dake (2290m), Hokkaidō's highest peak. Those on a tight schedule should at least try to get to Asahidake Onsen for a quick peek, but try to give yourself two days, maybe three, if possible. It's spectacular.

Buses come to the peak from Asahikawa, Biei, Furano (all are to the west), Kamikawa (north), Kitami (east) and Obihiro (south). All have hiking information available at their tourist information offices. There is a very detailed map series (in Japanese) called *Daisetsuzan Attack* (¥1000), and Lonely Planet's *Hiking in Japan* gives thorough coverage of Daisetsuzan's most spectacular hikes and how to best prepare for them.

Furano 富良野

☎ 0167 / pop 25,230

Famous for its lavender fields, delicious melons, excellent skiing and the late-July **Heso Matsuri** (へそ祭り; Navel Festival). If you've been pining for a place where you can strip off your shirt and have a scary traditional mask painted onto your torso before you go revelling, you've come to the right festival. *Tobiiri odori* ('jump right in' dancing is part of the fun; as with sumō, it helps to be heavy.

In case you're scratching your head trying to figure out the connection between this town and belly buttons, it's because Furano is in the geographical centre of Hokkaidō: the middle.

INFORMATION

Outside Furano station there are two **information offices** (☎ 23-3388; ☀ 9am-6pm). Across the station you can hire bicycles for ¥250 per hour. Free internet terminals (15 minutes only) in the offices show the town's saintly goodwill towards weary internet junkies.

SIGHTS & ACTIVITIES

For many people, **Furano** (☎ 22-111; www.prince hotels.co.jp/ski/furano_e/index.html; lift tickets full day/night only ¥4000/2700; ☀ day 8.30am-3pm, night 3-9pm) is all about the ski slopes. The FIS World Cup and Snowboarding World Cup are held here yearly at the **Furano Ski Jō** (Map p606) at the Shin Furano Prince Hotel. The slopes are a mix between beginner and intermediate, with a small section devoted to advanced. The fastest gondola in Japan whisks you to the top, where 24 runs cover three mountainsides, all with perfect powder snow. Night skiing is available. Snowboarding is allowed on all slopes; skis, snowboards, boots and poles can

all be rented at the Shin Furano Prince Hotel (p606), either as a set (¥4200) or individually (price varies). Outerwear is also available for an extra charge. The season runs from late November to early May.

If you're not going skiing or getting behind the wheel, the **Furano Wine Factory** (ふらのワイン工場; ☎ 22-3242; ☀ 9am-4.30pm Jun-Aug, 9am-6pm Sep-May) is about 4km northwest of the station, and offers tours explaining the wine-making process. A **Grape Juice Factory** (ふらのぶどう果汁工場; ☎ 23-3033; ☀ 9am-4.30pm Jun-Sep) is nearby, about 1.5km away. Gourmands could then continue on to the **Furano Cheese Factory** (Map p606; ☎ 23-1156; ☀ 9am-5pm May-Oct, 9am-4pm Nov-Apr, closed 1st & 3rd Sat & Sun of month Nov-Apr), which has select tastes – try the squid ink brie, among others. Admission also includes the **Ice Milk Factory** (ふらのアイスミルク工房; ☀ 9am-5pm May-Oct). All have free admission and (excluding the Ice Milk Factory) free cheese and milk samples. Japanese signage only, but it is fairly self-explanatory: just insert desired edible into your open mouth, then chew or swallow. For those who feel far from the farm there's even a robotic milking cow; for ¥100 you can grab a teat and go at it, but the recorded moo: *priceless*.

From June to September there are infrequent buses to most of Furano's attractions, including the stunning lavender fields at **Farm Tomita** (Map p606; ☎ 39-3939; www.farm-tomita.co.jp /e/index.html; admission free; ☀ 9am-4.30pm Oct–late Apr, 8.30am-6pm late Apr-Sep), or the summer-only **Lavender Farm station** (ラベンダー畑駅; ☀ Jun-Oct), where a purple, lavender-flavoured, soft-serve ice-cream cone costs ¥250.

Also in September is the **Furano Wine Festival**, with tasting and buccholic merriment. A barbecue lets you buy local produce and then grill it for yourself, while costumed revellers stamp barefoot on grapes in a barrel.

SLEEPING & EATING

Minshuku, ryokan, hotels and pensions abound, but if you're planning a skiing trip it's best to book lodging through an agent, as often they have very cheap packages that include lift tickets, accommodation and sometimes train fare.

Furano Youth Hostel (ふらのユースホステル; ☎ 44-4441; www4.ocn.ne.jp/~furanoyh/english.htm; dm ¥3360; ☐) Comfy and close to the station, it's in a big farmhouse with an expansive deck. Meals feature many homegrown vegetables.

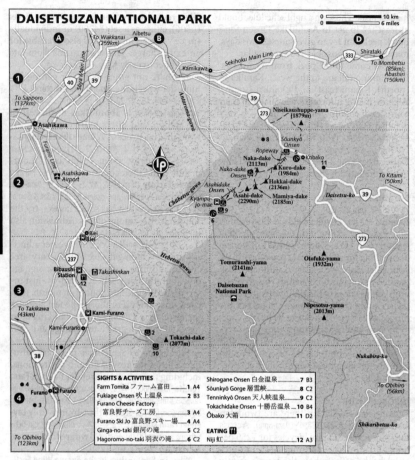

DAISETSUZAN NATIONAL PARK

SIGHTS & ACTIVITIES	
Farm Tomita ファーム富田	1 A4
Fukiage Onsen 吹上温泉	2 B3
Furano Cheese Factory 富良野チーズ工房	3 A4
Furano Ski Jo 富良野スキー場	4 A4
Ginga-no-taki 銀河の滝	5 C2
Hagoromo-no-taki 羽衣の滝	6 C2
Shirogane Onsen 白金温泉	7 B3
Sōunkyō Gorge 層雲峡	8 C2
Tenninkyō Onsen 天人峡温泉	9 C2
Tokachidake Onsen 十勝岳温泉	10 B4
Ōbako 大箱	11 D2

EATING 🍴	
Niji 虹	12 A3

For travellers with disabilities, the hostel is also barrier free.

Alpine Backpackers (アルパインバックパッカーズ; ☎ 22-1311; fax 23-4385; www.alpn.co.jp/english/index.html; bunk beds per person with shared bathroom Apr-Oct/Dec-Mar ¥2500/2700; 🖳) Cosy, clean little place with a youth-hostel feel. Only a few minutes' walk from the Kitanomine lift, so it's a great choice for anyone on a budget who's planning on mainly spending time on the slopes.

Rokugō Furarin Youth Hostel (ろくごうふらりんユースホステル; ☎ 29-2172; www2.odn.ne.jp /rokugo-furalin/in Japanese; dm ¥3360) This place really feels like home. It's airy and un-institutional with simple decorations that seem more like a kid's room than a hostel. Rooms have bathrooms with basins. The breakfast is buffet style (¥600) and most ingredients are organic and locally produced. From Furano station it's a 15-minute bus ride to the terminus at Rokugō, but you can get a free lift from the station if you phone ahead.

Sumire Ryokan (すみれ旅館; ☎ 23-4767; 4-30 Asahi-machi; r per person ¥3800, incl 2 meals ¥6000; 🖳) An informal standby, with cats and washing machines, that's only five minutes on foot from Furano station.

Shin Furano Prince Hotel (新富良野プリンスホテル; ☎ 22-1111; www.princehotels.co.jp/ski/furano_e /access.html; d per person from ¥16,200; 🖳) Right at the base of the gondola, recently remodelled, this top-end hotel has snazzy rooms and a variety of restaurants, bars, and souvenir stands. Ski-included winter packages are as low as ¥8000 per person.

If you're looking to unwind after a long day at a place that's not a Japanese snack-style pub, check out **Furano Bar Bocco** (フラノバー Bocco; ☎ 22-1010; www10.plala.or.jp/bocco/English/index .htm; cocktails ¥500-700; ❀ 6pm-2.30am; E), a fun watering hole that sometimes has 'English-speaker' get-togethers; offers a good selection of both international and local alcohols. Closes on irregular days.

GETTING THERE & AROUND

Most lodgings will help you arrange transport to the ski lifts and back. You can also hoof it most of the time, as many places are close to Furano station.

On the JR Furano line, *kaisoku* trains from Asahikawa reach Furano in 1¼ hours (¥1040), some continuing on to Obihiro (¥2420) in another two hours. Frequent local trains along this line stop at Kami-Furano (¥350, 20 minutes) and Biei (¥620, 40 minutes). *Futsū* trains go to Takikawa (¥1040, 67 minutes) where you can catch *tokkyū* to Sapporo (¥3410, one hour). Fairly frequent buses connect Furano with the rest of Hokkaidō as well: Asahikawa (¥860, 95 minutes, eight per day) and Sapporo (¥2100, two hours and 51 minutes, four per day) are common destinations. A *Lavender Express* special seasonal train runs direct from Sapporo (¥4340, two hours) to Furano, daily from early June to 31 August, and on weekends and holidays from September to the end of October.

Biei 美瑛
☎ 0166 / pop 11,700

With the dramatic Daisetsuzan mountains in the background, Biei is an artist's and nature-lover's mecca. The open fields, often covered in lavender or poppies, are so different from the rest of the mainland that you'll wonder if you have left Japan and somehow ended up in rural France. The ubiquitous tour buses will bring you back to reality, particularly in late June and July when the flowers peak. It's a fun place to visit any time: walking and cycling the dirt roads in summer, enjoying the autumn leaves, then cross-country skiing and snowshoeing in winter. If you want to sit down and relax, there are many coffee shops and art galleries.

INFORMATION

The **tourist information building** (美瑛町観光 協会; ☎ 92-4378; www.eolas.co.jp/hokkaido/sikibiei/;

❀ 8.30am-7pm May-Oct, 8.30am-5pm Nov-Apr) is outside Biei station. Staff here and at lodgings can supply you with cycling maps and a tourist booklet, *Hokkaidō Town of Hills Biei*, which contains an English-language map and details of local sights, outdoor activities and even art classes if Van Gogh starts whispering in your ear. Bike hire is available at several places, including **Gaido no Yamagoya** (ガイドの山小屋; ☎ 95-2277; www.yamagoya.jp; ❀ 8am-6pm), which has electrically assisted bicycles (great for those up-down hills!) for ¥600 per hour, as well as normal shopping bikes for ¥200 per hour. Across from Biei station, try **Matsuura Co** (松浦商店; ☎ 92-1415; ❀ 8am-7pm), which has both electric bicycles (¥600 per hour) and normal bicycles (¥200 per hour). Whether you walk or ride, stick to the paths and roadsides: don't tramp through the farmers' fields or steal tastes of the produce that peoples' livelihood depends upon.

SIGHTS

There are numerous art galleries and museums in the area. One of the most famous is **Takushinkan** (拓真館; ☎ 92-3355), a lovely museum dedicated to the internationally known photographer Shinzō Maeda (1922–98), whose stunning photographs of the Tokachi area are famous for their unusual colour and composition. The museum is a 10km-drive by car or taxi from Biei in the direction of Bibaushi. The road is full of panoramic vistas of pretty hills covered at different times of year with sunflowers, lavender, white birches or snow.

SLEEPING & EATING

Most of the lodgings are set in gorgeous areas among fields or flowers, but they're not close to the station. Many will arrange to pick you up at the station if you call ahead.

our pick **Biei Potato-no-Oka Youth Hostel** (美瑛 ポテトの丘ユースホステル; ☎ 92-3255; www .potatovillage.com/hpeng/engtop.html; dm ¥3800) Friendly English-speaking staff and comfortable bunks. Meals (extra cost) are available, but they are quite fancy, and usually feature Hokkaidō meats or produce. Star-gazing is included in the hostel's list of activities, and bikes can be hired by those looking to get away from it all. Pick-up to go to the hostel must be arranged at the station.

Hotel L'Avenir (ホテル　ラブニール; ☎ 92-5555; www.biei-lavenir.com in Japanese; r per person incl 2 meals from ¥5500; 💻) Turn left out of JR Biei station, pass the tourist info booth, and L'Avenir Is Just beyond: a clean, modern place with Western-style rooms and hands-on crafts and activities, such as making your own butter, cheese, bread or ice cream.

Auberge Hermitage (オーベルジュ・エルミタージュ; ☎ 92-0991; http://lilac.hokkai.net/~erumi/ in Japanese; r per person incl 2 meals from ¥17,500) A comfortable place plopped in the middle of gorgeous fields. Sophisticated, and with lovely Western-style rooms, it also has delicious aromas wafting from the kitchen (all of the meals are homemade by the chef on premises). The 24-hour Jacuzzi with a large picture window is a swanky addition, made better by the fact that you can reserve it for private use and thus not have to share. This upscale hotel only has six rooms, so book ahead.

Niji (Map p606; ☎ 95-2492; meals from ¥800; 🕐 lunch-dinner Fri-Wed) Surely a great example of the international ideal: an American-style log cabin up on the Biei farmland hills, serving up authentic Korean dishes: sizzling stone *bibimbap* or spicy soups. It has great views, too. No English menu, but the owner gladly makes suggestions or points out daily specials.

GETTING THERE & AWAY

Biei is on the JR Furano line between Asahikawa (*futsū* ¥530, 30 minutes) and Furano (¥620, 40 minutes). From near Biei station there are frequent buses to Asahikawa (¥520, 50 minutes).

Tokachi-dake, Fukiage & Shirogane Onsens 十勝岳　吹上温泉　白金温泉

Northeast of Furano, these remote hot-spring villages are less crowded than most other areas and offer good bases for hikes into Daisetsuzan National Park. You can climb the peak **Tokachi-dake** (十勝岳; 2077m) in a day; some tracks extend as far as Tenninkyō Onsen or the peak Asahi-dake, though these require three to four days of hiking. About 3km from Tokachi-dake Onsen, on the road to Shirogane Onsen, Fukiage Onsen has a free, public *rotemburo* overlooking a gorge. Locals say there have been some thefts of items left in cars, so lock your doors.

For accommodation, camping is the cheapest way to go (per person ¥500).

Kamihoro-sō (カミホロ荘; ☎ 0167-45-2970; r per person incl 2 meals ¥10,390), in Tokachi-dake, has large Japanese-style rooms and pleas-

ant hot-spring baths with a great view of the surrounding mountains. If coming by bus, get off at Kokumin Shukusha Mae; the bus drops you off almost right in from of Kamihoro-sō.

Very close to Fukiage Onsen's public *rotemburo*, **Hakugin-sō** (白銀荘; ☎ 0167-45-4126/3251; dm ¥2750) is a dorm-style place with a kitchen (though no meals are served, guests can cook for themselves) and beautiful baths, which are open to the public for day use (¥600, 10am to 10pm).

An inexpensive option at Shirogane Onsen is **Shirogane Onsen Shirakaba-sō** (白金温泉白樺荘; ☎ 0166-94-3344; r per person ¥3050); rates include access to the hot-spring baths.

From Kami-Furano station, it's a 45-minute bus ride to Tokachi-dake Onsen (¥500). Buses to Shirogane Onsen leave from Biei frequently (¥600, 30 minutes). There are also up to four buses a day direct from Asahikawa to Shirogane Onsen (¥1100, 1½ hours).

Asahidake Onsen 旭岳温泉

☎ 0166

This cosy, forested, hot-springs resort consists of some 10 small inns at the foot of Asahi-dake. At the end of the road, **Asahidake ropeway** (cable car; ☎ 68-9111; www.asahidakeropeway.com; one way/return Jul–mid-Oct ¥1500/2800, mid-Oct–Jun ¥1000/1800) runs to within easy hiking distance of the peak. Though Asahidake Onsen is not overdeveloped, it can become quite crowded, particularly during autumn when the leaves begin to change colour. An *onsen* map is available at the ropeway, listing the locations, prices and hours of the various baths.

SIGHTS & ACTIVITIES

Even if you're not a hiker, don't miss a chance to visit this area. It's simply spectacular, and the ropeway gives a good taste of the view. Those who enjoy hiking will love the variety of tracks, many of which wind through very unique terrain that offers a mix of volcanic activity, fields, forests and foliage.

Hiking

There are dozens of hiking options in this area. The **Asahidake Visitors Centre** (☎ 97-2153; www.town.higashikawa.hokkaido.jp/vc/ in Japanese; 🕐 9am-5pm Jun-Oct, 9am-4pm Tue-Sun Nov-May) has excellent maps that the staff will mark with daily track conditions. From June to August the flowers are at their peak; foliage turns the hills crimson and gold shortly thereafter, peaking in mid- to late September.

One popular hike follows tracks from the Asahidake ropeway via several peaks to Sōunkyō Onsen. The ropeway is open from 6am to 7pm from late June to August and shorter hours for the remainder of the year.

For those without a lot of time, there is also a 1.7km loop track that leads for about 50 minutes around the area before returning to the ropeway's upper terminal. On a clear day the views are spectacular, but even if it's cloudy or foggy the area has an ethereal, mystical quality that is awe-inspiring, passing lakes (some of which contain the elusive Ezo-salamander), boiling pools and wildflowers. It's easy to see why this area was one of the first places to be made a national park.

There are *rotemburo* off the northern route at Nakadake Onsen; branch left at Na-kadake-bunki just before ascending Naka-dake. Beware: the water in Yudoku Onsen is poisonous; don't touch it. From Asahidake Onsen there's also a 5.5km track leading through the forest in about two hours to Tenninkyō Onsen, a small hot-springs resort with a scenic gorge and the beautiful **Hagoromo-no-taki** (Angel's Robe Waterfall). In winter, cross-country skiing is possible on many of the tracks, too.

Onsen

This area is famous for *onsen* for a reason, and visitors luxuriate in the area's many baths. Most *onsen*, even at the higher-end hotels, are open for day use to the general public, but times and prices vary considerably. A useful map and guide is available from the tourist info booth at the ropeway's lower terminal. Prices range from ¥500 up to ¥1500. Bringing your own wash cloth and towel can save the additional ¥200 to ¥500 hire fee.

SLEEPING

If you're planning to do lengthy day hikes, staying overnight here will be much better than wasting all morning on the bus from Asahikawa.

Daisetsuzan Shirakaba-sō (大雪山白樺荘; ☎ 97-2246; http://park19.wakwak.com/~shirakaba; dm ¥6450, r per person incl 2 meals ¥7500) Both a hostel and ryokan, with separate pricing structures. Near the ropeway's lower terminal, this lodge-style place has both Japanese- and Western-style rooms and a large kitchen where you can cook

if you prefer not to have the included meals. Has indoor and outdoor *onsen*.

Lodge Nutapukaushipe (ロッジ・ヌタプカウシペ; ☎ 97-2150; r per person incl 2 meals from ¥7350; ✗) One of the few nonsmoking options in Japan. A cosy, log-cabin style place, it has indoor and outdoor baths with a ¥500 day-use option. It's also a *rāmen* shop, with a yummy *kitopiro rāmen* topped with Ainu scallion.

Asahidake Manseikaku Hotel Beamonte (旭岳万世閣ホテルベアモンテ; ☎ 97-2321; tw per person double occupancy ¥13,275-22,200; [P] ✗) A fancy resort hotel with giant indoor and outdoor baths, several restaurants, a well-appointed lounge, massage chairs, and pleasant Western- or Japanese-style rooms. Prices vary substantially depending on the season, and it can be quite full at times; calling ahead is a good plan. Visiting the bath only is possible for ¥1500.

GETTING THERE & AWAY

For much of the year (mid-October to mid-June) the bus from Asahikawa station to Asahidake Onsen and Tenninkyō Onsen is actually *free*. In the high season the price jumps to ¥1000, but if you spend more than ¥2000 at Asahidake Onsen (that includes lodging, a ¥2800 ropeway ticket, food…anything – just save your receipts), you can get a coupon for a free return, available at the ropeway station's information counter. Buses from Asahikawa are infrequent and quite inconvenient for those wishing for a nice Daisetsuzan day hike: take the 9.10am bus at stop 4 or you'll find yourself without a lot of time. The first bus from Asahidake Onsen departs at 9.15am, the last bus is a frustratingly early 5.05pm, so keep your eye on the clock if you need to get a bus back to Asahikawa. Buses between Asahidake Onsen and Tenninkyō Onsen are always free.

Sōunkyō Onsen 層雲峡温泉
☎ 01658

The town of Sōunkyō Onsen, known for its *onsen*, is a gateway for forays into the interior of the park as well as the gorge, Sōunkyō, but hikers may wish to continue to Asahidake Onsen instead of stopping here. It's mainly tracks, a few seasonal attractions and some scenic views – some of which are disappointing.

The **tourist information office** (☎ 5-3350; ☉ 10.30am-5pm), on the 1st floor of the public bath Kurodake-no-yu, has several maps and English-language pamphlets. Its booking service may be useful if you arrive in high season. Just up the hill, **mountain-bike hire** is available for ¥2000 per day. Next to the ropeway terminus, the park **visitor centre** (☎ 9-4400; http://sounkyovc.town.kamikawa.hokkaido.jp in Japanese; 9am-5pm Jun-Oct, 9am-5pm Tue-Sun Nov-May) can provide information on park conditions.

After a hard day of cycling or hiking, **Kuro-dake-no-yu** (黒岳の湯; ☎ 5-3333; admission ¥600; 10am-9pm Thu-Tue) offers handsome hot-spring baths (including *rotemburo*). It's on the town's main pedestrian street. You can also soothe your aching feet in the free **ashi-no-yu** (foot bath), next to the Ginsenkaku Hotel.

SIGHTS & ACTIVITIES
Sōunkyō 層雲峡
This **gorge** (Map p606) stretches for about 8km beyond Sōunkyō Onsen and is renowned for its waterfalls – **Ryūsei-no-taki** (流星の滝; Shooting Stars Falls) and **Ginga-no-taki** (Milky Way Falls; Map p606) are the main ones – and for two sections of perpendicular rock columns that give an enclosed feeling; hence their names, **Ōbako** (Big Box) and **Kobako** (小箱; Little Box).

Until recently it was possible to walk the entire 8km, but the riverside foot/bike path collapsed and has not been rebuilt, and cycling is not recommended because of hazardous tunnels. One bus runs daily to Ōbako (¥350, 35 minutes, 12.50pm) and returns about 30 minutes later, giving you almost no time to enjoy Ōbako's (albeit modest) charms.

Hiking
The combination of a **ropeway and chairlift** (☎ 5-3031) provides fast access to **Kuro-dake** (黒岳; 1984m) for hikers and sightseers. One-way/return tickets on the ropeway cost ¥900/1750 and on the chairlift ¥400/600. Hours of operation vary seasonally (8am to 7pm in July and August, closed intermittently in winter).

In fair weather, a popular hike goes to **Asahi-dake** (旭岳; 2290m) from either Sōunkyō Onsen or Asahidake Onsen. You can arrange to leave your baggage at either end and pick it up later or, better yet, take advantage of the coin lockers inside Asahikawa station before heading into the park. You could also do day hikes from the top of the Sōunkyō lift station to nearby peaks.

From July to the end of September, one bus a day goes to Ginsen-dai, where the trailhead **Aka-dake** (赤岳; 2078m) is located. The bus leaves Sōunkyō Onsen at 6.02am and returns from Ginsen-dai at 2.15pm (¥800, one hour), leaving you plenty of time for your ascent and descent.

A short, steep and very pretty track runs up to Soūbakudai, a scenic overlook of the two waterfalls, Ryūsei-no-taki and Ginga-no-taki. Look for the steps leading up the hill directly behind where the bus stops. It takes about 20 minutes to reach the top.

FESTIVALS & EVENTS
Hyōbaku Matsuri (氷瀑まつり; Ice-Waterfall Festival) From the end of January to the end of March, this festival features ice sculptures, tunnels and domes, some lit up.

Kyōkoku Hi Matsuri (峡谷火まつり; Kyōkoku Fire Festival) This celebration on the last Saturday in July is meant to purify the hot springs and appease the mountain and fire deities. Revellers perform traditional Ainu owl dances and drumming, climaxing with archers shooting flaming arrows into the gorge.

SLEEPING
Sōunkyō Youth Hostel (層雲峡ユースホステル; ☎ 5-3418; www.youthhostel.or.jp/sounkyo/; dm ¥2940; Jun-Oct) Dwarfed by the Prince and Taisetsuzan hotels, this hostel is about a 10-minute walk uphill from the bus station. Mostly bunk-bed accommodation, it has information on the walking tracks in the park, organises hikes and hires out gear for braving the elements. Bike hire costs ¥500 per day.

Ginsenkaku (銀泉閣; ☎ 5-3003; www.ginsenkaku .com; r per person incl 2 meals high/low season from ¥15,900/10,500) Ginsenkaku is a professional operation across from Minshuku Midori that has some English-speaking staff, Japanese-style rooms with full facilities (ie bathroom with bath, toilet and basin) and warm, steamy common baths, including *rotemburo*.

GETTING THERE & AWAY
Buses from Sōunkyō Onsen run approximately every two hours via JR Kamikawa station to Asahikawa (¥1900, 1¾ hours). Rail pass holders may want to do part of the trip by train and get off at Kamikawa, thus reducing the bus fare to ¥770. Up to four buses a day run direct to Kitami (¥2500, 1¾ hours), where you can transfer for connections to Bihoro (¥860, 43 minutes). From May to October, there are up to three buses a day from Bihoro to Kawayu Onsen in Akan National Park (¥1920, 2¼ hours).

From Sōunkyō Onsen there are two buses a day to Kushiro (¥4790, five hours and 20 minutes) via Akan Kohan (¥3260, 3½ hours) in Akan National Park. There are also two buses a day to Obihiro (¥2200, 80 minutes), which follow a scenic route via Nukabira-ko.

DŌ-TŌ (EASTERN HOKKAIDŌ) 道東

ABASHIRI 網走

☎ 0152 / pop 40,600

To most Japanese, Abashiri is as synonymous with the word prison as Alcatraz is to Westerners. Mention of the prison (still in operation) once sent chills through the spines of even the most hardened criminals. Winters here are as harsh as they come, yet this is exactly why the area's become a tourist attraction. Looking out at a snow-white plain of frozen ice floes is a surreal experience, and the sound of icebergs grinding together from the force of the sea's currents make a deep impression on all who hear it. Appreciation for nature's grandness, even for its bleakness, is very Japanese.

The town's economy now depends on fishing, tourism and trade with Russia, its nearest neighbour.

The closest major city to Shiretoko, Abashiri is a good hub for hikers but the winter ice floes, the September coral grass, its Abashiri Prison Museum (not to be confused with the prison itself) and its Northern Peoples' Museum are also worthwhile.

In the dead of winter, when up to 80% of the sea is ice-clogged, **Aurora icebreaker sightseeing boats** (流氷観光砕氷船オーロラ; ☎ 43-6000) depart four to six times a day from Abashiri port for one-hour cruises (¥3000) into the Sea of Okhotsk. In summer, the northern coastal areas are a pretty, easy walk, perfect for photography, with lots of sand dollars and other small shells.

Information

The **tourist information office** (☎ 44-5849; www2s .biglobe.ne.jp/~abashiri/e/index_e.html; ⏰ 9am-5pm) outside Abashiri station has the excellent English-language *Okhotsk Abashiri Tourist Guide*, maps and discount coupons for several of the local attractions.

QUIRKY HOKKAIDŌ EVENTS

- Sapporo's Yuki Matsuri (Snow Festival) – spectacular ice sculptures grace the streets (p577)
- Marimo Matsuri in Akan Kohan – return fuzzballs of algae to Akan-ko (p616)
- Orochon-no-Hi (Fire Festival) in Abashiri – fire dancers gyrate in flames (p612)
- Japan Cup National Dogsled Races in Wakkanai – watch as dogs dash and fur flies (p599)
- The Kyōkoku Hi Matsuri (Fire Festival) at Sōunkyō Onsen – flaming arrows are shot into a gorge (opposite)
- 'Come Back Salmon' night in Abashiri – grill seafood while watching salmon return to spawn (p612)
- Heso Matsuri (Navel Festival) in Furano – celebrate innies and outies in style (p605)

Sights & Activities

Tento-zan, the main mountain presiding over Abashiri (207m), is steep enough that its 5km climb will leave you winded unless you're going by bus or car. At the top, however, are some excellent views, a park and several interesting museums. A cycling road runs for 25km from Abashiri proper to the coral-grass viewing areas and beyond, providing some beautiful views of the area's lakes, forests and pumpkin fields.

Abashiri Prison Museum (網走監獄博物館; ☎ 45-2411; www.kangoku.jp/world/index.htm; admission ¥1050; ⏰ 8am-6pm Apr-Oct, 9am-5pm Nov-Mar) details many of the reasons that this prison was so feared. Inmates braved brutally cold winters with thin bedding and very little heat: one lone pipe ran the length of the corridors, providing almost no heat for those in the cells but a decent amount for the wardens. Unfortunately, the English signs here are quite difficult to understand (as is the website, although the pics are useful), making it harder to get the most from the exhibitions, which are worthwhile.

Abashiri Prison (網走刑務所), across the river and still a working penitentiary, has a **gift shop and tiny museum** (☎ 43-3167; ⏰ 9am-4pm) where crafts made by inmates can be purchased. It's also possible to walk around outside the prison walls, though further entry and photographs are prohibited.

HOKKAIDŌ

Museum of Northern Peoples (北方民族博物館; ☎ 45-3888; www.hoppohm.org/english/index.htm; admission ¥450; ⊙ 9.30am-4.30pm Tue-Sun) is a few minutes' walk downhill from the summit of Tento-zan. It is a state-of-the-art place with numerous exhibits of Ainu culture, as well as Native American, Aleutian and other indigenous peoples. An English pamphlet and small signs help visitors make the most of their tour.

Recently renovated, the unique **Okhotsk Ryūhyō Museum** (オホーツク流氷館; Museum of Ice Floes; ☎ 43-5951; www.ryuhyokan.com in Japanese; admission ¥520; ⊙ 8am-6pm Apr-Oct, 9am-4.30pm Nov-Mar) has odd ice-related exhibits. One of the more interesting is a display relating to the tiny *kurione* (aka Sea Angels), a funky relative of the sea slug, which is sort of an Abashiri mascot.

Tartaruga (タルタルーガ; ☎ 61-5201; www .tar2uga.co.jp; per day, 2 dives ¥30,000; ⊙ Jan-Mar) will bring you face-to-face with that odd mollusc, the *kurione*. Non-*kurione* dives are possible the rest of the year, too.

Stare out at the frozen landscape while grilling your preferred foods and drinking an alcoholic beverage of your choice on the **Ryūhyō Norokko Sightseeing Train** (流氷のろっこ観光列車; admission ¥810; ⊙ late Jan–mid-Mar). The train slowly runs through a field of utter white snow, and from the window you can see the frozen Sea of Okhotsk. It stops at Kitahama station (right at the coast) for 10 minutes, and travellers can get a close look at what these waters become in wintertime. Steel yourself for the cold (dress warmly) and for the aroma of dried toasted *surume* (squid), as both are part and parcel of this interesting ride.

Wakka Gensei Kaen (ワッカ原生花園; ⊙ May-Oct), the biggest coastal wildflower garden in Japan, is 20km long and up to 700m wide and boasts more than 300 species. It's an hour's bus ride from Abashiri station; take a bus from stop 2.

If you're looking to spend a day on the slopes, you'll find powder at **Kamui Ski Links** (カムイスキーリンクス; ☎ 72-2311; www.kamui -skilinks.com; lift ticket ¥2500; ⊙ 9am-5pm Dec-Apr). This top-rated resort is the site of several snow-boarding competitions and has an even mix of beginner, intermediate and advanced slopes, including one of Japan's longest – 3500m. Eight lifts and 10 courses help to keep crowds down, though at times it gets windy, especially at the top. There's no night skiing here, but Kamui is less pricey than some of its southern competitors, and much less crowded than any of the resorts outside Sapporo.

Festivals

Orochon-no-Hi (オロチョンの火) A fire festival held on the last Saturday in July, derived from the shamanistic rites of the indigenous Gilyak people, who once lived in the Abashiri area.

Coral Grass Viewing (サンゴ草群落地) Known as salt pickle or glasswort in other parts of the world, this humble marsh plant gets its 15 minutes of fame in mid-September, when it turns bright red. Busloads of tourists flock to a few boardwalk-viewing spots. Nature lovers will enjoy the bird life, as the marshes attract not only seagulls, but curlews, terns, egrets, herons and more.

Come Back Salmon Night (カムバックサーモンナイト) A welcome to the lake's most famous (and delicious!) fish. Each year (mid-October to mid-December, depending on the fishes' schedule) the salmon run upstream, greeted by bright spotlights that illuminate the fish as they pass into Abashiri Lake. Nearby grilling stations serve *sanma* (a dark, oily and delicious seasonal fish that's distantly related to mackerel, but smaller), scallops, squid and venison, often with free tastes. Salmon – the guest of honour – is *not* served…not *that* night anyway.

Sleeping

Minshuku Hokui 44 (民宿ほくい４４; ☎ 44-4325; www11.plala.or.jp/hokui44/in Japanese; dm incl 2 meals ¥4300) This *minshuku* is a Toho network member and offers dorm-style beds. The rate includes free admission (and a ride) to the nearby *onsen* hotel. If you phone ahead, someone will pick you up at the station and save you the 20-minute walk; however, no English is spoken.

Abashiri Gensei-kaen Youth Hostel (網走原生花園ユースホステル; ☎ 46-2630; http://sapporo .cool.ne.jp/genseikaen; dm incl 2 meals ¥5200) In the middle of a wildflower reserve, the hostel offers views of Shari-dake and Shiretoko-hantō. It is a good idea to call ahead as the opening hours vary.

Abashiri Central Hotel (網走セントラルホテル; ☎ 44-5151; www.abashirich.com; s/tw ¥7350/ 12,000; P ⊠ ⌨) Another nearby option, with LAN access in all rooms. Rooms are equipped with fridge, PJs, slippers, and even shaving kits. Unlike some hotels, this place accepts all major credit cards.

Eating

There are small eateries – the usual *rāmen* shops, *izakaya* and *yakiniku* places – in the side streets along the main arcade that runs the length of Abashiri, but the ones that aren't snack/whiskey bars close early.

Kandō Asa-ichi fish market (感動朝市; ☎ 43-7666; ☺ 6.30-9.30am Mon-Fri, 6.30-10.30am Sat & Sun mid-Jul–15 Oct) A great option for fresh fish lovers: select your own seafood and cook it on one of the open-air grills. Free shuttles leave from several major hotels; ask your lodging for details. Salmon (which can be fished right out of the river!) is superb.

Abashiri Beer Kan (網走ビール館; ☎ 45-5100; meals ¥700-2000; ☺ lunch & dinner) A microbrewery with various flavours on tap; offers mainly Western-style food, but some Japanese dishes, including a crab special, are also available. No English menu, but pics make things easy. The jumbo croquette (korokke) is tasty comfort food.

Murakami (むらかみ; ☎ 43-1147; www.drive-net .com/murakami/ in Japanese; from ¥945) Delicious sushi in a small, Japanese-style place. The owner changes the menu daily based on what's fresh from the boat each morning. In season, sanma, a thin, oily fish somewhat like mackerel, is fantastic. No English menu.

Getting There & Away

Memanbetsu airport links Abashiri with Sapporo, Fukuoka, Nagoya, Osaka and Tokyo. Airport buses (¥750, 30 minutes) are approximately timed to flights and run from the bus station via Abashiri station (they're about 1km apart) to the airport.

Abashiri is the terminus for the JR Sekihoku main line, which runs across the centre of Hokkaidō to Asahikawa (tokkyū ¥7750, 3¾ hours). Local trains run along the same route and stop at Bihoro (¥530, 30 minutes) and Kitami (¥1040, 50 minutes). From May to October there are up to three buses a day from Bihoro to Kawayu Onsen in Akan National Park (¥1920, about 2½ hours). From Kitami you can catch buses to towns near Daisetsuzan National Park (¥2500, two hours).

Abashiri is the terminus for the JR Senmō main line, which runs east to Shiretoko-Shari station and then south to Kushiro. One direct bus daily links Abashiri and Shari (¥1120, 65 minutes).

Direct buses from Abashiri to Sapporo (¥6210, six hours) leave from the bus terminal, a 10-minute ride east of Abashiri station. Between June and mid-October there are three buses from Memanbetsu airport via Abashiri

to Utoro in Shiretoko National Park (¥3000, 2½ hours).

Hiring a car may be the best option for those who want to get to the more remote sections of Shiretoko-hantō or Akan. Car-rental agencies such as **JR Hokkaido Rent a Lease** (ジェイアール北海道レンタリース; ☎ 43-6197; car hire per day from ¥6000; ☺ 8am-6pm Jan-Apr & Nov-Dec, 8am-8pm May-Oct) are located near the station, and you will need a valid International Driving Permit.

A ¥900 ticket gives all-day entry on a tourist-loop bus which stops at many of the major sites, including the museums (not the coral grass), as well as the bus and train terminals. Bikes may also be hired from **JR Hokkaido Rent a Lease** (ジェイアール北海道レンタリース; ☎ 43-6197; bike rental per hr ¥500; ☺ 8am-6pm Jan-Apr & Nov-Dec, 8am-8pm May-Oct), right in front of the station, though you should make sure the tyres have been inflated well if you're heading up Tento-zan or out to the coral grass areas.

AKAN NATIONAL PARK 阿寒国立公園

This expansive park (905 sq km) contains volcanic peaks, large caldera lakes and thick forests. Its scenic views attract over 6.6 million visitors per year, but it is big enough that even at peak times there are ways to get away from it all, particularly if you're looking to hike or meander around the forest tracks. There are numerous day-hike options and a few longer ones. Bears are a possible problem, and foxes, both common and cunning, often steal unguarded food or even sleeping bags.

The main access points are Abashiri and Bihoro to the north, and Kushiro to the south. Kawayu Onsen and Akan Kohan are its two main towns. Teshikaga (aka Mashū Onsen) is a useful transport hub.

Akan Bus Company (www.akanbus.co.jp in Japanese) provides tours and a running commentary (in Japanese) about the sights and attractions, stopping here and there for picture taking at some of the most scenic viewpoints. If that's unappealing to you, hire a car and don't look back. With your own wheels you'll be free to travel anywhere, even to hop over to Shiretoko National Park.

Kawayu Onsen 川湯温泉
☎ 015

A quiet onsen town, Kawayu has numerous ashiyu (foot onsen) where travellers can soak tired feet in hot water, in addition to the usual

HOKKAIDŌ

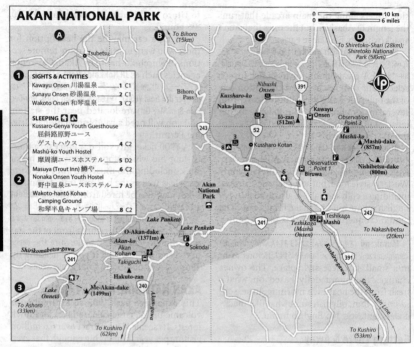

AKAN NATIONAL PARK

SIGHTS & ACTIVITIES	
Kawayu Onsen 川湯温泉 1	C1
Sunayu Onsen 砂湯温泉 2	C1
Wakoto Onsen 和琴温泉 3	C2

SLEEPING	
Kussaro-Genya Youth Guesthouse	
屈斜路原野ユース	
ゲストハウス 4	C2
Mashū-ko Youth Hostel	
摩周湖ユースホステル 5	D2
Masuya (Trout Inn) 鱒や.........................6	C2
Nonaka Onsen Youth Hostel	
野中温泉ユースホステル 7	A3
Wakoto-hantō Kohan	
Camping Ground	
和琴半島キャンプ場 8	C2

---

spas. Often free, they are sprinkled throughout the town and there is even one in the town's JR station. This area is accessible by train from Kushiro city, a do-able day trip.

The **tourist information office** (☎ 483-2255; 🕙 9am-6.30pm Jun-Sep, 9am-5pm Oct-May) is about 10 minutes on foot from the Kawayu bus station, and a good source of information. Pick up a copy of the English-language *Teshikaga English Guide Map* and, if you need to, ask the staff to help you book accommodation. Mashū, a little further south, is an alternative access point for the park and may actually be closer to some of the following attractions.

SIGHTS & ACTIVITIES

Sumo fans will enjoy **Koki Taiho Sumō Memorial Hall** (川湯相撲記念館; ☎ 483-2924; admission ¥400; 🕙 9am-9pm Jun-Sep, 9am-5pm Oct-May), a small museum dedicated to a hometown hero.

Iō-zan (硫黄山; 512m) is a hellish mountain with steaming vents, sunshine-yellow sulphur and *onsen*-steamed eggs. You'll hear the sellers calling *Tamago! Tamago! Tamago! Tamago!* (Eggs!) even before you reach the carpark. Though highly touted and a sickly

brownish-green, they don't taste much different from a regular kitchen-boiled egg.

The walk from Kawayu JR station to Kawayu Onsen (4km) is very pretty and passes Iō-zan along the way (1.5km). Its birches, stunted pines and other greenery can be pretty any time of year but are particularly nice in the autumn months of August and September.

Considered by many to be Japan's most beautiful lake, **Mashū-ko** (摩周湖) once held the world record for water clarity, with visibility of 35m. The island in the middle was known by the Ainu as 'Isle of the Gods'.

Kussharo-ko (屈斜路湖), the other major lake, is famous for its swimming, boating and volcanically warmed sands. Naka-jima is the aptly named 'middle island' that's in the centre of the lake, which has its own version of the Loch Ness monster, named 'Kusshi'. No one has yet claimed it to be a hoax, so if you're a Nessie fan, at least here in Hokkaidō you still have hope.

Sunayu Onsen (Map p614), a stretch of hot sand along the edge of Kussharo-ko, has too many souvenir stands, paddle boats and tourist-trap kitsch to really be relaxing, but it's nonetheless quite popular.

Wakoto Onsen (Map p614) is special not for what it *has*, but for what it *doesn't*; it just doesn't get any simpler than this: a scalding hot pool in the middle of nowhere on the southern shore of a beautiful lake. Best reached by car or bicycle, Wakoto Onsen has none of the razzle-dazzle of most spa resorts. There's no electricity, no soap, no buckets, not even any doors on the bathhouse: you just strip, dip and enjoy. Not for everyone, but true *onsen* buffs will appreciate it. It has a view of the western side of Lake Kussharo and, in season, snow geese fly overhead as the sun slips behind the mountains. Not for the modest either, as it's a *konyoku* (mixed sex) bath and there's algae on the rocks, which makes getting in and out a slippery affair. If it's too hot when you stick a toe in, try moving further away (towards the lake, not the bathhouse) and you'll find it's a slightly cooler shade of scalding.

A **Museum of Ainu Folklore** (斜路コタンアイヌ民族資料館; ☎ 484-2128; admission ¥310; ☯ 9am-5pm mid-Apr–Oct) at Kussharo Kotan displays tools and crafts.

SLEEPING

Camping is an option, as there are seven camping grounds in the vicinity.

Wakoto-hantō Kohan Camping Ground (☎ 484-2350; tent sites ¥450, cabins ¥4500; ☯ mid-May–Oct) One of the nicest camping grounds, it also has Spartan cabins. Canoes and kayaks are available for hire. Accessible by bus from Mashū, Bihoro and Kawayu Onsen.

Mashū-ko Youth Hostel (☎ 482-3098; www.masyuko.co.jp; dm ¥3900; ☐) A handsome farmhouse south of Mashū-ko. Internet access available (30 minutes for ¥100). If you know you will arrive after 4pm, call ahead for a lift. Opening hours may vary in December.

Kussharo-Genya Youth Guesthouse (☎ 484-2609; www.gogogenya.com/intro/e-intro.htm; dm from ¥4700; ☯ Jan-Mar May-Oct; ☐) Fancier than the average hostel and surrounded by pretty farmland. Unlike many comparable places, here it's OK to pay by credit card.

Masuya (Trout Inn; ☎ 482-5489; dm incl 2 meals ¥5700; ☐) Toho network member. The owner loves trout fishing and is happy to talk shop with fellow flycasters. Call ahead to be collected from Mashū station.

Onsen Minshuku Nibushi-no-Sato (温泉民宿にぶしの里; ☎ 483-2294; www1.ocn.ne.jp/~kussie; r per person incl 2 meals ¥8550; wi-fi) Log-cabin feel and casual, with mountain bikes for hire and an indoor, lake-view, hot-springs bath.

Misono Hotel (御薗ホテル; ☎ 483-2511; www.misonohotel.com in Japanese; high/low season incl 2 meals ¥10,650/8550; ☐) Luxurious hot-spring baths, private facilities (bath, toilet and sink) and a choice of Western- or Japanese-style rooms. A free *ashiyu* outside marks the carpark.

EATING

Genpei (源平; ☎ 483-3338; 1-5-30 Kawayu Onsen; dishes ¥600-1000; ☯ dinner) Across from the tourist centre, this is an atmospheric *izakaya*: follow the aromas of *robatayaki* and *rāmen*. Yum!

Marukibune (丸木舟; ☎ 484-2644; dishes ¥400-1500; ☯ 11am-7.30pm) Next door to the Museum of Ainu Folklore in Kussharo Kotan. The 'white *rāmen*' (noodles in milk broth) is unique and fun. Gourmands looking for adventure will enjoy the sashimi of *parimono* (a local river fish): so fresh that the head arrives still moving. Ainu music performances (¥3000) are given on certain Saturday nights: be sure to call for a reservation as seating is limited.

Great Bear (グレートベア; ☎ 482-3830; breakfast ¥800, dinner ¥1000-1500) The 'de facto' hall of the Mashū-ko Youth Hostel. Serves a variety of food, including steaks and curry with rice, but make sure your dinner is ordered before 7pm.

GETTING THERE & AROUND

The JR Senmō main line runs north from Kawayu Onsen to Shiretoko-Shari (*kaisoku* ¥900, 53 minutes) and south to Kushiro (*kaisoku* ¥1790, 111 minutes) via Mashū station. Kawayu Onsen station is a 10-minute bus ride from the town centre (¥280) but the buses are infrequent, and while they are timed to meet most of the trains there is not much time to transfer. A soak in the *ashiyu* or a quick trip to the toilet may leave you with a long wait…or walk instead.

From Kawayu Onsen bus station there are up to three buses a day to Bihoro (¥1920, about 2½ hours). The Bihoro service runs via scenic Bihoro Pass, and some of these buses continue onward to the Memanbetsu Airport. These buses also pass Nibushi, Sunayu and Wakoto Onsen.

Between May and October a sightseeing bus service runs four times a day from Kawayu Onsen bus station via the main sights in the park to Akan Kohan (¥2100, 2¼ hours). It stops for sightseeing and picture taking (all the major places are covered). If you're low on time and don't mind a tour, this is a nice way to see the area.

Buses between Kawayu Onsen and Mashū station cost ¥1080. Direct buses between Mashū Onsen and Wakoto-hantō (¥880, 35 minutes) pass the turn-offs for the Trout Inn, Sussharo Genya Youth Guesthouse and the camping ground at Wakoto-hantō.

Between Mashū station and Akan Kohan is a particularly scenic stretch on Rte 241, with an outstanding lookout at Sokodai that overlooks the lakes Penketō and Panketō.

Cycling is a good way to get around – but check distances carefully before a lengthy ride. Mashū-ko is a steep climb…and a quick return. Bikes can be hired at the bus station, Kawayu Onsen JR station or at the petrol station down the street (two hours for ¥600).

Akan Kohan 阿寒湖畔
☎ 0154

Busy Akan Kohan has one of the largest Ainu *kotan* settlements in Hokkaidō and is a hot spot for anyone interested in the ancient culture. The resort area isn't scenic, but the walking tracks are a great getaway. The **tourist information office** (☎ 67-3200; 2-1-15 Akan-ko Onsen; ◷ 9am-6pm) has pamphlets about the park in English, including excellent alpine trail guides with contour maps of O-Akan-dake and Me-Akan-dake.

SIGHTS & ACTIVITIES

The Ainu village is on the western side of town, with woodcrafts, leatherwork and other handmade items on sale. At the top of the hill is the **Ainu Seikatsu Kinenkan** (イヌ生活記念館; Ainu Lifestyle Memorial Hall; ☎ 67-2727; admission ¥300; ◷ 10am-10pm May-Oct), but it's small – perhaps a disappointment if you've already seen other Ainu exhibitions elsewhere. **Onnechise** (オンネチセ; admission ¥1000) is next door and better value: Ainu dance performances take place six times a day in the high season. Shows are at 11am, 1pm, 3pm, 8pm, 9pm and 10pm from April to October, and at least once a day the rest of the year (there are only one or two shows at night during winter). The **Akan Forest & Lake Culture Museum** (森と湖の藝術館; ☎ 67-2001; admission ¥500; ◷ 10am-5pm May-Oct) has more Ainu displays and the friendly staff are happy to explain exhibits, run the slide show and offer you a cup of coffee.

Akan-ko is famous for *marimo (Cladophora aegagropila)*, spheres of algae that are both biologically interesting (it takes as much as 200 years for them to grow to the size of a baseball) and very *kawaii* (cute). Only growing in a few places in the world, Akan *marimo* became endangered after being designated a national treasure: suddenly, everyone in Japan wanted one. The building of a power plant (which lowered the lake level several inches) did not help the plight of these green benthic fuzzballs. The Ainu finally came to the rescue by starting the **Marimo Matsuri** (まりも祭り), held in mid-October, which returns *marimo* to Akan-ko, one by one. Their numbers are growing but they are sometimes affected by natural disasters: typhoons can push as much as 50% of them out of the lake. Luckily, locals quickly return them to the water as soon as the winds have subsided.

The **Akan Kohan Eco-Museum Centre** (阿寒湖畔エコミュージアムセンター; ☎ 67-4100; admission free; ◷ Wed-Mon) is a good way to see *marimo* up close without spending a bundle on the boat trip (☎ 67-2511; www.akankisen.com in Japanese; 1hr trip ¥1350); there is an option of a 45-minute or one-hour trip, but only the hour-long boat trips include 15 minutes of *marimo* viewing. The museum has well-maintained exhibits with lots of photographs, and a number of *marimo* in aquarium tanks. It also has hiking maps and displays about the local flora and fauna. The *bokke* (bubbling clay pools) walk makes a shaded, breezy loop out to the lake and back through some pine forest, with views of obliging tufted-eared squirrels, chipmunks and birds.

Hiking

About 6km east of Akan Kohan is **O-Akan-dake** (雄阿寒岳; Male Mountain; 1371m). Buses to Kushiro pass the Takiguchi trail entrance five minutes out of Akan Kohan. The ascent takes a fairly arduous 3½ hours and the descent takes another 2½ hours. From the peak there are very fine views of the lakes Penketō and Panketō, and in summer the top is covered with alpine wildflowers. On clear days one can even see as far as Daisetsuzan National Park.

The highest mountain in the park, **Me-Akandake** (雌阿寒岳; Female Mountain; 1499m), is an active volcano and is often closed due to emissions of poisonous gas. Ask at the tourist information office about current conditions and pay careful attention to noxious effects of sulphur fumes as you hike.

The shorter climb to the observation platform on Hakutō-zan (650m) affords fine views of the lakes and the surrounding peaks. Starting at the Akan Kohan skiing ground 2km south of town, the ascent takes about an hour, winding through birch and fir forests and past several groups of bubbling sulphur hot springs (too hot to bathe in: don't try!).

SLEEPING

There are several small *minshuku* in the Akan Kohan area.

Nonaka Onsen Youth Hostel (Map p614; ☎ 0156-29-7454; Ashoro-chō Moashoro 159; dm ¥2910) Provides Japanese-style rooms, its own *onsen* and a base for climbing. Often booked in advance, so make reservations early.

Yamaguchi (山口; ☎ 67-2555; www.tabi-hokkaido .co.jp/~yamaguchi; 5-3-2 Akan Onsen; r per person incl 2 meals ¥5925) Clean and friendly with (yep, there's a theme here...) nice hot-spring baths with a high mineral content. Don't get confused and think the water's dirty; the colour comes from the minerals in the water itself. It's family run and one of the few places that's still quite reasonably priced. It has Japanese-style rooms and a fancier meal option (costs extra) is also offered.

Minshuku Kiri (民宿桐; ☎ 67-2755; www10.plala .or.jp/kiriminsyuku/in Japanese; 4-3-26 Akanko Onsen; r per person incl 2 meals ¥6500) Above a souvenir shop, opposite the Emerald Hotel. Famous for its hot-spring baths.

New Akan Hotel Shangri-la (ニュー阿寒ホテルシャングリラ; ☎ 67-2121; www.newakanhotel .co.jp/english/index.htm; d per person incl 2 meals ¥11,700) The luxurious multipooled baths here rotate genders daily (meaning what's used by men one day is used by women another, allowing guests who stay multiple nights a chance to see all the baths, despite the fact they're gender segregated), and it has both Japanese- and Western-style room options. A fake planetarium in the lobby – though impressive – is a bit over the top.

KUSHIRO SHITSUGEN NATIONAL PARK 釧路湿原国立公園

Japan's largest expanse of undeveloped marshland (269 sq km), this wetland is nearly the size of Tokyo and provides shelter for thousands of different species of wildlife. Among them is the *tanchō-zuru* (red-crested white cranes),

a traditional symbol of both longevity and Japan. They're also just plain cool, and several viewing areas let you watch these enormous birds in relative comfort as they land, feed, tend their young or do their mating dance. The peak crane season is winter to early spring, but even in August a few stragglers may be around if you're lucky. Binoculars are a must for any serious bird-watchers. If you're staying at the Kushiro Shitsugen Tōro Youth Hostel, you can use their spotting scope for free.

The park has a slow scenic train (with wood-finished cars) that runs along the eastern edge and provides good views of the marsh; the *futsū* train also follows the same tracks. Sit on the left for unhindered glimpses of the marsh.

Deer are so common in this area that the trains have a special *shika-bue* (deer whistle) to scare them off. To see even more wildlife, take a night train and stand in the front to look straight out at the tracks. You're sure to see deer; foxes are common and you could see other animals as well. It's an unorthodox but effective way to see wildlife and (usually) the beasts have the sense to stay off the tracks as the train passes by.

The park is best reached by train or car from Kushiro, the nearest large city, about 20 minutes away. You can take either a scenic train or a regular train to **Hosooka Observatory** (細岡展望台; ☎ 40-4455; admission free; ☉ 9am-7pm summer, 9am-5pm winter) on the eastern side, or a bus (¥660, 40 minutes) to the **Kushiro Observatory** (釧路湿原展望台; ☎ 56-2424; admission ¥360; ☉ 8.30am-6pm summer, 9am-5pm winter) on the west. The former is atop an overlook where one can appreciate the grand scale of this wetland preserve. Kushiro station also has an **information booth** (☎ 22-8294; ☉ 9am-noon & 1pm-5.30pm) and a **Postal ATM** (☉ 9am-7pm Mon-Fri, 9am-5pm Sat & Sun).

Sleeping & Eating

Kushiro has a number of inns, hotels, *minshuku* and ryokan. It is also the birthplace of *robatayaki* (meat or seafood slow-grilled over hot charcoal) and is the sister city of Burnaby, Canada.

The breakfast, served on the top floor of **Kushiro Royal Inn** (釧路ロイヤルイン; ☎ 31-2121; www.royalinn.jp; low season s/d internet booking ¥5000/7200; P ⊠ □), is wonderful. The rooms are what one expects in a business hotel, small but efficient, and it's (literally) a stone's throw from the station.

Redone and very spick-and-span, the comfortable, cosy **Kushiro Shitsugen Tōro Youth Hostel** (釧路湿原とうろユースホステル; ☎ 87-2510; www.sip.or.jp/~tohro/sub1.htm in Japanese; dm ¥3360) is more like a *minshuku*, and as such is a great deal. Meals are delicious and the bunk-style rooms are big enough for you not to feel cramped. A viewing deck and excellent train station access make it even more convenient, though it can be (infrequently) noisy due to its proximity to the tracks.

Kawamura (川村　かわむら; ☎ 22-5692; 12-1 Suehirochō; meals ¥1500-2500) is where salarymen come when they're sick of *izakayas* and want good Japanese cooking. It's packed after 6pm… for good reason: platters of specialities are set around the counter, easy to point at when something looks good. Sake is served the way it should be: overflowing into a *masu* (measuring cup made of *hinoki* wood). The mackerel-in-miso *(miso saba)* is superb. From the station, turn left and look for the small alley behind Tōkyū Inn (on your right). Follow the alley and turn left at the first intersection. Kawamura is on your right, just after you turn.

Just to the right of Kushiro station on the corner after Lawson convenience store, the impressive **Washō Market** (和商市場; ☎ 22-3226; www.washoichiba.com; 25-13 Kurokane-chō; items from ¥200; ⏰ 8am-6pm Mon-Sat) features every possible seafood one can imagine, plus a food court of *bentō* boxes and other prepared dishes. It's a great place to buy a rice bowl and add your own toppings as *o-bāsan* (grandmotherly women) hand out treats for you to try.

SHARI 斜里

☎ **0152 / pop 13,310**

Shari is the closest train stop to Shiretoko-hantō (an hour's ride away). Unless you miss the bus, you probably won't need to stay here, but the **tourist information office** (☎ 23-2424; 17 Minato-machi; ⏰ 10am-5pm mid-Apr–mid-Oct) near the train station can provide maps and book accommodation.

Koshimizu Gensei Kaen (小清水原生花園; ☎ 63-4187; admission free; ⏰ closed Nov-Apr) is an 8km stretch of wildflowers along the coast, only 20 minutes from Shiretoko Shari. Visit in late June to catch it at its peak: over 40 flowers simultaneously blooming.

If you need to spend the night, there a few options. The inexpensive **Kurione Rider House** (クリオネライダーハウス; ☎ 23-1889; tent & 1 person ¥1000) is about 25 minutes' walk from the station and has its own onsen. Bring your own bedding and expect things to be very casual. Another option that's right near the station is **Ryokan Tanakaya** (旅館たなかや; ☎ 23-3165; www.ryokan-tanakaya.com; r per person incl 2 meals from ¥7350). The **Shari Central Hotel** (斜里セントラルホテル; ☎ 23-2355; r per person from ¥5800) is well maintained, and credit cards are accepted.

Infrequent trains connect Shiretoko-Shari station with Abashiri (*futsū* ¥810, 45 minutes) and Kushiro (*kaisoku* ¥2730, 2½ hours). Shari's bus centre is to the left as you exit the station. There are between five and nine buses daily, all year round, to Utoro (¥1490), but only three in summer that continue on as far as Iwaobetsu (¥1770, 70 minutes).

SHIRETOKO NATIONAL PARK 知床国立公園

Shiretoko-Hantō, the peninsula that makes up Shiretoko National Park was known in Ainu as 'the end of the world', and it's aptly named. As remote as Japan gets, this magnificent park has no sealed roads within its boundaries save for a short northwest–southeast road that connects

ACCIDENTAL TOURISTS

As remote as they are, Hokkaidō's indigenous species have recently been facing threats from accidentally introduced non-native animals and plants. Up north, Shiretoko's native *tanuki* (raccoon dog) is now competing with the robust non-native racoon and, in the south lakes such as Tōya, introduced crayfish are taking over habitat that once belonged to native creatures.

Paradoxically, foreign visitors can often identify feral species more quickly than a Japanese tourist (many of whom haven't seen a lot of wildlife), so you can help by reporting to rangers any animals or plants that look just like the ones you see at home. A Shiretoko ranger said that Japanese people often misidentify a raccoon as a *tanuki* and don't bother to report it. If you're in doubt, look at the tracks – a raccoon has five toes on its front paws, the *tanuki* only has four.

Taking the time to rinse off your hiking boots and carefully check your hiking gear for stray seeds prior to a trip overseas can help minimise your own effects on the planet.

SHIRETOKO-HANTŌ

HOKKAIDŌ

p620) and foxes. The latter can be dangerous too, so don't take any chances: some have been known to steal food or sleeping bags. In addition, fox faeces have contaminated the water with the parasite echinococcus, which can be deadly. Don't drink any water that hasn't been properly purified.

Unfortunately, Iwaobetsu Onsen (岩尾別温泉) and Kamuiwakka-no-taki (カムイワッカの滝), a stunning *rotemburo* waterfall, are closed for five years for maintenance and restoration, but Shiretoko-go-ko (知床岬; Shiretoko Five Lakes) offers hiking with beautiful views of the ponds and mountains behind them.

Sleeping

Shiretoko Iwaobetsu Youth Hostel (☎ 24-2311; www.noah.ne.jp/shiretoko-ax/; dm ¥4300; ☺ Mar-Nov) is in Iwaobetsu, a small village within the park and is a good spot for those wanting to hike. It offers briefings on hikes and also has mountain bikes for hire, but is closed much of December and April, so call ahead. **Iwaobetsu Nature Lodge** (岩尾別ネイチャーロッジ; ☎ 24-2311; www.noah.ne.jp/shiretoko-ax/; dm ¥4300; ☺ Mar-Nov) is another option on the premises of the youth hostel. Things are casual, even shabby, but the chance to see wildlife is unparalleled. Bear, deer and fox are all regulars in the surrounding woods, and the staff know exactly when is the best time to see them.

Kinoshita-goya (木下小屋; ☎ 24-2824; dm ¥1575; ☺ Jun-Sep) is a mountain hut offering very basic accommodation right at the Rausu-dake trailhead. It is often booked solid, so call ahead.

Getting There & Around

Do yourself a favour and hire a car in Kushiro if at all possible, as public transport is scarce (and comparably expensive). From late April

the town of Utoro (on the northwestern edge) with Rausu (on the southern side); two-thirds of the park has no roads at all. The hiking tracks to Shiretoko-misaki (知床岬) are for expert hikers only: remote and poorly maintained, they wind over slippery boulders and disappear at times on cliff sides. If the weather turns frigid or you slip and break an ankle, you'll need to hope that a passing fishing boat spots you before the bears do. Hiking must be arranged in advance: there are steep fines for anyone caught hiking off limits or after hours.

Boat rides (☎ 24-2147; trips ¥6000) can be an option for those who want to see Cape Shiretoko but can't make the hike. It's expensive, but the 3¾-hour trip may be your only way to see the spectacular cliffs that Shiretoko is famous for. Otherwise, postcards will have to suffice.

The **Shiretoko Nature Centre** (☎ 24-2114; info@shiretoko.or.jp; slide show ¥500; ☺ 8am-5.40pm mid-Apr–mid-Oct, 9am-4pm mid-Oct–mid-Apr) has maps, info and a 20-minute slide show about the peninsula. So few people get here that humans haven't ruined it yet: hikers will see pristine forests, remote vistas without a sign of habitation and lots of wildlife, including bears (see

HOKKAIDŌ

WARNING: BEAR ACTIVITY

The peninsula, Shiretoko-hantō, is home to around 600 brown bears, one of the largest bear populations in Japan. Park pamphlets warn visitors that, once they enter Shiretoko National Park, they should assume that bears could appear at any time. Favourite bear haunts include Shiretoko-go-ko (知床岬; Shiretoko Five Lakes) and the falls Kamuiwakka-no-taki.

Hikers are strongly advised not to go into the forest in the early morning or at dusk, and to avoid hiking alone. Carrying a bell or some other noise-making device is also recommended (bears don't like surprises). If you're camping, tie up your food and do not bury your rubbish. Bear activity picks up noticeably during early autumn, when the creatures are actively foraging for food ahead of their winter hibernation. Visitors should be especially cautious at this time.

---

to October buses run four times daily from Utoro (¥900, 50 minutes) along the northern side of the peninsula, passing the nature centre, the youth hostel, Shiretoko Go-ko and Kamuiwakka-no-taki before terminating at Shiretoko-ōhashi. For the rest of the year, buses run only as far as the nature centre. From mid-June to mid-October there are also buses four times daily to Rausu via the dramatic Shiretoko-Toge pass (¥1310, 55 minutes). Overnight buses direct from Chitose or Sapporo to Utoro (¥8000, seven hours and 25 minutes) or other nearby cities.

The one-way journey to Shiretoko-ōhashi takes 50 minutes, including breaks for gawking at deer, foxes and possibly bears. A few buses a day continue on to Utoro.

RAUSU 羅臼
☎ 0153

This fishing village once grew wealthy on the herring industry, though there's not much here now other than a few very beautiful hikes. A challenging but well-marked track to Rausu-dake starts a few kilometres outside of town towards Shiretoko-Toge, near the (free) camping ground at **Kuma-no-yu Onsen** (熊の湯温泉) – yes, that's 'Bear's Boiled Water', you heard right!

Hiking out to the tip of the peninsula is no longer possible: you will be heavily fined if rangers catch you on the unmaintained track, which is often eroded beyond recognition.

From Rausu, head towards the tip and keep an eye out for a large overhang on the left, marked by a small carpark. Peek under the overhang at **phosphorescent moss**, which humbly glows a bright shade of green and is visible even in daylight.

There are not many reasons to stay overnight in Rausu, but right by the seaside the well-regarded ryokan **Marumi** (☎ 88-1313; www

.shiretoko-rausu.com in Japanese; r per person incl 2 meals ¥9300; 🖵) has Japanese rooms, lovely seafood meals, a *rotemburo* and sauna.

From mid-June to mid-October four buses a day (¥1310, 55 minutes) run between Utoro and Rausu via Shiretoko-Toge. From Rausu, buses run five times daily (¥4740, 3½ hours) all year round to Kushiro. Hiring a car and driving from Kushiro will save you a lot of time.

NEMURO 根室
☎ 0153 / pop 31,940

This tiny town's main attraction is its view of several islands, which (though a subject of heated debate) currently belong to Russia. It's the easternmost part of Japan, so those travellers who like to collect '-mosts' should be sure to come here. That said, there's not much else to do, and if the weather doesn't cooperate you end up looking at fog. On a clear day you get a view of some islands in the distance: the Hoppōryōdo islands are in dispute mainly because of their prime fishing grounds below the surface. English signage is limited, mainly plaques protesting the donation of these lands to Russia. Loudspeakers often blare from black trucks with *hi-no-maru* (the rising sun flags, discarded post-WWII) flags on them calling for the islands' return.

Sights & Activities

At the tip, Nosappumisaki, you will find a pricey souvenir shop, a **museum centre** (根室市観光物産センター; ☎ 28-2445; ⊗ 9am-5pm Mar-Oct, 9am-4pm Nov-Feb) with information in Japanese only, a **viewing tower** (ノサップ岬平和の塔; ☎ 28-3333; admission ¥900; ⊗ 8.30am-15 min after sunset) and a few restaurants.

The bus between Nemuro JR station and Nosappumisaki passes a number of interesting kelp-drying areas, which are self-explanatory if kelp is being dried: it looks like black strips of twisted leather stretched in rows on the ground; otherwise, these areas look like well-maintained gravel carparks.

To the south of Nemuro there are several pretty rock formations in what is by all measures a quite spectacular coastline. The **Wheel Rock** (車石) is the most famous. To get there take the (infrequent) train between Kushiro and Nemuro, getting off at the unmanned Hanasaki station. It's a 3km-walk to Hanasaki lighthouse and the rock is nearby.

Those on the train will only get a passing glimpse of it, but the estuary between Akkeshi and the mainland is a good place to see hawks, kites, herons and even sea eagles (which are easy to mistake for hawks until the two are together and you'll realise just how darn big they are!). A car makes stopping here for a picnic or picture a possibility.

Akkeshi, on the train route between Kushiro and Nemuro, is famous for oysters, seal watching and canoeing. Info about all three can be derived from **Akkeshi Mikaku Terminal Konkirie** (厚岸味覚ターミナルコンキリエ; ☎ 52-4139; www.conchiglie.net; 9am-9pm Tue-Sun Apr-Oct, 10am-9pm Tue-Sun Nov-Mar). Reserve three days in advance for the active sports.

Getting There & Around

Renting a car in Kushiro for a trip to Nemuro really makes sense and will allow more freedom for those who want to explore. The bus ride from the Nemuro JR station out to the Nosappumisaki is long (50 minutes) and comparatively expensive (one way/return ¥1040/1900). A discount coupon (buy it at the info centre *before* boarding the bus) knocks a few yen off the return price. It is timed to just barely meet the train, so make sure you don't dally at the station or you'll miss it. Buses leave Nosappumisaki about every two hours until 6.35pm.

TOKACHI 十勝

OBIHIRO 帯広
☎ 0155 / pop 171,600

Once an Ainu stronghold, Obihiro – a modern city squeezed in between the Hidaka and Daisetsuzan mountain ranges – was founded in 1883 by the Banseisha, a group of 'land reclaimers' (colonial settlers) from Shizuoka Prefecture. It's a friendly, laid-back city without much for tourists, but it makes a convenient back door to Daisetsuzan National Park; you may also find yourself passing through en route to Ikeda or Erimomisaki.

Tokachi Tourist Information (☎ 23-6403; 9am-7pm) is on the 2nd floor of the Esta shopping mall at the new Obihiro station. It can assist with various tourist-related issues and has a pamphlet for tourists with Obihiro info, including a *butadonburi* (see below) map.

Onsen buffs (or the very filthy) will enjoy a trip to Tokachikawa Onsen, about 20 minutes outside the city. It's a cluster of resort-style *onsens* and hotels along the Tokachi River. Most are open for day use, and some are quite snazzy. **Haniu-no-yado** (はにうの宿; ☎ 46-2225; www11.plala.or.jp/haniunoyado/no105.html; onsen bath ¥320; 2-9pm Mon, Tue, Fri & Sat, 10am-9pm Wed, Thu & Sun) is a middle-of-the-road option that's open until 9pm.

Obihiro has a number of restaurants and hotels around the station. As the city is less frequented by travellers, you should have an easier time booking accommodation. **Toipirka Kitaobihiro Youth Hostel** (トイピルカ北帯広ユースホステル; ☎ 30-4165; http://homepage1.nifty.com/TOIPIRKA/english/main_eng.htm; dm ¥4360) is an attractive log house with Western-style beds and nightly tea time. It's near Tokachigawa Onsen, so you'll need to take a bus there. Staff can pick you up at the station if you phone ahead.

Those who want a business hotel with reasonable rates and Japanese-style rooms should try **Hotel Musashi** (ホテル ムサシ; ☎ 25-1181; www.hotel-musashi.net in Japanese; s/tw ¥5091/8190;). From the bus/taxi/parking area in front of the station go diagonally to the right, heading for Mazda Rentacar (on the corner). With Mazda on your left, go parallel to the tracks for two blocks, turn right and look for Musashi on the right. Step outside the station and look up if you need other business hotels – just about every popular chain has an Obihiro location; almost all are within sight of the station.

Butadonburi (barbecued pork over rice) is an area speciality. If you're short on time, **Kikyō** (桔梗; ☎ 27-3771; dishes ¥750; 10am-10pm) is right in the station in Esta shopping mall and is a popular choice for salarymen and commuters. **Panchō** (ぱんちょう; ☎ 22-1974; dishes ¥850-1300) is across from the station, and *butadonburi* is all that's on the menu. Expect long queues during peak times.

HOKKAIDŌ

HOKKAIDŌ

Flights connect Obihiro with Tokyo, Osaka and Nagoya. Buses leaving from the front of Obihiro JR station are timed to meet most flights. *Tokkyū* trains run from Obihiro to New Chitose Airport (¥5900, 2 hours) and Sapporo (¥7020, 2½ hours). The JR Nemuro main line runs east to Ikeda (*kaisoku*, ¥440, 30 minutes) and Kushiro (*tokkyū* ¥4680, 1½ hours).

Buses leave in front of the station for Sapporo (¥3670, 4½ hours), Kushiro (¥2240, 2½ hours) and Asahikawa (¥3150, 3¾ hours). Those to Asahikawa go around Daisetsuzan to the north or to the west, passing either Sōunkyō Onsen or Furano/Biei, respectively. Local buses to Ikeda (¥590) take about an hour.

IKEDA 池田
☎ 015 / pop 8470

In the eastern Tokachi plain, Ikeda is a small farming town that became famous when the municipal government began making wine there in the 1960s. The name Tokachi is as synonymous with wine in Japan as Napa or Beaujolais is for Westerners, but oenophiles should decide for themselves whether to pull out a bottle of Ikeda when they have company. Judging by the giant corkscrew sculpture in the station, the folk here hope you will. Even if wine's not your thing, it's fun coming here just to stop someone on the street and ask, 'Can you tell me where Happiness is?' and have them answer (without batting an eyelash), 'Oh, just ahead on the right' (see below).

Town maps are available at the **tourist information desk** (☎ 572-2024; ☯ 10am-5pm Apr-Oct) inside the JR Ikeda station.

Wines are made at the **Wain-jō** (ワイン城; wine castle; ☎ 572-2467; www.tokachi-wine.com in Japanese; 83 Kiyomi, Ikeda-chō; admission free; ☯ factory tours 9am-5pm) on a hillside overlooking the town; head for the Ferris wheel. A tour guides you through the production process and there's a tasting afterwards. To get here head south along the train track from the station you will see the hill on your left shortly afterwards.

Happiness Dairy (ハッピネスデーリィ; ☎ 572-2001; http://happiness.presen.to/index.html in Japanese; 104-2 Kiyomi, Ikeda-chō; admission free; ☯ 9.30am-5.30pm Mon-Fri, 9.30am-6pm Sat & Sun & holidays in summer, 9.30am-5pm Mon-Fri, 9.30am-5.30pm Sat & Sun & holidays in winter) is a pleasant walk through wheat fields. It sells ice-cold gelato (¥250) and fresh cheese. From Wain-jō head east on Rte 39 about 200m, then

turn left at the T-junction, head 500m north and turn right at the cross section. Go 300m, and the shop is on your right. The brandy and rum-raisin flavour is to die for.

Moon Face Gallery & Cafe (画廊喫茶ムーンフェイス; ☎ 572-2198; 132 Kiyomi, Ikeda-chō; admission free; ☯ 10am-6pm Wed-Mon) displays works by local artists. **Spinner's Farm Tanaka** (スピナーズファーム・タナカ; ☎ 572-2848; in Japanese; admission free; ☯ 10am-6pm Apr-Oct, 10am-5.30pm Nov-Mar, closed 2nd Sat of each month) is an Ikeda wool-weaving workshop.

Friendly management and delicious dinners (¥1000, including a glass of wine) make **Ikeda Kita no Kotan Youth Hostel** (池田北のコタンユースホステル; ☎ 572-3666; www.11.plala.or.jp/kitanokotan/ in Japanese; dm incl meals ¥5620; ✗) a treat. You can hire a bike, but the hostel is within easy walking distance of the Toshibetsu station, one stop west of Ikeda (¥200). From the station take the main road south, turn left at the first intersection and the hostel is where the road ends. The entire place is nonsmoking.

Ikeda is 30 minutes by local train from Obihiro (¥440). Frequent buses run between Ikeda and Obihiro (¥590, 55 minutes). On the privately owned Furusato–Ginga Line there are four trains daily to Kitami (¥3410, 2½ to three hours), from where you can catch buses to Sōunkyō Onsen in Daisetsuzan National Park or take the JR Sekihoku main line east to Bihoro and Abashiri.

ERIMO MISAKI 襟裳岬
☎ 01466

This remote cape is far off the beaten path, but with its windswept cliffs and dramatic ocean vistas, and kelp strung up to dry like giant shoelaces, it's a good day trip for anyone with a car and a little extra time. The history of this unique place is something of an ecological miracle. Beginning in the Meiji era, the hills surrounding this kelp-farming community were gradually deforested, so by the 1950s it was nicknamed 'Erimo Desert'. Sand blew into the ocean, destroying the kelp, and the community faced a stark choice: reforest or leave. Thanks to the locals' perseverance and a vast number of seedlings, the hills now boast a Japanese black pine forest. Those same great offshore winds and Pacific swell make for spectacular surfing breaks for anyone daring enough to bring along a board and wetsuit, but check with locals about rips and safety before paddling out into the waves. Across from the deserted JR bus stop there's a small bluff that makes a good spot to take a snapshot of the fishing boats below. A lone post office and Postal ATM is near the city hall.

Ten minutes' drive further, at the cape itself, are a lighthouse and a wind museum, **Kaze-no-Yakata** (風の館 襟裳岬「風の館」; ☎ 3-1133; www9.ocn.ne.jp/~kaze/ in Japanese; 366-3 Tōyō, Erimo-chō; admission ¥500; ☒ 8.30am-6pm May-Sep, 9am-5pm Oct-Apr, closed Dec-Feb), with weather-related films and displays; you can also be blasted by gale-force winds inside a manmade wind tunnel. During calm seas, Kuril seals bask all year round on the rocks below, while nearby fishing boats harvest the kelp beds, which have finally returned. The seals are called *zenigata-azarashi* (money-shaped) because the white spots on their black bodies are reminiscent of old Japanese coins. You can pick out your own crab or conch and have it grilled at the restaurant-shacks beside the carpark. Bring a windbreaker: outside feels just as gusty as the wind tunnel does.

A 20-minute walk from the cape, **Minshuku Senba** (民宿仙庭; ☎ 3-1144; http://homepage2.nifty .com/erimorie/ in Japanese; 236-6 Erimo-misaki, Erimo-chō; dm from ¥2900; r per person from ¥3900) offers rustic accommodation and seafood dinners. Prices include two meals. **Minshuku Misaki-sō** (民宿 みさき荘; ☎ 3-1316; www.goodinns.com/misakiso/ in Japanese; Erimo-misaki Tōdaimoto, Erimo-chō; r per person ¥4200, incl breakfast ¥5250, incl 2 meals ¥6300-8400) is another homey option nearby. Prices vary according to choice of dishes. Credit cards not accepted.

There's also a **camping ground** (百人浜オートキャンプ場; ☎ 4-2168; camping per person ¥300; ☒ 20 Apr-20 Oct) on the beach at Hyakunin-hama, 8km northeast of the cape, right near the lighthouse.

Erimo Misaki is pretty darn remote and hiring a car or motorcycle would make sense for many travellers. Those without transport will have to make do with a lone daily bus from Sapporo (¥3500, four hours), which arrives at 8.15pm and leaves at 5.30am, or trains from Tomakomai to Samani (¥3150, 3½ hours, five daily) and take a bus from there (¥1300, one hour, five daily).

Shikoku 四国

For more than a millennium, *o-henrō* (pilgrims) have walked clockwise around Shikoku in the footsteps of the great Buddhist saint Kōbō Daishi (774–835), who achieved enlightenment on the island of his birth. Known as the '88 Sacred Temples of Shikoku', the 1400km journey is Japan's best known pilgrimage and oldest tourist trail, though much has changed in recent centuries.

Before the publication of the first guidebook in 1685, pilgrims frequently disappeared forever in Shikoku's rugged and mountainous interior. Before the advent of modern conveniences such as weather forecasts, mobile phones (cell phones) and convenience stores, pilgrims frequently fell ill and perished along the journey. Nowadays, hardship is not a factor as *o-henrō* buzz around the island in air-conditioned vehicles while giving little thought to the trials and tribulations of the past. In recent years, however, disenchantment with modern life has led to an increase in the number of Japanese who strike out on foot in search of meaning and self-realisation.

Like the rest of Japan, Shikoku is a land of contradictions – lightning-fast trains race alongside lumbering fishing boats while mountaintop shrines are lit up by walls of vending machines. More than other destinations, however, Shikoku is home to that elusive bit of lost Japan that seems virtually absent from the modern cityscape. Today, travellers can still hike age-old trails that bear the footprints of countless others who set out in that ever-elusive search for enlightenment.

HIGHLIGHTS

- Tread time-worn paths on a pilgrimage to the **88 Sacred Temples of Shikoku** (p630)
- Get off the beaten path in the stunning **Iya Valley** (p632), one of Japan's three 'Hidden Regions'
- Take a peaceful soak in the historic **Dōgo Onsen** (p649), located in the capital city of Matsuyama
- Trek up 1368 granite steps to pay homage at **Kompira-san** (p656) in the town of Kotohira
- Climb the sacred peak of **Ishizuchi-san** (p654), the highest mountain in western Japan
- Stroll through Takamatsu's exquisite Edo-period walking garden, **Ritsurin-kōen** (p658)

History

In Japan's feudal past, the island of Shikoku was divided into four regions – hence the name *shi* (four) and *koku* (region). The provinces of Awa, Tosa, Iyo and Sanuki became the modern-day prefectures of Tokushima-ken, Kōchi-ken, Ehime-ken and Kagawa-ken. The old names are still in common use in their prefectures.

Despite its geographical proximity to the historical centres of power of Osaka and Kyoto, Shikoku has always been considered somewhat remote throughout Japanese history. Getting there required a boat ride – until three bridge links to Honshū were built over the last couple of decades.

Shikoku is a rugged land. In the 12th century, defeated Heike warriors disappeared into the mountainous interiors to escape their Genji pursuers. Until very recently, the 88 Temples pilgrims returned from Shikoku with stories of extreme hardship that had to be overcome in their search for enlightenment.

It is natural that Shikoku's northern coast is more developed. The southern coast was cut off by the island's mountainous topography, ensuring that it lagged behind the northern coast in terms of development. As a result the people of Kōchi have historically been considered tough, hardy and independent.

Climate

Shikoku has amazing variations of climate for a small island. Summer can be stiflingly hot, while in winter the higher peaks are snow-capped. Typhoons regularly pound the Pacific coast from June until October. The village of Monobe in Kōchi-ken prefecture claims to have the highest rainfall levels in Japan, while the protected northern side of the island often suffers water shortages. The landscape of Kagawa-ken is pockmarked with *tame-ike* (water-collection ponds).

Getting There & Away

Before 1986 Shikoku was considered much more remote, with access being mainly by ferry. Today, however, there are a total of three bridge systems linking Shikoku with Honshū. Heading east to west, the Akashi Kaikyō–Ōhashi is west of Kōbe and leads to Tokushima (via Awaji-shima island). The Seto–Ōhashi bridge connects Okayama to Sakaide, which is west of Takamatsu. Finally, the Kurushima Kaikyō–Ōhashi island-hops along the Shimanami Hwy (Shimanami-kaidō) from Onomichi in Hiroshima-ken prefecture to Imabari in Ehime-ken.

As a result of the improved infrastructure, ferry services are on the decline, though Shikoku is still linked to a few major ports on Kyūshū and the San-yō coast of Honshū. However, most visitors arrive on the island either by train from Okayama or highway bus from Osaka, Kyoto and Tokyo. Air services also connect major cities in Shikoku with Tokyo, Osaka and other major centres.

Getting Around

This chapter's coverage follows the same order that most of Shikoku's visitors have used to travel around the island over the past 1000 years – in a circle starting in Tokushima and moving through Kōchi, Ehime and Kagawa prefectures. However, Shikoku's only train connection with Honshū is via the Seto-Ōhashi, so if you arrive by rail, your first prefecture will be Kagawa-ken (p655).

For more information on visiting the 88 Sacred Temples of Shikoku, see the boxed text (p630).

TOKUSHIMA-KEN 徳島県

Home to the first 23 of the 88 temples, the prefecture of Tokushima is known to *o-henro* as *Hosshin-no-dōjō*, the 'place to determine to achieve enlightenment'. The first 10 temples are more or less on an east–west line spanning about 25km on the north side of the Yoshino-gawa river valley. In the days of old, they were considered a mini-pilgrimage, and remain a worthy alternative if you don't intend to complete the full 88-temple circuit.

Noteworthy temples in Tokushima-ken include Temple 1, Ryōzen-ji (see p630), which is the pilgrimage's traditional starting point on the island of Shikoku. The walk from temples 11 to 12, which winds through the mountains of the Yoshino-gawa valley, has the reputation of being the steepest and hardest climb on the pilgrimage. Temple 19, Tatsue-ji, is a barrier temple – only those who are 'pure of intention' can pass.

Other notable attractions include the lively Awa-odori festival (Awa Dance Festival) in Tokushima, the mighty channel whirlpools of the Naruto Channel (Naruto-kaikyō), the pristine scenery of the Iya Valley and the surf beaches of the southern coast.

SHIKOKU

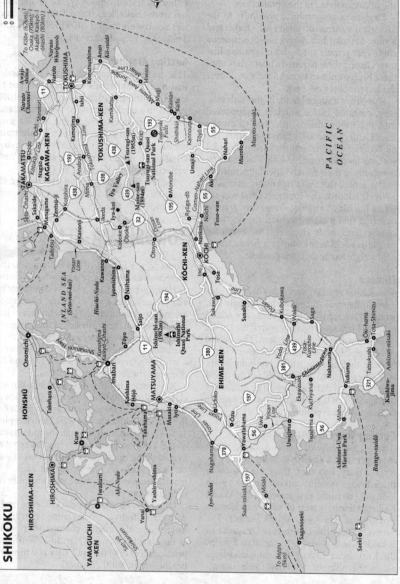
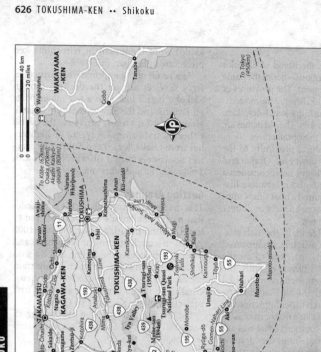

TOKUSHIMA 徳島

☎ 088 / pop 270,000

Flanked by forest-covered mountains and centred on a palm tree–lined promenade, the bustling modern city of Tokushima is best known for its annual Awa-odori festival in August. Tokushima also boasts a number of interesting attractions, and is a convenient base for exploring the nearby Naruto whirlpools. To most *o-henrō*, however, Tokushima serves as the gateway to the island, and as the jumping-off point for the first group of temples.

Orientation

Tokushima is defined by its two hills. The first, Shiroyama (城山), is dotted with castle ruins and is directly behind the train station. The second, Bizan (火山), is at the end of Shinmachibashi-dōri, which runs southwest from the station. The entertainment district and main shopping arcade are west of the river Shinmachi-gawa.

Information

The **tourist information office** (☎ 622-8556; ⏰ 9am-8pm), in a booth outside the JR Tokushima station, has English brochures and maps, and can help with booking accommodation.

The extremely helpful **Tokushima Prefecture International Exchange Association** (TOPIA; ☎ 656-3303; www.topia.ne.jp; ⏰ 10am-6pm) is on the 6th floor of the station building, and has an English-speaking staff that can also help you book accommodation. Internet access is available (¥50 for 10 minutes), and you can leave your bags here during the day.

There are coin lockers at the station, and the ATMs at the **post office** (1st fl, Sogō department store) accept international cards. **Kinokuniya Books** (8th fl, Sogō department store) has a smallish English-language books corner.

For more information, check out the useful website www.city.tokushima.tokushima.jp/english/index.html.

Sights & Activities

BIZAN 眉山

At the southwestern end of Shinmachibashi-dōri is the **Awa Odori Kaikan** (☎ 611-1611; 1-20 Banchi; admission free; ⏰ 9am-5pm, closed 2nd & 4th Wed of month), which features extensive exhibits relating to the local dance, namely the Awa-odori. There's also a modest municipal museum (admission ¥300) on the 3rd floor as well as a dance hall on the 2nd floor where

you can watch daily performances (day/night ¥500/700). From the 5th floor, a **ropeway** (cable car; ☎ 652-3617; one way/return ¥600/1000; ⏰ 9am-6.30pm, 9am-9pm Fri & Sat in summer) whizzes you to the 280m-high summit of Bizan for fine views over the city and sea. A combined ticket for all the attractions will cost you ¥1500.

At the top of the hill is a small park centred on a peace pagoda, which was erected in 1958 as a memorial to local soldiers who died in Burma (Myanmar) during WWII, and the **Wenceslão de Morães Museum** (☎ 623-5342; 1-26 Banchi; admission ¥200; ⏰ 9.30am-5pm, closed 2nd & 4th Wed each month). Morães was a Portuguese naval officer who lived in Japan from 1893 until his death in 1929, and is famous for his multi-volume study of the country. If the weather is nice, you can hike to the base of the hill along several paths in about 15 minutes.

AWA PUPPET THEATRE 人形浄瑠璃

For hundreds of years, *bunraku* (classic puppet theatre), known in the region as *ningyō jōruri*, thrived in the farming communities in and around Tokushima as a popular form of amusement (while the wealthy were entertained by the likes of kabuki – stylised theatre). Unfortunately, the region's puppet theatres have all but vanished, though local puppet dramas can still be seen at the **Awa no Jūrobei Yashiki** (阿波十郎兵衛屋敷; ☎ 665-2202; 1-84 Honura; tickets ¥400; ⏰ 8.30am-7pm). This museum, 5km northeast of the JR Tokushima station, is the former residence of the samurai Jūrobei, whose tragic Edo-era life story forms the material for the drama *Keisei Awa no Naruto*. A section from this puppet drama is performed daily by local women, generally at 3pm. Inquire at the tourist information booth or TOPIA for details.

It's also worth visiting the **Awa Deko Ningyō Kaikan** (阿波木偶人形会館; Awa Puppet Hall; ☎ 665-5600; 1-84 Honura; admission ¥400; ⏰ 8.30am-5pm), next door to the museum, which features puppet displays and demonstrations of their manufacture and use.

To reach the museum, take a Naruto-bound bus from the JR Tokushima station to the Jūrobei Yashiki-mae bus stop (¥270, 15 minutes).

CHŪŌ-KŌEN 中央公園

Northeast of the train station on the slopes of Shiroyama is **Chūō-kōen** (☎ 621-5295; admission free), which houses the ruins of Tokushima-jō castle. Built in 1586 for the clan of Hachisuka

SHIKOKU

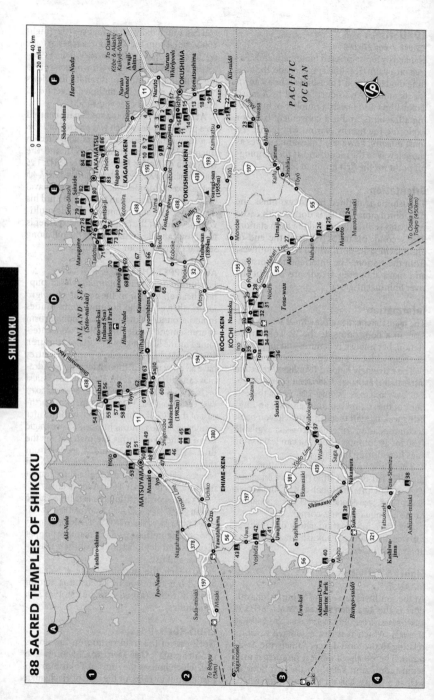

88 SACRED TEMPLES OF SHIKOKU

Iemasa, the castle was largely destroyed during the Meiji Restoration, though the remaining walls and moat provide an atmospheric backdrop to the gardens, bridges and walking trails in the park. If you're having problems imagining the former grandeur of the site, the **Tokushima Castle Museum** (☎ 656-2525; admission ¥300; ⏱ 9.30am-4.30pm Tue-Sun) has an impressive reconstruction of the castle as well as several informative exhibits. Just south of the ruins is the attractively landscaped **Senshūkaku-teien** (admission ¥50), an intimate garden that was laid out in the late 16th century.

ASTY TOKUSHIMA アスティ徳島

Located 4km southeast of the JR Tokushima station, this **exhibition hall** (☎ 624-5111; admission ¥910; ⏱ 9am-5pm) spotlights regional culture, particularly puppet drama and pottery. The highlight of the complex is the **Kōgei-mura** (工芸村; ☎ 624-5000; admission free; ⏱ 9.30am-5pm Wed-Mon) arts village where you can observe and participate in a variety of traditional arts and crafts including *aizome* (indigo dyeing), *washi* (paper-making) and pottery.

Direct buses run from the JR Tokushima station to ASTY (¥270, 15 minutes).

Festivals & Events

Tokushima plays host to one of the premier good-time events in Japan, the annual **Awa-odori festival** (阿波踊り; Awa Dance Festival), which is the largest and most famous 'bon' dance in Japan. Every night from 12 to 15 August, men, women and children don *yukata* (light cotton kimono) and take to the streets to dance to the samba-like rhythm of the theme song 'Yoshikono', accompanied by the sounds of *shamisen* (three-stringed guitars), *taiko* (drums) and *fue* (flutes). Dancing and the accompanying mayhem last into the wee hours of the morning! Plan early because accommodation is at a premium during the festival (more than a million people turn up each year!).

Sleeping

Sakura-sō (☎ 652-9575; fax 652-2220; 1-25 Terashima-honchō-higashi; s/d ¥3500/6000; P ⚹) The best budget option in town is conveniently located next to the tracks just three blocks east of the station, though you can expect an early wake-up call in the form of an express train. This humble *minshuku* (family-run budget accommodation) offers modest Japanese-style rooms

SHIKOKU

EXPLORING THE 88 SACRED TEMPLES OF SHIKOKU

During his lifetime, the great saint Kōbō Daishi was known as Kūkai, which translates to 'the sky and the sea'. Following his death, however, he was awarded his present name in honour of reaching enlightenment – *kōbō* means 'to spread widely the Buddhist teachings' while *daishi* means 'great teacher' or 'saint'. Although he was not the only person to receive the title of *daishi*, the Japanese have a saying that 'Kōbō stole the title of *daishi*', and when anyone talks of 'the *daishi*', everyone knows who is being referred to.

Kōbō Daishi founded the Shingon sect or 'Esoteric Buddhism', which is the only major sect that believes that enlightenment can be achieved in this lifetime. He is also credited with, among other things, putting together the first Chinese-Japanese dictionary, and creating *hiragana*, the system of syllabic writing that made it easier for Japanese to put their language into writing.

Kōbō Daishi is enshrined at the Kōya-san temple complex (see p417) in Wakayama-ken prefecture on the island of Honshū. It is a tradition that pilgrims start and end their journey at Kōya-san, asking for Kōbō Daishi's support and blessing for their upcoming journey, and thanking him for that support and their safety on their return. Pilgrims never walk alone: Kōbō Daishi is always by their side.

If you have the time and the inclination, the best way to see and experience Shikoku is to journey around the 88 Sacred Temples. Shikoku is a very special place, but a lot of people rush through and leave without really understanding what it has to offer. This is an opportunity to immerse yourself in Japan, and to experience something utterly unique. The pilgrimage is considered non-sectarian, and some pilgrims aren't even Buddhists – just people in search of themselves. With the right attitude, the pilgrimage is as big an adventure today as it was in the past.

Allow 30 to 60 days if walking (depending on your fitness), two weeks to a month on a bicycle, four to five days by motorised transport (though that would defeat the purpose of the visit). One point to remember: there are actually 89 temples. All pilgrims should travel back from Temple 88 to Temple 1 and complete the circle, for a circle is never-ending, just like the search for enlightenment.

If you're interested, all the gear you need is at Temple 1, Ryōzen-ji, which is located north of Tokushima (p627) in the city of Bandou (坂東). Frequent trains on the JR Kōtoku line connect Tokushima to Bandou (¥260, 20 minutes). Once arriving in Bandou, exit the station, cross over the railway tracks and continue straight for 100m until you reach the T-junction. Next, turn left and continue for 500m until you see the post office – now turn right and continue straight for another 200m until you reach the temple.

The temple has a shop where you can buy everything you need for the journey including maps and hiking guides as well as traditional walking sticks, prayer beads and religious trinkets. Like other temples along the circuit, Ryōzen-ji also has a **shukubō** (temple lodging; ☎ 088-689-1111; per person with meals ¥7000), which is an excellent opportunity to converse with other pilgrims while spending the night in peaceful surroundings.

For more information, pick up three English-language books: Oliver Statler's *Japanese Pilgrimage* is a classic academic work on the pilgrimage and its history; Ed Readicker-Henderson's *The Traveller's Guide to Japanese Pilgrimages* has information on each temple; and Craig McLachlan's *Tales of a Summer Henro* retells the adventures of a walking *gaijin henrō*.

And of course, always remember the words of Kōbō Daishi – 'Do not just walk in the footsteps of the men of old, seek what they sought'.

with shared bathrooms, and the friendly management will make you feel welcome.

Agnes Hotel Tokushima (☎ 626-2222; www.agneshotel.jp in Japanese; 1-28 Terashima-honchō-nishi; s/d ¥6500/13,000; P ⊗) This chic business hotel features spotless Western-style rooms with modern, minimalist design schemes. Three blocks west of the station, it's located above a chintzy European pastry shop that's perfect for a lazy breakfast.

Tokushima Tōkyū Inn (☎ 626-0109; www.tokyuhotels.co.jp/ja/TI/TI_TOKUS/plan/Tokyu_Hotels-t-tn_1147040315192.html in Japanese; 1-24 Motomachi; s/d from ¥7600/13,000; P ⊗) This reliable business hotel in the popular Tōkyū Inn chain is above the Sogō department store – convenient for all your impromptu shopping needs. Western-style rooms are small but functional, and the location really can't be beat.

Hotel Clement Tokushima (☎ 656-3111; www .hotelclement.co.jp/english.html; Terashima-honchō-nishi, 1-chōme; s/tw ¥11,000/14,000; P ⊠) Part of the new redeveloped JR Tokushima station complex, the Hotel Clement boasts 18 floors and 250 comfortable, spacious Western-style rooms, and proudly upholds its status as the top hotel in town. Although it's more expensive than other business hotels, your extra yen gets you a whole smattering of amenities including a top-notch spa and restaurant floor.

Eating

There is an expansive delicatessen area in the basement of Clement Plaza (inside the JR Tokushima station) as well as a variety of eateries on the 5th floor.

The following listings can be easily identified by their English signs.

Nakasu Ichiba (☎ 652-4569; ⏱ 5am-6pm Mon-Sat) This open-air market started out as Tokushima's fish stalls, but now offers an incredible variety of local food products for sale. A lively spot with the cheapest and freshest food in town, Nakasu Ichiba is about 1km southeast of JR Tokushima station alongside the Shinmachi river.

Masala (☎ 654-7122; Terashima-honchō-nishi, 1-chōme; ⏱ 7am-10pm; V ; E) On the 5th floor of the Clement Plaza, this Indian restaurant is an excellent choice for the Japanese language–wary traveller. English menus and an English-speaking staff make ordering a cinch, and there are a good variety of curries (from ¥800) on offer to please vegetarian and carnivorous patrons alike.

Shangri-La (☎ 626-0528; 1-24 Motomachi; ⏱ 7am-10pm; E) On the 1st floor of the Tokushima Tōkyū Inn building, Pan Asian–influenced Shangri-La has a popular buffet lunch (¥1000) as well as an excellent evening offer

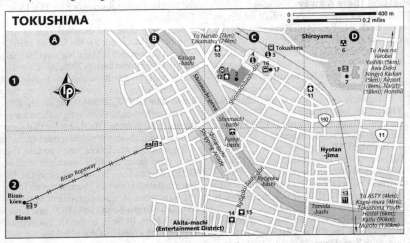

TOKUSHIMA

0 — 400 m
0 — 0.2 miles

SHIKOKU

INFORMATION		
Kinokuniya Books 紀伊国屋	(see 2)	
Post Office 中央郵便局	**1**	C1
Sogō Department Store		
そごう百貨店	**2**	C1
Tokushima Prefecture International		
Exchange Association		
徳島県国際交流センター	**3**	C1
Tourist Information Office		
駅前観光案内所	**4**	C1

SIGHTS & ACTIVITIES		
Awa Odori Kaikan		
阿波踊り会館	**5**	B2
Chūō-kōen 中央公園	**6**	D1

Senshūkaku-teien		
千秋閣庭園	**7**	D1
Tokushima Castle Museum		
徳島城博物館	**8**	D1
Wenceslão de Moraes Museum		
モラエス記念館	**9**	A2

SLEEPING		
Agnes Hotel Tokushima		
アグネスホテル徳島	**10**	C1
Hotel Clement Tokushima		
ホテルクレメント徳島	(see 3)	
Sakura-sō さくら荘	**11**	D1
Tokushima Tōkyū Inn		
徳島東急イン	**12**	C1

EATING		
Masala マサラ	(see 3)	
Nakasu Ichiba 中州市場	**13**	D2
Shangri-La シャングリラ	(see 12)	

DRINKING		
ACTY 21 アクテ 2	**14**	C2
Hung Loose ハングルース	**15**	C2
Roppongi 7 六本木7	(see 14)	

TRANSPORT		
Bus Terminal		
バスターミナル	**16**	C1
Rental Bicycles		
貸し自転車	**17**	C1

of *tabehōdai, nomihōdai* (all-you-can-eat and drink) for ¥3500/4000 per woman/man.

Drinking & Entertainment

Nightlife in Tokushima centres on the ACTY 21 building, which is an easily identifiable landmark in the Akita-machi entertainment district on the southwest side of the Shinmachi-gawa.

Hung Loose (☎ 623-3255; Tōjō Bldg 2F, 20-1 Ryōgokubashi; ⏰ 8pm-4am; E) On the opposite corner from ACTY 21 is this Hawaiian-style surfer bar, which serves margaritas and frozen cocktails (from ¥800) in a tropical setting complete with palm trees and deck chairs.

Roppongi 7 (☎ 652-7099; ACTY 21, Akitamachi, 1-chōme; cover charge ¥3000; ⏰ 8pm-4am Mon-Sat; E) Located on the 6F of the ACTY 21 building is this popular bar and discotheque, where locals get smashed and dance until the wee hours of the morning.

Getting There & Away

Tokushima's airport, 8km north of the city, is easily reached by bus (¥430, 25 minutes, hourly) from the front of the JR Tokushima station. There are direct flights to/from Tokyo (JAS/SKY, ¥23,950, 70 minutes, five daily), Nagoya (NAL, ¥16,000, one hour, two daily) and Fukuoka (JAC, ¥20,300, 85 minutes, two daily).

Tokushima is one hour from Takamatsu (¥1410), 2½ hours from Kōchi (¥3080) and 3½ hours from Matsuyama (¥4760) by the hourly *tokkyū* (limited express).

Overnight JR highway buses connect Tokushima with Tokyo (¥10,000) and Nagoya (¥6600), and there are frequent buses each day to/from Osaka (¥3600, 2½ hours) and Kyoto (¥4100, three hours). Note that the JR Pass is not valid for these connections.

Ferry services have all but disappeared, though there are still regular daily connections with **Nankai Ferry** (☎ 0120-732-156) between Tokushima and Wakayama (¥2400, about two hours). Ferries depart/arrive at Okinosu port, 3km east of the town centre, and can be reached by bus (¥240, 10 minutes, hourly) from the front of the JR Tokushima station. From Tokyo is the long-distance **Ocean Tōkyū Ferry** (☎ 5128-0109) going to Tokushima (¥9000, 18 hours).

Getting Around

It's easy to get around Tokushima on foot – it's only about 700m from the JR Tokushima station to the Bizan cable-car station. If you're looking to be a little more mobile, however, **free rental bicycles** (☎ 622-8556; deposit ¥3000; ⏰ 9am-4.30pm) are available from the underground bike-parking area to your left as you leave the station.

AROUND TOKUSHIMA

Naruto Whirlpools 鳴門のうず潮

At the change of tide, sea water whisks through the narrow Naruto Channel (which separates Shikoku from Awaji-shima island) with such velocity that ferocious **whirlpools** are created. The *naruto-no-uzu-shio* are one of the region's most famous attractions, though unfortunately they're not as easy to see as the tourist literature would have you believe.

In addition to knowing the tidal schedule, it also helps if you can time your visit to coincide with the full moon, which is when the whirlpools reach their peak intensity. To save yourself any disappointment, consult with the tourist information office or TOPIA in Tokushima.

For an up-close and personal view of the whirlpools (this is not for the faint of heart), you can venture out into the Naruto Channel on one of the **tourist boats** (¥2000, 30 minutes), which depart from the waterfront in Naruto. For a bird's-eye view, you can hike along the **Uzu-no-michi** (渦の道; ☎ 088-683-6262; admission ¥500; ⏰ 9am-6pm Tue-Sun), a 450m-long walkway underneath the Naruto-Ōhashi bridge that puts you just 45m above the swirling maelstrom.

To visit the whirlpools, you can take the local train from the JR Tokushima station (¥350, 40 minutes, hourly), though the JR Naruto station is about a 15-minute walk from the waterfront. A more convenient option is to take a Naruto-bound bus (¥600, one hour, hourly) from in front of the JR Tokushima station to the Naruto-Ōhashi bridge.

IYA VALLEY 祖谷渓

The remote Iya Valley, one of Japan's three 'Hidden Regions', is a welcome escape from the hustle and bustle of urban Japan. With its houses perched high on hillsides and its air of isolation, Iya has been dubbed the 'Tibet of Japan'.

The earliest record of the valley describes a group of shamans fleeing persecution in Nara in the 9th century. Iya later became a refuge for defeated Heike warriors, fleeing the Genji clan in the 12th-century civil wars.

The steep mountain topography and Japan's deepest gorges have ensured that Iya remains a refuge to this day.

Along with its famed *kazura-bashi* (vine bridges) and emerald green rivers, Iya boasts some classic folk architecture, with traditional farmhouses nestled into the hills.

The Iya region is a nature and adventure-sports haven, with superb hiking around Tsu-rugi-san mountain, white-water rafting in the

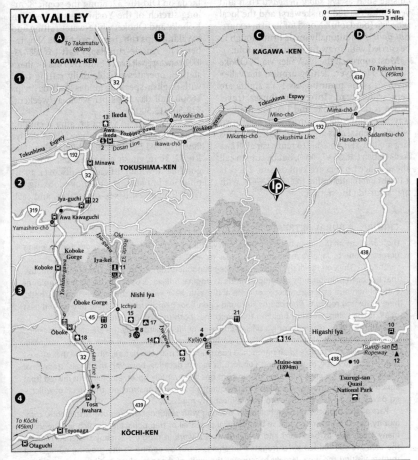

IYA VALLEY

SHIKOKU

stunning Ōboke and Koboke Gorges and great – if hilly – cycling opportunities. Worn-out travellers can reward themselves at the end of the day by soaking in top-notch *onsen* (mineral hot springs) and sampling Japanese mountain cuisine such as Iya *soba*, *dengaku* (fish and vegetables roasted on skewers) and the local *ishi-dofu* (hard tofu). Noted for its firm texture, *ishi-dofu* is traditionally made firm enough to be carried with straw tied around the tofu.

Most approach the Iya Valley via JR Ōboke station. However, getting around the valley involves some planning, as Iya's sights are very widespread. Infrequent buses travel between Ikeda, Ōboke and Iya, but the best way to explore the region is with your own wheels – rental cars are available in Shikoku's larger cities. It is possible to rent a car at **JR Awa Ikeda station** (☎ 0883-72-0809), but be sure to call ahead, since no cars are kept on site. There is a **tourist information office** (☎ 0883-72-7620) with maps outside the station.

Ōboke & Koboke 大歩危・小歩危

Ōboke literally means 'Great Danger Walking' (Koboke means 'Little Danger Walking'), and judging by the steep topography around here, it's no wonder why. South of Ikeda on Old Rte 32, along the scenic 8km-long stretch of the Yoshino-gawa between Koboke and Ōboke, white-water rafting and kayaking trips run from April to late November. The Aussie-run **Happy Raft** (☎ 0887-75-0500; www.happyraft.com), beside JR Tosa Iwahara station, operates reliable daily rafting trips with English-speaking guides (half-day trips ¥6500, full-day trips per weekday/weekend ¥12,500/13,500).

A great place to warm up after a chilling plunge down the Yoshino-gawa is at the **Iya Onsen** (☎ 0883-75-2311; ¥1500), which is along Old Rte 32. Here, guests can ride a self-propelled gondola down a cliff-side to discover a sulphurous but steamy *onsen* overlooking the river. The *onsen* is sex-segregated, and each

---

CHIIORI – A RURAL RETREAT

High on a mountainside in the remote Iya Valley, looking out over forested hillsides and plunging gorges, is one of Japan's most unusual places to visit.

Chiiori – 'The Cottage of the Flute' – is a once-abandoned 18th-century thatched-roof farmhouse that has been painstakingly restored towards its original brilliance. Unlike many such examples of cultural heritage in Japan, where concrete and plastic have wrecked the architectural aesthetic, here glistening red-pine floorboards surround open-floor hearths under soaring rafters. And best of all, it is a living, working building that welcomes both guests and volunteers.

Until the 1970s, residents of Iya preserved a way of life untainted by the effects of modernity. Set amid steep hillsides dotted by thatched houses and forests strewn with narrow mountain paths, Iya was an example of an untouched coexistence of man and nature, albeit one that offered residents little hope of wealth and comfort. In recent decades, however, the locals' traditional lifestyle and the balance with the environment has been rapidly upset; employment moved from agriculture to government-subsidised and frequently pointless construction, the effects of which – eg paved riverbeds – can be seen from almost any roadside.

Part of the project's mission has been working with residents to promote sustainable, community-based tourism and realise the financial potential of traditional life – which until recently many locals saw as backward and valueless. It is a work in progress – many thatched roofs in the area are still hidden by corrugated tin sheets – but by adding to the growing numbers of tourists visiting the area, largely because of the work of those involved in Chiiori, visiting here helps to encourage those conservation efforts.

Perhaps ironically given the Japanese tendency towards national pride, this place is the fruit of the work of two Americans. The house was bought as a ruin by the author and aesthete Alex Kerr in the early 1970s, and he went on to romanticise the Iya Valley – and feature Chiiori – in his award-winning book *Lost Japan*. Travel writer and photographer Mason Florence bought a half-share in the house in 1997, and managed the project until the middle of 2007.

Public transport is available to the bottom of the mountainside from the nearest train station, JR Ōboke – about 30km away – but buses are infrequent, and having your own vehicle is a better option. Chiiori itself can sometimes arrange pick-ups.

To learn more about the project log onto www.chiiori.org.

side has a small but extremely pleasurable hot spring-fed pool.

Just north of the *onsen* is the famous **Peeing Boy Statue**, which is placed at the same spot that passing motorists dare each other to stand for a rest stop. Standing on the highway barrier and peeing into the valley below may not seem dangerous at first, though you'll want to finish your business before the winds pick up!

Lapis Ōboke (☎ 0883-84-1489; admission ¥500), 1km north of JR Ōboke station, is a noteworthy geology museum featuring a fine collection of precious stones. It also serves as a tourist information centre.

An excellent Japanese-style budget-inn near JR Ōboke station is the riverside **Ku-Nel-Asob** (☎ 090-9778-7133; www.k-n-a.com; dm ¥2600; **P**). Accommodation is in simple but attractive communal tatami rooms, and the friendly English-speaking owners can provide free pick-ups/drop-offs at JR Ōboke station. A kitchen is available, and food can be bought at Bokemart, 30m from the train station. Since the house doesn't have a bath, a ride to the nearby Iya Onsen is offered for ¥500, including entry to the *onsen*.

Another good option is the **Awa Ikeda Youth Hostel** (☎ 0883-72-5277; dm ¥2850; **P**), which is part of the Mitsugon-ji mountain-temple complex in Ikeda. Rooms are a bit on the Spartan side, though the real appeal here is the ambience provided by the attached mountain-temple. Book ahead if you need a pick-up at JR Awa Ikeda station (6pm only). It's up a very steep mountain, so don't try to walk there.

Perched high above the river near JR Iya-guchi station, **Woody Rest** (☎ 0887-87-2211; lunch/dinner from ¥700/1000; ⏰ 11am-9pm; E) is a great place to sample the local specialities. The friendly, English-speaking couple can help you choose the perfect meal set, and they're also a great source of local travel information. Look for the English sign.

There is spectacular scenery in the deep canyons along Old Rte 32 – public buses (¥880, 55 minutes, three daily) between Ikeda and Iya Valley ply this narrow route. However, you can go at your own pace and really appreciate the beauty of the region if you have your own wheels.

Nishi Iya 西祖谷

Nishi Iya is popular for crossing the **Kazura-bashi** (¥500; ⏰ 9am-5pm) vine bridge. Rivers in Shikoku's mountainous interior were

once commonly spanned by these perilous catwalks, which could conveniently be cut down to prevent pursuing enemy clans from crossing. Nearby, **Biwa-no-taki** is an impressive, 50m-high waterfall.

Kazura-bashi Camping Village (☎ 090-1571-5258; tent sites ¥500 plus ¥200 per person, bungalows for up to 4-5 people from ¥5200; **P**) is an excellent camping ground 500m upriver from the vine bridge. The atmosphere is pleasant and rustic, and the basic facilities are well cared for.

If you're looking for more upscale accommodation, head no further than **Hotel Kazura-bashi** (☎ 0883-87-2171; www.kazurabashi.co.jp; per person with meals from ¥15,900; **P** ✂ 🖳), which is a few kilometres north of the bridge. Hotel Kazura-bashi offers minimalist Japanese-style rooms with terrific mountain views. The hilltop *onsen* here boasts equally terrific views, and is open to nonguests (¥1000). The *onsen* is sex-segregated, and is highlighted by its cliff-top *rotemburo* (open-air hot spring).

For great local chow, it's worth seeking out **Senkichi** (☎ 0883-87-2733; ⏰ 10.30am-5pm Fri-Wed Apr-Nov), on Rte 45, which serves home-made Iya *soba* for only ¥520. The stylish interior resembles a traditional Iya farmhouse. The exterior of the building is nondescript, though it's easy to spot if you look for the red waving flags advertising *soba*.

Higashi Iya 東祖谷

To escape the throngs of Japanese tourists at the vine bridge in Nishi Iya, head 30km east to the spectacular **Oku Iya Kazura-bashi** (¥500) in Higashi Iya. Set in a pristine natural environment, the secluded *fufu-bashi* (husband-and-wife vine bridges) hang side by side, high over the river gorge. Near the self-propelled, wooden cable-cart (a must-try!), there's a small public camping area.

The worthwhile **Higashi Iya Folk Museum** (☎ 0883-88-2286; admission ¥300; ⏰ 8.30am-5pm) is housed in the large red building in Kyōjo, and displays historic artefacts from the region.

Several kilometres up a narrow, winding road near Kyōjo, **Buke Yashiki** (☎ 0883-88-2893; admission ¥300; ⏰ 9am-5pm Wed-Mon) is an enormous thatched-roof samurai house–cum–museum commanding spectacular views of the valley. Beside the house is a pleasant Shintō shrine that is home to a massive cedar tree dating back more than 800 years.

Memme Juku (☎ 0883-88-2170; www.iya.jp/takumi /e.htm) is a nature- and field-studies school led by villagers who offer courses in Iya's traditional arts, crafts and customs. The school is in the village and tricky to find – either phone ahead or check the web for directions.

Mampu Lodge (☎ 0883-88-5001; cabins per person ¥4000; **P**) at Ryūgūgake-kōen park rents out comfy forest cabins complete with mini-kitchens. This is a great option for self-caters looking for a quiet, rural escape.

our pick **Iyashi no Onsen-kyo** (☎ 0883-88-2975; per person with meals ¥12,000; **P** **✕** **▣**) on Rte 438 is a beautiful hotel and hot-springs complex with some cutesy thatched-roof houses, a commendable restaurant serving local cuisine and an attractively designed *onsen* (¥800 for non-guests). The *onsen* is a large sex-segregated complex, designed with natural wood, which features a variety of indoor and outdoor baths and Jacuzzis.

At **Soba Dōjō** (☎ 0883-88-2577; ☷ 11am-9pm), also on Rte 438, you can sample a bowl of Iya *soba* (¥500) and even make your own (¥2500). From the road, look for the red waving flags advertising *soba*.

Tsurugi-san 剣山

This mountain's name translates to Sword Peak, although it is gently rounded rather than sharp-edged. At 1955m, Tsurugi-san is the second-highest mountain in Shikoku and provides excellent short and long hiking opportunities, as well as snowboarding in winter. A chairlift goes midway up, from which it is a leisurely 40-minute walk to the summit, but bona fide hikers start from **Ōtsurugi-jinja**, the shrine near the car park.

Information on the popular multi-day hike between Tsurugi-san and Muine-san (1894m), as well as mountaintop accommodation and other detailed regional hiking information, can be found in Lonely Planet's *Hiking in Japan*.

SOUTHERN TOKUSHIMA-KEN
徳島県南部

Tokushima's spectacular southern coastline is highlighted by its rocky scenery, near-empty beaches and picturesque fishing villages. In addition to the last temple in Tokushima, the region is also home to several of the island's best surf spots.

The JR Mugi line runs down the coast as far as Kaifu, just short of the border with Kōchi-ken prefecture. From Kaifu, the private Asa Kaigan railway runs two stops to Kannoura

in Kōchi-ken. There is a train line to Nahari from Kōchi city – but there is no train around Muroto-misaki. Kannoura is at the end of the line for train travel from Tokushima. You can continue by bus or thumb to the cape at Muroto-misaki and on to Kōchi city.

Hiwasa 日和佐
☎ 0884

If you're doing the pilgrimage, you'll be visiting **Yakuō-ji** (薬王寺), Temple 23 and the last temple in Tokushima. In this tiny fishing town, Yakuō-ji is a *yakuyoke-dera*, a temple specialising in warding off bad luck during unlucky years. Although there are a number of designated unlucky years, the unluckiest age for men is 42, while for women it is 33. The stairway up to the temple is split. The men's side has 42 steps, while the women's has 33. Pilgrims approach on the appropriate side and put a coin on each step – if you turn up at a busy time, the steps are virtually overflowing with money!

If you're hoping to rest those travel-worn bones, the town's best accommodation option is in Yakuō-ji's **shukubō** (☎ 77-1105; per person with meals ¥7000; **P** **✕**). Small but attractive Japanese-style tatami rooms are perfect for slowing down and contemplating the beauty of the temple complex.

If you have your own wheels, forget Rte 55 and take the spectacular **Minami-Awa Sun-line** (南阿波サンライン) coastal road, which runs south to Mugi. There is little traffic as the 18km road to Mugi snakes its way around the coast revealing spectacular views out to sea.

Kainan, Kaifu, Shishikui & Tōyō
海南 • 海部 • 宍喰 • 東洋

The next few towns are 'surf city' Japan – Kainan, Kaifu, Shishikui and Tōyō in neighbouring Kōchi-ken prefecture are where it's at in Shikoku for surfers. The coastline is spectacular, and there are superb beaches and colourful characters. National and international surfing contests are occasionally held in the area.

Each of the towns boasts sweeping yellow-sand and boulder stone beaches where you can carve a few waves, though it's best to inquire locally about specific surf spots. Be advised that the coastline is rocky in parts, and the waves and surge can really pick up in this region.

Visitors with wheels can head inland on Rte 193 from Kainan for about 25km to Shikoku's highest waterfall, the 55m-high **Todoroki Falls** (轟の滝), where there is good hiking in the surrounding area.

A 15-minute walk east of Kaifu station is the extremely enjoyable 4km-long **Atago-yama walking trail** (愛宕山遊歩道), which features sweeping views of the surrounding coastline.

At Shishikui Beach, take the hourly glass-bottomed boat cruise run by **Blue Marine** (ブルーマリン; ☎ 0884-76-3100; cruises per person ¥1800; ⏰ 9am-4pm Wed-Mon) to see the area's sea life.

A popular accommodation spot for surfers is the **Koku-minshuku-sha Mitoko-so** (国民宿舎みとこ荘; ☎ 0884-76-3510; fax 0884-76-3609; per person with meals ¥6500; P 🐕), a few kilometres southwest of Shishikui, out on the coast. It's a government-run lodging house with modest Japanese- and Western-style rooms, though the best features of the Mitoko-so are its great views and a big communal bath.

KŌCHI-KEN 高知県

The largest of Shikoku's four prefectures, Kōchi-ken spans the entire Pacific coastline from east of the cape at Muroto-misaki to west of the cape at Ashizuri-misaki. Historically known as the land of Tosa, the region was always considered wild and remote as it's cut off from the rest of Japan by a barrier of rugged mountains on one side and the Pacific Ocean on the other. To o-henrō, Kōchi-ken is known as *Shūgyō-no-dōjō* (the place of practice) and has a notorious reputation as the pilgrimage's testing ground.

Although the trip through Tosa makes up more than a third of the pilgrimage, only 16 of the 88 temples are located in the province. In fact, there are 84km between the last temple in Tokushima-ken at Hiwasa and the first temple in Kōchi-ken at Muroto-misaki. Furthermore, the distance from Temple 37 (Iwamoto-ji) in Kubokawa to Temple 38 (Kongōfuku-ji) at Ashizuri-misaki is 87km, the longest distance between temples on the pilgrimage. Since there are few places this remote in all Japan, o-henrō tend to breathe a sigh of relief after moving on to Ehime-ken prefecture.

Kōchi-ken is also regarded as an exquisite destination for outdoor lovers. Whether your passion is surfing, whale-watching, canoeing, rafting, hiking or camping, Kōchi-ken brims with scenic spots, especially along the Shi-manto-gawa, one of the last naturally flowing rivers in Japan.

TOKUSHIMA TO KŌCHI

If you've just come down the coast from Tokushima, you're literally at the end of the line at Kannoura as you pass into Kōchi-ken prefecture. This is the end of the train line, and if you want to carry on down to Muroto-misaki, you'll either have to take the bus or use your thumb. The good news is that the coast and its beaches and rocky headlands are about as scenic as they come.

The most popular spot along the coast for surfers is **Ikumi Beach** (郁美ビーチ), which also has free **camping**. If you're looking for slightly more comfortable accommodation, **Minami Kaze** (みなみかぜ; ☎ 0887-29-3638; per person ¥3000) is right on the beach at Ikumi, and is extremely popular with surfers. This basic *minshuku* has a collection of 10 simple Japanese-style rooms with shared toilets and showers. Meals and draught beer are also available.

Infrequent buses run to/from Kannoura from/to Muroto-misaki (¥1680, one hour) and Kōchi city (¥2950, 2½ hours). For the last 40km to the cape, the road hugs the coast, hemmed in by mountains on one side and the sea on the other.

Muroto-misaki 室戸岬
☎ 0887

One of Shikoku's two great capes that jut out into the Pacific, Muroto-misaki is famed in Japanese literature as one of the wildest spots in the nation, and as the doorway to the land of the dead. To pilgrims, it is the place where Kōbō Daishi achieved enlightenment. On a calm day, the Pacific is like a millpond; in bad weather Muroto is pounded by huge waves and buffeted by the wind. Visitors can explore Kōbō Daishi's bathing hole among the rock pools, or the cave where he once meditated.

A few kilometres northeast of the cape, a 5.5m-high white statue of the saint stares out to sea. Temple 24, **Hotsumisaki-ji** (最御崎寺; also known as Higashi-dera), sits on top of the hill directly above the point. The temple complex here has a basic **youth hostel** (☎ 23-0024; dm ¥3200) with threadbare Western-style dormitories. Meals and draught beer are available.

There are regular buses from Muroto to Kōchi station (¥3050, 2½ hours, seven daily).

A FOOD LOVER'S GUIDE TO SHIKOKU

Stretching from the ice-capped mountains of Hokkaidō to the subtropical islands of Okinawa, the Japanese archipelago is striking in its regional variation. With this incredible diversity of landscape, it should come as no surprise that each region of Japan boasts its own signature dishes and **meibutsu** (名物; local delicacies). Needless to say, the island of Shikoku is no different.

The island's most famous dish is **sanuki-udon** (さぬきうどん), a type of *udon* noodle that comes from Kagawa-ken (which was historically known as Sanuki), and is renowned for its silky texture and *al dente* firmness. According to legend, *udon* was first brought to Kagawa from China in the 9th century by Shikoku's most famous son, Kōbō Daishi (p630). Since the prefecture doesn't receive enough rainfall to enable full-scale rice production, Kagawa-ken relies heavily on wheat as a staple crop. In fact, it's estimated that *udon* consumption in Kagawa-ken is nearly seven times the national average. *Sanuki-udon* is traditionally served as **kake-udon** (かけうどん; noodles in hot soup), **zaru-udon** (ざるうどん; cold noodles with dipping sauce) and *kame-age* (釜揚げ; hot noodles with dipping sauce).

Another famous Shikoku delicacy is **iya-soba** (祖谷そば), a type of buckwheat noodle that comes from the Iya Valley in Tokushima-ken, and is renowned for its rough-hewn texture and rich flavour. Due to its cool, mountain climate, the region is perfectly suited for buckwheat production as opposed to rice. Iya-soba is best served as **zaru-soba** (ざるそば; cold noodles with dipping sauce), **kake-soba** (かけそば; noodles in hot soup) or as a complement to **iya-dofu** (祖谷豆腐; Iya tofu), a hard yet creamy variant of tofu.

In Tokushima-ken, the ferocious surge of the Naruto Whirlpools (p632) results in a special variant of **wakame** (わかめ; a type of seaweed) that is especially thick and textured. *Wakame* is typically harvested in the springtime, and is preserved according to traditional drying techniques that originated during the Edo period. After being laid out in the sun to dry, charcoal is sprinkled over the top, which facilitates the preservation process. In Shikoku, *wakame* features prominently in most soups and stocks, and is easily identified by its bright green colour.

The Naruto Whirlpools also have a pronounced effect on local fish, especially on the **tai** (鯛; sea bream), which is particularly lean and light in texture. In Shikoku, tai is usually served with **sudachi** (すだち; a small citrus fruit) and **sansho** (山椒; a tangy spice).

In Kōchi-ken, keep an eye out for **katsuo-no-tataki** (かつおのたたき), a famous dish of lightly charcoal-braised bonito that is left raw in the middle, served as sliced sashimi and usually accompanied by a light vinegar and soy sauce mix. The perfect follow-up to *katsuo-no-tataki* is its salted offal, which is called **shutō** (酒盗), or 'sake-theft', as it accompanies the drink so well that sake-less gastronomes are forced to turn to crime.

Finally, if you're travelling along the Shimanto-gawa, there's no shortage of unique local dishes including **tennen-ayu-no-shio-yaki** (天然鮎の塩焼き; salted and grilled wild sweetfish), **masu** (鱒; trout capriccio with capers and red peppers) and **magani** (まがに; boiled river crab).

Ryūga-dō 龍河洞
☎ 0887

Accessible by bus from Noichi station on the Gomen–Nahari line is the impressive limestone cave **Ryūga-dō** (☎ 53-2144; www.ryugadou.or.jp in Japanese; admission ¥1000; ⏱ 8.30am-5pm). Designated as a national natural monument, the cave has characteristic stalactites and stalagmites, and traces of prehistoric habitation. About 1km of the 4km of cave is toured in the standard visit. If you're into caves and book ahead, you can do the 'adventure course' (¥3000) and don overalls for a two-hour exploration of the cave's more inner reaches.

Ryūga-dō can also be reached by bus from Tosa-Yamada station (¥440, 20 minutes, hourly).

KŌCHI 高知
☎ 088 / pop 335,000

As the former capital of Tosa province, the castle town of Kōchi played a prominent role in the Meiji Restoration. Today, however, humble Kōchi is simply a prefectural capital, though there are a number of interesting sights in town, including its small but original castle. The city is also a good spot for resting your tired bones and indulging in modern conveniences before venturing out to the next set of temples.

Orientation

Kōchi city is centred on Harimayabashi-dōri, which runs from north to south and is serviced by a tramline. This street crosses the Obiyamachi shopping arcade near Hari-maya-bashi, a recently rebuilt replica of a historic bridge.

Information

The helpful **tourist information office** (☎ 882-7777; 9am-8pm), at the JR Kōchi station, provides English maps and brochures, and can help you book accommodation.

Also well worth visiting for local information, maps and friendly advice is the **Kōchi International Association** (KIA; ☎ 875-0022; www.kochi -f.co.jp/kia; 4-1-31 Honmachi; 8.30am-5.15pm Mon-Sat, closed Sat Aug), on the south side of the castle. It offers free internet access, a library, TV and English newspapers. Check out the association's website for information and events.

Coin lockers and a left-luggage office are in the station, while international ATMs are available at the post office next to the station.

Sights & Activities

KŌCHI-JŌ 高知城

Unlike other concrete reconstructions, Kōchi's **castle** (☎ 824-5701; admission ¥400; 9am-4.30pm) is the real thing. Building on the site dates back to the 14th century, though the original castle was built between 1601 and 1611, burnt down in 1727 and later rebuilt in 1753. By this time, however, the peaceful reign of the Tokugawa shōgunate was well established, and castles were scarcely necessary except as a symbol of a feudal lord's power. Therefore, the Kōchi lord rebuilt the castle with his *kaitokukan* (living quarters) on the ground floor, with doors opening into the garden. As a result, Kōchi-jō is a rather cosy little castle, and unlike those that were strongly fortified against enemy attack.

GODAISAN 五台山

Several kilometres east of the town centre on a stand-alone hill is **Godaisan-kōen** (五大山公園; dawn-dusk), which has excellent views over the city from its *tenbōdai* (viewpoint). At the top of the hill in the park is **Chikurin-ji** (竹林寺; ☎ 882-3085; admission to Treasure House & Gardens ¥400; 8.30am-5pm), Temple 31 on the

88 Sacred Temple Circuit, which has pleasant gardens, a five-storey pagoda and a small Treasure House. On the south side of the hill are the **Kōchi Prefectural Makino Botanical Gardens** (高知県立牧野植物園; ☎ 882-2601; admission ¥500; 9am-5pm Tue-Sun), which features more than 3000 different plant species. Frequent buses from the Harimaya-bashi bus terminal run directly to Godaisan (¥150, 10 minutes).

KATSURA-HAMA 桂浜

Katsura-hama is a popular **beach** located 13km south of central Kōchi at the point where Kōchi's harbour empties out into Tosa-wan. A five-minute walk west and up from the beach is the **Sakamoto Ryōma Memorial Museum** (高知県立坂本竜馬記念館; ☎ 841-0001; 8-30 Jōsan; admission ¥400; 9am-5pm), which tells the life story of this local hero in miniature dioramas. Although it was the progressive samurai class of Kagoshima and Hagi that played a major part in the dramatic events of the Meiji Restoration, the citizens of Kōchi claim it was their hometown hero Sakamoto who brought the two sides together. His assassination in Kyoto in 1867 at the age of 32 cemented his romantic yet tragic image, and he appears – looking distinctly sour – on countless postcards and other tourist memorabilia in Kōchi. In addition to the museum, there is an impressive **statue** of Sakamoto Ryōma by Katsura-hama beach. Frequent buses run from Kōchi station to Katsura-hama (¥610, 30 minutes).

SUNDAY MARKET 日曜市

If you're in Kōchi on a Sunday, don't miss the colourful **street market** (5am-6pm Sun Apr-Sep, 6am-5pm Sun Oct-Mar) along the road leading to the castle. The market, which has been going for some 300 years, has everything from fruit, vegetables and goldfish to antiques, knives and large garden stones.

Festivals

Kōchi's lively **Yosakoi-matsuri** (よさこい祭り) on 10 and 11 August perfectly complements Tokushima's Awa-odori festival (12 to 15 August; p629). There's a night-before event on 9 August and night-after effort on 12 August, but 10 and 11 August are the big days. Needless to say, a lot of alcohol disappears in the sweltering summer heat, and a lot of fun is had by all.

Recent festivals have attracted about 20,000 dancers in around 200 teams, including one

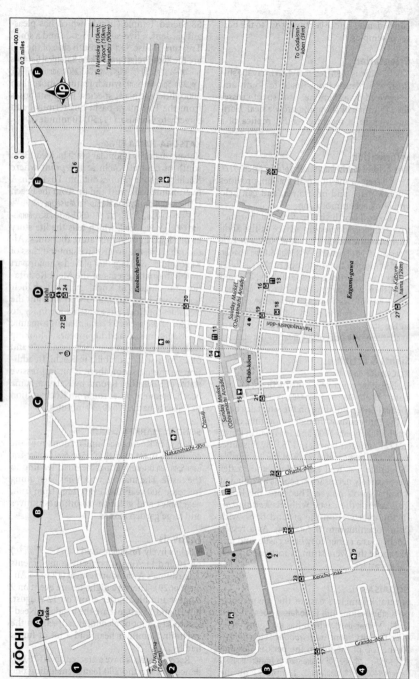

KŌCHI

team of foreigners. If you're keen to take part, contact the Kōchi International Association (p639), though it's best to get things sorted out early as accommodation is a nightmare to find on the day.

Sleeping

Big 1 (☎ 883-9603; www.big-1japan.co.jp in Japanese; 3-9-45 Kitahonmachi; per person ¥3700; P ✱ ✱ ✱) As hinted at by its English name, this men-only capsule hotel has no shortage of big capsules, though it's the attractive extras such as swimming pool, *onsen* and relaxation space that make the Big 1 a good choice. The hotel is conveniently located just 300m west of the station along the main road.

Tosa Bekkan (☎ 883-5685; fax 884-9523; 1-11-34 Sakura-chō; per person ¥4000; P ✱) The best deal in town is this homey *minshuku*, which is run by a warm family and features spacious Japanese-style rooms complete with en-suite facilities. If it's a particularly hot day, don't be surprised if the *obachan* (grandmother) offers you a frosty ice cream when you arrive! To reach the Tosa Bekkan, follow the train lines from the station and turn left when you see the English sign for the Green Hotel.

Hotel No 1 Kōchi (☎ 873-3333; www.hotelno1.jp/kochi in Japanese; 16-8 Nijōdai-chō; s/d ¥6000/8000; P ✱ ✱) Three blocks north of Hirome Ichiba (see right), this spick-and-span business hotel is within stumbling distance of Kōchi's entertainment quarter. Western-style rooms are a bit on the small side, though the rooftop *rotemburo* (open-air bath) is a nice touch.

Kōchi Palace Hotel (☎ 825-0100; www.kochipalace.co.jp in Japanese; 1-18 Nijūdai-machi; s/d ¥6500/8500; P ✱ ✱) Weighing in at 262 rooms, the Kōchi Palace Hotel is the largest in the prefecture. Although the Western-style rooms are your standard sterile business offering, there is an excellent smattering of on-site bars and restaurants. The hotel is two blocks west of the north–south tram line on the south side of the river, and is fairly easy to spot (it is the largest hotel in town!).

our pick **Sansuien** (☎ 822-0131; www.sansuien.co.jp in Japanese; 1-3-35 Takajō-machi; per person with meals from ¥15,000; P ✱) Three blocks south of the castle along Kencho-mae is this top-class ryokan, which is adjacent to a series of historic buildings on the grounds of the Kōchi *daimyō* (regional lord under the shōgun). Traditional Japanese-style rooms are refined and elegant, and guests also have free access to the attached gardens and private *onsen*.

Eating

Kōchi's top eating area is around the Obiyamachi shopping arcade, near the Harimayabashi junction, where the tram lines meet.

Hirome Ichiba (☎ 822-5287; 2-3-1 Obiyamachi; ✸ 8am-11pm) Even if it's not Sunday, this boisterous market just east of the castle (look for the English sign) is always a good choice for cheap eats and abundant drinks. Be on the look-out for *gomoku rāmen*, which is a nourishing mix of *rāmen* noodles and Kōchi's abundant fresh seafood.

Hakobe (☎ 822-5287; 1-2-5 Obiyamachi; ✸ 8am-11pm, closed Wed) At the eastern end of the Obiyamachi arcade, this hole-in-the-wall joint is a quick and easy way to fill up. The house special is *okonomiyake* (mixed pancake of egg, cheese, onions and meat; ¥500), which you cook yourself at the tabletop oven. If you're a bit of an aspiring chef, try to make your

SHIKOKU

meal look as nice as the plastic food models outside.

Tokugetsurō (☎ 882-0101; 1-17-3 Minami-harimaya-chō; from ¥5000; ☽ lunch & dinner) Open since 1870, this is the place to come to if you have a fat wallet and want to try immaculately presented *Tosa-ryōri* (local cuisine). Unfortunately, this can be a difficult place to visit if you don't read Japanese as the kanji-heavy menu changes daily, though you can always choose which *setto-cossu* (set course) you'd like based on the price. It's in a traditional building directly across from the Dentetsu Taminaru-biru Mae tram stop.

Drinking & Entertainment

Kōchi's entertainment area is also located around the Obiyamachi shopping arcade.

Tosa-no-izakaya Ippon-tsuri (☎ 825-3676; 1-5-5 Obi-yamachi; sake from ¥450; ☽ 7pm-midnight) In the middle of the Obiyamachi shopping arcade (look for the red lanterns outside), this popular *izakaya* (Japanese pub/eatery) features sake from each of the prefecture's 19 sake producers – make sure you know how to find your way home if you intend to try all of them.

Viva (☎ 823-6362; 1-1-11 Honmachi; drinks from ¥500; ☽ 6pm-1am Sun-Thu, 6pm-5am Fri-Sat; E) On the western edge of Chūō-kōen (look for the English sign) is this trendy dining bar, which has over 100 cocktails and beers on offer from all over the world. On weekends, Viva really gets kicking when the tables are pushed to the walls and the music is turned up.

Getting There & Away

Kōchi's airport, 10km east of the city, is easily reached by bus (¥700, 35 minutes, hourly) from the front of the JR Kōchi station. There are direct flights to/from Tokyo (ANA/JAS, ¥25,800, 1¼ hours, six daily), Nagoya (JAIR, ¥21,000, one hour, three daily), Osaka (ANK, ¥13,000, 40 minutes, six daily) and Fukuoka (JAC, ¥20,500, one hour, three daily).

Kōchi is on the JR Dosan line, and is connected to Takamatsu (¥4440, 2½ hours, hourly) via *tokkyū*. Trains also run westward to Uwajima (¥4340, three hours, hourly) where you can continue north to Matsuyama, though it's faster to travel by bus (¥3800, 2½ hours, hourly).

Tokkyu Ferry (☎ 622-1826) has regular ferry connections between Kōchi and Osaka (¥5000, nine hours, daily) and Kawasaki (¥11,500, 16 hours, weekly). Ferries depart/arrive at Kōchi

port, which is a few kilometres south of the town centre, and can be reached in 15 minutes by tram (see below).

Getting Around

Kōchi's colourful tram service (¥180 per trip) has been running since 1904, and consists of carriages from all over the world, including Germany, Norway and Portugal. There are two lines – the north–south line from the station intersects with the east–west tram route at the Harimayabashi junction. Pay when you get off, and ask for a *norikae-ken* (transfer ticket) if you have to change lines.

The tourist information office (p639) has free bicycles that visitors can use from 10am to 5pm, and overnight if they book accommodation in the city.

KŌCHI TO ASHIZURI-MISAKI

There are all sorts of interesting things going on between Kōchi and Ashizuri-misaki, particularly the closer you get to the cape. You can whale-watch, kayak and canoe on the last free-flowing river in Japan, while there's an exquisite beach at Ōki-hama and, at the cape itself, intriguing history and picturesque scenery.

The train line from Kōchi parts at Wakai. The JR Yodo line heads west through the mountains to Uwajima in Ehime-ken, while the Tosa-kuroshio line heads south to Nakamura, then west to Sukumo. There is also a regular bus service that goes to Ashizuri-misaki from Nakamura station (¥1970, one hour). You can continue around the cape and on to Sukumo and Uwajima by bus or thumb.

There are **whale-watching trips** (¥5000, three hours) on offer in Saga (☎ 55-3131) and Ōgata (☎ 43-1058) from spring to autumn, but you might want to call ahead to see if they are running.

The region's best accommodation option is the hard-to-get-to but often-raved-about **Shimanto-gawa Youth Hostel** (四万十川ユースホステル; ☎ 54-1352; www16.plala.or.jp/shimanto-yh in Japanese; dm ¥3150; P ☒). Accommodation is in basic Western-style dorms, though the hostel is the perfect destination for travellers who really want to get away from it all. The location is incredibly rustic and picturesque, and the hostel runs canoeing trips (¥5500 per person, including all tuition and gear). Meals and draught beer are available.

To reach the hostel, get off at Ekawasaki station, and take the bus to Kuchiyanai (¥850, 30 minutes). The youth hostel is 4.5km away across the river, but the manager will come and pick you up if you call and ask nicely.

Nakamura 中村

☎ 0880

Nakamura is a good place to organise trips on the beautiful **Shimanto-gawa** (四万十川), one of the last free-flowing rivers in Japan. Staff at the **tourist information office** (☎ 35-4171; ⏰ 10am-7pm) at Nakamura station can provide information on kayaking and canoe trips, camping and outdoor activities.

Dragonfly lovers will go bananas at the **Shimanto-gawa Gakuyūkan** (四万十川学遊館; ☎ 37-4111; admission ¥840; ⏰ 9am-5pm Tue-Sun) where over 3000 dragonflies from Japan and around the world are on display. There's a dragonfly park where living dragonflies cruise around, and a great display of fish from Shimanto-gawa.

About 40 minutes south of Nakamura on the bus to Ashizuri-misaki is **Ōki-hama** (大岐浜), a 2km-long stretch of sandy white beach backed by pine trees that is likely to have you blinking in disbelief and reaching for your swimming gear. It's possible to camp here, and although local surfers don't want to advertise it, it is an excellent surfing spot.

THE GENTLE JAPANESE ART OF ZAZEN (坐禅) *Melissa Wilson*

After sushi and Sony, perhaps one of Japan's most well-known contemporary exports is that of Zen Buddhism. However, Western associations of the word Zen – with minimalist interiors, water features and trays of sand with miniature rakes – have perhaps lost the *kokoro* (heart) of Zen somewhat. For example, at the heart of Zen Buddhism is the practice of *zazen* meditation, which focuses on deep breathing from the *hara* (abdomen) with the goal of emptying your mind of its 'outer layers' in search of enlightenment, or *satori*. Overwhelmed by the endless clutter of Japan, I set out on a pilgrimage in search of some spiritual calm.

In the early evening twilight surrounded by solemn forest, we entered a great wooden temple to the sound of chirping crickets. Having neatly stowed our shoes, we sat on cushions in tidy lines across the tatami matted floor of the hall. We began by bowing to the cushions and to one another, while the monk calmly struck two bells, the first a small chiming sound, and the second, a deeply resonant dong. Night fell outside; nearby temple buildings were bathed in deep turquoise light, stoic trees so still, the air cool. Only a gentle breeze permeated the hall, where the warm light and sandalwood incense was more than enough to put me in a meditative mood.

The monk was young, fresh faced and friendly. He wore a long elegantly cut kimono made of heavy blue fabric. His head was shaven; he wore no ornamentation, and he spoke freely while pacing the room, explaining the techniques we were to practise. Sitting in either the full lotus, half lotus or with legs crossed in front, we were to keep our spines relaxed but straight, heads level, eyes half closed. It is important not to fall asleep, but through concentration to empty your mind. In a foetal state of calm, I was blithely enjoying the sound of clearing of throats, the gentle padding of the monk's feet as he paced about the room, his robes rustling.

The first session began with three chimes and presently I was aware of a sharp *thwacking* sound. From the corner of my eye, my meditative emptiness was promptly displaced by an awareness that the monk was not only pacing the room wielding a long wooden stick, but also stopping now and then to beat practitioners on the back with it. 'That's not very Zen,' I thought to myself! Alarmed, I worried that I would be his next victim.

However, what they call 'punishment' is invited by the practitioner. With hands clasped, a small bow is followed by a submissive bow, at which point the monk delivers two hits to each shoulder. Although supposed to help focus the mind of the practitioner, I was surprised to see small children and old men alike, asking for it. All the while, the monk smiled calmly. Rather than my idea of Zen, this invoked associations with masochistic Japanese game shows. Although my Japanese friends assured me it did not hurt, I was nonetheless content to meditate without motivational aid!

Melissa Wilson is a freelance writer who focuses on comparative cultures and ritualistic traditions in Asia.

SHIKOKU

ASHIZURI-MISAKI 足摺岬
☎ 0880

Like Muroto-misaki, Ashizuri-misaki is a wild, picturesque promontory that is famous for its other-worldly appearance and violent weather. Ashizuri means 'foot stamping' – the cape got its name from the story of an old monk who stamped his foot in anguish when his young disciple set off looking for the promised land of Fudaraku in a boat. Fudaraku was believed to be the blessed realm of Kannon, goddess of mercy, and many set forth from the cape in their search for paradise in this lifetime, never to be heard from again. Centuries later, Ashizuri is famous for suicides, with stories such as that of a young geisha who danced off the edge onto the beckoning rocks below.

On the cape at Ashizuri-misaki, there is a large statue and a **museum** (ジャーンマン博物館; ☎ 88-1136; admission ¥300; ☑ 9am-4pm Fri-Wed) in honour of the locally born hero John Manjirō. Born in 1836 as Nakahama Manjirō, the young fisherman was swept onto the desolate shores of Tori-shima island, 600km off Tokyo Bay, in 1841. Five months later, he and his shipmates were rescued by a US whaler, and granted safe passage to Hawaii. After moving to Massachusetts and learning English, navigation and the ways of the West, 'John' returned to Japan to become one of the country's first true statesmen. Manjirō's intrepid journey is recounted in Masuji Ibuse's *Castaways*.

Ashizuri-misaki is also home to Temple 38 or **Kongōfuku-ji** (金剛福寺; ☎ 88-0038; ☑ 7am-5.30pm), which has breathtaking views of the promontory and the Pacific Ocean. If you want to linger in these desolate and lonely surroundings, nearby is the **Ashizuri Youth Hostel** (足摺ユースホステル; ☎ 88-0324; dm ¥3200; ℗ ☒), which has basic but well-cared-for Western-style dormitories. Meals and draught beer are available.

EHIME-KEN 愛媛県

Occupying the northwestern region of Shikoku, Ehime-ken is known to *o-henrō* as *Bodai-no-dōjō* (the place of attainment of wisdom) and has the largest number (27) of pilgrimage temples. Like Tosa, the southern part of the prefecture was always considered to be wild and remote, though *o-henrō* revel upon arrival in Shikoku's largest city, Mat-

suyama, as they know that the hard work of the pilgrimage has been done.

Perhaps the most famous temple in Ehime-ken is Temple 45, Iwaya-ji, which hangs high on a cliff-side above a valley floor. There are also large clusters of temples around Matsuyama and the Shimanami-kaidō bridge system, which links Shikoku to Honshū. However, perhaps more than other prefectures in Shikoku, Ehime-ken lures in travellers with its long list of noteworthy sights.

Prefectural highlights include the notorious sex shrine and museum in Uwajima, the immaculately preserved feudal castle and historic Dōgo Onsen in Matsuyama, and the sacred peak Ishizuchi-san (1982m), the tallest mountain in western Japan.

UWAJIMA 宇和島
☎ 0895 / pop 62,000

Were it not for its somewhat controversial sex shrine and museum, Uwajima would be just another rural town in Shikoku. Although there's not too much going on in town to hold your interest, a visit to Taga-jinja will definitely redefine your conceptions of Shintō shrines.

Information

The **tourist information office** (☎ 22-3934; ☑ 8.30am-5pm Mon-Fri, 9am-5pm Sat & Sun) is across the road from JR Uwajima station, and offers free internet access. The staff can also make accommodation bookings for you and will, of course, feign surprise when you ask the way to the sex museum.

There are coin lockers at the station and, for money, international ATMs at the post office, a few blocks west of the train station.

Sights & Activities
TAGA-JINJA & SEX MUSEUM 多賀神社
Once upon a time, numerous Shintō shrines had a strong connection to fertility rites, though this aspect was comprehensively purged when Puritanism was imported from the West following the Meiji Restoration. Nevertheless, a handful of these shrines including **Taga-jinja** survived, and today remain totally dedicated to sex. The grounds of Taga-jinja are home to tree-trunk phalluses and various other amusing statues and stone carvings, though the star attraction is the three-storey **sex museum** (☎ 22-3444; www1.quolia.com/dekoboko in Japanese; admission ¥800; ☑ 8am-5pm).

Inside, the museum is packed floor to ceiling with everything from explicit Peruvian pottery to Greek vases; from the illustrated Kamasutra to Tibetan Tantric sculptures; from South Pacific fertility gods to a showcase full of leather S&M gear; and from early Japanese *shunga* (explicit erotic prints) to their European Victorian equivalents, not to mention a healthy collection of modern porn magazines.

Watching the reactions of Japanese visitors here is almost as interesting as inspecting the intriguing exhibits. Even if you're sick to death of temples and shrines, this is one to put on the 'to visit' list. For a sneak preview, check out the website.

In case you're too embarrassed to ask for directions, fear not as the shrine is well signed (in English and Japanese), and is just across the bridge over the Suka-gawa.

UWAJIMA-JŌ 宇和島城

Dating from 1601, **Uwajima-jō** (☎ 22-2832; admission ¥200; 🕘 9am-4pm) is a small but interesting three-storey castle atop an 80m-high hillock in the middle of town. This castle once stood by the sea, and although land reclamation has moved the water well back, it still has good views over the town. Inside the castle grounds are photos of its restoration and of other castles in Japan and overseas. The surrounding park, **Shiroyama Kōen** (城山公園), is open from sunrise to sunset, and is a pleasant place for an afternoon stroll or relaxing picnic.

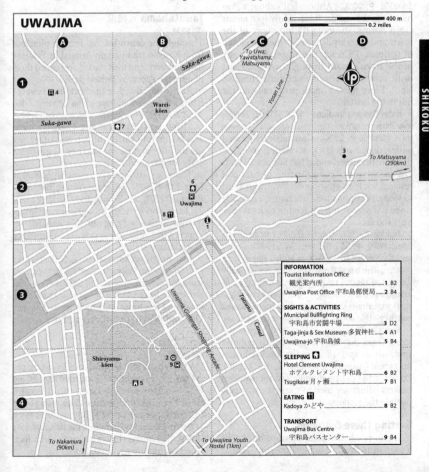

UWAJIMA

0 — 400 m
0 — 0.2 miles

To Uwa;
Yawatahama;
Matsuyama

Suka-gawa

Warei-kōen

Suka-gawa

Yosan Line

To Matsuyama
(290km)

Uwajima

Uwajima Gintengai Shopping Arcade

Tatsuno Canal

Shiroyama-kōen

To Nakamura
(90km)

To Uwajima Youth
Hostel (1km)

INFORMATION
Tourist Information Office
観光案内所 **1** B2
Uwajima Post Office 宇和島郵便局 **2** B4

SIGHTS & ACTIVITIES
Municipal Bullfighting Ring
宇和島市営闘牛場 **3** D2
Taga-jinja & Sex Museum 多賀神社 **4** A1
Uwajima-jō 宇和島城 **5** B4

SLEEPING 🛏
Hotel Clement Uwajima
ホテルクレメント宇和島 **6** B2
Tsugikase 月ヶ瀬 **7** B1

EATING 🍴
Kadoya かどや **8** B2

TRANSPORT
Uwajima Bus Centre
宇和島バスセンター **9** B4

SHIKOKU

BULLFIGHTS

Tōgyū is a sort of bovine sumō where one animal tries to shove the other out of the ring (actually, victory is achieved when one animal forces the other to its knees, or when one forces the other to turn and flee from the ring). Fights are held at Uwajima's **municipal bullfighting ring** (admission ¥3000), and you can sometimes hook up with a tour group that's paid for a special performance (see the tourist information office). Otherwise, fights are held on: 2 January, the first Sunday of April, 24 July, 14 August and the fourth Sunday of October.

Sleeping & Eating

Uwajima Youth Hostel (宇和島ユースホステル; ☎ 22-7177; www2.odn.ne.jp/~cfm91130 in Japanese; dm ¥3300; P ✕ ▣) Although it's about a 2km hike from the station, this friendly spot boasts clean dorms, stunning hilltop views of the town and a tranquil location near a clutch of temples. To reach the hostel, follow any of the town's main throughways southeast until you reach Uwatsuhiko-jinja (English sign). From here, a small path leads up the hill to the hostel.

Hotel Clement Uwajima (☎ 23-6111; fax 23-6666; www.shikoku.ne.jp/clement-uwajima/index.shtml in Japanese; s/d ¥6400/8400; P ✕ ▣) Conveniently located within the new JR Uwajima station complex, this newish business hotel has fair-sized Western rooms and a good offering of bars and restaurants. It's a great option if you only want to stop in Uwajima for a few hours, especially since it'll save you from having to haul your bags too far.

Tsukigase (☎ 22-4788; fax 22-4787; r per person with 2 meals ¥9500; P ✕) Between Warei-kōen park and the bridge to Taga-jinja is this family-run ryokan, which features a handful of traditionally decorated tatami rooms. Guests can take advantage of the stunning on-site *onsen* complete with mountain views, as well as the delicious country-style cooking of the welcoming hosts.

Kadoya (☎ 22-1543; ☽ 11am-9pm) Across the street from the train station is this popular spot, which specialises in the local delicacy, *tai-meshi* (steamed snapper with rice; ¥1600). Look for the plastic models and the wooden baskets (which are used to steam the snapper) outside the restaurant.

Getting There & Around

You can reach Uwajima by train on the JR Yosan line from Matsuyama via Uchiko (¥2030, three hours, hourly) and on the JR Yodan line from Kōchi via Kubokawa (¥3190, four hours, hourly). You can hire bicycles (¥100 per hour) from the tourist information office.

UWAJIMA TO MATSUYAMA

The stretch of Shikoku's western coast between Uwajima and Matsuyama is peppered with interesting towns such as Ōzu, with its newly reconstructed castle, and Uchiko, with its interesting old street, Yōkaichi. If you've come from points further south, you're back in the land of trains. From Uwajima, there's a choice of the JR Yodo line heading back to Kubokawa and Kōchi, or the JR Yosan line heading north to Matsuyama.

Yawatahama 八幡浜
☎ 0894

Through the centuries, 88-Temple pilgrims from Kyūshū traditionally arrived in Yawatahama by ferry, and then started and ended their pilgrimage at nearby **Meiseki-ji** (明石寺).

At the port, be sure to check out Yawatahama's fish market, **Dōya-ichiba** (どーや市場; ☎ 24-7147; ☽ 7-11am Sun-Fri), which is comprised of a lively set of 26 fish shops. There is a huge and fascinating variety of fish and other sea life on offer and up for sale here – get there early for the good stuff.

There are still ferry services with **Nankai Ferry** (☎ 0120-732-156) from Yawatahama to Beppu (¥1770, 2½ hours) and Usuki (¥1320, 2¼ hours) on Kyūshū, though they are infrequent and slowly dying out. Yawatahama-kō port is a five-minute bus ride (¥150) north of Yawatahama station.

Just north of Yawatahama, Sada-misaki extends about 50km towards Kyūshū, and from Misaki, near the end of the cape, car and passenger ferries (¥610 per person) make the crossing a few times daily to Saganoseki (near Oita and Beppu) in just over an hour.

Ōzu 大洲
☎ 0893

On the Yosan line northeast of Yawatahama is Ōzu, where traditional **cormorant river fishing** (うかい; *ukai*) takes place on the Hiji-kawa from 1 June to 20 September. **Sightseeing boats** (やかた船; yakata-bune; ☎ 24-2029; cruises per person ¥3000; ☽ 6.30-9pm Jun-Sep) follow the fishing boats down the river as the cormorants catch fish. Reservations are required.

Ōzu also boasts Japan's newest castle, **Ōzu-jō** (大洲城), which was recently reconstructed using as much of the original material as possible. At the time of research it was not open for inspection, though the castle makes an impressive sight above the river at the southern end of town.

The region's most popular accommodation option is the **Ōzu Kyōdokan Youth Hostel** (大洲郷土館ユースホステル; ☎ 24-2258; http://homepage3 .nifty.com/ozuyh; dm ¥3200; ℙ ✖), which has spick-and-span Western-style dorms and a friendly, communal atmosphere. The hostel is in the southwest part of town near the castle and adjacent to the Honmachi bus stop. Meals and draught beer are available.

Uchiko 内子
☎ 0893
During the late Edo and early Meiji periods, Uchiko was an important centre for the production of a vegetable wax known as *rō*, which has numerous industrial applications ranging from cosmetics to polishes. As the town began to prosper, wealthy *rō* merchants constructed a number of exquisite houses along Yōkaichi street, the majority of which are still standing today.

INFORMATION
There's a **tourist information booth** (☎ 43-1450; ◷ 9am-4pm Thu-Tue) on your right as you leave JR Uchiko station where you can pick up an English brochure/map on the town. If you're hauling your luggage, there are coin lockers at the station.

SIGHTS
Note that a combined ticket to Kama-Hagatei, Uchiko-za and the Museum of Commerce & Domestic Life costs ¥700 (a ¥200 saving).

Yōkaichi 八日市
Uchiko's picturesque main street, which extends for around 1km, has a number of interesting old buildings including houses, museums, souvenir stalls, craft shops and teahouses. Buildings on the street have cream-coloured plaster walls and 'wings' under the eaves that serve to prevent fire spreading from house to house. In recent years, residents have banded together to preserve the street, and to make sure that any renovations strictly comply with the traditional characteristics of the buildings.

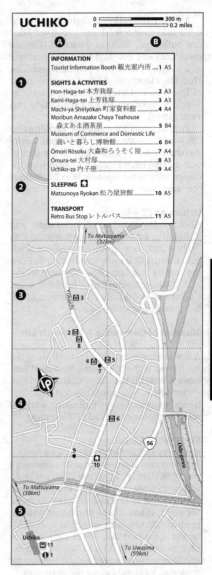

UCHIKO 0–300 m / 0–0.2 miles

INFORMATION
Tourist Information Booth 観光案内所 **1** A5

SIGHTS & ACTIVITIES
Hon-Haga-tei 本芳我邸 **2** A3
Kami-Haga-tei 上芳我邸 **3** A3
Machi-ya Shiriyōkan 町家資料館 **4** A4
Moribun Amazake Chaya Teahouse
　森文あま酒茶屋 **5** B4
Museum of Commerce and Domestic Life
　商いと暮らし博物館 **6** B4
Ōmori Rōsoku 大森和ろうそく屋 **7** A4
Ōmura-tei 大村邸 **8** A3
Uchiko-za 内子座 **9** A4

SLEEPING 🛏
Matsunoya Ryokan 松乃屋旅館 **10** A5

TRANSPORT
Retro Bus Stop レトロバス **11** A5

SHIKOKU

Opposite the Moribun Brewery at the end of the street is **Moribun Amazake Chaya Teahouse** (☎ 44-3057; ◷ 9am-5pm), where you can sample the local sake. A bit further up the street is **Ōmori Rōsoku** (☎ 43-0385; ◷ 9am-5pm Tue-Thu & Sat & Sun), Uchiko's remaining traditional candle maker, which has demonstrations of *rō* candle-making.

As the road makes a slight bend, there come into view several well-preserved Edo-era buildings, such as **Ōmura-tei** (Ōmura residence) and **Hon-Haga-tei**, a fine example of a wealthy merchant's private home. The Hon-Haga family established the production of fine wax in Uchiko, winning awards at World Expositions in Chicago (1893) and Paris (1900).

Further on is the exquisite **Kami-Haga-tei** (☎ 44-2771; admission ¥400; 9am-4.30pm), a wax merchant's house within a large complex of wax-making related buildings. Admission includes entry to the Japanese Wax Museum at the same location.

Uchiko-za 内子座

About halfway between the station and Yōkaichi is **Uchiko-za** (☎ 44-2840; admission ¥300; 9am-4.30pm), a magnificent traditional kabuki theatre. Originally constructed in 1915, the theatre was completely restored in the mid-1980s, complete with a revolving stage. Call ahead to find out if performances are being held during your visit.

Museum of Commerce & Domestic Life
商いと暮らし博物館

A few minutes' walk further north along the main road is the interesting **Museum of Commerce & Domestic Life** (☎ 44-5220; admission ¥200; 9am-4.30pm), which exhibits historical materials and wax figures portraying a typical merchant scene of the early 20th century.

SLEEPING & EATING

Matsunoya Ryokan (☎ 44-5000; www.dokidoki.ne.jp /home2/matunoya in Japanese; per person without/with 2 meals ¥8000/12,000; P) While Uchiko is probably best visited on a day trip, this traditional Japanese ryokan is a pleasant place to spend the night. It has a large number of well-appointed tatami rooms as well as a small attached restaurant that serves simple dishes such as *zaru-soba* (cold *soba*, ¥600) during the day. Matsunoya is located midway between the station and Yōkaichi along the main road.

GETTING THERE & AROUND

You can reach Uchiko by train on the JR Yosan line from Matsuyama (¥740, one hour, hourly). Yōkaichi is 1km walk north of Uchiko station, and is well signposted in English. Although it's a pleasant enough stroll, you might want to consider taking the **Retro Bus** (レトロバス; ☎ 43-1450; tickets ¥800; 9.30am-6pm), a 1920s English bus that seats nine and shuttles back and forth from the station. You can also rent bikes (¥500 for two hours, plus a ¥2000 deposit) from the tourist information office.

MATSUYAMA 松山
☎ 089 / pop 513,000

Shikoku's largest city is a bustling transport hub that boasts all the chic and flair of its sister cities on Honshū. However, Japanese and foreign tourists alike are principally drawn to Matsuyama for its famous sights, namely Matsuyama-jō, one of the country's finest feudal-era castles, and Dōgo Onsen Honkan (see boxed text, p649), a multi-level public bath house. If you're journeying around the 88 Sacred Temples, Matsuyama is home to seven temples, including Ishite-ji, one of the most famous stops on the pilgrimage. Matsuyama is also well set up for foreign visitors, easy to navigate via its historic tram system and home to two of the island's most enjoyable youth hostels.

Orientation

Most visitors arrive at the JR Matsuyama station, which is about 500m west of the castle's outer moat. From here, the city centre is immediately south, and is centred around the Matsuyama City station on the private Iyotetsudō line. Dōgo Onsen Honkan is 2km east of the city centre in the suburb of Dōgo, while the ferry port is north of Matsuyama in the city of Takahama.

Information

The main **tourist information office** (☎ 931-3914; 8.30am-8.30pm) is the JR Matsuyama station branch. The helpful staff can help you book accommodation and offer a good English brochure on the city. There is also an excellent **tourist information office** (☎ 921-3708; 8am-4.45pm) near the tram terminus for Dōgo Onsen as well as a small information counter at the ferry terminal (see p654 for information on hydrofoils).

Another good spot for infomation on the city is the **Ehime Prefectural International Centre** (EPIC; ☎ 943-6688; www.epic.or.jp; 8.30am-5pm Mon-Sat), which provides friendly advice, free internet access and English newspapers. EPIC is near the Minami-machi or Kenmin Bunkakaikan-mae tram stop. Although it is set back off the main road, it's easy to spot if you look for the giant red question mark.

AN INSIDER'S GUIDE TO DŌGO ONSEN 道後温泉

According to legend, Dōgo Onsen was discovered during the ancient age of gods when a white heron was found healing itself in the spring. Since then, Dōgo has featured prominently in a number of literary classics, and garnered a reputation for the curative properties of its waters. The mono-alkaline spring contains sulphur, and is believed to be particularly effective at treating rheumatism, neuralgia and hysteria.

The main building, **Dōgo Onsen Honkan** (道後温泉本館; ☎ 089-921-5141; 5-6 Dōgo-yunomachi; ⏰ 6am-11pm), was constructed in 1894, and designated as an important cultural site in 1994. The three-storey, castle-style building incorporates traditional design elements, and is crowned with a statue of a white heron in commemoration of its legendary origins. Although countless famous people have passed through its doors, Dōgo Onsen Honkan rose to popularity following its inclusion in the famous 1906 novel *Botchan,* which was authored by Sōseki Natsume, the greatest literary figure in Japan's modern age.

Even if you're well versed in the ins and outs of *onsen* culture, Dōgo can be a bit confusing as there are two separate baths (and four pricing options) to choose from. The larger, and more popular of the two baths, is the *kami-no-yu* (Water of the Gods), which is separated by sex and adorned with heron mosaics. A basic bath costs ¥300, while a bath followed by tea and *senbei* (rice crackers) in the 2nd-floor tatami room costs ¥620, and includes a rental *yukata* (light cotton kimono). A rental towel and soap will set you back a further ¥50. The smaller and more private of the two baths is the *tama-no-yu* (Water of the Spirits), which is also separated by sex and adorned with simple tiles. A bath followed by tea and *dango* (sweet dumplings) in the 2nd-floor tatami room costs ¥980, while the top price of ¥1240 allows you to enjoy your snack in a private tatami room on the 3rd floor. In case you're confused about which path to follow, Sōseki Natsume writes in *Botchan* that it's always wise to go 1st class.

Although there are English-language pamphlets on hand to clarify the correct sequence of steps, Dōgo Onsen can still be a bit intimidating if you don't speak Japanese. After paying your money outside, you should enter the building and leave your shoes in a locker. If you've paid ¥300, go to the *kami-no-yu* changing room (signposted in English) where you can use the free lockers for your clothing. If you've paid ¥620 or ¥980, first go upstairs to receive your *yukata,* and then return to either the *kami-no-yu* or *tama-no-yu* (also signposted in English) changing room. After your bath, you should don your *yukata* and retire to the 2nd-floor tatami room to sip your tea and gaze down on the bath-hoppers clip-clopping by in *geta* (traditional wooden sandals). If you've paid ¥1240, head directly to the 3rd floor where you will be escorted to your private tatami room. Here, you can change into your *yukata* before heading to the *tama-no-yu* changing room, and also return after your bath to sip tea in complete isolation.

Regardless of which path you choose, you are allowed to explore the building after taking your bath. On the 2nd floor, there is a small **exhibition room** that displays artefacts relating to the bath house including traditional wooden admission tickets. For an extra ¥210, you can also take a guided tour (in Japanese) of the private **imperial baths,** which were last used by the royal family in 1950, though they have been preserved for the public interest. On the 3rd floor, the corner tatami room (which was the favourite of Sōseki Natsume) has a small **display** (in Japanese) on the life of the celebrated author.

Dōgo Onsen is 2km east of the centre of Matsuyama, and can be reached by the regular tram service, which terminates at the start of the spa's shopping arcade. This arcade is lined with small restaurants and souvenir stores, and leads directly to the front of the Honkan.

Note that Dōgo can get quite crowded, especially on weekends and holidays, though dinner time is usually empty as most Japanese tourists will be dining in their respective inns. If you really want to escape the crowds, however, one minute on foot from the Honkan (through the shopping arcade) is **Tsubaki-no-yu** (椿の湯; admission ¥300; ⏰ 6am-11pm), which is Dōgo Onsen's hot-spring annexe, and is frequented primarily by locals. If you don't want a full bath, there are also nine free **ashi-yu** (足湯; foot baths) scattered around Dōgo Onsen where you can take off your socks and shoes and warm your feet. The most famous one is located in Hojoen Sq just opposite the station at the start of the arcade. Here, you can also check out the **Botchan Karakuri Clock** (坊ちゃんからくり時計), which was erected as part of Dōgo Onsen Honkan's centennial in 1994, and features figures that re-enact a scene from *Botchan* each hour from 8am to 10pm.

MATSUYAMA

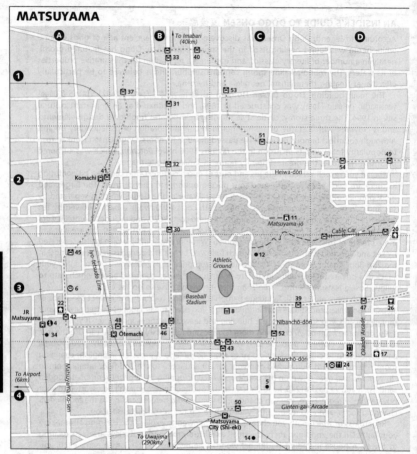

ATMs that accept international cards can be found at the central post office and at the post office a couple of minutes' walk north of JR Matsuyama station.

There are coin lockers and a left-luggage counter at JR Matsuyama, from where you can also hire bicycles (see p654).

English-language books can be found on the 4th floor of the **Kinokuniya bookshop** (☎ 932-0005; ☽ 10am-7.30pm), near Matsuyama City station.

Sights

MATSUYAMA-JŌ 松山城

Picturesquely sited atop a hill (Katsuyama) that virtually erupts in the centre of town, **Matsuyama-jō** (☎ 921-4873; admission ¥500; ☽ 9am-

5pm) is one of Japan's finest original surviving castles. However, it only squeaks by with the 'original' label as it was restored just before the end of the Edo period.

Although the original castle was built in 1602–03 with five storeys, it burnt down and was subsequently rebuilt in 1642 with only three storeys. In 1784, the castle burnt down once again after being struck by lightning. Surprisingly, the decision to rebuild the castle was not made until 1820, and it took another 34 years for the reconstruction to be completed! Between the years 1968 and 1986, the castle was completely restored to its present grandeur.

If the summer sun is particularly oppressive, you don't have to climb the steep hill up to the

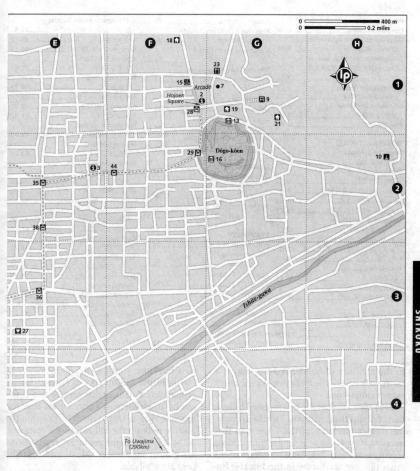

castle – a ropeway (¥160 return) will whisk you up the hill. However, there is a pleasant path to the top of the summit that starts from the ropeway building. Also consider walking down the back slopes of the castle hill to stroll around the **Ninomaru Shiseki Tei-en** (☎ 921-2000; admission ¥100; ☻ 9am-5pm) gardens, which were built in the outer citadel of the castle, and consist of various pools, gardens, rockeries and waterfalls. From here, it's a short wander to the **Ehime Museum of Art** (☎ 932-0010; 3-3 Ichibanmachi; admission ¥500; ☻ 9.40am-6pm Tue-Sun), which features rotating exhibitions of 20th-century Japanese art.

ISHITE-JI 石手時

About 2km east of Dōgo Onsen is **Ishite-ji**, number 51 of the 88 Sacred Temples, noted for

its Kamakura architecture. *Ishite* means 'stone hand', and is derived from a legend about a Matsuyama lord born with a stone in his hand. The temple has a three-storey pagoda, and is overlooked by a Buddha figure on the hill. It's said to be the second busiest of the 88 temples after Zentsū-ji (p655) in Kagawa-ken, which was Kōbō Daishi's boyhood home.

OTHER SIGHTS

Just south of Matsuyama City station in the temple grounds of Shoshu-ji is **Shiki-dō** (☎ 945-0400; admission ¥50; ☻ 8.30am-5pm), a replica of the humble house of the legendary haiku poet Shiki Masaoka (1867–1902).

Shiki Memorial Museum (☎ 931-5566; 1-30 Dōgo-kōen; admission ¥300; ☻ 9am-5pm Tue-Sun) is dedicated to the memory of Shiki Masaoka, and is a short walk east of the tram stop on the north side of Dōgo-kōen.

Dōgo-kōen (道後公園) is a forested hillock that contains the remains of Yuzuki-jō castle, the former residence of the Kōno clan that oversaw Iyo province in feudal times. More recent excavations here have revealed various relics that are on display in the **Yuzuki-jō Museum** (☎ 941-1480; admission free; ☒ 9am-5pm Tue-Sun) near the west entrance of the park.

Isaniwa-jinja (☎ 947-7447), 1km east of Dōgo Onsen Honkan, was built in 1667, and is the third-largest shrine of its kind in Japan. A national cultural treasure, the shrine was built to resemble Kyoto's Iwashimizu-Hachimangu.

Sleeping

Matsuyama has three accommodation areas: the JR Matsuyama station area, the city centre and the atmospheric Dōgo Onsen area.

BUDGET

our pick **Matsuyama Youth Hostel** (☎ 933-6366; www.matsuyama-yh.com/english/index.html; 22-3 Dōgo-himezuka-otsu; dm ¥3360; P ☒ ▣) Regularly top-

ping the Japan youth-hostel popularity poll, this beautiful hilltop spot is famous for its immaculate dorms, stellar service and communal atmosphere. It's also a great base for multiple visits to Dōgo Onsen as it's only a 10-minute walk up the hill east of the complex. Although you might get lucky, reservations are almost mandatory. Meals and draught beer are available.

Matsuyama Downtown Youth Hostel (☎ 986-8880; www.hihostels.com/dba/hostel032180.en.htm; 3-8-3 Ōkaitō; dm ¥3360; ☒ ▣) A good back-up option if the Matsuyama Youth Hostel is fully booked, this downtown spot has a funky vibe and spick-and-span dorm rooms to boot. It's also located smack-dab in the middle of the city, directly across from the ropeway leading to the castle. Although it's not as popular as its sister hostel, reservations are still a good idea. Meals and draught beer are available.

Check Inn Matsuyama (☎ 998-7000; www.check in.co.jp/matsuyama in Japanese; 2-7-3 Sanban-chō; s/d ¥5250/7750; P ☒ ▣) Although it's a self-proclaimed business hotel, the atmosphere at the Check Inn is anything but sterile and characterless. Modern rooms brim with swish

SHIKOKU

amenities including mini-fridges, hot pots and plasma TVs, and there is even a 10th-floor 'onsen-with-a-view' where you can scope out the cityscape. Located just one block east of the Ōkaidō throughway (look for the sparkling English sign), the Check Inn is convenient to the city centre action.

Terminal Hotel Matsuyama (☎ 947-5388; www .th-matsuyama.jp in Japanese; 9-1 Miyata-chō; s/d ¥5500/8000; **P** **⊠** **▣**) Virtually right outside JR Matsuyama station, the Terminal Hotel sure is convenient – even if it does lack personality. Standard-issue business rooms aren't anything special, but you can rest easy at night knowing that you won't have to carry your bags far in the morning. Note that 'special rates' here are often displayed on banners outside the building.

TOP END
Reservations at the following accommodation options are mandatory.

Funaya (☎ 947-0278; www.dogo-funaya.co.jp in Japanese; 1-33 Yunomachi; per person with meals from ¥20,000; **P** **⊠**) Next to the Shiki Memorial Museum, this ryokan has been in continual operation since 1626, and was one of Sōseki Natsume's favourite spots. Despite its simple exterior, Funaya is centred on an exquisite garden, and features elegant tatami rooms and a private *onsen* for guests.

ourpick Dōgo Kan (☎ 941-7777; www.dogokan.co .jp in Japanese; 7-26 Dōgo Takochō; per person with meals from ¥25,000; **P** **⊠**) Behind Tsubaki-no-yu, the Dōgo Kan hotel is worth the splurge if you're looking for world-class sophistication with a healthy smattering of opulence. Rooms of varying styles and influences are simply gorgeous, though the star attraction here is the private *onsen,* which consists of an elaborate series of indoor and outdoor baths.

Eating
The area around the Ginten-gai and Ōkaidō shopping arcades in central Matsuyama is teeming with interesting eating options.

Goshiki Sōmen Morikawa (☎ 933-3838; 5-4 Sanban-chō; meals ¥700-1500; ☽ 11am-8.30pm) Adjacent to the main post office is this Matsuyama institution, which specialises in *goshiki somen* (thin noodles of five different colours). This place is easily recognisable by the colourful plastic models in the window as well as the throngs of Japanese tourists snatching up sets of uncooked noodles (¥350) for their friends and family back home.

Kushihide Tori-ryōri-honten (☎ 921-1587; 3-2-8 Niban-chō; ☽ 4.30-11pm) Located down a side street adjacent to the Ōkaidō arcade (look for the chicken on the sign) is this speciality restaurant where you can feast on fresh and tasty free-range Ehime chicken dishes. Although there aren't any plastic models, the speciality of the house is the *tori sashimi* (raw chicken; ¥850). Check your hesitations at the door and dig in – it's delicious!

Dōgo Bakushukan (☎ 945-6866; 20-13 Dōgo-yunomachi; ☽ 11am-10pm) The Japanese love their mass-produced lagers, though beer drinkers with a more discerning palette know that you can't beat Dōgo Bakushukan's award-winning *korushu* (kolsch; ¥450). Alternate sips of sweet nectar with slivers of raw fish from the house *sashimi setto* (sashimi set; ¥1050) and you've got yourself a meal. Directly across from Dōgo Onsen, this spot is easily recognisable by the huge plastic beer mug outside.

Drinking & Entertainment
There's no shortage of bars and clubs in Matsuyama, though you'll find the greatest concentration of establishments in the city centre.

Dish & Bar After Glow (☎ 945-5453; 2-5-25 Ichiban-chō; glass of wine from ¥450; ☽ 5.30pm-3.30am; E) A few blocks east of the Ōkaidō tram stop (look for the English sign) is this excellent bistro, which boasts more than 200 varieties of wine from all over the world. Although it's tempting to choose some of the more familiar names, you can't go wrong with a chilled white from Yamanashi-ken.

Jett Rockbar (☎ 933-0001; 1-8-4 Niban-chō; drinks from ¥500; ☽ 5.30pm-4am; E) Needless to say, this basement bar specialises in rock 'n' roll, and there's a good chance that you can catch live music here on the weekends. Located next to the Washington Hotel, this place is easy to spot – just look for the English sign.

Getting There & Away
Matsuyama's airport, 6km west of the city, is easily reached by bus (¥330, 20 minutes, hourly) from the front of the JR Matsuyama station. There are direct flights to/from Tokyo (JAL/ANA, ¥28,600, 80 minutes, six daily), Nagoya (NAL, ¥16,400, 40 minutes, three daily), Osaka (ANA/JEX, ¥18,400, 50 minutes, four daily) and Fukuoka (JAL/JAC, ¥18,600, 55 minutes, four daily).

The JR Yosan line connects Matsuyama with Takamatsu (¥3400, 2½ hours, hourly), and there are also services across the Seto-Ōhashi to Okayama (¥3810, 2¾ hours, hourly) on Honshū. Trains also run southwest from Matsuyama to Uwajima and then east to Kōchi (¥5080, four hours).

There are also frequent JR Highway buses that run to/from Osaka (¥7800, seven hours) and Tokyo (¥12,200, 12 hours). Note that the JR Pass is not valid for these connections.

There are regular hydrofoil connections with **Super Jet** (☎ 575-1020) between Matsuyama and Hiroshima (¥6300, 1¼ hours, 15 daily). The Hiroshima to Matsuyama ferry (¥2500 to ¥2900, 2¾ hours, 10 daily) is also a popular way of getting to/from Shikoku. To reach Matsuyama port, take the Iyo-tetsudō private train line from Matsuyama City or Ōtemachi stations to the end of the line at Takahama (¥400, 25 minutes, hourly). From Takahama, a connecting bus (free) whisks you to the port.

Getting Around
Matsuyama has an excellent tram service costing a flat ¥150 (pay when you get off), though purchasing a day ticket for ¥300 is definitely your best option. There's a loop line and major terminus at Dōgo Onsen and outside Matsuyama City station. The Ōkaidō stop outside the Mitsukoshi department store is a good central stopping point.

Lines 1 and 2 are loop lines, running clockwise and anticlockwise around Katsuyama (the mountain the castle is on). Line 3 runs from Matsuyama City station to Dōgo Onsen, line 5 goes from JR Matsuyama station to Dōgo Onsen and line 6 from Kiya-chō to Dōgo Onsen.

If you're lucky with timing, you can ride the Botchan Ressha (坊ちゃん列車), the original small trains that were imported from Germany in 1887, and ran continuously for 67 years. They're back in use, and are named after Sōseki Natsume's famous novel.

For a more self-propelled option, the left-luggage counter at the JR Matsuyama station rents out **bicycles** (☎ 943-5002; per day ¥600; ☯ 8.50am-6pm Mon-Sat).

AROUND MATSUYAMA
There are a number of interesting day trips to be had from Matsuyama.

Kashima 鹿島
☎ 0899
Kashima is a pleasant little island popular with locals, and makes an easy day trip from

Matsuyama. It's so close that you could virtually swim there, but there is a return **ferry** (☎ 93-3010; ☯ 7am-9pm) for ¥300. The island has resident deer, an *onsen*, a nice beach, camping and several *minshuku* if you plan to stay overnight. Hourly trains from JR Matsuyama station reach Iyo-Hōjō station (¥240) in 20 minutes; from here it's a short walk to the ferry (fashioned with a plastic deer on top).

Saijo 西条
☎ 0897
Saijo is home to the **Asahi Brewery** (アサヒビール四国工場; ☎ 53-7770; ☯ 9.30am-3pm) where visitors can tour the factory and sample freshly brewed Super Dry for free. Call ahead as reservations are required.

The **Asahi beer garden** (アサヒビール園; ☎ 53-2277; ☯ 11am-9pm) next door has all-you-can-eat barbecued mutton, and beer. There are various *tabe-nomihōdai* (all-you-can-eat, all-you-can-drink) options, ranging in price from ¥3200 to ¥4000.

Saijō matsuri (西条祭り), the annual festival held from 14 to 17 October, is a rollicking affair that attracts visitors from all over Japan. About 80 teams push and pull *danjiri* (festival floats) and carry *mikoshi* (portable shrines) around town. For more information, check out www.city.saijo.ehime.jp/english/index.htm.

Hourly trains from JR Matsuyama station reach Iyo-Saijo station (¥240) in 20 minutes.

Ishizuchi-san 石鎚山
At 1982m, Ishizuchi-san is the highest peak in western Japan, and is considered by many to be a holy mountain. Ishizuchi attracts pilgrims and climbers alike, particularly during the July and August climbing season. During the winter (late December to late March), Ishizuchi also serves as a popular local ski slope.

To get to the Nishi-no-kawa cable-car station (on the northern side of the mountain), take the direct bus (¥990, 55 minutes, four daily) from Iyo-Saijo station.

You can climb up one way and down the other or make a complete circuit from Nishi-no-kawa to the summit, down to Tsuchi-goya and then back to Nishi-no-kawa. Allow all day and an early start for the circuit. For detailed information on hiking Ishizuchi-san mountain, snap up a copy of Lonely Planet's *Hiking in Japan*.

KAGAWA-KEN 香川県

Formerly known as Sanuki, Kagawa-ken is the smallest of Shikoku's four regions, and the second smallest of the country's 47 prefectures. To *o-henrō*, Kagawa-ken is known as *Nehan-no-dōjō* or 'the Place of Completion' as it has the last 22 of the 88 pilgrimage temples.

The region's hospitable weather and welcoming people have always been of great comfort to *henrō* as they complete their journey. However, if you're following the pilgrimage properly, remember that the journey is not complete when you get to Ōkubo-ji, Temple 88 – it's still a 40km journey back to Temple 1 in Tokushima to complete the circle.

Kagawa-ken also serves as the major arrival point on Shikoku since the only rail link with Honshū is via the Seto-Ōhashi bridge to Okayama. Highlights of the region include the celebrated shrine of Kompira-san at Kotohira, the beautiful gardens of Ritsurin-kōen at Takamatsu and the folk village of Shikoku-mura at Yashima.

MATSUYAMA TO TAKAMATSU

This stretch of country is home to a few noteworthy temples on the pilgrimage circuit including Kanonji, the boyhood home of Kōbō Daishi.

The JR Yosan line runs around the coast between Takamatsu and Matsuyama. At Tadotsu, the JR Dosan line splits off it and runs south to Zentsū-ji and Kotohira, through the Iya Valley (p632) and eventually to Kōchi (p638). Most trains for the Dosan line start in Takamatsu, can be joined in Tadotsu and end their journey at Kotohira; to continue south on the line will require a change of trains there.

Kanonji 観音寺
☎ 0875

If you've come from Ehime-ken on the pilgrimage or on the train, the first town of consequence in Kagawa-ken is Kanonji, noted for having two of the 88 temples in the same place: Temple 68, **Jinne-in** (神恵院) and Temple 69, **Kanon-ji** (観音寺). It's also known for **Zenigata** (銭形), a 350m-circumference outline of a square-holed coin dating from the 1600s. The coin's outline and four kanji characters are formed by trenches, which it is said were dug by the local population as a warning to

their feudal lord not to waste the taxes they were forced to pay him. The huge coin is beside the sea, at the foot of Kotohiki Hill in Kotohiki-kōen park, 1.5km northwest of Kanonji station.

Tadotsu 多度津
☎ 0877

Tadotsu is known throughout Japan as the national headquarters for the martial art of **Shorinji-kempo** (諸臨時健保). If you're extremely keen to watch training, call ☎ 33-1010 (in Japanese) and ask politely.

Tokkyu Ferry (☎ 088-622-1826) offers direct ferry connections from Tadotsu to Fukuyama (¥1530, 1¾ hours, six daily) in Hiroshima-ken. The ferry terminal is about 15 minutes' walk west of the station.

Marugame 丸亀
☎ 0877

An interesting detour from the 88-Temple circuit is in Marugame, which is home to the unique **Marugame-jō** (丸亀城; ☎ 24-8816; admission ¥100; ⌚ 9am-4.30pm). The castle dates from 1597, and has one of only 12 original wooden donjon (heavily fortified central tower) remaining of more than 5000 castles in Japan. The castle also contains stepped-stone walls, which tower over 50m high.

In the streets just to the north of the castle, there is a weekly **market** (⌚ 7am-4pm Sun) with local produce, delicacies and arts and crafts for sale.

At the **Uchiwa-no-Minato Museum** (うちわの港ミュージアム; ☎ 24-7055; admission free; ⌚ 9.30am-5pm Tue-Sun) there are displays and craft demonstrations of traditional Japanese *uchiwa* (paper fans). Marugame is responsible for about 90% of the country's paper-fan output, making it a logical place to pick one up.

Zentsū-ji 善通寺
☎ 0877

Zentsū-ji (善通寺; ☎ 62-0111) is Temple 75 of the 88 Sacred Temples, and holds a special significance as the boyhood home of Kōbō Daishi. It is also the largest temple – most of the other 88 could fit in its car park. The temple boasts a magnificent five-storey pagoda and giant camphor trees. To get into the Buddhist spirit, visitors can venture into the basement (admission ¥500) and traverse a 100m-long passageway in pitch darkness: by moving along with your left hand pressed to the wall (which is painted with mandalas, angels and lotus flowers), you are said to be safely following Buddha's way.

Zentsū-ji's other claim to fame is as the home of the cube watermelon, an ingenious square-sided Japanese modification that enables watermelons to fit into refrigerators more efficiently. Of course, convenience comes at a price, so you can expect to dig deep into your pockets if you want to sample this bizarre creation.

Kotohira 琴平

☎ 0877

The small mountain village of Kotohira is home to Kompira-san, a Shintō shrine that is dedicated to seafarers, and is one of Shikoku's most famous tourist attractions. If you mention to a Japanese person that you've visited Kotohira, you will almost certainly be asked if you made it to the top of the shrine. Although it's not a major mission (the official count is 1368 steps), half the fun of visiting Kompira-san is exaggerating its difficulty while psyching yourself up for the climb.

ORIENTATION

Kotohira is small enough to make navigation quite straightforward. Beginning a few streets southeast of the two stations, a busy shopping arcade lined with the inevitable souvenir shops stretches to the shrine entranceway. Those seeking to truly immerse themselves in the Japanese experience might like to buy a walking stick at one of the shops for the trek up to the shrine.

INFORMATION

There is a **tourist information centre** (☎ 75-3500; 🕑 9.30am-8pm) along the main road between JR Kotohira station and Kotoden Kotohira station. Staff can provide an English-language brochure and accommodation information. They also rent out bikes (¥100/500 per hour/day).

There are coin lockers at the station, and the ATMs at the post office accept international money cards.

SIGHTS

Kompira-san 金刀比羅宮

Kompira-san or, more formally, Kotohira-gū, was originally a Buddhist and Shintō temple dedicated to the Guardian of Mariners, though it became an official Shintō shrine after the Meiji Restoration. The shrine's hilltop position affords superb views over the countryside, and there are some interesting reminders of its maritime connections.

A big fuss is made about how strenuous the climb is to the top but, if you've got this far in Japan, you've probably completed a few long ascents to shrines already. If you really blanch at the thought of climbing all those steps, you can always dish out ¥6500 and be carried up and down in a palanquin.

The first notable landmark on the long climb is the **Ō-mon**, a stone gateway that leads to the **Hōmotsu-kan** (Treasure House; admission ¥500; 🕑 8.30am-4.30pm). Nearby you will find five traditional-sweets vendors at tables shaded by large white parasols. A symbol of ancient times, these *Gonin Byakushō* (Five Farmers) are the descendants of the original families permitted to trade within the grounds of the shrine. Further uphill is the **Shoin** (Reception Hall; admission ¥500; 🕑 8.30am-4.30pm), a designated National Treasure that dates from 1659 and has some interesting screen paintings and a small garden.

Continuing the ascent, you eventually reach the large **Asahino Yashiro** (Shrine of the Rising Sun). Built in 1837, this large hall is dedicated to the Sun Goddess Amaterasu, and is noted for its ornate woodcarving. From here, the short final ascent, which is the most beautiful leg of the walk, brings you to the **Gohonsha** (Gohon Hall) and **Ema-dō** (Ema Pavilion). The latter is filled with maritime offerings ranging from pictures of ships and models to modern ship engines and a one-person solar sailboat hull donated to the shrine after its round-the-world navigation. From this level, there are spectacular views that extend right down to the coast and over the Inland Sea.

If you're still feeling *genki* (energetic), incurable climbers can continue for another 500-odd steps up to the **Oku-sha** (Inner Shrine), which features stone carvings on the side of a cliff.

Other Sights

Built in 1835, the **Kanamaru-za** (☎ 73-3846; admission ¥300; 🕑 9am-5pm) is Japan's oldest kabuki playhouse, though it had a lengthy stint as a cinema before being restored in 1976. Inside, you can wander backstage and see the changing room, an old wooden bath, the revolving-stage mechanism, basement trap doors and a tunnel out to the front of the theatre. The playhouse is 200m west of the main approach to Kompira-san.

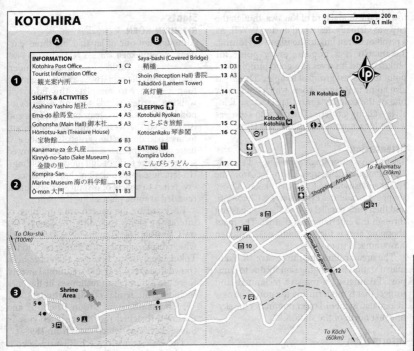

KOTOHIRA

Also of interest is the Marine Museum (☎ 73-3748; admission ¥400; 9am-5pm), situated along the main approach to Kompira-san, and displaying numerous ship models and maritime exhibits. If your throat is feeling a little parched, the **Kinryō-no-Sato** (☎ 73-4133; admission ¥310; 9am-4pm) sake museum, located outside the shopping arcade along the main approach, offers sake tasting for ¥100 – but don't be surprised if a few drinks sap your will for the climb. Finally, note the curious 26.7m-high **Takadōrō** lantern tower beside the Kotoden Kotohira station, which was traditionally lit in times of trouble.

SLEEPING & EATING
our pick Kotobuki Ryokan (☎ 73-3872; www.town.kotohira.kagawa.jp/onsen/kotobuki/kotobuki.html in Japanese; r per person with/without 2 meals ¥7000/4500; P) Conveniently situated by the riverside and next to the shopping arcade, this historic ryokan blends traditional design elements with congenial service. This is a great place to spend the night as Kotohira really starts to work its magic once the day-trippers leave.

Kotosankaku (☎ 75-1000; www.kotosankaku.jp/index_en.html; r per person with 2 meals ¥12,000; P) Weighing in at nearly 225 rooms, Kotosankaku is one of the island's largest ryokans, though it's still an immensely elegant place. Attractive Japanese-style rooms are complemented by a rooftop pool and a stunner of an onsen.

Kompira Udon (☎ 73-5785; 8am-5pm) This place is just short of the first set of steps leading up Kompira-san (look for the giant udon bowl outside). Here you can watch the noodles being made a few minutes before you consume them. The house speciality is shōudon (¥650), which is udon served with a hot dipping sauce.

GETTING THERE & AWAY
You can reach Kotohira by train on the JR Dosan line from Kōchi (¥3810, 1¼ hours, hourly) and on the private Kotoden line from Takamatsu (¥610, one hour, hourly). The JR Kotohira station is about 500m north and 500m east of the town centre, while the Kotoden station is just 200m west of the JR station.

TAKAMATSU 高松
☎ 087 / pop 425,000
Takamatsu was founded during the rule of Toyotomi Hideyoshi (1537–98) as the castle

town of the feudal lord of Kagawa, though the city was virtually destroyed during WWII. As a result of its rail link to the island of Honshū, Takamatsu is a popular entry point for Shikoku, and it serves as a good jumping-off point for the last group of temples. The city is also home to Ritsurin-kōen, which is arguably one of the country's most spectacular Edo-style walking gardens. The city also serves as a base for a number of unique day trips.

Orientation

Takamatsu is surprisingly sprawling – it's nearly 2km along the main street, Chūō-dōri, from the JR Takamatsu station to Ritsurin-kōen. A busy shopping arcade area extends across Chūō-dōri, and then runs parallel to it to the east, passing through the entertainment district. The main shopping area is further south near Kotoden Kawaramachi train station.

The area around the impressive JR Takamatsu station is changing rapidly due to 'Sunport Takamatsu', a massive reclaimed-land project that is modernising the port. The new Takamatsu Symbol Tower dominates the skyline just north of the station.

Information

The city is well set up to help foreign visitors. There's an excellent **tourist information office** (☎ 851-2009; ☾ 9am-6pm) directly outside the station where the helpful staff provide useful leaflets and maps, and can help you book accommodation.

In the northwest corner of Chūō-kōen is the **Kagawa International Exchange** (I-PAL Kagawa; ☎ 837-5901; www.i-pal.or.jp in Japanese; 1-11-63 Banchō; ☾ 9am-6pm Tue-Sun). This superb resource centre has a message board, foreign books and magazines, international phone and fax access, satellite TV and free internet access.

Visitors can pick up the free Kagawa Welcome Card at Kagawa International Exchange and the tourist information office (you'll need to show your passport). The card provides minor discounts around town, and comes with a mini-guidebook and fold-out city map.

There are coin lockers and a left-luggage office at JR Takamatsu station, and international ATMs available at the central post office (located near the northern exit of Marugamemachi Arcade).

English-language books and magazines can be found on the 5th floor of **Miyawaki Shoten Bookstore** (☎ 851-3732; ☾ 9am-10pm).

Sights

RITSURIN-KŌEN 栗林公園

Although not one of Japan's 'big three' gardens, **Ritsurin-kōen** (☎ 833-7411; admission ¥400; ☾ sunrise-sunset) could easily be a contender. Dating from the mid-1600s and taking more than a century to complete, this Edo-style walking garden winds around a series of ponds with lookouts, tearooms, bridges and islands. To the west, Shiun-zan mountain forms a backdrop to the garden, but to the east there is some much less impressive 'borrowed scenery' in the form of dull modern buildings. (In Japanese garden design, 'borrowed scenery' refers to a view of distant scenery that is revealed at some place along the path.)

Enclosed by the garden are a number of interesting sights including the **Sanuki Folk-craft Museum** (admission free; ☾ 8.45am-4.30pm), which displays local crafts dating back to the Tokugawa dynasty. If you're a fan of *matcha* (powdered green tea) and traditional sweets, there are a number of teahouses in the park including the feudal-era **Kikugetsu-tei** (菊月亭; Chrysanthemum Moon Pavilion) and the lovely thatched-roof **Higurashi-tei** (日暮亭; Sunset Pavilion), which dates from 1898.

The easiest way to reach Ritsurin-kōen is to take the frequent direct bus (¥230, 15 minutes) from the JR Takushima station

TAKAMATSU-JŌ 高松城

Although little remains of Takamatsu's castle, the castle grounds form a pleasant park, **Tamamo-kōen** (高松公園; ☎ 851-1521; admission ¥200; ☾ sunrise-sunset), which are only one-ninth of their original size. When the castle was built in 1588, the moat was filled with sea water, with the sea itself forming the fourth side. The castle ruins are next to Kotoden Chikkō station.

Sleeping

Hotel No 1 Takamatsu (☎ 812-2222; www.hotelno1 .jp/takamatsu in Japanese; 2-4-1 Kankō-dōri; s/d ¥5140/7740; P ☒ ⌨) Three blocks east and three blocks south of Kotoden Kawaramachi station, this sparkling business hotel is our top pick. Although smallish rooms are pretty much your standard business issue, the rooftop *rotemburo* affords a sweeping view of the city, particularly when the neon lights are blazing at night.

Takamatsu Terminal Hotel (☎ 822-3731; www .webterminal.co.jp in Japanese; 10-17 Nishinomaru-chō; s/d

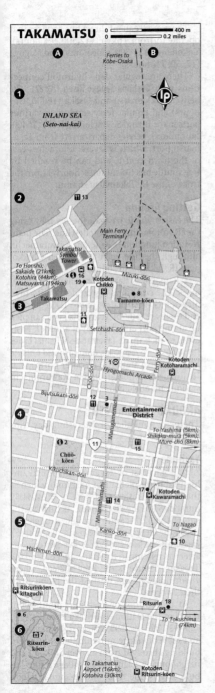

SHIKOKU

¥6500/8500; **P** **☒** **▯**) Just two blocks south and
three blocks east of the JR Takamatsu station,
this attractive business hotel is notable for
its offering of simple Japanese-style tatami
rooms, which are a nice change from the usual
Western-style cubicle. There is also a good
selection of on-site restaurants if you're not
up for venturing into town.

ANA Hotel Clement Takamatsu (☎ 811-1111;
fax 811-1100; 1-1 Hamano-chō; per person from ¥12,000;
P **☒** **▯**) This ultra-modern business hotel is
certainly eye-catching, especially since it's one
of the first buildings you see as you exit the
JR Takamatsu station. Spacious rooms incorporate chic minimalist design elements, and
there is a top-notch offering of sophisticated
bars and restaurants that all boast sweeping
views of the Inland Sea.

Eating & Drinking

Restaurants and bars cluster in the covered
arcades and entertainment district to the west
side of the tracks between Kotoden Kotohara-
machi and Kawaramachi stations.

Udonya Goemon (☎ 821-2711; 13-15 Furubaba-chō;
🕒 6pm-3am Mon-Sat) Just around the corner
from the southern exit of the Hyogomachi

Arcade, this no-nonsense spot is perfect for sampling the region's famous *sanuki udon* noodles – our favourite is the delicious *asari udon* (shellfish *udon*; ¥650). Although there's no English menu, there is a fairly detailed plastic food model display outside, which also makes finding this spot a breeze.

Kanaizumi (☎ 822-0123; 9-3 Konyamachi; ☿ 11am-9pm, closed Wed) *Sanuki udon* noodles are serious business in Takamatsu, and it's considered *de rigueur* to sample a few different dishes of the stuff before leaving the region. Four blocks north of Chūō-kōen, this popular spot offers self-service noodles (¥500) on the 1st floor and table service (¥1000) on the 2nd floor. As with Udonya Goemon, this place is pretty easy to spot – just look for the almost edible plastic food model displays outside.

Mikayla (☎ 811-5357; 8-40 Sunport; from ¥1500; ☿ 11am-10pm) At the northern end of the Sunport Takamatsu (north of the station), this seaside restaurant has an outdoor terrace and serves fresh fish straight out of the Inland Sea. If you're after the freshest fish, just ask for *kyou-no-osusume* (today's catch).

Tokiwa Saryō (☎ 861-5577; 1-8-2 Tokiwa-chō; drinks from ¥450; ☿ 11am-10pm) This historic ryokan, which occupies a traditional building one block south of the Tokiwa Arcade, now functions as an atmospheric *izakaya*. After indulging in an ice-cold sake (or two), be sure to explore the premises, particularly the stunning banquet room.

Getting There & Away

Takamatsu airport, 16km south of the city, is easily reached by bus (¥740, 35 minutes, hourly from the front of the JR Takamatsu station). There are direct flights to/from Tokyo (ANA/JAS, ¥24,500, one hour, six daily) and Fukuoka (JAC, ¥28,500, 70 minutes, two daily).

The rail line crossing the Seto-Ōhashi has brought Takamatsu much closer to the main island of Honshū. From Tokyo, you can take the *shinkansen* (bullet train) to Okayama (four hours), where you can change trains for Takamatsu (¥1470, 55 minutes, hourly). From Takamatsu, the JR Kōtoku line runs southeast to Tokushima (¥2560, one hour, hourly), the JR Yosan line runs west to Matsuyama (¥5500, 2½ hours; hourly) and the JR Dosan line runs to Kōchi (¥4440, 2½ hours, hourly). The private Kotoden line also runs direct to Kotohira (¥830, one hour, hourly).

There are frequent direct bus services that operate to/from Tokyo (¥12,500, 9½ hours), Yokohama (¥11,500, nine hours) and Nagoya (¥7550, 7¾ hours).

There are regular daily hydrofoil connections with **Goshima Sangyo Kisen** (☎ 821-9436) between Takamatsu and Osaka (¥6000, two hours) and regular ferry services to various ports in the Inland Sea including Kōbe (¥6400, four hours). Ferries depart/arrive from Takamatsu port, which is several kilometres east of the town centre, and can be reached by free shuttle bus (35 minutes, hourly) from the front of the JR Takamatsu station.

Getting Around

The easiest way to navigate the city is by using the JR Kōtoku line or Kotoden line. The main Kotoden junction is Kotoden Kawaramachi, although the line ends at Kotoden Chikkō, near JR Takamatsu station.

Takamatsu is flat and excellent for rental bikes. The city offers a great deal on its 'blue bicycles' (¥100 per day; photo ID required), and there are four 'bicycle ports'; you can pick up at one port and drop off at another. Easiest is to pick up at **Takamatsu-shi Rental Cycles** (☎ 821-0400; ☿ 7am-10pm), underground outside JR Takamatsu station. The other ports are at JR Ritsurin station, Kotoden Kawaramachi station and at Kajiyamachi.

AROUND TAKAMATSU

There are a number of interesting day trips from Takamatsu.

Yashima 屋島

About 5km east of Takamatsu is the 292m-high tabletop plateau of Yashima, which is the home of **Yashima-ji** (屋島寺; ☎ 841-9418), number 84 of the 88 temples. As this was the site of the 12th-century titanic struggle between the Genji and Heike clans, the temple's **Treasure House** (admission ¥500; ☿ 9am-5pm) exhibits artefacts relating to the battle. Just behind the Treasure House is the **Pond of Blood**, where victorious warriors washed the blood from their swords.

At the bottom of Yashima, about 500m north of the station, is **Shikoku-mura** (四国村; ☎ 843-3111; 9-1 Shimanaka; admission ¥800; ☿ 9am-6pm), an excellent village museum that houses old buildings brought from all over Shikoku and neighbouring islands. The village's fine kabuki stage came from Shōdo-shima (p465),

---

SEA KAYAKING ON THE INLAND SEA

For a bit of adventure, physical exertion and an enjoyable day out, you might like to try sea kayaking off the northeast coast of Kagawa-ken on the Inland Sea. **Noasobiya** (☎ 0879-26-3350; www.noasobiya.jp/noasobi/en/index.html) runs a thoroughly professional operation out of Ōchi, east of Takamatsu. Head guide Ryū holds New Zealand sea kayak–guiding qualifications and spends his off-seasons guiding in New Zealand's Abel Tasman National Park. Noasobiya ventures out to small uninhabited islands in the Inland Sea and offers half-/full-day options for ¥7350/12,600, including all gear.

The operation is run out of a large log cabin that was once used as a rest house for Emperor Hirohito, and there are cabins next door where visitors can stay (¥16,000 for up to four people). There is also a hotel nearby with a large *onsen* for an after-trip soak. Tours can be run in English, and staff will pick you up at the JR Sanbonmatsu station if you pre-request it. Depending on the weather, trips run from April to November; check out the English website for details.

---

which is famed for its traditional farmers' kabuki performances. Other interesting buildings include a border guardhouse from the Tokugawa era (a time when travel was tightly restricted) and a bark-steaming hut that was used in paper-making. There's also a water-powered rice-hulling machine and a fine old stone storehouse. English displays are present.

Hourly trains from Kotoden Chikkō station connect Takamatsu to Yashima station (¥270, 15 minutes). From here you can take the funicular railway to the top (¥700/1300 one way/return, five minutes), or hike up in about 30 minutes. At the top you can rent a bicycle (¥500) to pedal around the attractions.

Isamu Noguchi Garden Museum
イサムノグチ庭園美術館

Consider an excursion to the town of Murechō, east of Takamatsu, to witness the legacy of noted sculptor Isamu Noguchi (1904–88). Born in Los Angeles to a Japanese poet and an American writer, Noguchi set up a studio and residence here in 1970. Today the **complex** (☎ 870-1500; www.isamunoguchi.or.jp; 3-5-19 Murechō; admission ¥2100) is filled with hundreds of Noguchi's works, and holds its own as an impressive art installation. Inspiring sculptures are on display in the beautifully restored Japanese buildings and in the surrounding landscape.

Entry is decidedly worth it, but you've got to get your act together early if you want to visit here. One-hour tours are conducted at 10am, 1pm and 3pm on Tuesday, Thursday and Saturday; visitors should fax or email ahead for reservations at least two weeks in advance (check out the website).

To reach the museum, take the Kotoden train to Yakuri station (¥330, 30 minutes, hourly), from where the museum is a 20-minute walk towards the town centre or a five-minute taxi ride.

Megi-jima 女木島

Just offshore from Yashima is the small island of Megi-jima (population 250), also known as Oniga-shima, or Demon Island. Several homes on the island are surrounded by picturesque *ōte*, which are high stone walls built to protect a house from waves, wind and ocean spray. It was here that Momotarō, the legendary Peach Boy (p444), met and conquered the mythical demon. You can tour the impressive **caves** (☎ 873-0728; admission ¥500; ☯ 8.30am-5pm) where the demon was said to have hidden, but they've been a bit ruined by the fake demons put there, supposedly to make it more realistic. Five or six boats a day run to Megi-jima from Takamatsu (¥340, 20 minutes), departing from the docks on the northern edge of the city.

SHIKOKU

Kyūshū 九州

Kyūshū has long been Japan's most internationally minded region. Coinciding with the decline of the samurai tradition, young Kyūshū intellectuals of the Meiji Restoration led a reluctant Japan into the modern world. Today the cosmopolitan city of Fukuoka is a major international arrival point. At night, the city's charms come alive – from the packed riverside food stalls to the hip jazz and dance clubs of the Tenjin district. Nearby Nagasaki, Japan's first gateway to the West, continues to lead in the arts and commerce.

To the south, unusual hiking opportunities abound in the rugged mountains of the stunning Kirishima volcano chain. The eerie volcanic landscape of Aso-san awaits hikers and photographers alike, while smouldering Sakurajima looms over the port city of Kagoshima, at times showering the town with fine ash which the residents casually respond to with open umbrellas. With plentiful volcanic ash, Kyūshū also boasts numerous pottery villages, especially around Karatsu and Arita. Coastal Beppu is one of Japan's major hot-spring centres. Further inland, the hot mineral waters of Yufuin and Unzen promise a tranquil dip in a forested getaway setting.

The southern cities of Kagoshima and Miyazaki are known for their balmy climate and for the quality of their *shō-chū*, a popular drink distilled from sweet potatoes and other grains. The Miyazaki region is also the mythical home of the sun goddess Amaretsu, who took refuge on Kyūshū, hiding in a remote cave and plunging the world into darkness. Only after her fellow gods lured her out did light and warmth return to earth and the land of the rising sun.

HIGHLIGHTS

- Join the night owls for beer and *yakitori* at the *yatai* food stalls in **Fukuoka** (opposite)
- Gaze into the calm face of a 1000-year-old stone Buddha in **Usuki** (p727)
- Clamber across lava-fields of active **Sakurajima** (p716) with your ash umbrella
- Take an intimate soak in a Meiji-era *onsen* in **Beppu** (p727)
- Hike among rare azaleas and stunning views in **Kirishima-Yaku National Park** (p706)
- Experience the hospitality of **Nagasaki** (p681), which survived the atomic bomb
- Get covered in hot volcanic sand in **Ibusuki** (p718)
- Check out history at the space-age Kyushu National Museum in **Dazaifu** (p674)
- Drink distilled sweet-potato *shō-chū* in **Kagoshima** (p708)

★ Fukuoka
★ Dazaifu

Beppu ★

Usuki ★

Nagasaki ★

Kirishima-Yaku National Park ★

Kagoshima ★ ★ Sakurajima

★ Ibusuki

History

Kyūshū history is synonymous with Japan's most ancient origins. Very recent excavations near Kagoshima suggest that southern Kyūshū was the earliest home to Jōmon culture, which gradually spread north beginning 10,000 years ago.

Japan's centuries-old trade with China and Korea began in Kyūshū. In more recent times, Japan's 'Christian Century' (1549–1650) is notable for tales of secret Christians who, to escape persecution, altered their images of Christ and the Virgin to make them look like Buddhist icons.

In 1868 the Meiji Restoration ended the military shōgunate's policy of isolation, marking the birth of modern Japan. During the ensuing Meiji Era (1868–1912), the rapid rise of industrialisation led to profound social and political change. Saigō Takamori, a revered samurai and early Meiji leader from Kagoshima, is the subject of Ken Watanabe's 2003 film, *The Last Samurai*.

Guns first appeared in Japan in the 16th century, compliments of Portuguese merchants aboard a Chinese ship that was blown off course just south of Kagoshima. The new weapon changed the way feudal armies did battle, effectively ending the samurai tradition across Japan. August 9, 1945, marks the day that Nagasaki, long renowned for its early trade and cultural contacts with the West, became better known as the unfortunate second city to suffer the tragic effects of the atomic bomb.

Climate

Kyūshū, while more southern than much of Japan, has extremes that vary tremendously season to season. In the winter it can be quite cold, near freezing at night, and many of the mountains retain their snowcaps for much of the year. During the rainy season the island is inundated with heavy, often torrential rain. Travellers should bring layers and a waterproof rain shell, as it is often too windy to use an umbrella. Summer is hot and humid, and autumn regularly brings typhoons, along with the surfers who follow.

Getting There & Away

AIR

There are major airports at Fukuoka, Ōita (Beppu), Kitakyūshū, Nagasaki, Kagoshima, Kumamoto and Miyazaki. There are also flights to islands off the coast of Kyūshū and to the islands southwest of Kagoshima down to Okinawa. The most frequent routes depart from Fukuoka (to Tsushima, Goto, Amakusa and Naha), Nagasaki (to Tsushima, Iki and Goto), Kumamoto (to Amakusa) and Kagoshima (to Tanegashima, Yakushima, Kikaijima, Amamioshima and Tokunoshima).

BOAT

There are numerous sea connections to Kyūshū from Honshū, Shikoku and Okinawa. Local ferry services operate between Kyūshū and islands off the northwest and southern coasts.

TRAIN

The *shinkansen* (bullet train) line from Tokyo and Osaka crosses to Kyūshū from Shimonoseki and ends at Hakata station (Fukuoka).

Getting Around

Major cities in Kyūshū are connected by *tokkyū* (limited express) train services, along with an extensive highway bus system. Major cities and offshore islands are served by several domestic airlines.

FUKUOKA-KEN 福岡県

The northern prefecture of Fukuoka will be the arrival point for most visitors to Kyūshū, whether they cross over by road or tunnel from Shimonoseki or fly straight into Fukuoka city's international airport. The city of Kitakyūshū (population 1,000,150) is northernmost, but most travellers will want to head directly to less industrialised areas, starting with Fukuoka.

FUKUOKA 福岡・博多

☎ 092 / pop 1,358,765

Fukuoka is the biggest city in Kyūshū, and a rising star in Japanese commerce and tourism. Once upon a time it was two separate towns – the lordly Fukuoka castle town to the west of the river Naka-gawa, and to the east, the common folks' Hakata. When the two merged in 1889, the label Fukuoka was applied to both towns, but subsequent development has mainly been in Hakata and many residents still refer to the town that way. The airport is known as Fukuoka, the train station as Hakata.

KYŪSHŪ

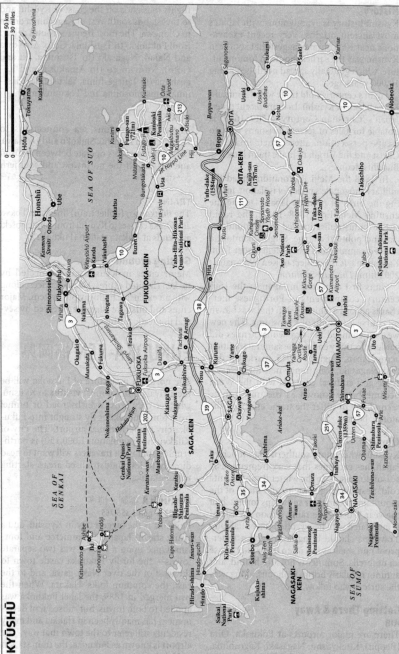

50 km
30 miles

To Hiroshima

To Hiroshima

Kudamatsu
Tokuyama
Hōfu
Ube
Onoda

Honshū

Kanmon
Straits
Shimonoseki

SEA OF SUO

Kitakyūshū Airport
Kanda
Yukuhashi
Buzen
Nakatsu

Usa-jingū
Usa

Yaba-Hita-Hikosan
Quasi-National Park

Hita

FUKUOKA-KEN

Shingū-gawa

Kurume

Saga-gawa

Tachiarai
Amagi

Yame

Amagi Cycling Route

SAGA-KEN

SEA OF GENKAI

Genkai Quasi-
National Park

Itoshima
Peninsula

Nokonoshima

Hakata-wan

FUKUOKA
Fukuoka Airport

Dazaifu
Chikushino
Kasuga
Nakagawa

Tosu

SAGA

Okawa
Yanagawa

Kashima

Ariake-kai

Takeo Onsen

Takeo
Taku

Imari

Ōki

Higashi-
Matsuura
Peninsula
Karatsu

Cape Hatomi
Yobuko

Imari-wan
Hirado-guchi

Hirado-shima
Hirado

Kujūku-
shima

Saikai
National Park

Kita-Matsuura
Peninsula
Sasebo

Huis Ten
Bosch

Sakai

Nishisonogi
Peninsula

Ōmura
Ōmura-wan

Nagasaki
Airport

Higashisonogi

Nagayo

NAGASAKI-KEN

*SEA OF
SUMŌ*

Nagasaki
Peninsula

NAGASAKI

Tachibana-wan

Obama
Unzen
Unzen-dake
(1359m)

Shimabara
Peninsula
Arie

Isahaya

Kazusa

Nomo-zaki

Kitakyūshū
Yahata

Iizuka

Nogata
Munakata
Okagaki
Nakama
Fukuma
Koga

Tagawa

3

202

3

39

38

Kokura

Kita-gawa

Kunisaki
Aki
Ōta
Airport

Kunisaki
Peninsula
Kunimi
Matama

Futago-san
(721m)
Futago-ji
Taketsu-ji
Magaibutsu
Kumano

Kabaji

Bungotakada
Usa

213

10

Beppu-wan

ŌITA

Beppu

Yufuin
Hiji

Yufu-dake
(1584m)

111

Kusu

Kunkawa
Onsen
Sentomo

Sanrindō
Youth Hostel

Senomoto

ŌITA-KEN

Kujū-san
(1787m)

Taka-dake
(1592m)

Aso-san

Ichinomiya
Aso

57

Ōita

JR Nippō Line

Taketa
Takamori

Takachiho

57

Kyūshū-Chūōsanchi
National Park

Yabe

Aso National
Park

Kikuchi
Gorge
Kikuchi
Onsen

Kumamoto
Airport

Mashiki

KUMAMOTO

Yamaga Onsen

3

37

Ōmuta
Arao

Tamana

Ueki

Uto

Misumi

Uki

Shimabara-wan

Shimabara

Fukae

57

251

Takaoki

Ariake-kai

Kashima

35

34

Saganoseki

Tsukumi

Saeki

Kamae

Nobeoka

10

10

Usuki
Notsu
Mie

Oka-jo

**Usuki
Stone
Buddhas**

**Kunisaki
Peninsula**

Hakusui

Nagasaki Airport

Tsuchibana-wan

Aso-san

Katsumoto

Ashibe

Iki

Indōji

Gononoura

Karatsu-wan

Maebaru

Hirado-guchi

Ōita

Ōkawa

Hijū-dake

Kamae

KYŪSHŪ

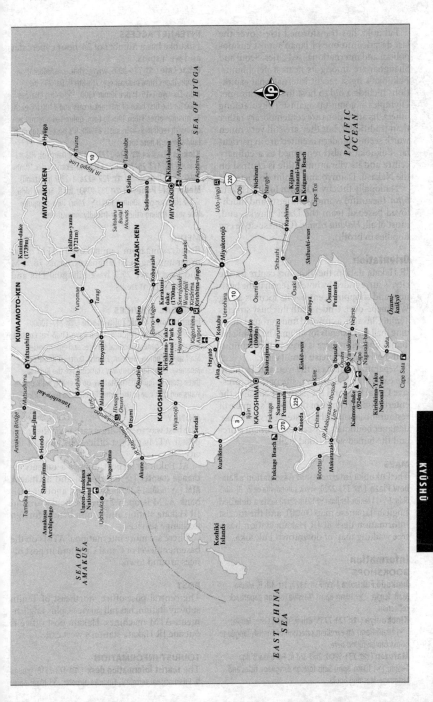

Fukuoka has transformed itself over the last decade into one of Japan's most cosmopolitan and internationalised cities. Seoul and Shanghai are among its nearest neighbours. Fukuoka's most recent international aspirations include a bid to host the 2016 Summer Olympics – going up against Tokyo among others. Its attractions are contemporary rather than traditional, but they are still very much worth seeing, modern architecture in particular. Fukuoka is also renowned as a culinary centre and its vibrant nightlife is centred on the Nakasu, Daimyo and Tenjin districts.

Nationally the city is known for its 'Hakata *bijin*' (beautiful women), its feisty and much-loved baseball team the Daiei Hawks, and, most of all, *Hakata rāmen* (Chinese-style egg noodles in broth).

Orientation

JR Hakata station, the transport centre for the city, is surrounded by hotels. Tenjin is the business and shopping centre – its focus is along Watanabe-dōri. Underneath this busy street is Tenjin Chikagai, a crowded underground shopping mall that extends for 400m. The Nishitetsu Tenjin bus centre here is close to the terminus of the private Nishitetsu Ōmuta line.

Separating Hakata to the west and Tenjin to the east is the Naka-gawa, site of the impressive Canal City and the island of Nakasu, the entertainment centre of the city. It's a maze of restaurants, strip clubs, hostess bars, cinemas, designer boutiques, upscale department stores and the famed *yatai* (food stalls).

MAPS

The Fukuoka International Association's **Rainbow Plaza** (☎ 733-2220; www.rainbowfia.or.jp; 8F, IMS Bldg, 1-7-11 Tenjin, Tenjin; 10am-8pm) sells a detailed English-Japanese map (¥600), and the tourist information desk at JR Hakata station has a free walking map of downtown Fukuoka.

Information

BOOKSHOPS

Junkudō Fukuoka (☎ 738-3322; 1st-4th fl, Media Mall, Tenjin; 10am-8pm) Massive foreign paperback collection.

Kinokuniya (☎ 721-7755; 6th fl, Tenjin Core, Tenjin; 10am-8pm) An excellent selection of English-language books can be found here.

Maruzen (☎ 731-9000; 2nd-3rd fl, Fukuoka Bldg, Tenjin; 10am-8pm) Sells foreign-language titles and language-learning books.

INTERNET ACCESS

Fukuoka has a number of 24-hour cybercafés and wi-fi spots:

Cybac Café (☎ 724-8005; www.cybac.com/infomation/tenjin/index.html in Japanese; 7th-8th fl, Dai 21 Line Bldg, Daimyo 1-15-1; per 30min ¥300; 24hr) Charges ¥600 for the first hour of internet access and ¥100 for each 15 minutes after. From 1am to 8am, unlimited internet access with reclining chairs costs ¥1980. It's possible to crash (and shower!) here too.

Kinko's Akasaka (☎ 724-7177; 2-12-12 Daimyo); Hakata-ekimae (☎ 473-2677; 2-19-24 Hakata-ekimae; per 10min ¥200; 24hr); Tenjin (☎ 722-4224; 1-22-7 Imaizumi)

Media Café Popeye (☎ 283-9393; 8th fl, Spoon Bldg, 5-1-7 Nakasu; per 30min ¥300; 24hr) Two-computer love seats among other user-friendly innovations.

MEDIA

Broadcasting from Tenjin, Love 76.1FM offers programming in 10 languages. Cross 78.7FM and Free Wave 77.7 have bilingual DJs and entertainment news.

MEDICAL SERVICES

International Clinic Tojin-machi (☎ 717-1000; http://internationalclinic.org; 1-4-6 Jigyo, Chūō-ku) Contact this clinic for general medical services and emergencies. Staff speak English, German, French, Dutch, Chinese and Japanese. From Tenjin subway station, take the Kuko line three stops to Tojin-machi station, go to exit 1, walk up the stairs and continue in the same direction for two blocks.

MONEY

The best way to withdraw cash is via the many postal ATMs at post offices throughout the city.

At Fukuoka airport, there's a **currency exchange counter** (8.30am-9pm) and a **Citibank ATM** (6.30am-9.30pm). In Tenjin another Citibank ATM is open 24 hours. Banks around JR Hakata station and Tenjin handle foreign exchange services.

There are more international ATMs on the basement level of Canal City, and in post offices around town.

POST

The central post office, northeast of Tenjin subway station, has full services, plus English-menu ATM machines. Hakata post office is outside JR Hakata station's west exit.

TOURIST INFORMATION

The **tourist information desk** (☎ 473-2518; ground fl, international terminal, Fukuoka airport; 10am-6pm) is beside a **reservations desk** (☎ international 483-7007, ☎ domestic 621-6059; ☯ 8am-9.30pm or last flight) that can arrange hotel accommodation and car rentals.

Useful local English-language publications include **Fukuoka Now** (www.fukuoka-now.com), a free monthly 'what's on' guide with up-to-date city maps and features, and *Rainbow*, the Fukuoka International Association's current events cultural newsletter.

ACROS Fukuoka (☎ 725-9200; www.acros.or.jp; 2nd fl, cultural centre, 1-1-1 Tenjin, Tenjin; ☯ 10am-7pm, closed 2nd & 4th Mon each month) Has plenty of English-language information on the surrounding prefecture.

Rainbow Plaza (☎ 733-2220; www.rainbowfia.or.jp; 8th fl, IMS Bldg, 1-7-11 Tenjin, Tenjin; ☯ 10am-8pm) The Fukuoka International Association's Rainbow Plaza has free 30-minute internet access, books on Japan, magazines, international newspapers and a notice board for events, accommodation and job ads. Bilingual staff is extremely helpful.

Tourist information desk (JR Hakata station; ☯ 8am-8pm) Has limited information and maps in English. Ask for the free 'Fukuoka Welcome Card' entitling visitors to discounts at hotels, attractions, shops and restaurants.

TRAVEL AGENCIES

No 1 Travel (☎ 761-9203; www.no1-travel.com/fuk/index.html; 3rd fl, ACROS Fukuoka Bldg, 1-1-1 Tenjin; ☯ 10am-6.30pm Mon-Fri, 11am-4.30pm Sat) For cut-rate international airfares and reliable information in English.

NZ Life Tours & Travel (☎ /fax 751-8670; www.nzlifetours.com; 1-4-15-103 Yakuin, Chūō-ku) Offers discounted international flights and tours.

Sights & Activities

CANAL CITY キャナルシティ

Sleek, streamlined and photogenic, the curvy-modern six-building shopping mall and entertainment complex **Canal City** (☎ 282-2525; www.canalcity.co.jp) overlooks an artificial canal with a fountain symphony. There are 13 cinema screens, a playhouse, two major hotels and innumerable boutiques, bars and bistros.

Canal City is 500m southeast of the Nakasu-Kawabata subway stop, or you can take one of many city buses to Canal City-mae.

TENJIN 天神

Tenjin has historic Western-style buildings, like the 1910 **Former Prefectural Hall & Official Guest House** (☎ 751-4416; 6-29 Nishinakasu; ☯ 9am-5pm Tue-Sun) in Tenjin Chūō-kōen. Copper-turreted **Akarenga Bunka-kan** (Akarenga Cultural Centre; admission free; ☯ 9am-9pm Tue-Sun) has simple historical exhibits and a charming coffee shop.

FUKUOKA ASIAN ART MUSEUM
福岡アジア美術館

This modern, expansive **museum** (☎ 263-1100; http://faam.city.fukuoka.jp; 7th-8th fl, Hakata Riverain, 3-1 Shimokawabata-machi; admission ¥200, special exhibitions from ¥1000; ☯ 10am-8pm Thu-Tue) showcases fine contemporary Asian art and rotating exhibits on the 7th floor. Cutting-edge shows by area artists-in-residence are staged in the 8th-floor gallery. The 7th-floor café next to the museum shop has skyline views out the floor-to-ceiling windows.

HAKATA MACHIYA FURUSATO-KAN
博多町家ふるさと館

This small **folk museum** (☎ 281-7761; www.hakatamachiya.com; 6-10 Reisen-machi; admission ¥200; ☯ 10am-5.30pm) opposite Kushida Shrine recreates a bit of old Japan with restored merchants houses, historic photos and displays of traditional Hakata culture. You can even hear recordings of impenetrable *Hakata-ben* dialect through antique telephones, or try your hand at *Hakata-ori* (traditional weaving for kimono cloth). An English brochure is available, and inexpensive souvenirs for sale in the museum shop.

FUKUOKA REKISHI NO MACHI 大名地区

This **history-theme village** (☎ 806-0505; 545-1 Tokunaga, Nishi-ku, Fukuoka-ken; adult/student ¥600/400; ☯ 10am-5pm) gathers over 30 working potters, weavers and paper makers, plus a souvenir shop to sell their wares. From Tenjin, take the JR train to Kyudai Gakuen toshi station (25 minutes).

SHRINES & TEMPLES

Tōchō-ji has impressively carved Kannon (goddess of mercy) statues and, upstairs, the largest wooden Buddha in Japan.

Shōfuku-ji is a Zen temple founded in 1195 by Eisai, who introduced Zen and tea to Japan. Don't confuse it with Sōfuku-ji (p685), once the temple of a feudal lord, with one gate taken from the original Fukuoka castle.

Kushida-jinja has displays of Hakata festival floats on the grounds, and a local **history museum** (☎ 291-2951; 1-41 Kamikawabata; admission ¥300; ☯ 10am-4.30pm).

Sumiyoshi-jinja (☎ 262-6665; 2-10-7 Sumiyoshi, Hakata; admission ¥100; ☯ 6am-9pm) is a garden and teahouse built by a Meiji-era merchant, with an intact garden wall, known as Rakusuien.

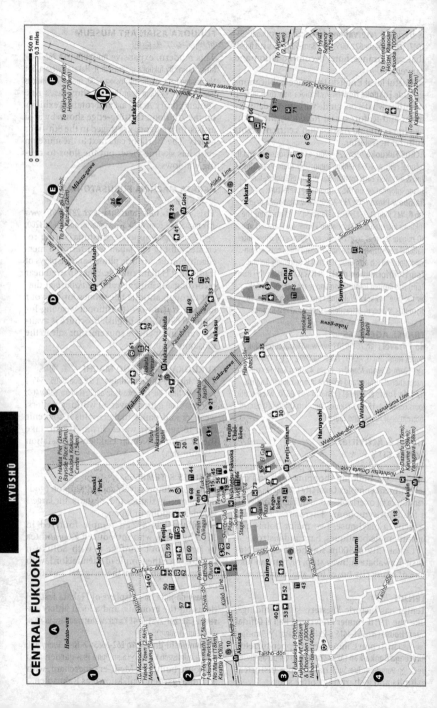

CENTRAL FUKUOKA

KYŪSHŪ

FUKUOKA-JŌ & ŌHORI-KŌEN
福岡城・大濠公園

Only the walls of Fukuoka-jō remain in what is now Maizuru-kōen, but the castle's hilltop site provides fine views of the city.

Ōhori-kōen, which is adjacent to the castle grounds, has a traditional (though recently constructed) Japanese garden, **Nihon-teien** (☎ 741-8377; admission ¥240; ☒ 9am-4.45pm Tue-Sun Sep-May, to 5.45pm Tue-Sun Jun-Aug).

Nearby, the **Fukuoka Art Museum** (☎ 714-6051; www.fukuoka-art-museum.jp/english; 1-6 Ōhori-kōen, Chūo-ku; admission ¥200; ☒ 9.30am-5pm Tue-Sun Sep-May, to 7pm Tue-Sat & to 5pm Sun Jul & Aug) has ancient pottery and Buddhist guardians on one floor, with works by Andy Warhol and Salvador Dali upstairs, and an interior garden to help soften the transition.

MOMOCHI DISTRICT 百浜
Further out in the west of the city you'll find the 234m-tall **Fukuoka Tower** (☎ 823-0234; www.fukuokatower.co.jp; admission ¥800; ☒ 9.30am-10pm Apr-Sep, to 9pm Oct-Mar). At 120m, the 4th-floor café **Sky Lounge Refuge** (☎ 833-8255) is a great place to view the city, especially at dusk.

The state-of-the-art **Fukuoka City Museum** (☎ 845-5011; http://museum.city.fukuoka.jp/english/ec/ec_fr2.html; 3-1-1 Momochi, Sawara-ku; admission ¥200; ☒ 9.30am-5pm Tue-Sun) displays local history and culture that make it obvious why Kyūshū residents have such fierce pride in their island.

The most precious treasure is an ancient golden snake seal with an inscription proving Japan's historic ties to China.

HAWKS TOWN ホークスタウン

Something of a seafront Canal City, **Hawks Town** (www.hawkstown.com) is set on reclaimed land near Momochi-kōen. This entertainment and shopping complex is also the location of the luxury **JAL Resort Sea Hawk Hotel & Resort** and the giant **Yahoo Dome**, home to the local Daiei Hawks baseball team. The highlight is Sea Hawk's indoor jungle atrium, complete with waterfalls and screeching tropical birdcalls, as well as bird's-eye views of the city.

Hawks Town is less than 1km northwest of Tōjin-machi station. There are frequent direct buses to Yahoo Dome from Tenjin bus station (about 15 minutes).

OFFSHORE ISLANDS

Nokonoshima, famous for its flower fields, is only about 10km in circumference. There's a swimming **beach** and **camping ground** at the northern end of the island. Buses 300 and 301 depart frequently from Nishitetsu Tenjin bus centre (¥360, 20 minutes). Ferries depart from Meinohama Municipal Ferry Terminal, west of the city centre near Meinohama station (¥220, 10 minutes).

Summer sightseeing cruises depart from Bayside Place. Ferries to delightfully rural **Shikanoshima** (志賀島), where fresh seafood restaurants line the harbourside streets, depart every 40 minutes (¥650, 33 minutes). Shikanoshima also has a **fishing shrine** (志賀海神社; ☎ 603-6501) decorated with deer antlers and is famed for its *kyūdō* (Japanese archery) meets, and a popular **beach** about 5km east of the shrine.

Festivals & Events

Hakozaki-gū Tamaseseri (箱崎宮) On 3 January, two groups of young men clad in loincloths raucously chase a wooden ball in the name of good fortune. Near Hakozaki-gū station at Hakozaki-gū shrine.

Hakata Dontaku Matsuri (博多どんたく祭り) On 3 and 4 May, Fukuoka's Meiji-dōri vibrates to the unique percussive shock of *shamoji* (wooden serving spoons for rice) being banged together like castanets, accompanied by *shamisen* (three-stringed instrument). The name Dontaku was added during the Meiji period (late 19th century) from the Dutch word *zontag*, meaning 'holiday'.

Hakata Yamagasa Matsuri (博多山笠祭り) The city's main festival is held from 1 to 15 July. The climax

starts at 4.59am on the 15th, when seven groups of men all converge at Kushida-jinja, just north of Canal City, and then race on a 5km-long course through the city carrying huge *mikoshi* (portable shrines). According to legend, the festival originated after a 13th-century Buddhist priest was carried aloft, sprinkling holy water over victims of a plague.

Kyūshū Bashō sumō tournament (大相撲九州場所) Held at the Fukuoka Kokusai Centre during mid-November, spanning a two-week period. Limited same-day tickets (*tojitsu-ken*; ¥3100 to ¥14,000) are available starting at 8am, and people start lining up at dawn for one of Japan's major sumō events. Good luck.

Sleeping

Fukuoka is a popular city for business and tourism alike, and has dozens of cut-rate business hotels and ryokan along with several unique upscale hotels.

BUDGET

International Hostel Khaosan Fukuoka (☎ 404-6035; www.khaosan-fukuoka.com; 11-34 Hakata-ku; dm ¥1800-2400, s/tw ¥4000/2600; ✖ ⊠ ☐) This sparkling 19-room hostel is Kyūshū's newest. Rooms are light and comfortable, the share kitchen is well stocked, and there's no curfew.

Hotel New Simple (☎ 411-4311; fax 411-4312; 1-23-11 Hatataekimae; dm/s/tw ¥3000/4200/7140, all incl breakfast; ⊠) One of Fukuoka's cheapest places to stay, this is a spotless gem and a 10-minute walk from Hakata station.

Hakata JBB (☎ 263-8300; fax 263-8301; 6-5-1 Reisen-machi, Hakata-ku; s/d ¥4500/6000; ⊠) Lace curtains and a lobby fax machine set the homey tone here. It's only a minute's walk from the Folk Museum, and the English-speaking owner provides free coffee all morning.

Amenity Hotel in Hakata (☎ 282-0041; fax 282-0044; 14-25 Kami-Kawabata; r incl light breakfast from ¥4900; ⊠) Near the Fukuoka Asian Art Museum, its rooms are on the small side but spotless and attractive. There is a helpful English-speaking staff.

Hotel Etwas Tenjin (☎ 737-3233, fax 737-3266; 3-5-18 Fukuokashi, Chūō-ku; s from ¥5145; ✖ ⊠ ☐) This smart and simple business hotel is a good budget choice, clean and quiet, even with busy Oyafuko-dōri around the corner.

MIDRANGE

our pick **Ryokan Kashima Honkan** (☎ 291-0746; r per person with shared bathroom ¥6000; ☐ ✖ ⊠ ☐) In the Gion district just northeast of Canal City, this wholly unpretentious ryokan is pleasantly faded and has its own enclosed garden – you expect a Meiji-period novelist to pop up at any moment. A hearty breakfast is available (Western ¥525; Japanese ¥1050). The owner speaks English.

Fukuoka Arty Inn (☎ 724-3511; fax 714-3200; 5-1-20 Watanabe-dōri; s/d from ¥6300/10,500; ✗ ✗ 🖳) Look for the English sign high above the building at this charming mid-sized option between bustling Tenjin and the river. The reception staff is unerringly helpful.

Plaza Hotel Tenjin (☎ 752-7600; www.plaza-hotel .net/; 1-9-63 Daimyo, Chūō-ku; s/tw from ¥7140/11.500; 🅿 ✗ ✗ 🖳) Like the Daimyo district it occupies, this renovated boutique hotel has it all – style, price and convenience. Dark-wood furnishings and bookshelves give rooms a lived-in feel.

Plaza Hotel Premier (☎ 734-7600; www.plaza-hotel .net/; 1-14-13 Daimyo, Chūō-ku; s/tw from ¥7980/13,125; 🅿 ✗ ✗ 🖳) Like its nearby twin, the Plaza Hotel Tenjin, the Premier is classy and good value. Both service and amenities match much pricier hotels.

Hotel Twins Momochi (☎ 852-4800; fax 845-8637; 1-7-4 Momochihama, Sawara-ku; s/d from ¥8000/10,080; 🅿 ✗ ✗ 🖳) Near Yahoo Dome, the Momchi is refreshingly different and good value. Spacious designer rooms have a spare, modernist feel, plus king-sized beds. Guests share kitchenettes and coin laundry.

TOP END

Hotel Il Palazzo (☎ 716-3333; www.ilpalazzo.jp in Japanese; 3-13-1 Haruyoshi, Chūō-ku; s/d/Japanese ste from ¥15,015/25,410/57,750; 🅿 ✗ ✗ 🖳) One of Fukuoka's most stylish hotels, this Italianate gem is worth a look even if you stay elsewhere. It's striking on the outside, and curvy and shadowy inside.

Hyatt Regency (ハイアット・リージェンシー; ☎ 412-1234; www.hyattregencyfukuoka .co.jp; 2-14-1 Hakataeki Higashi, Hakata-ku; s/tw/ste from ¥19,635/28,875/69,300; 🅿 ✗ ✗ 🖳) A five-minute walk from Hakata station brings you to another of Fukuoka's architectural showpieces, with the postmodern theme extending to spacious, well-appointed rooms and lounges.

Grand Hyatt Fukuoka (☎ 282-1234, 0120-51-2343; http://fukuoka.grand.hyatt.com; 1-2-82 Sumiyoshi; s/d from ¥28,000/42,000, Japanese-style ste ¥92,000; 🅿 ✗ ✗ 🖳 🐾 ; wi-fi) This bustling luxury property seems to anchor Canal City, with a rooftop garden and modern rooms that combine hi-tech amenities with *shōgi* (sliding rice-paper screens) touches.

ourpick **With the Style** (☎ 433-3900; www.withthestyle .com; 1-9-18 Kakataeki-minami; d/ste from ¥31,185/63,525; 🅿 ✗ ✗ 🖳) This designer boutique hotel manages to be swank and intimate at the same time. Reserve one of its 16 rooms and you're in for a treat. There's an excellent sushi restaurant and lively bar scene as well.

Also recommended:

Hakata Riverside Hotel (☎ 291-1455, 0120-20-8102; s/tw from ¥4200/8000; ✗) Choose one of the four rooms overlooking the river.

Nishitetsu Grand Hotel (☎ 781-0711; www.grand-h .jp; 6-60 Daimyo, 2chome, Chūō-ku; s/tw/ste from ¥13,860/25,410/57,750; 🅿 ✗ ✗ 🖳) Fukuoka's oldest luxury hotel.

Hotel Okura (☎ 262-1111; www.fuk.hotelokura.co.jp /english; 3-2 Shimokawabata-machi; s/d/ste from ¥19,950/25,200/84,000; 🅿 ✗ ✗ 🖳) Handsome and upscale, adjacent to the Fukuoka Asian Art Musuem.

Eating

To the vast majority of Japanese, Hakata means *rāmen*. In particular it means *tonkotsu-rāmen*, noodles in a distinctive, whitish broth made from pork bones. The telephone book lists hundreds of *rāmen* shops; discovering your own *rāmen* shop is all part of the fun. And there are even more *yatai* (food stalls on wheels, complete with portable kitchen and stools, drinks and chatty cooks) that are not listed.

The majority of the *yatai* are along the riverbanks in Nakasu and in front of Canal City and on the streets around Tenjin station, especially where Oyafuko-dōri meets Shōwa-dōri. Most open as dusk approaches; poke your nose in a few until you see what you like.

West (☎ 281-0560; 1-8 Kawabata Shōtengai; dishes ¥400-760) Near the Hakata-gawa, this is a steamy noodle shop with excellent tempura.

Hakata Ippudo Ramen (☎ 738-7061; 1-13-13 Tenjin, Chūō-ku; gyōza ¥400, rāmen bowls ¥500-750; ⏰ 11am-2am; E) Look for the big red lantern at the entrance to this cosy and bustling *rāmen* shop, one of several branches in town. The English menu boasts of Hakata-style *gyōza* (dumplings), traditionally made small so dainty Hakata women would not have to suffer the indignity of opening their mouths too wide to eat them.

Ichiran Chūō-ku (☎ 736-5272; 1-10-25 Tenjin; rāmen bowls ¥600-980; ⏰ 24hr; E); Rāmen Stadium (5F, Canal City) Customers here eat at individual cubicles, and fill out forms requesting precisely how they want their noodles prepared. Flavour strength, fat content, noodle tenderness, 'secret sauce'

KYŪSHŪ

and garlic content can all be regulated. Many branches of this famous Chūō-ku noodle shop can be found around town, including at Rāmen Stadium, where noodle lovers queue to slurp bowls of soup prepared in famous styles hailing from Hokkaidō all the way to southern Kyūshū.

Nazuki (☎ 715-1516; Beans Bldg, 1-8-40 Maizura; dishes from ¥650; ☽ lunch & dinner) This snappy Oyafuko-dōri eatery makes excellent cold Korean *rāmen* and fried rice bowls.

If you fancy eating something other than *rāmen*, the following places may well hit the spot.

Pik's Coffee Shop (☎ 781-0246; 2-18 Tenjin, 3 Chūō-ku; meals from ¥500-900; ☽ 4pm-3am Mon-Fri, 6pm-3am Sat; E) For bacon and eggs with a uniquely Japanese spin, head for this retro-'50s diner where the music and the menu are straight out of Kansas City, but the cook and clientele are local. Plus root beer and free coffee refills.

Yamasaki (☎ 762-6668; 1-8-11 Chestnut Bldg; meals around ¥1750; ☽ lunch & dinner) Just off busy Oyafuko-dōri, this traditional eatery serves up excellent fish, salads and *teishoku* (set meals). Grilled *sanma* (mackerel) or *netsuke* (red snapper), a salad and beer will cost you about ¥1750. There's no English sign; look for the small 'Chestnut' signboard. A picture menu is available.

CHINA (☎ 282-1234; 1st fl Grand Hyatt Hotel, Canal City; dim sum ¥2800; ☽ lunch) A Cantonese banquet hall offering all-you-can-eat dim sum.

The **IMS building** (1-7-11 Tenjin, Chūō-ku) in Tenjin has prime skyline views from its 12th- and 13th-floor restaurants, including **No No Budo** (☎ 714-1441; buffet ¥1575/2100; ☽ lunch & dinner), a busy 'all-you-can-eat' buffet, with fresh fish and meat dishes, noodles, salads, soups and desserts.

Nearby is **Pietro Corte** (☎ 733-2065; pasta & salad bar from ¥900) and, with beer on tap, **Kirin Sow-Sow Grill** (☎ 733-2073; seafood plates ¥350-1800); **Mrs Elizabeth Muffin** (☎ 733-2083; pastries from ¥150) in the basement food court sells sweet muffins with free coffee refills!

Drinking

The weekend starts on Thursday night in party-friendly Fukuoka. Most of the city's clubs, bars and pubs stay open until at least 3am. Pick a spot, hang out there for a good part of the evening and you're sure to make a friend or two. The main drag of Oyafuko-dōri roughly translates as 'street of unruly children' –

DAIMYO DISTRICT 大名地区

The narrow streets and lanes of the Daimyo district are home to many of Fukuoka's newest bars and eateries, and perfect for a late meal and a drink. **Bar Garasu** (☎ 712-8251; 1-12-28 Daimyo, Chūō-ku) draws a hip, hole-in-the-wall crowd, while nearby **Alohana** (☎ 724-0111; Donpa Bldg, 1-11-4 Daimyo, Chūō-ku) serves up Hawaiian-Japanese fusion plates, and the elegant **Bar Oscar** (☎ 7721-5352; 6th fl 1-10-29 Daimyo), named for jazz luminary Oscar Peterson, appeals to the swank Fukuoka set.

---

named for the old *Juku*, or cram schools, that once lined the road.

Off Broadway (☎ 724-5383; 2nd fl Beans Bldg) Close to the action with a bit of its own as well, overlooking busy Oyafuko-dōri. There's a full bar, pizza, R&B, salsa and hip-hop DJs, plus live music on weekends.

Uprising (☎ 716-6364; 2nd fl 1-3-4 Maizuru, Chūō-ku) A popular backstreet bar reflecting the personality of its Ghanaian owner, Hector. Mellow music with a reggae beat and good drinks make this place a pleasure.

Bōkairō (望海楼; ☎ 844-8000; 35th fl, Sea Hawk Hotel & Resort) Upscale neo-Chinese cocktail lounge in Fukuoka's seaside Momochi district, with lipstick red plush lounge seats and stellar night views. Cocktails start at ¥1000.

Van Beeru (☎ 282-9191; 5-2-3 Nakasu, Hakata-ku; draught mugs from ¥300; ☽ 6pm-6am) Just over the bridge on Nakasu island, this lively pub brags of over 1000 beers. Free popcorn and decent pub food.

Seattle's Best Coffee (☎ 737-3232; 1-11-1 Tenjin, Chūō-ku; wi-fi) Opposite Junkudō bookstore, SBC offers the usual coffee and sweets, plus free wi-fi.

International Bar (☎ 714-2179; 4th fl Urashima Bldg, 3-1-13 Tenjin) Free karaoke on Tuesdays is a hoot at Fukuoka's first international bar.

Entertainment

CLUBS

Nakasu Island is one of the most popular entertainment districts in Japan, but you need to go with a Japanese regular unless you're prepared to spend a fortune. Tenjin, and especially Oyafuko-dōri, are a better bet for a night on the town. Generally clubs have a weekend cover charge of ¥1000 to ¥3000, usually with a free drink or two.

Juke Joint (☎ 762-5596; 1-9-23 Maizuru, Chūō-ku) Customers can select the tunes at this unusual and intimate lounge. The music ranges from jazz and reggae to rock, blues and funk. Good drinks from ¥500, plus spicy seafood gumbo; owner Ko Matsumoto led a local relief fund for Hurricane Katrina victims.

Dark Room (☎ 725-2989; 8th fl Bacchus-kan; ☽ 6pm-2am) This hip urban rock bar offers darts, pool, dancing and Iron Butterfly vibes – along with a great sound system and killer *quesadillas*. In summer, check out the rooftop patio.

Voodoo Lounge (☎ 732-4662; 3rd fl, Tenjin Centre Bldg; 9pm-3am) Chilled-out and spacious, Voodoo is known for good live bands and DJs most nights, quality drinks at the long wooden bar and ¥100 beer on Thursday nights from 9pm to 10pm.

Sam & Dave (☎ 713-2223; www.samanddave.jp; 3rd fl, West Side Bldg, Tenjin Nishidōri) Named for the '60s soul duo, this roomy lounge with strobes, red neon and dancing throbs with hip-hop and R&B. On weekends, it's a meat market for 20-somethings.

Club Lab-Z Remix (☎ 711-1004; 6th fl, Okabe Bldg, 3-6-12 Tenjin, Chūō-ku) This small and sophisticated R&B club on Oyafuko-dōri grooves till the wee hours.

KABUKI

Hakata-za (☎ 263-5555; 2-1 Shimokawabata-machi, Hakata-ku; admission ¥5000-18,600) Fans of classical kabuki (stylised Japanese theatre) will swoon over this 1500-seat state-of-the-art theatre, above Nakasu-Kawabata subway stop. Actors enter and exit the stage via the raised *hanamichi* pathway through the audience.

Shopping

Clay *Hakata Ningyō* (Hakata dolls) depicting women, children, samurai and geisha are a popular Fukuoka craft. Hakata obi, the silk sashes worn with a kimono, are another local product. Try the Mitsukoshi or Daimaru department stores in Tenjin (see p667).

Hundred Yen Shop (4th fl Hakata station bus terminal; ☽ 10am-10pm) For last-minute bargain gift shopping, head for this sprawling shop opposite JR Hakata station.

Shopping, or at least window shopping, in Tenjin's high-rise and underground labyrinthine complexes is a popular Fukuoka pastime. Packed along a sparkling three-block section of Tenjin's Watanabi-dōri, **Tenjin Core** (☎ 721-7755), **Mitsukoshi** (☎ 724-3111), **Daimaru** (☎ 712-8181), **Solaria Plaza** (☎ 733-7004), subterra-

nean **Tenjin Chikagai** (☎ 721-8436) and **IMS building** (☎ 733-2001) are all favourite spots. The latter gets bonus points for a rooftop terrace, open 11am to 9pm, weather permitting.

Getting There & Away

AIR

Fukuoka is a major international gateway with flights to and from many major cities in Japan and Asia. Domestic flights go to Tokyo (¥27,900, 1½ hours, Haneda airport/Narita International Airport 45/four flights daily). Other domestic routes include Osaka (¥16,200, one hour, six flights daily) and Okinawa (Naha, ¥20,300, 1½ hours, 12 flights daily). ANA and JAL are the two most common carriers, and both have offices here.

Japan's only independent cut-rate carrier, **Skymark** (☎ 736-3131, in Tokyo 03-3433-7026) flies to Tokyo's Haneda airport (¥15,000, nine flights daily).

BOAT

Ferry services from Hakata connect to Okinawa and other islands off Kyūshū. An international high-speed hydrofoil service run by JR Kyūshū called **Biitoru** (say 'beetle'; ☎ in Japan 092-281-2315, in Korea 051-442-6111; www.jrbeetle.co.jp/english) connects Fukuoka with Busan in Korea (¥13,000, three hours, four daily). The **Camellia line** (☎ in Japan 092-262-2323, in Korea 051-466-7799; www.camellia-line.co.jp in Japanese & Korean) has a regular ferry service from Fukuoka to Busan (¥9000, six hours, daily at noon). In Fukuoka, the Beetle and the Camellia depart from Fukuoka Port International Terminal via bus 11, 19 or 50 from JR Hakata station (¥220), or bus 80 from Tenjin (Solaria Stage-mae; ¥180). From Busan, both the Beetle (Won 9000, three hours, four daily) and the Camellia (Won 80,000, overnight) depart from the International Ferry Port, approximately 200m from Jungang-dong subway station.

BUS

Long-distance buses (☎ English information 733-3333) depart from the Kōtsū bus centre near JR Hakata station and also from the Tenjin bus centre. Destinations include Tokyo (¥15,000, 14½ hours), Osaka (¥10,000, 9½ hours), Nagoya (¥10,500, 11 hours) and many other places around Kyūshū.

TRAIN

JR Hakata station (☎ English information 471-8111, JR English info-line 03-3423-0111) is the western terminus

KYŪSHŪ

of the 1175km-long Tokyo–Osaka–Hakata *shinkansen*. There are services to/from Tokyo (¥21,720, five to six hours), Osaka (¥14,590, 2½ to three hours) and Hiroshima (¥8700, 1½ hours). Prices are slightly higher for the Nozomi *shinkansen*.

JR lines also fan out from Hakata to other parts of Kyūshū. The Nippō line runs through Beppu and Miyazaki; the Kagoshima line runs through Hakata, Kumamoto and Kagoshima; and both the Nagasaki and Sasebo lines run from Hakata to Saga and Sasebo or to Nagasaki. The newest *shinkansen* line in Kyūshū runs from Shin-Yatsushiro to Kagoshima (¥6350, one hour); eventually it will extend up to Hakata. You can also travel by subway and JR train to Karatsu and continue from there to Nagasaki by train.

Getting Around
TO/FROM THE AIRPORT
Fukuoka airport is conveniently close to the city centre. The airport has three domestic terminals and an international terminal, all connected by a free shuttle bus.

The subway from the domestic terminals takes just five minutes to reach JR Hakata station (¥250) and 11 minutes to Tenjin (¥250). Buses run frequently between JR Hakata station and the international terminal.

Airport taxis cost around ¥1600 to Tenjin/Hakata.

BUS
City bus services operate from the Kōtsū bus centre in Hakata and the Tenjin bus centre. Nishitetsu buses have a flat ¥100 rate for city-centre rides.

From stand E opposite JR Hakata station at the Kōtsū bus centre, bus 11 or 19 goes to Hakata Pier International Terminal (¥220), while bus 47 or 48 reaches Bayside Place for ferries to islands.

SUBWAY
There are three subway lines in Fukuoka. The Kūkō (airport) line runs from Fukuoka domestic airport terminal to Meinohama station via Hakata, Nakasu-Kawabata and Tenjin stations. The Hakozaki line runs from Nakasu-Kawabata station to Kaizuka. The Nanakuma line runs from Tenjin-minami to Hashimoto. Fares around town start at ¥200; a one-day pass costs adult/child six to 11 ¥600/300. Trains run from 5.30am to 12.25am.

DAZAIFU 太宰府
☎ 092 / pop 66,308

Dazaifu, once the governmental centre of Kyūshū, is an amiable place for a day visit. Japan's newest national museum, a beautiful cluster of temples and a shrine make Dazaifu a rewarding day trip from Fukuoka. The **tourist information office** (☎ 925-1880; ☽ 9am-5.30pm) at Nishitetsu-Dazaifu station has helpful staff and an excellent English-language brochure map that details outlying ruins, temples and minor sights.

Sights
KYŪSHŪ NATIONAL MUSEUM
九州国立博物館

Japan's fourth national **museum** (☎ 918-2807; www.kyuhaku.com/eng/; 4-7-2 Ishizaka, Dazaifu City; adult/student ¥420/210; ☽ 9.30am-5pm, closed Mon) opened in 2005, the country's first since 1900. This stunningly modern structure in the tranquil hills of Dazaifu resembles a massive space station for the arts. Highlights include a fascinating Silk Road exhibit, stone carvings of AD 1st-century women with spears on horseback and a delicate 13th-century oil-spot *tenmoku* tea bowl. Free self-guided audio tours and HD video theatre.

TENMAN-GŪ 天満宮
Poet and scholar Sugawara-no-Michizane was a distinguished figure in the Kyoto court until he fell foul of political intrigue and was exiled to distant Dazaifu, where he died two years later. Subsequent disasters that struck Kyoto were blamed on his unfair dismissal and he became deified as Tenman Tenjin, the god of culture and scholars. **Tenman-gū** (☎ 922-8225; www.dazaifutenmangu.or.jp; 4-7-1 Saifu), his shrine and burial place, attracts countless visitors, among them students in hope of passing their college entrance exams. The *honden* (main hall) was rebuilt in 1591.

Behind the shrine is the **Kankō Historical Museum** (菅公歴史館; admission ¥200; ☽ 9am-4.30pm Wed-Mon) with dioramas showing events in Tenjin's life. The **treasure house** (宝物殿; admission ¥300; ☽ 9am-4.30pm Tue-Sun) has artefacts connected with his life and the shrine.

Every other month the shrine hosts an *omoshiro-ichi* (literally 'interesting market'), a giant flea market selling everything from antique kimonos to Mickey Mouse telephones. Dates vary, so check with tourist information at the station.

KŌMYŌZEN-JI 光明禅寺

Secreted away inside this small **temple** (☎ 922-4053; admission by donation ¥200; ☯ 9am-4.30pm) is an exquisite jewel of a Zen garden. It's a peaceful contrast to the crowds at the nearby shrine. It's on the southern edge of Dazaifu.

OTHER SIGHTS

The **Kyūshū Historical Museum** (九州歴史資料館; ☎ 923-0404; admission free; ☯ 9am-4pm Tue-Sun) is not far beyond Kōmyōzen-ji (above), with items mostly from the Stone Age to the Middle Ages.

Hidden out among the rice fields, **Kaidan-in** (戒壇院) dates from 761 and was one of the most important ordination monasteries in Japan. Adjacent **Kanzeon-ji** (観世音寺; ☎ 922-1811) dates from AD 746 but only the great bell, said to be the oldest in Japan, remains from the original construction. Its **treasure hall** (宝蔵; admission ¥500; ☯ 9am-4.30pm) has an impressive collection of statuary, most of it wood, dating from the 10th to 12th centuries. Many of the items show Indian or Tibetan influence.

Dazaifu Exhibition Hall (大宰府展示館; ☎ 922-7811; admission ¥150; ☯ 9am-4.30pm Tue-Sun) displays finds from local archaeological excavations. Nearby are the **Tofurō ruins** (都府楼), foundations of the ancient government buildings. **Enoki-sha** (榎社) is where Sugawara-no-Michizane died. His body was transported from here to its burial place, now Tenman-gū, on the ox cart that appears in so many local depictions.

Eating

O Cha Cha (お茶々; ☎ 929-0626; ☯ 11am-6pm) For a perfect sweet snack of *He-ko-yaki* (crepes with sesame and black sugar; ¥500) or *mochi* (pounded rice made into cakes and eaten at festive occasions), and of course *ma-cha* (traditional green tea) or freshly ground coffee made to order. It's located towards Lawsons.

Hiyori (日和; ☎ 929-0626; teishoku sets from ¥1300; ☯ lunch & dinner) Near the station and temple grounds, Hiyori offers excellent food and gracious service. Dinner reservations recommended. To find Hiyori, exit the station and cross the street to Lawson's, and walk 30m to the right. No English sign, but look for traditional wooden front and landscaping. Some English is spoken, plus a picture menu.

Getting There & Around

The private Nishitetsu line connects Tenjin in Fukuoka (p673) with Dazaifu (¥390, 25 minutes), but a change of trains at Nishitetsu-Futsukaichi station is required.

Bicycles can be rented (per three hours/day ¥300/500) at Nishitetsu Dazaifu station.

FUTSUKAICHI ONSEN 二日市温泉

☎ 092

About 300m south of JR Futsukaichi station, this small, unassuming *onsen* (mineral hot spring) town has public baths grouped together in the old main street. Favoured by traditionalists, **Gozen-yu** (御前湯; ☎ 928-1126; admission ¥200; ☯ 9am-9pm, closed 1st & 3rd Wed each month) is the most characteristic. From JR Futsukaichi station, cross back over the tracks, then follow the road under the torii (shrine gate) and across the stream.

TACHIARAI 大刀洗

☎ 0942

Even locals don't know about **Tachiarai Heiwa Kinenkan** (太刀洗平和記念館; ☎ 23-1227; admission ¥500; ☯ 9.30am-5pm), a tiny memorial museum established by ex-aviators and residents of Tachiarai, a small farmland village near Ogōri. The museum commemorates Japanese killed in WWII, including kamikaze pilots and Tachiarai locals who died when USAF B-29s bombed the military air base on 27 March 1945.

It's a strangely affecting place, with wartime memorabilia and a Japanese fighter plane, retrieved from nearby Hakata Bay where it crashed in 1942. Little is labelled in English.

KURUME 久留米

☎ 0942

The town of Kurume, south of Dazaifu, is noted for its crafts, including splash-dyed indigo textiles, paper making, lacquerware and bamboo work. Its rubber industry is responsible for *jika-tabi*, the floppy split-toed boots worn by labourers all over Japan, as well as for Bridgestone tyres.

Narita-san (成田山; ☎ 21-7500; ☯ 7am-5pm), a branch of the more famous temple outside Tokyo (see p229), is the town's biggest attraction, both literally and metaphorically speaking. Its 62m-high statue of the goddess of mercy, Kannon, stands beside a miniaturised replica of Borobudur. Inside the statue you can climb up past Buddhist treasures and religious dioramas right into the divine forehead.

Ishibashi Museum of Art (石橋美術館; ☎ 39-1131; www.ishibashi-museum.gr.jp; adult/child ¥500/300;

⊙ 10am-5pm, closed Mon) boasts an excellent private collection of Asian and Western art assembled by the founder of Bridgestone, who felt strongly that art should always be publicly accessible rather than being hidden away. The museum is 1km from the Nishitetsu–Kurume station.

Going to Kurume from Fukuoka takes 30 minutes, either on the JR Kagoshima line or the private Nishitetsu line (¥600).

SAGA-KEN 佐賀県

KARATSU 唐津

☎ 0955 / pop 132,330

One of Japan's world-renowned pottery towns, Karatsu is a must-see for *yakimono* (pottery or ceramic ware) fans. Already a well-known pottery town, Karatsu's Korean influences elevated it from useful ceramic ware to art. Karatsu-made vessels are some of the finest in Japan. Not surprisingly, they are also some of the priciest: a small *sakazuki* (sake cup) can easily go for ¥20,000, a modest vase for ¥5,000,000. Even if you're not in the market for a piece to add to your collection, meandering about the exquisite gardens and displays is a wonderful way to spend an afternoon. At JR Karatsu station, the **tourist information office** (☎ 72-4963; ⊙ 9am-6pm) has a good English-language map booklet. Staff can book accommodation, but little English is spoken.

Sights & Activities

A modern reconstruction, **Karatsu-jō** (☎ 72-5697; admission ¥400; ⊙ 9am-5pm) is picturesquely perched on a hill overlooking the sea. Inside are antique ceramics, samurai armour and archaeological displays.

Karatsu-jinja (☎ 72-2264) is a scenic shrine in the centre of the city, near the **Hikiyama Festival Float Exhibition Hall** (☎ 72-8278; admission ¥300), which contains the 14 floats used in the Karatsu Kunchi Matsuri (opposite). Designs include the Aka-jishi (Red Lion), samurai helmets, a dragon and a chicken.

Around town there are a number of **kilns and studios** where you can see local potters at work, and there are also ceramic shops along the street between Karatsu train station and the town centre. The most famous kiln-gallery

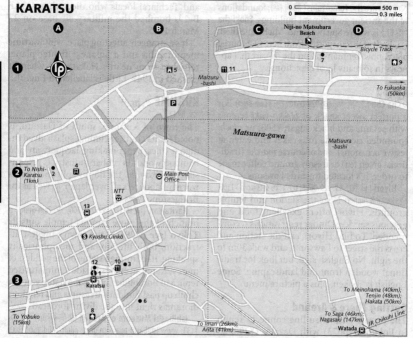

is that of **Nakazato Tarōemon** (☎ 72-8171; admission free). It's about 350m southeast of Karatsu station. Other inviting galleries are nearby, and you can feel free to peep into the well-manicured gardens. Most potters feel strongly that their art is not only a work in itself, but that it is a part of the surroundings. The gallery owners try hard to display their wares as attractively as possible – and with photos, it's best to ask permission before you shoot. Many also offer a complimentary tea service.

Just next to Karatsu station, **Karatsu Ware Federation Exhibition Hall** (☎ 73-4888; 2nd fl, Arupino Bldg) not only gives a taste of what the area's potters are producing, but also provides local contact information. Many of the items on display are for sale from ¥500.

A bicycle track cuts through the pine trees planted behind the 5km-long Niji-no Matsubara Beach Hotel. Each morning there is a busy **asa-ichi** (morning market) at the west end of the beach, from dawn until 9am.

For **surfing**, head to the middle of the beach where Karatsu catches good swells in late summer, especially around typhoon season. Karatsu's resident Rastafarian, Nishimura Eiji, knows all about it and his efficient little **Surf Camp shop** (☎ 72-1207) opposite the beach has boards and diving gear, along with a camper trailer (see right).

Festivals & Events

Doyō-yoichi (観光案内所; night market) On four consecutive Saturdays in late July and early August; held in the town centre with much singing and dancing.

Karatsu Kunchi Matsuri (唐津くんち祭り) Taking place from 2 to 4 November, this spectacular festival dates from 1592.

Sleeping & Eating

Surf Camp shop (☎ 72-1207; per person ¥1000) Has a funky camper trailer opposite the beach with five lumpy bunk beds and free use of the leopard-skin TV.

Business Hotel SOLA (☎ 72-3003; www.hotel-sola .com in Japanese; s incl breakfast ¥4900; P X X) This attractive and modern business hotel offers single rooms only. The generous breakfast buffet is a plus.

our pick Niji-no-Matsubara Hotel (☎ 73-9111, 0120-73-9100; fax 75-9991; s/d/tw ¥5000/8400/10,500, Japanese-style r ¥15,000; P X X 🖥) You can't get much closer to the ocean than at this well-managed budget gem a short bus (¥160) or taxi (¥900) ride from Karatsu station. Single rooms have ocean views, though twin rooms face inland. A full breakfast buffet runs to ¥900.

Kiage (☎ 73-8080; ⏲ lunch & dinner) Next to the ticket turnstile at Karatsu station, Kiage serves up tasty noodles, *gyōza* and other hearty station fare. A generous pork *rāmen* and fried rice combo costs ¥750 (picture menu).

Mambō (☎ 75-1881; dishes ¥500-2000; ⏲ lunch & dinner) Pick up a bento box for the train, or sit down for squid *shūmai teishoku* (set meal; ¥1500) at this Karatsu station eatery.

Kawashima Tōfu (☎ 72-2423; www.zarudoufu.co.jp in Japanese; set meals ¥1500-2500; ⏲ 8am & noon only, by reservation) Close by the station, Kawashima Tōfu has been making fresh bean curd since the Edo period. *Zaru-dōfu*, its speciality, is scooped like ice cream and served with set meals on *Karatsu-yaki* plates (see p678).

Early risers can check out the *asa-ichi* nearby the water for seafood and other delicacies.

Getting There & Around

From Fukuoka (p663), take the Kūkō subway line from Hakata or Tenjin to the end of the line at Meinohama, then change to the JR Chikuhi line to reach Karatsu (¥1110, 80 minutes). From Karatsu to Nagasaki (¥2830, 2½ hours) take the JR Karatsu line to Saga, and the JR Nagasaki line from there.

KYŪSHŪ

From the **Ōtemachi bus centre** (☎ 73-7511), highway buses depart for Fukuoka (¥1000, 70 minutes) and Nagasaki (¥2400, two hours).

Tourists are able to borrow bicycles for free from the **Arupino** (☎ 75-5155) building. For excursions around Saga-ken, **Eki-mae Rent-a-Car** (☎ 74-6204) is located in front of Karatsu station, with half- and full-day rentals.

HIGASHI-MATSUURA PENINSULA 東
松浦半島

Karatsu is at the base of Higashi-Matsuura Peninsula, with its dramatic coastline, dotted at night with the flickering lights of fishing boats heading out to sea. During the day, a string of dramatic sea caves are evidence of the pounding waves rolling in from the Sea of Genkai.

Yobuko 呼子

A busy fishing port with a wonderful **morning market** for fish and produce; the main action is over by 8am. A series of modern wooden ryokan, charging from around ¥9500 per person (including meals), lines a narrow lane alongside the waterfront; rooms look straight out onto the bay. Prices drop 10% on weekdays. Squid sashimi and tempura are the local delicacies. Shōwa buses run from Karatsu to Yobuko (¥730, 30 minutes).

Nagoya-jō 名護屋城

En route to Cape Hatomi, buses stop at this now-ruined **castle** (admission ¥100), from which Toyotomi Hideyoshi launched his unsuccessful invasions of Korea. Look for the model of the castle in its glory days. Excellent views over the ruins are available from inside the

prefectural museum (名護屋城博物館; ☎ 0955-82-4905; admission free; ⏰ 9am-6pm), which holds everything from Buddhas to fishing boats. Highlights include a 14th-century scroll painting of Kannon, and Toyotomi's lavishly embroidered overcoat.

IMARI 伊万里
☎ 0955 / pop 58,900

Although Imari is the name commonly associated with pottery from this area, the pottery is actually produced outside town. At JR Kurume station, check with the friendly English-speaking staff at **Imari City Information** (☎ 23-3479; ⏰ 8.30am-6pm) for local maps and tips.

Ōkawachiyama (大川内山), where 20 pottery kilns operate today, is a 20-minute bus ride from Imari (¥150). Buses are frequent from Monday to Friday, but do not run on weekends. Arrive by midday to allow time for exploring. The **bridge** entering Ōkawachiyama is spectacularly decorated with shards of *Imari-yaki* and large vases. The bus stops right near the bridge and the village is on the surrounding hillsides on both sides of the river. At the bottom of the hill where the village begins is **Kataoka Tsurutarō Kōgeikan** (片岡鶴太郎工芸館; ☎ 22-3080; admission ¥300) gallery, an austere structure dedicated to the intense work of potter-genius Sawada Chitōjin, whose name means 'pottery-crazy person'. Uphill, **Nabeshima Hanyō-kōen** (鍋島藩窯公園; ☎ 23-1111) shows the techniques and living conditions of feudal-era potters.

Inside a narrow shopping arcade near the train station, **Akira Kurosawa Memorial Satellite Studio** (黒澤明記念館サテライトスタジオ;

KYŪSHŪ POTTERY TOWNS

In mountainous Kyūshū many villages had difficulty growing rice and turned towards other ways to make a living. Easy access to good clay, forests and streams made pottery-making a natural substitute, and a number of superb styles can be found here, many of Korean origin.

Imari and Arita are the major pottery towns of Saga-ken. From the early 17th century pottery was produced in this area using captive Korean potters, experts who were zealously guarded so that the secrets of their craft did not slip out. Pottery from this area, with its brightly coloured glazes, is still highly esteemed in Japan.

- Karatsu (p676): rough and groggy, marked by subtle earth tones; Karatsu-yaki (Karatsu pottery) is particularly prized for use in the tea ceremony (Saga-ken).

- Arita (opposite): a highly decorated porcelain ware, usually with squares of blue, red, green or gold (Saga-ken).

- Imari (above): similar to Arita, highly prized white-and-blue porcelain (Saga-ken).

☎ 22-9630; admission ¥500; ⊘ 9am-5.30pm, closed 2nd & 4th Mon each month) has little English labelling, but it matters not to fans of one of cinema's greatest visionaries. Explore three floors of film memorabilia and directors' sketches of the legendary filmmaker and glimpse behind-the-scenes documentaries and rare outtakes from masterpieces like *Rashomon* (1950) and *Shichinin no Samurai* (Seven Samurai; 1954), which show continuously. There is also a lunch and wine bar.

Karatsu is connected with Imari (*futsū*, ¥630, 50 minutes) by the JR Chikuhi line. Local buses to Ōkawachiyama depart hourly from the main bus terminal, a few blocks west of the train station, where you can also catch direct buses to Fukuoka (¥2150, two hours).

ARITA 有田

☎ 0955 / pop 21,570

Kaolin clay was discovered here in 1615 by Ri Sampei, a naturalised Korean potter, enabling the manufacture of fine porcelain in Japan for the first time. By the mid-17th century it was being exported to Europe. The **tourist information desk** (☎ 42-4052; www.arita.or.jp/index_e.html; ⊘ 9am-5pm) inside Arita train station can help orient visitors with maps and bus schedules.

An annual **pottery fair** is held from 29 April to 5 May.

Shops line the main street leading out from the station towards the **Kyūshū Ceramics Museum** (九州陶磁文化館; ☎ 43-3681; admission free; ⊘ 9am-4.30pm Tue-Sun), a converted warehouse well worth a visit for its fine overview of the development of ceramic arts in Kyūshū. Pottery connoisseurs are sure to find the modest **Imaemon Gallery** (今衛門ギャラリー; ☎ 42-5550; admission ¥300; ⊘ 9.30am-4.30pm Tue-Sun), **Kakiemon Kiln** (柿右衛門窯; ☎ 43-2267; admission free; ⊘ 9am-5pm) and **Genemon Kiln** (源衛門窯; ☎ 42-4164; admission free; ⊘ 8am-5.30pm Mon-Sat) interesting, and there are dozens of other workshops to visit.

For the full treatment, join the Japanese package tours at **Arita Porcelain Park** (有田ポーセリンパーク; ☎ 41-0030; adult/student ¥1000/500; ⊘ 10am-5pm Mar-Nov, to 4pm Dec-Feb), a 10-minute bus ride (¥150) from the train station, or shop for **Fukagawa** porcelain at **China on the Park** (チャイナオンザパーク; ☎ 46-3900; ⊘ 9am-5.30pm) gallery 5km west of town on Rte 202, where you can watch the firing process.

A taxi from Arita train station costs about ¥1000. An Arita bus (¥150, four daily from

9.30am) can take you to the clay mines as well. Walk back to the station from the mines, about an hour's stroll if the many galleries don't tempt you. Along the way, note the house walls in some of the back streets: leftover pottery was often used in bricks and some of the older buildings show this quite well.

A short hop east of Arita, **Takeo Onsen** (武雄温泉) is a modern hot-springs town. The traditional baths are said to have refreshed the armies of Toyotomi Hideyoshi. Look for the lacquered Chinese-style gate, which was built without nails.

Takeo Onsen Youth Hostel (武雄温泉ユースホステル; ☎ 0954-22-2490; fax 0954-20-1208; dm member/nonmember incl breakfast ¥3300/4300) is a good option, but the last bus to the hostel (¥250, seven minutes) leaves Takeo Onsen station at 4pm.

From outside JR Arita station, private Matsuura-tetsudō trains depart for Imari (¥400, 25 minutes). JR *tokkyū* trains between Hakata (Fukuoka) and Sasebo stop at Arita, and also Takeo Onsen. Takeo Onsen is also connected to Arita by local trains (¥270, 20 minutes). Around town, community bus routes (¥150) cover most sights, departing hourly from Arita station. Rental bicycles are only ¥300 per day, at the train station.

NORTHWEST ISLANDS

Five large and many smaller islands lie to the northwest of Kyūshū and are accessible from Fukuoka, Sasebo and Nagasaki, but reaching them is not cheap. These are strictly islands for those who want to get far away from it all. Some are part of Saga-ken, but all of those below are part of Nagasaki-ken.

IKI 壱岐

☎ 09204 / pop 32,310

Attractive Iki, an island off Kyūshū's northern coast, has an area of 138 sq km and lies closer to Karatsu than Fukuoka. As well as being home to fine beaches, it's also relatively flat and a decent place for cyclists. Toyotomi Hideyoshi fortified **Gonoura**, the busiest port and a base for exploring the island. **Ondakejinja**, north of Ashibe, features stone statues dedicated to a half-monkey deity. These eroded figures were carved by a local lord, and were originally intended to bring health to the island's livestock. **Yunomoto Onsen** on the west coast is the island's only hot spring.

KYŪSHŪ

Other minor sights include burial mounds, Buddhist rock carvings and historic ruins.

The gorgeous little **beach** near Katsumoto on the island's north side also has a camping ground nearby. At the hot springs, the *kokumin-shukusha* (people's lodge) **Ikishima-sō** (壱岐島荘; ☎ 43-0124; r with 2 meals ¥6660) is good value. Cheerful **Tomita-sō** (富田荘; ☎ 47-0011; r with 2 meals ¥5800) is in Gonoura. At Gonoura ferry terminal, the **information desk** (☎ 47-3700) can help book other *minshuku* (Japanese B&B), pension and ryokan accommodation around the island.

ORC Air has flights from Nagasaki to Iki (¥8000, 30 minutes, two daily). Jetfoils run year-round from Hakata to Gonoura or Ashibe (¥4680, 70 minutes, three daily) on Iki. Ordinary car ferry services take twice that long (¥1930, two daily). On Iki, rental cars start at ¥3000 per three hours, costing ¥10,000 for two days. They can be rented at all of the ferry ports. Try friendly **Genkai Kotsū Rent-a-Car** (☎ 44-5658). Bike rental is possible from **Kawabe Motors** (☎ 44-6636; ¥1000), near the ferry terminal; for an extra ¥1000 you can have the bike dropped to you anywhere on the island.

HIRADO-SHIMA 平戸島
☎ 0950 / pop 39,077

Blessed with sunshine and verdant tea fields, Hirado-shima's proximity to the mainland makes it easy – and cheap – to access. The island has interesting historical sights, beckoning white-sand beaches, two noteworthy festivals, and a little-known collection of erotic drawings.

The **tourist information centre** (☎ 22-2015; ◷ 8am-5pm), on the waterfront by the bus terminal, sometimes has English-language brochures and can book accommodation.

The island, close to Sasebo and actually joined to Kyūshū by a toll bridge (¥100) from Hirado-guchi, the nearest train station (a private line, Matsuura Tetsudō), has had an interesting European history. Portuguese ships first landed on Hirado-shima in 1549 and, a year later, St Francis Xavier visited the island (after his expulsion from Kagoshima). It was not until 1584 that the Portuguese formally established a trading post, but they were soon followed by the Dutch and the British. Relations between the British and Dutch became so acrimonious that, in 1618, the Japanese had to restore law and order on the island. In 1621 the British abandoned Hirado-shima

and Japan, and turned their full attention to India.

The main town, Hirado, is small enough to navigate on foot. The **Matsuura Historical Museum** (松浦史料博物館; ☎ 22-2236; admission ¥500; ◷ 8am-5.30pm) is housed in the residence of the Matsuura clan, who ruled the island from the 11th to the 19th centuries. Among the esteemed treasures is **Kanun-tei**, a *chanoyu* (tea-ceremony) house for the unusual Chinshin-ryū warrior-style tea ceremony that is still practised on the island today. **Hirado Christian Museum** (平戸切支丹資料館; ☎ 28-0176; admission ¥200; ◷ 8am-5pm Jan-Nov) displays some items relating to the island's history, including a Maria-Kannon statue that the 'hidden Christians' used in place of the Virgin Mary image.

Hirado-jō (平戸城; ☎ 22-2201; admission ¥500; ◷ 8.30am-5.30pm) presides over the town, with an enormous number of rebuilt structures. Inside you'll see traditional armour and clothing, and a few artefacts from the hidden Christian era. There are fine views over the islands of the Gotō-rettō from **Cape Shijiki**. About midway down the beautiful west coast of the island, **Neshiko Beach** is a lovely and long stretch of sand, while **Senri-ga-hama** is renowned for windsurfing. **Hotel Ranpu** (ホテル蘭風; ☎ 23-2111), near the beach, rents windsurfing gear.

Jangara Matsuri (ジャンガラ祭り), a folk festival held on 18 August, is particularly colourful. It is quite different from mainland festivals and is reminiscent of Okinawa or Korea. Arrive in Hirado by late morning, if possible, for the afternoon events. From 24 to 27 October, the **Okunchi Matsuri** (おくんち祭り) has dragon and lion dancing at Kameoka-jinja.

Over in Hirado-guchi, the closest mainland town, there's a camping ground and a beautiful **youth hostel** (たびら平戸口ユースホステル; ☎ 57-1443; dm ¥3360) with two attractive *rotemburo* (open-air or outdoor baths), one for men facing the sea, and another for women with mountain views. They also make excellent meals on request, and at night you can glimpse the twinkling lights of the squid boats. The kind staff will also pick you up at the station if you call ahead, and may even detour for groceries.

Hirado-guchi (aka Tabira) is accessible by bus from Sasebo (¥1150, 1¼ hours), and by train (¥1190, 1½ hours). Local buses cross the bridge to Hirado town (¥260, 10 minutes). Express buses (¥1450, 1½ hours) and trains (¥1600, 1½ hours) run from Nagasaki to Sasebo.

GOTŌ-RETTŌ 五島列島

The two main islands in the Gotō-rettō group are **Fukue-jima** and **Nakadōri-shima**, but there are three other medium-sized islands plus over 100 small islands and islets. At one time these islands were a refuge for Japanese Christians fleeing the Edo government's anti-Christian repression; today the main attraction is their natural beauty.

Fukue, the fishing port on the island of the same name, is the main town in the group. The town's **Ishida-jō** was rebuilt in the 1860s. There's a street of samurai houses nearby. **Ondake**, about 800m from Fukue, is a cotyloid volcano (315m) covered by grass and with an astronomical observatory. **Dozaki Tenshudō** (堂崎天主堂; ☎ 0959-73-0705; admission ¥300; ☺ 9am-4.30pm) has exhibits of artefacts from the 'hidden Christian' era, and is the oldest church in the Gotō islands. It's a 30-minute bus ride from Fukue. The island's most popular **beaches** are on the north central coast.

All Nippon Koku (ANK) has flights to Gotō-Fukue airport from Fukuoka (¥16,350, 35 minutes, three daily). Jetfoils leave Nagasaki for Fukue two to five times daily (¥6630, 1½ hours); regular car ferry services depart three times daily (¥2700, 3½ hours). Bicycles and cars can be rented on Fukue-jima.

NAGASAKI-KEN 長崎県

NAGASAKI 長崎

☎ 095 / pop 451,738

Nagasaki is a vibrant city, but its fate as the second atomic bomb target overshadows its early history of contact with the Portuguese and Dutch. Despite the tragic events of WWII, Nagasaki has a wealth of activities, state-of-the-art museums, delicious food, and natural beauty that rivals far more visited parts of Japan. Schedule at least a few days here to take advantage of all the city has to offer.

History

Nagasaki's role in Japan's emergence as a modern nation is as layered as it is tragic. Starting with the dramatic events of the 'Christian Century' (1549–1650), Nagasaki became Japan's first gateway to the West, as well as its nearer neighbours in Asia. The arrival of an off-course Chinese ship in 1543, with guns and Portuguese adventurers aboard, signalled the start of Nagasaki's long period as Japan's principal connection with the West.

The first visitors were soon followed by the missionary St Francis Xavier in 1560, one of many to follow. Although their visits were brief, these Portuguese contacts were to have far-reaching effects. Among the first Japanese to be converted to Christianity by the visitors was a minor *daimyō* (regional lord), Ōmura Sumitada, in northwestern Kyūshū. Under Ōmura, Nagasaki became the main arrival point for Portuguese trade ships. Although the Portuguese principally acted as intermediaries between China, Korea and Japan, the trade was mutually profitable, and Nagasaki quickly became a fashionable and wealthy city.

However, by 1587 Japanese authorities, who had begun to perceive the growing influence of Christianity as a threat, implemented a policy of persecution, expelling the Jesuits, and in 1597 crucifying 26 European and Japanese Christians. The upstart religion was officially banned in 1614. Catholic Portuguese and Spanish traders were expelled in favour of the Protestant Dutch, who were perceived as being more interested in trade and less in religion.

The final chapter of the 'Christian Century', the Shimabara peasant uprising of 1637–38, led the authorities to forbid any contact with foreigners, and to ban all travel outside Japan. The single exception, however, was the closely watched Dutch enclave on the island of Dejima in Nagasaki harbour. Through this small outpost a trickle of Western science and culture found its way into Japan, and by 1720, Nagasaki had become an important scientific and artistic centre. When Nagasaki reopened to the West in 1859, it quickly re-established itself as a major economic force, particularly in shipbuilding, the industry that made it a target on 9 August 1945 (for details see the boxed text, p684).

Orientation

About 1km south of Nagasaki station, the Hamano-machi arcade and Shian-bashi entertainment area make up Nagasaki's central city area. Nagasaki is relatively compact and it's

KYŪSHŪ

NAGASAKI

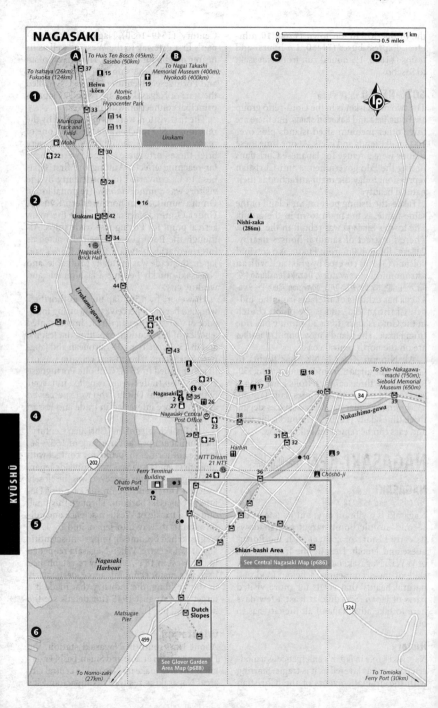

To Huis Ten Bosch (45km);
Sasebo (50km)

To Isahaya (26km);
Fukuoka (124km)

To Nagai Takashi
Memorial Museum (400m);
Nyokodō (400km)

Heiwa-
kōen

Atomic
Bomb
Hypocenter Park

Urukami

Municipal
Track and
Field

Mobil

Nishi-zaka
(286m)

Urakami

Nagasaki
Brick Hall

Urukami-gawa

To Shin-Nakagawa-
machi (150m);
Siebold Memorial
Museum (650m)

Nagasaki

Nakashima-gawa

Nagasaki Central
Post Office

Harbin

NTT Dream
21 NTT

Chōshō-ji

Ferry Terminal
Building

Ōhato Port
Terminal

Nagasaki
Harbour

Shian-bashi Area
See Central Nagasaki Map (p686)

Matsugae
Pier

Dutch
Slopes

See Glover Garden
Area Map (p688)

To Nomo-zaki
(27km)

To Tomioka
Ferry Port (30km)

0 — 1 km
0 — 0.5 miles

KYŪSHŪ

quite feasible to walk all the way south to the Dutch slopes and Glover Garden. The atomic bomb hypocentre is in the suburb of Urakami, about 2.5km north of JR Nagasaki station by streetcar (Matsuyama station).

Information
BOOKSHOPS
Kinokuniya (Map p682; ☎ 811-4919; 4th fl, Yume-saito Bldg, 10-1 Motofune-chō) Offers large selection of English and foreign titles, plus CDs, software, DVDs and maps.

INTERNET ACCESS
Chikyū-shimin Hiroba (Map p682; ☎ 842-2002; 2nd fl, Nagasaki Brick Hall; per hr ¥100; ☿ 9am-8pm) Five minutes' walk from Urakami station.

Cybac Café (Map p686; ☎ 818-8050; 3rd-4th fl, Hashim-oto Bldg, 2-46 Aburaya-chō; membership fee ¥300, per 15min ¥100; ☿ 24hr) Internet, darts, drinks, foot spa and more.

Internet Café Shin (Map p686; ☎ 822-7824; 5-25 Fu-rukawamachi, Hamano-machi; per 30min ¥210; ☿ 8am-8pm) Chinatown, opposite Minato Park.

Kinko's (Map p682; ☎ 818-2522; Amu Plaza; per 10min ¥210; ☿ 8am-10pm) Next to 18-Bank.

MONEY
All postal savings ATMs accept internationally issued cards, and there's one inside Nagasaki station. Several branches of the 18-Bank handle (slowly!) foreign-currency exchange.

TOURIST INFORMATION
City tourist information centre (Map p682; ☎ 823-3631; Nagasaki station; ☿ 8am-8pm) Can assist with finding accommodation, though little English is spoken.
Nagasaki Prefectural Tourist Information Center (Map p682; ☎ 828-7875; center@ngs-kenkanren.com; 3-1 Daikoki-machi; ☿ 9am-5.30pm, closed for Nenmatsu Nenshi holiday 27 Dec-3 Jan) Has detailed information on the city and prefecture and extremely helpful English-speaking staff. From the station, cross the pedestrian walkway to enter the prefectural building on the 2nd floor.

Sights
URAKAMI 浦上
Urakami, the hypocentre of the atomic explosion, is today a prosperous, peaceful suburb with modern shops, restaurants, cafés and even a couple of love hotels just a few steps from the hypocentre. Nuclear ruin seems comfortably far away.

Atomic Bomb Hypocenter Park (Map p682) has a smooth, black, square stone column (reminiscent of the monolith from Stanley Kubrick's *2001: A Space Odyssey*) marking the exact point above which the bomb exploded. Nearby are bomb-blasted relics, including a section of the wall of the Urakami Cathedral. The Matsuyama-machi tram stop on tram routes 1 or 3 is near the site.

KYŪSHŪ

THE ATOMIC EXPLOSION

When the United States Air Force (USAF) B-29 bomber *Bock's Car* set off from Tinian in the Marianas on 9 August 1945 to drop the second atomic bomb on Japan, the target was Kokura (near Kitakyūshū) on the northeastern coast of Kyūshū. Fortunately for Kokura it was a cloudy day and, despite flying over the city three times, the bomber's crew could not sight the target, so a course was set for the secondary target, Nagasaki.

The B-29 arrived over Nagasaki at 10.58am but again visibility was obscured by cloud. When a momentary gap appeared in the cloud cover, the Mitsubishi Arms Factory, not the intended Mitsubishi shipyard, was sighted and became the target. The 4.5-ton 'Fat Man' bomb had an explosive power equivalent to 21 kilotons of TNT, far more than the 13 kilotons of Hiroshima's 'Little Boy'.

The bomb missed its intended target and scored a near-direct hit on the largest Catholic church in Asia (Urakami Cathedral; below). The explosion took place at 11.02am, at an altitude of only 500m, completely devastating the Urakami suburb of northern Nagasaki and killing 75,000 of Nagasaki's 240,000 population. Most victims were women, children and senior citizens, as well as 13,000 conscripted Korean labourers and 200 allied POWs. Another 75,000 people were injured and it is estimated that as many people again have subsequently died as a result of the blast. Everything within a 1km radius of the explosion was destroyed and after the resulting fires, a third of the city was wiped out.

For details of the atomic bomb that devastated Hiroshima, see p457.

The **Nagasaki Atomic Bomb Museum** (Map p682; ☎ 844-1231; www1.city.nagasaki.nagasaki.jp/na-bomb/museum; 7-8 Hirano-chō; admission ¥200, audio guide rental ¥150; ⏰ 8.30am-5pm) exhibits begin with live footage of the bomb blast, then move through the city's destruction and loss of human life. The bent hands of a twisted clock stuck at 11.02 recall the moment when the bomb exploded above the city's neighbourhoods. These riveting exhibits also cover Japan's 15 years of military aggression prior to the war. A depressing, if must-see, experience, made more bearable by the streams of cheerful school kids who visit from all around Kyūshū.

Heiwa-kōen (平和公園; Peace Park) is north of the hypocentre, and is presided over by the **Nagasaki Peace Statue** (Map p682) and includes the Peace Symbol Zone, an unusual sculpture garden with contributions from around the world. An annual antinuclear protest is held at the park on 9 August.

Urakami Cathedral (Map p682; ☎ 844-1777; 1-79 Motoo-machi; ⏰ 9am-5pm Tue-Sun), the largest church in the East, was completed in 1914 after three decades, then flattened in three seconds in 1945. The replacement cathedral was completed in 1959.

The courage of Dr Nagai Takashi in the face of overwhelming adversity is the subject of the extraordinary **Nagai Takashi Memorial Museum** (永井隆記念館; ☎ 844-3496; 22-6 Ueno-chō; admission ¥100; ⏰ 9am-5pm). Already suffering from leukaemia, and having lost his wife during the atomic explosion, Dr Nagai devoted himself to the treatment of bomb victims until he died in 1951. Even after he became bedridden, Dr Nagai continued to write prolifically and secure donations for survivors and orphans from the international community. Next door, Dr Nagai's small hut **Nyokodō** (如己堂) is preserved as a memorial.

The **One-Pillar Torii** (Map p682) is southeast of the hypocentre. The blast knocked down one side of the entrance arch to the Sanno-jinja, but the other pillar is still stands to this day.

Just short walk from the torii you'll find the **Nagasaki Museum of History & Folklore** (Map p682; ☎ 847-9245; admission free; ⏰ 9am-4.30pm Tue-Sun), which exhibits antique household items such as fishing lures, dolls, cookware and so on, which otherwise one rarely gets to see. A 'hands on' room allows children of all ages to play around.

NAGASAKI STATION AREA

The **26 Martyrs Memorial** (Map p682) is a memorial wall with reliefs of the 26 Christians crucified in 1597, commemorating a harsh crackdown when six Spanish friars and 20 Japanese were killed. The youngest killed were boys aged 12 and 13. Behind the memorial is a simple **museum** (☎ 822-6000; 7-8 Nishisaka-machi; admission ¥250) with Christianity-related displays.

The memorial is five minutes' walk from JR Nagasaki station.

Fukusai-ji Kannon (Nagasaki Universal Kannon Temple; Map p682; ☎ 823-2663; 2-56 Chikugo-machi; admission ¥200; ⏰ 8am-4pm) is in the form of a huge turtle carrying an 18m-high figure of the goddess Kannon on its back. Inside, a Foucault pendulum (demonstrating the rotation of the earth on its axis) hangs from near the top of the hollow statue. Only St Petersburg and Paris have larger examples.

The original temple, Chinese in origin, was built in 1628 but was completely burnt by the A-bomb fire. The replacement was built in 1976. The temple bell tolls at 11.02am daily, the exact time of the explosion (see opposite).

Nearby, the serene gardens of **Shōfuku-ji** (Map p682; ☎ 823-0282; 3-77 Tamazono-machi) temple, not to be confused with Sōfuku-ji (see right), contain an arched stone gate dating from 1657. The main building was reconstructed in 1715 in the ornate Chinese style of the time. The *onigawara* (ogre-covered) wall is particularly interesting, as is the book-burning kiln. There are clear views of Nagasaki port from here.

Just west is another temple, **Kanzen-ji** (Map p682), with one of the biggest camphor *(kusunoki)* trees in Nagasaki.

SUWA-JINJA 諏訪神社

Between 7 and 9 October, this enormous **shrine** (Map p682; ☎ 824-0445; 18-15 Kaminishiyama-machi) comes to life with the dragon dance of Kunchi Matsuri (p689), Nagasaki's most important annual celebration. Inside you will find a number of cutesy *komainu* (prayer dogs!). Be sure to see the *kappa-komainu* (water-sprite dog, which you pray to by dribbling water on the plate on its head) and the *gan-kake komainu* (turn-table dog). The latter was used by prostitutes, who prayed that storms would arrive soon, forcing the sailors to stay at the port another day.

Suwa-jinja was established in 1625 and its forested hilltop setting is meditative indeed. Tram lines 3, 4 and 5 run to the Suwa-jinja-mae stop.

NAGASAKI MUSEUM OF HISTORY & CULTURE 長崎歴史文化博物館

Just east of famous Sōfuku-ji temple you'll find Nagasaki's newest **museum** (☎ 818-8366; www.nmhc.jp; 1-1-1 Tateyama; adult/child 6-12/student ¥600/300/400; ⏰ 8.30am-7pm, closed 3rd Tue of month). Newly opened in 2005, this handsome structure focuses on Nagasaki's proud history of overseas exchange, including common items imported on Dutch and Chinese ships, plus a protective deity of navigation. The main gallery is a partial reconstruction of the Edo-period Nagasaki Magistrate's Office which, fittingly enough, controlled trade and diplomacy. There's a free English audio guide (two hours). From Sakuramachi tram stop, it's a five-minute walk.

TERA-MACHI (TEMPLE ROW) 寺町

Between the Shian-bashi entertainment area and the smaller of the city's two rivers, Nakajima-gawa, the justly famous Tera-machi (literally 'temple street') is anchored at either end by Nagasaki's two best-known temples, Sōfuku-ji and Kōfuku-ji, both Chinese in origin. The path connecting them is home to several smaller temples and famous gravesites and makes for a relaxing stroll.

An Ōbaku (the third-largest Zen sect after Rinzai and Sōtō) temple, **Sōfuku-ji** (Map p686; ☎ 823-2645; 7-5 Kajiya-machi; admission ¥300; ⏰ 8am-5pm) was built in 1629 by Chinese monk Chaonian. Its red entrance gate *(Daiippo-mon)* exemplifies Ming dynasty architecture. Inside the temple you can admire a huge cauldron that was used to prepare food for famine victims in 1681, and a statue of Maso, goddess of the sea, worshipped by early Chinese seafarers.

Continuing north along the path from Sōfuku-ji, steep steps lead up to **Daikō-ji** (Map p686; ☎ 822-2877; 5-74 Kajiya-machi), famous for somehow avoiding fires, even atomic ones, since its founding in 1614. Near the bottom of the road, turn right and take a few steps to **Hosshin-ji bell** (Map p686; ☎ 823-2892; 5-84 Kajiya-machi), which has the oldest temple bell in Nagasaki, cast in 1438. Then climb the stairs to the large Kuroganemochi tree at the entrance to **Daion-ji** (Map p686; ☎ 824-2367; 5-87 Kajiya-machi) and follow the path that heads to the grave of Matsudaira Zushonokami. He had been magistrate of Nagasaki for a year when, in 1808, the British warship HMS *Phaeton* sailed into Nagasaki harbour and seized two Dutch hostages. The British and Dutch were on opposite sides in the Napoleonic War at that time. Unable to oppose the British, Zushonokami capitulated to their demands for supplies, then promptly disembowelled himself.

A short distance further on, turn down the path to **Kōtai-ji** (Map p686; ☎ 823-7211; 1-1 Tera-machi),

CENTRAL NAGASAKI

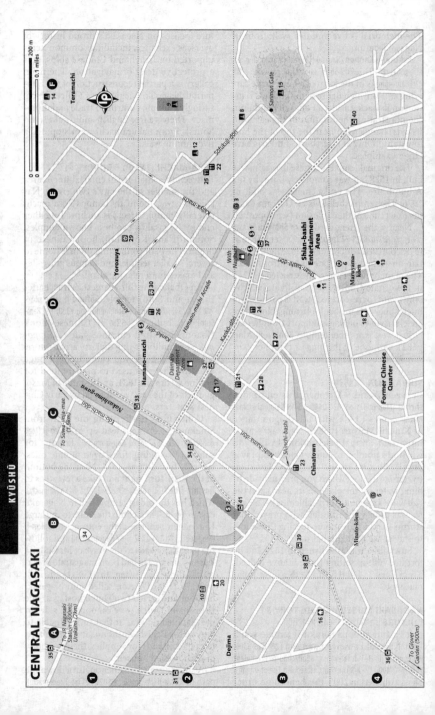

KYŪSHŪ

0   200 m
0   0.1 miles

Teramachi

Sōfuku-ji-dōri

Kaiya-machi

Shian-bashi
Entertainment
Area

Shian-bashi-dōri

Maruyama-kōen

Former Chinese
Quarter

Yorozuya

Hamano-machi Arcade

Kankō-dōri

Hamano-machi

Kabō-dōri

Arcade

Daimaru
Department
Store

Nishi-hama-dōri

Nakashima-gawa

Shinchi-bashi

Chinatown

Edo-machi-dōri

Arcade

To Suwa-jinja-mae
(1.5km)

Minato-kōen

To IR Nagasaki
Station (300m);
Urakami (2km)

Dejima

To Glover
Garden (500m)

INFORMATION			SLEEPING			DRINKING		
18 Bank 十八銀行	**1**	E3	Fukumoto Ryokan 福本旅館	**16**	A3	Albert's Diablo		
18 Bank 十八銀行	**2**	B2	Holiday Inn			アルバーツプレイス	**27**	D3
Cybac Café サイバックカフェ	**3**	E3	ホリデイイン長崎	**17**	C2	Moonshine ムーンシャイン	**28**	C3
International ATM 国際ATM	**4**	D2	Nishiki-sō にしき荘	**18**	D4			
Internet Café Shin しん	**5**	B4	Sun Road Inn サンロードイン	**19**	D4	ENTERTAINMENT		
Maruyama Police Box			Tredia Hotel Dejima			Ayer's Rock エアーズ・ロック	**29**	E1
丸山町交番	**6**	D4	トレディアホテル出島	**20**	A2	Panic Paradise		
Shinwa Ginkō 親和銀行	**7**	D3				パニックパラダイス	**30**	D2
			EATING					
SIGHTS & ACTIVITIES			Fukusaya Castella Cake Shop			TRANSPORT		
			福砂屋本家	(see 11)		Dejima 出島	**31**	A2
Daikō-ji 大光寺	**8**	E3	Ginnabe 銀鍋	**21**	C3	Kankō-dōri 観光通り	**32**	C2
Daion-ji 大音寺	**9**	F2	Hamakatsu Shippoku			Nishi-Hamano-machi 西浜町	**33**	C1
Dejima Museum 出島資料館	**10**	A2	卓袱浜勝	**22**	C2	Nishi-Hamano-machi 1		
Fukusaya Castella Cake Shop			Kagetsu 花月	(see 13)		西浜町	**34**	C2
福砂屋本家	**11**	D3	Kairaku-en 会楽園	**23**	C3	Ōhato 大波止	**35**	A1
Hosshin-ji Bell 発心寺	**12**	E2	Unryūtei 雲龍亭	**24**	D3	Ōura-kaigan-dōri		
Kagetsu 花月	**13**	D4	Wine Cellar Rosenthal			大浦海岸通り	**36**	A4
Kōtai-ji 皓台寺	**14**	F1	ローゼンタール	**25**	E2	Shian-bashi 思案橋	**37**	E3
Sōfuku-ji 崇福寺	**15**	F3	Yosso 吉宗	**26**	D2	Shimin-Byōin-mae		
						市民病院前	**38**	B3
						Shinchi Bus Terminal		
						新地バスターミナル	**39**	B3
						Shōkakuji-shita 正覚寺下	**40**	F4
						Tsuki-machi 築町	**41**	B3

the only temple in Nagasaki with active monks-in-training and a favourite with local artists; it has a notable bell dating from 1702. The final temple along the temple-row walk, **Kōfuku-ji** (Map p682; ☎ 822-1076; 4-32 Tera-machi; admission ¥200; ☺ 6am-6pm), dates from the 1620s and is noted for the Ming architecture of the main hall. Like Sōfuku-ji, it is an Ōbaku Zen temple – and the oldest in Japan.

Megane-bashi めがね橋
Parallel to the temple row is the river, the Nakashima-gawa, which is crossed by a picturesque collection of 10 17th-century stone bridges. At one time, each bridge was the distinct entranceway to a separate temple. The best known is the double-arched **Megane-bashi** (Spectacles Bridge; Map p682), so called because the water and the arches come together to form a reflection in the water, creating a 'spectacles' effect. Six of the 10 bridges, including Megane-bashi, were washed away on 23 July 1982, but restored using the recovered stones.

SHIAN-BASHI AREA 思案橋
The Shian-bashi tram stop marks the site of the bridge over which pleasure-seekers would cross into the Shian-bashi quarter. The bridge's name loosely translates to 'Bridge of Pondering': men might stop here one last time, debating whether to seek a night of pleasure or to return home. The bridge and

the elegant old brothels are long gone but this is still the entertainment area of Nagasaki.

In between the bars, restaurants and clubs, Shian-bashi still has a few reminders of those old days. A walk south from the southern tram stop on Shian-bashi-dōri will bring you to the **Fukusaya Castella Cake Shop** (Map p686; ☎ 821-2938; www.castella.co.jp; 3-1 Funadaiku-machi), in business since 1624, and a must for history buffs and those with a taste for Japanese sweets. Turn left at this junction, pass the police post and you come to the driveway to **Kagetsu** (p691), now an elegant and expensive restaurant, but at one time an even more elegant and expensive brothel.

DEJIMA AREA 出島地区
From the mid-17th century until 1855, the small isolated Dutch trading post of Dejima provided Japan its only peephole to the world outside; the Dutch were cordoned off and only allowed contact with their Japanese trading partners and courtesans. The area around **Dejima Wharf** (Map p682) was the focal point for much of this activity, and has recently been converted into an open-air collection of restaurants, bars, shops and galleries, all facing the bay and well worth a visit.

Dejima Museum 出島資料館
The small **museum** (Map p686; ☎ 822-2207; www1.city.nagasaki.nagasaki.jp/dejima/main.html; 8-21 Dejima; admission ¥300; ☺ 9am-5pm), a cluster of small buildings, has exhibits on the Dutch and other foreign

KYŪSHŪ

contact with Nagasaki, and free walking-tour maps of the entire site. Although the island was submerged during 19th-century land-reclamation projects, the trading post, now a national historic site, has been restored.

CHINATOWN AREA 中国街

Theoretically, during Japan's long period of seclusion Chinese traders were just as circumscribed in their movements as the Dutch, but in practice they were relatively free. Only a couple of buildings remain from the old area (Map p686), but Nagasaki still has an energetic Chinese community that has had a great influence on the city's culture, architecture, festivals and cuisine.

GLOVER GARDEN AREA グラバー園周辺
Glover Garden

At the southern end of Nagasaki, some former homes of the city's pioneering Meiji period European residents have been reassembled in this hillside **garden** (Map p688; ☎ 822-8223; 8-1 Minami-yamatemachi; adult/student ¥600/300; ☺ 8am-9.30pm 27 Apr-9 Oct, to 6pm 10 Oct-26 April). The series of moving stairways up the hill, along with the koi ponds and fountains, gives it the air of a cultural theme park (ever popular in Japan). The stylish houses are the main draw here, along with the interesting history and superb views across Nagasaki.

The garden takes its name from Thomas Glover (1838–1911), whose arms-importing operations played an important part in the Meiji Restoration; he built the first train line in Japan and he helped establish the country's first modern shipyard.

The best way to explore the hillside garden is to take the walkways to the top and then walk back downhill. At the top of the park is **Mitsubishi No 2 Dock building** with displays about the city's important shipyard. Going down the hill you come to **Walker House**, the **Ringer** and **Alt Houses** and finally **Glover House**. Halfway down the hill, above Glover House, is the renowned **statue** of the Japanese opera singer Miura Tamaki, often referred to as Madame Butterfly. You exit the garden through the **Nagasaki Traditional Performing Arts Museum**, which has a display of dragons and floats used in the colourful Kunchi Matsuri.

Ōura Catholic Church 大浦天主堂

Just below Glover Garden is this hilltop **church** (Map p688; ☎ 823-2628; www9.ocn.ne.jp/~oura/in Japa-

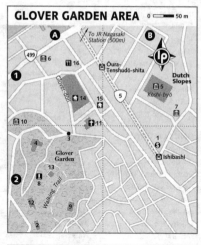

nese; admission ¥300; ☺ 8.30am-5pm). Soon after it opened its doors in 1864 to Nagasaki's foreign community, a group of Japanese arrived to announce that Christianity had been maintained among the Urakami community throughout the 250 years it had been banned. Their timing could not have been worse. Japan was anxious about contacts with the West, and when this news leaked out, thousands of Urakami residents were exiled to other parts of Japan before Christianity was legalised in 1873. The church is dedicated to the 26 Christians crucified in 1597 (see p681 for more information).

Dutch Slopes オランダ坂
The gently inclined flagstone streets known as the Dutch Slopes (Oranda-zaka; Map p688) were once lined with wooden **Dutch houses**. Several buildings have been beautifully restored and offer glimpses of Japan's early interest in the West. **Koshashin-shiryōkan** (Map p688; ☎ 820-3386; 6-25 Higashi Yamatemachi; combined admission ¥100; ☑ 9am-5pm Tue-Sun) has a collection of vintage photographs (including a rare one of the Meiji-era hero Sakamoto Ryoma), while **Maizō-shiryōkan** has archaeological artefacts. 'Oranda-zaka' comes from the name foreigners were given: Oranda-san, people from Holland.

Other Sights
Behind the jauntily coloured **Kōshi-byō**, a Confucian shrine, the **Historical Museum of China** (Map p688; ☎ 824-4022; 10-36 Ōuramachi; admission ¥525; ☑ 8.30am-5pm) has exhibits on loan from Beijing. The original shrine dates from 1893, but was destroyed in the fires following the A-bomb explosion.

The historic **Hong Kong & Shanghai Bank Nagasaki Branch Museum** (Map p688; ☎ 827-8746; 4-27 Matsugaemachi; admission ¥100; ☑ 9am-5pm) is also worth a peek. It has high ceilings, burnished wood banisters, several displays, and signage in English, French and Chinese.

SIEBOLD MEMORIAL MUSEUM
シーボルト記念館
Near Shin-Nakagawamachi tram stop is the site of **Dr Siebold's house** (☎ 823-0707; www1.city .nagasaki.nagasaki.jp/siebold/; 2-7-40 Narutaki; admission ¥100; ☑ 9am-5pm Tue-Sun), an imposing Western-style structure set in a leafy residential neighbourhood of narrow lanes and flower boxes. The doctor helped introduce Western medicine and scientific learning to Japan between 1823 and 1829, though he was eventually expelled for trying to smuggle Japanese goods. His daughter Ine was one of Japan's first female obstetricians.

INASA-YAMA LOOKOUT 稲左山展望台
From the western side of the harbour, a **cable car** (ropeway; Map p682; ☎ 861-6321; return ¥1200; ☑ 9am-10pm Mar-Nov, to 9pm Dec-Feb) ascends every 20 minutes to the top of 333m-high Inasa-yama, offering superb views over Nagasaki,

particularly at night. Buses 3 and 4 leave from outside JR Nagasaki station; get off at the Ropeway-mae stop and walk up the stone steps through the grounds of Fuchi-jinja.

Tours
Nagasaki Harbour Cruises (Map p682; ☎ 822-5002; Nagasaki Harbour Terminal Bldg) offers a great way to glimpse picturesque Nagasaki (¥1200, one hour). From 20 July to 31 August, join the one-hour midnight cruise (¥1600), then stroll over to Dejima Wharf for a drink or late bite.

Festivals & Events
Peiron dragon boat races Colourful races introduced by the Chinese in the mid-1600s, and held to appease the god of the sea, still take place in Nagasaki Harbour in late July.

Shōrō-nagashi On 15 August in this beautiful event, lanternlit floats are carried down to the harbour in honour of one's ancestors. The boats are handcrafted from a variety of items (bamboo, wood, rice stems etc) and vary in size depending on the family or individual. Eventually they are carried out to sea and destroyed by the waves. The best viewpoint is at Ōhato (Map p686).

Kunchi Matsuri Held 7–9 October, an energetic festival that features more Chinese dragons, this time dancing all around the city but especially at Suwa-jinja. The festival is marked by elaborate costumes, fireworks, cymbals, and giant dragon puppets on poles.

Sleeping
Nagasaki has a wide range of accommodation possibilities stretching from the A-bomb site to Glover Garden. Central Nagasaki, convenient for both walking and catching public transport around town, has a number of affordable hotels, ryokan and *minshuku*.

BUDGET
Fukumatsu Ryokan (Map p682; ☎ 823-3769; 4-18 Daiko-kumachi; r ¥3500; ✦) A block behind Kenei bus station, this small and friendly budget choice has five rooms, clean and bright, with shared bathroom. Look for the small red oval sign, just opposite a small shrine.

Minshuku Tanpopo (Map p682; ☎ 861-6230; www .tanpopo-group.biz/tanpopo; 21-7 Hoeimachi; s/d/tr with shared bathroom ¥4000/7000/9000; ✦ ✕ 🖳) Close to JR Urakami station, this smart budget choice and Japanese Inn Group member features common bathrooms with mineral spring waters. Breakfast (¥600) and dinner (¥1500) are optional extras.

KYŪSHŪ

Nagasaki Ebisu Youth Hostel (Map p682; ☎ 824-3823; www5a.biglobe.ne.jp/~urakami; 6-10 Ebisumachi; dm incl/excl meals ¥4300/2500; ✖) Run by a friendly family with years of experience helping travellers. There are three Japanese-style dorm rooms, and one more with bunk beds. Curfew is 11pm.

Fukumoto Ryokan (Map p686; ☎ 821-0478; 3-8 Dejimamachi; r incl/excl 2 meals ¥6000/4500; ✖) Located in front of the Matsuda Cars building, this welcoming spot is a cross between a ryokan and a business hotel, with both Japanese-style and Western-style rooms.

MIDRANGE

Nishiki-sō (Map p686; ☎ 826-6371; 1-2-7 Nishikojima; r incl breakfast ¥4000-4500; ✖) The pick of the pack for charm, this is a creaky old building with 11 rooms, most Japanese style. The helpful staff can direct you around town, and there's an in-house *ofuro* bath and laundry. Check out the massive *kushinoki* (camphor tree) around the corner.

Tredia Hotel Dejima (Map p686; ☎ 826-4176; www .tredia-h.com in Japanese; 1-25 Dejimamachi; s/tw from ¥6100/10,500; P ✖ ✖ 🖳) This smart 133-room hotel near the port is just opposite Dejima Museum and good value. Rooms are long and light, and come with wide desks

Toyoko Inn Nagasaki Ekimae (Map p682; ☎ 825-1045; 5-45 Gotōmachi; s/d/tw incl breakfast ¥5460/7560/7560; ✖ ✖ 🖳 wi-fi) This popular, well-managed business hotel gets points for small but efficient rooms, service and location between the bay and Nagasaki station.

JR Kyūshū Hotel Nagasaki (Map p682; ☎ 832-8000; fax 832-8001; 1-1 Onoukemachi; s/tw/tr ¥6900/12,600/16,200; P ✖ ✖ 🖳) Typical JR value, with small stylish lobby, and unusually large rooms, many overlooking Nagasaki.

ourpick Holiday Inn (Map p686; ☎ 828-1234; fax 828-0178; 6-24 Dozamachi; s/d/tw from ¥10,000/14,000/15,000; P ✖ ✖ 🖳) Near the Shian-bashi entertainment area on a quiet alleyway, this 88-room inn is easily one of the best value in town. The lobby is cosy and inviting; service, room size and furnishings match far more expensive choices.

TOP END

Best Western Premier Hotel Nagasaki (Map p682; ☎ 821-1111; www.bestwestern.com/premier; 2-26 Takaramachi; s/d/ste from ¥15,000/23,000/45,000; P ✖ ✖ 🖳) Nagasaki's most elegant hotel features a black marble lobby, complete with fireplace and grand piano. Rooms are large and handsome,

many with harbour views. Opposite tram stop Takara-machi.

Sakamoto-ya (Map p682; ☎ 826-8210; 2-13 Kanayamachi; r per person with 2 meals from ¥15,750; ✖) A magnificent old (1890s) and very well-kept ryokan, with traditional touches, a beautiful garden, and only 12 rooms.

Hotel New Nagasaki (Map p682; ☎ 826-8000; www.newnaga.com; s/d/from ¥21,700/27,700/30,000; P ✖ ✖ 🖳) Next to JR station, this well-regarded hotel sports a massive marble lobby, along with spacious rooms, modern furnishings and satellite TV. All rooms have bay or hillside city views.

Other recommendations:

Sun Road Inn (Map p686; ☎ 821-5039; fax 827-7724; 2-11 Yoriai-Machi; s/tw from ¥5700/9500; ✖) Good value on quiet street, just past small car park.

Hotel Monterey Nagasaki (Map p688; ☎ 827-7111; nag@hotelmonterey.co.jp; 1-22 Ōuramachi; s/tw from ¥9000/18,000; P ✖ ✖ 🖳) Comfy Portuguese-styled hotel with antique lamps to match, near Glover Garden.

ANA Hotel Nagasaki Glover Hill (Map p688; ☎ 818-6601; www.ana-gloverhill.co.jp in Japanese; 1-18 Minami Yamatemachi; s/tw from ¥12,700/23,000; P ✖ ✖) Renovated upscale complex overlooking Glover Garden.

Eating

Like Yokohama and Kōbe, Nagasaki has the reputation of being a culinary crossroads. The city's diverse influences come together in *shippoku-ryōri*, a banquet-style offering (the more diners the better) that rolls together Chinese, Japanese and Portuguese influences. *Champon*, the local *rāmen* speciality (inexpensive and very popular) is made with squid, octopus, pork, *kamaboko* (white and pink fish-based patty) and veggies in a white, salt-based broth. *Sara-udon* is the stir-fried equivalent.

Unryūtei (Map p686; ☎ 823-5971; 3-15 Motoshikkui-machi; plate of gyōza ¥300; ◷ dinner) A Nagasaki stand-by tucked away at the end of Shianbashi Gourmet St, this place only seats six and specialises in cheap and tasty *gyōza* (dumplings), excellent with beer.

Tabibitojaya (Map p682; ☎ 822-9916; 6-15 Daikokumachi; lunch from ¥520; ◷ breakfast, lunch & dinner; E) This charming and tiny café makes perfect sandwiches, fresh juices and coffee that the regulars drink from pottery cups facing the counter. Look for the word 'coffee' and more cups in the window.

Kairaku-en (Map p686; ☎ 822-4261; 10-16 Shinchimachi; dishes ¥700-1000) Famed for its *champon* and *sara-udon*, this is among the best of several southern Chinese eateries clustered around the Nagasaki Washington Hotel. It's a three-minute walk from Tsuki-machi tram stop, just inside the Chinatown gate.

Shikairō (Map p688; ☎ 822-1296; set meals ¥900-1100) An imposing Chinese-style restaurant near Glover Garden, credited as the creator of *champon*. It has been in operation since 1899.

Yosso (Map p686; ☎ 821-0001; 8-9 Hama-machi; set meals from ¥1050; ⊗ lunch & dinner, closed 2nd & 4th Tue of month; ⊗ Ⓥ ⓐ) From the old grandfather clock on the wall to the traditional *chawan-mushi* (egg custard with veggies), Yosso is very Nagasaki – relaxed, welcoming and good value. Look for the string of red lanterns high above the dark-wood exterior.

Ginnabe (Map p686; ☎ 821-8213; 7 Douza-machi; set meals ¥1500; ⊗ lunch & dinner; E) Combining modern and traditional, Ginnabe stands out in Hamano-machi for its style and good value, with generous *teishoku* such as *unagi* (eel; ¥1365) or tempura and sushi (¥1575).

Hamakatsu Shippoku (Map p686; ☎ 826-8321; 6-50 Kajiya-machi; per person around ¥3000) Banquet-style *shippoku*. Last order is at 8.30pm.

Kagetsu (Map p686; ☎ 822-0191; 2-1 Kajiya-machi; set meals ¥5200-15,000; ⊗ lunch & dinner) A *shippoku* restaurant that dates back to 1642 when it was a high-class brothel; today it's a rabbit warren of private and pricy dining rooms and tiny gardens.

Beside JR Nagasaki station, **Amu Plaza** (Map p682; 5th fl; meals from ¥650) has a surprisingly varied restaurant arcade. Follow the lunch crowd to the locally owned **Sushi Katsu** (☎ 808-1501; 5th fl, Amu Plaza; sushi plates from ¥200). Look for white lanterns out front and moving sushi inside. **Daichi no Table** (☎ 818-2388; 5th fl, Amu Plaza; lunch/dinner ¥1200/1500; ⊗ lunch & dinner; ⊗ Ⓥ ⓐ) is a busy natural-food all-you-can-eat Japanese buffet featuring sashimi, *champon*, soup and three kinds of rice. Watch the time, too; you're given 90 minutes. **Dragon Deli** (basement, Amu Plaza; items from ¥300) is an import grocery shop selling goodies from all across Asia and the West, and a good place to pick up a gift. A few steps away is a branch of famous **Fukusaya bakery** (☎ 808-2938), which has been making Portuguese pound cake since 1624.

Drinking

Nagasaki's nightlife tends to centre on the narrow lanes of Hamano-machi.

Albert's Diablo (Map p686; 90-4992-3407; 2nd fl, Azuma Bldg, 15-13 Douza-machi; draughts & cocktails from ¥600) Pacific Islander Albert draws a late crowd to this mellow music bar. You'll hear blues, jazz, reggae, plus the occasional TV sporting event.

Moonshine (Map p686; ☎ 823-9186; 2nd fl, Ebisu Bldg, 10-9 Douza-machi; dishes from ¥700, drinks from ¥500) Set above a *rāmen* shop, the menu includes Western, Chinese and Japanese cuisine. After 10pm the long bar starts to fill up; by midnight it's usually packed.

Entertainment

Panic Paradise (Map p686; ☎ 824-6167; basement, Nagatoshokai Bldg, 5-33 Yorozuya-machi; drinks from ¥600) Cool, cosy and friendly, this tight basement bar with open-pipe décor features nightly DJ rock, blues and reggae.

Ayer's Rock (Map p686; ☎ 828-0505; basement, Hananoki Bldg, 6-17 Marya-machi; admission Fri & Sat ¥1500) This cosy basement bar thumps with techno DJs, bongos and beer. Popular with local musicians, it's a good place to scope out the local scene.

Shopping

There are displays of local crafts and products at 3-1 Daikoku-machi, directly opposite JR Nagasaki station on the same floor as the Nagasaki Prefectural Tourist Information Center. You'll also find lots of shops along the busy Hamano-machi shopping arcade. Do your best to ignore Nagasaki's tortoiseshell crafts: turtles still need their shells too.

Getting There & Away

There are flights between Nagasaki and Tokyo (Haneda airport, ¥34,700), Osaka (¥23,000) and Naha (¥25,000, 1½ hours) in Okinawa, plus flights to other Kyūshū cities.

From the Kenei bus station opposite JR Nagasaki station, buses depart for Unzen (¥1900, 1¾ hours), Sasebo (¥1450, 1½ hours), Fukuoka (¥2900, 2¾ hours), Kumamoto (¥3790, three hours) and Beppu (¥4500, 3½ hours). Night buses for Osaka (¥11,000, 10 hours) leave from both the Kenei bus station and the highway bus station next to the Irie-machi tram stop.

JR lines from Nagasaki head for Sasebo (*kaisoku*, ¥1600, 1¾ hours) or Fukuoka (*tokkyū*, ¥4410, two hours).

There are ferries from a few places around Nagasaki, including Ōhato terminal, south of JR Nagasaki station.

To travel between here and the Amakusa Archipelago, take bus 10 to Mogi port from the South Exit at Nagasaki station (¥160, 30 minutes), then the ferry to Tomioka on Amakusa island (one way ¥1600, 70 minutes).

Getting Around

TO/FROM THE AIRPORT

Nagasaki's airport is about 40km from the city. Airport buses (¥800, 45 minutes) operate from stand 4 of the Kenei bus station opposite JR Nagasaki station (Map p682). A taxi costs about ¥9000.

BICYCLE

Bicycles can be rented (40% discount for JR Pass holders) from **JR Nagasaki station** (Map p682; ☎ 826-0480) at the Eki Rent-a-Car. Some are even electric powered. Rates are reasonable (per two hours/day ¥500/1500).

BUS

A greater area is covered by buses than by trams (with buses reaching more of the sights directly) but the Japanese script on the bus service is more difficult to decipher than that on the tram service.

TRAM

The best way of getting around Nagasaki is on the easy-to-use tram service. There are four colour-coded routes numbered 1, 3, 4 and 5 (No 2 is for special events). Most stops are signposted in English. It costs ¥100 to travel anywhere in town, but you can only transfer to another line at the Tsuki-machi stop if you have a ¥500 all-day pass for unlimited travel. These passes are available from the shop beside the station information counter, from the Nagasaki Prefectural Tourist Information Center (p683) across the road, or from most hotels. Most trams stop running before 11.30pm.

Around Nagasaki

HUIS TEN BOSCH ハウステンボス

This 'virtual-Holland' **theme park** (☎ 095-627-0526; www.english.huistenbosch.co.jp/index.html; adult/child/student from ¥3200/1000/2000; ☺ 9am-9pm) exemplifies Japan's long fascination with the West. Huis Ten Bosch (house in the forest) often delights Dutch visitors, who are intrigued by the mirror image it presents. The rambling replica of an old Dutch town, complete with horse-drawn carriages and windmills, faces Hirado island, where a Dutch trading post opened in 1609.

SHIMABARA PENINSULA 島原半島

The most popular route between Nagasaki and Kumamoto is via the hilly roads of Shimabara *hondō* (main route). Local bus services connect with ferries from Shimabara to the Kumamoto coast, and tour buses operating between Nagasaki and Kumamoto explore the peninsula.

It was an uprising on the Shimabara peninsula that led to the suppression of Christianity in Japan and the country's subsequent two centuries of seclusion from the West. The peasant rebels made their final valiant stand against overwhelming odds (37,000 versus 120,000) at Hara-jō, at almost the southern tip of the peninsula. The warlords even chartered a Dutch man-of-war to bombard the hapless rebels, who held out for 80 days before being slaughtered.

On 3 June 1991, the 1500m peak of Unzen-dake erupted after lying dormant for 199 years, taking the lives of 43 journalists and scientists. Over 12,000 people were evacuated from nearby villages before the lava flow reached the outskirts of Shimabara.

UNZEN 雲仙

☎ 0957 / pop 51,100

Unzen is a very active volcanic centre. Home to Japan's first national park (1934), Unzen's woodsy walks and paths are clearly signposted in English and you can explore the town and nearby trails in an afternoon. For town maps and help with accommodation, check with the resourceful **Unzen Tourist Association** (雲仙観光協会; ☎ 73-3434; ☺ 9am-5pm).

The bubbling and spurting *jigoku* (hells; actually boiling mineral hot springs) currently boil nothing more sinister than the popular wayside snack of eggs, known as *onsen tamago*; a few centuries ago the same fate was reserved for 30 stubborn Christian martyrs who were tossed into bubbly Oito Jigoku.

Today you can voluntarily boil yourself at any of the resort's luxury hotels, though budget travellers will likely prefer the three excellent public baths, all within walking distance of the bus station:

Kojigoku (小地獄温泉館; ☎ 73-3273; admission ¥400; ☉ 9am-9pm)

Shin-yu (新湯温泉; ☎ 0957-73-3545; admission ¥100; ☉ 9am-11pm, closed Wed)

Yunosato (湯の里温泉; ☎ 73-2576; admission ¥100; ☉ 9am-10.30pm, closed 10th & 20th each month)

The ultramodern **Unzen Spa House** (雲仙スパハウス; ☎ 73-3131; admission ¥800; ☉ 9am-6pm), next to the Unzen Tourist Association office, even has a glass-blowing workshop (lessons ¥2000 to ¥3000 per 10 to 15 minutes, enough time to make something to break on your way home).

From the town there are popular walks to Kinugasa, Takaiwa-san and Yadake, all situated within the **Unzen-Amakusa National Park**, Japan's oldest national park. The **Unzen Visitors Centre** (雲仙お山の情報館; ☎ 73-3636; ☉ 7am-6pm 10 Apr-2 Nov, 9am-5pm 3 Nov-9 Apr, closed Thu), opposite the Kyūshū Hotel, has excellent displays on flora and fauna and plentiful information in English, especially about hiking trails. Around town, the 1300-year-old temple, **Manmyō-ji** (満明寺; ☎ 73-3422), rebuilt in 1638, and the screeching, geyserlike **Daikyōkan Jigoku** are worth seeing.

Outside town, reached via Nita Pass, is **Fugen-dake** (1359m), part of the Unzen-dake range, with its popular hiking trail. The views of the lava flow from the summit are incredible.

The bus to Nita-tōge parking area, the starting point for the Fugen-dake walk, operates regularly between 9am and 3pm (¥370, 20 minutes) from Unzen's **Shimatetsu bus station** (☎ 74-3131); the last bus back to Unzen leaves the Nita Pass car park at 4.30pm. A **cable car** (ropeway; ☎ 73-3572; ticket each way ¥610; ☉ 8.55am-5.30pm) whisks you in three minutes close to a shrine and the 1333m-high summit of **Myōken-dake**, from where the hike to Fugen-dake via **Kunimi-wakare** takes just under two hours return. You can also walk the 3.5km back from the shrine to Nita via the village and valley of Azami-dani. For a longer excursion (three hours), you can detour to **Kunimi-dake** (1347m). Along the way you can get a good glimpse of Japan's newest mountain, the smoking lava dome of **Mount Heisei Shinzan** (1486m) (literally 'new mountain'), created in November 1990, when Fugen-dake blew its stack.

Sleeping & Eating

Unzen has numerous hotels, *minshuku* and ryokan with nightly rates from around ¥7500, including dinner and brekkie. You can easily visit as a day-tripper, but staying overnight makes for a refreshing stop between Nagasaki (p608) and Kumamoto (p695). On Saturdays and holidays, expect to pay a surcharge.

Shirakumo-no-ike camping ground (白雲の池キャンプ場; ☎ 73-2642; camp sites from ¥300; ☉ 10 Jul-31 Aug) This picturesque summer camp site next to Shirakumo Pond is about a 600m walk downhill from the post office; tent hire is available (¥500).

Unzen Sky Hotel (雲仙スカイホテル; ☎ 73-3345; fax 73-3349; r per person incl/excl 2 meals from ¥9600/5250; ℗) Between Yusanota public *onsen* and Manmyō-ji, this smart budget option has Japanese-style and Western rooms, and an attractive sulphur *rotemburo*.

Yumoto Hotel (湯元ホテル; ☎ 73-3255; fax 73-2126; r per person with 2 meals/breakfast ¥12,800/8000; ℗ ✕) A hive of activity in the town centre, Unzen's oldest hotel has 70 rooms, a sauna, *rotemburo* and traditional Japanese garden. Anyone can use for free its *ashiyu* (foot bath) outside the front lobby, or the handsome *onsen* for only ¥150.

Unzen Tabi-no-Biru-kan (雲仙旅の麦酒館; ☎ 73-3113; ☉ lunch & dinner; ⓔ E) Overlooking woodsy Unzen, this lively local brewpub pours a local favourite, 'Unzen Yuagari Biru' (after-bath beer). It also serves up pizza and a popular beer curry with salad (¥950).

Getting There & Away

Direct buses between Nagasaki and **Shimatetsu bus station** (☎ 74-3131) in Unzen take almost two hours (¥1900). Buses run more frequently from the town of Isahaya, which is 35 minutes by *kaisoku* train (¥450) from Nagasaki. From Isahaya to Unzen, buses take another 80 minutes (¥1400). Onward buses from Unzen to Shimabara (¥810, 45 minutes) stop at Shimabara's port (p695) and castle before arriving at Shimabara train station.

SHIMABARA 島原

☎ 0957 / pop 50,800

The ferry route to nearby Kumamoto, Shimabara is famous for its clear springs, which first appeared following the 1792 eruption of Mt Unzen.

The **tourist information office** (☎ 62-3986; ☉ 8.30am-5.30pm) is on the 1st floor of the port terminal complex (with various shops and the bus station). Shimabara's castle, samurai street and reclining Buddha are the town's main attractions.

KYŪSHŪ

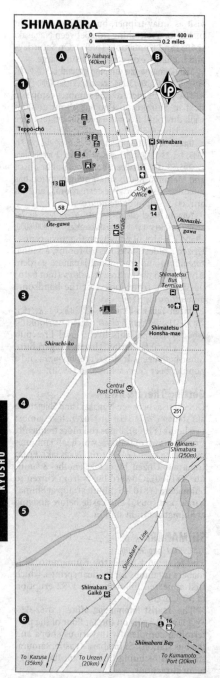

Sights

Built between 1618 and 1625, **Shimabara-jō** (☎ 62-4766; ⊗ 9am-5pm) played a part in the Shimabara Rebellion and was rebuilt in 1964 during Japan's nationwide spate of castle reconstruction. Walk around its expansive grounds to see carp ponds, tangled gardens, mossy walls and picturesque pines. The **tearoom** features a traditional bark roof.

The castle itself houses a few **museums** (☎ 62-4766; combined admission adult/child ¥520/260; ⊗ 9am-5pm). The **Shimabara cultural hall** displays items relating to the Christian uprising, the **Fugen-dake museum** details Fugen-dake's pyrotechnic exploits (including the colossal explosion of 1792 in which 15,000 people died, most from the resulting tsunami) and a third, the **sculpture museum**, is dedicated to the artwork of Seibō Kitamura, who sculpted the Nagasaki Peace Statue. Another small **folk museum** (admission free) is stuffed with antiques from the Edo, Meiji and Shōwa periods.

In the Teppō-chō area, northwest of the castle, is a *buke-yashiki*, or collection of **samurai houses** that line a picturesque street with an unusual feature: a channel in the centre, which once carried water to the households. Three of the houses are open to the public, and a free rest area serves tea and the local traditional sweet. Just south of the town centre, near the Shimatetsu bus station, is a **carp stream** with over 1500 colourful fish and a small park.

At Kōtō-ji is the rather beautiful **Nehan-zō**, or 'Nirvana Statue'. At 8.6m, it's the longest **reclining Buddha** in Japan.

Festivals & Events

The town **water festival** is held in early August.

Sleeping

There's a variety of inexpensive hotels, *minshuku* and ryokan in the castle area.

Shimabara Youth Hostel (☎ 62-4451; dm HI member/nonmember ¥2850/3450) A short walk north of Shimabara-Gaikō station will lead you to what looks like a misplaced ski chalet. There are both bunk beds and futons.

Business Hotel Chidori (☎ 62-4845; r from ¥4200; P ❷) This hotel has clean, bright rooms. Look for the brick façade and white railing above.

Hotel & Spa Hanamizuki (☎ 62-1000; s/tw ¥6000/9800; P ❷ ❷ 🖳) This bright and modern 42-room hotel caters to both business travellers and tourists. There is a large modern *o furo* (traditional Japanese bath), an excellent Japanese breakfast (¥840) and the staff speaks some English.

Eating

Shimabara's best-known dish is *guzōni*, a thick soup made from seafood, veggies, and *mochi* (pounded rice). The soup got its start in 1637 when Amakusa Shirou and his followers took over Shimabara castle and the central government cut off their supply lines. People put anything they could find into clear broth, along with *mochi*, which takes longer to spoil.

Himematsu-ya (☎ 63-7272; meals ¥760-2100; ⏰ 10am-8pm; 🚹) serves Shimabara's speciality, *guzōni* (¥1100), and several types of tasty *rāmen* (try *robuke-e soba*). The restaurant is, appropriately enough, in front of Shimabara-jō. There is a picture menu.

Drinking

Shimabara Mizuyashiki (☎ 62-8555; www.mizuyashiki .com in Japanese; admission/tea & sweets free/¥500) This Meiji-era private teahouse and museum features a beautiful Japanese garden and collection of *maneki-neko* (beckoning cat designed to bring prosperity).

Near Shimabara-jō, there's a cluster of good *izakaya* (pubs), among them **Izakaya Unzen** (☎ 64-2708; E) featuring ¥100 skewers, ¥350 beer mugs and *teishoku* sets from ¥700

to ¥1500. Look for the round window with bamboo design.

Getting There & Around

JR trains on the Nagasaki line run from Nagasaki to Isahaya (*kaisoku*, ¥450, 25 minutes), which then connect with the private Shimabara-tetsudō line trains departing hourly to Shimabara (*futsū*, ¥1450, 1¼ hours). Shimabara station is about 350m east of the castle.

Ferries to the Kumamoto coast depart frequently from Shimabara port between 7am and 7pm. There's a jet ferry (adult/child ¥800/400, 30 minutes) and the slower car ferry (adult/child ¥680/340, one hour). All boats are bound for Kumamoto Port, which is a 30-minute bus ride from the city (¥420).

Local buses shuttle between Shimabara station and the ferry terminal (¥100); a taxi is about ¥900. Bikes can also be rented at the ferry terminal and at the train station (per hour ¥150).

KUMAMOTO-KEN 熊本県

KUMAMOTO 熊本

☎ 096 / pop 669,558

Kumamoto, the city that brought you *kobori* (a traditional technique for swimming upright wearing a suit of armour, often to fire arrows at an attacker), has one of Japan's finest reconstructed castles and a magnificent garden. These days it also has an active nightlife, live music, and a variety of restaurants, museums and galleries.

Orientation & Information

The JR Kumamoto station is some distance southwest of Kumamoto's city centre, which is where you'll find banks, hotels, restaurants, the bus centre and the entertainment area, along with the castle and other attractions.

On the northwest side of JR Kumamoto station is a postal ATM. Higo Bank in central Kumamoto has currency-exchange facilities.

Cybac Café (Map p699; ☎ 24-3189; www.cybac.com; 5th-6th fl, Carino Shimotori, 1-2 Anesi-machi; membership fee/15min ¥300/100; ⏰ 24hr) A city-centre location.

Kinokuniya Bookstore (Map p699; ☎ 322-5531; 1-7-18 Shimotori) Stocks foreign-language titles, maps and newspapers.

Kumamoto City International Centre (Map p699; ☎ 359-2020; 4-8 Hanahatachō; ⏰ 9am-8pm Mon-Sat, to 7pm Sun & holidays) Has free 30-minute internet use,

KYŪSHŪ

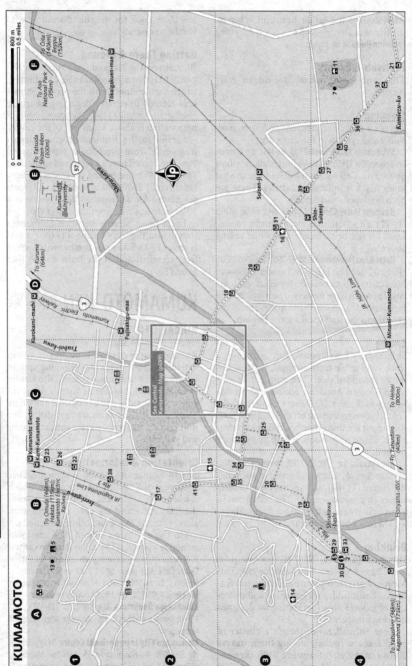

KYŪSHŪ

KUMAMOTO

CNN news and English-language magazines on the 2nd floor.

Tourist information desk JR Kumamoto station (Map p696; ☎ 352-3743; ⏰ 8.30am-7pm); Kumamoto Castle parking area (Map p699; ☎ 322-5060; ⏰ 9am-5pm) Has helpful English-speaking assistants.

Sights

KUMAMOTO-JŌ 熊本城

Kumamoto's **castle** (Map p699; ☎ 352-6820; Honmaru; admission ¥500; ⏰ 8.30am-5.30pm Apr-Oct, to 4.30pm Nov-Mar) dominates the centre of town. The closer you get, the more impenetrable it seems. A free tour (in English, ☎ 322-5900) is available.

Built between 1601 and 1607, Kumamoto-jo was once one of the great castles of feudal Japan. Its architect, Katō Kiyomasa, was a master of castle design and some of his ingenious engineering, including slots for dropping stones and other missiles onto attackers, can be seen in the 19th-century reconstruction.

Nevertheless, in 1877 during the turmoil of the Satsuma Rebellion (a postscript to the Meiji Restoration) the castle was besieged and burnt in one of the final stands made by samurai warriors against the new order. The rebel samurai held out for 50 days before finally being overcome. For more on the rebellion and its leader, Saigō Takamori, see the boxed text, p715.

Beyond the castle is the **Former Hosokawa Gyōbutei** (Map p696; ☎ 352-6522; 3-1 Kyō-machi; admission incl/excl castle ¥640/300; ⏰ 8.30am-5.30pm Apr-Oct, to 4.30pm Nov-Mar), a spacious samurai villa with

grounds pleasant for wandering. The Hosokawa clan came into being around 1632 and held sway until the Meiji Restoration.

Closer to the main road, the **Kumamoto Prefectural Museum of Art** (Map p696; ☎ 352-2111; 2 Ninomaru; admission ¥260; ⏰ 9.30am-4.30pm Tue-Sun, closed 25 Dec-4 Jan) has ancient Buddhist sculptures and modern paintings. **Kumamoto Prefectural Traditional Crafts Centre** (Map p696; ☎ 324-4930; 3-35 Senjōmachi; admission ¥200; ⏰ 9am-5pm Tue-Sun, closed 28 Dec-4 Jan) has displays of local Higo inlay, Yamaga lanterns, porcelains and woodcarving.

SUIZENJI-KŌEN 水前寺公園

Southeast of the city centre, originating with a temple in 1636, this extensive strolling **garden** (☎ 383-0074; www.suizenji.or.jp/E-index.htm; 8-1 Suizenji-kōen; admission ¥400; ⏰ 7.30am-6pm Mar-Nov, 8.30am-5pm Dec-Feb) represents the 53 stations of the Tōkaidō (the old road that linked Tokyo and Kyoto), and the miniature Mt Fuji is instantly recognisable. The 400-year-old **Kokin Denju-no-Ma Teahouse** (Map p696; tea & Hosokawa sweets ¥500-600) was where the young emperor was tutored in poetry at the Kyoto Imperial Palace (the teahouse building was moved here in 1912 and has serene views across the ornamental lake). Turn the other way and you will see somewhat less scenic souvenir stalls.

HONMYŌ-JI 本妙寺

To the northwest of the centre, on the hills sloping up from the river, is the temple and mausoleum of **Katō Kiyomasa** (Map p696), the architect of Kumamoto's great castle. A steep

KYŪSHŪ

flight of 176 steps leads up to the mausoleum that was designed to be at the same height as the castle's donjon (fortified central tower). There's also a **treasure house** (Map p696; ☎ 354-1411; 4-13-20 Hanazono; admission ¥300; ⏱ 9am-5pm Tue-Sun) next to the temple with Kiyomasa's crown and other personal items.

WRITERS' HOMES

Right in the centre of town, behind the Tsu-ruya department store, is writer **Lafcadio Hearn's former home** (Map p699; ☎ 354-7842; 2-6 Ansei-machi; admission ¥200; ⏱ 9.30am-4.30pm Tue-Sun, closed 29 Dec-3 Jan); he was known to the Japanese as Koizumi Yakumo. Hearn also had a Japanese residence in Matsue (see p489).

The former home of famed Meiji-era novelist Sōseki Natsume is preserved as the **Sōseki Memorial Hall** (Map p696; ☎ 325-9127; 4-22 Tsubo-machi; admission ¥200; ⏱ 9.30am-4.30pm Tue-Sun). Sōseki lived here as an English teacher, but only for a few years. (For more on Sōseki, see p64.) Among his classic tales is *Botchan* (1906), which begins 'A great loser have I been ever since a child, having a rash, daring spirit, a spirit I inherited from my ancestors...'

OTHER SIGHTS

Continue north up the hill beyond the ryokan, *minshuku* and love hotels until you reach the white **Bussharito** (a traditional stupa said to hold the Buddha's ashes; Map p696) atop the hill, with superb views over the town.

The delightful **Shimada Art Museum** (島田美術館; Map p696; ☎ 352-4597; 4-5-28 Shimazaki; admission ¥500; ⏱ 9am-5pm Thu-Tue) collects works pertaining to Miyamoto Musashi, mainly calligraphy and scrolls. The museum is within walking distance of Honmyō-ji (p697).

Northeast of the town centre, **Tatsuda Shizen-kōen** (立田自然公園; Tatsuda Nature Park; ☎ 344-6753; 4-610 Kurokami; admission ¥200; ⏱ 8.30am-4.30pm, closed 29-31 Dec) contains the 1646 Taishō-ji. The grave of Hosokawa Gracia (1563–1600) is in the temple grounds. She was an early convert to Christianity but her husband arranged her death to prevent his enemies from capturing her. To get there, take a Musashigaoka-kita line bus from platform 28 at Kumamoto Kōtsū bus centre (Map p699; ¥190, 20 minutes).

Festivals & Events

Takigi Nō (薪能) Traditional performances at Suizenji-kōen are performed by torchlight on the first Saturday in August (from 6pm), usually in Kumamoto-jō.

Hi-no-kuni Matsuri (火の国まつり; Land of Fire Festival) Lights up Kumamoto with fireworks and dancing in mid-August.

Autumn festival From mid-October to early November the Kumamoto-jō has its grand festival, with *taiko* drumming and cultural events.

Sleeping
BUDGET

Suizen-ji Youth Hostel (Map p696; ☎ 371-9193; fax 371-9218; 1-2-20 Hakuzan; dm member/nonmember ¥2900/3900; ✕ ✕) You face a 10pm curfew at this clean and friendly five-room hostel, just a five-minute walk from JR Shin-Suizen-ji station.

Higoji Minshuku (Map p696; ☎/fax 352-7860; r per person from ¥3500; ✕) On the hill behind Kumamoto station, Kumamoto's best-value traditional option is a small and welcoming inn with superb night views. The kind owner will pick you up from the station if you call first.

Minshuku Kajita (Map p696; ☎/fax 353-1546; 1-2-7 Shinmachi; s/d ¥4000/7200; ✕ ✕) This 10-room ryokan-style hotel with shared bathroom is clean, quiet and great value. Breakfast (¥700) and dinner (¥2000) are available. Look for 'Minshuku' in English outside. You'll know you're in the right place when you spot the Marilyn Monroe posters inside.

MIDRANGE & TOP END

Kumamoto Castle Hotel (Map p699; ☎ 326-3311; fax 326-3324; 4-2 Jōtōmachi; s/tw/d from ¥10,300/18,500/19,650, Japanese-style r ¥30,000; ℗ ✕ ✕) Overlooking the castle, this classy Kumamoto stand-by gets points for excellent service and clerks in formal kimono. The best views are from the twin or double rooms.

Maruko Hotel (Map p699; ☎ 353-1241; 11-10 Kamidōrimachi; d incl 2 meals from ¥12,600; ✕) This charming century-old Japanese-style inn in the town centre features an *o-furo* with good views. Look for the English sign inside the covered arcade.

Hotel Nikko Kumamoto (Map p699; ☎ 211-1111; www.nikko-kumamoto.co.jp; s/tw from ¥16,170/30,030; ℗ ✕ ✕ ▯) Kumamoto's smartest upscale hotel is subdued, elegant, centrally located and adjacent to the Contemporary Art Museum. Rooms are spacious and well appointed with reading lamps, roomy bathrooms, high ceilings and city views.

Other recommendations:

Kumamoto Kōtsū Center Hotel (Map p699; ☎ 326-8828; 3-10 Sakuramachi; s/d/tr from ¥5700/13,000/16,500; ✕ ✕ ▯) Remodelled business hotel, good location.

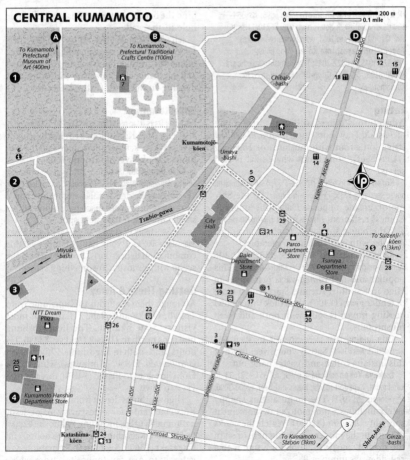

CENTRAL KUMAMOTO

KYŪSHŪ

JR Kyūshū Hotel Kumamoto (Map p696; ☎ 354-8000; kumamoto@jrk-hotels.com; s/tw ¥6210/11,340; ✗ ⚡ 💻) New in 2003, with corner twin rooms.

Toyoko Inn Karashima Kō-en (Map p699; ☎ 322-1045; fax 322-2045; 1-24 Kouyaima-machi; s/d ¥6090/8190; ✗ ⚡ 💻 wi-fi) Two tram stops from Kumamoto-jō.

Eating

Adventurous diners will want to try a bite of *basashi* (raw horsemeat), *karashi-renkon* (fried lotus root with mustard) or *Higo-gyū* (Higo beef). Sometimes whalemeat is also served.

Kōran-tei (Map p699; ☎ 352-7177; 5-26 Anseimachi; house speciality ¥735; ☽ lunch & dinner) In the Shimotori arcade, opposite Daiei, this longtime Chinese restaurant serves good *teishoku* deals. Try the house speciality, *taipīen* (*harusame* noodles with cuttlefish and vegetables).

Ramen Komurasaki (Map p699; ☎ 325-8972; 8-16 Kamitōri-machi; meals from ¥900; ☽ lunch & dinner; E) This popular and fast *rāmen-ya* is just opposite Higo in Kamitōri Arcade. Start with a plate of tender *gyōza* (¥400), then tuck into a bowl of King *rāmen* (¥560), with pork and fresh mushrooms.

Cafe Anding (Map p699; ☎ 352-6701; 4th fl, 4-10 Kamidōri; dishes ¥1000) Satisfy your sweet tooth at this upstairs coffee-and-pastry hang-out.

Izakaya Yokobachi (Map p699; ☎ 351-4581; 11-40 Kaminoura, Kamidori-machi; meals incl beer ¥2000-3000; ☽ dinner; ♿ Ⓥ E) The menu at this snappy eatery includes Kumamoto's raw-horsemeat speciality, *basashi* (¥1000). Watch the cooks at work in the modern open kitchen, or sit in the shaded courtyard. Look for a sign with a red sideways number '8'.

Jang Jang Go (Map p699; ☎ 323-1121; 12-10 Hana-hatacho; per person around ¥2500; ☽ lunch & dinner; E) Kumamoto's trendiest date spot serves neo-Chinese cuisine from a bustling open kitchen in this mock-colonial-style eatery that seats over 200.

Drinking

Kumamoto has a sprinkling of decent bars and clubs that attract both *gaijin* (foreigners) and local Japanese. The Nami Kizaka-dōri area, at the north end of the Kamitōri Arcade, is worth exploring.

Shark Attack (Map p699; ☎ 090-6299-1818; 8th fl, 6-3 Ansei-machi; beer, shōchū, cocktails ¥500-700; ☽ closed Tue) Despite the name, the mood is mellow here. A sandy floor, surfboards and tiki lamps behind the bar set the tone at this cosy 8th-floor hole-in-the-wall.

Jeff's World Bar (Map p699; ☎ 090-9405-0867; 2nd fl, 1-4-3 Shimotori) A mix of *gaijin* and Japanese frequent this 2nd-floor pub boasting 25 Japanese and international beers, a lively darts scene, and dancing on weekends (with ¥2500 cover).

Entertainment

Rock Bar Days (Map p699; ☎ 323-7110; BF1-C, Shimotori 1-4-18) The DJ at Kumamoto's coolest basement dive plays rock, blues and requests till the wee hours. Drinks average around ¥600.

Euro Dance Bar (Map p699; ☎ 354-0803; basement, Shanse Sinagawa Bldg, 11-18 Hanabata; admission ¥400; ☽ 8pm-6am) Friday is salsa night, but you'll hear everything from disco to hip-hop at this small Ginza-dōri basement spot.

Bar Sanctuary (Map p699; ☎ 325-5634; 4-16 Eba Bldg; admission ¥500) Get your hand stamped at this combination dance, darts, drinks and karaoke scene with a mostly 20-something crowd.

Getting There & Away

Although there are flights to Kumamoto from Tokyo, Osaka and Naha (Okinawa), most visitors come by train. The JR Kagoshima line runs north to Hakata (*tokkyū*, ¥3440, 1½ hours) and south to Kagoshima-Chūō station (*shinkansen*, ¥5850, 70 minutes), while the JR Hōhi line goes to Beppu (¥4830, three hours) via Aso town.

Highway buses depart from the Kumamoto Kōtsū bus centre for almost every major destination in Kyūshū, including Fukuoka (¥2000, two hours), Kagoshima (¥3650, 3½ hours) and Nagasaki (¥3600, 3¼ hours). Kumamoto is a gateway to Aso-san (opposite), from where you can continue to Beppu (p727).

Getting Around

TO/FROM THE AIRPORT

Buses to and from the airport (¥670, 50 minutes) stop at the Kumamoto Kōtsū bus centre and JR Kumamoto station.

BUS

One-day tram passes are also valid for travel on green-coloured Shiei buses (but not other city buses), which are handy for connecting between the tram and outlying sights or zooming between JR Kumamoto station and the bus centre.

The small Castle Loop Bus (¥130) connects Kumamoto Kōtsū bus centre with all the sights in the castle area at least every half hour, between 8.30am and 5pm daily. A one-day loop pass (¥300) will get you a discount at the museum and other establishments.

TRAM
Kumamoto's tram service connects with all the major sights. Single fares range from ¥130 to ¥200. A one-day pass (¥500) allows unlimited travel, and can be bought on the trams or in front of Kumamoto station.

YAMAGA & KIKUCHI ONSEN
山鹿温泉・菊池温泉
☎ 0968 / pop Yamaga Onsen 33,559, Kikuchi Onsen 52,681

These popular hot-springs towns northeast of Kumamoto spring to life during the spectacular **Yamaga Chōchin Matsuri** held on 15 and 16 August. *Taiko* drums signal the beginning of this famous lantern festival in rustic Yamaga Onsen. For two nights the women of the town, clad in summer kimonos, dance through the streets to the sound of *shamisen* (a three-stringed traditional Japanese instrument that resembles a banjo), wearing *washi* paper lanterns on their heads. **Yamaga Tourism Office** (☎ 43-2952), opposite the Plaza shops, can help with accommodation.

Yamaga Cycling Terminal (山鹿サイクリングターミナル; ☎ 43-1136; r per person incl 2 meals ¥5200), on a traffic-shielded 34km cycling route from Kumamoto via Ueki, has large communal tatami rooms and a huge bath. Without a bike, it's a 10-minute taxi ride (¥1500) from the centre of Yamaga Onsen.

Kikuchi Information Centre (☎ 23-1155), near the bus station, has maps and brochures in English.

Outside Kikuchi Onsen, **Kikuchi Gorge** (菊池渓谷; donation ¥100; ☿ mid-Apr–Nov), formed by Mt Aso's outer edge, has **walking trails** that follow the Kikuchi-gawa's cool and clear waters through groves of elm, camphor and refreshingly cool waters. Back in town, the hot-springs ryokan, *minshuku* and hotels are clustered together on a quiet maze of streets, just downhill from an imposing **statue** of a feudal lord on horseback.

Day-trippers should try the riverside **onsen** (¥500) at **Iwakura Ryokan** (☎ 27-0026).

Getting There & Around
From JR Kumamoto station or the Kumamoto Kōtsū bus centre (see opposite), there are buses throughout the day to either Yamaga Onsen (¥870, 70 minutes) or Kikuchi Onsen (¥820, 70 minutes). For a day trip to Yamaga Onsen, ask the driver for an *ichi nichi furii joshaken* (round-trip pass ¥1200). There are frequent buses Monday to Saturday (¥430, 30 minutes) between the two *onsen* towns.

ASO-SAN AREA 阿蘇山
☎ 0967 / pop 29,948

In the centre of Kyūshū, halfway from Kumamoto to Beppu, is the gigantic Aso-san volcano caldera. There has been a series of eruptions over the past 300,000 years but the explosion that formed the outer crater about 90,000 years ago must have been a big one – the crater has a 128km circumference and accommodates towns, villages and train lines.

It's still the largest active caldera in the world – in 1979 an eruption of Naka-dake killed a woman on her honeymoon. The last major blast was in 1993, but the summit is frequently declared off limits due to toxic gas emissions. Check with the tourist information office (below) for continuous updates. Officials may close the summit for a day or just an hour; it all depends on wind conditions.

Aso-san has literary value as well; in addition to its being used as the backdrop for a number of movies (those of Akira Kurosawa among them), it has been a key site for writers, artists and other literati to visit as well. Among them was Akiko Yosano, one of Japan's first feminists and a gifted writer, who toured this area, staying in local ryokan and writing poems as she went along. In one of her *tanka* poems, she wrote, 'In the faint mist covering Daikambo-san, the beauty of the morning glories stands out at the hotel, in the mountains of Aso.'

Orientation & Information
Rtes 57, 265 and 325 make a circuit of the outer caldera, and the JR Hōhi line runs across the northern section. Daikanbō Lookout is one of the best places to see Aso from afar. Aso is the main town in the crater but there are other towns, including Takamori, on the southern side. There are roads running into the centre of the crater and to the five 'modern' peaks within the one ancient outer peak.

Next to JR Aso station in the Eco building, there is a helpful English-speaking **tourist information office** (☎ 34-0751; ☿ 9am-6pm) offering

KYŪSHŪ

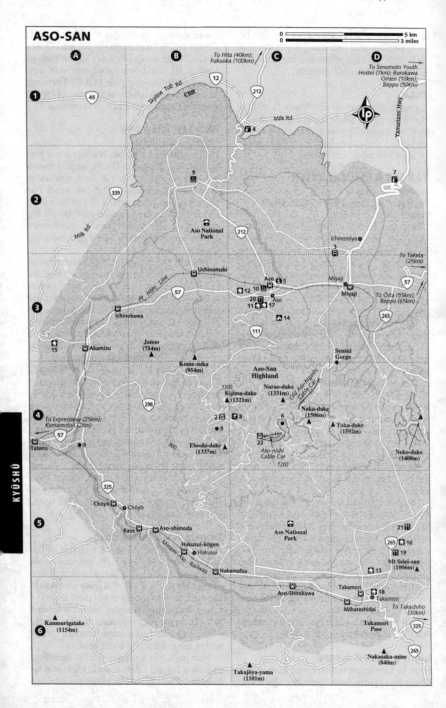

ASO-SAN

KYŪSHŪ

free hiking and road maps, and information on local accommodation. Coin lockers are available. A postal ATM is 100m south, across Hwy 57.

Sights

ASO-GOGAKU 阿蘇五岳

The **Five Mountains of Aso** are the five smaller mountains within the outer rim. They are Eboshi-dake (1337m), Kijima-dake (1321m), Naka-dake (1506m), Neko-dake (1408m) and Taka-dake (1592m). Naka-dake is currently the active volcano in this group. Neko-dake, furthest to the east, is instantly recognisable by its craggy peak but Taka-dake, between Neko-dake and Naka-dake, is the highest.

ASO VOLCANIC MUSEUM 阿蘇火山博物館

This state-of-the-art **museum** (☎ 34-2111; www
.asomuse.jp/in Japanese; admission incl/excl cable-car return
¥1480/840; ⏰ 9am-5pm) has real-time footage, compliments of a camera mounted inside the active crater wall. You can point the camera with a remote control from inside the mu-

seum! There's an English brochure available plus a 17-minute big-screen video (with English audio) on Aso and other volcanoes from around the world, all strutting their stuff.

KUSASENRI & KOME-ZUKA 草千里 • 米塚

Opposite the volcanic museum is **Kusasenri** (1000km of grass), a grassy meadow with two lakes in the flattened crater of an ancient volcano. It's a postcard-perfect picture on a clear day.

Just off the road that runs from the museum to the town of Aso is the perfectly shaped small cone of **Kome-zuka** (954m), another extinct volcano. The name means 'rice mound'.

NAKA-DAKE 中岳

Naka-dake (1506m) has been very active in recent years. The cable car to the summit was closed from August 1989 to March 1990 due to eruptions, and it had only been opened for a few weeks when the volcano erupted again in April 1990, spewing dust and ash over a large area to the north.

In 1958, following an unexpected eruption that killed 12 onlookers, concrete shelters were built around the rim for sightseers to take shelter (in an emergency). Nevertheless, an eruption in 1979 killed three visitors over 1km from the cone, in an area that was thought to be safe. This eruption destroyed a cable car that used to run up the northeastern slope of the cone.

From the Aso Volcanic Museum (left), it's 3km up to the cable-car station. When Naka-dake is not misbehaving, the **cable car** (ropeway; each way ¥410; ⏰ 9am-5pm) whisks you up to the summit in just four minutes. From there, the walk to the top takes less than 30 minutes. The 100m-deep crater varies in width from 400m to 1100m and there's a walk around the southern edge of the crater rim. Arrive early in the morning to glimpse a sea of clouds hovering inside the crater, with Kujū-san (1787m) on the horizon.

Activities

From the top of the cable-car run you can walk around the crater rim to the peak of Naka-dake and on to the top of Taka-dake. From there you can descend to Sensui Gorge (Sensui-kyō), which blooms with azaleas in mid-May, or to the road that runs between Taka-dake and Neko-dake. Either way will

KYŪSHŪ

lead you to Miyaji, the next express train station east of Aso. The direct descent to Sensui Gorge is very steep, so it's easier to continue back from Taka-dake to the Naka-dake rim and then follow the old Aso-higashi cable-car route down to Sensui Gorge. Allow four to five hours from the Aso-nishi cable-car station walking uphill to Sensui Gorge, then another 1½ hours for the descent.

Shorter walks include the easy ascent of Kijima-dake from the Aso Volcanic Museum, about 25 minutes to the top. You can then return to the museum area or take the branch trail to the Naka-dake ropeway in about 30 minutes. You can also climb to the top of Eboshi-dake in about 50 minutes. All the peaks offer superb views, as do several lookout perches on the crater's outer rim, including Shiroyama Tembōdai on the Yamanami Hwy, and Daikanbō near Uchinomaki Onsen.

Perfect after a long hike, **Yume-no-yu Onsen** (☎ 35-5777; admission ¥400; ⏰ 10am-10pm), just in front of Aso station, has wonderful indoor and outdoor pools and a large sauna.

Festivals & Events

A spectacular fire festival, **hi-furi-matsuri**, is held at **Aso-jinja** (☎ 22-0064) one day in mid-March (dates vary). The shrine, dedicated to the 12 gods of the mountain, is about a 300m walk north of JR Miyaji station, and is one of only three shrines in Japan with its original *mon* (gate). The drinking water here is said to be delicious, and at dusk residents can be seen filling 20L canteens to take home with them.

Sleeping & Eating

Over 50 places to stay make finding a bed in the Aso-san area easy. Most are in Aso town, Akamizu and Takamori village; most provide meals. Away from Aso town, accommodation is scattered and hard to reach by public transport. There's a cluster of eateries on Hwy 57 near Aso station, plus one inside the station, just right for catching the nearby bus to the ropeway cable car.

ASO TOWN

Bōchū Kyampu-jo (☎ 34-0351; camp sites per person ¥310; ⏰ Jun-Sep) Reached via a path that veers off the highway below the youth hostel, the camp has good facilities and tent rentals (¥600).

Aso Youth Hostel (☎ 34-0804; dm ¥2450; P ☒) This friendly 10-room hostel is a 20-minute walk from JR Aso station uphill towards the mountain, past small Saigenden-ji, which dates from AD 726. Buses up to the cable-car station stop outside the hostel. A kitchen is available and the owners will happily discuss hiking in the area.

ourpick **Aso-no-Fumoto** (☎ 34-0624; r per person ¥4200; P ☒ ☒) Great value, this well-managed *minshuku* is approximately 350m from the station; the owner will also pick you up. Breakfast (¥500) and dinner (¥1000) are available.

Shukubou Aso Minshuku (☎ 34-0194; fax 34-1342; r per person incl/excl 2 meals ¥12,000/6000; P ☒ ☒) This traditional *minshuku* with modern touches is set in the trees, less than 500m from Aso station, and good value.

Sanzoku-Tabiji (☎ 34-2011; set meals from ¥950; ⏰ 11am-7pm; V ♿) On Hwy 57, five minutes' walk from Aso station, just past Lawson store; has very good *teishoku*.

TAKAMORI

On the outskirts of Takamori is *pension mura* (pension village) charging rates of around ¥8000 per person, with two meals. Inquire at the tourist information counter next to Aso station.

Takamori-Murataya Ryokan Youth Hostel (☎ 62-0066; dm HI member/nonmember ¥2700/3700) In Takamori town, this is quite pleasant, though the toilets are Japanese-style only. The owner will meet you at the station.

Bluegrass (☎ 62-3366; fax 62-3022; r per person incl/excl 2 meals ¥7000/4000; P E) This rustic ranch house and inn manages to serve both Western-style barbecue and Japanese cuisine (meals from ¥1500; open 11am to 8pm, closed Tuesday).

AKAMIZU

Kumamoto YMCA Aso Camp (☎ 35-0124; dm ¥3000-3200; P) With clean, modern and comfortable cabins. It's about 600m west of JR Akamizu station, across the river.

Kyūkamura Minami-Aso (☎ 62-2111; r per person from ¥5500; P) A national vacation village that gets crowded in July and August. Inquire at the information counter next to Aso station.

Dengaku-no-Sato (☎ 62-1899; set meals from ¥1800; ⏰ lunch & dinner) At this old farmhouse restaurant, you cook your own kebablike *dengaku* (hardened *mochi* rice dipped in miso) on individual *hibachi* (barbecue).

Getting There & Around

Aso is on the JR Hōhi line between Kumamoto (*tokkyū*, ¥2180, 70 minutes) and Ōita (*tokkyū*,

¥3490, two hours). Some buses from Beppu (¥3080, 2¾ hours) continue to the Aso-nishi cable-car station (an extra ¥1130).

To get to Takamori on the southern side of the crater, transfer from the JR Hōhi line at Tateno (¥360, 30 minutes) to the scenic Minami-Aso private line, which terminates at Takamori (¥470, 30 minutes). Buses from Takamori continue southeast to the mountain resort of Takachiho (¥1280, 70 minutes, three daily).

Buses operate approximately every 90 minutes from JR Aso station via the youth hostel and volcano museum to Aso-nishi cable car station (¥470, 35 minutes). The first bus up leaves at 8.37am, with the last return trip down from the cable-car station at 5pm.

Bike rentals are available at Aso station (¥300, two hours). Cars can be rented for the day at **Eki Rent-a-Car** (☎ 34-1001; www.ekiren.co.jp in Japanese), opposite the tourist information office adjacent to the train station, from ¥6000.

A toll (¥560) is required on a portion of the road skirting the crater. If you hire a car, there's only one toll road in the area, from Aso-nishi to Kato-nishi (¥560, 1.5km).

KUROKAWA ONSEN 黒川温泉
☎ 0967 / pop 400

A real treasure. A few dozen ryokan lie along a steep-sided valley beside the Kurokawa, some 6km west of the Yamanami Hwy. Considered one of the best *onsen* villages in Japan, Kurokawa is everything a resort town should be without accompanying kitsch or ugliness. While it's well frequented and you certainly won't be alone, this low-key resort still seems like it's a tiny, forgotten village that you've been lucky to stumble upon.

The enlightened Onsen Association has also made it affordable: an 'onsen passport' (¥1200) from the **tourist information desk** (☎ 44-0076; ☯ 9am-6pm) and from several ryokan allows access to three baths (8.30am to 9pm) of your choice. Kurokawa is especially famous for its 23 *rotemburo*. Among local favourites are Yamamizuki, Kurokawa-sō and the magnificent Shimmei-kan, with its cave baths and riverside *rotemburo*. Many places offer *konyoku* (mixed bathing) and separate male and female baths.

Sleeping

Between Miyagi and Kurokawa Onsen, **Aso Senomoto Youth Hostel** (阿蘇瀬の本ユースホステル; ☎ 44-0157; www.jyh.gr.jp/aso/next.html; dm HI member/nonmember ¥2415/2940) has English information about hiking Kujū-san and other high peaks in the area. Breakfast and dinner are available.

The *onsen* ryokan at Kurokawa are well worth splurging on – not cheap, but good value and unique.

At secluded **Sanga Ryokan** (山河旅館; ☎ 44-0906; www.sanga-ryokan.com/in Japanese; r per person incl 2 meals from ¥13,800) several of the 15 rooms have private *onsen* attached. Nearby **Okyakuya Ryokan** (御客屋旅館; ☎ 44-0454; fax 44-0551; r per person incl 2 meals from ¥12,000) overlooks a serene garden. English is spoken at both ryokan, and a station pick-up service is provided.

Getting There & Away

There are five buses daily from JR Aso station (Map p702) to Senomoto-Kogen (¥810), Senomoto Youth Hostel (¥830) and Kurokawa Onsen (¥960, one hour). The last bus to return to Aso departs at 5.55pm. If you miss it, you can take a taxi out to the Yamanami Hwy (¥1000) and take a bus from the Senomoto bus stop to Aso. A taxi between Kurokawa and Aso costs around ¥7000 (40 minutes). The last bus leaves Kurokawa for Kumamoto at 8.30pm (¥1430, one hour); the last bus to Beppu departs at 7pm (¥2350, two hours).

SOUTH OF KUMAMOTO

About 90km south of Kumamoto, the **coastal wetlands** at Izumi are the winter home to 85% of the global population of hooded cranes.

The nearby port of **Minamata** became infamous in the late '60s when it was discovered that a nearby chemical factory had been dumping waste containing high levels of mercury into the sea, contaminating the fish eaten by local residents, leading to high rates of illness and birth defects. The company's efforts to suppress the story led to outrage in Japan. In the early '70s, W Eugene Smith's heart-rending documentary photos focused worldwide attention on the town's tragedy.

AMAKUSA ARCHIPELAGO 天草諸島
☎ 0969

South of the Shimabara Peninsula are the islands of the Amakusa-shotō. The islands were a stronghold of Christianity during Japan's 'Christian Century' and the grinding poverty here was a major factor in the Shimabara

KYŪSHŪ

Rebellion of 1637–38. It's still one of the least developed regions of Japan.

Around the islands, there are opportunities for diving and dolphin-watching cruises. **Hondo** is the main town and has exhibition halls relating to the Christian era. **Amakusa Youth Hostel** (天草ユースホステル; ☎ 22-3085; dm HI member/nonmember ¥2780/3780) is about a 300m walk uphill from the bus terminal. Tamioka, where Nagasaki ferries berth, has castle ruins; this west-coast area is particularly interesting.

Getting to the islands usually involves a ferry from various places in Nagasaki-ken or along the Kumamoto coast. Amakusa Five Bridges links the island directly with Misumi, southwest of Kumamoto.

KAGOSHIMA-KEN
鹿児島県

Kyūshū's southernmost prefecture is dominated by the majestic volcano of Sakurajima, which overlooks the bustling city of Kagoshima across the bay. To the south is the Satsuma Peninsula, and to the north Kirishima-Yaku National Park with its superb volcanoes and hiking. Here is where the Meiji Restoration began, initially under the leadership of Saigō Takamori (see the boxed text, p715). Famous also for its dialect, the prefecture's Kagoshima-ben is so difficult that it was used as code in WWII much the way the Native American Navajo language was used by the USA.

Atop an unimpressive bluff in Kokubu city, 40 minutes north of Kagoshima, a construction crew digging a hotel foundation stumbled upon what would be identified as the oldest Jōmon-era remains ever found. Almost 10,000 years ago primitive civilisation arrived here and stayed long enough to leave relics of its passing. The site at Uenohara boasts a small museum and a research station, well worth a stop if you're heading in that direction.

KIRISHIMA-YAKU NATIONAL PARK
霧島

The day walk from Ebino-kōgen (Ebino Plateau, not to be confused with the town of Ebino down on the plains) to the summits of a string of volcanoes is one of the finest volcanic hikes in Japan. Parts of the park are in Miya-

zaki-ken, but much of it is in Kagoshima-ken. It's 15km from the summit of Karakuni-dake (1700m) to the summit of Takachiho-no-mine (1574m) and there's superb scenery – if the peaks aren't being lashed by thunderstorms or shrouded in fog, which is common during the rainy season (mid-May through June). Shorter walks, such as a lake stroll on the plateau or up and down Karakuni-dake or Takachiho-no-mine, are great too. The area is known for its wild azaleas, hot springs and the impressive 75m waterfall, **Senriga-taki**.

Orientation & Information
A centre at each end of the volcano walk has bilingual maps and hiking information.

Ebino-kōgen Eco Museum Centre (☎ 0984-33-3002; ☺ 9am-5pm) This has most of the hotels, restaurants and camping facilities, and also has displays on local wildlife and geology, plus an indoor rest area with vending machines. Staff sells topographic hiking maps, and dispenses local advice for free.

Takachiho-gawara Visitors Centre (☎ 0995-57-2505; ☺ 9am-5pm)

Sights & Activities
EBINO PLATEAU WALKS
The Ebino-kōgen lake circuit is a relaxed 4km stroll around a series of volcanic lakes – **Rokkannon Mi-ike** has an intense blue-green colour. Across the road from the lake, Fudō-ike, at the base of Karakuni-dake, is a steaming *jigoku*. The stiffer climb to the 1700m summit of **Karakuni-dake** skirts the edge of the volcano's deep crater before arriving at the high point on the eastern side. The panoramic view to the south is superb, taking in the perfectly circular caldera lake of Ōnami-ike, rounded **Shinmoe-dake** and the perfect cone of Takachiho-no-mine. On a clear day, you can see Kagoshima and the smoking cone of Sakurajima. Naka-dake is another nice half-day walk, and in May and June it offers good views of the Miyama-Kirishima azaleas.

LONGER WALKS
The long views across the lunarlike terrain of volcano summits are otherworldly. If you have six or seven hours, you can continue from Karakuni-dake to Shishiko-dake, Shinmoe-dake, Naka-dake and Takachiho-gawara, from where you can make the ascent of Takachiho-no-mine. Close up, Takachiho is a formidable volcano with a huge, gaping crater. The whole trek goes above and below the treeline on a

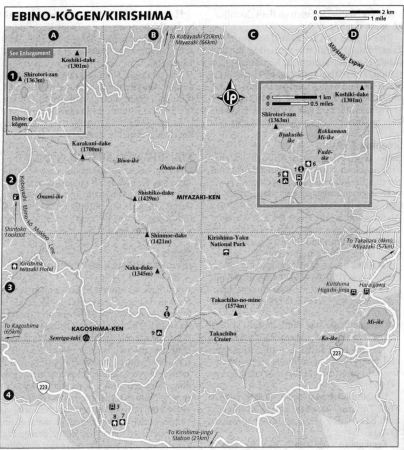

trail that can be muddy or dry, clear or foggy. But cheer up; some Kagoshima monks-in-training do this route daily.

If you miss the afternoon bus (3.49pm) from Takachiho-gawara to Kirishima-jingū; it's a 7km walk down to the village shrine area, or a ¥1000 taxi ride; a taxi up to Ebino-kogen is about ¥3500.

KIRISHIMA-JINGŪ 霧島神宮

Bright-orange **Kirishima-jingū** (☎ 0995-57-0001) is beautifully situated, picturesque, and offers nice views of the surrounding area. Though it dates from the 6th century, the present shrine was built in 1715. It is dedicated to Ninigi-no-mikoto, who, according to the *Kojiki* (a historical book compiled in 712), made his

INFORMATION
Ebino-kogen Eco-Museum Centre **1** C2
Takachiho-gawara Visitors Centre **2** B3

SIGHTS & ACTIVITIES
Kirishima-jingū 霧島神宮 **3** B4

SLEEPING 🏠 🏕
Ebino-kōgen Campground & Lodge
えびの高原キャンプ村 **4** C2
Highland Resort Ebino-kōgen-sō
ハイランドリゾートえびの高原荘 **5** C2
Karakuni-sō からくに荘 **6** D2
Minshuku Kirishima-ji 民宿きりしま路 **7** B4
Krishima Jingu-mae Youth Hostel
霧島神宮前ユースホステル **8** B4
Takachiho-gawara Camping Ground 高千穂河原
キャンプ場 **9** B3

TRANSPORT
Bus Centre バスセンター **10** C2

KYŪSHŪ

legendary landing in Japan on the Takachiho-no-mine summit.

The shrine can be visited en route to Takachiho-gawara. It's accessible by bus (¥240, 15 minutes) from JR Kirishima-jingū station. The festivals of **Saitan-sai** (1 January), **Ota-ue-sai** (mid-March) and the lantern festival of **Kontō-sai** (5 August) are worth seeing. If you're a temple fan, visit Kirishima Higashi-jinja for ancient cedars and scenic views.

Sleeping & Eating

Ebino-kōgen village (on the Miyazaki side) has a reasonable choice of accommodation, but not restaurants. Most village shops close by 5pm.

Ebino-kōgen Campground & Lodge (☎ 0984-33-0800, 0984-35-1111; camp sites/lodge cabins from ¥980/1560) About a 500m walk from the Eco-Museum Centre. Open year-round, tent and blanket hire is available. In July and August the room price at the lodge cabins jumps to ¥6000.

Takachiho-gawara camping ground (☎ 0995-57-0996; tent rental ¥1100; ☽ Jul & Aug) Camping items (tent etc) can be rented. A set-up tent, blankets, and cooking utensils for five people costs ¥2760.

Kirishima Jingū-mae Youth Hostel (☎ 0995-57-1188; dm HI member/nonmember ¥3500/4500; ✗) Southeast of Kirishima-jingū, this clean and comfy hostel has a liberal midnight curfew, and offers breakfast (¥500) and dinner (¥1000).

Minshuku Kirishima-ji (☎ 0995-57-0272; r per person ¥4500) This basic six-room ryokan with shared bath has a small *onsen*, and offers breakfast (¥700).

Karakuni-sō (☎ 0984-33-0650; fax 0984-33-4928; per person incl 2 meals ¥8600, annexe house s/d/tr ¥5000/8000/9000) This small, comfortable ryokan comes with deer nibbling around the grounds and a wonderful *onsen* that is also open to the public from 11am to 3pm (¥300).

Highland Resort Ebino-kōgen-sō (☎ 0984-33-0161; www.ebinokogenso.jp/in Japanese; r per person incl 2 meals from ¥12,000) This is a surprisingly elegant *kokumin-shukusha* with *rotemburo* and sauna. Stop by its good-value restaurant, Nokaidō (dishes ¥600 to ¥1200; open for lunch). The exquisite *rotemburo* is open to the public from 11.30am to 7.30pm (¥500).

Getting There & Away

The main train junctions are JR Kobayashi station, which is northeast of Ebino Plateau, and Kirishima-jingū station to the south.

However, a direct bus to Ebino-kōgen is by far the best way to go. From Kagoshima, Hayashida buses (four daily) make the 27km run to Ebino-kōgen starting at 10am (¥1570, 1¾ hours).

The approach from Miyazaki is more difficult – take the bus to Kobayashi (¥2000, 80 minutes). From there, you'll need to take a taxi (¥5000, 35 minutes), or hitch.

Schedules often change for travel to Ebino-kōgen; check before starting out.

KIRISHIMA-SHI KOKUBU 霧島市国分

Directly north of Sakurajima you'll find Kokubu, Kagoshima's second-largest city, which still seems like a small countryside town despite its growing population and several industries, such as Kyōcera and Sony, which have branches nearby.

Sights

UENOHARA JŌMON-ERA SITE 上の原縄文遺跡

If you have an interest in archaeology, you'll want to detour to see Uenohara. Once just a remote make-out spot with an empty parking lot and a few lonesome vending machines, Uenohara was transformed when – in the process of digging the foundation for a planned hotel – the oldest known Jōmon-era pottery shards were uncovered leading to entirely new views about how civilisation developed in Japan. It now appears that the first humans may have come from the south rather than the north, via canoes or rafts along the Ryūkyū island chain.

A re-created Jōmon-era village, demonstrations, tools and artefacts make this appealing **museum** (上野原縄文の森; ☎ 48-5701; admission ¥300; ☽ 9am-5pm Tue-Sun) a fascinating spot.

Getting There & Around

Kokubu can be easily reached by frequent trains from Kagoshima (see p715). Buses from Kokubu station (¥400, six daily) arrive at the Uenohara Jōmon Site in 24 minutes. The last bus leaves Uenohara for Kokubu station at 5.35pm. Car rentals can be made with **Toyota Renta Lease** (Toyota Renta Riisu; ☎ 47-0600; ☽ 8am-8pm), three minutes' walk from Kokubu station; turn left at the first street after the station.

KAGOSHIMA 鹿児島

☎ 099 / pop 604,367

Kagoshima is the southernmost major city in Kyūshū and a warm, sunny and relaxed place –

at least while looming Sakurajima volcano, just a stone's throw across the bay, is behaving itself. 'Dustfall' brings out the umbrellas in Kagoshima as frequently as rainfall in other parts of the world, coating cars, leaves, rooftops and, of course, any laundry left outside to dry.

History
Recent archaeological discoveries (see opposite) are showing that Kagoshima may actually be the birthplace of Jōmon civilisation, as its 10,000-year-old remains are some of Japan's oldest. For much of its history, Kagoshima prefecture was dominated by one family, the Shimazu clan, who held sway for 29 generations (nearly 700 years) until the Meiji Restoration. Even then, the clan continued to influence events. In 1865 the family helped to smuggle more than a dozen young men out of the country to study Western technology first-hand in the UK. A statue in front of JR Kagoshima station commemorates these 17 adventurers who defied a national ban on foreign travel.

In fact the Kagoshima region, known as Satsuma, had always been receptive to outside contact and for many years was an important centre for trade with China. St Francis Xavier first arrived here in 1549, making Kagoshima one of Japan's earliest contact points with Christianity and the West. Contact was also made with Koreans, whose pottery methods were influential in the creation of Satsuma-yaki (see p678).

Orientation
Kagoshima spreads north–south along the bayside and has two JR stations, the major one being Kagoshima-Chūō to the south. The town centre is at the point where the lively Tenmonkan-dōri shopping and entertainment arcade crosses the tram lines. The garden of Sengan-en (below), the town's principal attraction, is north of Kagoshima station but most other things to do are around the centre, north of the river (Kōtsuki-gawa), with frisky Sakurajima always in view.

Information
Numerous places in the city (including the tourist information office) carry an excellent English guide called (not surprisingly!) *Kagoshima*. It has maps, a host of activities, model excursions broken into three-hour, half-day and whole-day sections, all with detailed maps. Some highlights include visiting local pottery kilns, silk-weaving workshops, *shōchū* distilleries and even a Satsuma fish-paste factory! Also check out the excellent website www.synapse.ne.jp/update.

The postal savings ATM at the central post office (Map pp712–13) near JR Kagoshima-Chūō station accepts international cards.

International Exchange Plaza (Map p710; ☎ 221-6620; 14-50 Yamashita-chō; access per 30min free; ⏰ 8.30am-7pm, closed Mon) It also has CNN, magazines and books for browsing.

Internet Café Aprecio (Map pp712-13; ☎ 226-2077; 17-28 Nishisengoku-chō; per 30min ¥300; ⏰ 24hr) In Tenmonkan.

Joy Road (☎ 253-2201; www.jr.kyushu.co.jp/english/index.html; Kagoshima-Chūō station; ⏰ 8am-8pm) JR's own travel service inside the station, and can help with various travel needs.

Tourist information office (Map pp712-13; ☎ 253-2500; inside JR Kagoshima-Chūō station; ⏰ 8.30am-7pm) Has information in English. Pick up a copy of *Kagoshima Visitor's Guide*.

Sights
SENGAN-EN (ISO-TEIEN) 磯庭園仙巌園
Starting in 1658, the 19th Shimazu lord laid out this beautiful bayside **garden** (☎ 274-1551;

KYŪSHŪ

GUNS IN JAPAN
It's rare to see a gun in Japan, even though they've been around for centuries. The first guns appeared in 1543, when a Chinese trade ship bound for Macao was blown off course, drifting ashore on the southern island of Tanegashima. Among those aboard were a few Portuguese adventurers sporting primitive muskets. Military commanders at Kagoshima soon learned of the new weapon, and within 20 years Japan was manufacturing the highest-quality guns in the world.

The powerful samurai class was not impressed. Battles decided by guns rather than swords threatened a long tradition. Moreover, guns were a decidedly foreign invention. Restrictions on gun production grew and Japan gradually abandoned the technology it had perfected. The conflict between samurai culture and the new order is beautifully dramatised in Kurosawa's cinematic masterpiece *The Seven Samurai*.

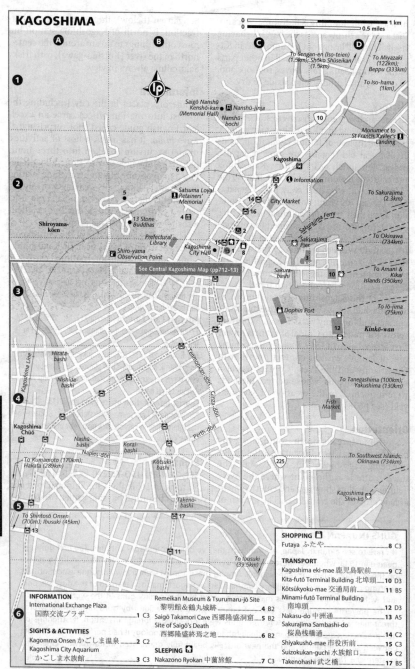

KAGOSHIMA

To Sengan-en (Iso-teien) (1.5km); Shōko Shūseikan (1.5km)

To Miyazaki (122km); Beppu (333km)

To Iso-hama (1km)

Monument to St Francis Xavier's Landing

Saigō Nanshū Kenshō-kan (Memorial Hall)

Nanshū-jinja

Nanshū-bochi

Kagoshima

Information

City Market

Satsuma Loyal Retainers' Memorial

Shiroyama-kōen

13 Stone Buddhas

Prefectural Library

Kagoshima City Hall

Shiro-yama Observation Point

To Sakurajima (2.3km)

Sakurajima Ferry

Sakurajima Pier

Sakura-bashi

To Okinawa (734km)

To Amani & Kikai Islands (350km)

See Central Kagoshima Map (pp712–13)

Dophin Port

To Iō-jima (75km)

Kinkō-wan

Hirata-bashi

Nishida-bashi

Kagoshima Chūō

Nashū-bashi

Naples-dōri

Korai-bashi

Kōtsuki-bashi

Takeno-bashi

Kagoshima Line

Tenmonkan-dōri

Ginza-dōri

Perth-dōri

To Kumamoto (170km); Hakata (289km)

To Shintosō Onsen (700m); Ibusuki (45km)

To Tanegashima (100km); Yakushima (130km)

Fish Market

To Southwest Islands; Okinawa (734km)

Kagoshima Shin-kō

To Ibusuki (39.5km)

KYŪSHŪ

9700-1 Yoshinochō; admission incl/excl guided villa tour & tea ceremony ¥1500/1000; 8.30am-5.15pm), incorporating one of the most impressive pieces of 'borrowed scenery' to be found anywhere in Japan – the fuming peak of Sakurajima. Look for the stream where the 21st Shimazu lord once held poetry parties – the participants had to compose a poem before the next cup of sake floated by (haiku verse was no doubt popular). The villa of **Shimazu-ke** was once a second home of the omnipotent Shimazu clan. Women in elegant kimonos guide you through the villa, after which you are served traditional tea and sweets. Look for a moment at the tea bowl's pattern or shape before you take a sip, if you want to be especially polite.

Other teashops around the garden sell *jambo* (pounded rice cakes on a stick).

The museum of **Shōko Shūseikan** (尚古集成館; admission free with garden ticket; 8.30am-5.15pm), adjacent to Sengan-en, once housed Japan's first factory, built in the 1850s. Exhibits relate to the Shimazu family – in fact most of the 10,000 items are precious heirlooms, including ancient scrolls, military goods and pottery. The art of *kiriko* (cut glass) has been revived at an on-site workshop.

MUSEUMS

Museum of the Meiji Restoration (Map pp712-13; 239-7700; 23-1 Kajiiya-chō; admission ¥300; 9am-5.30pm mid-Jul–Aug, to 4.30pm Sep–mid-Jul) has hourly performances by robotic Meiji reformers, including Saigō Takamori (see the boxed text, p715). Exhibits and historical hi-tech dioramas, labelled mostly in Japanese, laud Kagoshima Meiji-era firsts (Japan's first telegraph, first gas lighting, among others).

Kagoshima City Museum of Art (Map pp712-13; 224-3400; 4-36 Shiroyamachō; admission ¥200; 9.30am-6pm Tue-Sun) has a small, permanent collection of works by modern-day Kagoshima painters, as well as some 16th-century porcelains and wood-block prints. Be sure to see the collection of Sakurajima paintings.

Reimeikan (Kagoshima Prefectural Museum of Culture; Map p710; admission ¥300; 9am-4.30pm Tue-Sun) is on the former site of **Tsurumaru-jō** – the walls and the impressive moat are all that remain of the 1602 castle, and bullet holes in the stones are still visible. Inside you'll find interesting exhibits on Satsuma history and ancient sword-making displays.

OTHER SIGHTS

Kagoshima boasts no less than 50 public *onsen*. Local favourite **Nishida Onsen** (Map p712-13; 255-6354; 12-17 Takasu) is just a few minutes' walk from JR Kagoshima-Chūō. **Kagomma Sentō (Onsen)** (Map p710; 226-2688; 3-28 Yasui-chō; admission ¥360; 10am-1am) is five minutes' walk from the Sakurajima Port.

Kagoshima City Aquarium (Map p710; 226-2233; 3-1 Hon Minato Shinmachi; adult/child ¥1500/750; 9am-5pm) is well done, not least the examples of local marine life, giving glimpses of spectacular diving in the Southwest Islands. **Iso-hama**, the city's popular and kid-friendly beach getaway, is good for summer swimming and splashing about, with Sakurajima in view.

Festivals & Events

Sogadon-no-Kasayaki (Umbrella Burning Festival) One of Kagoshima's more unusual events in late July. Boys burn umbrellas on the banks of Kōtsuki-gawa in honour of two brothers who used umbrellas as torches in one of Japan's oldest revenge stories.

Isle of Fire Festival In late July on Sakurajima.

Ohara Festival Featuring folk dancing in the streets on 3 November; visitors are invited to join in.

Sleeping

our pick **Nakazono Ryokan** (Map p710; 226-5125; shindon@satsuma.ne.jp; 1-8 Yasuichō; s/d/tr ¥4200/8400/11,970;) You can find fancier and better-appointed places to rest your head, but you'll get a good taste of Kagoshima hospitality at this inn, used to dealing with the vagaries of *gaijin* clients. Part of the Japanese Inn Group, it is one of those gathering places filled with the personality of its owner, in this case the inimitable Shinichi Nakazono, who greets guests with a wry smile and a small pot of tea. He provides maps with handwritten notes highlighting Kagoshima's attractions, big and small. There's also a mineral-water *sentō* (public bathhouse) nearby, and the inn is walking distance to Tenmonkan. If you return late at night, Nakazono-san will show you the secret door entry. The ryokan is tucked down a narrow alley behind a temple, near the Shiyakusho-mae (City Hall) tram stop and a five-minute walk to Sakurajima pier.

Hotel Ishihara-sō (Map pp712-13; 254-4181; 4-14 Chūōchō; s/d ¥4725/8925;) This surprising 14-room urban oasis is only four minutes' walk from the station. There's a small elegant lobby with a good Satsuma-cuisine restaurant attached.

KYŪSHŪ

CENTRAL KAGOSHIMA

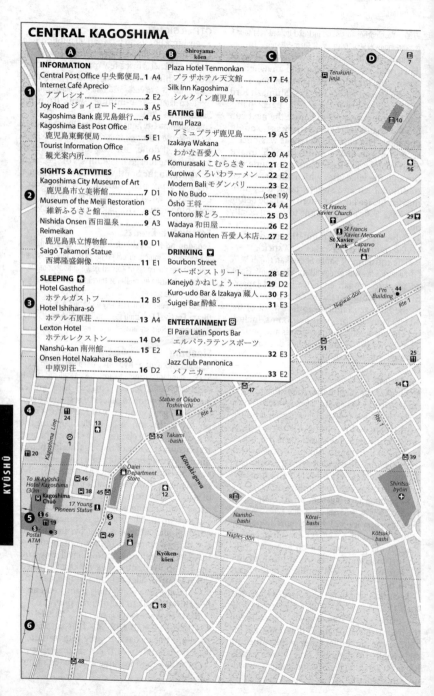

INFORMATION
Central Post Office 中央郵便局..**1** A4
Internet Café Aprecio
アプレシオ.................................**2** E2
Joy Road ジョイロード................**3** A5
Kagoshima Bank 鹿児島銀行......**4** A5
Kagoshima East Post Office
鹿児島東郵便局.........................**5** E1
Tourist Information Office
観光案内所...............................**6** A5

SIGHTS & ACTIVITIES
Kagoshima City Museum of Art
鹿児島市立美術館.....................**7** D1
Museum of the Meiji Restoration
維新ふるさと館.........................**8** C5
Nishida Onsen 西田温泉............**9** A3
Reimeikan
鹿児島県立博物館....................**10** D1
Saigō Takamori Statue
西郷隆盛銅像.........................**11** E1

SLEEPING
Hotel Gasthof
ホテルガストフ.......................**12** B5
Hotel Ishihara-sō
ホテル石原荘.........................**13** A4
Lexton Hotel
ホテルレクストン....................**14** D4
Nanshū-kan 南州館..................**15** E2
Onsen Hotel Nakahara Bessō
中原別荘...............................**16** D2

Plaza Hotel Tenmonkan
プラザホテル天文館................**17** E4
Silk Inn Kagoshima
シルクイン鹿児島...................**18** B6

EATING
Amu Plaza
アミュプラザ鹿児島................**19** A5
Izakaya Wakana
わかな吾愛人.........................**20** A4
Komurasaki こむらさき............**21** E2
Kuroiwa くろいわラーメン......**22** E2
Modern Bali モダンバリ..........**23** E2
No No Budo.........................(see 19)
Ōshō 王将..............................**24** A4
Tontoro 豚とろ.......................**25** D3
Wadaya 和田屋.......................**26** E2
Wakana Honten 吾愛人本店....**27** E2

DRINKING
Bourbon Street
バーボンストリート.................**28** E2
Kanejyō かねじょう................**29** D2
Kuro-udo Bar & Izakaya 蔵人...**30** F3
Suigei Bar 酔鯨.......................**31** E3

ENTERTAINMENT
El Para Latin Sports Bar
エルパラ・ラテンスポーツ
バー.....................................**32** E3
Jazz Club Pannonica
パノニカ...............................**33** E2

Hotel Gasthof (Map pp712-13; ☎ 252-1401; 7-1 Chūō-chō; s/d/tw/tr ¥5565/8400/8925/12,600; ⊠ ♻ 🖳) Old-world Europe meets urban Japan at this unusual 48-room central hotel, with big rooms and big furniture straight from Bavaria. There's also a gallery packed with Japanese and Chinese artwork and a swank basement restaurant.

Plaza Hotel Tenmonkan (Map pp712-13; ☎ 222-3344; fax 222-9911; 7-8 Yamanokuchi-cho; s/tw incl breakfast from ¥5700/9000; ⊠ ♻ 🖳) One of the best values in Tenmonkan, this well-managed business hotel has a narrow, inviting entry (with a tiny English sign). Rooms are smallish, but spotless. The breakfast buffet is generous.

Nanshū-kan (Map pp712-13; ☎ 226-8188; fax 226-9383; 19-17 Higashi-Sengo-kuchō; s/d from ¥6300/8400; Ⓟ ⊠ ♻) Excellent value and well located, the attractive and comfortable rooms combine Japanese and Western features. A breakfast buffet is available (¥840).

Lexton Hotel (Map pp712-13; ☎ 222-0505; www .nisikawa.net/lexton/english/dining/index.html; 4-20 Yamanokuchi-chō; s/d from ¥7350/10,080; Ⓟ ⊠ ♻ 🖳) This smart-looking hotel is one of Tenmonkan's newest. Rooms are large and well appointed with dark-wood furnishings. All rooms are smartly arranged around an open centre, with skylight above. This is excellent value in this range.

Onsen Hotel Nakahara Bessō (Map pp712-13; ☎ 225-2800; fax 226-3688; 15-19 Terukunichō; r per person incl/excl 2 meals ¥10,000/8000; Ⓟ ⊠ ♻) This family-owned Japanese-style accommodation dates from 1904. Ignore its boxy exterior; inside you'll find spacious rooms, a modern *rotemburo*, traditional artwork plus a good *Satsuma-ryōri* restaurant.

Also recommended:

Silk Inn Kagoshima (Map pp712-13; ☎ 258-1221; 19-30 Uenosonochō; s/d/tw from ¥6090/9975/10,500; Ⓟ ⊠ ♻ 🖳) Well-appointed business hotel near children's park.

JR Kyūshū Hotel Kagoshima (☎ 213-8000; kagoshima@jrk-hotels.com; 1-1-2 Take; s/tw ¥6900/12,600; ⊠ ♻ 🖳)

Eating

Side streets around Tenmonkan and JR Kagoshima-Chūō station have an abundance of eateries, many featuring Kagoshima *Satsuma-ryōri* – the food of the Satsuma region. Dishes to try: *tonkotsu*, pork ribs seasoned with miso (fermented soybean paste) and black sugar; and *satsuma-age*, a deep-fried fishcake flavoured with sake.

KYŪSHŪ

Ōshō (Map pp712-13; ☎ 226-4718; Naka-machi; dishes ¥400-700; ⏱ lunch & dinner) Just around the corner from the central post office, with excellent (nongreasy!) chicken *kara-age*, a local favourite, fried rice and *gyōza* – it's cheap, good and fast. A picture menu is available.

Izakaya Wakana (Map pp712-13; ☎ 286-1501; 2-21-21 Nishida-chō; dishes from ¥600; ⏱ lunch & dinner) Just a two-minute walk from JR Kagoshima-Chūō station's west gate, this smart and busy eatery serves excellent, reasonably priced Japanese standards, including *nabe* (Japanese-style hot pot), *oden* and black pork. No English sign; look for the hanging red *noren* cloth. A picture menu is available from the helpful staff.

Modern Bali (Map pp712-13; ☎ 224-1338; 12-20 Higashi-Sengoku-chō; dishes from ¥600; admission ¥500; ⏱ dinner, closed Mon; E) This atmospheric eatery and bar serves authentic Indonesian favourites like *gado-gado* and *nasi goreng*.

Wakana Honten (Map pp712-13; ☎ 222-5559; 9-14 Higashi-Sengoku-chō; dishes from ¥700; ⏱ 5.30-11.15pm) Come early to avoid the wait at this popular eatery specialising in *miso-oden* (¥650), sashimi and black pork that you cook at your table.

No No Budo (Map pp712-13; ☎ 206-7585; 5th fl, Amu Plaza; lunch/dinner buffet ¥1600/2200; ⏱ lunch & dinner; ✕ Ⓥ ♿ E) Follow the after-work crowd to this natural-food all-you-can-eat buffet with a range of Japanese standards, sashimi and desserts. Hard to beat, and there's a real non-smoking section.

There's always a *rāmen* debate in the Tenmonkan area. You'll have to stand in line at **Tontoro** (Map pp712-13; ☎ 222-5857; 9-41 Yamanokuchi; rāmen dishes from ¥500; ⏱ until late), a hole-in-the-wall and one of Kagoshima's favourite new noodle shops. Both food and atmosphere are lively. Others in the area worth sampling include **Komurasaki** (Map pp712-13; ☎ 222-5707; 11-19 Higashi-Sengoku-chō; ⏱ lunch & dinner, closed Thu), **Kuroiwa** (Map pp712-13; ☎ 222-4808; 9-9 Higashi-Sengoku-chō; ⏱ lunch & dinner) and **Wadaya** (Map pp712-13; ☎ 226-7773; 11-2 Higashi-Sengoku-chō; bowls ¥630-800; ⏱ lunch & dinner), another Tenmonkan favourite.

Drinking

There's a lot happening in Tenmonkan – shot bars, discos, karaoke boxes and retro coffee shops. Most dance clubs don't get going until around 11pm. Many bars have an admission charge (average ¥500 to ¥1000).

Suigei Bar (Map pp712-13; ☎ 227-7707; Tanaka Bldg, 14-15 Sennichi-chō; E) Named 'Drunken Whale' in Japanese, this appealing, low-key pub has a cluster of small tables and stools, with *shōchū* and other drinks from ¥500, small meals like rice salad from ¥600.

Bourbon Street (Map pp712-13; ☎ 224-6854; 13-18 Higashi-Sengoku-chō; admission free; ⏱ until late) Listen to mellow jazz and blues at this smart basement shot bar, just opposite Tenmonkan-dō tram stop.

Kanejyō (Map pp712-13; ☎ 223-0487; 2nd fl, 7-20 Higashi-Sengoku-chō) Small Asian café by day; atmospheric jazz bar by night.

Kurō-udo Bar & Izakaya (☎ 227-0960; 5th fl, Rodan Bldg, 13-3 Sennichi-chō) Over 200 kinds of *shōchū*, swank bamboo décor and cool jazz make this an inviting spot.

Entertainment

Jazz Bar Pannonica (Map pp712-13; ☎ 216-3430; 2nd fl, 7-12 Higashi-Sengoku-chō; admission ¥500-1000) This cool jazz bar often features live vocalists.

El Para Latin Sports Bar (Map pp712-13; ☎ 223-3464; 2nd fl, Diamond Bldg, 11-7 Yamanokuchi-chō) Catch your big sports game here, or indulge in beer and darts. Features a killer menu of *tapas* (small-plate Spanish appetisers).

De'Nile (Map pp712-13; ☎ 222-4970; admission incl 2 free drinks ¥1000-3000; ⏱ Sat & Sun) This is another subterranean dance spot with different DJs every night, located behind Taka-Pla.

DRINKING SHŌCHŪ

The drink of choice throughout Kyūshū is *shōchū*, and the island's southern region claims the highest per-capita consumption in Japan of this distilled liquor. Each prefecture is known for its own particular variety. In Kumamoto, it's usually made from rice; in Oita, barley is the favourite. But in the *izakaya* bars of southern Kyūshū, the first choice is the sweet potato. Ask for *imo-jō-chū*. You can drink it straight, with soda or over ice, but the most traditional way is to sip it warm (*oyu-wari*) from a stone pot, heated over glowing coals, and poured into a tiny cup. From this, you taste modestly, while enjoying your meal. If you lose count (a common risk), you generally begin to glow like the coals.

SAIGŌ TAKAMORI 西郷隆盛

Although the Great Saigō had played a leading part in the Meiji Restoration in 1868, in 1877 he had second thoughts about the curtailment of samurai power and status, and this led to the ill-fated Satsuma Rebellion. Kumamoto's magnificent castle was burnt down during the rebellion but when defeat became inevitable, Saigō retreated to Kagoshima and committed *seppuku* (ritual suicide by disembowelment).

Despite his mixed status as both a hero and villain of the Restoration, Saigō is still a towering figure in the history of Japan. His square-headed features and bulky stature are instantly recognisable, and Kagoshima, like Ueno-kōen, Tokyo (see p133), also has a famous Saigō statue, as well as a memorial hall. Displays at the **Saigō Nanshū Kenshō-kan** (☎ 099-247-1100; 2-1 Kami Tatsuochō; admission ¥100; ☻ 9am-5pm, closed Mon) tell of the failed rebellion.

Shopping

Satsuma specialities include a variation on the *ningyō* (Japanese doll), *kiriko* and cards printed with inks produced from Sakurajima volcanic ash. Sakurajima ash is used in the making of Sakurajima pottery, but the main ceramic wares are white and black Satsuma-yaki. *Imo jōchū* (see the boxed text, opposite) is the drink of choice. There's another *asa-ichi* at the smaller Kagoshima station.

Futaya (Map p710; ☎ 222-5261; 5-20 Yasui-chō) For vintage kimonos and inexpensive gifts; near Nakazono Ryokan.

Asa-ichi (morning market; Map p712-13; ☻ 6am-noon Mon-Sat) Kagoshima's *asa-ici* is just south of JR Kagoshima-Chūō station. It's a raucous, lively event.

You can shop for quality goods at Sengan-en (Iso-teien), p709, and **Kagoshima Brand Shop** (Map pp712-13; ☎ 892-0821; 9-1 Meizan-chō; ☻ 9am-5pm) in Tenmonkan.

Getting There & Away
AIR

Kagoshima's airport has international connections with Shanghai and Seoul, as well as domestic flights to Tokyo (¥34,700, 95 minutes), Osaka (¥24,000, 70 minutes), Fukuoka (¥16,700, 45 minutes) and other Kyūshū destinations. Kagoshima is also the major jumping-off point for flights to the Southwest Islands and Okinawa (¥23,300, 85 minutes).

BICYCLE

Bikes can be rented reasonably (per two hours/day ¥500/1500) at Kagoshima-Chūō station and returned at a number of participating hotels (¥300). JR pass holders get a 40% discount. Ask at the tourist information office for details (p709).

BOAT

Ferries shuttle every 10 to 30 minutes across the bay to Sakurajima (¥150, 15 minutes). Jetfoils depart from Kita-futō (north wharf) to Yakushima (¥9000, three hours). Regular ferries to Yakushima depart from Minami-futō (south wharf; ¥5400, 13 hours). For details on ferry services to Yakushima, see p743.

From Kagoshima Shin-kō (Kagoshima New Port), **Queen Coral Marix Line** (☎ 225-1551) has ferries to Naha (Okinawa) via the Amami archipelago (¥14,200, 24 hours).

BUS

Most long-distance buses leave from the Express Bus Center in the Nangoku Nissei Building, opposite Amu Plaza at Kagoshima-Chūō station. There are myriad highway bus stops, mostly found around Kagoshima-Chūō station and Yamakataya (Map pp712–13) in Tenmonkan.

Typical services include Miyazaki (¥2700, 2¾ hours), Fukuoka (¥5300, four hours), Oita (¥5500, six hours) and overnight to Osaka (¥12,000, 12 hours).

Hayashida buses to Ebino-kōgen (¥1550, two hours) depart from opposite Taka-Pla department store in Tenmonkan or JR Kagoshima-Chūō station.

TRAIN

Most trains arrive and depart from Kagoshima-Chūō station. Additionally, the JR Kagoshima line heads north to Kumamoto (*shinkansen*, ¥5850, 75 minutes) and Fukuoka-Hakata (¥8920, four hours). Also stopping at Kagoshima station, the JR Nippō line goes to Miyazaki (*tokkyū*, ¥3790, two hours) and Beppu (¥9460, five hours).

Trains also run south from Kagoshima to the popular hot-spring resort of Ibusuki (p718) and continue partway around the Satsuma Peninsula (*kaisoku*, ¥970, 55 minutes).

Getting Around

TO/FROM THE AIRPORT
Express buses to Kagoshima airport depart every 20 minutes from JR Kagoshima Chūō station (¥1200, 40 minutes).

BUS
There's a comprehensive city bus network, though trams are usually simpler.

For tourists, the City View Bus (¥180) does a loop of all the major sights, departing every 30 minutes throughout the day, from 9am to 5pm daily. You get on and off when you want. A one-day pass (¥600) is also valid on trams – a great deal compared to single tickets (¥180).

Bus tours (per person ¥4500) are organised through the **tourist information office** (Map pp712-13; ☎ 253-2500; inside Kagoshima-Chūō station; ☺ 8.30am-7pm).

CAR
Cars can be rented for trips around Satsuma Peninsula from **Nankyu Senpaku** (☎ 422-1083) and **Kagoshima Shosen** (☎ 334-0012).

TRAM
The tram service in Kagoshima is easy to understand and operates frequently. Rte 1 starts from Kagoshima station, goes through the centre and on into the suburbs. Rte 2 diverges at Takami-baba to Kagoshima-Chūō station and terminates at Korimoto. Either pay the flat fare (¥160) or buy a one-day travel pass (¥600) from the tourist information office or on the tram.

SAKURAJIMA 桜島
☎ 099 / pop 5800
Dominating the skyline from Kagoshima is the brooding cone of this spectacular active volcano. Since 1955 there has been an almost continuous stream of smoke and ash. The most violent eruption was in 1914, when the volcano poured out over three billion tonnes of lava, overwhelming numerous villages and converting the island to a peninsula.

Among Sakurajima's three peaks, only Minami-dake (1040m) is active. Visitors are not permitted to climb the volcano, but there are several good lookout points with walkways across a small corner of the immense lava flow. While some parts of Sakurajima are covered in deep volcanic ash or crumbling lava, other places have exceptionally fertile soil. Huge *daikon* (radishes) weighing up to 35kg and tiny *mikan* (oranges) only 3cm in diameter are locally grown.

Information
Information desk (ferry terminal building; ☺ 8.30am-5pm) For maps.
Sakurajima Visitors Centre (☎ 293-2443; ☺ 9am-5pm) Located near the ferry terminal and has a variety of exhibits and videos about the volcano, its eruptions and its natural history. A working model showing the volcano's growth over the years is the centre's main attraction.

Sights & Activities
South of the visitors centre is **Karasujima Observation Point**, where the 1914 lava flow engulfed the small island that had once been 500m offshore. The same lava flow swallowed three villages, destroying over 1000 homes.

Continuing anticlockwise around the island, you come to a **monument** to writer Hayashi Fumiko, whose famous poem claimed that 'though a flower's life is short, its sufferings are many.'

Nearby is the splendid hot springs at **Furusato Onsen**. Furusato Kankō hotel has a seaside **rotemburo** (☎ 211-3111; admission ¥1050, rental locker & towel ¥410; ☺ for hotel guests 6am-10pm, onsen-only visitors 8am-8pm, closed Mon & Thu morning). As it is also a shrine, you'll be given a *yukata* (cotton kimono), thus allowing both men and women to bathe here. Closer to the ferry terminal, **Rainbow Sakurajima Hotel Onsen** (☎ 293-2323; admission ¥300; ☺ 8am-8pm) is excellent, and located just before Sakurajima Visitors Centre.

At **Kurokami Buried Torii**, only the top third of a 3m-high torii emerges from the volcanic ash. On the north coast you can soak in the very hot and earthy waters of **Shirahama Onsen Centre** (☎ 293-4126; admission ¥300; ☺ 10am-9pm).

Tours
Sightseeing bus tours of Sakurajima leave from JR Kagoshima-Chūō station (see Map pp712–13) at 8.50am (adult/child ¥4000/2000, six hours). While these involve listening to the guide's running discussion of sights (Japanese only), there is an English transcription book available, and the tours provide the only way to see the island if you're pressed for time.

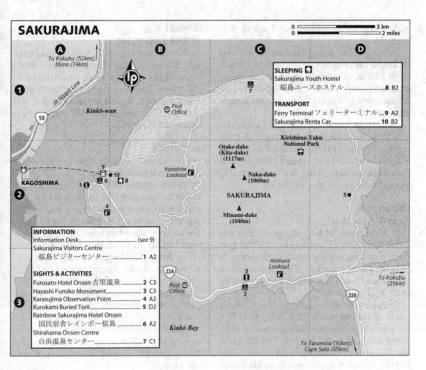

SAKURAJIMA

SLEEPING 🛏
Sakurajima Youth Hostel
桜島ユースホステル **8** B2

TRANSPORT
Ferry Terminal フェリーターミナル..**9** A2
Sakurajima Renta Car.........................**10** B2

To Kokubu (52km);
Ebino (74km)

JR Nippō Line

Kinkō-wan

Post
Office

Kirishima-Yaku
National Park

Otake-dake
(Kita-dake)
(1117m) ▲

▲ Naka-dake
(1060m)

Yunohira
Lookout

KAGOSHIMA

SAKURAJIMA

Minami-dake
(1040m)

Arimura
Lookout

To Kokubu
(25km)

Post
Office

Kinkō Bay

To Tarumizu (10km);
Cape Sata (65km)

INFORMATION
Information Desk..................................(see 9)
Sakurajima Visitors Centre
桜島ビジターセンター **1** A2

SIGHTS & ACTIVITIES
Furusato Hotel Onsen 古里温泉.......**2** C3
Hayashi Fumiko Monument................**3** C3
Karasujima Observation Point...........**4** A2
Kurokami Buried Torii.........................**5** D2
Rainbow Sakurajima Hotel Onsen
国民宿舎レインボー桜島 **6** A2
Shirahama Onsen Centre
白浜温泉センター **7** C1

Sleeping

There's a simple, seasonal camping ground across the road from the visitors centre.

ourpick Sakurajima Youth Hostel (☎ /fax 293-2150; dm incl/excl 2 meals ¥3870/2650; **P** ✕ ♨ 🖥) Less than 500m from the ferry terminal, this cheery, well-managed hostel has an *onsen* for both men and women (just flip the English sign by the door to indicate your gender and it's all yours!). Make sure you catch the 9pm ferry from Kagoshima to arrive before reception closes.

Getting There & Around

A 24-hour passenger and car ferry service shuttles frequently back and forth between Kagoshima and Sakurajima (¥150, 15 minutes); pay at the Sakurajima end.

The Sakurajima ferry terminal is a short bus ride from JR Kagoshima-Chūō station. Take the City View Bus or any bus bound for the aquarium and get off at Suizokukan-mae (¥180, half-hourly).

Getting around Sakurajima without your own transport can be difficult. Bicycles can be rented from **Sakurajima Renta Car** (☎ 293-2162;

1/2hr ¥400/600) near the ferry. Cars are available as well (per two hours ¥6500).

Local buses operate regularly on the island until about 8pm. JR buses from the ferry terminal pass Furusato Onsen (¥290) and run up to the Arimura lookout. Otherwise, the Furusato Kankō Hotel at Furusato Onsen offers a limited free shuttle service to and from the port, departing roughly every half hour except during lunchtime and on Monday and Thursday mornings when the *onsen* closes.

SATSUMA PENINSULA 薩摩半島

This peninsula south of Kagoshima city has fine rural scenery, well-preserved samurai houses, a kamikaze pilots' museum, the hot-spring resort of Ibusuki (famous for its hot-sand baths) and the conical peak of Kaimon-dake. On the other side of Kinkō-wan is Cape Sata, the southernmost point of Japan's main islands.

Exploring the peninsula by train and bus is possible, but quite time-consuming. The JR Ibusuki–Makurazaki line operates south from Kagoshima to Ibusuki and then turns west to Makurazaki, from where you can

KYŪSHŪ

make your way by local bus back to Kagoshima.

Renting a car is a good alternative, and **Eki Rent-a-Car** (www.ekiren.co.jp in Japanese; 12hr from ¥4720); JR Kagoshima-Chūō station (☎ 258-1412; 2nd fl tourist information booth; ✆ 8am-8pm); Ibusuki (☎ 0993-23-3879; JR Ibusuki station, 1-1-1 Minata; ✆ 8am-5pm) is the easiest option.

Daily bus tours to Ibusuki and Chiran depart from Kagoshima-Chūō station. A daily sightseeing bus (¥4550) heads off to Chiran at 8.50am, whizzes you around the sights and then does the same thing in Ibusuki, ending the day with a soak in a hot spring.

Chiran 知覧
☎ 0993 / pop 13,453

Just 34km south of Kagoshima, Chiran has a fine collection of samurai houses and gardens, plus a fascinating museum memorial to WWII's kamikaze pilots. Chiran was one of the major bases from which fighters left on their final missions.

All seven of the residences along Chiran's street of **samurai houses** (武家屋敷; ☎ 83-2511; admission ¥500; ✆ 9am-5pm), dating from the mid-Edo period, are noted for their gardens. Look for the use of 'borrowed scenery', particularly in No 6. Water is usually symbolised by sand or gravel. A well-stocked carp stream runs parallel to the samurai street.

Taki-An (高城庵) is a traditional house and garden on the samurai street where you can sit on tatami mats to eat a bowl of hot *soba* (buckwheat noodles; ¥600) and sip Chiran's famous green tea.

Another kind of warrior is commemorated in the **Kamikaze Peace Museum** (知覧特攻平和会館; Chiran Tokkō Heiwa-Kaikan; ☎ 83-2525; admission ¥500; ✆ 9am-4.30pm), 2km west of town; a collection of aircraft, mementos, and photos of young, fresh-faced men who were selected for the Special Attack Corps in WWII. It's difficult to see these young men as different from any other country's soldiers: young, idealistic, hoping to defend their country. It's a moving tribute. There's a helpful English brochure.

Kagoshima Kōtsū buses to Chiran (¥920, 80 minutes) and Ibusuki run from JR Kagoshima-Chūō station and the Yamakataya bus station in Tenmonkan. From Chiran, there are three buses per day to Ibusuki (¥940, 65 minutes), leaving from stops along the highway.

Ibusuki 指宿
☎ 0993 / pop 46,124

At the southeastern end of the Satsuma Peninsula, 50km from Kagoshima, is the hot-spring resort of Ibusuki. It's quiet, especially in the off-season, and more especially after dark. At Ibusuki station, the **information desk** (☎ 22-2111; ✆ 8.30am-5.15pm Mon-Fri) has basic maps and can assist with directions.

ACTIVITIES

On the beachfront is Ibusuki's *raison d'etre*, the **Tennen Sunamushi Kaikan** (天然砂蒸し会館; ☎ 23-3900; admission ¥900; ✆ 8.30am-noon & 1-9pm). Pay at the entrance (the fee includes a *yukata* and towel), change downstairs, and wander down to the beach where the burial ladies are waiting, shovel in hand, to cover you in wonderfully hot volcanic sand. Reactions range from claustrophobic to euphoric; 15 minutes is usually recommended, but many stay longer. Now and then, the ladies may gently mop your brow, while the quiet wash of the bay plays with your senses. When you're through, head back up to the bath, discard the sand-covered *yukata* and stay for as long as you like in the regular *onsen*. For hot-springs aficionados, Ibusuki's sand baths are a must.

The sand baths are less than 1km southeast of Ibusuki station.

SLEEPING & EATING

Tamaya Youth Hostel (圭屋ユースホステル; ☎ 22-3553; dm incl 2 meals/breakfast ¥4200/3200) Of the two youth hostels in town, this is the closest to the sand baths. Look for the palm tree out front.

Minshuku Marutomi (民宿丸富; ☎ 22-5579; fax 22-3993; r incl 2 meals from ¥7000) A small but very popular inn, famous for its fresh seafood, caught by the owner who would rather be fishing.

Ryokan Ginshō (旅館吟松; ☎ 22-3231; www.ginsyou.co.jp in Japanese; r per person incl 2 meals from ¥15,000; P ✕) The seaside *rotemburo* at this upscale ryokan has romantic, lanternlit shower stalls.

Aoba (青葉; ☎ 22-3356; dishes from ¥750; ✆ lunch & dinner, closed Tue & Wed; ✕) Tasty Japanese standards with a beautiful aquarium (for viewing only), and it's next to the station.

Iwasaki Hotel (いわさきホテル; ☎ 22-2131) From July through September, it has a beer garden.

GETTING THERE & AWAY

Ibusuki is less than two hours from Kagoshima by bus (¥850). A bit faster is JR's Nano-Hana Deluxe train (¥1000, 60 minutes).

AROUND SATSUMA PENINSULA

West of Ibusuki, **Ikeda-ko** is a beautiful volcanic caldera lake, inhabited by giant eels that grow 2m long. South of the lake is **Cape Naga-saki-bana**, from where offshore islands can be seen on a clear day.

Tōsenkyō-kōen Sōmen Nagashi (唐船峡公園 そうめん流し; ☎ 0993-32-2143; dishes from ¥500; ♨ 8.30am-6pm) is a 10-minute taxi ride (¥1500) from JR Kaimon station. This place is fun: *sōmen* noodles whirl around in a plexiglass table-top trough; you simply dip your chopsticks in and let the current do the rest – then dip them in sauce and slurp.

The beautifully symmetrical 924m cone of **Kaimon-dake** can be climbed in two hours from the Kaimon-dake bus stop, or also from JR Jamakawa station and JR Kaimon station. Start early and you'll be rewarded with views of Sakurajima, Cape Sata, and tropical islands Yakushima and Tanegashima.

At the southwestern end of the peninsula is **Makurazaki**, a busy port famous for *katsuo* (bonito) and the terminus for the train line from Kagoshima. Just beyond Makurazaki is **Bōnotsu**, a fishing village that was an unofficial trading link with the outside world via Okinawa during Japan's two centuries of seclusion. About 35km north of Bōnotsu is **Fukiage Beach. Fukiage-hama Youth Hostel** (吹上 浜ユースホステル; ☎ /fax 0992-92-3455; dm ¥3750) has just a dozen beds; no English is spoken. It's a 1.5km walk from JR Ijūin station.

ŌSUMI PENINSULA

The southernmost point on the main islands of Japan, **Cape Sata** is on the opposite side of Kagoshima, the Ōsumi Peninsula, and is marked by the oldest lighthouse in Japan. You can reach the cape from the Kagoshima side of Kinkō-wan by taking the ferry from Yamakawa, a stop south of Ibusuki, to Nejime on the other side. However, public transport onward is nearly impossible. An 8km bicycle track leads down to the end of the cape.

If you're bent on getting here, another option is to rent a car in Kagoshima (p716) and drive. At the cape's tip, the **Sata-Day-Go** (☎ 0994-27-3355; 30min tours adult/child ¥2000/1000), a glass-bottomed boat, offers views of the underwater fish and coral. Sea turtles, sharks or dolphins may swim by. You will certainly see plenty of *fugu* (pufferfish), which are plentiful (and deadly if prepared incorrectly!).

There is a ferry (¥600, 50 minutes) connecting Yamakawa (Satsuma) to Nejime (Ōsumi).

MIYAZAKI-KEN 宮崎県

Rte 222 from Miyakonojō to Obi and Nichinan on the coast is a superb road, twisting and winding over the hills along the sea. Although there is train and bus service, renting a car to explore this rugged coastline south of Miyazaki will allow you greater freedom.

AOSHIMA 青島
☎ 0985

This is a beach resort famed for its small island covered in betel palms, fringed by spectacularly unique washboard rock formations and connected to the mainland by a thin causeway. A short walk east of Aoshima station is photogenic **Aoshima-jinja** (青島神社; Ogre's Washboard Temple; ☎ 65-1262), reputedly good for matchmaking, and the scene of two exciting **festivals**. On the second Monday in January, loincloth-wearing locals dive into the ocean while on 17 June there's more splashing as *mikoshi* are carried through the shallows to the shrine. Nearby is a **botanical garden** (青島 熱帯植物園; ☎ 65-1042; admission ¥200) that boasts 64 different species of fruit trees. Wandering around the grounds and garden is free. While you're in Aoshima, check out the Aoshima Palm Beach Hotel for a version of Florida in the Pacific.

Aoshima is on the JR Nichinan line from Miyazaki (¥360, 30 minutes). Buses from Miyazaki train station stop at Aoshima (¥670, 40 minutes, hourly) en route to Udo-jingū .

UDO-JINGŪ 鵜戸神宮

If you walk through this brightly painted coastal **shrine** (☎ 0987-29-1001) to the end of the path, you'll find yourself in an open cavern overlooking an unusual rock formation. A popular sport is to buy five *undama* (luck stones), make a wish and try to hit the shallow depression on top of one of the turtle-shaped rocks. Wishes are usually related to marriage and childbirth, possibly because the boulders in front of the cavern are said to represent Emperor Jimmu's mother's breasts!

Hourly buses from Aoshima (¥990, 40 minutes) and Miyazaki (¥1440, 1½ hours) stop on the highway. From the bus stop, an approximately 700m walk to the shrine will take you past wonderful rock formations, more washboards and picturesque fishing boats.

OBI 飫肥

From 1587 the wealthy Ito clan ruled this town from the castle for 14 generations, surviving the 'one kingdom, one castle' ruling in 1615. The clan eventually dissolved as the Meiji Restoration ended the feudal period.

Sights & Activities

Only the walls of the original castle remain, but the grounds of Obi-jō (飫肥城; ☎ 0987-25-4533; combined admission ¥600; ☻ 9.30am-4.30pm) contain a number of interesting buildings, including the impressive gate, Ōte-mon. The castle museum has a collection relating to the Ito clan's long rule over Obi, with everything from weapons and armour to traditional clothes and household equipment. Matsuo-no-Maru, the lord's private residence, has been reconstructed. When the lord visited the toilet at the far end of the house, he was accompanied by three pages – one to lead the way, one to carry water for washing, and one to fan him during the summer months!

Yōshōkan, formerly the residence of the clan's chief retainer, stands just outside the castle entrance and has a large garden incorporating Atago-san as 'borrowed scenery'.

Shintoku-dō, the hall adjacent to the castle, was established as a samurai school in 1831. Up the hill behind Shintoku-dō is Tanoue Hachiman-jinja; the shrine is shrouded by old-growth trees and reached by a steep flight of steps.

On the western side of the river, Ioshi-jinja has a pleasant garden and the Ito family mausoleum.

Getting There & Around

The JR Nichinan line connects Obi with Miyazaki (kaisoku, ¥910, 65 minutes) via Aoshima. From Obi station, it's a short bus ride (¥140) plus about a 500m walk to the castle, reached by turning left outside the station. Buses from Miyazaki (¥1990, 2¼ hours, last return bus 4pm) stop along the main road below the castle entrance. Bikes are the best way to visit,

and can be rented (¥300 for three hours) at the train station.

NICHINAN-KAIGAN & CAPE TOI
日南海岸都井岬

The beautiful 50km stretch of coast from Nichinan to Miyazaki offers stunning views, picturesque coves, interesting stretches of washboard rocks and heavy traffic at holiday times. Like Cape Sata, the ocean views from Cape Toi are superb.

On the last weekend in September Cape Toi hosts a dramatic fire festival. The cape is also famed for its herds of wild horses, but don't come expecting galloping stallions and frisky mares: it's essentially a grassy park, and the horses seem rather friendly.

Just off the coast from the beach at Ishi-nami-kaigan, the tiny island of Kō-jima is home to a group of monkeys that apparently rinse their food in the ocean before eating. To stay overnight in the area, head to Koigaura Beach, a popular surfing beach, about 5km from Cape Toi or 7km from Kōjima. Try Minshuku Tanaka (☎ 0987-76-2096; per person incl 2 meals from ¥6000) or Koigaura Minshuku (☎ 0987-76-1631; per person incl 2 meals from ¥4500).

MIYAZAKI 宮崎
☎ 0985 / pop 311,098

Due to the warm offshore currents, the city of Miyazaki has a balmy climate and some of the best surfing in Japan, particularly at Kizaki-hama and other beaches further north towards Hyūga. The warm weather also brings five professional baseball teams here for spring training. Many areas around Miyazaki played an important part in early Japanese civilisation, and are recorded in Japan's oldest chronicle, the Kojiki. Interesting excavations can be seen at Saitobaru (p724).

Information

There's a 24-hour internet café above Cafe Lanai (p724) charging ¥480 for the first hour, or ¥1900 for unlimited access between midnight and 8am, including soft drinks.

There's an international ATM at the south end of Miyazaki station, and also at the central post office, five minutes' walk up Takachiho-dōri from Miyazaki station.

At the tourist information centre (☎ 22-6469; inside Miyazaki station; ☻ 9am-6.30pm), the helpful staff speaks English and has maps of the city and surroundings. Make sure you pick up the excellent *Discovering Miyazaki: A Travel Guide* or *Let's Go Miyazaki City* guidebook and pullout map.

The **Miyazaki Prefectural International Plaza** (☎ 32-8457; 8th fl, Carino Bldg; ⏰ 10am-7pm Mon-Sat) opposite the main post office has CNN and English-language newspapers and magazines, but no internet access.

Sights

MIYAZAKI SCIENCE CENTRE
宮崎科学技術館

A short walk from Miyazaki station, this hi-tech science **museum** (☎ 23-2700; 38-3 Miyawakichō; admission with sky show ¥730; ⏰ 9am-4pm Tue-Sun) (aka Cosmo Land) topped by a gleaming silver dome, boasts one of the world's largest planetariums and interactive displays. English-language pamphlets are available.

MIYAZAKI-JINGŪ & MUSEUM
宮崎神宮　宮崎総合博物館

Three kilometres north of the town centre in the village of Koguya, this **shrine** (☎ 27-4004; 2-4-1 Jingū) honours the Emperor Jimmu, the semi-mythical first emperor of Japan and founder of the Yamoto court. There are 600-year-old wisteria vines covering the thickly forested grounds. Just north of the shrine grounds, the **Miyazaki Prefectural Museum of Nature & History** (☎ 24-2071; 2-4-4 Jingū; admission free; ⏰ 9am-4.30pm, closed Tue) has kid-friendly exhibits on local history, archaeological finds, festivals and folkcrafts. Behind the museum is the interesting **Minka-en** (民家園; admission free), with four traditional-style Kyūshū farmhouses.

The shrine is located about a 500m walk from Miyazaki-jingū station, one stop north of Miyazaki. Several buses from Miyazaki station and Tachibana-dōri run directly to the shrine (¥160, 10 minutes).

HEIWADAI-KŌEN 平和台公園

The centrepiece of **Heiwadai-kōen** (Peace Park; ☎ 24-5027; admission free) is a 37m-high tower constructed in 1940, a time when peace in Japan was about to disappear. **Haniwa Garden**, within the park, is dotted with reproductions of the curious clay *haniwa* (earthenware figures found in Kōfun-period tombs) that have been excavated from the Saitobaru burial mounds (p724).

Heiwadai-kōen is about 1.5km north of Miyazaki-jingū. There are frequent buses there from along Tachibana-dōri (¥270, 20 minutes).

SEAGAIA シーガイア

About 10km north of town at the sprawling Seagaia resort, **Ocean Dome** (オーシャンドーム; ☎ 21-1111; www.seagaia.co.jp/english/odr/; Hamayama Yamasakichō; adult/child ¥2000/10000; ⏰ 10am-5pm) is a water-based theme park with a variety of razzle-dazzle attractions. But beware; it's kid-friendly to the point of exhaustion!

KAEDA GORGE 加江田渓谷

An 8km **hiking path** at Kaeda Gorge follows a sparkling stream filled with big boulders and hidden swimming holes, banana palms and mountain cedars. About 1km from the car park, poke your nose into a lovely middle-of-nowhere pottery **gallery** (きまぐれ陶芸かん).

Festivals & Events

Yabusame (samurai-style horseback archery) You can witness this at Miyazaki-jingū (left) on 2 and 3 April.

Fireworks show Kyūshū's largest, lighting up the summer sky over the Oyodo-gawa in early August.

Erekocha Matsuri (えれこっちゃみやざき) Miyazaki's newest festival with dancers and *taiko* drummers filling Tachibana-dōri in mid-August.

Miyazaki-jingū Grand Festival (Jimmu-Sama) In late October; brings in the fall season with horses and *mikoshi* being carried through the streets.

Sleeping

Fujin-kaikan Youth Hostel (☎ 24-5785; 1-3-10 Asahi; dm ¥2750; ✕ ✕) A well-managed Japanese-style hostel that doubles as a rec centre during the day, requiring that you not be around from 10am to 3pm. Aside from that, and the 10pm curfew, it's quite inviting! Japanese breakfast is available (¥500).

Business Hotel Royal (☎ 25-5221; fax 29-1103; 2-5-20 Segashira; s/d/tw from ¥4200/6000/7000; P ✕ 🖳) Close to Miyazaki station on a quiet side street, this 32-room hotel has a cosy lobby filled with greenery, a coffee bar and a parakeet.

Hotel Kensington (☎ 20-5500; www.face.ne.jp /kensington in Japanese; 3-4-4 Tachibanadōri-higashi; s/d ¥6300/10,000; ✕ ✕ 🖳) Look for the British suit of armour in the lobby that seems to be waiting for the lift. Small but spotless rooms – plus an excellent breakfast (with *Hiya-jiru* porridge) and lunch buffet – make this good value.

Hotel Mirieges (☎ 26-6666; www.merieges.co.jp in Japanese; 1-11 3-chome Tachibana-dōri-Nishi; s/d from ¥8100/12,600; P ✕ ✕ 🖳) Excellent value in this price range, it offers large sparkling

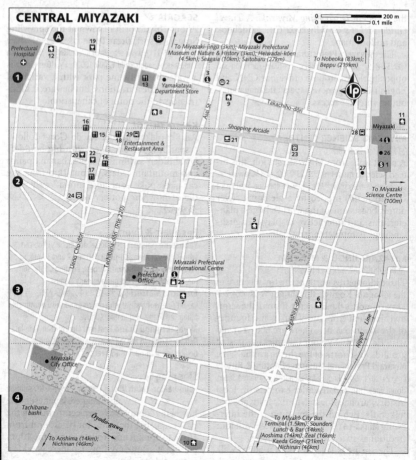

CENTRAL MIYAZAKI

0 ___ 200 m
0 ___ 0.1 mile

Prefectural Hospital

To Miyazaki-jingū (3km); Miyazaki Prefectural Museum of Nature & History (3km); Heiwadai-kōen (4.5km); Seagaia (10km); Saitobaru (27km)

To Nobeoka (83km); Beppu (219km)

Yamakataya Department Store

Takachiho-dōri

Aoi St

Shopping Arcade

Miyazaki

Entertainment & Restaurant Area

To Miyazaki Science Centre (100m)

Ueno Cho-dōri

Tachibana-dōri (Rte 220)

Miyazaki Prefectural International Centre

Prefectural Office

Sasshira-dōri

Nippō Line

Miyazaki City Office

Asahi-dōri

Tachibana-bashi

Ōyodo-gawa

To Aoshima (14km); Nichinan (46km)

To Miyako City Bus Terminal (1.5km); Sounders Lunch & Bar (14km); Aoshima (14km); Zeal (16km); Kaeda Gorge (21km); Nichinan (46km)

rooms, satellite TV, handsome rattan furnishings and good service throughout. The lobby is on the 3rd floor past the wedding shops.

On the riverside are Miyazaki's top-end hotels, with the **Miyazaki Kankō Hotel** (☎ 32-5920; www.miyakan-h.com in Japanese; 1-1-1 Matsuyama; s/d from ¥7710/14,000, Japanese-style r ¥8400-18,000; P ✕ ✕ ▯), easily the best of the lot, with stylish rooms, *onsen* and a baby grand in the lobby. Ask for a river-view room.

Also recommended:

Business Family Hotel Miyako (☎ 27-9991; fax 27-0023; 13-21 Miyatachō; r per person ¥3675; ✕) Large tatami rooms. No English; look for the white picket fence in window!

Toyoko Inn Miyazaki Ekimae (☎ 32-1045; www.toyoko-inn.com; 2-2-31 Oimatsu; s/tw incl breakfast ¥5250/7770; P ✕ ✕ ▯ ; wi-fi) Free lobby phones, clerks in pastel.

Roynet Hotel Miyazaki (☎ 60-0055; fax 60-2000; 2-2-3 Miyazaki-Eki Higashi; s/d/tw from ¥6900/8800/12,000, all incl breakfast buffet; P ✕ ✕ ▯) Smart business hotel behind Miyazaki station.

Eating

Hiya-jiru is a cold summer soup made from baked tofu, fish, miso paste and cucumbers, served over rice. Miyazaki is also known for *yuzu-kosho*, a tangy citrus spice. At Miyazaki station, a favourite *bentō* for the train is *shiitake ekiben*, a boxed lunch featuring mushrooms. Be aware that many eateries in the entertainment district add a 'table charge' of around ¥300, which usually gets you a small appetiser.

KYŪSHŪ

INFORMATION	Roynet Hotel Miyazaki ロイネットホテル....11 D1	**ENTERTAINMENT**
ATM....1 D2	Tokoyo Inn Miyazaki Ekimae 東横イン宮崎駅前....12 A1	Cafe Lanai カフェラナイ....(see 19)
Internet Café キャフェラナイ....(see 19)	**EATING**	Jazz Spot Lifetime ライフタイムジャズバー....23 C2
Main Post Office 中央郵便局....2 C1	Bon Belta (East Building) ボンベルタ東館....13 B1	Planet Café Sports プラネットカフェ....24 A2
Miyazaki Prefectural International Plaza 宮崎県国際交流センター....3 B1	Den Den Den でんでんでん本店....14 A2	**SHOPPING**
Tourist Information Centre 観光案内所....4 D2	Don Don Ju どんどんじゅ....15 A2	Miyazaki Prefectural Products Promotion Exhibition Hall みやざき物産館....25 B3
SLEEPING	Izakaya Seoul 居酒屋ソウル....16 A1	**TRANSPORT**
Business Family Hotel Miyako ビジネスファミリー都ホテル....5 C2	La Dish Gourmet & Deli....17 A2	Eki Rent-a-Car 駅レンタカー....26 D2
Business Hotel Royal ビジネス宮崎ロイヤルホテル....6 D3	Restaurant-Bar De-meté-r デーメテール....18 B2	Mazda Rent-a-Car マツダレンタカー....27 D2
Fujin-kaikan Youth Hostel 婦人会館ユースホステル....7 B3	**DRINKING**	Miyazaki Ekimae Bus Center 宮崎交通....28 D2
Hotel Kensington ホテルケンジントン....8 B1	Cafe Lanai カフェラナイ....19 A1	Tachibana-dōri 3-chome Bus Stop 橘通り三丁目バス停....29 B2
Mirieges ホテルメリージュ....9 C1	One Coin Bar ワンコインバー....20 A2	
Miyazaki Kankō Hotel 宮崎観光ホテル....10 B4	Pari No Okashiyasan パリのお菓子屋さん....21 C2	
	Suntory Shot Bar サントリーショットバー....22 A2	

La Dish Gourmet & Deli (☎ 32-7929; 1-1 Chuōdōri; 🕑 11am-3am Mon-Sat, 6pm-1am Sun) Amid the hustle of the entertainment district, this import grocery store sells both cold and hot deli items, plus a good selection of wines, cheeses and desserts.

Den Den Den (☎ 24-3825; 3-2-10 Tachibana-dōri-nishi; 🕑 6pm-2am) This boisterous *izakaya* specialises in *kushiage* (deep-fried seafood on skewers from ¥150) and generous *teishoku* from ¥1000. Owner-cook speaks English. Look for dark-wood exterior.

Restaurant Bar De-meté-r (☎ 29-0017; 2nd fl, 3-8-18 Tachibana-dōri-nishi; dishes ¥450-1400, pizzas ¥700-1200; 🕑 dinner) Popular for its brick-oven pizza, this place features an endless bilingual menu, draught beer and no cover charge.

Sounders Lunch & Bar (サウンダーズ; ☎ 65-0767; 1-6-23 Aoshima; set meals from ¥600; 🕑 lunch & dinner; E) The owners of this Hawaiian surf bar near Aoshima cook up spinach and bacon salads, burgers and tacos with a Japanese twist. Set lunches and dinners start at ¥600. There's live music most weekends.

Izakaya Seoul (☎ 29-8883; 7-26 Chūōmachi; 🕑 dinner; E) This tiny no-nonsense Korean-Japanese restaurant features great *nabe* dishes from ¥1000.

Zeal (ジール; ☎ 65-1508; 6411 Kaeda; buffet adult/child ¥1300/800; 🕑 lunch Sat, Sun & holidays) On the road to Kaeda (15km), this macrobiotic lunch spot with outdoor tables offers a constantly changing menu of fresh pasta, veggies, desserts etc.

Don Don Ju (☎ 31-8929; basement, 3-10-36 Tachibanadōri-nishi; set meals ¥2200-3600; 🕑 lunch & dinner) This eatery specialises in *Miyazaki-gyū* (Miyazaki beef), which is the real thing, and has English-speaking staff and menus.

Bon Belta has an 8th-floor restaurant arcade (lunch sets under ¥1000) and a variety of takeaway is available from its basement marketplace. Don't miss the *onigiri* (rice-ball snack) counter.

Drinking

Locals claim that Miyazaki has some 3500 bars, which may be a bit of an exaggeration, or perhaps not. Avoid the 'snack bars' where the customer is the snack.

One Coin Bar (☎ 31-1152; 8-21 Chūō-dōri; 🕑 closed Tue) All drinks are ¥500 (one coin!) at this smart eight-stool hole-in-the-wall where you can't help but rub elbows with other customers, while gracious English-speaking owner Hideki Yano makes your drink.

Suntory Shot Bar (☎ 0985-25-4665; 1-13-1F, Chūōdōri) Good for a quiet, inexpensive beer, and the owner speaks some English – ask him for his 'special'.

Pari No Okashiyasan (☎ 29-3507; 1-68 Hiroshima; 🕑 10am-8pm) This French-style place offers pastries, sweets and coffee near the station.

In summer Bon Belta department store has a rooftop beer garden.

Entertainment

Miyazaki has a surprising nightlife, and the establishments range from the quiet and relaxing to the wild and crazy. The downtown Ichibangai area and the train station are both alive with the sounds of street musicians.

Jazz Spot Lifetime (☎ 27-8451; www1.ne.jp/~life time; 2nd fl, 2-3-8 Hiroshima; admission Fri ¥500; ☻ 11.45am-2pm & 5pm-12.30am, closed Sun) Modern jazz is alive and well in Miyazaki where near-nightly jams at this upstairs bistro-bar feature top bop musicians. When the band isn't jamming, English-speaking owner Kenjiro plays classics from Miles to Coltrane. Drinks start at ¥600, with coffee, snacks and steaks on the menu.

Cafe Lanai (☎ 23-3412; 2-1-1 Shimizu) This mellow pub, with a surf-and-aloha groove, has a great selection of Hawaiian slack-key music plus surfing videos above the full bar. Dishes (from ¥700) also have an island flair.

Planet Café Sports (☎ 32-5064; 8-25 Kamino-machi) Come for the sports, stay for the great *Jidori*, a grilled chicken dish that goes great with beer or *shōchū*.

Shopping

Miyazaki Prefectural Products Promotion Exhibition Hall (☎ 22-7389; 1-6 Miyatachō; ☻ 9.30am-7pm Mon-Fri, 10am-6.30pm Sat & Sun) Sells handwoven *tetsumugi* textiles, clay *haniwa* and Takachiho *kagura* masks.

Getting There & Away

AIR
Miyazaki is connected by air with Tokyo (¥32,700), Osaka (¥21,000), Okinawa (¥25,200), Fukuoka (¥17,700) and other cities around Kyūshū.

BOAT
There are ferry services linking Miyazaki with Osaka (2nd class ¥10,000, 13 hours) and Kawasaki (¥12,640, 21 hours). For reservations contact **Marine Express** (☎ in Kyūshū 0982-55-9090, in Osaka 06-6616-4661, in Miyazaki 22-8895).

BUS
Most long-distance buses originate at the **Miyakō City bus terminal** (☎ 52-2200) south of the river, near JR Minami-Miyazaki station, including to Kagoshima (¥2700, 2¾ hours), Kumamoto (¥4500, 3¼ hours), Nagasaki (¥6500, 5½ hours) and Fukuoka (¥6000, four hours).

Many buses run along Tachibana-dōri, but if you don't read Japanese you may be better off heading down to the Miyakō City bus terminal. There is also **Miyazaki Ekimae Bus Center** (☎ 53-1000) opposite Miyazaki station.

TRAIN
The JR Nippō line runs down to Kagoshima (*tokkyū*, ¥3790, two hours) and up to Beppu (*tokkyū*, ¥5770, three hours). The JR Nichinan line runs slowly along the coast south to Aoshima (¥360, 30 minutes) and Obi (¥910, 65 minutes).

Getting Around
Miyazaki's airport is connected to the city centre by bus (¥400, 30 minutes) or train (¥340, 10 minutes) from JR Miyazaki station. Although most bus services start and finish at the Miyakō City bus terminal, many run along Tachibana-dōri in the centre. Only a few depart from outside Miyazaki station.

There are several car-rental companies around Miyazaki station and at the airport.

AROUND MIYAZAKI 宮崎周辺
Saitobaru 西都原
☎ 0983
If the *haniwa* in Miyazaki piqued your interest in the region's archaeology, then you should head north 27km to the **Saitobaru Burial Mounds Park**, where several square kilometres of fields and forest are dotted with over 300 *kofun* (burial mounds). The mounds, dating from AD 300 to 600, range from insignificant little bumps to hillocks large enough to appear as natural creations.

The interesting small **Saitobaru Archaeological Museum** (西都原考古博物館; ☎ 41-0041; http://saito-muse.pref.miyazaki.jp/home.html; admission free; ☻ 10am-6pm Tue-Sun) has displays of archaeologi-

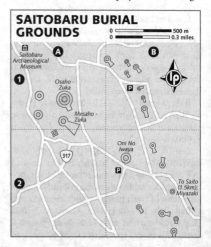

SAITOBARU BURIAL GROUNDS

cal finds, including ancient swords, armour, jewellery, *haniwa* and much more.

The park area is always open. Buses run frequently to Saitobaru from along Tachibana-dōri in Miyazaki (opposite) and also from Miyakō City bus terminal (¥1040, one hour). You'll need your own transport if you want to explore the mound-dotted countryside, or you should plan to walk a lot.

Saitobaru is just outside the town of Saito, where the unique **Usudaiko dance festival**, with drummers wearing odd pole-like headgear, takes place in early September. The equally interesting **Shiromi Kagura** performances are on 14 and 15 December, part of a harvest festival that lasts from 12 to 16 December.

TAKACHIHO 高千穂
☎ 0982 / pop 15,840

The mountain resort town of Takachiho is about midway between Nobeoka on the east coast and Aso-san in the centre of Kyūshū. Just north of the bus station in the centre of town is the **Takachiho Tourism Association** (☎ 72-1213; ⏰ 8.30am-5pm); visit for reliable information in English about events and lodgings in and around Takachiho.

Sights
TAKACHIHO-KYŌ 高千穂峡

Takachiho's magnificent gorge, with its waterfall, overhanging rocks and sheer walls was formed over 100,000 years ago by a double volcanic eruption. During the autumn, trees seem to burst into the colours of the season. There's a 1km-long nature trail above the gorge, but it is best viewed up close in a **rowboat** (☎ 73-1213; per 30min ¥1500; ⏰ 8.30am-5pm). The gorge is about 1km from the centre.

TAKACHIHO-JINJA 高千穂神社

Takachiho-jinja, close to the train and bus stations, is set in a grove of cryptomeria pines. From late November to February the local *iwato kagura* **dances** (☎ 73-2413; tickets ¥500) are performed for an hour each evening from 8pm (see the boxed text, right, for details).

AMANO IWATO-JINJA 天岩戸神社

The Iwato-gawa splits **Amano Iwato-jinja** (☎ 74-8239) into two parts. The main shrine, Nishi Hongū, is on the west bank of the river while on the east bank is Higashi Hongū, at the cave where Shintō myth holds that the sun god-

dess Amaterasu hid until she was lured out by the bawdy performance of another goddess, Uzume (see the boxed text, below).

A short walk from the Amano Iwato-jinja beside a picture-postcard stream takes you to the **Amano Yasugawara** cave where Amaterasu finally emerged, bringing light to the world again. The shrine is 8km from Miyakō. Buses from Miyakō bus centre depart hourly (¥370, 17 minutes).

Festivals & Events

Important *iwato kagura* festivals are held from 10am to 10pm on or around 2 and 3 May, 22 to 23 September and 3 November (dates change every year) at the Amano Iwato-jinja (left). There are also all-night performances in farmhouses from mid-November to mid-February and a visit can be arranged by inquiring at the shrine. In all, 33 dances are performed from 6pm until 9am the next morning. If you brave the cold until morning, prepare to be caught up in a wave of excitement.

Sleeping & Eating

Takachiho has over 30 hotels, ryokan, *minshuku* and pensions. Every place in town can be booked out during peak holiday periods.

Many visitors just eat at their ryokan or *minshuku,* but Takachiho also has plenty of *yakitori-ya* where you can order *kappo-zake,* local sake heated in bamboo stalks.

Takachiho Youth Hostel (☎ /fax 72-3021; dm HI member/nonmember ¥2800/3800; Ⓟ) About 2km from

---

TAKACHIHO LEGENDS

Ninigi-no-mikoto, a descendant of the sun goddess Amaterasu, is said to have made land fall in Japan on top of the legendary mountain Takachiho-yama in southern Kyūshū. In Takachiho the residents insist that it was in their hamlet that the sun goddess's grandson arrived. They also lay claim to Ama-no-Iwato, or the boulder door of heaven. Here Amaterasu hid and night fell across the world. To lure her out, another goddess performed a dance so comically lewd that the sun goddess was soon forced to emerge from hiding to find out what the merriment was about. That dance, the *iwato kagura,* is still performed in Takachiho today, characterised by masks with unusually long…noses.

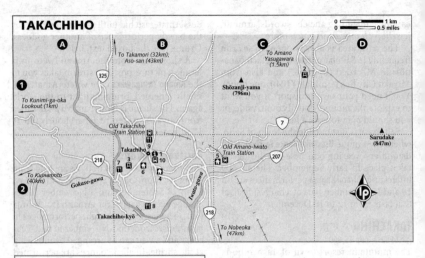

TAKACHIHO

the centre, near Amano-Iwato station. Clean and efficient, with bunk beds and breakfast.

Yamatoya Ryokan (☎ 72-2243; fax 72-6868; r per person incl 2 meals ¥8000-15,000; P ☒ ☒) All rooms are traditional ryokan style, and there's helpful English-speaking staff. Look for the masked *iwato kagura* dancer painted on the front.

Folkcraft Ryokan Kaminoya (☎ 72-2111; fax 72-5040; r incl 2 meals ¥9975-12,075; P ☐) Just downhill from the bus station, right in the centre of Takachiho, this well-managed ryokan is good value, especially for two. Rooms are spacious with large *shōji*-style windows. Look for the blue wooden sign.

Young Echo (☎ 72-4948; dishes from ¥600; ☺ breakfast, lunch & dinner) This reliable eatery is a good spot to plot your next move. The outdoor summer beer garden is open from 5pm to 10pm.

Several *sōmen-nagashi* (thin noodles served in running water, then dipped in a soy-based broth) places offer a light, refreshing change. Try **Chiho no Le** (千穂の家; ☎ 72-2115; ☺ breakfast & lunch) or **Onoroko Chaya** (おのころ茶屋; ☎ 72-3931; ☺ breakfast & lunch). You catch noodles with your chopsticks as they float by in halved bamboo rafts.

Getting There & Around

From Miyakō bus centre, about a 500m walk downhill from the old train station (trains no longer serve Takachiho), there are buses to Takamori (¥1280, 70 minutes, three daily), near Aso-san, and Kumamoto (¥2300, 2¾ hours).

Although you can walk to the gorge and Takachiho-jinja, the other sites are some distance from town and public transport is a problem. Regular tours leave from the bus station: the 'A Course' (¥2000) covers everything, while the 'B Course' (¥1500) skips Amano Iwato-jinja. Bicycles can be rented next to the old station in Takachiho (two/four/eight hours ¥700/1200/2000).

ŌITA-KEN 大分県

Ōita-ken offers Japanese *onsen* mania, Beppu and the traditional town of Yufuin. The region also bears some traces of Japan's earliest civilisations, particularly on the Kunisaki Peninsula. The office of **Tourism Ōita** (Map p730; ☎ 0977-26-6250;

(🕙 9am-5pm) at the west end of JR Beppu station has helpful English-speaking staff.

USUKI 臼杵
☎ 0972 / pop 43,051

About 5km from Usuki is a superb collection of thousand-year-old **Buddha images** (臼杵石仏; ☎ 65-3300; admission ¥530; 🕙 8.30am-4.30pm). Four clusters comprising 59 Buddha images lie in a series of niches in a ravine. Some are complete statues, whereas others have only the heads remaining, but many are in wonderful condition. The **Dainichi Buddha head** (古園石仏) is considered the finest stone Buddha statue in all of Japan. Some of the faces are so well preserved that they almost seem alive. Serene and spectacular, it's a must-see well worth making a special detour for.

Usuki also has several temples and well-preserved traditional houses. On the last Saturday in August, the town hosts a **fire festival**, and there are other festivities throughout the year. Ask for details at the **tourist information office** (☎ 64-7130; 🕙 8.30am-5pm) adjacent to Usuki station. Internet users can log on for free at **Sala de Usuki** (サーラデ臼杵; ☎ 64-7271), the town civic/rec centre.

Local restaurants boast the best *fugu* in Japan; expect to pay about ¥8000 for a dinner set, including sake.

The town of Usuki is about 40km southeast of Beppu. Take the JR Nippō line to Usuki station (*tokkyū*, ¥1430, 55 minutes), from where it's a 20-minute bus ride to the ravine site. Bikes can also be rented for free from Usuki station (☎ 63-8955) or the town centre (☎ 64-7130).

BEPPU 別府
☎ 0977 / pop 122,814

Understanding the working spa town of Beppu is in some ways to understand Japan. Quaint yet crowded, traditional and modern, Beppu remains what it always has been: a place to which people escape. For some that's hedonistic fun in the pleasure district, for others it's relaxing soaks in one of hundreds of baths. The recent arrival in 2000 of **Ritsumeikan Asia Pacific University** in the foothills north of town has brought a welcome influx of both Japanese and international students to Beppu.

Orientation & Information

Beppu is a sprawling town and the hot-spring areas are spread out, often some distance from the town centre. The adjacent town of Ōita is virtually contiguous with Beppu, although it lacks any notable attractions. The tiny but beautiful *onsen* village Myōban (p729) is a quieter place to soak if you're so inclined.

At Beppu station, the **Foreign Tourist Information Office** (Map p730; ☎ /fax 23-6220; 12-13 Ekimae-machi; 🕙 9am-5pm) has helpful English-speaking personnel with an arsenal of English-language information on Beppu and its environs. They can happily recommend accommodation, itineraries and more. Another **Foreign Tourist Information Office** (☎ 23-1119; fax 25-0455; cnr Ekimae-dōri & Ginza Arcade; 🕙 9am-5pm) is a five-minute walk from the station, and also has free internet use.

International ATM machines can be found at the Kitahama post office (Map p730) and the nearby the Cosmopia shopping centre. Ōita Bank handles foreign exchange services.

Sights & Activities
HOT SPRINGS

Beppu has two types of hot springs, and they pump out more than 100 million litres of hot water every day. *Jigoku* are hot springs for looking at. *Onsen* are hot springs for bathing. If you go to a high spot such as Myōban (p729) where you can look down over Beppu, you'll see the white plumes (called '*yunoka*') of hundreds of steam vents.

The Hells

Beppu's most hyped attraction is the 'hells' or *jigoku*, a collection of **hot springs** (Map p728; each hell ¥400; 🕙 8am-5pm) where the water bubbles forth from underground, often with unusual results. You can purchase a ¥2000 coupon that covers all except two (Hon Bōzu Jigoku and Kinryū Jigoku). Unlike Unzen (p692), where you see the geothermal wonders natural, raw and unadorned, these have been turned into mini–amusement parks, each with a different theme. If you're pressed for time and unsure if this is your cup of, er, *onsen* water, peek at the postcard pack in the station, which has good pictures, and you'll know instantly whether these are worth your time.

The hells are in two groups – eight at Kannawa, over 4km northwest of Beppu station, and two more several kilometres away. In the Kannawa group, **Umi Jigoku** (Sea Hell), with its large expanse of steaming artificially blue water, and **Shiraike Jigoku** (White Pond Hell) may be worth a look. **Kinryū Jigoku** (Golden

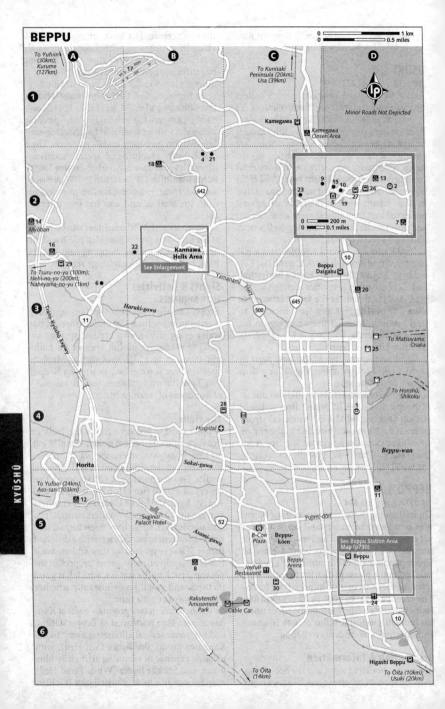

BEPPU

0 ___ 1 km
0 ___ 0.5 miles

To Yufuin
(30km);
Kurume
(127km)

17

To Kunisaki
Peninsula (20km);
Usa (39km)

Minor Roads Not Depicted

Kamegawa

Kamegawa
Onsen Area

18

4 21

642

9

15

13

23

10

26

2

5

19

27

7

0 ___ 200 m
0 ___ 0.1 miles

14
Myōban

16

22

**Kannawa
Hells Area**

See Enlargement

**Beppu
Daigaku**

10

29

To Tsuru-no-yu (100m);
Hebi-no-yu (200m);
Nabeyama-no-yu (1km)

6

Yamanami Hwy

20

Haruki-gawa

11

500

645

To Matsuyama;
Osaka

25

Trans-Kyūshū Expwy

To Honshū;
Shikoku

28

1

3

Hospital

Horita

Sakai-gawa

Beppu-wan

To Yufuin (24km);
Aso-san (103km)

12

11

Suginoi
Palace Hotel

52

Asami-gawa

8

B-Con
Plaza

**Beppu-
kōen**

Fujimi-dōri

See Beppu Station Area
Map (p730)

Beppu

Beppu
Arena

Joyfull
Restaurant

30

24

Rakutenchi
Amusement
Park

Cable Car

10

Higashi Beppu

To Ōita
(14km)

To Ōita (10km);
Usuki (20km)

KYŪSHŪ

Dragon Hell) and **Kamado Jigoku** (Oven Hell) have dragon and demon figures overlooking the pond. Kinryū features tropical fruit trees, compliments of the steamy tropical surroundings. Skip the **Oni-yama Jigoku** (Devil's Mountain Hell) and **Yama Jigoku** (Mountain Hell), where a variety of animals are kept under shamefully bad conditions.

The smaller pair has **Chi-no-ike Jigoku** (Blood Pool Hell), with its photogenically red water, and **Tatsumaki Jigoku** (Waterspout Hell), where a geyser performs regularly. The final two hells, not included in the group's admission ticket, are **Hon Bōzu Jigoku** (Monk's Hell) with its collection of hiccupping and belching hot-mud pools up the long hill from the main group of hells, and **Kinryū Jigoku** with its 'dragon-spitting' steam vent, for the easily impressionable.

From the bus stop at JR Beppu station, buses 5, 9, 41 and 43 go to the main group of hells at Kannawa. There are buses every 20 minutes but the round trip (¥820) costs virtually the same as an unlimited-travel day pass (¥1000).

Jigoku tour buses regularly depart from the JR Beppu station (¥3000, including admission to all hells).

Onsen

The hells, though mildly interesting, shouldn't distract you from the *real* hot springs. Scattered around the town are eight *onsen* areas. *Onsen* enthusiasts spend their time in Beppu moving from one bath to another – experts consider at least three baths a day *de rigueur*. Costs range from ¥100 to ¥1000, though many (and two of the best) are free. Bring your own soap, washcloth and towel, as many places don't rent them. There's an **onsen festival** during the first weekend in April. Some of the baths alternate daily between male and female so that each gender can appreciate each side.

Near JR Beppu station, the classic **Takegawara Onsen** (Map p730; ☎ 23-1585; 16-23 Motomachi; admission ¥100, sand bath ¥1000; ⏰ 6.30am-10.30pm, sand bath 8am-9.30pm) dates from the Meiji era. Its bath is very simple and *very* hot; simply scoop out water with a bucket, pour it over yourself, and jump in! It also has a relaxing sand bath where a *yukata* is provided. You lie down in a shallow trench and are buried up to your neck in heated sand, followed by an *onsen* dip and shower. The entire affair takes about 40 minutes.

North of the town, in the **Kannawa onsen area** (Map p728), near the major group of hells, is the popular and renovated **Mushi-yu steam bath** (Map p728; ☎ 67-3880; 1 Furomoto, Kannawa; admission ¥500, yukata ¥210; ⏰ 9am-6pm). **Hyōtan Onsen** (Map p728; ☎ 66-0527; 159-2 Kannawa; admission ¥700; ⏰ 8am-9pm) has a *rotemburo* and also offers sand baths (*yukata* rental ¥200). Most ryokan and *minshuku* also have public baths.

Shibaseki onsen baths (Map p728; ☎ 67-4100; 4 Noda; admission ¥210; ⏰ 7.20am-8pm, closed 2nd Wed of each month) are near the smaller pair of hells. You can also rent a private *kazoku-buro* (private family or couples bath) for ¥1570 per hour. Between JR Beppu station and the **Kamegawa onsen area**, try the very popular **Shōnin-ga-hama sand bath** (Map p728; ☎ 66-5737; admission ¥1000; ⏰ 8.30am-6pm Apr-Oct, 9am-5pm Nov-Mar); it has a great beach location and English is spoken.

In the hills northwest of the town centre is the **Myōban onsen area** (p728). Quieter and quite hilly, you will find numerous baths as well as

KYŪSHŪ

odd thatched-roof huts that are Edo-era replicas of the huts in which bath salts were made. You can go inside (the salts resemble yellow-brown mould), wander the 'hell' outside, and even purchase salts for a bath from hell when you return home. Nearby, **Onsen Hoyōland** (Map p728; ☎ 66-2221; 5-1 Myōban; admission ¥1050; ☧ 9am-8pm) has wonderful giant mud baths, as well as mixed-gender and open-air bathing.

For an *onsen* experience next to the beach, head to **Kitahama Termas Onsen** (Map p728; ☎ 24-4126; admission ¥500; ☧ 10am-8pm) . There are separate baths for men and women; the outside *rotemburo* mixes it up, but you'll need a bathing suit.

Ekimae Kōtō Onsen (Map p730; ☎ 21-0541; 13-14 Ekimae-machi; admission ¥300) is very simple and hot, and just a couple of minutes' walk from the station.

HIDDEN BATHS
Tsuru-no-yu, Hebi-no-yu & Nabeyama-no-yu 鶴の湯 ヘビん湯 鍋山の湯
The Myōban area has some wonderful baths, some tucked away out of the public eye. Locals built and maintain **Tsuru-no-yu** (the easiest to

reach), a lovely free *rotemburo* on the edge of Ogi-yama. In July and August, a natural stream emerges to form the milky blue bath. Take a bus to Konya Jigoku-mae bus stop (25 minutes northwest from JR Beppu station). Walk up the small road that hugs the right side of the grave-yard until the road ends. Dive into the bushes to your left, and there's the bath. Higher in the mountain greenery is another free *rotemburo*, the **Hebi-no-yu** (Snake Bath). Continue further (about 1km) to reach **Nabeyama-no-yu**, the last of the wild *onsen* of Myōban. The Beppu station information desk ladies (volunteers all!) are also happy to make you a hand-drawn map.

Mugen-no-sato 夢幻の里
This collection of privately available small *rotemburo* is ideal for a romantic, secluded dip. Ask for a **kazoku-buro** (private bath; Map p728; ☎ 22-2826; 6 Hotta; admission ¥600; ☧ 9am-9pm). Take a bus 33, 34, 36 or 37 to Horita. Mugen-no-sato is five minutes' walk west.

Ichinoide Kaikan いちのいで会館
The owner of **Ichinoide Kaikan** (Map p728; ☎ 21-4728; 14-2 Ueharamachi) is an *onsen* fanatic, so

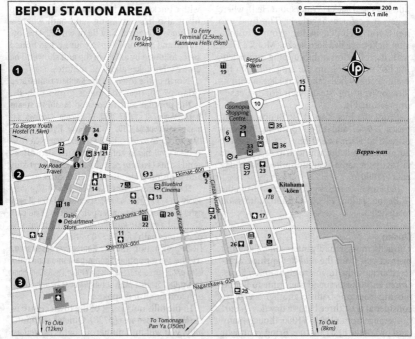

BEPPU STATION AREA

much so that he built three pool-sized *rotem-buro* in his backyard. The view, overlooking Beppu and the bay, is the city's finest. Bathing is free when you order a *teishoku* (¥1050), and the chefs prepare it while you swim. To get there by bus and walking, inquire at the Foreign Tourist Information Office. A shared taxi (from Beppu; ¥900) might be a good investment.

OTHER SIGHTS

Given all that sybaritic bathing, **Hihōkan Sex Museum** (Map p728; ☎ 66-8790; 338-3 Shibuyu, Kannawa; admission ¥1000; ☻ 9am-10pm) fits right in. Among the Kannawa hells, it hosts a bizarre collection of sex-related items ranging all the way from fine erotic *ukiyo-e* (wood-block prints) and zany porno to life-sized dioramas and kinky toys. There's an unfortunate paucity of postcards in the gift store, but plenty of surreal items with which to disturb the customs officials on the way home.

Near Takegawara Onsen, the **Hirano Library** (Map p730; ☎ 23-4748; 11-7 Motomachi; admission free; ☻ Mon-Sun) is a private institution with historical exhibits and photographs of the Beppu area.

The hands-on **Beppu Traditional Bamboo Crafts Centre** (Map p728; ☎ 23-1072; 8-3 Higashi-sōen) displays masterpieces dating from the Edo period, as well as incredible examples of what can be made with this versatile material. Seasonal hands-on demos allow you to try your own hand at making something. From Beppu station, take Kamenoi bus 25 to Dento Sangyo-mae, in front of the centre.

In 2000, Kyoto-based **Ritsumeikan Asia Pacific University** (Map p728; ☎ 78-1114; 1-1 Jūmonjihara) opened its landmark college in Beppu, with about half its undergraduates drawn from other parts of Asia and beyond – a unique situation in Japan. The campus overlooks the city from Jumonji-baru, a 30-minute bus trip from Beppu station (¥520).

Sleeping

Beppu Guest House (Map p730; ☎ 3967-9044; beppu .g.h@q.vodafone.ne.jp; 1-12 Ekimae-chō; dm/s/tw/tr ¥1500/2000/4000/6000; ☒ ☒ ☐) Newly opened in 2006, this is Beppu's cheapest lodging and good value. The atmosphere is upbeat, and there's a big kitchen to make meals in and chat with fellow travellers. You can choose dorm-style or private rooms, and the English-speaking owners can steer you to Beppu's bubbliest spots.

Hotel Annex Matsumi (Map p730; ☎ 25-5872; fax 25-3699; 6-28 Ekimae-honchō; s/tw/tr ¥4000/7000/10,000; ☐ ☒ ☒ ☐) Count on a converted love hotel to feature large rooms and good service at budget prices. Just behind Beppu station, the Matsumi also offers free lobby internet use.

Kokage International Minshuku (Map p730; ☎ 23-1753; www.tiki.ne.jp/~kokage; 8-9 Ekimae-machi; s/d/tr ¥4350/7650/1475) This cosy 10-room Japanese Inn group member feels old and friendly, starting with the small antique-filled sitting area where you can make tea and toast. There's an *onsen*, and the quietest rooms are over the entrance.

Beppu Youth Hostel (Map p728; ☎ 23-4116; 20-28 Nakajima; dm incl/excl 2 meals ¥4935/3360; P ⓧ) Just 1km from JR Beppu station, this hostel has a hot-springs bath and a bar, where travellers can trade *onsen* tips while sipping the owner's homemade Kabosu-*shōchū*.

ourpick **Nogami Honkan Ryokan** (Map p730; ☎ 22-1334; www008.upp.so-net.ne.jp/yuke-c/english.html; 1-12-1 Kitahama; r per person incl/excl breakfast ¥5500/4500; P ⓧ ⓧ ▣) Located near Takegawara *onsen*, 19 of the 24 tatami-style rooms have private bathrooms. And there's not one, but five small *onsen*; you can reserve your own for an hour at a time.

Hotel Arthur (Map p730; ☎ 25-2611; 1-2-5 Kitahama; s/d from ¥5500/9500; ⓧ ⓧ ▣) A grandfather clock and fresh flowers brighten up the lobby of this smart 100-room business-tourist hotel, less than five minutes' walk from Beppu station. You'll get city views from the 5th floor up.

Hotel Seawave Beppu (Map p730; ☎ 27-1311; www .coara.or.jp/seawave in Japanese; 12-8 Ekimae-chō; s/tw/ste from ¥6300/8400/17,800; P ⓧ ⓧ ▣) Just across the street from the station, the Seawave has smart-looking modern rooms, English-speaking staff and a breakfast buffet (¥800).

Also recommended:

Kamenoi Hotel (Map p730; ☎ 22-3301; www.kamenoi .com; 5-17 Chūōmachi; s/d/tw incl 2 meals from ¥6950/9000/10,100; P ⓧ ▣) Bustling tour group mecca with *onsen* and restaurants.

Hotel Seikaisō (Map p730; ☎ 22-0275; fax 23-4885; www.seikaiso.com; 14-3 Kitahama; r per person from ¥12,500; P ⓧ ⓧ ▣) Seaside Japanese-style inn with bed-tatami rooms and private rooftop onsen.

Eating

Beppu is renowned for its freshwater fish, for its *fugu* and for the wild vegetables grown in the mountains further inland. Also look out for *dango-jiru*, a *miso* soup with vegetables and dumplings.

ourpick **Eki Ichiba** (station market; Map p730; ⓨ 9am-5pm) To see a Beppu few travellers find, head to the long and winding shopping arcade under the tracks out the back of Beppu station. This is where local residents fill their grocery bags with fresh fish and veggies, and also pick up wonderful *eki-ben* (station lunch boxes) and hot meals to take home. You don't need much English to enjoy this bustling, workaday market, and get a good bargain while you're at it. It's great fun to wander from stall to stall,

savouring the *yobuko-ika* (squid tempura) or *futomaki sushi* (rice and seaweed roll). On weekends, you'll find lots of university students stocking up on provisions for the week ahead. During the week many elderly folks who live alone come here to pick up dinner. But you don't have to be an old-timer to take away a well-cooked meal, made to order, and perfect for a picnic on the beach at Kitahama-kōen.

Tomonaga Panya (Map p728; ☎ 23-0969; Chiomachi 2-29; ⓨ breakfast & lunch Mon-Sat) Tomonaga's hot-from-the-oven fresh rolls, breads and pastries are a treat worth waking up early for, and they go fast (phone orders accepted!). The walls are filled with photos going back to 1917 when it first opened.

Kuishinbō (Map p730; ☎ 21-0788; 1-1-12 Kitahama-dōri; dishes from ¥600; ⓨ dinner) A cheerful corner *izakaya* open till 2am serving unusual tofu and *daikon* steaks, and *chawan-mushi* (savoury custard), and ¥100 *yakitori* skewers – good for late-night snacking.

Toyotsune (Map p730; ☎ 22-2083; 3-7 Ekimae Hon-machi; ⓨ lunch & dinner, closed Thu) This reliable eatery just opposite Beppu station has no English menu, but the tempura rice bowl (*tendon*; ¥620) with huge prawns is the dish to get. Sashimi and chicken *kara-age teishoku* sets (¥1050) are also good choices.

Ureshi-ya (Map p730; ☎ 22-0767; 7-12 Ekimae-machi; ⓨ dinner, closed Mon) You'll get your money's worth at this friendly and busy *shokudō* (budget eatery) with *donburi* (dishes served over rice), sashimi, *oden* and noodle dishes from ¥750. Food models are displayed in the window.

Fugu Matsu (Map p730; ☎ 21-1717; 3-6-14 Kitahama; ⓨ lunch & dinner; E) This is the place to try *fugu* in style, if you're game (die-hards love it). Expect to pay from ¥3000.

Drinking & Entertainment

Beppu hides some one-of-a-kind coffee shops in the central shopping arcades.

Speakeasy (Map p730; ☎ 21-8116; 12-1 Motomachi; ⓨ closed Tue; E) Like speakeasies of old, you have to duck under a low door to enter this swank and friendly back-alley jazz bar. Tap beer and stronger stuff cost from ¥500.

Jin Robata & Beer Pub (Map p730; ☎ 21-1768; 1-15-7 Kitahama; ⓨ dinner; E) A flashing neon fish sign directs you to this welcoming pub with a good mix of APU students, salarymen and office ladies as the night goes on. There's plenty of good food to go with your beer, *shōchū* or sake. Pick a favourite from the rows of fresh fish on display, then watch it grilled (*robata*-style) behind the counter, or try a steaming bowl of *ocha-zuke* (green-tea *soba*).

World Sports Bar Small Eye (Map p730; ☎ 21-3336; 2nd fl, 1-10-12 Kitahama; drinks/snacks from ¥500/400; ⊗ closed Thu). You'll find a good mix of locals, APU students and *gaigin* at this Hawaiian-style bar with high ceilings, darts and beach umbrellas. Expect to hear hip-hop, reggae and classic Hawaiian tunes on the great sound system.

Natsume Kissa (Map p730; ☎ 21-5713; 1-4-23 Kitahama; ⊗ closed Wed) A good snack and dessert spot best known for its own *onsen kōhī* (¥530), coffee made with hot-springs water.

Shingai Coffee Shop (Map p730; ☎ 24-1656; 10-2 Kusumachi; ⊗ closed Mon) A mellow place with good coffee, plus antique maps and old photos of Beppu.

Getting There & Away

There are flights to Ōita airport from Tokyo Haneda (¥31,800), Osaka (¥17,300), Okinawa (¥27,000) and cities around Kyūshū. It's even possible to fly direct to Seoul (¥27,000).

The JR Nippō line runs from Hakata (Fukuoka) to Beppu (*Sonic tokkyū*, ¥5250, two hours) via Kitakyūshū, continuing down the coast to Miyazaki (¥6270, 3¾ hours). The JR Hōhi line connects Beppu with Kumamoto (¥5330, three hours) via Aso-san (¥3940, 1½ hours).

There's a Beppu Kyūshū Odan bus to Aso station (¥2950, three hours).

The **Ferry Sunflower Kansai Kisen** (☎ 22-1311) makes an overnight run between Beppu and Osaka (¥8800, 11 hours), stopping en route at Matsuyama (4½ hours) and Kōbe (10 hours). The evening boat departs at 7pm to western Honshū and passes through the Inland Sea, arriving at 6am the next morning. For the port, take bus 20 or 26 from Beppu station's west exit.

Getting Around

TO/FROM THE AIRPORT

Hovercraft (☎ 097-558-7180, 0120-81-4080) run from JR Ōita station to Ōita airport (¥2950, 25 minutes), located around the bay from Beppu on the Kunisaki Peninsula.

Beppu airport buses to Ōita-ken airport stop outside the Tokiwa department store (¥1450, 45 minutes, twice daily) and Beppu station.

BUS

Of the local bus companies, **Kamenoi** (☎ 23-5170) is the largest. Most buses are numbered. An unlimited 'My Beppu Free' travel pass for Kamenoi buses comes in two varieties: the 'minipass' (adult/student ¥900/700), which covers all the local attractions, including the hells, and the 'wide pass' (one/two days ¥1600/2400), which goes further afield to Yufuin and Ritsumeikan APU. Passes are available from the Foreign Tourist Information Office (p727) and at various lodgings around town. Buses 5, 9 and 41 take you to Myōban (20 to 30 minutes).

YUFUIN 湯布院

☎ 0977 / pop 36,407

About 25km inland from Beppu, picturesque Yufuin sits in the shadow of the majestic twin peaks of Yufu-dake. Tourism development has gradually increased in the past few years, and Yufuin is best avoided on holidays and weekends. It's still very much worth a stop en route to Aso, or on a day trip from Beppu.

The **Yufuin Hot Springs Tourist Information office** (☎ 84-2446; ⊗ 9am-7pm) inside the train station has some information in English, including an excellent and detailed walking map showing galleries, museums and *onsen*. There is a postal ATM next to the station. The station itself is a striking piece of architecture, and holds a small art gallery as well.

As in Beppu, making a pilgrimage from one *onsen* to another is a popular activity in Yufuin. **Shitan-yu** (下ん湯; admission ¥200; ⊗ 10am-9pm) is a thatched bathhouse on the northern shore of Kirin-ko, a lake fed by hot springs, so it's warm(ish) all year round. Yufuin is noted for its high-quality handicrafts. The town also has a few interesting temples and shrines; **tourist information** (☎ 85-4464) is available.

The double-peaked **Yufu-dake** (1584m) volcano overlooks Yufuin and takes about 90 minutes to climb. A few buses between Beppu and Yufuin stop at the base of Yufu-dake, Yufu-tozan-guchi (由布登山口; ¥700, 43 minutes). From Yufuin, the bus takes 16 minutes (¥360).

Sleeping & Eating

Yufuin has many *minshuku*, ryokan and pensions; most are upscale, with rates to match. Prices average 10% higher on weekends and holidays.

KYŪSHŪ

Yufuin Youth Hostel (湯布院ユースホステル; ☎ 84-3734; dm HI member/nonmember ¥3040/3565; Ⓟ) Almost 2.5km northeast of the train station, this peaceful hostel occupies a forested hillside with breathtaking views. Buses (¥180) run weekdays to the hostel, and on weekends the English-speaking owners will pick you up. Two meals are available for an extra ¥1750.

Pension Yufuin (ペンション湯布院; ☎ 85-3311; r incl breakfast from ¥6500; Ⓟ) This popular riverside guesthouse is patterned after *Anne of Green Gables*, and there's no shortage of cherub water fountains or angel-patterned wallpaper. The very kind owner speaks a bit of English.

Makiba-no-ie (牧場の宿; ☎ 84-2138; fax 85-4045; r per person incl 2 meals ¥8000-13,500; Ⓟ) Accommodation is available here in a series of thatched-roof huts around a large *rotemburo*. The antique-filled garden restaurant does chicken *jidori* and wild-boar *teishoku* meals from ¥1500 to ¥2700. Day visitors can make use of the lovely *rotemburo* for ¥525.

Hanayoshi (☎ 84-5888; 🕒 11am-4pm; Ⓥ 👶) Stop in at this superb *soba* restaurant for generous and steaming bowls of *soba* and *udon* (¥500 to ¥1000). Walk out 20m from the station, take the first right and it's opposite the bike shop. There's a picture menu.

Getting There & Away

Local trains on the JR Kyūdai line connect Beppu with Yufuin (¥1080, 1¼ hours), via Ōita. Limited express trains (¥1510) make the trip in 60 minutes. There is a special 'Yufuin no Mori' express train a few times daily (¥4400, 2¼ hours).

Buses depart JR Beppu station (p733) for Yufuin throughout the day (¥900). Continuing beyond Yufuin is not so simple. Buses go to Aso and Kumamoto but not year-round. There are also express buses (Kyūshū Sanko) to Fukuoka (¥3100).

KYŪSHŪ

YUFUIN TO ASO-SAN

The picturesque Yamanami Hwy extends 63km from the Aso-san region to near Yufuin; from there, Hwy 38 runs to Beppu on the east coast. You'll cross a high plateau and pass numerous mountain peaks, including **Kujū-san** (1787m), the highest point in Kyūshū.

Taketa 竹田

South of Yufuin, near the town of Taketa, are the **Oka-jō ruins**, which have a truly magnificent ridgetop position. The ruins are over 2km from JR Bungo-Taketa station. Taketa has some interesting reminders of the Christian period, as well as atmospheric temples and well-preserved traditional houses. **Taketa Onsen Hanamizuki** (花水月温泉; ☎ 0974-64-1126; admission ¥500; 🕒 9am-9pm) is a short walk from the station.

From Aso-san, it takes just under an hour by train on the JR Hōhi line to Bungo-Taketa (*futsū*, ¥820); from there it's just over an hour by train to Ōita (¥1250) – a little longer by bus.

KUNISAKI PENINSULA 国東半島

Immediately north of Beppu, Kunisaki-hantō bulges eastward from the Kyūshū coast. The region is noted for its early Buddhist influence, including some rock-carved images related to more famous images at Usuki (p727).

Sights

USA 宇佐

In the early post-WWII era, when 'Made in Japan' was no recommendation at all, it's said that companies would register in Usa so they could proclaim that their goods were 'Made in USA'! **Usa-jinja** (宇佐神社; ☎ 0978-37-0001; admission to treasure hall ¥300; 🕒 closed Tue), the original of which dates back over 1000 years, is connected with the warrior-god Hachiman, a favourite deity of Japan's right wing. It's a 10-minute bus ride from Usa station on the JR Nippō line from Beppu (*tokkyū*, ¥17200, 29 minutes).

OTHER SIGHTS

The 11th-century **Fuki-ji** (富貴寺; ☎ 0978-26-3189; admission ¥200) in Bungotakada is the oldest wooden structure in Kyūshū and one of the oldest wooden temples in Japan. Ōita Kōtsū buses from Usa station go to Bungotakada (¥810, 35 minutes); from there, it's a 10-minute taxi ride (around ¥1000).

In the centre of the peninsula, near the summit of Futago-san (721m), is **Futago-ji** (両子寺; ☎ 0978-65-0253; admission ¥200), dedicated to Fudō-Myō-o, the ferocious, fire-enshrouded, sword-wielding deity who shows the inner power of Buddha – able to repel attacks even while appearing calm outside.

Nearby **Taizō-ji** (☎ 0978-26-2070; admission ¥200; 🕒 8.30am-5pm) is known for its famously uneven stone stairs. Local legend says that they are so random and haphazard that the Oni (devils) must have created them in a single night, confirming that, even in mythology, it has always been hard to get good help.

Carved into a cliff behind Taizō-ji, 2km south of **Maki Ōdō**, there are two 8th-century Buddha images; a 6m-high figure of the Dainichi Buddha and an 8m figure of Fudō-Myō-o. Known as **Kumano Magaibutsu**, these are the largest Buddhist images of this type in Japan. Other stone statues, thought to be from the Heian period, are seen in Maki Ōdō. There are no buses here; get a taxi from Fuki-ji to Bungotakada, and then a bus to Usa (¥260).

Getting Around

Beppu's Ōita airport is on the peninsula, about 40km from Beppu. Kaminoie tour buses (reservations ☎ 0977-23-5170) pick up and drop off at Beppu station (¥6400); the excursion takes seven hours. Prices include admission to all the temples and even an *omiyage* (souvenir) to bring home. Otherwise try **Eki Rent-a-Car** (☎ 0977-24-4428; www.ekiren.co.jp in Japanese) in JR Beppu station.

Okinawa & the Southwest Islands

沖縄　南西諸島

Welcome to the other Japan, where pebble gardens and cherry blossoms give way to white-sand beaches and swaying palm trees. Despite centuries of mainland exploitation and horrific destruction during the closing months of WWII, Japan is in the midst of an Okinawa boom. Today, Japanese mainlanders, both young and old, are flocking to the islands in droves. And it's not difficult to see why – with a year-round balmy climate and plenty of sunshine, Okinawa and the Southwest Islands, or the Nansei-shotō, are the perfect destination for beachcombers, hikers and marine sports–lovers alike.

While package tourism is evident, independent travellers can easily search out unspoilt beauty and relative seclusion. Coastlines are dotted with beaches that run the spectrum from powder-white sand to *hoshi-suna* or 'star sand', which consists of the skeletal remains of tiny animals. Island interiors range from subtropical rainforest to mangrove jungles, while the underwater world teems with colourful fish and vibrant coral reefs. Okinawa and the Southwest Islands were also the centre of the Ryūkyū kingdom, and there are still traces of this rich cultural heritage in the region's architecture, language, music and cuisine.

Okinawa and the Southwest Islands comprise a string of subtropical islands that stretch for more than 1000km from the southern tip of Kyūshū to about 110km from Taiwan. Although the Nansei-shotō is one of the top domestic tourist destinations for Japanese, few foreigners explore this part of the country. It's unfortunate, as the region is brimming with sights, and a glimpse of tropical Japan is a wonderful complement to time spent exploring the mainland.

HIGHLIGHTS

- Commune with millennia-old cedar trees on the Unesco World Heritage island of **Yakushima** (p739)

- Take a deep breath through your regulator as you swim alongside schools of manta rays on **Ishigaki-jima** (p773)

- Trek through virgin jungles in search of the elusive *yamaneko* (mountain cat) on the lush mangrove island of **Iriomote-jima** (p776)

- Admire the *shiisa* (lion-dog rooftop guardian) statues, red-tiled roofs and coral walls of the 'living museum' that is **Taketomi-jima** (p779)

- Soak up the sun by day and kick it in the bars by night with an alternative cast of characters on the laid-back island of **Miyako-jima** (p763)

- Enjoy the tropical hustle and bustle of Naha's **Kokusai-dōri** (p751) before ferry-hopping around the **islands near Okinawa-hontō** (p759)

★ Yakushima

★ Okinawa-hontō
★ Naha

Iriomote-jima ★　　Miyako-jima
　　★ ★ Ishigaki-jima
Taketomi-jima

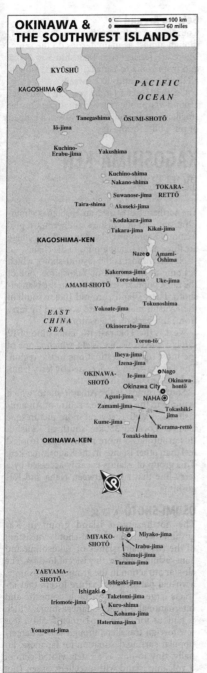

**OKINAWA &
THE SOUTHWEST ISLANDS**

0 ——— 100 km
0 ——— 60 miles

KYŪSHŪ

KAGOSHIMA

*PACIFIC
OCEAN*

Tanegashima   ŌSUMI-SHOTŌ

Iō-jima

Kuchino-
Erabu-jima   Yakushima

Kuchino-shima
Nakano-shima   TOKARA-
Suwanose-jima   RETTŌ
Taira-shima   Akuseki-jima

Kodakara-jima
Takara-jima   Kikai-jima

KAGOSHIMA-KEN

Naze   Amami-
Ōshima

Kakeroma-jima
Yoro-shima   Uke-jima
AMAMI-SHOTŌ

Tokunoshima

*EAST
CHINA
SEA*   Yokoate-jima

Okinoerabu-jima

Yoron-tō

Iheya-jima
Izena-jima
OKINAWA-   Ie-jima   Nago
SHOTŌ   Okinawa City   Okinawa-
hontō
Okinawa City
Aguni-jima   NAHA
Zamami-jima   Tokashiki-
jima
Kume-jima   Kerama-rettō
Tonaki-shima

OKINAWA-KEN

Hirara
Miyako-jima
MIYAKO-
SHOTŌ   Irabu-jima
Shimoji-jima
Tarama-jima
YAEYAMA-
SHOTŌ   Ishigaki-jima
Ishigaki   Taketomi-jima
Iriomote-jima   Kuro-shima
Kohama-jima
Hateruma-jima
Yonaguni-jima

History

For centuries, Okinawa and the Southwest Islands were ruled by *aji* (local chieftains), who battled for control of small fiefs, and struggled among themselves for power and fame. In 1429, however, the islands were united by Sho Hashi of the Chūzan kingdom, which led to the establishment of the Ryūkyū dynasty. During this era, Sho Hashi increased contact with China, which contributed to the flourishing of Okinawan music, dance, literature and ceramics. In this 'Golden Era', weapons were prohibited, and the islands were rewarded with peace and tranquillity.

With no weapons and little means of defence, the Ryūkyū kingdom was not prepared for war when the Shimazu clan of Satsuma (modern-day Kagoshima) invaded in 1609. The Shimazu conquered the Ryūkyū kingdom easily, and then established severe controls over their trade. While the rest of Japan closed its doors to the world prior to 1853, the Shimazu sustained trade with China under the guise of the Ryūkyū kingdom. The islands were controlled with an iron fist, and taxed and exploited greedily for the next 250 years.

With the restoration of the Meiji emperor and the abolition of the Japanese feudal system, the Ryūkyūs were annexed to Japan as Okinawa Prefecture in 1879. However, life hardly changed for the islanders as they were treated as foreign subjects by the Japanese government, just as they had been by the Shimazu. Furthermore, the Meiji government stamped out local culture by outlawing the teaching of Ryūkyū history in schools, and establishing Japanese as the official language.

As a consequence, Ryūkyū islanders paid a heavy price for their new citizenship in the closing stages of WWII as Okinawa became the only battlefield on Japanese soil. By the time the Battle of Okinawa was over, 12,500 US soldiers and an estimated quarter of a million Japanese had died. Even today, many locals feel that Okinawa was sacrificed to save the mainland.

The post-war history of the region has been characterised by the collusion between Washington and Tokyo, which has transformed the island of Okinawa-hontō into one of the most heavily armed places on earth. For more information, see p748.

Climate

Okinawa and the Southwest Islands experience a subtropical climate, and are much warmer than mainland Japan, particularly further south.

If you travel in the winter months of November to March, crowds are smaller, accommodation is less expensive and underwater visibility for divers is at its best. However, inter-island ferry services are culled outside the busy summer months.

Summer can be hot and crowded depending where you go. Typhoons, which can turn up at any time between June and October, wreak havoc with ferry schedules.

The average daily temperature in Okinawa in December is 20°C, while in July it is 31°C.

Language

Although the Ryūkyū islands used to have their own distinctive language, this has by and large disappeared. However, you may run into difficulties speaking standard Japanese with one of Okinawa's remarkable number of centenarians.

Getting There & Away

Okinawa and the Southwest Islands are easily accessible from mainland Japan.

While Naha is the hub, with direct flights to major mainland Japanese cities (p814), Amami-Ōshima, Miyako-jima and Ishigaki-jima also have daily direct flights to Tokyo and Osaka. Other outer islands such as Yonaguni-jima, Kume-jima and Zamami-jima can be reached by air with a change of flight in Naha.

If you're heading for the northern islands, it may be best to fly into Kagoshima on Kyūshū, then change to ferries or flights to the islands. There are daily direct flights from Kagoshima to Yakushima, Tanegashima, Amami-Ōshima, Tokunoshima, Yoron-tō and Okinoerabu-jima.

Ferries from Tokyo, Nagoya, Osaka, Kōbe and Kagoshima make their way with varying regularity to the Nansei-shotō. An incredible number of ferries ply the waters between the islands.

If you are arriving in Japan by air, it is worth noting that JAL and ANA both offer 'visit Japan'-type airfares for domestic flights within Japan – as long as they are bought outside Japan in conjunction with a ticket to Japan. Such tickets, if used to Okinawa, are an incredible saving from standard domestic airfares bought within Japan.

Getting Around

Countless aircraft buzz between the islands, though almost as many ferries do the same. There are ferries from Kagoshima to Naha and from Naha to Ishigaki-jima that stop at all the major islands in between.

On the larger islands, you can easily get around via public bus or rental car. On the smaller islands, you can always rent a moped or push bike for the day.

KAGOSHIMA-KEN
鹿児島県

The northern half of the Nansei-shotō is administratively part of Kyūshū's southernmost prefecture of Kagoshima. Heading southwest, there are three main island groups in the chain.

Northernmost is the Ōsumi-shotō, which is home to the island of Yakushima, one of the most popular destinations in the Nansei-shotō. These islands, around 100km south of the Kyūshū mainland, are accessed by ferry from, and back to, Kagoshima.

Next is the Tokara-rettō, consisting of 12 rarely visited volcanic islets, which is one of the most remote destinations in the region. The Tokara-rettō are accessed by ferry from, and back to, Kagoshima.

Southernmost is the Amami-shotō, which is home to the population centre of Amami-Ōshima as well as several more picturesque islands. Located 380km south of Kyūshū, this group has a more pronounced tropical feel than other islands in the Kagoshima-ken. This group of islands is easily accessed by a ferry line that runs between Naha and Kagoshima.

ŌSUMI-SHOTŌ 大隈諸島

The northernmost island group in Kagoshima-ken is the Ōsumi-shotō, consisting of the two main islands of Yakushima and Tanegashima and the tiny islet of Iō-jima. The all-star attraction in the group is Yakushima, a virtual paradise for nature lovers that attracts large numbers of both domestic and international travellers. Tanegashima, which is famous for its rocket-launch facility, sees few foreign travellers, though it is a fiercely popular surfing destination for Japanese. Finally, tiny Iō-jima is a rarely visited gem of a volcanic island with excellent *onsen* (hot

IN DEEP WATER

Although its popularity among the international diving community pales in comparison to other Asian countries such as Thailand, Indonesia and the Philippines, the Nansei-shotō is a diver's paradise. The waters surrounding Okinawa and the Southwest Islands are home to an outstanding variety of tropical fish and pelagic animals including dolphins, whale sharks, hammerheads and manta rays. There is also a good variety of hard and soft coral reefs as well as a healthy smattering of underwater wrecks, cavern systems and even the odd archaeological ruin. For a good introduction, check out www.divejapan.com/okinawainf.htm, which has maps, photos and information on different dive spots throughout the islands.

Here's the good news: each island is surrounded by a fair number of dive sites, which means that diving in the Nansei-shotō is significantly less crowded than other Asian destinations. Outside the more popular dive sites, it's sometimes possible to have an entire section of reef all to yourself. Here's the bad news: diving in the Nansei-shotō is significantly more expensive than other Asian destinations. Although prices vary slightly between operators, you can expect to pay between ¥8000 and ¥10,000 for two boat dives (including lunch), and between ¥2000 and ¥5000 for full equipment rental.

One of the biggest deterrents for foreign divers is the fact that few operators on the islands speak English. Although there are a handful of foreign-run dive shops on the island of Okinawa-hontō, it helps to have a basic understanding of the Japanese language if you're travelling elsewhere. Fortunately, Japanese divers use a significant number of English loan words, which means you certainly don't need to be bilingual to enter a dive shop. For a quick crash course in the local diving lingo, see boxed text (p777).

In order to dive around Okinawa and the Southwest Islands, you will need to be in possession of a valid dive card. Although most dive shops allow noncertified individuals to go on a 'Discovery Dive', divemasters may feel uncomfortable bringing a foreigner down if there is a significant language barrier. If you're renting equipment, you should know your weight in kilograms, your height in metres and your shoe size in centimetres.

Throughout this chapter, we list recommended dive operators and popular dive spots on each of the main islands. However, just to whet your appetite a bit, here's a list of our top five favourite *daibingu-supotto*; or 'dive spots'.

- **Manta Way** (p778) One of the most famous sites in the Nansei-shotō, Manta Way is located in the straits between Iriomote-jima and Kohama-jima, and is absolutely teeming with manta rays in late spring and early summer.

- **Manta Scramble** (p773) Located off the coast of Ishigaki-jima, this popular dive spot virtually guarantees a manta ray sighting, particularly in spring and summer.

- **Irizaki Point** (p782) If swimming alongside sharks doesn't absolutely terrify you, this famous spot off the coast of Yonaguni-jima is frequented by schools of hammerheads in winter.

- **Underwater Ruins** (p782) One of the most unusual dive spots in Nansei-shotō is also located off the coast of Yonaguni-jima, and is home to a mysterious underwater archaeological ruin of unknown origins.

- **Mini Grotto** (p764) This popular dive spot off the coast of Miyako-jima is home to an elaborate series of underwater caves, which beckon to be explored (assuming you have sufficient experience – and the right equipment).

---

springs), and it's fairly likely that you'll have plenty of elbow room here.

Yakushima 屋久島
☎ 0997 / pop 14,000

Justifiably designated as a Unesco World Heritage site (Japan's first) in 1993, Yakushima is one of Japan's most remarkable travel destinations. More than 75% of Yakushima is covered with thickly forested mountains, and while the high peaks are snowcapped in winter, the mangrove-dotted flat lands around the coastline remain subtropical. The island's towering terrain also manages to catch every inbound rain cloud, which gives Yakushima one of the wettest climates in Japan.

Yakushima has long been viewed by the Japanese as a mystical island. The old kanji (Chinese characters) for Yakushima meant 'Medicine Island', and the island's indigenous plants have been utilised by herbologists for centuries. In fact, *gajutsu*, a type of native ginger, is still harvested today for use in digestive medicines. However, it's the island's ancient *yaku-sugi* (屋久杉; *Cryptomeria japonica*) cedar trees that inspire most travellers to journey to this primeval wonderland.

Immortalised by Miyazaki's wildly popular anime Princess Mononoke, Yakushima's old-growth forests are an incredible destination for mountains hikers and outdoor enthusiasts. But even if you're not prepared to tackle some of the island's most difficult treks, there are plenty of easy day hikes at the lower elevations as well as a number of rural *onsen* and subtropical beaches to explore.

ORIENTATION

Yakushima's main port is Miyanoura, on the island's northeast coast. From here, a road runs around the perimeter of the island, passing through the secondary port of Anbō on the east coast, and then through the hot-springs town of Onoaida (尾の間) in the south. On the west coast, the road narrows to just one paved lane – drive slowly, and watch out for monkeys and falling rocks.

INFORMATION

Miyanoura's ferry terminal has a useful **information desk** (☎ 42-1019; ⏰ 8.30am-5pm) that can help find accommodation, and sells topographic hiking maps. In Anbō there's a small **tourist office** (☎ 46-2333; ⏰ 8.30am-5pm) on the main road just north of the river.

In Miyanoura, the **Environmental & Cultural Centre** (☎ 42-2900; admission & film ¥500; ⏰ 9am-5pm Tue-Sun, daily in summer) is at the corner of the ferry-terminal road. It has bilingual exhibits about the island's natural history and traditions. Subtitles are available upon request in several foreign languages for screenings of an inspiring 25-minute IMAX film.

SIGHTS & ACTIVITIES
Onsens

The following *onsens* have their own bus stops.

Onsen lovers will be in heaven at the **Hirauchi Kaichū Onsen** (admission ¥100), just west of Onoaida. Mixed outdoor baths are in the rocks by the sea, and usable only when the tide is out (tide charts are posted at the island's accommodation).

A tad further west is **Yudomari Onsen** (admission ¥100), which is also located beside the sea and usable when the tide is out. The small bath here has a divider if you're looking for a bit more privacy, though the view is somewhat fouled by the concrete jetty.

In the village of Onoaida is **Onoaida Onsen** (☎ 47-2872; admission ¥200; ⏰ 7am-10pm), which is a rustic bathhouse that is divided by gender. Note that the water here is scalding hot, so do as the locals do and pour buckets of cold water on yourself before entering the baths.

Hiking

There are some seriously awesome hikes in Yakushima's mountainous interior, though it's best to seek out local advice before setting out.

An excellent topographic map of the island is the *Yama-to-Kougen-no-Chizu- Yakushima* (山と高原の地図屋久島; ¥840), which is available at most major bookstores.

Although the summer sun may be shining on the coastline, you will need warm, waterproof clothing if you're heading up into the mountains. If you're planning on spending the night out in the wilderness, there is a network of mountain huts along each of the trails. Facilities are basic, and you will need to bring your own food, stove and sleeping bag.

Before heading up into the hills, be sure to alert someone at your accommodation of your intended route.

The granddaddy of hikes on Yakushima is the day-long strenuous outing to the 1935m summit of **Miyanoura-dake**, the highest point in southern Japan. To reach the summit, allow 10 hours return from **Yodogawa-tozanguchi** (1370m).

The most popular hike on the island leads to **Jōmon-sugi**, a monster of a *yaku-sugi* that is estimated to be at least 5000 years old. The discovery of this tree in the late 1960s ultimately led to the preservation of the island's forests. To reach the tree, allow at least five hours each way from the trailhead, **Arakawa-tozanguchi**.

If you have the proper supplies and equipment, there are also a number of two- and three-day treks across several mountain peaks. For the complete scoop on the island's hikes, pick up a copy of Lonely Planet's *Hiking in Japan*.

If you're feeling a little less adventurous, consider a visit to **Yaku-sugi Land** (admission ¥500; ⏱ 9am-5pm). Despite its theme park-esque name, Yaku-sugi Land is extremely well laid out, and offers shorter hiking courses over wooden boardwalks, and longer treks deep into the millennia-old cedar forest. Although the three shorter courses wind past a few thousand-year-

old trees, it's worth taking the 150-minute hiking course, which passes by the 2600-year-old **Jamon-sugi**. The preserve is a 30-minute drive inland and up from Anbō on a rough and rugged road. It's incredibly picturesque, and if you're lucky, you may see *yakuzaru,* the local species of monkey. There are two buses a day (¥720, 40 minutes) from Anbō.

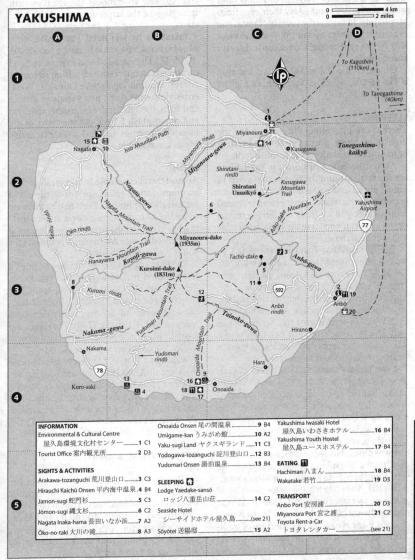

Based in Miyanoura, **Native Vision** (ネイティ
ブビジョン; ☎ 42-0091; www.native-vision.com in Japanese) runs all sorts of outdoor tours including
hiking, snorkelling and kayaking. Day trips
cost between ¥3000 and ¥7500.

Other Sights & Activities
On the northwest coast of the island is **Nagata
Inaka-hama**, a beautiful stretch of yellow sand
where sea turtles come to lay their eggs from
May to July. In the nearby town of Nagata, you
can visit the **Umigame-kan** (☎ 49-6550; admission
¥200; ☽ 9am-5pm Wed-Mon) for sea turtle displays
and exhibits.

On the west coast and at the last bus stop
is **Ōko-no-taki**, which is Yakushima's highest
waterfall at 88m.

SLEEPING
There is camping along the coast and in the
highland interior, plus an established system
of mountain huts along the summit trails.

Accommodation options on Yakushima
are scattered around the island, so it's best to
phone ahead and make a reservation before
arriving on the island. Most places will send
a car to pick you up from the ferry terminal
or the airport if you let them know what time
you will be arriving.

our pick **Yakushima Youth Hostel** (☎ 47-3751;
www.yakushima-yh.net; dm with/without meals ¥4400/2800;
ℙ ⊠ ▣) A short walk from the Hirauchi
Iriguchi bus stop just west of Onoaida is this
impeccably run youth hostel, which is entirely
constructed of local cedar. Accommodation
is in Western-style dorms that welcome you
with the inviting aroma of polished wood.
The hostel also rents out bicycles for trips to
nearby waterfalls and hot springs.

Lodge Yaedake-sansō (☎ 42-1551; fax 42-2673; r per
person with meals ¥7500; ℙ ⊠) This secluded *minshuku* (family-run budget accommodation)
features Japanese-style rooms in rustic riverside cabins that are all connected by wooden
walkways. There's also a private hot-springs
bath where you can soak up the beauty of your
surroundings. The lodge is located inland upriver on the Miyanoura-gawa, but if you make
a booking they'll pick you up in Miyanoura.

Sōyōtei (☎ 45-2819; http://soyote.ftw.jp/u44579.html
in Japanese; r per person with meals ¥12,600; ℙ ⊠) On
the northwest of the island near Inaka Beach,
this stunning ryokan has a collection of traditional Japanese-style rooms that boast private
verandas and ocean views. Guests can also

take advantage of the open-air hot-springs
bath where you can close your eyes and listen
to the sounds of the crashing surf.

Seaside Hotel (☎ 42-0175; www.ssh-yakushima.co.jp
in Japanese; d from ¥13,000; meals available; ℙ ⊠ ▣)
Overlooking the ferry port in Miyanoura, this
popular resort hotel is extremely convenient.
Accommodation is in a variety of Western-
and Japanese-style rooms, though it's worth
splurging for the larger rooms with harbour
views.

Yakushima Iwasaki Hotel (☎ 47-3888; http://
yakushima.iwasakihotels.com in Japanese; d from ¥20,000;
ℙ ⊠ ▣) The island's most expensive hotel
commands an impressive view from its mountaintop location high above Onoaida. Western-style rooms come in a variety of shapes
and sizes, though they're incredibly spacious
and oh-so-plush (check out the views of the
forests below from the window-side Jacuzzis).
Meals are available.

EATING
As most travellers choose to take meals at their
accommodation, eating options on the island
are surprisingly limited. Fortunately, there are
a handful of convenience stores and a supermarket in each of the main towns. Also, most
accommodations can prepare a *bentō* box for
you if you're going hiking.

Hachiman (☎ 33-8322; ☽ 11am-9pm) Located a
few hundred metres west of the Yakushima
Youth Hostel in Onoaida, this all-wood bis-
tro-style restaurant (look for the red flags
outside) serves up an excellent *yakizakana
teishoku* (grilled fish set; ¥750). The restaurant
is on the ocean side of the road while the parking lot is located on the opposite side.

Wakatake (☎ 46-3172; ☽ 6-9pm) Overlooking
the river in Anbō (look for the hanging red
lanterns), this boisterous *izakaya* (Japanese-
style pub) is a great spot for chatting with locals
and swapping hiking tips with other travellers.
Try a fresh *sashimi-setto* (sashimi set; ¥1250)
or an ice-cold *nama-birru* (tap beer; ¥450).

GETTING THERE & AWAY
Air
JAC, part of the JAS network, flies from Kagoshima to Yakushima (¥11,000, 40 minutes,
six daily). Yakushima's airport is on the northeastern coast between Miyanoura and Anbō.
Hourly buses stop at the airport, though you
can usually phone your accommodation for
a pick-up or take a cab.

Boat

The fastest way to reach Yakushima is by the hydrofoil, though you will need to make a reservation in advance with **Toppy** (☎ 099-255-7888). You can also stop by the ferry terminal a day in advance to buy tickets. Hydrofoils run from Kagoshima's Kita-Futō terminal to Miyanoura and Anbō (one way/return ¥7000/12,600, 2½ hours, four daily). Keep in mind that the jet foils stop running at the slightest hint of inclement weather.

Orita Kisen (☎ 099-226-0731) runs the scenic ferry route between Kagoshima's Minami-Futō and Miyanoura (one way/return ¥5000/8000, four hours, once daily). The ferry departs from Kagoshima at 8.35am, and leaves Miyanoura at 1.20pm.

GETTING AROUND

Local buses travel the coastal road part way around Yakushima roughly every hour, though only a few head up into the interior. However, your best option for getting around the island is to rent a car. **Toyota Rent-a-Car** (☎ 43-5180) is located near the terminal in Miyanoura.

Tanegashima 種子島
☎ 0997 / pop 36,000

A long narrow island standing north–south to the east of Yakushima, Tanegashima is known as the home of Japan's Space Centre, and as a year-round surfing mecca. It also has the dubious distinction of being the spot where firearms were first introduced to Japan by shipwrecked Portuguese in 1543. After the local lord copied the matchlock guns, the firearms spread throughout Japan, which completely changed the balance of power among the feudal lords (who were known as *tanegashimas* from then on).

The island's port of Nishi-no-omote (西の表) is located on the northwest coast of the island, while the airport is about halfway down the island near the west coast. There is a helpful **information office** (観光案内所; ☎ 22-1146; 🕑 8.30am-5.30pm) in the ferry building at the port. Check out www.tanegashima.info for more information in Japanese.

Tanegashima's **Space Centre** (宇宙センター), on the southeastern coast of the island, is open to the public for free. There is a large parklike complex with rocket-launch facilities as well as a **Space Technology Museum** (宇宙科学技術館; ☎ 26-9244; 🕑 9.30am-5.30pm Tue-Sun) that details the history of Japan's space

program. Note that the museum is closed on launch days.

The coastline in the immediate vicinity of the Space Centre is known as the **Takesaki-kaigan** (竹崎海岸), and is home to a beautiful stretch of white sand that is immensely popular with surfers. The **Nagahama-kaigan** (長浜海岸) on the west coast of Tanegashima is home to a 12km stretch of white sand that is equally popular with surfers. From early May to early August, Nagahama-kaigan plays host to sea turtles laying their eggs.

The **History and Folklore Museum** (中種子町立歴史民俗資料館; ☎ 27-2233; admission ¥160; 🕑 9am-7pm Tue-Sun), near Tanegashima's airport, has displays on the history and traditional lifestyles of the islanders.

A few blocks inland from Nishi-no-omote port, **Ryokan Miharu-sō** (旅館美春荘; ☎ 22-1393; r per person with meals ¥3700; 🅿 🐕) is the best choice on the island as the mellow owner also runs a surf shop, and is an incredible source of information. Accommodation is in basic but perfectly adequate Japanese-style tatami rooms, and the staff's cooking will certainly hit the spot after a long day out on the surf.

JAC, part of the JAS network, flies from Kagoshima to Tanegashima (¥11,000, 40 minutes, three daily). Fast-boat services by **Kagoshima Shosen** (☎ 099-255-7888) run from Kagoshima Main Port (Kagoshima-honkō; 鹿児島本港) to Nishi-no-omote (¥6000; 1¾ hours, four daily), and **Orita Kisen** (☎ 099-226-0731) runs a regular ferry service (¥2540, 3¾ hours, one daily).

Iō-jima 硫黄島
☎ 09913 / pop 115

Part of the Kirishima volcanic belt, Iō-jima is a gem of an island that is based around an active volcano, and is well known for its wild peacocks and remote *onsen*. Difficult access means that Iō-jima is rarely visited by foreign travellers, and the lack of public transportation on the island means that you're probably going to have to visit most of the sights on foot. However, being one of the most remote destinations in Japan, Iō-jima is the perfect destination if you really want to get away from it all.

For more about the island, the website www.mishimamura.jp has information in Japanese and some great photos.

The eastern end of the island is home to the often-smoking volcano **Iō-dake** (硫黄岳;

704m), while the port is on the southwestern coast.

There are a couple of superb *onsen* on the island that are free to those willing to walk to them. On the north coast, about a 5km walk from the port, is **Sakamoto Onsen** (坂本温泉), a rectangular pool built into the sea. Its depth reaches 1.5m when the tide is in, but when the tide is out test the temperature with your finger as the natural flow of hot water from the spring is around 50°C. On the south coast, about a 3km walk east of the port and right below Iō-dake, is **Higashi Onsen** (東温泉). It is a big, hot rock-pool next to the pounding waves that is a must for *onsen* connoisseurs.

Iō-jima has historical links and legends associated with the 12th-century struggles between the Genji and Heike clans to control Japan. At the northern tip of the island, about a 2km walk from Sakamoto Onsen, are the remains of a Heike **castle**.

Right next to the port, the Iō-jima **camping** area is free and open year-round – you can even borrow a tent for free. If you're looking for more comfortable surroundings, **Miyukisō** (みゆき荘; ☎ 2-2116; fax 2-2116; r per person with meals ¥6500; 🅿) is a friendly, family-run *minshuku* that is also located next to the port. Accommodation is in cosy Japanese-style tatami rooms, and there's a good chance that the island's famous seafood will be on your dinner plate.

KAGOSHIMA TO NAHA BY SEA

Daily cargo ferries ply the waters between Kagoshima city on Kyūshū and Naha, the main city in Okinawa. These ferries are in good shape, reasonable in cost and an excellent way to either travel directly to Naha or to island-hop along the Amami-shotō. A 2nd-class ticket admits travellers to a large tatami room that is shared with others, while tickets for a private room are considerably more expensive.

Ōshima Unyu (☎ Tokyo 03-5643-6170, Kagoshima 099-222-2338, Naha 098-861-1886; www.minc.ne.jp/aline in Japanese) and **Marix Line** (☎ Tokyo 03-3274-0502, Kagoshima 099-225-1551, Naha 098-868-9098; www .marix-line.co.jp) operate to the following schedule on alternate days (ie between them, there is a daily departure in each direction).

For ¥14,200 you can travel 2nd-class on either company's ferry directly from Kagoshima to Naha or vice versa. Alternatively, you can get off and on at any of the ports listed below, though you will have to buy a new ticket each time you board the ferry. Note that this costs slightly more than travelling directly between Kagoshima and Naha or vice versa – disembarking at each of the ports along the way would cost a total of ¥18,700.

Southbound

Day	Time	Destination
Day 1	1800	Kagoshima-shinkō
Day 2	0550	Amami-Ōshima (Naze)
Day 2	0940	Tokunoshima (Kametoku)
Day 2	1200	Okinoerabu-jima (Wadomari)
Day 2	1400	Yoron-tō
Day 2	1650	Okinawa (Unten-kō in Motobu)
Day 2	1840	Okinawa (Naha-kō in Naha)

Northbound

Day	Time	Destination
Day 1	0700	Okinawa (Naha-kō in Naha)
Day 1	0910	Okinawa (Unten-kō in Motobu)
Day 1	1200	Yoron-tō
Day 1	1410	Okinoerabu-jima (Wadomari)
Day 1	1630	Tokunoshima (Kametoku)
Day 1	2020	Amami-Ōshima (Naze)
Day 2	0630	Kagoshima-shinkō

Iō-jima is accessed by ferry from Kagoshima Main Port. **Mishima Soneisen** (☎ 099-222-3141) runs three to four ferries a week, depending on the season, generally leaving Kagoshima at 9.30am and arriving at Iō-jima four hours later (¥3500).

TOKARA-RETTŌ トカラ列島

099 / pop 700

The Tokara group is made up of seven inhabited and five uninhabited volcanic islands, which are strung out between Yakushima and Amami-Ōshima. Since the total population of the island chain is only 700, the islands are virtually untouched, and covered with dense subtropical vegetation and plentiful natural hot springs. In terms of travel in Japan, this is real get-away-from-it-all stuff.

If you're planning a visit, you will need to be self-sufficient as there is virtually no tourist infrastructure in place. At the bare minimum, you should bring a tent, sleeping bag and basic supplies. For more information in Japanese, www.tokara.jp has pictures of each of the islands as well as useful tips for visitors.

Toshima Soneibune (☎ 222-2101) has a ferry that leaves Kagoshima Main Port on Mondays and Fridays, and stops at each island down the chain to Takara-jima (the Monday departure continues on to Naze on Amami-Ōshima). The return trip leaves Takara-jima on Wednesdays and Sundays. Check departure dates and times before turning up as they can vary and are affected by typhoons.

For ¥15,600 you can travel 2nd-class from Kagoshima to Amami-Ōshima. Alternatively, you can get off and on at any of the ports listed below, though you will have to buy a new ticket each time you board the ferry. Note that this option costs slightly more than travelling directly between Kagoshima and Amami-Ōshima.

Travelling from north to south, the ferry visits Kuchino-shima (口之島), Nakano-shima (中之島), Taira-jima (平島), Suwanose-jima (諏訪之瀬島), Akuseki-jima (悪石島), Kodakara-jima (小宝島) and Takara-jima (宝島).

AMAMI-SHOTŌ 奄美諸島

The southernmost island group in Kagoshima-ken is the Amami-shotō, which is based around the island of Amami-Ōshima, the region's main population centre. The island is also a renowned destination for outdoor pursuits, especially ocean kayaking. Heading south, Tokunoshima has excellent diving, Okinoerabu-jima has intriguing coral-based land formations and Yoron-tō is a popular beach destination. Unfortunately, difficult access means that this island group is not as popular as other destinations in the Nansei-shotō, though there are some amazing experiences to be had here if you're willing to get off the beaten path.

Amami-Ōshima 奄美大島

☎ 0997 / pop 70,000

Amami-Ōshima, the main island of the Amami group, is 380km south-west of Kagoshima, and is Japan's third-largest offshore island after Okinawa-hontō and Sado-ga-shima in Niigata prefecture. It has a mild subtropical climate year-round and is home to some unusual flora and fauna, including tree ferns, mangrove forests and the rare Amami black rabbit. Although it serves as the main population centre in the Amami-shotō, it's also a popular destination for outdoor enthusiasts, especially sea kayakers.

The main city and port is Naze (名瀬), which is on the northwest coast and surrounded by hills. The island's tiny airport is 55 minutes away by bus (¥750, hourly) on the northeast coast. There's a small **tourist information office** (☎ 63-2295) at the airport that opens for incoming flights, but nothing at the ferry terminal. For more information in Japanese, check out www.amami.or.jp.

For an excellent view of Naze and its harbour, head 1km south of the port to **Og-amiyama-kōen** (おがみ山公園), a park with walking trails and viewing areas.

A few blocks north of the bus centre is the **Amami Habu Centre** (奄美観光ハブセンター; ☎ 52-1505; admission ¥750; ⏰ 8am-6pm) where you can learn all about the Nansei-shotō's infamous venomous snake, the habu (p760).

Just 15 minutes west of Naze by direct bus (¥280, hourly) is the **Ohama-Kaihin-Kōen** (大浜海浜公園), a beautiful beach park known for its white sands and stunning sunsets. The park is popular for swimming, snorkelling and sea kayaking in summer, and camping is possible here for ¥300.

Island Service (アイランドサービス; ☎ 52-5346; www.synapse.ne.jp/~island-s/in Japanese) runs a guided sea-kayaking tour (¥12,000, eight hours) and mangrove canoe experience (from ¥2500, from two hours). If you ring up, they can arrange for a pick-up and drop you off at your accommodation.

A few blocks inland from the ferry port in Naze is the **Tatsuya Ryokan** (たつや旅館; ☎ 52-0260; r per person with/without meals ¥4500/3000; P ✖), which has a handful of attractive Japanese-style tatami rooms complete with satellite TV and en-suite facilities. The owner is also chock-full of information about the island – phone ahead for a pick-up.

Amami-Ōshima is serviced by JTA (part of the JAL network) and ANK (part of the ANA network), with daily direct flights to/from Tokyo (from ¥40,000, 2½ hours, one daily), Osaka (from ¥32,000, one hour 50 minutes, one daily) and Kagoshima (from ¥16,500, 55 minutes, five daily).

There are between five and seven ferries running to/from Tokyo (¥18,500, 37 hours) and Osaka (¥13,500, 28 hours) each month that carry on to Naha. Ferries also operate daily from Kagoshima and Naha (see boxed text, p744).

Amami-Ōshima has an excellent public bus system and buses run to all corners of the main island from the bus centre in Naze. Rental cars, scooters and bicycles are readily available in Naze.

Tokunoshima 徳之島
☎ 0997 / pop 28,000

Tokunoshima is the second-largest island in the Amami-shotō, and is famous for its spectacular natural landscapes. The coastline is awash with rock formations, particularly jagged volcanic rocks jutting towards the sky, while the interior is composed of rugged mountains. Tokunoshima's year-round mild climate also makes it a popular destination for divers. Although the seas around the island aren't as tropical as those further south, there is a healthy reef system of soft and hard corals around much of Tokunoshima.

On the island's east coast is the main port of **Kametoku-shinkō** (亀徳新港) and the main town of **Kametsu** (亀津). Tokunoshima's airport is on its west coast, not far from the secondary port of **Hetono** (平土野). A small **tourist information office** (☎ 82-0575; ☉ 9am-6pm Mon-Sat) is at the ferry building.

Tokunoshima has a history of tōgyū (闘牛大会; bovine sumō) dating back more than 600 years. While there are 13 official fight sites on the island that hold around 20 tournaments a year, the island championships are held at **Dōmu Tōgyū-jō** (ドーム闘牛場) in the southeast of the island, not far from Kametsu. The big three events for the year are held on 3 January, 5 May and either the first or second Sunday in October – call the tourist office to confirm details.

At the northeastern tip of the island is the **Kanami Sotetsu Tunnel** (金見ソテツトンネル), an impressive 200m-long tunnel of 400-year-old cycad trees leading out to the viewpoint at Cape Kanami. At the northwestern tip is **Mushirose** (ムシロ瀬), an amazing rippled rock formation that disappears into the sea. The **Megane-iwa** (メガネ岩), with two huge holes in the rock that look like a pair of glasses, is on the west coast.

Villa Takakura (ヴィラ高倉; ☎ 84-1185; r per person with/without meals ¥5500/3500) is a popular diver's hotel that organises trips to the island's dive sights. Accommodation is in attractive maritime-themed Western-style rooms with en-suite facilities, though the real reason you're here is to take advantage of the on-site dive shop. Villa Takakura is located near Kedoku on the east coast – phone ahead for a pick-up.

Tokunoshima is serviced by JTA and ANK, with daily direct flights to/from both Kagoshima (from ¥25,000, one hour, two daily) and Amami-Ōshima (from ¥18,500, 35 minutes, two daily).

Daily ferries (see boxed text, p744) head both southward to Naha and northward to Kagoshima.

There are bus stations at the ports of Hetono and Kametoku, and a good public bus system to all parts of the island. Rental cars, scooters and bicycles are readily available in Kametsu.

Okinoerabu-jima 沖永良部島
☎ 0997 / pop 15,000

A raised coral island to the southwest of Tokunoshima, Okinoerabu-jima is known for its intriguing land formations, which include around 300 caves and caverns. Extensive flower farming, especially of lilies, means that from March to May the island is covered in yellow and white flowers.

The airport is at the eastern tip of the island, with **Wadomari-kō** (和泊港), the main port and town, 6km away on the east coast. There is a small **tourist information booth** (☎ 92-1111; ☉ 8.30am-5.30pm) at Wadomari port on the 2nd floor of the terminal building.

The island has many impressive geographical landforms. **Taminamisaki** (田皆崎), at the northwest tip of the island, has ancient coral that has been uplifted to form a 40m cliff. Over the years, natural erosion caused by the wind, rain and sea has made the point a rugged yet beautiful spot. At the island's northeast tip, **Fūcha** (フーチャ) is a blowhole in the limestone rock that shoots water 10m into the air on windy days.

Although the island's caves are all open to 'unofficial' exploration, organised tours are given at **Shōryūdō** (昇竜洞; ☎ 93-4536; admission ¥1000; ☉ 8.30am-5pm), a few kilometres inland from the southwest coastal road.

The legendary Saigō Takamori (see boxed text, p715) was exiled on Okinoerabu-jima for two years in 1862. He helped foster the islanders' desires to be self-sustaining, and is honoured by a statue in Wadomari's **Nanshū-jinja** (南州神社) temple.

A convenient, comfortable base on the island is the **Kankō Hotel Higashi** (観光ホテル東; ☎ 92-1283; www5.synapse.ne.jp/khotel-azuma in Japanese; r per person with/without meals from ¥6500/4500; P ✂), which is next to the ferry port and close to the action in Wadomari. Accommodation is in a variety of Japanese- and Western-style rooms – ask for the ones in the front, which have nice views of the ships coming into port.

Okinoerabu is serviced by JTA and ANK, with direct flights to/from Kagoshima (from ¥24,000, one hour 40 minutes, three daily), Amami-Ōshima (from ¥13,000, 35 minutes, one daily) and Yoron-tō (from ¥7400, 25 minutes, one daily).

Daily ferries (see boxed text, p744) operate services south to Naha and north to Kagoshima.

The island has a good public bus system, and rental cars, scooters and bicycles are readily available in Wadomari.

Yoron-tō 与論島 • ヨロン島

☎ 0997 / pop 6000

Shaped like a huge angelfish, Yoron-tō is the southernmost island in Kagoshima-ken. On a good day, Okinawa-hontō's northernmost point of Hedo-misaki is clearly visible just 28km to the southwest. Fringed with picture-perfect white sand beaches, Yoron-tō has a reputation as a tropical paradise, and is the most popular destination in the Amami-shotō for domestic travellers.

The harbour is next to the airport on the western tip of the island, while the main town of **Chabana** (茶花) is just a couple of kilometres east. Beside the city office in Chabana is the useful **tourist information office** (☎ 97-5151; ☉ 8.30am-5.30pm), which provides maps, an English pamphlet and can make accommodation bookings. Check out www.yoron.jp in Japanese for more information.

On the eastern side of the island, Yoron's best beach is the popular **Oganeku-kaigan** (大金久海岸), which also features an attractive **camping area** (sites per person per night ¥610) complete with sparkling facilities. Just offshore from Oganeku-kaigan is **Yurigahama** (百合ヶ浜), a stunning stretch of white sand surrounded by a hard coral reef that disappears completely at high tide. Boats (¥1000 return) putter back and forth, ferrying visitors out to it.

The **Southern Cross Centre** (サザンクロスセンター; ☎ 97-3396; admission ¥200; ☉ 9am-6pm), a short walk from the Ishini (石仁) bus stop 3km south of Chabana, is so named as Yoron-tō is the northernmost island in Japan from which the Southern Cross can be seen. The centre also serves as Yoron-tō's museum, and has displays on the history and culture of the Amami islands. The remains of **Yoron Castle** (与論城跡), which was half-built by the Hokuzan king in the 15th century, can be seen next door.

The **Yunnu Rakuen** (ユンヌ楽園; ☎ 97-2341; admission ¥400; ☉ 9am-6pm) is a tropical botanical garden with more than 300 types of plants including hibiscus, bougainvillea, plumeria and golden shower. It's a great place to chill out and breathe in the tropical mood.

Just up the road from the tourist information office is the convenient **Minshuku Nankai-sō** (民宿南海荘; ☎ 97-2145; fax 43-0888; r per person with/without meals ¥5500/3000; P ✂), with simple Japanese-style accommodation, shared bathrooms and a laid-back communal atmosphere. It's a fairly easy spot to find, though the staff will pick you up if you phone ahead.

Yoron-tō is serviced by JTA and ANK, with direct flights to/from Kagoshima (from ¥26,000, 1¾ hours, one daily) and Naha (from ¥9500, 35 minutes, one daily).

Daily ferries (see boxed text, p744) head south to Naha and north to Kagoshima.

The island has a good public bus system, and rental cars, scooters and bicycles are readily available in Chabana.

OKINAWA-KEN 沖縄県

pop 1.35 million

The southern half of the Nansei-shotō is Okinawa-ken, which is the furthest south of Japan's prefectures. Heading southwest, there are three main island groups in the chain.

Northernmost is the Okinawa-shotō, centred around Okinawa-hontō and the prefectural capital of Naha. Due to the large presence of American military bases (below), this is undoubtedly the most Westernised destination in the Nansei-shotō. Naha is Okinawa-ken's transport hub, and is easily accessed by flights to/from the mainland and outlying islands as well as by inter-island ferries.

Located 300km southwest of Okinawa-hontō, Okinawa-ken's middle group of islands is Miyako-shotō, which is home to the popular beach destination of Miyako-jima. This group

is best accessed by direct flights from the mainland, or by plane or ferry from Naha.

The southernmost island group is the Yaeyama-shotō, a further 120km southwest, though the westernmost island of Yonaguni-jima is only 110km from Taiwan. This island group, which includes the coral-fringed island of Ishigaki and the nearby jungle-clad Iriomote-jima, is one of the top domestic tourist destinations in Japan. This group is also best accessed by direct flights from the mainland, or by plane or ferry from Naha.

OKINAWA-HONTŌ 沖縄本島
☎ 098

Okinawa-hontō is the largest island in the Nansei-shotō, and the historic seat of power of the Ryūkyū dynasty. Although its cultural differences with mainland Japan were once evident in its architecture, almost all traces were completely obliterated in WWII. For-

---

THE AMERICAN ISSUE

After the war, Okinawa had to be restored from complete destruction. While Japan recovered its sovereignty in 1953, Okinawa remained under the control of the US Military Occupation Government, which appropriated whichever land it wanted for military bases. Local protests finally forced Okinawa's return to Japan in 1972. Because of its strategic location, however, collusion between Tokyo and Washington maintained a heavy US military presence in the islands, much to the displeasure of many Okinawans – especially those who had lost their land.

Okinawans found it hard to understand why, with less than 1% of Japan's landmass, they had to play host to 75% of the American military presence in Japan. The thorny issue sputtered along through the Vietnam and Cold Wars, then peaked in 1995 when three servicemen were found guilty of raping a 12-year-old Okinawan schoolgirl. In the aftermath, Governor Ōta Masahide was voted into power on a pledge to end the American military presence. Ōta's demands made little headway in Tokyo though, and in 1998 he was beaten by Inamine Keniichi, a 'pro-American base' politician who argued that the poor Okinawan economy needed the cash that the American bases brought with them. Inamine's attitude was rewarded by Tokyo when Okinawa hosted the G8 Summit in July 2000.

At the time of research, Tokyo had recently decided that the burden of American bases should be shared more evenly around Japan, but was having problems finding prefectures and towns willing to play host. As a result, the American issue featured prominently in the November 2006 Okinawan gubernatorial elections. At the heart of the campaign was the government-sponsored plan to construct a new V-shaped runway near Camp Schwab in northern Okinawa, which was rumoured to be an environmentally disastrous project.

Candidate Keiko Itokazu, who was campaigning to become Okinawa's first female governor, was opposed to the construction of the runway, and went as far as proclaiming that the American bases should be moved out of Japan altogether. However, she was narrowly defeated by Hirokazu Nakaima, a candidate supported by Japan's ruling coalition, who won the ballot on a platform of improving the region's economy. Although he is opposed to the relocation plan, Hirokazu said he would negotiate with the central government on the issue and avoid confrontation. Unfortunately, Okinawans opposed to the US presence view Hirokazu Nakaima's promises as empty political rhetoric, especially considering that the Americans are the lifeblood of the island's economy.

tunately, Allied bombing wasn't powerful enough to completely stamp out other remnants of Okinawan culture, and today the island is home to a unique culinary, artistic and musical tradition.

Throughout the past several decades, however, Okinawa-hontō has also played host to a different breed of cultural influence, namely in the form of American imperialism. Today, there are more than 25,000 American military personnel stationed on the island, and their impact on the island's economy and culture cannot be overstated. The highways along the island are lined with used-car dealers, strip malls and fast-food outlets, all of which wouldn't look too out of place in suburban America. In fact, the Westernisation of the island has resulted in a bizarre tourism industry whereby mainland Japanese families visit the island in order to experience American-style steakhouses and to buy American products.

This island is home to Okinawa-hontō's prefectural capital and largest city, Naha, which serves as a transportation hub for the other islands in the group and for the prefecture as a whole. War memorials are clustered in the south of the island, while the central area is home to the military bases, a few historic ruins and some interesting cultural attractions. If you're keen on snorkelling and diving, head straight to the Motobu Peninsula (for info on the best dive spots, see p755) – the further north you go, the more rural things become.

The island also serves as the jumping-off point for several smaller subtropical islets in the Okinawa-shotō, which offer a healthy mix of white-sand beaches, swaying palm trees and blissful seclusion (for more information, see p759).

Naha 那覇
pop 320,000

Although it was completely flattened during WWII, the prefectural capital of Naha was rapidly rebuilt and is presently in the midst of a population explosion. Today, the city sports a swish new overhead monorail and a rapidly expanding skyline of modern high-rise apartments. However, the heart of the city is still very much Shuri-jō, the castle ruins of the erstwhile Okinawan capital that grace the backside of the new ¥2000 bill.

Naha also has a reputation for its boisterous (if at times scandalous) nightlife. Of course,

this shouldn't come as too much of a surprise as American GIs, mainland tourists and college students make for quite a heady mix. The action centres on Kokusai-dōri (International Blvd), a colourful and energetic 2km main drag of hotels, restaurants, bars, clubs and just about every conceivable type of souvenir shop.

Assuming you can find the strength to go easy on the drink, Naha is also home to several interesting areas including the Tsuboya pottery district and a historic series of Asian-style covered markets.

ORIENTATION

Naha is fairly easy to navigate, especially since its main sights and attractions are located in the city centre. The city is also easy to get around thanks to its cheap and efficient monorail system. The line starts from the airport in the south of the city, terminates in the suburbs in the northeast and runs parallel-ish to Kokusai-dōri.

The main drag in the city centre is Kokusai-dōri, while the Tsuboya Pottery district is to the southeast via a series of covered arcades. The Shuri district is located about 3km to the east of the city centre, and can be reached via the monorail.

Note that some of the listings in this section are located near Ōnoyama Park just south of the Kokuba-gawa river, which is about a 20-minute walk from the southeastern end of Kokusai-dōri.

INFORMATION

The prefectural **tourist information office** (Map p752; ☎ 857-6884; ⏰ 9am-9pm) is in the arrivals terminal at Naha Airport. This office and its staff are extremely helpful, so you should definitely take advantage of their services before heading into town. English is spoken, and there are English-language brochures, maps of the islands in the Okinawa prefecture and accommodation lists in English.

The city **tourist information office** (Map p752; ☎ 868-4887; ⏰ 8.30am-8pm Mon-Fri, 10am-8pm Sat & Sun) has free maps and staff members speak some English. It's just off Kokusai-dōri on the corner with Starbucks. For information online check out the Okinawa Tourism & Convention Bureau's website www.ocvb.or.jp.

Post office ATMs accept international money cards; Naha Central Post Office is next to Tsubokawa monorail station, Tomari-kō Post Office (Map p752) is in the port building,

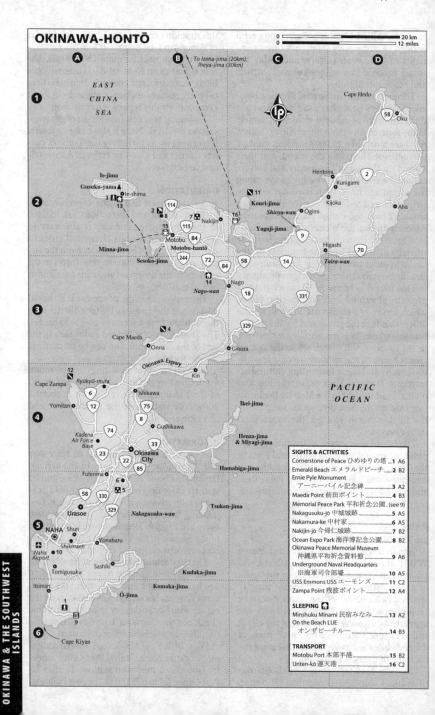

OKINAWA-HONTŌ

0 ————— 20 km
0 ————— 12 miles

EAST CHINA SEA

To Izena-jima (20km);
Iheya-jima (30km)

Cape Hedo

Oku

Hentona

Kunigami

Kijoka

Aha

Ie-jima

Gusuku-yama▲

Ie-shima

Kouri-jima

Shioya-wan

Ōgimi

Higashi

Nakijin

Yagaji-jima

Motobu

Motobu-hantō

Minna-jima

Sesoko-jima

Taira-wan

Nago

Nago-wan

Cape Maeda

Onna

Ginoza

Okinawa Expwy

Kin

Ikei-jima

PACIFIC OCEAN

Cape Zampa

Ryūkyū-mura

Ishikawa

Yomitan

Gushikawa

Henza-jima & Miyagi-jima

Kadena Air Force Base

Okinawa City

Hamahiga-jima

Futenma

Urasoe

Nakagusuku-wan

Tsuken-jima

NAHA

Shuri

Shikinaen

Yonabaru

Naha Airport

Sashiki

Tomigusuku

Kudaka-jima

Itoman

Komaka-jima

Ō-jima

Cape Kiyan

SIGHTS & ACTIVITIES
Cornerstone of Peace ひめゆりの塔	**1**	A6
Emerald Beach エメラルドビーチ	**2**	B2
Ernie Pyle Monument アーニーパイル記念碑	**3**	A2
Maeda Point 前田ポイント	**4**	B3
Memorial Peace Park 平和祈念公園	(see 9)	
Nakagusuku-jō 中城城跡	**5**	A5
Nakamura-ke 中村家	**6**	A5
Nakijin-jō 今帰仁城跡	**7**	B2
Ocean Expo Park 海洋博記念公園	**8**	B2
Okinawa Peace Memorial Museum 沖縄県平和祈念資料館	**9**	A6
Underground Naval Headquarters 旧海軍司令部壕	**10**	A5
USS Emmons USS エーモンズ	**11**	C2
Zampa Point 残波ポイント	**12**	A4

SLEEPING
Minshuku Minami 民宿みなみ	**13**	A2
On the Beach LUE オンザビーチルー	**14**	B3

TRANSPORT
Motobu Port 本部半港	**15**	B2
Unten-kō 運天港	**16**	C2

and the Kokusai-dōri Post Office (Map p752) is around the corner from Makishi monorail station.

Net Café (Map p752; ☎ 941-2755; 2-4-14 Makishi; ☿ 9.30am-midnight) on Kokusai-dōri charges ¥300/480 for the first half-hour/hour of internet access, including free soft drinks and snacks.

There are heaps of travel agencies around Kokusai-dōri. **Nice Ticket** (Map p752; ☎ 866-8988; 2-16-10 Makishi; ☿ 10am-7pm Mon-Fri, 10am-5pm Sat) sells discounted airline tickets.

SIGHTS & ACTIVITIES
Central Naha 那覇中心街

The city's main artery, **Kokusai-dōri** (国際通り), makes a colourful walk, day or night. Turning south opposite Mitsukoshi department store leads you down **Heiwa-dōri** (平和通り), a bustling Asian-style covered shopping arcade.

If you take the left fork at the first major junction, a short walk beyond the shopping arcade brings you to the **Tsuboya pottery area** (壺屋). More than a dozen traditional potteries still operate in this compact neighbourhood, which has served as a centre of ceramic production since 1682, when Ryūkyūan kilns were consolidated here by royal decree. Most shops sell all the popular Okinawan ceramics including *shiisā* (lion-dog roof guardians) and containers for serving *awamori,* the local firewater.

In the neighbourhood is the worthwhile **Tsuboya Pottery Museum** (Map p752; ☎ 862-3761; 1-9-32 Tsuboya; admission ¥300; ☿ 10am-6pm Tue-Sun), which contains some truly exquisite masterpieces. Here, you can also inspect potters' wheels and appreciate *arayachi* (unglazed) and *jōyachi* (glazed) pieces.

At the eastern end of Kokusai-dōri, a left turn will take you to the reconstructed gates of **Sōgen-ji** (Map p752). The original stone gates once led to the 16th-century temple of the Ryūkyū kings, though it was unfortunately destroyed in WWII.

On the north side of Tomari port is the fascinating **international cemetery** (Map p752), which has a small monument commemorating Commodore Perry's 1852 landing in Naha. The US naval officer subsequently used Okinawa as a base while he forced the Tokugawa shōgunate to finally open Japanese ports to the West.

Garden fans should take a stroll through Chinese-style **Fukushū-en** (Map p752; ☎ 869-5384; 2-29 Kume; admission free; ☿ 9am-6pm Thu-Tue). All materials were brought from Fuzhou, Naha's sister city in China, including the pagoda that sits atop a small waterfall.

Nami-no-ue beach (Map p752; ☿ 9am-6pm), near the **Naminoue-gu shrine**, is a small city beach where you can relax without leaving town. It comes complete with lifeguards, jellyfish/shark nets, showers and toilets.

There are countless small karate training places around Naha. For more information, see boxed text (p757).

Shuri Area 首里

Shuri was the original capital of Okinawa, though the title was surrendered to Naha in 1879 just prior to the Meiji Restoration. Shuri's temples, shrines, tombs and castle were all destroyed in WWII, although some impressive reconstructions and repairs, with meticulous attention to detail, have been made. To reach the complex, take the Yui-rail monorail to its eastern terminal, Shuri station.

The reconstructed old residence of the Okinawan royal family, **Shurijō-kōen** (首里城公園; Map p752; ☎ 886-2020; www.shurijo-park.go.jp/index_e.html; admission ¥800; ☿ 9am-5.30pm Mar-Nov, 9am-5pm Dec-Feb), is well worth a visit. There is an excellent brochure in English highlighting the attractions.

The castle's walls have numerous gates, but the pick is the Chinese-influenced **Shurei-no-mon** (首里の門) which appears on Japan's ¥2000 banknote. As the ceremonial entrance to the castle, the gate was originally constructed some 500 years ago, though it was completely rebuilt in 1958. Today, it's considered to be *the* symbol of Okinawa.

Also on the grounds is the modest **Okinawa Prefectural Museum** (沖縄県立博物館; Map p752; ☎ 884-2243; 1-1 Ōnaka-chō; admission ¥200; ☿ 9am-5pm Tue-Sun), which has a number of interesting displays on Okinawan lifestyle, history, culture and natural environment.

Around Naha 那覇周辺

Around 1.6km east of the city is the **Shikina-en** (識名園; ☎ 855-5936; admission ¥300; ☿ 9am-5pm Thu-Tue), a Chinese-style garden containing stone bridges, a viewing pavilion and a villa that belonged to the Ryūkyū royal family. Despite its flawless appearance, everything had to be painstakingly rebuilt after WWII. To reach the garden, take bus 1 or 5 to the Shikinaen-mae stop (¥400, 20 minutes).

A three-minute walk from Akamine monorail station (follow the English signs) is the **Naha**

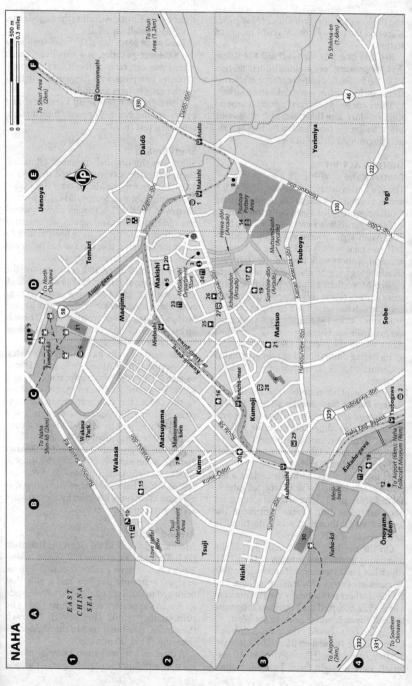

NAHA

Folkcraft Museum (那覇市伝統工芸館; ☎ 858-6655; 1-83-1 Bannari; admission ¥300; ☻ 9am-5.30pm Wed-Mon), which houses a detailed collection of traditional Okinawan crafts. Staff members are on hand to demonstrate glass-blowing, weaving and pottery-making in the workshops.

FESTIVALS & EVENTS
Dragon-boat races are held in early May, particularly in Itoman and Naha. With Chinese origins dating back several centuries, these races – called *hari* – bless the luck and prosperity of fishing families.

In October, the **Dai-Ryūkyū Matsuri** (大琉球祭り) brings together more than a dozen festivals and special events celebrating Okinawan culture. The **Tsunahiki Matsuri** (綱引き祭り) takes place in Naha on the 10th, and features large teams that compete in the world's biggest tug-of-war, using a gigantic 1m-thick rope weighing over 40 tonnes.

SLEEPING
Naha is the most convenient base for exploring Okinawa-hontō – not surprisingly, the island's accommodation options are concentrated in the city centre. In the busy summer season, a number of city residents run informal guesthouses (look for flyers inside the ferry terminal and in the airport). The following places are on Map p752.

Base Okinawa (☎ 868-2968; www.baseokinawa.net /en/index.html; 1-17-5 Wakasa; dm ¥1000, r per person ¥3000; P ⌘ ▣) Housed in a bright pink building (look for the English sign) next to Asahigaoka Park, Base Okinawa is most likely the island's cheapest guesthouse. However, this is our top choice as spick-and-span dorms and modest Japanese-style rooms are centred on two funky chill-out room where all sorts of interesting characters congregate. Guests can also take advantage of the roof-lounge as well as the free bikes, free laundry, free internet, free snorkel gear, free fishing rods, etc (the list goes on and on). Discounted weekly and monthly rates are available.

Kashiwaya (☎ 869-8833; www.88smile.com/kasiwaya; 2-12-22 Wakasa; dm ¥1500, r per person ¥3000; P ⌘ ▣) Conveniently located just off Kokusai-dōri and right behind the Kōsetsu Market, this quaint, cosy guesthouse has simple but airy dorms and Western-style private rooms. The real appeal, however, is its central location and laid-back atmosphere – check out the tatami chill-out room complete with mounted guitars and *sanshin* (an Okinawan traditional stringed instrument). Discounted weekly and monthly rates are available.

Ukishima Towns Ryokan (☎ 869-1010; fax 869-5059; www.shinkin-1.net in Japanese; 2-12-7 Matsuo; r per person with/without bathroom ¥3500/3000; P ⌘) Just off Kokusai-dōri, above an African-themed café and pub, this popular ryokan is housed in a converted apartment building, and offers a mix of clean and comfortable Western- and Japanese-style rooms. This is a good choice if you're looking for a bit of privacy, or if you're travelling in a large group as the bigger apartments can take up to 10 guests.

Okinawa International Youth Hostel (☎ 857-0073; www.jyh.gr.jp/okinawa/english.htm; 51 Ōnoyama; dm ¥3150; P ⌘ ▣) Located in Ōnoyama-kōen, a five-

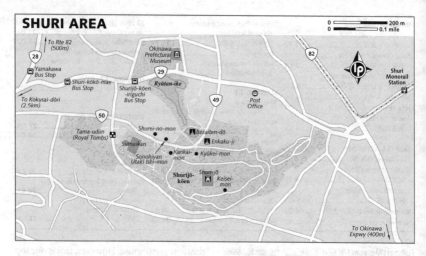

SHURI AREA

minute walk from the Tsubogawa monorail stations, the island's youth hostel is more along the lines of a deluxe backpacker resort. Although it's definitely pricier than other budget options, dorms here are absolutely spotless, and there are some nice added perks including an on-site *onsen*, rooftop lounge and 24-hour key-card access.

Tōyoko Inn Naha Izumisaki Kōsaten (☎ 951-1045; www.toyoko-inn.com/hotel/00076/in Japanese; 2-1-20 Kume; s/d from ¥5500/7500; P X ☒) Just a short walk north of Kokusai-dōri, this newish hotel in the reputable chain of Tōyoko business hotels is a good choice if you're a fan of your creature comforts. Western-style rooms are well-decorated with modern furnishings, and the rooms on the higher floors boast impressive views of the downtown action.

Hotel Sun Palace (☎ 863-4181; www.palace-okinawa .com in Japanese; 2-5-1 Kumoji; s/d from ¥7500/9500; P X ☒) Overlooking a canal just north of the Palette Kumoji building, the Hotel Sun Palace is one of the nicest city-centre business hotels. Standard Western-style rooms are transformed into something special with the addition of landscaped balconies – the perfect spot to watch the sunset while sipping a cold Orion lager. The Sun Palace also has an excellent offering of on-site bars and restaurants.

EATING

Naha is the perfect spot to sample the full range of Okinawan classics. For a quick rundown of what's cooking, see boxed text (p769). The following places are on Map p752.

If you're looking for cheap eats, try browsing along the shopping arcade Heiwa-dōri, where you can buy anything from fresh seafood to *andagi* (Okinawan deep-fried doughnuts).

Unlike other islands in the Nansei-shotō, the presence of American GIs on Okinawa-hontō means that most restaurants will have at least one staff member who can speak English. Likewise, the vast majority of restaurants will offer English menus to foreign guests.

Daitō Soba (☎ 867-3889; 1-4-59 Makishi; ⏱ 11am-10pm; E) This dinky little noodle house is the perfect spot for sampling your first bowl of *okinawa-soba* (Okinawan-style noodles; ¥450). We like ours with extra *shima-tōgarashi* (pickled hot peppers in sesame oil). It's one block north of Kokusai-dōri on Midori-ga-oka Park (look for the red banners and plastic food models).

Asian Dining (☎ 859-6530; 50 Ōnoyama; ⏱ 5pm-3am; E) Sure, it's a bit tacky, but there is definite novelty value in eating dinner at the top of a three-storey plastic banyan tree, and the views of the nearby port aren't too shabby. The speciality of the house is Southeast Asian cuisine, though there's also a good offering of Okinawan specialities and other Japanese fare. The tree (which isn't too hard to miss) is right around the corner from the Okinawa International Youth Hostel.

Yakiniku Station Bambohe (☎ 861-4129; 1-3-47 Makishi; ⏱ 11am-11pm; E) If you've got a big appetite and quantity is important, head here where an all-you-can-eat *yakiniku* (grilled meat over table-top hibachi grills), including dessert and soft drinks, will only set you back ¥2000. The restaurant is just off of Kokusai-dōri, across from the covered arcades, and is easily recognised by its bright yellow English sign.

DRINKING & ENTERTAINMENT

There is no shortage of drinking and dancing establishments on and around Kokusai-dōri. It seems every little side street harbours a couple of hidden-away drinking spots. The following places are on Map p752.

China (☎ 861-8451; 1-1-9 Makishi; ☉ 5pm-3am; E) This hip *izakaya* offers a great deal – for the first 45 minutes, frosty Orion beers and *awamori* cost ¥100 assuming you order one food plate per person. With the full range of Okinawan delicacies on offer, you shouldn't have too many problems choosing what to eat. China is 100m off Kokusai-dōri on Ichigin-dōri – look for the English sign and hanging red flags.

Helios (☎ 863-7227; 1-3-24 Makishi; drinks from ¥450; ☉ 5-11pm; E) If you have a discerning palette, head straight for this Kokusai-dōri drinking establishment (look for the plastic beer models outside). Although there's nothing wrong with Orion lager, it's got nothing on the expertly crafted microbrews on tap here.

Chakura (☎ 869-0283; 1-2-1 Makishi; cover ¥3000; ☉ 7pm-1am) In the heart of Kokusai-dōri, Chakura is a celebrated 'live house' run by local music maverick Kina Shōkichi. Kina-san and his band, Champloose, perform here nightly (when not touring), starting at 8pm. Although there is a small English sign, Chakura is fairly nondescript, though it's famous enough that most locals can point it out to you if you're having problems finding it.

Club Cielo (☎ 861-9955; 1-1-1 Ryubo; cover ¥3000; ☉ 11pm-late; E) Smart and sophisticated, Club Cielo is one of the hottest spots in downtown Naha. Although it's going to be a pricey night out, this is a good choice for top-quality music ranging from the latest in American hip-hop to the hottest Euro-electronica tracks. The club is on the 6F across the street from the Okinawan Prefectural Assembly Hall.

SHOPPING

The Japanese love of *omiyage* (souvenirs) is evident the moment you set foot on Kokusai-dōri – whether you're looking for a Hello Kitty beach towel or a plastic habu (see p760) for the kids, chances are you'll walk away with something.

Kitschy tourist junk aside, Okinawa is renowned for its colourful Ryūkyū glassware, a relatively modern folk art that originated after WWII by recycling soda pop and juice bottles used by US occupation forces. Okinawa also has its own distinctive textiles, particularly the brightly coloured *bingata* and *ryūsen* fabrics.

Much of the Tsuboya pottery is in the form of storage vessels, but look for *shiisā*, the guardian lion-dog figures that can be seen perched on the rooftops of many traditional Okinawan buildings.

GETTING THERE & AWAY
Air

There are direct flights operating into Naha's airport from 20 Japanese mainland cities as

---

DIVING ON OKINAWA-HONTŌ

Okinawa's most famous dive spot is the wreck of the **USS Emmons** (Map p750), a US Navy Gleaves-class destroyer that sunk in 1944 around 1km off Kouri-jima, a small island lying northeast of the Motobu Peninsula. Divers can make out the hulk from the depth of 25m, though strong currents, low visibility and the presence of unexploded ordinance make this a challenging dive.

Another popular spot is **Maeda Point** (Map p750), off Cape Maeda, which has a drop-off wall that attracts numerous species of tropical fish including batfish, parrotfish, barracudas and clown-fish. For more advanced divers, **Zampa Point** (Map p750), near Zampa Cape, features a huge wall that bottoms out at more than 90m. Be advised, however, that currents can really pick up here.

Although there's no shortage of dive operators on the island, two foreign-owned, English-speaking dive shops are **Reef Encounters** (リーフエンカウンター; ☎ 098-968-4442; www .reefencounters.org) and **IANTD Okinawa** (IANTD 沖縄; ☎ 090-7585-2348; www.iantdokinawa.com). Both shops are in Naha's suburban sprawl and are difficult to find – if you phone ahead, they can arrange a pick-up from your accommodation.

For a quick crash course on scuba diving in Okinawa and the Southwest Islands, see p739.

well as from Seoul, Manila, Shanghai and Taipei. Since Naha serves as the principal transport hub in the Nansei-shotō, flights depart to the major Japanese cities virtually every hour.

Fares are dependent on availability and seasonality – as a general rule, prices are the highest in the summer months, and you can save a considerable amount of money if you book two weeks prior to your flight. Flights to the mainland range from ¥15,000 to ¥40,000 while inter-island flights are typically ¥10,000 to ¥20,000.

Boat

Various operators have ferry services to Naha from Tokyo, Nagoya, Osaka, Kōbe, Kagoshima and other ports. The schedules are complex (and subject to weather delays), and there is a wide range of fares that vary according to season and availability. Check out **Ōshima Unyu** (☎ Tokyo 03-5643-6170, Kagoshima 099-222-2338; www.minc.ne.jp/aline in Japanese) as well as boxed text (p744).

Long-distance ferries run to/from Miyako-jima (¥4250, nine hours) and to/from Ishi-gaki-jima (¥5350, 14 hours). Note that these services are not daily, and travel times vary depending on the season and the weather. Ferries are culled in the winter months and cut completely at the first sign of bad weather. Call **Arimura Sangyō** (☎ in Japan 869-1980, in Taiwan 07-330-9811) for weekly schedules.

Arimura Sangyō operates a weekly ferry service between Naha and Taiwan, sometimes via Ishigaki and Miyako in Okinawa-ken. The Taiwan port alternates between Keelung and Kaohsiung. Departure from Okinawa is on Thursday or Friday; departure from Taiwan is usually on Monday (2nd class one way ¥15,200/4235TWD, 20 hours).

Naha is also the hub for ferries to other islands in the Okinawa-shotō – for more information, see p759.

There are three ports in Naha, and this can be confusing. From Naha-kō (Naha Port; Map p752), ferries head north to Fukuoka/Hakata and Kagoshima, while Naha Shin-kō (Naha New Port) has ferries to Nagoya, Kōbe, Osaka and Tokyo. Ferries to Taiwan, Miyako-jima and Ishigaki-jima may depart from either place. From Tomari-kō (Tomari Port; Map p752) on Rte 58, ferries operate to a number of the smaller islands around Okinawa-hontō, including Kume-jima, Zamami-jima and Aka-

jima. Naha's ferry terminals can be easily accessed by the monorail or bus (see below).

GETTING AROUND

Naha's impressive new Yui-rail monorail makes things easy for getting around Naha. At one end of the line is Naha airport, at the other end, Shuri. The prices range from ¥200 to ¥290 depending on how far you go. Kenchō-mae station is at the western end of Kokusai-dōri, while Makishi station is at its eastern end.

Naha-kō is a 10-minute walk from Asahi-bashi station, while Tomari-kō is a similar distance north from Miebashi station. Bus No 101 from Naha bus terminal heads further north to Naha Shin-kō (20 minutes, hourly).

When riding on local town buses, simply dump ¥200 into the slot next to the driver as you enter. For longer trips, collect a ticket showing your starting point as you board and pay the appropriate fare as you disembark. Buses run from Naha to destinations all over the island.

Okinawa-hontō is a good place to get around in a rented vehicle, although traffic can be heavy. Numerous car hire agencies around Naha charge from around ¥5000 per day. Ask at hotels, guesthouses or youth hostels about hiring bicycles, scooters or motorcycles.

Southern Okinawa-hontō
沖縄本島の南部

During the closing days of the Battle of Okinawa, the southern part of the island bore the brunt of the American 'typhoon of steel'. Although southern Okinawa-hontō is now a heavily populated residential area, there are some striking reminders of those terrible days.

Note that this section of the island is best visited as a day trip from Naha.

The **Memorial Peace Park** (☾ dusk-dawn), on the southern coast of the island, is a sobering tribute that should not be missed – a reflective stroll through the park reveals war memorials from every prefecture in Japan. The centrepiece of the park is the **Okinawa Peace Memorial Museum** (Map p750; ☎ 997-3844; admission ¥300; ☾ 9am-4.30pm Tue-Sun), which focuses on the Okinawan suffering at the hands of both the Japanese military and subsequent US occupation authorities. Also of interest is the **Cornerstone of Peace** (Map p750; ☉ dusk-dawn), which is inscribed with the names of everyone who died in the Battle of Okinawa, controversially listing Okinawan civilians and foreign military personnel right alongside Japanese military commanders. To reach the park, take bus 32, 33, 46 or 89 from Naha bus terminal to Itoman (¥500, one hour, hourly), from where you transfer to bus 82, which goes to Heiwa Kinen-kōen (¥400, 25 minutes, hourly).

Directly south of Naha in Kaigungo-kōen is the **Underground Naval Headquarters** (Map p750; ☎ 850-4055; admission ¥450; ☉ 8.30am-5pm) where 4000 men committed suicide as the battle for Okinawa drew to its prolonged and bloody conclusion. Only 250m of the tunnels are open, but you can wander through the maze of corridors, see the commander's final words on the wall of his room and inspect the holes and scars in other walls from the grenade blasts that killed many of the men. To reach the sight, take bus 33, 46 or 101 from Naha bus station to the Tomigusuku-kōen-mae stop (¥230, 20 minutes, hourly). From there it's a 10-minute walk – follow the English signs.

Central Okinawa-hontō 沖縄本島の中部

This heavily populated stretch, which is home to the island's American military bases, is centred on **Okinawa City** (沖縄市). Just a village before the war, Okinawa has mushroomed to a town of more than 120,000 people, and has all the hallmarks of US influence from pizzerias to army surplus stores. The area is also home to an amazing number of artificial tourist attractions where thousands of

---

OKINAWA: THE HOME OF KARATE

During the 'golden era' of King Sho Shin-O (1477–1526), when trade and culture flourished with China, a law was passed that banned the carrying of weapons in the Ryūkyū kingdom. A century later in 1609, when the Shimazu from Satsuma (now called Kagoshima) on Kyūshū invaded, the weapon less locals could not defend themselves against a well-armed adversary and were conquered easily. The Shimazu exploited the Ryūkyūs greedily and strictly enforced the edict of no weapons for the next 250 years. It was during this period that the *te,* or unarmed fighting techniques of the native Ryūkyūans, began to be developed and refined in secrecy.

As the Shimazu kept up trade with China under the front of the Ryūkyū kingdom, many traders and sailors from China settled in Naha, including many Chinese martial arts exponents. Local *te* practitioners had the chance to practise with, and learn from these people. Later, Okinawans headed to China to study the Chinese fighting arts. The celebrated Higaonna Kanryō and then his successor and top student Miyagi Chōjun spent time studying in Fuzhou in southern China in the late 1800s and early 1900s.

What we now know as the martial art of karate is a mixture of traditional Okinawan *te* and techniques introduced from China. While the original characters for *karate* meant 'Chinese hand', when the martial art was introduced to mainland Japan in the 1920s, the characters 空手 (meaning 'empty hand') were used.

In the years before WWII, karate gained increasing popularity on mainland Japan. After the war, occupying troops took the martial art home to America with them. Hollywood became involved and karate's popularity spread around the globe.

Traditional training continues in Okinawa. There are many styles and countless small *dōjō* (training places) around Naha. The **Okinawa Prefectural Budōkan** (沖縄県立武道館; Martial Arts Hall; Map p752; ☎ 858-2700; 52 Okutakeyama; ☉ 9am-9pm) is a stunning architectural masterpiece in Onoyama Kōen in Naha. It has three floors of training rooms for all martial arts, not only karate, and welcomes visitors. It is a five-minute walk from the monorail's Tsubogawa station.

One style that has become truly international is Okinawa Goju-Ryu. The **Okinawan International Goju-Ryu Karate Federation** (IOGKF; www.iogkf.com) has 45 member countries and is based in Naha. In July 2004 its World Budosai event attracted 750 karate practitioners from 35 countries to Naha for a week. The IOGKF is headed by Higaonna Morio Sensei, who also runs the **Higaonna Karate Dōjō** (東恩空手道上; Map p752; ☎ 864-1673; 65 Makishi; ☉ 8pm-late Mon-Sat). From the monorail's Asato station, walk south on Himeyuri-dōri. After the monorail curves away to the right you'll see a sign for the Higaonna Dōjō just before the Esso gas station on the right-hand side of the road.

yen could easily be squandered on entry fees. While there are a few interesting attractions, you will have to search them out.

Note that this section of the island is best visited as a day trip from Naha or from the Motobu Peninsula (below).

On the east coast of the island and just south of Okinawa City are the castle ruins of **Nakagusuku-jō** (Map p750; ☎ 895-5719; admission ¥300; ◷ 8.30am-5pm). Commanding an enviable position overlooking the coast, Nakagusuku-jō predated stone construction of this type on the mainland by at least 80 years. Although the castle was destroyed in 1458, the remaining foundation hints at its former grandeur. A 10-minute walk uphill is **Nakamura-ke** (Map p750; ☎ 935-3500; admission ¥300; ◷ 9am-5.30pm), which is probably the best-preserved traditional Okinawan house on the island. Although the Nakamura family's origins in the area can be traced back to the 15th century, the foundation dates from around 1720. Notice the substantial stone pigsties, the elevated storage area to deter rats and the trees grown as typhoon windbreaks. Both sights are a 10-minute taxi ride from Futenma, which can be accessed via bus 25 from Naha (¥500, one hour, hourly).

Two-thirds of the way up the island is the city of **Nago** (名護), which serves as the junction town for buses to the Motobu Peninsula, and is home to a few interesting sights. The city is centred on a fine old banyan tree, Himpun Gajumara, which is a useful landmark. The small **Nago Museum** (名護博物館; ☎ 0980-53-1342; 2-11 Tōedo; admission ¥150; ◷ 10am-6pm Tue-Sun), south of the banyan tree, has some interesting old photographs of traditional *hejichi* (women's tattooing). Next door is the **Orion Brewery** (オリオンビール名護工場; ☎ 0980-52-2137; 2-12 Tōedo; admission free; ◷ 9-11am & 1-4pm Mon-Fri), which offers tours and tastings of Okinawa's much loved brew. Nago is best accessed by the direct express bus from Naha (¥2000, two hours, hourly). Buses 66 and 65 run anticlockwise and clockwise respectively around the Motobu peninsula.

Motobu-hantō 本部半島

Jutting out to the northwest of Nago, hilly Motobu-hantō is home to some of the most attractive stretches on the island, mainly because it's nowhere near as densely populated as the central and southern regions. Motobu-hantō also serves as the jumping-off point for

Okinawa's rugged northern region and for several nearby islets.

SIGHTS
Offshore Islands
Sesoko-jima (瀬底島), which is connected to the peninsula by a 762m bridge south of Motobu, has good beaches and well-developed free camping facilities. The island is famous for its tasty watermelons, which are available from May to September in small stalls. While Okinawa is known for its bovine sumō, Sesoko-jima has its own local goat sumō version that can be seen in May and November.

Tiny **Minna-jima** (水納島), just 15 minutes from Motobu town by ferry, is riddled with fabulous beaches and snorkelling spots, and is popular as a day trip. The **Minna Kaiun** (☎ 47-5179) ferry service (round trip ¥1600, three to eight daily) pulls in right beside the main beach, which is well developed for day-trippers, and has toilets, showers and food stalls.

The **Ie-jima Sonei** (☎ 49-2255) ferry will take you to the popular offshore island of **Ie-jima** (伊江島) from Motobu-kō (¥580, 30 minutes), 1.5km south of Motobu town. Ie-jima's main attraction is the wonderful view from the top of **Gusuku-yama** (172m), which is a straightforward 45-minute walk from the ferry. Around 10 minutes' walk west of the pier is a **monument** (Map p750) to the US war correspondent Ernie Pyle, who was killed on the island during the early days of the Battle of Okinawa. Buses around the 8km-by-3km island are irregular, though bicycles and scooters can be rented at the pier. There are also two ferries a day from Naha's **Tomari-kō** (Asahi Kankō; ☎ 868-1174) in summer (¥3400, 1¼ hours).

Other Sights
A couple of kilometres north of Motobu town is the **Ocean Expo Park** (Map p750; ☎ 48-3748; admission free; ◷ 9.30am-7pm Fri-Wed Jun-Aug, 9.30am-5.30pm Fri-Wed Sep-May), which was the site of the 1975 International Ocean Exposition. Worthwhile sights in the park include the 10,000-tonne **aquarium** (admission ¥1800), home to an enormous whale shark; the **Oceanic Culture Museum** (admission ¥170), which displays cultural artefacts drawn from all over Polynesia, Melanesia, Micronesia and Southeast Asia; and a **Native Okinawan Village** (admission free), with traditional houses and indigenous plants. This park also boasts the lovely **Emerald Beach** (Map p750), which is a

popular weekend destination for Okinawan families looking for a little fun under the sun. From Nago, bus 70 runs directly to the park (¥800, 45 minutes). Both peninsula loop lines (buses 65 and 66) stop outside.

Set back from the peninsula's north coast and winding over a hilltop, the 14th-century walls of **Nakijin-jō** (Map p750; ☎ 56-4400; admission ¥150; 8.30am-5.30pm) look especially wonderful when the cherry trees bloom. The ruins were once visited by Commodore Perry, who compared its stone gate to ancient Egyptian architecture. In the past, this was the head castle of the unruly Hokuzan kings, and contained shrines and sacred houses for *noro* (hereditary priestesses). From the summit of the hill, there are superb views out to sea. Both peninsula loop lines (buses 65 and 66) stop outside.

SLEEPING

There are several free camp sites located on Minna-jima, Ie-jima and Sesoko-jima.

On the Beach LUE (Map p750; ☎ 47-3535; www .luenet.com in Japanese; 26-26-1 Motobu; s/tw/condos from ¥5000/8000/12,000; P) This positively adorable beach-side hotel, just a few kilometres south of the bridge to Sesoko-jima, offers a variety of bright, sunny Western-style rooms that all overlook the beach. If you're travelling in a group of three to four people, the detached condos are an excellent deal, especially since they feature well-stocked kitchens. The hotel also has an on-site dive shop and a laid-back beachfront restaurant that serves Western-style fast food and Okinawan seafood cuisine (meals from ¥500). The restaurant is open from 11.30am to 9pm.

Minshuku Minami (Map p750; ☎ 49-2910; fax 49-2910; r per person with meals ¥5500;) If you're planning to spend the night on Ie-jima, this low-key family-run *minshuku* is conveniently located next to the ferry port. Accommodation is in surprisingly spacious Japanese-style tatami rooms with shared facilities, and there's a good chance that the area's famous seafood will appear on the dinner table.

GETTING THERE & AROUND

Motobu-hantō is served by frequent loop lines from Nago – buses 66 and 65 respectively run anticlockwise and clockwise around the peninsula.

From Unten-kō (Unten Port; Map p750), ferries depart for the offshore islands of Iheya-jima and Izena-jima (p761).

If you rented a car in Naha, and managed to emerge unscathed from the congestion of southern and central Okinawa-hontō, Motobu-hantō is a great place to explore via your own set of wheels.

Northern Okinawa-hontō
沖縄本島の北部

The northern part of Okinawa-hontō is largely undeveloped and comparatively wild and rugged. Because of its hilly terrain, thousands of Okinawan families escaped the obliteration in the south of the island at the end of WWII by hiding out here.

Note that this section of the island is best visited as a day trip from Naha or from the Motobu Peninsula. Since there is no public transportation in the north, you will need a rental car – there is some seriously scenic driving to be had up here.

A narrow road hugs the west coast all the way up to **Cape Hedo** (辺戸岬), which marks the northern end of Okinawa. The point is an incredibly scenic spot backed by hills, with rocks rising from the dense greenery. On a good day, Yoron-tō, the southernmost island in the Amami-shotō, is easily seen only 28km to the northeast. From Cape Hedo, the road wraps around the tip of the island and heads down the east coast. For the next stretch of the drive, the road skirts alongside several fine-looking sandy beaches, though be advised that there are strong currents and rips here. The road then turns inland, though it seems to take forever to get back to what passes as a town – the contrast with southern Okinawa-hontō could not be more extreme.

Islands around Okinawa-hontō

The outer islands of the Okinawa-shotō are a world away from the hustle and bustle of the main island. Life is more relaxed, there is still evidence of traditional Ryūkyū culture and you won't be consistently bombarded with signs of Americana. The islands around Okinawa also offer superb white sand beaches, clear emerald seas and excellent diving and snorkelling.

The closest islands to Okinawa-hontō are the **Kerama-rettō** (慶良間列島), which are just 30km offshore from Naha, and include the main islands of Zamami-jima, Aka-jima and Tokashiki-jima. The Kerama-rettō, particularly Zamami-jima, are a popular destination

---

HABU SNAKES

Any discussion of the Nansei-shotō eventually gets around to 'deadly' habu snakes. Perhaps it's a reflection of Japan's severe shortage of real dangers, but you could easily get the impression that the poor habu, a species of pit viper, is the world's most dangerous snake, and that there's one waiting behind every tree, shrub, bush and bar stool on the islands. They're hardly so prolific – the most likely place to see one is at a mongoose-versus-habu fight put on for tourists, or floating in a jar of very expensive (and slightly poisonous) sake.

Nevertheless, they are venomous! It's not a good idea to go barefoot when stomping through the bushes, though you should stomp – the vibrations will scare any snakes away. If you do get bitten, take it seriously and seek immediate medical advice as fatalities (though rare) can occur if antivenin is not administered.

---

for Japanese day-trippers who visit from Naha, though you'll appreciate the islands more if you spend the night.

Usually thought of as a pair, Iheya-jima and Izena-jima are 20km offshore to the northwest of Okinawa-hontō, and are the northernmost islands in Okinawa prefecture. Because they are accessed from Unten-kō on the northern side of the Motobu-hantō, Iheya-jima and Izena-jima are not as popular as the Kerama-rettō, though the island pair is a spectacular destination for hikers.

Ninety kilometres to the west of Okinawa-hontō, Kume-jima is the largest of the offshore islands, and perhaps the most popular destination in the outer islands. Although the island is most often accessed from Naha, there are direct flights to Kume-jima from Tokyo during the busy summer months.

ZAMAMI-JIMA 座間味島
☎ 098 / pop 1050

Zamami-jima has a deserved reputation as an island paradise with some of the clearest waters you will ever see – not surprisingly, the diving and snorkelling here is tops. However, most visitors to Zamami are happy to stay on the boat and keep an eye out for humpback whales, which have returned to the waters in recent years. If you only have time to visit one of the islands in the Kerama-rettō, this is definitely the one.

There is a **tourist information office** (☎ 987-2277; ☯ 8.30am-5.30pm) at the port. More information in Japanese is available at www.vill .zamami.okinawa.jp.

Furuzamami Beach (古座間味島ビーチ), approximately 1km east from the port, is a stunning stretch of white sand that is fronted by clear waters full of bright coral heads. The beach is also well developed for day-trippers,

and has toilets, showers and food stalls. You can also rent snorkelling gear here (¥1000).

Whale-watching is possible between the months of January and March. For more information, either inquire at the tourist information office or call the **whale-watching office** (☎ 896-4141). Tours run once or twice a day, last about two hours and cost ¥5000.

Natureland Kayaks (ネイチャーランドカヤク; ☎ 987-2187), a three-minute walk from the Zamami port (follow the English signs), operates excellent sea kayak trips. Day trips with everything included cost ¥11,000 and half-day trips ¥7000.

Small fishing boats can also be chartered at the port for a negotiable price (from ¥1000) to take you out to the smaller, uninhabited islands.

The waters around Zamami are home to an impressive number of hard coral heads that are teeming with tropical reef fish. Although there's no shortage of dive shops on the island, a recommended operator is **Joy Joy** (☎ 987-2445), which is run out of the *minshuku* of the same name.

Zamami-jima makes a great day trip from Naha, though you'll escape the crowds and mellow out a bit more if you stay on the island for two days. A good spot to call home for the night is **Joy Joy** (ジョイジョイ; ☎ 987-2445; r per person with meals ¥5500; ☒) in the northwest corner of the village – if you phone ahead, the staff will pick you up from the ferry terminal. Accommodation is in simple Japanese-style tatami rooms that surround a small garden, though the real appeal of staying here is the on-site dive shop.

RAC, part of the JAL network, has one flight a day from Naha to the Kerama Airport (from ¥7000, 20 minutes), which is on Fukachi-jima, south of Aka-jima. There are boat connections to Zamami-jima from the airport. **Zamami Sonei** (☎ 098-868-4567) has two or three fast ferries a day (¥2750, 50 minutes) and one regular ferry (¥1860, 1¾ hours) from Naha's Tomari-kō.

There are no buses or taxis on Zamami-jima, though nothing is too far away. Rental cars, scooters and bicycles are readily available all over the main town.

TOKASHIKI-JIMA 渡嘉敷島
☎ 098 / pop 750

The largest island of the Kerama-rettō is Tokashiki-jima, a long, skinny, north–south standing island that is famous for its outstanding beaches. Tokashiki is also the closest island in the group to Okinawa-hontō, and predominantly caters to beach-loving day-trippers.

Ferries arrive at the port of Tokashiki (渡嘉敷) on the east coast. For more information on the island, check out www.vill.tokashiki .okinawa.jp in Japanese.

The island's most attractive strips of sand are **Tokashiku Beach** (とかしくビーチ) and **Aharen Beach** (阿波連ビーチ), both of which are located on the west coast, and just a few minutes by bus from the port. Aharen is particularly good for snorkelling, while Tokashiku is predominantly a swimming beach. As with Zamami, both beaches are well developed for tourism, and have toilets, showers, food stalls and shops where you can rent snorkelling gear (¥1000).

A popular activity for Japanese tourists is a 40-minute ride on the **Yellow Submarine** (☎ 987-2010; ¥2000), which runs from Aharen Beach. Actually, it's not really a submarine but rather a glass-bottom boat, though you'll still get to see a good variety of coral heads and reef fish.

Tokashiki is an easy day trip from Naha, though Aharen has a relaxed beach scene at night that's worth checking out. Practically on the beach is the **Pension Southern Cross** (ペンションサザンクロス; ☎ 987-2258; r per person with/without meals ¥6500/4000; 🅿), a completely chilled-out family-run inn where it's easy to slow down for a bit and soak up the ambience. Accommodation is in a mix of breezy Western- and Japanese-style rooms, the majority of which have great ocean views.

Only 35 minutes from Naha by fast ferry, Tokashiki-jima is an ideal day trip from Naha. **Tokashiki Sonei** (☎ 098-987-2537) operates two fast ferries a day (¥2210, 35 minutes) and

one regular ferry (¥1470, one hour 10 minutes) from Naha's Tomari-kō.

There is a bus network that runs from Tokashiki to the beaches, though it's a beautiful island to cycle around. Bicycles, cars and scooter, are available all over town.

AKA-JIMA 阿嘉島
☎ 098 / pop 330

Only a couple of kilometres south of Zamami-jima, Aka-jima is a largely undeveloped island of rugged hills and a rocky coastline that sees few visitors. However, Aka is a good destination for divers, and it's certainly one of the quietest islands in the Kerama-rettō.

If you keep your eyes open around dusk you might spot a **Kerama deer** (慶良間シカ), descendants of deer that were brought by the Satsuma from Kagoshima when they conquered the Ryūkyūs in 1609. The deer are smaller and darker than their mainland cousins, and have been designated a national treasure.

The best beach on the island is **Nishibama** (ニシバマビーチ), which has fine yellow sand and is located on the east coast. However, if you're after beaches, you're better off heading to Zamami-jima or Tokashiki-jima.

Pension Shiisa (ペンションシーサー; ☎ 987-2973; www.seasir.com in Japanese; r per person with meals ¥6500; 🅿) is a popular dive-and-stay operation that will pick you up at the ferry terminal. Accommodation is in basic Japanese-style tatami rooms, and the owner is a wealth of information on the local diving scene.

RAC, part of the JAL network, has one flight a day from Naha to the Kerama Airport (from ¥7000, 20 minutes), which is on Fukachi-jima, south of Aka-jima. There are bus connections from the airport to Aka-jima along the inter-island bridge.

Zamami Sonei (☎ 098-868-4567) has two or three fast ferries a day (¥2750, 50 minutes) and one regular ferry (¥1860, 1¾ hours) from Naha's Tomari-kō. These ferries stop at Aka-jima either before or after docking at Zamamji-jima.

There are no buses or taxis on Aka-jima, though nothing is too far away. Rental cars, scooters and bicycles are readily available all over the main town.

IHEYA-JIMA & IZENA-JIMA
伊平屋島・伊是名島
☎ 0980 / pop 1600 & 1900

The island pair of Iheya-jima and Izena-jima complement one another with a good blend of sandy beaches, unique natural attractions and ample opportunities for hiking and camping. However, since the islands are accessed from Unten-kō in Motobu-hantō (p759) instead of from Naha, they see significantly fewer travellers than the Kerama-rettō.

Iheya-jima, to the north, is long and skinny, while Izena-jima, 5km to the south, is shaped more like a ball. Ferries arrive in Iheya-jima at Mae-domari (前泊) while ferries arrive in Izena-jima at Nakata (中田). For information in Japanese, look up www.vill.iheya.okinawa .jp and www.izena-okinawa.jp.

Hillier than its southern neighbour, with five 'mountains' over 200m along its spine, Iheya-jima has some impressive natural assets. For excellent views, you can climb **Torazu-iwa** (虎頭岩; Tiger's Head Rock), the landmark that guards Mae-domari harbour. At the northern end of the island, **Kumaya Dōkutsu** (クマヤ洞窟) is a huge natural cavern nearly 50m deep and 15m tall at its highest point. Next door is the free Kumaya camping ground, which has basic facilities. A couple of kilometres south, **Nentōhiramatsu** (念願平松) is a 300-year-old pine tree that has been trained to look like an umbrella. At the southern tip of Iheya-jima is the island's top beach, **Yonesaki Beach** (米崎ビーチ), an attractive wilderness beach that also has a free camping area.

Izena-jima has historical links to the Ryūkyū rulers – check out the island's traditions and culture at the **Folklore Museum** (伊是名村ふれあい民俗館; ☎ 45-2165; admission ¥200; ⏰ 9am-5pm Wed-Sun) in Nakata. One-third of the island is the **Izenayama Forest Park** (伊是名山森林公園), which protects vast groves of Ryūkyū pines, and has a number of well-maintained walking trails. On the south coast, the **Futamigaura-kaigan** (二見が浦海岸) is a striking stretch of coastline that is home to some towering standing rocks.

On Iheya-jima, **Minshuku Uchima-sō** (民宿内間荘; ☎ 46-2503; r per person with/without meals ¥5000/4000; 🅿) is a few blocks inland from the Mae-domari port, though the staff will pick you up if you phone ahead. This comfortable family-run *minshuku* has a handful of Japanese-style tatami rooms that are tastefully decorated with traditional furnishings.

On Izena-jima, the **Nakagawakan** (なか川館; ☎ 45-2100; r per person with/without meals ¥5000/4000; 🅿) is about a five-minute walk from Nakata port near the town centre, though the staff here will also pick you up if you phone ahead.

This traditional ryokan offers spacious Japanese-style tatami rooms with private facilities, and the friendly owner is a good person to talk to about hikes in Izenayama Forest Park.

Iheya Sonei (☎ 0980-46-2177) operates two ferries each day to Maedomari-kō on Iheya-jima from Unten-kō on the main island (¥2380, 1¼ hours). Similarly, **Izena Sonei** (☎ 0980-56-5084) has two ferries a day to Nakata-kō on Izena-jima from Unten-kō (¥1760, one hour). Unten-kō can be reached by bus from Nago.

KUME-JIMA 久米島
☎ 098 / pop 9600

The furthest flung of the outer islands, Kume-jima is a hopping destination in the summer months, though it's not too hard to see why. With palm-fringed beaches, interesting geographical features and excellent locally produced *awamori*, Kume has all the essential ingredients for the perfect Okinawan holiday. Unlike the other islands in the Okinawa-shotō, however, Kume cannot be visited as a day trip from Okinawa-hontō.

The airport is at the western extreme of the island, while the main port of Kaneshiro (兼城) is on the southwest coast. For more information in Japanese check out the website www .kumejima.info.

The action on Kume-jima centres on **Ifu Beach** (イーフビーチ), on the east coast of the island. *Ifu* means 'white' in the local Kume dialect, and not surprisingly, the beach is known for its powdery white sand. Well developed for tourism, this beach has toilets, showers, stalls and shops where you can rent snorkelling gear for ¥1000. Another attractive beach is **Shinri-hama** (シンリ浜), on the west coast near the airport, which is known for its sunsets over the East China Sea. There is a camping area here.

Hate-no-hama (はての浜) beach is something special. A 20-minute boat ride from the Kume-jima main island, Hate-no-hama is a 7km-long sandbar surrounded by emerald green seas. The best way to get there is on an excursion with **Hatenohama Kankō Service** (☎ 090-8292-8854), which runs a tour with lunch included for ¥4500. If you book in advance, staff members can pick you up from your accommodation.

On tiny Ō-jima, which is connected to Kume-jima's east coast by a causeway, you'll find the intriguing **Tatami-ishi** (畳石), a natural formation of pentagon-shaped rocks that covers the seashore. Note that Tatami-ishi can only be seen at low tide.

If you're looking for a cool (alcoholic) drink, **Kumejima-no-Kumesen** (久米島の久米仙; ☎ 985-2276; ⏰ 10am-noon & 1-4pm) offers the opportunity to check out a real *awamori* factory, which converts local spring water into its headache-inducing product. There are 50 different labels of *awamori* in the factory shop – *kampai!*

Ifu Beach is the place to stay, and there are plenty of choices along the 1.5km waterfront. Although some of the accommodation here can get quite pricey, an affordable yet surprisingly comfortable spot is the **Minshuku Shirahama** (民宿しらはま; ☎ 985-8336; r per person ¥3000; ⊠), which offers basic Japanese-style tatami rooms with shared facilities. This *minshuku* is just a few minutes' walk along the coast from the Ifu Beach bus stop.

JTA, part of the JAL network, has five flights a day between Naha and Kume-jima (from ¥9500, 30 minutes), and from June to September a daily flight from Tokyo (¥20,000 to ¥45,000, 2½ hours). **Kume Shosen** (☎ 098-868-2686) runs a daily ferry from Naha's Tomari-kō to Kume-jima's Kaneshiro-kō (¥2650, four hours).

Kume-jima has an efficient bus system, though there are also taxis, rental cars, scooters and bicycles for rent in the main town.

MIYAKO-SHOTŌ 宮古諸島

About 300km southwest of Okinawa and directly en route to the Yaeyama-shotō is the eight-island Miyako group, which includes the main islands of Miyako-jima, Irabu-jima and Shimoji-jima as well as a scattering of tiny islets. Edging closer to the Tropic of Cancer, the Miyako-shotō is the quintessential beach destination, though divers will find ample opportunities for a little underwater fun. The islands are also extremely popular among Japanese *freeters* (alternative lifestylers), which has resulted in a slowly burgeoning reggae scene.

Although Miyako-shotō is experiencing a boom in domestic tourism, few foreigners make it south of Okinawa-hontō. But if you have the time, it makes an excellent stopover en route to the Yaeyama-shotō, guaranteeing a little fun in the sun. The islands are incredibly laid-back, and they're refreshingly Japanese, which is a welcome change if you're coming from Okinawa-hontō.

Miyako-jima 宮古島
☎ 0980 / pop 49,000

Miyako-jima serves as the major transport hub for the Miyako-shotō, and is the most populated and developed island in the group. From the main city of Hirara, boat services fan out to Irabu-jima while the islands of Ikema-jima and Kurima-jima are connected to Miyako via bridges.

In addition to serving as your port of entry to the Miyako-shotō, Miyako-jima is also the main tourist destination in the island group. Unlike the majority of other islands in the Nansei-shotō, Miyako-jima is completely flat, which makes the island perfectly suited for the cultivation of sugar cane. As a result of this unique topography, Miyako hosts the Strongman All-Japan Triathlon, which attracts more than 1500 triathletes every April. However, if you're looking for a more laid-back holiday, you'll be happy to know that Miyako's beaches and dive spots are among the finest in the Nansei-shotō, and the islanders are also famous for their hospitality as well as their love of the drink (see p767).

ORIENTATION
Hirara, Miyako-jima's main population centre, is on the eastern coast of the island. Although it's rather sprawling, Hirara is centred on the rough square formed by McCrum-dōri, Shimozato-dōri and Ichiba-dōri. If you think McCrum-dōri is an unusual name for a Japanese street, you are absolutely correct. McCrum, the American in charge of Miyako-jima after the war, bulldozed a wide road from the port to his inland weather station – the road still bears his name.

A series of highways branch out from Hirara and head along the coastline and into the interior. There are several small population centres along the southern coast, though most of the interior of the island is comprised of sugar cane plantations.

INFORMATION
The **tourist information office** (Map p766; ☎ 73-1881; ⏰ 9am-6pm Mon-Sat) is helpful, though it can be a little difficult to find (head south on a side street parallel to Shimozato-dōri). The friendly staff can help you book accommodation around the islands, and can provide the useful English-language *Okinawa Miyako Islands Guide*. There's also an **airport information desk** (☎ 72-0899) that is open for all flight arrivals.

It's possible to access the internet for free on the 2nd floor of the **public library** (Map p766; cnr McCrum-dōri & Chūō-dōri). The ATMs at the **post office** (Map p766; Ichiba-dōri) accept foreign ATM cards.

SIGHTS

Hirara 平良

Travellers to Miyako-jima have problems prying themselves away from the island's beaches, though there are a few modest sights worth checking out.

Near the harbour is the **mausoleum** (Map p766) of Nakasone Tōimiyā, the 15th-century hero who not only conquered the Yaeyama-shotō, but also prevented an invasion from the north. Also near the harbour is the **Hakuai (Kaiser Wilhelm) Monument** (Map p766), which was presented as a gesture of gratitude for the rescue of the crew of a typhoon-wrecked German merchant ship in 1873.

Around 500m north of town along the coastal road is the **Nintōzeiseki** (人頭税石), a 1.4m-high stone used to determine who was required to pay taxes during the heavy-handed rule of the Shimazu, who invaded from southern Kyūshū in the early 1600s.

Next to the small town shrine of Miyako-jinja is the **Miyako Traditional Arts & Crafts Centre** (Map p766; ☎ 72-8022; admission free; ☉ 9am-6pm Mon-Sat), which displays traditional island crafts – be sure to check out the *minsā* weaving looms on the 2nd floor.

Six kilometres east of Hirara harbour is the worthwhile **Hirara City Sōgō Museum** (Map p765; ☎ 73-0567; admission ¥300; ☉ 9am-4pm Tue-Sun), which screens documentary videos of fast-disappearing Okinawan religious rites and traditional island festivals.

Just 200m north of the museum are the **Hirara Tropical Botanical Gardens** (Map p765; ☎ 72-3751; admission free; ☉ 8.30am-6pm), which are home to more than 40,000 tropical trees and plants.

Beaches

Although Miyako is full of secret little spots, there are several large beaches that are popular with tourists and locals alike.

Just a short walk south of the ferry terminal is the surprisingly attractive **Painagama Beach** (Map p765), which is a good place to do a little swimming. Because Painagama is the closest beach to Hirara, locals frequently host late-night beach parties here.

North of Hirara is the lovely **Sunayama Beach** (Map p765), where you can clamber over a dune and watch the sunset through a giant stone arch. Unfortunately, the scene is slightly tainted (in true Japanese fashion) by the huge safety net that is strung over the arch.

On the southwest coast, beautiful white-sand **Maehama Beach** (Map p765) is often called the finest beach in Japan. Here, a huge sweeping crescent of white sand is met by crystalline turquoise water that's perfect for swimming.

On the southeast corner of the island is **Bo-raga Beach** (Map p765), which is a popular spot for snorkelling and kayaking. From here, it's a great walk out to the cape at **Higashi Henna-misaki** (東平安名崎).

If you're looking for a more relaxed beach scene, **Yoshino Beach** and **Aragusuku Beach** (both Map p765) on the east coast are laid-back, and are good places to do a bit of snorkelling.

There are also good wilderness beaches on **Ikema-jima** (池間島), off the northernmost point of Miyako-jima, and on **Kurima-jima** (来間島) to the south. Both islands are linked to the main island by a bridge.

ACTIVITIES

Diving

For a quick crash course on scuba diving in Okinawa and the Southwest Islands, see boxed text (p739).

Miyako-jima is a wildly popular diving centre, with more than 50 dive sites and a dynamic range of underwater drop-offs and overhangs. The waters around Miyako-jima are also home to an elaborate system of underwater caves, which can be explored if you're an experienced diver. One popular sight off the west coast of nearby Irabu-jima is the **Mini Grotto** (Map p765), which is a large calcareous cave with impressive rock formations. Other popular spots are the **Yaebishi** reef (Map p765) just north of Ikema-jima and the **Tōri-ike** underwater tunnels (Map p765) off the western coast of nearby Shimoji-jima (also see p768).

A recommended dive operator is the **Good Fellas Club** (グードフェラークラブ; ☎ 73-5483; www.goodfellas.co.jp), around 1.1km south of Hirara town centre. If you have your own wheels, it's across from the Family Mart just east of the intersection between routes 390 and 192. If not, phone ahead and the staff can pick you up from your accommodation.

SLEEPING

Accommodation options on Miyako-jima are spread out around the island, so it's best to

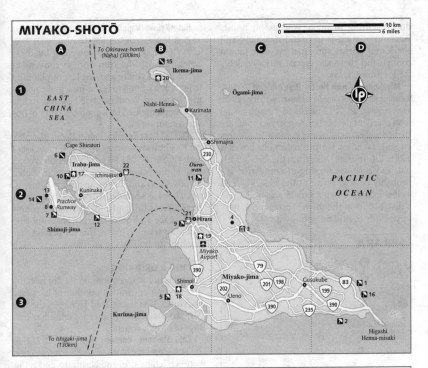

MIYAKO-SHOTŌ

phone ahead and make a reservation before arriving on the island. Most places will send a car to pick you up from the ferry terminal or the airport if you let them know what time you will be arriving.

There are free camping grounds at many beaches, including Maebama, Boraga and Aragusuku. In the busy summer season, a number of Hirara residents run informal guesthouses (look for flyers inside the ferry terminal and in the airport).

Guesthouse Miyako-jima (☎ 76-2330; www2.mi yako-ma.jp/yonaha/index.html; dm ¥2000, 1 week ¥12,000, r per person ¥3000, 1 week ¥15,000; 🅿 ❄) This bright and cheery guesthouse has a scenic location near Maehama Beach, and is perfectly set up for budget travellers. Accommodation is in cosy Western-style dorms and private rooms with shared facilities, and there are special rates available for long-term stays. Guests can also borrow bicycles and scooters for free.

Hirayaya (Map p765; ☎ 0980-75-3221; www.miyako -net.ne.jp/~hiraraya/index2.html; dm ¥2000, 1 week ¥12,000, r per person ¥3000, 1 week ¥18,000; meals available; 🅿 ❄) Located in central Hirara just one block north of Miyako-jinja (look for the light blue curtain that says guesthouse), this laid-back spot is run by a charming young woman who will do everything to make you feel at home. Accommodation is in brand-new (and still sparkling) dorms and Japanese-style tatami rooms, and there are special rates available for long-term stays.

Miyakojima Youth Hostel (Map p765; ☎ 73-7700; www.mco.ne.jp/~miyakoyh/in Japanese; r per person ¥3000; meals available; P X) The island's youth hostel is an excellent deal as Japanese-style rooms are surprisingly spacious, and come with spotless en-suite facilities. Unfortunately, the hostel is a 2km (30-minute) hike from the ferry terminal, and is slowly waning in popularity. It's probably best to arrive at the hostel by cab as it is located down a small backstreet quite a distance from the town centre, and is near impossible to find on your own.

Hotel Kyōwa (Map p766; ☎ 73-2288; www.hotelkyowa .co.jp in Japanese; s/d/tr/q with breakfast ¥6000/9000/ 12,000/15,000; P X) This towering business hotel, just off McCrum-dōri, is convenient to the port if you're arriving late or planning to get a quick jump to Irabu-jima in the morning. Standard Western-style business rooms are complemented by a good selection of on-site restaurants.

OURPICK Raza Cosmica Tourist Home (Map p765; ☎ 75-2020; www.raza-cosmica.com; r per person with 2 meals ¥10,000; P X) Run by a friendly young couple, this charmingly eclectic inn, which blends Asian and European design elements, sits above a secluded little beach cove on Ikema-jima. Romantic Western-style rooms offer peace and quiet in truly beautiful surroundings, which makes this the perfect destination for holidaying couples.

EATING & DRINKING

Hirara is home to a good number of restaurants and an enormous number of bars (see opposite). If you can read Japanese, the free *Miyako-jima-Taun-gaido* magazine has listings of local favourites.

Koja Shokudō Honten (Map p766; ☎ 72-2139; ✆ 10am-10pm) One block west of the intersection between Ichiba-dōri and Nishizato-dōri is this nondescript noodle house (look for the plastic food models), which is something of a local legend. For more than 50 years, Koja has been serving up steamy bowls of *Miyako-soba* (¥650), the local variant of the Okinawan classic.

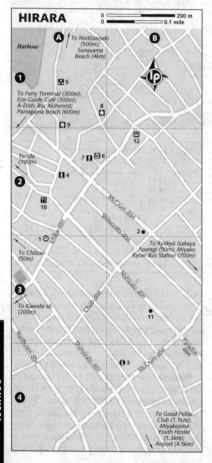

HIRARA

0 ——— 200 m
0 ——— 0.1 mile

Harbour

To Nintōzeiseki (500m); Sunayama Beach (4km)

To Ferry Terminal (300m); Eco-Guide Café (300m); A-Dish; Bar Alchemist; Painagama Beach (600m)

To Isla (100m)

To Chūzan (50m)

To Kawata-sō (200m)

To Ryūkyū Izakaya Aparagi (50m); Miyako Kyoei Bus Station (700m)

To Good Fellas Club (1.1km); Miyakojima Youth Hostel (1.3km); Airport (4.5km)

McCrum-dōri
Shimozato-dōri
Nishizato-dōri
Chūō-dōri
Ichiba-dōri
Paradise-dōri
Nunbouse-dōri

THE 'COMMUNICATION DRINK'

The friendly people of Miyako-jima have earned a reputation for drinking, and the Izato entertainment area in the town of Hirara is said to have more bars per capita than any other town in Japan.

Miyako even has its unique local drinking custom, called *otori*. This group ritual involves making a speech, filling your own glass (usually with potent *awamori*, the local liquor) and then filling the glasses of all in the room. Everyone drinks up, the leader makes a short closing speech, picks the next victim and the routine starts all over again. Miyako's *otori* is so notorious that even hard-livered Okinawans from neighbouring islands are said to fear the ritual.

If you happen to end up lured into an *otori* and want to sneak out before getting plastered, one local veteran boozer advises, 'Never say goodbye. Just head for the toilet and don't come back!'

A-Dish (チーシュ; ☎ 72-7114; dishes from ¥750; ☯ 6pm-midnight Tue-Sat; E) A short walk southwest of the ferry terminal (look for the English sign and the funky decorations), A-Dish is a hip little spot that is heaven for discerning gourmands. In addition to exquisitely prepared Okinawan classics, A-dish also serves up delicious pastas and pizzas featuring fresh local ingredients.

Chūzan (中山; ☎ 73-1959; ☯ 6pm-midnight) Two blocks west of the central post office (look for the hanging lanterns outside), this popular *izakaya* is a great spot that offers a variety of locally caught seafood. You can't go wrong with the *sashimi-setto* (¥1250), which washes down perfectly with a tall glass of *nama-birru* (¥450).

Bar Alchemist (バーアルケミスト; ☎ 82-4278; drinks from ¥450; ☯ 6pm-4am Tue-Sat; E) Upstairs from the A-Dish, this eclectic bar is decorated with all sorts of random paraphernalia, though that shouldn't distract you from the stunning sunset views. A few times each month, Bar Alchemist features live acts performing anything from Okinawan traditional ballads to Jamaican-style reggae.

Isla (イスラー; ☎ 74-3451; drinks from ¥450; ☯ 9pm-4am; E) One block west of the traffic light on Nishizato-dōri (look for the Jamaican flag), this Caribbean-themed bar hosts live reggae acts as well as the occasional salsa night. The charismatic English-speaking owner, Chiharu, is a legend behind the bar and on the dance floor.

GETTING THERE & AWAY

Air

Miyako-jima is serviced by JTA and ANK, and has direct flights to/from Tokyo (three hours, three daily), Osaka (2½ hours, three daily),

Naha (45 minutes, 12 daily) and Ishigaki-jima (20 minutes, four daily).

Fares are dependent on availability and seasonality – as a general rule, prices are the highest in the summer months, and you can save a considerable amount of money if you book two weeks prior to your flight. Flights to the mainland range from ¥15,000 to ¥40,000 while inter-island flights are typically ¥10,000 to ¥20,000.

Boats

Long-distance ferries to/from Naha (¥4250, nine hours) and to/from Ishigaki-jima (¥2070, 5½ hours) depart/arrive from the harbour. Note that these services are not daily, and travel times vary depending on the season and the weather. Ferries are culled in the winter months and cut completely at the first sign of bad weather. Call **Arimura Sangyō** (☎ 098-860-1980) or **Ryūkyū Kaiun** (☎ 098-868-1126) for more information.

Miyako-jima is also the departure/arrival point for ferries to Irabu-jima and Shimoji-jima (p768).

GETTING AROUND

Miyako-jima has a sporadic bus network that is not very useful for tourists. In fact, there are no buses between the airport and Hirara – taxis cost ¥1000. However, infrequent buses do run from the Yachiyo bus terminal (八千代バスターミナル; Map p766) to Ikema-jima (¥450, 35 minutes), and from the Miyako Kyōei bus station (宮古協栄バスターミナル), 700m east of town, to Higashi-Henna-misaki (¥650, 50 minutes).

The island's flat terrain is perfectly suited to biking, though you'll get around much quicker on a scooter. **Tomihama Motors** (Map p766;

☎ 72-3031; ⏰ 9am-6pm) on Nishizato-dōri (look for the English sign) has scooters for ¥2000 a day, and it's possible to circle the island in about three to four hours.

Irabu-jima & Shimoji-jima
伊良部島 • 下地島

A 10-minute ferry ride from Miyako-jima brings you to Irabu-jima and Shimoji-jima, which are pleasantly rural islands covered with fields of sugar cane and linked by a series of six bridges. Like Miyako, Irabu and Shimoji are a beach-lovers' paradise, and there are ample opportunities for swimming, snorkelling or simply sprawling out underneath the tropical sun.

The islands are best visited as a day trip from Hirara, though there are a handful of low-key guesthouses on the island as well as plenty of free camp sites.

Although there's no shortage of sandy coastline, the best beaches in the area are **Sawada-no-hama** and **Toguchi-no-hama** on Irabu-jima's west coast. With fine yellow sands and turquoise waters, you'd be hard-pressed to find more beautiful spots for an afternoon swim. Both beaches also have small shops where you can rent snorkelling equipment and kayaks; as well there are free camp sites with basic facilities. If you're planning to do a bit of snorkelling, the best spot is **Naka-no-shima**, on the west coast of Shimoji-jima. After walking across an attractive beach of crushed coral, you can snorkel around a series of hard coral heads that are protected by a high-walled bay.

Another interesting sight is **Tōri-ike**, a series of enormous pools on the west coast of Shimoji-jima that are linked to the sea by hidden tunnels. This is a great spot to walk around, though the best place to experience it is underwater. Not surprisingly, this is a popular diving destination for operators on nearby Miyako-jima. About 800m south of the pools is **Obi-iwa**, a 13m-high rock that was thrown up from the sea floor by a tsunami after a massive earthquake in 1771.

If you fly over Shimoji-jima, take a look down at the airport below – the runway appears to be longer than the island itself. This is because it's used as a **practise runway** by JAL and ANA for touch-and-go training. Although the airport is closed to visitors, a great way to spend an hour or two is to park along the northern end of the runway, and

simply watch the planes take off right before your eyes.

ourpick If you're really looking to chill out and slow things down for a night or two, the totally mellow **Guesthouse Birafuya** (☎ 78-3380; www.birafuya.com in Japanese; dm ¥2000, s/d ¥3000/5000; 🅿 🐾 🖳) is a few blocks inland from Sawada-no-hama beach. Built almost entirely out of polished wood, Birafuya features dormitories, Western-style rooms and a communal lounge that are soothing on the eye and completely calm-inducing. The best part about staying here are the delightful staff members, who work hard to foster a warm environment by making everyone feel at home. If you phone ahead, you can arrange to be picked up at the ferry terminal. Bikes are also available for rent; discounted weekly and monthly rates are available.

From the marine terminal in Hirara, **Miyako Ferry** (☎ 72-3263) and **Hayate Kaiun** (☎ 78-3337) operate a total of 30 speedboats a day (¥410, 10 minutes) to Irabu-jima.

The best way to explore the island is by scooter or rental car, which can be hired from **San Rent-a-Car** (☎ 78-5071). To reach its office, turn right at the main road after exiting the ferry and walk straight for about 300m.

YAEYAMA-SHOTŌ 八重山諸島

At the far southwestern end of the Nansei-shotō are the islands of the Yaeyama group, which include the two main islands of Ishigaki-jima and Iriomote-jima as well as a scattering of 17 isles between and beyond. Located near the Tropic of Cancer, the Yaeyama-shotō are renowned for their spectacular beaches, superb diving and lush landscapes. The islands are also a haven for Japanese *freeters* (alternative lifestylers), which means you're bound to meet an intriguing cast of characters during your travels here.

Much like the Miyako-shotō, the Yaeyama islands are experiencing a boom in domestic tourism, though few foreigners make it this far south. This is a shame as the Yaeyama group is arguably the top destination in the Nansei-shotō, and you could easily spend weeks indulging in the diverse sights and activities that the islands have to offer. Increased transportation links have also made the main island of Ishigaki easier to access than ever, and there's an elaborate inter-island ferry network to help facilitate your island-hopping fantasies.

A FOOD LOVER'S GUIDE TO OKINAWA & THE SOUTHWEST ISLANDS

In the culinary lexicon of Japanese food, if *kansai-ryōri* (Kansai cuisine) is a different dialect, then Okinawan cuisine is a different language. Reflecting its geographic and historical isolation – Naha is closer both geographically and culturally to Taipei than Tokyo – the food of Okinawa and the Southwest Islands shares little in common with that of mainland Japan. Since it was only approximately 130 years ago that the Ryūkyū kingdom was incorporated into the country, the southern islands still have a strong sense of being caught between the two behemoth cultures of China and Japan.

Okinawan cuisine originated from the splendour of the Ryūkyū court and from the humble lives of the impoverished islanders. Healthy eating is considered to be extremely important. Indeed, island thought has long held that medicine and food are essentially one and the same. The Okinawan language actually splits foodstuffs into *kusui-mun* (medicinal foods) and *ujinīmum* (body nutritious foods). Today, the island's staple foods are pork, which is acidic and rich in protein, and *konbu* (a type of seaweed), which is alkaline and calorie-free.

The humble pig often features in Okinawan food, and every part of the animal is used from top to bottom. **Mimigā** (ミミガー), which is thinly sliced pig's ears marinated in vinegar, might not be at the top of every gourmand's must-try list. However, on a hot, sweltering night in Naha, it's the perfect accompaniment to a cold glass of **Orion** (オリオンビール), the extremely quaffable local lager. **Rafutē** (ラフテー), which is very similar to the mainland **buta-no-kakuni** (豚の角煮), is pork stewed with ginger, brown sugar, rice wine and soy sauce until it falls apart. If you're looking for a bit of stamina, you should also try an inky-black bowl of **ikasumi-jiru** (イカスミ汁), which is stewed pork in black squid ink. Finally, try the **inamudotchi** (イナムドーチ), a hearty stew of pork, fish, mushrooms, potatoes and miso that is said to be reminiscent of eating wild boar.

While stewing is common, Okinawans prefer stir-frying, and refer to the technique as **chanpurū** (チャンプルー). Perhaps the best known stir-fry is **goya-chanpurū** (ゴーヤチャンプルー), which is a mix of pork, bitter melon and the island's unique tofu, **shima-dōfu** (島豆腐). *Shima-dōfu* is distinguished from the mainland variety by its sturdy consistency, which makes it especially suited to frying. Occasionally, you will come across an unusual variant known as *tōfuyō* (豆腐痒), which is sorely fermented, violently spicy and fluorescent pink – try small amounts from the end of a toothpick and do not eat the whole block!

The Okinawan working folks' food is **okinawa-soba** (沖縄そば), which is actually *udon* noodles served in a pork broth. The most common variants are **sōki-soba** (ソーキそば), which contains pork spare ribs; and **shima-tōgarashi** (島とうがらし; pickled hot peppers in sesame oil) and **yaeyama-soba** (八重山そば), which contain thin white noodles akin to *sōmen*.

Others dishes to look out for include **hirayāchi** (ヒラヤーチ), which is a thin pancake of egg, vegetables and meat that is similar to the mainland **okonomiyaki** (お好み焼き). **Yagi-jiru** (山羊汁; goat soup) is an invigorating (albeit stinky) reminder of a past era when goats were traditionally slaughtered to celebrate the construction of a new house. On the island of Miyako-jiima, look for **umi-budō** (海ぶどう), literally 'sea grapes', an oddly-textured seaweed that is often described as 'green caviar'. Finally, there's nothing quite like a scoop (or two) of **Blue Seal** (ブルーシール) ice cream, an American favourite that was introduced to the island following WWII.

Okinawans are a gregarious and cheerful bunch who love their food almost as much as their drink. While travelling through the Nansei-shotō, be sure to sample the local firewater, namely **awamori** (泡盛), which is distilled from rice, and has an alcohol content of 30% to 60%. Although it's usually served **mizu-wari** (水割り; diluted with water), this is seriously lethal stuff, especially the **habushu** (ハブ酒), which comes with a small habu snake (see boxed text p760) coiled in the bottom of the bottle. If you're hitting the *awamori* hard, take our advice and cancel your plans for the next day (or two).

Ishigaki-jima 石垣島

☎ 0980 / pop 50,000

Located 110km southwest of Miyako-jima, Ishigaki-jima serves as the major transport hub for the Yaeyama-shotō, and is the most

populated and developed island in the group. From Ishigaki City (the southernmost city in Japan), boat services fan out to nearby islands while flights depart for cities throughout the Nansei-shotō and on the mainland.

YAEYAMA-SHOTŌ

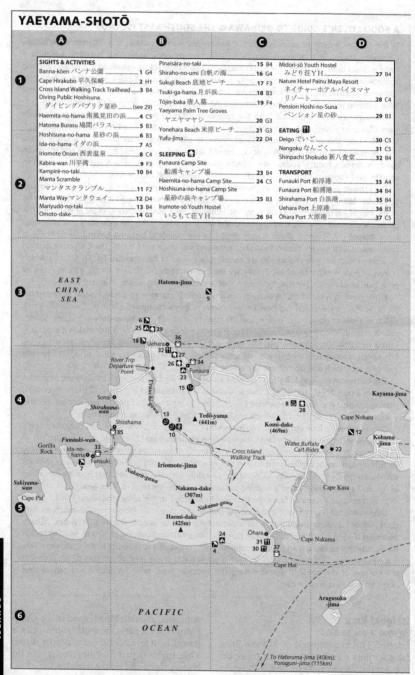

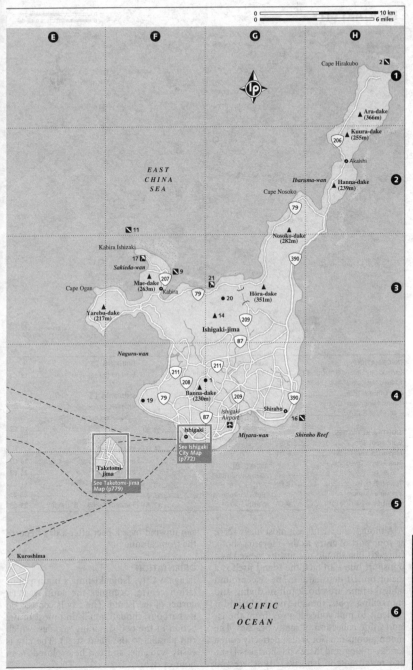

0   10 km
0   6 miles

Cape Hirakubo   2 **E1**

Ara-dake
(366m)

206   **Kuura-dake**
(255m)

Akaishi

Ibaruma-wan   **Hanna-dake**
(239m)
Cape Nosoko   79

EAST
CHINA
SEA

390

Nosoko-dake
(282m)

11 **E**

Kabira Ishizaki
17 **E**   9 **E**
Sakieda-wan   207
Mae-dake   Kabira   21 **E**
(263m)   79   **Hōra-dake**
Cape Ogan   20   **(351m)**

14   209

Yarebu-dake   *Ishigaki-jima*
(217m)   87

Nagura-wan   211

211
208   1
19   79   **Banna-dake**   209   390
(230m)   **Shiraho**
87   *Ishigaki*   16 **E**
Airport
Ishigaki   *Miyara-wan*   *Shiraho Reef*
See Ishigaki
City Map
(p772)

Taketomi-
jima
See Taketomi-jima
Map (p779)

Kuroshima

PACIFIC
OCEAN

OKINAWA & THE SOUTHWEST
ISLANDS

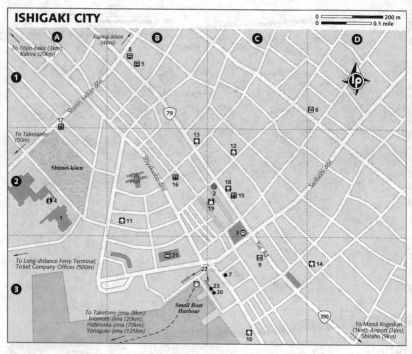

ISHIGAKI CITY

| 0 | 200 m |
| 0 | 0.1 mile |

Although the island will most likely serve as your port of entry to the Yaeyama-shotō, Ishigaki-jima should not just be viewed as a transport hub – in fact, the island itself is a major tourist destination. The seas around Ishigaki-jima are chock-full of diving and snorkelling spots, though you might find it difficult to pull yourself away from the island's fine collection of sandy beaches. The mountainous interior is also perfectly suited for day-hiking, and there's no shortage of bars and restaurants in Ishigaki City where you can unwind over a beer after a day beneath the tropical sun.

ORIENTATION

Ishigaki City, Ishigaki-jima's main population centre, occupies the southwestern corner of the island. The city is centred on its harbour, though you'll find most of the action in the two shopping arcades, which run parallel to the main street. The city is easily walkable, and can be explored in an hour or two.

A series of highways branch out from Ishi-gaki City and head along the coastline and into the interior. There are several small population centres near the coast, though most of the interior of the island is comprised of rugged mountains and patches of farmland.

INFORMATION

The **tourist information office** (Map p772; ☎ 82-2809; ☺ 8.30am-5.30pm Mon-Fri) occupies the 2nd floor of the building next to the library, and has a friendly English-speaking staff. They can help you book accommodation around the islands as well as provide you with an English-language brochure on the Yaeyama-shotō. If you arrive on the island by plane, there's a small but helpful **information booth** (☎ 88-0638; ☺ 8am-8pm) in the airport. For information in Japanese, check out the website www .yaeyama.or.jp.

Internet access is available at **Ishigaki Net Café** (Map p772; ☎ 83-8684; ☺ noon-3am) and the are international ATM at the post office (200m up the main road heading inland from the port).

SIGHTS

Ishigaki City 石垣市

Ishigaki-jima's sights are more of the natural kind, though there are a few interesting spots in and around the city that are worth checking out if you have the time and inclination.

Located 100m southeast of the post office is the modest **Yaeyama Museum** (Map p772; ☎ 82-4712; admission ¥100; ☺ 9am-4.30pm Tue-Sun), which has exhibits on the culture and history of the island, and displays coffin palanquins, dugout canoes, island textiles and festival photographs.

Although the Nansei-shotō didn't really have samurai, **Miyara Dōnchi** (Map p772; ☎ 82-2767; admission ¥200; ☺ 9am-5pm Wed-Mon) is essentially a samurai-style house that dates from 1819, and is the only one left in the whole island chain. To reach the house, walk north along Sanbashi-dōri until you see signs (in English) pointing to the house.

Founded in 1614, the Zen temple of **Tōrin-ji** (Map p272), near the intersection of Shimin-kaikan-dōri and Rte 79, is home to the 18th-century statues of Deva kings, which serve as the guardian deities of the islands. Adjacent to the temple is **Gongen-dō** (Map p272), a small shrine originally built in 1614, which was rebuilt after being destroyed by a tsunami in 1771.

About 3km northwest of the city along the coastal highway is **Tōjin-baka** (Map pp770–1),

a colourful cemetery that commemorates the Chinese labourers who sought refuge on Ishigaki-jima after escaping from British and American taskmasters during their voyage to California.

About 4km north of the city along Rte 208 is **Banna-kōen** (Map pp770-1; admission free), a mountainside botanical garden that boasts more than 2500 species of tropical flora.

Beaches

There's no shortage of sun-kissed beaches, where you can snorkel along the offshore reef or just take a dip before working on your tan.

North of Ishigaki City along Rte 79 is **Yonehara Beach** (Map pp770–1), a famed spot among underwater photographers, and home to a vibrant reef that teems with tropical fish. You can rent snorkel gear (¥1000) at any of the shops along the main road. If you have your own gear, there is a free camp site with basic facilities right beside the beach.

Just west of Yonehara is the equally famous **Kabira-wan** (Map pp770–1), a sheltered bay with fine sand, though swimming here is discouraged due to the local cultured black-pearl industry. However, if you want to check out what lies on the ocean floor, **Kabira Marine** (☎ 88-2335) runs glass-bottom-boat tours (¥1000, one hour) every hour.

Over the peninsula is the white-sand **Sukuji Beach** (Map pp770–1), perhaps the best swimming spot on the island, and the perfect place to kick back and scope out the beach scene.

If you've got a little time on your hands, there are a number of unnamed sandy stretches along the coastline to explore.

ACTIVITIES

Diving

For a quick crash course on scuba diving in Okinawa and the Southwest Islands, see boxed text (p739).

The sea around Ishigaki-jima is famous among the diving community for its large schools of manta rays, particularly in spring and summer. The most popular place is **Manta Scramble** (Map pp770–1), off the coast of Kabira Ishizaki. Although it's likely that you'll be sharing with a fair number of dive boats, you're almost guaranteed to see a manta (or four).

Another worthwhile trip is **Shiraho-no-umi** (Map pp770–1), off the coast of Shiraho, which is home to rare patches of Ao and Hama corals. Other good dive spots include the mazelike tunnels at **Kabira-wan** and the reefs off **Yonehara Beach** and **Cape Hirakubo** (all on Map pp770–1).

There are a number of dive shops on Ishigaki-jima, and two recommended places are **Tom Sawyer Dive Shop** (☎ 83-4677; ⏰ 8am-8pm), north of the harbour in Ishigaki City; and **Umicoza** (海講座; ☎ 88-2434; ⏰ 8am-8pm), next to the beach in Kabira.

Hiking

There are plenty of great hiking trails in Ishigaki-jima's mountainous interior, though it's best to seek local advice before heading out.

An excellent topographic map of the island is the *Yama-to-Kougen-no-Chizu-Ishigakijima* (山と高原の地図石垣島; ¥840), which is available at most major bookstores.

Omoto-dake (於茂登岳; Map pp770–1), at 526m, is the highest point in Okinawa-ken, with good views of the island from the large boulder at the top. The mountain can be accessed via a small road branching off Rte 87.

On the slopes between Omoto-dake and Yonehara Beach are the **Yaeyama Palm Tree Groves** (Map pp770–1), the perfect place for a leisurely walk. The 15m- to 25m-tall palms grow wild only in the Yaeyama group, and have been designated a national natural monument.

Good hiking exists on **Nosoko-dake** (野底岳; 282m), the eroded core of a volcano, where a steep 45-minute trek takes you to the summit for excellent views, particularly of the island's northern peninsula. The mountain can be accessed via a small road that branches off Rte 79.

SLEEPING

Ishigaki City serves as the island's principal accommodation centre – the following listings are all within walking distance of the ferry terminal.

our pick Yashima Ryokan Youth Hostel (Map p772; ☎ 82-3157; www.jyh.or.jp/english/kyushu/yaesu/index.html; dm ¥2600; P ✕ 🖳) East of the Yaeyama Museum, this cosy youth hostel is in a traditional Ryūkyū-style house. Accommodation is in several communal Japanese-style tatami rooms with shared facilities, and there's a (free!) nightly 'Awamori Hour' where guests and staff commune around a long wooden table.

Rakutenya (Map p772; ☎ 83-8713; www3.big.or.jp/~erm8p3gi/english/english.html; r per person ¥3000; P ✕ 🖳) This warm and inviting spot is two blocks north of the covered markets, and has

attractive Western- and Japanese-style rooms in a rickety, old wooden house. The managers are a friendly Japanese couple who speak a little bit of English, and are a fantastic source of local information.

Pension Yaima-biyōri (Map p772; ☎ 88-5578; www.yaima-well.net/ybiyori/index.htm in Japanese; r per person ¥3000; ✕) Two blocks northwest of the bus station, this welcoming pension offers simple but spacious Western- and Japanese-style rooms with shared facilities. A bonus of staying here is a 'free drink' coupon for Mori-no-Kokage (see opposite), a superb little *izakaya* run by the owner's wife.

Hyper Hotel Ishigaki-jima (Map p772; ☎ 82-2000; www.hyper-ishigaki.co.jp/index.shtml in Japanese; s/d/tr with light breakfast ¥5200/6200/7200; P ✕ 🖳) Just east of the harbour along the waterfront, this newish business hotel is a good choice if you're looking for a little privacy or if you just want to crash for the night before catching an early morning ferry. Sizable Western-style rooms feature extra-wide beds and spotless bathrooms – ask for one with a harbour view.

Super Hotel Ishigaki (Map p772; ☎ 83-9000; www.infinix.co.jp/sh/in Japanese; s with light breakfast ¥6000; P ✕ 🖳) Four blocks northeast of the city hall is this entirely automated business hotel, which caters exclusively to single business travellers. Minimalist Western-style rooms are fitted with ultra-modern furnishings and stylish trimmings, which makes the Super Hotel ideal if you're in the mood for a little comfortable seclusion.

EATING & DRINKING

Ishigaki City has a good mix of boutique tourist restaurants, cheap but atmospheric local dives and boisterous watering holes (islanders love their drink). If you can read Japanese, the free *Tanoshima* (楽島) magazine has listings of local favourites.

Eifuku Shokudō (Map p772; ☎ 82-5838; ⏰ 8.30am-11pm) This hole-in-the-wall, one block northwest of the covered arcade, is easy to find if you look for the plastic models of tasty-looking noodle dishes. Not surprisingly, this is one of the cheapest places on the island for *yaeyama-soba* (¥300), though we recommend the stinky (but oh-so-delicious!) *yagi-soba* (goat soba; ¥500).

Takesantei (たけさん亭; ☎ 88-0704; ⏰ 5pm-midnight Mon-Sat) A few blocks south of the park is this intimate *izakaya*, which is one of Ishigaki-jima's most famous spots. Okinawan cuisine is the reason why you're here – our recommendation is the locally caught *gurukun* (rockfish; ¥850), which is pan-fried and served with a lime. Although its exterior is completely nondescript, the view of the bustling interior through its windows makes Takesantei easy to spot.

Mori-no-Kokage (Map p772; ☎ 83-7933; Yui Rd; 5pm-midnight Mon-Sat) Just north of the covered arcade (look for the twinkling Christmas lights), this superb little *izakaya* is our top pick for its warm and natural ambience – there's nothing like the look and feel of real wood. There is a generous selection of local specialities on offer including *Ishigaki-gyuu* (Ishigaki beef; from ¥1200) and the local microbrew, *Ishigaki-shima-nari* (¥450).

Asian Kitchen KAPI (Map p772; ☎ 82-2026; meals ¥1200-1500; 5pm-midnight Mon-Sat; E) Next door to Mori-no-Kokage (look for the English sign), this trendy Pan-Asian bistro is a good choice if your Japanese is limited. In addition to the local cuisine, KAPI also offers an impressive range of Asian favourites, from Korean-style hot pots to fiery Indonesian curries.

Misushi (Map p772; ☎ 82-3708; 5.30-11pm) On the corner of the park (look for the coral statues out front), this high-class sushi spot serves impeccable sushi platters amid refined and traditional surroundings. If you're having problems deciding what to order, you can't go wrong with the *sushi-setto* (¥2000).

SHOPPING
Japanese travellers love to shop for *omiyage*, especially locally produced food products and liquors. Not surprisingly, Ishigaki-jima is a shopper's dream, and there's no shortage of potential purchases including sea salt, tropical fruits, Ishigaki beef, seashells and *awamori*.

A good place to shop for *omiyage* is the main shopping arcade, which also has a public market. Upstairs from the market is the **Ishigaki City Special Products Centre** (Map p772; ☎ 88-8633; 10am-7pm), which lets visitors sample traditional herbal teas, and browse textiles and pearl jewellery.

Also worth a look is the **Minsā Kōgeikan** (みんさー工芸館; ☎ 82-3473; 9am-6pm), which is a weaving workshop and showroom with exhibits on Yaeyama-shotō textiles. The building is located between town and the airport, and can be reached via the airport bus (be sure to tell the driver you want to stop here).

GETTING THERE & AWAY
Air
Ishigaki-jima is serviced by JTA and ANK, and has direct flights to/from Tokyo (3½ hours, three daily), Nagoya (three hours, one daily), Osaka (2¾ hours, three daily) and Fukuoka (2¼ hours, one daily). In summer, there are also several daily flights to/from Naha (one hour), Miyako-jima (30 minutes), Yonaguni-jima (25 minutes) and Hateruma-jima (25 minutes).

Fares are dependent on availability and seasonality – as a general rule, prices are the highest in summer, and you can save a considerable amount of money if you book two weeks prior to your flight. Flights to the mainland range from ¥15,000 to ¥40,000 while inter-island flights are typically ¥10,000 to ¥20,000.

Boat
Long-distance ferries to/from Miyako-jima (¥1890, five hours) and Naha (¥5350, 14 hours) depart/arrive at a terminal west of the harbour (a 15-minute walk along the waterfront). The Okinawa–Taiwan ferry also operates via Ishigaki (see p756 for details). Note that these services are not daily, and travel times vary depending on the season and the weather. Ferries are culled in the winter months and cut out completely at the first sign of bad weather. Telephone **Arimura Sangyō** (☎ 098-860-1980) or **Ryūkyū Kaiun** (☎ 098-868-1126) for the weekly schedules.

Ishigaki-jima is also the centre for all the Yaeyama-shotō ferries, and its small boat harbour south of the city centre is a real hive of activity. The two main ferry operators are **Yaeyama Kankō** (☎ 82-5010) and **Anei Kankō** (☎ 83-0055).

GETTING AROUND
The bus station is across the road from the harbour in Ishigaki City. There are hourly buses to the airport (¥200, 15 minutes) as well as a few daily buses to Kabira-wan (¥580, 40 minutes), Yonehara Beach (¥720, one hour) and Shiraho (¥350, 30 minutes).

Rental cars, scooters and bicycles are readily available at shops throughout the city centre. If you're comfortable on a scooter, it's a scenic four- to five-hour cruise around the island, though you should plan for longer if you want to spend some time relaxing on the island's beaches.

OKINAWA & THE SOUTHWEST ISLANDS

Iriomote-jima 西表島

☎ 0980 / pop 2000

Although it's just 20km west of Ishigaki-jima, Iriomote-jima could easily qualify as Japan's last frontier. Dense jungles and mangrove forest blanket more than 90% of the island, and are home to a variety of exotic wildlife including the rare *yamaneko*, a nocturnal and rarely seen wildcat.

Needless to say, Iriomote-jima is the perfect destination for outdoor enthusiasts, and the island's rugged cross-island trail is one of the most rewarding (and difficult) treks in the Nansei-shotō. The island is also crisscrossed by a series of muddy rivers (which wouldn't look at all out of place in the Amazon). They're easily explored by river boat or kayak. Add to the mix sun-drenched beaches and spectacular diving, and it's easy to see why Iriomote-jima is one of the most popular destinations in the Nansei-shotō for domestic travellers.

In true Japanese fashion, Iriomote-jima plays host to countless day-trippers from Ishigaki-jima, though few people stay on the island long enough to fully appreciate its charms. Although half a day is enough time for a quick river trip, two or three nights on the island will give you enough time to fully explore one of the least-developed corners of the country.

ORIENTATION & INFORMATION

Iriomote-jima has a 58km-long perimeter road that runs about halfway around the coast. No roads run into the interior, which is virtually untouched. Boats from Ishigaki-jima either dock at Funaura or Uehara on the north coast, which are closer to the main points of interest, or at Ōhara on the southeast coast.

If you arrive by ferry in Funaura, there is a small **information booth** (☎ 82-9836; ☉ 8am-8pm) inside the terminal that can help you book accommodation.

SIGHTS

Most travellers to Iriomote-jima are too busy indulging in outdoor pursuits to go sightseeing, though there are a few interesting spots on the island as well as an impressive collection of tropical beaches.

Beaches

The majority of the island's beaches are rocky and have shallow waters, though they are impossibly scenic and nearly always abandoned. If you are hoping to swim, **Tsuki-ga-hama** (Moon Beach; Map pp770–1) is a crescent-shaped yellow-sand beach at the mouth of the Urauchi-gama on the north coast.

If you're looking to do a bit of snorkelling, head to **Hoshisuna-no-hama** (Star Sand Beach; Map pp770–1) on the northwestern tip of the island. The beach is named after its star sand, which actually consists of the dried skeletons of tiny creatures.

From **Shirahama** (白浜), at the western end of the north coast road, there are four daily boats to the end-of-the-line settlement of **Funauki** (船浮; ¥410). Once there, it's a mere 10-minute walk on to the gorgeous **Ida-no-hama** (Map pp770–1), which pretty much meets all expectations of a picture-perfect tropical beach.

If you want to have a sandy beach to yourself, head to **Haemita-no-hama** (Map pp770–1), at the extreme western end of the south coast road. The beach wraps around the coast for kilometres on end, and consists of yellow sand strewn with massive boulders. On a clear day, you can see the island of Hateruma-jima (p781) to the south.

Other Sights

If outdoor activities are rained out, a good back-up plan is the **Iriomote Onsen** (Map pp770-1; ☎ 85-5700; admission ¥1500; ☉ 10am-10pm), on the east coast of the island. The *onsen* consists of sex-separated indoor and outdoor baths, a sauna, a mixed *rotemburo* (outdoor baths) and a pool. The grounds are attractively landscaped, and there are nice views of the nearby jungle-clad mountains.

Further south on the coastal road, carts drawn by water buffalo roll through the shallow shoreline over to **Yufu-jima** (由布島; Map pp770-1; ☎ 85-5470; cart ride & park admission ¥1300; ☉ 9am-5pm), a small islet with an excellent botanical garden.

ACTIVITIES

Whether your passion is boating, hiking or diving, chances are you'll find what you're looking for on Iriomote-jima.

River Trips

Iriomote's number one attraction is a trip up the **Urauchi-gawa** (浦内川), a winding brown river that is reminiscent of a tiny stretch of the Amazon. From the mouth of the river, **Urauchi-gawa Kankō** (☎ 85-6154) offers river tours (¥1500,

---

LEARNING THE LINGO

Feeling a little tongue-tied? The following glossary will have you speaking like a local diver in no time:

Getting Started

I'd like to…	…shitai no desu ga.	…したいのですが。
…go diving.	daibingu o…	ダイビングを…
…explore caves.	kēbu o tanken…	ケーブを探検…
…explore wrecks.	chimbotsusen o tanken…	沈没船を探検…
…go night diving.	naito daibingu o…	ナイトダイビングを…
…go snorkelling.	shunōkeringu o…	シュノーケリングを…
…join a diving tour.	tsuā ni sanka…	ツアーに参加…
…learn to dive.	daibingu o shūtoku…	ダイビングを習得…

Equipment Rental

I want to hire (a)…	…o rentaru shitai no desu ga.	…をレンタルしたいのですが。
…diving equipment.	daibinguyōgu…	ダイビング用具…
…regulator.	regurētā…	レギュレーター…
…buoyancy vest.	Bīshīdī…	BCD…
…tank.	tanku…	タンク…
…weight belt.	wētoberuto…	ウェイトベルト…
…wetsuit.	wettosūtsu…	ウェットスーツ…
…mask.	masuku…	マスク…
…flippers.	fin…	フィン…
…snorkel.	shunōkeru…	シュノーケル…
What is your weight?	taijū wa nan kiro desu ka?	体重は何キロですか。
What is your height?	shinchū wa nan senchi desu ka?	身長は何センチですか。
What is your shoe size?	kutsu no saizu ha ikutsu desu ka?	くつのサイズはいくつですか。
I need an air fill.	tanku jūten ga hitsuyō desu.	タンク充填が必要です。

On the Boat

Is the visibility good?	shikai wa īdesu ka?	視界はいいですか。
How deep is the dive?	fukasa wa dono kurai desu ka?	深さはどのくらいですか。
Are there currents?	kairyū ga arimasu ka?	海流がありますか。
Are there…	…ga imasu ka?	…がいますか。
dolphins?	iruka…	イルカ…
sharks?	same…	サメ…
whales?	kujira…	クジラ…
turtles?	umigame…	ウミガメ…
manta rays?	oniitomakiei…	オニイトマキエイ…
moray eels?	utsubo…	ウツボ…
garden eels?	chananago	チンアナゴ…
octopuses?	tako…	タコ…
lion fish?	minokasago…	ミノカサゴ…
clown fish?	kumanomi…	クマノミ…

---

three hours), which include a stop at the nearby waterfalls, **Mariyudō-no-taki** (マリユドゥの滝; Map pp770–1) and **Kampirē-no-taki** (カンピレ ーの滝; Map pp770–1). Here, you can hike around the base of the falls, and take a refreshing dip in a number of swimming holes.

From close to the Ōhara docks it is also possible to take cruises with **Tōbū Kōtsū** (☎ 85-5304; ⏰ 8.30am-5.30pm) up Iriomote's second-largest river, the **Nakama-gawa** (仲間川). The one-hour tour (¥1260) passes through lush mangroves and thick vegetation, and is much less touristy (and a bit more relaxing) than the Urauchi-gawa excursion.

If you're the independent type, you can rent kayaks and canoes (¥4000 per day) near both departure points for the river tours.

Hiking

There are some great walks in Iriomote-jima's jungle-clad interior, though it's best to seek local advice before setting out.

An excellent topographic map of the island is the *Yama-to-Kougen-no-Chizu-Iriomote-jima* (山と高原の地図西表島; ¥840), which is available at most major bookstores.

Pinaisāra-no-taki (ピナイサーラの滝; Map pp770–1) is Okinawa's highest waterfall. On the hills behind the lagoon, it is visible from boats coming into Funaura. When the tide is right, you can paddle a kayak across the shallow lagoon, and then follow the river up to the base of the falls. A path branches off and climbs to the top of the falls, from where there are superb views down to the coast. The walk takes less than two hours, and the falls are great for a cooling dip.

Just past Kampirē-no-taki, which is located at the end of the Urauchi-gawa trip, is the trailhead for the challenging **cross-island walking track**, which cuts through the island's interior to Ōhara in the south. The 18km hike takes a full day, though it can be tricky to find your way as past trekkers have inadvertently created a confusing network of false trails.

All you need to know about exploring Iriomote-jima on foot is found in Lonely Planet's *Hiking in Japan*.

Diving

For a quick crash course on scuba diving in Okinawa and the Southwest Islands, see boxed text (p739).

Although Iriomote-jima is not as developed for diving as nearby Ishigaki-jima, there is no shortage of dive sites including the famous **Manta Way**. Located in the straits between Iriomote-jima and Kohama-jima, Manta Way is home to large schools of manta rays, especially in late spring and early summer. Another popular spot is the hard coral reef at **Hatoma Burasu**, between Iriomote-jima and Hatoma-jima, where divers can see lion fish, squid, clown fish and moray eels.

A recommended dive operator is **Diving Public Hoshisuna** (Map pp770–1; ☎ 85-6488), which is run out of the Pension Hoshi-no-Suna and

can pick you up from your accommodation if you phone ahead.

SLEEPING

Iriomote-jima's accommodation is spread out around the island, so it's best to phone ahead and make a reservation before arriving on the island. Most places will send a car to pick you up from the ferry terminal if you let them know what time you will be arriving.

If you're looking to save a few thousand yen, there are free camping grounds with basic facilities at Hoshisuna-no-hama, Haemita-no-hama and close to the ferry terminal in Funaura.

Irumote-sō Youth Hostel (Map pp770–1; ☎ 85-6255; www.ishigaki.com/irumote in Japanese; dm ¥3000; P ✗ 💻) A top choice is this impeccably run youth hostel, which has a stunning hilltop location overlooking the Funaura port. Accommodation is in comfortable Western-style dorms with shared facilities, and guests can take advantage of the communal kitchens and chill-out lounges. Meals are also available. To reach the hostel, follow the uphill road from the Funaura ferry for a few hundred metres (look for the English signs).

Midori-sō Youth Hostel (Map pp770–1; ☎ 85-6526; www.yasigani.net/yado/midori/midori.htm in Japanese; dm ¥3000; P ✗) Midori-sō, 200m south of Uehara port, lacks the personality of the Irumote-sō, but it's hard to beat its central location. It's still a relaxed place where you can easily meet other backpackers, and has basic but adequate Western-style dorms, share communal facilities and a small kitchen.

ourpick Pension Hoshi-no-Suna (Map pp770–1; ☎ 85-6448; www.making.com/hoshinosuna/in Japanese; r per person with/without meals ¥5500/4000; P ✗) With hilltop views of Hoshisuna-no-hama, this welcoming pension is a superb choice if you don't mind being a little far from the ferry port. Western- and Japanese-style accommodation is available in a series of cute beachside bungalows complete with private en-suite facilities. There is also a small on-site bar and restaurant that is perfect for a sundowner as well as a small gift shop and a dive shop.

Nature Hotel Painu Maya Resort (Map pp770–1; ☎ 85-5700; fax 85-5099; d from ¥14,500; P ✗ 💻 🍴) If you're looking for a splurge, this tasteful resort is a good option, emphasising natural materials over concrete (a rarity in Japan). Spacious Western-style rooms are bright and airy, and guests can take advantage of the on-site swimming pool, *onsen* and bar-restaurant. The hotel is on the northeast corner of the island.

EATING
With few restaurants on the island, most travellers prefer to take meals at their accommodation (or self-cater). However, there are a few notable spots worth checking out. If you can read Japanese, the free *Yaeyama Navi* (や えやまなび) magazine has listings of local favourites.

Shinpachi Shokudō (新八食堂; Map pp770-1; ☎ 85-6078; ⏲ lunch & dinner) Just 200m south of the port in Uehara (look for the red banners outside), this no-frills noodle shop is the perfect spot for a hot bowl of *sōki soba* (¥550).

Nangoku (Map pp770-1; ☎ 85-5253; ⏲ 11am-9pm) Opposite the Midori-sō Youth Hostel in Uehara port (look for the red banners outside), Nangoku specialises in Okinawan fare. The *champuru* (stir-fry) for ¥650 is filling, though if you feel like splashing out, you can't go wrong with the *inoshishi teishoku* (wild pigmeat set) for ¥1800.

Deigo (Map pp770-1; ☎ 85-5477; ⏲ 11am-9pm) Just past the Eneos gas station in Ōhara (look for the English sign) is this adorable bistro, run by a friendly young couple. There's no shortage of delicious local dishes, though our recommendation is a bowl of *ika-sumi-soba* (¥700), delicious squid ink–flavoured noodles.

GETTING THERE & AROUND
Yaeyama Kankō (☎ 82-5010) and **Anei Kankō** (☎ 83-0055) run ferries to Ōhara (¥1540, 35 minutes), Uehara (¥2000, 40 minutes) and Funaura (¥2000, 40 minutes) from Ishigaki-jima. Although there are several ferries per day to each of the ports, frequency is dependent on the season and the weather.

A few buses each day run between Ōhara and Shirahama (¥1040, 1¼ hours), though it's probably worth renting your own set of wheels. Fortunately, there are plenty of rental agencies near each set of ports. The island's youth hostels also rent out bicycles, motor scooters and cars to guests. With plenty of alternative lifestylers on the island, your thumb is also a quick and easy way of getting around.

Taketomi-jima 竹富島
☎ 0980 / pop 300
A mere 10-minute boat ride from Ishigaki-jima, the tiny islet of Taketomi-jima is a 'living

museum' of Ryūkyū culture. Centred on a flower-bedecked village of traditional houses complete with red *kawara* (tiled) roofs, coral walls and *shiisa* (lion-dog rooftop guardian) statues, Taketomi is a breath of fresh air if you're sick of concrete.

In order to preserve the island's historic ambience, residents (one-third of whom are over 70 years old) have joined together to ban signs of modernism such as asphalt. As a result, the island is criss crossed by a series of crushed-coral roads that are ideally explored by the humble push bike. Taketomi is also refreshingly free of other eye-sores such as the ubiquitous convenience store, though there are plenty of adorable 'Mom & Pop' shops scattered around the island.

TAKETOMI-JIMA

INFORMATION	
Taketomi Post Office 竹富郵便局	1 B2
Yugafu-kan 竹富ゆがふ館	2 B1

SIGHTS & ACTIVITIES	
Kihōin Shūshūkan 喜宝院蒐集館	3 A2
Nagomi-no-dai なごみの台	4 A2
Nishitō Utaki 西塘御嶽	5 B2
Taketomi Mingei-kan 竹富民芸館	6 B1

SLEEPING	
Minshuku Izumiya 民宿泉屋	7 A1
Ōhama-sō 大浜荘	8 B2
Takana Ryokan 高那旅館	9 B2

EATING	
Painu-jima ぱいぬ島	10 B1
Shinmēnābi しんめえなばび	11 A2

TRANSPORT	
Maruhachi Rentals 丸八レンタサイクル	12 B2
Taketomi Port 竹富港	13 B1
Water Buffalo Rides 水牛車乗り場	14 A2

OKINAWA & THE SOUTHWEST ISLANDS

Taketomi-jima is besieged by Japanese day-trippers in the busy summer months, though the island is blissfully quiet at night. If you have the chance, it's worth spending a night here as Taketomi truly weaves its spell after the sun dips below the horizon.

ORIENTATION & INFORMATION

Ferries arrive at the small port (竹富港) on the northeast corner of the island, while Taketomi village is located in the centre. Only 7km long and 2km wide, Taketomi-jima is easily explored on foot or by bicycle.

There's a small **information desk** (🕐 8am-5pm) in the port building, but for the full scoop on Taketomi-jima, head next door to the **Yugafukan** (竹富ゆがふ館; ☎ 85-2488; 🕐 8am-5pm) visitor centre, which has excellent displays and exhibits on the island.

SIGHTS

There are a number of modest sights in Taketomi cillage, though the main attraction here is simply wandering around and soaking up the ambience. On this otherwise pancake-flat island, the ladder-like lookout, **Nagomi-no-dai** (なごみの台) has good views over the red-tiled roofs. **Nishitō Utaki** (西塘御嶽) is a shrine dedicated to a 16th-century ruler of the Yaeyamashotō who was born on Taketomi-jima. **Kihōin Shūshūkan** (喜宝院蒐集館; ☎ 85-2202; admission ¥300; 🕐 9am-5pm) is a private museum with a diverse collection of folk artefacts. **Taketomi Mingei-kan** (竹富民芸館; ☎ 85-2302; admission free; 🕐 9am-5pm) is where the island's woven *minsā* belts and other textiles are produced – the *minsā* fabrics used to be woven by young women as a sign of love.

Taketomi-jima is also heaven for beach lovers, especially since the island is virtually free of the tacky shops and restaurants that plague other Okinawan destinations. Most of the island is fringed with beach, and although the water is very shallow, Taketomi is a great place to bring your snorkelling gear. At **Kondoi Beach** (コンドイビーチ) on the west coast, you'll find the best swimming on the island. Just south is **Gaiji-hama** (カイジ浜), which is the main *hoshi-suna* (star sand) hunting ground. Although you are requested not to souvenir more than a few grains (which are actually the dried skeletons of tiny creatures), it's sold in bulk at local shops.

SLEEPING & EATING

Many of the traditional houses around the island are Japanese-style ryokan that serve traditional Okinawan cuisine. However, don't turn up on the last ferry expecting to find accommodation. Taketomi fills up quickly, so be sure to book ahead.

Takana Ryokan (高那旅館; ☎ 85-2151; www.kit.hi-ho.ne.jp/hayasaka-my/in Japanese; dm with/without meals ¥3880/2600, r per person with meals ¥8500; 🖳) Opposite the tiny post office, Takana actually consists of a basic youth hostel and an attached upmarket ryokan. Basic Western-style dorms in the youth hostel are a great option if you're on a budget, though the charming Japanese-style tatami rooms in the ryokan are a romantic choice if you're travelling with a loved one.

Ōhama-sō (大浜荘; ☎ 85-2226; fax 85-2226; r per person with/without meals ¥5500/3500; 🖳) Also beside the post office, this family-run *minshuku* has a light and jovial atmosphere, especially when the owner starts to entertain on the *sanshin* after dinner. Accommodation is in simple yet comfortable Japanese-style tatami rooms with shared facilities.

Minshuku Izumiya (民宿泉屋; ☎ 85-2250; www.wbs.ne.jp/bt/matsuzaki/yado/izumiya.htm in Japanese; r per person with/without meals ¥5500/3500; 🖳) On the northwest edge of the village, this intimate *minshuku* is centred on a stunning traditional garden. Japanese-style tatami rooms with shared facilities are inviting, though ask the owners if it's possible to stay in the nearby thatched house.

Painu-jima (ぱいぬ島; ☎ 85-2505; 🕐 10am-6pm) Opposite the Taketomi Mingei-kan (look for the red banners), this dinky little noodle house serves excellent *shima-soba* (Okinawan-style noodles) for ¥550.

Shinmēnābi (しんめえなあび; ☎ 85-2772; 🕐 11am-11pm) Located near the western edge of the village, this laid-back *izakaya* (look for the white lanterns) serves up hot and steamy bowls of tasty *rafute* (¥650), a traditional Okinawan pork stew.

GETTING THERE & AROUND

Yaeyama Kankō (☎ 82-5010) and **Anei Kankō** (☎ 83-0055) run fast, frequent ferries from Ishigaki-jima (round trip ¥1100, 10 minutes, every 15 minutes).

Rental bicycles are great for exploring the crushed-coral roads. **Maruhachi Rentals** (丸ハレンタサイクル; ☎ 85-2260; 🕐 8am-6pm) has bicycles for ¥300 per hour and runs a free shuttle between its shop and the port. For Japanese visitors, a popular method of seeing the island is by taking a tour (¥1000, 30 minutes) in a cart drawn by **water buffalo** (水牛車乗り場; ☎ 85-2103; ⏱ 8.30am-5pm).

Hateruma-jima 波照間島
☎ 0980 / pop 600

Sixty kilometres south of Iriomote-jima is the tiny islet of Hateruma-jima, Japan's southernmost piece of inhabited real estate. Just 15km around, Hateruma-jima has some stunning contrasts in geographical features, and is an increasingly popular destination for Japanese travellers who really want to get away from it all.

Ferries arrive at the small port on the northwest corner of the island, while Hateruma village is in the centre. Slightly larger than Taketomi-jima, Hateruma-jima is easily explored by bicycle or scooter. There's a small **information desk** (⏱ 8am-5pm) in the port building and in the airport that can help you find accommodation on the island.

A few minutes' bicycle ride west of the port on the northwest coast is **Nishihama** (ニシ浜), a perfect beach of snow-white sand where it is fairly easy to while away a day in the sun. Here, you will find free public showers, toilets and a camping ground. In the opposite southeast corner of the island, directly south of the airport, is the impressive **Takanasaki** (高那崎), a 1km-long cliff of Ryūkyū limestone that is pounded by the Pacific Ocean. At the western end of the cliffs is a small monument marking **Japan's southernmost point** (日本最南端の碑), which is an extremely popular photo spot for Japanese visitors.

Although there's no shortage of family-run accommodation on the island, an excellent choice is the popular **Minshuku Minoru-sō** (民宿みのる荘; ☎ 85-8438; http://park14.wakwak.com/~minoruso/in Japanese; r per person with/without meals ¥5000/2500; ✕) near the town centre. The friendly owners rent out bicycles, scooters and snorkelling gear, and can also arrange a boat for troll fishing (from ¥50,000). Accommodation is in cosy Japanese-style tatami rooms, accented with traditional fixtures. If you make a reservation, the owners can pick you up from the ferry port.

Ryūkyū Air Commuter (RAC) has one flight a day from Ishigaki to Hateruma-jima (from ¥6500, 25 minutes). Ferries run by **Anei Kankō** (☎ 83-0055) and **Hateruma Kaiun** (☎ 82-7233) each have three ferries a day to Hateruma-jima from Ishigaki (¥3000 and ¥3050 respectively, one hour). There is no public transport on the island, but rental bicycles and scooters are readily available for hire.

Yonaguni-jima 与那国島
☎ 0980 / pop 1800

About 125km west of Ishigaki and 110km east of Taiwan is the islet of Yonaguni-jima, Japan's westernmost piece of inhabited real estate. Although Yonaguni is about as far-flung as you can imagine in Japan, the island is incredibly popular with domestic travellers. Renowned for its strong sake, small horses and marlin fishing, the island is also home to the jumbo-sized 'Yonaguni atlas moth', the largest moth in the world.

However, it's what lies beneath the waters around Yonaguni that continues to lure travellers to the island in droves. Following the discovery of deep water ocean ruins by divers in 1985, Yonaguni was firmly put on the map as one of Okinawa's best diving destinations. Of course, seasoned scuba vets have always known about Yonaguni, especially since the waters around the island are a favourite haunt of hammerhead sharks.

Yonaguni used to be known as *Dunan,* meaning 'hard to reach' – it's still not an easy place to get to, though you'll certainly be rewarded for your time and effort.

ORIENTATION & INFORMATION

The ferry port of Kubura (久部良) is at the island's western extreme, with the airport between it and the main township at the port of Sonai (租内) on the north coast.

There are small **information desks** (⏱ 8am-5pm) in both the port building and the airport, which can help you find accommodation. For more information on the island, check out www.town.yonaguni.okinawa.jp (in Japanese).

SIGHTS

Just as Hateruma-jima has a monument to mark Japan's southernmost point, Yonaguni-jima has a rock (from Taiwan!) to mark the country's **westernmost point** (日本最西端の碑) at **Irizaki** (西崎). If the weather is perfect, the mountains of Taiwan are visible far over the sea, and the country's last sunset of the day is always a beautiful sight.

Yonaguni has an extremely rugged landscape, and the coastline is marked with great rock formations, much like those on the east coast of Taiwan. The most famous of these are **Tachigami-iwa** (立神岩), literally Standing-God Rock, **Gunkan-iwa** (軍艦岩) and **Sanninu-dai** (サンニヌ台) on the east coast. At the eastern tip of the island, Yonaguni horses graze in the pastures leading out to the lighthouse at **Agarizaki** (東崎).

The giant moths, which have a wingspan of 25cm to 30cm and are affectionately known as *Yonaguni-san,* can be seen at **Ayamihabiru-kan** (アヤミハビル館; ☎ 87-2440; admission ¥500; ⏰ 10am-4pm Wed-Sun), just south of Sonai.

If you want to sample Hanazake, the island's infamous local brew, head to one of the island's three factories in Sonai. **Irinamihira Shuzō** (いりなみひら酒造; ☎ 87-2431; ⏰ 8.30am-5.30pm), **Sakamoto Shuzō** (坂本酒造; ☎ 87-2417; ⏰ 8am-5pm) and **Kokusen Awamori** (国選泡盛; ☎ 87-2315; ⏰ 8am-5pm) are bunched together in Sonai, and each offers free tastings and sales on site.

ACTIVITIES
Diving
Washed by the rich Kuroshio Current, the seas around Yonaguni-jima are perfectly suited to diving. For a quick crash course on scuba diving in Okinawa and the Southwest Islands, see boxed text (p739).

Local divers have long known about the thrills that await at **Irizaki Point** (西崎ポイント), off the coast of Cape Irizaki. In the winter months, the deep waters here are frequented by large schools of hammerhead sharks. Despite their ferocious appearance and ill-repute, hammerheads are docile and shy when confronted by divers. Although it's fairly safe to jump in the water here, you will need to summon up the courage to not completely lose your cool, especially since hammerheads can reach sizes of nearly 6m.

The most popular dive spot near Yonaguni is the **underwater ruins** (廃墟), which were discovered by chance in 1985 by the Japanese marine explorer, Kihachirou Aratake. According to a group of scientists from the University of the Ryūkyūs in Naha, vestiges of the ruins are comparable to the pyramids of Egypt, Mesopotamia, Mexico and Peru. In fact, several analyses also indicate that one of the structures is nearly 8000 years old, which would go against the accepted chronological history of humanity.

Numerous archaeologists, including John Anthony West and Robert Schoch, argue that the ruins could be largely explicable by ocean erosion and coral reef settlements. Geologists familiar with the area maintain that the structures are mere geologic processes of natural origin, and are consistent with other known geological formations. Whether you believe that the ruins are remnants of the legendary ancient civilisations of Mu or merely a peculiar underwater rock formation, they are still one of the most unusual dive spots you're bound to come across.

There are numerous dive operators on the island, though most people choose to book through their accommodation. One recommended shop is **Yonaguni Diving Service** (与那国ダイビングサービス; ☎ 87-2658; www2.icb.ne.jp/~yds), which is run in conjunction with the Minshuku Yoshimarusō (below).

Fishing
In addition to diving, the seas off Yonaguni are also renowned for **marlin fishing**, and the All-Japan Billfish Tournament is held here each year in June or July. If you're interested in trolling, boats in Kubura can be chartered from ¥50,000 a day – call the **Yonaguni Fishing Co-operative** (☎ 87-2803 in Japanese) for information.

SLEEPING & EATING
Although there are several sleeping options around the island, it's best to phone ahead as Yonaguni is quite a distance to travel without a reservation. The following places will pick you up at either the airport or the ferry terminal.

Minshuku Yoshimarusō (民宿よしまる荘; ☎ 87-2658; www.yonaguniyds.com/html/1p/yosimaru/yosimaru.htm in Japanese; r per person with meals ¥5500; ✱) Near the ferry terminal in Kubura, Yoshimarusō is ideal for divers, as the friendly owners also operate the on-site Yonaguni Diving Service (above). Simple Japanese-style tatami rooms with shared facilities have nice views of the nearby port, though the real appeal of this *minshuku* is the owners' local diving expertise.

Hotel Irifune (ホテル入船; ☎ 87-2311; www.yonaguni.jp in Japanese; r per person with meals ¥6000; ✱) If you want to be a little closer to the action in Sonai, this simple business hotel is located near the main post office. Irifune offers fairly standard Japanese- and Western-style rooms, though it's a good option if you're looking for a little bit of privacy.

Fujimi Ryokan (ふじみ旅館; ☎ 87-2143; fax 87-2956; r per person with meals ¥6500; ✕) One block inland from the Hotel Irifune in Sonai, this intimate ryokan is a good choice if you're looking for more traditional accommodation. Attractive Japanese-style tatami rooms are decorated with local crafts, and the welcoming owners definitely know how to serve a feast.

Hate (はて; ☎ 87-3255; ⏱ 11.30am-11pm) Five blocks west of Sonai's only traffic light (look for the bright lanterns outside), this unpretentious *izakaya* is the perfect spot for *namabirru* (tap beer; ¥450) and *sashimi* (¥500) after diving.

GETTING THERE & AROUND

RAC has two flights a day to Yonaguni-jima from Naha (from ¥20,000, 1½ hours) and two flights a day from Ishigaki (from ¥10,000, 30 minutes).

Fukuyama Kaiun (☎ 87-2555) operates two ferries a week from Ishigaki to Kubura port (¥3460, four hours).

There are public buses and taxis on Yonaguni-jima, though the best way to get around the island is by rental car or scooter. **Yonaguni Honda** (☎ 87-2376) in central Sonai will send a car to meet you at the airport or the ferry terminal if you phone ahead.

Directory

CONTENTS

ACCOMMODATION

Japan offers a wide range of accommodation, from cheap guesthouses to first-class hotels. In addition to the Western-style accommodation, you'll also find distinctive Japanese-style places like ryokan (traditional Japanese inns; see p788) and *minshuku* (inexpensive Japanese guesthouses; see p787).

In this guide, accommodation listings have been organised by neighbourhood and price. Budget options cost ¥6000 or less; midrange rooms cost between ¥6000 and ¥15,000; and top-end rooms will cost more than ¥15,000 (per double).

Of course, there are some regional and seasonal variations. Accommodation tends to be more expensive in big cities than in rural areas. Likewise, in resort areas like the Izu-hantō, accommodation is more expensive during the warm months. In ski areas like Hakuba and Niseko, needless to say, accommodation prices go up in winter and down in summer.

Reservations

It can be hard to find accommodation during the following holiday periods: Shōgatsu (New Year) – 31 December to 3 January; Golden Week – 29 April to 5 May; and O-Bon – mid-August. If you plan to be in Japan during these periods, you should make reservations as far in advance as possible.

Tourist information offices at main train stations can usually help with reservations, and are often open until about 6.30pm or later. Even if you are travelling by car, the train station is a good first stop in town for information, reservations and cheap car parking.

Making phone reservations in English is usually possible in most major cities. Providing you speak clearly and simply, there will usually be someone around who can get the gist of what you want. For more information on making accommodation reservations in Japan, see the Japanese Accommodation Made Easy boxed text (p786).

The **International Tourism Center of Japan** (formerly Welcome Inn Reservation Center; www.itcj .or.jp/indexwel.html) is a free reservation service that represents hundreds of *minshuku*, ryokan, inns and pensions in Japan. It oper-

---

BOOK ACCOMMODATION ONLINE

For more accommodation reviews and recommendations by Lonely Planet authors, check out the online booking service at www.lonelyplanet.com. You'll find the true, insider lowdown on the best places to stay. Reviews are thorough and independent. Best of all, you can book online.

PRACTICALITIES

- **Newspapers & Magazines**: There are three main English-language daily newspapers in Japan: the *Japan Times, Daily Yomiuri* and *Asahi Shimbun/International Herald Tribune*. In the big cities, these are available at bookstores, convenience stores, train station kiosks and some hotels. In the countryside, you may not be able to find them anywhere. Foreign magazines are available in the major bookshops in the bigger cities.

- **Radio**: Recent years have seen an increase in the number of stations aimed specifically at Japan's foreign population. InterFM (76.1FM) is a favourite of Tokyo's expat community, and the Kansai equivalent is FM Cocolo (76.5FM).

- **Electricity:** The Japanese electric current is 100V AC. Tokyo and eastern Japan are on 50Hz, and western Japan, including Nagoya, Kyoto and Osaka, is on 60Hz. Most electrical items from other parts of the world will function on Japanese current. Japanese plugs are the flat two-pin type.

- **Video Systems**: Japan uses the NTSC system.

- **Weights & Measures**: Japan uses the international metric system.

ates counters in the main tourist information offices in Tokyo (see p109) and Kyoto (see p313), and at the main tourist information counters in Narita and Kansai airports. You can also make reservations online through its website (which is also an excellent source of information on member hotels and inns).

The **Japanese Inn Group** (www.jpinn.com/index.html) is a collection of foreigner-friendly ryokan and guesthouses. You can book member inns via its website or phone/fax. Pick up a copy of its excellent mini-guide to member inns at major tourist information centres in Japan.

If you make a reservation and then change your plans, be sure to cancel the reservation. One reason foreigners occasionally have a hard time with accommodation is because others who have gone before them have made reservations and then pulled no-shows. It is common courtesy to cancel a reservation if you change your plans and it makes things easier for those who come after you.

Camping

Camping is possible at official camping grounds across Japan, some of which are only open during the summer high season of July and August. Camping is also possible year-round (when conditions permit) at camping grounds in the mountains or around certain mountain huts (p787). 'Wild' or unofficial camping is also possible in many parts of rural Japan, but we recommend asking a local person about acceptable areas before setting up your tent.

Cycling Terminals

Cycling terminals (*saikuringu tāminaru*) provide low-priced accommodation of the bunk-bed or tatami-mat variety and are usually found in scenic areas suited to cycling. If you don't have your own bike, you can rent one at the terminal.

Cycling terminal prices compare favourably with those of a youth hostel: at around ¥3000 per person per night or ¥5000 including two meals. For more information, check out the website of the **Bicycle Popularization Association of Japan** (www.cycle-info.bpaj.or.jp/english/begin/st.html).

Hostels

Japan has an extensive network of youth hostels, often located in areas of interest to travellers. The best source of information on youth hostels is the *Zenkoku Youth Hostel no Tabi* booklet, which is available for ¥1365 from **Japan Youth Hostels, Inc** (Map pp112–13; JYHA; ☎ 03-3288-1417; www.jyh.or.jp/english; 9th fl, Kanda Amerex Bldg, 3-1-16 Misaki-chō, Chiyoda-ku, Tokyo 100-0006). Many youth hostels in Japan sell this handbook.

The best way to find hostels is via the JYHA website, which has details in English on all member hostels, and allows online reservations. Another option is the *Youth Hostel Map of Japan*, which has one-line entries on each hostel. It's available for free from JNTO and travel information centres (TICs) in Japan.

MEMBERSHIP, PRICES & REGULATIONS

You can stay at youth hostels in Japan without being a member of either the JYHA or

---

JAPANESE ACCOMMODATION MADE EASY

More than one foreign traveller has turned up unannounced in a ryokan or *minshuku* and been given a distinctly cold reception, then concluded that they have been the victim of discrimination. More than likely, they simply broke one of the main rules of Japanese accommodation: don't surprise them. Unlike some countries, where it's perfectly normal to rock up at a place with no reservation, in Japan, people usually make reservations, often months in advance. With this in mind, here are a few tips to help you find a bed each night in Japan. Note that these also go for hotels, although these are generally a little more flexible than traditional accommodation.

■ **Make reservations whenever possible** – Even if it's a quick call a few hours before arriving, if you give the place a little warning, you'll vastly increase your chances of getting a room.

■ **Fax** – The Japanese are much more comfortable with written than spoken English. If you fax a room request with all your details, you will find a warm welcome. You can always follow it up with a call, once you're all on the same page.

■ **The baton pass** – Get your present accommodation to call ahead and reserve your next night's accommodation. This will put everyone at ease – if you're acceptable at one place, you'll be just fine at another. Remember: this is a country where introductions are everything.

■ **Tourist information offices** – In even the smallest hamlet or island in Japan, you'll find tourist information offices, usually right outside train stations or ferry terminals. These people exist just to help travellers find accommodation (OK, they also give brilliant directions). They will recommend a place and call to see if a room is available, and then they will tell you exactly how to get there. This is another form of introduction.

Lastly, there will be times when you just have to slide that door open and hope for the best. Even the surprise-averse Japanese have to resort to this desperate move from time to time. The secret here is to try to minimise the shock. Smile like you're there to sell them insurance, muster your best *konbanwa* (good evening) and try to convince them that you actually prefer futons to beds, green tea to coffee, chopsticks to forks, and baths to showers.

---

the International Youth Hostel Federation (IYHA). You can purchase a one-year IYHA membership card at youth hostels in Japan for ¥2800.

Hostel charges currently average ¥3000 per night; some also add 5% consumption tax (see p799 for more information). Private rooms are available in some hostels from ¥3500 per night. As a friendly gesture, some hostels have introduced a special reduction – sometimes as much as ¥500 per night – for foreign hostellers.

Average prices for meals are ¥500 for breakfast and ¥900 for dinner. Almost all hostels require that you use a regulation sleeping sheet, which you can rent for ¥100 if you do not have your own. Although official regulations state that you can only stay at one hostel for three consecutive nights, this is sometimes waived outside the high season.

Hostellers are expected to check in between 3pm and 8pm to 9pm. There is usually a curfew of 10pm or 11pm. Checkout is usually before 10am and dormitories are closed between 10am and 3pm. Bath time is usually between 5pm and 9pm, dinner is between 6pm and 7.30pm, and breakfast is between 7am and 8am.

Hotels

You'll find a range of Western-style hotels in most Japanese cities and resort areas. Rates at standard midrange hotels average ¥9000 for a single and ¥12,000 for a double or twin. Rates at first-class hotels average ¥15,000 for a single and ¥20,000 for a double or twin. In addition to the 5% consumer tax that is levied on all accommodation in Japan, you may have to pay an additional 10% or more as a service charge at luxury hotels in Japan.

BUSINESS HOTELS

These are economical and practical places geared to the single traveller, usually lesser-ranking business types who want to stay somewhere close to the station. Rooms are clean, Western style, just big enough for you to turn around in, and include a miniature bath/WC unit. Vending machines replace room service.

Cheap single rooms can sometimes be found for as low as ¥4500, though the average rate is around ¥8000. Most business hotels also have twin and double rooms, and usually do not have a service charge.

CAPSULE HOTELS

One of Japan's most famous forms of accommodation is the *capseru hoteru*. As the name implies, the 'rooms' in a capsule hotel consist of banks of neat white capsules stacked in rows two or three high. The capsules themselves are around 2m by 1m by 1m – about the size of a spacious coffin. Inside is a bed, a TV, a reading light, a radio and an alarm clock. Personal belongings are kept in a locker room. Most capsule hotels have the added attraction of a sauna and a large communal bath. The average price is ¥3800 per night.

Capsule hotels are common in major cities and often cater to workers who have partied too hard to make it home or have missed the last train. The majority of capsule hotels only accept male guests, but some also accept women (see p148 and p151).

LOVE HOTELS

As their name indicates, love hotels are used by Japanese couples for discreet trysts. You can use them for this purpose as well, but they're also perfectly fine, if a little twee, for overnight accommodation.

To find a love hotel on the street, just look for flamboyant façades with rococo architecture, turrets, battlements and imitation statuary. Love hotels are designed for maximum privacy: entrances and exits are kept separate; keys are provided through a small opening without contact between desk clerk and guest; and photos of the rooms are displayed to make the choice easy for the customer.

During the day, you can stay for a two- or three-hour 'rest' (*kyūkei* in Japanese) for about ¥4000 (rates are for the whole room, not per person). Love hotels are of more interest to foreign visitors after 10pm, when it's possible to stay the night for about ¥6500, but you should check out early enough in the morning to avoid a return to peak-hour rates. There will usually be a sign in Japanese (occasionally in English) outside the hotel, announcing its rates. Even if you can't read Japanese, you should be able to figure out which rate applies to a 'rest' and which applies to an overnight stay.

Most love hotels are comfortable with foreign guests, but some travellers have reported being turned away at the odd place. Same-sex couples may have more trouble than one man and one woman.

Kokumin-shukusha

Kokumin-shukusha (people's lodges) are government-supported institutions offering affordable accommodation in scenic areas. Private Japanese-style rooms are the norm, though some places offer Western-style rooms. Prices average ¥5500 to ¥6500 per person per night, including two meals.

Minshuku

A *minshuku* is usually a family-run private lodging, rather like a Western-style B&B, except that you get both breakfast *and* dinner at a *minshuku*, making them extremely convenient for the traveller. The average price is around ¥6000 per person per night (with two meals). *Minshuku* are particularly common in rural areas and on the outer islands of Japan, where they may be the only accommodation option. For information on staying in a *minshuku*, see p788.

Mountain Huts

Mountain huts (*yama-goya*) are common in many of Japan's hiking and mountain-climbing areas. While you'll occasionally find free emergency shelters, most huts are privately run and charge for accommodation. These places offer bed and board (two meals) at around ¥5000 to ¥8000 per person; if you prepare your own meal that figure drops to ¥3000 to ¥5000 per person. It's best to call ahead to reserve a spot (contact numbers are available in Japanese hiking guides and maps, and in Lonely Planet's *Hiking in Japan*), but you won't be turned away if you show up without a reservation.

Pensions

Pensions are usually run by young couples offering Western-style accommodation based on the European pension concept. They are common in resort areas and around ski fields. Prices average ¥6000 per person per night, or ¥8500 including two meals.

Rider Houses

Catering mainly to touring motorcyclists, rider houses (*raidā hausu*) provide extremely basic shared accommodation from around ¥1000 per night. Some rider houses are attached to local *rāmen* restaurants or other eateries, and may offer discounted rates if you agree to eat there. You should bring your own sleeping bag or ask to rent bedding from the owner. For bathing facilities, you will often be directed to the local *sentō* (public bath).

Rider houses are most common in Hokkaidō, but you'll also find them in places like Kyūshū and Okinawa. If you can read some Japanese, spiral-bound *Touring Mapple* maps, published by Shobunsha and available in Japan, mark almost all of the rider houses in a specific region, as well as cheap places

to eat along the way. Japanese readers will also find the **Rider House Database** (www.tabizanmai.net/rider/riderdate/k_db.cgi) useful.

Ryokan

Ryokan are traditional Japanese lodgings, usually fine wooden buildings with traditional tatami-mat rooms and futons for bedding. Ryokan range from ultra-exclusive establishments to reasonably priced places with a homey atmosphere. Prices start at around ¥4000 (per person per night) for a no-frills ryokan without meals and climb to ¥100,000 for the best establishments. For around ¥10,000 per person, you can usually find a very good

...'G IN A RYOKAN OR MINSHUKU

...it: a hotel is a hotel wherever you go. Just as you want to try local food when you're ...ad, you probably also want to try a night in traditional local accommodation. Unfortunately, in most of Asia, this is a lot more difficult than it sounds. Sure, if you happen to be on the steppes of Mongolia, you can bed down in a *gher* without too much trouble, but try finding good traditional accommodation in, say, Thailand, Vietnam or China. Fortunately, Japan is the exception here. Indeed, Japan may be the only country in Asia where you can easily sleep in traditional local accommodation.

In Japan you'll find two kinds of traditional accommodation: ryokan and *minshuku*. Ryokan (written with the Japanese characters for 'travel' and 'hall') are usually fine old wooden Japanese buildings, with tatami mats, futons, gardens, deep Japanese bathtubs, traditional Japanese service and kitchens that turn out classic Japanese cuisine. *Minshuku* (written with the Japanese characters for 'people' and 'accommodation') are simpler versions of the same, sometimes private Japanese homes that have a few rooms given over to guests, other times purpose-built accommodation.

Due to language difficulties and unfamiliarity, staying in a ryokan or *minshuku* is not as straightforward as staying in a Western-style hotel. However, with a little education, it can be a breeze, even if you don't speak a word of Japanese. Here's the basic drill:

When you arrive, leave your shoes in the *genkan* (foyer area) and step up into the reception area. Here, you'll be asked to sign in and perhaps show your passport (you pay when you check out). You'll then be shown around the place and then to your room where you will be served a cup of tea, or shown a hot water flask and some tea cups so you can make your own. You'll note that there is no bedding to be seen in your room – your futon is in the closet and will be laid out later. You can leave your luggage anywhere except the *tokonoma* (sacred alcove), which will usually contain some flowers or a hanging scroll. If it's early enough, you can then go out to do some sightseeing.

When you return, you can change into your *yukata* (lightweight Japanese robe) and be served dinner in your room or in a dining room. In a ryokan, dinner is often a multi-course feast of the finest local delicacies. In a *minshuku*, it will be simpler but still often very good. After dinner, you can take a bath. If it's a big place, you can generally bathe anytime in the evening until around 11pm. If it's a small place, you'll be given a time slot. While you're in the bath, some mysterious elves will go into your room and lay out your futon so that it will be waiting for you when you return all toasty from the bath.

In the morning, you'll be served a Japanese-style breakfast (some places these days serve a simple Western-style breakfast for those who can't stomach rice and fish in the morning). You pay on check-out, which is usually around 11am.

The only problem with staying in a good ryokan is that it might put you off hotels for the rest of your days! Enjoy.

place that will serve you two excellent Japanese meals.

See the websites of the **International Tourism Center of Japan** (formerly Welcome Inn Reservation Center; www.itcj.or.jp/indexwel.html) and the **Japanese Inn Group** (www.jpinn.com/index.html) for information about the ryokan booking services they offer. For information on staying in a ryokan, see the boxed text (opposite).

Shukubō

Staying in a *shukubō* (temple lodging) is one way to experience another facet of traditional Japan. Sometimes you are allocated a simple room in the temple precincts and left to your own devices. Other times you may be asked to participate in prayers, services or *zazen* (seated meditation). At some temples, exquisite vegetarian meals *(shōjin ryōri)* are served.

Tokyo and Kyoto TICs produce leaflets on temple lodgings in their regions. Kōya-san (p417), a renowned religious centre in the Kansai region, includes more than 50 *shukubō* and is one of the best places in Japan to try this type of accommodation. The popular pilgrimage of Shikoku's 88 sacred temples also provides the opportunity to sample *shukubō* (see p630 for more information).

Over 70 youth hostels are located in temples or shrines – look for the reverse swastika in the JYHA handbook. The suffixes *-ji*, *-in* or *-dera* are also clues that the hostel is a temple.

Toho

The **Toho network** (www.toho.net/english.html) is a diverse collection of places that has banded loosely together to offer a more flexible alternative to youth hostels. Most of the network's 90 members are in Hokkaidō, although there are a few scattered around Honshū and other islands further south. Prices average ¥4000 per person for dormitory-style accommodation, or ¥5000 with two meals. Private rooms are sometimes available for about ¥1000 extra.

ACTIVITIES

Japan may be best known for its cultural attractions, but it's also a great place to ski, climb, trek, dive, snorkel and cycle. And, needless to say, it's a great place to pursue martial arts like jūdō, aikidō and karate.

Cycling

Bicycle touring is fairly popular in Japan, despite the fact that most of the country is quite mountainous. See p815 for more information on cycling in Japan. See also p785 for information on places to stay.

Diving & Snorkelling

Popular diving destinations include the Okinawan islands (p736), in the far southwest of Japan, and the chain of islands south of Tokyo, known as Izu-shotō (Izu Seven Islands; p231). Other dive sites in Japan include the waters around Tobi-shima (p546), off northern Honshū, and the Ogasawara-shotō (p235).

As you would expect, diving in Japan is expensive. Typical rates are ¥12,000 per day for two boat-dives and lunch. Courses for beginners are available in places like Ishigaki-jima (p773) and Iriomote-jima (p778) in Okinawa, but starting costs are around ¥80,000. Instruction will usually be in Japanese.

Hiking & Mountain Climbing

The Japanese are keen hikers, and many national parks in Japan have hiking routes. The popular hiking areas near Tokyo are around Nikkō (p187) and Izu-shotō (p231). In the Kansai region, Nara (p400), Shiga-ken (p367) and Kyoto (p309) all have pleasant hikes.

Japan comes into its own as a hiking destination in the Japan Alps National Park, particularly in Kamikōchi (p267), the Bandai plateau (p505) in northern Honshū, and Hokkaidō's national parks (p567).

While rudimentary English-language hiking maps may be available from local tourism authorities, it's better to seek out proper Japanese maps and decipher the kanji. Shobunsha's *Yama-to-Kōgen No Chizu* series covers all of Japan's most popular hiking areas in exquisite detail. The maps are available in all major bookshops in Japan.

Serious hikers will also want to pick up a copy of Lonely Planet's *Hiking in Japan*, which covers convenient one-day hikes near major cities and extended hikes in more remote areas.

Martial Arts

Japan is the home of several of the world's major martial arts: aikidō, jūdō, karate and kendō. Less popular disciplines, such as *kyūdō* (Japanese archery) and sumō, also attract devotees from overseas. It is possible for foreigners to study all these disciplines here, although it's sometimes difficult to do so as a traveller. If you are really keen, we suggest living for a short spell near your *dōjō* (training place) of choice.

All Japan Jūdō Federation (Zen Nihon Jūdō Renmei; ☎ 03-3818-4199; www.judo.or.jp in Japanese; c/o Kōdōkan, 1-16-30 Kasuga, Bunkyō-ku, Tokyo)

All Japan Kendō Federation (☎ 03-3211-5804; www .kendo-fik.org/english-page/english-top-page.html; c/o Nippon Budokan, 2-3 Kitanomaru-kōen, Chiyoda-ku, Tokyo)

All Nippon Kyūdō Federation (☎ 03-3481-2387; www.kyudo.jp/english/index.html; 4th fl, Kishi Memorial Hall, 1-1-1 Jinnan, Shibuya-ku, Tokyo)

International Aikidō Federation (☎ 03-3203-9236; www.aikido-international.org; 17-18 Wakamatsu-chō, Shinjuku-ku, Tokyo)

Japan Karate Association (☎ 03-5800-3091; www .jka.or.jp/english/e_index.html; 2-23-15 Kōraku, Bunkyō-ku, Tokyo)

Japan Karate-dō Federation (☎ 03-3503-6640; www.karatedo.co.jp/index3.htm; 6th fl, No 2 Nippon Zaidan Bldg,1-11-2 Toranomon, Minato-ku, Tokyo)

Nihon Sumō Kyōkai (☎ 03-3623-5111; www.sumo .or.jp/eng; c/o Ryōgoku Kokugikan, 1-3-28 Yokoami, Sumida-ku, Tokyo)

Skiing

Japan is the best place to ski in Asia and it boasts some of the most reliable snow in the world. For more information, see the Skiing in Japan chapter (p80).

BUSINESS HOURS

Department stores usually open at 10am and close at 6.30pm or 7pm daily (with one or two days off each month). Smaller shops are open similar hours but may close on Sunday. Large companies usually work from 9am to 5pm weekdays and some also operate on Saturday morning.

Banks are open 9am to 3pm weekdays. For information on changing money, see p798.

Restaurants are usually open from 11am to 2pm and from 6pm to 11pm, with one day off per week, usually Monday or Tuesday. Some stay open all afternoon. Cafés are usually open 11am until 11pm, with one day off per week, usually Monday or Tuesday. Bars usually open around 5pm and stay open until the wee hours.

CHILDREN

Japan is a great place to travel with kids: it's safe and clean and there's never a shortage of places to keep them amused. Look out for *Japan for Kids* by Diane Wiltshire Kanagawa and Jeanne Huey Erickson, an excellent introduction to Japan's highlights from a child's perspective. In addition, Lonely Planet publishes *Travel with Children*, which gives the lowdown on getting out and about with your children.

Practicalities

Parents will find that Japan is similar to Western countries in terms of facilities and allowances made for children, with a few notable exceptions. Cots are available in most hotels and these can be booked in advance. High chairs are available in many restaurants (although this isn't an issue in the many restaurants where everyone sits on the floor). There are nappy-changing facilities in some public places, like department stores and some larger train stations; formula and nappies are widely available, even in convenience stores. Breast feeding in public is generally not done. The one major problem concerns child seats for cars and taxis: these are generally not available. Finally, child-care agencies are available in most larger cities. The only problem is the language barrier: outside Tokyo, there are few, if any, agencies with English-speaking staff.

Sights & Activities

Tokyo has the most child-friendly attractions in Japan, including Tokyo Disneyland (p142); for more information, see Tokyo for Children (p144). In Kansai, popular attractions for the young 'uns include Osaka's Universal Studios Japan (p383), Osaka Aquarium (p382) and Nara-kōen (p401) in Nara, with its resident deer population.

Children who enjoy the beach and activities like snorkelling will adore the islands of Okinawa (p736) and the Izu-shotō (p231).

CLIMATE

The combination of Japan's mountainous territory and the length of the archipelago (covering about 20° of latitude) makes for a complex climate. Most of the country is located in the northern temperate zone, which yields four distinct seasons. In addition, there are significant climatic differences between Hokkaidō in the north, which has short summers and lengthy winters with heavy snowfalls, and the southern islands, such as Okinawa in Nansei-shotō (Southwest Archipelago), which enjoy a subtropical climate.

In the winter months (December to February), cold, dry air-masses from Siberia move

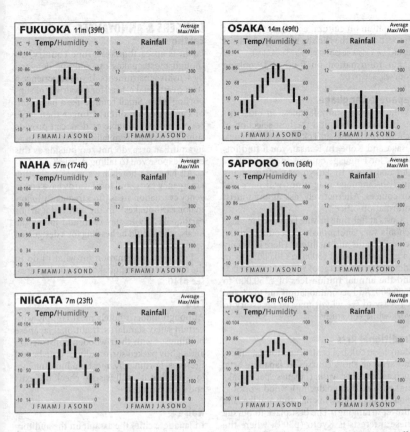

down over Japan, where they meet warmer, moister air-masses from the Pacific. The resulting precipitation causes huge snowfalls on the side of the country that faces the Sea of Japan. The Pacific Ocean side of Japan receives less snow but can still be quite cold, while the big cities of Honshū like Tokyo, Osaka, Nagoya and Kyoto have winters with highs in the single digits or even low teens and lows a few degrees above zero (Celsius). The odd January or February day will be colder, but these cold snaps usually don't last.

The summer months (June to August) are dominated by warm, moist air currents from the Pacific, and produce high temperatures and humidity throughout most of Japan (with the blissful exception of Hokkaidō). In the early part of summer, usually mid-May to June, there is a rainy season lasting a few weeks that starts in the south and gradually works its way northward. Although it can be inconvenient, this rainy season is not usually a significant barrier to travel. August, September and October is typhoon season, which can make travel in Okinawa, the Izu-shotō and Ogasawara-shotō difficult.

In contrast to the extremes of summer and winter, spring (March to May) and autumn (September to November) in Japan are comparatively mild. Rainfall is relatively low and the days are often clear. These are, without a doubt, the very best times to visit the country.

COURSES

A course is a great way to deepen your appreciation of Japanese culture. Kyoto and Tokyo are the best places to find courses taught in English. Cultural activities visas require applicants to attend 20 class-hours per week. Those wishing to work while studying need to apply for permission to do so. For more

DIRECTORY

information on cultural activities visas, visit the website of the **Ministry of Foreign Affairs of Japan** (www.mofa.go.jp/j_info/visit/visa/04.html).

For information on food and cooking courses, see p102.

Japanese Language

While you can study Japanese in most cities in Japan, you'll find the best selection of schools and courses in Tokyo, Kyoto, Nagoya, Osaka and Kōbe. In Kansai, you'll find lots of ads for language courses in *Kansai Time Out* magazine. In Tokyo, any of the many English-language magazines will have ads for courses. Alternatively, ask at any tourist information office.

Costs at full-time private Japanese language schools vary enormously depending on the school's status and facilities. There is usually an application fee of ¥5000 to ¥30,000, plus an administration charge of ¥50,000 to ¥100,000 and the annual tuition fees of ¥350,000 to ¥600,000. Add accommodation and food, and it is easy to see why it may be necessary to work while you study.

Traditional Arts

Many local cultural centres and tourist offices can arrange short courses in Japanese arts, such as ceramics, *washi* (Japanese papermaking), *aizome* (indigo dyeing), wood working, *shodō* (calligraphy), ink painting and ikebana (flower arranging). The best place to pursue these interests is Kyoto (p309), where the TIC (p313) or the International Community House (p312) can put you in touch with qualified teachers.

CUSTOMS

Customs allowances include the usual tobacco products plus three 760mL bottles of alcoholic beverages, 56mL of perfume, and gifts and souvenirs up to a value of ¥200,000 or its equivalent. You must be over the age of 20 to qualify for these allowances. Customs officers will confiscate any pornographic materials in which pubic hair is visible.

There are no limits on the importation of foreign or Japanese currency. The export of foreign currency is also unlimited but there is a ¥5 million export limit for Japanese currency.

Visit **Japan Customs** (www.customs.go.jp/index _e.htm) for more information on Japan's customs regulations.

DANGERS & ANNOYANCES
Earthquakes

Japan is an earthquake-prone country, although most quakes can only be detected by sensitive instruments. If you experience a strong earthquake, head for a doorway or supporting pillar. Small rooms, like a bathroom or cupboard, are often stronger than large rooms but even a table or desk can provide some protection from falling debris. If you're in an urban area, do not run outside as this could expose you to falling debris.

All Japanese hotels have maps indicating emergency exits, and local wards have emergency evacuation areas (fires frequently follow major earthquakes). In the event of a major earthquake, try to stay calm and follow the locals, who should be heading for a designated safe area.

For more information on what to do in the event of an earthquake in the Tokyo area, see p110.

Fire

Although modern hotels must comply with certain safety standards, traditional Japanese buildings – with their wooden construction and tightly packed surroundings – can be real firetraps. Fortunately, most old buildings are low-rise, but it's still wise to check fire exits and escape routes.

Noise

In Japanese cities the assault on the auditory senses can be overwhelming: you'll hear announcements on buses, escalators, elevators, on sidewalks, in shopping malls, even at popular beaches and ski resorts. Earplugs can help, particularly when you're trying to sleep.

Size

Even medium-sized foreigners need to mind their heads in Japanese dwellings. The Western frame may make it hard to fit into some seats and those with long legs will often find themselves wedged tight. Toilets in cramped accommodation necessitate contortions and careful aim (be warned!). Bathtubs are also sometimes on the small side and require flexibility on the part of the bather.

Theft

The low incidence of theft and crime in general in Japan is frequently commented on. Of course, theft does exist and its rarity is no reason for carelessness. It's sensible to take the normal precautions in airports and on the crowded Tokyo rail network, but there's definitely no need for paranoia.

Lost-and-found services do seem to work; if you leave something behind on a train or other mode of transport, it's always worth inquiring if it has been turned in. The Japanese word for a lost item is *wasure-mono,* and lost-and-found offices usually go by the same name. In train stations, you can also inquire at the station master's *(eki-chō)* office.

DISCOUNT CARDS
Hostel Cards

See p785 about obtaining a youth hostel membership card.

Museum Discount Card

The **Grutt Pass** (www.museum.or.jp/grutto/about-e.html) is a useful ticket that allows free or discounted admission to almost 50 museums in the Tokyo area. For more information see p109.

Senior Cards

Japan is an excellent place for senior travellers, with discounts available on entry fees to many temples, museums and cinemas. To qualify for widely available senior discounts, you have to be aged over 60 or 65, depending upon the place/company. In almost all cases a passport will be sufficient proof of age, so senior cards are rarely worth bringing.

Japanese domestic airlines (JAS, JAL and ANA) offer senior discounts of about 25% on some flights (for airline contact details, see p814). Japan Rail (JR) offers a variety of discounts and special passes, including the **Full Moon Green Pass** (www.japanrail .com/JR_discounttickets.html#a4), which is good for travel in Green Car (1st-class) carriages on *shinkansen* (bullet trains), regular JR trains and sleeper trains. The pass is available to couples whose combined age exceeds 88 years (passports can prove this). The pass costs ¥80,500/99,900/124,400 per couple for five/ seven/12 consecutive days of travel. They are available at major JR stations within Japan from 1 September to 31 May, and they are valid for travel between 1 October and 30 June (with the exception of 28 December to 6 January, 21 March to 5 April, and 27 April to 6 May). Note that these dates may change slightly from year to year. See the above website for details.

Student & Youth Cards

Japan is one of the few places left in Asia where a student card can be useful, though some places only offer discounts to high school students and younger, not to university and graduate students. Officially, you should be carrying an International Student Identity Card (ISIC) to qualify for a discount, but you will often find that any youth or student card will do.

EMBASSIES & CONSULATES
Japanese Embassies & Consulates

Diplomatic representation abroad:

Australia Canberra (embassy; ☎ 02-6273 3244; www .japan.org.au; 112 Empire Circuit, Yarralumla, Canberra, ACT 2600); Brisbane (consulate; ☎ 07-3221 5188); Melbourne (consulate; ☎ 03-9639 3244); Perth (consulate; ☎ 08-9480 1800); Sydney (consulate; ☎ 02-9231 3455)

Canada Ontario (embassy; ☎ 613-241 8541; www .ca.emb-japan.go.jp; 255 Sussex Dr, Ottawa, Ontario K1N 9E6); Calgary (consulate; ☎ 403-294 0782); Montreal (consulate; ☎ 514-866 3429); Toronto (consulate; ☎ 416-363 7038); Vancouver (consulate; ☎ 604-684 5868)

France (☎ 01 48 88 62 00; www.fr.emb-japan.go.jp; 7 ave Hoche, 75008 Paris)

Germany (☎ 493-021 09 40; www.de.emb-japan .go.jp/index.html; Hiroshimastrasse 6, 10785, Berlin)

Hong Kong (consulate; ☎ 852-2522 1184; www .hk.emb-japan.go.jp/eng/index.html; 46-47/F, One Exchange Sq, 8 Connaught Pl, Central, Hong Kong)

Ireland (☎ 01-202 8300; www.ie.emb-japan.go.jp; Nutley Bldg, Merrion Centre, Nutley Lane, Dublin 4)

Netherlands (☎ 70-346-95-44; www.nl.emb-japan .go.jp; Tobias Asserlaan 2 2517 KC, Den Haag)

New Zealand Wellington (embassy; ☎ 04-473 1540; www.nz.emb-japan.go.jp; Level 18 & 19, The Majestic Centre, 100 Willis St, PO Box 6340, Wellington); Auckland (consulate; ☎ 09-303 4106)

South Korea (☎ 822-2170 5200; www.kr.emb-japan .go.jp; 18-11, Jhoonghak-dong, Jhongro-gu, Seoul)

UK (☎ 020-7465 6500; www.uk.emb-japan.go.jp; 101-104 Piccadilly, London, W1V 9FN)

USA Washington DC (embassy; ☎ 202-238 6700; www .us.emb-japan.go.jp; 2520 Massachusetts Ave, NW, Washington, DC 20008); Los Angeles (consulate; ☎ 213-617 6700); New York (consulate; ☎ 212-371 8222)

Embassies & Consulates in Japan

Diplomatic representation in Japan:

Australia Tokyo (embassy; Map pp112-13; ☎ 03-5232-4111; www.australia.or.jp/english; 2-1-14 Mita, Minato-ku, Tokyo); Fukuoka (consulate; ☎ 092-734-5055; 7th fl, Tenjin Twin Bldg, 1-6-8 Tenjin, Chūō-ku, Fukuoka); Osaka (consulate; ☎ 06-6941-9271; 16th fl, Twin 21 MID Tower, 2-1-61 Shiromi, Chūō-ku, Osaka)

DIRECTORY

Canada Tokyo (embassy; ☎ 03-5412-6200; www.canada
net.or.jp/english.shtml; 7-3-38 Akasaka, Minato-ku,
Tokyo); Fukuoka (consulate; ☎ 092-752-6055; 9th fl, FT
Bldg, 4-8-28 Watanabe-dōri, Chūō-ku, Fukuoka); Osaka
(consulate; ☎ 06-6212-4910; 12th fl, Round Cross Shinsaibashi Bldg, 2-2-3 Nishi Shinsaibashi, Chūō-ku, Osaka)

France Tokyo (embassy; Map pp112-13; ☎ 03-5420-
8800; www.ambafrance-jp.org; 4-11-44 Minami Azabu,
Minato-ku, Tokyo); Osaka (consulate; ☎ 06-4790-1500;
10th fl, Crystal Tower, 1-2-27 Shiromi, Chūō-ku, Osaka)

Germany Tokyo (Map pp112-13; ☎ 03-5791-7700; www
.tokyo.diplo.de/ja/Startseite.html; 4-5-10 Minami Azabu,
Minato-ku, Tokyo); Osaka (consulate; ☎ 06-6440-5070;
35th fl, Umeda Sky Bldg Tower East, 1-1-88 Ōyodonaka,
Kita-ku, Osaka)

Ireland Tokyo (embassy; Map pp112-13; ☎ 03-3263-
0695; www.embassy-avenue.jp/ireland/index_eng.html;
Ireland House, 2-10-7 Kōji-machi, Chiyoda-ku, Tokyo); Osaka
(consulate; ☎ 06-6204-2024; c/o Takeda Pharmaceutical
Company Limited, 4-1-1,Doshō-machi, Chūō-ku, Osaka)

Netherlands Tokyo (embassy; Map pp119; ☎ 03-5401-
0411; www.oranda.or.jp/index/english/index.html; 3-6-3
Shiba-kōen, Minato-ku, Tokyo); Osaka (consulate; ☎ 06-
6944-7272; 33rd fl, Twin 21 MID Tower, 2-1-61 Shiromi,
Chūō-ku, Osaka)

New Zealand Tokyo (embassy; Map pp112-13; ☎ 03-
3467-2271; www.nzembassy.com/home.cfm?c=17; 20-40
Kamiyama-chō, Shibuya-ku, Tokyo); Osaka (consulate;
☎ 06-6373-4583; Umeda Centra Bldg, 2-4-12 Nakazaki-
nishi Kita-ku, Osaka 530-8323)

South Korea Tokyo (embassy; Map pp112-13; ☎ 03-
3452-7611; www.mofat.go.kr/ek/ek_a001/ek_jpjp/ek
_02.jsp; 1-2-5 Minami Azabu, Minato-ku, Tokyo); Fukuoka
(consulate; ☎ 092-771-0461; 1-1-3 Jigyōhama, Chūō-ku,
Fukuoka)

UK Tokyo (embassy; Map pp112-13; ☎ 03-5211-1100;
www.uknow.or.jp/index_e.htm; 1 Ichiban-chō, Chiyoda-
ku, Tokyo); Osaka (consulate; ☎ 06-6120-5600; 19th fl,
Epson Osaka Bldg, 3-5-1 Bakuromachi, Chūō-ku, Osaka)

USA Tokyo (embassy; Map pp119; ☎ 03-3224-5000;
http://japan.usembassy.gov/t-main.html; 1-10-5 Akasaka,
Minato-ku, Tokyo); Fukuoka (consulate; ☎ 092-751-9331;
2-5-26 Ōhori, Chūō-ku, Fukuoka); Osaka (consulate; ☎ 06-
6315-5900; 2-11-5 Nishitenma, Kita-ku, Osaka)

FESTIVALS & EVENTS

A *matsuri* (festival) is often the highlight
of a trip to Japan. It is a chance to see the
Japanese at their most uninhibited, and get
some insight into the ancient traditions and
beliefs of the country. In addition to *matsuri*,
there are several important annual events,
which are often Buddhist imports from China
or more recent imports from the West (eg
Christmas).

The Japanese often welcome foreigners
to participate in their local *matsuri*. You
might help carry a portable shrine around
a neighbourhood, march in a parade or just
dance around a fire. If you'd like to join a
local *matsuri*, the best thing to do is ask at the
local tourist information office. If you happen
upon a *matsuri*, you can usually ask one of the
participants if it would be OK to join in. Be
warned: participation in a *matsuri* usually also
means participation in the drinking session
that inevitably follows the festival – or is the
main part of the festival!

Some of the most important annual
events:

January

Shōgatsu (New Year) The celebrations from 31 December
to 3 January include much eating and drinking, visits to
shrines or temples and the paying of respects to relatives
and business associates.

Seijin-no-hi (Coming-of-Age Day) Second Monday in
January. Ceremonies are held for boys and girls who have
reached the age of 20.

February–May

Setsubun (3 or 4 February) To celebrate the end of winter
(last day of winter according to the lunar calendar) and
drive out evil spirits, the Japanese throw beans while
chanting '*fuku wa uchi, oni wa soto*' (In with good fortune,
out with the devils).

Hanami (Blossom Viewing) The Japanese delight in the
brief blossom-viewing season from February to April. The
usual sequence is plum in February, peach in March and
cherry in late March or early April.

Hina Matsuri (Doll Festival; 3 March) During this festival
old dolls are displayed and young girls are presented with
special dolls *(hina)* that represent ancient figures from the
imperial court.

Golden Week (29 April to 5 May) Golden Week takes
in Midori-no-hi (Green Day; 29 April), Kempō Kinem-bi
(Constitution Day; 3 May) and Kodomo-no-hi (Children's
Day; 5 May). This is definitely not a time to be on the move
since transport and lodging in popular holiday areas can
be booked solid.

Kodomo-no-hi (Children's Day; 5 May) This is a holiday
dedicated to children, especially boys. Families fly paper
streamers of carp *(koi-nobori)*, which symbolise male strength.

July–August

Tanabata Matsuri (Star Festival; 7 July) The two stars
Vega and Altair meet in the Milky Way on this night.
According to a myth (originally Chinese), a princess and a
peasant shepherd were forbidden to meet, and this was
the only time in the year when the two star-crossed lovers

could organise a tryst. Children copy out poems on streamers, and love poems are written on banners that are hung out on display. An especially ornate version of this festival is celebrated from 6 to 8 August in Sendai.

Fuji Rock Festival (late July) Held in Naeba, in Niigata-ken, this is Japan's biggest rock festival and it always draws some top-shelf acts from abroad. It's a world-class event and is worth planning a trip around. For more information see p564.

O-Bon (Festival of the Dead; 13 to 16 July, and mid-August) According to Buddhist tradition, this is a time when ancestors return to earth. Lanterns are lit and floated on rivers, lakes or the sea to signify the return of the departed to the underworld. Since most Japanese try to return to their native village at this time of year, this is one of the most crowded times of year to travel or look for accommodation.

November

Shichi-Go-San (Seven-Five-Three Festival; 15 November) Traditionally, this is a festival in honour of girls who are aged three and seven and boys who are aged five. Children are dressed in their finest clothes and taken to shrines or temples, where prayers are offered for good fortune.

FOOD

In the bigger cities, the restaurants that appear in the Eating sections of this guide are divided by neighbourhoods and type of cuisine (Japanese or international). Outside the bigger cities, eating options are generally presented in one section. For more information about Japan's cuisine, see p85.

GAY & LESBIAN TRAVELLERS

With the possible exception of Thailand, Japan is Asia's most enlightened nation with regard to the sexual preferences of foreigners. Shinjuku-ni-chôme in Tokyo is an established scene where English is spoken and meeting men is fairly straightforward. In provincial areas there may be one 'snack' bar, where you pay about ¥1500 for the first drink, entry and the snack. Staying in hotels is simple as most have twin rooms but love hotels are less accessible; if you know someone Japanese and can overcome the language barrier, a stay in a love hotel may be possible, but some are not particularly foreigner-friendly (see p787). Gay saunas double as late-night crash spots if you, unwittingly or otherwise, miss the last train home – so ask your barman for details.

The lesbian scene is growing in Japan but is still elusive for most non-Japanese speaking foreigners. Outside Tokyo you may find it difficult to break into the local scene unless you spend considerable time in a place or have local contacts who can show you around.

Given Japan's penchant for convenience the internet has been a boon for the gay and lesbian scene. **Utopia** (www.utopia-asia.com) is the site most commonly frequented by English-speaking gays and lesbians. For information about gay and lesbian venues in Tokyo, see p174.

There are no legal restraints to same-sex sexual activities of either gender in Japan. Public displays of affection are likely to be the only cause for concern for all visitors – gay, straight or otherwise.

HOLIDAYS

Japan has 15 national holidays. When a public holiday falls on a Sunday, the following Monday is taken as a holiday. If that Monday is already a holiday, the following day becomes a holiday as well. And, if two weekdays (say, Tuesday and Thursday) are holidays, the day in between (Wednesday) will also become a holiday.

You can expect travel and accommodation options to be fully booked during the New Year festivities (29 December to 6 January), Golden Week (29 April to 6 May) and the mid-August O-Bon festival. See opposite for more details of these festivals and events.

Japan's national holidays:

Ganjitsu (New Year's Day) 1 January
Seijin-no-hi (Coming-of-Age Day) Second Monday in January
Kenkoku Kinem-bi (National Foundation Day) 11 February
Shumbun-no-hi (Spring Equinox) 20 or 21 March
Showa-no-hi (Shôwa Emperor's Day) 29 April
Kempô Kinem-bi (Constitution Day) 3 May
Midori-no-hi (Green Day) 4 May
Kodomo-no-hi (Children's Day) 5 May
Umi-no-hi (Marine Day) Third Monday in July
Keirô-no-hi (Respect-for-the-Aged Day) Third Monday in September
Shûbun-no-hi (Autumn Equinox) 23 or 24 September
Taiiku-no-hi (Health-Sports Day) Second Monday in October
Bunka-no-hi (Culture Day) 3 November
Kinrô Kansha-no-hi (Labour Thanksgiving Day) 23 November
Tennô Tanjôbi (Emperor's Birthday) 23 December

INSURANCE

A travel insurance policy to cover theft, loss and medical problems is a good idea. Some policies will specifically exclude 'dangerous activities', which can include scuba diving, motorcycling and even trekking; if you plan to engage in such activities, you'll want a policy that covers them.

You may prefer a policy that pays doctors or hospitals directly rather than have you pay on the spot and claim later. If you have to claim later, make sure you keep all documentation. Some policies ask you to call (reverse-charge) a centre in your home country where an immediate assessment of your problem is made. Check that the policy covers ambulances or an emergency flight home.

Some insurance policies offer lower and higher medical-expense options; choose the high-cost option for Japan. Be sure to bring your insurance card or other certificate of insurance to Japan; Japanese hospitals have been known to refuse treatment to foreign patients with no proof of medical insurance.

For information on car insurance, see p818. For information on health insurance, see p826.

INTERNET ACCESS

If you plan on bringing your laptop to Japan, first make sure that it is compatible with Japanese current (100V AC; 50Hz in eastern Japan and 60Hz in western Japan). Most laptops function just fine on Japanese current. Second, check to see if your plug will fit Japanese wall sockets (Japanese plugs are flat two pin, identical to most ungrounded North American plugs). Both transformers and plug adaptors are readily available in electronics districts, such as Tokyo's Akihabara (Map pp112–13), Osaka's Den Den Town (Map p375) or Kyoto's Teramachi-dōri (Map p322).

Modems and phone jacks are similar to those used in the USA (RJ11 phone jacks). Conveniently, many of the grey IDD pay phones in Japan have a standard phone jack and an infrared port so that you can log on to the internet just about anywhere in the country if your computer has an infrared port. In this book, an internet symbol (🖳) indicates that this accommodation option has at least one computer with internet for guests' use. A wi-fi symbol indicates a place with wi-fi somewhere on its premises. You'll find internet cafés and other access points in most major Japanese cities. Rates vary, usually ranging from ¥200 to ¥700 per hour. As a rule, internet connections are fast (DSL or ADSL) and reliable in Japan. Most accommodation options also have some way of getting online, with terminals in the lobby, wi-fi or LAN access.

See p25 for some useful websites on Japan.

LEFT LUGGAGE

Only major stations have left-luggage facilities, but there are almost always coin-operated storage lockers costing ¥100 to ¥500 per day, depending on their size. The lockers are rented until midnight (not for 24 hours). After that time you have to insert more money before your key will work. If your bag is simply too large to fit in the locker, ask someone '*tenimotsu azukai wa doko desu ka*' (Where is the left-luggage office?).

LEGAL MATTERS

Japanese police have extraordinary powers compared with their Western counterparts. For starters, Japanese police have the right to detain a suspect without charging them for up to three days, after which a prosecutor can decide to extend this period for another 20 days. Police can also choose whether to allow a suspect to phone their embassy or lawyer, though if you find yourself in police custody you should insist that you will not cooperate in any way until allowed to make such a call. Your embassy is the first place you should call if given the chance.

Police will speak almost no English; insist that an interpreter (*tsuyakusha*) be summoned. Police are legally bound to provide one before proceeding with any questioning. Even if you do speak Japanese, it's best to deny it and stay with your native language.

If you have a problem, call the **Japan Helpline** (☎ 0570-000-911), an emergency number that operates 24 hours a day, seven days a week.

MAPS

If you'd like to buy a map of Japan before arriving, both Nelles and Periplus produce reasonable maps of the whole country. If you want more detailed maps, it's better to buy them after you arrive in Japan.

The Japan National Tourist Organization's (JNTO) free *Tourist Map of Japan*, available at JNTO-operated tourist information centres inside the country and JNTO offices abroad, is a reasonable English-language map that is suitable for general route planning. If you'd like something a little more detailed, both

ADDRESSES IN JAPAN

In Japan, finding a place from its address can be difficult, even for locals. The problem is two-fold: first, the address is usually given by an area rather than a street; and, second, the numbers are not necessarily consecutive, as prior to the mid-1950s numbers were assigned by date of construction.

In Tokyo very few streets have names – so addresses work by narrowing down the location of a building to a number within an area of a few blocks. In this guide, Tokyo addresses are organised as such: area number, block number and building number, followed by area and ward. For example, 1-11-2 Ginza, Chūō-ku.

In Kyoto, addresses are simplified. We either give the area (eg Higashiyama-ku, Nanzen-ji) or we give the street on which the place is located, followed by the nearest cross street (eg Karasuma-dōri-Imadegawa). In some cases, we also give additional information to show where the place lies in relation to the intersection of the two streets mentioned. In Kyoto, the land usually slopes gently to the south; thus, an address might indicate whether a place lies above or north of (*agaru*) or below or south of (*sagaru* or *kudaru*) a particular east–west road. Thus, 'Karasuma-dōri-Imadegawa' simply means the place is near the intersection of Karasuma-dōri and Imadegawa-dōri; Karasuma-dōri-Imadegawa-sagaru indicates that it's south of that intersection. An address might also indicate whether a place lies east (*higashi*) or west (*nishi*) of the north–south road.

In Sapporo, a typical address would be S17W7-2-12 Chūō-ku. The 'S17W7' is the South 17, West 7 block. The building is in the second section at number 12.

Elsewhere in this guide, addresses list area number, block number and building number, followed by area and ward. This is the more common presentation in English. For example, '1-7-2 Motomachi-dōri, Chūō-ku'. Where given, the floor number and building name are listed first.

To find an address, the usual process is to ask directions. Have your address handy. The numerous local police boxes are there largely for this purpose. Businesses often include a small map in their advertisements or on their business cards to show their location.

Most taxis and many rental cars now have satellite navigation systems which make finding places a breeze, as long as you can program the address or phone number into the system. Needless to say, you'll have to be able to read Japanese to input the address, but phone numbers should be no problem.

Shobunsha and Kodansha (Japanese publishers) publish a series of bilingual fold-out maps (prices start at around ¥700).

The *Japan Road Atlas* (Shobunsha) is a good choice for those planning to drive around the country. Those looking for something less bulky should pick up a copy of the *Bilingual Atlas of Japan* (Kodansha). Of course, if you can read a little Japanese, you'll do much better with one of the excellent *Super Mapple* road atlases published by Shobunsha.

MONEY

Despite being a thoroughly modern country, it is not always easy to get cash in Japan. This is because the vast bulk of the country's ATMs only work with Japan-issued bank cards and credit cards. However, Japan's post office ATMs accept most foreign-issued bank cards (see the following ATMs section for details). If your card is not a member of one of the networks accepted by Japanese postal ATMs, you will have a hard time getting cash in Japan and you'll have to bring a lot of cash or travellers cheques to exchange.

The currency in Japan is the yen (¥) and banknotes and coins are easily identifiable. There are ¥1, ¥5, ¥10, ¥50, ¥100 and ¥500 coins; and ¥1000, ¥2000, ¥5000 and ¥10,000 banknotes (the ¥2000 notes are very rarely seen). The ¥1 coin is an aluminium lightweight coin, the ¥5 and ¥50 coins have a punched hole in the middle (the former is coloured bronze and the latter silver). Note that some vending machines do not accept older ¥500 coins (a South Korean coin of much less value was often used in its place to rip off vending machines).

The Japanese pronounce yen as 'en', with no 'y' sound. The kanji for yen is: 円.

For information on costs in Japan, see p22. For exchange rates, see the inside front cover of this guide.

DIRECTORY

WARNING: JAPAN IS A CASH SOCIETY!

Be warned that cold hard yen (¥) is the way to pay in Japan. While credit cards are becoming more common, cash is still much more widely used, and travellers cheques are rarely accepted. Do not assume that you can pay for things with a credit card; always carry sufficient cash. The only places where you can count on paying by credit card are department stores and large hotels.

For those without credit cards, it would be a good idea to bring some travellers cheques as a back-up. As in most other countries, the US dollar is still the currency of choice in terms of exchanging cash and cashing travellers cheques.

ATMs

Automated teller machines are almost as common as vending machines in Japan. Unfortunately, most of these do not accept foreign-issued cards. Even if they display Visa and MasterCard logos, most accept only Japan-issued versions of these cards.

Fortunately, Japanese postal ATMs accept cards that belong to the following international networks: Visa, Plus, MasterCard, Maestro, Cirrus American Express and Diners Club cards. Check the sticker(s) on the back of your card to see which network(s) your card belongs to. You'll find postal ATMs in almost all post offices, and you'll find post offices in even the smallest Japanese village.

Most postal ATMs are open 9am to 5pm on weekdays, 9am to noon on Saturday, and are closed on Sunday and holidays. Some postal ATMs in very large central post offices are open longer hours.

Note that the postal ATMs are a little tricky to use: first press 'English Guidance' on the lower right-hand side of the screen and then press the withdrawal button. The post office has a useful online guide to using its ATMs at www.yu-cho.japanpost.jp/e_index .htm. Click 'International ATM service' for an explanation of postal ATMs.

In addition to postal ATMs, you will find a few international ATMs in big cities like Tokyo, Osaka and Kyoto, as well as major airports like Narita and Kansai International Airport. International cards also work in Citibank Japan ATMs. Visit www.citibank .co.jp/en/branch/index.html for a useful branch index.

Credit Cards

Except for making cash withdrawals at banks and ATMs, it is best not to rely on credit cards in Japan. While department stores, top-end hotels and some restaurants do accept cards, most businesses in Japan do not. Cash-and-carry is still very much the rule. If you do decide to bring a credit card, you'll find Visa the most useful, followed by MasterCard, Amex and Diners Club.

The main credit-card offices are in Tokyo:

Amex (☎ 0120-020-120; 4-30-16 Ogikubo, Suginami-ku; ⏰ 24hr)

MasterCard (Map p117; ☎ 03-5728-5200; 16th fl, Cerulean Tower, 26-1 Sakuragaoka-chō, Shibuya-ku)

Visa (Map p119; ☎ 03-5275-7604; 7th fl, Hitotsubashi Bldg, 2-6-3 Hitotsubashi, Chiyoda-ku)

Exchanging Money

Banks, post offices and discount ticket shops will change all major currencies and travellers cheques. As with most other countries, you'll find that US dollars are the easiest to change, although you should have no problems with other major currencies. Note, however, that the currencies of neighbouring Taiwan (New Taiwan dollar) and Korea *(won)* are not easy to change, so you should change these into yen or US dollars before arriving in Japan.

You can change cash or travellers cheques at most banks, major post offices, discount ticket shops, some travel agents, some large hotels and most big department stores. Note that discount ticket shops (known as *kakuyasu kippu uriba* in Japanese) often have the best rates. These can be found around major train stations.

INTERNATIONAL TRANSFERS

In order to make an international transfer you'll have to find a Japanese bank associated with the bank transferring the money. Start by asking at the central branch of any major Japanese bank. If they don't have a relationship with your bank, they can usually refer you to a bank that does. Once you find a related bank in Japan, you'll have to give your home bank the exact details of where to send the money: the bank, branch and location. A credit-card cash advance is a worthwhile alternative.

Taxes

Japan has a 5% consumer tax. If you eat at expensive restaurants and stay in top-end accommodation, you will encounter a service charge which varies from 10% to 15%.

Tipping

There is little tipping in Japan. If you want to show your gratitude to someone, give them a gift rather than a tip. If you do choose to give someone a cash gift (a maid in a ryokan, for instance), place the money in an envelope first.

PHOTOGRAPHY

Japan is one of the world's best places to buy cameras (digital or film), photographic equipment, memory and anything else that you can possibly think of to help you record your trip. Japan's photo shops also offer a wide range of services for digital photographers, such as high-quality prints from digital files. The typical cost for printing digital photos is ¥35 per print.

For more information on buying cameras and other photographic equipment, see p801.

POST

The Japanese postal system is reliable, efficient and, for regular postcards and airmail letters, not markedly more expensive than other developed countries.

Postal Rates

The airmail rate for postcards is ¥70 to any overseas destination; aerograms cost ¥90. Letters weighing less than 25g are ¥90 to other countries within Asia, ¥110 to North America, Europe or Oceania (including Australia and New Zealand) and ¥130 to Africa and South America. One peculiarity of the Japanese postal system is that you will be charged extra if your writing runs over onto the address side (the right side) of a postcard.

Sending & Receiving Mail

The symbol for post offices is a red T with a bar across the top on a white background (〒). District post offices (the main post office in a ward) are normally open from 9am to 7pm weekdays and 9am to 3pm Saturday, and are closed Sunday and public holidays. Local post offices are open 9am to 5pm weekdays, and are closed Saturday, Sunday and public holidays. Main post offices in the larger cities may have an after-hours window open 24 hours a day, seven days a week.

Mail can be sent to, from or within Japan when addressed in English (Roman script).

Although any post office will hold mail for collection, the poste restante concept is not well known and can cause confusion in smaller places. It is probably better to have mail addressed to you at a larger central post office. Letters are usually only held for 30 days before being returned to sender. When inquiring about mail for collection ask for *kyoku dome yūbin*.

It should be addressed as follows:

Darren O'CONNELL
Poste Restante
Central Post Office
Tokyo, JAPAN

SHOPPING

Japan is truly a shopper's paradise, and it is not as expensive as you might imagine. As well as all the electronic gadgetry available in Japan, there is a wide range of traditional crafts to choose from, all of which make great souvenirs. The big department stores often have the best selections of Japanese gift items, and they usually have English speakers on hand.

Bargaining

Bargaining is largely restricted to flea markets (where anything goes) and large discount electronics shops (where a polite request will often bring the price down by around 10%).

Computer Equipment

Computers, computer accessories and software are widely available. Unfortunately for the foreign traveller, most of what's out there – operating systems, keyboards and software – is in Japanese and not of any use unless you intend to work with the Japanese language. However, if you're after hardware like peripherals, chips and the like, where language isn't a factor, you will find lots to choose from, including second-hand goods at unbelievably low prices. The world's biggest selection of computer equipment can be found in Japan's major electronics districts: Akihabara in Tokyo and Den Den Town in Osaka (see following Electronics section).

Electronics

Nowhere in the world will you find a better selection of electronics than in Tokyo's

Akihabara district (p179) and Osaka's Den Den Town (p389). Keep in mind though that much of the electrical gadgetry on sale in Japan is designed for Japan's curious power supply (100V at 50Hz or 60Hz) and may require a transformer for use overseas. The safest bet is to go for export models – the prices may be slightly higher but, in the long run, you'll save the expense of converting the equipment to suit the conditions in your own country.

Japanese Arts & Crafts

As well as all the hi-tech knick-knacks produced by the Japanese, it is also possible to go home loaded with traditional Japanese arts and crafts. Anything from carp banners to kimono can make good souvenirs for the Japanophile.

KASA (JAPANESE UMBRELLAS)

A classic souvenir item, *kasa* (Japanese umbrellas) come in two forms: *higasa*, which are made of paper, cotton or silk and serve as a sunshade; and *bangasa*, which are made of oiled paper and keep the rain off. Department stores and tourist shops are your best bet for finding *kasa*.

KATANA (JAPANESE SWORDS)

A fantastic souvenir – good *katana* (Japanese swords) are going to cost more than all your other travel expenses put together! The reason for their expense is both their mystique as the symbols of samurai power, and the great care that goes into making them. Sword shops that sell the real thing will also stock *tsuba* (sword guards), and complete sets of samurai armour. Some department stores, on the other hand, stock realistic (to the untrained eye at least) imitations at affordable prices.

KIMONO & YUKATA

A good kimono is perhaps the ultimate souvenir of a trip to Japan, and prices for new kimono start at around ¥60,000. Keep in mind that you'll have to go for at least one fitting and wait for around a week before the finished item is ready to pick up. A used kimono is a good solution if you don't have the time or money to spend on a new one. Used-clothing shops usually stock a variety of kimono ranging in price from ¥1500 to ¥9000. Another good place to pick up a used kimono is a flea market, where you can find a huge variety of often very fine kimono for less than ¥2000.

Yukata (light summer kimono or bathrobes) are another great souvenir and new ones can be had for as low as ¥2000. Unlike kimono, these are easy to put on and can be worn comfortably around the house. These are available from tourist shops and department stores in Japan.

KOINOBORI (CARP BANNERS)

The lovely banners that you see waving in the breeze on Kodomo-no-hi (Children's Day; 5 May) throughout Japan are called *koinobori*. The carp is much revered for its tenacity and perseverance, but you might like the banners for their simple elegance.

NINGYŌ (JAPANESE DOLLS)

Not for playing with, Japanese dolls are usually intended for display. Often quite exquisite, with coiffured hair and dressed in kimono, *ningyō* make excellent souvenirs or gifts. Also available are *gogatsu-ningyō*, dolls that are dressed in samurai suits used as gifts on Kodomo-no-hi. The most well-known dolls are made in Kyoto and are known as *kyō-ningyō*.

Ningyō can be bought in tourist shops, department stores and special doll shops. In Tokyo, Edo-dōri in Asakusa (p181) is well known for its many doll shops.

POTTERY

Numerous pottery villages still exist in Japan; many feature pottery museums and working kilns that are open to the public. Of course, it is also possible to buy examples of stoneware and porcelain. Sources of different pottery styles abound: there's Bizen (p446), near Okayama in western Honshū, which is famed for its Bizen-yaki pottery; and Karatsu (p676), Imari (p678) and Arita (p679) in Kyūshū (the home of Japanese pottery).

Department stores are a surprisingly good place to look for Japanese pottery, and Takashimaya (see p179 for details) often has bargain bins where you can score some real deals. For even better prices try some of Japan's flea markets.

SHIKKI (LACQUERWARE)

Another exquisite Japanese craft is *shikki* (lacquerware). The lacquerware-making process, involving as many as 15 layers of lacquer, is used to create objects as diverse as dishes and furniture. As you might expect, examples of good lacquerware cannot be had for a song, but smaller items can be bought at affordable prices from department stores. Popular, easily transportable items include bowls, trays and small boxes. Department stores often have good selections of lacquerware in their housewares sections.

UKIYO-E (WOOD-BLOCK PRINTS)
Originating in the 18th century as one of Japan's earliest manifestations of mass culture, wood-block prints were used in advertising and posters. It was only later that *ukiyo-e* was considered an art form. The name (literally, 'pictures from the floating world') derives from a Buddhist term indicating the transient world of daily pleasures. *Ukiyo-e* uniquely depicts such things as street scenes, actors and courtesans.

Today, tourist shops in Japan stock modern reproductions of the work of famous *ukiyo-e* masters such as Hokusai, whose scenes of Fuji-san are favourites. It is also possible to come across originals by lesser-known artists at prices ranging from ¥3000 to ¥40,000.

WASHI (JAPANESE PAPER)
For more than 1000 years, *washi* (Japanese paper) has been famous as the finest handmade paper in the world. Special shops stock sheets of *washi* and products made from it, such as notebooks, wallets and so on. As they're generally inexpensive and light, *washi* products make excellent gifts and souvenirs. You'll find them in the big department stores. See p363 for suggestions on places to buy *washi*.

Pearls
The Japanese firm Mikimoto developed the technique of producing cultured pearls by artificially introducing an irritant into the pearl oyster. Pearls and pearl jewellery are still popular buys for foreign visitors. The best place in Japan to buy pearls is Mikimoto's home base: Toba, in Mie-ken (p438).

Photographic Equipment
Tokyo is an excellent hunting ground for photographic equipment. As almost all of the big-name brands in camera equipment are locally produced, prices can be very competitive. The prices for accessories, such as motor drives and flash units, can even be compared to Singapore and Hong Kong. In addition, shopping in Japan presents the traveller with none of the rip-off risks that abound in other Asian discount capitals.

Tokyo's Shinjuku area is the best place for buying camera equipment, although Ginza also has a good selection of camera shops (see p181 for details). Second-hand camera equipment is worth checking out. In Tokyo, both Shinjuku and Ginza have a fair number of second-hand shops where camera and lens quality is usually very good and prices are around half what you would pay for new equipment. In Osaka, the area just south of Osaka station has used-camera shops as well (see p389).

Tax-Free Shopping
Shopping tax-free in Japan is not necessarily the bargain that you might expect. Although tax-free shops enable foreigners to receive an exemption from the 5% consumption tax (*shōhi-zei*) levied on most items, these still may not be the cheapest places to shop. Shops that offer this exemption usually require that you pay the consumption tax and then go to a special counter to receive a refund. You will often need to show your passport to receive this refund. Tax-free shops will usually have a sign in English that announces their tax-free status.

Toys
Tokyo has some remarkable toy shops. See p180 for more information. Elsewhere, look out for some of the traditional wooden toys produced as regional specialities – they make good souvenirs for adults and children alike.

SOLO TRAVELLERS
Japan is an excellent place for solo travellers: it's safe, convenient and friendly. Almost all hotels in Japan have single rooms, and business-hotel singles can cost as little as ¥4000. Ryokan usually charge by the person, not the room, which keeps the price down for the single traveller. The only hitch is that some ryokan owners balk at renting a room to a single traveller, when they might be able to rent it to two people instead. For more on accommodation, see p784.

Many restaurants in Japan have small tables or counters which are perfect for solo travellers. *Izakaya* (Japanese-style dining pubs) are also generally welcoming to solo travellers, and you probably won't have to wait long before you're offered a drink and roped into a conversation, particularly if you sit at the counter. Finally, the 'gaijin bars' in the larger cities are generally friendly, convivial places; if you're after a travel partner or just an English-speaking conversation partner, these are good places to start.

TELEPHONE

Japanese telephone codes consist of an area code plus a local code and number. You do not dial the area code when making a call in that area. When dialling Japan from abroad, dial the country code ☎ 81, followed by the area code (drop the '0') and the number. For a list of area codes for some of Japan's major cities and emergency numbers, see the inside front cover of this guidebook. Numbers that begin with the digits ☎ 0120, ☎ 0070, ☎ 0077, ☎ 0088 and ☎ 0800 are toll-free.

Directory Assistance

For local directory assistance dial ☎ 104 (the call costs ¥100), or for assistance in English ring ☎ 0120-364-463 from 9am to 5pm weekdays. For international directory assistance dial ☎ 0057.

International Calls

The best way to make an international phone call from Japan is to use a prepaid international phone card (see right).

Paid overseas calls can be made from grey international ISDN phones. These are usually found in phone booths marked 'International & Domestic Card/Coin Phone'. Unfortunately, these are very rare; try looking in the lobbies of top-end hotels and at airports. Some new green phones found in phone booths also allow international calls. Calls are charged by the unit, each of which is six seconds, so if you don't have much to say you could phone home for just ¥100. Reverse-charge (collect) overseas calls can be made from any pay phone.

You can save money by dialling late at night. Economy rates are available from 7pm to 8am. Note that it is also cheaper to make domestic calls by dialling outside the standard hours.

To place an international call through the operator, dial ☎ 0051 (KDDI operator; most international operators speak English). To make the call yourself, dial ☎ 001 010 (KDDI), ☎ 0041 010 (SoftBank Telecom)

or ☎ 0033 010 (NTT) – there's very little difference in their rates – then the international country code, the local code and the number.

Another option is to dial ☎ 0038 plus your country code for home country direct, which takes you straight through to a local operator in the country dialled. You can then make a reverse-charge call or a credit-card call with a telephone credit card valid in that country.

PREPAID INTERNATIONAL PHONE CARDS

Because of the lack of pay phones from which you can make international phone calls in Japan, the easiest way to make an international phone call is to buy a prepaid international phone card. Most convenience stores carry at least one of the following types of phone cards: KDDI Superworld Card, NTT Communications World Card and SoftBank Telecom Comica Card. These cards can be used with any regular pay phone in Japan.

Local Calls

The Japanese public telephone system is very well developed. There are a great many public phones and they work almost all the time. Local calls from pay phones cost ¥10 per minute; unused ¥10 coins are returned after the call is completed but no change is given on ¥100 coins.

In general it's much easier to buy a telephone card (*terefon kādo*) when you arrive rather than worry about always having coins on hand. Phone cards are sold in ¥500 and ¥1000 denominations (the latter earns you an extra ¥50 in calls) and can be used in most green or grey pay phones. They are available from vending machines and convenience stores, come in a myriad of designs and are also a collectable item.

Mobile Phones

Japan's mobile phone networks use 3G (third generation) cell phone technology on a variety of frequencies. Thus, non-3G cell phones cannot be used in Japan. This means that most foreign cell phones *will not work* in Japan. Furthermore, SIM cards are not commonly available in Japan. Thus, for most people who want to use a cell phone while in Japan, the only solution is to rent a mobile phone.

Several companies in Japan specialise in short-term mobile phone rentals, a good option for travellers whose own phones won't work in Japan, or whose own phones would be prohibitively expensive to use here. The following companies provide this service:

Mobile Phone Japan (☎ 075-361-8890; www .mobilephonejp.com) This company offers basic mobile phone rental for as low as ¥2900/week. Incoming calls, whether international or domestic, are free, and outgoing domestic calls are ¥2 per second (outgoing domestic calls vary according to country and time of day). Free delivery anywhere in Japan is included and a free prepaid return envelope is also included.

Rentafone Japan (☎ 090-9621-7318; www.rentafone japan.com) This company rents out mobile phones for ¥3900 per week and offers free delivery of the phone to your accommodation. Call rates are the same as above.

Useful Numbers

If you're staying long-term, adjusting to life in Japan can be tough; but there are places to turn to for help. **Metropolitan Government Foreign Residents' Advisory Center** (☎ 03-5320-7744; 9.30am-noon & 1-4pm Mon-Fri) is a useful service operated by the Tokyo metropolitan government. Otherwise, try the 24-hour **Japan Helpline** (☎ 0120-461 997).

TIME

Despite the distance between Japan's east and west, the country is all on the same time: nine hours ahead of Greenwich Mean Time (GMT). Sydney and Wellington are ahead of Japan (+1 and +3 hours, respectively), and most of the world's other big cities are behind Japan (New York -14, Los Angeles -17 and London -9). Japan does not have daylight savings time (also known as summer time). For more information see World Time Zones (pp866-7).

TOILETS

In Japan you will come across Western-style toilets and Asian squat toilets. When you are compelled to squat, the correct position is facing the hood, away from the door. Make sure the contents of your pockets don't spill out! Toilet paper isn't always provided, so carry tissues with you. You may be given small packets of tissue on the street in Japan, a common form of advertising.

In many bathrooms in Japan, separate toilet slippers are often provided just inside the toilet door. These are for use in the toilet only, so remember to change out of them when you leave.

It's quite common to see men urinating in public – the unspoken rule is that it's accept-

able at night time if you happen to be drunk. Public toilets are free in Japan. The katakana script for 'toilet' is トイレ, and the kanji script is お手洗い.

You'll often also see these kanji:
Female 女
Male 男

TOURIST INFORMATION

Japan's tourist information services are first-rate. You will find information offices in most cities, towns and even some small villages. They are almost always located inside or in front of the main train station in a town or city.

A note on language difficulties: English speakers are usually available at tourist information offices in larger cities. Away from the big cities, you'll find varying degrees of English-language ability. In rural areas and small towns you may find yourself relying more on one-word communication and hand signals. Nonetheless, with a little patience and a smile you will usually get the information you need from even the smallest local tourist information office.

Japan National Tourist Organization (JNTO)

The **Japan National Tourist Organization** (JNTO; www .jnto.go.jp, www.japantravelinfo.com) is the main English-language information service for foreign travellers to Japan. JNTO produces a great deal of useful literature, which is available from both its overseas offices and its Tourist Information Center in Tokyo (p109). Most publications are available in English and, in some cases, other European and Asian languages. JNTO's website is very useful in planning your journey.

Unfortunately for foreign travellers, JNTO is pulling out of the business of operating tourist information centres inside Japan. The sole remaining domestic office is the Tokyo office.

JNTO has a number of overseas offices:
Australia (☎ 02-9251 3024; Level 18, Australia Sq Tower, 264 George St, Sydney, NSW 2000)
Canada (☎ 416-366 7140; 165 University Ave, Toronto, ON M5H 3B8)
France (☎ 01 42 96 20 29; 4 rue de Ventadour, 75001 Paris)
Germany (☎ 069-20353; Kaiserstrasse 11, 60311 Frankfurt am Main)
UK (☎ 020-7734 4290; Heathcoat House, 20 Savile Row, London W1S 3PR)

USA Los Angeles (☎ 213-623 1952; 515 South Figueroa St, Suite 1470, Los Angeles, CA 90071); New York (☎ 212-757 5640; One Rockefeller Plaza, Suite 1250, New York, NY 10020)

Other Information Offices

There are tourist information offices (*kankō annai-sho*; 観光案内所) in or near almost all major railway stations, but the further you venture into outlying regions, the less chance you have of finding English-speaking staff.

TRAVELLERS WITH DISABILITIES

Japan is a relatively easy country in which to travel for travellers with disabilities. Many new buildings in Japan have access ramps, traffic lights have speakers playing melodies when it is safe to cross, train platforms have raised dots and lines to provide guidance and some ticket machines in Tokyo have Braille. Some attractions also offer free entry to disabled persons and one companion. On the negative side, many of Japan's cities are still rather difficult for disabled persons to negotiate, often due to the relative lack of normal sidewalks on narrow streets.

If you are going to travel by train and need assistance, ask one of the station workers as you enter the station. Try asking: '*karada no fujiyuū no kata no sharyō wa arimasu ka?*' (Are there train carriages for disabled travellers?).

There are carriages on most lines that have areas set aside for people in wheelchairs. Those with other physical disabilities can use the seats set near the train exits, called *yūsen-zaseki*. You will also find these seats near the front of buses; usually they're a different colour from the regular seats.

The most useful information for disabled visitors is provided by the **Japanese Red Cross Language Service Volunteers** (☎ 03-3438-1311; http://accessible.jp.org/title2-e.html; c/o Volunteers Division, Japanese Red Cross Society, 1-1-3 Shiba Daimon, Minato-ku, Tokyo 105-8521, Japan). Its website has online guides for disabled travellers to Tokyo, Kyoto and Kamakura.

For information on negotiating Japan in a wheelchair, see the website for **Accessible Japan** (www.wakakoma.org/aj).

Eagle Bus Company (☎ 049-227-7611; www.new-wing.co.jp/koedo/Nostalsic%20Little%20Edo/index.htm) has lift-equipped buses and some English-speaking drivers who are also licensed caregivers. It offers tours of Tokyo and around for travellers with disabilities. However, the number of English-speaking drivers/caregivers is limited, so it is necessary to reserve well in advance. Group bookings are possible. It also offers English-language tours of Kawagoe, a small town outside Tokyo, which is sometimes known as little Edo.

VISAS

Generally, visitors who are not planning to engage in income-producing activities while in Japan are exempt from obtaining visas and will be issued a *tanki-taizai* visa (temporary visitor visa) on arrival.

Stays of up to six months are permitted for citizens of Austria, Germany, Ireland, Mexico, Switzerland and the UK. Citizens of these countries will almost always be given a 90-day temporary visitor visa upon arrival, which can usually be extended for another 90 days at immigration bureaux inside Japan (for details see opposite).

Citizens of the USA, Australia and New Zealand are granted 90-day temporary visitor visas, while stays of up to three months are permitted for citizens of Argentina, Belgium, Canada, Denmark, Finland, France, Iceland, Israel, Italy, the Netherlands, Norway, Singapore, Spain, Sweden and a number of other countries.

Japan requires that visitors to the country entering on a temporary visitor visa possess an ongoing air or sea ticket or evidence thereof. In practice, few travellers are asked to produce such documents, but to avoid surprises it pays to be on the safe side.

For additional information on visas and regulations, contact your nearest Japanese embassy or consulate, or visit the website of the **Ministry of Foreign Affairs of Japan** (www.mofa.go.jp). Here you can find out about the different types of visas available, read about working-holiday visas and find details on the Japan Exchange & Teaching (JET) program, which sponsors native English speakers to teach in the Japanese public school system.

Alien Registration Card

Anyone, and this includes tourists, who stays for more than 90 days is required to obtain an Alien Registration Card (*Gaikokujin Torokushō*). This card can be obtained at the municipal office of the city, town or ward in which you're living or staying.

You must carry your Alien Registration Card at all times as the police can stop you and ask to see the card. If you don't have the card, you may be taken back to the station and will have to wait there until someone fetches it for you.

Visa Extensions

With the exception of those nationals whose countries have reciprocal visa exemptions and can stay for six months, the limit for most nationalities is 90 days or three months. To extend a temporary visitor visa beyond the standard 90 days or three months, apply at the nearest immigration office (for a list of immigration bureaux and regional offices visit www.immi-moj.go.jp/english/soshiki/index.html). You must provide two copies of an Application for Extension of Stay (available at the immigration office), a letter stating the reasons for the extension, supporting documentation and your passport. There is a processing fee of ¥4000.

Many long-term visitors to Japan get around the extension problem by briefly leaving the country, usually going to South Korea. Be warned, though, that immigration officials are wise to this practice and many 'tourist visa returnees' are turned back at the entry point.

Work Visas

Unless you are on a cultural visa and have been granted permission to work (see p143), or hold a working-holiday visa, you are not permitted to work in Japan without a proper work visa. If you have the proper paperwork and an employee willing to sponsor you, the process is straightforward, although it can be time-consuming.

Once you find an employer in Japan who is willing to sponsor you, it is necessary to obtain a Certificate of Eligibility from the nearest immigration office. The same office can then issue you your work visa, which is valid for either one or three years. The whole procedure usually takes two to three months.

Working-Holiday Visas

Australians, Britons, Canadians, Germans, New Zealanders and South Koreans between the ages of 18 and 25 (the age limit can be pushed up to 30 in some cases) can apply for a working-holiday visa. This visa allows a six-month stay and two six-month extensions. It is designed to enable young people to travel extensively during their stay; although

employment is supposed to be part-time or temporary, in practice many people work full-time.

A working-holiday visa is much easier to obtain than a work visa and is popular with Japanese employers. Single applicants must have the equivalent of US$2000 of funds, a married couple must have US$3000, and all applicants must have an onward ticket from Japan. For details, inquire at the nearest Japanese embassy or consulate (see p793).

VOLUNTEERING

For obvious reasons, Japan doesn't have as many volunteer opportunities as some other Asian countries. However, there are positions out there for those who look. One of the most popular volunteering options in Japan is provided by **Willing Workers on Organic Farms Japan** (WWOOF Japan; fax 011-780-4908; www.wwoofjapan.com/index_e.shtml; Honcho 2-jo, 3-chome 6-7, Higashi-ku, Sapporo 065-0042, Japan). This organisation places volunteers on organic farms around the country, where they help with the daily running of the farms and participate in family or community life. This provides a good look into Japanese rural life, the running of an organic farm and a great chance to improve your Japanese-language skills.

Alternatively, you can look for volunteer opportunities once you arrive in Japan. There are occasional ads for volunteer positions in magazines like *Kansai Time Out* in Kansai and the various English-language journals in the Tokyo area. Word of mouth is also a good way to search for jobs. Hikers, for example, are sometimes offered short-term positions in Japan's mountain huts (see p787).

WOMEN TRAVELLERS

Japan is a relatively safe country for women travellers, though perhaps not quite as safe as some might think. Women travellers are occasionally subjected to some form of verbal harassment or prying questions. Physical attacks are very rare, but have occurred. Long-term foreign women residents of Japan have been victims of stalking, harassment and worse, and have often found the local police to be unwilling to help them prosecute offenders.

The best advice is to avoid being lulled into a false sense of security by Japan's image as one of the world's safest countries and to take the some precautions you would in your home country. If a neighbourhood or establishment looks unsafe, then treat it that way. Never give your address or the name of your accommodation out to an unfamiliar man and never invite an unfamiliar man to your place or go to his. As long as you use your common sense, you will most likely find that Japan is a pleasant and rewarding place to travel.

Several train companies in Japan have recently introduced women-only cars to protect female passengers from *chikan* (men who feel up women and girls on packed trains). These cars are usually available during rush-hour periods on weekdays on busy urban lines. There are signs (usually pink in colour) on the platform indicating where to board these cars, and the cars themselves are usually labelled in both Japanese and English (again, these are often marked in pink).

If you have a problem and find the local police unhelpful, you can call the **Japan Helpline** (☎ 0570-000-911), an emergency number that operates 24 hours a day, seven days a week.

Finally, an excellent resource available for any woman setting up in Japan is Caroline Pover's book *Being A Broad in Japan,* which can be found in bookstores and can also be ordered from her website at www.being-a-broad.com.

WORK

Japan is an excellent and rewarding place to live and work and all major cities in Japan have significant populations of expats doing just that. Teaching English is still the most common job for Westerners, but bartending, hostessing, modelling and various writing/editorial jobs are also possible.

The key to success in Japan is doing your homework and presenting yourself properly. You will definitely need a proper outfit for interviews, a stack of *meishi* (business cards) and the right attitude. If you don't have a university degree, you won't be eligible for most jobs that qualify you for a work visa. Any qualification, like an English-teaching qualification, will be a huge boost.

Finally, outside of the entertainment, construction and English-teaching industries, you can't expect a good job unless you speak good Japanese (any more than someone could expect a job in your home country without speaking the *lingua franca*).

Bartending

Bartending does not qualify you for a work visa; most of the foreign bartenders in Japan are either working illegally or are on another kind of visa. Some bars in big Japanese cities hire foreign bartenders; most are strict about visas but others don't seem to care. The best places to look are 'gaijin bars', although a few Japanese-oriented places also employ foreign bartenders for 'ambience'. The pay is barely enough to survive on – usually about ¥1000 per hour. The great plus of working as a bartender (other than free drinks) is the chance to practise speaking Japanese.

English Teaching

Teaching English has always been the most popular job for native English speakers in Japan. A university degree is an absolute essential as you cannot qualify for a work visa without one (be sure to bring the actual degree with you to Japan). Teaching qualifications and some teaching experience will be a huge plus when job hunting.

Consider lining up a job before arriving in Japan. Big schools, like Nova for example, now have recruitment programs in the USA and the UK. One downside to the big 'factory schools' that recruit overseas is that working conditions are often pretty dire compared with smaller schools that recruit within Japan.

Australians, New Zealanders and Canadians, who can take advantage of the Japanese working-holiday visa (p805), are in a slightly better position. Schools are happier about taking on unqualified teachers if they don't have to bother with sponsoring a teacher for a work visa.

There is a definite hierarchy among English teachers and teaching positions in Japan. The bottom of the barrel are the big chain *eikaiwa* (private English conversation schools), followed by small local *eikaiwa,* inhouse company language schools, and private lessons, with university positions and international school positions being the most sought after. As you would expect, newcomers start at the lower rungs and work their way up the ladder.

ELT News (www.eltnews.com/home.shtml) is an excellent site with lots of information and want ads for English teachers in Japan.

GOVERNMENT SCHOOLS

The program run by **Japan Exchange & Teaching** (JET; www.jetprogramme.org) provides 2000 teaching assistant positions for foreign teachers. The job operates on a yearly contract and must be organised in your home country. The program gets very good reports from many of its teachers.

Teachers employed by the JET program are known as Assistant Language Teachers (ALTs). Although you will have to apply in your home country in order to work as an ALT with JET, it's worth bearing in mind that many local governments in Japan are also employing ALTs for their schools. Such work can sometimes be arranged within Japan.

Visit the JET website or contact the nearest Japanese embassy or consulate (p793) for more details.

INTERNATIONAL SCHOOLS

Major cities with large foreign populations, such as Tokyo and Yokohama, have a number of international schools for the children of foreign residents. Work is available for qualified, Western-trained teachers in all disciplines; the schools will usually organise your visa.

PRIVATE SCHOOLS

Private language schools *(eikaiwa)* are the largest employers of foreign teachers in Japan and the best bet for the job-hunting newcomer. The classifieds section of the Monday edition of the *Japan Times* is the best place to look for teaching positions. Some larger schools rely on direct inquiries from would-be teachers.

Tokyo is the easiest place to find teaching jobs; schools across Japan advertise or recruit in the capital. Heading straight to another of Japan's major population centres (say Osaka, Fukuoka, Hiroshima or Sapporo), where there are smaller numbers of competing foreigners, is also a good bet.

Hostessing

A hostess is a woman who is paid to pour drinks for and chat with (usually) male customers in a so-called 'hostess bar'. Although hostessing does involve a lot of thinly veiled sexual innuendos and the occasional furtive grab at thighs or breasts, it is not a form of prostitution. At some of the seedier places, however, there may be some pressure to perform 'extracurricular activities'.

Work visas are not issued for hostesses. Rates for Western women working as hostesses typically range from ¥3000 to ¥5000 per hour (plus tips), with bonuses for bringing customers to the club. An ability to speak Japanese is an asset, but not essential – many Japanese *salarymen* want to practise their English.

Proofreading, Editing & Writing

There is a huge demand for skilled editors, copywriters, proofreaders and translators (Japanese to English and, less commonly, vice versa) in Japan. And with the advent of the internet, you don't even have to be based in Japan to do this work. Unfortunately, as with many things in Japan, introductions and connections play a huge role, and it's difficult simply to show up in Tokyo or plaster your resume online and wind up with a good job.

You'll need to be persistent and do some networking to make much in this field. Experience, advanced degrees and salesmanship will all come in handy. And even if you don't intend to do translation, some Japanese-language ability will be a huge plus, if only for communicating with potential employers and clients. If you think you've got what it takes, check the Monday edition of the *Japan Times* for openings.

For more information about proofreading and editing in Japan, visit the webpage for the **Society of Writers, Editors & Translators** (SWET; www.swet.jp).

Ski Areas

Seasonal work is available at ski areas in Japan and this is a popular option for Australian and Kiwi travellers, who want to combine a trip to Japan, a little skiing and a chance to earn a little money. A working-holiday visa (see p805) makes this easier, although occasionally people are offered jobs without visas. The jobs are typical ski town jobs – ski lift attendants, hotel workers, bartenders, and, for those with the right skills (language and skiing), ski instructors. You won't earn much more than ¥1000 per hour unless you're an instructor, but you'll get lodging and lift tickets. All told, it's a fun way to spend a few months in Japan.

Transport

CONTENTS

TRANSPORT

GETTING THERE & AWAY

ENTERING THE COUNTRY

While most travellers to Japan fly via Tokyo, there are several other ways of getting into and out of the country. For a start, there are many other airports in Japan, which can make better entry points than Tokyo's somewhat inconvenient Narita International Airport. It's also possible to arrive in Japan by sea from South Korea, China, Russia and Taiwan.

Passports

A passport is essential. If your passport is within a few months of expiry, get a new one now – you will not be issued a visa if your passport is due to expire before the visa. For information on visas, see p804.

AIR

There are flights to Japan from all over the world, usually to Tokyo, but also to a number of other Japanese airports. Although Tokyo may seem the obvious arrival and departure point in Japan, for many visitors this may not be the case. If you plan on exploring western Japan or the Kansai region, it might be more

> **THINGS CHANGE**
>
> The information in this chapter is particularly vulnerable to change. Check directly with the airline or a travel agent to make sure you understand how a fare (and ticket you may buy) works and be aware of the security requirements for international travel. Shop carefully. The details given in this chapter should be regarded as pointers and are not a substitute for your own careful, up-to-date research.

convenient to fly into Kansai International Airport (KIX) near Osaka.

Airports & Airlines

There are international airports situated on the main island of Honshū (Nagoya, Niigata, Osaka/Kansai and Tokyo Narita), and on Kyūshū (Fukuoka, Kagoshima, Kumamoto and Nagasaki), Okinawa (Naha) and Hokkaidō (Sapporo).

TOKYO NARITA INTERNATIONAL AIRPORT

With the exception of China Airlines, all international flights to/from Tokyo use **Narita International Airport** (NRT; www.narita-airport.or.jp/airport_e). Since Narita is the most popular arrival/departure point in Japan, flights via Narita are usually cheaper than those using other airports. Of course, if you can get a cheap flight into another airport, particularly one close to your area of interest, then there's no reason to use Narita.

OSAKA/KANSAI INTERNATIONAL AIRPORT

All of Osaka's international flights now go via **Kansai International Airport** (KIX; www.kansai-airport.or.jp/en/index.asp). It serves the key Kansai cities of Kyoto, Osaka, Nara and Kōbe. Airport transport to any of these cities is fast and reliable (though it can be expensive if you're going all the way to Kyoto).

CHŪBU INTERNATIONAL AIRPORT CENTRAIR

Conveniently located between Tokyo and Osaka is Japan's newest major airport: **Chūbu**

International Airport Centrair (NGO; www.centrair
.jp). From Nagoya, flights connect with Australia, Canada, China, Guam, Hong Kong,
Indonesia, Malaysia, New Zealand, the Philippines, Saipan, Singapore, South Korea, Taiwan, Thailand and the USA.

FUKUOKA INTERNATIONAL AIRPORT
Fukuoka, at the northern end of Kyūshū,
is the main arrival point for western Japan.
Fukuoka International Airport (FUK; www.fuk-ab.co
.jp/english/frame_index.html), conveniently located
near the city, has flights to/from the following
cities: Seoul, Busan, Beijing, Dalian, Shanghai,
Guangzhou, Hong Kong, Taipei, Singapore,
Bangkok, Manila, Guam and Ho Chi Minh
City.

NAHA AIRPORT
Located on Okinawa-hontō (the main island
of Okinawa), **Naha Airport** (OKA; www.naha-airport
.co.jp in Japanese) has flights to/from Seoul, Manila, Shanghai and Taipei.

NIIGATA AIRPORT
Located north of Tokyo, **Niigata Airport** (KIJ;
www.niigata-airport.gr.jp in Japanese) has flights
to/from Irkusk, Vladivostok, Khabarovsk,
Seoul, Shanghai, Harbin, Xian, Honolulu
and Guam.

OTHER AIRPORTS
On Kyūshū, **Kagoshima Airport** (KOJ; www.koj-ab.co
.jp in Japanese) has flights to/from Shanghai and
Seoul; **Kumamoto Airport** (KMJ; www.kmj-ab.co.jp in
Japanese) has flights to/from Seoul; and **Nagasaki Airport** (NGS; www.nabic.co.jp/english) has flights
to/from Shanghai and Seoul.

On Hokkaidō, **New Chitose Airport** (CTS; www
.new-chitose-airport.jp/language/english/index.html)
has connections with Shanghai, Taipei and
Shenyang.

AIRLINES FLYING TO/FROM JAPAN
Aeroflot (code SU; ☎ 03-5532-8701; www.aeroflot
-japan.com/eng/index.asp; hub Sheremetyevo International Airport, Moscow)

Air Canada (code AC; ☎ 03-5405-8800, toll-free 0120-
048-048; www.aircanada.ca/e-home.html; hub Toronto
Pearson International Airport, Toronto)

Air China (code CA; ☎ 03-5520-0333; www.china-air
lines.com/en/index.htm; hub Beijing Capital International
Airport, Beijing)

Air France (code AF; ☎ 03-3475-2210; www.airfrance
.com; hub Charles de Gaulle International Airport, Paris)

Air India (code AI; ☎ 03-3508-0261; www.airindia.com;
hubs Chhatrapati Shivaji International Airport, Mumbai, &
Indira Gandhi International Airport, Delhi)

Air New Zealand (code NZ; ☎ 03-5521-2744, toll-free
0120-300-747; www.airnewzealand.co.nz; hub Auckland
International Airport, Auckland)

CLIMATE CHANGE & TRAVEL
Climate change is a serious threat to the ecosystems that humans rely upon, and air travel is the
fastest-growing contributor to the problem. Lonely Planet regards travel, overall, as a global benefit, but believes we all have a responsibility to limit our personal impact on global warming.

Flying & Climate Change
Pretty much every form of motor travel generates CO_2 (the main cause of human-induced climate
change) but planes are far and away the worst offenders, not just because of the sheer distances
they allow us to travel, but because they release greenhouse gases high into the atmosphere.
The statistics are frightening: two people taking a return flight between Europe and the US will
contribute as much to climate change as an average household's gas and electricity consumption over a whole year.

Carbon Offset Schemes
Climatecare.org and other websites use 'carbon calculators' that allow jetsetters to offset the
greenhouse gases they are responsible for with contributions to energy-saving projects and
other climate-friendly initiatives in the developing world – including projects in India, Honduras,
Kazakhstan and Uganda.

Lonely Planet, together with Rough Guides and other concerned partners in the travel industry,
supports the carbon offset scheme run by climatecare.org. Lonely Planet offsets all of its staff
and author travel.

For more information check out our website: lonelyplanet.com.

Air Niugini (code PX; ☎ 03-5216-3555; www.airniugini
.com.pg/main.htm; hub Jacksons International Airport,
Port Moresby)

Air Tahiti Nui (code TN; ☎ 03-6267-1177; www.air
tahitinui.com; hub Faa'a International Airport, Faaa)

Air Pacific (code FJ; ☎ 03-5208-5171, toll-free 0120-
489-311; www.airpacific.com; hub Nadi International
Airport, Nadi)

Alitalia (code AZ; ☎ 03-5166-9123; www.alitalia.com;
hubs Malpensa Airport, Milan, Leonardo da Vinci International Airport, Fiumicino)

All Nippon Airways (code NH; ☎ 03-5435-0333, toll-
free 0120-029-333; www.anaskyweb
.com; hubs Narita International Airport, Tokyo, Kansai
International Airport, Osaka)

American Airlines (code AA; ☎ 03-4550-2111, toll-
free 0120-000-860; www.aa.com; hub Dallas/Fort Worth
International Airport, Dallas)

Asiana Airlines (code OZ; ☎ 03-5812-6600; http://us
.flyasiana.com; hub Incheon International Airport, Seoul)

Austrian Airlines (code OS; ☎ 03-5222-5454;
www.aua.com/us/eng; hub Vienna International Airport,
Vienna)

Biman Bangladesh Airlines (code BG; ☎ 03-3502-
7922; www.bimanair.com; hub Zia International Airport,
Dhaka)

British Airways (code BA; ☎ 03-3570-8657; www.brit
ishairways.com; hub London Heathrow Airport, London)

Cathay Pacific Airways (code CX; ☎ 03-5159-1700;
www.cathaypacific.com; hub Hong Kong International
Airport, Hong Kong)

China Eastern Airlines (code MU; ☎ 03-3506-1166;
www.ce-air.com/cea2/en_US/homepage; hub Shanghai
Pudong International Airport, Shanghai)

China Southern Airlines (code CZ; ☎ 03-5157-8011;
www.cs-air.com/en; hub Guangzhou Baiyun International
Airport, Guangzhou)

Continental Airlines (code CO; ☎ 03-5464-5100,
toll-free 0120-242-414; www.continental.com; hub George
Bush Intercontinental Airport, Houston)

Continental Micronesia (code CS; ☎ 03-5464-5050;
www.continental.com; hub Guam International Airport,
Guam)

Delta Air Lines (code DL; ☎ 03-3593-6666, toll-free
0120-333-742; www.delta.com; hub Hartsfield-Jackson
Atlanta International Airport, Atlanta)

Deutsche Lufthansa (code LH; ☎ 03-4333-7656,
toll-free 0120-051-844; www.lufthansa.com; hub Frankfurt
International Airport, Frankfurt)

Dragon Air (code KA; ☎ 03-5159-1715; www.dragonair
.com; hub Hong Kong International Airport, Hong Kong)

EgyptAir (code MS; ☎ 03-3211-4524; www.egyptair
.com.eg; hub Cairo International Airport, Cairo)

Finnair (code AY; ☎ 03-3222-6801, toll-free 0120-700-915;
www.finnair.com; hub Helsinki-Vantaa Airport, Helsinki)

Garuda Indonesia (code GA; ☎ 03-3240-6161; www
.garuda-indonesia.com; hub Soekarno-Hatta Airport,
Jakarta)

Iberia Airlines (code IB; www.iberia.com; hub Barcelona
International Airport, Barcelona)

Iran Air (code IR; ☎ 03-3586-2101; www.iranairjp.com;
hub Mehrabad International Airport, Tehran)

JALWAYS (code JO; ☎ 03-5460-0511, toll-free 0120-
255-931; www.jalways.co.jp/english; hub Narita International Airport, Tokyo)

Japan Airlines (code JL; ☎ 03-5460-0511, toll-free
0120-255-931; www.jal.com/en; hubs Narita International
Airport, Tokyo, Kansai International Airport, Osaka)

Japan Asia Airways (code EG; ☎ 03-5460-0533, toll-
free 0120-747-801; www.japanasia.co.jp in Japanese; hubs
Narita International Airport, Tokyo, & Kansai International
Airport, Osaka)

KLM-Royal Dutch Airlines (code KL; ☎ 03-3570-
8770; www.klm.com; hub Amsterdam Schiphol Airport,
Amsterdam)

Korean Air (code KE; ☎ 03-5443-3311; www.koreanair
.com; hub Incheon International Airport, Seoul)

Malaysia Airlines (code MH; ☎ 03-5733-2111; www
.malaysiaairlines.com; hub Kuala Lumpur International
Airport, Kuala Lumpur)

Northwest Airlines (code NW; ☎ 0476-31-8000;
www.nwa.com; hub Minneapolis-St Paul International
Airport, Minneapolis)

Pakistan International (code PK; ☎ 03-3216-6511;
www.piac.com.pk; hub Jinnah International Airport,
Karachi)

Philippine Airlines (code PR; ☎ 03-5157-4361; www
.philippineairlines.com; hub Ninoy Aquino International
Airport, Manila)

Qantas (code QF; ☎ 03-5593-7000; www.qantas.com;
hub Sydney Kingsford Smith Airport, Sydney)

Scandinavian Airlines System (code SK; ☎ 03-
5400-2331; www.flysas.com; hub Copenhagen Airport,
Copenhagen)

Shanghai Airlines (code FM; ☎ 06-6945-8666; www
.shanghai-air.com/ywwy/home.htm; hub Shanghai Pudong
International Airport, Shanghai)

Singapore Airlines (code SQ; ☎ 03-3213-3431;
www.singaporeair.com; hub Singapore Changi Airport,
Changi)

Sri Lankan Airlines (code UL; ☎ 03-3431-6611; www
.srilankan.aero; hub Bandaranaike Airport, Colombo)

Swiss International Airlines (code LX; ☎ 03-5156-
8252; www.swiss.com; hub Zurich International Airport,
Zurich)

Thai Airways International (code TG; ☎ 03-3503-
3311; www.thaiairways.com; hub Suvarnabhumi Airport,
Bangkok)

Turkish Airlines (code TK; ☎ 03-5251-1551; www.thy
.com; hub Atatürk International Airport, Istanbul)

United Airlines (code UA; ☎ 03-3817-4411, toll-free 0120-114-466; www.united.com; hub Chicago O'Hare International Airport, Chicago)

US Airways (code US; ☎ 03-3597-9471; www.usairways .com; hub Philadelphia International Airport, Philadelphia)

Uzbekistan Airways (code HY; ☎ 03-3500-1355; www.uzbekistanairways.nl; hub Yuzhny Airport, Tashkent)

Vietnam Airlines (code VN; ☎ 03-3508-1481; www .vietnamairlines.com; hub Tan Son Nhat International Airport, Ho Chi Minh City)

Virgin Atlantic Airways (code VS; ☎ 03-3499-8811; www.virgin-atlantic.com; hub London Heathrow Airport, London)

Tickets

The price of your ticket will depend to a great extent on when you fly. High-season prices are determined by two sets of holidays and popular travel times: those in the country you're flying from and those in Japan. Generally, high season for travel between Japan and Western countries is in late December (around Christmas and the New Year period), late April to early May (around Japan's Golden Week holiday), as well as July and August. If you must fly during these periods, book well in advance.

Australia

Garuda, Malaysian Airlines and Cathay Pacific usually have good deals for travel between Australia and Japan. Return fares start at around A$1200 with Garuda, which allows a stopover in Bali. Direct flights to Japan with airlines including Qantas and Japan Air Lines (JAL) are more expensive – expect to pay at least A$1600 for a return fare.

Two well-known agencies for cheap fares are **STA Travel** (☎ 134 782; www.statravel.com.au), which has offices in all major cities; and **Flight Centre** (www.flightcentre.com.au), which has dozens of offices throughout Australia. For online bookings, try www.travel.com.au.

Canada

Return fares between Vancouver and Tokyo start at around C$1000, while return fares between Toronto and Tokyo start at around C$1300. Carriers to check include Japan Airlines, All Nippon Airways, Air Canada, United, American, Delta and Northwest Airlines.

Travel Cuts (☎ 800-667-2887; www.travelcuts.com) is Canada's national student travel agency. For online bookings, try www.expedia.ca and www.travelocity.ca.

China

There are several daily flights between Japan and Hong Kong on Cathay Pacific, as well as on JAL and All Nippon Airways (ANA). In Hong Kong try **Four Seas Tours** (☎ 2200-7777; www.fourseas travel.com/fs/en). There are also flights between Japan and Beijing, Shanghai, Guangzhou, Harbin, Shenyang, Xian and Dalian.

Continental Europe

Most direct flights between Europe and Japan fly into Tokyo but there are also some flights into Kansai. Typical low-season return fares from major European cities are Frankfurt–Tokyo €500, Rome–Tokyo €700 and Paris–Tokyo €580.

The following are recommended travel agencies in continental Europe:

FRANCE
Anyway (☎ 08 92 89 38 92; www.anyway.fr in French)

Lastminute (☎ 08 99 78 50 00; www.fr.lastminute .com in French)

Nouvelles Frontières (☎ 08 25 00 07 47; www .nouvelles-frontieres.fr in French)

OTU Voyages (☎ 01 55 82 32 32 www.otu.fr in French) This agency specialises in student and youth travellers.

Voyageurs du Monde (☎ 08 92 23 56 56; www.vdm .com in French)

GERMANY
Expedia (☎ 01805-007146; www.expedia.de in German)

Just Travel (☎ 089-747 33 30; www.justtravel.de)

STA Travel (☎ 069-743 032 92; www.statravel.de) For travellers under the age of 26.

ITALY
CTS Viaggi (☎ 064 41 11 66, www.cts.it in Italian)

NETHERLANDS, THE
Airfair (☎ 0900-771 77 17; www.airfair.nl in Dutch)

SPAIN
Barcelo Viajes (☎ 902 20 04 00; www.barceloviajes .com in Spanish)

Nouvelles Frontières (☎ 902 12 42 12; www.tui.es /VIA/Inicio)

Japan

In most of Japan's major cities there are travel agencies where English is spoken. For an idea of the latest prices in Tokyo check the travel ads in the various local English-language publications, and in Kansai check *Kansai Time Out*. In other parts of Japan check the *Japan Times*. For more details on city-based travel agencies, see relevant sections under Tokyo (p109), Osaka (p376) and Kyoto (p313).

New Zealand

Return fares between Auckland and Tokyo start at around NZ$1500. Airlines that fly this route include Malaysian Airlines, Thai International, Qantas and Air New Zealand. You'll save money by taking one of the Asian airlines via an Asian city rather than flying direct.

Both **Flight Centre** (☎ 0800 243 544; www.flight centre.co.nz) and **STA Travel** (☎ 0508 782 872; www.statravel.co.nz) have branches throughout New Zealand.

South Korea

Numerous flights link Seoul and Busan with Japan. A Seoul–Tokyo flight purchased in Seoul costs around US$200/400 one way/return. From Tokyo, flights to Seoul are the cheapest way out of Japan. Low-season return fares start as low as ¥30,000.

In Seoul, try the **Korean International Student Exchange Society** (Kises; ☎ 02-733-9494; www.kises.co.kr in Korean; 5th fl, YMCA Bldg, Chongno 2-ga).

See opposite for information on sea-travel bargains between Korea and Japan.

Taiwan

Return flights from Taipei to Tokyo start at around NT10,000. Flights also operate between Kaohsiung and Osaka or Tokyo.

UK

Expect to pay from UK£500 to UK£600 for a return ticket with a good airline via a fast route. ANA and JAL offer direct flights between London and Japan. Air France is a reliable choice for flights to Japan (usually Tokyo), but you'll have to change in Paris. For a less convenient trans-Asian route, it's about UK£350. The following travel agencies are recommended:

Flight Centre (☎ 087-0499 0040; www.flightcentre .co.uk)

Flightbookers (☎ 087-1223 5000; www.ebookers.com)

North-South Travel (☎ 01245 608291; www.north southtravel.co.uk) North-South Travel donates part of its profit to projects in the developing world.

Quest Travel (☎ 087-1423 0135; www.questtravel.com)

STA Travel (☎ 087-1230 0040; www.statravel.co.uk) For travellers under the age of 26.

Trailfinders (☎ 084-5058 5858; www.trailfinders .co.uk)

Travel Bag (☎ 080- 0082 5000; www.travelbag.co.uk)

USA

From New York during the low season you can find discount return fares to Japan for as low as US$700. Some carriers to check include Korean Air, JAL and ANA, United Airlines and Northwest Airlines. From the US west coast, low-season discount return fares are available from as little as US$500. High-season discount fares will just about double these figures.

STA Travel (☎ 800-781-4040; www.statravel.com) is a good place to start your ticket search in the USA. **IACE Travel USA** (☎ 800-872-4223, 212-972-3200; www.iace-usa.com) is a travel agency specialising in travel between the USA and Japan which can often dig up cheap fares. San Francisco's **Avia Travel** (☎ 800-950-2842, 510-558-2150; www.avia travel.com) is a favourite of Japan-based English teachers and can arrange tickets originating in Japan.

The following agencies are recommended for online bookings:

- www.cheaptickets.com
- www.expedia.com
- www.itn.net
- www.lowestfare.com
- www.orbitz.com
- www.sta.com (for travellers under the age of 26)
- www.travelocity.com

Other Asian Countries

There are daily flights between Bangkok and Japan on Thai Airways International, ANA and JAL, with fares starting at about 18,000B return in the low season. From Singapore, return tickets cost approximately S$800; from Indonesia (Jakarta/Denpasar), a return flight costs around US$800.

From the Philippines (Manila) a return flight to Japan is around US$550 and from Malaysia (Kuala Lumpur) it's around RM2500 return. From Vietnam (Ho Chi Minh City) a return flight costs around US$650.

Other Asian countries with limited flights to Japan include India, Nepal and Myanmar (Burma).

Other Regions

There are also flights between Japan and South America (via the USA and Europe),

Africa (via Europe, south Asia or Southeast Asia) and the Middle East.

LAND
Trans-Siberian Railway

A little-used option of approaching or leaving Japan is the Trans-Siberian Railway. There are three Trans-Siberian Railway options, one of which is to travel on the railway to/from Vladivostok in Russia and take the ferry between Vladivostok and Fushiki in Toyama-ken. The cheaper options are the Chinese Trans-Mongolia and Russian Trans-Manchuria routes, which start/finish in China, from where there are ferry connections to/from Japan via Tientsin, Qingdao and Shanghai.

See below for information on ferry connections between Japan, Russia and China.

More detailed information is also available in a good number of publications – see Lonely Planet's *Trans-Siberian Railway: A Classic Overland Route*. Those making their way to Japan via China (or vice versa) should pick up a copy of Lonely Planet's *China* guide, which has invaluable information on travel in China as well as information on Trans-Siberian travel.

SEA
China

The **Japan China International Ferry Company** (in Japan ☎ 06-6536-6541, in China ☎ 021-6325-7642; www.fune.co.jp/chinjif in Japanese) links Shanghai and Osaka/Kōbe. A 2nd-class ticket costs around US$180. The journey takes around 48 hours. A similar service is provided by the **Shanghai Ferry Company** (in Japan ☎ 06-6243-6345, in China ☎ 021-6537-5111; www.shanghai-ferry.co.jp in Japanese). For more information on both of these, see p389.

The **China Express Line** (in Japan ☎ 078-321-5791, in China ☎ 022-2420-5777; www.celkobe.co.jp in Japanese) operates a ferry between Kōbe and Tientsin where 1st-/2nd-class tickets cost US$240/210. The journey takes around 48 hours. For more information, see p397.

Orient Ferry Ltd (in Japan ☎ 0832-32-9677, in China ☎ 0532-8387-1160; www.orientferry.co.jp in Japanese) runs between Shimonoseki and Qingdao, China, with three departures a week. The cheapest one-way tickets cost around US$130. The trip takes around 27 hours. See p477 for details.

Russia

FKK Air Service (☎ 0766-22-2212; http://fkk-air.toyama -net.com in Japanese) operates ferries between Fushiki in Toyama-ken and Vladivostok.

One-way fares start at around US$250. The journey takes around 36 hours. The ferry operates from July until the first week of October. For more details, see p238.

An even more exotic option is the summertime route between Wakkanai (in Hokkaidō) and Korsakov (on Sahkalin Island), operated by the **East Japan Sea Ferry Company** (in Japan ☎ 0162-23-3780, in Russia ☎ 4242-42-0917; www.kaiferry.co.jp in Japanese). One-way fares start at around ¥22,500 (around US$190) and the journey takes around six hours. The ferry operates from mid-May to the end of October. For more details, see p571.

South Korea

South Korea is the closest country to Japan and has several ferry connections.

BUSAN–SHIMONOSEKI

Kampu Ferry (in Japan ☎ 0832-24-3000, in Korea operating under Pukwan Ferry ☎ 051-464-2700; www.kampuferry.co.jp in Japanese) operates the Shimonoseki–Busan ferry service. One-way fares range from around US$85 to US$180, and the journey takes around 12 hours. See p477 for more details.

BUSAN–FUKUOKA

An international high-speed hydrofoil service, known as the Biitoru (say 'beetle'), is run by **JR Kyūshū** (in Japan ☎ 092-281-2315, in Korea ☎ 051-465-6111; www.jrbeetle.co.jp/english) and connects Fukuoka with Busan in Korea (around US$110 one

---

BAGGAGE FORWARDING

If you have too much luggage to carry comfortably or just can't be bothered, you can do what many Japanese travellers do: send it to your next stop by *takkyūbin* (express shipping companies). Prices are surprisingly reasonable and overnight service is the norm. Perhaps the most convenient service is Yamato Takkyūbin, which operates from most convenience stores. Simply pack your luggage and bring it to the nearest convenience store; they'll help with the paperwork and arrange for pick-up. Note that you'll need the full address of your next destination in Japanese, along with the phone number of the place. Alternatively, ask the owner of your accommodation to come and pick it up (this is usually possible but might cost extra).

way, three hours). **Camellia Line** (in Japan ☎ 092-262-2323, in Korea ☎ 051-466-7799; www.camellia-line.co.jp in Japanese & Korean) also has a regular daily ferry service between Fukuoka and Busan (around US$80, six hours from Fukuoka to Busan, 11 hours from Busan to Fukuoka). See p673 for more details.

Taiwan

Arimura Sangyō (in Japan ☎ 098-869-1980, in Taiwan ☎ 07-330-9811) operates a weekly ferry service between Naha (Okinawa) and Taiwan, sometimes via Ishigaki and Miyako in Okinawa-ken. The Taiwan port alternates between Keelung and Kaohsiung. Departure from Okinawa is on Thursday or Friday; departure from Taiwan is usually on Monday. The journey takes about 20 hours. One-way fares cost around US$140 in 2nd class.

GETTING AROUND

Japan is justifiably famous for its extensive, well-organised and efficient transportation network. Schedules are strictly adhered to and late or cancelled services are almost unheard of. All this convenience comes at a price, however, and you'd be well advised to look into money-saving deals whenever possible (see p823).

AIR

Air services in Japan are extensive, reliable and safe. In many cases, flying is much faster than even *shinkansen* (bullet trains) and not that much more expensive. Flying is also an efficient way to travel from the main islands to the many small islands around Japan.

Airlines in Japan

Japan Airlines (JAL; ☎ 03-5460-0522, 0120-255-971; www.jal.co.jp/en) is the major international carrier and also has a domestic network linking the major cities. **All Nippon Airways** (ANA; ☎ 03-3490-8800, 0120-029-709; www.ana.co.jp/eng) is the second largest international carrier and operates a more extensive domestic system. **Japan Trans Ocean Air** (JTA; ☎ 03-5460-0522, ☎ 0120-255-97; www.jal.co.jp/jta in Japanese) is a smaller domestic carrier that mostly services routes in Okinawa and the Southwest Islands.

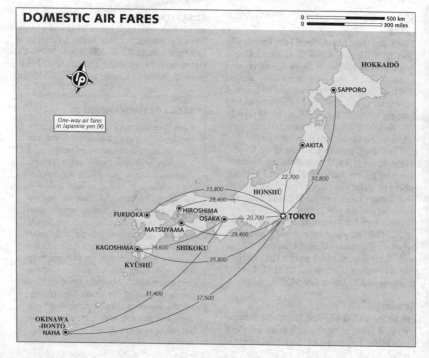

DOMESTIC AIR FARES

In addition to these, **Skymark Airlines** (SKY; ☎ 03-3433-7670; www.skymark.co.jp/en) is a recent start-up budget airline and **Shinchūō Kōkū** (☎ 0422-31-4191; www.central-air.co.jp in Japanese) has light-plane flights between Chōfu Airport, outside Tokyo, and the islands of Izu-shotō.

The Domestic Air Fares map (p814) shows some of the major connections and one-way fares. Note that return fares are usually around 10% cheaper than buying two one-way tickets. The airlines also have some weird and wonderful discounts if you know what to ask for. The most useful of these are the advance-purchase reductions: both ANA and JAL offer discounts of up to 50% if you purchase your ticket a month or more in advance, with smaller discounts for purchases made one to three weeks in advance. Seniors over 65 also qualify for discounts on most Japanese airlines, but these are sometimes only available if you fly on weekdays.

ANA also offers the Star Alliance Japan Airpass for foreign travellers on ANA or Star Alliance network airlines. Provided you reside outside Japan, purchase your tickets outside Japan and carry a valid international ticket on any airline, you can fly up to five times within 60 days on any ANA domestic route for only ¥11,550 per flight (a huge saving on some routes). Visit www.ana.co.jp/wws/us /e/travelservice/reservations/special/airpass .html for more details.

BICYCLE

Japan is a good country for bicycle touring and several thousand cyclists, both Japanese and foreign, traverse the country every year. Favourite bike touring areas include Kyūshū, Shikoku, the Japan Alps (if you like steep hills!), Noto-hantō and Hokkaidō.

There's no point in fighting your way out of big cities by bicycle. Put your bike on the train or bus and get out to the country before you start pedalling. To take a bicycle on a train you may need to use a bicycle carrying bag, available from good bicycle shops.

See p818 for information on road maps of Japan. In addition to the maps mentioned in that section, a useful series of maps is the *Touring Mapple* (Shobunsha) series, which is aimed at motorcyclists, but is also very useful for cyclists.

For more information on cycling in Japan, you can check out the excellent website of **KANcycling website** (www.kancycling.com).

Guided Bicycle Tours

For more information about guided bicycle tours in Kyoto, see p366. There is talk of a similar service being offered in Tokyo in the near future – a web search should turn up the operator once they're up and running.

Hire

You will find bicycle rental shops outside the train or bus stations in most of Japan's popular tourist areas, as well as near the ferry piers on many of the country's smaller islands. Typical charges are around ¥200/1000 per hour/day. Kyoto, for example, is ideally suited to bicycle exploration and there are plenty of cheap hire shops to choose from.

Note that the bicycles for rent are not usually performance vehicles. More commonly they're what the Japanese call *mama chari* (literally 'mama's bicycles'): one- or three-speed shopping bikes that are murder on hills of any size. They're also usually too small for anyone over 180cm in height.

Many youth hostels also have bicycles to rent – there's a symbol identifying them in the *Japan Youth Hostel Handbook*. 'Cycling terminals' found in various locations around the country also rent out bicycles. For more on cycling terminals, see p785.

Purchase

In Japan, prices for used bikes range from a few thousand yen for an old shopping bike to several tens of thousands of yen for good mountain bikes. New bikes range anywhere from about ¥10,000 for a shopping bike to ¥100,000 for a flash mountain or road bike.

Touring cycles are available in Japan but prices tend to be significantly higher than you'd pay back home. If you're tall, you may not find any suitably sized bikes in stock. One solution for tall riders, or anyone who wants to save money, is to buy a used bike; in Tokyo check the English-language publications and in Kansai check *Kansai Time Out*.

BOAT

Japan is an island nation and there are a great many ferry services both between islands and between ports on the same island. Ferries can be an excellent way of getting from one place to another and for seeing parts of Japan you might otherwise miss. Taking a ferry between Osaka (Honshū) and Beppu (Kyūshū), for example, is a good way of getting to Kyūshū and – if you choose the right departure time – seeing some of the Inland Sea (Seto-nai-kai; p463) on the way. Likewise, the ferry run up and down the Izu-shotō (p231) can be incredibly scenic.

The routes vary widely, from two-hour services between adjacent islands to 1½-day trips in what are in fact small ocean liners. The cheapest fares on the longer trips are in tatami-mat rooms where you simply unroll your futon on the floor and hope, if the ship is crowded, that your fellow passengers aren't too intent on knocking back the booze all night. In this basic class, fares are usually lower than equivalent land travel, but there are also more expensive private cabins. Bicycles can always be brought along and most ferries also carry cars and motorcycles.

Information on ferry routes, schedules and fares is found in the *JR Jikokuhyō* (p825) and on information sheets from the Japan National Tourist Organisation (JNTO; p803). Some ferry services and their lowest one-way fares, as well as major ferry companies, appear in the table below.

BUS

Japan has a comprehensive network of long-distance buses. These 'highway buses' are nowhere near as fast as the *shinkansen* but the fares are comparable with those of normal *futsū* trains. The trip between Tokyo and Sendai (Northern Honshū), for example, takes about two hours by *shinkansen*, four hours by *tokkyū* and nearly eight hours by bus. Of course, there are also many places in Japan where trains do not run and bus travel is the only public transport option.

Bookings can be made through any travel agency in Japan or at the Green Window in large Japan Rail (JR) stations. The Japan Rail Pass is valid on some highway buses, but in most cases the *shinkansen* would be far preferable (it's much faster and more comfortable). Note that the storage racks on most buses are generally too small for large backpacks,

FERRY FARES & TIMES		
Hokkaidō–Honshū	**Fare**	**Duration (hr)**
Otaru–Niigata	¥6200	18
Otaru–Maizuru	¥9600	20
Tomakomai–Hachinohe	¥4080	7
Tomakomai–Sendai	¥7300	14½
Tomakomai–Ōarai	¥8000	19
Tomakomai–Nagoya (via Sendai)	¥9400	38½
Departing from Tokyo	**Fare**	**Duration (hr)**
Tokushima (Shikoku)	¥9310	18
Shinmoji (Kitakyūshū)	¥14,000	34
Naha (Okinawa)	¥23,500	47
Departing from Osaka/Kōbe	**Fare**	**Duration (hr)**
Imabari (Shikoku)	¥5400	7
Matsuyama (Shikoku)	¥6300	9½
Shinmoji (Kitakyūshū)	¥7400	12
Beppu (Kyūshū)	¥8800	12
Ōita (Kyūshū)	¥8800	12
Miyazaki (Kyūshū)	¥10,400	13
Shibushi (Kyūshū)	¥10,700	14
Naha (Okinawa)	¥18,800	39
Departing from Kyūshū	**Fare**	**Duration (hr)**
Kagoshima-Naha (Okinawa)	¥14,200	25

but you can usually stow them in the luggage compartment underneath the bus.

Costs
Some typical long-distance fares and travel times out of Tokyo include the following:

Destination	Fare (one way)	Duration (hr)
Aomori	¥4000	10½
Hakata	¥9900	16
Hiroshima	¥8000	11½
Kyoto	¥4200	9
Nagoya	¥3000	7
Niigata	¥3000	7
Osaka	¥4200	10
Sendai	¥3300	7

Night Services
Night buses are a good option for those on a tight budget without a Japan Rail Pass. They are relatively cheap, spacious (allowing room to stretch out and get some sleep) and they also save on a night's accommodation. They typically leave at around 10pm or 11pm and arrive the following day at around 6am or 7am.

CAR & MOTORCYCLE
Driving in Japan is quite feasible, even for just the mildly adventurous. The major roads are signposted in English; road rules are generally adhered to and driving is safer than in other Asian countries; and petrol, while expensive, is not prohibitively so. Indeed, in some areas of the country it can prove much more convenient than other forms of travel and, between a group of people, it can also prove quite economical.

Automobile Associations
If you're a member of an automobile association in your home country, you're eligible for reciprocal rights with the **Japan Automobile Federation** (JAF; ☎ 03-6833-9000, 0570-00-2811; www .jaf.or.jp/e/index_e.htm; 2-2-17 Shiba, Minato-ku, Tokyo 105-0014). Its office is near Onarimon Station on the Tōei Mita line. JAF publishes a variety of publications, and will make up strip maps for its members.

Driving Licence
Travellers from most nations are able to drive in Japan with an International Driving Permit backed up by their own regular licence. The international permit is issued by your national automobile association and costs around US$5 in most countries. Make sure it's endorsed for cars and motorcycles if you're licensed for both.

Travellers from Switzerland, France and Germany (and others whose countries are not signatories to the Geneva Convention of 1949 concerning international driver's licences) are not allowed to drive in Japan on a regular international licence. Rather, travellers from these countries must have their own licence backed by an authorised translation of the same licence. These translations can be made by their country's embassy or consulate in Japan or by the JAF. If you are unsure which category your country falls into, contact the nearest JNTO office (p803).

Foreign licences and International Driving Permits are only valid in Japan for six months. If you are staying longer, you will have to get a Japanese licence from the local department of motor vehicles. To do this, you will need to provide your own licence, passport photos, Alien Registration Card and the fee, and also take a simple eye test.

Expressways
The expressway system will get you from one end of the country to another but it is not particularly extensive. Also, since all the expressways charge tolls, it is uniformly expensive – about ¥24.6 per kilometre. Tokyo to Kyoto, for example, will cost about ¥10,050 in tolls. The speed limit on expressways is 80km/h but seems to be uniformly ignored. At a steady 100km/h, you will still find as many cars overtaking you as you overtake, some of them going very fast indeed.

There are good rest stops and service centres at regular intervals. A prepaid highway card, available from tollbooths or at the service areas, saves you having to carry so much cash and gives you a 4% to 8% discount in the larger card denominations. You can also pay tolls with most major credit cards. Exits are usually fairly well signposted in romaji but make sure you know the name of your exit as it may not necessarily be the same as the city you're heading towards.

Fuel & Spare Parts
You'll find *gasoreen sutando* (petrol stations) in almost every town in Japan and in service stations along the country's expressways. The cost of petrol ranges from ¥95 to ¥140 per litre.

Spare parts are widely available in Japan for Japanese cars. For foreign cars, you may have to place a special order with a garage or parts store.

Hire

You'll usually find car-rental agencies clustered around train stations and ferry piers in Japan. Typical hire rates for a small car are ¥6825 to ¥9450 for the first day and ¥5775 to ¥7875 per day thereafter. Move up a bracket and you're looking at ¥11,550 to ¥14,700 for the first day and ¥9450 to ¥11,550 thereafter. On top of the hire charge, there's a ¥1000 per day insurance cost.

It's also worth bearing in mind that car hire costs go up during high seasons – 28 April to 6 May, 20 July to 31 August, and 28 December to 5 January. The increase can make quite a difference to costs. A car that costs ¥8800 a day will usually go up to ¥9700 during any of the peak times.

Communication can be a major problem when hiring a car. Some of the offices will have a rent-a-car phrasebook, with questions you might need to ask in English. Otherwise, just speak as slowly as possible and hope for the best.

Two of the main Japanese car-rental companies and their Tokyo phone numbers are **Hertz** (☎ 0120-489-882) and **Toyota Rent-a-Lease** (☎ 0070-8000-10000).

MOTORCYCLE HIRE & PURCHASE

Hiring a motorcycle for long-distance touring is not as easy as hiring a car, although small scooters are available in many places for local sightseeing.

Although Japan is famous for its large-capacity road burners, most bikes on the road are 400cc or less. This is because a special licence is required to ride a bike larger than 400cc, and few Japanese and even fewer foreigners pass the test necessary to get this licence.

The 400cc machines are the most popular large motorcycles in Japan but, for general touring, a 250cc machine is probably the best bet. Apart from being large enough for a compact country like Japan, machines up to 250cc are also exempt from the expensive *shaken* (inspections).

Smaller machines (those below 125cc) are banned from expressways and are generally less suitable for long-distance touring, but people have ridden from one end of Japan

to the other on little 50cc 'step-thrus'. An advantage of these bikes is that you can ride them with just a regular driving licence, so you won't need to get a motorcycle licence.

The best place to look for motorcycles in Japan is the Korin-chō motorcycle neighbourhood in Tokyo's Ueno district. There are over 20 motorcycle shops in the area and some employ foreign salespeople who speak both Japanese and English. For used bikes in Kansai check *Kansai Time Out*, *Kansai Flea Market*, or the message board in the Kyoto International Community House (p312).

Insurance

When you own a car, it is necessary to get compulsory third-party insurance (*jidosha songai baishō sekinin hoken*). This is paid when your car undergoes the compulsory inspection (*shaken*). It is also recommended that you get comprehensive vehicle insurance (*jidosha hoken*) to cover any expenses that aren't covered by the compulsory third-party insurance.

Maps & Navigation

Get yourself a copy of the *Road Atlas Japan* (Shōbunsha, ¥2999). It's all in romaji with enough names in kanji to make navigation possible even off the major roads. If you're really intent on making your way through the back blocks, a Japanese map will prove useful even if your knowledge of kanji is nil. The best Japanese road atlases by far are the *Super Mapple* series (Shōbunsha), which are available in bookshops and some convenience stores.

There is a reasonable amount of signposting in romaji so getting around isn't all that difficult, especially in developed areas. If you are attempting tricky navigation, use your maps imaginatively – watch out for the railway line, the rivers, the landmarks. They're all useful ways of locating yourself when you can't read the signs. A compass will also come in handy when navigating.

These days, many rental cars come equipped with satellite car navigation systems, which can make navigation a snap, provided you can figure out how to work the system (ask the person at the rental agency to explain it and be sure to take notes). With most of these systems, you can input the phone number of your destination, which is easy, or its address, which is just about impossible if you don't

TRANSPORT

ROAD DISTANCES (KM)

This is a triangular road-distance chart. Each origin city (left) lists road distances (km) to the destination cities named along the diagonal.

Origin \ Destination	Aomori	Fukuoka	Fukushima	Hiroshima	Kagoshima	Kanazawa	Kitakyūshū	Kōbe	Kōchi	Kyoto	Maebashi	Matsue	Matsuyama	Mito	Miyazaki	Morioka	Nagano	Nagasaki	Nagoya	Niigata	Osaka	Sapporo	Sendai	Shizuoka	Tokushima	Tokyo	Tottori	Toyama	Urawa
Fukuoka	1746																												
Fukushima	481	1495																											
Hiroshima	1463	283	1212																										
Kagoshima	2067	1816	1212	604																									
Kanazawa	798	321	948	665	1269																								
Kitakyūshū	1679	67	1428	216	388	881																							
Kōbe	1151	595	900	312	916	353	528																						
Kōchi	1436	618	1185	335	939	638	551	285																					
Kyoto	1066	680	815	397	1001	268	613	85	370																				
Maebashi	714	1211	285	928	1532	392	1144	616	901	531																			
Matsue	1380	409	1134	185	730	582	342	313	439	343	874																		
Matsuyama	1449	631	1198	348	952	651	564	298	121	383	914	452																	
Mito	658	1328	223	1045	1649	539	1261	733	1018	147	991	1031																	
Miyazaki	2019	407	1768	556	142	1221	340	868	891	953	648	1484	1601																
Morioka	213	1664	268	1381	1985	716	1597	1069	1354	121	1298	904	445	1937															
Nagano	695	1084	414	801	1405	263	1017	489	774	383	984	1367	787	276															
Nagasaki	1920	174	1669	457	314	1122	241	769	792	854	553	682	1357	805	1937	613													
Nagoya	957	822	673	539	1143	272	755	227	512	142	404	553	276	805	568	996	476												
Niigata	481	1265	235	982	1586	317	1198	670	955	51	968	899	332	699	214	1439	803	193	636										
Osaka	1117	629	866	346	950	319	34	319	51	582	347	233	585	968	902	1035	455	1838	1258	764	1400								
Sapporo	283	2029	764	1746	2350	1081	1962	1434	1719	562	1663	1349	997	941	2302	496	978	2203	1240	949	380	681							
Sendai	398	1578	83	1295	1899	635	1511	983	1268	368	1217	1281	260	1851	185	497	1752	756	318	1250	1528	1090	569						
Shizuoka	967	1009	486	726	1330	459	942	414	699	329	316	672	712	754	277	1183	187	491	380	128	1054	545	373	508					
Tokushima	1245	994	557	878	447	490	94	224	179	710	378	238	827	830	583	731	321	764	576	353	1077	196	251	704					
Tokyo	771	1205	290	922	1526	492	1138	610	895	525	120	868	908	123	1478	558	229	1379	383	358	220	1536	1040	196	512				
Tottori	1253	536	1007	309	857	455	469	186	312	216	747	127	864	809	1171	620	710	1187	249	772	384	436	570	221	729	741			
Toyama	733	1013	487	730	1334	65	946	418	703	333	327	647	474	933	651	198	252	1404	328	220	601	545	409	512	427	705	402		
Urawa	757	1230	276	947	1551	467	1163	635	920	95	893	933	138	872	1503	544	265	1343	408	328	1404	1016	359	221	512	25	766	463	61
Yokohama	807	1169	326	886	1490	528	1102	574	859	489	832	872	159	1442	574	594	347	389	540	1090	540	36	668	160	1090	520			

read Japanese (although you can always ask for help here, too).

Motorcycles

For citizens of most countries, your overseas licence and an International Driving Permit are all you need to ride a motorcycle in Japan (see p817 for details on which nationalities require additional documentation). Crash helmets are compulsory and you should also ensure your riding gear is adequate to cope with the weather, particularly rain. For much of the year the climate is ideal for motorcycle touring, but when it rains it really rains.

Touring equipment – panniers, carrier racks, straps and the like – is readily available from dealers. Remember to pack clothing in plastic bags to ensure it stays dry, even if you don't. An adequate supply of tools and a puncture repair kit can prove invaluable.

Riding in Japan is no more dangerous than anywhere else in the world, which is to say it is not very safe and great care should be taken at all times. Japan has the full range of motorcycle hazards from single-minded taxi drivers to unexpected changes in road surface, heedless car-door openers to runaway dogs.

Parking

In most big cities, free curbside parking spots are almost nonexistent, while in rural areas you'll be able to park your car just about wherever you want. In the cities you'll find that you usually have to pay ¥200 per hour for metred street parking, or anywhere from ¥300 to ¥600 per hour for a spot in a multistorey car park. You'll find car parks around most department stores and near some train stations. Fortunately, most hotels have free parking for guests, as do some restaurants and almost all department stores.

Road Rules

Driving in Japan is on the left. There are no real problems with driving in Japan. There are no unusual rules or interpretations of them and most signposts follow international conventions. JAF (p817) has a *Rules of the Road* book available in English and five other languages for ¥1000.

HITCHING

Hitching is never entirely safe in any country in the world, and we don't recommend it. Travellers who decide to hitch should understand that they are taking a small but potentially serious risk. In particular, Japan is a very dangerous place for solitary female hitchhikers; there have been countless cases of solitary female hitchers being attacked, molested and raped. People who do choose to hitch will be safer if they travel in pairs and let someone know where they are planning to go.

Provided you understand the risks and take appropriate precautions, Japan can be a good country for hitchhiking. Many hitchhikers have tales of extraordinary kindness from motorists who have picked them up.

The rules for hitchhiking are similar to anywhere else in the world. Dress neatly and look for a good place to hitch – expressway onramps and expressway service areas are probably your best bet.

Truck drivers are particularly good for long-distance travel as they often head out on the expressways at night. If a driver is exiting before your intended destination, try to get dropped off at one of the expressway service areas. The *Service Area Parking Area* (SAPA) guide maps are excellent for hitchers. They're available free from expressway service areas and show full details of each interchange (IC) and rest stop. These are important orientation points if you have a limited knowledge of Japanese.

For more on hitching in Japan pick up a copy of the excellent *Hitchhiker's Guide to Japan* by Will Ferguson. In addition to lots of general advice, this book details suggested routes and places to stay on the road. All in all, it's just about invaluable for anyone contemplating a long hitch around Japan.

LOCAL TRANSPORT

All the major cities offer a wide variety of public transport. In many cities you can get day passes for unlimited travel on bus, tram or subway systems. Such passes are usually called an *ichi-nichi-jōsha-ken*. If you're staying for an extended period in one city, commuter passes are available for regular travel.

Bus

Almost every Japanese city has an extensive bus service but it's usually the most difficult public transport system for foreign travellers to use. The destination names are almost always written in kanji and often there are no numbers to identify which bus you want.

Fares are either paid to the driver on entering or as you leave the bus and usually operate on one of two systems. In Tokyo and some other cities, there's a flat fare regardless of distance. In the other system, you take a ticket as you board which indicates the zone number at your starting point. When you get off, an electric sign at the front of the bus indicates the fare charged at that point for each starting zone number. You simply pay the driver the fare that matches your zone number. There is often a change machine near the front of the bus that can change ¥100 and ¥500 coins and ¥1000 notes.

In many tourist towns there are also *teiki kankō basu* (tour buses), often run from the main railway station. Tours are usually conducted in Japanese but English-language tours are available in popular areas like Kyoto and Tokyo. In places where the attractions are widespread or hard to reach by public transport, tours can be a good bet.

Taxi

Taxis are convenient but expensive and can even be found in quite small towns; the train station is the best place to look. Fares are fairly uniform throughout the country – flagfall (posted on the taxi windows) is ¥600 to ¥660 for the first 2km, after which it's around ¥100 for each 350m (approximately). There's also a time charge if the speed drops below 10km/h. During the day, it's almost impossible to tell if a moving taxi is occupied (just wave at it and it will stop if it's free); at night, vacant taxis are distinguishable by an illuminated light on the roof – an occupied taxi will have its light turned off.

Don't whistle for a taxi; a simple wave should bring one politely to a halt. Don't open the door when it stops; the driver does that with a remote release. The driver will also shut the door when you leave the taxi.

Communication can be a problem with taxi drivers in Japan, but perhaps not as much as you fear. If you can't tell the driver where you want to go, it's useful to have the name written down in Japanese. At hotel front desks there will usually be business cards complete with name and location, which can be used for just this purpose. Of course, Japanese script is provided on map keys in this guidebook, too.

Tipping is not necessary. A 20% surcharge is added after 11pm or for taxis summoned by radio. There may also be an added charge if you summon the taxi by phone or reserve the taxi.

Train & Subway

Several cities, especially Osaka and Tokyo, have mass transit rail systems comprising a loop line around the city centre and radial lines into the central stations and the subway system. Subway systems operate in Fukuoka, Kōbe, Kyoto, Nagoya, Osaka, Sapporo, Sendai, Tokyo and Yokohama. They are usually the fastest and most convenient way to get around the city.

For subways and local trains you'll most likely have to buy your ticket from a machine. They're pretty easy to understand even if you can't read kanji as there is a diagram explaining the routes; from this you can find out what your fare should be. If you can't work the fare out, a solution is to buy a ticket for the lowest fare. When you finish your trip, go to the fare adjustment machine (*seisan-ki*) or counter before you reach the exit gate and pay the excess. JR train stations and most subway stations not only have their names posted above the platform in kanji and romaji but also the names of the preceding and following stations.

Tram

Many cities have tram lines – particularly Nagasaki, Kumamoto and Kagoshima on Kyūshū, Kōchi and Matsuyama on Shikoku, and Hakodate on Hokkaidō. These are excellent ways of getting around as they combine many of the advantages of bus travel (eg good views) with those of subways (it's easy to work out where you're going). Fares work on similar systems to bus travel and there are also unlimited-travel day tickets available.

TRAIN

Japanese rail services are among the best in the world: they are fast, frequent, clean and comfortable. The services range from small local lines to the *shinkansen* super-expresses or 'bullet trains' which have become a symbol of modern Japan.

The 'national' railway is **Japan Railways** (JR; www.japanrail.com), which is actually a number of separate private rail systems providing one linked service. The JR system covers the country from one end to the other and also provides local services around major cities like Tokyo and Osaka. There is more than 20,000km of railway line and about 20,000 services daily. JR operates the *shinkansen* network throughout Japan. *Shinkansen* lines are totally separate from the regular railways and, in some places, the *shinkansen* stations are a fair distance from the main JR station (as is the case in Osaka). JR also operates buses and ferries, and ticketing can combine more than one form of transport.

In addition to JR services, there is a huge network of private railways in Japan. Each large city usually has at least one private train line that services that city and the surrounding area, or connects that city to nearby cities.

Services

TYPES OF TRAINS

The slowest trains stopping at all stations are called *futsū* or *kaku-eki-teisha*. A step up from this is the *kyūkō* (ordinary express), which stops at only a limited number of stations. A variation on the *kyūkō* trains is the *kaisoku* (rapid) service. Finally, the fastest regular (non-*shinkansen*) trains are the *tokkyū* services, which are sometimes known as *shin-kaisoku*.

SHINKANSEN

The fastest and best-known train services in Japan are JR's *shinkansen*. The *shinkansen* reach speeds of up to 300km/h and some experimental models have gone significantly faster. In addition to being incredibly fast, *shinkansen* are also incredibly safe: in more than 30 years of operation, there has never been a fatality.

The service efficiency starts even before you board the train. Your ticket indicates your carriage and seat number, and platform signs indicate where you should stand for that carriage entrance. The train pulls in precisely to the scheduled minute and, sure enough, the carriage door you want is right beside where you're standing.

On most *shinkansen* routes, there are two or three types of service: faster express services stopping at a limited number of stations, and slower local services stopping at all *shinkansen* stations. There is no difference in fare with the exception of the super-express Nozomi service on the Tōkaidō/San-yō *shinkansen* line. There are, however, regular and Green Car (1st-class) carriages.

There are a limited number of *kin'en-sha* (nonsmoking carriages); request one when booking or ask on the platform for the *kin'en-sha-jiyū-seki* (unreserved nonsmoking cars).

Unreserved carriages are available on all but the super-express Nozomi service, but at peak holiday periods they can be very crowded and you may have to stand for the entire trip.

For prices on specific *shinkansen* routes, see below.

Classes

Most long-distance JR trains, including the *shinkansen*, have regular and Green Car carriages. The seating is slightly more spacious in Green Car carriages, but most people will find the regular carriages perfectly acceptable.

Train Types

shinkansen	新幹線	bullet train
tokkyū	特急	limited express
shin-kaisoku	新快速	JR special rapid train
kyūkō	急行	express
kaisoku	快速	JR rapid or express
futsū	普通	local
kaku-eki-teisha	各駅停車	local

Other Useful Words

jiyū-seki	自由席	unreserved seat
shitei-seki	指定席	reserved seat
green-sha	グリーン車	1st-class car
ōfuku	往復	round trip
katamichi	片道	one way
kin'en-sha	禁煙車	nonsmoking car
kitsuen-sha	喫煙車	smoking car

Costs

JR fares are calculated on the basis of *futsū-unchin* (basic fare), *tokkyū-ryōkin* (an express surcharge levied only on express services) and *shinkansen-ryōkin* (a special charge for *shinkansen* services). The following are some typical fares from Tokyo or Ueno, not including the Nozomi super express (prices given for *shinkansen* are the total price of the ticket):

Destination	Basic Fare	Shinkansen
Fukushima	¥4620	¥8190
Hakata	¥13,440	¥21,210
Hiroshima	¥11,340	¥17,540
Kyoto	¥7980	¥12,710
Morioka	¥8190	¥13,640
Nagoya	¥6090	¥10,070
Niigata	¥5460	¥9760
Okayama	¥10,190	¥15,850
Shin Osaka	¥8510	¥13,240
Sendai	¥5780	¥10,080
Shin Shimonoseki	¥12,810	¥20,060

TRANSPORT

SURCHARGES

Various surcharges may be added to the basic fare. These include reserved seat, Green Car, express service and *shinkansen* surcharges. You may also have to pay a surcharge for special trains to resort areas or for a seat in an observation car. The express surcharges (but not the *shinkansen* super-express surcharge) can be paid to the train conductor on board the train.

Some of the fare surcharges are slightly higher (5% to 10%) during peak travel seasons. This applies mainly to reserved seat tickets. High-season dates are 21 March to 5 April, 28 April to 6 May, 21 July to 31 August, and 25 December to 10 January.

Further surcharges apply for overnight sleepers, and these vary with the berth type, from approximately ¥9800 for various types of two-tier bunks, and ¥20,000 for a standard or 'royal' compartment. Note that there are no sleepers on the *shinkansen* services as none of these run overnight. Japan Rail Pass users must still pay the sleeper surcharge (for more on the Japan Rail Pass, see below). Sleeper services mainly operate on trains from Tokyo or Osaka to destinations in Western Honshū and Kyūshū.

The Nozomi super express has higher surcharges than other *shinkansen* services and cannot be used with a Japan Rail Pass. As a guideline, the Nozomi surcharge for Tokyo–Kyoto is ¥300; for Tokyo–Hakata it's ¥600 (seat reserve fee).

Passes & Discount Tickets

If you plan to do any extended travel in Japan, a Japan Rail Pass is almost essential. Not only will it save you lots of money, it will also spare you the hassle of buying tickets each time you want to board a train.

In addition to the Japan Rail Pass, there are various discount tickets and special fares available. The most basic is the return fare discount: if you buy a return ticket for a trip which is more than 600km each way, you qualify for a 10% discount on the return leg.

JAPAN RAIL PASS

One of Japan's few real travel bargains is the Japan Rail Pass, which *must be purchased outside Japan*. It is available to foreign tourists and Japanese overseas residents (but not for-eign residents of Japan). The pass lets you use any JR service for seven days for ¥28,300, 14

days for ¥45,100 or 21 days for ¥57,700. Green Car passes are ¥37,800, ¥61,200 and ¥79,600, respectively. The pass cannot be used for the super express Nozomi *shinkansen* service, but is OK for everything else (including other *shinkansen* services).

The only surcharge levied on the Japan Rail Pass is for overnight sleepers. Since a one-way reserved seat Tokyo–Kyoto *shinkansen* ticket costs ¥13,220, you only have to travel Tokyo–Kyoto–Tokyo to make a seven-day pass come close to paying off. Note that the pass is valid only on JR services; you will still have to pay for private train services.

In order to get a pass, you must first purchase an 'exchange order' outside Japan at JAL and ANA offices and major travel agencies. Once you arrive in Japan, you must bring this exchange order to a JR Travel Service Centre (these can be found in most major JR stations and at Narita and Kansai airports). When you validate your pass, you'll have to show your passport. The pass can only be used by those with a temporary visitor visa, which means it cannot be used by foreign residents of Japan (those on any visa other than the temporary visitor visa).

The clock starts to tick on the pass as soon as you validate it. So don't validate if you're just going into Tokyo or Kyoto and intend to hang around for a few days.

For more information on the pass and over-seas purchase locations, visit the JR website's **Japan Rail Pass section** (www.japanrailpass.net/eng /en001.html).

JR EAST PASS

This is a great deal for those who only want to travel in eastern Japan. The passes are good on all JR lines in eastern Japan (including Tōhoku, Yamagata, Akita, Jōetsu and Nagano *shinkansen*, but not including the Tōkaidō *shinkansen*). This includes the area around Tokyo and everything north of Tokyo to the tip of Honshū, but doesn't include Hokkaidō.

Prices for five-day passes are ¥20,000/ 16,000/10,000 for adults over 26/youths 12 to 25/children aged six to 11. Ten-day passes are ¥32,000/25,000/16,000 for the same age groups. Four-day 'flexible' passes are also available which allow travel on any four consecutive or non-consecutive days within any one-month period. These cost ¥20,000/16,000/10,000 for the same age

TRANSPORT

groups. Green Car passes are available for higher prices.

As with the Japan Rail Pass, this can only be purchased outside Japan (in the same locations as the Japan Rail Pass) and can only be used by those with temporary visitor visas (you'll need to show your passport). See the preceding Japan Rail Pass section for more details on purchase places and validation procedures.

For more information on the JR East Pass, visit the website's **JR East Pass section** (www.jreast.co.jp/e/eastpass/top.html).

JR WEST SAN-YŌ AREA PASS

Similar to the JR East Pass, this pass allows unlimited travel on the San-yō *shinkansen* line (including the Nozomi super express) between Osaka and Hakata, as well as local trains running between the same cities. A four-day pass costs ¥20,000 and an eight-day pass costs ¥30,000 (children's passes are half-price). These can be purchased both inside Japan (at major train stations, travel agencies and Kansai airport) and outside Japan (same locations as the Japan Rail Pass) but can only be used by those with a temporary visitor visa. The pass also entitles you to discounts on hiring cars at station rent-a-car offices. For more information on this pass, see the JR West website's **San-yo Area Pass section** (www.westjr.co.jp/english/global.html).

JR WEST KANSAI AREA PASS

A great deal for those who only want to explore the Kansai area, this pass covers unlimited travel on JR lines between most major Kansai cities, such as Himeji, Kōbe, Osaka, Kyoto and Nara. It also covers JR trains to/from Kansai airport but does not cover any *shinkansen* lines. One-/two-/three-/four-day passes cost ¥2000/4000/5000/6000 (children's passes are half-price). These can be purchased at the same places as the San-yō area rail pass (both inside and outside Japan) and also entitle you to discounts on station hire-car offices. Like the San-yō Area Pass, this pass can only be used by those with a temporary visitor visa. For more information, see the JR West website's **Kansai Area Pass section** (www.westjr.co.jp/english/global.html).

JR KYŪSHŪ RAIL PASS

This pass is valid on all JR lines in Kyūshū with the exception of the *shinkansen* line. A five-day pass (the only option) costs ¥16,000

(children's passes are half-price). It can be purchased both inside Japan, at Joyroad Travel Agencies in major train stations in Kyūshū, and outside Japan, at the same locations as the Japan Rail Pass (see p823 for purchase details). It can only be used by those on a temporary visitor visa. If you purchase an exchange order overseas, you can pick up your pass at major train stations in Kyūshū. For more information, visit the website of **JR Kyūshū** (www.jrkyushu.co.jp/english/kyushu_railpass.html).

SEISHUN JŪHACHI KIPPU

If you don't have a Japan Rail Pass, one of the best deals going is a five-day Seishun Jūhachi Kippu (literally a 'Youth 18 Ticket'). Despite its name, it can be used by anyone of any age. Basically, for ¥11,500 you get five one-day tickets valid for travel anywhere in Japan on JR lines. The only catches are that you can't travel on *tokkyū* or *shinkansen* trains and each ticket must be used within 24 hours. However, even if you only have to make a return trip, say, between Tokyo and Kyoto, you'll be saving a lot of money. Seishun Jūhachi Kippu can be purchased at most JR stations in Japan.

The tickets are intended to be used during Japanese university holidays. There are three periods of sale and validity: spring – which is from 20 February to 31 March and valid for use between 1 March and 10 April; summer – from 1 July to 31 August and valid for use between 20 July and 10 September; and winter – from 1 December to 10 January and valid for use between 10 December and 20 January. Note that these periods are subject to change. For more information, ask at any JR ticket window.

If you don't want to buy the whole book of five tickets, you can sometimes purchase separate tickets at the discount ticket shops around train stations.

For more on the Seishun Jūhachi Kippu, see the JR East website's **Seishun Jūhachi Kippu section** (www.jreast.co.jp/e/pass/seishun18.html).

KANSAI THRU PASS

See p311 for details on this excellent pass, which allows unlimited travel on all non-JR private train lines and most bus lines in Kansai.

SHŪYŪ-KEN & FURII KIPPU

There are a number of excursion tickets, known as *shūyū-ken* or *furii kippu* (*furii* is

Japanese for 'free'). These tickets include the return fare to your destination and give you unlimited JR local travel within the destination area. There are *shūyū-ken* available to travel from Tokyo to Hokkaidō and then around Hokkaidō for up to seven days. A Kyūshū or Shikoku *shūyū-ken* gets you to and from either island and gives you four or five days of travel around them. You can even go to Kyūshū one way by rail and one way by ferry. These tickets are available at major JR stations in Japan. For more information on these and other special ticket deals, see the JR East website's **Useful Tickets and Rail Passes for Visitors to East Japan** section (www.jreast .co.jp/e/pass/index.html).

Discount ticket shops are known as *kaku-yasu-kippu-uriba* in Japanese. These stores deal in discounted tickets for trains, buses, domestic plane flights, ferries, and a host of other things like cut-rate stamps and phone cards. You can typically save between 5% and 10% on *shinkansen* tickets. Discount ticket agencies are found around train stations in medium and large cities. The best way to find one is to ask at the *kōban* (police box) outside the station.

Schedules & Information

The most complete timetables can be found in the *JR Jikokuhyō* (book of timetables; available at all Japanese bookstores; written in Japanese). The JNTO, however, produces a handy English-language Railway Timetable booklet which explains a great deal about the services in Japan and gives timetables for the *shinkansen* services, *JR tokkyū* (limited express services) and major private lines. If your visit to Japan is a short one and you will not be straying far from the major tourist destinations, this booklet may well be all you need.

Major train stations all have information counters, and you can usually get your point across in simplified English.

If you need to know anything about JR, such as schedules, fares, fastest routes, lost baggage, discounts on rail travel, hotels and car hire, call the **JR East Infoline** (☎ 050-2016-1603; www.jreast.co.jp/e/info/index.html; ☷ 10am-6pm, closed during the year-end/new-year period). Information is available in English, Korean and Chinese. More information can be found on the website.

Tickets & Reservations

Tickets for most journeys can be bought from vending machines or ticket counters/reservation offices. For reservations of complicated tickets, larger train stations have *midori-no-madoguchi* (green counters) – look for the counter with the green band across the glass. Major travel agencies in Japan also sell reserved-seat tickets, and you can buy *shinkansen* tickets through JAL offices overseas if you will be flying JAL to Japan.

On *futsū* services, there are no reserved seats. On the faster *tokkyū* and *shinkansen* services you can choose to travel reserved or unreserved. However, if you travel unreserved, there's always the risk of not getting a seat and having to stand, possibly for the entire trip. This is a particular danger at weekends, peak travel seasons and on holidays. Reserved-seat tickets can be bought any time from a month in advance to the day of departure.

Information and tickets can be obtained from travel agencies, of which there are a great number in Japan. Nearly every railway station of any size will have at least one travel agency in the station building to handle all sorts of bookings in addition to train services. JTB (Japan Travel Bureau) is the big daddy of Japanese travel agencies. However, for most train tickets and long-distance bus reservations, you don't need a travel agency – just go to the ticket counters or *midori-no-madoguchi* (green counters) of any major train station.

Health Dr Trish Batchelor

CONTENTS

Japan is a wealthy industrialised country with a high standard of medical care. The level of care in rural areas, however, is not usually up to the same high standards as in the major cities. Food and water sanitation is generally good, though there is some risk of disease transmission through eating certain raw or undercooked foods. There is a low risk of catching an insect-borne disease such as Japanese encephalitis, Lyme disease and tick-borne encephalitis in specific areas at certain times of the year. Medical care is expensive, so ensure you have adequate travel insurance.

BEFORE YOU GO

Prevention is the key to staying healthy while abroad. A little planning before departure, particularly for pre-existing illnesses, will save trouble later. See your dentist before a long trip, carry a spare pair of contact lenses and glasses, and take your optical prescription with you. Bring medications in their original, clearly labelled containers. A signed and dated letter from your physician describing your medical conditions and medications, including generic names, is also a good idea. If carrying syringes or needles, be sure to have a physician's letter documenting their medical necessity. If you have a heart condition bring a copy of a recent electrocardiogram (ECG/EKG). If you take any regular medication carry extra supplies in case of loss or theft – it may be difficult to get exactly the same medications in Japan. In particular it can be difficult to get oral contraceptives.

Although medical care in most of Japan is quite reasonable, it is still wise to carry a basic medical kit suitable for treating minor ailments. Recommended items include simple painkillers, antiseptic and dressings for minor wounds, insect repellent, sunscreen, antihistamine tablets and adequate supplies of your personal medications.

INSURANCE

Even if you are fit and healthy, don't travel without specific travel health insurance – accidents can happen. If your health insurance does not cover you for medical expenses while abroad, get supplemental insurance. Find out in advance if your insurance plan will make payments directly to providers or reimburse you later for overseas health expenditures. Take a higher medical expense option as health costs in Japan are high. If you are seeing a doctor as an outpatient in Japan you will usually be expected to pay up front. If you're admitted to hospital, your insurance company may be able to pay the hospital directly; however, this is much easier if the company actually has an office in Japan.

RECOMMENDED VACCINATIONS

No vaccinations are required for Japan. However, you should be aware that Japan scrupulously checks visitors who arrive from countries where there is a risk of yellow fever and other similar diseases.

The World Health Organization (WHO) recommends that all travellers be covered for diphtheria, tetanus, measles, mumps and rubella, regardless of their destination. Since most vaccines don't produce immunity until at least two weeks after they're given, visit a physician at least six weeks before departure. Specialised travel medicine clinics are your best source of information as they will be able to give you personalised information for you and your trip. The doctors will take into account factors like your medical history, past vaccination history, the length of your trip, time of year you are travelling, and any activities you may be undertaking, as any of these factors can alter general recommendations. Ensure you receive an International Certificate of Vaccination (the yellow booklet), which lists the vaccines you have received.

Adult diphtheria/tetanus (ADT) A booster is recommended if it is more than 10 years since your last shot. Side effects include a sore arm and a fever.

Measles/Mumps/Rubella (MMR) Two doses of MMR are recommended unless you have had the diseases. Many adults under the age of 35 require a booster. Occasionally a rash and flu-like illness can occur about a week after vaccination.

Varicella (Chickenpox) If you have not had chickenpox you should discuss this vaccine with your doctor. Chickenpox can be a serious disease in adults with complications such as pneumonia and encephalitis. As an adult you require two shots, six weeks apart (usually given after a blood test to prove you have no immunity).

Under certain circumstances, or for those at special risk, the following vaccinations are recommended. These should be discussed with a doctor specialised in travel medicine.

Hepatitis A The risk in Japan is low but travellers spending extensive amounts of time in rural areas may consider vaccination. One injection gives almost 100% protection for six to 12 months; after a booster at least 20 years' protection is provided. This vaccine is commonly combined with the hepatitis B vaccine in the form of 'Twinrix'.

Hepatitis B For those staying long term or who may be exposed to body fluids by sexual contact, acupuncture, dental work etc, or for health-care workers. Three shots are required, given over six months (a rapid schedule is also available).

Influenza If you are over 50 years of age or have a chronic medical condition such as diabetes, lung disease or heart disease, you should have a flu shot annually. Side effects include a mild fever and a sore arm.

Japanese B encephalitis There is no risk in Tokyo, but there is risk in rural areas of all islands. The risk is highest in the western part of the country from July to October. Three shots are given over the course of a month, with a booster after two years. Rarely, allergic reactions can occur, so the course is best completed 10 days prior to travel.

Pneumonia (pneumococcal) This vaccine is recommended to travellers over the age of 65 or with chronic lung or heart disease.

Tick-borne encephalitis This is present only in the wooded areas of Hokkaido and is transmitted from April to October. This vaccine is readily available in Europe but can be difficult or impossible to find elsewhere.

INTERNET RESOURCES

There is a wealth of travel health advice on the internet. For further information, the Lonely Planet website, at www.lonelyplanet.com, is a good place to start. WHO publishes a superb book called *International Travel and Health*, which is revised annually and is available free online at www.who.int/ith/. Other websites of general interest are MD Travel Health at www.mdtravelhealth.com, which provides complete travel-health recommendations for every country; the Centers for Disease Control and Prevention has a good site at www.cdc .gov; and Fit for Travel at www.fitfortravel .scot.nhs.uk has up-to-date information about outbreaks and is very user-friendly.

It's also a good idea to consult your government's travel-health website before departure, if one is available.

Australia (www.dfat.gov.au/travel/)
Canada (www.travelhealth.gc.ca)
New Zealand (www.moh.govt.nz)
UK (www.dh.gov.uk)
USA (www.cdc.gov/travel/)

FURTHER READING

For those spending an extended period of time in Japan the best book is the *Japan Health Handbook* by Meredith Maruyama, Louise Picon Shimizu and Nancy Smith Tsurumaki. It gives an excellent overview of the Japanese medical system for expats. Lonely Planet's *Healthy Travel Asia & India* is a useful pocket-sized guide to travel health. *Travel with Children* from Lonely Planet is useful if you are taking children with you. Other recommended general travel-health references are *Traveller's Health* by Dr Richard Dawood and *Travelling Well* by Dr Deborah Mills – check out the website www .travellingwell.com.au for other trips.

IN TRANSIT

DEEP VEIN THROMBOSIS (DVT)

Blood clots may form in the legs during plane flights, chiefly because of prolonged immobility. The longer the flight, the greater the risk. The chief symptom of DVT is swelling or pain of the foot, ankle or calf, usually but not always on just one side. If a blood clot travels to the lungs it may cause chest pain and breathing difficulties. Travellers with any of these symptoms should immediately seek medical attention.

HEALTH

To prevent the development of DVT on long flights you should walk about the cabin, contract the leg muscles while sitting, drink plenty of fluids and avoid alcohol. If you have previously had DVT speak with your doctor about preventive medications (usually given in the form of an injection just prior to travel).

JET LAG & MOTION SICKNESS

To avoid jet lag (common when crossing more than five time zones) try drinking plenty of nonalcoholic fluids and eating light meals. Upon arrival, get exposure to natural sunlight and readjust your schedule (for meals, sleep and so on) as soon as possible.

Antihistamines such as dimenhydrinate (Dramamine), prochlorperazine (Phenergan) and meclizine (Antivert, Bonine) are usually the first choice for treating motion sickness. The main side effect of these medications is drowsiness. A herbal alternative is ginger.

IN JAPAN

AVAILABILITY & COST OF HEALTH CARE

Medical care in Japan is significantly better in the major cities compared to rural areas. Outside urban areas it may be difficult to access English-speaking doctors, so try to take a Japanese speaker with you to any medical facility. Japan has a national health insurance system, but this is only available to foreigners if they have long-term visas in Japan. Be aware that medical facilities will require full payment at the time of treatment or proof that your travel insurance will pay for any treatment that you receive. Insurance companies in the West are comfortable with the facilities in Japan's major urban centres, but have found variable standards of care in the country areas.

Tourist offices operated by Japan National Tourist Organization (JNTO; p803) have lists of English-speaking doctors and dentists, and hospitals where English is spoken. You can contact your insurance company or embassy to locate the nearest English-speaking facility.

Dental services are widespread and of good standard; however, they are very expensive so make sure you have a check-up before you leave home.

Drugs that require a prescription in the West also generally require one in Japan. En-sure you bring adequate supplies of your own medications from home.

There are certain medications that are illegal to bring into Japan, including some commonly used cough and cold medications such as pseudoephedrine (found in Actifed, Sudafed etc) and codeine. Some prescription medications not allowed into Japan include narcotics, psychotropic drugs, stimulants and codeine. If you need to take more than a one-month supply of any other prescription drug, you should check with your local Japanese embassy as you may need permission. Ensure you have a letter from your doctor outlining your medical condition and the need for any prescription medication.

Pregnant women should receive specialised advice before travelling. Some vaccines are definitely not recommended, others are only prescribed after an individual risk/benefit analysis. The ideal time to travel is during the second trimester (between 15 and 28 weeks), when the risk of pregnancy-related problems are at their lowest and pregnant women generally feel at their best. During the first trimester there is a risk of miscarriage and in the third trimester problems such as premature labour and high blood pressure are possible. Always travel with a companion, have a list of quality medical facilities available at your destination and ensure you continue your standard antenatal care while you travel. Avoid travel to rural areas with poor transport and medical facilities. Most importantly, ensure your travel insurance covers you for pregnancy-related problems, including premature labour. There have recently been reports of hepatitis E in Japan, contracted from undercooked pork liver, boar and deer meat (see p829).

Supplies of sanitary products are readily available in Japan. It can be very difficult to get the oral contraceptive pill so ensure you bring adequate supplies of your own pill from home.

Japan is a safe country to travel with children. Ensure they are up to date with their basic vaccinations prior to travel.

INFECTIOUS DISEASES
AIDS & STDs

AIDS and STDs can be avoided completely only by abstaining from sexual contact with new partners. Condom use in Japanese society is low. HIV is still relatively uncommon in Japan, but the incidence is slowly increasing.

In the year 2000, 78% of new cases were contracted via sexual contact. Condoms can help prevent some sexually transmitted infections, but not all. If you have had sexual contact with a new partner while travelling, or have any symptoms such as a rash, pain or discharge, see a doctor for a full STD check-up.

Hepatitis B

Hepatitis B is a virus spread via body fluids, eg through sexual contact, unclean medical facilities or shared needles. People who carry the virus are often unaware they are carriers. In the short term hepatitis B can cause the typical symptoms of hepatitis – jaundice, tiredness and nausea – but in the long term it can lead to cancer of the liver and cirrhosis. Vaccination against hepatitis B is now part of most countries' routine childhood vaccination schedule and should be considered by anyone travelling for a long period of time or who may have contact with body fluids.

Hepatitis E

Hepatitis E is a virus spread via contaminated food and water. There have been a number of cases reported from Japan, linked to eating boar and deer meat, and most recently undercooked pork liver. The disease causes jaundice (yellow skin and eyes), tiredness and nausea. There is no specific treatment and those infected usually recover after four to six weeks. However, it can be a disaster in pregnant women, with a death rate of both mother and baby of up to 30% in the third trimester. Pregnant women should be particularly careful to avoid eating any undercooked foods. There is no vaccine yet available to prevent hepatitis E.

Influenza

Influenza is generally transmitted between November and April. Symptoms include high fever, muscle aches, runny nose, cough and sore throat. It can be a very severe illness in those aged over 65 or with underlying medical conditions such as heart disease or diabetes. Vaccination is recommended for these high-risk travellers or for anyone who wishes to reduce their risk of catching the illness. There is no specific treatment for 'the flu', just rest and paracetamol.

Japanese B Encephalitis

Japanese B encephalitis is a viral disease transmitted by mosquitoes. It is a rare disease in travellers and the vaccine is part of the routine childhood vaccination schedule in Japan. Risk exists in rural areas of all islands, but is highest in the western part of the country. In western Japan the risk season is from July to October. On Ryuku Island (Okinawa) the risk season runs from April to December. Vaccination is recommended for travellers spending more than a month in rural areas during the transmission season. Other precautions include general insect avoidance measures such as using repellents and sleeping under nets if not in screened rooms. Although this is a rare disease, it is very serious - there is no specific treatment and a third of people infected will die and a third will suffer permanent brain damage.

Lyme Disease

Lyme disease is spread via ticks and is present in the summer months in wooded areas. Symptoms include an early rash and general viral symptoms, followed weeks to months later by joint, heart or neurological problems. The disease is treated with the antibiotic doxycycline. Prevent Lyme disease by using general insect avoidance measures and checking yourself for ticks after walking in forested areas.

Tick-Borne Encephalitis

Tick-borne encephalitis occurs on the northern island of Hokkaidō only, and, as its name suggests, is a virus transmitted by ticks. The illness starts with general flu-like symptoms, which last a few days and then subside. After a period of remission (about one week) the second phase of the illness occurs with symptoms such as headache, fever and stiff neck (meningitis), or drowsiness, confusion and other neurological signs such as paralysis (encephalitis). There is no specific treatment, and about 10% to 20% of those who progress to the second phase of illness will have permanent neurological problems. You can prevent this disease by using insect avoidance measures and checking yourself for ticks after walking in forested areas. A vaccine is available in Europe but is very difficult if not impossible to find elsewhere. Two doses are given four to 12 weeks apart with a third shot after nine to 12 months. Boosters are required every three years to maintain immunity.

TRAVELLER'S DIARRHOEA

There is a low risk of traveller's diarrhoea in Japan, only 10% to 20% of travellers will experience some stomach upset. If you develop diarrhoea, be sure to drink plenty of fluids, preferably an oral rehydration solution (eg Dioralyte). A few loose stools don't require treatment, but if you start having more than four or five stools a day you should start taking an antibiotic (such as norfloxacin, ciprofloxacin or azithromycin) and an anti-diarrhoeal agent (such as loperamide). If diarrhoea is bloody, persists for more than 72 hours, is accompanied by fever, shaking, chills or severe abdominal pain, or doesn't respond quickly to your antibiotic, you should seek medical attention.

ENVIRONMENTAL HAZARDS

Air Pollution

Air pollution can be a problem in major centres such as Tokyo if you have an underlying lung condition. If you have a pre-existing lung condition speak with your doctor to ensure you have adequate medications to treat an exacerbation.

Altitude Sickness

Altitude sickness could develop in some people when climbing Mt Fuji (for more information, see p200) or some of the higher Japanese alps. Altitude sickness is best avoided by slowly acclimatising to higher altitudes. If this is impossible, the medication Diamox can be a helpful preventative if taken on a doctor's recommendation. The symptoms of altitude sickness include headache, nausea and exhaustion and the best treatment is descending to a lower altitude. We recommend that you familiarise yourself with the condition and how to prevent it before setting out on any climb over 2000m. Rick Curtis's *Outdoor Action Guide to High Altitude: Acclimatization and Illness* (www.princeton.edu/~oa/safety/altitude.html) provides a comprehensive overview.

Hypothermia

Hypothermia is possible if walking or climbing in the alps. It is surprisingly easy to progress from very cold to dangerously cold due to a combination of wind, wet clothing, fatigue and hunger, even if the air temperature is above freezing. It is best to dress in layers; silk, wool and some of the new artificial fibres are all good insulating materials. A hat is important, as a lot of heat is lost through the head. A strong, waterproof outer layer (and a space blanket for emergencies) is essential. Carry basic supplies, including food containing simple sugars to generate heat quickly and fluid to drink. Symptoms of hypothermia are exhaustion, numb skin (particularly the toes and fingers), shivering, slurred speech, irrational or violent behaviour, lethargy, stumbling, dizzy spells, muscle cramps and violent bursts of energy. Irrationality may take the form of sufferers claiming they are warm and trying to take off their clothes. To treat mild hypothermia, first get the person out of the wind and/or rain, remove their clothing if it's wet and replace it with dry, warm clothing. Give them hot liquids – not alcohol – and some high-calorie, easily digestible food. The early recognition and treatment of mild hypothermia is the only way to prevent severe hypothermia, which is a critical condition.

Insect Bites & Stings

Insect bites and stings are not a common problem in Japan. You should, however, follow general insect avoidance measures if you are hiking in the woods or are in rural areas during the summer months. These include using an insect repellant containing 20% to 30% DEET (diethyl-M-toluamide), covering up with light-coloured clothing and checking yourself for ticks after being in the forest. When removing ticks ensure you also remove their heads. Some people have an allergic reaction to ticks so it is a good idea to carry an antihistamine with you.

Water

The water is generally safe to drink in Japan.

TRADITIONAL MEDICINE

The two most well-known forms of traditional Japanese medicine are shiatsu and *reiki*.

Shiatsu is a type of massage that emerged in Japan out of traditional Chinese medicine. It is a form of manual therapy incorporating gentle manipulations and stretches derived from physiotherapy and chiropractic, combined with pressure techniques exerted through the fingers or thumbs. The philosophy underlying shiatsu is similar to many traditional Asian medical systems and involves the body's *ki* (vital energy) flowing through the body in a series of channels known as meridians. If the *ki* is blocked from flowing freely, illness can occur. The technique is used to improve the flow of *ki*. Shiatsu was officially recognised by the Japanese government as a therapy in its own right in the mid-1900s.

Reiki claims to heal by charging this same life force with positive energy, thus allowing the *ki* to flow in a natural, healthy manner. In a standard treatment, *reiki* energy flows from the practitioner's hands into the client. The practitioner places their hands on or near the clients' body in a series of positions that are held for three to 10 minutes. People become practitioners after receiving an 'attunement' from a *reiki* master.

If you do decide to have any traditional medical treatments make sure you tell your practitioner if you are taking any Western medicines.

Language

CONTENTS

Japanese is the language spoken across all of Japan. While the standard language, or *hyōjungo*, is understood by almost all Japanese, regardless of their level of education, many Japanese speak strong local dialects (known as *ben*, as in the famous dialect of Kansai, *Kansai-ben*). These dialects, particularly in rural areas, can be quite difficult to understand, even for Japanese from other parts of the country. Luckily, you can always get your point across in *hyōjungo*.

In this language guide you'll find a selection of useful Japanese words and phrases. For information on food and dining, including words and phrases that will help in deciphering menus and ordering food in Japanese, see p85. For information on language courses available in Japan, see p792.

GRAMMAR

To English speakers, Japanese language patterns often seem to be back to front and lacking in essential information. For example, where an English speaker would say 'I'm going to the shop' a Japanese speaker would say 'shop to going', omitting the subject pronoun (I) altogether and putting the verb at the end of the sentence. To make

---

TRYING ENGLISH IN JAPAN

Visitors to Japan should be warned that many Japanese do not speak or understand much English. Although English is a required subject in both junior high school and high school, and many students go on to study more of it in university, several factors conspire to prevent many Japanese from acquiring usable English. These include the nature of the English educational system, which uses outdated methods like translation; the extreme difference between English and Japanese pronunciation and grammar; and the typical reticence of the Japanese, who may be shy to speak a language that they haven't mastered.

There are several ways to facilitate communication with Japanese who may not have a mastery of spoken English:

- Always start with a smile to create a sense of ease.

- Speak very slowly and clearly.

- When asking for information, choose people of university age or thereabouts, as these people are most likely to speak some English. Also, Japanese women tend to speak and understand English much better than Japanese men.

- If necessary, write down your question; Japanese are often able to understand written English even when they can't understand spoken English.

- Use the sample phrases in this chapter and, if necessary, point to the Japanese phrase in question.

---

matters worse, many moods which are indicated at the beginning of a sentence in English occur at the end of a sentence in Japanese, as in the Japanese sentence 'Japan to going if' – 'if you're going to Japan'.

Fortunately for visitors to Japan, it's not all bad news. In fact, with a little effort, getting together a repertoire of travellers' phrases should be no trouble – the only problem will be understanding the replies you get.

WRITTEN JAPANESE

Japanese has one of the most complex writing systems in the world, which uses three different scripts – four if you include the increasingly used Roman script, romaji. The most difficult of the three, for foreigners and Japanese alike, is kanji, the ideographic script developed by the Chinese. Not only do you have to learn a couple of thousand of them, but unlike Chinese many Japanese kanji have wildly variant pronunciations depending on context.

Due to the differences between Chinese and Japanese grammar, kanji had to be supplemented with a 'syllabary' (an alphabet of syllables), known as hiragana. And there is yet another syllabary that is used largely for representing foreign loan words such as *terebi* (TV) and *biiru* (beer); this script is known as katakana. If you're serious about learning to read Japanese you'll have to set aside several years.

If you're thinking of tackling the Japanese writing system before you go or while you're in Japan, your best bet would be to start with hiragana or katakana. Both these syllabaries have 48 characters each, and can be learned within a week, although it'll take at least a month to consolidate them. Once in the country, you can practise your katakana on restaurant menus, where such things as *kōhii* (coffee) and *kēiki* (cake) are frequently found. Practise your hiragana on train journeys, as station names are usually indicated in hiragana (in addition to English and kanji). If you fancy continuing on to learn the kanji, be warned that it'll take quite a few years.

ROMANISATION

The romaji used in this book follows the Hepburn system of romanisation. In addition, common Japanese nouns like *ji* or *tera* (temple) and *jinja* or *jingū* (shrine) are written without an English translation.

Silent Letters

Hepburn romaji is a direct system of Romanisation that doesn't fully reflect all elements of spoken Japanese. The most obvious of these is the tendency in everyday speech to omit the vowel 'u' in many instances. In this language guide, and in Useful Words & Phrases on p102, these silent letters have been retained to provide accuracy in the written Romanisations, but they have been enclosed in square brackets to aid accurate pronunciation.

LANGUAGE BOOKS

Lonely Planet's *Japanese Phrasebook* gives you a comprehensive mix of practical and social words and phrases that should cover almost any situation confronting the traveller to Japan.

If you'd like to delve deeper into the intricacies of the language, we recommend *Japanese for Busy People* for beginners, *Introduction to Intermediate Japanese* (Mizutani Nobuko) for intermediate students, and *Kanji in Context* (Nishiguchi Koichi and Kono Tamaki) for more advanced students. One of the best guides to the written language, for both study and reference, is *Kanji & Kana* (Wolfgang Hadamizky and Mark Spahn).

PRONUNCIATION

Unlike other languages in the region with complicated tonal systems, such as Chinese, Vietnamese and Thai, Japanese pronunciation is fairly easy to master.

The following examples reflect British pronunciation:

a	as in 'father'
e	as in 'get'
i	as in 'macaroni'
o	as in 'bone'
u	as in 'flu'

Vowels appearing in this book with a macron (or bar) over them (ā, ē, ō, ū) are pronounced in the same way as standard vowels except that the sound is held twice as long. You need to take care with this as vowel length can change the meaning of a word, eg *yuki* means 'snow', while *yūki* means 'bravery'.

Consonants are generally pronounced as in English, with the exception of the few listed below:

f	this sound is produced by pursing the lips and blowing lightly
g	as in 'get' at the start of word; and nasalised as the 'ng' in 'sing' in the middle of a word
r	more like an 'l' than an 'r'

LANGUAGE

ACCOMMODATION

I'm looking for a ...
... o sagashite imas[u]
...を探しています。

camping ground
kyampu-jō
キャンプ場

family-style inn
minshuku
民宿

guesthouse
gesuto hausu
ゲストハウス

hotel
hoteru
ホテル

inn
ryokan
旅館

Japanese-style inn
ryokan
旅館

youth hostel
yūsu hosuteru
ユースホステル

Do you have any vacancies?
aki-beya wa arimas[u] ka?
空き部屋はありますか?

I don't have a reservation.
yoyaku wa shiteimasen
予約はしていません。

single room
shinguru rūmu
シングルルーム

double room
daburu rūmu
ダブルルーム

twin room
tsuin rūmu
ツインルーム

Japanese-style room
washitsu
和室

Western-style room
yōshitsu
洋室

Japanese-style bath
o-furo
お風呂

room with a (Western-style) bath
basu tsuki no heya
バス付きの部屋

How much is it (per night/per person)?
(ippaku/hitori) ikura des[u] ka?
(一泊/一人)いくらですか?

Does it include breakfast/a meal?
chōshoku/shokuji wa tsuite imas[u] ka?
(朝食/食事)は付いていますか?

I'm going to stay for one night/two nights.
hito-ban/futa-ban tomarimas[u]
(一晩/二晩)泊まります。

Can I leave my luggage here?
nimotsu o azukatte itadakemasen ka?
荷物を預かっていただけませんか?

CONVERSATION & ESSENTIALS

The all-purpose title *san* is used after a name as an honorific and is the equivalent of Mr, Miss, Mrs and Ms.

Good morning.
ohayō gozaimas[u]
おはようございます。

Good afternoon.
konnichiwa
こんにちは。

Good evening.
kombanwa
こんばんは。

Goodbye.
sayōnara
さようなら。

See you later.
dewa mata
ではまた。

Please/Go ahead. (when offering)
dōzo
どうぞ。

Please. (when asking)
onegai shimas[u]
お願いします。

Thanks. (informal)
dōmo
どうも。

Thank you.
dōmo arigatō
どうもありがとう。

Thank you very much.
dōmo arigatō gozaimas[u]
どうもありがとうございます。

Thanks for having me. (when leaving)
o-sewa ni narimash[i]ta
お世話になりました。

You're welcome.
dō itashimashite
どういたしまして。

No, thank you.
iie, kekkō des[u]
いいえ，けっこうです。

Excuse me/Pardon.
sumimasen
すみません。

Excuse me. (when entering a room)
o-jama shimas[u]/shitsurei shimas[u]
おじゃまします。/失礼します。

I'm sorry.
gomen nasai
ごめんなさい。

What's your name?
o-namae wan na des[u] ka?
お名前は何ですか？

My name is ...
watashi wa ... des[u]
私は...です。

This is Mr/Mrs/Ms (Smith).
kochira wa (Sumisu) san des[u]
こちらは(スミス)さんです。

Pleased to meet you.
dōzo yorosh[i]ku
どうぞよろしく。

Where are you from?
dochira no kata des[u] ka?
どちらのかたですか？

How are you?
o-genki des[u] ka?
お元気ですか？

Fine.
genki des[u]
元気です。

Is it OK to take a photo?
shashin o totte mo ii des[u] ka?
写真を撮ってもいいですか？

Cheers!
kampai!
乾杯！

Yes.
hai
はい。

No.
iie
いいえ。

No. (for indicating disagreement)
chigaimas[u]
違います。

No. (for indicating disagreement; less emphatic)
chotto chigaimas[u]
ちょっと違います。

OK.
daijōbu (des[u])/ōke
だいじょうぶ(です)。/オーケー。

Requests

Please give me this/that.
kore/sore o kudasai
(これ/それ)をください。

Please give me a (cup of tea).
(o-cha) o kudasai
(お茶)をください。

Please wait (a while).
(shōshō) o-machi kudasai
(少々)お待ちください。

SIGNS	
Information	
annaijo	案内所
Open	
eigyōchū	営業中
Closed	
junbichū	準備中
Entrance	
iriguchi	入口
Exit	
deguchi	出口
Toilets	
o-tearai/toire	お手洗い/トイレ
Male	
otoko	男
Female	
onna	女

Please show me the (ticket).
(kippu) o misete kudasai
(切符)を見せてください。

DIRECTIONS

Where is the ...?
... wa doko des[u] ka?
...はどこですか？

How far is it to walk?
aruite dono kurai kakarimas[u] ka?
歩いてどのくらいかかりますか？

How do I get to ...?
... e wa dono yō ni ikeba ii des[u] ka?
...へはどのように行けばいいですか？

Where is this address please?
kono jūsho wa doko des[u] ka?
この住所はどこですか？

Could you write down the address for me?
jūsho o kaite itadakemasen ka?
住所を書いていただけませんか？

Go straight ahead.
massugu itte
まっすぐ行って。

Turn left/right.
hidari/migi e magatte
(左/右)へ曲がって。

near/far
chikai/tōi
近い/遠い

HEALTH

I need a doctor.
isha ga hitsuyō des[u]
医者が必要です。

LANGUAGE

How do you feel?
kibun wa ikaga des[u] ka?
気分はいかがですか？

I'm ill.
kibun ga warui des[u]
気分が悪いです。

It hurts here.
koko ga itai des[u]
ここが痛いです。

I have diarrhoea.
geri o shite imas[u]
下痢をしています。

I have a toothache.
ha ga itamimas[u]
歯が痛みます。

I'm ...
watashi wa ...　　　　私は...
　diabetic
　tōnyōbyō des[u]　　　糖尿病です。
　epileptic
　tenkan des[u]　　　　てんかんです。
　asthmatic
　zensoku des[u]　　　喘息です。

I'm allergic to antibiotics.
kōsei-busshitsu ni arerugii ga arimas[u]
抗生物質にアレルギーがあります。

I'm allergic to penicillin.
penishirin ni arerugii ga arimas[u]
ペニシリン）にアレルギーがあります。

antiseptic
　shōdokuyaku　　　　消毒薬
aspirin
　asupirin　　　　　　アスピリン
condoms
　kondōmu　　　　　　コンドーム
contraceptive
　hinin yō piru　　　　避妊用ピル
dentist
　ha-isha　　　　　　歯医者
doctor
　isha　　　　　　　　医者
hospital
　byōin　　　　　　　病院
medicine
　kusuri　　　　　　　薬
pharmacy
　yakkyoku　　　　　　薬局
tampons
　tampon　　　　　　タンポン
(a) cold
　kaze　　　　　　　　風邪

EMERGENCIES

Help!
tas[u]kete!
助けて！

Call a doctor!
isha o yonde kudasai!
医者を呼んでください！

Call the police!
keisatsu o yonde kudasai!
警察を呼んでください！

I'm lost.
michi ni mayoi mash[i]ta
道に迷いました。

Go away!
hanarero!
離れろ！

diarrhoea
　geri　　　　　　　　下痢
fever
　hatsunetsu　　　　　発熱
migraine
　henzutsū　　　　　　偏頭痛

LANGUAGE DIFFICULTIES

Do you speak English?
eigo ga hanasemas[u] ka?
英語が話せますか？

Does anyone speak English?
donata ka eigo o hanasemas[u] ka?
どなたか英語を話せますか？

Do you understand English/Japanese?
ei-go/nihon-go wa wakarimas[u] ka?
（英語／日本語）はわかりますか？

I don't understand.
wakarimasen
わかりません。

I can't speak Japanese.
nihongo wa dekimasen
日本語はできません。

How do you say ... in Japanese?
nihongo de ... wa nan to iimas[u] ka?
日本語で...は何といいますか？

What does ... mean?
... wa donna imi des[u] ka?
...はどんな意味ですか？

What is this called?
kore wa nan to iimas[u] ka?
これは何といいますか？

Please write in Japanese/English.
nihongo/eigo de kaite kudasai
（日本語／英語）で書いてください。

Please speak more slowly.
mō chotto yukkuri itte kudasai
もうちょっとゆっくり言ってください。
Please say it again more slowly.
mō ichidō, yukkuri itte kudasai
もう一度，ゆっくり言ってください。

NUMBERS

0	zero/rei	ゼロ/零
1	ichi	一
2	ni	二
3	san	三
4	yon/shi	四
5	go	五
6	roku	六
7	nana/shichi	七
8	hachi	八
9	kyū/ku	九
10	jū	十
11	jūichi	十一
12	jūni	十二
13	jūsan	十三
14	jūyon/jūshi	十四
20	nijū	二十
21	nijūichi	二十一
30	sanjū	三十
100	hyaku	百
200	nihyaku	二百
1000	sen	千
5000	gosen	五千
10,000	ichiman	一万
20,000	niman	二万
100,000	jūman	十万
one million	hyakuman	百万

QUESTION WORDS
What?
nani? なに?
When?
itsu? いつ?
Where?
doko? どこ?
Who?
dare? だれ?

SHOPPING & SERVICES
bank
ginkō 銀行
embassy
taishi-kan 大使館
post office
yūbin kyoku 郵便局
market
ichiba 市場

a public telephone
kōshū denwa 公衆電話
toilet
o-tearai/toire お手洗い/トイレ
the tourist office
kankō annaijo 観光案内所

What time does it open/close?
nanji ni akimas[u]/shimarimas[u] ka?
何時に(開きます/閉まります)か?
I'd like to buy ...
... o kaitai des[u]
... を買いたいです。
How much is it?
ikura des[u] ka?
いくらですか?
I'm just looking.
miteiru dake des[u]
見ているだけです。
It's cheap.
yasui des[u]
安いです。
It's too expensive.
taka-sugi mas[u]
高すぎます。
I'll take this one.
kore o kudasai
これをください。
Can I have a receipt?
ryōshūsho o itadakemasen ka?
領収書をいただけませんか?

big
ōkii 大きい
small
chiisai 小さい
shop
mise 店
supermarket
sūpā スーパー
bookshop
hon ya 本屋
camera shop
shashin ya 写真屋
department store
depāto デパート

TIME & DAYS
What time is it?
ima nan-ji des[u] ka? 今何時ですか?

today
kyō 今日
tomorrow
ash[i]ta 明日

yesterday
  kinō　　　きのう
morning/afternoon
  asa/hiru　　　朝/昼

Monday
  getsuyōbi　　　月曜日
Tuesday
  kayōbi　　　火曜日
Wednesday
  suiyōbi　　　水曜日
Thursday
  mokuyōbi　　　木曜日
Friday
  kinyōbi　　　金曜日
Saturday
  doyōbi　　　土曜日
Sunday
  nichiyōbi　　　日曜日

TRANSPORT

What time does the next ... leave?
  tsugi no ... wa nanji ni demas[u] ka?
  次の...は何時に出ますか?
What time does the next ... arrive?
  tsugi no ... wa nanji ni tsukimas[u] ka?
  次の...は何時に着きますか?

boat
  bōto/fune　　　ボート/船
bus (city)
  shibas[u]　　　市バス
bus (intercity)
  chōkyoribas[u]　　　長距離バス
tram
  romen densha　　　路面電車
train
  densha　　　電車
bus stop
  basutei　　　バス停

station
  eki　　　駅
subway (train)
  chikatetsu　　　地下鉄
ticket
  kippu　　　切符
ticket office
  kippu uriba　　　切符売り場
timetable
  jikokuhyō　　　時刻表
taxi
  takushi　　　タクシー
left-luggage office
  nimotsu azukarijo　　　荷物預かり所
one way
  katamichi　　　片道
return
  ōfuku　　　往復
non-smoking seat
  kin'en seki　　　禁煙席

How much is the fare to ...?
  ... made ikura des[u] ka?
  ...までいくらですか?
Does this (train, bus, etc) go to ...?
  kore wa ... e ikimas[u] ka?
  これは...へ行きますか?
Please tell me when we get to ...
  ... ni tsuitara oshiete kudasai
  ...に着いたら教えてください。
I'd like to hire a ...
  ... o karitai no des[u] ka
  ...を借りたいのですが。
I'd like to go to ...
  ... ni ikitai desu
  ...に行きたいです。
Please stop here.
  koko de tomete kudasai
  ここで停めてください。

Also available from Lonely Planet:
Japanese Phrasebook

Glossary

ageya – magnificent banquet halls where artists, writers and statesmen gathered in a 'floating world' ambience of conversation, art and fornication

aimai – ambiguous and unclear

Ainu – indigenous people of Hokkaidō and parts of northern Honshū

aka-chōchin – red lantern; a working man's pub marked by red lanterns outside

ama – women divers

Amaterasu – sun goddess and link to the imperial throne

ama-zake – sweet sake served at winter festivals

ANA – All Nippon Airlines

ANK – All Nippon Koku

annai-sho/annai-jo – information office

arubaito – from the German *arbeit*, meaning 'to work', adapted into Japanese to refer to part-time work; often contracted to *baito*

asa-ichi – morning market

awamori – local alcohol of Okinawa

ayu – sweetfish caught during *ukai*

bangasa – rain umbrella made from oiled paper

banzai – 'hurrah' or 'hurray'; in the West this exclamation is, for the most part, associated with WWII, although its more modern usage is quite peaceful; literally '10,000 years'

bashō – *sumō* tournament

basho-gara – fitting to the particular conditions or circumstances; literally 'the character of a place'

bentō – boxed lunch, usually of rice, with a main dish and pickles or salad

bonsai – the art of growing miniature trees by careful pruning of branches and roots

boso-zoku – 'hot-car' or motorcycle gangs, usually noisy but harmless

bottle-keep – system whereby you buy a whole bottle of liquor in a bar, which is kept for you to drink on subsequent visits

bugaku – dance pieces played by court orchestras in ancient Japan

buke yashiki – *samurai* residence

bunraku – classical puppet theatre using huge puppets to portray dramas similar to *kabuki*

burakumin – traditionally outcasts associated with lowly occupations such as leather work; literally 'village people'

bushidō – a set of values followed by the *samurai*; literally 'the way of the warrior'

butsudan – Buddhist altar in Japanese homes

champuru – stir-fry with mixed ingredients such as *goya* and *fū*

chaniwa – tea garden

chanoyu – tea ceremony

charm – small dish of peanuts or other snack food served with a drink at a bar – it's often not requested but is still added to your bill

chikan – men who feel up women and girls on packed trains

chimpira – *yakuza* understudy; usually used pejoratively of a male with *yakuza* aspirations

chizu – map

chō – city area (for large cities) between a *ku* and *chōme* in size; also a street

chōchin – paper lantern

chōme – city area of a few blocks

chōnan – oldest son

chu – loyalty

daibutsu – Great Buddha

daifuku – sticky rice cakes filled with red bean paste and eaten on festive occasions; literally 'great happiness'

daimyō – regional lords under the *shōgun*

daira/taira – plain

danchi – public apartments

danjiri – festival floats

dantai – a group of people

dengaku – fish and vegetables roasted on skewers with a sweet miso sauce

donko – name for local trains in country areas

eboshi – black, triangular *samurai* hat

eki – train station

ekiben – *bentō* lunch box bought at a train station

ema – small votive plaques hung in shrine precincts as petitions for assistance from the resident deities

engawa – traditional veranda of a Japanese house overlooking the garden

enka – often described as the Japanese equivalent of country and western music, these are folk ballads about love and human suffering that are popular among the older generation

enryō – individual restraint and reserve

ero-guro – erotic and grotesque *manga*

fu – urban prefecture

fū – gluten

fude – brush used for calligraphy

fugu – poisonous blowfish or pufferfish

fundoshi – loincloth or breechcloth; a traditional male garment consisting of a wide belt and a cloth drawn over the genitals and between the buttocks. Usually seen only at festivals or on *sumō* wrestlers.

furigana – Japanese script used to aid pronunciation of *kanji*
furii kippu – one-day open transport ticket
fusuma – sliding screen
futon – traditional quilt-like mattress that is rolled up and stowed away during the day
futsū – a local train; literally 'ordinary'

gagaku – music of the imperial court
gaijin – foreigners; literally 'outside people'
gaijin house – cheap accommodation for long-term foreign residents
gaman – to endure
gasoreen sutando – petrol stations
gasshō-zukuri – an architectural style; literally 'hands in prayer'
gei-no-kai – the 'world of art and talent'; usually refers to TV
geisha – woman versed in arts and dramas who entertains guests; not a prostitute
gekijō – theatre
genkan – foyer area where shoes are removed or replaced when entering or leaving a building
geta – traditional wooden sandals
giri – social obligations
giri-ninjō – combination of social obligations and personal values; the two are often in conflict
go – board game; players alternately place white and black counters down, with the object to surround the opponent and make further moves impossible; probably originated in China, where it's known as *weiqi*
goya – bitter melon

habu – a venomous snake found in Okinawa
hachimaki – headband worn as a symbol of resolve; *kamikaze* pilots wore them in WWII, students wear them to exams
haiku – 17-syllable poems
hanami – blossom viewing (usually cherry blossoms)
haniwa – earthenware figures found in Kōfun-period tombs
hanko – stamp or seal used to authenticate any document; in Japan your *hanko* carries much more weight than your signature
hantō – peninsula
hara – marshlands
hara-kiri – belly cutting; common name for *seppuku* or ritual suicide
hara-kyū – acupuncture
hari – dragon-boat races
hashi – chopsticks
hatsu-mōde – first shrine visit of the new year
heiwa – peace
henrō – pilgrims on the Shikoku 88 Temple Circuit
higasa – sunshade umbrella

higawari ranchi – daily lunch special
Hikari – express *shinkansen*
hiragana – phonetic syllabary used to write Japanese words
hondō – main route
honsen – main rail line

ichi-go – square wooden sake 'cups' holding 180ml
ichi-nichi-jōsha-ken – day passes for unlimited travel on bus, tram or subway systems
IDC – International Digital Communications
ijime – bullying or teasing; a problem in Japanese schools
ikebana – art of flower arrangement
imobō – a dish consisting of a local type of sweet potato and dried fish
irezumi – a tattoo or the art of tattooing
irori – hearth or fireplace
itadakimasu – an expression used before meals; literally 'I will receive'
ITJ – International Telecom Japan
ittaikan – feeling of unity, of being one type
izakaya – Japanese version of a pub; beer and sake and lots of snacks available in a rustic, boisterous setting

JAC – Japan Air Commuter
JAF – Japan Automobile Federation
JAL – Japan Airlines
JAS – Japan Air System
jigoku – boiling mineral hot springs, which are definitely not for bathing in; literally 'hells'
jika-tabi – split-toe boots traditionally worn by Japanese carpenters and builders
jikokuhyō – timetable or book of timetables
jinja – shrine
jitensha – bicycle
jizō – small stone statues of the Buddhist protector of travellers and children
JNTO – Japan National Tourist Organization
JR – Japan Railways
JTB – Japan Travel Bureau
jujitsu – martial art from which judo was derived
juku – after-school 'cram' schools
JYHA – Japan Youth Hostel Association

kabuki – a form of Japanese theatre based on popular legends, which is characterised by elaborate costumes, stylised acting and the use of male actors for all roles
kaikan – hotel-style accommodation sponsored by government; literally 'meeting hall'
kaiseki – Japanese cuisine which obeys very strict rules of etiquette for every detail of the meal, including the setting
kaisha – a company, firm
kaisoku – rapid train
kaisū-ken – a book of transport tickets
kaiten-zushi – sushi served at a conveyor-belt restaurant (also the name of such a restaurant)

kakizome – New Year's resolutions

kami – Shintō gods; spirits of natural phenomena

kamidana – Shintō altar in Japanese homes

kamikaze – typhoon that sunk Kublai Khan's 13th-century invasion fleet and the name adopted by suicide pilots in the waning days of WWII; literally 'divine wind'

kampai – 'Cheers!'

kampō – Chinese herbal medicines that were dominant in Japan until the 19th century, when Western pharmaceuticals were introduced

kana – the two phonetic syllabaries, *hiragana* and *katakana*

kani-ryori – mainly steamed crab

kanji – Chinese ideographic script used for writing Japanese; literally 'Chinese script'

Kannon – Buddhist goddess of mercy (Sanskrit: Avalokiteshvara)

kannushi – chief priest of a Shintō shrine

karakasa – oiled paper umbrella

karakuri – mechanical puppets

karaoke – bars where you sing along with taped music; literally 'empty orchestra'

kasa – umbrella

kashiwa-mochi – pounded glutinous rice with a sweet filling, wrapped in an aromatic oak leaf

katakana – phonetic syllabary used to write foreign words

katamichi – one-way transport ticket

katana – Japanese sword

katsuo-bushi – thin flakes of *katsuo* (bonito) fish often used as a flavouring for broth or as a condiment

KDD – Kokusai Denshin Denwa (International Telephone & Telegraph)

keigo – honorific language used to show respect to elders or those of high rank

keiretsu – business cartels

ken – prefecture

kendō – oldest martial art; literally 'the way of the sword'

ki – life force, will

kimono – brightly coloured, robe-like traditional outer garment

kin'en-sha – nonsmoking carriage

kissaten – coffee shop

kōban – police box

kōgen – general area, plain

koi – carp; considered to be a brave, tenacious and vigorous fish. Many towns have carp ponds or channels teeming with colourful ornamental *nishiki-goi* (ornamental carp).

koinobori – carp banners and windsocks; the colourful fish pennants that are flown in honour of sons whom it is hoped will inherit a carp's virtues. These wave over countless homes in Japan in late April and early May for Boys' Day, the final holiday of Golden Week. These days, Boys' Day has become Children's Day and the windsocks don't necessarily simply fly in honour of the household's sons.

kokki – Japanese national flag

kokumin-shukusha – peoples' lodges; an inexpensive form of accommodation

kokuritsu kōen – national park

kokutetsu – Japanese word for Japan Railways (JR)

Komeitō – Clean Government Party; third-largest political party

kotatsu – heated table with a quilt or cover over it to keep the legs and lower body warm

koto – 13-stringed instrument that is played flat on the floor

ku – ward

kuidaore – eat until you drop (Kansai)

kūkō – airport

kura – mud-walled storehouses

kyakuma – drawing room of a home, where guests are met

kyōiku mama – a woman who pushes her kids through the Japanese education system; literally 'education mother'

kyūkō – ordinary express train (faster than a *futsū*, only stopping at certain stations)

live house – nightclub or bar where live music is performed

machi – city area (for large cities) between a *ku* and *chōme* in size; also street or area

machiya – traditional Japanese townhouse

maiko – apprentice *geisha*

mama-san – woman who manages a bar or club

maneki-neko – beckoning cat figure frequently seen in restaurants and bars; it's supposed to attract customers and trade

manga – Japanese comics

matcha – powdered green tea

matsuri – festival

meinichi – the 'deathday' or anniversary of someone's death

meishi – business card

mentsu – face

miai-kekkon – arranged marriage

mibun – social rank

miko – shrine maidens

mikoshi – portable shrines carried during festivals

minshuku – the Japanese equivalent of a B&B; family-run budget accommodation

miso-shiru – bean-paste soup

MITI – Ministry of International Trade & Industry

mitsubachi – accommodation for motorcycle tourers

mizu-shōbai – entertainment, bars, prostitution etc

mochi – pounded rice made into cakes and eaten at festive occasions

mōfu – blanket

morning service – *mōningu sābisu*; a light breakfast served until 10am in many *kissaten*

mura – village

nagashi-somen – flowing noodles
nengajō – New Year cards
N'EX – Narita Express
NHK – Nihon Hōsō Kyōkai (Japan Broadcasting Corporation)
Nihon – Japanese word for Japan; literally 'source of the sun'
nihonga – term for Japanese-style painting
ningyō – Japanese doll
ninja – practitioners of *ninjutsu*
ninjutsu – 'the art of stealth'
Nippon – see *Nihon*
nō – classical Japanese drama performed on a bare stage
noren – cloth hung as a sunshade, typically carrying the name of the shop or premises; indicates that a restaurant is open for business
norikae – to change buses or trains; make a connection
norikae-ken – transfer ticket (trams and buses)
NTT – Nippon Telegraph & Telephone Corporation

o- – prefix used to show respect to anything it is applied to; see *san*
obanzai-ryōri – home-style cooking
o-bāsan – grandmotherly type; an old woman
obi – sash or belt worn with a *kimono*
o-cha – tea
ofuku – return ticket
o-furo – traditional Japanese bath
o-jōsan – young college-age woman of conservative taste and aspirations
okashi-ya – sweet shops
okiya – *geisha* quarters
okonomiyaki – cabbage pancakes
OL – 'office lady'; female employee of a large firm; usually a clerical worker – pronounced 'ō-eru'
o-miai – arranged marriage
o-miyage – souvenir
onnagata – male actor playing a woman's role (usually in *kabuki*)
onsen – mineral hot-spring spa area, usually with accommodation
origami – art of paper folding
o-shibori – hot towels provided in restaurants
o-tsumami – bar snacks or *charms*
oyaki – wheat buns filled with pickles, squash, radish and red-bean paste

pachinko – popular vertical pinball game, played in *pachinko* parlours
puripeido kādo – 'prepaid card'; a sort of reverse credit card: you buy a magnetically coded card for a given amount and it can be used for certain purchases until spent. The prepaid phonecards are the most widespread but there are many others such as Prepaid Highway Cards for use on toll roads.

raidā hausu – basic shared accommodation/houses, catering mainly to those touring on motorcycles
rakugo – Japanese raconteurs, stand-up comics
reien – cemetery
reimen – *soba* noodles served with *kimchi* (spicy Korean pickles)
reisen – cold mineral spring
Rinzai – school of Zen Buddhism which places an emphasis on *kōan* (riddles)
rō – vegetable wax
robatayaki – *yakitori-ya* with a deliberately rustic, friendly, homy atmosphere; see also *izakaya*
romaji – Japanese roman script
rōnin – students who must resit university entrance exams; literally 'masterless *samurai*'
ropeway – Japanese word for a cable car or tramway
rotemburo – open-air or outdoor baths
ryokan – traditional Japanese inn
ryōri – cuisine

sadō – tea ceremony; literally 'way of tea'
saisen-bako – offering box at Shintō shrines
sakazuki – sake cups
sakoku – Japan's period of national seclusion prior to the Meiji Restoration
sakura – cherry blossoms
salaryman – standard male employee of a large firm
sama – even more respectful suffix than *san*; used in instances such as *o-kyaku-sama* – the 'honoured guest'
samurai – warrior class
san – suffix which shows respect to the person it is applied to; see also *o-*, the equivalent honorific. Both can occasionally be used together as *o-kyaku-san*, where *kyaku* is the word for guest or customer.
sansai – mountain vegetables
san-sō – mountain cottage
satori – Zen concept of enlightenment
seku-hara – sexual harassment
sembei – flavoured rice crackers often sold in tourist areas
sempai – one's elder or senior at school or work
sensei – generally translates as 'teacher' but has wider reference
sentō – public baths
seppuku – ritual suicide by disembowelment
setto – set meal
seza – a kneeling position
shamisen – a three-stringed traditional Japanese instrument that resembles a banjo
shi – city (to distinguish cities with prefectures of the same name eg Kyoto-shi)
shiken-jigoku – the enormously important and stressful entrance exams to various levels of the Japanese education system; literally 'examination hell'
shikki – lacquerware

shinkansen – ultra fast 'bullet' trains; literally 'new trunk line', since new train lines were laid for the high speed trains

Shintō – the indigenous religion of Japan

shirabyōshi – traditional dancer

shitamachi – traditionally the low-lying, less affluent parts of Tokyo

shōchū – strong distilled alcohol often made from potatoes; sometimes wheat or rice is used

shodō – Japanese calligraphy; literally the 'way of writing'

shogekijō – small theatre

shōgi – a version of chess in which each player has 20 pieces and the object is to capture the opponent's king

shōgun – former military ruler of Japan

shōgunate – military government

shōji – sliding rice-paper screens

shōjin ryōri – vegetarian meals (especially at temple lodgings)

Shugendō – offbeat Buddhist school, which incorporates ancient Shamanistic rites, Shintō beliefs and ascetic Buddhist traditions

shūji – a lesser form of *shodō*; literally 'the practice of letters'

shukubō – temple lodgings

shunga – explicit erotic prints; literally 'spring pictures', the season of spring being a popular Chinese and Japanese euphemism for sexuality

shuntō – spring labour offensive; an annual 'strike'

shūyū-ken – excursion train ticket

soapland – Japanese euphemism for bathhouses that offer sexual services

soba – buckwheat noodles

soroban – abacus

Sōtō – a school of Zen Buddhism which places emphasis on *zazen*

sukiyaki – thin slices of beef cooked in sake, soy and vinegar broth

sumi-e – black-ink brush paintings

sumō – Japanese wrestling

tabi – split-toed Japanese socks used when wearing *geta*

tadaima – a traditional greeting called out upon returning home; literally 'now' or 'present'

taiko – drum

tako – kite

tanin – outsider, stranger, someone not connected with the current situation

tanka – poems of 31 syllables; see *waka*

tanuki – racoon or dog-like folklore character frequently represented in ceramic figures

tarento – 'talent'; generally refers to musical performers

tatami – tightly woven floor matting on which shoes are never worn. Traditionally, room size is defined by the number of tatami mats.

tatemae – 'face'; how you act in public, your public position

TCAT – Tokyo City Air Terminal

teiki-ken – discount commuter passes

teishoku – set meal

tekitō – suitable or appropriate

tennō – heavenly king, the emperor

TIC – Tourist Information Center

to – metropolis, eg Tokyo-to

tosu – toilet

tokkuri – sake flask

tokkyū – limited express; faster than an ordinary express (*kyūkō*) train

tokonoma – alcove in a house in which flowers may be displayed or a scroll hung

torii – entrance gate to a Shintō shrine

tsukiai – after-work socialising among salarymen

tsunami – huge tidal waves caused by an earthquake

tsuru – cranes; a symbol of longevity often reproduced in *origami* and represented in traditional gardens

uchi – has meanings relating to 'belonging' and 'being part of'; literally 'one's own house'

uchiwa – paper fan

udon – thick white noodles

ukai – fishing using trained cormorants

ukiyo-e – wood-block prints; literally 'pictures of the floating world'

umeboshi – pickled plums thought to aid digestion; often served with rice in *bentō* sets

wa – harmony, team spirit; also the old *kanji* used to denote Japan, and still used in Chinese and Japanese as a prefix to indicate things of Japanese origin; see *wafuku*

wabi – enjoyment of peace and tranquillity

wafuku – Japanese-style clothing

waka – 31-syllable poem; see *tanka*

wanko – lacquerware bowls

waribashi – disposable wooden chopsticks

warikan – custom of sharing the bill (among good friends)

wasabi – Japanese horseradish

washi – Japanese handmade paper

yabusame – horseback archery

yakimono – pottery or ceramic ware

yakitori – charcoal-broiled chicken and other meats or vegetables, cooked on skewers

yakitori-ya – restaurant specialising in *yakitori*

yakuza – Japanese mafia

yamabushi – mountain priests (Shugendō Buddhism practitioners)

yama-goya – mountain huts

yamato – a term of much debated origins that refers to the Japanese world

yamato damashii – Japanese spirit, a term with parallels to the German Volksgeist; it was harnessed by the militarist government of the 1930s and 1940s and was identified with unquestioning loyalty to the emperor

yamato-e – traditional Japanese painting

yanqui – tastelessly dressed male, with dyed hair and a cellular phone

yatai – festival floats/hawker stalls

YCAT – Yokohama City Air Terminal

yōfuku – Western-style clothing

yukar – epic poems

yukata – light cotton summer *kimono*, worn for lounging or casual use; standard issue when staying at a *ryokan*

zabuton – small cushions for sitting on (used in *tatami* rooms)

zaibatsu – industrial conglomerates; the term arose prior to WWII but the Japanese economy is still dominated by huge firms like Mitsui, Marubeni and Mitsubishi, which are involved in many different industries

zazen – seated meditation emphasised in the Sōtō school of Zen Buddhism

Zen – introduced to Japan in the 12th century from China, this offshoot of Buddhism emphasises a direct, intuitive approach to enlightenment rather than rational analysis

Behind the Scenes

THIS BOOK

This 10th edition of *Japan* was written by a team of authors led by Chris Rowthorn. Kenneth Henshall wrote the History chapter; Dr Trish Batchelor wrote the Health chapter. Chris Rowthorn wrote all the other front chapters, all of the back chapters, and the Kansai chapter. Ray Bartlett (Hokkaidō and Northern Honshū), Andrew Bender (Around Tokyo and Central Honshū), Michael Clark (Kyūshū), Matthew Firestone (Shikoku and Okinawa & the Southwest Islands), Tim Hornyak (Western Honshū), and Wendy Yanagihara (Tokyo) all contributed tirelessly to this edition. Simon Bartz wrote the boxed text 'Rock Festivals in Japan' on p565 and Morgan Pitelka wrote 'Japanese Tea Culture' on p100. Chris Rowthorn coordinated the 8th and 9th editions. This guidebook was commissioned in Lonely Planet's Melbourne office, and produced by the following:

Commissioning Editor Rebecca Chau
Coordinating Editor Justin Flynn
Coordinating Cartographer Ross Butler
Coordinating Layout Designer Wibowo Rusli
Managing Editors Katie Lynch, Melanie Dankel
Managing Cartographers Julie Sheridan, David Connolly
Managing Layout Designer Sally Darmody
Assisting Editors Susie Ashworth, Janice Bird, Jacqueline Coyle, Anne Mulvaney, Kristin Odijk
Assisting Cartographers James Bird, Jessica Deane, Diana Duggan, Daniel Fennessey, Kusnandar, Jolyon Philcox, Sophie Richards, Jody Whiteoak
Cover Designer Nic Lehman
Language Content Coordinator Quentin Frayne
Project Manager Chris Love

Thanks to Brooke Lyons, Margot Kilgour, Evan Jones, Laura Stansfeld, Jeanette Wall, Fionnuala Twomey, Glenn van der Knijff, Susan Paterson, Yvonne Byron, Celia Wood

LONELY PLANET: TRAVEL WIDELY, TREAD LIGHTLY, GIVE SUSTAINABLY

The Lonely Planet Story

The story begins with a classic travel adventure: Tony and Maureen Wheeler's 1972 journey across Europe and Asia to Australia. There was no useful information about the overland trail then, so Tony and Maureen published the first Lonely Planet guidebook to meet a growing need.

From a kitchen table, Lonely Planet has grown to become the largest independent travel publisher in the world, with offices in Melbourne (Australia), Oakland (USA) and London (UK). Today Lonely Planet guidebooks cover the globe. There is an ever-growing list of books and information in a variety of media. Some things haven't changed. The main aim is still to make it possible for adventurous individuals to get out there – to explore and better understand the world.

The Lonely Planet Foundation

The Lonely Planet Foundation proudly supports nimble nonprofit institutions working for change in the world. Each year the foundation donates 5% of Lonely Planet company profits to projects selected by staff and authors. Our partners range from Kabissa, which provides small nonprofits across Africa with access to technology, to the Foundation for Developing Cambodian Orphans, which supports girls at risk of falling victim to sex traffickers.

Our nonprofit partners are linked by a grass-roots approach to the areas of health, education or sustainable tourism. Many projects we support – such as one with BaAka (Pygmy) children in the forested areas of Central African Republic – choose to focus on women and children as one of the most effective ways to support the whole community.

Sometimes foundation assistance is as simple as helping to preserve a local ruin like the Minaret of Jam in Afghanistan; this incredible monument now draws intrepid tourists to the area and its restoration has greatly improved options for local people.

Just as travel is often about learning to see with new eyes, so many of the groups we work with aim to change the way people see themselves and the future for their children and communities.

BEHIND THE SCENES

THANKS
CHRIS ROWTHORN

I would like to thank the following people: Hiroe Kamine, Keiko Hagiwara, Anthony Weersing, Paul Carty, KS and HS, Divyam, Ian Ropke, Rebecca Chau, Julie Sheridan, Corinne Waddell, Marian Goldberg, Yoko Tanaka, Andy Bender, Wendy Yanagihara, Matt Firestone, Michael Clark, Tim Hornyak and Ray Bartlett. I would also like to thank all the readers of Lonely Planet Japan books who sent in letters and emails with information about Japan – your input really helps and I've tried to use as much of it as possible!

RAY BARTLETT

I am so thankful to so many special people who helped and supported me during the creation of this book. Just a list of names – you know who you are and how grateful I am to have had your help, friendship, support, and love. Kana and Nobu, Shino, Hisako and Kayoko, Chris R and Rebecca C, Miss 'Jump' and Miss Megumi, Matt, Kageyama, Koguma, Maki and Mieko, Ben McB and Felicia, Rumiko and Ikeda-san, Mun, 'Shippo' and Felicia, Sharon and TC, Risa, Alisa, Maki, Yoshimi and Mayumi and Shizuka, Tom J, Luke and Noriko, my family and friends, and of course, the incomparable Ezoshimarisu. Most of all, a heart-felt thank you to the kind, good-hearted, generous people of Japan – may you treat each traveller on your precious land the same way you've treated me.

ANDREW BENDER

First thanks go to Yohko Scott, Marutani Noriko, Marian Goldberg and Kawaguchi Etsuko of the JNTO in the USA. In Japan, thanks to spirit guides too many to mention, but here's a go: Kawazoe Kyòsuke and Nozawa Yoneko, Kinta Tendò, Kimura Kenichi and Matsunaga Kimiko, Ozawa Keiichi, Kimura Tarò, Sugai Yukiko, Watanabe Kazufumi and Andrew Smith, Gomi Kikuhiro, Seino Fumitaka, Kojima Hiromi, Satō Eiichi, Nomura Yoshihiko, Hashimoto Yasuyo, Hayakawa Yoshinobu. And last but not least, thanks to Rebecca Chau, Chris Rowthorn and Justin Flynn for their fine judgment and good cheer.

MICHAEL CLARK

My time in Kyushu was a joy, primarily due to the help of the kind and generous Kyushu residents I met every day. In particular, Misuzu Nishikawa in the Nagasaki TIC office; Yukie Onisuka, Aki Ueda and Stephen Kuhlke in Kumamoto; Michiko-san in Aso; Yuki and Megumi, Brad Simcock & Like Lokon, Ed & Naomi Rummel, Brendan & Kaori Rodda of

Miyazaki; Koji, Tomoko Takamizawa, Kaori Yano, Nick Szasz, and Lewis & Tomoko in Fukuoka; Nao Yoshida in Dazaifu; in Kagoshima, Mikiko Morita, Brian Pedersen; and in Beppu, Keiko Hirano, Gato-san and Okuma Asuka. In addition, fellow travellers offered frequent tips, insights and conversation, in particular Ian Hodge; Jim and Sian Samuel; and Paul and Rosalyn for discovering the majestic camphor tree of Nagasaki, and Udo & Hellen de Boer for introducing me to Donut-san. Thanks too friends Taku Imagawa, Alan McCornick and Avalon Evans for poetic inspiration, and Mirei Sato for script assistance. Special thanks to fellow Japan author and Kyoto resident Chris Rowthorn, and Rebecca Chau at Lonely Planet Melbourne who managed to pull it all together. Back home, love and kisses to my wife Janet, and kids Melina and Alex for hanging in there!

MATTHEW D FIRESTONE

First and foremost, I'd like to thank my wonderful family. To my mother and father, thank you for not worrying too much about me and instead focusing on the important things in life – like hitting the jackpot on the nickel machines and taking another card on a soft 17. To my sister, thank you for continuing to be rich and powerful as I've got lots of ideas for where I want to retire. Second, I'd like to give a big shout out to the entire Lonely Planet team. I'd especially like to thank Rebecca for giving me the chance to work for Lonely Planet, and to Chris for his professional mentorship. Finally, I'd like to thank the weird and wonderful cast of characters that made this trip to Japan so special. To Drew, Greg and Alban, the illustrious members of TM, I hope Japan was everything you hoped it would be. To Aki, thank you for opening up my eyes to the wonder and beauty of your country.

TIMOTHY N HORNYAK

I'd like to thank Chris Rowthorn and LP staff, Takuya Karube, Amy Chavez, Masashi Iesako, Alexander Wilds, Masahiko Kitamura & family, Shinji Ohno, Mayuka, Jackie Hoffart, and all the tourist information staff who helped along the way. And of course, my family and friends for their support.

WENDY YANAGIHARA

I cannot thank my family enough for their love and support in and out of Japan – and to Dad and Jason for coming to visit during my research. Many thanks to Kenichi-san for the seeker's perspective, Yamada-san for the dinner chat, Kuro for the milonga and especially Mariko for the excellent photos and help on the ground. To Marie, Miguel,

Alberto, Midori and Naoya, *muchas gracias* for diligently helping me research *izakaya*!

OUR READERS

Many thanks to the travellers who used the last edition and wrote to us with helpful hints, useful advice and interesting anecdotes:

A Shahjahan Ali, Graham Apthorpe, Jackie Arnold, James Arthur, Scott D Ash **B** Brett Bardsley, Marge Beard, Rafael Belliard, Claudia Bergeron, Walter Bertschinger, Jessica Bertuzzi, Chris Bethell, Henryk Blasinski, Valentino Boccato, Shawna Bohlender, Renzo Bonroy, Tony Boulton, Mark Brady, Margaret Briffett, Laura Brown, Tamar BrüGgemann, Chris Buchman, Felix Buchner, Trent Bulgin, Lauren Bull, Mary Beth Bursey **C** Deborah Chaikind, Fen Chiam, Paula Chiu, Clement Chu, Jeremy Churchill, Jessica Cichy, Norma Jean Clark, Garth Clarke, Michael Clemens, Jodi Concepcion, Andrew Coppin, Fredrik Coulter, Anthony Cross, Nathan Cruz, Catherine Cullen, Rory Cusack, Daniel Cutler **D** Justin Dabner, Paolo Dardanelli, Liam Davenport, Nicolas Delerue, Peter Dinges, Sally Dipell, Nigel Dixon, Esther Dohijo, David Dolley, Lorenz Dopplinger, Luis Ducla Soares, Tyler Durden **E** Dominic Edsall, Niek Eleveld, Peter Endriss, Brian Engel, Bodil Enoksson, Brad Ensminger, Meredith Erochko, Rachel Evans **F** Jorge Juan FernáNdez GarcíA, Bryan Foggo, May Fong, Bryan Forbes, Carla Francis, Daniel Friedrich, Tetsuya Fujimoto **G** Matt Gardner, Danielle Gleeson, Sophie Godefroy, Fabio Goto, Stefan Groetsch, Alexia Guillois, Thomas Gumpenberger **H** Emily Haas, Bodo Hansen, Bodo Hansen, Adam Hardy, Maureen Harris, Karen Hastings, Richard Haynes, Sophie Haynes, Brigitte Hein, Pierre Heisbourg, Tim Herborn, Ilona Hilkovsky, Michael Kovensky, Stuart Hodgson, Michael Hoefele, Michael Howson, Todd Hull **I** Ran Inbar, Nassir Isaf **J** Tess Jenkin, Brendan Jenkin, Nakajima Jiro, Kelly Jones, Natalie Jordaan **K** Toyoda Kenjiro, Natascha Kadlubowski, Tina Kafarnik, Koko Kato, Alexandra Kaufman, Irene Kawahara, Takafumi Kawakami, Peter Keres, Jessica Kingsley, Natalia Kirgetova, Tanya Knight-Olds, Brian Knox, Dr Thomas Kohl, Lill Kristiansen **L** C L, Darren Lambie, Richard Lang, Alasha Lantinga, Terry Lawless, Marianne Lee, Mrs C Lee, Brian Lee, Kyle Leonard, Jed Levine, Harry Lewis, Khee Boon Lim, Keri Lim, Swee Ching Lim, M K Loke, Isobel Long, Kevin Lorette, Chris Louie, Laurent Lugand, Jeffrey Lum **M** Craig Macnab, Robert Marks, Kay Martin, Alex Matskevich, Annerose Matsushita-Bader, Henning Maurer, Rob Mc, Gregory Mcelwain, Sean Mckelvey, D Mcnulty, Susie Mee, Petra Meier, Dora Mesic, Mark Messer, Matthew Middleman, Stephen Mintz, Nanako Miyamoto, Lars Moberg, Ian Morris, Jean-Philippe Mulet, Ann Murphy, Alexandra Murray **N** Ines Nadais, Hitomi Nagata, Ron Nash, Lucy Nuttall **O** Diane Olsen, Ivan Orlov, Olivia Ott **P** Adam Pasley, Alice Pater, Elly Perkins, Bart Peters, Julia Phipps, Francesco Pogaccini, Michael Polansky, Bradford Pomeroy, Ric Powell, Lisa Powell, Helen Pugh **R** Peter Reed, Ine Reijnen, Jake Reiner, Lionel Renggli, Jenny Richens, Barbara Rimington, Bernhard Riniker, Michael Rossiter, Shawn Stewart Ruff, Matthew Russell **S** Helen Sales, Julian Satterthwaite, Naoko Schaal, Chris Schwen, Hugh Selby, Bettina Selig, Erin Shew, Rita Silek, Gitte Sindbjerg, Suzy Small, Nienke Smith, Andrew Smyth, Jamie Snashall, Dschun Song, Kathleen Sparkes, Holly Star, Pauline Stavrakis, Stephanie Stipernitz, Richard Szostak **T** Masami Takahashi, Manabu Takanaka, Yutaka Takayama, Robert Tamarua, Amanda Tarzwell, Stephen Taylor, Nicole Thompson, Derek Tokashiki, Sarah Tunik Ttuunniikk, Andrew Tweed, Charlie Tyack **V** Bryan Venti **W** Luke Waddington, Katharina Wagner, Steve Ward, Robert Waterman, David Weber, Simon Wellington, Jane Wolfers, Andy Wong, Tricia Woo, Keith Woodend **Y** Terh Kuen Yii, Shomi Yoon, Briony Yorke, Edwin Zaccaï, Peter Zihla, Herbert Aspevig, Fabrizio Beverina, Chris Chamberlin, Chris De Fries, Dirk Den Ouden, Murray Dickson, Neil Gunther, Matthew Mac Gabhann, Daniel Macdougall, Chris Mather, Gregor Murray, Marion Penaud, Hans Van Der Veen, Katherine Vera, Matt Wilksch, Takasi Yasuda

SEND US YOUR FEEDBACK

We love to hear from travellers – your comments keep us on our toes and help make our books better. Our well-travelled team reads every word on what you loved or loathed about this book. Although we cannot reply individually to postal submissions, we always guarantee that your feedback goes straight to the appropriate authors, in time for the next edition. Each person who sends us information is thanked in the next edition – and the most useful submissions are rewarded with a free book.

To send us your updates – and find out about Lonely Planet events, newsletters and travel news – visit our award-winning website: **www.lonelyplanet.com/contact**.

Note: we may edit, reproduce and incorporate your comments in Lonely Planet products such as guidebooks, websites and digital products, so let us know if you don't want your comments reproduced or your name acknowledged. For a copy of our privacy policy visit www.lonelyplanet.com/privacy.

ACKNOWLEDGMENTS

Many thanks to the following for the use of their content:

Globe on title page ©Mountain High Maps 1993 Digital Wisdom, Inc.

Tokyo metro map: Tokyo Metro Co., Ltd. & copy; 2007.1

Osaka transport map: Osaka Subway System Map © Osaka Municipal Transportation Bureau 2006.

Index

INDEX

INDEX

000 Map pages
000 Photograph pages

INDEX

INDEX

000 Map pages
000 Photograph pages

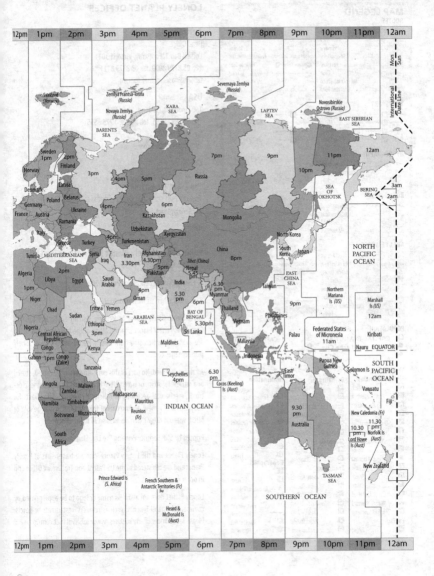

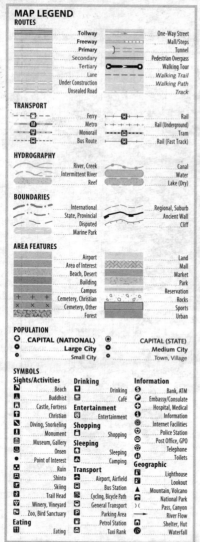

MAP LEGEND

(map legend symbols and key)

LONELY PLANET OFFICES

Australia
Head Office
Locked Bag 1, Footscray, Victoria 3011
☎ 03 8379 8000, fax 03 8379 8111
talk2us@lonelyplanet.com.au

USA
150 Linden St, Oakland, CA 94607
☎ 510 893 8555, toll free 800 275 8555
fax 510 893 8572
info@lonelyplanet.com

UK
72–82 Rosebery Ave,
Clerkenwell, London EC1R 4RW
☎ 020 7841 9000, fax 020 7841 9001
go@lonelyplanet.co.uk

Published by Lonely Planet Publications Pty Ltd
ABN 36 005 607 983

© Lonely Planet Publications Pty Ltd 2007

© photographers as indicated 2007

Cover photograph: Geisha in kimono signing autograph for fan, Greg Elms/Lonely Planet Images. Many of the images in this guide are available for licensing from Lonely Planet Images: www.lonely planetimages.com.